JUVENILE DELINQUENCY

COMIC BOOKS

✦

MOTION PICTURES

✦

OBSCENE AND
PORNOGRAPHIC MATERIALS

✦

TELEVISION PROGRAMS

GREENWOOD PRESS, PUBLISHERS
NEW YORK

Originally published in 1955-1956, Washington, D.C.

First Greenwood Reprinting 1969

Library of Congress Catalogue Card Number 77-90720

SBN 8371-2774-2

PRINTED IN UNITED STATES OF AMERICA

84TH CONGRESS \
1st Session ∫   SENATE   ∫ REPORT \
                                              No. 62

COMIC BOOKS AND JUVENILE DELINQUENCY

INTERIM REPORT

OF THE

COMMITTEE ON THE JUDICIARY

PURSUANT TO

S. Res. 89 and S. Res. 190
(83d Cong. 1st Sess.)   (83d Cong. 2d Sess.)

A PART OF THE INVESTIGATION OF JUVENILE DELINQUENCY IN THE UNITED STATES

COMMITTEE ON THE JUDICIARY

HARLEY M. KILGORE, West Virginia, *Chairman*

JAMES O. EASTLAND, Mississippi
ESTES KEFAUVER, Tennessee
OLIN D. JOHNSTON, South Carolina
THOMAS C. HENNINGS, JR., Missouri
JOHN L. McCLELLAN, Arkansas
PRICE DANIEL, Texas
JOSEPH C. O'MAHONEY, Wyoming

ALEXANDER WILEY, Wisconsin
WILLIAM LANGER, North Dakota
WILLIAM E. JENNER, Indiana
ARTHUR V. WATKINS, Utah
EVERETT McKINLEY DIRKSEN, Illinois
HERMAN WELKER, Idaho
JOHN MARSHALL BUTLER, Maryland

SUBCOMMITTEE TO INVESTIGATE JUVENILE DELINQUENCY IN THE UNITED STATES

ESTES KEFAUVER, Tennessee, *Chairman*

THOMAS C. HENNINGS, JR., Missouri
OLIN D. JOHNSTON, South Carolina

WILLIAM LANGER, North Dakota
ALEXANDER WILEY, Wisconsin

JAMES H. BOBO, *General Counsel*

NOTE.—Former Senator Robert C. Hendrickson, New Jersey, served as chairman of this subcommittee until December 13, 1954.
Senator Johnston and Senator Wiley did not participate in this report, having been appointed to the subcommittee on February 7, 1955.

II

CONTENTS

		Page
I.	Introduction	1
	Scope of this interim report	2
II.	A brief history of the development of the comic-book industry	3
	First comic book appeared in 1935	3
	An overview of the organization and operation of the comic-book industry	4
III.	The nature of crime and horror comic books	7
	Specific examples of material dealt with at New York hearings	7
	Methods utilized in crime and horror comics to portray violence	10
IV.	Crime and horror comics as a contributing factor in juvenile delinquency	11
	Crime and horror comics and the well-adjusted and normally law-abiding child	12
	Crime and horror comics may appeal to and thus give support and sanction to already existing antisocial tendencies	13
	Techniques of crime are taught by crime and horror comics	14
	Criminal careers are glamorized in crime and horror comic books	15
	Defenders of law and order frequently represented as all-powerful beings who kill and commit other crimes to defend "justice"	15
	Excessive reading of crime and horror comics is considered symptomatic of emotional pathology	16
	Need exists for more specific research to fully ascertain the possible effects of this type of reading material upon children	16
V.	Other questionable aspects of comic books	17
	Weapons and pseudomedical nostrums advertised in comic books designed for children	17
	Misuse of mailing lists compiled through comic-book advertisements	18
	The exportation of crime and horror comic books	20
VI.	Comic books as a medium of communication	22
VII.	Where should responsibility for policing crime and horror comic books rest?	23
	Comic books and authority	23
	Responsibility of parents, assisted by citizens' groups	24
	Role of Child Study Association as an evaluator of comics	25
	Responsibility of the comic-book industry for self-regulation	27
	Newsdealers unable to assume adequate responsibility	27
	Wholesalers are not most feasible parties to regulate content	28
	Printer cannot feasibly regulate content	28
	Distributor holds one of the key positions in comic-book industry	28
	Publisher has primary responsibility for subject and treatment	29
	Past attempts at industry self-regulation	30
	Current efforts at industry self-regulation	32
VIII.	Conclusions	32
	Only one part of investigation into the mass media of communication	33

	Page
Appendix	34
Senate Resolution 89 (83d Cong., 1st sess.)	34
Senate Resolution 190 (83d Cong., 2d sess.)	34
Section of the United States Code requiring statement of ownership to be filed annually with postmaster	35
Code of the National Cartoonists Society	35
Code of the Association of Comics Magazine Publishers, 1948	35
Code of the Comics Magazine Association of America, Inc., adopted October 26, 1954	36
Correspondence from the Committee on Evaluation of Comic Books, Cincinnati, Ohio	38
List of comic book publishers and comic-book titles, spring, 1954	39
Chart showing the organization of the comic-book industry in the United States, according to distributor, comic group, and publisher, in the spring of 1954	44

COMIC BOOKS AND JUVENILE DELINQUENCY

A PART OF THE INVESTIGATION OF JUVENILE DELINQUENCY IN THE UNITED STATES

MARCH 14 (legislative day, MARCH 10), 1955.—Ordered to be printed

Mr. KEFAUVER, from the Committee on the Judiciary, submitted the following

INTERIM REPORT

[Pursuant to S. Res. 89, 83d Cong., 1st sess., and S. Res. 190, 83d Cong., 2d sess.]

I. INTRODUCTION

The Subcommittee To Investigate Juvenile Delinquency, pursuant to authorization in Senate Resolution 89, 83d Congress, 1st session, and Senate Resolution 190 of the 2d session of said Congress, has been making a "full and complete study of juvenile delinquency in the United States," including its "extent and character" and "its causes and contributing factors." In addition to a number of community hearings that have been held in major cities, the subcommittee has undertaken studies of various special problems affecting juvenile delinquency.

Over a period of several months the subcommittee has received a vast amount of mail from parents expressing concern regarding the possible deleterious effect upon their children of certain of the media of mass communication. This led to an inquiry into the possible relationship to juvenile delinquency of these media.

Members of the subcommittee have emphatically stated at public hearings that freedom of speech and freedom of the press are not at issue. They are fully aware of the long, hard, bitter fight that has been waged through the ages to achieve and maintain those freedoms. They agree that these freedoms, as well as other freedoms in the Bill of Rights, must not be abrogated.

The subcommittee has no proposal for censorship. It moved into the mass media phase of its investigations with no preconceived opinions in regard to the possible need for new legislation.

Consistent with this position, it is firmly believed that the public is entitled to be fully informed on all aspects of this matter and to know all the facts. It was the consensus that the need existed for a thorough, objective investigation to determine whether, as has been

1

alleged, certain types of mass communication media are to be reckoned with as contributing to the country's alarming rise in juvenile delinquency. These include: "crime and horror" comic books and other types of printed matter; the radio, television, and motion pictures.

In its investigations of mass media, as in its investigation of other phases of the total problem, the subcommittee has not been searching for "one cause." Delinquency is the product of many related causal factors. But it can scarcely be questioned that the impact of these media does constitute a significant factor in the total problem.

Juvenile delinquency in America today must be viewed in the framework of the total community-climate in which children live. Certainly, none of the children who get into trouble live in a social vacuum. One of the most significant changes of the past quarter century has been the wide diffusion of the printed word, particularly in certain periodicals, plus the phenoménal growth of radio and television audiences.

The child today in the process of growing up is constantly exposed to sights and sounds of a kind and quality undreamed of in previous generations. As these sights and sounds can be a powerful force for good, so too can they be a powerful counterpoise working evil. Their very quantity makes them a factor to be reckoned with in determining the total climate encountered by today's children during their formative years.

SCOPE OF THIS INTERIM REPORT

The first phase of the subcommittee's investigation of the mass media of communication dealt with so-called comic books. This report is an interim one dealing with certain aspects of the findings to date of the investigation in this field. While it is not presumed to be comprehensive of the material that can be explored in this field, this interim report is based upon the public hearings in New York City on April 21, 22, and June 4, 1954, and upon research by members of the staff of the subcommittee. Because of the limited extent of the studies that exist on this subject, due in part to the comparatively recent introduction of comic books, there remains a considerable area which deserves careful and scientific exploration.

When looking at the question: What are "comic books?" we find that many, including all those with which the subcommittee's investigation was concerned, were found to be neither humorous nor books. They are thin, 32-page pamphlets usually trimmed to 7 by 10½ inches. Most of them sell for 10 cents a copy. They are issued monthly, bimonthly, quarterly, semiannually or as one-time publications. They are wire-stitched in a glossy paper cover on which, in the crime and horror type, there has been printed in gaudy colors an often grim and lurid scene contrived to intrigue prospective purchasers into buying them. The inside pages contain from 3 to 5 stories told in pictures with balloon captions. The pictures are artists' line drawings printed in color, intended to tell part of the story by showing the characters in action. In the case of crime and horror comic books, the story and the action are often quite horrendous.

Not all comic books were considered in this investigation. The subcommittee was concerned only with those dealing with crime and horror. It was estimated that by the spring of 1954 over 30 million copies of crime and horror comic books were being printed each month.[1] If only 50 percent of that number were sold by the retailers, the annual gross from crime and horror comics had reached $18 million. These constituted approximately 20 percent of the total output of comic books. The inquiry was not concerned in this phase with the comic strips that appear daily in most of our newspapers.

The methods utilized in investigating the possible effects of crime and horror comic books included several steps. These included the sending of samples of such books to psychiatrists and psychologists to obtain their opinions as to the possible effects of this type of printed matter upon children. The staff of the Library of Congress prepared a useful summarization of articles and books pertaining to the subject.[2] The subcommittee's staff conducted extensive research into the organization of the comic-book industry and interviewed many individuals concerned with that industry. This was done prior to the public hearings in New York.

II. A Brief History of the Development of the Comic Book Industry

The first comic strip to appear in a newspaper was Outcault's "Yellow Kid" which was introduced in the New York World in 1896. The concept, however, of an entire publication devoted to comics was not developed until 1911 when the Chicago American offered reprints of Bud Fisher's Mutt and Jeff in pamphlet form as a premium for clipping coupons from six daily issues.

FIRST COMIC BOOK APPEARED IN 1935

The pattern for present-day comic books was set in 1935 when New Fun, a 64-page collection of original material printed in four colors, was put on the newsstands. Action Comics were put on sale in 1938, and Superman Quarterly Magazine appeared in 1939. The number of comic book publishers has increased and the circulation figures have risen astonishingly since that time.

It has been estimated conservatively that in 1940 publishers of at least 150 comic-book titles had annual revenues of over $20 million. Ten years later, in 1950, about 300 comic-book titles were being published with annual revenues of nearly $41 million. The upswing in the next 3 years brought the number of titles to over 650 and the gross to about $90 million.[3] Average monthly circulation jumped from close to 17 million copies in 1940 to 68 million in 1953.

---

[1] This estimate is slightly different from the estimate prepared by the staff of the subcommittee prior to the New York hearings on April 21 and 22, 1954.

[2] See Hearings Before the Subcommittee To Investigate Juvenile Delinquency (Comic Books) of the Committee on the Judiciary, U. S. Senate, 83d Cong., 2d sess., pp. 12–23, Washington: Government Printing Office, 1954.

[3] No accurate figures are available. Many of the newer publishers of comic books do not report to the Audit Bureau of Circulations nor to the Controlled Circulation Audits, the two firms that compile circulation figures. The subcommittee, in making the above estimate, took the most conservative estimate. It assumed that 300,000 copies of each comic-book title were printed, even though information given to the subcommittee indicated that this is a minimum print order and that some print orders are close to the million mark. It was also assumed that one-half of the comic books printed were sold, even though information given was to the effect that the "break-even" point for the average publisher would more likely be closer to 65 percent. And finally it was assumed that one-half of the comic books were published monthly and that the remainder were published bimonthly, even though information furnished by the publishers themselves indicated that more than one-half of the comic books were published monthly. See McNickle, Roma K., Policing the Comics, Editorial Research Reports, 1205 19th St. NW., Washington, D. C., vol. I, 1952, pp. 229–230. See also N. W. Ayer & Son's Directory of Newspapers and Periodicals for the years 1945 through 1953.

In the years between 1945 and 1954, two striking changes took place in the comic-book industry. The first was the great increase in the number of comic books published and the number of firms engaged in their publication. The second was the increased number of comic books dealing with crime and horror and featuring sexually suggestive and sadistic illustrations. This increase of materials featuring brutality and violence is being offered to any child who has the 10-cent purchase price. That these examples of crime and horror are aimed at children is clearly evident from the advertisements with which each issue is replete.

AN OVERVIEW OF THE ORGANIZATION AND OPERATION OF THE COMIC-BOOK INDUSTRY

On first impression, the present comic-book industry would seem to comprise many different publishing firms with no apparent relationship of one to another. On closer scrutiny, however, it is found that the picture is entirely different.

Information obtained by the subcommittee indicates that, while there are 112 seemingly separate and distinct corporations engaged in the publication of comic books, these corporations, through such devices as common-stock holders and officer and family ties, are in actual fact owned and controlled by a relatively small group of men and women. Thus the 676 comic-book titles are published by 111 corporations owned by only 121 persons or families in addition to 1 corporation which has many stockholders.[4]

The majority of these publishers maintain editorial offices in New York City. While the editorial content of comic books is determined in New York City, the actual printing, binding and distribution usually takes place at printing establishments often located in other States and far removed from the editorial offices.

A view of the steps involved in producing and distributing a comic book affords some insight into the problems confronting the industry in determining an editorial content acceptable for reading by children.

While ultimate responsibility for editorial content rests with the publishers, their training and backgrounds vary widely. One, for example, combines publication of comic books with an active law practice. Some publish "girlie" magazines and comic books from the same editorial office. Some publish well-known pocket-size book editions. One man publishes both comic books and the pseudomedical type of sex books. Several include pseudoscience books among their publications. One fact is clearly noted: A background in knowledge of child education and development is not a requisite to becoming a publisher of crime and horror comic books designed for children.

Neither the editor, the script writer nor the artist is required to possess such a background. A majority of the comic-book publishers employ one or more editors. Some also employ writers and artists on a permanent basis, although more frequently they utilize such persons on a free-lance arrangement.

The publisher, and his editor, establish the general theme and tone of a particular comic book. The idea for the story is then conceived by the editor or writer. Once the idea is firmed-up, the writer prepares a short synopsis. This is reviewed by the editor who

[4] Listing of publishers and titles shown on pp. 39–44 of appendix to this report.

directs such changes as he sees fit. In some of the smaller publishing firms, the publisher himself may sit in on this story conference. In the larger firms, the publisher does not attempt detailed review of story content.

After the synopsis is agreed upon, the writer prepares a script which sets forth, panel by panel, the action to be illustrated and dialogue for the "balloons." The editor again reviews the script and indicates the revisions to be made. The artist, following directions in the script, then prepares black and white drawings which are reviewed by the editor who orders such changes as he wants. The drawings are not colored by the original artist, but by other persons in the employ of the publisher, or by the printer under instructions from the editor.

Three or four stories are then grouped together to form a comic book of 32 pages. Not all of these pages contain illustrated stories. Some may be used for advertising space. Others may be used for short stories without illustration for "fan" clubs or correspondence.

The layout for the comic books, complete with original drawings and color scheme, is then sent to the printer according to a prearranged time schedule. Inside pages are printed on "newsprint" and the cover is printed on a slightly heavier, glossy paper. These two operations are sometimes accomplished at different printing plants.

The minimum print order for any one issue of a comic book is approximately 300,000, although press runs of 750,000 for a single issue are not uncommon. The publishers' experience has shown that this minimum is necessary to assure such widespread coverage as will provide the opportunity for sufficient sales to cover costs and, hopefully, result in profits on that particular issue. With 95,000 to 110,000 newsdealers in the country, a press run of 300,000 would put only 3 copies of the comic book on the shelves of each dealer, if evenly distributed.

After an issue of a comic book is printed, the copies are not shipped to the distributor as one might expect, but directly to the local wholesaler. Shipments are made by mail, freight, express, and truck. Such shipments are made by the printing concern at the direction of and in accordance with the instructions supplied by the distributor. The wholesaler then supplies the newsdealer, who is the retailer from whom the public buys.

Virtually every community of appreciable size in the United States has at least one independently owned wholesaler who distributes comic books for one or a number of the independent national distributors. It is estimated the 950 independent wholesalers operate within the United States. In addition, the American News Co. maintains its own 400 company-owned-and-operated branches, in the capacity of wholesale concerns. Moreover, a subsidiary of the American News Co., called the Union News Co., has branches which supply newsstands at railway stations, subways, and some hotels.

If the printer and the wholesaler perform the physical function of distributing comic books, who then is the distributor and what is his role in the total industry picture? Thirteen national distributors handle comic books within the continental United States. Some distributors are also publishers and handle their own publications. Others do not publish but deal with a number of independent publishers. The American News Co. sends materials only to its company-owned wholesalers. The other 12 distributors route materials to independently owned wholesalers.

The distributor is a cross between a financier, a statistician, and a publishers' salesman or representative. His financial function is performed through the advance payments he makes to the publisher. He will often advance up to 25 percent against the final accounting, which will take place (3 or 4 months later) when the total sales of a particular issue can be computed. His statistical function consists of determining those wholesalers to whom a given comic book can most profitably be routed, including the number of copies to be supplied to each. His function as salesman consists of directing "on the road" representatives who seek to maintain satisfactory customer relations with the wholesaler. This agent urges the wholesaler to carry and to push the sales of a larger number of the publications carried by the distributor whom he represents.

The distributor maintains a record for each wholesaler with whom he does business. He lists the title and the issue of each comic book delivered, the quantity shipped, the quantity sold, and the number eventually returned unsold. Future calculations are made on the basis of past performance. As each new issue is prepared, the distributor gages sales possibilities. He then orders a given number of shipping labels bearing the name and address of each wholesaler and the number of copies to be sent to that wholesaler. These labels are delivered to the printer.

Thus the comic book, conceived by the editor and writer, given concrete form by the artist, and put into mass production by the printer on order of the publisher, reaches the business of a wholesaler in a particular area, having been shipped there by the printer under a label prepared by a national distributor. It is now ready for its journey onto the shelves of the newsdealer.

The wholesaler also maintains records as to the sales made by newsdealers serviced by him. On the basis of these records, the wholesaler makes up a bundle for his newsdealers. It is a mixed bundle. It contains a number of copies of each of the comic books he has received for distribution since his last distribution day. The bundle might also contain copies of "girlie" magazines, men's, sports, popular scientific publications, motion picture and television periodicals, and other types of literary, news, and household publications. In other words, the bundle prepared for delivery to the newsdealer can and does run the gamut of many types of magazines, depending on what the wholesaler distributes. The bundle is then delivered by a truckdriver to the retailer who operates a newsstand in a small store, on the street, or in a station, to drugstores, candy stores, and other retail outlets.

The widely diverse assortment of publications, which might be routed by the distributor to the wholesaler and in turn to the retail newsdealer, was shown in the prepared exhibits of some of the magazines distributed by the Kable News Co. These exhibits, which were introduced at the New York hearings, included such titles as: Suppressed, The Facts About Modern Bootlegging, Mysteries, Billy Bunny, Exhibit Homes, Haunted Thrills, Zip, Romance Time, Nifty, Homecraft, Mystery Tales of Horror and Suspense, Picture Scope, Magazine Digest, Masked Ranger, Gala, Danger, Voodoo, The Children's Hour, Wham, Radio-Electronics, Pack O' Fun, Strange

Fantasy, Exclusive, Dare, Frolic, Child Life, Fantastic Fears, Universe, Tops, He, Hunting and Fishing, Danger, and Tab. The covers of many of these publications carried pictures of scantily clad females in suggestive poses. The titles of some of the article as featured on the covers were: "The Lady Is a Man," "All-Year Vacation Home," "Sex Before Marriage," "I Was Forced Into Russia's Fifth Column," "I Sold Myself in the Marriage Racket," "Athletes Are Lousy Sports," "What's New in Transistors," "Babes in Boyland," "The Prodigal Son," "Backstage at Burlesk," "The Smart Drummer," "Rica Rita— Pantie Model," "Angel of the Battlefields," "Sexie Tessie Up North," "Joseph and His Brothers," "Tommy's Bedroom Secret," "Dead End Kids of Space," "Are Bosomy Beauties a Fad?" "Are Vets Freeloading Medical Care?" "Sixty Lady-Killers on the Loose," "Evelyn West vs. Kinsey," "Are Our Churches Really Red?" "The Beauty Is a Witch," "Slaves to Beauty," "Trouble in Morocco," "Court of Immoral Women," "Backlashes? Try Educating Your Thumb," and "Where Bad Girls Make Good."

The newsdealer is charged for the entire contents of the bundle he receives. However, the newsdealer may return the comic books, if they remain unsold, as in the case of other items, and receive credit. The wholesaler may route the returns to other dealers. When it is finally determined that certain returns are not salable, the wholesaler returns them to the distributor, for use in his accounting with the publisher, returning either the comic books themselves or their covers. There is also a practice in the industry of putting groups of returned comic books into thicker books, and reissuing them under a new title and cover for a sale price of 25 cents.

The distributor and the publisher complete their accounting on the basis of the returns—either of the covers or the entire comic books— and payment is made to the publisher for the copies sold. The amount retained by the distributor is a small percentage of the total amount of the sales.

III. The Nature of Crime and Horror Comic Books

It has been pointed out that the so-called crime and horror comic books of concern to the subcommittee offer short courses in murder, mayhem, robbery, rape, cannibalism, carnage, necrophilia, sex, sadism, masochism, and virtually every other form of crime, degeneracy, bestiality, and horror. These depraved acts are presented and explained in illustrated detail in an array of comic books being bought and read daily by thousands of children. These books evidence a common penchant for violent death in every form imaginable. Many of the books dwell in detail on various forms of insanity and stress sadistic degeneracy. Others are devoted to cannibalism with monsters in human form feasting on human bodies, usually the bodies of scantily clad women.

SPECIFIC EXAMPLES OF MATERIAL DEALT WITH AT NEW YORK HEARING

To point out more specifically the type of material being dealt with, a few typical examples of story content and pictures were presented at the New York hearings on April 21, 1954. From the few following examples, it will be clearly seen that the major emphasis of the material then available on America's newsstands from this segment of the comic book industry dealt with depraved violence:

STORY No. 1

BOTTOMS UP (STORY COMICS)

This story has to do with a confirmed alcoholic who spends all his wife can earn on alcohol. As a result their small son is severely neglected. On the day the son is to start in the first grade in school the mother asks the father to escort him to the school building. Instead, the father goes to his favorite bootlegger and the son goes to school by himself. En route the child is struck and killed by an automobile. Informed of the accident, the mother returns home to find her husband gloating over his new supply of liquor. The last four panels show the mother as she proceeds to kill and hack her spouse to pieces with an ax. The first panel shows her swinging the ax, burying the blade in her husband's skull. Blood spurts from the open wound and the husband is shown with an expression of agony. The next panel has a montage effect: the husband is lying on the floor with blood rushing from his skull as the wife is poised over him. She holds the bloody ax, raised for more blows. The background shows an enlargement of the fear-filled eyes of the husband, as well as an enlargement of the bloody ax. To describe this scene of horror the text states that—"And now the silence of the Hendrick's apartment is broken only by the soft humming of Nora as she busies herself with her 'work'." She then cuts his body into smaller pieces and disposes of it by placing the various pieces in the bottles of liquor her husband had purchased. She then returns the liquor to the bootlegger and obtains a refund. As she leaves, the bootlegger says: "*HMMN, funny*! I figured that *rye* would be *inside* Lou by now!" The story ends with the artist admonishing the child readers in a macabre vein with the following paragraph, "*But* if Westlake were to examine the remainder of the case more closely he'd see that it is Lou who is inside the liquor! *Heh, heh*! Sleep well, kiddies!" We then see three of the bottles—one contains an eye, one an ear, and one a finger.

STORY No. 2

FRISCO MARY (ACE COMICS)

This story concerns an attractive and glamorous young woman, Mary, who gains control of a California underworld gang. Under her leadership the gang embarks on a series of holdups marked for their ruthlessness and violence. One of these escapades involves the robbery of a bank. A police officer sounds an alarm thereby reducing the gang's "take" to a mere $25,000. One of the scenes of violence in the story shows Mary poised over the wounded police officer, as he lies on the pavement, pouring bullets into his back from her submachinegun. The agonies of the stricken officer are clearly depicted on his face. Mary, who in this particular scene looks like an average American girl wearing a sweater and skirt and with her hair in bangs, in response to a plea from one of her gang members to stop shooting and flee, states: "We could have got twice as much if it wasn't for this frog-headed rat!!! I'll show him!"

STORY No. 3

WITH KNIFE IN HAND (ATLAS COMICS)

A promising young surgeon begins to operate on wounded criminals in order to gain the money demanded by his spendthrift wife. After he has ruined his professional career by becoming associated with the underworld, a criminal comes to get help for his girl friend who has been shot by the police. In the accompanying panels the girl is placed upon the operating table; the doctor discovers that the criminal's girl friend is none other than his own wife. The scene then shows the doctor committing suicide by plunging a scalpel into his own abdomen. His wife, gasping for help, also dies on the operating table for lack of medical attention. The last scene shows her staring into space, arms dangling over the sides of the operating table. The doctor is sprawled on the floor, his hand still clutching the knife handle protruding from his bloody abdomen. There is a leer on his face and he is winking at the reader, connoting satisfaction at having wrought revenge upon his unfaithful spouse.

Story No. 4

HEAD ROOM (ENTERTAINING COMICS)

The female keeper of a decrepit hotel gives special attention to one of her male boarders. She attempts to win his affection by giving him lower rates, privileges, etc. Since he is in his room only at night, she rents the same room for daytime use to a gruesome-looking man, shown on the first page of the story. There are repeated reports over the radio of a homicidal maniac at large, the "Ripper." She comes to suspect the daytime boarder and is shown searching his room and finding seven gruesome, bloody heads hanging in his closet. Her privileged boarder comes into the room and she tells him of her findings. He is then shown transformed into the gruesome daytime boarder. The last picture shows him as he decapitates her.

Story No. 5

ORPHAN (ENTERTAINING COMICS)

This is the story of a small golden-haired girl named Lucy, of perhaps 8 or 10 years of age, and the story is told in her own words. Lucy hates both her parents. Her father is an alcoholic who beats her when drunk. Her mother, who never wanted Lucy, has a secret boy friend. The only bright spot in Lucy's life is her Aunt Kate with whom she would like to live. Lucy's chance to alter the situation comes when the father, entering the front gate to the home, meets his wife who is running away with the other man, who immediately flees. Snatching a gun from the night table, Lucy shoots and kills her father from the window. She then runs out into the yard and presses the gun into the hands of her mother, who has fainted and lies unconscious on the ground. Then through Lucy's perjured testimony at the following trial, both the mother and her boy friend are convicted of murdering the father and are electrocuted. These are pictures that show, first, "Mommie" and then "Stevie" as they sit strapped to the electric chair as the electric shock strikes them. Other pictures show Lucy's joyous contentment that it has all worked out as she had planned and she is now free to live with her Aunt Kate. The last picture shows her winking at the reader and saying, "* * * which is just the way I'd hoped it would work out when I shot daddy from the front bedroom window with the gun I knew was in the night table and went downstairs and put the gun in mommy's hand and started the crying act."

Story No. 6

HEARTLESS (STORY COMICS)

This is the story of a petty gangster, Bernie Kellog. He is in a cheap, small-town hotel, when he starts to have chest pains and calls a physician. The doctor gives Bernie a drug to calm his nerves. The drug makes Bernie feel like talking and he tells the doctor that he is in the hotel waiting for a woman to bring him $50,000 in blackmail money. He tells the doctor how the woman begged to be "let off the hook" because her husband didn't have that much money. Bernie insists, however, so the woman goes home and commits suicide. As it turns out, the woman, Elaine, is the doctor's wife. One of the pictures then presented shows the doctor sitting dazedly on the edge of the bed * * * And, stretched across the bed, we find Bernie with his heart cut out. Bernie is shown lying dead on the bed with a gaping hole in his chest, a rib protruding, blood flowing over the bed onto the floor, his face fixed in a death mask as he stares at the reader.

Story No. 7

STICK IN THE MUD (STORY COMICS)

An extremely sadistic schoolteacher gives special attention to one of her pupils in order to curry favor with the boy's rich, widowed father. In a year she succeeds in marrying the man, but he turns out to be a miser. She stabs him to death with a butcher knife approximately a foot and a half in length and 3 inches wide. The picture shows the body of the old man, limbs askew, falling to the floor, emitting a gurgle. There is a large hole in his back and blood is squirting in all directions. The wife is behind him clutching the bloody butcher knife. She says: "You stupid old fool! I've stood for your miserly, penny-pinching ways long enough! From now on it'll be my money * * * and I'll spend it my way! Die, Ezra * * * die!" She then covers up her crime by throwing him into a pen with a wild bull that gores his body to pieces. She now has the money, but also the stepson whom she hates. The boy suspects that she killed his father and makes her chase him around the farm by calling her names. He leads her to some quicksand and she falls in. Several pictures show her as she begs the boy to get help. He promises to do so if she confesses to him that she killed his father. She does so, and he then lets her sink to her death. A closeup is shown of the terrified woman, sunk into the quicksand which is flowing into her open mouth. The boy is quite satisfied with himself and walks about the farm humming a tune while others search for his "lost" stepmother.

It is appropriate to point out that these were not the only, nor the worst, pictures and stories gathered by the subcommittee during the investigation. In fact, they constitute a small sampling of the total array of crime and horror comic books available to the youth of this Nation.

METHODS UTILIZED IN CRIME AND HORROR COMICS TO PORTRAY VIOLENCE

Physical acts shown in the foregoing pictures are not the only means for portraying violence in the crime and horror type of comic books. Violence is frequently demonstrated by the type of character, plot, and setting of a story; as well as by the sequence of events and by the language used in the "balloons." The following are a few examples of some of the devices used in the portrayal of violence and horror:

1. Character, plot, and setting

The majority of fantasy stories, which pictorially depicted relatively few physical acts of violence, dealt with supernatural people and events. More frequently the supernatural phenomena involved werewolves, vampires, zombies, witches, people returning from the dead, and animal monsters. Physical violence usually occurred in only 1 or 2 frames. The total extent of violence, however, cannot be measured by counting isolated frames taken out of context. Each frame contributed to the story buildup of horror and suspense.

One method of portraying horror relates supernatural phenomena with real people and things. In this type of story, horror was portrayed by making use of fantastic supernatural powers and by identifying these powers with people and animals that really exist. By association, it is suggested that real policemen may be ghouls who prey on the citizens of a city. The next-door neighbor may be a zombie secretly plotting with other zombies, also neighbors, to take over the world. Ordinary house pets are actually man's enemies awaiting the opportunity to destroy him.

Another resource for portraying horror places supernatural beings, such as werewolves and vampires in highly realistic setting. Therefore, horror is identified not only with real people but also with real situations. An example of this type was pointed out in the hearings by Richard Clendenen, subcommittee executive director. It was the story of a small orphan who was adopted by two individuals ostensibly devoted to the child. After having fattened him up, they entered his room at night, fangs bared, and it is seen that they were vampires. The boy, however, is turned into a werewolf and attacks the two and claws them. Thus, violence and horror are not restricted in comic books to the isolated action shown in each frame. Though there are no frames with physical violence in some instances, a whole story may create horror by its selection of characters, sequence of events and situations.

2. *Language*

Words alone, or in conjunction with pictures, may describe violence and horror more vividly than the graphic techniques. In comic books, language is utilized to contribute to horror in several ways. It may be used to (*a*) stimulate the reader's anticipation of horrible things to come; (*b*) reinforce a belief in supernatural monsters; (*c*) describe desires impossible of being shown graphically; and (*d*) describe killings.

One of the more frequent functions of language in crime comics is to replace graphic portrayals of brutal killings. In such instances the pictures do not show the weapons in contact with the victims, nor are the victims' mangled bodies exposed to the reader. The acts of killing, however, and their effects on the victims are imaginatively described in the texts. The following serves as an illustration of this technique:

A man is shown lifting an ax preparatory to striking his wife on the floor. In the next frame he lowers the ax, the wife is not shown but the caption reads: "Bertha squealed as Norman brought the ax down. The swinging of steel and the thud of the razor-sharp metal against flesh cut the squeal short." In the next frame he holds the ax poised again, the body still is not exposed and the caption reads: "He brought the ax down again and again, hacking, severing, dismembering."

In cases similar to the above, violence is portrayed to the reader by words instead of pictures.

Other symbols are often used to signify violence and horror. The red background of a picture is used as symbolic of blood. This may be noted in the following example:

The caption reads: "His (the victim's) shrieks died to a bubbling moan * * * then a final death rattle. * * * You did not stop swinging the chair until the thing on the floor was a mass of oozing scarlet pulp." No body is shown but the entire frame is colored red.

3. *Sequence*

Another method in which the impressions of horror or violence may be conveyed is by the sequence of events. Stories may be so constructed that each frame stimulates the imagination of the reader up to a shocking climax in the last frame. The sequence may be carried out through the use of words and pictures which, in themselves, are unrelated to horror. One of the more subtle instances where violence was portrayed by neither action, words, nor color, is the following:

The story is about a man who gets entangled in a swamp. One frame shows him in the swamp and a huge vulture circling above the doomed man. The next frame shows the man being carried out on a stretcher with bandages over his eyes.[5]

IV. Crime and Horror Comic Books as a Contributing Factor in Juvenile Delinquency

Inquiring into the relationship of crime and horror comic books to juvenile delinquency, the subcommittee approached this question without preconceived convictions. It was not assumed that comic

---

[5] Acknowledgment for this section on methods of portraying violence in comic books is due Mrs. Marilyn Graalfs of the department of sociology of the University of Washington who prepared A Survey of Comic Books in the state of Washington (mimeographed), Seattle, 1954. This was a report made to the Washington State Council for Children and Youth, having been prepared in cooperation with the research and statistics section of the department of public institutions.

books are a major cause of juvenile delinquency. On the other hand, care was taken to avoid stating categorically that these crime and horror comic books have no effect in aggravating the problem.

However, there are many who accept the idea of the cause and effect relationship between comic-book reading by children and antisocial behavior. Many judges have pointed to crime and horror comic books and have cited cases of children who have explained their delinquent acts by claiming they got the ideas from such comic books. This kind of evidence is largely discounted by the behavioral scientists, who point out that children can hardly be expected to understand their own behavior, much less explain it. A child may ascribe his behavior to a comic he has read, but such explanations without substantiating findings can scarcely be considered scientific evidence of causation.

The behavioral sciences are as yet far from exact. Therefore, it is not surprising to note some diversity of opinion even among experts in the fields of criminology, psychology and sociology. Responsible observers of the American social pattern are in general agreement that juvenile delinquency has many causes, not just one.

Today there are many who consider themselves experts who persist in explaining all delinquency solely as a product of personality maladjustment, while at the other extreme, there are those who find the influence of the slum to be the source of all the difficulties. Others point solely to the influence of crime and horror comic books. These people overlook the fact that no one personality trait or social background distinguishes delinquent children. The endless variations of circumstance, opportunity, and personal history must be taken into account. When doing this, it is necessary to determine the effects in each case of all the contributing factors.

A study of crime and horror comic books should consider their effects upon children in the total setting of the child's behavior pattern. It was the concern of the subcommittee to inquire into expert opinion of the relationship between this material and the delinquent behavior of children who are (a) considered to be emotionally stable and (b) those thought of as emotionally maladjusted. The following is a brief summary of professional opinion in which the attempt is made to reflect some of the divergencies where they exist:

CRIME AND HORROR COMICS AND THE WELL-ADJUSTED AND NORMALLY
LAW-ABIDING CHILD

Attention has been given by some experts to the influence of crime and horror comics on well-adjusted children who normally are not in conflict with society. Majority opinion seems inclined to the view that it is unlikely that the reading of crime and horror comics would lead to delinquency in a well-adjusted and normally law-abiding child.

A different view is held by Dr. Frederic Wertham, consulting psychiatrist, Department of Hospitals, New York City. He maintains that it is primarily the "normal" child upon whom the comics have their greatest detrimental effects, and thus it is this type of individual who is "tempted" and "seduced" into imitating the crime portrayed in the story. Dr. Wertham has been termed the "leading crusader against comics." Although stating that he does not adhere to a single factor theory of delinquency causation, he does attribute a large portion of juvenile offenses to the comics.[6]

A critique of the position that has been held by Dr. Wertham for many years is found in an article by Prof. Frederic M. Thrasher entitled, "The Comics and Delinquency: Cause or Scapegoat." This article, which appeared in 1949, pointed to alleged weaknesses in Dr. Wertham's approach, the major one being that his propositions are not supported by adequate research data.[7] Professor Thrasher asserted that Dr. Wertham's major claims rest upon a selected group of extreme cases. Although Dr. Wertham has since declared that his conclusions are based upon a study of thousands of children, he has not offered the statistical details of his study. He says that he used control groups, i. e., compared his groups of delinquents with a similar group of nondelinquents, but he has not described the groups to prove that the difference in incidence of comic-book reading is other than a selective process. In conclusion, Professor Thrasher writes:

* * * it may be said that no acceptable evidence has been produced by Wertham or anyone else for the conclusion that the reading of comic magazines has, or has not, a significant relation to delinquent behavior.

A summarization of Professor Thrasher's contention is, that in 1949, the case against comic books had not been proved pro or con. His presentation points out the need for more study and research on that subject which has not yet been done.

CRIME AND HORROR COMICS MAY APPEAL TO AND THUS GIVE SUPPORT AND SANCTION TO ALREADY EXISTING ANTISOCIAL TENDENCIES

Dr. Harris Peck, director of the bureau of mental health services for the New York City Court of Domestic Relations, indicated in his testimony that there is a possible relationship of crime and horror comic books to juvenile delinquency through appealing to and thus giving support and sanction to already existing antisocial tendencies.[8] While pointing out that it is unlikely that comic books are a primary cause of juvenile delinquency, he stated that it should not be overlooked that certain comic books may aid and abet, as it were, delinquent behavior which has been set in motion by other forces already operating on the child. Dr. Harris has also noted the preoccupation with comics of many delinquents with whom he has come in contact. This observation should be weighed with reference to the fact that there are many nondelinquents who are avid comic-book readers.

It is appropriate that a distinction be made between the "emotionally maladjusted" delinquent to which reference has been made and the "normally adjusted" delinquent. It is quite possible for an individual to be both socially and psychologically adjusted within his own group of delinquent companions. While the group may commit acts of delinquency and be completely out of joint with society as a whole, the individual members may have the same normal feelings and needs as members of a law-abiding group of the same age. Therefore, even though these delinquent youths are deemed emotionally stable,

[6] See Wertham, Frederic, Seduction of the Innocent, New York; 1954.
[7] Thrasher, Frederic M., The Comics and Delinquency: Cause or Scapegoat, in The Journal of Educational Sociology, December 1949, pp. 195–205.
[8] See Peck, Harris, testimony in hearings before the Subcommittee To Investigate Juvenile Delinquency of the Committee on the Judiciary, U. S. Senate, 83d Cong., 2d sess., pp. 63–69, Washington: Government Printing Office 1954.

the content of crime comic books may coincide with the attitudes and values of the group and give support to the group's delinquent activities.

This leads to the conclusion that in both the "emotionally abnormal" and the "emotionally normal" delinquent, the contents of crime and horror comic books may become a part of the youth's total experience and operate as another of the many supports of antisocial behavior present today in our society.

There exists a minority opinion that suggests a possible cathartic effect can be achieved by reading about or looking at a violent action; that is, a period of calm, or relaxation results. The possibility was suggested that this effect may become desirable for certain individuals and may develop into a mechanism by which they can relieve everyday tensions which cannot otherwise be coped with satisfactorily. However, even among authorities in the field of child development who agree that such material does have a cathartic effect, some believe that the same kind of effect might be achieved more safely through other means for the vicarious expression of aggression.

TECHNIQUES OF CRIME ARE TAUGHT BY CRIME AND HORROR COMICS

Another aspect of the contribution of comic books to juvenile delinquency, in the opinion of a number of experts, was the indication that the more serious forms of delinquency incorporate knowledge of specific techniques which many comic books provide. This was considered to be another valid criticism of comic books, i. e., they offer juveniles a comprehensive written and pictorial presentation of both methods and techniques of criminal activities. Dr. Robert H. Felix, director of the National Institute of Mental Health, attributed this negative feature to comic books when he wrote:

They might well be instructive in the techniques of criminal activity and of the avoidance of detection.[9]

Offering an example of this practice of teaching crime techniques via crime through comic books, Dr. Wertham testified:

* * * I had no idea how one would go about stealing from a locker in Grand Central, but I have comic books which describe that in minute detail and I could go out now and do it.

Dr. Wertham was the first psychiatrist to call attention of the American people to crime and horror comics. It is incontrovertible that he has exerted far-reaching influence through alerting parents' and citizens' groups to the extent of bestiality and depravity being dispensed to children through such comics.

Content analysis of crime comics by the subcommittee indicated that in most instances the crimes as portrayed in these books were committed with little finesse or imagination. Guns were the most frequent weapon for murder. "Holdups," safeblowing and payroll seizures were among the methods employed in robberies. However, there were stories in which utilization was made of the following: lead pipes, kitchen knives, wet rawhide belts (tied around a man's neck to dry in the sun, thereby shrinking and strangling him), whips, hot coffee thrown in a person's face, wrenches, jagged edges of bottles,

⁹ Hearings before the Subcommittee To Investigate Juvenile Delinquency Comic Book of the Committee on the Judiciary, U. S. Senate, 83d Cong., 2d sess., p. 11, Washington: Government Printing Office 1954.

and acid (for "melting a person's face"). In a few stories more sophisticated methods of crime were described. For example, it was explained that it is easier to pick pockets in a cafeteria because "a man hesitates to drop a tray of food to see if his pockets have been picked"; and it was suggested that tires can be stolen from one junkyard and sold to another.

CRIMINAL CAREERS ARE GLAMORIZED IN CRIME AND HORROR COMIC BOOKS

A number of impressions were obtained from reading how the criminal moves in his cultural pattern as depicted by the crime comics. For example, crime may have brought wealth and fame even though it was sometimes temporary. Large monetary rewards from crime were shown through scenes of cash being counted or money being spent on luxurious living. Through committing bizarre crimes, individuals became widely known figures and sometimes they became idols, eulogized through the publicity accorded them in the newspapers. Many of the stories included texts which described the sensation experienced by a killer. Killing was described as the means of acquiring a high degree of self-confidence, giving the individual a feeling of strength and power. A highly pleasing physical sensation was also described as resulting from killing.

Some stories in comic books showed that membership in the criminal underworld was dependent upon certain personal characteristics highly valued by experienced criminals. These attributes were mainly physical. Criminals were admired for their "toughness," their hatred for "cops" and a willingness to commit any type of crime regardless of the risk involved. In their interpersonal relationships, comic-book criminals never exhibited such human virtues as consideration of others, charity and the like. Furthermore, to reinforce the behavior expected of the potential criminal, names suggestive of toughness were assigned to him.

In some of the stories, murder for revenge was justified under certain conditions. The murderers were not apprehended and there was no suggestion that they would be taken in custody at a future date. The end of the criminal's career came about, if at all, through chance factors or by superhuman beings or other ideal types. As the latter two do not exist in reality, the obvious interpretation from these stories is that crime does pay if one is ruthless and clever to a sufficient degree.

However, defenders and hired apologists for the crime and horror comic books constantly point out that in the majority of crime and horror comics, the villain came to a well-deserved end.

DEFENDERS OF LAW AND ORDER FREQUENTLY REPRESENTED AS ALL-POWERFUL BEINGS WHO KILL AND COMMIT OTHER CRIMES TO DEFEND "JUSTICE"

There were a number of comics of the type which pictured the hero as some sort of supernatural being always impervious to any physical harm. In these comic books the crime was always real and the superhuman's triumph over good was unreal. Commenting on this, Dr. Wertham singled out the superman comic books as being injurious to the ethical development of children. Dr. Wertham believes these books arouse phantasies of sadistic joy in seeing other people repeatedly punished while the hero remains immune. He called this the superman complex. Another witness referred to this idea when she gave examples of institutionalized children injuring themselves by jumping off high places in attempts to fly like the comic-book characters.

Members of the subcommittee believe that in this respect content of the comic books can be criticized. In many crime comics, law and order are maintained by supernatural and superhuman heroes, and officers of the law, ineffective in apprehending criminals, must depend on aid from fantastic characters. The law-enforcement officials who do solve cases often succeed through "accidental events." In contrast, actual law-enforcement officials are at a disadvantage in terms of prestige and the small part they play in apprehending criminals. The impressions obtained from the comic books are contrary to the methodical routine work characteristic of police investigation.

Discussing the ethical content of comic books, Dr. Wertham took to task the oft-reiterated statement that in these books good wins over evil and that law and order always win in the end.[10] He pointed out that there are whole comic books in which every single story ends with the triumph of evil, with a perfect crime unpunished and actually glorified.

EXCESSIVE READING OF CRIME AND HORROR COMICS IS CONSIDERED SYMPTOMATIC OF EMOTIONAL PATHOLOGY

Surveying the work that has been done on the subject, it appears to be the consensus of the experts that comic-book reading is not the cause of emotional maladjustment in children. Although comic-book reading can be a symptom of such maladjustment, the emotionally disturbed child because of abnormal needs may show a greater tendency to read books of this kind than will the normal child. This theory appears as valid as the thinking that alcoholism is a symptom of an emotional disturbance rather than its cause.

It has also been suggested that the child with difficulties may find in comic books representations of the kinds of problems with which he is dealing, and that comic books will, therefore, have a value for him which they do not have for a child who is relatively free of these troubles. Further, it is stated that the kinds of comic books a child chooses often provides the child psychiatrist with some clues to the kinds of problems faced by the child.

NEED EXISTS FOR MORE SPECIFIC RESEARCH TO FULLY ASCERTAIN THE POSSIBLE EFFECTS OF THIS TYPE OF READING MATERIAL UPON CHILDREN

Although the inquiry revealed the marked differences of opinion among experts, the need for careful, large-scale research studies was repeatedly made apparent. Samples of crime and horror comics were sent to Carl H. Rush, Jr., Ph.D., executive assistant of the American Psychological Association, and to Dr. R. H. Felix, Director of the

---

[10] It should be pointed out that there are innumerable stories of this nature. But in stories containing 32 picture panels, the criminal often lived splendidly off the fruits of his crimes. It is not until the last panel that he met his doom at the hands of a fantasy character or by some stupid mistake.

National Institute of Mental Health, so that they could study them and give their professional opinions as to the possible effects this type of reading material might have on children. Both of these individuals commented upon the need for scientific research in this field.

The few approaches already taken and the reasons for the scarcity of sound findings on this topic have been indicated by Dr. Rush.[11] It is evident from his brief summary of some studies in this topic area that research has been concerned with segmental aspects of the problem. Juvenile delinquency is a developmental problem and for that reason research should be conducted on a longitudinal basis in which the subjects of the investigation are examined periodically over a span of several years. Research of this type is beyond the means of individual investigators. The financial support of a foundation or institution is required if the scope of study is to be adequate.

There can be little question that research is much needed on these problems. If we are to fully understand the impact of crime and horror comic books upon the behavior of normal and emotionally disturbed children, a broad program of research must be undertaken and means for its support must be provided. Furthermore, it seems desirable that such research be but one of a number of controlled studies, each to be directed to one of the facets of the problem of juvenile delinquency. The influence of comic books is but one aspect of a larger program which has as its ultimate objective the determination of the multiple causes of juvenile delinquency.

V. Other Questionable Aspects of Comic Books

Considerable concern has been expressed regarding the type of advertising often carried in comic books. The responses by children to such ads sometimes results in the development of mailing lists that are later rented to other concerns for the direct-mail solicitation of such children for the purchase of salacious materials.

WEAPONS AND PSEUDOMEDICAL NOSTRUMS ADVERTISED IN COMIC BOOKS DESIGNED FOR CHILDREN

Among the more objectionable advertisements that came to the attention of the subcommittee was a full-page advertisement, labeled "Sportsman's Paradise," operated by a concern listing a New York address, which shows a variety of weapons that may be purchased by mail order. Several might be a threat to the safety of children. Although one line of the coupon reads, "Note: Not sold to minors under 17, state age," it is needless to say that no real proof of age was required.

The illustrations in the advertisement introduced at the New York hearings showed at least 10 dangerous articles that would appeal to a minor, ranging from a powerful hunting crossbow, a throwing dagger and a "fireball" slingshot, to a .22-caliber automatic (not available to New York residents) and an army training rifle. Their descriptions leave little for the imagination. For example, "Oriental battle knife— designed for long-distance throwing, it is made to *split a board at 30*

---

[11] Rush, Carl H., letter in hearings before the Subcommittee To Investigate Juvenile Delinquency Comic Book of the Committee of the Judiciary, U. S. Senate, 83d Cong., 2d sess., pp. 162–164, Washington: Government Printing Office, 1954.

feet and is *balanced to stick* * * *"; "Commando knife—real 'Commando' weapon. An all-metal, *needle-pointed, razor-sharp* 12-inch knife that *may save your life* * * *"; the " 'Fireball' slingshot—silent, sweet shooting. Extra powerful—you get that 'feel of accuracy' with your first shots * * *"; "Throwing dagger. An exciting sport that provides fun and thrills—indoors or outdoors. This knife is light in weight and expertly balanced to stick. Tempered steel blade with double bevel edges * * *"; "Arrow sling gun. A new thrill in hunting. Powerful sling gun sends 12-inch metal-tipped arrows through metal-guide barrel to 300-inch range. Swift. Silent. Accurate. Kills all small game. Five arrows included * * *"; or "Finnish hunting knife, handmade in Finland. Richly engraved blade with deep blood grooves. Flashy horse-head handle * * *."

Numerous pseudomedical advertisements in comic books and love magazines are aimed at the teen-ager's desire to glorify his personal appearance or to improve his physique through easy measures: a tablet to put on weight; a tablet or chewing gum to take off weight; hair and scalp formula; skin cleanser or treatment for pimples; an electrically operated "spot reducer"; a course of exercises to develop muscles.

An example in point is the advertisement of Kelpidine chewing gum, supposedly useful in enabling one to reduce weight. Sales of the article are essentially conducted by mail order. The Post Office Department advised the subcommittee that it has been interested in this product for some time. Examination and analysis of Kelpidine chewing gum by the Food and Drug Administration indicated that it consists essentially of small squares of chewing gum containing a small amount of powdered kelp (seaweed). The presence of the kelp ingredient has no particular significance in the article, and there was found no reason to believe it was harmful. On the other hand, there was found no valid reason for concluding that the article has any particular effectiveness for enabling one to reduce weight—the primary representation on which it is offered for sale.

Action has been taken by the Federal Trade Commission against some of the concerns making false advertising claims. In a number of instances the Food and Drug Administration has taken exception to the labeling of a product. Nor are the prices of these temptingly advertised goods within comfortable reach of youth in the deteriorated areas of large cities where certain types of crime and horror comics are most often found.

MISUSE OF MAILING LISTS COMPILED THROUGH COMIC-BOOK ADVERTISEMENTS

Many business firms making sales by direct mail obtain the names and addresses of persons from lists which are purchased from brokers who have in turn secured these lists from still other mail-order houses. A firm wishing to sell auto seat covers might be interested in purchasing a mailing list of people who had made mail-order purchases of auto compasses.

Attention has been called to the fact that juveniles in this country receive large quantities of direct-mail advertising for salacious and sexually stimulating materials. In some instances it has been pointed out that such advertising was received following a youngster's response to an advertisement appearing in a comic book.

The Post Office Department informed the subcommittee that the mails had been used to advertise and sell a book entitled "The Illustrated Encyclopedia of Sex," by Dr. A. Willy and others; of 297 complaints received over a period dating from April 1951, 93 concerned mailings to minors. Although the book was not considered obscene, the methods of advertising by the publisher included blaring advertisements in numerous magazines, showing pictures of scantily clad young women in sexually provocative poses.

Parents from many States complained to the subcommittee that teen-age sons, daughters, and friends had received advertisements which flagrantly describe obscene material. In the New York investigation it was discovered that Samuel Roth, who for many years has been engaged in using the mails to advertise lewd and lascivious printed materials, had purchased mailing lists that contained the names of many teen-agers. Roth refused to testify before the subcommittee, claiming his rights under the fifth amendment to the Constitution.

It was found that Roth purchased 136,567 names and addresses from Robert B. Vallon of the Mapleton Service Co. Many of those names were obtained through correspondence with comic-book readers. A sample circular, mailed out by Roth to a 16-year-old high-school student, advertised such books as Wild Passion, Wanton by Night, Waterfront Hotel, and The Shame of Oscar Wild, all of which have been declared nonmailable under the postal obscenity law. Roth's advertisements also carried descriptions of "seven books of pleasure and sexual excitement calculated to keep you on blissful heights for days and days. * * *"

The development of mailing lists and their sale is now a large-scale practice. Members of the subcommittee expressed concern that some purveyors of salacious literature may deliberately seek to secure mailing lists of juveniles for direct-mail solicitation. One publisher, Alex Segal, testified that "by mistake" one of his trays of addressograph plates bearing the names of 400 children was routed to the publisher of sex literature. Segal himself advertises and sells a book called How to Hypnotize—A Master Key to Hypnotism. This advertisement appeared in Quality Comics and portrayed a male looking at a young female with the caption "Want the thrill of imposing your will on someone? Stravon Publishers will tell you how." Upon receipt of the book on hypnotism, a child also received a list of other purchasable material—including sex literature. Advertisements of such nature have been received by juveniles as young as 9 years old.

This matter has been under study by the subcommittee, and we have called it to the attention of the Attorney General, the Postmaster General, and the Committees on Post Office and Civil Service of the Senate and the House. If such actions constitute violation of the laws dealing with the mails to offer for sale obscene, lewd, lascivious, or filthy material, when consideration is given to the fact the offer is being made to persons of immature years, then we are at a loss to understand why something has not been done to apprehend the offenders. If the existing statutes are found to be inadequate to meet this situation, a study will be made to determine what changes will be necessary in existing legislation to prohibit such practices.

To summarize, although some of the advertising in comic books is of acceptable standards, many advertisements are directed toward the

sale of articles that are potentially harmful to children, or are fraudulent in that the articles are unable to effect the physical changes
claimed. Because of the manner in which mailing lists are sold, some
juveniles who have answered advertisements appearing in comic books
have been solicited by publishers of obscene or salacious materials.
The question has been raised regarding the responsibility publishers
of comic books should assume for protecting their young readers, both
from the wrong kind of advertising and from any misuse of resulting
mailing lists which might accrue through the acceptance of advertising
from other than reliable firms.

THE EXPORTATION OF CRIME AND HORROR COMIC BOOKS

It has been repeatedly affirmed that the comic book, native product
of the United States, is provoking discussion in other countries.
Many Americans have expressed indignation over the influence these
books may have upon the children and young adults in other parts of
the world.

Some hold the view that there is no way in which we could give the
young people abroad a more unfavorable and distorted view of American values, aspirations, and cultural pattern than through crime and
horror comics. The destructive potentials of the comic book must be
recognized both within our domestic society and in consideration of our
relationship to peoples abroad. Publishers of undesirable comic books
should be made aware of the negative effects these books may exert
upon the thinking and conduct of persons who read them throughout
the world and of the deplorable impression of the United States gained
through their perusal.

Several considerations stem from the impact of the comic books
abroad. They are:

1. Information gathered by United States Department of State
personnel in many countries reveals public concern over the spread of
crime and horror comic book reading. As far as can be ascertained
by the subcommittee, concern has been expressed in almost every
European country over the problem posed by the introduction of
American comics, or comics of that pattern, since World War II.

2. Crime and horror comic books introduce to foreign cultures a
lowered intellectual milieu. Detective and wierd stories, American
style, present a hardened version of killing, robbery, and sadism.

3. Comic books are distributed in many countries where the population is other than Caucasian. Materials depicting persons of other
races as criminals may have meanings and implications for persons of
another race which were unforeseen by the publisher.

4. There is evidence that comic books are being utilized by the
U. S. S. R. to undermine the morale of youth in many countries by
pointing to crime and horror as portrayed in American comics as one
of the end results of the most successful capitalist nation in the world.

In Great Britain, where importation of comic books is restricted
because of limitations on dollar exchange, comic books are published
locally from United States copy or stereotypes. An example of
British thought on comic books was expressed on July 17, 1952, in the
House of Commons when American style comics were the subject of
pointed criticism. Mr. Maurice Edelman, of the Labor Party, asserted:

It is perfectly true that they were brought to this country in the first instance
by American forces. They were widely read by American troops, but very rapidly

it was found by publishers * * * that there was a considerable market for this type of horror and sadistic literature; literature which glorifies the brute, literature which undermines the law simply because it suggests that the superman is the person who should take the law into his own hands and mete out justice in his own way. The most sinister thing about these publications is that they introduce the element of pleasure into violence. They encourage sadism; and they encourage sadism in association with an unhealthy sexual stimulation.

Other members of the House of Commons who were present and participating in the debate referred to "the crude and alien idiom to which all of us take exception"; to the "anxiety among the parents of this country"; and to the "emphasis upon violence as such."

Repeated recommendations have been made in various parts of the United Kingdom either to prohibit comic books of this sort or to establish a semiofficial advisory group to provide guidance to parents and teachers regarding this type of printed matter.

A Communist magazine, printed in East Germany and devoted to bitter criticism of the United States, appeared under the name, "USA im Wort und Bild" (USA in Word and Picture). The publication ridicules comic books and similar American attempts to present the classics in simple form. Some of the phrases read:

Shakespeare in Yankee dialect is the latest "cultural triumph" * * *. The "cultural" achievement of the publishers is expressed on the jacket of the pamphlet: "You can quote the best quotations of Shakespeare and impress your friends, without reading the play."

One example of racial antagonism resulting from the distribution of American-style comic books in Asia is cited by the former United States Ambassador to India, Chester Bowles, in his recent book, Ambassador's Report. He reports on page 297 the horrified reaction of an Indian friend whose son had come into possession of an American comic book entitled The Mongol Blood-Suckers. Ambassador Bowles describes the comic book as depicting a—

superman character struggling against half-human, colored Mongolian tribesmen who had been recruited by the Communists to raid American hospitals in Korea and drink the plasma in the blood banks. In every picture they were portrayed with yellow skins, slanted eyes, hideous faces, and dripping jaws.

At the climax of the story, their leader summoned his followers to an attack on American troops. "Follow me, blood drinkers of Mongolia," he cried. "Tonight we dine well of red nectar." A few panels later he is shown leaping on an American soldier with the shout, "One rip at the throat, red blood spills over white skins. And we drink deep." Ambassador Bowles commented:

The Communist propagandists themselves could not possibly devise a more persuasive way to convince color sensitive Indians that Americans believe in the superior civilization of people with white skins, and that we are indoctrinating our children with bitter racial prejudice from the time they learn to read.[12]

Soviet propaganda cites the comic book in support of its favorite anti-American theme—the degeneracy of American culture. However, comic books are but one of a number of instruments used in Soviet propaganda to illustrate this theme. The attacks are usually supported with examples drawn from the less-desirable American motion pictures, television programs, literature, drama, and art.

It is represented in the Soviet propaganda that the United States crime rate, particularly the incidence of juvenile delinquency, is largely incited by the murders, robberies, and other crimes portrayed

---

[12] Bowles, Chester, Ambassador's Report, New York, 1954, p. 297.

in "trash literature." The reason such reading matter is distributed, according to that propaganda, is that the "imperialists" use it to condition a generation of young automatons who will be ready to march and kill in the future wars of aggression planned by the capitalists.

VI. COMIC BOOKS AS A MEDIUM OF COMMUNICATION

Crime and horror comic books constitute but a segment, although quite a substantial segment, of the total comic-book industry in the United States. There are some publishers in this field who have not produced crime and horror comic books and do not intend to do so. The members of the subcommittee were particularly interested in certain aspects of the industry which relate to communication, education, and public opinion. In those areas, it appears that there are possibilities for positive contributions.

Joseph W. Musial, educational director of the National Cartoonists Society, testified as a witness on the use of comics in informational programs. Appearing with Musial before the subcommittee were Walt Kelly, president of the National Cartoonists Society, and Milton Caniff, artist. They pointed to the widespead adaptation of cartoons and comics as a medium of communication. They spoke of contributions the artists in their society had made in the public interest, and presented several exhibits of materials prepared for this purpose.

Mr. Musial in an article described the increasing use of comic books in communicating messages in public relations. According to him the techniques used in the comics are especially suited to exert such mass appeal:

> So packed with condensed presentation is the cartoon, that, although physically static, it may be said to be in motion a highly specialized art, it suggests movement, evokes hordes of other images, tells a story. It tells not of *a* man but of *men;* not of *a* wedding or *a* picnic or *a* fear or *an* appetite, but of weddings, picnics, fears, appetites *in general.* Employing a tremendously painstaking, exacting art of its own, the cartoon "hits home" to everyone because its topic and situation are grasped at once by all who view it. Unlike literal illustration, the cartoon employs exaggerated measurements and actions and values, and presents not only truth but universal, recognizable, appreciable truth. Universal truth is transformed by the cartoon into universal appeal, and thus the success of the cartoon is accounted for.[13]

Mr. Musial, Mr. Kelly, and Mr. Caniff, presenting the view of the National Cartoonists Society, offered a rather convincing case for the subtlety and humaneness of the deft cartoon or comic strip. They pointed out that the comic-book artist is usually not at the top of his career, but generally a beginner in the field. Mr. Kelly asserted that the code of the society[14] precluded from membership any artist who produces indecent or obscene matter or in any way proves himself to be an objectionable citizen.

The consensus is that the comic art has genuine appeal for a large segment of the American public. It is apparent that comic books have assumed major importance in the reading diet of thousands of American youths. For that reason, it is important that the artwork be of a high level. Although the cartoonists are not responsible for the accompanying script, it should measure up to some standards. Mr.

---

[13] Musial, J. W., in Public Relations Journal, November 1951.
[14] The text of the code of the National Cartoonists Society appears on p. 35 of the appendix of this report.

Kelly pledged the Cartoonists Society to continually improving their own material, but the society—

views as unwarranted any additional legislative action that is intended to censor printed material.

One of the objections that has been made repeatedly to comic books is that they contribute to limiting the reading ability and the reading experience of a vast portion of our youthful population. This thought was dealt with by Robert Warshow in a recent article. He said:

* * * We are left above all with the fact that for many thousands of children comic books, whether bad or "good," represent virtually their only contact with culture. There are children in the schools of our large cities who carry knives and guns. There are children who reach the last year of high school without ever reading a single book. Even leaving aside the increase in juvenile crime there seem to be larger numbers of children than ever before who, without going over the line into criminality, live almost entirely in a juvenile underground largely out of touch with the demands of social responsibility, culture, and personal refinement, and who grow up into an unhappy isolation where they are sustained by little else but the routine of the working day, the unceasing clamor of television and the jukeboxes, and still, in their adult years, the comic books. This is a very fundamental problem; to blame the comic books, as Dr. Wertham does, is simple minded. But to say that the comics do not contribute to the situation would be like denying the importance of the children's classics and the great European novels in the development of an educated man.[15]

After hearing the presentation of Mr. Musial, Mr. Kelly, and Mr. Caniff to the effect that government and private agencies and philanthropic organizations have recognized the comic book as an effective medium of communication for worthwhile objectives, it is apparent too that the comic book can also be an effective medium for unworthy objectives. The comic book is recognized as a means of publicizing crime and horror. There was no plausible reason offered as to why this medium should be less impressive when dealing with one kind of subject matter than with another.

VII. WHERE SHOULD RESPONSIBILITY FOR POLICING CRIME AND HORROR COMIC BOOKS REST?

The subcommittee believes that this Nation cannot afford the calculated risk involved in the continued mass dissemination of crime and horror comic books to children.

Where does the responsibility rest for preventing the distribution of such materials?

With the comic book industry?

With the parents, assisted by educational campaigns of civic organizations?

With governmental censorship either at the Federal, State, or local levels?

COMIC BOOKS AND AUTHORITY

The subcommittee flatly rejects all suggestions of governmental censorship as being totally out of keeping with our basic American concepts of a free press operating in a free land for a free people.

Canadian experience seems to indicate the futility of such an approach. Evidence introduced during the subcommittee's hearings indicated that in 1949 the Canadian Parliament passed a law making it an offense to print, publish, or sell a crime comic.[16] According to

[15] Warshow, Robert; Paul, The Horror Comics and Dr. Wertham, in Commentary, June 1954.
[16] See Hearings Before the Subcommittee To Investigate Juvenile Delinquency (Comic Books) of the Committee on the Judiciary, U. S. Senate, 83d Cong., 2d sess., p. 256, Washington: Government Printing Office, 1954.

the Honorable E. D. Fulton, member of the Canadian House of Commons, within a year or so following the enactment of the Canadian legislation, the crime comic as such almost completely disappeared from Canadian newsstands. Into the void poured such a flood of love, sex, and girlie magazines that the Canadian Senate established a special committee to look into the sale and distribution of salacious literature.

After a bit, however, there crept into Canada the crime comic in its original form. It also began to appear in an alternative form, i. e., the horror comic. Mr. Fulton ascribed many reasons for the reappearance on the Canadian newsstands of crime and horror comics, despite the criminal statute: inability to reach a major publisher for prosecution since they are, in the main, in the United States; relaxation of public vigilance so that there was no longer the constant supervision of newsstands to pick out offensive publications and bring them to the attention of the authorities and demand prosecution; and, inability and unwillingness of customs officials to act as censors.

Legislation has been enacted by three States, New York, New Jersey, and Idaho, to prohibit what is known as tie-in sales practices. There was testimony before the subcommittee that some newsdealers handle crime and horror comic books because they fear they will be penalized by the wholesaler if they refuse to do so. This penalty frequently takes the form of withholding more popular periodicals from the newsdealer who refuses to sell crime and horror comics or other objectionable publications. Evidence heard by the subcommittee indicated that such practices are geographically widespread but scattered.

Testimony was also presented to the subcommittee that these restrictive practices did not exist.

It was suggested to the subcommittee that Federal legislation prohibiting tie-in sales on all printed matter involved in interstate commerce would be of marked assistance. However, while the subcommittee is of the opinion that such a Federal statute is not needed at this time, this matter has been brought to the attention of the Attorney General to determine if the charges of tie-in sales, if substantiated, constitute violations of the antitrust laws as presently enacted.

RESPONSIBILITY OF PARENTS, ASSISTED BY CITIZEN GROUPS

There is no doubt that much can and has been accomplished toward eliminating crime and horror comic books from newsstands through vigorous citizen action in local communities. Children can be guided away from the purchase of crime and horror stories. Complaints directed to the vendor and wholesaler, if repeated, will frequently result in the removal of particular publications from the newsstands.

Effective steps of this nature have been taken in several parts of the United States. For example, the citizens of Hartford, Conn., spurred on by the Hartford Courant, have been successful in cleaning up the newsstands of their city. Another example of effective citizen action was the formation several years ago in Cincinnati, Ohio, of a committee on evaluation of comic books.[17] Its purpose is to make a

---

[17] See evaluations of comic books by that committee in Hearings Before the Subcommittee To Investigate Juvenile Delinquency (Comic Books) of the Committee on the Judiciary, United States Senate, 83d Cong., 2d sess., pp. 36–53, Washington: Government Printing Office, 1954.

study of comics in the spring of each year, and to pass on findings to parents. The Cincinnati committee points out that more than 80 prominent citizens are members of the committee. It publishes an annual list of comic books, together with a rating of each comic.

William M. Gaines, publisher of Entertaining Comics Group, ridiculed the efforts of parents' groups to restrain their children from reading crime and horror comics. Gaines, who published some of the most sadistic crime and horror comic books with monstrosities that nature has been incapable of, issued a page which was reprinted with the testimony from the New York hearings.[18] Under the heading, "Are You a Red Dupe?" Gaines prints the story of Melvin Blizunken-Skovitchsky, who lived in Soviet Russia and printed comic books, but some people did not believe that other persons possessed sufficient intelligence to decide what they wanted to read. Consequently, the secret police came, smashed poor Melvin's four-color press and left Melvin hanging from a tree. Gaines' message at the end reads:

So the next time some joker gets up at a PTA meeting, or starts jabbering about "the naughty comic books" at your local candy store, give him the once-over. We are not saying he is a Communist. He may be a dupe. He may not even read the Daily Worker. It is just that he's swallowed the Red bait—hook, line and sinker.

The subcommittee does not ridicule such efforts. It believes that parents have a full measure of responsibility for the reading material reaching their children and that civic organizations can do a worthy job by calling the attention of parents to those materials offered for children's reading that fall below the American standard of decency by glorifying crime, horror, and sadism.

The tempter of children cannot excuse his attempts to gain personal wealth through disregard of cultural values by crying that the parents should have been more vigilant. The simple fact remains that all this constant vigilance on the part of parents and civic organizations would not have been necessary if the persons responsible for producing and distributing comic books had exercised that measure of self-restraint and common decency which the American people have a right to expect from an industry aiming its product so largely at the young and impressionable minds of our children.

ROLE OF CHILD STUDY ASSOCIATION AS AN EVALUATOR OF COMICS

The Child Study Association of America includes among its functions the provision of guidance to parents and teachers on reading materials for children. In its review of such reading material, the association has, quite commendably, concerned itself with comic books.

In 1943 and again in 1948 surveys of comic books were made by the association. These surveys were carried out by members of the association's book committee. Miss Josette Frank of the association's staff served as editorial adviser. Some attention to comic books has been given in various other materials produced by the association and members of its staff.

Although some objections are voiced to certain aspects of comic book publications—exploitation of horror and sex, poor drawings, illegible lettering and bad taste—these statements fall far short, in

---

[18] Hearings before the Subcommittee To Investigate Juvenile Delinquency (Comic Books) of the Committee on the Judiciary, U. S. Senate, 83d Cong., 2d. sess, p. 62, Washington: Government Printing Office, 1954.

the opinion of the subcommittee, of presenting a realistic picture either of the percentage of comic books devoted to crime and horror or of the volume of competent opinion which is concerned with their effects upon children.

These statements were given particularly close scrutiny during the subcommittee's hearing since the Child Study Association has received financial donations from a major comic book publisher, National Comics, and Miss Josette Frank is also a salaried consultant to the same firm. This means that in reviewing and commenting upon comic books as reading materials for children, the association was in fact passing judgment upon a product from which it and a member of its staff were receiving financial benefits.

Moreover, the character of the comic-book industry's output has undergone change since 1943 and 1948. The percentage of comic books devoted to crime and horror had increased materially by the spring of 1954.

In a book issued in the spring of 1954 on children's reading materials, Miss Josette Frank, its author, devotes one chapter to the comics. This material, although current, devotes but 2 of its 12 pages to a review of objections to comic books as reading materials for children. The opinions of psychiatrists and psychologists cited are selected from those secured in connection with the 1948 survey of comic books conducted by the Child Study Association of America.

It is probably theoretically possible for an organization to be objective in evaluating the products of a company which contributes to its support and retains one of its staff members. The subcommittee believes, however, that in fairness to the parents who look to the association for guidance, the association should make known in any evaluation of comic books, its affiliations with the comic-book industry.

In drawing conclusions relative to this "conflict in interest," the subcommittee wishes to be entirely fair and clearly understood. After careful review of all available data the subcommittee specifically finds:

(1) That the Child Study Association is to be commended in including comic books within its evaluative activities.

(2) That there is no reason to criticize a publisher for employing qualified consultants.

(3) That the association's statements on comic books and those of its staff member concerned do not adequately reflect either the character of the total present-day product of the industry or the substance of qualified opinion fearing its effects.

(4) That, although the Child Study Association maintains that the contributions it received from the publishers did not color its judgment, a reasonable doubt as to the association's objectivity in this matter is raised by the fact that, in the face of a rising tide of crime and horror comic books, the association continued to distribute evaluations which inadequately and unrealistically reflected the current situation.

(5) That the Child Study Association is confronted with a serious ethical question in relation to these practices and that it cannot fairly represent itself as an objective, impartial reporter on reading materials for children so long as they continue.

RESPONSIBILITY OF THE COMIC-BOOK INDUSTRY FOR SELF-REGULATION

The subcommittee believes that the American people have a right to expect that the comic-book industry should shoulder the major responsibility for seeing to it that the comic books placed so temptingly before our Nation's children at every corner newsstand are clean, decent, and fit to be read by children. This grave responsibility rests squarely on every segment of the comic-book industry. No one engaged in any phase of this vast operation—from the artists and authors to the newsstand dealers, from the publisher to printer to distributor to the wholesaler—can escape some measure of responsibility. A few persons engaged in this business have it within their power to do more than others to insure that this reading matter is suited to children. But many of those in the comic-book industry who had the opportunity to act to prevent abuses harmful to children have failed to do so.

In short, neither the comic-book industry nor any other sector of the media of mass communications can absolve itself from responsibility for the effects of its product. Attempts to shift all responsibility to parents are unjustified. Claims of the absolute right of an industry to produce what it pleases unless it is proven "beyond a reasonable doubt" that such a product is damaging to children, are unjustified. Parents have a right to expect that the producers of materials that may influence their children's thinking will exercise a high degree of caution. They have a right to expect the highest degree of care. And the American people have a right to demand that this degree of care be exercised at all times, in all ways, and with respect to all mass media.

What kind of responsibility for content can and should be assumed by each segment of the comic-book industry?

NEWSDEALERS UNABLE TO ASSUME ADEQUATE RESPONSIBILITY

In larger cities such as New York or Chicago, the newsdealer offers for sale as many as 600 to 1,000 titles. Time does not permit him to sort and inspect these magazines at the moment of delivery. He is restricted as to space. So far as he is aware of the contents of a particular publication he, if he wishes, may "keep that magazine from moving," either by placing it below the counter or by hanging it in an obscure spot. But frequently, he is unaware of the contents. He may also be hampered in his efforts to prevent certain publications from moving by pressures exerted by the wholesaler or his representative. Such pressures may take the form of delays in the refunds he receives for his unsold magazines or delays in the delivery of bundles or routing of his bundles to the wrong address. Evidence presented to the subcommittee also indicated that in some instances he may be subjected to the additional pressures of tie-in sales, that is, if he refuses to handle crime and horror comics his supply of the best selling and more profitable periodicals is withheld or drastically reduced. The newsdealer is usually operating on small capital and is often a disabled veteran. He has not been in a position to select the periodicals on his shelves, and therefore he is not in a position to assume effective responsibility for eliminating crime and horror comics from the channels of distribution.

These facts do not mean that the newsdealer should not make every effort to discontinue handling publications which he knows to be objectionable; or that he should not make known his objections to such publications through such channels as exist for him, perhaps through a local organization of newsdealers.

WHOLESALERS ARE NOT MOST FEASIBLE PARTIES TO REGULATE CONTENT

The wholesaler receives cartons containing thousands of copies of the publications he is to distribute. The carton has an outside label which designates the contents. It would be possible for the wholesaler to refuse to handle certain titles. He could return a carton to the national distributor or to the publisher, unopened. However, there are in the United States approximately 950 independent wholesalers and some 400 branches of the American News Co. The suggestion that these 1,350 firms be utilized as censors to cut off the supply of crime and horror comic books to the newsstands would appear to be highly impractical and wasteful.

It is not presumed to say that the wholesaler should be absolved of all responsibility for the printed matter offered for sale. Both as individuals and as members of 1 of the 8 organizations of wholesalers in this country, the wholesaler can and should make his influence felt in efforts to curtail distribution of objectionable reading materials for children.

The subcommittee notes with approval that the parent body of these organizations, the Bureau of Independent Publishers and Distributors, has given some attention to offensive reading materials on newsstands. It is hoped that further attention will be given the matter and that concerted action will be taken.

PRINTER CANNOT FEASIBLY REGULATE CONTENT

The printer of crime and horror comics may be responsible for doing only a portion of a printing job. One printer may do the covers and another the inside pages. A single publisher may use several different printers for his work. For these reasons, it would seem impractical to suggest that the printer be thrust into a screening role. Once again, however, it does not seem unreasonable to expect a reputable printer to refuse to print material, the reading of which in his estimation may influence children negatively.

DISTRIBUTOR HOLDS ONE OF THE KEY POSITIONS IN COMIC-BOOK INDUSTRY

There are only 13 national distributors of comic books.[19] Although the distributor does not have an opportunity for review of individual issues prior to publication, it is not unrealistic to assume that he should be able to maintain familiarity with the general nature of the publications he handles month after month. Indeed, through a system of advances, the national distributor is frequently in the position of being the financial backer, in part, of the publications he distributes.

It is the opinion of the subcommittee that because of his key position in the industry, a major responsibility falls upon the national

19 Listing of comic book distributors by groups and publishers appears in the appendix of this report, pp. 44–50.

distributor for the content of the printed matter he distributes. The subcommittee is glad to note a majority of the distributors have expressed agreement with this point of view. Some of the 13 distributors have never handled crime and horror comic books. Others, since the subcommittee hearings, have taken the initiative in discontinuing the handling of certain crime and horror comic titles. In certain instances they have worked with publishers to the end of changing the character of the contents of comic books. The subcommittee notes these developments with approval. It will be even more reassured when those distributors who have been carrying large numbers of crime and horror titles permanently discontinue such publications.

The responsibility of the national distributor to guard against distributing reading materials to children which are detrimental to their welfare, cannot be discharged, however, by discontinuing a few titles when public furor arises. As responsible members of the community, and as persons engaged in an industry which plays a large part in molding the impressionable minds of youth, they should maintain constant, continuing supervision over the publications they distribute.

PUBLISHER HAS PRIMARY RESPONSIBILITY FOR SUBJECT AND TREATMENT

Within the industry, primary responsibility for the contents of each comic book rests squarely upon the shoulders of its publisher. The publisher can be discriminating. He is the creator of the comic book and he shapes his own editorial policy. The writers and artists who work on the contents are employed by him and are under his direction. The attitude of the owners is reflected in the tenor of the work of the writers and artists.

Vast differences exist between the types of comics produced by publishers in this field. The largest single publisher of comic books does not list crime or horror comics among its nearly 100 comic-book titles, and never has. At the other extreme is the publisher who at the time of the New York hearings specialized in crime and horror and whose only standard regarding content was in terms of "what sells."

It has already been indicated that a large number of undesirable comic-book titles have been discontinued or revamped. Initiative for this change has come from the individual publisher as well as from the distributor. Several publishers have written to the subcommittee regarding their desire to be absolved of the criticism of in any way contributing to juvenile delinquency through their publications. One publisher has notified his readers that he is discontinuing his crime and horror line in favor of other and less controversial themes.

Again the subcommittee feels that this is progress in the right direction. As in the case of the distributors, however, the subcommittee also feels that the publishers of children's comic books cannot discharge their responsibility to the Nation's youth by merely discontinuing the publication of a few individual titles. It can be fully discharged only as they seek and support ways and means of insuring that the industry's product permanently measures up to its standards of morality and decency which American parents have the right to expect.

PAST ATTEMPTS AT INDUSTRY SELF-REGULATION

In 1948, public indignation at the flood of crime, sex, and horror comic books made itself heard in ever louder tones. It was in that year that the National Association of Prosecuting Attorneys added its voice to that of many other organizations and agencies by passing a resolution strongly recommending "that legislation be adopted designed to prohibit the sale of objectionable crime, sex, and horror books to juveniles." Ordinances designed to curb the sale of crime and horror comics to juveniles were in fact passed by some communities. This was at a time when there were only 34 publishers of comic books whose monthly sale of about 270 titles amounted to approximately 50 million copies. And at that time, too, the number of titles dealing with crime and horror were relatively few compared to the increasing numbers that have appeared on the newsstands in succeeding years.

On July 1, 1948, the comic-book industry—or at least a part of it—reacted to this mounting criticism. An Association of Comics Magazine Publishers (ACMP) was formed in New York City and it adopted a six-point code of editorial practices.[19] At the time, the New York Times reported:

> The self-policing, in an industry that has been meeting a growing criticism from educators' and parents' groups, marks only the first step in a plan for raising the moral tone of comic magazines * * *.

However, the then president of the newly formed association, Mr. Phil Keenan, denied that the code could be—

> attributed to any single piece of unfavorable criticism or to the legal curbs that have been placed on the sale of certain comic books in a number of cities.

Even from the beginning, the association was plagued by lack of unity of purpose and objectives within the industry itself. Only 12 major publishers joined the association and they were responsible for publishing only one-third of the comic books issued. Two other publishers agreed to abide by the code. Many of the publishers who did not join the association or adhere to the code were sincerely motivated. They believed that since the materials they published did not deal with crime or horror there was no need for them to participate in the organization.

Mrs. Helen Meyer, vice president of Dell Publications, testified:

> With regard to Dell's refusal to belong to the Comic Book Association, Dell had no other alternative. When the association was first introduced, we, after thorough examination, saw that Dell would be used as an umbrella for the crime comic publishers. Dell, along with these publishers, would display the same seal. How could the newsdealer afford the time to examine the contents of each comic he handled? The parents and children, too, would suffer from misrepresentation. Dell didn't need a code set down by an association, with regard to its practices of good taste. We weren't interested in trying to go up to the marginal line in our comic-book operation, as we knew we were appealing, in the main, to children.

Undaunted by not having all the publishers as members, the association went ahead with its original concept. An advisory committee that included educators, the superintendent of schools of New York City, and the New York State librarian met with publishers with a view to raising the language levels and improving the story content

---

[20] See the code of the Association of Comics Magazine Publishers, p. 35 in the appendix of this report.

of comic magazines.   A seal signifying conformity with the six-point code of editorial practices was adopted and issued to members.

However, this effort at self-regulation of the industry was doomed to failure for a variety of reasons.   Not only were not all the publishers members from the very beginning, but many of those who originally were members resigned from the association.   They resigned for various reasons.

Mr. Henry Edward Schultz, attorney for the association, stated two of the reasons for the defections:

> Some of them felt that they should not be associated with some of the elements in the industry that they felt were publishing products inferior to theirs and there is also, in passing, a great deal of internecine warfare in this industry, a lot of old difficulties which mitigated a strong, well-knit attempt to organize.   In addition, other publishers such as William Gaines resigned from the association rather than meet the standards of the code.

Finally, in 1950, to quote Mr. Schultz:

> the defections became so bad we could not afford to continue * * * (the) pre-censorship arrangement and that has been discarded.   Today we do no self-regulation at all except as it may exist in the minds of the editors and they proceed in their daily work * * *.   The association, I would say, is out of business and so is the code.

Meanwhile, however, those publishers who continued as members also continued to imprint on the covers of their comic books the seal of approval which bore the words: "Authorized ACMP.   Conforms to the Comics Code."   This practice was continued even though the association was for all intents and purposes defunct and even though none of the comics were reviewed at any point by or for the association.   As a matter of fact, some highly objectionable comic books dealing with crime and horror were introduced at the subcommittee hearings bearing such an imprint.   The subcommittee believes that this practice was highly questionable and most assuredly calculated to mislead the parents of the children buying such comic books.

Why did this attempt at self-regulation in the industry fail?   There were many reasons and they offer some lessons in judging future attempts at industry self-regulation.

It is the subcommittee's opinion that, if self-regulation by an industry such as the comic book industry is to succeed, there are certain attributes and certain mechanisms which it must have.   This earlier attempt of the comic-book industry at self-regulation lacked many of these.

In the first place, the code itself must be clear and explicit.

In the second place, there must be wide public education of the code and the meaning it has for the public when making purchases.

In the third place, the public must be sold this idea of restricting purchases of comics to those carrying the seal of approval.   This, of course, becomes difficult if numerous publishers do not subscribe to the code and particularly, if some of the nonsubscribers are major publishers of good, clean comic books.   Such a course of action permits the unscrupulous publisher, who is unwilling to meet the standards of the code, to hide behind the skirts, so to speak, of the reputable publisher who does not display the seal for other reasons.   If those who are not adherents to the code are numerous enough, then adherence or nonadherence is meaningless in the public eye and enforcement machinery breaks down.

Finally, there must be established enforcement machinery to make certain that the code's standards are adhered to. This machinery should have sufficient, well-trained staff imbued with the spirit that theirs is a task which, if well performed, can help the children of our Nation. If it is not well performed, it can affect them adversely. In addition, this enforcement machinery should be so established and operated that it is independent of the publishers whose materials it is set up to judge. This independence of thought and action should be maintained at all times lest the entire endeavor become beclouded with suspicion.

CURRENT EFFORTS AT SELF-REGULATION

Following the hearings of the subcommittee on the effects of crime and horror comic books and intensified community action throughout the country in protesting to objectionable comic books, establishment of the Comics Magazine Association of America was announced. A code was adopted on October 26, 1954.[21] Charles F. Murphy, formerly a city magistrate in New York, was named code administrator. John Goldwater, president of the Comics Magazine Association of America, said that a staff of professional reviewers will be selected to assist the code administrator in inspecting all comic books before they are printed. The code provides for a ban on all horror and terror comic books but not on crime comic books. A seal of approval will be printed on all comic books approved by the code administrator.

It is the consensus of the subcommittee that the establishment of this new association, the adoption of a code, and the appointment of a code administrator are steps in the right direction. This effort at self-regulation on the part of the comic book industry is in accordance with suggestions made by the subcommittee. Whether the fact that not all publishers of comic books are members of the association will impair the effectiveness of this latest attempt at self-regulation, as it did in the previous attempt, remains to be seen. However, since the association and the code authority have so recently been organized, it is still too early to form a judgment as to either the sincerity or the effectiveness of this latest attempt at self-regulation by the comic book industry. The subcommittee intends to watch with great interest the activities of this association and will report at a later date on this effort by the comic book industry to eliminate objectionable comic books. At any rate, the subcommittee is convinced that if this latest effort at industry self-regulation does not succeed, then other ways and means must—and will—be found to prevent our Nation's young from being harmed by crime and horror comic books.

VIII. Conclusions

While not attempting to review the several findings included in this report, the subcommittee wishes to reiterate its belief that this country cannot afford the calculated risk involved in feeding its children, through comic books, a concentrated diet of crime, horror, and violence. There was substantial, although not unanimous, agreement among the experts that there may be detrimental and delinquency-producing effects upon both the emotionally disturbed child and the emotionally normal delinquent. Children of either type may gain suggestion, support, and sanction from reading crime and horror comics.

[21] See the code of the Comics Magazine Association of America, pp. 36–38 in the appendix of this report.

There are many who believe that the boys and girls who are the most avid and extensive consumers of such comics are those who are least able to tolerate this type of reading material. The excessive reading of this kind of materials is viewed by some observers as sometimes being symptomatic of some emotional maladjustment, that is, comic book reading may be a workable "diagnostic indicator" of an underlying pathological condition in a child.

It is during childhood that the individual's concepts of right and wrong and his reactions to society's standards are largely developed. Those responsible for the operation of every form of the mass media of communication, including comic books, which cater to the education or entertainment of children have, therefore, a responsibility to gear their products to these special considerations.

Standards for such products, whether in the form of a code or by the policies of individual producers, should not be aimed to eliminate only that which can be proved beyond doubt to demoralize youth. Rather the aim should be to eliminate all materials that potentially exert detrimental effects.

To achieve this end, it will require continuing vigilance on the part of parents, publishers and citizens' groups. The work that has been done by citizens' and parents' groups in calling attention to the problem of crime and horror comics has been far-reaching in its impact.

The subcommittee notes with some surprise that little attention has been paid by educational and welfare agencies to the potential dangers, as well as benefits, to children presented by the growth of the comic book industry. As spokesmen in behalf of children, their responsibility requires that they be concerned for the child and the whole world in which he lives. The campaign against juvenile delinquency cannot be won by anything less than an all-out attack upon all conditions contributing to the problem.

The interest of our young citizens would not be served by postponing all precautionary measures until the exact kind and degree of influence exerted by comic books upon children's behavior is fully determined through careful research. Sole responsibility for stimulating, formulating and carrying out such research cannot be assumed by parents' or citizens' groups. Rather it must also be assumed by the educational and social welfare agencies and organizations concerned.

In the meantime, the welfare of this Nation's young makes it mandatory that all concerned unite in supporting sincere efforts of the industry to raise the standards of its products and in demanding adequate standards of decency and good taste. Nor should these united efforts be relaxed in the face of momentary gains. Continuing vigilance is essential in sustaining this effort.

ONLY ONE PART OF INVESTIGATION INTO THE MASS MEDIA OF COMMUNICATION

The subcommittee wishes to call particular attention to the fact that its exploration of crime and horror comic books as a contributing factor to juvenile delinquency is only one part of its investigation into the mass media of communication.

A future report of the subcommittee will contain certain additional recommendations which will deal with the several media and, as such, will have further bearing upon the problem of crime and horror comics.

APPENDIX

SENATE RESOLUTION 89

(83d Cong., 1st sess.)

Resolved, that the Committee on the Judiciary, or any duly authorized subcommittee thereof, is authorized and directed to conduct a full and complete study of juvenile delinquency in the United States. In the conduct of such investigation special attention shall be given to (1) determining the extent and character of juvenile delinquency in the United States and its causes and contributing factors, (2) the adequacy of existing provisions of law, including chapters 402 and 403 of title 18 of the United States Code, in dealing with youthful offenders of Federal laws, (3) sentences imposed on, or other correctional action taken with respect to, youthful offenders by Federal courts, and (4) the extent to which juveniles are violating Federal laws relating to the sale or use of narcotics.

SEC. 2. The committee, or any duly authorized subcommittee thereof, is authorized to sit and act at such places and times during the sessions, recesses, and adjourned periods of the Senate, to hold such hearings, to require by subpenas or otherwise the attendance of such witnesses and the production of such books, papers, and documents, to administer such oaths, to take such testimony, to procure such printing and binding, and, within the amount appropriated therefor, to make such expenditures as it deems advisable. The cost of stenographic services to report hearings of the committee or subcommittee shall not be in excess of 40 cents per hundred words. Subpenas shall be issued by the chairman of the committee or the subcommittee, and may be served by any person designated by such chairman.

A majority of the members of the committee, or duly authorized subcommittee thereof, shall constitute a quorum for the transaction of business, except that a lesser number to be fixed by the committee, or by such subcommittee, shall constitute a quorum for the purpose of administering oaths and taking sworn testimony.

SEC. 3. The committee shall report its findings, together with its recommendations for such legislation as it deems advisable, to the Senate at the earliest date practicable but not later than January 31, 1954.

SEC. 4. For the purposes of this resolution, the committee, or any duly authorized subcommittee thereof, is authorized to employ upon a temporary basis such technical, clerical, and other assistants as it deems advisable. The expenses of the committee under this resolution, which shall not exceed $44,000, shall be paid from the contingent fund of the Senate upon vouchers approved by the chairman of the committee.

SENATE RESOLUTION 190

(83d Cong., 2d sess.)

Resolved, That section 3 of S. Res. 89, Eighty-third Congress, agreed to June 1, 1953 (authorizing the Committee on the Judiciary to make a study of juvenile delinquency in the United States), is amended to read as follows:

"SEC. 3. The committee shall make a preliminary report of its findings, together with its recommendations for such legislation as it deems advisable, to the Senate not later than February 28, 1954, and shall make a final report of such findings and recommendations to the Senate at the earliest date practicable but not later than January 31, 1955."

SEC. 2. The limitation of expenditures under such S. Res. 89 is increased by $175,000, and such sum together with any unexpended balance of the sum previously authorized to be expended under such resolution shall be paid from the contingent fund of the Senate upon vouchers approved by the chairman of the committee.

34

TITLE 39—U. S. CODE

SEC. 233. SWORN STATEMENTS RELATING TO NEWSPAPERS AND OTHER PUBLICATIONS.

It shall be the duty of the editor, publisher, business manager, or owner of every newspaper, magazine, periodical, or other publication to file with the Postmaster General and the postmaster at the office at which said publication is entered, not later than the 1st day of October of each year, on blanks furnished by the Post Office Department, a sworn statement setting forth the names and post-office addresses of the editor and managing editor, publisher, business managers, and owners, and in addition, the stockholders, if the publication be owned by a corporation; and also the names of known bondholders, mortgagees, or other security holders; and also, in the case of daily and weekly, semiweekly, triweekly newspapers, there shall be included in such statement the average of the number of copies of each issue of such publication sold or distributed to paid subscribers during the preceding twelve months: *Provided*, That the provisions of this paragraph shall not apply to religious, fraternal, temperance, and scientific, or other similar publications: *Provided further*, That it shall not be necessary to include in such statement the names of persons owning less than 1 per centum of the total amount of stock, bonds, mortgages, or other securities. A copy of such sworn statement shall be published in the second issue of such newspaper, magazine, or other publication printed next after the filing of such statement. Any such publication shall be denied the privileges of the mail if it shall fail to comply with the provisions of this paragraph within ten days after notice by registered letter of such failure. (August 24, 1912, ch. 389, sec. 2, 37 Stat. 553; March 3, 1933, ch. 207, 47 Stat. 1486; July 2, 1946, ch. 533, 60 Stat. 416.)

AMENDMENTS

1946—Act July 2, 1946, amended section by inserting "and weekly, semiweekly, triweekly" between "daily" and "newspapers" in first sentence.

CODE OF THE NATIONAL CARTOONISTS SOCIETY

We, the members of the National Cartoonists Society, believe:
1. That we should preserve our present high standards of artistic achievement and good taste in our relationship with the public and with those agencies that distribute cartoons for professional use.
2. That our work should comply with the established standards of morality and decency; and we should condemn any violations of such standards.
3. That promising talent should be encouraged and guided to the fullest extent.
4. That cartoonists, as creators of characters, symbols, and ideas, which become tangible financial properties are entitled to the protection and just rewards those properties deserve.
5. In the freedoms guaranteed by our Government and pledge ourselves to resist any attempt to interfere with these freedoms.

CODE OF THE ASSOCIATION OF COMICS MAGAZINE PUBLISHERS, 1948

1. Crime should not be presented in such a way as to throw sympathy against law and justice or to inspire others with the desire for imitation. No comics shall show the details and methods of a crime committed by a youth. Policemen, judges, Government officials, and respected institutions should not be portrayed as stupid or ineffective, or represented in such a way as to weaken respect for established authority.
2. No scenes of sadistic torture should be shown.
3. Sexy, wanton comics should not be published. No drawing should show a female indecently or unduly exposed and in no event more nude than in a bathing suit commonly worn in the United States.
4. Vulgar and obscene language should never be used. Slang should be kept to a minimum and used only when essential to the story.
5. Divorce should not be treated humorously nor represented as glamorous or alluring.
6. Ridicule or attack on any religious or racial group is never permissible.

CODE OF THE COMICS MAGAZINE ASSOCIATION OF AMERICA, INC.

Adopted October 26, 1954

PREAMBLE

The comic-book medium, having come of age on the American cultural scene, must measure up to its responsibilities.

Constantly improving techniques and higher standards go hand in hand with these responsibilities.

To make a positive contribution to contemporary life, the industry must seek new areas for developing sound, wholesome entertainment. The people responsible for writing, drawing, printing, publishing, and selling comic books have done a commendable job in the past, and have been striving toward this goal.

Their record of progress and continuing improvement compares favorably with other media in the communications industry. An outstanding example is the development of comic books as a unique and effective tool for instruction and education. Comic books have also made their contribution in the field of letters and criticism of contemporary life.

In keeping with the American tradition, the members of this industry will and must continue to work together in the future.

In the same tradition, members of the industry must see to it that gains made in this medium are not lost and that violations of standards of good taste, which might tend toward corruption of the comic book as an instructive and wholesome form of entertainment, will be eliminated.

Therefore, the Comics Magazine Association of America, Inc. has adopted this code, and placed strong powers of enforcement in the hands of an independent code authority.

Further, members of the association have endorsed the purpose and spirit of this code as a vital instrument to the growth of the industry.

To this end, they have pledged themselves to conscientiously adhere to its principles and to abide by all decisions based on the code made by the administrator.

They are confident that this positive and forthright statement will provide an effective bulwark for the protection and enhancement of the American reading public, and that it will become a landmark in the history of self-regulation for the entire communications industry.

CODE FOR EDITORIAL MATTER

General standards—Part A

(1) Crimes shall never be presented in such a way as to create sympathy for the criminal, to promote distrust of the forces of law and justice, or to inspire others with a desire to imitate criminals.

(2) No comics shall explicitly present the unique details and methods of a crime.

(3) Policemen, judges, Government officials and respected institutions shall never be presented in such a way as to create disrespect for established authority.

(4) If crime is depicted it shall be as a sordid and unpleasant activity.

(5) Criminals shall not be presented so as to be rendered glamorous or to occupy a position which creates a desire for emulation.

(6) In every instance good shall triumph over evil and the criminal punished for his misdeeds.

(7) Scenes of excessive violence shall be prohibited. Scenes of brutal torture, excessive and unnecessary knife and gunplay, physical agony, gory and gruesome crime shall be eliminated.

(8) No unique or unusual methods of concealing weapons shall be shown.

(9) Instances of law-enforcement officers dying as a result of a criminal's activities should be discouraged.

(10) The crime of kidnaping shall never be portrayed in any detail, nor shall any profit accrue to the abductor or kidnaper. The criminal or the kidnaper must be punished in every case.

(11) The letters of the word "crime" on a comics-magazine cover shall never be appreciably greater in dimension than the other words contained in the title. The word "crime" shall never appear alone on a cover.

(12) Restraint in the use of the word "crime" in titles or subtitles shall be exercised.

General standards—Part B

(1) No comic magazine shall use the word horror or terror in its title.

(2) All scenes of horror, excessive bloodshed, gory or gruesome crimes, depravity, lust, sadism, masochism shall not be permitted.

(3) All lurid, unsavory, gruesome illustrations shall be eliminated.

(4) Inclusion of stories dealing with evil shall be used or shall be published only where the intent is to illustrate a moral issue and in no case shall evil be presented alluringly, nor so as to injure the sensibilities of the reader.

(5) Scenes dealing with, or instruments associated with walking dead, torture, vampires and vampirism, ghouls, cannibalism, and werewolfism are prohibited.

General standards—Part C

All elements or techniques not specifically mentioned herein, but which are contrary to the spirit and intent of the code, and are considered violations of good taste or decency, shall be prohibited.

Dialogue

(1) Profanity, obscenity, smut, vulgarity, or words or symbols which have acquired undesirable meanings are forbidden.

(2) Special precautions to avoid references to physical afflictions or deformities shall be taken.

(3) Although slang and colloquialisms are acceptable, excessive use should be discouraged and, wherever possible, good grammar shall be employed.

Religion

(1) Ridicule or attack on any religious or racial group is never permissible.

Costume

(1) Nudity in any form is prohibited, as is indecent or undue exposure.

(2) Suggestive and salacious illustration or suggestive posture is unacceptable.

(3) All characters shall be depicted in dress reasonably acceptable to society.

(4) Females shall be drawn realistically without exaggeration of any physical qualities.

NOTE.—It should be recognized that all prohibitions dealing with costume, dialog, or artwork applies as specifically to the cover of a comic magazine as they do to the contents.

Marriage and sex

(1) Divorce shall not be treated humorously nor represented as desirable.

(2) Illicit sex relations are neither to be hinted at nor portrayed.   Violent love scenes as well as sexual abnormalities are unacceptable.

(3) Respect for parents, the moral code, and for honorable behavior shall be fostered.   A sympathetic understanding of the problems of love is not a license for morbid distortion.

(4) The treatment of live-romance stories shall emphasize the value of the home and the sanctity of marriage.

(5) Passion or romantic interest shall never be treated in such a way as to stimulate the lower and baser emotions.

(6) Seduction and rape shall never be shown or suggested.

(7) Sex perversion or any inference to same is strictly forbidden.

CODE FOR ADVERTISING MATTER

These regulations are applicable to all magazines published by members of the Comics Magazine Association of America, Inc.   Good taste shall be the guiding principle in the acceptance of advertising.

(1) Liquor and tobacco advertising is not acceptable.

(2) Advertisement of sex or sex instruction books are unacceptable.

(3) The sale of picture postcards, "pinups," "art studies," or any other reproduction of nude or seminude figures is prohibited.

(4) Advertising for the sale of knives or realistic gun facsimiles is prohibited.

(5) Advertising for the sale of fireworks is prohibited.

(6) Advertising dealing with the sale of gambling equipment or printed matter dealing with gambling shall not be accepted.

(7) Nudity with meretricious purpose and salacious postures shall not be permitted in the advertising of any product; clothed figures shall never be presented in such a way as to be offensive or contrary to good taste or morals.

(8) To the best of his ability, each publisher shall ascertain that all statements made in advertisements conform to fact and avoid misrepresentation.

(9) Advertisement of medical, health, or toiletry products of questionable nature are to be rejected. Advertisements for medical health, or toiletry products endorsed by the American Medical Association, or the American Dental Association, shall be deemed acceptable if they conform with all other conditions of the Advertising Code.

CORRESPONDENCE FROM THE COMMITTEE ON EVALUATION OF COMIC BOOKS, CINCINNATI, OHIO

The work of the committee on evaluation of comic books at Cincinnati, Ohio, is an example of what can be accomplished by citizen action in dealing with the problem of comic books. The Cincinnati committee has been a nonprofit group and is not subsidized by the comic-book industry. It is composed of public-spirited citizens who have sought to be objective. The committee's evaluations, prepared by a staff of 84 trained reviewers, have been widely reprinted and circulated. The Reverend Jesse L. Murrell is chairman of the executive committee of the committee on evaluation of comic books.

On page 41 of the comic book hearings before the Subcommittee To Investigate Juvenile Delinquency, the July 1953 list of the Cincinnati committee's evaluation of comic books was accurately reprinted. Since that time Ham Fisher, cartoonist, who draws "Joe Palooka Adventures" comic books, submitted the following correspondence from the committee on evaluation of comic books with the request that it be printed:

COMMITTEE ON EVALUATION OF COMIC BOOKS,

Cincinnati, Ohio, November 4, 1954.

Mr. HAM FISHER,
        New York, N. Y.

DEAR MR. FISHER: In answer to your telephone inquiry of Wednesday, November 3, I have looked up our files on Joe Palooka Adventures, and find that the issue which our reviewers read was March 1954. It is No. 82. This issue is pretty well devoted to prizefighting, and the criticism seems to fall with the second story, where on the seventh page, I believe it is, Joe is being so pommeled by his opponent that he sees in his vision, or semiconsciousness, the terrible ordeal of somebody, perhaps himself, hung up by his wrists and being lashed by a whip. This situation occurs in at least four frames, and our reviewers feel that this, together with the very rough pommeling that is going on in the whole story, would give to a small child a horrible feeling of man's cruelty to man. It would therefore fall into the area of morbid emotionality, and as you will notice in the enclosed list of evaluated comic books where, at the end, we have our criteria, it shows that Joe Palooka is objectionable, because of No. 29. You will see that that is, "Stories and pictures that tend to anything having a sadistic implication or suggesting use of black magic."

I do not read the comic-book magazines for pleasure, and therefore do not know what you have in Joe Palooka from time to time, but I would suggest that you attempt to avoid such situations as described here, even though they are the imagination of someone who is suffering, for the reason that, to a child it is all in the picture.

I have looked over copies of the eight evaluations we have made of comic books since the summer of 1948, and find that we have rated Joe Palooka each time except July 1952. In the July 1951 review, Joe Palooka rated "No objection." In the year 1948, the spring of 1949, December 1949, August 1950, and July 1953, it rated "Some objection" which in our category does not militate against a comic book's use by children or young people, but has some minor characteristic which the reviewers would like to see improved. This usually has to do with physical setup. In the April 1954 review this comic book was rated "Objectionable" for the reason of its sadistic implications in the second story.

It is fair to say that our committee considers Joe Palooka to be a very good comic book.

        Yours cordially,

JESSE L. MURRELL.

COMMITTEE ON EVALUATION OF COMIC BOOKS,.
Cincinnati, Ohio, November 8, 1954.

Mr. FISHER: I sent the telegram to Newsweek according to your request and here is the copy:

"NEWSWEEK MAGAZINE,
New York City:

"Having heard that the March issue of Joe Palooka Adventures comic book which the committee on evaluation of comic books in Cincinnati had rated objectionable has caused quite a stir. I desire to advise you that we have been reviewing copies of this magazine since 1948 and that this is the first issue that has received the objectionable rating. We consider this comic one of the very good ones but it so happened that this particular issue carried four frames that our reviewers thought would be frightening to small children.

"JESSE L. MURRELL, *Chairman.*"

I trust this will help to put you and your product in the proper light and I am very sorry that you have been disturbed.

We appreciate your zeal for our common cause of better comic books and your efforts in behalf of clean young manhood.

Cordially,

JESSE L. MURRELL.

COMIC BOOK PUBLISHERS AND COMIC BOOK TITLES, SPRING 1954

A. A. Wyn, Inc., 23 West 47th Street, New York, N. Y. (Ace):
Glamorous Romances, Hand of Fate, Love Experiences, Real Love, Web of Mystery
Ace Magazines, Inc., 23 West 47th Street, New York, N. Y. (Ace):
Complete Love, Ten Story Love
Allen Hardy Associates, 500 Fifth Avenue, New York, N. Y. (Allen Hardy):
Danger, Death Valley, Dynamite, House of Horror, Love and Kisses, Weird Terror
Animirth Comics, Inc., 270 Park Avenue, New York, N. Y. (Atlas):
Adventures Into Weird Worlds, Homer Hooper, Marines in Battle, 3D Action, Riot, Western Outlaws
Archie Comic Publications, Inc., 241 Church Street, New York, N. Y.:
Archie Comics (7 titles), Pep Comics, Wilbur Comics
Aragon Magazines, Inc., 175 Fifth Avenue, New York, N. Y. (Stanley P. Morse):
Mister Mystery
Arnold Publications, Inc., 347 Madison Avenue, New York, N. Y. (Quality):
Buster Bear, Marmaduke Mouse
Atlas News Co., Inc., 270 Park Avenue, New York, N. Y. (Atlas):
Buck Duck, Lovers, Police Action
Avon Periodicals, Inc., 575 Madison Avenue, New York, N. Y. (Avon):
All True Detective Cases, Eerie, Funny Tunes, Jesse James, Merry Mouse, Peter Rabbit, Peter Rabbit Jumbo Book, Realistic Romance, Romantic Love, Sensational Police Cases, Space Comics, Space Mouse, Space Thrillers, Spotty The Pup, Super Pup, Wild Bill Hickok
Bard Publishing Corp., 270 Park Avenue, New York, N. Y. (Atlas):
Patsy Walker
Best Syndicated Features, Inc., 45 West 45th Street, New York, N. Y. (ACG):
Adventures Into The Unknown, The Kilroys, Romatic Adventures.
Better Publications, Inc., 10 East 40th Street, New York, N. Y. (Standard):
Exciting War, Popular Romances
Beverly Publishing Co., 480 Lexington Avenue, New York, N. Y.:
Secret Hearts
Broadcast Features Publications, Inc., 270 Park Avenue, New York, N. Y. (Atlas):
Girls' Life, My Friend Irma
Canam Publishers Sales Corp., 270 Park Avenue, New York, N. Y. (Atlas):
Arrow Head, Black Rider, Journey Into Mystery, 3D Tales of the West.
Chipiden Publishing Corp., 270 Park Avenue, New York, N. Y. (Atlas):
Human Torch, Strange Tales
Classic Syndicate, Inc., 270 Park Avenue, New York, N. Y. (Atlas):
Crazy

Close-Up, Inc., 241 Church Street, New York, N. Y. (Archie):
    Archie's Girls Betty & Veronica, Ginger Comics, Katy Keane Comics, Laugh
      Comics, Super Duck Comics, Suzie Comics
Comic Combine Corp., 270 Park Avenue, New York, N. Y. (Atlas):
    Men's Adventures, Sub Mariner, The Outlaw Kid
Comic Favorites, Inc., 347 Madison Avenue, New York, N. Y. (Quality):
    Gabby, Jonesy
Comic Magazines, 347 Madison Avenue, New York, N. Y. (Quality):
    Blackhawk, Brides Romances, Candy, G. I. Combat, G. I. Sweethearts, Heart
      Throbs, Love Confessions, Love Letters, Love Secrets, Plastic Man, T-Man,
      True War Romances, Web of Evil, Wedding Bells
Cornell Publishing Corp., 270 Park Avenue, New York, N. Y. (Atlas):
    Crime Fighters, Spaceman
Crestwood Publishing Co., Inc., 1790 Broadway, New York, N. Y. (Prize):
    Black Magic, Young Love
Current Detective Stories, Inc., 270 Park Avenue, New York, N. Y. (Atlas):
    Navy Action
Dell Publishing Co., Inc., 261 Fifth Avenue, New York, N. Y. (Dell):
    Monthlies: Edgar Rice Burroughs' Tarzan, Gene Autry Comics, Loony Tunes
      and Merrie Melodies Comics, Marge's Little Lulu, Roy Rogers Comics,
      The Lone Ranger, Tom and Jerry Comics, Walter Lantz New Funnies
    Bimonthlies: Bugs Bunny, Carl Anderson's Henry, Cisco Kid, Howdy Doody,
      Little Iodine, MGM's Lassie, Porky Pig, Walter Lantz Andy Panda,
      Walter Lantz Woody Woodpecker
    Quarterlies: Ben Bowie & His Mountain Men, Flying A's Range Rider,
      Henry Aldrich, Hi-Yo Silver, I Love Lucy, Indian Chief, Jace Pearson—
      Texas Rangers, King of the Royal Mounted, Marge's Tubby, Popeye,
      Queen of the West—Dale Evans, Rex Allen, Rin Tin Tin, Rootie Kazootie,
      Sergeant Preston of the Yukon, Tom Corbett—Space Cadet, Tonto,
      Trigger, Tweety & Sylvester, Walt Kelly's Pogo Possum, Western Round-
      up, Wild Bill Elliott, Zane Grey's Picturized Editions
    Semi-annuals: Andy Hardy, Beany & Cecil, Bozo The Clown, Buck Jones,
      Francis The Talking Mule, Gerald McBoing Boing, Johnny Mack Brown,
      Krazy Kat, Little Scouts, Max Brand's Silvertip, Oswald The Rabbit,
      Zorro
    Annuals: Beetle Bailey, Bugs Bunny (Album, Christmas Funnies, Halloween
      Parade, Vacation Funnies) Charlie McCarthy, Daffy, Double Trouble
      With Goober, Elmer Fudd, Ernest Haycox's Western Marshal, Flash
      Gordon, Frosty The Snowman, Gypsy Colt, Jungle Jim, Knights of the
      Round Table, Little Beaver, Marge's Little Lulu—Tubby Annual, Milton
      Caniff's Steve Canyon, Napoleon, Prince Valiant, Rageddy Ann & Andy,
      Rhubarb The Millionaire Cat, Rivets, Rusty Riley, Santa Claus Funnies,
      Son of Black Beauty, Spike N'Tyke, Super Circus, Susie Q. Smith, The
      Brownies, The Green Hornet, The Little King, The Lone Ranger's Western
      Treasury, Tom & Jerry (Summer Fun, Winter Carnival), 3D Flukey
      Kazootie, 3D Rootie Kazootie, Uncle Wiggly, Walt Kelly's Pogo Parade,
      Walter Lantz Woody Woodpecker Back to School
Educational Comics, Inc., 225 Lafayette Street, New York, N. Y. (EC):
    Mad
Excellent Publications, Inc., 30 East 60th Street, New York, N. Y. (Farrell):
    Billy Bunny, Swift Arrow
Fables Publishing Co., Inc., 225 Lafayette Street, New York, N. Y. (EC):
    Haunt of Fear, Two-Fisted Tales, Weird Science-Fantasy
Family Comics, Inc., 1860 Broadway, New York, N. Y. (Harvey):
    Casper
Famous Authors, Ltd., 101 Fifth Avenue, New York, N. Y. (Classics Illus-
    trated):
    Classics Illustrated, Junior Series: No. 501—Snow White and The Seven
      Dwarfs, No. 502—The Ugly Duckling, No. 503—Cinderella, No. 504—The
      Pied Piper, No. 505—Sleeping Beauty, No. 506—The Three Pigs, No.
      507—Jack and The Beanstalk, No. 508—Goldilocks and The Three Bears,
      No. 509—Beauty and The Beast, No. 510—Little Red Riding Hood
Famous Funnies Publications, 500 Fifth Avenue, New York, N. Y. (Famous):
    Famous Funnies, New Heroic Comics, Personal Love
Farrell Comics, Inc., 30 East 60th Street, New York, N. Y. (Farrell):
    Haunted Thrills, Lone Rider, Strange Fantasy

Fawcett Publications, Inc., 67 West 44th Street, New York, N. Y. (Fawcett):
  Captain Marvel Adventures, Funny Animals, Hopalong Cassidy, Lash LaRue, Marvel Family, Rocky Lane, 6–Gun Heroes, Tex Ritter, This Magazine Is Haunted
Feature Publications, Inc., 1790 Broadway, New York, N. Y. (Prize):
  Frankenstein, Prize Western Comics, Young Brides, Young Romance
Fiction House, Inc., 1658 Summer Street, Stamford, Conn. (Fiction House):
  Ghost Comics
Fight Stories, Inc., 1658 Summer Street, Stamford, Conn. (Fiction House):
  Fight Comics
Flying Stories, Inc., 1658 Summer Street, Stamford, Conn. (Fiction House):
  Knockout, Monster
Foto Parade, Inc., 270 Park Avenue, New York, N. Y. (Atlas):
  Battle
Four Star Publications, Inc., 30 East 60th Street, New York, N. Y. (Farrell):
  Fantastic Fears, Voodoo
Gem Publications, Inc., 270 Park Avenue, New York, N. Y. (Atlas):
  Patsy & Hedy
Gilberton Co., Inc., 101 Fifth Avenue, New York, N. Y. (Classics Illustrated):
  Classics Illustrated: No. 1—The Three Musketeers, No. 2—Ivanhoe, No. 3—Count of Monte Cristo, No. 4—Last of the Mohicans, No. 5—Moby Dick, No. 6—A Tale of Two Cities, No. 7—Robin Hood, No. 10—Robinson Crusoe, No. 11—Don Quixote, No. 12—Rip Van Winkle and The Headless Horseman, No. 13—Dr. Jekyll and Mr. Hyde, No. 15—Uncle Tom's Cabin, No. 17—The Deerslayer, No. 18—The Hunchback of Notre Dame, No. 19—Huckleberry Finn, No. 20—The Corsican Brothers, No. 21—3 Famous Mysteries, No. 22—The Pathfinder, No. 23—Oliver Twist, No. 24—A Connecticut Yankee in King Arthur's Court, No. 25—Two Years Before the Mast, No. 26—Frankenstein, No. 27—Adventures of Marco Polo, No. 28—Michael Strogoff, No. 29—Prince and The Pauper, No. 31—Black Arrow, No. 32—Lorna Doone, No. 34—Mysterious Island, No. 37—The Pioneers, No. 39—Jane Eyre, No. 40—Mysteries by Edgar Allan Poe, No. 42—Swiss Family Robinson, No. 46—Kidnapped, No. 47—Twenty Thousand Leagues Under The Sea, No. 48—David Copperfield, No. 49—Alice In Wonderland, No. 50—The Adventures of Tom Sawyer, No. 51—The Spy, No. 52—The House of Seven Gables, No. 54, Man In The Iron Mask, No. 55—Silas Marner, No. 57—The Song of Hiawatha, No. 58—The Prairie, No. 62—Western Stories, No. 64—Treasure Island, No. 67—The Scottish Chiefs, No. 68—Julius Caesar, No. 69—Around The World In Eighty Days, No. 70—The Pilot, No. 72—The Oregon Trail, No. 75—Lady of The Lake, No. 76—Prisoner of Zenda, No. 77—The Iliad, No. 78—Joan of Arc, No. 79—Cyrano De Bergerac, No. 80—White Fang, No. 83—The Jungle Book, No. 85—The Sea Wolf, No. 86—Under Two Flags, No. 87—A Midsummer Night's Dream, No. 88—Men of Iron, No. 89—Crime and Punishment, No. 90—Green Mansions, No. 91—The Call of the Wild, No. 92—The Courtship of Miles Standish and Evangeline, No. 93—Pudd'nhead Wilson, No. 94—David Balfour, No. 95—All Quiet On The Western Front, No. 96—Daniel Boone, No. 97—King Solomon's Mines, No. 98—The Red Badge of Courage, No. 99—Hamlet, No. 100—Mutiny On The Bounty, No. 101—William Tell, No. 102—The White Company, No. 103—Men Against The Sea, No. 104—Bring 'Em Back Alive, No. 105—From the Earth to The Moon, No. 106—Buffalo Bill, No. 107—King of The Khyber Rifles, No. 108—Knights of The Round Table, No. 109—Pitcairn's Island, No. 110—A Study In Scarlet, No. 111—The Talisman, No. 112—Kit Carson, No. 113—The Forty-Five Guardsmen, No. 114—The Red Rover, No. 115—How I Found Livingstone, No. 116—The Bottle Imp, No. 117—Captains Courageous, No. 118—Rob Roy, No. 119—Soldiers of Fortune, No. 120—The Hurricane
  Picture Progress (issued monthly during school year).
Gillmor Magazines, Inc., 175 Fifth Avenue, New York, N. Y. (Stanley P. Morse):
  Radiant Love, Weird Mysteries
Glen-Kel Publishing Co., 1658 Summer Street, Stamford, Conn. (Fiction House):
  Jungle Comics, Kaanga Jungle King
Harvey Enterprises, Inc., 1860 Broadway, New York, N. Y. (Harvey):
  Dotty Dripple, First Love, Little Dot
Harvey Picture Magazines, Inc., 1860 Broadway, New York, N. Y. (Harvey):
  Little Audry, Warfront

Harvey Publications, Inc., 1860 Broadway, New York, N. Y. (Harvey):
  Blondie Comics, Dagwood Comics, Daisy and Her Pups, Dick Tracy Comics,
  Joe Palooka Comics, Little Max Comics, Sad Sack Comics, Tomb of Terror
Harvey Publications, 1860 Broadway, New York, N. Y. (Harvey):
  Jiggs & Maggie, Katzenjammer Kids, Rags Rabbit, Ripley's Believe It or Not
Headline Publications, Inc., 1790 Broadway, New York, N. Y. (Prize):
  Dixie Dugen, Fighting America, Headline Comics, Justice Traps the Guilty
Hercules Publishing Corp., 270 Park Avenue, New York, N. Y. (Atlas):
  Ringo Kid, Spy Cases, Two Gun Kid
Home Comics, Inc., 1860 Broadway, New York, N. Y. (Harvey):
  Black Cat, First Romance, Hi-School Romance, Love Problems, Teen Age
  Brides
I. C. Publishing Co., 225 Lafayette Street, New York, N. Y. (EC):
  Tales From The Crypt
Illustrated Humor, Inc., 1860 Broadway, New York, N. Y. (Harvey):
  Flip
Interstate Publishing Corp., 270 Park Avenue, New York, N. Y. (Atlas):
  Outlaw Fighters, Wild, Young Men
Jay Jay Corp., 316 North Eighth Street, St. Louis, Mo.:
  Judo Joe
Joseph A. Wolfert, 32 Broadway, New York, N. Y.:
  Algie, Animal Adventures, Blazing Western, Crime Detector, Police Against
  Crime
Junior Books, Inc., 23 West 47th Street, New York, N. Y. (Ace):
  Crime Must Pay The Penalty
K. K. Publications, Inc., Poughkeepsie, N. Y. (Dell):
  Red Ryder Comics, Walt Disney Comics and Stories
Key Publications, Inc., 45 West 45th Street, New York, N. Y. (Stanley P. Morse):
  Hector, Ideal Romance, Peter Cottontails, Weird Chills
Leading Magazine Corp., 270 Park Avenue, New York, N. Y. (Atlas):
  Kid Colt Outlaw
Leverett S. Gleason, 114 East 32d Street, New York, N. Y. (Lev Gleason):
  Black Diamond, Boy Illustories, Boy Loves Girl, Buster Crabbe, Crime
  Does Not Pay, Crime and Punishment, Daredevil, Lovers Lane, Squeeks
Literary Enterprises, Inc., 10 East 40th Street, New York, N. Y. (Standard):
  Buster Bunny, Lucky Duck, Sniffy The Pup, Supermouse
L. L. Publishing Co., Inc., 225 Lafayette Street, New York, N. Y. (EC):
  Crime Suspen Stories, The Vault of Horror
Love Romances Publishing Co., Inc.. 1658 Summer Street, Stamford, Conn.
  (Fiction House):
  Planet Comics
Magazine Enterprises, 11 Park Place, New York, N. Y. (ME):
  Badmen of the West, Best of the West, Cave Girl, Dream Book of Love,
  Dream Book of Romance, Durango Kid, Ghost Rider, Great Western,
  Home Run, Hot Dog, Muggsy Mouse, Red Fox, Red Hawk, Straight
  Arrow, Tim Holt (now Red Mask), Undercover Girl, White Indian
Male Publishing Corp., 270 Park Avenue, New York, N. Y. (Atlas):
  Justice, Spellbound, World's Greatest Songs
Manvis Publications, Inc., 270 Park Avenue, New York, N. Y. (Atlas):
  True Secrets
Marjean Magazine Corp., 270 Park Avenue, New York, N. Y. (Atlas):
  My Own Romance
Marvel Comics, Inc., 270 Park Avenue, New York, N. Y. (Atlas):
  Marvel Tales
Master Comics, Inc., 11 East 44th Street, New York, N. Y.:
  Dark Mysteries
Mikeross Publications, Inc., 55 West 42d Street, New York, N. Y.:
  Get Lost, Heart and Soul
Miss America Publishing Corp., 270 Park Avenue, New York, N. Y. (Atlas):
  Miss America
Mystery Publishing Co., Inc., 500 Fifth Avenue, New York, N. Y. (Allen Hardy):
  All True Romance, Dear Lonely Hearts, Horrific, Noodnik
National Comics Publications, Inc., 480 Lexington Avenue, New York, N. Y.
  (Superman—DC):
  Action Comics, Adventure Comics, All American Men of War, All Star
  Western, Animal Antics, Batman, Big Town, Bob Hope (the Adventures
  of), Buzzy, Comic Cavalcade, Date With Judy, Detective Comics, Every-

thing Happens to Harvey, Flippety and Flop, Fox and Crow, Funny Folks,
Funny Stuff, Gang Busters, Here's Howie, Hopalong Cassidy, House of
Mystery, Leading Comics, Leave it to Binky, Martin and Lewis, Mr.
District Attorney, Mutt and Jeff, Mystery in Space, Our Army at War,
Peter Panda, Peter Porkchops, Real Screen Comics, Rex the Wonder Dog,
Star Spangled War Stories, Strange Adventures, Superboy, Superman,
Tomhawk, Western Comics, Wonder Woman, World's Finest Comics
Newsstand Publications, Inc., 270 Park Avenue, New York, N. Y. (Atlas):
    Man Comics
Official Magazine Corp., 270 Park Avenue, New York, N. Y. (Atlas):
    Battleground, Bible Tales for Young Folk, Little Lizzie, Lorna The Jungle
    Girl, Mystic, Wendy Parker
Our Publishing Co., 114 East 32d Street, New York, N. Y.:
    Love Diary, Love Journal
Periodical House, Inc., 23 West 47th Street, New York, N. Y. (Ace):
    Baffling Mysteries, Love at First Sight
Pflaum, George A., 38 West 5th Street, Dayton, Ohio:
    The World Is His Parish, Treasure Chest of Fun and Fact
Postal Publications, Inc., 270 Park Avenue, New York, N. Y. (Atlas):
    Battlefront, Patsy and Her Pals
Premier Magazines, Inc., 11 East 44th Street, New York, N. Y. (PM):
    Animal Fun, Horror from the Tomb, Masked Ranger, Nuts, Police Against
    Crime, True Love Confessions
Prime Publications, Inc., 270 Park Avenue, New York, N. Y. (Atlas):
    Captain America, Uncanny Tales
Real Adventures Publishing Co., Inc., 1658 Summer Street, Stamford, Conn.
    (Fiction House):
    The Spirit, 3D Sheena, 3D Circus, The First Christmas
Regis Publications, Inc., 45 West 45th Street, New York, N. Y. (ACG):
    Cookie Comics, Funny Films, Lovelorn
Ribage Publishing Corp., 480 Lexington Avenue, New York, N. Y.:
    Crime Mysteries, Youthful Romances
St. John Publications, 545 Fifth Avenue, New York, N. Y. (Preferred):
    Abbott & Costello, Authentic Police Cases, Basil, Bingo The Monkey Doodle
    Boy, Crime on the Run, Cinderella Love, Daring Adventures, Diary
    Secrets, Dinky Duck, Fightin' Marines, Fly Boy, Gandy Goose, Heckle
    and Jeckle, House of Terrors, Invisible Boy, Kid Cowboy, Kid Carrots,
    Little Eva, Little Ike, Little Roqufort, Lucy the Real Gone Gal, Mighty
    Mouse Adventure Stories, Meet Miss Pepper, Mopsy, Nightmare, North
    West Mounties, 1,000,000 Years Ago, Paul Terry, Pictorial Romances,
    Perfect Love, Romantic Marriage, Teen Age Romances, Teen Age Temp-
    tations, Terrytoons, The Hawk, The Whack, Three Stooges, Tor & Chee
    Chee, True Love Pictoral, Wartime Romances, Western Bandit Trails,
    Weird Horrors, Wild Boy. 3D–series: 9 of the above titles.
Scope Magazines, Inc., 45 West 45th Street, New York, N. Y. (ACG):
    Giggle Comics, Ha Ha Comics, Out of the Night.
Signal Publishing Co., 125 East 46th Street, New York, N. Y.:
    Girls' Love Stories, Girls Romances.
Song Hits, Inc., Division Street, Derby, Conn. (CDC):
    Atomic Mouse, Cowboy Western, Crime and Justice, Eh!, Funny Animals,
    Haunted, Hot Rods and Racing Cars, Lash La Rue Western, My Little
    Margie, Packet Squad In Action, Rocky Lane Western, Romantic Story,
    Six-Gun Heroes, Space Adventures, Stange Suspense Stories, Sweethearts,
    Tex Ritter Western, The Thing, True Life Secrets, TV Teens, Zoo Funnies.
Sphere Publishing Co., 270 Park Avenue, New York, N. Y. (Atlas):
    Combat Kelly, Millie the Model Comics.
Sports Action, Inc., 270 Park Avenue, New York, N. Y. (Atlas):
    Combat Casey.
Standard Magazines, Inc., 10 East 40th Street, New York, N. Y.:
    Intimate Love, Thrilling Romances.
Stanhall Publications, Inc., 480 Lexington Avenue, New York, N. Y.:
    Broadway-Hollywood Blackouts, Farmers Daughter, G. I. Jane, Muggy
    Doo, Oh Brother.
Stanmor Publications, Inc., 175 Fifth Avenue, New York, N. Y. (Stanley P.
    Morse):
    Battle Cry.

Star Publications, Inc., 545 Fifth Avenue, New York, N. Y. (Star):
  All Famous Police Cases, Confessions of Love, Confessions of Romances,
  Frisky Animals, Fun Comics, Ghostly Weird Stories, Mighty Bear, Popu-
  lar Teen Agers, Shocking Mystery Cases, Spook, Startling Terror Tales,
  Super Cat, Terrifying Tales, Terrors of The Jungle, The Horrors, The
  Outlaws, Top Love Stories, True to Life Romances, Unsane.
Sterling Comics, Inc., 480 Lexington Avenue, New York, N. Y.:
  The Informer, The Tormented.
Story Comics, Inc., 11 East 44th Street, New York, N. Y.:
  Fight Against Crime, Mysterious Adventures
Timely Comics, Inc., 270 Park Avenue, New York, N. Y. (Atlas):
  Love Romances, Secret Story Romances
Tiny Tot Comics, Inc., 225 Lafayette Street, New York, N. Y. (EC):
  Panic, Shock Suspen Stories
Titan Publishing Co., 45 West 45th Street, New York, N. Y. (ACG):
  Forbidden Worlds, Funny Films, Atomic Sub
Toby Press, Inc., 17 East 45th Street, New York, N. Y. (Toby):
  Billy The Kid, Felix and His Friends, Felix The Cat, Gabby Hayes, Great
  Lover Romances, He-Man, John Wayne, Johnny Danger, Lil Abner,
  Meet Merton, Return of the Outlaw, Sorority Secrets, Super Brat, Tales
  of Horror, With the Marines
Trojan Magazines, 125 East 46th Street, New York, N. Y.:
  Beware
20th Century Comic Corp., 270 Park Avenue, New York, N. Y. (Atlas):
  Astonishing, Mystery Tales
USA Comic Magazine Corp., 270 Park Avenue, New York, N. Y. (Atlas):
  War Comics
United Feature Syndicate, Inc., 220 East 42d Street, New York, N. Y. (United
  Feature):
  Comics On Parade, Fritzi Ritz, Sparkle Comics, Sparkler Comics, Tip-Top
  Comics, Tip Topper Comics
Unity Publishing Corp., 23 West 47th Street, New York, N. Y. (Ace):
  The Beyond
Visual Editions, Inc., 10 East 40th Street, New York, N. Y. (Standard):
  Adventures Into Darkness, Dennis The Menace, Joe Yank, Kathy, New
  Romances, Out of the Shadows, Ricky, The Unseen
Western Fiction Publishing Co., 270 Park Avenue, New York, N. Y. (Atlas):
  Journey Into Unknown Worlds, Wild Western
Witches Tales, Inc., 1860 Broadway, New York, N. Y. (Harvey):
  Chamber of Chills, Witches Tales
Wings Publishing Co., Inc., 1658 Summer Street, Stamford, Conn. (Fiction
  House):
  Indians, Wings Comics
Zenith Publishing Corp., 270 Park Avenue, New York, N. Y. (Atlas):
  Girl Confessions, The Monkey and The Bear
Ziff-Davis Publishing Co., 366 Madison Avenue, New York, N. Y.:
  G. I. Joe

ORGANIZATION OF THE COMIC BOOK INDUSTRY IN THE UNITED STATES ACCORD-
ING TO DISTRIBUTOR, COMIC GROUP, AND PUBLISHER, IN THE SPRING OF 1954

DISTRIBUTOR

Ace News Corp., 23 West 47th Street, New York, N. Y.; A. A. Wyn, president; 5 publishers, 11 comic titles.

Comic groups, publishers, and number of comic-book titles

Ace Fiction Group, 23 West 47th Street, New York, N. Y.   Owners: A. A.
  Wyn, Rose Wyn.

Publisher:	Number of titles
A. A. Wyn, Inc	5
Ace Magazines, Inc	2
Junior Books, Inc	1
Periodical House, Inc	2
Unity Publishing Corp	1

(The) American News Co., Inc., 131 Varick Street, New York, N. Y.; P. O'Connell, president; 26 publishers, 287 comic titles.

Comic groups, publishers, and number of comic-book titles

Archie Comic Group, 241 Church Street, New York, N. Y. Owners: Maurice Coyne, John L. Goldwater, Louis H. Silberkleit.

	Number of titles
Publisher:	
Archie Comic Publications, Inc_____	9
Close-Up, Inc_____	6

Dell Comic Group, 261 Fifth Avenue, New York, N. Y. Owners: George T. Delacorte, Jr., Margarita Delacorte, 687 stockholders of Western Printing & Lithographing Co.

	Number of titles
Publisher:	
Dell Comics_____	88
K. K. Publications, Inc_____	19

Famous Funnies Group, 500 Fifth Avenue, New York, N. Y. Stockholders: James H. Darcey, David S. Hibbard, Sylvia S. Hibbard, Eric Pape, William B. Pape, William J. Pape, E. Robert Stevenson, Elizabeth E. Stevenson, Robert I. Stevenson, J. Warren Upson.

	Number of titles
Publisher:	
Famous Funnies Publications_____	3

Fiction House, Inc., 1658 Summer Street, Stamford, Conn. Owner: J. G. Scott.

	Number of titles
Publisher:	
Fiction House, Inc_____	1
Fight Stories, Inc_____	1
Flying Stories, Inc_____	2
Glen-Kel Publishing Co., Inc_____	2
Love Romances Publishing Co., Inc_____	1
Real Adventures Publishing Co_____	4
Wings Publishing Co., Inc_____	2

Jay Jay Publications, 316 North 8th Street, St. Louis, Mo. Owners: B. M. Hirsch, R. Grable, R. Messing, Sr., R. Messing, Jr.

	Number of titles
Publisher:	
Jay Jay Corp_____	1

Magazine Enterprises, 11 Park Place, New York, N. Y. Owner: Vincent Sullivan.

	Number of titles
Publisher:	
Magazine Enterprises_____	17

Preferred Comics Group, 545 Fifth Avenue, New York, N. Y. Owner: Archer St. John.

	Number of titles
Publisher:	
St. John Publications_____	55

Quality Romance Group, 347 Madison Avenue, New York, N. Y. Owners: Everett M. Arnold, Claire C. Arnold.

	Number of titles
Publisher:	
Arnold Publications, Inc_____	2
Comic Favorites, Inc_____	2
Comic Magazines_____	14

Standard Comics Group, 10 East 40th Street, New York, N. Y. Owner: Ned L. Pines.

	Number of titles
Publisher:	
Better Publications, Inc_____	2
Literary Enterprises, Inc_____	4
Standard Magazines, Inc_____	2
Visual Editions, Inc_____	8

Star Publications, 545 Fifth Avenue, New York, N. Y. Owner: J. Kramer.

	Number of titles
Publisher:	
Star Publications, Inc_____	19

Toby Press Group, 17 East 45th Street, New York, N. Y.   Owner: Elliott A. Caplin.

	Number of titles
Publisher:	
Toby Press, Inc_____	16

United Feature Comic Group, 220 East 42d Street, New York, N. Y.   Owners: Karl A. Bickel, Winifred Scripps Ellis, Margaret C. Hawkins, W. W. Hawkins, Jack R. Howard, Margaret R. Howard, Roy W. Howard, Charles E. Scripps, Edward W. Scripps, Florence Scripps Kellogg, John P. Scripps, Robert P. Scripps, The Ellen Browning Scripps Foundation.

	Number of titles
Publisher:	
United Feature Syndicate, Inc_____	6

Ziff-Davis Publishing Co., 366 Madison Avenue, New York, N. Y.   Owners: B. G. Davis, Sylvia Davis, Amelia Ziff.

	Number of titles
Publisher:	
Ziff-Davis Publishing Co_____	1

DISTRIBUTOR

Atlas Magazines, Inc., 270 Park Avenue, New York, N. Y.; Martin Goodman, president; 31 publishers, 64 comic titles.

Comic groups, publishers, and number of comic-book titles

Magazine Management Co., Marvel Comic Group (Atlas), 270 Park Avenue, New York, N. Y.   Owners: Martin Goodman, Jean Goodman.

	Number of titles
Publisher:	
Animirth Comics, Inc_____	6
Atlas News Co., Inc_____	3
Bard Publishing Corp_____	1
Broadcast Features Publications, Inc_____	2
Canam Publishers Sales Corp_____	4
Chipiden Publishing Corp_____	2
Classic Syndicate, Inc_____	1
Comic Combine Corp_____	3
Cornell Publishing Corp_____	2
Current Detective Stories_____	1
Foto Parade, Inc_____	1
Gem Publications, Inc_____	1
Hercules Publishing Corp_____	3
Interstate Publishing Corp_____	3
Leading Magazine Corp_____	1
Male Publishing Corp_____	8
Manvis Publications, Inc_____	1
Marjean Magazines Corp_____	1
Marvel Comics, Inc_____	1
Miss America Publishing Corp_____	1
Newsstand Publications, Inc_____	1
Official Magazine Corp_____	6
Postal Publications, Inc_____	2
Prime Publications, Inc_____	2
Sphere Publications, Inc_____	2
Sports Action, Inc_____	1
Timely Comics, Inc_____	2
20th Century Comic Corp_____	2
USA Comic Magazine Corp_____	1
Western Fiction Publishing Corp_____	2
Zenith Publishing Corp_____	2

DISTRIBUTOR

Capital Distributing Co., Derby, Conn.; Robert A. Baker, circulation director; 1 publisher, 21 comic titles.

Comic groups, publishers, and number of comic book-titles

Charlton Comics Group, Division Street, Derby, Conn.   Owners: Edward Levy, John Santangelo.

	Number of titles
Publisher:	
Song Hits, Inc_____	21

DISTRIBUTOR

Curtis Circulation Co., Independence Square, Philadelphia, Pa.; Benjamin Allen, president; 2 publishers, 103 comic titles.

Comic groups, publishers, and number of comic book-titles

William E. Kanter, 101 Fifth Avenue, New York, N. Y. Owners: Albert L. Kanter, Hal Kanter, Maurice Kanter, Rose Kanter, William E. Kanter.

Publisher:	*Number of titles*
Famous Authors, Ltd_____	10
Gilberton Co., Inc_____	93

DISTRIBUTOR

Fawcett Publications, Inc., 67 West 44th Street, New York, N. Y.; Roger Fawcett, vice president; 1 publisher, 9 comic titles.

Comic groups, publishers, and number of comic book-titles

Fawcett Publications, Inc., Fawcett Place, Greenwich, Conn. Stockholders: Claire Sue Bagg, James Wesley Bagg, Marion Fawcett Bagg, William Bagg, Gordon W. Fawcett, Helen Aline Fawcett, John Fawcett, John Roger Fawcett, Mary Blair Fawcett, Michael Blair Fawcett, Roger Fawcett, Roscoe K. Fawcett, Marie F. Fawcett, Thomas Knowlton Fawcett, Vivian D. Fawcett, W. H. Fawcett, Jr., W. H. Fawcett III, William Blair Fawcett, Mrs. Virginia Kerr, (Estate of) Mira King, Gloria Fawcett Leary, Mrs. Eva Roberts.

Publisher:	*Number of titles*
Fawcett Publications, Inc_____	9

DISTRIBUTOR

Gilberton Co., Inc., 101 Fifth Avenue, New York, N. Y.; William E. Kanter, vice president; 1 publisher, 1 comic title.

Comic groups, publishers, and number of comic-book titles

Gilberton Co., Inc., 101 Fifth Avenue, New York, N. Y. Owners: Albert L. Kanter, Hal Kanter, Maurice Kanter, Rose Kanter, William E. Kanter.

Publisher:	*Number of titles*
Gilberton Co., Inc_____	1

DISTRIBUTOR

Hearst Magazines (International Circulation Division of), 250 West 55th Street, New York, N. Y.; R. E. Haig, vice president; 1 publisher, 16 comic titles.

Comic groups, publishers, and number of comic-book titles

Avon Comics Group, 575 Madison Avenue, New York, N. Y. Owners: Joseph Meyers, Maurice Diamond, Harry Rebell.

Publisher:	*Number of titles*
Avon Periodicals, Inc_____	16

DISTRIBUTOR

Independent News Co., 480 Lexington Avenue, New York, N. Y.; Paul H. Sampliner, president; 10 publishers, 65 comic titles.

Comic groups, publishers, and number of comic-book titles

American Comics Group, 45 West 45th Street, New York, N. Y. Owners: Frederick H. Iger, Frances Sanger.

Publisher:	*Number of titles*
Best Syndicated Features_____	3
Regis Publications, Inc_____	3
Scope Magazines, Inc_____	3
Titan Publishing Co_____	3

Beverly Publishing Co., 480 Lexington Avenue, New York, N. Y. Owners:
Gizella F. Frank, Sonia Iger, George H. Levy.

Publisher: *Number of titles*

    Beverly Publishing Co_____ 1

National Comics Group, 480 Lexington Avenue, New York, N. Y. Owners:
A. Donenfeld, G. Donenfeld, H. Donenfeld, I. Donenfeld, S. Donenfeld, J. I.
Golinko, F. Iger, J. S. Liebowitz, R. Liebowitz. A. I. Menin, P. H. Sampliner,
S. U. Sampliner.

Publisher: *Number of titles*

    National Comics Publications, Inc_____ 40

Prize Comic Group, 1790 Broadway, New York, N. Y. Owners: Michael M.
Bleier, Paul Epstein.

Publisher: *Number of titles*

    Crestwood Publishing Co., Inc_____ 2
    Feature Publications, Inc_____ 4
    Headline Publications, Inc_____ 4

Signal Publishing Co., 125 East 46th Street, New York, N. Y. Owners: Avrum
Ben-Avi, Irwin Donenfeld, Harry C. Lieb.

Publisher: *Number of titles*

    Signal Publishing Co_____ 2

DISTRIBUTOR

Kable News Co., 500 Fifth Avenue, New York, N. Y.; Samuel James Campbell,
chairman of board; 11 publishers, 36 comic titles.

Comic groups, publishers, and number of comic book-titles

Farrell Comic Group, 30 East 60th Street, New York, N. Y. Owners: Robert
W. Farrell, S. Lichtenbert.

Publisher: *Number of titles*

    Excellent Publications, Inc_____ 2
    Farrell Comics, Inc_____ 3
    Four Star Publications, Inc_____ 2

Allen Hardy, 500 Fifth Avenue, New York, N. Y. Owners: Philip Birch, Jerry
Feldmann, Allan Hardy, Harry Lutz. Coowner of Mystery Publishing Co.,
Inc.: Samuel J. Campbell.

Publisher: *Number of titles*

    Allen Hardy Associates_____ 6
    Mystery Publishing Co., Inc_____ 4

Stanley P. Morse, 175 Fifth Avenue, New York, N. Y. Owners of Aragon,
Gillmor and Stanmor: Gilbert Singer, Michael Morse, Stanley P. Morse.
Owners of Key: S. Lichtenbert, Stanley P. Morse.

Publisher: *Number of titles*

    Aragon Magazines, Inc_____ 1
    Gillmor Magazines, Inc_____ 2
    Key Publications, Inc_____ 4
    Stanmor Publications, Inc_____ 1

Premier Magazines, Inc., 11 East 44th Street, New York, N. Y. Owner: Lew
A. Stricoff.

Publisher: *Number of titles*

    Premier Magazines, Inc_____ 6

Joseph A. Wolfert, 32 Broadway, New York, N. Y. Owner: Joseph A. Wolfert.

Number of titles

Publisher:

    Joseph A. Wolfert_____ 5

DISTRIBUTOR

Leader News Co., Inc., 114 East 47th Street, New York, N. Y.; Michael Estrow, president; 12 publishers, 24 comic titles.

Comic groups, publishers, and number of comic-book titles

Entertaining Comics Group, 225 Lafayette Street, New York, N. Y.   Owners: William M. Gaines, Jesse K. Gaines.   Coowner of Tiny Tot: Virginia E. MacAdie.

	Number of titles
Publisher:	
Educational Comics	1
Fables Publishing Co., Inc	3
I. C. Publishing Co., Inc	1
L. L. Publishing Co	2
Tiny Tot Comics	2

Master Comics, Inc., 11 East 44th Street, New York, N. Y.   Owners: Michael Estrow and Stanley M. Estrow as agents for Leader News Co.

	Number of titles
Publisher:	
Master Comics, Inc	1

Mikeross Publications, Inc., 55 West 42d Street, New York, N. Y.   Publishers: Ross Andru, Michael Esposito.

	Number of titles
Publisher:	
Mikeross Publications, Inc	2

Ribage Publishing Corp., 480 Lexington Avenue, New York, N. Y.   Owners: Michael Estrow and Stanley M. Estrow as agents for Leader News Co.

	Number of titles
Publisher:	
Ribage Publishing Corp	2

Stanhall Publications, Inc., 480 Lexington Avenue, New York, N. Y. Owners: Michael Estrow and Stanley M. Estrow as agents for Leader News Co.

	Number of titles
Publisher:	
Stanhall Publications, Inc	5

Sterling Comics, Inc., 480 Lexington Avenue, New York, N. Y.   Owners: Sidney Chenkin, Eleanor Grupsmith, Peter V. D. Voorhees, Martin Smith.

	Number of titles
Publisher:	
Sterling Comics, Inc	2

Story Comics, Inc., 11 East 44th Street, New York, N. Y.   Owners: William K. Friedman, Morton Myers.

	Number of titles
Publisher:	
Story Comics, Inc	2

Trojan Magazines, Inc., 125 East 46th Street, New York, N. Y.   Owners: Ann Estrow, Michael Estrow.

	Number of titles
Publisher:	
Trojan Magazines, Inc	1

DISTRIBUTOR

George A. Pflaum, 38 West 5th Street, Dayton, Ohio; George A. Pflaum, Jr.; 1 publisher, 2 comic titles.

Comic groups, publishers, and number of comic-book titles

George A. Pflaum, 38 West 5th Street, Dayton, Ohio.   Owners: Mrs. Mary Pflaum Fischer, George A. Pflaum, Sr., Mrs. George A. Pflaum.

	Number of titles
Publisher:	
George A. Pflaum, Publisher	2

Publishers Distributing Corp., 1841 Broadway, New York, N. Y.; I. S. Man-
heimer, president; 10 publishers, 37 comic titles.

Comic groups, publishers, and number of comic-book titles

Lev Gleason Comics, 114 East 32d Street, New York, N. Y. Owners: Leverett S.
Gleason, Carol L. Rosenthal, Edward Rosenthal, Ellen J. Rosenthal, Jane
Rosenthal, Judy Rosenthal, Morton Rosenthal, Pat Rosenthal, Peter Rosenthal,
Rosalind Rosenthal.

	Number of titles
Publisher:	
Leverett S. Gleason	9

Harvey Comics Group, Inc., 1860 Broadway, New York, N. Y. Owners: Alfred
Harvey, Leon Harvey, Robert B. Harvey.

	Number of titles
Publisher:	
Family Comics, Inc	1
Harvey Enterprises, Inc	3
Harvey Picture Magazines, Inc	2
Harvey Publications	4
Harvey Publications, Inc	8
Home Comics, Inc	5
Illustrated Humor, Inc	1
Witches Tales, Inc	2

Our Publishing Co., 114 East 32d Street, New York, N. Y. Owner: Ray R.
Hermann.

	Number of titles
Publisher:	
Our Publishing Co	2

○

JUVENILE DELINQUENCY

(MOTION PICTURES)

HEARINGS

BEFORE THE

SUBCOMMITTEE TO INVESTIGATE JUVENILE DELINQUENCY

OF THE

COMMITTEE ON THE JUDICIARY UNITED STATES SENATE

EIGHTY-FOURTH CONGRESS

FIRST SESSION

PURSUANT TO

S. Res. 62

INVESTIGATION OF JUVENILE DELINQUENCY IN THE UNITED STATES

JUNE 15, 16, 17, AND 18, 1955

Printed for the use of the Committee on the Judiciary

COMMITTEE ON THE JUDICIARY

HARLEY M. KILGORE, West Virginia, *Chairman*

JAMES O. EASTLAND, Mississippi
ESTES KEFAUVER, Tennessee
OLIN D. JOHNSTON, South Carolina
THOMAS C. HENNINGS, JR., Missouri
JOHN L. McCLELLAN, Arkansas
PRICE DANIEL, Texas
JOSEPH C. O'MAHONEY, Wyoming

ALEXANDER WILEY, Wisconsin
WILLIAM LANGER, North Dakota
WILLIAM E. JENNER, Indiana
ARTHUR V. WATKINS, Utah
EVERETT McKINLEY DIRKSEN, Illinois
HERMAN WELKER, Idaho
JOHN MARSHALL BUTLER, Maryland

SUBCOMMITTEE TO INVESTIGATE JUVENILE DELINQUENCY IN THE UNITED STATES

ESTES KEFAUVER, Tennessee, *Chairman*

THOMAS C. HENNINGS, JR., Missouri
PRICE DANIEL, Texas

WILLIAM LANGER, North Dakota
ALEXANDER WILEY, Wisconsin

JAMES H. BOBO, *General Counsel*

II

CONTENTS

Page

Statement of—
Albright, Roger, director, Department of Educational Service, Motion Picture Association of America, Washington, D. C_____ 210
Boggs, John, consultant, Human Relations Committee, Los Angeles, Calif_____ 65
Breitenbach, member of the board, California Youth Authority_____ 55
Brown, Harry Joe, producer and director, Producers-Actors Corp., Hollywood, Calif_____ 136
Daly, Emmet, assistant attorney general, State of California_____ 18
Ford, John Anson, member, board of supervisors, Los Angeles, Calif__ 145
Freeman, Y. Frank, vice president, Paramount Pictures, Inc., Hollywood, Calif_____ 118
Frym, D. Marcel, director of criminology and chief of staff, the Hacker Foundation, Beverly Hills, Calif_____ 102
Gilford, Max M., general counsel, National Society of Television Producers, Los Angeles, Calif_____ 182, 239
Greenspan, Lou, executive secretary, Motion Picture Industry Council, Los Angeles, Calif_____ 147
Griffin, Rev. Andy, pastor, Emmanuel Methodist Church, Los Angeles, Calif_____ 34
Hacker, Dr. Frederick J., chief of staff, the Hacker Foundation, Beverly Hills, Calif_____ 96
Jacobs, Paul, chairman, Civil Liberties Union, Los Angeles, Calif____ 225
Johnson, Mr. Ralph, superintendent, Twin Pines Ranch, Banning, Calif_____ 36
Lindquist, Rev. Raymond I., pastor, Hollywood First Presbyterian Church, Hollywood, Calif_____ 23
Miley, Arthur F., read statement of John Anson Ford_____ 32
Mooring, William, motion picture and television editor, Catholic Tidings, Los Angeles, Calif_____ 75
Murphy, George, actor, official, Screen Actors Guild, Hollywood, Calif_____ 139
Ochoa, Rinaldo, director, Federation of Social and Car Clubs, Los Angeles, Calif_____ 73
Parker, R. E., chief of police, Pomona, Calif_____ 50
Parker, William H., chief of police, Los Angeles, Calif_____ 5
Reagan, Ronald, free lance actor, Hollywood, Calif_____ 92
Richards, Richard, California State senator, Los Angeles, Calif_____ 178
Roy, Leon, executive secretary, Catholic Big Brother Organization, Los Angeles, Calif_____ 44
Sanders, Nort, chief, community services division, probation department_____ 46
Schary, Dore, vice president in charge of production, Metro-Goldwyn-Mayer, Hollywood, Calif_____ 106
Shurlock, Goeffrey, director, Production Code Administration, Motion Picture Association of America, Los Angeles, Calif_____ 185
Tutak, John, executive director, Los Angeles Times Boys Club, Los Angeles, Calif_____ 67
Wald, Jerry, executive producer, Columbia Studios, Hollywood, Calif_ 132
Warner, Jack L., producer and vice president, Warner Brothers Pictures, Inc., Hollywood, Calif_____ 124
White, Gordon S., director, advertising code administration of the Motion Picture Association of America, New York, N. Y_____ 154
Whitfield, M. G., county parks recreational facilities for the county of Los Angeles, Los Angeles, Calif_____ 183
Wyman, Mrs. Rosalind Weiner, councilwoman, fifth district, Los Angeles, Calif_____ 27

EXHIBITS

(Number and summary of exhibits)

Page

1. Los Angeles Police Department weekly administrative report for the week ending midnight June 5, 1955_____ [2] 8
2. Los Angeles Police Department Form 15.81.11: Juvenile Arrests, Booked and Nonbooked, May 1955_____ [2] 9
3. Copy of brochure, Twin Pines Ranch, by Superintendent Ralph Johnson_____ [2] 39
4. Harnessing the Hot Rodders, article written by Ralph E. Parker_____ [2] 53
5. Copy of Youth Authority publication, planning handbook for town meetings on delinquency and delinquency prevention_____ [2] 57
6. Report to Senate Subcommittee on Juvenile Delinquency, Current Trends and Effects in Motion Pictures and Television and Their Potential Bearing Upon Juvenile Delinquency, by William H. Mooring_____ [2] 86
7. Investigator Says Youth Not Damaged by Movies, article submitted by Lou Greenspan_____ [2] 152
8. Photograph of scene from Warner Brother's film, East of Eden_____ [1] 165
9. Movie advertisement section of New York Times, Washington Post and Times Herald, Chicago Daily Tribune, and the Denver Rocky Mountain News_____ [1] 169
10. An advertising code for motion pictures and regulations for its administration_____ [2] 169
11. California Legislature assembly bill No. 183, an act to add section 299 to the penal code, relating to comic books and magazines_____ [2] 180
12. A code to govern the making of motion pictures, the reasons supporting it and the resolution for uniform interpretation_____ [2] 200
13. Copy of letter from the Joint Estimates of Current Entertainment Films_____ [2] 233
14. Copy of letter from the National Legion of Decency_____ [2] 234

[1] On file with the subcommittee.
[2] Printed in the record.

JUVENILE DELINQUENCY

(Los Angeles, Calif.)

WEDNESDAY, JUNE 15, 1955

United States Senate,
Subcommittee of the Committee on the
Judiciary To Investigate Juvenile Delinquency,
Los Angeles, Calif.

The subcommittee met, pursuant to notice, at 1:25 p. m., in room 518, Federal Building, Los Angeles, Calif., Senator Estes Kefauver (chairman) presiding.

Present: Senator Kefauver.

Also present: James H. Bobo, general counsel; William Haddad, consultant; and Harold Lane, field representative for Congressman Chet Holifield.

Chairman Kefauver. The subcommittee meeting will please come to order.

Today the Senate Subcommittee To Investigate Juvenile Deliquency begins the first of 3 days of hearings on the problem of juvenile delinquency.

Before I discuss our purpose in these hearings, let me take this opportunity of expressing my personal thanks to many civic officials—State, city, and county—and the many organizations that have cooperated with the subcommittee staff during the past few days. That staff tells me that the friendliness and the assistance of both the local and State officials, and others, have greatly enhanced our work.

I want to particularly express my appreciation to some of the officials of the General Services Administration and Internal Revenue Department—Mr. Stillwell, Mr. Campbell, and Mr. Kroger, and to the field representative of Congressman Chet Holifield. Congressman Holifield gave us his assistant, Mr. Harold Lane.

This subcommittee is composed of Senator Wiley of Wisconsin, Senator Hennings of Missouri, Senator Langer of North Dakota, Senator Daniels of Texas.

We had planned that three members of the committee would be here today, but at the last minute, it was impossible for Senator Hennings and Senator Langer to come for this first meeting. We do hope that Senator Langer will be here tomorrow, because personally I do not like to hold one-man committee hearings. But we had our arrangements made, and we feel that we must carry on.

Last year this subcommittee held three hearings in California. We visited San Francisco, Los Angeles, and San Diego. At that time the candidness of California public officials and private citizens enabled us to collect valuable information, on the causes of delinquency,

1

which have been included in the official report of the Senate, and have been of much assistance to us in considering legislation.

I want to assure all of the witnesses that their testimony will be read and thoroughly studied by the members of this subcommittee and by the United States Senate.

From these California hearings and other hearings across this country we have been able to piece together the pattern of juvenile crime. We learned that juvenile crime manifests itself in many ways: Some children take to narcotics; some children run away from home and get into trouble; others join teen-age gangs and plunder and frighten the whole communities. Vandalism and robbery are other outlets for juvenile frustrations.

This year we are investigating the various forms of juvenile delinquency which we found occurring in community after community. Although only about 4 or 5 percent of our Nation's children get into trouble with the authorities, this is still far too many for the advanced status of our society—a society with the know-how, the ability, and the interests necessary to overcome this menace.

Our subcommittee found that in 1953 over 435,000 youngsters came before the juvenile courts. But this figure represents only part of the total number of children who come into conflict with the law. Conservative authorities estimate that over a million and a quarter adolescents get into some kind of trouble each year. Most of these children are, of course, released by the authorities.

I wish I could report that the situation has altered for the better in 1954. According to the statistics, it did not. But we have had some encouraging reports that there have been fewer number of conflicts with the law among juveniles here in California last year than in preceding years.

Children under 21, as of the present time, commit 72.6 percent of all automobile thefts, 62.9 percent of all burglaries, 54 percent of all thefts, and 51 percent of all arrests of property offenses. Even 36.3 percent of all men arrested for rape are boys under 21 years of age. Incidentally, sex crimes in the last 12 years have increased something like 110 percent throughout the Nation.

What accounts for this sordid picture?

The causes of juvenile delinquency are as complex as are our society. A Nation torn between war and peace presents additional threats to the security of our young people. I think of delinquency as the scum that rises to the top from the imperfections within our society. As the imperfections are cleared, delinquency will decrease.

I want to tell you that all of the picture is not sordid, because in the last year and a half I have never seen as much interest in any subject matter, any problem as that which has been manifested by public officials of all levels of government and what is more important, by individual parents, citizens, church, school, and the home, in getting at the cause and taking action at the local level, and trying to give our young people a better opportunity and to eradicate to the extent we can juvenile delinquency.

I think I should say also that no nation ever had a finer bunch of youngsters than we have in this country today: 95 or 96 percent of our teen-agers, are intelligent, physically strong, morally good, training to be good and useful citizens. But the number that we have that are not are too many.

In our earlier report we recommended several ways in which the Federal Government could speed along this decrease in delinquency. For instance, we reported that inadequately staffed schools contributed to the delinquency problem. Crowded classrooms and meager counseling staffs prohibited the schools from carrying out its role in preventing delinquency. We say that the community has the choice of paying out money now for better schools or paying out more money in the future for bigger jails and larger police forces. We also made recommendations for better housing and better mental health programs.

Some 25 other bills have been introduced by this subcommittee to correct other more specific aspects of the juvenile delinquency program.

But when Congress handed us our assignment it asked us to do more than just draft a legislation; it instructed us to probe into the causes and cures of juvenile delinquency—to make a nationwide survey. It ordered us to focus public attention on juvenile delinquency, and this we are trying to do. We are here in Los Angeles today to focus attention on how California is meeting the challenge of rising juvenile delinquency.

Today we will hear from the public officials who have the final responsibility for caring for California's young people. Many fine efforts have been undertaken and carried out in California, which we will discuss later, and many in Los Angeles. Their experience with juvenile delinquency control makes them especially qualified to speak to us and to the Nation about their work.

I have long admired California's enlightened approach to this serious situation. Your youth authority, your ranch and forestry camps, all are activities which other interested groups should know about.

But for all the fine work here in California, it takes more than just State and local authorities to handle this complicated problem. A part of the solution rests with other institutions.

Three institutions exert a major influence on the course a child will follow in later life: that is, of course, the home, the church, and the school.

Although a child who comes from an insecure home can grow into a fine outstanding citizen, he will nevertheless, have been handicapped by this earlier environment. In the last analysis, it is the parent who can exercise the strongest authority in the development of the well-adjusted personality. The witnesses today, I am advised, will show how the parent can better meet this responsibility.

The church, too, has an added responsibility. The church is no longer a 1-day-a-week affair. Society expects the church to extend its influence and activities into every day of the week. The citizen has now looked to the church as a weeklong gathering place. This is especially true of the children of this country. Churches with progressive attitudes on the handling of teen-agers can and do exercise a strong preventive hand in curbing juvenile delinquency.

Today church representatives will tell us of their activities to prevent delinquency, prevent children from going wrong.

One last word about delinquency: In our national hearings we found that one of the weakest links in the attack on this problem was the lack of proper rehabilitation programs. It is true today that 100,000 young people who have been convicted of some kind of crime are in jails along with hardened criminals. There is no special training or schools for them. It is true that in 98 percent of the cases there is very little rehabilitation to get them adjusted back into a normal productive life. But here in California the work of the youth authority and the special projects like ranch and forestry camps present one of the most encouraging approaches to this rehabilitation program.

If adequate care and attention be given to the child once he goes wrong, he can again be set on the right track. The saving to society will not only be in terms of dollars and cents but also in the terms of human life.

Tomorrow our subcommittee will study the relationship of crime and violence movies to juvenile crime.

I am happy to say that we have had the finest possible cooperation from all parts of the movie industry in our approach to this problem in getting this information that we want and need.

On Friday we shall continue the investigation of the relationship of pornographic materials to delinquency.

Mr. James Bobo, this small young man at my left, is our chief counsel. Mr. Bobo, do you have any comments or any information that you wish to present before we call our first witness?

Mr. Bobo. Yes, Mr. Chairman, I have two resolutions I would like the record to show. The first is the resolution authorizing the sitting of this committee.

Chairman KEFAUVER. The first is Senate Resolution No. 62, which will be read into the record at this point, which is the resolution creating this subcommittee. The second is a resolution passed by this subcommittee authorizing the chairman and such other committee members as may be present to hold these hearings here on June 15, 16, and 17. This will also be read into the record:

Calendar No. 54, 84th Congress, 1st session, Senate Resolution 62 (Rept. No. 51), in the Senate of the United States, February 21, 1955. Mr. Kilgore, from the Committee on the Judiciary, reported the following resolution; which was refered to the Committee on Rules and Administration. March 10, 1955. Reported by Mr. Green, with amendments.

RESOLUTION

Resolved, That in holding hearings, reporting such hearings, and making investigations as authorized by section 134 of the Legislative Reorganization Act of 1946, and in accordance with its jurisdictions specified by rule XXV of the Standing Rules of the Senate insofar as they relate to the authority of the Committee on the Judiciary to conduct a full and complete study of juvenile delinquency in the United States, including (*a*) the extent and character of juvenile delinquency in the United States and its causes and contributing factors, (*b*) the adequacy of existing provisions of law, including chapters 402 and 403 of title 18 of the United States Code, in dealing with youthful offenders of Federal laws, (*c*) sentences imposed on, or other correctional action taken with respect to, youthful offenders by Federal courts, and (*d*) the extent to which juveniles are violating Federal laws relating to the sale or use of narcotics, the Committee on the Judiciary, or any subcommittee thereof, is authorized from March 1, 1955, through July 31, 1955, (1) to make such expenditures as it deems advisable including no more than $2,000 for obligations outstanding and incurred pursuant to Senate Resolution 49, agreed to February 4, 1955; (2) to employ on a temporary basis such technical, clerical, and other assistants and consultants as it deems advisable; and (3) with the content of the heads of the department or agency concerned, to utilize the reimbursable services, information, facilities, and personnel of any of the departments or agencies of the Government.

SEC. 2. The expense of the committee under this resolution, which shall not exceed $125,000, shall be paid from the contingent fund of the Senate by vouchers approved by the chairman of the committee.

SEC. 3. This resolution shall be effective as of March 1, 1955.

RESOLUTION

Resolved by the Subcommittee of the Committee on the Judiciary to Study Juvenile Delinquency in the United States, That pursuant to subsection (3) of rule XXV, as amended of the Standing Rules of the Senate (S. Res. 180, 81 Cong., 2d sess., agreed to Feb. 1, 1950) and committee resolutions of the Committee on the Judiciary adopted January 20, 1955, That Senator Estes Kefauver, Democrat of Tennessee, and such other members as are present, are authorized to hold hearings of this subcommittee in Los Angeles, Calif., on June 15, 16, and 17, and such other days as may be required to complete these hearings, and to take sworn testimony from witnesses.

Signed by Senators Kefauver, Langer, Wiley, Hennings, and Daniel.

Mr. BOBO. We also have a communication, Mr. Chairman, from Governor Knight which reads as follows:

Regret impossible to be with you today, and all the more so because of my deep interest in subjects which committee will discuss extensively. Have asked California Youth Authority to be present and to represent State. As you are aware, California last year, despite its tremendous growth in population, had no increase in juvenile delinquency. The Youth Authority is vested by law to handle this subject at State level. Accordingly I am sure that the committee authority's testimony illuminating and beneficial.

Cordially,

GOODWIN J. KNIGHT, *Governor.*

Chairman KEFAUVER. I think the mayor will probably be here later, and will either have a message or a personal appearance from the attorney general of the State, the Honorable Pat Brown, who has also been invited to come and testify. Is there anything else, Mr. Bobo?

Mr. BOBO. That is all at this time.

Chairman KEFAUVER. Mr. Bobo, who is our first witness?

Mr. BOBO. Our first witness is Chief W. H. Parker of the Los Angeles Police Department.

Chairman KEFAUVER. Chief Parker, we are glad to have you with us, and it is good to see you again.

Mr. PARKER. Shall I take the oath?

Chairman KEFAUVER. We don't think we will swear some of the witnesses, unless you are going to talk about other people. You might be going to talk about some others.

Mr. PARKER. I usually do.

Chairman KEFAUVER. I guess it would be better to swear you, then.

TESTIMONY OF WILLIAM H. PARKER, CHIEF OF POLICE, LOS ANGELES, CALIF.

Mr. PARKER. First, Senator, the mayor has asked me to convey his respects to you and the committee and has also requested that in my capacity as chief of police of the city of Los Angeles that I am representing him here today in this hearing.

Chairman KEFAUVER. Chief Parker, how long have you been chief of police of Los Angeles? I have been coming out here for some time, and you have been here a good many years to my knowledge.

Mr. PARKER. Well, I guess a number of years as chief. I have been chief of police since August 9, 1950.

Chairman KEFAUVER. And you have jurisdiction over all of Los Angeles County?

Mr. PARKER. Just the city of Los Angeles.

Chairman KEFAUVER. Just the city of Los Angeles?

Mr. PARKER. That's right. There are 46 cities in the county.

Chairman KEFAUVER. How large is Los Angeles now?

Mr. PARKER. Los Angeles has an area of about 460 square miles, and a population in excess of 2,100,000 people. Of course, we serve an area of over 5 million people, and a great deal of the travel in the area is through the city of Los Angeles by many of the people who do not live in it, as they go about their daily business.

Chairman KEFAUVER. The metropolitan area of Los Angeles is about what, now?

Mr. PARKER. Of course, the civic center portion of the city is following the trend of all large American cities, the population is actually decreasing, and it is increasing in the suburban areas. For instance, in the San Fernando Valley at the present time it is considerably in excess of 600,000 people who are living there. It is estimated that we will have a population of 1 million in that area by 1970.

Chairman KEFAUVER. Mr. Bobo, do you want to ask Chief Parker any preliminary questions before he testifies?

Mr. BOBO. Chief, we would like to know something of the juvenile squad that you have in Los Angeles at the present time.

Chairman KEFAUVER. Perhaps you are going to tell us about that in your general statement.

Mr. PARKER. Perhaps we might start, if I might suggest, with the general picture from the police viewpoint in connection with the subject matter before the committee.

Chairman KEFAUVER. Why don't you tell us first about your general organizational setup to deal with juvenile delinquency.

Mr. PARKER. There is a juvenile division in the Los Angeles Police Department that is part of the control bureau. There are 212 police officers of various ranks assigned to the juvenile division. They are represented in all of the geographical divisions of the department as well as in the central headquarters. And working with the other forces of the department all cases involving juveniles, either by reason of the conduct of the juvenile or by reason of a juvenile being the victim of criminal conduct on the part of an adult, are investigated by the personnel of the juvenile division.

Chairman KEFAUVER. What is the age of a juvenile?

Mr. PARKER. Well, under the law in this State anyone under the age of 18. That is the age demarcation that we utilize.

Chairman KEFAUVER. If they are over 18 they are treated as other adults?

Mr. PARKER. They are treated as other adults. As far as the police department is concerned, but that might not be the ultimate situation after the court has opportunity to handle the individual. They may be committed to the youth authority's care at a greater age, but that is a determination to be made by the court. We treat all persons over the age of 18 years or of the age of 18 as adults as far as discharging our responsibilities are concerned.

There is also a section of the juvenile division that we call the youth service section. They are concerned with the activities that the department is engaged in, such as the auxiliary police program and the Junior Band and Boy Scout activities. That is a part of the juvenile division.

Of course, that is a phase of the department that is not necessarily its responsibility.

Perhaps we would make that quite clear if I might become technical for a moment, the term "crime prevention" is used rather broadly and loosely. In reality it divides into two terms: crime prevention and crime repression. Crime prevention activities are those things that are done to prevent people from becoming criminals, and that is not the essential responsibility of the police. Crime repression are those activities that the police engage in to discourage persons with criminal tendencies from committing crimes. And I think it should be made quite clear that the primary responsibility of a police department is crime repression. Although we do engage in the crime prevention field, either formally through department activity or individually through members of our department who in their community may be engaged in youth activity work.

Chairman KEFAUVER. Go right on.

Mr. PARKER. The situation in Los Angeles, as far as the problem of the juvenile is concerned, is somewhat encouraging. So that you may have the exact data, I am reading from a report that indicates crime and arrest trends from the 1st of January 1955 to and including June 12, 1955, and a comparison of those trends over the same period in 1954.

It is interesting to note in that period that arrests of adults in the city of Los Angeles increased 9.1 percent over the same period last year while arrests of juvenile increased 4.1 over the same period last year. That trend has been quite constant, and it would indicate to me that the juvenile behavior is superior to the adult behavior on a ratio basis.

Of course, I have long been convinced we are making a serious error when we attempt to separate the juvenile problem from the problem of society as a whole, because I believe that the troubles that we have with the youth of the community are those that arise from the patterns that have been set by the adults. And we well know that a child patterns after the adults with whom he is brought in constant contact.

So that actually we have a greater adult delinquency problem in the city of Los Angeles today than we do a juvenile delinquency problem.

Some trends are interesting, and if the committee would care for a copy——

Chairman KEFAUVER. Will you give us the numbers that you are talking about in this 9.4 percent?

Mr. PARKER. Yes; I will. Arrests of all types, excluding traffic citations, for the period from January 1, 1955, through June 12, 1955, for adults, amounted to 92,657. That means that that many times an individual was temporarily deprived of his liberty and booked in a police station or jail.

That compares with the figures of 84,953 for the same period of 1954, and that gives us the increase of 9.1 percent.

In the juvenile situation for this period, that is, during 1955, there were 4,297 juveniles investigated and booked. They were placed on the record of the department as having been arrested.

That compares with 4,126 for the same period last year, or an increase of 4.1 percent.

If the committee would be interested, I have one copy of this general statistical report.

Chairman KEFAUVER. Yes; we are interested, and we will file that as a part of our record.

(The document referred to was marked "Exhibit No. 1," and reads as follows:)

EXHIBIT No. 1

Los Angeles Police Department weekly administrative report, week ending midnight June 5, 1955

Offense	Crimes reported				Arrests			
	Last week	Year to date	Last year to date	Percentage of change	Last week	Year to date	Last year to date	Percentage of change
Robbery	51	1,305	1,812	−28.0	50	1,762	2,061	−14.5
Felonious assault	92	1,867	1,992	−6.3	47	1,193	1,129	+5.7
Burglary	312	7,209	8,513	−15.3	76	2,304	2,326	−.9
Burglary and theft from auto	260	6,562	7,936	−17.3	9	355	476	−25.4
Grand theft	35	813	818	−.6	24	668	622	+7.4
Pickpocket	20	518	629	−17.6	2	32	44	−27.3
Purse snatch	11	173	269	−35.7		3	7	−57.1
Petty theft	199	5,150	5,341	−3.6	32	1,185	1,103	+7.4
Auto theft	150	3,160	3,348	−5.6	41	809	851	−4.9
Worthless checks	128	3,875	4,467	−13.3	26	632	710	−11.0
Total [1]	1,258	30,632	35,125	−12.8	307	8,943	9,329	−4.1

[1] Includes attempts and juveniles.

	Last week	Year to date	Last year to date	Percentage of change
Arrests:				
Drunk	1,981	42,160	36,907	+14.2
Vice	195	4,799	4,164	+15.2
Narcotics	55	1,910	1,716	+11.3
Sex offenses	69	1,335	1,262	+5.8
Other misdemeanors	926	28,079	24,314	+15.5
Other felonies	45	1,896	3,914	−51.6
Total	3,271	80,179	72,277	+10.9
Grand total	3,578	89,122	81,606	+9.2
Juvenile activity:				
Investigated—booked	155	4,152	3,979	+4.3
Investigated—not booked	45	957	(1)	(1)
Adults handled by juvenile	22	521	709	−26.5
Total	222	5,630		
Traffic accidents reported:				
Property damage	380	9,806	9,352	+4.9
Personal injury	356	8,425	7,813	+7.8
Fatal	2	140	126	+11.1
Total	738	18,371	17,291	+6.2
Citations issued:				
Moving	11,063	242,606	226,393	+7.2
Nonmoving	2,247	48,132	48,128	+.0
Parking	7,131	170,317	153,592	+10.9

[1] Not accumulated on daily basis in 1954.

NOTE.—Officers on military leave, 60; vacancies: officers 94, civilians 73 (30 miscellaneous, 43 substitutes). Source: Statistics Unit, Planning and Research Division.

Mr. PARKER. Now, I have more copies of this report that I would like to talk about.

Chairman KEFAUVER. Do you have sufficient copies for the press?

Mr. PARKER. No, I haven't. I don't know whether I have sufficient or not, but at least there are some here.

Chairman KEFAUVER. Well, we have some extra ones here.

(The document referred to was marked "Exhibit No. 2," and reads as follows:)

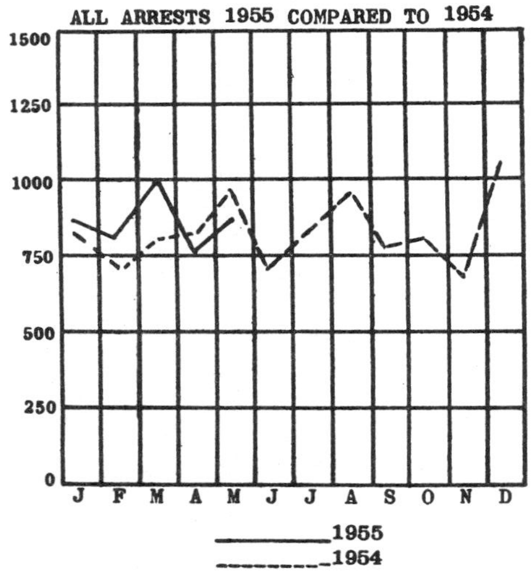

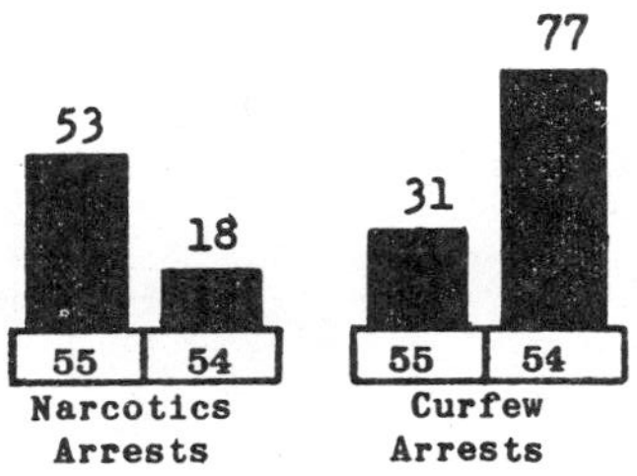

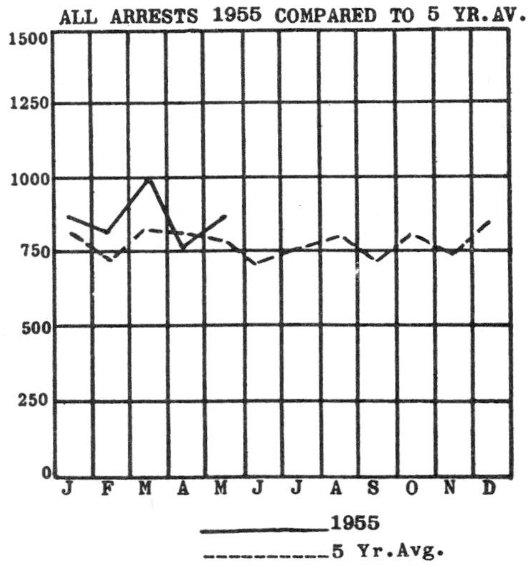

LAPD Form 15.81.11
March 1955

JUVENILE ARRESTS

Booked & Non-booked

May 1955

ALL ARRESTS 1955 COMPARED TO 1954
1500
1250
1000
750
500
250
0
J F M A M J J A S O N D
1955
1954

53
18
55
54
Narcotics Arrests
31
77
55
54
Curfew Arrests

ALL ARRESTS 1955 COMPARED TO 5 YR.AV.
1500
1250
1000
750
500
250
0
J F M A M J J A S O N D
1955
5 Yr.Avg.

BOOKED JUVENILES

Divisions	Cent.	Hwd.	Wils.	W. L. A.	Val.	Ven.	Univ.	Hobk.	Harb.	Hl. Pk.	77th	Newt.	Outside	Total
Division of arrest:														
This month	106	27	27	59	121	84	100	74	62	23	100	51	30	864
Current 12	1,452	370	481	326	1,237	500	1,059	608	564	524	1,118	598	333	9,180
Previous 12	1,753	381	398	282	1,027	341	1,038	585	494	608	1,107	680	327	9,021
Delinquency charges:														
This month	53	24	21	48	107	66	77	61	40	14	73	36	23	643
Current 12														
Previous 12														
Dependency charges:														
This month	53	3	6	11	14	18	23	13	22	9	27	15	7	221
Current 12														
Previous 12														

NONBOOKED JUVENILES

Divisions	Cent.	Hwd.	Wils.	W. L. A.	Val.	Ven.	Univ.	Hobk.	Harb.	Hl. Pk.	77th	Newt.	Outside	Total
Division of residence:														
This month	11	2	4	10	2	4	7	5	3	18	6	7	8	87
Current 12														
Previous 12														

Mr. PARKER. Now; this report you have before you is a little complex and it needs some interpretation. The graphs are somewhat self-explanatory in that they purport to show first the following: The graph on the upper left of the page indicates all the arrests, juvenile arrests, that is, during 1955 as compared with 1954. Then, of course, the 1954 picture represented by the broken line is complete, while you will note that the black solid line representing 1955 breaks with the month of May, which is the period covered by this report, that is, the year through the close of the month of May.

I think it is interesting to note in that graph that in the months of April and May, arrests of juveniles were actually lower than in 1954. There you will note that the blank line has dipped down beyond the broken line in both of those months.

Now, the graph to the right compares to the juvenile arrests so far in 1955, that is, through the month of May, with the 5-year average. While we are talking about 5-year averages, we must realize that the population growth in the Los Angeles area is continuing at a very rapid rate, and these figures are not translated in terms of population ratio. Of course, we realize, of course, there are more people in here today than there ever were before in the history of the city. Nevertheless, in month of April the juvenile-arrest activity was actually below the average for the preceding 5 years; which begins to support my contention that the problem in Los Angeles as far as the police phase of coping with the juvenile delinquency is concerned, is not alarming when you consider the increase in population and the increase in adult delinquency.

We purport to show in the center of this report trends in two specific types of arrests. And you will note that one column shows the number of narcotic arrests in the first 5 months of 1955 as compared with the number of narcotic arrests in the first 5 months of 1954. It is rather alarming in view of the general trend to find that there were 53 arrests in narcotics, that is, 53 juveniles arrested for narcotic offenses in the first 5 months of this year as compared with only 18 arrested on such offenses for the same period of 1954.

Mr. BOBO. Referring to those narcotic arrests, Chief Parker, were they for the possession, sale, or peddling of marihuana, heroin, or what?

Chief PARKER. They cover the whole field: Possession, transportation, sale, or addiction.

Mr. BOBO. Do you find a great many juveniles involved in the sale?

Mr. PARKER. Well, no. Juveniles are involved more in the using of narcotics rather than its actual sale. But this presents a very serious problem to us, and I would like to bring this comparison out again: On curfew arrests we know just the reverse, that there were only 31 such arrests in the first 5 months of 1955 as compared with 77 such arrests in the first 5 months of 1954.

But a situation has arisen in this State that has seriously interfered with the ability of the police to cope with the narcotic problem. The Supreme Court of the State of California in the case of *People* v. *Charles H. Cahan and others* handed down a decision—I don't have the date of the decision—it was a couple of months ago, in which for the first time in the history of this State they have invoked the evidence exclusionary rule in criminal cases, because they said in effect that if in the opinion of the court the evidence was obtained in any manner inconsistent with the guaranties in the fourth amendment to the Constitution, or the constitution of the State, that evidence will not be entertained regardless of the crime with which the individual is charged or regardless of the degree of guilt.

We have had a number of cases dismissed recently in our local courts on the basis of that decision, and I am talking now about narcotic cases, cases involving substantial amounts of narcotics where the guilt of the defendant was not in question at all, but merely the manner in which the evidence was obtained.

Now, I don't want to leave any impression that I am against the Constitution—quite to the contrary—but I don't believe that the interpretation that is being placed upon the fourth amendment is a true interpretation. I am talking now about the portion of the amendment that is a guaranty against unreasonable searches and seizures, and I mean that in terms of present-day conditions that these searches that have resulted in the seizures of this evidence have not been unreasonable despite the fact that a great many judges and prosecutors do not agree with me.

I would like to illustrate what I mean by an actual case. The police officers working in the narcotic field know that an individual is a narcotic peddler. Now, that is a known fact to them. So they place him under surveillance. At that time we were aware that considerable amounts of heroin were coming into this area from the east coast, and we were totally unable to determine how it was being shipped. While they had this peddler's house under surveillance the postman came by and took from his bag a package, looked at it, and tossed it up on the porch, and proceeded on. The known peddler recognized by the officers came out and retrieved the package and went into the house with it. Shortly after that the officers entered the house and found the package in the closet that contained a kilo of pure heroin, about 2 pounds and 2 ounces, or about $300,000, of heroin on the market that had been shipped second-class mail from the Bronx in New York. That peddler was convicted.

But under the interpretation of the Cahan decision he would have been turned loose by the court and released from custody and put back on the street; because they would have held that that heroin was seized in an unreasonable search.

Now, from the standpoint of getting a search warrant, without laboring this committee with our local problems, that presents a very complex legal problem, because you must be able to describe not only the place to be searched, but the things to be seized. And you first have to know that it is there before you can even apply for a warrant.

But that sort of thing has given us considerable trouble and it will reflect itself in this juvenile field because if we cannot successfully stop the peddling of narcotics, why, they are going into the hands of juveniles.

This decision has been so technically construed that we are precluded from proceeding in criminal prosecutions where evidence is found in an automobile unless we can establish that it was there before we searched for it.

The attorney general of California has appointed a committee of 10 people of which I am proud to be a member, to study this situation from the standpoint of remedial legislation. For the purpose of clarification the Supreme Court of California in handing down its decision in the Cahan case quoted with approval the Supreme Court of the United States, who when applying the exclusionary rule, said:

It is not a command of the fourth amendment but is a judiciary created rule of evidence which Congress might legate.

In other words, it is not a duty placed upon the Court by the fourth amendment at all; it is a gratuitous act on their part to do what they termed "curb the lawlessness of the police."

Chairman KEFAUVER. Can you give us the citation of that case, or a copy of the opinion?

Mr. PARKER. I will be pleased to leave a copy with the committee.

Now, in that same connection I would like to quote from a prosecutor, Bradford M. Crittender, district attorney of San Juaquin County, who in a speech, called the Decision We Asked For, which was given at a peace officers' convention, the peace officers of the State of California in their convention on May 21 last, talking about this decision said, and I would like to quote in part from his speech:

In the San Francisco Examiner for May 4, 1955, one of the justices of our State supreme court is quoted as saying, in commenting on the decision, "The individual should have liberties to know that as long as he does not openly violate the law that he is safe." This opens up a new field and concept. As long as you break the law secretly it is all right. Such a position is incredulous and amazing. I wonder if the justice thinks crimes are committed in the public square or on the courthouse steps? Has he never heard of the stealth, secrecy, and high degree of security in operations of the Communist Party in this country? Sabotage and violent revolution are not planned in the open forum of a schoolhouse or auditorium. Bookmakers don't set up their business in the public parks, or in the courtrooms of our halls of justice. Crime, Mr. Justice, is planned in secrecy and executed where? Under those circumstances most conducive to avoiding detection.

Now, once again those are not my words. I am quoting you the speech delivered by District Attorney Bradford M. Crittenden, of San Joaquin County, and he ably states the dilemma in which we find ourselves.

I bring that to your attention merely to point out that until this matter is straightened out either by an additional explanation from the Supreme Court—because you see, they did not explain the decision—they did not draw the lines of the areas in which they believe we can work without coming in conflict with the fourth amendment; they merely said, "From this day forward the exclusionary rule is in effect in California period."

They also say in the dictum, "You need not necessarily follow the Federal decisions."

So that you can readily see that we have guides, in that the State of California did not have the exclusionary rule until the Cahan case, and there is no case law on those areas. Because it has been immaterial on criminal prosecutions in the past as to how the evidence was obtained. And at the end, the court, in its dictum said, "We need not necessarily follow the Federal rule."

We find ourselves in a veritable quandary. We are not going to try to work our way out of it, and we are not going to give up, that is why we are striving to get some Federal legislation. But it is an important point and I believe that this narcotic thing, which is one of the areas in which we are hindered the most, is going to have its effect upon the juvenile situation in this community until something can be done to give the police the proper authority with which to combat this narcotic menace.

I think that's probably all I should say about that.

Mr. YOUNG. Mr. Senator, I wonder if I may——

Chairman KEFAUVER. Wait just a minute, please.

Mr. PARKER. Once again, I want to reiterate that I am not quarreling with obeying the Constitution. I am a lawyer, as you know, Senator, and I have been since 1930, and I am an officer of the court as such and I have taken an oath to uphold the law and defend the Constitution not only as a lawyer but as a police officer. But it is the right to differ that makes this country what it is, with the interpretations that men place upon things. And I am dealing with the word, "reasonable." I don't believe it is unreasonable to go into a narcotic peddler's house, whom you have reason to believe has bought a kilo of narcotics that was just delivered to him—you would never get it under a warrant—it wouldn't be there when you got back if you did get the warrant. That's my whole point.

Chairman KEFAUVER. I have read the California case. Does it follow the general cases of the Supreme Court of the United States?

Mr. PARKER. Well, they merely invoked the exclusionary rule such as United States has long since done, but then in the dictum they said we need not necessarily follow the Federal decisions.

Chairman KEFAUVER. So there is some confusion about it now?

Mr. PARKER. There are some cases that have been appealed by the district attorney where they were dismissed on motion without going to trial, and we are hoping that the supreme court of this State will give us some clarification on it in some of these cases that are coming up now, and if not, we can get something out of the legislature at the special session next year clarifying the laws of search and seizure and the laws of arrests.

Chairman KEFAUVER. Well, I know that the Supreme Court rule may place some burden or hardship on enforcement officers, but I have always thought it fairly clear in following the Constitution—I am not familiar with this matter here——

Mr. PARKER. Well, I just wanted to call that matter to your attention. I am not asking at all that the committee do anything. I can tell you frankly that I seem to be in the minority on this question, but I believe eventually I will prevail.

Chairman KEFAUVER. We are glad to have your explanation of what the condition is.

Mr. PARKER. Well, that just about sums up about all I have to say unless the committee has some further questions.

Chairman KEFAUVER. Do you have any, Mr. Bobo?

Mr. BOBO. Chief, there is one question that I would like to ask relative to one situation: What is the situation on automobile thefts in California? It is shown on one of the charts.

Mr. PARKER. It is shown on the chart here. We had a very satisfactory decrease in crime in this area in general until this certain situation came along, then our arrests have dropped considerably since then. But the auto theft situation is reflected in this report you have before you, and it indicates that from January 1 through June 12, 1955, there was a decrease of 4.8 percent in auto thefts. However, that general decrease has reflected in all of our major crimes and to a greater extent in auto thefts. Of course, auto thefts will always be a problem because of the vast number of cars available, the exposure of the car, the facility with which you can get to them, and the ingenuity with which you can start them even without keys. So that we will probably always be faced with the that problem. And in those cities where there is a large concentration of automobiles, such as Detroit and Los Angeles, you will find that the rate is quite high.

Mr. BOBO. I noticed that you mentioned that there was a great increase in the importation of heroin from the east coast. Have you noticed it in any decrease in the importation in narcotics, either marijuana or heroin, from the Mexican border area?

Mr. PARKER. I was not singling out the east coast, but we happen to know from particular information we had that this particular peddler was getting his supply from the east coast, although a great deal of our narcotics come from the Orient and some from Mexico. They are coming in from three different directions. But this particular case, which is a factual case did involve the supply from the east coast.

Chairman KEFAUVER. Chief Parker, I am interested in this youth service squad that you speak of in the police department that has responsibility over trying to foster interest in the Boy Scouts, junior band, things of that sort. How many do you have in that service, or about how many?

Mr. PARKER. There are about 30 people involved in that activity.

Chairman KEFAUVER. Just what then do they do?

Mr. PARKER. They have a deputy auxiliary police program which consists of about 3,000 young people in its organized activity, we have a camp in the mountains and they are taken up there for 4 weeks outing in the summer and also in the winter. And then they are broken down by our police divisions, as we call them, and they have social activities and instructions in athletic activities. The things that are generally done in youth group activities. But they are identified as a group sponsored by the Los Angeles Police Department. We have thirty-some Boy Scout troops. In fact, I understand that we sponsor a greater number of Boy Scout troops than any other police department. And we also have men working in the field in these troublesome areas working and attempting to find out what is causing the friction, primarily, racial friction, they are out there not waiting for trouble to develop, but out there attempting to find out what the irritations are and alleviate them before something happens.

Chairman KEFAUVER. What kind of penal facilities do you have for youngsters?

Mr. PARKER. Well, the police department——

Chairman KEFAUVER. Of course, that is not in your jurisdiction.

Mr. PARKER. We have some of our own. That is, we have holding cells at the juvenile headquarters, and no other persons are kept there. And then, of course, we have to have an order from the court before there can be any detention, any hearing, and then, of course there is the juvenile hall which is under the control of the county of Los Angeles. They are getting ready to build a new one with more adequate facilities. But we have no problem as far as the police department itself is concerned in the way of adequate facilities or for the temporary custody and segregation of the juveniles from the adult persons.

Chairman KEFAUVER. If a juvenile is convicted and sent to a training school or is to be placed in incarceration, where does he go?

Mr. PARKER. Well, the committed juvenile is committed to the youth authority, and I believe you have someone here from the youth authority. Then they have a number of different places that they might send a juvenile, depending upon the individual himself. I believe they can tell you more accurately just what they do. We don't have the problem such as they are having in Michigan where 15-year-old boys are going to the penitentiary. We don't have that.

Chairman KEFAUVER. Well, you have the youth authority and you have pretty good training schools for them. Then, as I get your testimony, you are holding your own or maybe doing a little better than holding your own insofar as handling the juvenile problem and juvenile delinquency is concerned, considering your population is slightly on the decrease in the city of Los Angeles, you would say?

Mr. PARKER. No, the population——

Chairman KEFAUVER. I say considering the population——

Mr. PARKER. I would say that while there might be a slight rise—— of course the chart shows that there is a fluctuation, but the last two months would indicate that we dropped below. So that the most recent information indicates that we are doing better than holding our own. In spite of the increase of the population there were less juvenile arrests in the first 5 months of this year as compared to what they were in 1954. So if we can take that as a trend there is considerable improvement.

Chairman KEFAUVER. Well, as a law enforcement officer and chief of police for quite a number of years is there any word of counsel you would like to take this opportunity to give to the people and to the organizations and clubs and service groups that are trying to cooperate to give our children a better chance and to lessen juvenile delinquency?

Mr. PARKER. Yes, Senator, I have some ideas on this problem, not only as the result of years of experience in police service, amounting to almost 28—it will be 28 years as of August—but I think many times we have lost sight of the fact that there has been a catastrophic change in the pattern of American living, and we have gone a long way from the type of rural life that I know I enjoyed, I might say, as a young boy. Now I think that has left its mark upon the behavior pattern of children. I do believe that the pace in which we live, the habits of our people are such that they are not conducive to a healthy atmosphere in which to raise children in many cases. I believe that parents are thoughtless in many cases because they do things they don't want their children to do, I mean, in the presence of their children and they expect the child will not emulate them. Perhaps the husband was talking about the winning or losing of a bet on a horse race, and yet he doesn't want the child to gamble. Perhaps they don't think anything of drinking in front of the child, but they don't expect the child to drink alcoholic liquor. It is a danger that there is a trend among parents to turn to agencies of government and private organizations for assistance in discharging the parental obligations.

There is one factor that I think is not impressed enough upon all of our people, and that is morality and ethics. I believe that many of us have forgotten what the words mean. And once again I will not segregate, I will not separate, rather the juvenile problem from the adult, because I think they are one. If we make an artificial barrier on age and say "This is one group of people and this is another one," they are not; they are one. In talking at one of the universities about 25 years to come I was asked if I had any suggestions of how they could improve their curriculum, and I said, "Yes, I believe in everything you teach that the ethics of the situation should be taught."

I think it is time that the Ameican people took stock in themselves, that they looked in mirrors at themselves, and not at other people to find out what is causing their children to misbehave. That's about all I care to say.

Chairman KEFAUVER. It is difficult to expect no juvenile delinquency where you have so much adult delinquency?

Mr. PARKER. That's my entire point.

Chairman KEFAUVER. Thank you very much, Chief Parker, for your contributions and your suggestions and advice on this committee. We want you to know that we are anxious to cooperate to help in any way that we can on the Federal level, and we would be very happy hearing from you and obtaining your suggestions or recommendations at any time they are pertinent.

Mr. PARKER. Well, sir, you will probably be hearing from me.

Chairman KEFAUVER. I want to thank you and all of your staff.

Mr. YOUNG. Mr. Senator, would I be out of order in asking a question to Chief Parker and the committee here?

Chairman KEFAUVER. What is your name?

Mr. YOUNG. Jack R. Young.

Chairman KEFAUVER. What is your business?

Mr. YOUNG. 335 South Cloverdale Avenue, Los Angeles 36.

Chairman KEFAUVER. What is it you want to ask the committee?

Mr. YOUNG. I am a motion picture cameraman by profession, I have been for over 30 years, and 25 years in the city of Los Angeles. And I have lived here and in our State of California. It was with reference to the juvenile delinquency here pertaining to the motion picture industry as well as the juvenile delinquent——

Chairman KEFAUVER. Get down to your point. What is the matter you wish to bring out?

Mr. YOUNG. With all due respect to police commissioner—Chief Parker—and police and law enforcement officers, as a law-abiding citizen and as a loyal American—and I say that without fear of contradiction——

Chairman KEFAUVER. We don't want you to make a speech. If you have some questions you want to ask, do so.

Mr. YOUNG. Chief Parker stated as to the amendment of violating the homes on the narcotic evidence. I am quoting the press that it has been ruled that the police department was in violation in our city and State and throughout the United States as to violating a home and entering without a search warrant. The attorney general so accepts that decision. Chief Parker still defies that decision. Chief Parker failed to state that one of our juries in our city court, here, told the police department that they could easily obtain a search warrant within a short space of time to enter such homes when they had that evidence. And it has been ruled that they are in violation, and as an American I stand on that violation. And I state as a loyal American, not a Communist—that I am opposed to communism—thank you, sir.

Chairman KEFAUVER. Thank you very much for your contribution, Mr. Young.

Our next witness is Mr. Emmet Daly, the assistant attorney general of California who is here from San Francisco. He is from the office of Attorney General Pat Brown, and he has to catch a 3:30 plane. You may make it yet, Mr. Daly.

We will change our order to allow Mr. Daly to tell us what we can do about juvenile delinquency.

TESTIMONY OF EMMET DALY, ASSISTANT ATTORNEY GENERAL, STATE OF CALIFORNIA

Mr. DALY. My name is Emmet Daly, and I am assistant attorney general of the State of California. My headquarters are in San Francisco.

Chairman KEFAUVER. Mr. Daly, you are here to represent Mr. Brown?

Mr. DALY. That's correct.

Chairman KEFAUVER. You are his assistant?

Mr. DALY. I am assistant and in charge of our crime prevention bureau of the attorney general's office, and in that capacity very much interested in the subject of the inquiry before the committee.

Chairman KEFAUVER. How long have you been in this position?

Mr. DALY. I have been with Mr. Brown in that particular capacity almost 4 years. Prior to that I was assistant district attorney with him in San Francisco. Prior to that I had 5 years with the FBI throughout the United States.

Chairman KEFAUVER. All right, Mr. Daly, we will be glad to have your opinion about this problem and how you are getting along in California and what the difficulties are, and what suggestions you have for this committee.

Mr. DALY. I don't have any statistical data to give you because I know that you are going to have various heads of the departments, such as the department of correction, the youth authority, and others. Mr. Brown has told me to tell you that if there are any specific statistics which you would care to have that our bureau of statistics can furnish you with, just let us know and we will get that for you. He wants to cooperate in every possible way with your committee.

Now, the subjects that have just been discussed by Mr. Parker, I might direct your attention to one phase, which is that of narcotics, because there has been so much talk about it.

About a year and a half ago the attorney general set up two committees, one in San Francisco and one in Los Angeles, of outstanding professional and lay citizens to engage in a study of that specific question of narcotics. Following a year study we prepared a report which was submitted to him, and as a result of that report, we have now presented to the recent legislature in Sacramento a bill known as assembly bill 2334. That bill in substance sets up for the first time in California a commission on narcotics.

I might say that in our study we went to San Quentin Pentitentiary. We went down to Chino to the correctional institution for men, and we talked to a number of addicts and peddlers, and from them we learned this one important fact: that most men who were addicts and peddlers told us that if something had been done for them when they were young, when they first started their addiction, when they first started marihuana—because that seems to be the pattern—they take very innocently a cigarette of marihuana and maybe a few more, and gradually they want something stronger, and end up as an addict.

Chairman KEFAUVER. Many times thinking it is smart to smoke marihuana?

Mr. DALY. That's right. That's right. It is done either as a dare or because the party is inquisitive, one or the other. Rarely is it just a desire to smoke marihuana.

However, we found that through the testimony given to us by the various addicts, it seemed to be rather universal that if something had been done at that stage of their addiction—other words when they were 17, 18, and 19—they might have prevented going on to the ultimate end that we saw when we saw them up in such a place as San Quentin.

So this new bill which I have just referred to, 2334, is going to set up for the first time a treatment facility, and it is aimed particularly at the juvenile. The treatment facility will work substantially as follows: If a boy or girl is arrested for narcotic addiction he may go before the court and on being convicted he may be placed on probation, and then as a term of that probation he can be committed to a treatment facility.

Those treatment facilities will be operated by the State in various parts of the State, and we believe that through the medical help of psychiatrists and trained conscientious personnel who will be assigned to that work, that we may prevent a lot of these youngsters from going on into the more serious forms of addiction.

I just want to say that to you.

Chairman KEFAUVER. Well, I think that's a wonderful thing to do, Mr. Daly. We have at Lexington, Ky., as you know, the Federal Hospital for Narcotic Addiction.

Mr. DALY. Yes.

Chairman KEFAUVER. Where many young people who do become addicted are treated, and many of them are cured and get over their addiction. Our experience has been, in the first place, that this is not known of and it is not used and that is generally as it should be, and in the next place it is in the eastern side of the United States. There is no similar Federal facility in this part of the country. I think this treatment facility that you are talking about will do much to restore life and health to many, many young people, and I hope the bill passes.

Mr. DALY. It has passed, Senator, and I believe is on the desk of the Governor now for his signature.

There is one thing that I would like to comment on very briefly because I am intensely interested in it, and that is the effect which alcoholism has on deliquency. When I was with Mr. Brown as assistant district attorney we had a problem of some 85 percent of all arrests in the city and county of San Francisco coming directly, shall we say, from the abuse of the handling of liquor. Mr. Brown asked me to make a survey, and as a result of that survey we set up a clinic which is known as the Adult Guidance Center in San Francisco. We are getting on an average of about 100 cases a day. It has been in existence now since 1948 and it is known as the 150 Otis Street Clinic. We have trained psychiatrists and medical personnel there who take the alcoholic and attempt to do something with him. We are actually turning them back into profitable work again, back to their families within 10 days; whereas the usual format in the old days was to arrest them and to use the parlance of the police, kick them out the next morning, or give them 6 months in the county jail.

So we do feel that the work done up there has been very helpful. It has shown that something can be done in the field of alcoholism if you treat the person who is an alcoholic and treat him medically and give them an opportunity to become rehabilitated.

The reason I want to mention it in relation to delinquency is this: We have a followup program on most of the persons who go through the clinic, and if I recall correctly, the figure is around about 65 percent of the men and women who have gone through the clinic, who tell us that looking back over their case histories, their problems came from an alcoholic parent. In other words, either the mother or the father was an alcoholic to a point where the family was broken up, and the child then seems to automatically follow in that footstep.

So if we can do something intelligently from a medical viewpoint in the treatment of the alcoholic, we believe that we might in days to come or years to come, do something profitable in preventing a great many from becoming alcoholics.

Chairman KEFAUVER. Mr. Daly, those treatments were followed up by the case workers to see what happened?

Mr. DALY. Yes. We had quite a bit of that work done.

Chairman KEFAUVER. What percentage of restorations have you found?

Mr. DALY. On the first group of persons that went through the clinic we had a 6-month followup when we could see what could be done, and 52 percent of the men and women—and incidentally these persons had been taken right out of skid row—the ones I am referring to now, as they say, were the bottom-of-the-barrel type of alcoholic— every one of them had come from skid row—and so it is generally said that you can't do anything with that type of person—nevertheless, a 6-month followup of them showed that 52 percent were working and sober 6 months after they got out of the clinic.

Chairman KEFAUVER. That's a remarkable percentage.

Mr. DALY. That was a very fine record.

Chairman KEFAUVER. This is being done in San Francisco?

Mr. DALY. This is being done in San Francisco.

Senator KEFAUVER. Is that the only county where it is being done?

Mr. DALY. Along that line, yes; but may I also say this, Senator, that you may be interested in knowing that the State legislature has set up now a State alcoholic rehabilitation commission, and at the last legislature they have agreed upon a budget of $204,000 for the coming year. They are going to set up, I understand, a comparable clinic in Los Angeles; and $50,000 has been allocated for that, and the commission, as I understand, will sort of model itself after the work that is being done in San Francisco. So we are making some progress.

Chairman KEFAUVER. Mr. Daly, that's one of the things our committee is interested in, is getting experiences that are worthwhile that people in other cities know about as to the result of some successful experience in a large city like San Francisco. We are glad to know about it. Is there anything else you want to tell us?

Mr. DALY. There are so many phases to this problem—I might say this: That having read as much as I can on it, there is a great authority, Sir Bert, who has stated that there is some 160 separate reasons why we have delinquency, and any one of them may be the dominant cause of delinquency. And the longer I study it, the more I am convinced that that is true. That we have to come down to certain overall things, and I believe, as Chief Parker has stated, your family, your parents, and again, shall I say in your alcoholic picture, where we know that delinquency comes from alcoholic parents— and another thing we have to realize in California is this new population that is coming in at an average—I believe the rate is today— of 1,000 a day. Another thing being that there is so many families moving. I believe the average move is six times a year in California. It is rather hard for a child growing up from any age up to 17 and 18, if his family is moving on an average of 6 or 8 times a year, to get any roots in the community.

Chairman KEFAUVER. You don't mean that the average family in California moves 6 or 8 times in a year?

Mr. DALY. There are statistics to that effect.

Chairman KEFAUVER. That's a lot of moves.

Mr. DALY. Yes.

Chairman KEFAUVER. Anyway, 160 causes, one may be dominant as to this child and one may be an important thing as to another?

Mr. DALY. Yes. Lack of religious training and lack of education. And it can be biological, some difficulties the boy has.

Chairman KEFAUVER. Mr. Bobo, any questions that you want to ask Mr. Daly?

Mr. BOBO. No questions.

Chairman KEFAUVER. Well, you give the attorney general our best wishes, and we thank you very much for your contribution.

Mr. DALY. I am very happy to be here. Thank you, sir. I was very happy to meet you, Mr. Bobo.

Mr. FRIEDMAN. May I have the attention of the committee for a moment?

Chairman KEFAUVER. What is your name?

Mr. FRIEDMAN. Phillip Friedman.

Chairman KEFAUVER. Phillip Friedman?

Mr. FRIEDMAN. That's right. I listened to Chief Parker and Attorney General Daly, and they confined most of their remarks to crime amongst adults and what was being done or what was not being done, and quoted statistics. And we are well aware that there are two kinds of lies——

Chairman KEFAUVER. Well, Mr. Friedman, just a minute, please. What is the question you wish to ask?

Mr. FRIEDMAN. The question is, The two speakers have not mentioned anything in the line of prevention or what has been done by the two gentlemen in the departments that they represent to remove the power of suggestion to the young delinquent in becoming an addict.

Chairman KEFAUVER. Mr. Friedman, I don't think your point is well taken.

Mr. FRIEDMAN. I understand the committee is interested in juvenile delinquency and not in crime.

Chairman KEFAUVER. They have given experiences that are useful to the committee. In our hearings we will try to deal with all aspects and phases of it, and if you feel that you have anything that may be worth while to the committee we invite you to see one of our staff members and tell him what you have on your mind. And there is a tall gentlemen there, just tell him what you have in mind, and if it will be worth while, we will call you too.

Mr. FRIEDMAN. Thank you.

Chairman KEFAUVER. I understand that Mayor John M. Lawson of Glendale, Calif., is here. Mr. Lawson was to be a witness, but I heard that he didn't have any testimony that he wanted to give. But I understand you want to be recognized, Mr. Lawson?

Mr. LAWSON. Thank you, Senator. We have a little test here. I am supposed to be dead now because of this atomic-bomb test.

Chairman KEFAUVER. Are you already dead or are you going to be buried by the test later on? Do you have to leave, Mr. Lawson, to go back to Glendale?

Mr. LAWSON. I will have a rather close schedule.

Chairman KEFAUVER. Well, we appreciate your presence here, and we will be glad if you will let us know of any suggestions or any comments you have. If later on you wish to testify, we will give you an opportunity to do so.

Mr. LAWSON. Thank you.

Chairman KEFAUVER. Rev. Raymond I. Lindquist, pastor of the Hollywood First Presbyterian Church.

Mr. LINDQUIST. Thank you, sir.

Chairman KEFAUVER. Reverend Lindquist, you are the pastor of the Hollywood First Presbyterian Church, is that correct?

Mr. LINDQUIST. Yes.

Chairman KEFAUVER. How many do you have in your congregation?

Mr. LINDQUIST. We presently have 6,300.

Chairman KEFAUVER. How long have you been pastor?

Mr. LINDQUIST. For 2 years, sir.

Chairman KEFAUVER. You have been pastor somewhere before that time?

Mr. LINDQUIST. I was in Orange, N. J., in the historical Presbyterian Church there for 19 years.

Chairman KEFAUVER. That's longer than I would have expected.

Mr. LINDQUIST. Thank you, sir.

Chairman KEFAUVER. Are there any preliminary questions that you want to ask, Mr. Bobo?

Mr. BOBO. I don't think so.

Chairman KEFAUVER. We are glad to have you with us, and we appreciate that the churches of all denominations have perhaps next to the family the greatest influence in this problem that we are concerned with, and it has been very heartening to us to see the broader approach to the problem of child opportunity by all of the churches, all denominations. We certainly will be glad to have your comments and recommendations, or anything you have to tell us.

STATEMENT OF REV. RAYMOND I. LINDQUIST, PASTOR, HOLLY-WOOD FIRST PRESBYTERIAN CHURCH, HOLLYWOOD, CALIF.

Mr. LINDQUIST. We are trying in the First Presbyterian Church in Hollywood to meet that very situation that was brought up by a person in this audience today: In other words, a preventive approach, but along with that we have a rehabilitation program. We have a Sunday school numbering about 6,500; naturally in that group we draw many boys and girls who are potential juvenile delinquents. We have made a study of the membership of our Sunday school in terms of parental background, and in 1 of our groups we find that 52 percent of the group comes from broken homes.

Now, this program indoctrinating the youth of our country with deep and abiding faith in God and in country and in themselves, too, Senator, we find that helps them, gives them the kind of foundation that will overcome the background of a broken home. Among the 79 young men that we have studying for the Christian ministry right now, many of them come out of broken homes, but they have overcome that initial difficulty because of the kind of program that they have.

We use a club approach for the week-day activities. You spoke a little while ago, Senator, of the fact that the church today is no longer expected to be of a simply a 1-day a Sunday affair and at our institution we are constantly working every day in the week. We have now 27 different clubs for boys and girls. And in these clubs we find that 50 percent of the memberships comes right out of the community and outside of the boundary of our church and Sunday school religionships. And because of this we find that the preventive method of helping, combined with the rehabilitation program, work out pretty well.

I can cite, for example, a number of cases——

Chairman KEFAUVER. Reverend, just tell us of your experience and what you know.

Mr. LINDQUIST. Yes; just this last week we had a certain call, a call from a certain school in our area, where 2 fifth-grade boys had gotten into a great deal of difficulty; 1 of them on the way home from school had gotten into a fight with another boy and had completely disfigured him. That boy is in the hospital and will be for some time. But, we have already sent one of our members to that school, and he is very quietly studying this boy on the playground and in the school. He will quite accidentally meet up with him today or tomorrow. He will invite him over to our week-day activities program, and especially to our skating rink. We have just built a $12,000 skating rink. The boy will get started there. We will give him a little job, perhaps repairing skates. From that he will go into a club, perhaps into the King's Men or 1 of the other 27 clubs, but the point that we try to accomplish, to get another boy, an older boy, interested in him to pal up with him to prove to him that somebody really cares that he amounts to something. We have learned that as soon as the boy finds out he is wanted, somebody cares for him, he begins to respond, and he wants to measure up to what that other fellow thinks of him.

Chairman KEFAUVER. You mean, Reverend Lindquist—I have four children so I know something about it—that he is going to look up to someone, whether it is a Dillinger, a racketeer, or a good person? They are going to find someone to look up to and emulate?

Mr. LINDQUIST. A young person seems to be incurably romantic. He has hero worship in his very bones. Of course, we have a number of athletes on our staff. For example, right now working at our place, back from Princeton Theological Seminary, is Don Wilmont, all-American football player, and naturally, these boys flock around a fellow like that. They see this great big chap and they find out he has a definite interest in them. Well, they respond at once, and get right in and go to work.

We have brought back for this staff this very week six additional young men from universities and from seminaries around the country who are at work on this matter. If we can face the insecurity of those boys and girls and help them realize that that insecurity isn't the basic condition of their character and of their life, they have a marvelous way of responding.

Just 2 years ago we had a young man—I have forgotten what particular grade he was in in high school—but he had a police record—the police got in touch with the director of our weekday activities, Mr. James Ferguson, a former star athlete at UCLA, and he very quietly arranged it so he would bump into this boy. They got to know each other, and then Mr. Ferguson invited him over and said, "Would you like to play basketball? We have a good gym."

And they brought him over and inside of a year and a half that boy had not only left this area of delinquency, but he was a positive force for good.

Now he is the associate director of one of our clubs and has signified his intention of going into the Christian ministry.

We have 3 young men studying for the ministry now out of the 79 young men, as I said before, who have former police records, and have been rehabilitated through this program in which we try to place every boy with another person. We don't believe it is possible for us to have the wholesale approach; we have got to work with them individually. But once we get them into the club, it seems that it is just a short while before they are interested in doing something for the club, maybe helping to organize another club, and helping to advance the fortunes of the club. For example, three clubs this past week voted to undertake the complete support of several Korean orphans.

Chairman KEFAUVER. You mean the kids themselves?

Mr. LINDQUIST. Yes, the kids themselves. The kids who have been in trouble are now trying to help other people out of trouble.

Chairman KEFAUVER. Let's see, Reverend Lindquist: You have 6,000 in Sunday School?

Mr. LINDQUIST. Yes, a little more.

Senator KEFAUVER. And out of that number you say that you form clubs. How many clubs do you have?

Mr. LINDQUIST. Now we have 27 clubs, but those clubs aren't necessarily formed out of the Sunday school group. The Sunday school group, you see, meets on Sunday, and they are a type of person who rarely gets into juvenile delinquency problems. What we are doing is to help to man to a certain extent these clubs with boys and girls from Sunday school; constituting a corps of fellowship to which we can invite the delinquents. The delinquents come in and get enjoyment, and, to use the theological term, "regenerated."

Chairman KEFAUVER. Reverend Lindquist, you work in your neighborhood regardless of what their religion may be?

Mr. LINDQUIST. It doesn't matter what religion or what color or what race. We have within the confines of our church Negroes, Koreans, Japanese, Spanish speaking people, and Chinese. So the great majority, by the very nature of our background as a church, are the type of person that we have in this city, the American folk who come out and settled in this part of the country.

Chairman KEFAUVER. How do you finance the staff for these clubs?

Mr. LINDQUIST. Well, we put it right into our church budget. I was figuring up today that in actual cash outlay we put about $26,000 a year. This doesn't seem very much, but for a church that's quite a bit; because it comes right out of the voluntary giving of the people. We don't have any type of underwriting for it. We have no great group to give us large amounts of money. But, in addition to that amount of cash that we put out, we probably have another twenty-five, thirty, or forty thousand dollars in terms of service.

Chairman KEFAUVER. You mean volunteer service?

Mr. LINDQUIST. Volunteer services of all kinds.

Chairman KEFAUVER. You mean volunteer service?

Mr. LINDQUIST. Volunteer service of all kinds.

Chairman KEFAUVER. And that is important, isn't it?

Mr. LINDQUIST. Well, we find that that is very good for the person servicing, and it is very splendid for the people who are served.

Chairman KEFAUVER. Reverend Lindquist, we have been told, and I think it is true—that in the past, that particularly one of the shortcomings of the church as far as juvenile delinquency was concerned that there has been too much reliance just upon the sermon, however good it may be, and Sunday school, however good that may be, and may be some Bible meeting once a week; and an absence of setting up these functions which children can take an interest and join in to bring them into the religious life. Do you think that is true?

Mr. LINDQUIST. I think you are absolutely right, Senator, we are trying to get these boys and girls—the girls don't give us the same problem in this area that they used to give us in the East—we are trying to get them expressing their own personality style. Therefore we have all kinds of trips away to the mountains, out to the shore, horseback trips, and like activities in addition to our athletic contests and that kind of work. I find that it doesn't take very long— and there is no pressure in that regard—before a boy begins to ask, "What is the angle in this? Why are you interested in me? Nobody has ever taken any interest in me before. Here you have just come out of the blue?"

In fact, we have some boys up at the church this afternoon from a high school club that is notorious. Two former members of that high school club are in San Quentin right now. We have given those boys gymnasium space.

Chairman KEFAUVER. You mean the high school gang?

Mr. LINDQUIST. High school club. It is an organized club.

Chairman KEFAUVER. Yes.

Mr. LINDQUIST. And, of course, one thing to do in the high school— and the people there know it—would be to suppress it, but then they will go underground. But this particular club has been given space at the church for their basketball activities and for skating and out of that group already there has began to appear some of these fruits that we have began to expect out of this kind of work.

Now, what happens really—and this is the main business of the church—it is not simply to rehabilitate young people who have gone wrong, it is not simply the going wrong of young people who seem to be all right now—but what we are trying to do is to build something infinitely greater, and that is an underlying faith upon which they can build solid character and true home life; so that they will not repeat this endless frustrating pattern which we find in evidence now, and they can take a real step forward, and when they have children they will be able to give them the kind of homes they ought to have.

Chairman KEFAUVER. A great step in checking juvenile delinquency, do you agree with me, if churches and schools generally would recognize that in this 20th century living, particularly in the cities, that they must be more and more the center of wholesome activity meeting together, getting young people together for some purpose other than letting them go out on their own and get into trouble?

Mr. LINDQUIST. Yes. I think there is a twofold problem with the young person today: One is the problem of the insecurity, just basic insecurity which drives a young person to a feeling of frustration. He gets out on the town and he starts coming home later and later and nobody is there—both parents are working maybe on the night shift, and then he goes to school tired the next morning, and pretty soon he is on edge and he gets into a fight and he starts his long downward journey. But unfortunately there are juvenile delinquents in homes that seem to be perfectly all right, in homes on the right side of the track, for example. And these people, the young people, are out for the "kicks," they are out for adventure. So you have two different tugs at their interest: One is the sense of insecurity and the other is the sense of boredom. Well, there is nothing to do. We will grab this car. It is standing in front of the church, let us say, and somebody did a year ago, drive down to the beach, have a swim, leave the car there, take another car back and park it where they had left the first car. Or, as the 14-year-old boy did in New York, grabbed a car, drove it all the way out here, and had a whole series of car thefts in his record.

But somehow we have gotten him into a club. As far as I can tell he is completely rehabilitated at the present time.

Chairman KEFAUVER. That's wonderful.

Mr. LINDQUIST. Of course, it isn't very dramatic and the numbers aren't as large as one would like. We are trying constantly to increase that number. But I think in the cases where this program takes hold we have someone who is really on the way to start a new generation and more than that, several generations of law-abiding character and church center of activity and self-respecting personalities.

Chairman KEFAUVER. Anything else, Mr. Bobo?

Mr. BOBO. That is all.

Chairman KEFAUVER. Reverend Lindquist. Thank you very much, and we follow with interest your good work.

Mr. LINDQUIST. Thank you, sir.

Chairman KEFAUVER. Mrs. Rosalind Weiner Wyman.

STATEMENT OF MRS. ROSALIND WEINER WYMAN, COUNCIL-WOMAN, FIFTH DISTRICT, LOS ANGELES, CALIF.

Chairman KEFAUVER. Mrs. Wyman is a councilwoman of the fifth district of Los Angeles. It has been the privilege of the chairman to know Mrs. Wyman for a number of years. We are certainly privileged to have her testify before our committee.

Mrs. WYMAN. Thank you, Senator.

Chairman KEFAUVER. To add a little charm and grace to the hearings.

Mrs. WYMAN. Thank you, very much.

Chairman KEFAUVER. Mrs. Wyman, how long have you been a councilwoman now?

Mrs. WYMAN. Well, Senator, counting back it will be 1 year and 10 months.

Chairman KEFAUVER. In addition to being a councilwomen you have a family?

Mrs. WYMAN. No, I have been married only 10 months. I am on my 10th month of being married. I have no family yet.

Chairman KEFAUVER. Well, in this country, we always look to the future.

Mrs. WYMAN. That's true. I also draw my experience in going through college. While I was going through college I worked my way on the playground so I have had some experience with young people of the community in that way.

Chairman KEFAUVER. We certainly will be glad to have your statement, including your suggestions and your counsel.

Mrs. WYMAN. Senator Kefauver, I draw my experiences firstly from the councilmanic district that I represent. And, although actually it is brief, it is somewhat of a good story in reference to juvenile delinquency. I think this is based on the fact that the district or the area that I represent is the middle and the upper middle class. I think when we find that there is proper housing and there is the least amount of broken homes, and where there are added church facilities, recreational facilities, available to the teen-agers that the crime ratio is down and I think basically that we key our recreational facilities for the very young person. In other words we have swings and slides and we have the various things on our playgrounds, but the teen-ager is not interested in slides and swings and ping-pong and these various sports. I think this is basically where we have missed with them. I think it is not reaching them.

I found out when I was on the playground as well as in my work here, that the teen-ager is at the age maybe where he is dating or maybe where he is interested in his own activities. And I find that if we help them in supervised activities such as, let us say, coke parties, or recording sessions, or something like that, then we are reaching the teen-ager and can draw them into supervised activities.

Chairman KEFAUVER. Mrs. Wyman, your district includes the Bellair and Westwood areas?

Mrs. WYMAN. Yes, it does. I have Bellair and Westwood at the extreme western end of my area, and of course this is the upper and middle class. I have what we call 2 subdivisions or 2 police stations from which the police would arrest these juveniles; one is the Wilshire station and one is the West Los Angeles station.

Looking at our statistics for 1954 we find such crimes as offenses against family and children. You find none in our area and you find none also out in the West Los Angeles area along those lines.

I would like to feel that it is a fact here that the parents are giving good supervision, because I don't think any witness will testify before you and not say that it is up to the parents primarily to give good leadership to their children. And I don't care who you are you just can't give what a parent can give if they are willing to give to their children. We have hired professionals to try to fill the vacuum and sometimes they have to, and I am glad that today we are at least expending a little money for that. Of course, there is a lot of argument that we spend money this way, but I would rather be spending it in preventing than later saying that we have to put them in penal institutions. Of course, this is an old argument as to where you are spending your money. And looking down at the figures in my district we find that for crime—I'll give you an example of it—on the east side or the central area we have a total of the various crimes such as homicide, burglary, auto thefts, assault, and all the crimes with which you are familiar. I found in an area such as the central area, which would be more or less down here, that we have about 1,500 committed. In our area you will find crimes amounting to 467 in comparison. So you see, there is quite a difference. As I say, I think it is due to the fact that we have proper housing and we have proper facilities. Someday maybe we will get to the realization that we need more police officers and various influences around in the areas where there are broken homes and where there are people who have no place to play—no recreation. I don't think a kid wants to bring a friend home unless he has a place to bring them. He would rather hang out on the street, which I think is a very bad situation.

Chairman KEFAUVER. Don't you usually find that in slum areas you have a much higher juvenile delinquency rate?

Mrs. WYMAN. Yes, much higher, Senator; and that is why I said "overall," in my councilmanic district, where you have proper facilities, the crime ratio goes down.

There is also a great move by the younger people toward religion, and I think this is probably one of the healthiest things we have seen in a long time.

I was listening to Reverend Lindquist very closely. I happened to know him, and he and his group are doing an excellent job. I think we will find that over the last 5 years the adult groups and church groups have increased, and I think every church should have a teen-age or a young adult group. I think the tendency has been to take care of the very young or the old and to forget the teen-agers. For example, we have the deputy auxiliary police group in the city which is doing a fine job, but it is not getting to this group of youngsters. In other words, these 15-, 16-, and 17-year-olds need someone to look up to as a leader, and they can't get into organizations like the deputy auxiliary police group, and I do feel that we must provide recreation for these teen-agers.

As chairman for the parks and recreation committee in the city, I am trying to do what I can along these lines.

Chairman KEFAUVER. You are the chairman of the recreation and parks committee of this council?

Mrs. WYMAN. Yes, that is true.

Chairman KEFAUVER. And you are the second chairman of the health and welfare committee?

Mrs. WYMAN. Yes.

Chairman KEFAUVER. I think your point is well made, and I say that from my own experience.

Mrs. WYMAN. They don't want to go on a swing or down a slide, and they have to have something else.

And, Senator, I think sometimes there is a great hesitancy, which is a natural expression around 13 or 14, where the children want to mix and want to start to have coeducational activities. And, if properly supervised, I think that is the time certainly when they should be taught to engage in such activities as dancing and coke parties. We tried these at my playground, and I tell you, I don't think anything was more successful, including some of the rougher boys who thought first that it was sissy stuff, and they felt that they were still going to go and lift things off cars. They needed other boys to look up to, and we later found out that it turned out to be the boy who was a good ballroom dancer in the affair that the other boys were looking up to. I think this type of experience is an excellent one for youngsters, and I think we should encourage it under proper supervision.

I don't know whether anybody has spoken of this yet, but we have a new experience in connection with the hot rods. I don't know if you follow this much as yet.

Senator KEFAUVER. I haven't heard about it out here.

Mrs. WYMAN. Let me briefly tell you about it.

We know that boys in hot rods are dangerous going down city streets, and they were cutting in and out, and they could leave everybody at the signal. They would be away by the time you are just starting up. I mean, they cruise, which is the term they use when they start off, at about 60 miles an hour, which is pretty good for any car. And really they have worked hard on these hot rods. These are not proper things to be used in the city streets, and it has just been recently that we have finally gotten an area where on Saturdays and Sundays they can go out under supervision, which is always the right way to do it, if you can get them supervised. And now there are groups that go out to Hansen Dam and they have the hot-rod races which are conducted under proper supervision and the boys are learning the safety rules in reference to the track, and it is taking them off the streets. This, of course, is a step forward. But it took many years for people to feel that we should let them have this form of expression. In other words, it again means this: Do you encourage this expression or do you say "No"? I think the minute you say "No" just blankly and flatly then they are going to do it some other way.

But in this way you have a proper supervised place for them, which is the way to do it, I feel. I think we have progressed along these lines. I think many times if you give the young teen-ager an opportunity their mind will work out their own problems pretty well in a group situation, and I have found in some areas that there are some pretty bad children. I don't know. It seems like the old democratic principle that they learn nothing through their ears, they go on growing up finding out the democratic way, and that self-discipline among themselves. And if they are given a chance at some type of a program that they can themselves work out, sometimes they come up with very good ideas and very good solutions. I guess maybe I am giving a little different testimony. I don't feel that it has been too long since I have been in that teen-age stage, and I have been close to them, and I have enjoyed my work very much in connection with the recreation for young people.

Chairman KEFAUVER. Mrs. Wyman, don't you feel that among our people generally there is more interest in activities along the lines you are talking about than there has been in the past years?

Mrs. WYMAN. Yes, I feel that there is a great deal of improvement, and I think that we are beginning to become aware that this is somewhat of a problem that we do have to cope with. I certainly hope that the young person does not get into a penal institution such as was rather prominently displayed—I think it was in Mississippi—where 15-year-olds were incarcerated with hardened criminals away up in years.

Chairman KEFAUVER. Well, that happens in a lot of places in the United States.

Mrs. WYMAN. That's true. I think we can be very proud of what is going on in California with our youth authority and our juvenile hall. I don't know if the representative of the supervisors spoke of that, but it is an excellent place, our juvenile hall, because this is usually the first step where the youngsters meet officers of the law. And I think our juvenile hall is certainly a step forward, because the children are treated with such kindness that they realize the law is not necessarily something to fear. I think the first contact with the child, especially first-offense children, who are teen-agers when they first come in, is so important, that very first contact with them. And I think that in all areas if they could have something like our juvenile hall, which is a special place where there are only juveniles in there and they are treated with kindness, and learn that you don't have to fear a police officer, that it would be a wonderful thing.

Chairman KEFAUVER. That's very important.

Mrs. Wyman, you have a report. May I see it?

Mrs. WYMAN. Yes, I have a breakdown in all the various areas of the city by precincts, where the stations are.

Chairman KEFAUVER. This is a report showing the number of arrests in the various precincts in the city of Los Angeles, is that true?

Mrs. WYMAN. The section that I was referring to—I was trying to show you the breakdown where the better section is with proper homes and no slum areas. You will see at the bottom of each column the totals there.

Chairman KEFAUVER. Then you have the age and the offense. I think this is a good report. I have seen one of these. May we have this and we will file it as an exhibit?

Mrs. WYMAN. Senator, may I return this to you. I borrowed this from the library. I have to return it on my library card.

Chairman KEFAUVER. You tell the library we will get one.

Mrs. WYMAN. I will get one for you which shows the breakdown and what I am trying to prove with reference to slum areas which I think are very rare.

Chairman KEFAUVER. How many members of the council are there?

Mrs. WYMAN. There are 15 of us. We just had a very hot session yesterday.

Chairman KEFAUVER. What happened?

Mrs. WYMAN. We lost—well, I don't know how to put it. It was defeated. We had a very long session. I don't know how many hours long it was, but it sort of set a precedent for us.

Chairman KEFAUVER. How much of your time do you give to being a councilwoman?

Mrs. WYMAN. Senator, it is a full-time job. We meet 5 days a week, and we are the only legislative body in the world that has no provision for recess or adjournment. Our trems are 4 years and we are supposed to have no vacation. There is no provision in our city charter for it. And we serve on three committees. As I say, we meet 5 days a week. It is a full-time job—if you do it properly—every single member of the city council is serving on the basis of it being a full-time job.

Chairman KEFAUVER. Is there anything else, Mr. Bobo?

Mr. BOBO. No, sir.

Chairman KEFAUVER. Thank you very much.

Mrs. WYMAN. I am sorry about our weather. I wish I could do better for you. Don't hold it against us, and come and see us soon.

Chairman KEFAUVER. Well, I think you have less smog this time than you had before when I was here. Of course I was here one day when I didn't see anything but smog.

Mrs. WYMAN. That's a county problem.

Chairman KEFAUVER. We will take about a recess for 15 minutes.

(A short recess was taken.)

Chairman KEFAUVER. The committee is glad there are present here a number of men and women who are either presidents or chairmen of various organizations who have programs or are trying to do something in the interest of opportunity for our young people to control and lessen juvenile delinquency, and we appreciate your presence.

Among those who are here are Mrs. Neff, who is president of the Lawyers' Wives of Los Angeles and Mrs. Krug, who is chairman of the juvenile delinquency division of that agency.

I am aware of the efforts that these ladies and their organizations and others here are making, and we appreciate your being here.

Mr. Miley is here to bring a word from Commissioner John Anson Ford.

Mr. Miley, will you come forward?

Mr. ARTHUR F. MILEY. I am here to represent Supervisor John Anson Ford.

Chairman KEFAUVER. Sit down, Mr. Miley. The chairman has known Mr. Arthur F. Miley, the field representative for the Honorable John Anson Ford and the board of supervisors, third district of Los Angeles, and we appreciate your interest in our work and your greetings from Mr. Ford.

We will be glad to have you state whatever you wish, Mr. Miley.

Mr. MILEY. First I would like to say that Supervisor Ford, because of previous engagements, which have tied him up at the present time, wishes to extend greetings to you and the committee, and, of course, a very pleasant stay in our city. We hope that the weather gets better for you.

The reason why he asked me to appear here was because I have been a field deputy for him for 17½ years. Primarily my interest in the office as it was divided up was people and all their problems—old people, young people, sick and poor and alcoholics, and so forth.

I retired on January 1, but because of the fact that that has been my assignment for some 17 years he asked me to appear and read a statement for him. So he has given me a statement to read which I will read.

Chairman KEFAUVER. How long is that statement, Mr. Miley?

Mr. MILEY. Oh, about 2 or 3 minutes.

Chairman KEFAUVER. All right, sir. Will you read it fast?

STATEMENT OF JOHN ANSON FORD, MEMBER, LOS ANGELES COUNTY BOARD OF SUPERVISORS (READ BY ARTHUR F. MILEY)

Mr. FORD. The causes and cure of juvenile delinquency present one of the most complex social problems of our day. As indicated below, many factors not present when life was simpler contribute to the departure of boys and girls from normal living patterns.

My comments are based largely on more than 20 years service as a supervisor for the largest county government operation in this country. During most of these years the county probation department, the county's five juvenile forestry camps, El Retiro School for Girls, and the county's detention home, known as Juvenile Hall, have been part of my committee assignments. Years of observing the administration of these projects have given me a broad field for observing delinquency.

Basically city life is not wholly normal or natural for a young growing boy, or even a girl, whose nature more naturally responds to life in the wide-open spaces. Unavoidably city restraints in a score of ways irk the growing youngsters.

Youth found it hard, particularly a few years ago, to change from the war psychology of hate and destruction for the enemy, to a psychology of tolerance and cooperation for the gang in the next block or the crowd from another elementary or high school. Undoubtedly war has contributed indirectly to many of our youth problems.

While small children have little or no regard for differences of race or color, adolescent youth and very young men and women are apt to give much emphasis to these differences, in an intolerant spirit. From this, much strife and even bloodshed results.

Los Angeles colored youth and those of Mexican ancestry find themselves in difficult social situations. Economic necessity and/or language handicaps tend to make many of these youth drop out of school before graduation. Unequipped for trade and with few if any skills, they increasingly resent being forced into unskilled work; they become sensitive and resentful of alleged social inferiority. Integration into self-support and self-respect in a society dominated by a middle class Anglo-Saxon psychology is not easily achieved by them. Even Boy Scouting and YMCA connections are shunned by many who are resentful of what life has brought them.

It should be emphasized also that the many-sided social changes taking place disconcertingly and simultaneously in all classes are resulting in delinquency of boys and girls for reasons quite distinctive from those cited above. Vandalism is one of the inexplicable offenses occurring in alarming proportions. Automobiles produce temptations to violate speed laws and moral laws. Violence dominates too many movie and television plots. The appalling percentage of divorces in this county (almost equal to the number of marriages) is one of the greatest contributors to delinquency. No child can escape suffering when the two persons who are his first and greatest sources of love and security divorce and discredit each other.

To meet all these conditions and many more not enumerated, our socially minded leaders, far too small in numbers, have tried heroically, almost desperately, to combat these trends. Youth centers, well equipped and manned, are being multiplied. The YMCA has revised its procedure to emphasize neighborhood activities rather than branch YMCA buildings; the Jewish people are fostering a social program which is family-centered; the Catholic Church has successfully furthered Boys Scouts and Catholic youth programs, etc. Many Protestant Churches are devoting special emphasis to youth activities both on Sunday and weekdays. The value of these religious inspired efforts cannot be overemphasized. But the tragic part is that thousands of homes have no church contacts. The American Legion, the Masons and other fraternal orders are bringing a percentage of their own youth into well-ordered programs for young people.

Los Angeles County, through the probation department, has assigned 10 socially trained deputies to be gang leaders—leaders who really befriend and guide many gangs otherwise without the pale of accepted society.

As others doubtless will relate, the county's boys' camps and the State youth authority camps are doing much to restore and rescue a percentage of the boys who have taken first steps in the wrong direction.

From what I have touched on here, the remedies for delinquency may be summed up by saying: Our homes must do much more; our schools are not yet meeting the full need; and our churches are not yet going into the byways and bringing in these unfortunate youth. The harvest is truly plentious but the real laborers are too few.

Chairman KEFAUVER. That's a very fine statement, and it has some good recommendations, and you tell Mr. Ford that we appreciate it very much, Mr. Miley.

Mr. MILEY. I might say one more thing. As Mr. Daly, the assistant attorney general, spoke on the Governor's committee on alcoholism, the board of supervisors has appointed a committee on alcoholism, of which I am a member, trying to implement something along the line of alcohol clinics in southern California. So what will become of it, I do not know. The committee is a new committee just started, and we hope that the county through the clinic will be able to do something which will relieve some of the alcoholic problems which have been cited here before as the cause in the homes by example of juvenile delinquency. That's about all I have to say.

Chairman KEFAUVER. Thank you very much, Mr. Miley. We appreciate your coming.

Mr. MILEY. Thank you.

Chairman KEFAUVER. The next witness will be the Rev. Andy Griffin, pastor of Emmanuel Methodist Church, Los Angeles.

STATEMENT OF REV. ANDY GRIFFIN, PASTOR, EMMANUEL METHODIST CHURCH, LOS ANGELES, CALIF.

Chairman KEFAUVER. Is that right, Reverend?

Mr. GRIFFIN. That's correct, at 830 South Herbert Avenue, Los Angeles.

Chairman KEFAUVER. How large is your church and how long have you been a pastor?

Mr. GRIFFIN. My church is located in an area in which my constituency belongs to another major denomination, and consequently on Sunday mornings our congregation is a very small congregation— 30 or 40 people. However, we work in and our major ministry is with the youth groups in the community that attend other churches.

Chairman KEFAUVER. Will you tell us all about it, Reverend?

Mr. GRIFFIN. That church is located in an area where there is an apparent need for concern for the behavior problems of young people. This is our major ministry. We are only one of the several institutions and agencies maintained by the Methodist Church in this area.

Concerning the recognition, the theoretical, and the basic comments regarding the delinquency, I concur with Dr. Lindquist and Supervisor Ford and others who have added their comments.

Ninety-eight percent of the teen-agers and young adults that we are working with are members of another major denomination. Of course, financial support cannot come from the very small congregation of the church. For this reason the Missionary Society of our denomination and the service clubs of southern California, as a result of lectures I have made in those organizations, are the basis of our financial support.

Facilities are very small and in state of bad repair. Private homes, a hospital executive's conference rooms, and county recreational facilities furnished the settings for our activities.

At the moment I recognize these facts about the youth situation in our area. For one thing, there is a very significant growth in the kind of group that is not identified with any established agency, public or private, but rises spontaneously out of the community and becomes autonomous and entirely gregarious in its own rights. These groups are not anti-authority groups. Actually, they seem to be searching for supervision acceptable to their particular needs. They accept behavior-problem youth and behavior-problem youth accepts them. In other words, this particular group seems to fill a void that I have felt. The kind of group that will accept the kind of kid that is not acceptable in the so-called youth groups, the difference between that kind of a group and the gang group, this seems to be the void.

No. 2. The supervisors or sponsors of these groups are being drawn from the ranks of the average citizen. These folks are ready to help but are conscious of their inadequacy in handling behavior-problem youth. A very significant group has developed in the county probation department called the group guidance section. These men, probation officers under the direction of Carl Holton, probation officer of the county, are helping to supplement the efforts of these unskilled sponsors for these groups.

To make it very short, it seems to me that the need to help kids that the average citizen wants, has had for some time, is being met by these men out of the probation department, the group guidance section, that are coming out and helping us and supplementing our own inadequacy with skilled guidance. To meet this is one of the most significant developments and growing aids to deliquency situations.

No. 3. The new developments in supervision have somewhat lessened the skepticism of public facilities in permitting groups to have activities and to function where they once had skepticism bordering on fears; in other words, do we let the behavior-problem group or the groups bordering on behavior problems use facilities where the masses of youth attend?

No. 4. I have the privilege of serving as 1 of 9 appointive commissioners of public welfare in this county, and one of the duties of this group is the granting of permits to conduct teen-age dances. Now, this body has developed the policy of interviewing sponsors and teen-agers belonging to clubs that are appearing for a teen-age dance license. And out of these interviews have come significant hints as to their problems. The commission then has instructed one of the commissioners to visit with these groups that are getting licenses and to go over some of their problems with them. In this way it comes to the attention of society and agencies representing society that these groups do exist in the community and then we in turn act as referral agencies to the other groups that can help them with their problems.

I feel there is a need for an agency which will have a good rapport with such groups as these, to be composed of men and women who have had, by virtue of personal experience or association with behavior-problem youth, an adequate background to deal with them. In the vernacular of the community, let me say, Senator, that some of our groups in areas where behavior problems are prevalent, just don't dig squares, that is all.

And there is a need for this kind of a coordinating effort. Such a group could keep close contact with club patterns and problems.

The previously mentioned group guidance section of the probation department seems to be working toward this end. Precedent values of this kind of an organization have been established by groups known as the Federation of Social and Car Clubs of California and the East Los Angeles League of Clubs; who, with only the help of citizens from the community, have taken groups once hostile in their behavior toward one another and found common grounds for them to coordinate their efforts on. And in so doing do away with the hostile feelings. And this has resulted in an emphasis on kids spending the money that they make on their teen-age dances on charitable activities. For instance, the city of Hope had recently much of their income come from these car clubs that were out soliciting funds throughout the Los Angeles area. And I feel that not all of them but many that I know of, the vast majority of them, the kind of kids that are in these groups could very easily be borderline behavior problems if they didn't have somewhere to channel their activities.

Incidentally, these groups are earning their own money. They don't seem to be bothering Mr. Ochoa or Mr. Nevada's group particularly, the federation. Mr. Ochoa and Mr. Nevada are here today.

They have not asked any money from merchants in the community. They haven't solicited the community. They are using money from their teen-age dances to buy their jackets—other group meetings that they have.

Recapping quickly some of the things: Liquor continues to be a growing problem. School dropouts represent a serious problem. However, the laws of California provide for youth over 18 to enter college without taking full high school courses. The East Los Angeles Junior College has made rapid strides in their area, and many young people who never finished high school in the east Los Angeles area particularly are going to school now and seeking an education at the college level.

Generally speaking I echo the optimism of Chief Parker. However, I feel that the general tone is still tense, and with this tenseness comes a great opportunity to work with youth groups which seem to be rapidly taking the place of the old gang pattern.

Chairman KEFAUVER. Thank you very much, Reverend Griffin, for your interest and your statement. We appreciate your observations very much.

Are there any questions, Mr. Bobo?

Mr. BOBO. No.

Chairman KEFAUVER. Thank you very much.

Mr. Ralph Johnson, superintendent of the Twin Pines Ranch, Banning, Calif., will be our next witness. Mr. Johnson has to go back to Banning here very shortly. It is good to see you, sir.

Mr. JOHNSON. Thank you. How do you do.

STATEMENT OF RALPH JOHNSON, SUPERINTENDENT, TWIN PINES RANCH OF BANNING, CALIF.

Chairman KEFAUVER. Mr. Bobo, will you ask Mr. Johnson the preliminary questions?

Mr. BOBO. Mr. Johnson, you are superintendent of Twin Pines Ranch in Banning, Calif.?

Mr. JOHNSON. That is right.

Mr. BOBO. How long have you been superintendent there?

Mr. JOHNSON. Seven years.

Mr. BOBO. And prior to that time your experience was with youth or some other service?

Mr. JOHNSON. I was with the United States Indian Service at a youth boarding school for Indians in Riverside, Calif.

Mr. BOBO. And what type of a ranch camp is Twin Pines? What type of program.

Mr. JOHNSON. Twin Pines Ranch is a high school for youth with problems, youth which you refer to as delinquents. We started with 2 boys and at the present time we have 64. There has been some 250 boys go through the ranch program. Out of our ranch program we now boast, if you want to call it boast—but we are very happy to say—that there is an 82 percent rehabilitation of these youths from the ages of 15 years and 9 months through 18 years.

It is entirely different, and it is a new approach to the treatment of youth with problems, in that we, as Chief Parker mentioned, have gotten away from the rural way of living. But that is not so at Twin Pines. We have gone back to the rural way of living.

Mr. BOBO. Twin Pines is operated by the State or by the county?

Mr. JOHNSON. By Riverside County and subsidized by California Youth Authority. That's the State of California.

In building this program we found it necessary to first make a home for the boy; secondly, to get him back on his education, because so many of them were boys who had left school for different reasons, and many of them were habitual truants.

We have a very fine academic program which is a credit. It is a credit even to a point that we belong to an athletic league which is a member of the California Athletic Board or whatever it is.

The next thing we thought about was, if this was going to be a good home we would give them the academic subjects and next would be to teach them to use their hands profitably and we started out on just a little old ranch; at the present time we are constructing all of our buildings, which are made out of cement blocks which are also made at the school itself. And to do this we couldn't get the traditional type of counselor. We had to get a counselor who was a craftsman, an artisan at the trade, a man who was sympathetic toward boys with problems, a man who could teach the boys to use their hands properly and a man who could use a lot of horsesense in his counsel. And it has paid dividends. Of course, we also have special trades besides the building trades, and then we have a very fine agricultural program. The next was religious guidance and we left that up to the Ministerial Association at Banning and the priest of the parish. The priest comes up on Saturday morning and conducts his service and on Sunday morning occasionally we have a pastor come from below. But the boys would much rather conduct their own services right at the school. And if you ever want a spiritual lift come up to the ranch on a Sunday morning right after a good ranch breakfast and see what the boys can do in conducting their own program.

We had to give the boys many, many traditional niceties that makes for a good home; that is, on Easter Sunday, a basket of Easter eggs in front of their plate; on a boy's birthday a cake and everybody sings Happy Birthday; on Mother's Day, cards to send home, or Father's Day cards, if it is that day, and a big Christmas. Those are not paid for by the county; they are paid for by the people of Riverside County who have been very nice to us. And I must say this, that the social contact we have with the public has been one of the big features toward rehabilitation at Twin Pines.

We lean toward dramatics also. Everybody has a bit of dramatics in them. They like pageantry and so we go to pageantry.

Speaking about rural living, on the day a new boy comes to Twin Pines Ranch he is met at the gate by an old ranch surrey pulled by two beautifully matched horses. And he is met at the gate where it says "Howdy Partner" with a warm handshake because we feel at Twin Pines that a warm handshake is the helping hand that the boy has been looking for.

And then with the superintendent the boy rides down a tree-lined dusty road toward the ranch, and he is told what is expected of him; that there are no rules and regulations; that we live on tradition at Twin Pines; there are no fences, there are no locks, that there are no barred cells, and there are no guards. There is no punishment, there are no rollcalls, that we live as a person would live in a good home.

Runaways are very, very few. Of course, if a boy leaves the ranch he understands he never comes back. But the boy understands all of this by the time he reaches the office where he is registered. And he

is not committed to the ranch; he is placed at the ranch because we
do everything we can to relieve any stigma being attached to the ranch.

Mrs. Johnson and I work constantly—we have to. Right at the
present time we are receiving invitations anywhere from Blyth, Calif.,
to Ontario and from Barstow to Newport Beach, inviting us to attend
the commencement exercises of boys who are going to graduate. It is
pretty hard to set yourself that far, but we do our best.

Chairman KEFAUVER. You mean boys that have been to the ranch
and who have gone back to school?

Mr. JOHNSON. Who have gone back to school, who would never have
graduated had they not had the benefits of the Twin Pines program.

I would like to invite you on Friday afternoon and the rest of your
team to come out and see 14 boys mount a stage, an outdoor stage,
dressed in caps and gowns to the tune of an organ, playing in the
mountains, and receive their diplomas like any boy in any public
school would receive them. I would like very much to have you come
and see that.

On graduation exercises that we see in so many institutions they
ask, "Is the boy ready to leave?" The party that is going to take the
boy away from that facility picks up the boy and before the boy has an
opportunity to say goodbye to some of friends he is taken away.

At Twin Pines Ranch we do differently. On the day of graduation
we hitch the hitching rack outside the bunkhouse and there are many
horses bridled, and we do have horses there too—What is a ranch
without a horse?—on that morning the horses are saddled and bridled
and hitched to the hitching rack outside the bunkhouse. That is
indicative of how near the boy is going to leave that day. Over the
breakfast table, after the dishes are cleared away, the superintendent
announces who is going to graduate, and then each staff member talks
to the boy. Sometimes it is an admonition, but mostly always praise.

And it goes on that way through the day until the noon hour, when
we have the boy seated at the guest table with his guests. It is an
honor table. After the meal is over, he is presented with a farewell
gift, which is a wallet and the next presentation is made by the superintendent, and that is the money he has saved while he has been at the
ranch. We do pay them 25 cents a day for their labor there, for
their work. We then go to the corral, which is some quarter of a mile
away from the boys' bunkhouse, and around the old ranchhouse, and
there in the center of the corral is a huge white snubbing. And around
that snubbing post we form a human wagon—the men do and the
boys—and in the meantime the superintendent, riding in the surry,
and the graduates riding on their favorite horses, ride up to that area.
When we get there, the buggy is racked some 40 yards down the road
headed out, and the graduates hitch their horses to a hitching rack
outside the tack room which is adjacent to the corral gate.

We then go in and join this wagon wheel. As soon as this forms,
it starts whirling around to the tune of Roll on Wagon Wheel. The
song ended, the boys and the wheel breaks and we separate all over the
corral. And then as they reform the wheel spoke by spoke, with the
graduates standing a short distance away, the first boy walks in and
the last boy turns and admonishes that "T" stands for truth—always
be truthful. The next boy walks in, the last boy turns and admonishes
the youth who is leaving "W" stands for "Winner," always be a winner
and so on until all the letters of Twin Pines Ranch have been used.

The wheel formed again with the new boys in it, they start rolling again to the tune of Roll on Wagon Wheel. The wagon wheel breaks this time and they form a gauntlet at the corral gate. The graduates walk out through the gauntlet and unsaddle and unbridle their horses and hang their gear in the tack room for the last time, and lead their horses down the gauntlet and turn them back into the corral. And then as they go out they have an opportunity to shake hands and bid goodby to every fellow on the ranch, staff members and ranch hands included. The superintendent meets them at the gate, and then as we walk to the ranch surry, which you have pictured there some 40 yards down the road, all the ranch hands and staff members lean over the fence singing a farewell song. I can't sing it, but I can repeat it:

> We sure do hate to see you go,
> To us you have been a pal, you know,
> But go if you must, we'll watch the dust
> As you ride on down the road.
> It's been swell to have had you here,
> So so long and be of good cheer
> You hear us all say, "So long partner."

And then as we step up in the buggy we all shout "So long partner." And away we go to this huge ranch gate where it says "So long, partner," and it is there that the superintendent bids goodby to this fellow who spent a little while where surely God must have spent a lot of time.

I have just a few of these. It is an entire quotation of the ranch.

Chairman KEFAUVER. These and your pictures will be made exhibits. This is a marvelous effort, Mr. Johnson, even if it affects only a few boys.

(The document referred to was marked "Exhibit No. 3," and reads as follows:)

EXHIBIT No. 3

TWIN PINES RANCH, RALPH JOHNSON, SUPERINTENDENT

Nestled in a picturesque little valley on the northern slope of stately and majestic old Mount San Jacinto peacefully lies Twin Pines Ranch, a resident high school for boys with problems. This ranch home is 11 miles southeast of Banning, Calif., and is under the jurisdiction of the Riverside County Probation Office. There are 320 acres of land within its borders, 40 of which are set aside for the proposed physical plant; another 50 or 60 acres are suitable for and will be devoted to agricultural projects. The remainder of the land blends from rolling hills to rough mountainous terrain, wild with chaparral, scrub oak, sycamore and pine trees.

The sole purpose of Twin Pines Ranch, its general program and curriculum, is the true rehabilitation of the boy. Therefore, if the four basic needs of a boy with problems are love, attention, recognition, and adventure, then this ranch with its mountains, valleys, rocks, trees, and lakes is ideally situated for the youth to find adventure.

Staff members are selected for their ability to work with boys that are socially maladjusted. They are men who are sympathetic, understanding, patient, and can teach them to use their hands for legitimate, profitable gain. A boy who has confidence in an adult with these qualities cannot but feel that he is wanted, is recognized and loved. That type of staff member gives the youth the attention needed to reestablish the confidence within himself so vitally needed to carry him through his adjustment period.

Inasmuch as the curriculum is suited to the needs of youth whose maladjustment to society often manifests itself in intense dislike of traditional schooling, it is of the utmost importance that our curriculum be one that is suited to the needs of the boy, rather than attempting to mold him into a pattern which he has already shown no desire to follow. Since its inception, much lipservice has been paid to the educational philosophy of "learning by doing," but in actual practice, this ideal fell far short of fulfillment. Certainly the opportunity to make "learning by doing" a reality has been achieved at Twin Pines Ranch to a degree seldom possible in the usual school situation. Any curriculum which failed to take advantage of such an opportunity would therefore be little more than useless, and all our aims are toward vital and functional teaching which would help these boys better to make their peace with themselves and their environment.

In all cases, we attempt to relate closely the academic subjects we teach to the vocational education with which we hope better to equip these boys to get along and gain recognition without recourse to antisocial means. Such a curriculum must of necessity be highly flexible in order to fit into the needs of the individual, and in order to help him to find out for himself the field in which to find his greatest worth and happiness. In the event we find individuals whose aptitudes and abilities are such as to warrant higher education than the secondary level, we stand ready to help them achieve such a goal.

In vocational education, we attempt to use every possible means to teach useful skills by actual work on jobs necessary to the building and maintenance of a well-run ranch, so that the boy can look to his finished job and know that he has really made a contribution to the general welfare. We purposely avoid "pseudowork" hastily put together for instructional purposes, and just as easily demolished as soon as completed. Under the guidance and instruction of our counselor instructors, the students in vocational education construct the buildings in which they eat, sleep, attend school, work, and play. Besides the building trades classes, there are several special trades, which the boy may select as his vocation. These special trades are machine shop, both types of welding, tin and coopersmithing, auto mechanics, cooking and baking, and laundry operation. Vocational agriculture is an important part of our educational system. Here, also, the practical application is productive as well as instructive.

On the academic side of the curriculum, we believe that mathematics can best be taught by helping the boy to see for himself the necessity for its use in planning and completing work within the broader skills we are attempting to teach. Our aim in English is to help the boy express himself satisfactorily, both orally and in writing, so as to establish better communication between the boy and his ranch and his home environment. Under social studies, good citizenship, of course, can best be learned by being a real contributing member to the everyday life of the ranch. But since we cannot live in a vacuum, we believe that we should help the boy to become aware of what is going on in the world today, and the possible effects of those occurrences upon himself. Also, being a citizen of democracy, we should create in the boy a reasoning respect for the rights of others regardless of nationality, color, or creed.

Although we will be hampered for some time to come by lack of equipment and modern playing fields, we believe that we do best to concentrate almost entirely on games with a great deal of carry-over value for the individual so that he can continue to work off surplus "steam" through worthwhile recreational activities even after leaving the ranch. Physical education is a required subject in the regular educational curriculum. In order that our boys be given wholesome contacts with the community at large, as well as lose some of their selfish devotion to themselves by participating in team sports, we are very fortunate to have been invited to be a member of the Arrowhead League. Our participation in this league makes us a member of the California Interscholastic Federation (C. I. F.).

In the rehabilitation of the boys through the educational process of social living, our aim is to give each individual boy the guidance necessary to help him evaluate his abilities and preferences, and to make his own decisions as to what occupational and formal school work will be of the greatest help to himself while at the ranch, as well as to his future success in life. The boy must learn to make his own decisions if the rehabilitation program is to be of lasting value. Methods used to carry out this purpose:

(1) Counseling and guidance by ranch supervisors and the teachers through personal interviews and in group instruction in the classroom and on the job. The teachers help each boy to find a new attitude toward books and the classroom. By patient instruction, they will endeavor to get the boy to discover for himself that he is able to do the basic or elementary subjects that before seemed impossible. Thus, confidence is gained and self-expression realized. The work supervisors help the boy to discover and develop his occupational interests and

abilities through trial and error, and by the supervision of his efforts on a particular job.

(2) Correlation of classroom and field work accomplished by daily coordination of their specific activities by teachers and work supervisors. The boys are thus made to realize in concrete form the connection between their classroom studies and their work projects.

(3) Orientation period of testing the boy for the most effective placement in the school and work program. Also, he is given an opportunity to choose his vocation:

(a) Time—3 weeks more or less.

(b) Temporary assignment of each boy to a job in order to learn his aptitudes and preferences.

(c) Formal tests given by the teachers to help the boy to find out for himself what his deficiencies in school work are and what he must do to correct them. Also, they help to uncover the boy's particular interests and abilities.

The boys are granted high school credit for formal instruction and occupational experiences at the Twin Pines Ranch High School. In creating a new social environment, it is proven that self-direction on the part of the boy is essential to true rehabilitation, work and study on a voluntary basis; rewards rather than punishment; learning by doing.

The newcomer to the ranch is immediately a part of the program by his acceptance on the part of the group. He is not placed in an indoctrination group to do the dirty work until he is replaced by another new boy, nor is he ever placed in a punishment work group. This is an educational institution and it is impossible to truly educate by punitive tactics. Difficult jobs are manned by rotating boys from different shops and cleanup is done by all boys the first period after breakfast. All boys make dirt, so all boys clean up the ranch grounds. Home atmosphere builds confidence and self-expression through the feeling that each boy has a place and is wanted. Such an atmosphere fosters the realization that each boy has his own special contribution to make to the enjoyment and welfare of the ranch as a whole. Fewer rules and regulations, minimum supervision, less restriction, and no staff coercion have been replaced by group control, which is the outgrowth of self-direction, confidence, and appreciation. The boy must be impressed with a sense of responsibility toward the group, that all the liberty and attention he receives is not carte blanche to infringe upon the rights of others.

The ranch attempts to provide a homelike atmosphere for him by providing him those traditional niceties that a good home provides by helping him celebrate his birthday, and holidays, particularly Christmas. These special events are no longer just accepted; they are appreciated and looked forward to. Ranch atmosphere will give the zest of concrete things to do, love of out-of-doors, a wholesome channel for a boy's natural love of adventure and achievement. What is a ranch without horses, and what are youth years without the advantage or privilege of caring for or riding horses? Twin Pines Ranch has its stables, tack room, corrals, pastures, and horses. Riding in the hills atop his favorite horse, a boy is at peace with the world. Swimming, fishing, hiking, and horseback riding—all these, plus regular hours, plenty of good food, plenty of sunshine, and a chance to be clean tend to make him a better physical specimen, which in turn helps his mental state. For once in his life, he is finding himself in an environment relatively free from anxiety.

While at the ranch, the boys receive a small daily wage with which they must purchase personal necessities, i. e., toilet articles, writing materials, haircuts, etc., and confections and soft drinks. By this method, staff members have an opportunity to teach them the value of a dollar and how to save because, when leaving the program, they receive their savings, which can be a helping hand as they start life anew away from the ranch.

During the slow steady growth of the boy population, as well as the physical plant, traditions have infiltrated into the program to the extent that they are now a potent power which not only directs the boy at the ranch, but also guides him when he returns to society. Many of the traditions are purposely dramatized to stir his emotions, making lasting impressions upon the youth.

At the entrance to the ranch, a large white ranch gate has been erected upon which has been carved the words "Howdy Pahdner." The superintendent greets each new student ranch hand beneath this huge gate with a hearty handshake. Perhaps that handshake is the helping hand that the boy has long been looking for. The boy and the superintendent drive to the ranch house, about one-half mile away, in a ranch surrey drawn by two well-matched paint horses. During the drive, the superintendent tells the youth "Why Twin Pines Ranch," and the results that will be attained if the boy forgets his past and builds only for the future. If the boy comes to us in a rebellious state, fearful of the new environment into which he has been thrust, he cannot help but lose that fear on this buggy ride down a tree-lined country road past the glistening waters of the lake upon which white ducks are resting. At the end of the road, the sight of the rustic old ranch houses appeals to the inner soul of the boy which edges out much of the "inner rebellion" ; this is the objective of a good ranch therapeutic program.

Arriving at the ranch office, his parents' address is verified so that a personal letter may be sent notifying them of his arrival. He, then, is introduced to a chief counselor, who fits him out with his ranch outfit and assigns him to his "brand." The brand leader takes over, shows him the ranch and acquaints him with the other brand members with whom he will be identified while at the ranch. To round out his reception, at his first meal, the boy is introduced and made welcome by the entire group singing the ranch welcome song. Seeing and hearing the entire student body participate in his welcome has a stabilizing effect, making him feel that he is accepted.

Each boy is assigned to a counselor to whom he may go for advice, consolation, and guidance. However, realizing that there are clashes of personalities between individuals, the youth is told that he is privileged to go to any counselor that he finds to his liking. On-the-spot counseling is effective and is in keeping with the homelike atmosphere, but by far the most effective and impressing counseling is over the chuck-wagon tables, after meals, to the entire group.

So much freedom and so little supervision during the boys' free time does not mean that the staff members have a lackadaisical attitude such as "out of sight, out of mind." They believe a disturbed youth must work out his own problems ; therefore, he shall supervise himself and his actions. Little acts which might be considered antisocial can be straightened out by group control.

Social contact with the public away from the ranch is attained by attending the theater in the village every Saturday. This is not a reward for the conformist, but everyone's treat. When we say this is not a punitive but educational institution, we mean just that. Some boys just cannot do everything right; should they be punished for this? Is it not better to teach a boy that he is entitled to all benefits as any other boy and not to put forth his right foot occasionally to selfishly gain benefits, but rather show his appreciation for our kindness by an honest endeavor to do right?

Visitation of service clubs who hold dinner meetings at the ranch has been a wonderful social contact. Businessmen and women taking time out to come up and break bread with the boys take away that self-planted stigma and replant the seed of self-respect and confidence. Occasionally, groups of young people come to the ranch for community sings and folk dancing. Music hath charms; so does a wholesome young lady who will spend her evening that a disturbed youth may enjoy dancing and singing.

There comes a time when the ranch program has completed its work and the staff members feel that a youth is ready to go back to society. Without graphs, charts, or a file crammed full of useless scribblings on paper, how do we know when a boy is ready for graduation? Some people facetiously call it the intuitive system. But who cares what it is called? Ours is a feeling that he is ready. This day is one long to to be remembered by the graduate, the staff members and the remaining ranch hands. If a program such as ours is actual and not the "lip service" type, then members of the staff have learned to love the boy, and his absence from the ranch program is surely and sincerely to be felt.

It is a tradition that any morning when the boys arise and find horses saddled and bridled hitched to the hitching post outside the bunkhouse, that is graduation day. The number of horses is indicative of the number of boys graduating. After the breakfast dishes have been cleared away, the superintendent announces the names of the graduates. Then while all are assembled in the chuck wagon, the staff members each say their parting words to the graduate. Sometimes they are admonished, perhaps counseled or advised. The words spoken, good or bad, are always as the staff members look at the boy and his future—above all else, they are truthful. This is sort of a "pop to boy" deal at the time of breaking family ties. The remaining ranch hands go to the regular program while the graduating boys invariably go to the stable, saddle their favorite horse and ride over the hills. On their return, they usually confer with their adviser and best friends for a few moments, then go to the ranch office and receive the statistical report on their payroll account.

At lunch time, the graduating boys are seated at a special table. When lunch is over and the tables cleared, the boys' best friends present them with a traditional graduation gift, a wallet. The superintendent then presents the check covering their savings. Guests are called upon to say a few words, and after that the graduates are given an opportunity to say what is in their minds. The next person called upon to say something to the graduates is a boy selected at random (usually a fairly recent arrival), to say a few words in behalf of those who are staying at the ranch.

This particular session at an end, the staff members and ranch hands gather in the corral and form a human wagon wheel around the snubbing post. The superintendent, driving in the surrey, and the graduates riding alongside astride their favorite horses, go into the corral, join the wagon wheel, which rolls around as the boys sing Wagon Wheels. The wagon wheel breaks, and as it is re-formed, spoke by spoke, with new hands joining in, the graduates standing near-by are admonished by the last boy in each spoke—"T" stands for truth, always be truthful; "W" stands for winner, always be a winner, and so on until all the letters of Twin Pines Ranch have been used as admonitions to the graduates. Twin Pines Ranch is spelled by the spokes which again rolls on. The boys form a gauntlet pronounces the words and the wheel again rolls on. The boys form a gauntlet to the corral gate through which the graduates walk to their horses. They unsaddle and unbridle the horses and hang the gear in the tack room for the last time, turn their horses into the corral and as they walk out through the gauntlet, they receive that friendly slap on the back or a farewell handshake. The superintendent meets them at the corral gate and walks with them to the surrey, and as they walk, the entire group, leaning on the corral fence, sing these words: "We sure do hate to see you go, to us you've been a pal you know, but go if you must and we'll watch the dust as you ride down the road. It's been swell to have you here, so smile and be of good cheer, for as you ride away, you'll hear us all say * * * " (and as the boys step up in the surrey), the boys at the fence about, "So long, pahdner!"

The superintendent drives the boys in the surrey past the old rustic ranch house by the lake with the ducks swimming gracefully about, up the tree-lined road to the ranch gate where upon its huge beam is carved these words: "So long, pahdner." Beneath this gate, the superintendent bids so long to those young men who spent a while where surely God must have spent a little more time than elsewhere.

Mr. JOHNSON. That is what I am here for.

Chairman KEFAUVER. If it is done here and there it amounts to a whole lot.

Mr. JOHNSON. I would like to see these all over the country.

Chairman KEFAUVER. How long would a boy stay?

Mr. JOHNSON. That is up to him. When he comes to the ranch we say it is up to him, and when we feel that he is ready we will send him out. The average length of stay is about 11 months. There are some who have left at 6½ months.

Chairman KEFAUVER. And where do the boys come from?

Mr. JOHNSON. From Riverside, Orange, and San Bernardino Counties.

Chairman KEFAUVER. How do you get them?

Mr. JOHNSON. They come from the juvenile courts, from the probation departments and they are placed there by the juvenile judges of the courts.

Chairman KEFAUVER. And it is financed by the county with some assistance from the youth division of the State?

Mr. JOHNSON. That's right, sir. And a lot of our money—that is what makes the ranch very appealing and a success—is the help that we are getting from the communities.

Chairman KEFAUVER. This is a great record that you are making, but I wish we had more Twin Pines Ranches.

Mr. JOHNSON. I hope so too, sir.

Chairman KEFAUVER. Thank you very much. Good luck. If any of you good people have an opportunity you would do well to go out to Twin Pines Ranch.

You are Leon Roy, executive secretary of the Catholic Big Brother organization?

Mr. ROY. That's right, of Los Angeles.

Chairman KEFAUVER. Of Los Angeles.

Mr. Bobo, do you wish to ask any preliminary questions?

Mr. BOBO. Mr. Roy, how long have you been with the staff of the Big Brothers?

Mr. ROY. Four and a half years.

Mr. BOBO. You deal specifically with youth?

Mr. ROY. Youth who are in trouble or who in the opinion of the authorities are heading for trouble.

Mr. BOBO. Would you tell us something about it?

STATEMENT OF LEON ROY, EXECUTIVE SECRETARY, CATHOLIC BIG BROTHER ORGANIZATION, LOS ANGELES, CALIF.

Mr. ROY. Yes. I will be very brief.

Our agency, too, is interested in juvenile delinquency, and more specifically in the Catholic boy who is behaving in a manner which is not acceptable to the community at large. Our primary interest is with the boy who, in the opinion of these authorities, is in danger of becoming a delinquent in the more serious sense of this word. Our goal is responsible citizens for tomorrow, and to this extent our agency does not differ substantially from most others which come to your attention. How we reach our goal, however, is unique in the Big Brother movement, which is nationwide with offices in many of the principal cities. We have in Los Angeles also a Jewish Big Brothers, and a third nonsectarian agency which is in the process of being organized.

We are particularly fortunate in that we have at our immediate disposal in this city over 100 men who are sufficiently interested in the welfare of youth to spend a few hours each week or so with the boy who has been brought to our agencies. These are professional and businessman who recognize that their community responsibilities transcend their own lawabiding contact and financial support of State and private welfare institutions. These men are willing and able to make an additional contribution, and it would be a serious loss to the welfare of this community should they not be afforded the opportunity to do so.

But it is not only for the sake of using this important resource in manpower that we introduce these men to an individual boy; our primary concern remains with the boy who also benefits from this type of association. Experience has shown us, as has been said earlier here this afternoon, that a boy in the process of his development seeks to pattern himself after someone or his ideal. This is a well recognized process, and probably is at the core of this investigation, because boys are susceptible to pictures and influences. It is their need to imitate just as it is their need for an idol and some recognition, and, of course, boys will satisfy these needs one way or another.

It is in recognition of these facts that we introduce our boys to a big brother, such a man as I have described, who by frequent and close association wins the boy's friendship and respect, and eventually becomes his idol. This process whereby a well motivated and able man exerts his influence on a boy has proven its worth many times over, not only in our own agency but throughout the country.

An element necessary in the success of this work, and one which we enjoy, is the cooperation and help of our county juvenile court and juvenile police departments. It is the basic understanding of children's behavior on the part of the representative of some of these departments that makes our contributions toward better citizens of tomorrow possible.

We are interested in boys between the ages of 8 and 18. We are particularly interested in having these boys referred to an agency such as ours from the police who are generally in the position of having these boys first come to their attention when they behave in a manner which is not entirely acceptable.

I believe that briefly explains our program.

Chairman Kefauver. Thank you very much, Mr. Roy. I know we are all interested in the Big Brothers' effort. It is a wonderful influence all over this country. You have 100 men who are willing to give some of their time and thought and effort to this cause?

Mr. Roy. That's right, and who give considerable of their time and considerable of their thought and patience to these boys.

Chairman Kefauver. How many boys, let us say, in the course of a year, do you reach in this way?

Mr. Roy. Last year we were able to work with 758 boys.

Chairman Kefauver. Just how do you do it? Do you meet every so often and meet with their Big Brothers and the Big Brothers keep in touch with what they are doing?

Mr. Roy. Exactly, sir. I think you have heard of this program through an investigation in Washington where a representative of our national organization spoke to you on the committee.

A boy who needs this type of association, comes to our attention, and we find in his immediate neighborhood a man who is willing and able and has sufficient patience—because it does take patience to assume this responsibility—to spend some time with this boy. He will do various activities with this boy of a nature which are interesting to both. Through these activities, which are only a method of reaching this boy, he will win the boy's friendship and his respect and his confidence, and he, the Big Brother, will become the person that every boy needs to look up to at some time in that boy's life.

These associations will last frequently on a lifetime basis. We have a big brother who some years ago acted as a big brother to a little brother, and in addition to standing up for him in the process of his marriage, he is now serving as a godfather at his child's baptism.

Chairman Kefauver. It is important and wonderful because it is the giving of one's own thought and time and attention to the child. We think this is one of the marvelous efforts throughout our Nation, and we certainly want to encourage you in what you are doing. I think it has meant much to tens of thousands of kids all through this country. We thank you very much.

Mr. Roy. Thank you, Senator.

Chairman KEFAUVER. We are glad to see.

A little while ago Mr. Ed Ladeck who has been helping the committee and who is Congressman Roosevelt's fieldman was here, and I just wanted to tell him how grateful we are for his assistance.

Mr. Nort Sanders is our next witness.

Mr. SANDERS. My name is Nort Sanders and my position is chief, Community Services Division, Probation Department, Los Angeles County.

Chairman KEFAUVER. Mr. Bobo, will you ask Mr. Sanders the preliminary questions? Then give Mr. Sanders an opportunity to tell us what he knows about this situation.

Mr. BOBO. Mr. Sanders, how long have you been with the Probation Department of Los Angeles County?

Mr. SANDERS. Sir, since January 1939.

Mr. BOBO. And you work under the direct supervision of Mr. Carl Holton, is that correct?

Mr. SANDERS. That's right.

Mr. BOBO. The function of your department would be to accept from the juvenile courts those who are committed to the probation department by the juvenile courts?

STATEMENT OF NORT SANDERS, CHIEF, COMMUNITY SERVICES DIVISION, PROBATION DEPARTMENT, LOS ANGELES COUNTY

Mr. SANDERS. Well now, the particular division of work that I have is our community services and that includes the crime and delinquency prevention work in my department. In my particular office of work we do not handle the investigation and supervision of cases for the juvenile court; we have the community organization program, the coordinating council program for developing community interest into a concerted effort in correcting community factors that contribute to delinquency. We have the group guidance program, incidentally the staff that Andy Griffin referred, to that are assigned out into the so-called gang areas of the county. That staff works full time and exclusively in these so-called gang areas with very hard to reach youth. We also staff the county committee on juvenile relations and provide the county coming-home program.

Mr. BOBO. Would you tell us something about the work that your community services division does with youth gangs and relative to them?

Mr. SANDERS. Yes, sir. Our department has taken responsibility in this field since 1941. That was at the time that there was considerable gang warfare, the so-called zuit-suit or pauchuca-riot days. We entered the field because all agencies at that time were asked to help in any way they were equipped to do so because of the community crises. We also faced very real problems in our juenvile-court work in handling the case of a boy who would be brought before the court involved in gang activities. Very frequently, or usually would not be the youngster who precipitated the difficulty, but one who happened to be picked up. And in returning him to the community with directions that he should not associate with boys with whom he has been in trouble, he should have certain restrictions that would put him in direct conflict with the prevailing pattern of life in the community where he lived posed such problems such that we were anxious to do it for that reason. We also felt that principally in all fields and certainly in the welfare and youth field prevention must be in inseparable partner of treatment. And we hear a lot now about detached workers, progressive casework, and protective services, and actually these have been the basic elements of our program since 1941. It was essentially an experimental project, and because of your time factor 1 won't go into details, except to say that this staff of 10 positions encompass and are assigned to work in the various gang areas of the county.

We took on as a responsibility group cases that would parallel our particular responsibility to individual youngsters. There are many youthful problems, parents who need help in counseling, but that is not the responsibility of the probation department. It is to take only those cases where the problem is so acute that for the welfare of the individual and the public government has a definite responsibility. Therefore, the gang referrals that our department takes are only those in situations where investigation has shown that the youth groups are beyond the reach or resources of existing programs. The situation in the county has had its ups and downs in the gang-warfare situation. These clubs, and hostility between them, has been mostly broken down because of a countywide federation of the youth clubs. So that in fact in all instances these particular groups have been converted into a club type of operation. They have their membership cards. They have learned to elect leaders by the democratic process rather than by the leader taking over.

I am telescoping this very briefly because in many instances it took many months to gain the confidence and support of these youngsters, most of whom are members of our minority groups.

At the present time, we can say that in the county the gang type of violence, the gang type of delinquency, is well down and has maintained a low-frequency situation for quite a period of time. I think that 1 of the reasons, 1 of the main reasons contributing to that, Senator and Mr. Bobo, has been the fact that experience has shown that the best way to approach this type of problem is, of course, an early detection. But it is the integration of effort on the part of the various agencies.

We find that law enforcement now in effect talks the same language as our staff persons, as does, for instance, church influences, such as Reverend Griffin's with the private agencies. Therefore, in the community we have been able to accomplish more of the team approach to meet the needs of these youngsters.

I think that that has been one of the very significant constructive trends in the field of work, has been the demonstration of our various agencies to cooperate as a team and mutually approach this particular problem.

We now are working, incidentally, with about 26 groups in 19 areas throughout the county. One of the main changes that happens is that instead of these groups being all localized in the downtown or eastside area we have found that they have gone out very frequently more to the periphery, because our outskirts now have become so densely populated that youth faces the same problems there that they used to face in downtown Los Angeles.

Mr. Bobo. You find in any of your gang problems here that adults are in any way leading these youth groups or youth gangs?

Mr. Sanders. I would say, sir, only to the extent that these are very naturally loose groupings. They are loosely structured gangs. In other words, they are an accumulation of those youth and young adults who happen to live in the neighborhood or community.

In response to your question, insomuch as some of the young people in these areas are what we would call legal age, adult age—maybe they are over 18—maybe 21 or 23—but so far as adult leadership for positive criminal activity is concerned, I would say there has been in our experience a total absence of that. In fact, our gang warfare out here has not been the predatory type for committing planned criminal acts; it has primarily been an expression of their hostility and insecurity by competing for status with other comparable groups. Most of their overt criminal actions have been in reference to other groups of youths such as themselves, rather than against public individuals or the public generally.

Mr. Bobo. In the California youth gang situation, then, you don't have a condition where you will have one block gang interlocked with a district gang, interlocked with a city gang, as we have found?

Mr. Sanders. No. We don't have that type of situation. Most of the grouping here actually results, I would say, in—this is a field for security by these youngsters, and you will find that the constituents of the groups, the individuals, actually do not desire to get into a fight. They personally don't want to. But there is this esprit de corps; there is this feeling of being chicken; there is the feeling of loss of status if they don't show at least at some levels that they can be superior to some people. But it is not an organized process such as you refer to.

Mr. Bobo. And the detached program which you use is used effectively to combat youth gangs?

Mr. Sanders. Yes. From the very beginning we recognized certain things, that you have to meet these young people at the level where they are and under the conditions where they are. You can't expect them to come into a building centered program. You have to go out on the street corners and you have to go out to the neighborhoods and you have to establish rapport by gaining their confidence, which is pretty slow, but gradually it can be done, and then using the influence to divert their type of group expressions away from those that endanger public welfare.

The only other thing that I would be inclined to say is this: I heard you earlier talking about the matter of statistics in reference to the delinquency pattern. I know that we have been quite alarmed by the reading of such things as over a 4-year period, 1948 to 1952, it increased 29 percent, over the Nation about 5 times the ratio of the youth population, and then the Bureau of Census tells us that in 1960 the youth population will be 40 percent more than it is in 1952; that these are pretty discouraging factors. With no smugness whatsoever, we can at least indicate that I think likely through community effort, citizenry interest, and agency responsibility—we do know that in the first 5 months of this year as against the first 5 months of last year the records of the juvenile division of the police department show approximately a 3 percent increase in juvenile arrests.

Now, when we check our school enrollment, the youth normally of the delinquency age, junior high school and high school, at the same time we had a 3 percent increase in juvenile arrests we had a 9.1 increase in the enrollment numerically of youth in our high schools and junior high schools, which I think may be more or less a tribute to the agency than it is a tribute to the community.

One of the things that I think I might mention, and which I think is very pertinent, is that we are finding that there is a real eagerness on the part of youth to be involved in that very democratic process, to be involved in planning for affairs that affect them. In our 94 coordinating councils throughout the county they have developed a youth coordinating council where high school youths are meeting and are taking responsibility for sharing, and how they can contribute constructively to community betterment. I think it is developing future community leaders, and we have found that the youths have a real eagerness to participate. And I think when we face the drop of figures in many of our youth problems and so forth we must realize that youth of the high school age has a real potential and will earnestly accept the challenge if we in the field can provide it for them.

Chairman KEFAUVER. Mr. Lane, are there any questions you wish to ask Mr. Sanders?

Mr. LANE. Yes. Mr. Sanders, you said that these young people would not respond to a building type program and you had to go out into the streets and invite them to come in.

Mr. SANDERS. Yes.

Mr. LANE. Do you mean that that is a particular type of youngster, or would you mind elaborating on that situation?

Chairman KEFAUVER. Let's talk louder. Nobody can hear what is going on here.

Mr. SANDERS. The question was whether we found that we did have to go to meet the youth rather than utilize the existing facilities or expect them to come in. That was very consistently a factor, yes, sir.

As I mentioned, the gang activity that we referred to, involving the minority group youth, is also related to the youth in the less dense areas of the community. These youths were never oriented into being personally able to feel that they could successfully participate in constructive recreational programs and programs of other types. They felt that they were not wanted, and they felt that they did not belong, and they felt less secure. And they wanted to belong to a larger group as something to be attached to. And it was very necessary to go right out and meet the youths and accept them where they were with their existing problems, establish the relationship, and then use that gradually to work with them and develop a confidence and a willingness to accept some of these other things that are more readily available to people of average means in our community.

Chairman KEFAUVER. Thank you very much for your statement, Mr. Sanders. We appreciate your telling us about what you are doing.

Our next witness is Chief R. E. Parker, chief of police of Pomona, Calif.

I swore Chief Parker of Los Angeles, and I think I had better swear you, too.

TESTIMONY OF R. E. PARKER, CHIEF OF POLICE, POMONA, CALIF.

Chairman KEFAUVER. You are Chief R. E. Parker of the city of Pomona, chief of police of that city?

Mr. PARKER. Yes.

Chairman KEFAUVER. Mr. Bobo, will you ask him any preliminary questions you wish?

Mr. BOBO. Chief Parker, how long have you been chief of police of Pomona, Calif.?

Mr. PARKER. About 5½ years; since December 9, 1949.

Mr. BOBO. How large a city is Pomona?

Mr. PARKER. Approximately 50,000.

Mr. BOBO. On your police force how many officers do you have assigned?

Mr. PARKER. We have 59 uniformed personnel.

Mr. BOBO. Are any of these assigned specifically to juvenile delinquency work?

Mr. PARKER. Yes, three.

Mr. BOBO. Three officers are assigned to that work?

Mr. PARKER. Yes.

Mr. BOBO. Do you have any type of juvenile program within the police department, such as a PAL Club or Boy Scout activities?

Mr. PARKER. Yes, we do have a well-rounded program. We feel we are keeping abreast of juvenile delinquency in Pomona.

Chairman KEFAUVER. You are a big man, Mr. Parker, and will you just turn this way so that everybody can hear you?

Mr. PARKER. I said we do feel that we are keeping abreast of juvenile delinquency in the city of Pomona in the use of a positive-type program. I would like to point out that the honorable councilwoman of the city of Los Angeles almost scooped me on one of them.

In 1950 the city of Pomona had a lot of problems, hot-rod problems created by hotrod racing, and every night we were receiving calls from irate citizens who were demanding that these disturbances and the danger to their homes be taken away. It didn't take us long to realize that we couldn't quell the exuberances of youth. We put on extra officers and we couldn't chase them down.

And so in an effort to bring the hotrodders under control we decided to join them. We certainly couldn't beat them. So one of the officers, who is a racing enthusiast himself, went to the clubs and explained the nature of the complaints and because of his enthusiasm in the sport was able to become a member of the club. And at a later date the officers of the city of Pomona let them use their local clubroom as a meeting place.

We had organized activities for the hotrod clubs. We had what we call contests for car cleanliness, car safety, and so forth. The club members would lose points by having their car unsafe or unsightly.

Chairman KEFAUVER. Have you got a place where they can race or run out there?

Mr. PARKER. Yes; we do. In 1950 the club members said, "Well, you policemen don't want us to race, but where can we race?"

So we started looking around for a place for them, and we finally found an old airport in San Bernardino County that had been abandoned, and after meeting with the San Bernardino County Board of Supervisors we did obtain permission to use that. I think ours was the first law-enforcement agency in the United States to sponsor such a track. We did receive inquiries from the boys to join the hot rods. After several difficulties in getting insurance we did open up in 1951, and the opening date was such a success that there were hotrodders that came from as far away as San Diego and camped on the strip all night to run the next day.

Since that time the program has been such a wonderful success that the city of Pomona, in cooperation with the Los Angeles County Fair Association, formed a league in the city of Pomona and contributed $5,000 and put a well-organized strip in the parking lot of the Los Angeles County Fairgrounds. Since that time the calls coming into the police department complaining about hotrod racing are practically nonexistent. Before that they used to drive into the local drive-ins and drink beer and curse and create a disturbance, and then the police were chasing them down the street, and that certainly has been alleviated.

The annual statistical report of the California Highway Patrol disclosed that since 1950 there has been approximately a 10 percent increase in accidents each year involving youths under the age of 18, 18 or unquestionably under the age of 20. While the city of Pomona has had approximately a 21-percent increase in population, our accident rate in that category has been less than 9 percent. We feel that that has a very direct reference as to how well the program is working.

Also, the youths around drive-ins, who formerly created a very great disturbance, have ceased such activity, and that condition has been alleviated. And at the same time they have contributed over $20,000—they are incorporated as nonprofit—these donations go to the city of Hope, the March of Dimes, and so forth, the Children's Home. And they have also given prizes and trophies to other types of clubs that have that activity.

We feel in the city of Pomona that if you give youths a chance, that they will come through, and we feel that the American people have an inherent desire for individualism. We feel that the youth certainly strives to get recognition such as any other person. We have a well-supervised program, and we have channeled their enthusiasm, and we feel that youth will come through.

Referring to the problem of seasonal activities by youths, and particularly Halloween, in 1952 they practically burned the city of Pomona down. These groups would go out and set fire to palm trees and burn telephone lines. And in one section to the south, they turned on so many hydrants, fire hydrants, that the fire department was unable to fight the fire, and generally destruction was caused throughout the city. We realized that this couldn't be an annual program for the youth; we decided to create a regular Halloween committee. The committee was composed of members of the PTA, the YMCA service clubs, and so forth. Plans were immediately drawn for a safe and sane Halloween. This blueprint included the organization of parties not only available to, but attractive to every boy and girl of junior and senior high school age. For the junior high schools, the parties were of the carnival type with games and other means of group activity, and a dance was provided for the members of the senior high school.

A few days prior to Halloween of 1953 a member of the police department and of the fire department appeared at assemblies at these high schools and made a straightforward appeal to the young citizens to participate in the planned activities and to refrain from destructive type of celebration.

The activities of this program can be quickly summarized by saying that since its initiation Halloween has become an enjoyable event in Pomona, looked forward to by adults as well as children. No extra policemen are required for patrol duty on Halloween nights, and our businessmen no longer expect to find their store windows soaped the morning following Halloween. In fact, as a result of these activities we haven't had one window soaped or one fire hydrant opened or one bit of vandalism on Halloween. This is certainly an indication of what youth can do if given an opportunity and if given recognition.

We had a gang problem in the city of Pomona. In February 1952 two elements of Pomona's youthful society were readied for open warfare. Because of a series of circumstances beginning with an insulting handshake, the situation grew to warlike proportions. This department was in receipt of inside information indicating that nearly 200 youths were about to set upon a Mexican neighborhood with such weapons as rifles, shotguns, sidearms, hand grenades, dynamite, and homemade bombs. One skirmish between these two factions resulted in several cars being nearly demolished and the hospitalization of at least two individuals with serious injuries.

Because of the imminence of the crisis, the idea of a truce meeting between the factions was hit upon and successfully carried out. Since that time there has been no group violence between Caucasian and Mexican-American groups.

Chairman KEFAUVER. Chief Parker, I don't like to interrupt, but the people in the back can't hear you at all, so they are misbehaving a little bit back there. Will you speak louder? If you would speak louder, may be you would have better attention from the back row.

Mr. PARKER. The leaders and the outstanding members of each group did come down to the police department, and we did appeal to them to settle their differences in a democratic manner, and as a result we talked them into forming clubs and so forth, in which the county probation department, as Mr. Sanders pointed out, has done a wonderful job. Our local merchants and our local service clubs have followed through, and the same boys that were wielding bicycle chains, clubs, can openers, knives, and so forth, at each other, are now getting first prizes on their floats in the parades. One of them was a float made upon a religious theme called "United Under God," and it was certainly wonderful to see those same fellows, who were booing the police department and creating these disturbances, riding down one of our main streets on a float.

One of our officers was killed in the line of duty, and one of these clubs donated a considerable sum to the officer's widow, as well as making good donations to charitable groups.

We feel that by the police department taking the initiative in establishing fellowship among the youths is certainly putting us well on the way in crime prevention.

The police department has several programs in which they put on dances for the youths, sponsor baseball leagues, and they also send one man to the California Boys' League in Sacramento as a counselor.

I believe that is about all I have to offer today.

Mr. Bobo. Chief, I wonder if in a city the size of Pomona you ever have any narcotic problem with marihuana or heroin?

Mr. Parker. Yes, we have had, but it has been at a very minimum. Recently, I think—it was about a year and a half ago that we had our major case wherein we had one boy who was selling marihuana to very young juveniles. We were able to apprehend the subject as well as the boys who did smoke marihuana, and as a result of investigation he is in prison now.

Through informants, through friends we made through organized activities we have the names of every juvenile who has ever bought or smoked marihuana, and we do keep a good file and record of that, and through adequate counseling we feel that the marihuana problem is well on its way to solution in Pomona.

Chairman Kefauver. Well, Chief, we are very glad to know of the activities over in Pomona as you aspire to carry it out with such success, and we appreciate your coming and being with us today. I think it an appropriate place in the record to insert Chief Parker's article, Harnessing the Hot Rodders.

(The article referred to was marked "Exhibit No. 4," and reads as follows:)

Exhibit No. 4

Harnessing the Hot Rodders

Over the fireplace in our old family home where I was born, hung an old family heirloom, a tapestry in which was woven the following inscription:

"There is so much good in the worst of us,
And so much bad in the best of us,
That it ill-behooves any of us,
To try and find fault with the rest of us."

In those days, while I could read the words, I never understood exactly what they meant and the important philosophy hidden in them. Their truth didn't really sink in until later years, especially when I entered the field of law enforcement.

"There is good in the worst of us and bad in the best of us."

Every city and village in this fast-moving age of the automobile, the airplane and supersonic travel, have had their trouble with speed—speed on the highway—speed causing death by the thousands each year—speed that involves mature grownups as well as juveniles. The hot rodder is only one aspect of the major problem of our age, and for the most part we have not intelligently recognized this; consequently we have gone off the beam in trying to solve the hot-rod problem.

In Pomona we finally woke up and applied a little psychology and homespun remedy to get the kids on our side—the side that would enable them to let off steam in an orderly and controlled fashion without endangering life and limb of us oldsters, who were every bit in need of a safety belt in our day as the kids are now.

First of all, we became aware of the fact that the kids with their "souped up" hot rods were not all bad. They were a nuisance, a hazard, and a menace, but somewhere and somehow was an answer to their problem. How to let them have their fun—let off steam—yet not do it where lives would be in jeopardy and where the law enforcement would have to be continually tracking them down, giving them the feeling they were lawbreakers, delinquents, and that the cops were against them.

In reality, the kid driving and "revving up" a hot rod was not a criminal or a juvenile delinquent. We knew that from the arrests we had made. When we looked at their crimes in the light of what we had done in our teen-age years, we had a guilty conscience.

Society and congestion had grown up around the kids, but society had not learned how to harness the devilment, exuberance, and tack their boisterous sails along orderly lines.

Every negative approach had been tried. We had so many laws and ordinances on the books even the officers couldn't keep track of them. There were speeches galore on the subject of the hot rodder. You are all familiar with the literature in the field, yet the answer was not to be found in roundtable discussions alone, but positive, intelligent, and understanding action was necessary. As a last resort we dropped the idea of trying to "beat" the hot rodders and decided to "join" them, gain their confidence, and by so doing lend respectibility to their sport.

The hot rod problem has been with us for a long time. All brought by a keen spirit of competition between each owner of a hot rod, an extremely hazardous condition resulted by the use of city streets during dark hours for race track activities. As you are all aware, this caused many complaints from irate citizens demanding the hazards to their safety and the disturbance to their peace and quiet, be stopped. Public sentiment, aroused by lack of control, caused large-scale drives against hot rodders by law enforcement officers in southern California. The problem was of such magnitude the California State Legislature enacted laws making it illegal for any person to participate or be in attendance at such races. This had just the opposite effect and hot rod activities increased. Many fatal accidents occurred as the result of a young hot rod enthusiast trying out his "souped-up buggy" at every opportunity. Several spontaneous hot rod clubs were formed, but they lacked organization and purpose and continued on their merry way of giving the public and police officials a constant headache.

A traffic officer of the Pomona Police force, a racing enthusiast himself, was appointed liaison officer between the Pomona Police Department and the hot rodders. In contacting the different clubs and explaining the nature of complaints received by the police department, yet showing an interest in their activities, this officer was able to gradually establish a spirit of understanding and fellowship among them. Some progress was noted in the initial stages. At one of the many meetings, the police department offered to donate the use of the officers' club rooms one evening a week for the hot rod club to use as a meeting place. The offer was accepted. This move proved to be mutually advantageous as it brought the hot rodders and the police department closer together, and afforded an opportunity for each to gain a more thorough understanding of the other's problems.

Efforts were made to find a place for a hot rod track. No one would listen to our plea. Finally, "we cracked the ice" at an old abandoned airfield in San Bernardino County. Another setback—insurance; we finally, after many discouragements, obtained a policy from Lloyds of London. We were open for business, and our opening Sunday was a huge success. Several hundred cars came to watch those "rambling wrecks" roar down the track.

And, let me tell you this—the old adage, "nothing succeeds like success" is true. People flocked to our aid—prizes, timers, and all were offered. We were a going concern and "off to the races" in every sense of the word.

We later, through the help of the city of Pomona, leased the parking lot at the Los Angeles County Fair Ground. The track is better and the attendance is continually increased.

An extensive safety program was initiated into the club's curriculum and added life was given to the club's activities through the medium of supervised "poker-runs", time runs, secret-destination runs, and planned group tours. To stimulate interest further, an activity chart was set up to bring out the spirit of competition. A point system was established wherein the club members could gain or lose points according to their degree of participation in the program. The incentive used to stimulate interest in acquiring the most points was in the shape of a large perpetual activity trophy which is awarded to the winner semiannually. There was such high competitive spirit and interest among the club members that the membership was tripled in a short time. The activity chart and point system were largely instrumental in decreasing the number of citations issued to "hot rodders" and complaints received. The hot rodders have become a forceful group for the promoting of a sound safety program throughout the community. Their spirit and desire to be helpful have accrued to the benefit of everyone. The energy of this youthful group has been channeled along sound and progressive lines. It can be proudly stated that through the cooperative program carried on between the hot rodders and the local police department, there has been a sharp decline in accidents involving the younger drivers. Also, nightly calls received by the police from complaining citizens concerning racing hot rods on the city streets have become practically nonexistent. Whatever problems still existing is usually caused by those who have no knowledge of the program.

The alliance between the police and hot rodders has caused the young drivers to use more consideration in their driving habits toward the public, and the public has responded by taking a keener interest in the hot-rod program. This is further reflected by the attendance at the "Drag Races" held each Sunday on a well laid-out, properly supervised drag strip. The hot rodder is no longer a problem in Pomona—he is part of a program.

The annual statistical report in the State of California Department of Highway Patrol disclosed that, since 1950 there has been approximately 10 percent increase in accidents each year involving drivers under the age of 20. During the same period in Pomona we have decreased accidents involving those under 20 by 9 percent. "Operation Dragstrip," deserves most of the credit for this record of which our department is mighty proud. It is even more remarkable when it is realized that Pomona's population in the 1952–53 period has increased over 20 percent.

One question that has been asked by numerous law enforcement agencies considering the use of a hot-rod program in their respective communities is, "What are the future possibilities of a program of this type in relation to traffic safety"?

The future of such a program depends entirely upon the way the activities of these clubs are conducted in the future. In order to insure proper activities of these clubs, there must be proper supervision and organization. This supervision, if carried out by the police on a friendly basis, can serve as the means of assuring a well-regulated program. If the youthful driver of today is trained properly in his driving habits during the early part of his driving career, and members of law enforcement are participating in his education, then there is a good chance that his future driving habits will be better regulated, and thus, guarantee a safer traffic future for his community.

If the youth of today can be taught safety now through the use of such a program, as the supervised hot-rod program, then drivers of tomorrow will not be as accident prone as the drivers of today are. Not only will many lives be saved, but insurance rates will be decreased, both which society is interested in. Gaining the cooperation of the hot-rodder in today's traffic safety program is tomorrow's insurance for greater safety on our highways. With this program, not only has law enforcement succeeded in suppressing traffic problems, but the close relationship formed between young people and the police will serve as a deterrent to juvenile delinquency in other respects.

And so, if the old adage, "There is so much good in the worst of us and so much bad in the best of us," is true, it behooves us, the law enforcement agencies, through our planned prevention programs to try and bring out and accentuate the good and to control and correct the bad. If we find, through the use of some type of program, we have successfully converted a troublesome element into a cooperative and law abiding segment of society, then we, as members of law enforcement, are doing our job.

If you have the same problem in your community and the hot-rodder has exhausted your patience, scared your citizens, and "raised Cain" in general, why don't you try to join them and by leadership and enthusiasm guide them along accepted channels without throttling the spirit that has made America the great nation that she is.

Chairman KEFAUVER. Who is our next witness, Mr. Bobo?

Mr. BOBO. Mr. Eugene Breitenbach.

STATEMENT OF EUGENE BREITENBACH, MEMBER, CALIFORNIA YOUTH AUTHORITY

Chairman KEFAUVER. All right, Mr. Breitenbach.

Mr. Bobo, will you ask Mr. Breitenbach some preliminary questions?

Mr. BOBO. Mr. Breitenbach, you are with the California Youth Authority?

Mr. BREITENBACH. I am a member of the California Youth Authority; yes, sir.

Mr. BOBO. You are a member of the board of the California Youth Authority?

Mr. BREITENBACH. That is correct, sir.

Mr. Bobo. For how long have you been with the California Youth Authority?

Mr. Breitenbach. Since June 28, 1953, sir.

Mr. Bobo. Will you tell us something about the composition of the California Youth Authority?

Mr. Breitenbach. The California Youth Authority is composed of a director and four members of the board appointed by the Governor with a confirmation by the State senate.

Mr. Bobo. And it has jurisdiction over all youth institutions?

Mr. Breitenbach. We have the responsibility for the classification, segregation, and parole of youthful offenders who are under the age of 21 at the time of apprehension.

Mr. Bobo. Mr. Breitenbach, I believe that the youth authority has instituted 1 or 2 outstanding programs within the last year. Would you tell us something about those programs?

Mr. Breitenbach. Yes; I will be very happy to, and I should state preliminarily that I am appearing here today at the request of the Honorable Goodwin J. Knight, Governor of the State of California, and the Honorable H. G. Stark, director of the California Youth Authority.

We are all mighty pleased that this committee is interested in learning more about the problem of juvenile delinquency in California, and are, of course, very glad to cooperate with the committee to the very best of our ability.

The most significant development in California in the way of preventing juvenile delinquency and crime occurred just recently. Gov. Goodwin J. Knight inaugurated a few weeks ago this most significant development in the history of the prevention of delinquency in this State.

On April 27, 1955, Governor Knight promulgated a program of statewide town meetings in a letter addressed to the mayors of all incorporated cities in California and to the chairmen of the county boards of supervisors throughout the State.

I would like for the record, if the committee please, to read this brief letter into the record.

Chairman Kefauver. Either read it or we will have it printed in the record at this place, Mr. Breitenbach.

Mr. Breitenbach. The only reason that I request that I read it is because it draws the outlines of this program, and I will read it.

Chairman Kefauver. Suppose you read it, then.

Mr. Breitenbach. This is addressed to the mayor from the Governor:

My Dear Mayor: California held the line on juvenile delinquency in 1954. While the Nation generally reported increases up to 15 percent during the year, statewide statistics just compiled by the youth authority show that the delinquency rate has actually decreased in California. This has been accomplished by neighborhood and community agencies which have done an effective job of coping with the problems facing our children.

The California Youth Authority has provided outstanding leadership in the field of delinquency prevention and youth rehabilitation. Although we held the line last year, delinquency is still a matter of major concern to our citizens, and I am convinced that we can make further progress by immediate statewide community action. Now is the time to attack the problem by early detection and local treatment of delinquents and potential delinquents.

I am requesting that you and all mayors. and all chairmen of boards of supervisors call together in an old-fashioned town meeting the interested agencies and organizations in our community to evaluate existing facilities and programs and to study the local aspects of delinquency and delinquency prevention. Such an old-fashioned New England town meeting as I am suggesting, to be successful, must bring together in free gathering all groups and individuals in the community who have direct or indirect interest in children, or have facilities or programs to assist them.

The tradition of citizens gathering together to express their individual ideas about matters of common concern is as old as the history of our country, and continues as a sturdy manifestation of our inherited passion for free speech and political action.

I am sure the citizens of your community will welcome your leadership in naming a group to plan a town meeting for your city. Many communities already have mayors' committees on juvenile delinquency which could plan the program. Where these do not now exist, they might well be formed, or an established organization such as the community council or the welfare council, et cetera, might serve as a planning committee for your town meeting.

Anticipating that you will join this program I have directed the field officers of the youth authority to give every assistance in planning these meetings. Their services and specially prepared technical material may be obtained by writing to Mr. Heman G. Stark, director of the youth authority, directly in Sacramento.

I plan to call a statewide council in April of 1956 to study the reports of these town meetings and to develop a master plan for the improvement of these services in California.

In preparation for this conference I am asking the Governor's advisory committee on children and youth, and interested State departments, to prepare a statewide balance sheet on youth services so that the conferences may have this material available. Upon completion of your meeting I would appreciate receiving a copy of your findings and recommendations.

Cordially,

GOODWIN J. KNIGHT, *Governor.*

Now, if the committee please, to date more than 200 communities have already indicated that they would hold such town meetings. The program is taking hold in a wonderful way. This is a grassroots program to combat juvenile delinquency at the local level, where we believe it can best be handled.

Under the governor's direction the youth authority is getting out two publications. One is entitled "Planning Handbook for Town Meeting." And I would like to submit for the purpose of the record a copy of it.

Chairman KEFAUVER. It is a very useful exhibit and will be made a part of our record.

(The document referred to was marked "Exhibit No. 5," and reads as follows:)

EXHIBIT NO. 5

PLANNING HANDBOOK FOR TOWN MEETINGS ON DELINQUENCY AND DELINQUENCY PREVENTION

THE TOWN MEETING TRADITION

Many changes are taking place in community life today. People are moving about more freely than ever before. Community ties are fewer and roots are more shallow. Life generally is more complex. Families are finding it more difficult to remain strong and united. As our cities steadily increase in size, their problems rapidly multiply. Citizens tend to leave the development of community life to chance, or to shift the total responsibility to government.

Throughout California thinking people are seeking ways and means of strengthening local community life through increased citizen knowledge and participation. Everywhere there is a growing eagerness to learn from one another. The tradition of free and open discussion is as old as the history of our country. It is perhaps for this reason that the New England Town Meeting has persisted in only slightly altered form for nearly two centuries.

Juvenile delinquency is a serious and continuing aspect of community life. Gov. Goodwin J. Knight has reported that we have "held the line" in California in 1954 while the Nation was reporting increases in delinquency up to 15 percent. We can be proud of our record in controlling delinquency last year, but we must face the fact that the problem is still large and serious. We must further recognize that the prevention and control of juvenile delinquency, to be effective, must be pursued primarily in the community. Only by constant community vigilance will we be able to keep delinquency within bounds. Only by concerted community action can we make further progress through a more effective local attack on the problem.

PURPOSE OF THE TOWN MEETING

The town meeting's main function should be to clarify viewpoints on problems relating to delinquency prevention and control; to present and study new ideas; to encourage citizen thinking and discussion; and to stimulate community planning and action to combat delinquency. Free discussion by the group should be the focus of the meeting, rather than lectures in which the audience participates passively.

The results of your town meeting will also make a valuable contribution to delinquency prevention and control throughout the State. Governor Knight has asked that the findings and recommendations of each town meeting be submitted to him as early as possible, in preparation for a statewide conference he will call in April 1956, at Sacramento. The reports and recommendations of the town meetings will serve as a framework for this Governor's Conference, will provide the springboard for discussions at that meeting, and will be used to develop a master plan for improvement of services to youth in California.

PLANNING THE TOWN MEETING

The following outline of duties and responsibilities for town meeting leaders is not intended as a complete check list but only as a general guide.

Prior to any assignment of responsibilities, the board of supervisors and the mayor or city council should direct heads of county or city departments related to youth services to give full cooperation to town meeting planning committees.

Mayor or chairman of board of supervisors

Informally discusses idea of town meeting with others likely to be interested. Clarifies understanding why town meeting is to be held—its value, purpose, and objective.

Selects tentative date after conferring with others to avoid any conflicts.

Looks for existing sponsoring group, such as a mayor's committee or county-wide committee, coordinating council, or welfare council, to plan and carry out town meeting.

If no such group exists, appoints a broadly representative planning committee. Appoints planning committee chairman.

Looks for possibility of an existing community agency to furnish staff service to the planning committee and the town meeting itself.

Obtains financing for necessary expenses: mailing, printing or mimeographing announcements, programs, and final reports. This may be done by a small appropriation of public funds or by a 50-cent meeting registration fee.

Planning committee chairman

Accepts overall responsibility of town meeting leadership, planning, and management in behalf of mayor or chairman of board of supervisors.

Confers with mayor or chairman of board of supervisors and other interested people in the community for ideas and suggestions regarding the town meeting.

Convenes the committee and assists mayor or chairman of board of supervisors in familiarizing the committee with the town meeting idea, the focus, preliminary objectives, and purpose of the meeting, and tentative plans developed to date.

Keeps the mayor or chairman of board of supervisors advised of developments and gets his approval on matters where needed or advisable.

Coordinates or obtains full committee approval of the work of subcommittees.

Planning committee

Prepares a statement on the purposes and objectives of the meeting.

Reaches agreement on date and location of the meeting.

Makes decision on scope of attendance, how public is to be informed at the meeting, and who is to receive invitations.

Agrees on the use to be made of, and the time to be allotted to, the opening session, discussion meetings for smaller groups, and the closing session. Considers use to be made of consultants (individually or in panels) at discusion meetings.

Determines the number of section meetings or discussion groups, what the subject matter for discussion will be in each group, the size to which groups will be limited, and the method to be used for assigning participants to a specific section.

Develops a program in detail:
Time general sessions and section meetings are to be held.

Determines need for, and responsibilities of, discussion leaders, recorders for section and general session meetings, section coordinators, and any other necessary meeting personnel. Section coordinators and discussion leaders should be selected as early as possible and invited to susbequent planning committee meetings.

Decides on topic for general session speaker, if one is to be used.

Considers such matters as welcoming remarks, invocation, color ceremony, national anthem, introduction of special guests, and announcements for the opening session.

Determines whether luncheon or dinner meetings are to be held.

Agrees on method and technique to be used in obtaining reports from the individual sections, in reporting findings and recommendations of individual sections to the general meeting at the closing session, and in preparing an overall report or proceedings of the meeting for submission to the board of supervisors, the mayor, and the governor.

Authorizes subcommittees to be appointed by a planning committee chairman. These might include:
Arrangements: Responsible for obtaining meeting rooms for general sessions and section meetings, seeing that they are properly set up for the meetings, that necessary equipment and other facilities are available, et cetera.

Editorial: Responsible for getting program mimeographed and preparing final report or proceedings.

Publicity: Responsible for press, radio, and television publicity before, during, and after the town meeting.

Registration: Responsible for planning and carrying out pre-meeting registration and meeting registration, or otherwise obtaining a list of those attending, their affiliations, and addresses. (This may be assigned to a local civic group.)

Discussion leader

Helps group to define and select the problems that it wishes to discuss, to see that all points of view are given a chance to be aired, and to keep the discussion directed toward the problems under consideration.

Clarifies and summarizes the progress of the group from time to time and tries to maintain an atmosphere in which the maximum number of people can participate in the discussion. Sometimes this requires limiting opinions or statements to two minutes.

Assists recorder in the preparation of a summary of group discussion for presentation at the closing session and in preparing a final written report of the section for the proceedings.

Recorder

Functions of the recorder are to put down on paper the major points developed by group thinking. One convenient way to do this is to develop an outline such as:
Main issues or problems brought out.
Main differences of opinion among group members.
General conclusions agreed upon.
Specific final recommendations made and to whom they were directed.
Other information.

Develops significant highlights of the group discussion for use by newspaper reporters or publicity chairman.

Works with the discussion leader to prepare section report for the editorial committee or those responsible for preparing the final report.

Section coordinator

Meets with planning committee to become familiar with town meeting plans.
Responsible for making final check on physical arrangements for his section:
    Public address.
    Heating, lighting, and ventilation.
    Seating arrangements to facilitate discussion.
    Charts, visual aids, exhibits, blackboards.
Maintains attendance lists.

TRAINING OF TOWN MEETING LEADERS

A good planning committee trains its corps of assistants before the meeting
begins. Some of these assistants, such as the recorders and coordinators, will be
assigned personnel from participating agencies, and they may have prior experience in conference participation. Others will have no previous experience. In
such a situation, team training becomes essential. This training need take only
a few hours for a small town meeting, but it may require a full day for larger
programs. Training should be the responsibility of someone from the planning
committee who is thoroughly familiar with the town meeting plan and method
of operation. It should include a full description of the nature and purpose of
the town meeting.

General sessions

The first general session explains to the group the organization and plan for
the town meeting. Productive thought and discussion will be reached more
quickly if the opening session:
Creates an atmosphere in which the participant feels that he is important to
the success of the meeting. It is important that the participants be made aware
that all major decisions will be made by them.
Reviews some of the problems leading to the calling of the town meeting. The
participants should understand that the meeting will consider both their suggested problems as well as the leader's suggestions.
A good town meeting takes time for a final session which is as important as
the opening session. Here the entire group gets the essence of the program and
a clear sense of the findings of the town meeting through hearing the reports
of the individual section meetings. They make any necessary final decisions,
and plan ways to carry out those decisions through group or individual efforts.
Public commitment leads people to carry good intentions into action. The final
session then should become a commitment session in which those attending
publicly endorse the findings of the meeting and, at least by implication, declare
that they will carry out its recommendations.

Town meeting followup

A successful meeting requires some kind of followup. A preliminary decision
as to the type of organization needed to follow up on the town meeting should
be made by the planning committee. This plan or an alternate plan should be
detailed and endorsed by those attending the closing session. Some of the recommendations will be directed to specific organizations and agencies. No permanent
new organization should be created unless no representative coordinating group
exists in the community capable of furthering the recommendations.
The followup committee might have the following functions:
To forward reports of the meeting to the mayor, to the board of supervisors,
and to the governor.
To carry on the work of stimulating community action on the recommendations
of the meeting.
To develop plans for reassembly of the town meeting from time to time, to assay
results and lay new community plans for effective action.
To plan for the creation of a county committee on children and youth, advisory
to the board of supervisors.

Mr. BREITENBACH. And the other is a workbook for those attending
town meetings, entitled "An Outline of a Community Program for
the Prevention of Juvenile Delinquency." This is still in the course
of printing, and we will be happy to present it to the committee for
inclusion as an exhibit.

What we desire is to learn the local problems and local conditions
which revolve around the causes and prevention of juvenile delin-

quency at the local level. As an important part of this town-meeting program each community will prepare a balance sheet setting forth the positive and negative factors on such items as health, welfare, recreation, and so forth, for youths in each local community. This information will be assembled following the town meeting.

In Los Angeles County alone two community agencies have joined forces already and have offered assistance to the mayors of their communities for the holding of almost 100 town meetings throughout this county and the preparing of balance sheets from the information obtained. The coordinating council, who actually hold these meetings, and the Los Angeles County Welfare Planning Council will then compile balance sheets on youth for each community. These reports will then be integrated in a statewide report based on the world of all the other counties which will be presented and discussed at a statewide conference to be held in April of 1956.

The mayors, county supervisors, courts, probation officers, and enforcement agencies throughout the State of California have cooperated 100 percent with the Governor in carrying out this town-meeting program to date. It is believed that this has tremendous possibilities for the prevention of juvenile delinquency and crime.

Now, if the committee please, I would like to present one or two brief statements regarding why we believe what the factors are which have enabled us in California to hold the line, as it were, against further increase of juvenile delinquency during the past year. They are three in number:

No. 1. These figures are based upon a decline of police arrests.

No. 2. They are based upon a decline in probation cases.

No. 3. They are based upon a decline in the number of commitments to the youth authority in proportion to the approximate 5 percent increase in population during the same period of time.

We believe that the holding of the line in California has been accomplished through at least two developments peculiar to California, which we believe your committee will feel are also noteworthy contributions to this field.

No. 1 is the provision of a forestry camp program for boys, which has been so successful that people all over the world are visiting us to study it. You have heard this afternoon the dramatic story from the director of the camp at Twin Pines.

The other development has been the spirit of cooperation between all the agencies in this field, such as the courts, the probation department, law-enforcement agencies, schools, and local community meetings. This spirit of cooperation is one of the very wonderful factors in our work as a State agency, and has led to making possible such things as the town-meetings program in which we are engaged.

There is one other matter that I have been asked by our committee to comment upon, and that is the matter of the effect of television programs upon certain aspects of juvenile delinquency.

Now, it is our belief that television is one of the greatest media for the dissemination of constructive information programs. The overall majority of the programs are instructive and entertaining. While we have made no specific study of this particular problem here, it is reasonable to assume that certain impressionable and easily suggestible youngsters are influenced in a damaging way by scenes of assault, violence, and the actual modus operandi of violent crime such as robbery, mayhem, assault, and similar offenses. It is the considered opinion of some of us working in this field that programs that fail to promote respect for law are often injurious to such young people. Likewise, programs that show someone being knocked out in various episodes frequently tend to make that type of behavior acceptable to impressionable young minds.

However, we feel that certain television programs when properly presented have a very constructive influence on the lives of children and can be a great factor in the prevention of juvenile delinquency and crime. And we are encouraged to see more of these programs being developed, and we are hopeful that the entire field in the prevention of juvenile delinquency and crime will be increasingly presented and interpreted in an educational and constructive fashion.

I would like to comment briefly, if I may, on certain pending legislation which we feel has great promise in this particular field. We are pleased to learn that there is pending in the Congress of the United States constructive legislation dealing with the prevention of juvenile delinquency and crime. We believe that House bill No. 3771, Senate bill 894, and the Kefauver bill, Senate bill No. 728, are very constructive.

There are three additional suggestions that we would like to make at this time regarding the latter piece of legislation. These are very minor, but we feel that they might be helpful.

First, we feel that the provision for some group administration through the Federal Advisory Council on Juvenile Delinquency should be changed. We believe that group administration is not as strong as centralized administration. In other words, the Federal Advisory Council, we feel, should be an advisory power only, and that no administrative power be given to it.

Secondly, we feel that youth training schools should be represented on the Federal Advisory Council.

No. 3, we feel that specific agencies should administer the grants and aid. In other words, we believe it should be the counterpart of the youth authority in the various jurisdictions, since an agency of this sort deals with field services and is familiar with the problems of local delinquency prevention.

I would like to comment on one further thing. Mr. Phillip Green, newly appointed chief of the bureau of delinquency prevention services in the Federal Children's Bureau, was formerly chief probation officer of San Francisco County. We are happy to see that the Children's Bureau has recognized at this date the work that he has accomplished in this field, by choosing three of our State people for important positions in delinquency prevention under this bureau, including Mr. Phil Green, who is heading up this project.

Gentlemen of the committee, I believe that concludes my presentation here today.

Chairman KEFAUVER. Unless there are some questions this committee would like to ask Mr. Breitenbach, we are certainly grateful for your coming here and for this report. I want to say that I think the suggestion for townhall meetings to study and consider problems at a local level, allied with the townhall process, is a very, very good one. We on this committee have been trying to get started a so-called capital city program in which we get the governors of the States working with the mayors of the capital cities to try to make a model of cooperation of all of the agencies and groups dealing with delinquency in the capital cities; feeling that from the capital cities the information would disseminate to the other cities of the States, and the members of the legislature could come in and they would go back to their communities and they would carry the message as to what is being done in the capital city. Of course, it is a long-range program, just like the townhall meetings, but I certainly want to commend Governor Knight on this townhall meeting plan, and I suggest, of course, in the townhall meetings in something is decided upon it is followed through and other meetings held to see that the program works.

Mr. BREITENBACH. That is correct. We plan on holding committee meetings and meetings throughout the State for the purpose of implementation of the recommendations of the statewide meetings next April 1956.

Chairman KEFAUVER. You say that 200 cities or towns have already responded favorably?

Mr. BREITENBACH. That is correct, Senator Kefauver.

Chairman KEFAUVER. How many meeting have been held?

Mr. BREITENBACH. I couldn't give you the exact number of meetings that have been held, but a number of them have. One of the most successful developments has been in the city of San Francisco itself.

Chairman KEFAUVER. And then the forestry camp idea I think is an outstanding program. It has great possibilities. I hope it may be a program in which the Federal Government may be of some assistance by way of aid to the States in getting the forestry camps established and sustained.

How many camps do you now have like Twin Pines?

Mr. BREITENBACH. We have three camps that are operated by the California Youth Authority, in which we have the complete responsibility or, rather, for which we have the compete responsibility and control. In addition, we have throughout the State a great number of camps which are owned and operated by the local probation department, such as Twin Pines operated by the Riverside County Probation Department, to which we give a subsidy in the operation. These would number, I think, possibly 16 or 17. They are developing several youth camps this summer, and I would say the exact number is still changing from week to week.

Chairman KEFAUVER. Where are the three that are totally maintained locally?

Mr. BREITENBACH. The nearest one is Camp Gold, which, of course, is located in the Sierra Nevada Mountains near Yosemite National Park. The next nearest would be Camp Ben Lomond, which is near Santa Cruz on the coastal plain. A third camp is at Pine Grove, which is about 35 miles from Sacramento.

Chairman KEFAUVER. How many do you plan to have after the program gets under way?

Mr. BREITENBACH. I am not certain at this time whether we are contemplating the development of any additional forestry camps owned and operately exclusively by the California Youth Authority. That will depend entirely upon the increase in the number of commitments to the authority. But so far as the public is concerned, there are at the present time plans underway for the development of a camp in

Orange County, Santa Clara County, in the northern tier of counties north of Sacramento, and a number of others that are constantly being developed by the communities. As a result of these, the local agencies are able to handle those marginal cases that might otherwise have been committed to the California Youth Authority; leaving to the California Youth Authority those most difficult types of youngsters to rehabilitate. So it is a great saving from the standpoint of finances involved to the State, and is particularly a saving again in that it enables the people engaged in the program to train the youngsters near their own homes where it can be most effective and most convenient.

Chairman KEFAUVER. How many young people on the average do you have in these three camps that are around the State? I mean the total number. You don't need to necessarily break it down as to each place.

Mr. BREITENBACH. At Camp Gold our population as of April 1955 was 106; at Ben Lomond the population was 60; and at Pine Grove the population was 89.

This varies, of course, from time to time as releases are made and as new boys are transferred from our various correctional schools. I would say that the average number of boys that are being trained in the camps owned and operated by the local probation department would be in the neighborhood of between 50 and 60.

Chairman KEFAUVER. And what is the appropriated or budgeted funds for the camps that you have per year?

Mr. BREITENBACH. I would have to supply that from our budget, Senator. I could get it for you. It would be readily available.

Chairman KEFAUVER. If you would give us the information about the cost of the organizational set up and other details we will be very glad to have it.

Mr. BREITENBACH. Do you want the per capita cost and the total cost, Senator?

Chairman KEFAUVER. Yes.

Mr. BREITENBACH. Very well, sir.

Chairman KEFAUVER. Any other questions?

Mr. BOBO. No.

Chairman KEFAUVER. We certainly appreciate your coming and being with us, Mr. Breitenbach.

Mr. BREITENBACH. Thank you, gentlemen. It is certainly a pleasure to be here.

Mrs. KRUG. Senator, has any provision been made for girls? It seems as though all of these activities are directed toward the boys.

Chairman KEFAUVER. Well, I think that is a question which is very good, Mrs. Krug. And by the way, Mrs. Milton Krug is chairman of the juvenile delinquency committee of the California Lawyers' Wives Association, is that correct?

Mrs. KRUG. Yes.

Chairman KEFAUVER. Where did Mr. Breitenbach go to? I hope he is going to tell me that they don't have any girls to take this rehabilitation course.

Mr. BREITENBACH. I think that is an excellent question. I certainly agree.

Answering the question directly as to whether any provision is being made or contemplated for the handling of girls in minimum security facilities, such as camps, there is now in preparation and contemplation, I am informed, in the county of Santa Barbara, perhaps either acting alone or in cooperation with the county of Ventura, plans for the development of a facility for girls similar to these boys' camps that are now operated and owned by the probation department. The exact form that this facility will take I don't think is yet completely determined, but I think that it will be quite similar to our camps.

You may recall that at one time there was in the county of Los Angeles a number of years ago a camp for girls, but there were considerable difficulties encountered in the handling of the girls in the minimum security setting, and in the operation of that camp. We are going to observe with very great interest the development of these plans in the county of Santa Barbara and in the county of Ventura.

Chairman KEFAUVER. Mr. Breitenbach, you tell them that Mrs. Krug can go and get the story from you.

Mr. BREITENBACH. There are, of course, many cities—and I am sure Los Angeles has part-time day camps for girls and boys too.

Chairman KEFAUVER. I assume that there is a smaller percentage of girls in the group that needs some camp facility, but I think they ought to be provided for, too.

Mr. BREITENBACH. Well, I quite agree. The ratio between the number of girls and the number of boys in the youth authority will run approximately 87 percent boys and about 13 percent girls. That will give you some idea of the relative amount of difficulties which the girls and boys encounter in the group living together.

Chairman KEFAUVER. You might want to talk with Mrs. Krug sometime about her program.

Mr. BREITENBACH. I will be very happy to do so, yes, indeed.

Chairman KEFAUVER. Thank you.

Mr. BREITENBACH. Thank you, Senator.

STATEMENT OF JOHN BOGGS, CONSULTANT, HUMAN RELATIONS COMMITTEE, LOS ANGELES, CALIF.

Chairman KEFAUVER. You are Mr. John Boggs, consultant on the human relations committee of Los Angeles County?

Mr. BOGGS. Yes, sir.

Chairman KEFAUVER. We are very glad to have you with us.

Do you want to ask any preliminary questions, Mr. Bobo?

Mr. BOBO. Would you describe to us what the work of the human relations committee is?

Mr. BOGGS. The Los Angeles County Committee on Human Relations was established by the county board of supervisors in 1944, and at the time of its establishment it was given the responsibility of seeking out the causes of racial conflict and attempting to solve them by whatever means it could devise.

The committee at this time consists of 37 members; 25 lay people who are appointed by each of the county boards of supervisors from the districts they represent, and 12 heads or assistant heads of county departments.

Mr. BOBO. For how long are they appointed?

Mr. BOGGS. One year.

Mr. Bobo. And in what way does this deal with juvenile delinquency, and what is the effect of this committee in working with it?

Mr. Boggs. Well, it has been the feeling of those of us who have been concerned in the field of human relations that there is a very definite tieup and relationship between the poor human relations and juvenile delinquency, and very recently we have conducted a survey among the juvenile probation officers in the probation department, seeking to determine whether or not in their experience they have discovered a relationship existing between poor human relations and the activities of the juveniles and their delinquent acts. This survey is not yet completed, but I would like to give you some information that we have preliminarily gotten from it.

For example, these probations officers have indicated throughout this survey to our committee that in all 54 junior and senior high schools in Los Angeles County there is a definite relationship between juvenile delinquency and the relationship that exists between youngsters of different racial and cultural backgrounds.

For instance, they have indicated—21 of these men have indicated that gang fights can be directly related to poor human relations in many of the areas that they have observed, and that these gang fights come as a result of rumors circulating among youngsters indicating hate and prejudice on the part of all persons concerned, and the expression of attitudes on the part of adults—poor human relations attitudes with respect to persons of different racial groups; that these attitudes as expressed by adults find a sometimes responsive chord in the delinquent acts that the children of these people perpetrate in connection with their relations at school and on the street.

The groups that are for the most part indicated by these offices as being delinquent in their acts stemming from poor relations are Anglos versus Negroes, Anglos versus Mexicans, Mexicans versus Negroes, predominantly, and in each of the nine areas that the probation department has divided as a means of doing its work with facility, there is some indication that tensions are directly related in many instances to poor human relations, and the acts of juvenile delinquency come as a result of these attitudes.

Mr. Bobo. Do you have any program within the schools or among the juveniles to deal with improving the relations of humans?

Mr. Boggs. The Los Angeles County Committee on Human Relations, in cooperation with 60 private agencies in this community, are at present working with the city schools in assisting in the development of a program designed to relieve tensions between the various racial and cultural groups at those institutions. We have had several meetings with the assistant superintendent of the high schools and junior high schools, and just over the past 2 months we have had 6 or 7 meetings with high school principals, many of whom have asked these agencies to come in and assist them in setting up various programs for in-service training, training programs for teachers, perhaps designed to relieve them of some of their prejudices, and, secondly, to help them develop intercultural programs.

Mr. Bobo. Has there been any school or any area where this whole project was done on this type of work?

Mr. Boggs. Not to my knowledge in this county at this time.

Chairman KEFAUVER. In other words, Mr. Boggs, you think unquestionably a lot of the gang conflicts grow out of this antagonism of one against the other?

Mr. BOGGS. Yes.

Chairman KEFAUVER. And ·you feel that if you can get grownups to do right and understand, why, then the children are pretty likely to do that, also?

Mr. BOGGS. Yes. This we are trying to get over to the adult groups that our committee works with, and through the committee coordinating, possibly throughout the country, we feel that if we can get the adults in the community to realize the effect of the expression and attitudes many times on juvenile delinquency, that this problem will in some measure be recognized and steps taken to do something about it.

Chairman KEFAUVER. The only thing you can do is publicize the problem and do something about the educational process to remedy it.

Mr. BOGGS. That's about it.

Chairman KEFAUVER. Thank you very much, Mr. Boggs.

Mr. Tutak, would you come around, sir?

STATEMENT OF JOHN TUTAK, EXECUTIVE DIRECTOR, LOS ANGELES TIMES BOYS CLUB, LOS ANGELES, CALIF.

Chairman KEFAUVER. You are executive director of the Los Angeles Times Boys Club?

Mr. TUTAK. Yes, sir.

Chairman KEFAUVER. Will you tell us about it?

Mr. TUTAK. The Los Angeles Times Boys Club is one of some four-hundred-odd members of the Boys Clubs of America. We have these units all over the United States, and the vast majority of them are supported by the community chests in the cities in which these boys clubs are located. However, this one is supported completely by the Los Angeles Times charities. I don't know what the other papers are going to say about this, but as long as they will excuse me I will proceed with it.

Chairman KEFAUVER. We understand you are doing good work and we like to hear about good work, and I am sure they will appreciate it just like we do.

Mr. TUTAK. Incidentally, the philosophy and policies and the practices which we follow at the Times Boys Club are similar to those followed by the other boys clubs all over the country, which are supported by private funds.

Chairman KEFAUVER. But your club is supported——

Mr. TUTAK. Completely by the Los Angeles Times charities, yes.

Chairman KEFAUVER. By the Times charities?

Mr. TUTAK. That is correct.

Chairman KEFAUVER. How do you operate? How many boys do you have?

Mr. TUTAK. We started in 1944 in an old building on North Broadway, just a couple of miles up from here. Today we have a program housed in a facility for which the Times charities expended some $500,000, and last year we spent $108,000 in our operating budget. We have a membership, last year, of 2,001 boys and 356 girls. We have a very, very simple philosophy, sir. Basically it is that people need people. I think one of our great facts is that we as people haven't been able to convince one another how very important we are.

For example, I think that one of the most valuable assets which we have in this country—and I am sure we will all agree—are these kids, kids like this in every single community in the United States. There are millions of them. And I think if we look at these kids all over the United States and say that they all need to be loved and need to love, that they all need recognition, that they all need status, that they all need to be treated with respect and with dignity, and that every one of them has within himself something to contribute to some other individual of some other group, that many of the problems which face us in regard to juveniles will be eliminated.

Chairman KEFAUVER. This is a fine picture. Do you want to give it to the committee?

Mr. TUTAK. It is the only one I have.

Chairman KEFAUVER. I guess the answer is "No", then.

Mr. TUTAK. I think one of the other items that we believe in so thoroughly and try to practice to our own limits is that no matter what an individual makes it has value, whether it is something like this or something like this or this, or a mural, or this, or a mural 8 feet by 10 feet, which on canvas was painted by this boy over a period of 13 months. This mural and this drawing have exactly the same value. This is no worse or no better than is this mural. This we feel is a very, very important concept in working with people no matter who they are or no matter where they are.

For example, if we think of this guy here, who incidentally has been—there have been many of them like him who have been called a pacheco—he is a member of one of our group clubs—he is attending the Southern California Youth Association meeting, and he is listening so intently because he has to report back to his club at our agency.

We have all kinds of programs there, and these are pictures of them, if you care to look at them. But again I can't leave them with you. The program itself, no matter what it is all about, is what is important. And we have had everything from boxing, fencing, tackle football, social group clubs, and arts of every kind. We are open 62 weeks a year, 6 days a week, and the children may come at any time they want to after school.

Chairman KEFAUVER. You mean from anywhere in the city or any race, creed, or color?

Mr. TUTAK. Our membership is limited only on a geographical basis to those children between the ages of 6 and 20 who live in Lincoln Heights or the area served by the Nightingale Junior High and the Abraham Senior High School. The reason we chose this area is this: We found that back in 1944 and 1945 that practically all the gang fights which occurred in the community during those years—this was the pacheco gang warfare time, as you know—occurred among children who were going to either one of those two schools or back again, or even on the school grounds themselves.

I would like to refer back to a statement made by Mr. Sanders of the probation department. I am going to say it perhaps a little stronger than he did, because I am a worker in a private agency. I think that some of us have a tendency to follow a pattern of work which has outlived its usefulness in a large part. Now we have, I think, 15 social group clubs or gangs, as some people call them—they are going to become social groups—but they have many other groups also—there are a number of these groups that would not come to our boys club because they looked upon it as "sissy." So we sent out workers, just as the group in the probation department does. We sent out workers to those hills and to the east-side area, and met these groups right on the streets. One of these groups met last December in a locker room of a playground clubhouse, and that is as close as they would get into an agency program. This is a gang on its way to becoming a social group club. They are shown here in this picture working on a poster in our shop, on a poster for a dance they are holding. And here is their way of making a contribution as a group. This is their first attempt at a constitution. This is their club which we are helping them to form.

Chairman KEFAUVER. What you have been showing us are the elementary rules written out by the boys themselves?

Mr. TUTAK. That is correct, for their own behavior as a group. This is the first step that we are taking to help them, from within themselves, learn what are acceptable social values and attitudes and behavior patterns.

Chairman KEFAUVER. This is very interesting.

Mr. TUTAK. December 1954. A–1. Ice skating. That's the date. And then the next group. 15 cents a week for everyone.

Rules on the bus: No spitting outside of the bus or car. No hollering or yelling in the bus. No swearing, profane or abusive or obscene language. No pushing when skating.

Who may join club. Little Clover only. Only 25 may join. Club is to have a membership card. Club meets on Friday night. The name of the club is—they didn't decide on the name at that time, but they have it on the poster.

Here is another club. The Cobras up in Happy Valley. This is a gang. They wouldn't come to the club at all. And here were some rules that they made for their first camp trip to Sequoia.

Incidentally, for the teenagers—a teenager goes to camp that is sponsored by our group, he himself will take the opportunity and the effort to think and plan and organize his own camp group, and even plans so far as to set the fee. For instance, the Cobras went to the Sequoia farm last summer, and here is the way in which they planned that trip.

Chairman KEFAUVER. Well, it is too long to read, but No. 1 is no smoking in the bus except at breaks. No alcoholic drinking before or during trip. No night prowling in cabins. No knife-throwing at each other.

I think you might make a copy of that and give it to us.

(The copy referred was not received prior to printing.)

Mr. TUTAK. Here is another group. Incidentally, this group meets every Tuesday night. They met last night again. This group was started, incidentally, by a group of six junior high-school girls who were referred to us by the junior high in our community. They were such a disturbing influence that the girls' vice principal asked us if we wouldn't work together with the school to help these girls develop some acceptable social pattern of behavior. These girls call themselves by the name of "Killerettes." The club name has been changed now. It has become a coed club. And we just took that out of their notebook. Every club has its own notebook, which is kept in the group club supervisor's office.

That is a copy of a letter which they wrote. I think around a year ago or so one of the local groups wrote it.

Chairman KEFAUVER. Suppose you read that letter.

Mr. TUTAK. This is to the editor and it appeared in the Daily News of January 7, 1954:

> We are boys and girls of the Bebops Club. We would greatly appreciate it if you would not call us such names as punks, hoodlums, and ratpacks in your paper, because in our club we have different nationalities and we have respect for each other, not only in our club, but in our State, country, and other countries. Our parents wonder why you call us teenagers such rough names. They are losing confidence in us. In your paper you call us these names and it is getting us in bad with the people in our district. We want to be friends with all the people and we cannot unless you stop calling us all those names. When we walk down the street people call us such names as ratpacks and hoodlums, and by those names we are losing our reputation.
>
> MARY ESTEVAN,
> *Bebops Club Secretary.*

There are some 40 members in the Bebops Club.

Chairman KEFAUVER. We thank you very much for telling us about this. I think you are doing fine work.

Do you have anything else you want to add?

Mr. TUTAK. Yes, I do. I feel that if we consider that nothing in this country is more important than these kids in any community in the United States, this is perhaps one of the major ways in which we can help all of the people to develop positive and meaningful values and attitudes and behavior patterns in our society here, no matter where we are. I feel that we ought to have more money appropriated for research in the whole area of human growth and development, and, further, I feel that we ought to accept this fact: That it is an expensive job to work with people once they have developed these unhealthy social attitudes, and it is very, very expensive. However, it is more economical to start at whatever point they are in this negative development, and try to rehabilitate them than to just let them progress backward.

Chairman KEFAUVER. We agree with you fully about that.

We thank you very much, and we wish you good luck in your future work.

Mr. TUTAK. I hope you have time to come over and see our clubs.

Chairman KEFAUVER. If we have time we certainly will come. We are about to recess at this time until tomorrow morning, and we do have one other witness, Mr. Reynolds Ochoa. Mr. Ochoa, would you rather testify in the morning first thing or this afternoon?

Mr. OCHOA. At the committee's convenience. Whatever will be convenient to the committee.

Chairman KEFAUVER. We are going to start at 10 o'clock in the morning, but we will start 15 minutes earlier if you will come and be with us in the morning. We will appreciate that.

Mr. OCHOA. I certainly will.

Chairman KEFAUVER. If there is nothing else at this time, the committee will stand in recess until 9:45 tomorrow morning.

(Whereupon, at 5:15 p. m., Wednesday, June 15, 1955, the subcommittee recessed until Thursday, June 16, 11955, at 9:45 a. m.)

JUVENILE DELINQUENCY
(Motion Pictures)

THURSDAY, JUNE 16, 1955

United States Senate,
Subcommittee of the Committee on the
Judiciary To Investigate Juvenile Delinquency,
Los Angeles, Calif.

The subcommittee met, pursuant to recess, at 10:10 a. m., at room 518, United States Post Office and Courthouse building, Los Angeles, Calif., Senator Estes Kefauver presiding.

Present: Senator Kefauver.

Also present: James H. Bobo, counsel, and William Haddad and Carl Perian, consultants.

Chairman KEFAUVER. The subcommittee will come to order.

This morning the subcommittee is continuing its extensive study of the mass media in order to determine the impact of these media on the youth of our Nation.

Earlier this year the subcommittee issued a report on its study of crimes, brutality, horror, and sadism in comic books. In a short while we shall issue our report on the effects of crime and horror television programs on juvenile delinquency. Both of these subjects were part of this larger study of the mass media.

Today we will study the effect on juvenile delinquency of crime, violence, and sex in the movies. We will also examine the manner in which these movies are advertised.

I would like to make it clear at the outset that this subcommittee has no preconceived or final conclusions concerning the effects of movies on children. Above all, we do not wish to create the impression that we have censorship of the movie industry in mind.

We have continually denounced censorship in all forms. We have adhered to the concept of regulation by the industry itself, and the industry generally, I think, does do a fine job in regulating itself. As a result of our report, the comic book industry appointed a so-called czar to insure that "good" comic books were produced. And I hope that this program of the comic book industry works out.

I would like to reiterate this denunciation of censorship today. We honestly believe that the majority of the people in the film-making business, the great majority, are sincere in their efforts to make good products. I know they are presented with the problem of making products that attract audiences because, after all, they are in business, the free enterprise business to make money. They can't just have programs that will be altogether educational. They have got to have movies that will sell to the public.

71

The industry would readily agree that no harmful movies should be seen by American youngsters. The cooperation afforded us by the industry in our study attests to this fact. Eric Johnston and his office greatly assisted both my staff and myself in our study, and we have been in touch with them for several months now.

When our investigation was first announced, some industry representatives expressed concern about our purposes. As we progressed, however, their attitude toward us, toward our study, has changed. Now I think they are convinced that between us we can examine the trade and come up with some conclusions that will be beneficial both to the industry and to our investigation of the mass media.

In recent months, the subcommittee has been receiving an increasing amount of correspondence from intelligent people throughout the country. These people are concerned about an increase in what is felt to be unnecessary movie violence. They complain of excessive brutality, sadism, and illicit sexual behavior in motion pictures. Many of these letters link the increase in the brutal nature of many juvenile crimes with this increase in crime and violence in movies.

We on the subcommittee realize that to say bad movies create additional delinquency is far-fetched. You cannot say *a* child will see *a* movie and then commit *an* act of delinquency. But we do feel that with the prevailing world conditions, with the uncertainty of the draft, with the lurking thought of atomic destruction, with all of these as background an atmosphere of violence is being conveyed by the mass media.

While these media are, on the one hand, reflecting the behavior of the older generation, they are, in turn, forming the minds of the younger generation, and that is where our greatest danger lies.

While social scientists at this time cannot fully pinpoint the exact relationship between movies and children's behavior, they do feel that to allow the indiscriminate showing of scenes depicting violence or brutality constitutes at least a calculated risk to our young people; a risk we cannot afford to take. The same scientists strongly feel that these films are often viewed extensively by the type of children who can least afford to see them, that is, by emotionally unstable children who have already developed behavior of a sadistic or brutal nature. These children may gain support and ideas from a similar type of film.

While these contentions have not been proven by controlled experiments, scores of clinical psychologists and psychiatrists, surveyed and heard by the committee—men and women who have handled emotionally warped delinquents—feel that the mass media provide fertile material for furthering the antisocial behavior of their parents.

The subcommittee has also received numerous complaints about the advertising of motion pictures. Readers of even the most respectful family newspapers have noticed an increase in what they consider bad advertising. They report to us—sending us clips from newspapers all over the country—that these advertisements have reached a point close to the obscene in some few cases. By implication and innuendo these ads appear to remain within the bounds of discretion, but their total impact, especially on imprissionable young minds, can only be provactive. The technique will also be looked at today.

In these advertisements supercharged sex is sometimes the keynote. Purple prose is keyed to feverish tempo to celebrate the naturalness of seduction, the condonability of adultery, and the spontaneity of adolescent relations. Let me stress to you that these ads only represent a portion, and I think a small portion, of the total advertising content. Yet it is the portion the subcommittee is concerned with.

The rapid growth and acceptance of motion pictures and its influence on American morality and ethics has added to the responsibilities of the industry. These responsibilities present a direct social challenge to the industry here in Hollywood. The industry has willingly answered this challenge. Both the movie industry and the advertising people have, of their own free will, initiated a code to control their activities, which generally I think is a very good code.

Today we shall hear how this code is working. We shall also hear about the positive contributions of the movie industry to the betterment of our way of life. I am sure that the executives here today will point with justifiable pride to the many fine pictures which have helped to fight delinquency, even as the bad pictures might have helped to create delinquency.

In other words, I want to tell the members of the industry we are here not for the purpose of just trying to point out the bad. We want to recognize and appreciate the fact that the industry, generally, has been a fine influence for the good, great media for entertainment and education of our people, not only in the United States but throughout the world.

And it is our purpose to, in some little way, try to work with the industry for even the performance of a greater good, particularly in the field of juvenile delinquency and the impression that pictures make upon our young people.

Is Mr. Mooring our first witness?

Mr. Bobo. Yes.

Chairman KEFAUVER. Yesterday we had one other general witness on organizations, dealing with juvenile problems we didn't get to hear, so, Mr. Mooring. I will ask you to step aside a minute and we will call you back.

Mr. Mooring. Thank you.

STATEMENT OF RENALDO OCHOA, FEDERATION OF SOCIAL AND CAR CLUBS OF CALIFORNIA

Chairman KEFAUVER. How do you do. What is your name?

Mr. Ochoa. Renaldo Ochoa.

Chairman KEFAUVER. You may make your statement. You will make it brief, won't you, sir?

Mr. Ochoa. I will make it brief. It is just more or less an outline of what I have been doing.

Chairman KEFAUVER. Sit up closer and talk louder.

Mr. Ochoa. I just want to——

Chairman KEFAUVER. Tell us about your organization and what you have been doing.

Mr. Ochoa. The organization of Federation of Social and Car Clubs was organized in 1952.

Chairman KEFAUVER. The organization of what?

Mr. Ochoa. Federation of Social and Car Clubs of California. The reason for the organization was due to the fact——

Chairman KEFAUVER. What are you in the organization?

Mr. OCHOA. I am the founder and one of the directors of the organization. The reason for the organization was the fact that we were having much trouble with the automobile clubs here, hot rods and custom cars in dragging along the streets.

Mr. Navarro, cofounder of the organization, and myself got hold of some of the agencies, such as the Community Chest and others, to try and sponsor these car clubs, in order to give them leadership.

These organizations told us they were not here to handle anything such as car clubs, due to the fact of the liability they would construct.

Therefore, we found it and deemed it necessary to try and make some type of an organization to give them leadership; thus the foundation of this organization. The program of this federation is set by the kids themselves and not by the directors. They will tell us what they want to do and we, in turn, go out and help them and work along with them and see their program come through.

I will give you more or less right now what this program has been along the charitable lines. They have contributed to the March of Dimes. They have contributed to the Community Chest, to the City of Hope and, of course, the pet organization of this federation is the Sister Kenny Foundation, due to the fact they gave a party for the kids, and helping children 2 and 3 years suffering. They have actually taken this as their pet charity.

They have helped to establish a toy loan library in their district. They have given Christmas baskets. They have collected used toys and painted them and fixed them and given them out at Christmastime; the same at Thanksgiving.

It is nice to know that the teen-agers themselves, the kids themselves, have set aside four scholarships for theirs. They have given 1 to Roosevelt High, 1 scholarship to Garfield High School, 1 scholarship to a student from East Los Angeles Junior College, and another scholarship to a member of the federation.

The aims and purposes of this federation are mainly to establish drag strips and for better recreation and dance facilities. Drag strips were offered to us by many county officials, city officials and State officials as far back as 4½ years ago.

We haven't been able to get them as yet. The trouble mainly lies in trying to get the land. Finance backing is there, both by private enterprise and different agencies, for these drag strips.

So far as the dances are concerned, we have been using recreational facilities of the county. They are said to accommodate six to seven hundred kids. We have had as many as 1,700 kids at these dances, which goes to show if you give them clean and wholesome recreation they will attend that recreation, instead of going out and doing things they shouldn't be doing.

Another thing about that is of great importance here is the fact this federation is self-sustaining. All of the expenses are met through the media of the kids themselves in having sponsored different activities. The cooperation of many of the businessmen has been given greatly. Also, the sheriff's office and many of the county and city agencies. However, this cooperation has not been financial as much as it has been moral.

In conclusion, we feel this way about juvenile delinquency: We feel through resolution of the federation, and it is the kids themselves, that much of the juvenile delinquency is due to the fact of hanging out on street corners and out in the streets, because the playgrounds, the recreation department does not have a program—they have beautiful playgrounds, but they do not have a program that interest the kids enough to attend those programs.

We also feel that the educational system needs some revamping. We feel we need more trade schools after high school and more business schools, where the kids can attend at a minimum cost or at a cost to the government, and not making it compulsory to attend.

The liquor problem with the kids, as discussed in the federation, is such we feel the federation can only advise them to stay away from liquor. But the main problem lies in the State Board of Equalization and the liquor control districts to make the laws and legislation a little rougher on both giving and selling liquor to the kids.

That is about all.

Chairman KEFAUVER. We thank you very much. Mr. John Anson Ford has written that he has been in touch with your federation and it has been very successful. You have more than 20 clubs in the federation. Is that right?

Mr. OCHOA. That is right. A combined membership of about 2,000 kids.

Chairman KEFAUVER. 2,000 kids. That is very fine work you are doing and we appreciate your coming here.

Mr. OCHOA. I hope we have been of some use to the committee.

Chairman KEFAUVER. Thank you.

Mr. OCHOA. Thank you.

STATEMENT OF WILLIAM MOORING, MOTION PICTURE AND TELE-VISION EDITOR, CATHOLIC TIDINGS, LOS ANGELES, CALIF.

Chairman KEFAUVER. Mr. Mooring, you have a statement, don't you?

Mr. MOORING. I do, yes.

Chairman KEFAUVER. You can read your statement or you can file it and it will be printed in the record, or tell us what you want to tell us.

Mr. MOORING. As you already know, my name is William Mooring. I live in California. I was born in Britain and now am an American citizen.

I am the television and motion-picture editor of the Catholic Tidings, the local archdiocese and newspaper, and I am syndicated weekly to some 50 other Catholic newspapers throughout the United States and Canada and other parts.

I would say on this subject that criminal violence, human brutality, sadism, and other psychopathic disorders have been increasingly and majorly stressed in movies and on TV during the past 2 years. Mr. Eric Johnston of the Hollywood Producers has admitted this, has publicly admitted it. In many instances this viciousness, I think, has been accomplished by different treatments of sex. This however, the film and TV people seem anxious to deny.

As to the forms in which these and other recent films have been advertised, they have in many instances violated all tenets of public decency, fair play, and commercial honesty and seem to be approaching that line that suggests we only go from here to obscenity.

With apparently good reasons, the Hollywood producers have many times claimed that American films reflecting the better aspects of our national experience, our culture, our character and ideals have helped to create to the world favorable impressions of what we call very proudly "the American way of life." Thus the film people tacitly acknowledge the power of the movies toward public attitudes and thinking. Therefore, programs glorifying crimes and criminals, condoning loose morals or revealing low forms of living must have a correspondingly damaging effect or, at least, a potentiality that way. Perhaps more so because of the fascination of evil and the inequitable impact of violence on the imagination of young people.

There are films which polish the apple for America, so to speak. But they are not enough, if, as so often happens, it is the same old apple with which Eve temped Adam, and by this time has gotten rather rotten at the core.

Without discounting the highly dramatic and technical merits of some of the films that I could mention, I would cite Blackboard Jungle, The Wild One, Big House U. S. A., Kiss Me Deadly, Black Tuesday, Cell 2455, Death Row, among many films having a potentially harmful influence on behavior patterns, particularly those of young men and women at a high pitch of sexual curiosity and imitativeness.

It is difficult and fairly inaccurate to connect by documentation this increase of crime and immorality on the screen, with the current alarming rise in juvenile delinquency. However, my personal observations over some considerable period, borne out by the findings of some police investigators, turn up quite disturbing indications. When Marlon Brando in The Wild One was in release it played at many children's matinees. It attracted large numbers of young people, including youthful motorcycle parties, such as in the film, was shown terrorizing peaceful communities.

I saw young men at several of these shows dressed like Brando in leather jackets. It was clear they identified themselves with the arrogant character he played in the film. And they put on his swagger, and some of them went off recklessly on their motorcycles, just like the gang in the picture.

I wouldn't suggest that this impression was a deep or permanent one. I do say it was not a good one. It to some extent immediately undermined them with respect to the authority, at least to the management of the theater. And I think we have had, even before this chain of films, a number of films dealing with bad cops, bad policemen, in which the emphasis was developed against good law and order by lowering the respect of youth for police activities and personnel.

Now, Chief Parker told me himself that he felt that the effect was not only on juveniles here, but upon adults who, because they lost that respect and sense of cooperation with the law, might tend not to instruct children in such proper respect.

Now, more recently, among the large number of youths attending Blackboard Jungle, some of the theater managements reported unusually loud, noisy, belligerent behavior and some disturbances which followed on the parks or the streets. For obvious reasons it is more difficult to observe the direct effect, if any, of, say, that situation in Blackboard Jungle which dealt with an incorrigible teenage boy attempting rape against the teacher. Incidentally, she was shown to have offered some provocation. I doubt whether a film of this dramatic intensity can fail to arouse some imitative behavior. At least, it must set loose inherent tendencies to violence, even if, when it reaches constructive conclusions, is commensurate in dramatic power with its graphic exposures of violence and hoodlumism.

I do not think that Blackboard Jungle has this balance, although I will say it was an intelligent, well-directed, beautifully produced picture, technically, and in a certain sense artistically.

I might express an opinion—I do seem to be using the personal pronoun too much, Mr. Chairman—I believe youths already involved in crime and violence will immediately identify themselves with the ringleaders in Blackboard Jungle. And the measure of villainy shown in the film would suggest to their minds the measure as heroic leadership which they themselves imagine they have. I am not suggesting that expose about social structures or criticism about public institutions, such as schools, prisons, hospitals, et cetera, should not occur in screen drama, nor that some producers who choose such subjects lack a deep and proper sense of public responsibility.

I do suggest, however, that caution and sane dramatic balance are necessary when crime and juvenile or adult sex situations are realistically posed in movies and television. And I do not think this caution has been exercised during the past 2 years.

Some producers argue that since the screen enjoys the same constitutional right to freedom of expression as the press, that anything that can be described in print, in books or publications, newspapers, so forth, can, with equal freedom from all restraint, be safely and justifiably described in motion pictures. This takes no cognizance of the much more powerful impact motion pictures have on everyone, young and old, especially when they are conveyed to mass audiences, in the newly improved wide screen technique, with these wonderfully amplified sound effects.

Again it is sometimes argued in Hollywood for every picture dealing with crime, brutality, hidden sex, the movie industry turns out a dozen morally good and decent pictures. This poses to my mind a whole string of fair balance.

When someone takes poison, the sure antidote is not found by reaching down a bottle from a crowded shelf labeled "nonpoisonous." Imitative behavior undoubtedly can be inspired by films in which crime is validly presented with taste and restraint. This is an important admission to make, because we see that sometimes crime and such things are handled with restraint.

Now, on May 19, 1951, Johnny Belinda, an excellent film for adult audiences, was shown at a children's matinee in Buena Park, Calif.: it was a Saturday afternoon. In it a deaf and dumb girl was criminally attacked by a brute. The scene was sensitively played by two outstanding and capable actors, Jane Wyman and Stephen McNaulty. It was absolutely essential to the story. I believe the scene could not have been more delicately presented in view of its nature.

Yet, police records and theater timetables indicated to me that shortly after witnessing that scene on the screen a young man named

McCracken, since executed, followed a little girl out of that theater, waylaid, attacked, and murdered her.

Now, if criminal violence of this kind, chastely presented in well-balanced plays, can arouse murderous passions in borderline cases, such as this—I am thinking of police evidence that the man had a previous record of degeneracy—can we safely assume that the effect of ill-balanced sensational crime and sex films, such as are now on the increase, are having no serious effects at all upon many incipient offenders, and even to an extent upon the apparently normal but highly impressionable youngsters who are in the usual way well behaved.

I feel it must be true, also, that shocking details of crime and intimate sensational revelations of illicit sex adventure in the steady stream of movie and television shows plays a sinister part in enlarging, if not creating, a desire for what are sometimes called stag or party pictures, namely the type of pornography with which this subcommittee has been predominantly concerned.

As sure as marihuana leads to heroin, morally vicious pictures create a desire for pornography. And I would commend probabilities of such connections to investigation by this subcommittee and to the leaders of the motion picture and television industry, whom I would like to say I believe to be imbued with a fine sense of citizenship and responsibility to the public in the main.

From those who defend a policy of no restraints because movies and TV deal in intangible ideas and not tangible commodities, I have heard the argument that young people by habit have come to regard the show as something to be enjoyed, not necessarily believed and certainly not imitated. If this were true, would you think that so many people, especially the young ones, would take examples, say, from the happier aspects and characters currently popular?

We see that millions of youngsters now clamor for Dávy Crockett hats. And millions of children play gangsters with wooden guns and with an Edward G. Robinson snarl. It would be easy to say this is a passing craze, but do we know that; are we sure? Are we certain that these ideas which take root in the young mind do not bear fruit later? I think other matters prove that we would be wrong in taking that line.

Now, if it is important—and the commercials do tell us that it is—that the physical health of the children shall be protected by giving them the right kind of cereals for breakfast, it seems to me much more important that their moral health should be protected by giving them the right kind of ideas from the motion picture and television screens.

I acknowledge very freely that producers try to cater to every human type in Hollywood. The current emphases in screen drama are usually drawn from what the producers conceive to be subjects of major current interest to the public.

There is an identity, of course, upon stage plays and novels, and today it is sadly evident these sources, often with the aid and approval of many who would call themselves literary or dramatic critics, are increasingly politic. I would ascribe the present trend toward criminal violence and salaciousness in pictures and television partly to this pollution and partly to the following causes:

1. A vigorous and easily understandable competition between motion pictures and television, with the movie people insisting that television is getting away with it and why shouldn't they, and vice versa.

2. The design on Hollywood's part, sharpened by some limited success of some of the sensational foreign pictures which have been imported to this country, to strive for what they call a larger adult content in American motion pictures. Here I would say there is a prevailing fetish, however, that only those screenplays that deal intimately or sensationally with the sordid side of life contain the most desirable elements of adult appeal. I think this rather smears adults with adultery.

I think we have excellent examples in recent production of films, which could be described as of strong adult appeal, but which were made without any offense to anyone, and without twisting the bad in life to make it look good, honorable, or acceptable.

I could mention Marty, which deals with the life of a man living, rather, "boiling," and working hard—it is nice to see someone work on the motion pictures—yet found that he had ideals. He would hunt around with the boys—if that is what it is called—but he got tired of that. The picture shows what he desired stamped him as a man of high ideals. He wanted to find a good woman, not a pretty one, not a glamorous one. He wasn't looking for Marilyn Monroe. He was looking for a wife he could respect, love, admire, and stay with.

Then also East of Eden, also eminently adult in its view and well treated, I think, did not deal with the necessarily revealing facts in such a way as to play upon the emotions or to overstimulate the emotions of any young people or old who might see it.

However, where a pursuit generally is for this thing called adult or mature entertainment, the result most often evident to this critic is an adolescent preoccupation with sex or a false emphasis on human quirks and aberrations. And unless, as a result of this committee or some other influence, there is a change in the direction of this trend of crime and violence, we may soon find ourselves plunged into new horrors dealing with sexual and mental aberrations.

Then, too, thirdly, there is in Hollywood an increasing resistance to anything and everything identified with censorship. I understand that this committee has reached conclusions on that subject. And I am not surprised, because, as the word connotes interference by faultfinding busybodies with the rights of others to please themselves, censorship naturally is abhorrent to the American mind.

But too often no intelligent distinctions are drawn by the Hollywood producers between what is called bluenosed censorship and the very sane editorial restraints proposed by Hollywood's own voluntary production code. We here in this country are proud of a free press, but we know, too, that freedom does not confer upon editors the right to publish anything, and we know that they exercise their editorial prerogatives sometimes rather lightly, we think, to curtail offensive matter in newspapers.

What then is wrong—and some critics do allege there is something wrong—with the idea of a production code such as is in existence, but which I shall, in fairness, submit is not being properly operated today? I think it has become a little too indulgent.

I believe there is oppressing need for a voluntary code with teeth in it, and an administration with the will and know-how to enforce it and to regulate television programs. And I think here we have a key to the situation in which we find our motion pictures, because until and unless some control is achieved in television, movie producers with some apparent justification will continue to chafe against the reins of their own movie code and produce the kind of pictures we have been having in larger and larger numbers. Thus the vicious circle of competition on the lowest moral level may well continue.

While questions of personal judgment and opinion naturally are involved, I would say that many recent movies have violated the rules of the Motion Picture Production Code, either in letter or spirit, and sometimes in both. And I would include in this the picture Son of Sinbad, a picture without any appearance of any purpose to entertain, except in the same way that burlesque and other similar forms of exhibitionism are held to entertain. This I fail to see on the screen at all and I fail to see how it got by the code.

Not As a Stranger. This is a very excellent picture, think, about a young doctor, a young American fellow who is anxious to become a great doctor. He marries a woman, it is true, to get her money to get through medical college, and then later is drawn into some kind of mesalliances with an adventuress.

But the study of the human types involved is interesting, vivid, and well done. Yet in one particular spot there is introduced a symbolical connection between the natural urges of 2 animals and the sexual urges of 2 human beings. It is done by a pattern known to film people as crosscutting.

We first see the human characters coming together in obvious desire, and then we see the animals attempting to do so but separated by a gate. Eventually, cutting back and forth from this scene, which reaches a crescendo of emotional excitement, we see the man lean over the corral, release the latch, uniting the animals. Whereupon he closes in upon the female.

As a revelation of fact, I think it brings nothing to us we are not all familiar with. I don't think it shocks us. I am not thinking prudishly, I am trying to think prudently.

What does this convey to the young, impressionable mind? It clearly makes no distinction between humankind, which we believe to be governed and conditioned by reason and some conscience in these matters, and the lower animals whom nature and God have arranged shall be brought together purely by natural instinct. The inference to be drawn by youth then is that sex, being a powerful appetite, and in a particular case a youth feeling that urge shall indulge himself instinctively without exercising either his reason or his conscience or listening to his conscience.

I think that is bad. But I think those things should not be passed by the code, and I think it violates the tenet in the code wherein it says that low forms of sexual behavior shall not be held to be the generally accepted thing.

The Seven Year Itch. I tell you, I would scratch it if I could, because, while it may very well be filled with laughter and opportunities for laughter by sophisticated people, I think it is generally bad influence, that we laugh at the wrong things. There are certain things in my book, there are certain things at which we do not laugh.

We do not laugh at our mothers. We do not laugh at God. We do not laugh at the law if we are good citizens.

Now, these people laugh at the law and they laugh at some of those immutable principles which not only catholicwise—I am not speaking as a Catholic, although I happen to be one—but by Christians, Jews, and all good Americans, I think, are accepted as immutable principles. Chastity and fidelity are not to be laughed at, even in a motion picture.

Five Against the House is a story about college boys who, for fun—and here it is in the same milieu as The Seven Year Itch—for the sake of fun conceive of and start to plan and carry out a holdup in a Reno gambling joint. I don't have much respect for those kind of places, so if it is held up it is their own business, but the law says they shall not be. The law says no one shall do these things. Of course, these boys didn't need the money; they were only doing it for the "kicks." What message does that convey to the not-too-deeply-thinking youth who sees it? Doesn't it rather appeal the idea generally in a laughing way, because of the fact it creates laughter, that it is perfectly all right, as long as you are not serious about it and will give the money back afterward?

Kiss Me Deadly. I wouldn't dilate on that; no. The usual mixture of Mickey Spillane trash and crime and—I think they call them dames. The very word itself so often used in the advertising connotes exactly that disrespect for womanhood which I think these kind of films may tend seriously to increase.

Cell 2455—Death Row, the Caryl Chessman story. Everybody knows it because there is a credit on the screen which says it is his story. But the film gets by the code presumably because it technically does not offend against that rule which says that the criminal in modern times shall not be identified and referred to in this film.

Now, I always thought the credits were a part of the films. I stand corrected by the Motion Picture Association code authority, which passes this picture and this picture goes out as a justification, practically, in a sense, of what this man did. He tries to tell them not to do the same thing, but he also tells them that the reason why he became a juvenile criminal was because of adverse social conditions besetting his youth and his family was poor and he was an underprivileged boy, and here the film repeats this theme which has been used ab initio in films of this type, always imputing that a class matter is involved in this question of juvenile crime, when we know all the time it is not always poverty which breeds this kind of juvenile crime, unless one includes that kind of poverty one sometimes finds in very wealthy homes, the poverty of parental example and guidance.

Big House, U. S. A. Here again, on a technicality, we get a quite frightful story of childhood. It has always been held by the code that child kidnaping is a subject so urgent and so fearful in this country, in view of the criminal history, that it should not be too graphically presented or even presented at all on the motion-picture screen.

It is said that it shall not be presented. It is said in the code it shall not be presented as a theme. So here a producer conceived the idea of introducing what he called a major theme of prison break, relegating the theme of kidnaping, child kidnaping, to a secondary significance.

I submit that that would be impossible in any drama, because by its nature this type of kidnaping is bound to supervene or prevail over any theme in any particular picture, and in this case we see that the child is kidnaped, and the details of the kidnaping are given, how the ransom was collected. The only corrective applied throughout the whole theme is that corrective so often considered sufficient by so many people, which I think is very much inadequate, the conclusion of crime being punishment.

What is so interesting to me, also, at this time is that many drive-in theaters have recently turned to this type of crime and violence and sex picture. The drive-in was once regarded as practically sacrosanct to family entertainment, because the people could take the kids along in the car. It is changing very much, not only here on the coast, but I understand throughout the country. These very vicious pictures are now being booked with more and more frequency in drive-ins. And I am told this change in policy changes with an apparent change in clientele.

I have information that was given to me confidentially which indicates that some drive-ins here in California and elsewhere not only show the pictures that are calculated to provide emotional excitement for some young people, but they condone and even to a degree encourage behavior that obviously appeals for some police action. The general technique, as I understand it, that an eye is blinked at certain cars which are directed to certain parts of the amphitheater, and the understanding young patrons take along with them is they need not be overly concerned with the entertainment quality of the picture, that there will be no police patrol passing by and no interference from the manager.

Now, I think I have said all I should say and perhaps too diffusely. I would perhaps round up my talk this way, by saying it is my belief, and I believe this very strongly, that most of the major producers in Hollywood, and I believe in television, are sincerely desirous of providing good, well-balanced entertainment for the public. They are bound to do so, because—incidentally, I did fail to mention this: They are faced with problems abroad as well as at home. Some countries regulate the films that are shown to children. In Britain, for instance, they have three classifications. The British Board of Film Censors, a nonstatutory body, permits children unaccompanied to see only such pictures as are rated U, for universal exhibition.

Those rated A, for adult exhibition, may be seen by juveniles but only when accompanied by responsible adults, who obviously give parental or some such consent.

Films rated X, as horror, sex and crime films are rated, may not be shown in any circumstances to any person in Great Britain under the age of 18.

Now, this system or something of its kind may very well become an insistent demand on the part of a large segment of the American public, unless something is done to prevent young and impressionable children, even teen-agers, from seeing the type of film which is produced mainly for adult consumption.

I would leave you with the thought that I believe the industry does try to produce a variety, as it must, of films which deal with the varieties of life. There has been some preoccupation with these violent subjects, that in developing them there has been a great deal of indiscretion, that in advertising them there has been a flagrant disregard for good standards of taste and even of common decency.

I believe, not only the presence of this committee here in this town and the result of its inquiry, but also the facts that have now been brought to the minds of the leaders of the motion-picture industry, will result in improvement.

Thank you very much.

Chairman KEFAUVER. Thank you very much, Mr. Mooring. You have given us a carefully prepared and documented analytical statement, which we are grateful to you for.

Mr. MOORING. Thank you.

Chairman KEFAUVER. How many papers do you write for, Mr. Mooring?

Mr. MOORING. I think there are 47 in America and 3 in Canada, in addition to some supplied in Europe through various Catholic news agencies. I would say about 50 here and in Canada.

Chairman KEFAUVER. Do you have any questions, Mr. Bobo?

Mr. BOBO. Yes, sir.

Mr. Mooring, you have spoken of a great increase in crime and violence in the movies. To what do you attribute this increase in crime and violence?

Mr. MOORING. Well, to the three points. I would say to a tendency to confuse the provisions and operations of the production code, with censorship on the part of some producers. There is resentment against the code and they try not to—they try to avoid its objectives. That is one thing.

Violent and very well understandable competition between movies and television, because the movie people feel they have this additional competitor right in the homes. I am bound to say I agree with those who argue if it is proper to shoot crime and violence right in the drawing room or living room of an American home, then it isn't improper to show it on the motion-picture screen where at least there is an element of choice involved. On television it is thrown right at the people.

Something, it seems to me, must be done by the television people to clean this situation up, and I think, as a result of it, the movie people would take fresh courage and get back to making their own voluntary production code work.

Mr. BOBO. Do you think that the American public demands this type of picture or that the motion-picture industry sets the demand for the American public?

Mr. MOORING. It would be churlish for a critic to deny that box-office results of some of these pictures indicate that there is an element of public demand, but in my opinion that should not be the deciding factor.

While obviously the motion-picture and television people are in business to make money—quite obviously so—they do have an additional responsibility. They are not to consider themselves free to sell any kind of motion picture, and I don't think they really wish to feel free to sell any kind of motion picture.

They do want to give a picture which is popular to the largest possible number. I would say here that I think it is somewhat like a vein of coal in a mine, which might suddenly give out. We find that trends and demands for certain types of films give out. The public for a time has a run on this or that or the other.

I would say here that I believe that this crime and violence has to go in two directions. It either will peter out or it must become progressively worse. That places the motion-picture producer in a difficult position. Each succeeding producer who makes another, to add to this chain of crime and violence pictures, must make it more violent, he must make it more sexy, you see. And unless he does, then the appetite for that type of picture is satisfied, and some other type of picture for the time being becomes predominantly in demand.

I think that is proved by the history of the cycles in the motion-picture business, although I don't deny perhaps the aptitudes of the motion-picture people themselves, as well as the appearances of public demand, control the type of picture we are getting here and now and then.

For instance, if there is a certain type of play on Broadway dealing with, as now, certain miserable aberrations, somebody else will introduce it in another play on Broadway.

The fact that Hollywood draws very heavily upon Broadway results in Hollywood's attempt to bring that kind of thing to the motion-picture screen, and when one motion picture has been made on that subject others are made, until the sky is the limit. I thing very, very largely the trend we notice now has developed out of this cycle habit in motion-picture production.

Mr. Bobo. You spoke of a symbolism in a picture involving 2 animals and 2 actors at the corral. Do you think that a juvenile, a person of juvenile age would interpret a scene such as this in the same manner in which an adult would interpret, such as yourself?

Mr. Mooring. Yes, I do. I think—I am thinking now of knowledgable children. I would say that American youth generally is very well poised.

I am not one who subscribes to the idea it is inherent in the American nature, this passion for crime and sex. I believe that people in America are usually very well imbued with a fine sense of citizenship and decency. I think it is too bad on so many of them that this aspect of delinquency, in a minority sense, has to be so emphasized.

I think in this specific case an average intelligent youth, of average intelligence, would see this and what he would likely get from it would not be arrived at so much through—be arrived at so much through his mind as through his senses and his emotions. Down there would be implanted a feeling that instinct is important in these matters and there is nothing per se wrong in yielding to an urge.

Now, what I would suggest is that a picture should not convey that, because, as we must acknowledge, if we are not on the way to social anarchy, and fast, that we must acknowledge in these matters man is controlled and conditioned by reason and by conscience; neither of which have any effect or hold on an animal.

I hope I make that clear. I am giving a long answer. I do think that children are influenced, emotionally perhaps more than mentally, but, nevertheless, any boy who starts to think about it couldn't get any other conclusion than it was quite all right for Robert Mitchum, so why shouldn't it be quite all right for him.

Mr. Bobo. Do you think the cumulative effect of scenes such as this or scenes of violence and crime might have more of an impact than just viewing one scene such as this?

Mr. Mooring. Well, yes, obviously, because there is more opportunity for corrective thinking, and there is also a distraction from that major thing in a case where sex or a violent scene is posed briefly. The effect may be shocking. In fact, indeed, it is, I am sure. And I think it is put in for that purpose. But its effect might not be so permanent, might not be so deep, for the reason there is put in the film other things that distract.

Still, however, it is a fact that a large number of pictures I have not documented, but which I could so easily document have contained, while being excellent pictures otherwise, have contained unnecessarily brutal scenes of fighting.

Strange Lady In Town, there is a terribly brutal fight in it. Is it necessary to mix it up this roughly?

Chairman Kefauver. Mr. Mooring, what is your opinion of the voluntary code, of the Motion Picture Association's code?

Mr. Mooring. My opinion, Mr. Chairman, of the code is conditioned by my belief in the Ten Commandments from which it derives. I believe the code is a workable document. I believe it puts not the slightest hindrance against the development of the art and technique and craft of motion pictures.

That, to the contrary, by recognizing and outlining immutable principles and by particularizing as to how the drama can be developed in conformity with ideas and facts and principles which we accept, that the code helps the motion-picture artist who is in good faith and who cares to understand his moral philosophy.

I think that too few do understand that. I think perhaps very naturally, as so often happens to us all, this code has presented itself to the minds of many writers, producers, et cetera, as a list of taboos, of don'ts; don't do this and don't do that.

We know what happens to juveniles and we know what happens to Julio when we say, "Don't do that," he then wants to do it instantly. And I think that the code does, in a sense, invite on the part of the writers who don't care to study it from any other point of view, that it invites an effort to defeat it, to step around it, to write around it; and there is a challenge in it to that exent.

But if we could get them to understand, if they would trouble to understand that it can constructively help them to make drama more true to life and, therefore, more acceptable to people, then we should find that the code is a workable and quite wonderful instrument of self-regulation, far, far preferable to any kind of superimposed censorship which, in common with born Americans, I abhor.

Chairman Kefauver. Have you had an opportunity, sir, of studying the television industry's code?

Mr. Mooring. Yes, sir, I have made a study of it and I find it not different in its provisions from that of the motion-picture code. It is perhaps not in all respects as complete, and it should be made as complete.

More particularly, however, I have found what is lacking in television is an administration to enforce the code, and it seems to me from the programs I so often see that perhaps a copy of the television production code on most of the producers' and writers' desks in television is very near the bottom of the pile, and it is not too frequently consulted.

Now, in motion pictures we have an administration and I am sure we have an administrator of very high principles, Mr. Geoffrey Shurlock. I have disagreed with some of the findings he has reached, but I certainly would like to say here that I have the utmost admiration for his uprightness and his good judgment and his fine experience.

Now, in television there seems to be nobody doing that.

Chairman KEFAUVER. Mr. Mooring, in order to eliminate the competition in the extent of crime and violence between motion pictures and television, which is one of the elements that has led to some deterioration of both, I expect there is going to have to be substantially the same code and same strict enforcement or compliance with the code in both industries.

Mr. MOORING. Yes.

Chairman KEFAUVER. If that competition is going to be eliminated.

Mr. MOORING. Yes, indeed.

Chairman KEFAUVER. All right, sir. Anything else?

Mr. BOBO. That is all.

Chairman KEFAUVER. We appreciate your contribution.

Mr. MOORING. Yes.

Chairman KEFAUVER. You have made a digest of some important points which were not brought out in your statement, which will be printed in the record, Mr. Mooring.

Mr. MOORING. Thank you very much.

(The document referred to was marked "Exhibit No. 6," and reads as follows:)

EXHIBIT No. 6

STATEMENT OF WILLIAM H. MOORING ON CURRENT TRENDS AND EFFECTS IN MOTION PICTURES AND TELEVISION AND THEIR POTENTIAL BEARING UPON JUVENILE DELINQUENCY

GENERAL SURVEY

Criminal violence, human brutality, sadism, and other manifestations of psychopathic disorder, have increased noticeably in motion pictures and on television within the past 2 years.

Official Hollywood admission of overemphasis upon violence has been made by Eric Johnston of the Motion Picture (Producers) Association. (See Hollywood Reporter and Daily Variety, May 23, 1955.)

Concurrently and in many instances coincidentally, the treatment of sex in motion pictures and on television has been less restrained, although so far no admission of this has been made officially by the Hollywood motion-picture or television producers.

Direct effect of these trends, separately or combined, may be difficult to connect by documentation with prevalent increases of juvenile delinquency. Nevertheless fair argumentation, backed by some documentation, will suggest, if not prove, that behavior patterns, especially among juveniles at impressionable age levels, are immediately and directly conditioned by motion pictures and television programs of high emotional content and criminal or immoral suggestibility.

Motion picture producers have many times claimed that American films, incidental to their reflections of American culture, or what is commonly called the American way of life, inform and edify a worldwide public by and through their manifold representations of social, economic, and domestic advantages enjoyed by the American people at large.

This argument implicitly claims that movies in which American working people are shown driving elegant, late-model autos, living in comfortably modern-equipped homes, wearing good clothes, enjoying the best services of beauticians, medical doctors, dentists, etc., and indulging freely in an endless variety of sports and recreations, create throughout the world a powerful impression of a nation, economically prosperous and socially idealistic.

Allowing that many films take dramatic license to exaggerate the ease with which, for instance, a working girl acquires an enviable wardrobe or a laboring man sports an expensive car, it appears true that Hollywood's motion pictures have helped to create abroad some impressions of American well-being, self-reliance, and general knowledgability.

If this be true—and I firmly believe it is—then the power of constructive suggestion wielded by the motion picture is officially acknowledged and proudly claimed by American film producers.

It cannot reasonably be argued that this suggestibility in motion pictures ends there. We must recognize its destructive potentialities also.

Motion pictures dealing with social disorders within the American system (instance, The Blackboard Jungle, On the Waterfront, The Wild One) or with prevalent American crime patterns (instance, Big House, U. S. A., Black Tuesday, Cell 2455, Death Row, Riot in Cell Block 11) must be said likewise to impress the minds of spectators wherever they are seen.

Indeed, since evil has for many persons a stronger fascination than good, the impact of films featuring criminal violence, brutality and sexual immorality must be said to exercise correspondingly greater influence upon human behavior.

For youths especially, the personal element in pictures calls for consideration. A film projecting violence and antisocial rebellion among youthful characters may present greater dangers of exciting imitative behavior among the young when it is played out by a movie actor whom youths widely accept as a popular hero. (Instance, Wild One, starring Marlon Brando as the arrogant leader of a belligerent, antisocial gang of youthful motorcyclists who terrorized peaceful communities.)

During the public run of this film, I visited several theaters showing it. In each instance youths were predominant in the audience.

Some were in motorcycle parties; wore leather jackets like those shown in the film.

Either during or after performances, many affected the postures of Brando and his gang.

This film was shown at many matinees given especially for children and youths.

Youths have predominated at many of the more recent showings of the Blackboard Jungle. I have the assurance of one police investigator that at one Los Angeles suburban theater, where the management claimed the behavior of youngsters was usually good, this film was accompanied by noisy misbehavior. Youths left the theater affecting the swagger and diction of the hoodlum actors and disturbances among them followed on the streets and parking lots.

It is not suggested that this impression had taken permanent or even deep roots among the boys, but there appears no reason to doubt that the emotional effect of the film was strong.

In this district there have been many recent instances of vandalism in the schools: a situation directly corresponding to some in the film. If the effect of the film is not to increase such vandalism, at least it is arguable that it cannot be expected to decrease it.

For obvious reasons it is more difficult to observe any direct effect of a situation in the Blackboard Jungle, wherein an incorrigible, teen-age schoolboy was shown to attempt rape against a teacher (who offered some provocation). However, sex situations of this type, when they occur in a context of crime and violence, may strike the emotions of youthful spectators with momentous force while at a high pitch of excitement.

I do not suggest that films entertaining a spirit of inquiry or criticism toward our public institutions (schools, prisons, hospitals, et cetera) should not be made.

Nor that producers who make such films are lacking in a sense of social responsibility.

I do suggest that, allowing, for example, that the Blackboard Jungle was a powerfully dramatic and technically excellent example of screencraft (thus sharpening its potentiality as a conditioner of collective opinion or individual thought and behavior), it should have reached constructive conclusions commensurate in power with its graphic exposition of youthful gangsterism. In my opinion, it did not, although, unlike the Wild One, it did commit its heroic interest to a popular star (Glenn Ford) who was seen as on the side of law and order.

Moreover it implied, as have many other films bearing on the theme of juvenile delinquency (instance, the earlier Dead End films), that juvenile crime is attributable to social causes: poverty, bad housing, et cetera, whereas in fact police and court records will show that juvenile delinquency often flourishes in comfortable circumstances where only the poverty of parental love, guidance, and example, plus a surplus of financial advantage, can be offered as a cause for youthful graduation into crime.

Those who defend unrestrained realism in motion pictures and television have advanced the following arguments:

1. That the habit of moviegoing has accustomed youth (and others) to accept a film story as something to be enjoyed, not necessarily believed, let alone imitated.

2. That it is impracticable to gear the dramatic content of motion pictures to the quirks of a small minority (presumed) of "border-line" mentalities, viz, deviates, sadists, molesters, and so forth.

3. That what is true to life is wholly acceptable in films and is given expression through media such as books, newspapers, comics, and therefore is equally valid and safe for the screen.

This first argument appears to have some value, although it cannot be applied to all, or even with certainty, to a majority of young people who see movies and TV shows.

The second argument also projects an element of truth, although if, as it implicitly admits, the incipient criminal or social moron can be excited to imitative behavior, the same in varying degrees is true of us all. Everyone of us is subject to temptation and the incidence of persuasion from the screen must depend upon individual circumstances, conditions, and character qualities nobody can definitely fix.

The third argument takes no cognizance of the fact that dramatized images on a screen are far more powerful in their effect upon the human mind and imagination than the printed word. New and wonderful methods of picture magnification and sound fidelity employed in the latest movies have increased this power.

It is arguable that no precautions in presenting crime in motion pictures can guarantee that imitative criminal behavior will not result.

For instance, Johnny Belinda, an excellent motion picture produced in 1947–48, was shown at a children's matinee held in a Buena Park (Calif.) theater on May 19, 1951. In the film there occurred, with perfect dramatic validity, a scene of sexual attack against a deaf and dumb girl. This scene was filmed with the utmost restraint: it was essential to the story.

Yet on that afternoon, from that theater, within a short time after this attack was witnessed on the screen, a young man named McCracken followed a little girl out of the audience, lured her to his rooms, attacked and murdered her.

According to police evidence he was a typical "border line" case.

Motion-picture and television producers must cater to patrons of every human type. They must endeavor—and I believe do earnestly endeavor—to turn out a continuous stream of entertainment reflecting, in unlimited variety, the verities of life.

This leads them to cater to all tastes on as many levels of human intelligence and appreciation as they, and those they employ, can comprehend or share.

Their emphases are drawn from what they conceive currently to be subjects of major public interest. If crime and violence assume an upswing in our social and national experience, it follows that the Hollywod movies reflect that upswing in a corresponding increase of screenplays featuring violence.

This may presently indicate a vicious circle in which the motion picture and television borrow criminal color from current circumstance and passes it on to society, at some peril of increasing the momentum of the prevailing evil.

There is, at present, some evidence of increasing public demand for more effective restraints on the content of movies and TV, and of the low, suggestive, vulgar, and misleading advertising used in connection with many of them.

Censorship, as it connotes arbitrary suppression of ideas, is abhorrent to many Americans. Superficially film censorship is understod to involve a denial by a minority of faultfinders of the rights of others to choose freely what they shall see on the screen.

This oversimplification of the issue is attended by an absence of clear definitions.

It is not censorship if and when a film producer edits a screenplay for the purpose of making it more widely acceptable to the public.

The newspaper editor claims a right to exercise precisely the same function in giving us the news. Many feel that in these days certain elements of our free press indulge their liberties to a point of license, but at least it is never argued that we have a censored press.

In the early 1930's, the American motion-picture industry, through the MPPA, voluntarily adopted a Code of Production Standards.

This consisted of a number of rules with given reasons for each rule.

Based broadly on the Ten Commandments, these rules defined the moral and ethical principles by which matter involving crime, sex, vulgarity, profanity, costume, racial, and national sentiments should be evaluated and related to screen drama.

It is aparent that the current trend toward excessive crime and salacious sex treatment in films is partly attributable to some failure of performance on the part of film producers who are pledged to observe this code and the industry-appointed officials whose task it is to administer it.

There is a belief among some film producers that this code, in spirit and effect, is censorious. They complain that to observe it, letter and spirit, is to hamper the artistic expression and mature development of the motion picture.

Main arguments employed against the code are—

1. That it restricts production of films of adult appeal.

2. That, since TV producers are bound only by token acceptance of principles and practices embodied in the film code and do not maintain an administration strictly to apply them, TV is correspondingly freer than their movie competitors to engage in sensational appeal to the public.

3. That the Supreme Court has ruled that the screen enjoys the same constitutional rights to freedom of expression as the newspaper press and that therefore the public shall have the sole right to decide what is fit and acceptable in movie and TV entertainment.

The following counterarguments are offered:

1. The Production Code offers no restrictions to those engaged in producing, writing, or directing films who care to understand and give effect to its moral philosophies and ethical principles. To the contrary, it provides a key to validity in the drama by alining worldly conflicts between good and evil with immutable principles laid down by Judeo-Christian law. There prevails a common misconception that "adult" entertainment involves preoccupation with the sordid side of life. The result is that many so-called "adult" films (including some exploiting juvenile crime and violence) betray, on the part of those responsible for them, a palpably adolescent approach to sex problems and situations.

2. It is true that the TV industry, under its standard of practices and so-called Television Code, presently fails sufficiently to curb, either in quality or relative quantity, its representations of crime, violence, and sexual immorality. The result is fast-growing public resistance and a loss of public following (and consequently of partonage for commercial sponsors).

3. The Supreme Court has not ruled that the constitutional rights of a "free screen" or of a "free press" include the right to present any idea that may come to a film producer's or editor's mind. While the Supreme Court has handed down no legal definitions, it has tacitly acknowledged that that which is obscene, incites to violence, or otherwise jeopardizes law and order is subject to legal restraints on the screen as in everyday life.

FOREIGN COMPARISONS

Overseas importers of American films almost unanimously oppose those in which violence and brutality are dominant features.

The British Board of Film Censors, a nonstatutory body which commands the respect of the British film industry and the public at large, has recently banned public exhibition of:

The Wild One; Cell 2455, Death Row (based on the criminal case history of condemned kidnap-rapist Caryl Chessman); Black Tuesday (in which a condemned gangster escapes from the electric chair, takes hostages and coldly kills several of them); Wicked Woman; and Cry Vengeance—and Blackboard Jungle has been refused a certificate and negotiations are proceeding.

Other recent films have been subject to heavy eliminations resulting in damage to, or destruction of, story continuity.

Warning has been given by the British Board of Film Censors to the Hollywood producers that no film scenes involving excessive brutality, criminal violence, or extreme and salacious sex situations will be accepted for public exhibition in Great Britain.

It is worth noting that the British Board of Film Censors operates a system of film classifications.

Only films classified "U" may be seen by all. Those considered of purely adult, emotional appeal are certified "A" and may be seen by children only if and when accompanied by a responsible adult.

All films of a horrific nature, or which deal in brutality, sadism, cruelty or questionable situations involving sex, are certified "X" and may not, in any circumstance, be attended by persons under the age of 18.

That the British Board of Film Censors has refused several of these recent crime and sex pictures any kind of certification at all indicates the grave view they take of their likely effect upon the national culture and upon immediate problems of maintaining public morals and good law and order.

It is the official British view that the films mentioned as having been banned are not acceptable even for adults.

Yet here they have been or are being shown, without let or hindrance, to young and old alike.

Most of the continental European films which reflect a heavy emphasis on social unrest or moral turpitude, where these are accepted at all, are granted only the "X" certificate in Great Britain; hence youths under 18 do not see them.

This situation can be compared again with that existing in the United States. The most gravely condemnable motion pictures—morally and sometimes politically subversive—are imported into this country from Europe, Mexico, and other countries, to be shown to all and sundry: teen-agers, young children, and adults. That such films frequently are released only in so-called specialty theaters not generally patronized by youngsters offers the one faint hope that their poisons may not prove as virulent as if they were given blanket release, as are most Hollywood films, in the chain and neighborhood theaters.

We are led, however, at this point to observe the influence of these so-called realistic, adult dramas, imported from abroad, upon the minds of some Hollywood impresarios.

There is evidence that a class of filmgoer which for some inexplicable reason is identified with the intelligentsia attends specialty theaters by choice and habit. Many of these persons rarely go to regular run theaters.

It is to woo their patronage, or so it is argued, that many in Hollywood strive to invest their own screenplays with the type of adult appeal they acclaim in these foreign sex dramas. (Instance, One Summer of Happiness, a young couple swimming nude, then lying together with natural results; The Bed a group of sex episodes totally ignoring accepted and traditional American standards; LaRonde a roundabout of sex exchanges among a group of lustful characters—and many others.)

That some artistic quality is evident in some of these films may be admitted without any acceptance of the theory that they may, with public prudence, be made available to the young people of America. Or that, with any sense of responsibility to the mass American movie public, Hollywood producers may accept the mores common to the European screen drama, in pressing this sin and crime trend to ultimate developments.

CONCLUSIONS

That a dangerous trend in crime and sex treatments has recently taken shape.

That it can and should be checked by intelligent and respectful application of the existing Motion Picture Production Code.

That the television industry should adopt and practice an identical code of ethics and morals, and set up an administration with teeth in it, to accomplish uniform and constant controls.

That the only alternative to these steps is censorship by State or civic bodies (within such limits as are set by law).

That if and when such limits should prove inadequate, there will arise a public clamor for remedial legislation.

That while it is happily true that many motion pictures and TV programs originating in Hollywood exercise benefic effect upon millions, it is fallacious to reason that the good they do balances the harm which results from a smaller number of crime and sex films.

By making a woman house-proud or beauty conscious, you do not minimize any traits she may have toward shop-lifting.

Feeding junior from a gleaming ice-box or giving him a lift in a late-model Cad will not stop him from holding up the gas station on the corner.

Crime does not have to pay as long as it holds thrills.

DOCUMENTATION

While interpretation of production code rules involves matters of opinion, there seems little room to doubt that the following films were in violation of code rules, either as to letter or spirit, and in many instances, both (Mr. Mooring's accusations) :

Black Tuesday.—Introduced brutal killings, a new and unique trick for concealing a gun, a perfect pattern for crime (escape from the just process of law), and excessive brutality. All these are expressly forbidden by the production code.

Big House, USA.—Dealt with the kidnaping of a child (which became a main theme despite efforts to cover the fact by introducing prison break as a secondary theme). It also introduced excessive brutality and gave details of the crime of kidnaping in violation of the production code.

Cell 2455, Death Row.—Dealt with the life of a notorious criminal of current times and identified him in the screen titles, thus, while side-stepping the rule against use of the criminal's name in the film, it violated the express purpose of the rule. It also contained intimate reference to sexual intercourse detailed partly by pictorial means then confirmed by sound effects.

Son of Sinbad.—Exploits seminudity which the production code forbids, coming under the heading of immoral actions. It also presents dances identifiable with sexual actions and, after the fashion of burlesque, is intended to excite the emotional reaction of an audience through exposure and movement : all code violations.

Kiss Me Deadly.—Viciously combines criminal brutality and sex salaciousness in violation of the production code.

Five Against the House.—Presents a pattern of crime conceived by four young college men (one of them popular film-TV hero, Guy Madison) and executed for fun by methods most calculated to inspire others with a desire for imitation, contrary to the production code. It also highly suggests reference to sex.

Violent Saturday.—Powerful dramatically and technically of high caliber, explicitly details the methods of a bank robbery crime in violation of production code. Some scenes also appear to break the rule against excessive brutality.

Not As a Stranger.—Links animal mating by direct symbolism with an illicit sex adventure between a man and woman, thus imputing instinctive animalistic nature to humankind and inferring that low forms of sex relationship are the accepted thing (by implying they are not subject to reason but only to animal instinct).

Many other examples are available.

It is noticeable also that of late, drive-in theaters, once regarded as almost sacrosanct to family entertainment, have shown with increasing frequency the worst examples in crime and sex films.

Reliable information suggests that this trend is not accidental, but coincides in some instances with conditions that invite immediate police action.

At certain drive-ins cars occupied by young couples are directed to specific parts of the theater where it is understood their behavior will be subject to no interference by theater attendants.

DOCUMENTATION B

Son of Sinbad.—Appears to present nothing of appeal to mature-minded adults, is described in a Hollywood trade press critique as "an affront to the public intelligence." Its burlesque-type parade of seminude females may very well excite the passion of young men at impressionable stages of sex curiosity. Moreover the film appears to be designed on exhibitionist lines for that specific purpose.

The Seven Year Itch.—Deals with adultery and illicit sex as subject for fun. The technique employed, rather common of late, is to presume that the illicit adventures existed only in the imagination of the characters and did not in fact occur. This method permits of the characters talking about, and going through the forms of sexual promiscuity without any restraints. If the film is aimed at adults, the fact is that adolescents will be free to attend and many may be impressed that sexual promiscuity is an easy, acceptable, laughing matter; not violation of the virtues.

STATEMENT OF RONALD REAGAN, FREE LANCE ACTOR, HOLLYWOOD, CALIF.

Chairman KEFAUVER. Mr. Ronald Reagan will be our next witness. Sit down, Mr. Reagan. How are you?

Mr. REAGAN. Thank you.

Chairman KEFAUVER. Mr. Reagan, we are glad to have you with us. Mr. Bobo, will you ask Mr. Reagan some preliminary questions?

Mr. BOBO. Mr. Reagan, would you tell us within what capacity you are associated with the motion picture industry?

Mr. REAGAN. I am what is termed a free-lance actor. This is the status of most of the actors in the motion picture business. There is very little continued employment; only a few hundred out of our 8,000 actors are under contract with studios. The rest of us work when we in the studio and the producer get together on a script. In addition to that I have served as an officer and am presently serving as an officer of the Screen Actors Guild which is the actors union.

Mr. BOBO. As an actor, Mr. Reagan, and in the motion picture industry, I am sure you have heard recently of some of the complaints or suggestions about too much crime and violence or brutality within motion pictures.

I wonder, would you give us your feelings on this subject as an actor?

Mr. REAGAN. Well, Mr. Bobo, if I could correct you slightly, I have been in the picture business since 1937 and I have never known a time at which the picture business wasn't being criticized for something. Lately they seem to be dwelling more on crime and violence. I don't know how I could answer that without perhaps getting kind of lengthy or talking about personal references.

I just finished a western movie in which I did a scene, I administered quite a drubbing to my partner in this picture. The story is about a misunderstanding between those of us—the two of us who are good friends. Now, a very great dramatic part of this picture depends in the fact I, misunderstanding my friend, start the fight and he won't fight back.

My principal concern with pictures is that they are a part of the theater. They are theatrical entertainment, and while there are very few rules that hold for theatrical entertainment, one I have always subscribed to and I believe is basic is that you cannot have successful theater unless your audience has an emotional experience of some kind. If it is comedy, they must laugh. If it is tragedy, they must cry.

Now, I don't know how you can get over the dramatic point of a story of two partners who come to a misunderstanding that leads almost to blood enmity or killing between them, and then find them or see them find their way back to their friendship, without showing the extent of their hatred at this one point for each other. And to do that we have a scene that, of course, will appear to be brutal.

This is taken from a story by Bret Harte. I think Bret Harte was a pretty good writer of the particular period of the mining days in early California.

I think the heritage of our country is based a great deal on those early days of violence here in the West. I don't know how you portray accurately without trying realistically to show what took place.

A little while ago I was in a picture based on the Korean war, called Prisoner of War. It came from the stories of the first 60 repratriated prisoners.

Some people complained because the picture was too brutal. Well, a lot of American kids went over to the war and a lot of them went through and lived through in reality what we tried to portray.

I am sorry, but I don't see what is wrong with letting the American public, who are free to either buy the ticket or not buy the ticket—what is wrong with letting them come in and see a sample of what the American kids in the Armed Forces went through, who had to fight that war for them. You can't do that by flashing a notice on the screen and saying, "We don't want to show you this, it is terrible, but awful things happened to this fellow," and then go on with the story. You have to portray what took place and what happened to him.

As I say, to try and answer this I have to ramble all around. We are in the field, as I said, of theatrical entertainment.

I remember some years ago when the rackets were running rampant in this country, that we did a picture out here supposed to show the protection racket in the Midwest in the food markets. How the gangsters would threaten and if you didn't pay protection they would come in and ruin the stock.

There is political censorship in the State of Ohio. In Ohio these censors cut out of this picture every scene that showed what the racketeers did. The result was that your picture went out the window, because you had a wonderful picture about the FBI and policemen who were chasing gangsters, but you never saw anything that the gangsters did. The result was the audience didn't know what the fuss was all about or why they were bad men, because they never saw them being bad.

In all of our crime and violence pictures there is one thing that I believe is true, has to be true, and is true of every picture that has ever been made in Hollywood: crime never pays. Right always triumphs.

Now, if we are going to try, and in a picture in addition to entertainment we are going to try and instill in the audience respect for law and order, and the idea that right is to triumph, you certainly have got to go some distance in showing how evil the wrongdoers are; and I think this basically we have done. Naturally, there are going to be some men who are not going to produce pictures with the same good taste as others.

I think the greatest mistake the critics of the motion picture industry make is to refer to it as an industry, and think that when they talk to us they are talking to General Motors or General Electric, one company, that if they can get one person or one board of directors to make a decision the problem is solved.

The Screen Actors Guild has over 400 signatories to our contract, over 400 individual producers or producing companies making motion pictures. These men are a cross section of American life. And it stands to reason that some of them are not going to have the same ideas, the same principles, the same good tastes as others.

We have a voluntary production code. I don't care what other witnesses have said, I believe that in all the years I have been connected with the picture business by and large 99 percent of the time we subscribe to that code, and I believe it is a voluntary censorship. It is a program of self-restraint that is unequaled in any other form of communications in our land or in the world. I know of no publishing industry, I know of no records firm, I know of no radio or television station, no other form in the communications industry that has the same self-restraint as does the motion picture industry.

Well, I had better stop and let you ask another question.

Mr. Bobo. I think no one would take exception with you that in a picture we must portray certain activity. We can go at times beyond the bounds in a picture by too much killing to get across our point, or too much crime, wouldn't you think, in some pictures?

Mr. Reagan. Yes. As I say, there are bound to be individuals who I think, no matter with what sincerity or good intentions their idea of telling the story, let us say, do not have the same good taste that another producer might have or another director or writer.

In the last analysis, however, isn't the American citizen, with his money at the box office, the best judge of what he wants to see?

Mr. Bobo. I think that is probably true. We are speaking more here today in the realm of juveniles, those 16 and under. We sometimes wonder whether or not they are capable of making their minds up as to what would be good or what would be bad.

Mr. Reagan. Well, then, I wonder if the program begins with the motion picture industry, because I have never pinned down the percentage, but I think that by and large the greatest majority of our pictures come from published stories, books and plays that have already been staged. There are very few original stories in the overall percentage that account for some 350 pictures a year.

Now, I read in the paper this morning that one of the pictures that was going to be mentioned was Blackboard Jungle. I saw Blackboard Jungle. Before I saw it, I read it in the Saturday Evening Post. It was available on the newsstands to anyone that wanted to read it for 15 cents. As a matter of fact, I read an editorial comment of what a forceful story it was, how powerful. I thought the picture very faithfully portrayed the story. They did not exaggerate or take over at any time and go off on any tangent. They stuck to the story.

Now, in seeing the picture, sure, there was violence. But I think any one of us realizes this situation does prevail in certain educational institutions in the country. And you have to look at the end result, and I think the end result to any youngster that was in there had to be, as it was with me—I am certainly not a youngster any more—had to be a feeling of disgust for the boys who were on the wrong side of the fence. There had to be a certain feeling of triumph when the one boy was won over and became a leader for the right.

And as a sort of a sideline, I thrilled to another message I read in the picture. I thought it was a great tribute for a very much maligned and misunderstood and abused segment of American humanity, the schoolteacher. I thought it portrayed this very dedicated group of people we don't pay enough, don't do enough for; it showed their selflessness in dealing with this problem and sticking with it.

Mr. Bobo. You would say as an actor, Mr. Reagan—I notice you mentioned the story was in the Saturday Evening Post—that possibly if you were portraying a part on the screen that I probably would derive more of an emotional experience watching you portray it than reading the story, and it would have more of an impact upon me.

Mr. REAGAN. Yes; I hope so. If not, we are all out of work.

Mr. BOBO. There was another question I was interested in. You also have a television program, which I saw the other night.

Mr. REAGAN. That is right.

Mr. BOBO. Do you think in choosing the material for the television program there is any more restraint put upon the subject matter that you would choose for a television program than what you would choose for a motion picture?

Mr. REAGAN. Yes, there very definitely is. Of course, there is also a very definite economic reason there. You have in television a different kind of censorship. You have to get your script past the sponsor, so you very quickly learn what sort of thing the sponsor wants and doesn't want, and this is the way you read stories and submit them to him.

I think the element enters in, in television that you are going into a home. I think you select stories on the basis of the hour of the evening. In our program, we realize that the children are still up and they are going to be sitting with their parents. It isn't a matter of whether we are going to be moral or immoral on the screen. We try to pick a story that we think won't cause a family fight; that mom and pop and the kids will all agree that they can at least look at it and get something out of it.

Mr. BOBO. I think that is all.

Chairman KEFAUVER. Thank you very much, Mr. Reagan.

Mr. REAGAN. May I impose on you for just one more statement? I have been hearing some of the testimony this morning and—I am imposing, because I know this is not the proper province of your committee, but there is something that has always disturbed me and disturbs me very much right at the moment, and that is about this hue and cry about the motion picture industry and what effect it might have on youth.

I happen to be a parent. I am as concerned as any other parent with whether my children see things that are vulgar or obscene or brutal. I realize I can't wrap them in cotton wool in this day and age; that they only have to go as far as the front page of their daily newspaper to see the seamier side of life.

I think as a parent my obligation at home is to bring my children up in such a way that when they are exposed to vulgarity and obscenity and brutality they will be able to properly evaluate it and make a decision and put it in its right place.

The thing that worries me very much about what is being done to the motion-picture industry, or what is being talked to the motion-picture industry is something I can't lick with my children at home. Ours is a first-generation business, and I am very much worried about my children and all the other children their age, an entire generation that is going to grow up taking it for granted it is all right for someone to tell them what they can see and hear from a motion-picture screen, because when they grow up and take our places as adults I am afraid they will be mentally conditioned to where then somebody can tell them it is all right to tell them what they can read and what they can hear from a speaking platform, and what they can say and what they can think. If that day comes, of course, we have lost the cold war.

Thanks very much.

Chairman KEFAUER. Thank you, Mr. Reagan.

We will have about a 5- or 6-minute recess and then carry on about 25 minutes more before lunchtime.

(Short recess taken.)

STATEMENT OF DR. FREDERICK J. HACKER, CHIEF OF STAFF, THE HACKER FOUNDATION, BEVERLY HILLS, CALIF.

Chairman KEFAUVER. Dr. Hacker, we know you are a well-known, eminent psychiatrist. I believe you are chief of staff of the Hacker Foundation for Psychiatric Research and Education. Is that correct?

Dr. HACKER. Yes, sir.

Chairman KEFAUVER. Will you tell us a little more about your background, experience, and training?

Dr. HACKER. I was born and raised in Vienna, and went to medical school and graduated in Switzerland and had all my postgraduate training in medicine and psychiatry in this country at Columbia University, and particularly at the medical clinic at Topeka, Kans. The last 11 years I have had my own clinic here in Beverly Hills. Attached to it is a psychiatric foundation which is dedicated to research and education. It just so happened this last year our main topic has been juvenile delinquency, the various causes and reasons and forms of expression of it.

Right now the committee catches me at the right time, because I am still full of a whole year of discussion of it. As a result of that, I made only a very small, short statement. Otherwise I would have to give a series of seminars. I don't want to impose to such an extent, so I made just a very short statement about what I consider to be the main points of the situation at the moment.

Chairman KEFAUVER. Dr. Hacker, do you wish to read your statement or file your statement and speak orally?

Dr. HACKER. Well, psychiatrists are usually much better in answering questions and arguing on whatever it may be. But if you want me to read this very short statement, it will just take 2 minutes.

Chairman KEFAUVER. You read your statement, Doctor.

Dr. HACKER. Social scapegoating attempts to single out the modern media of mass communication—movies, television, comic books, and so forth—as the main culprits responsible for all that ails the world. Obviously, no such simple cause-and-effect relationship exists. In the intricate pattern of modern society, every so-called effect is produced by innumerable related causes and itself gives rise to manifold other effects.

Therefore, it cannot be stated with any degree of dispassionate scientific accuracy that movies or other mass media cause juvenile delinquency, but innumerable clinical observations prove that they not only describe but often contribute to, or at least shape the content of, criminal activity.

Movies, as a whole much more adult and restrained than television or comic books, show awareness of social responsibility by voluntary submission to a code. This expresses the basic conviction that even entertainment and realism have to live up to some minimal educational and moral standards. Pictures may have become better than ever, but, while only a few of them stimulate and exploit vile aggressive impulses, many of them depict extreme brutality as a natural function of ordinary living, and most of them rely heavily on the outcome of physical combat as an eminently satisfactory means of solving human problems.

The technical perfection of the movies provides an excellent identification and crystallization model for the vague and unformed attitudes of the adolescent. The often-prevailing general atmosphere of violence in movies and other media of mass communication promotes hero-worship of the criminal, ridicule of thoughtfulness or sensitivity or any type of intellectual pursuit, and thus produces the confusion of brutality with rugged masculinity. The code's strictly enforced taboo against overt salaciousness frequently permits the uninhibited display of orgies of brutality, which are, in fact, hostile manifestations of a perverse sexuality. This deterioration of the noble American dedication to action into violence for its own sake represents a distinct social danger, and there is probably a definite, though extremely complex, parallelism between the general brutalization of our youth and the increased violence in media of mass communication.

To investigate in detail these relationships may be one of the most important tasks of psychological and sociological research of the immediate future.

Chairman KEFAUVER. Mr. Bobo.

Mr. BOBO. Doctor, do you feel that in crime-and-violence movies youngsters will have a tendency to seek out this particular type of movie?

Dr. HACKER. Yes, and I believe some studies indicate that—and this speaks not against the movies—about twice as many delinquents— that among the compulsive movie attendants there are twice as many delinquents than those boys and girls that are not delinquents. In other words, there is a relationship between moviegoing and delinquency or between a very insistent television-viewing habit and delinquency.

However, I would like to state emphatically I do not mean to imply by that the movies produce the crimes or that there is a parallelism between the attendance of movies and that this has the causal effect of producing the crime. It is much more so that the criminally more inclined are those that are more exposed to that, that do not know what to do with themselves and therefore seek very often this kind and form of entertainment.

Mr. BOBO. Do you feel an emotionally disturbed child may gain ideas from brutal scenes or scenes of sadism or scenes of illicit sex?

Dr. HACKER. I think there is no question about it, because I see it daily in my practice, that they actually copy some of the violence as depicted in movies. Of course, it could be argued, on the other hand, if they would not copy that pattern they possibly might copy another one.

That, therefore, the description of violence in the movies may just act as a trigger mechanism and not be an essential cause.

But we certainly do see in our clinical practice, without a question of a doubt, innumerable crimes are distinctly influenced in their conception, in their perpetration and even in some details by certain models that were gained by the mass media of communication, movies, television, comic books, et cetera.

Mr. Bobo. The visual coupled with the sound media of communication, would it have more of a serious impact on emotionally disturbed youngsters than reading a comic book or reading a story in a magazine?

Dr. Hacker. It undoubtedly has. I think the very marvelous and technically very admirable combination and blending of auditory and visual stimuli, of hearing and seeing, produces certainly a heightened and cumulative effect, so that I would think that movies and television, but particularly also movies, are in their social effect much more important than all reading matter taken together.

Mr. Bobo. Dr. Hacker, how many children or juvenile delinquents have you come in contact with in your practice?

Dr. Hacker. I think in the course of my practice I have certainly seen many hundreds of them as patients individually and maybe in groups and so on. I have been in some therapeutic contact with many thousands of them, because that has been so much in Dr. Frym's and my own field of interest in the immediate past.

Mr. Bobo. Do you think that children by looking at the scenes of crime and violence might receive some vicarious outlet for their own inward feelings in watching these movies?

Dr. Hacker. Yes, I think again there is no doubt about the fact that there is sometimes some relief of some tension or anxiety or some vicarious gratification, as you put it. But it is very doubtful whether that is a very therapeutic measure, because this relief that is provided in that manner usually doesn't last for a very long time.

But I think since maybe, today, at least, I appear as the only psychiatrist on the witness list, it is fair to state beyond my own opinion, that the psychiatric opinion is such—it is maybe not surprising—it is somewhat divided on the issue, as they are on most issues— as most people are on most issues.

And you know, there is the one opinion that will have it that insofar as there is a definite relationship between mass communication and crime, and that insofar as mass communication is at least one thing that one can alter, presumably, that one should very strictly censor these media and subject them to either voluntary or involuntary censorship. Of course, there is the other point of view that claims this is a surface manifestation of social ills altogether, and it is doing an injustice to mass media to single them out and to treat something, you know, very much on the surface, and one should rather attack the underlying causes for those things, and from their point of view there is, of course, a great fear of censorship that was voiced today by some witnesses before your committee, too.

So, I mean, even among phychiatrists there is a somewhat divided opinion as to what to do about it, though there is, I think, little disagreement about the fact that in a very fundamental way the media of mass communication does shape and influence criminal activity, though they do not cause it.

Mr. Bobo. Do you think that in building up this vicarious outlet that they might have, that the tendency might come for them to act this out in a more brutal form, having received their outlet there, that it was only temporary.

Dr. HACKER. Yes, I think that is a very distinct danger. I think another witness pointed out that with the tremendous voraciousness of modern mass media that swallows up material at a tremendous rate, that the only way that some producers help themselves is to constantly raise the emotional angle. In order to produce the same effect of emotional impact they have to make the scene so vile it is more and more emphatic and more and more distinct and more and more overt, and that may then lead, not only may lead, but very frequently does lead to a stimulation of an otherwise predisposed youngster.

Mr. BOBO. We have talked about the predisposed youngster. Under the tension of the times in which we live, with our mass media of television and movies and also reading it in stories and books, might a normal youngster be led into an emotionally disturbed youngster by this constant diet of crime and violence and brutality.

Dr. HACHER. I think that is quite correct. As you probably know, though it has been said every generation feels that way about the subsequent one, many older people now would consider the normal so-called adolescent emotionally disturbed. So the dividing line between the so-called normal and so-called emotionally disturbed one is sometimes very hard to draw, particularly in adolescence, which is traditionally and one could almost say physiologically for all of us a rather disturbed and disturbing period. These influences may be very decisive.

But, naturally, one should say—and maybe I am only adding that for my own, because I have my own professional ax to grind, that sociological conditions alone are never responsible for any kind of emotional distress, and also not for crime. There has to be a certain individual psychological predisposition or disturbance connected with it, too.

Mr. BOBO. In your capacity as a phychiatrist and with the foundation, in recent years have you noticed any increase in the number of emotionally disturbed youngsters that come before you or come to you for treatment?

Dr. HACKER. I am not in possession of large-scale statistics that could decisively answer that question, but it is our distinct impression that particularly crimes of violence have increased tremendously, that such—I say that with all due caution—that such acts of seemingly unmotivated violence, as you see them in wolfpacks and such, are really almost a novel phenomena. That form of a gang organization of violence for violence's sake is something new that has been added, and particularly, and this may be the thing I want to stress most, there is an increased toleration of brutality and violence, even of the so-called normal adolescent or person.

I mean, it may be one thing that the movies and television and comic books have certainly done is to make us all impervious to violence. In other words, as I tried to state in my statement, we accept that as a part of normal, ordinary life and do not particularly protest against it.

This brutalization, even of the so-called normal—forgetting about the emotionally disturbed for a moment—in terms of social engineering may be the greatest and most distinct danger.

Mr. BOBO. Are we becoming immune to human suffering?

Dr. HACKER. Yes, and accept brutality and violence as part of ordinary human living. And particularly also to feel—this is something I believe everybody connected with the movie industry will frankly admit, though he may say he does it for dramatic reasons—that to constantly describe the so-called hero, meaning the one that gets the girl in the end, is the one who is particularly good in physical combat and who usually wins the last fight, as if that makes him eligible not only for the possession of the girl, but also for the heroic solution of all other problems that may confront him in life.

So that implicitly, without actually saying it, an atmosphere is created in which there is emphasis placed on a kind of brutal ruggedness that appears of doubtful value in the solution of national, social, international, or any other kind of conflict.

Mr. BOBO. You stated that extreme brutality and wolf gangs were a new phenomena. Do you have any opinion as to the reason for this?

Dr. HACKER. Well, I think there again a great variety of reasons probably contribute to that. It is probably a certain social conditioning, the frequent loss of parental authority and of the binding morals of either state or church and so on, that predisposes this kind of gang formation. And then the absence of any particular premium on thinking and intellectual activities very frequently drives the youngster into doing something for doing's sake, in order to just pass the time.

They constantly have to, again here, too, raise the threshold of their excitement and pretty soon they may engage in violence that doesn't take any particular account of what damage it may do. This is a very primitive explanation, but there are many, many more factors. But I am sure it is something of a sequence of that nature.

Mr. BOBO. We couldn't produce pictures in this country without showing some form of life or some form of violence, as everyday life is lived?

Dr. HACKER. Certainly not. I certainly do not want to protest for, not squeamish morals, but squeamish psychiatric reasons, for the suppression of anything that is realistic.

But in movies, for instance, a great, great number of things that are perfectly realistic are not shown; never shown and never will be shown, and maybe they should never be shown.

For instance, certain intimate scenes, certain eliminative functions, certain eliminative scenes of the human being that are perfectly natural, they are perfectly human and certainly occur every moment are certainly not shown in movies.

Why not? Because it is not believed this is a representative function of the human being and odd in any form. It is not only description as it was told today, but it is also representative description.

And I believe it is indeed a social danger to consider the young healthy normal American male as being representatively described by his combative efforts and by his brutality. Though it may occur, this is not, I think, a sufficient explanation or excuse for showing it all the time.

Mr. BOBO. Do you think, Doctor, that same of the increase in sex crimes, especially among juveniles, which has increased 110 percent in the last 12 years, could be attributed to the looseness of sex as is displayed not only in motion pictures, but at times in television and magazines and stories we read?

Dr. HACKER. For that, certainly, however, the movies cannot be blamed, because the few movies I do see seem to pay much more attention to the elimination of these sexual factors and to measure the plunging necklines of the ladies, rather than the seeming deleterious expressions of violence.

I am quite sure, however, that the constant stimulation by other media of mass communication has maybe also something to do with keeping this kind of abnormal sexual excitement alive.

Chairman KEFAUVER. Well, Doctor, as I understand, in summary, you feel that the movie industry has shown some awareness as to its public responsibility, as evidenced by the fact it has voluntarily adopted a very good code and most of the pictures are wholesome and educational and entertaining without being deleterious.

Dr. HACKER. I would think so.

Chairman KEFAUVER. In your experience as a psychiatrist, you have had young patients who have committed acts which were based, you feel, to some extent, at least, upon what they had seen or been subjected to through the media of communication, movies or television.

Dr. HACKER. Yes.

Chairman KEFAUVER. Is that correct?

Dr. HACKER. That is correct.

Chairman KEFAUVER. You don't claim the movies or the television were the cause. They were already of the nature where they might get into trouble, and this was just a——

Dr. HACKER. Trigger.

Chairman KEFAUVER. A trigger or a manifestation.

Dr. HACKER. Correct.

Chairman KEFAUVER. And you think that while the movies have done a very good job, that in the field of crime and violence and portraying as the hero the fellow who is the most violent on occasions, that they could have a better influence upon our young people.

Dr. HACKER. That is correct. I would say that since the principle of the code has been adopted by the movie industry anyway, regardless of whether that is a correct or incorrect principle, and it is hard to see why the main force of this code should be directed against—you know, against only, let's say, various expressions of sexuality, rather than also being directed against the equally dangerous or much more dangerous forms of brutality and violence, since the existing instruments of the code would already permit it.

One has almost the impression—almost—that the suppression of overt sexuality and sensuality and so on is compensated for by increased emphasis on physical violence.

Chairman KEFAUVER. Dr. Hacker, your statement is a great help to us. We know that you have no ax to grind, that you have had great experience. You do take a broad public interest view of this matter.

Dr. HACKER. Yes.

Chairman KEFAUVER. I am certain your statement will be of assistance to the movie industry, also, and to those who are concerned with the type of picture they produce and show. We appreciate very much your coming in.

Dr. HACKER. Thank you very much.

Chairman KEFAUVER. While we have a lot of fine witnesses yet, and we are going to hear all of our witnesses, even if we have to carry this part of the hearing over until the morning; it is now 12 o'clock, and I think we had better stand in recess until 2 o'clock.

(Whereupon, at 12 noon, a recess was taken until 2 p. m. of the same day.)

(Whereupon, the hearing was resumed at 2:15 o'clock p. m.)

Chairman KEFAUVER. We are delighted to have Mayor Poulson with us for a while this afternoon. The mayor and I served in the House of Representatives for many years together. Although we were of different political faiths, we were close friends. One time I took him down to see the Tennessee Valley Authority, trying to get him to vote for the TVA. We spent the weekend at Lookout Mountain Hotel. This was in 1947. I wasn't quite running for the Senate, but I was getting ready to, so Mayor Poulson started managing my campaign for the Senate, and thought he was doing pretty well. But we ascertained we were over in the State of Georgia and he had been campaigning with citizens of Georgia and not Tennessee so it didn't work out. But I appreciated his good efforts, anyway.

We are glad to have Mr. William Rosenthal, who is a member of the general assembly, and whom I have known pleasantly for some time.

Mayor, we had one of your representatives here yesterday, Chief Parker, and other officials, who told us about conditions in Los Angeles. If you have anything to add, we will be glad to give you an opportunity to speak.

Mayor POULSON. I think Chief Parker, as he stated, was testifying in my behalf because, after all, this is a matter which experts have to deal with, that it is a problem that comes under his jurisdiction, and I feel that the proper method of approaching these problems is to have the general interest in the problem, but at the same time it must be handled primarily by the department heads who are responsible for it.

For that reason I asked Chief Parker to testify. I did come here today solely to pay a personal visit to a personal friend of mine of many years' standing and one whom I have always enjoyed his friendship. One thing about it, politics never made any difference with us.

Chairman KEFAUVER. That is right. Thank you very much. You stay with us as long as you can.

Our first witness this afternoon is Dr. Marcel Frym.

STATEMENT OF DR. MARCEL FRYM, DIRECTOR OF CRIMINOLOGY AND CHIEF OF STAFF OF THE HACKER FOUNDATION, BEVERLY HILLS, CALIF.

Chairman KEFAUVER. Dr. Frym, you are the director of criminology, or the research in criminology, at the Hacker Foundation.

Dr. FRYM. That is right.

Chairman KEFAUVER. Mr. Bobo, do you wish to ask Dr. Frym any preliminary questions about his experience and background?

Mr. BOBO. Yes. Where did you receive your training, Doctor?

Dr. FRYM. I want to correct a mistake on your background sheet, gentlemen. I am not an M. D. I am not practicing medicine. I am a doctor of jurisprudence, which means a doctor of law, with special training in criminology and legal medicine, and now 10 years' experience in psychiatric work with the Hacker Psychiatric Clinic.

I am a member of the faculty of the University of Southern California, School of Public Administration, where I have been teaching law enforcement officers in criminology for the last 2 years. I am also teaching classes and graduate seminars in correction and psychology and criminology.

Mr. Bobo. Have you done any extensive work in the realm of mass media?

Dr. Frym. Yes, I have been treating, the correction of psychotherapies, a member of the staff of the psychiatric clinic, delinquents, and specifically juvenile delinquents for many years.

It was a topic of special interest for me in all these years, and also as a research man, to establish correlation between mass media and delinquency.

Mr. Bobo. Doctor, in your study of the relationship of mass media to juvenile delinquency, what have been some of your conclusions and findings?

Dr. Frym. Well, I agreed with those authorities in our field who state that there is a relation between certain exhibitions of mass media and delinquency. I believe it cannot be denied that certain criminology from juveniles is extremely affected, as Dr. Hacker pointed out today, by signs, by character description in movies and in TV shows. It cannot be denied and I wish there would be more research material available to endorse his view. I am personally quite concerned, quite convinced that these mass media are a very serious contributor to delinquency. I would like to explain this briefly, if I may.

Any type of criminality is an act of aggression, a rebellion against restrictions imposed by law and by moral codes.

Now, we have learned in modern psychology, that is, extreme aggression and rebellion is usually generated by fears, by states of anxiety, by insecurity, and very often by anxieties related to the sexual position of the human being, if the man is sufficiently masculine and the woman is sufficiently feminine.

As a matter of fact, I would like to state in this connection that in my opinion most vicious and extremely brutal crimes have a strong underlay of homosexual intentions. It is not necessary the person has had, has ever had any homosexual experience, but they have had, at least been tortured deep below the level of their consciousness about the insecurity about their sexual position. And therefore I want to say unwittingly and unknowingly it is in pictures and other mass media which stimulates and overstimulates this basic mechanism.

I want to say I am extremely opposed to those views which would try to censor mass media at large. I want to point to the tremendous importance of pictures like, for instance, Snake Pit, which has demonstrated very outrageous conditions in mental hospitals and alarmed the public to these conditions.

For instance, a picture like Caged, dealing with most deplorable conditions in women's prisons in the United States, and I wish there would be more pictures that would be made to point to the conditions in the United States prisons. By the United States prisons I do not mean Federal prisons, but prisons in the United States which are, in my opinion, too many of them a disgrace to our country.

I believe it is not the job of movies just to produce or present sugar-coated unrealities. It should show caste conditions and alarm public indignation, but I personally am very, very leery about those pictures which have no message whatsoever, or just pretend a message and really only capitalize on viciousness and brutality.

Mr. BOBO. In the relationship among our juveniles of today and juveniles in adolescence, where many of them don't receive any type of sexual education in the home or in the school or through the church, do you think it would eventually be possible from the mass media of communication for them to learn about sex or get the wrong attitude about sex from some of the media of communication?

Dr. FRYM. Yes. By all means. You see, our basic concepts of right and wrong behavior are shaped in accordance to suggestive examples, and the characters that are created and depicted in a mass communication media are very suggestive examples of right and wrong.

The hero is not the good guy in this type of picture we are now concerned about. Actually glamorized is the brutal, vicious guy who succeeds only by muscular strength.

Mr. BOBO. In view of some of the biological drives which we have and some of the social controls we have over sex today, do you feel that the mass media may stimulate sex desires in youth, and in view of the existing social controls, these desires probably would not be properly satisfied, and might account for some of the sex crimes?

Dr. FRYM. Yes, sir, Mr. Bobo. But I cannot conceive how this could or should be presented, except if we accept in a limited way, at least, the technique used in most European countries.

I think one of the witnesses today pointed to regulations in England, and they exist in many other countries in Europe, that juveniles are not admitted to adult pictures. I prefer this by far to reducing pictures to an unreality, to a childlike quality, just in order to protect youth. I don't know whether this is financially feasible. This is not an angle which I can discuss, but I am worried that kids, especially of relatively tender age, are admitted here in our country to any type of pictures.

When I traveled 2 years ago extensively in Europe as a criminologist, visiting law enforcement agencies and penal institutions and especially being concerned with juvenile delinquecy, I was really surprised how lower the incidents in juvenile delinquency are in Europe as compared to the United States.

We must consider that Europe has suffered tremendously on destructive warfare and financial distress, and our country has been spared in that regard. Still there is so much less delinquency there it should make us more and more aware of all of the contributing factors, and one of them definitely is some irresponsible productions in mass media.

Mr. BOBO. Do you think that criminally disposed or an emotionally upset youngster, by going to a movie, could pick up the outlines for a crime which would cause him to have an outlet to perform this crime?

Dr. FRYM. Well, as was said before today it could trigger such a certain recognition or proneness of the boy. We could, of course, argue that something else completely different, something he may have read in the newspapers, picture in a newspaper or magazine, or a scene on the street might equally have triggered his mechanism or he must be prone, and if he came out bad, outlaw all trigger mechanisms, I don't believe this.

What I would really suggest, if I may, my personal opinion, I am very proud of our production code administration. I think they are doing an outstanding job and very intelligently and in good taste.

But I would like to see a kind of advisory board to this agency or to another agency to be created for TV, consisting of experts in human behavior, for instance, educators, psychologists, psychiatrists, and even criminologists.

Mr. Bobo. The purpose of this being to interpret for them what the impact of a certain scene or a certain series of scenes might be.

Dr. Frym. Yes. I believe very much that human behavior is no longer a matter of concern only to the layman. Of course, everybody misbehaving as a human being believes himself therefore, to be an expert.

I was a prosecutor in the old days and I still can't understand what I did to human beings just out of ignorance, out of the lack of knowledge of the mechanisms of human beings.

I feel all who are concerned about delinquency, especially juvenile delinquency, should avail themselves of more knowledge in the field of the dynamics of human behavior. And only experts can assist those entrusted with this job in doing the right thing.

I am very worried about the censorship, it could be hypocritical and moralistic and very insincere. But I think this can be prevented by choosing the right members to an advisory board.

Mr. Bobo. We oftentimes read in the newspaper when a controversial picture is being played of a group of juveniles, one or more, performing an act, and saying they had received the idea from seeing a certain picture or reading a certain magazine or seeing a certain television show.

Do you think it possible for children, so viewing one picture, to pick up an idea and go out and commit a crime of violence?

Dr. Frym. I would mistrust very much these statements. I want to point out that it is equally wrong to believe that the motivations which a human being offers, what he believes to be his motivating force, is usually not a true dynamic factor in his behavior.

On the other hand, we should listen to it. It is very possible that in one individual case a boy really may have, especially if he is a feebleminded boy, been tremendously impressed by something that stimulated and touched at his weak spots.

On the other hand, many may deny this, many kids might say no, "the movies and the TV shows I have been watching, they have no bearing on what I did," and it might just in this case have been a very important dynamic factor. We must realize that the human behavior really originates on the unconscious level. A person doesn't know why he does something. And it is time that we learned this.

Mr. Bobo. We couldn't say that the movie he saw would be the cause of his performing a certain act.

Dr. Frym. In my experience this would be just an excuse of the youngster. He wants to use it, just as a type of any other excuse. I wouldn't trust this statement.

Chairman Kefauver. Have you given any special study, Doctor, to advertisements for movies, such as you see here?

Dr. Frym. Well, I must admit—I am almost ashamed to admit I do not read funnies and do not look at these posters. But here, this is a very impressive series, I must say. I think they are very bad, indeed. They are terrible and they shouldn't be permitted.

Chairman KEFAUVER. Some of them are much worse than the movies; aren't they?

Dr. FRYM. They certainly are. In defense of the movies, you must say this. I believe it is another section of the movie industry which is responsible for these posters, rather than the men who produce the pictures.

Chairman KEFAUVER. Anything else, Mr. Bobo?

Mr. BOBO. Do you think that the impact of some of these particular posters could have an effect, a lasting effect on a child more so than a movie would have?

Dr. FRYM. Well, yes, they could have a very strong dynamic effect, but only as a trigger mechanism. I believe even adults should be protected from this kind of trash.

Chairman KEFAUVER. Then, Doctor, summing up, do you feel a lot of movies are wholesome, educational, entertaining, and a good influence on children generally?

Dr. FRYM. Yes.

Chairman KEFAUVER. Some unfortunately are not. You feel that really the wholesome movies can be as attractive, attract as good houses as the other kind?

Dr. FRYM. I personally am an optimist. I believe this, Senator; yes.

Chairman KEFAUVER. We thank you very much for your statement to our subcommittee.

Dr. FRYM. Thank you.

Chairman KEFAUVER. We are glad to have Mr. Waters, the United States attorney, and Mr. Kinnison, with us. Mr. Kinnison was here sitting with us.

Mr. WATERS. Mr. Kinnison has been here and gone.

Chairman KEFAUVER. He came and he went.

STATEMENT OF DORE SCHARY, VICE PRESIDENT IN CHARGE OF PRODUCTION, METRO-GOLDWYN-MAYER, HOLLYWOOD, CALIF.

Mr. Dore Schary, vice president in charge of production, Metro-Goldwyn-Mayer.

Mr. Schary, we are glad to have you as a witness, and the chairman is privileged to know Mr. Schary a number of years. We appreciate your cooperation with our subcommittee. I thought that you had a written statement.

Mr. SCHARY. No, I don't have a written statement.

Chairman KEFAUVER. You have something written out there.

Mr. SCHARY. Well, I have some notes on information that may be of importance, depending on the questions. I figured that I'd best come in with a very open mind, and let's see what happens.

Chairman KEFAUVER. All right, Mr. Bobo, do you wish to ask Mr. Schary some preliminary questions?

Mr. BOBO. Mr. Schary, you are vice president in charge of production, and how long have you been with the movie industry, and in what capacity?

Mr. SCHARY. I have been working for films for 23 years in the capacity of a writer, a producer, and as an executive.

Mr. Bobo. As vice president in charge of production, it is more or less your responsibility to pass on the pictures that will be made, to make decisions on scripts as to what will be shown in the pictures?

Mr. Schary. That's right.

Chairman Kefauver. I think that we have a very good biographical background of Mr. Schary which shows his experience, some of the awards that he has won, some of the pictures that he introduced under his direction. Is this substantially correct? I think we will have it read into the record.

(The document referred to is as follows:)

Vice president in charge of production and head of studio operations, MGM. Newspaper and magazine columnist. Author alone and in collaboration on numerous pictures from 1932. Academy award, best original, 1938 (Boys' Town, MGM). In 1942 appointed an executive producer, MGM. In 1943 joined Vanguard Films, Inc., as producer executive vice president in charge production at RKO Radio Pictures, Inc.; January 1947, July 1948, vice president in charge of production, MGM.

Recent pictures: I'll Be Seeing You, Spiral Staircase, Till the End of Time, Farmer's Daughter, Bachelor and the Bobby-Soxer, Crossfire, Battleground, The Next Voice You Hear, Go For Broke, It's a Big Country, Westward the Women, Washington Story, Plymouth Adventure, Dream Wife, Take the High Ground.

Mr. Bobo. Mr. Schary, in the production of a motion picture, from the beginning of it in script form or book form, what is the attitude of the company with which you work with regard to crime and violence and brutality as are displayed in the movies that might be made?

Chairman Kefauver. Well first, Mr. Bobo, before he answers that question, Mr. Schary has been in this business for a long time and he knows about it; I think it would be interesting to those who read the record and certainly the Members of the Senate who read the hearings to have you state briefly just how a picture is produced from the beginning to the end, whose hands it goes through, and what happens.

Mr. Schary. I'll be glad to try and do that, Senator.

I think you should know that every picture has its own particular history and record. There are some 30,000 story ideas submitted during the course of an average year at a major studio. Those 30,000 ideas are probably sifted down to 1,000 which are considered the best by the reading department and/or the producer who may find the story, or the writer who may come in to discuss it with you, or director or the executive himself. I have to cover those thousand stories personally. Out of those 1,000 you pick then the 30 or 32 that will be the core of your production for a fiscal year. Those 30 or 32 are picked on the basis of balance of program, and hopefully on the artistic and commercial success of the picture.

Chairman Kefauver. Mr. Schary, are these 30,000 that are sent in by people all over the country?

Mr. Schary. They are sent in by agents. There are television shows that are covered. There are short stories covered in magazines. There are original ideas that are brought in by people to discuss them with you first by oral form and later on in script form. They come from a variety of sources.

Chairman Kefauver. Some of them are produced by your own writers?

Mr. Schary. That's right.

Chairman Kefauver. About what percentage are sent in and what percentage do your own people compose?

Mr. Schary. I'd better clarify it for you, sir. Of the 30 that are done or finished each year, I would say that no more than 5 come from within your organization. The other 25 usually come from without your organization from sources other than your own people, but your own people do the actual writing. The writers that you employ develop those ideas, or take the novel or the play and turn them into a screen play. It's only about, I would say 15 or 20 percent come from within your own organization, an idea that a producer may have for a picture, or a writer or a director. Does that clarify your question?

Chairman Kefauver. Yes, it does.

Mr. Schary. Now, the selection of those stories, as I say, is based on the balance you want in your program. You obviously can't make a series of pictures all on the same subject. You cannot make them all at the same cost. You have to balance cost and subject-material mostly in the interest of a balanced public, hopeful for the interest of a balanced public. Also another consideration today is the foreign business that our industry is doing, and we have to bear in mind the audience of other countries other than our own. This program is balanced in so-called action pictures, dramatic pictures, music pictures, color pictures, costume pictures, tropical pictures, and so on.

Chairman Kefauver. Now, the 32 that you have in a normal year, or was that last year that you produced 32?

Mr. Schary. Actually, last year we made 28. You usually prepare about 32 and you make 28.

Chairman Kefauver. Would you give a breakdown generally of the type of those 28 so that we can get some idea?

Mr. Schary. Well, last year we probably made 8 musical films, 4 costume pictures, I would say 8 so-called modern stories, and a couple of westerns, and the rest fell in those other categories in one way or another.

Chairman Kefauver. Very well. The idea, then, is accepted by you, and then what happens?

Mr. Schary. Well, after we agree to make the picture, the writer is assigned to develop it with a producer, sometimes with a director. They do a treatment of the story. During the arrangement of that treatment, they may see me and discuss the tone of the story. They may discuss the kind of a picture that it will be in terms of the size picture. After they have prepared the treatment, I will read it, and we will then have a discussion about it. We will have a discussion in terms of its dramatic integrity, its possibilities, its commercial aspects. They will then go and write a screen play, which is a regular continuity with all the dialog. Following completion of that screen play, we will have more discussion on the actual writing of the screen play. Once that is approved and put into final form, it is sent to a hundred-some-odd departments in the studio where it is analyzed for cost by these departments, screenery, costuming, and so on, and then the picture moves into its final stage of production, it is organized for production.

Probably much before that time, however, a director has been assigned to it; his ideas have been listened to and discussed with him, and then he takes over the active making of the picture, that is the shooting of the picture. The picture is put on the stage and shot. I will look at the film as it comes through, along with the producer and the director, and then we begin to assemble the picture; we begin to put those daily pieces of work together.

Following the shooting of the picture it is all strung together. We have what is called the rough cut, the rough showing. We look at it and we make our final decisions about it, do some cutting, perhaps some retaking of scenes that we do not like, and then the picture is handed over to the sound and music department where it is finally completed.

We then go out to preview the picture. If it is a good preview, we do very little; if it is a bad preview, we have to do a little bit more, and depending on the success of the first preview, we may or may not have a second preview, it is finally finished and given its final dubbing job, sound job, and then handed over to the various departments for sales and distribution.

Chairman KEFAUVER. Where is the script or the scenario submitted to the code committee?

Mr. SCHARY. Well, that is submitted in its very first form, and very often when we have a challenging story, a story that we feel may run into certain problems affecting the code, we will submit the story to them before we do the screenplay, and get their advice, and let them warn us as to where the sensitive points are, and that will guide us in the writing of the screenplay. Then we submit the screen play to them, the first act of the screenplay, and they send us a letter telling us what's wrong or what's right, telling us where the areas of danger are. If there seem to be points that need discussion, we will meet with Mr. Shurlock or his representatives and get everything straightened out.

Chairman KEFAUVER. Well then, after the first run or the rough film is made, does Mr. Shurlock or any members of the code committee review the picture as it——

Mr. SCHARY. They see the picture usually after we have previewed it. At that time it is still in very loose form and they call the corrections that they want to make. Sometimes they will see it before preview.

Chairman KEFAUVER. And then if they do have suggestions about changes, those are considered and usually made?

Mr. SCHARY. They are always made if they say they must be made.

Chairman KEFAUVER. And where is the advertising for the pictures prepared?

Mr. SCHARY. In the New York advertising office.

Chairman KEFAUVER. In your case by the Metro-Goldwyn-Mayer New York office?

Mr. SCHARY. That's right.

Chairman KEFAUVER. And each motion-picture producer has its own advertising department.

Mr. SCHARY. Each producing company.

Chairman KEFAUVER. Each producing company.

Mr. SCHARY. That's right.

Chairman KEFAUVER. There are some producing companies, though, that handle some advertising of some films for a number of independents, aren't there?

Mr. SCHARY. That's right. A company like United Artists handles independent productions, and in those cases I imagine that the independent producer has most to say about his own campaign.

Chairman KEFAUVER. Is there anything else you would like to tell about the industry generally or operations at Metro-Goldwyn-Mayer, before——

Mr. SCHARY. I think that covers generally our approach to finding our story material. I think perhaps as Mr. Bobo asks me some questions, we may get into other points that may be of interest.

Chairman KEFAUVER. All right. Go ahead, Mr. Bobo.

Mr. BOBO. Mr. Schary, you recently released a motion picture which has become rather controversial which is entitled "Blackboard Jungle." Would you give us your idea of the reasons for the production of this picture?

Mr. SCHARY. Well, we knew from the start that it would be a controversial film. When the book was circulated there was a good deal of interest in it. There were some people who were very shy about making the picture. We felt at M-G-M that it would make a very good report on a very serious problem of juvenile delinquency. I feel that if films do not make occasionally a controversial film, so-called controversial film, they will wither and die. It seems to be within the nature of good film making to occasionally make a film that will provoke talk and controversy, if you have a moral conviction that what you are provoking the controversy about is deserving of that attention. In the case of Blackboard Jungle, all of us have been aware of the increasing vandalism and of the increasing problems of juvenile delinquency.

I have a file here of dates, for instance, that we made before we bought the picture, which outlined for us the increasing damage that was being done by hoodlums not only in this State but through many States in the United States. I am sure you are all familiar, must be familiar, with the articles that appeared in magazines with Senate investigating committees that already reported that this was a very serious and terrible menace. We felt that Blackboard Jungle isolated dramatically a way of making a report to the Nation. As soon as we announced the production, there was a good deal of excitement about the picture. There were some souls who didn't want us to make it. That's perfectly all right, because that happens very often. There is hardly a successful picture, and I mean it when I say that hardly ever is a successful picture made that does not have in the background of its production a minority voice that pleads not to have it made, and that can go from as pleasant and certainly noncontroversial film as say Caruso to Blackboard Jungle. There is always somebody who has good reason why it should not be made. Usually when they are made they turn out fine, because they reflect actually a kind of interest in the subject, and in the case of Blackboard Jungle there were people, as I say, who didn't want it made. As I say, we felt we could be responsible and give an honest report. We believe at M-G-M that we have presented a very honest report. We are not frightened or intimidated or self-conscious about the controversy it stirred up, because we believe deeply and honestly that when the picture is reviewed a couple of years from now, it will be found that it did an awful lot of good, because it brought the subject into the public view.

Mr. Bobo. Is it your theory, Mr. Schary, that through the medium of motion pictures such as this that certain subjects such as this, the educational topic, the juvenile delinquency picture, can be brought to the attention of the public so that correction will be made?

Mr. Schary. That's right. You see, in the history of motion pictures—I wonder if I might take a few minutes to talk about public opinion in connection with pictures. Motion pictures very seldom—and I actually don't know of any cases where they anticipate public opinion or where they lead public opinion; in the main they reflect public opinion, and in some instances accelerate public opinion. This goes all the way back to motion picture making as far back as 1915 when the first so-called controversial film ever made was a picture stimulated by Theodore Roosevelt. It was called The Battle Cry of Peace, and it was a picture designed to alert American citizens to the dangers of Kaiserism. The picture provoked a good deal of interest. I am sure very few people have seen this picture, but I very definitely remember seeing it, and it did an awful lot to excite people and alert them to Kaiserism, and did a lot to fight the fight of the rather pro-German attitude that existed in America here as late as 1916, early 1916.

During the gangster era, our pictures again reflected public opinion. You remember those early gangster pictures, where the hero was mainly a young man who had come back from war, had been given a gun, had been taught how to kill, had his job taken away from him, and went into bootlegging because it was now a rather respectable business. That reflected public opinion because our attitude about the bootlegger in the early twenty's was very tolerant. He seemed to us to be kind of a nice guy. Sometimes he was our uncle or our cousin or our friend next door, and we had no feeling that he was doing anything highly immoral in terms of prohibition. Everybody was taking a drink whether there was a law or not, and we had a feeling that the bootlegger was a pretty nice guy, and that was reflected in our films.

It wasn't until the late twenties and early thirties when the menace of what had happened to the country suddenly became apparent. We became aware of the tremendous inroads that the Capone empire had made. We were made aware by Edgar Hoover's report that this was a serious condition. It was once compared by William Valeco, a writer, as the closest thing to a true underworld empire since the days of Catiline. And the public began to react to prohibition and to the gangster and the hoodlum element. Hoover got aid from the Government in terms of the FBI. We immediately reflected that public opinion too because our films changed. We went into a large group of G-men pictures at the time, and the very men who had played gangsters in some of our early pictures like Cagney, Robinson, Paul Muni, Pat O'Brien, et cetera, now were playing G-men, and they accelerated this public antipathy toward the gangster, and they did accelerate public opinion and did create a change.

This was certainly reflected by the interest the public had in those pictures. During the early days of nazism public opinion was very divided in the early thirties on the problem. Motion pictures actually did not deal with this subject until public opinion was quite clear about it. There were many of us in the industry who felt strongly about it, but we were not able to deal with it in terms of pictures because public opinion did not reflect a real serious anti-Nazi point of view. I think it was as late as 1937 when a poll taken revealed that a majority of the American people were not in favor of helping England at the expense of getting into a war with Germany. Then in 1939, a period of 2 short years, public opinion had switched itself, and a large portion of the public were willing to help England even at the risk of going to war. It was in that period when we began making the first anti-Nazi pictures, because we began to reflect that growing feeling in the United States that nazism was a very serious and dangerous menace. We perhaps did accelerate public opinion in connection with those pictures, and we helped reflect the public attitude toward this menace.

The same thing happened right after the war with the anti-Communist pictures that we made. There have been something like over 60 films made, anti-Communist pictures made, and I certainly think that they reflect again the public attitude, the public feeling about communism.

In connection with insulations against minority hatreds, pictures like Crossfire, Gentleman's Agreement, Pinky, Home of the Brave, Intruder in the Dust, they again reflected a public attitude against the hatred that suddenly broke out immediately after World War II when you had a little short, sharp rise of the Klan in America, and also the Columbus group; I think it was in Georgia, and they reflected the public revulsion against this type of hate, and we made those pictures that reflected that kind of hate.

In connection with Blackboard Jungle, I believe that what we have done is make a picture that again reflects a rise in public tide against the menace of delinquency that has gone too long unchecked.

Mr. Bobo. Do you think, Mr. Schary, that in sometimes reflecting the attitudes of the adult generation that we might at the same time be affecting the attitudes of the adolescent and juvenile generation?

Mr. Schary. I suppose that is a very reasonable point of view to take, and one would have to make a very definitive study, I think, however, to prove that what you say is true.

It would be my hunch, based on showings I have seen of Blackboard Jungle, that we are not doing any damage at all. We are associating younger people in terms of dramatic emphases with the schoolteacher and with those elements in the class that stand behind the teacher. I have seen a couple of runnings of the picture now—when I say "couple," by that I mean at least 5 or 6 runnings with audiences that have paid to see the picture—and their reactions are pretty much the same. One of the things is the usual demonstrations on the part of the kids towards the exciting music at the beginning, which now has that of a vogue, the rock-and-roll music, and in the early section they are laughing really at the teacher; they are with the gang. There is no doubt about that, and that's the way the picture was designed. But as the picture develops, and as the teacher's problem becomes dramatically clear, and as the attitude of the audience begins to switch away from the hoodlum elements in the class, they are with the teacher; they support those elements that support him, and in the showings I have seen they always applaud the end of the picture where the teacher triumphs over bad.

Mr. Bobo. Do you think it might be possible among some of the more hardened elements as were represented in that picture that they know that the picture itself in the last reel is going to turn out with the good triumphant, that they might have a tendency to emulate the type of character there, thinking it wouldn't happen to them?

Mr. SCHARY. Well, I don't know; I think what Dr. Frym said before is very interesting and it briught to mind an experiment we made some years ago when we were working with film in connection with experiments in impression. There was a short film made with the following scene, a very short scene in which a man on a street corner held a knife. A policeman came around the corner and grabbed the man, very hurriedly. The man took the knife, swung it at the policeman, the policeman then pushed him to one side, the man lunged at him again with the knife, and then ran away as another policeman approached. That was the scene. It was shown to people that we thought might be susceptible to another point of view. These were done without the people being aware they were part of an experiment. In an amazing amount of cases, almost 50 percent of the cases, some of the people reported that the policeman had come around the corner holding a knife and had tried to kill the man on the corner. Now, this is the exact same film that many of them saw, and I think it is very likely that there will be people wo go to see Blackboard Jungle or any other picture and come away with a point of view which they have brought to the picture themselves. They could see as harmless and has happy and as lovely a picture as Seven Brides and come away determined that the only way to get a girl is to kidnap her, and there is nothing much that we could do about that. I think that is the normal kind of risk that you make with a free screen and a free society.

Chairman KEFAUVER. Mr. Schary, it was reported in the Memphis paper, I am sure you have had an account of it,—I haven't seen Blackboard Jungle, but the report was that some girls went out and burned down the big barn at the fairgrounds for some unexplained reason, and when apprehended they said the reason they did it was they got the idea from Blackboard Jungle. What could be in the picture that could cause that?

Mr. SCHARY. Sir, I haven't the faintest idea. There is no fire in the picture; they can't pin that on us. I don't know, I'm inclined to believe that these girls arrested decided to associate themselves with some sort of a big headline subject.

Mr. Binford, as you know, had a point of view about the picture. And based on Mr. Binford's background, I am not so sure he wasn't a little irritated at the fact that one of the main characters was a Negro. That may not be fair to Mr. Binford; I don't know.

Chairman KEFAUVER. Mr. Binford is the man that passes on pictures in the city of Memphis?

Mr. SCHARY. Yes. For a while he refused us a license. But he has let the picture go by.

In any event, I just frankly believe it was an excuse. I don't believe it is a serious point of view.

Chairman KEFAUVER. Have you had any other reactions of that kind?

Mr. SCHARY. Well, I know there was one instance in New York City where a group of hoodlums were picked up and found with a copy of the book Blackboard Jungle in their pockets. I think that just happened to be a coincidence. They could have been found with any number of violent, busting novels available to them for sale at a very, very cheap price at most bookstores.

We have had many people who have written in about the picture, have said that the picture is very exciting, would provoke a change. There have been newspapers that have supported the picture and believe it will accomplish some good.

In New York City the recent study by the mayor's committee has revealed the exact points that the picture makes, that the problems of juvenile delinquency are reflections of the problems within the home, of a rather aching society, as a result of a series of wars that we have gone through and dislocations as a result of crowded city conditions, as a result of apathy on the part of the teachers to their student and as a result of apathy on the part of society to school-teachers.

There are so many contributing reasons and Blackboard Jungle doesn't pretend to be a panacea. It merely pretends—and I believe comes off well—to be an honest report of serious conditions.

Chairman KEFAUVER. Mr. Schary, you said in the case of Blackboard Jungle you were interested in a picture that would help in the juvenile delinquency problem. I know that was your intention and it is still a controversy among some people, as to just what the picture did do.

But who passes on matters of that kind, what advice do you have?

You gave an instance a few minutes ago of the different people that saw the police escapade in a different way.

Mr. SCHARY. Yes.

Chairman KEFAUVER. In the case of M-G-M do you have a kind of a committee or what kind of council do you have, or is there someone or some group for all the movie industry?

Mr. SCHARY. No. No, there isn't. In the case of Blackboard Jungle, that decision, whether good or bad, was my decision. Each person in the responsible position in the picture business has his own background and experience that he brings to making these decisions. If he makes enough bad ones, he gets fired. If he makes enough good ones, he remains in his job.

I have made some bad ones and will undoubtedly continue to make them, but they are my decisions. And in the case of Blackboard Jungle my decision was based on my own background, my own experience, my own knowledge about juvenile delinquency, and I know a little bit about it, and my own background with so-called controversial pictures.

The last one that involved me in a little bit of public struggle was a picture called Crossfire. There were many people that didn't want me to make this particular picture. They thought it would lead to more anti-Semitism. There were people that actually went into a trauma when they saw the picture, and believed, because the picture had violence in it, that it would encourage anti-Semites and bigots to start killing Semites, Jews, all through America.

We felt, on the other hand, it would insulate against anti-Semitism. We had tests made of the picture immediately following its release by psychologists from NYU, and that point of view was reaffirmed. The picture did insulate. And I think Blackboard Jungle will insulate against this, rather than accelerate it.

Chairman KEFAUVER. My point was, while you have good judgment, would it be of some help in a picture like Blackboard Jungle if you had actual experiences with the reaction of children themselves, or at least study of the picture before it is too far along, by psychiatrists and children experts?

Mr. SCHARY. Those studies are made, not quite as definitive perhaps as you are suggesting, Senator. But the subject material was discussed with people that I know, in the case of Blackboard Jungle, with 2 psychiatrists, 2 friends of mine.

The picture was then shown many times at previews. We previewed the picture four times, as a matter of fact, we showed it to a group of schoolteachers here in California, teachers who work here in California.

They had some points of view about it. We accommodated it for those points of view, because we felt they were valid. We made changes in this picture to accommodate for those reasonable points of view.

I don't want you to get the impression, in the case of any controversial film, that any one person or any one studio bulls his way along without listening to a rational point of view from someone else.

There were people consulted on Blackboard Jungle and there were people to advise us.

Chairman KEFAUVER. All right. Mr. Bobo.

Mr. BOBO. Mr. Schary, in the production of movies, to get across an emotional impact, may there sometimes be a tendency among directors or producers to put in extra scenes, say, of violence or brutality, or an extra fight to provide that extra emotional impact the audience might get, to make it sell?

Mr. SCHARY. I think that is possible, yes. I am sure that is possible. We are in a position to, in some instances, to correct that. In talking of pictures of violence, all of us must be aware there are certain pictures in which the scenes of violence actually are perfectly acceptable and very necessary to the audience. A case in point that comes to mind is a picture recently that we made called Bad Day At Black Rock. That picture had a very violent scene in it.

Our two toughest countries, in terms of violence, two countries that fight a good deal against violence, are India and Australia, and in both of these countries the picture was passed without a single solitary cut, which is very unusual. They felt that the picture, the violence in the picture was necessary to identify it with the cause of good.

Not every fight in the picture is bad. Not every bit of violence is damaging. I think it is very likely and certainly very possible that there are pictures in which there is too much violence and in which violence is done for violence's sake. I certainly would like to see less of that, but I don't know how possibly you could legislate that kind of bad judgment out of the making of motion pictures.

Chairman KEFAUVER. Mr. Schary, we had some testimony this morning with reference to the competition between television and movies, that television didn't act upon as strict a code basis and that when they had more violence, then there was the inclination of the movies to come up, or vice versa, whichever way it may be.

Have you noticed any evidences of that?

Mr. Schary. I don't think that is the accurate picture of the competitive function of TV. Actually, TV performs pretty much the same function that talking pictures provided in the theaters years ago. When talking pictures came along there was a whole group of people who believed the theater was through. Actually, the only thing through in the theater was a long list of mediocre plays that the motion picture business inherited, because we were able to make them cheaper and make them available to the public on a cheaper basis.

The theater at that time produced, I would guess, somewhere around 220 to 250 plays a year. Today there are only some 90 plays produced in the theater, but they are generally of a better caliber, they are more provocative, and they are much more successful and they run for a longer period of time, probably because there are less of them available to the public. Talking pictures took over that large amount of storymaking.

Television has taken over again from us a large number of these so-called budget pictures and smaller subject pictures. We used to make somewhere between 450 and 500 pictures in this business. I would guess that we will make somewhere around 300 or 350 and perhaps in years to come even less number, and that television has taken that other group of stories from us. We hope that they have inherited some of our mediocrity for the time being.

Chairman Kefauver. Mr. Schary, do you make any pictures for television?

Mr. Schary. No, sir, not at our studio.

Chairman Kefauver. Not at your studio?

Mr. Schary. No, sir.

Chairman Kefauver. Do any of the larger movie producers make any pictures for television?

Mr. Schary. As I understand it, Columbia Pictures, I believe, had a subsidiary that makes some film for TV; I don't know how much, though.

Paramount I know does not make any. Twentieth Century-Fox, I believe, has started a program of a small group of pictures that are designed primarily to export their own product on television. I don't think it is actual production for television. I am not sure of that.

Warner Bros. I think have the same kind of program as Twentieth-Fox. We at this point are not making any.

Chairman Kefauver. My next question has to do with a rather philosophical approach. I was interested in your remarks about the time the bootlegger was accepted, that he was rather favorably presented; that at the time that it was apparent that nazism was becoming a menace, that you probably accelerated the antagonism toward nazism and fascism. That, of course, is a tremendous responsibility that you take in your hands, in deciding whether something is good or bad.

Mr. Schary. Yes.

Chairman Kefauver. It may be that a very little minority position would be the correct position. Yet if public opinion were swinging the other way or was predominantly the other way, according to what you have just said, chances are your movies would reflect that predominant public opinion.

Mr. Schary. I think that is a very, very good question and legitimate. I thing it is a legitimate risk, sir. We can only hope there will be enough people in the motion picture industry constantly who will reflect the better and best and big majority point of view that exists in our democracy, which usually reflects, I believe honestly, those things for the best.

There is always room for minority opinion in the making of a picture, and the proof of that is the pictures are made that some people don't want made.

You must understand that when a picture becomes controversial and does reflect public opinion it may not at that time reflect a popular point of view, even though it may reflect public opinion.

I think that, as I said before, is a normal, healthy risk you have to take in a free society, free screen, and free press and free everything.

Chairman KEFAUVER. I can see that. I have frankly been somewhat worried, in our country usually when we start to take a position we go so far overboard usually in taking it, to such an extent that we sometimes lose the ability to reason about it.

Mr. SCHARY. I think that is very good, a very good observation. Unfortunately, you have a good protection against that, which is the public opinion. If the public opinion finally becomes surfeited they stop going. And as soon as they stop going we stop making them. You can depend on the public to always tip us off, whether we are out of line or not. They just won't go to see those pictures that they don't want to go to see.

Chairman KEFAUVER. But your pictures, though, tend to mold or keep in an attitude that public opinion might be in the national interest for it to be swinging back the other way.

Mr. SCHARY. I don't think that is true. I think again because we are always 5 or 6 months late, we are 5 or 6 months behind, we will shift in changes in public opinion. And if we have an opinion that is not in tune, in we are late, if we have guessed wrong, the public just is indifferent to the picture and they won't go.

We are not molding their opinion at all. They just dismiss the picture if they are, for instance, tired of being talked to on the subject of communism or fascism or lynching or anything else, why, they just won't go to see the pictures. We can make them and try and get them to have a point of view about it, but it won't do any good.

Chairman KEFAUVER. But you have already got your investment in them and you are trying to get your houses to show them.

Mr. SCHARY. That is right. Then we are out of luck, because the houses won't show them. There is no love lost generally between the exhibitor and the picturemaker. That is something you learn.

We can't show pictures that the public doesn't want to see. There has been no way found of getting the public to buy a picture they don't want to go to see. We can spend $5 million advertising it and they won't go. And the records are full and bloody with instances of that kind. They just won't go.

Chairman KEFAUVER. Mr. Schary, with all of the problem we have with juvenile delinquency, is MGM—I assume you will—continue to think about ways, as to the point of view, ideas you might have to curb delinquency, to get people to give our kids a better opportunity and create better attitudes on their part?

Mr. SCHARY. I hope we will continue to search for material, and I hope we can find material that will express other facets, other phases of this problem and perhaps other pictures that will have constructive points of view to make about ways of licking this problem. Those are very hard to find. We are always open for anything that we feel will do some good.

Chairman KEFAUVER. Do you have anything else that you would like to tell us about?

Mr. SCHARY. No, sir, I really don't think so.

I would only like to comment on something actually that you yourself commented on in your opening statement, and that refers to the list of pictures that were in the newspaper this morning.

I just had a little feeling that if we are to do a definitive study of juvenile delinquency or the effect of motion pictures on juvenile delinquency, it seems to me it would be like doing a study of how do newspapers affect juvenile delinquency, and in doing such a definitive study we would have to talk about all newspapers. We would have to discuss the highly responsible ones along with the ones that may not be responsible.

I felt if we were going to do a serious study of how movies affect the younger generation, we would have to make up a different list. We shouldn't just get the list of the 12 provocative and in some instances not highly representative pictures. I think you would have to deal with pictures like The Robe, Roman Holiday, Lili, Little Boy Lost, Rear Window, and a long list of other pictures that have a plus influence, and find out what kind of a balance we make on the young mind. I think the balance would turn out to be a very, very good one myself. I know it would be difficult to make such a study, but I think at the time we study the negative we must try and study the positive.

Chairman KEFAUVER. I certainly agree with you, and I hope we have not left the impression that we do not think a great predominance of the movies that come out are on the plus side. I think that is true.

Mr. SCHARY. As I say, sir, you made that as your statement.

Chairman KEFAUVER. A good part of them are good, but it doesn't mean we wouldn't like to see less of the undesirable ones, fewer and fewer undesirable ones.

Mr. SCHARY. I can assure you as a picturemaker I would also like to see less unsuccessful pictures.

Chairman KEFAUVER. Yes.

Mr. SCHARY. Thank you.

STATEMENT OF Y. FRANK FREEMAN, VICE PRESIDENT, PARAMOUNT PICTURES, INC., HOLLYWOOD, CALIF.

Chairman KEFAUVER. I have a brief biographical sketch of Mr. Freeman's business career, among which it says he was born in Georgia and went to the Georgia Tech.

Mr. FREEMAN. That is right.

Chairman KEFAUVER. And you have been with Paramount since 1926; is that correct?

Mr. FREEMAN. Since 1933.

Chairman KEFAUVER. We will make this biographical sketch a part of the record, which I feel fills in some details.

Vice president, Paramount Pictures, Inc., born Greenville, Ga., December 14, 1890. Educated Georgia Institute of Technology, Atlanta (EE).

With S. A. Lynch enterprises (theater), 1916–32 (division of Paramount from 1926).

Joined Paramount, New York, January 18, 1933; elected vice president of Paramount Pictures in charge of theater operations, 1935; in 1938 named vice president in charge of studio operations.

President, Association of Motion Picture Producers, Inc., 1940–44. Member, National Committee, WAC; chairman, Motion Picture Producers Association, 1947–48; chairman, Los Angeles branch, Federal Reserve Board, 1944–47; chairman, Research Council, Motion Picture Producers, Hollywood, 1945–47; director, deputy chairman, Federal Reserve Board, San Francisco, 1954–55.

All right, Mr. Bobo.

Mr. Bobo. Mr. Freeman, I think you as vice president in charge of Paramount Pictures have some definite ideas on the role of motion pictures in all the facets of human life, especially that dealing with juvenile delinquency.

Do you care to make a statement about your experience in the motion picture field?

Mr. Freeman. To start off, let me say that I speak pure Georgian English, and if the audience doesn't understand me, I know you and the Senator will, being from the neighboring State of Tennessee.

Mr. Bobo. Yes.

Chairman Kefauver. Yes, indeed.

Mr. Freeman, we will get these mikes closer so they can hear you, whether they understand you or not.

Mr. Freeman. All right. I have spent the last 17 years of my life in Hollywood. I spent the earlier part of my life in New York and Georgia and in the theatrical field.

When I came to Hollywood I had no knowledge whatsoever of the way or how or why you produced a motion picture. I was handed a studio and told to operate it. The mistakes were never caught up with because it took too long for them to find out just what I had done wrong.

In my years of association with people in the Hollywood branch of the motion-picture industry, that is, the branch that makes the pictures, I have found simply a cross section of America, and, let me say, of the world.

Our community is composed of about 25,000 workers in all fields and they come from all areas of the country, small towns, big towns, the country. They represent a cross section of the thinking, of the lives and the morals of the people of this country, and let me say, also, of other countries.

I would think that there are in our industry no less than 750 writers who work not all the time but at times in the development of stories and scripts for motion pictures.

I would say there are 300 directors who act in their individual capacity with reference to the direction of a motion picture. I would say that there are 150 producers, who also work in that capacity as producers of pictures.

All of these people, thinking individually and not collectively, nor dominated by any group that controls their thinking, that is, I think, the greatest safeguard that the American motion pictures have today.

God forbid that the time will ever come when the thinking of those people must be through a controlled channel, from whatever source it may originate. At that time you can rest assured the value, the effect of the motion picture ceases to exist, because the motion picture is a medium of entertainment. It represents a field of entertainment for the great masses of the people of the world. They are the quickest, the people, and they recognize propaganda as such immediately and they are not interested. And wherever in any country there has been an attempt to base a control on pictures with propaganda on the public, they are not successful.

I have found among these people that I have mentioned good men, the great majority good, and some bad ones, as you will find in your hometown or in any city or any place you may go. I have found that the majority of these people recognize that when they come into the motion-picture industry they have accepted a trust, a trust that imposes upon them an obligation much deeper than maybe the man, the average man in the street, or woman, layman, would feel they had, because through this medium that is at their disposal they recognize what they do, what they use in that medium can have its effect upon people throughout the world, and are finally conscious of this.

I think we are the one industry that has a separate code, production code. I am a great admirer of people that administer that code. I think it is a safeguard to the public, that a great majority of motion pictures will be in an area that is acceptable, in good taste and, certainly, never in an area where they simply know emotional impact or know excitement. If so, the picture, as Mr. Schary so aptly said, will not succeed, and the person who is responsible for the production of such pictures will soon be looking for another job.

For anyone to say that errors have not been made would be very foolish. They will continue to be made. The perfect man, as I understand, has never been found, or the perfect administrator, nor the fellow who can maybe make all the decisions right.

In the operation of the Paramount Studio it may differ somewhat from the operation of the Metro Studio, the same as Fox may differ, because there I do not have the experience that Mr. Schary has had in fields of writing and in actual production of motion pictures. My job has been as executive administrator, to employ the people that are creative and to have as my right-hand assistant a man who furnishes, as Mr. Schary does, in the way of supervising the actual production of the pictures.

However, no picture comes out of the Paramount Studios for which I can in any way deny responsibility. I have full charge of the studio and if an error is made, that error is mine, because I always have the right to say no, and I do not lay at the feet of the men who may make the picture a charge it was their fault or their responsibility. It is mine. I have made some mistakes, I have made many. I will continue to make more. And the man that sits at the desk where I sit, with an allocation of $35 million to be used in the making of 18 or 20 motion pictures—we do not make as many as Metro—having to reach a decision, and those pictures averaging anywhere from a million and a half to our latest one, which is $11 million, and make that decision upon a piece of paper which yet hasn't been developed into a screenplay or into a final motion picture, and spend that money that belongs to somebody else—it is not his money—it is a terrific responsibility, and one that you have to always, regardless of your personal opinion, rely somewhat upon the economic situation and what the possibility of box-office value is and the story or the idea you are thinking of might have at the box office, in order to see that stockholders, whose money you are spending, get a fair chance of their investment being safe and sound.

There are no peculiarities particularly in our business. I was born in Greenville, Ga., a town of 814. I came to Hollywood with all of the things that people say about Hollywood and Hollywood people, that a stranger there would last 3 months, 4 months, 5 months. And I have never found a more friendly, a more American, a more corial group of people than composed in the motion-picture industry, and a group that I will stand by and with at any time, any place, in defense of their deep sense of obligation to their community, to their public, and to the problems that exist in our country.

And doing that, I will tell you, Senator, I will still make a lot of mistakes, but we will do it forthrightly, we will do it courageously and we will take our penalty for the mistakes we make, without asking for any sympathy whatsoever. We will stand on our record of the job that has been done by American motion pictures in every section of the world, in carrying the American way of life to all peoples of the world, so that today 80 percent of the playing time on all theaters of the world are American motion pictures.

I think that is about my statement.

Chairman KEFAUVER. Mr. Freeman, we appreciate your forceful and good general statement. What particular considerations are you giving at Paramount to this problem we are investigating, as to the welfare of our children and the difficulty of juvenile delinquency? Do you have any or are you planning any particular pictures that will try to furnish leadership in bettering this general situation?

Mr. FREEMAN. Well, in the end result I hope so. We are preparing and trying to work out a story now that is on the delinquency of some parents in their homes, and what they do that brings about maybe a broken life and leads to greater contribution, I think, to juvenile delinquency than any other media.

I am one who believes that the fault does not lie in the newspapers, does not lie in television, does not lie in motion pictures. I am one of those fellows born in a country town, raised by parents who I think understood—and I think maybe you had the same experience, Senator,—what it meant for the children to recognize their mother and father and for the mother and father to live the kind of lives that would be something the children could respect, and bring them up in a way that the problem that you have today doesn't exist.

In my opinion, when you wind it all up and make all the examinations you can go through, all of the research you can make, it will come right back to the source of the foundation of our way of life in this country, and that is the home. Drinking liquor, divorce, we didn't start it; it starts at the source of the family heart.

Chairman KEFAUVER. Mr. Freeman, my hometown was not quite as big as Greenville, but I know what you are talking about.

Mr. FREEMAN. Good. You knew what a hickory switch was.

Chairman KEFAUVER. "Hells Island" which you produced has been criticized some, particularly the advertisements in connection with it.

Mr. FREEMAN. I think it is very bad; no excuse for it.

Chairman KEFAUVER. The advertisements?

Mr. FREEMAN. The advertisements.

Chairman KEFAUVER. You see it back there [indicating].

Mr. FREEMAN. I have seen it. If you could see my criticism of it, I don't think it would bear to go into the record.

Chairman KEFAUVER. How come you let the advertisement go through?

Mr. FREEMAN. I don't control it.

Chairman KEFAUVER. You don't control the advertisements?

Mr. FREEMAN. No, I do not. Advertising of all Paramount pictures is controlled out of New York, under the direction of the head of distribution and the general advertising manager. He can be honest in what he does.

Because I disagree with him and say what I do doesn't necessarily mean I am right and he is wrong. I don't mean that.

Chairman KEFAUVER. Don't you have the authority to change this man or direct what he does?

Mr. FREEMAN. No, I haven't. My problem here at the studio is in charge of production of the picture, the manufacture of the product. When I finish it I turn it over to New York, to the distributing department. It then takes charge of the sales policy and the advertising policy and the distribution of the picture.

Chairman KEFAUVER. Don't you think the code ought to apply to the advertising as well as to the picture itself?

Mr. FREEMAN. There is an advertising code.

Chairman KEFAUVER. But apparently it is not working too good.

Mr. FREEMAN. It is there in New York, in the office of the Motion Picture Producers Association, and I say it is my understanding that all ads and all stills have to be submitted to this code for approval before they are released; I say that is my understanding.

Chairman KEFAUVER. Well, it would seem that since you have the responsibility for the impression that Paramount pictures make for the good or the bad, that it is not quite fair to impose advertising that you don't agree with, upon the reputation of Paramount over which you have charge.

Mr. FREEMAN. Well, I think that one of the problems which is hard to understand, that exists in the making and in a company trying to produce 18 pictures a year, or see that they are produced, is that you have to delegate authority and you have to divide it up. No one man is mentally or physically able to supervise the responsibilities of all branches of producing, distributing and sales organization, such as Metro or Fox or Paramount or Warner or any other major studio.

I want to be fair, Senator, because I disagree on something and I don't think it is right, I am not going to say that my position is perfectly right and the other man's is perfectly wrong. There may be an honest difference of opinion. I only express my personal opinion.

Chairman KEFAUVER. Mr. Schary told how the code operated in connection with Metro pictures. Is that about the same arrangement or same system you have?

Mr. FREEMAN. I think it is exactly the same in every instance. The idea is you buy a story, you take it up to see if there is objectionable things with the code administrator. You follow it through with the first script and present it. If they have things they wish to suggest to you that are not according to the code, they do it and you change it, and then when you finally make the picture you present it to them for approval and if there are scenes still in the picture that don't come out just right, the code says it has to be changed, you argue it out with them, as to what changes, and finally decide on it.

Chairman KEFAUVER. With Paramount, does the opinion of the code always finally prevail?

Mr. FREEMAN. Paramount has never released a motion picture in its history, insofar as I know—and certainly not within my 17 years of experience here—that did not have the code approval, the code seal.

Chairman KEFAUVER. Mr. Bobo, are you going to bring out by some witness how many of the producers there are that are, and whether there are any or not, members of the code association?

Mr. BOBO. Yes, sir.

Chairman KEFAUVER. Do you have any questions, Mr. Bobo?

Mr. BOBO. I think that is all.

Chairman KEFAUVER. Thank you very much.

Mr. FREEMAN. I would, before closing, like to say—and this is: call it a plug for motion pictures, if you wish, but I think if you will think about the responsibility the industry has assumed, for instance, in making a picture like The Ten Commandments, which is possibly the biggest motion picture ever made by the industry, under the direction of a man like Mr. De Mille, you will find they do think in the area of what an impact a picture of this kind can have on the world today.

And also, in pointing up what Mr. Schary said, it just happens to be a Paramount picture, that Paramount is making The Ten Commandments. It would be just as good or as great if it were made by any other studio.

When you start to get ready to think of developing a story into a final motion-picture production, there can be a period of time from 15 to 24 months before that final product is seen on the screens of the country. So many things can happen in that interim period that had you known at the time you started you might have thought differently about it.

But today if I start to get ready to have a picture produced or made at the Paramount Studio an idea suggested, by the time the screenplay is finished, by the time it is possible to cast it and find all the different component parts necessary to make it, having completed the shooting schedule on it, the process then of editing and, as Mr. Schary said, going in for music and sound, finishing all of that and going, if it is a color picture, to your color laboratory to get what you call your answer print, and then find out from previews if it is right or not, and finally get your print out, and a period in between to advertise it, if you get it out within 18 to 20 months you have done a very good job.

There are times when things happen in between that would make you feel that maybe you wouldn't have done this had you known at that day you started what was going to happen in September 2 years later.

Chairman KEFAUVER. We thank you very much for your cooperation, for coming here and being with us, Mr. Freeman.

Mr. FREEMAN. Thank you.

Chairman KEFAUVER. The subcommittee will stand in recess for 10 minutes.

(Short recess taken.)

STATEMENT OF JACK L. WARNER, PRODUCER AND VICE PRESIDENT, WARNER BROS. PICTURES, INC., HOLLYWOOD, CALIF.

Chairman KEFAUVER. Mr. Warner, we appreciate your coming and giving us the benefit of your many years of experience and your views on the subject.

I have a biographical sketch here which tells all the good and bad things you have done.

Apparently, you started in the business back in 1918.

Mr. WARNER. Way back there. It was in 1905.

Chairman KEFAUVER. 1908. Entered distribution with formation Duquesne Amusement Co. at Pittsburgh in 1908.

Mr. WARNER. It was about 3 years before that. That is all right.

Chairman KEFAUVER. That was with your late brother, Sam Warner. This is a long experience you have had, and we will put this biographical sketch in the record at this point.

With late brother Sam produced "My Four Years in Germany" (1917). In 1918 took charge of Warner Sunset studios in Hollywood; 1919, with brothers pioneered in development of talking pictures; in charge of west coast studios since.

Academy awards for best production: "The Life of Emile Zola," 1937; "Casablanca," 1943.

In 1933, appointed by President Roosevelt chairman NRA board of California. Commissioned lieutenant colonel, United States Air Force. Many decorations.

Member: Committee for Economic Development, National Aeronautics Association, Air Patrol League, Southern California Symphony Association, Beverly Hills Community Council, Beverly Hills Chamber of Commerce, et cetera.

Now, you tell us about——

Mr. WARNER. Yes, sir. There is only one thing I would like to add as correction. I was born in London, Ontario, Canada. My parents moved to Lynchburg, Va. I want to get the southern feeling in this.

Chairman KEFAUVER. That is getting down in Davy Crockett territory.

Mr. WARNER. That is correct. I want to make sure that——

Chairman KEFAUVER. We had Georgia and South Tennessee and now Virginia.

Mr. WARNER. Yes. From Lynchburg we moved to Youngstown, Ohio, where they really claim me.

About Davy Crockett—I don't know whether this is supposed to be a pun or not—the local papers last Sunday carried a story of the love and life of Davy Crockett. I don't know whether it has anything to do with the order of business or not.

Chairman KEFAUVER. He is a great hero in Tennessee.

Mr. WARNER. He is all over the world. He is doing a big job.

Chairman KEFAUVER. I think it might be of interest in this argument whether Davy Crockett was born in Tennessee or North Carolina, he wasn't born in either State. Back in 1792, what is now Tennessee was created as the State of Franklin. It lasted three and a half or four years. That is when Davy was born.

Mr. WARNER. He has done a good job with his predecessors.

Chairman KEFAUVER. Yes, he is a fine man, Davy.

Mr. WARNER. He has a corner on all the coonskin caps.

I think I would rather be serious; if you don't mind a little spice of life occasionally, it is all right sometimes.

The cause you represent, I believe, is a serious one. I just tried to diagnose and think over to myself in the last day or two of what could have been, or what has caused the delinquency of juveniles throughout not only America, but I believe it is throughout the world, and I came across several phases, one in particular within the last 40 years, that there has been a complete change in the mode of life in our country.

That era, the prohibition era, when law and order were completely disregarded, tended to create not only juvenile delinquency, but there was much adult delinquency. I feel during that period of time of disrespect and disregard of law and order, we all know, especially all the older fellows, and girls as well, that everybody tossed aside—law meant nothing, to any degree, and particularly I am speaking of the prohibition era.

Therefore, I feel over the years there has come many, many children of the parents of the period who saw this lack of law and order, and the disrespect, it grew up into now what may be many of the juvenile delinquents, or it may be the parents of many of them. I feel that had something to do with it.

Along that very particular order we happened to, I believe, have made the first motion pictures that brought to the surface that very era; naming one, the first one was "Public Enemy." We showed conclusively just exactly the operation of the gangsters of the period, the prohibition operation, whatnot, whatnot. We made a picture "Little Caesar" and probably a half a dozen others, all with great, with what I thought had social contact, so much so that it sounds very much sort of a comic nature now, but at the time it was rather serious.

When I went to New York then one of our films was showing at our theater there and I went to some speakeasy and I met one of the boys I knew, and I said that I thought they were mad at me because we had been showing them up.

He said, "No, it is great. Me and my gal have been up here three times. We are going again to see it."

I felt, although that was humorous, the seriousness behind it these pictures brought to the surface, to the public, and to the hoodlums, just exactly what they were, and I feel had much to do with law and order taking hold again or at least steering it into an avenue, whatever it may be, and bringing it to the surface and stamping it out. It had a lot to do with it, as a matter of fact.

Another film we made at the time was called "G–Men." It was a history to a degree, more or less, of the G–man, J. Edgar Hoover, of the time; I think about 1928, 1930. Many of the things we showed in the film were things that Mr. Hoover was trying to get, such as his

FBI men being armed. They weren't permitted to carry arms at the time. We showed the arming of FBI men and how they could protect themselves and protect law and order, and whatnot. It all came to pass, which is now in existence.

I feel that motion pictures have done a great job in that respect. We have really shown life in the raw, shown the cause, shown the effect and we show the cure. In fact, the New York Times dubbed this as combining good citizenship with good picturemaking. In fact, we have used that slogan quite often ever since. In fact, it is quite a good one. Not only in just this type of film, but I mean in pictures of every walk of life, probably a thousand or more, in that number.

Chairman Kefauver. Pictures certainly have a great impact on the kind of citizens, good or bad, that we are going to have.

Mr. Warner. Yes. Another thing I felt, in addition to the prohibition debacle, which I believe apparently it turned out, so far as I am concerned, was the world wars that we have, both the hot and cold, over the period of about 32, 33, 34 or 35 years. That, too, has seen what I would say were life and human rights, where they were at the lowest ebb.

I happened to have been in the war, at the end of the war, in Dachau. I saw the operation of that particular camp, and there was no human rights whatsoever. Naturally, we depicted films—when I came back I happened to make a picture called "Hit or Live" where I redepicted the things I am mentioning here. I won't go into a long dissertation on it.

The world has, of course, been evolving around some very, very troublesome times. The matter, as I see it in the last 40 or 50 years of my life, has been that everybody—those years have been very, very tough years, and that had a lot to do with the planting of the seed of juvenile delinquency.

After all, if you are in a war or in peace, whatever it may be, you see law and order being disrespected, tossed aside, people getting off easy or getting off hard, whatever it may be, I think it has a lot to do with creating the juvenile delinquency problem we are facing today.

I feel committees of your kind, all American citizens who think right, can do a lot to eradicate and stamp out this; I know they can. Committees of your kind have done great jobs heretofore and I know you can do this one by the very idea of going around to citizens and bringing it to the attention of the people, the mothers and fathers and kids themselves realizing just what they are doing.

Let's show them in pictures, if we can do good, or show it in everything that is printed, if it does good. It does do good. There has been a bad one here and there, which there is in everything. But on the whole you will find—I have very rarely ever seen a film that hasn't had some kind of a moral, either for good or bad, but they have some kind of a moral. I feel the prohibition, the years of the wars has planted all this. Kids are tough. I, too, was brought up in Youngstown, Ohio. It wasn't an easy town. It was a mixture of all races and a pretty tough town; a steel town. I haven't been there in 30 years. I guess it is all right now.

When we make these films we must have this dramatic content or you just can't make a motion picture. You are not living in a tranquil world, Utopia, because it really doesn't exist. When you make a film you have to show the bad and good and how good triumphs. Unless you have a comparison, as I said before, you do not have the cause and effect. That is about all I can say on that.

About parents not giving their children guidance and so forth and so on, all that, that is every parent's own opinion. No doubt the fathers and mothers who told their children what to do, they think they are doing the right. That is only a personal opinion of the people, which I wouldn't have any control over. It is up to the people themselves.

I just made some notes here to try to guide myself. Other people have touched on the divorce problem of the homes and the environment, the confusion of children, and so forth, which is virtually the A. B. C. of the whole juvenile delinquency project, is the way I see it.

I feel that motion pictures do a great social service on the whole, and I heard Mr. Freeman say nobody is perfect. We have made many, many bad films. We have the majority of good films.

Not only—in addition to making motion pictures of feature lengths, we make short features, we make cartoons for children like "Bugs Bunny" and "Tweetie Pie" and, oh, all kinds of things, and patriotic films, and we have the Warner-Pathé newsreels.

Going back to 1918, my brother and I produced a silent film called My Four Years in Germany by Ambassador Girard at the time, depicting the coming of World War I. During World War II, oh, 50 films. To give you one or two, The Confessions of a Nazi Spy. I was the first man who made a picture showing nazism in all its raw form, who, under the threat of death in written form by the local German consul—not the word "death," he didn't use that, but words to that effect, "You better not do this." That was in 1932, called Confessions of a Nazi Spy. I have the letter.

Also recently we just made a picture, I Was a Communist for the FBI. We are always trying to do something for the good of our country. Not always do we make it as a matter of a commercial project. Many of these pictures do not succeed, but, however, being in a large business as we are we can afford to do something maybe the individual fellow can't. We can try to make things good for our country. Commercially, yes, and if not, nothing is lost.

Mr. Freeman put in what we term in the movies or motion pictures as sort of a "plug" for big pictures. I want to name 2; he only named 1. Two, so I give him two for one. We have one called The Land of the Pharaohs. We have over 45,000 people in it. We made it in Egypt and in Italy.

We have another called Helen of Troy equally as big; on a big scale, tremendous investment.

We hope that these pictures—they are educational. The Land of the Pharaohs is a great educational film and shows the building of the pyramids, and Helen of Troy is, of course, Homer's Iliad original love story.

I think I have about covered everything I have to say, other than I have been in this business all my life, ever since I was about 9 years old. I don't want to say how old I am now. But I have always found it a great pleasure. When things go bad, why, you feel a little down in the mouth. When things are good you are right up there smiling. If you do a good film that does good for your country, commercially, why, you feel wonderful, and if not, you keep trying.

Chairman KEFAUVER. How many pictures does Warner Bros. make a year?

Mr. WARNER. In the last 15 years we have made as high as 70 pictures. We are down now to where we do about 30.

Chairman KEFAUVER. And what particular attention do you give to the matter of juvenile delinquency—an opportunity for our kids— what contribution are you making to the cause we are talking about here?

Mr. WARNER. We are producing, just about finished the film called Rebel Without a Cause. It is not the book that we talked about the other day, but it is a story where we are trying—not trying, we have shown where the parents are at fault and probably switch it around and call it juvenile delinquency of parents.

Chairman KEFAUVER. That hasn't been released as yet?

Mr. WARNER. No.

Chairman KEFAUVER. We have had some calls saying this is not a good picture, from the viewpoint of influence on young people.

Mr. WARNER. They must be working from radar, because I myself haven't seen it put together. You mustn't believe everything you get by call—I guess you know that by now.

Chairman KEFAUVER. I don't believe everything I get by calls. Some of these people seem to know what they were talking about. One or two of them seemed right reliable. I thought I would ask you about it.

Mr. WARNER. They are not sore they didn't make the picture themselves, are they? Are these competitors?

Chairman KEFAUVER. No, I am very serious. No, they are not competitors. They are people interested in the public interest and welfare of people.

Mr. WARNER. All I will say is that the picture will stand for what it is. I am responsible for it personally. While I am not the producer or director or writer, as Mr. Freeman explained, it works virtually the same in all studios.

Chairman KEFAUVER. Do you pass on the pictures finally, before they are released?

Mr. WARNER. Final editing, we call it; yes, sir.

Chairman KEFAUVER. What group do you have in the way of psychiatrists or people that know something about the reaction of young people? What group do you have consider your pictures or the parts of them, from that viewpoint?

Mr. WARNER. Well, in fact, every film we go into we go into with expert advice. If we make a Navy, Marine film, whatever it is, we have officers assigned from the Department of Defense.

In this particular film, it is very prevalent with what we are naturally interested in. I would like to recite some of the people who have helped in making the picture.

Chairman KEFAUVER. You mean some of the people you have consulted with from the viewpoint of impact on youth?

Mr. WARNER. Not only did they help, but they aided and examined the scenario and I would say steered us to more or less the things they thought were not right, and we would naturally change it, from expert opinions.

The first name is Dr. Douglas Kelly, criminologist of the University of California at Berkeley, chief examining psychiatrist at the United

States Army, at the Nuremberg war trials, lecturer and adviser to the police department; and Dr. H. R. Brickman, California Youth Authority; Dr. Coudley, chief psychiatrist at the juvenile hall; Hon. Judge William B. McKesson; Dr. David Bogen, director of juvenile hall; Mr. Gentilli of the Boys' Group Movement; Carl Holtman, probation officer; Capt. Ben Stein, California Youth Authority.

Furthermore, I have a letter here from Dr. Kelly to the director of the film, stating that he had read the script, and so forth and so forth.

Here is one I brought from the youth authority for the State of California, signed Dr. H. R. Brickman. It says:

DEAR MR. URIS—

he was one of the writers—

I consider it a privilege to have been of some possible aid to your very worthwhile artistic undertaking. You most certainly did not overstay your welcome. As mentioned in our conversation, I would be most happy to be of any further assistance at any time. My best regards.

And so forth.

We very thoroughly go into specialization, with people who know their particular fields, when we do anything. And I would say in every film there is the story of Dien Bien Phu. We had a French colonel flown all the way from Dien Bien Phu.

We made a film called Jump Into Hell. Schary or Freeman said we were too late. Before we could make the film or put it out everybody had forgotten it, Dien Bien Phu. It was all washed out. However, we made the film and took the loss. We were very authentic, by the way, but nobody came to see it.

Mr. YOUNG. May I rise, as you suggested?

Chairman KEFAUVER. All right, sir. Tell us your name.

Mr. YOUNG. Young; Jack R. Young.

Chairman KEFAUVER. All right, Mr. Young. What do you arise for?

Mr. YOUNG. Mr. Warner, in stating of the pictures he has made, Mr. Warner has failed to state that the Warner Bros. studio, under his supervision, during the period of time, has made more gangster pictures than all major studios combined, so much so that the churches throughout the country had gotten together and preached to the congregation not to attend these pictures, gangster pictures, where they were shown.

And the late Mr. Will Hayes, who then was designated or engaged as the producers' representative, had insisted that a code be drawn up, whereby pictures of the nature of gangsters that would influence delinquency of children, as well as adults, be stopped.

For a while that code was adhered to, but since then, I regret to say, as a motion picture cameraman—and Mr. Warner has known me for many years, perhaps 30 or more—that that condition at this time is prevailing; that children, youths, are influenced by the presentation, such as was stated by Mr. Mooring, of Black Tuesday, whereby a police officer had helped a criminal plant a gun in the execution chamber under a chair.

That is not a true conviction of that criminal, but is exaggerated for the suspense in showing, where a police officer in a penal institution had planted a gun, a loaded gun in the presence——

Chairman KEFAUVER. Mr. Young, Mr. Warner is on the stand. You had something to say, and let's don't get off the subject.

Mr. YOUNG. That is right.

Chairman KEFAUVER. You said that Mr. Warner's company had produced more gangster pictures than all the rest of them put together, Mr. Hayes had a lot of trouble with them, and they complied with the code for a while, but had stopped complying with it now. Is that a summary of what you were saying?

Mr. YOUNG. That not only applies to Mr. Warner, but all the major, and independent studios.

Chairman KEFAUVER. All right, sir.

Mr. YOUNG. Thank you, sir.

Chairman KEFAUVER. You see, we have controversy, Mr. Warner. What do you say about that?

Mr. WARNER. I don't agree with him. As a matter of fact, I don't know how many pictures we have made that—whatever it was. I really don't know what the man is talking about, other than we made pictures, as I described. I named the real hard ones. I didn't name——

Chairman KEFAUVER. He said you knew him.

Mr. WARNER. I probably do know him.

Chairman KEFAUVER. Have you had any trouble with either the code under Mr. Hayes or under Mr. Johnson's dominion?

Mr. WARNER. No, we had no more trouble than anyone else. Everybody has trouble.

Chairman KEFAUVER. You do have arguments, and you finally abide by their decisions?

Mr. WARNER. Absolutely. There has never been a picture that our company has put out that hasn't had the proper seal and full respect of the code. I am highly in favor of the code, because they are doing a very monumental job.

Chairman KEFAUVER. Every picture you have put out has had the approval of the seal of the code since it has been in existence?

Mr. WARNER. Yes.

Chairman KEFAUVER. Mr. Bobo, do you have any questions you want to ask?

Mrs. GEORGE. May I ask a question?

Chairman KEFAUVER. You make your statement to me.

Mrs. GEORGE. Yes.

Chairman KEFAUVER. What is your name?

Mrs. GEORGE. Mrs. S. George.

Chairman KEFAUVER. Mrs. George?

Mrs. GEORGE. Yes. Mr. Warner has stated that 2 years later—he was 2 years too late in making a war picture, because the current topic wasn't interesting any more. But I would say this: If pictures like the Blackboard Jungle, where the kids, as they say, are all het up with turbulent emotions and crazy upside-down patterns of life, why profit in dollars and cents to bring forth pictures that we already know have hit home at families, and do not care to have it exploited by film companies?

That is not teaching you anything. We read it enough, and the familes have suffered; we all know what it is. Why go to see it?

For instance, the kids that are doing that, they have done it. But the other kids that haven't seen any part of it will go to see that, because most of the adults do not go to see that type of picture.

We don't want all that brutality, and showing how degraded the children are. But that will prove something to the children that are a little weaker in their emotions, and will go to the movies to see the picture, and probably do the same thing as they are doing in this motion picture.

Chairman KEFAUVER. Have you had that experience with your children or children you know?

Mrs. GEORGE. Well, I have heard from other mothers that have said they wouldn't allow their children——

Chairman KEFAUVER. Well, Mr. Warner didn't make Blackboard Jungle.

Mrs. GEORGE. No, no; I am not assuming he made that picture. But I am only bringing that as an example. If he has in mind something like that to profit by horror things, where the hcildren's emotions are turbulent now, why not keep them quiet or close down the studios with that kind of picture, and give the children a breath of air?

Chairman KEFAUVER. All right. Thank you, Mrs. George.

Mr. Warner, what do you think the Warner Bros. and other producers can do to help us in our problem? We are interested in working with you people to get your recommendations to us, and to try to to create public opinion for better movies. Movies have a great impact upon the thinking of young people.

Mr. WARNER. Yes.

Chairman KEFAUVER. What do you recommend?

Mr. WARNER. Well, I say, as I think—not to be repeating too much, but I feel your committee and others like it will bring these types of events to the surface, and you can only do good. I don't know how much good, but there will be a lot of good come out of this.

I feel right-thinking men in the film industry certainly welcome it. Certainly there will be mistakes. Naturally; everybody is human and will make mistakes.

But I feel that we can do a lot and we will do everything that we humanly can to cooperate and avoid repetition.

Chairman KEFAUVER. We have had some criticism of I Died a Thousand Lives. Is that on the board over there?

Mr. BOBO. No.

Mr. WARNER. That is just——

Chairman KEFAUVER. Have you had much criticism on that?

Mr. WARNER. That picture hasn't been shown yet. It is a rather inoffensive film, of very little consequence.

Chairman KEFAUVER. It hasn't been shown yet?

Mr. WARNER. No; it hasn't been shown to the public.

Mr. SMALL. May I ask a question?

Chairman KEFAUVER. You can make a statement to me.

Mr. SMALL. Of the last 30 pictures that Warner Bros. have put out, how many do not show excess drinking and smoking by women and juveniles?

Chairman KEFAUVER. What is your name, sir?

Mr. SMALL. Nathan Small.

Chairman KEFAUVER. Where do you live, sir?

Mr. SMALL. Los Angeles.

Mr. WARNER. I can only answer that by "Why do you beat your wife?" It is the same thing.

You must be living in a backwoods country, boy, because everybody is smoking and drinking nowadays in some form. You drink water or something.

A SPECTATOR. But not excessively.

Mr. WARNER. But you have to drink——

Chairman KEFAUVER. All right.

Thank you very much, Mr. Warner.

STATEMENT OF JERRY WALD, EXECUTIVE PRODUCER, COLUMBIA STUDIOS, HOLLYWOOD, CALIF.

Mr. Jerry Wald. What is your address, Mr. Wald?

Mr. WALD. Address or where do I work?

Chairman KEFAUVER. Where do you work?

Mr. WALD. I work—I am an executive producer at Columbia Studios.

Chairman KEFAUVER. You are an executive producer?

Mr. WALD. Yes.

Chairman KEFAUVER. All right. Mr. Bobo, do you want to ask any questions?

Mr. BOBO. We have a background statement of Mr. Wald.

Chairman KEFAUVER. You have been a radio editor, you have published books and various magazine articles.

Produced short subjects for RKO and made eight radio shorts for Warner called Rambling 'Round Radio Row.

You have written scenarios and have produced a number of pictures, some of which are Task Force, Storm Warnings, Blue Veil, Clash By Night, Lusty Men, Miss Sadie Thompson.

Mr. WALD. That doesn't cover it, Senator. I have been producing pictures and writing them for about 23 years. Among the pictures that I have been directly connected with in the production end were two pictures in this investigation. One was Caged, mentioned by Dr. Frym, and Johnny Belinda, which I understand was discussed this morning.

Now, what amazes me is that anybody would single out Johnny Belinda, because some person saw the film and raped a girl. The seeds for this destructive force were in this man obviously much before he saw the picture. But nobody here apparently took time out to recognize the force for good that this picture did. This picture dealt with the problems of the mutes all over the world. We found it did an immeasurable amount of good, because it gave a better understanding to the world and to audiences of the problems of the mutes all over the world.

On Caged, this was a picture I made at Warner's as a producer. We were very much concerned about the problem of the criminal code in California which allowed first offenders to be thrown into the same cell with second, third, and fourth offenders.

The picture was made with the cooperation of the penal authorities. We tried to point out the damage being done by allowing any person to be thrown into the same cell—a person who basically may have been a first-time offender, to be thrown into a cell and meet up with second, third, and fourth offenders, who were logically and obviously perverts and had all sorts of criminal records.

Now, the one thing I don't understand, Senator, is that nobody has stopped to take the time out to recognize the force for good. There was a gentleman here who was condemning Warner Bros. for the amount of gangster pictures they made. But this gentleman must be well aware of the pictures like Louis Pasteur, Zola, Midsummer Night's Dream, and the pictures that did a tremendous amount of good throughout our country and all over the world.

It showed one thing to the rest of the world. It showed we had the right to criticize ourselves, that we were a democratic nation, that we had the right to, if we didn't like something in our own country—that if we felt that what was being done was wrong, that we had the right to present it on the screen.

I have not seen any picture criticizing the Russian Government that has come out of Russia, and, in fact, I have never seen any film coming out of any European country which takes the problems of their own times and presents them on the screen, as we have done here.

I am connected with a company that in the last 2 years made a picture—has made several pictures that have caused—they haven't caused any uproar, but they were tremendous box office films. From Here To Eternity, On The Waterfront, Caine Mutiny, The Long Gray Line. Each of these films were forces for good, we think.

The Long Gray Line was a story of the United States Military Academy. It tried to tell the story of the responsibility of the boys in our country toward the Academy. The meaning of West Point and what good it could do for good.

Chairman KEFAUVER. Yes; I have heard much favorable comment about The Long Gray Line. Well, nobody is claiming, I don't think —even the most severe critics—that many pictures are not great forces for good. What we are dealing with here is the impact of certain pictures upon the youth of our Nation, whether the motion picture industry is doing all that it can do to help with our youth problems, whether some of the excessive violence and brutality we see at some movies is a good influence.

I don't know of anyone in the industry who will contend that some parts of some movies haven't been rather deleterious to young people. We are not diminishing the good that the industry has done. What we are anxious to know is how are you going to have better movies, insofar as the impact upon young people is concerned.

Mr. WALD. Senator, I have discovered in looking over the biggest box office pictures made that none of them have had violence in them for violence's sake. I have discovered that the greatest pictures—the biggest box office films—From Here To Eternity, The Best Years of Our Lives, Gone With The Wind, Going My Way—all these films, that were really big box office films, and films that did not have a limited audience—they were pictures that were made with good taste and did not violate any rules of the Breen office or the Johnston office, as it is called today.

And I have discovered, as a part of my responsibility in making pictures, that we have to really ride on two horses at one time. The first is not to make any story that will offend the innocent, and at the same time don't offend the intelligent picture-goers. Now, it is possible to ride on both horses. And it can be done with a piece of good material that is done with good taste.

And I am convinced that part of our job is to appreciate and continue all that is good in our own national life. There are many things that are wrong that we try to put on the screen, but it still has to be done in good taste.

I can well understand, having two boys of my own—and, Senator, you have a family of your own—that children are easily influenced. But, at the same time, I think the basic upbringing we give them in our own homes is what is the initial strength, so that they will withstand any of the temptations they pick up from the daily papers or motion pictures, perhaps, or from TV shows.

Chairman KEFAUVER. Well, I think we all appreciate the fact that home is and the parents are the big things. But, undoubtedly, what children read and see has a great influence on their lives.

Mr. WALD. Senator, do you think your children would be influenced if they saw Blackboard Jungle?

Chairman KEFAUVER. They haven't seen it. My daughter is 13 and we have a son 9. Some of the movies they have seen, they have come home and been very upset all night, emotionally disturbed. I don't think that is particularly good for a child.

Mr. WALD. No, it isn't, sir.

Chairman KEFAUVER. Do you have any questions, Mr. Bobo?

Mr. BOBO. Yes. I was interested in this point, Mr. Wald: Of course, the children of parents that are the right type of parents, that would go to the theater with their parents, or come home to their parents at night after seeing a motion picture, and have it explained to them as to any questions they might have, is one thing. But how about the large number of children who are probably the most avid moviegoers, who come from either broken homes or homes that have inadequate parents, the child that is likely to pick up the crime and violence, the techniques of crime as shown in the movies, is liable to have more of an emotional impact on his life. There are some million and a half of these youngsters in this country.

I think that is where our problem here would have to center. What is your feeling on that?

Mr. WALD. We would have to screen every child going to a movie, to find out if they come from a broken home or not. Our big problem, Mr. Bobo, is that you are making pictures for a mass audience. We can't stop to ask each individual patron, "What is your background and where do you come from? Are you emotionally disturbed?" It would be pretty tough to do that.

Mr. BOBO. Mr. Wald, would you not admit there are pictures that have violence in them for violence's sake? I didn't see the picture the other day, but I heard of one the other day that had—I can't recall the name—35 people killed in it. I saw one the other night myself that had 17 killed in it.

Mr. WALD. Undoubtedly you are correct, but Mr. Bobo, it is like branding the book industry as being indecent because we read a lot of paper-covered books, and we say, "My God." I read some detective stories that had 30 people killed and branded and kicked and gouged the first 40 pages. But I like to measure the book business by the good books that come out and not the bad ones.

Mr. BOBO. Well, I think that is the way the people will measure the motion-picture industry, by the good pictures that come out.

But certainly a number of people are disturbed about the crime and violence and sadism and the long fights. Some fights last as long as 6 and 8 minutes.

I think the code is constantly aware of this. And I think I saw an article of yours on Sunday on crime and violence in pictures.

Mr. WALD. I agree with you, Mr. Bobo. In fact, I don't understand how any normal audience will believe some of the fights that are on the screen. They run for 10 minutes. I don't think true prizefighters of the heavyweight talent could stand the—some of the punishment handed out in some of these pictures. I agree with you.

Mr. BOBO. I think in some of our gangster pictures, numerous times we have spoken of them as showing the gangster age; I think in a number of those pictures we portray the gangsters sometimes, and the children will go home and emulate that character, because he is a well-known movie star. I think maybe some of those things we should possibly guard against.

Mr. WALD. I have always told our writers this: If you look to read Hamlet carefully, you will find there are quite a number of killings in Hamlet. The killings there result directly from character, and it is not violence for violence's sake. I think some of the greatest literature that has lasted through the years has contained violence, but it is violence of a different caliber than we are talking about. I mean it is violence that comes out of a character study, out of character delineations, and character motivation.

I agree with you that a picture that uses violence primarily to act as a come-on for customers is in complete disagreement with the thinking that goes on by most of us in the motion-picture business.

Mr. BOBO. The question is, How do we get that minimized?

Mr. WALD. I think we have a very good code administrator and there isn't any picture we do that we don't work constantly with Mr. Shurlock. I know I do and I know everyone at the major studios does. But, like any other industry, there are always a few that try to slip in under the wire.

We have never released a picture that hasn't a seal. But yet I can't speak for the entire industry. You can't judge the theater by Minsky. You have to judge it by Rodgers and Hammerstein, for the good and not for the low points.

Mr. YOUNG. Mr. Senator——

Chairman KEFAUVER. You have to take an average.

Mr. YOUNG. Mr. Senator.

Chairman KEFAUVER. Just a minute, Mr. Young.

Does your question have to do with what Mr. Wald is saying?

Mr. YOUNG. Yes, sir. If I may again be permitted, with all due respect to Mr. Wald, Mr. Wald said a gentleman stated about the bad pictures Warner's made. It is true Warner's did make some fine pictures, too.

The same applies, Senator, when you questioned that hoodlum Mickey Cohen. It was stated that Mickey Cohen had contributed to various institutions charitably, but that did not condone the violations and the criminal acts he had committed, which he eventually was sent to a penal institution for; indicted, convicted. He is there now and may be convicted or indicted again.

I only refer to Caged that Mr. Jerry Wald had produced.

Mr. Jerry Wald—Senator, I wish you would ask Mr. Jerry Wald how old his children are he has referred to. I would like to know what age, whether they were permitted to see Caged in some of the outrageous scenes done in that particular picture pertaining to a women's penal institution that were vulgar and common of its nature, and it is not practiced in our penal institutions.

I, as a news photographer and motion-picture cameraman, for years I have been in various institutions—not permitted to photograph inside of them, but outside, and have without my camera been in them the same as any other newsman.

And I say that without the fear of contradiction, that Mr. Wald state to us as to the age of these children. Then let's ask him——

Chairman KEFAUVER. All right. We appreciate your contribution. We will let Mr. Wald have a chance to say what he has to say about it.

Mr. YOUNG. Yes.

Mr. WALD. My children weren't born at the time—one of them was, I guess. I have two boys, 9 and 12. Now, we will get over that point.

About Caged, the picture was passed by Mr. Shurlock's office here and it was passed by the penal institutions here. The picture received artistic awards all over the world. The young lady who played the lead in the picture received the Venice film award and other awards all over the country. The picture was wholeheartedly approved by the Federal Penal Board. We have had many, many thousands of compliments, complimentary letters.

I don't know if Mr. Young was ever in prison or not. I wasn't, either.

But I did do this, sir: I had a woman, a reporter, go into prison for 6 months. She worked there. Virginia Kellogg worked in prison and got all the statistical information right from the prison.

And we had as our technical adivsers three women wardens who were under instructions from us to constantly watch the film for any technical errors and to make sure we were duplicating prison life as it really existed.

When the picture was in script form, sir——

Chairman KEFAUVER. Well——

Mr. WALD. Just this one last thing. We had Dr. Frym, who is a psychiatrist for the California Criminal Board, read the script and come over and discuss it with us and he helped us remove any inaccuracies in the script.

Chairman KEFAUVER. Would you take your boys to see it?

Mr. WALD. I would show it to them today; yes, sir. It was made, I guess, 9 years ago. They were too young at that time.

Chairman KEFAUVER. Anything else, Mr. Bobo?

Mr. BOBO. No.

Chairman KEFAUVER. Thank you very much, Mr. Wald.

STATEMENT OF HARRY JOE BROWN, PRODUCER AND DIRECTOR, HOLLYWOOD, CALIF.

Mr. Brown, you are a producer and director; is that correct?

Mr. BROWN. Yes.

Chairman KEFAUVER. Who are you with?

Mr. BROWN. Our own company, Producers-Actors Corp.

Chairman KEFAUVER. Mr. Bobo, do you want to ask some questions?

Mr. BOBO. Yes.

Chairman KEFAUVER. Let's get down to the main points of Mr. Brown's testimony as soon as possible.

We have a biographical sketch about your experience, Mr. Brown. You came from Pittsburgh, Pa.; you have been in the industry a long, long time.

All right, Mr. Bobo.

Mr. BOBO. Mr. Brown, is your company a member of the Motion Picture Production Code?

Mr. BROWN. We are through our distributors, Columbia Pictures Corp.

Mr. BOBO. Are your scripts approved, scripts for your movies approved prior to the making of those movies?

Mr. BROWN. Yes.

Mr. BOBO. Your pictures are mostly westerns?

Mr. BROWN. At the present time they are; yes.

Mr. BOBO. Has there been any change in the western pictures in the last few years, that you can speak of, as to more crime or violence or more brutality shown in western pictures?

Mr. BROWN. I doubt it very much. I don't see any change or haven't seen any change in the western picture, the format, than the first days I made western pictures 35 years ago.

Mr. BOBO. Mr. Brown, the other night at Columbia Pictures Studio, I think it was, I saw the picture Ten Wanted Men, and in that picture there were some 17 persons killed.

Mr. BROWN. I doubt it.

Mr. BOBO. You know how many were killed?

Mr. BROWN. I would say—to my recollection, it has been a little while, but I would say 4 or 5. There are no 17. And every killing there was a reason for. There was a good came out of that killing. We never kill indiscriminately. We never kill just to kill. Any time there is a death in a western picture, you will fiind there is an awful big reason for it. There is a reason, good or bad, something to bring home to the child—and if I may interrupt here just for a moment before I forget it, I have listened all afternoon to what these gentlemen have had to say in the industry and what you gentlemen are seeking I believe is to find out.

The thought came to my mind—I suppose to you it is that you want to know what a child carries away after viewing a motion picture.

Now, it comes to my mind, what does a child carry away after viewing a western picture, say, one with taste; you know, the ordinary western picture. I am sure when he gets home he doesn't put on a black mustache and gloves and become the heavy. Rather, he puts on the coon cap and he becomes Davy Crockett. He becomes Bill Hickok. He becomes all that is good, the law-enforcing man. That is what he sees in the western picture; he sees a good Americano, like he would like to be; not the death.

I think the scenes, if they are violent or not, I think they are very soon forgotten in the mind of that child or the mind of the adult. But they carry away the good Americano. They carry away beautiful scenery in many instances, where they can't afford to go. They carry away the good and bad; they carry all those thoughts. And, therefore, I am a firm believer—believe me, I say this honestly—in a decent, good western picture; that it is great for the kids.

Mr. Bobo. Mr. Brown, and I hate to single out your one picture, but I did see it.

Mr. Brown. Yes.

Mr. Bobo. In that particular picture, where the brother of the leading man was shot and killed, he was shot in a very cold-blooded fashion, standing right close to him, once in the hand and once in the arm and once apparently through the chest. He had a very cold-blooded death.

Mr. Brown. Yes; it was.

Mr. Bobo. I don't know what the children took home from that picture. I am thinking about myself. I wonder if excessive violence in that form might have more impact than Randy Scott as the hero.

Mr. Brown. That was a great exception to the case. There was quite a battle over it with the Johnston office. It is very rare we do a thing like that.

But the message brought home of that particular killing was the great love that the father had for his son; that was more important than the killing. To bring home to the child what it means to have a parent that would go through hell for you, be shot four times rather than divulge the whereabouts of this boy, which these heavies wanted to find.

That is what I meant, that when you find killings in our pictures— I am not just speaking of our pictures, I am saying for most Westerns—there was a very valid reason, it should be brought out.

Mr. Bobo. Mr. Brown, in making Westerns—and I know here they are all referred to as just another Western by a number of people— isn't it true that most of the scripts run pretty much the same and that we have to have a little more violence or a little more impact or a little longer fight for there to be the audience—the reaction audience, which I think would be mostly children——

Mr. Brown. Well, I think I may disagree with you. I think that a very mistaken thought—that that is a very mistaken thought, that just children see Westerns.

Go to your theater in the evening, where the big crowds are. Our pictures fortunately play what we call at first-run theaters. For example, we play here in our city the Hill Street and the Pantages Theaters; two very up-to-date theaters.

You go there in the evenings, and I will venture to say there won't be 1 out of 10 which is a child maybe 10 or 12 years old. Your matinees take it down very little. The fact that children do go to Westerns I think is another good reason that folks sanction their going to them. After all, they must get that 30 or 40 cents to attend. Because I think the folks see what they see also in a Western, the good, and not the bad that has been brought up here.

But getting back to your question, as I say, this particular picture was an exception. There was more than we generally have, much more. But I can say—go down through the killings, if we had the time, and prove to you that each and every one was a great lesson for their child, if he took enough interest in that killing.

Chairman Kefauver. You said a part of your pictures were approved by the code, those you sold to——

Mr. BROWN. Oh, no; that is a mistake. All of our pictures have the same code regulation as any other picture by a major producing organization, because the fact that we——

Chairman KEFAUVER. Do you get the seal on all your pictures?

Mr. BROWN. We must get the seal on all our pictures, the same as the other companies.

Chairman KEFAUVER. All right. Thank you very much.

Mrs. ADAMS. May I ask a question?

Chairman KEFAUVER. What is your name?

Mrs. ADAMS. Mrs. Jean Adams.

Because of the havoc that has been brought on the youths and the adults because of this irresponsibility and the conscienceless work of the Hollywood production code, I think that we should have a Government-appointed board censoring all of these movies and television programs, and they can also at the same time see to it that pictures be eliminated which have to do with racial discrimination and racial hatred. I have seen so many of those. I think it is very necessary.

Chairman KEFAUVER. Thank you very much, lady.

Mrs. FOSTER. Could I make a statement?

Chairman KEFAUVER. Yes, ma'am.

Mrs. FOSTER. In 1947 I took a trip to a foreign land and on the ship there were many foreigners and juveniles. The picture that was shown was the Farmer's Daughter. Now, that showed a United States Senator drunk that was running for reelection. The farmer's daughter was a girl not out of high school, not educated, but she won the election. This United States Senator did everything crooked that he could to win that election.

I would like to know—I have listened all afternoon—how all these pictures are done for good—I would like to know how much good was done in this picture, how many juveniles respected the United States Senator and how many foreigners respected the United States Senator.

Chairman KEFAUVER. I didn't see it.

Mrs. FOSTER. You ought to see it. I had a brother at one time in the United States Senate.

Chairman KEFAUVER. I know you are very serious and your brother is in the United State Senate. I know Senator Watkins quite well, favorably.

I don't know the Farmer's Daughter, I didn't see the picture.

But I have seen many pictures that rather make fun of law-enforcement officials and of public officials, and I think this is one point of criticism not only of some pictures, but of some television shows which create some disrespect for law-enforcement officers and for public officials.

Mr. George Murphy will be our last witness this afternoon.

STATEMENT OF GEORGE MURPHY, ACTOR, OFFICIAL, SCREEN ACTORS GUILD, HOLLYWOOD, CALIF.

Mr. Murphy, we are appreciative for the cooperation you have given our subcommittee for coming here and testifying about the subject matter we are interested in.

We have a short biographical sketch of your life and of the movies that you have been in, beginning back in 1937, when you were on the stage, and then you came to the movie industry in 1934 in Kid Millions.

Mr. Murphy. That is right, sir.

Chairman Kefauver. In 1950 you were chairman of the Hollywood Coordinating Commission.

Mr. Murphy. Committee. That is the committee that channels the free appearance of the motion picture personalities; They started working in close conjunction with all the national charities and armed services. We send all the shows overseas. It is an offspring of what is called the War Activities Committee.

Chairman Kefauver. And your picture The Pilot's Girl won a special academy award for interpreting the motion picture industry correctly to the country at large.

Mr. Murphy. Actually, it wasn't the picture. I personally was given a unique Oscar for public relations work in connection with the industry.

As the Senator probably knows, over the years our business thrives on publicity and sometimes we are a little more in the spotlight than we should be. In many cases, as Mr. Freeman explained today, there are many writers here that write special stories about our people and personalities. Sometimes they run out of material and the stories get into the realm of imagination.

I found, traveling during the war, it was a very, very bad and a very wrong and false impression of Hollywood and its people and the people in the motion picture industry.

So that my boss at that time said, "If you feel that way about it, why don't you do something about it?" So since then I have done a great deal. I have appeared in practically every city in the United States, every large city, and before all sorts of groups and organizations and Rotary Clubs, and parent-teacher associations and ministers' groups and the rest, and explained actually what happens in the motion picture industry and to tell the true story of its people.

We are, of course, like any other community. We have 2 or 3 or 4 people that, unfortunately, break the rules now and then. But, by and large, I think we have a fine community. We have a great record, which I am sure my friend Ronald Reagan told you about when he appeared this morning. That has been the major part of my work for the last 7 or 8 years.

I have also been president of the Screen Actors Guild, so I have been a representative of the labor side. Presently I am in charge of public relations in M–G–M Studio.

Chairman Kefauver. Mr. Bobo, do you have some particular matter you want to bring up with Mr. Murphy?

Mr. Bobo. Yes. Mr. Murphy, we have been discussing some of the evil influences of television and the movies this afternoon. I think you have an idea for some real constructive force to help in educating the public on this problem and meeting it.

Mr. Murphy. I think there has been a great deal of talk here today, for instance, it has been clearly brought forward, the process of making a motion picture, the application of the code, which we are very, very proud of and we are very unique, being the only industry that has tried to guard our own morals.

It is true that once in a whole we will make mistakes and slip a little bit. But, by and large, our people try to employ their good moral sense. We realize the tremendous influence the motion picture has on the public morals and on the country at large, and particularly the international field.

I think that it has been well established here that if there has been any bad influence created by pictures, it was certainly not intended; that the intent was always good.

There were certain pictures, for instance, Blackboard Jungle, that has been mentioned here. I quite honestly, in the beginning, when I read the book, had some misgivings about Blackboard Jungle being made into a picture. And when I saw the picture I was very, very happy it had been made and proud our studio had made it, because I think by drawing attention to the actual stark reality—and I assure everyone on this committee that that picture was not overdrawn, that there are situations that happen right here in Los Angeles that are just as bad, if not worse, in some conditions, because I have spent a great deal of time talking to some of the juvenile officers and juvenile court people. I have also been quite active. I am on the local council of the Boy Scouts of America. I had the pleasure of making a motion picture of their jamboree which took place here 2 years ago.

I think the impact of the motion picture is tremendous. We have a great responsibility that goes with it and I think our people, our leaders are conscious of it.

As I say, if they make a mistake once in a while, it is not intentional. I am sure that the fact your committee has come here will probably act as a very good influence on their thinking, because it will make us conscious of the fact the job we have is a great and important one, and the moral responsibility that goes with it.

On the constructive side, which I think is more important than pointing the finger at who caused the trouble—what do you do to cause the trouble? I think that the motion picture and television could probably do the greatest service to this country if a concentrated effort were made to bring to the attention of the people actual cases based on case history. I know that 90 percent of the people in our city haven't the slightest idea what goes on in juvenile court, because they haven't taken the time to go down there and find out. I think every so often these things ought to be put on television, and let the people know.

I agree with the statements made here, and for a very good reason: the basis of the trouble generally starts in the home. The basis of the trouble is in the control of the parents. But I think this is a thing we can discuss interminably and come up with all sorts of answers.

I am certain of one thing. If there is a concentrated effort on the part of the motion-picture industry and on the part of television, to make constructive series of pictures to show exactly what is happening, and then at the end of each sequence to have a short piece by one of the outstanding juvenile court judges, with a little sort of a road map to tell people what to do, how to combat the problem, how to get active in it, what to do about it.

Of course, we get back to the simple basis. We all know of areas in Los Angeles where juvenile delinquency was at its highest, and when we got boys' clubs started or Boy Scout troops started in those areas, that juvenile delinquency goes down. I believe completely with old

Father Flanagan, that there is no bad boy. That sometimes through neglect, through his environment, that he doesn't have a chance to play baseball and football—any number of reasons—that maybe he gets into bad habits.

I think we can do a tremendous job and I am sure you will find, sir, that the leaders of our industry will be more than happy to cooperate in any way they can to bring this program before the public on a constructive basis. And I hope that we can find the solution to what is now a very, very grave national problem.

Chairman KEFAUVER. That is a very worthwhile suggestion, Mr. Murphy. I hope that all of the officials in the industry will be thinking about ways and means they can bring the actual picture home to our people. In a country—we have to live on the theory that if people know the facts they will do something about it. That is our great hope.

Anything else, Mr. Bobo?

Mrs. GEORGE. May I make another statement?

Chairman KEFAUVER. All right, lady.

Mrs. GEORGE. Mr. Murphy was very——

Chairman KEFAUVER. You ask me and I will decide whether I want to ask Mr. Murphy.

Mrs. GEORGE. Mr. Murphy brings out the point, as the other gentleman brought forth, that they have made a great many mistakes. Now, they are supposed to be very intelligent people and executives of their own companies. How many mistakes are they permitted to be very profitable to the disadvantage of the family and the children?

If it hadn't been for you, if the committee hadn't come and investigated, they would probably have gone on until the committee investigation, and then they come out and say they have made mistakes, which is a human element; which is not true.

We are assuming that the people that are at the head of the industry are intelligent. Now, what is to be done about that?

Chairman KEFAUVER. I think your point is that this is a very sensitive industry that we are dealing with. That we realize the importance of all mass media of communication, and particularly the impression of pictures, so that the producers and the people who run our studios, and the writers, must be constantly on the alert to try to see that they take into consideration the public welfare always.

Mrs. GEORGE. May I also ask, Senator, what are they going to do about these billboards, these posters that have all of the suggestiveness you would find in pornography. I mean, down at the movie theaters, where the children pass all the time with their mothers on shopping tours, what are they going to do about that?

I don't even want to look at them myself, and I am not a blue nose, not old-fashioned. What is the impact on the children of that, that passes down Broadway and sees all that nonsense, all those pictures? Is that art or is it just to arouse their emotions? Why don't they tear them down?

The children see these great big colorful posters, like the suggestive one on The Prodigal. Now, what are they going to do? Are they going to school and study history and algebra, or are they going to talk about that [indicating]?

I have seen pictures of it, where the students at John Marshall High School, on Los Feliz, there is a big billboard sign there, and

I saw those large suggestive poses. Maybe the motion pictures don't have it, but the posters suggest it. And those kids are not thinking of algebra when they go to school.

Chairman KEFAUVER. Well, I think your point is very, very well taken, lady. And I haven't heard any members of the industry defend a lot of these posters.

Mr. YOUNG. They have been——

Chairman KEFAUVER. Just a minute. Just a minute.

Mr. YOUNG. They have been evasive of the very fact, not only are these pictures exaggerated, but when they take still pictures—and Mr. Murphy knows. I worked with Mr. Murphy, although Mr. Murphy is a fine gentleman and clean, he comes from a clean family, sport minded, football. He knows I know that because I covered a story on his father, as to football. Is that correct, Mr. Murphy, at RKO?

Mr. MURPHY. Could be.

Mr. YOUNG. I am not citing Mr. Murphy, because I know his background is one of the finest of the gentlemen associated, and I had the pleasure of being associated with him.

But when they take 24 sheets, as it is termed, that will cover practically the wall of this room, and they show these, as the lady has stated, and then take featured players and take them over the sidelines and take still pictures of them, exaggerating their exposure in their seminudeness, and then send them out to these cheap, vulgar publications, to be used, as I have a record of right now in one of these little magazines.

But I will say this, Mr. Senator, and the committee, that since your arrival here—and I have made it a point to go to these 50 drugstores, to see these stands of these cheap publications, where children sit down and look at these things, that they have removed them since your presence here.

The question is, will they be replaced after you leave here?

Thank you, Mr. Senator.

Chairman KEFAUVER. You are talking about some of the magazines you have seen?

Mr. YOUNG. Yes, that show these featured players.

Chairman KEFAUVER. Mr. Murphy, you see what some of the people are saying about these posters, and the comments of people who are here. All that goes to make up public opinion. I am sure that is something you are going to be thinking about.

Mr. MURPHY. I have had a very broad experience in this field, Senator. As I say, I have traveled and gone to meeting of all types across the country. I have heard, as I have heard this afternoon, objection to too much violence in the pictures.

I assure you, if there is too much violence it is a case of bad judgment on the part of the director or the cutter, because I am certain nobody ever put violence in a picture to the degree it is going to offend the audience. The purpose for making the pictures is to please the audience.

If they go out and say the picture is a bad picture, then the business is bad and nobody comes to see it. If they go out and say it is a good picture, then more people come in and that is the object and that is what we are trying to do.

The question of whether the pictures have had a good or bad influence on children is one that has been discussed for many, many years. I have gone back in research—I have a statement here written by Judge Ben Lindsay, who is the originator of the juvenile courts, back in 1936, which would apply today. I would like to read the statement into the record, because I think it is a good one and I think it fits our case.

He had been asked about the effect of the motion picture on juvenile minds.

I can be much more definite and certain, in saying I know of thousands of children who have positively been elevated, inspired and made happier because of the movies, who have been kept off of streets, out of alleys, the vulgar story-telling of the barnyard, and the multitude of idle, evil associations by wholesome appeals, the family gatherings and educational opportunities afforded them by the movies. I really believe if we had never had any motion pictures at all we would probably have more crime among youth than we now have, or at least we would certainly have as much. Nothing in the last 50 years of this most eventful history of all times has perhaps done more to reduce sin and crime and add to the happiness, education and progress of the human race than the motion pictures. And if the right-minded, intelligent people of this country will support the producers in giving us wholesome amusement, they will certainly do more in this regard in the years to come.

I think that is a fair statement of fact from a man who was Judge Ben Lindsay, who certainly knew as much about this as any man I know of.

I think, as has been said here continually, we are human beings and we make mistakes. We will try to stop making the mistakes. We will try for perfection. We will probably never attain it, but it is my sincere belief that the motion picture has done much more good than bad, and in the future, Senator, I agree with Mr. Young, that your very visit to this city will probably jog our memories a little bit and make us a little more careful in our responsibilities. I sincerely hope it will, and will have that effect.

Chairman KEFAUVER. Mr. Murphy, we are depending on men like you to keep this issue before the picture people, and I know your influence will be wholesome.

Mrs. ADAMS. Mr. Senator, may I make one more question?

Chairman KEFAUVER. We have to adjourn now. We are too late. You come back in the morning, if you want to ask a question.

Mrs. ADAMS. Thank you.

Chairman KEFAUVER. We will stand in recess until 9 : 30 tomorrow morning. We will begin sharply at 9 : 30 in the morning.

(Whereupon, at 5 : 15 p. m., Thursday, June 16, 1955, the subcommittee recessed until Friday, June 17, 1955, at 9 : 30 a. m.)

JUVENILE DELINQUENCY
(Motion Pictures)

FRIDAY, JUNE 17, 1955

United States Senate,
Subcommittee of the Committee on the Judiciary,
To Investigate Juvenile Delinquency,
Los Angeles, Calif.

The subcommittee met, pursuant to recess, at 9:45 a. m., at room 518, United States Post Office and Court House Building, Los Angeles, Calif., Senator Estes Kefauver presiding.

Present: Chairman Kefauver.

Also present: James H. Bobo, counsel; and William Haddad and Carl Perian, consultants.

Chairman KEFAUVER. We will come to order, please.

The subcommittee is glad to have with us this morning—and I hope he will sit with us after he has made a few statements—an old, old dear friend of the chairman, a man who has contributed much to the social and political life of this section. He is well known throughout the United States. Supervisor John Anson Ford.

Mr. Ford has been of much assistance and help to our subcommittee and to our subcommitee's staff, and we are certainly appreciative of his presence here.

Mr. Ford, won't you come around and give us the benefit of any suggestions and advice.

We were pleased to have Mr. Miley, who has been associated with you, read your very excellent statement, but any other remarks or counsel for the subcommittee or for the people of this section, in dealing with the problem of juvenile delinquency, we will be very glad to hear from you.

STATEMENT OF JOHN ANSON FORD, MEMBER, BOARD OF SUPERVISORS, LOS ANGELES, CALIF.

Mr. FORD. Well, Senator Kefauver, I appreciate the opportunity to supplement my remarks of the other day, which were transcribed because my throat had given me a little trouble and I wasn't able to appear, as I had hoped to respond to your initial invitation.

If I were to say a supplementary word, Senator, it would be to emphasize the importance of concentrating upon that section of our younger population which feels that it is somewhat outcast. Part of our great problem here in southern California, with all our marvelous facilities for recreation and rehabilitation, arises from the fact that because of racial differences and language differences many of our younger folks feel they are outcasts, they are declassed. That in

145

many cases makes the YMCA, the Catholic Youth Organizations, the various social agencies which do such a wonderful job, it makes them, you might say, unavailable. These boys and girls, particularly the boys, develop a resentfulness which at its worst is manifested through zoot suit riots of a few years ago, but is always present in some degree, even to the point where they sometimes fight among themselves.

I think in our studies with the youth we have found that sometimes we don't appreciate the legitimate levels of their interests. These boys, like all boys, are very fond of automobiles. They are fond of mechanical gadgets.

And as you may or may not know—I don't know whether there has been testimony regarding it here or not—one of the real social forces among hundreds of these boys is the so-called car clubs. Boys delight to take an automobile and strip it down and rebuild it and give it more speed, more zip. I have shared with my colleagues on the board of supervisors in trying to provide a safe well-regulated, properly supervised race course or drag strip, as they like to call it, where these boys, after weeks of preparation with their cars, cannot engage in racing, but, rather, they can engage in a time and test—timing strip, they like to call it.

Strange to say, the public has resented the establishment of these supervised timing strips. At least, they have resented it to a certain extent. A few farsighted people, like some of the police officers, in Bell and Maywood, have organized an association and have agreed to underwrite the insurance for these boys, and agreed to write rules for them.

I cannot go into the details, Senator, but it is things of that sort which are very constructive in laying groundwork for a boy's confidence in his fellow man, a boy's appreciation that society does understand his interest and has a regard for him.

Chairman KEEAUVER. Well, we have had some testimony about the so-called——

Mr. FORD. Timing strips.

Chairman KEFAUVER. Timing strips. And we had the police chief from Pomona, and he told about how much better the situation is down there. Mr. Miley gave us some information about it. It seems to be working not only here, but in other parts of the country, for the better.

Mr. FORD. If I am not encroaching too much on the time I would like to emphasize this, Senator: I went to a meeting of about 25 of these clubs, time strip clubs, where the boys each had given his heart to the building up of a high speed car for testing purposes.

We met in the chambers of one of the local justices one evening and crowded the room full. We called the roll of these clubs and it was almost pathetic that one president after another got up and said, "What we need is some businessman who will sponsor our organization so we can have a standing in the community."

Chairman KEFAUVER. Well. I was very delighted to hear from Mr. Ochoa, the chairman of the federation. as to the amount of interest there is in these clubs throughout the State. But, as you say, in all of these activities they need some good citizen or citizens to sponsor them.

Thank you very much, Mr. Ford. We are delighted to have you here, and I hope you will come around and sit with us.

Mr. FORD. I would like to stay for a few minutes.

Chairman KEFAUVER. We have received a number of telegrams from organizations that we will read into the record. Others will be answered.

Mr. Bobo, you have a telegram from some group?

Mr. BOBO (reading):

Los Angeles Tenth District Parent Teachers Organization with a membership of more than 237,000 has long been concerned about Blackboard Jungle and protested its being shown in this city. We believe this and other similar films are detrimental and breed further delinquents in young people. As a volunteer organization interested in child welfare we commend you on your investigation and the interest of the protection of our youth. We are hopeful of positive results.

Mrs. L. S. BACA, *President.*

Chairman KEFAUVER. This morning we will continue our motion picture hearings. Our last witness yesterday was Mr. George Murphy.

Our first witness this morning is Mr. Lou Greenspan, executive secretary of the Motion Picture Industry Council.

STATEMENT OF LOU GREENSPAN, EXECUTIVE SECRETARY, MOTION PICTURE INDUSTRY COUNCIL, LOS ANGELES, CALIF.

Chairman KEFAUVER. Mr. Bobo, will you ask Mr. Greenspan preliminary questions?

We have a lengthy biographical sketch of Mr. Greenspan. It shows his background. That you, Mr. Greenspan, were educated at Northwestern University in theology, in journalism, literature, music and arts.

You have been a reporter, publisher, produced a number of shows. You have been with the movie industry since 1931, is that correct, Mr. Greenspan?

Mr. GREENSPAN. Yes. I have been here before. I was here originally in 1926.

Chairman KEFAUVER. Mr. Greenspan, you move up and talk louder. We will read into the record your long and distinguished career. [Reading:]

Journalist, associate producer. Born Chicago, Ill. Educated Northwestern University, theology, then journalism, literature, music and arts. Reporter, City News Bureau, then Associated Press correspondent, Chicago. Publisher and editor Heard and Seen, Chicago; editor Variety Weekly in Chicago, New York, and Hollywood.

Produced vaudeville acts and floor shows for night clubs, hotels, cafes, et cetera.

In 1931, to Hollywood as independent producer.

In 1932–35, executive producer assistant, Universal. In 1936, president and general manager, Motion Picture Advertising Corp., Hollywood. In 1936–38, executive producer assistant, Grand National. In 1939, special west coast representative for ASCAP. In 1939–42, editor, Hollywood Reporter. In 1942, associate producer RKO. Joined Motion Picture Society for Americans as assistant to Joseph I. Breen, 1943; resigned March 1945. Joined Lou Irwin Agency, April 1945, as executive associate. In 1946, associate producer Star Pictures. Now in public relations, Hollywood.

You are now in public relations, Mr. Greenspan, is that correct?

Mr. GREENSPAN. Yes. As the executive secretary of the Motion Picture Industry Council, I am concerned with the good public relations of the industry at large.

I might tell you a little bit about the Motion Picture Industry Council. It is a sort of a senate of the cinema, you might call it, or little "United Nations," as it represents all segments of the motion-picture industry, both labor and management. This includes all the guilds, all the unions, the various associations, et cetera.

I might also add that it is quite distinguished from other industries, in that it is the only organization of its kind. I don't know of any other industry in the world where management and labor can sit down at a table and discuss common problems, common purposes and ideals, for the good and welfare of that industry.

I am not talking about any labor discussions or conditions, or anything of the sort, except for the good and welfare of the industry itself. Our council has now been in effect for about 6 years.

Incidentally, Dore Schary was one of the founders of it, who was here yesterday.

That gives you a little of the background.

Chairman KEFAUVER. Mr. Greenspan, what do you mean by management and the workers?

Mr. GREENSPAN. I mean the representatives of the management and the representatives of the labor unions and guilds sit around a table and discuss common problems for the good and welfare of the industry.

Chairman KEFAUVER. That is the writers——

Mr. GREENSPAN. The writers, the actors, the art directors, A. F. of L. film unions, all the technical unions, cameramen, soundmen, and all the rest of them, as well as the Producers Association, the Independent Producers Association, and so forth.

Chairman KEFAUVER. That is very interesting. How many unions are there in the industry, incidentally.

Mr. GREENSPAN. There are about 26, I believe, unions, actually trade unions in the setup of the American Federation of Labor studio unions.

In addition to that, there are some half dozen or more guilds, some who are not affiliated, like the Screen Writers Guild or the Screen Directors Guild, the Art Directors Guild.

Mr. FORD. 27 organizations or 27 chapters?

Mr. GREENSPAN. No, unions. There are some 26 actual locals of the various crafts in the A. F. or L. film studio union setup. Altogether I would say there is approximately between twenty and twenty-five thousand people employed in the motion-picture industry.

Chairman KEFAUVER. Very well, Mr. Greenspan.

Mr. Bobo, you had some specific questions to ask?

Mr. BOBO. Yes.

Mr. Greenspan, in the meetings of the Motion Picture Industry Council, you say that you take up certain of the problems of the motion-picture industry, and how to better foster the motion-picture industry?

Mr. GREENSPAN. That is right.

Mr. BOBO. Do you take into consideration within these meetings the public disapproval of certain types of pictures and what can be done about that?

Mr. GREENSPAN. Well, we do from time to time, although this is not one of our main purposes. We are not concerned with attacks from the outside, outside the industry, as well as we are concerned with the good relations intra-industrywise among ourselves.

We try not to infringe on the autonomy of the various organization members of our group. The matter of, let us say, so-called censorship or attack on movies, of course, we are extremely interested in, because all public opinion is very, very important to us, because it helps us decide which way we are going. But we do not take any definite action. We can discuss it among ourselves and make suggestions, and perhaps even reprimand each other once in a while, or even more than that. But it remains in camera, more or less.

Mr. Bobo. As a motion picture industry councilman, representing all facets of the motion-picture industry, has your group given any thought or made any recommendations to the motion-picture industry within itself, as to types of pictures, as to content of pictures?

Mr. Greenspan. No, we have not.

Mr. Bobo. The purpose of the council then is what, Mr. Greenspan?

Mr. Greenspan. The purpose of the council is not to engage in film content to the extent of telling producers what they may or may not make, or what they should or should not make. We can only bring to them the reactions of the public and also the reactions of other people in the industry. But as to any decisions, the individual studios themselves must decide that.

Besides, we have the code, as you know, and all of the major companies, as well as the independents, subscribe to the Motion Picture Code. That is the organization where they do discuss film content, what may or may not, should or should not get on the screen. We have no jurisdiction or function in that direction.

Mr. Bobo. Mr. Greenspan, did you have a statement you wish to make?

Mr. Greenspan. Yes, I have several things here. It won't take too long. They are both my own opinions and observations, as well as some educated opinions.

I mean I have been here, as you know, the last couple of days, and I have listened very attentively to a great deal of it, and I think some of this has a bearing. I have a statement here that was made by the field director of the United States National Child Welfare Association. I will see if I can get his name here. If I may, I would like to read this, Senator.

Chairman Kefauver. How long is it, Mr. Greenspan?

Mr. Greenspan. Just a little thing.

Chairman Kefauver. Very well. Who is it by, sir?

Mr. Greenspan. The field director of the United States National Child Welfare Association.

Chairman Kefauver. Well, just tell us what it says. If we don't know who it is by, there is not much use of reading it.

Mr. Greenspan. He says:

Most have heard a great deal about the damage certain types of modern pictures are supposed to do to the minds of children. Reformers assure us that the gangster pictures might well lead a child along the path of wrongdoing. However, every once in a while someone familiar with the ways of children rises up and says it isn't so.

The director went on to say:

Even when a young delinquent himself puts the blame on a film, it doesn't necessarily mean anything. Children have an almost remarkable capacity for saying what they believe adults want to hear * * *. On being brought before some judge for committing some crime they begin searching for an excuse—an impressive excuse. The motion picture provides just that.

And then he went on:

Newspaper readers whose memories go back 50 or 60 years ago can remember when the dime novel, instead of moving pictures, was the scapegoat. It used to be said that children who read of the exploits of gunmen in dime novels would grow up to be gunmen themselves; the current charge against the movies is only an adaptation of that old complaint.

I think that covers what he has to say, but I would like to supplement that, if I may.

Mr. BOBO. Mr. Greenspan, on that one particular instance there, have you also brought along with you other instances where people might have taken a varying viewpoint with that person there?

Mr. GREENSPAN. A varying viewpoint?

Mr. BOBO. Yes.

Mr. GREENSPAN. No, I haven't.

Mr. BOBO. Has the council gone into any research?

Mr. GREENSPAN. The council has. We have gone into research from time to time, and our findings more or less reflect some of the statements that were made here yesterday by some our our studio heads.

For one thing, we agree and I personally agree that the public must share the responsibility as well as the credit that motion pictures reflect. Don't forget it is the same public, the same people who pay their money to see Blackboard Jungle, that also pay their money to see A Man Called Peter or a Davy Crockett or a Disney picture. It is the same people.

And we also know that "crime doesn't pay" has always been the keynote that has been sounded by motion pictures. In fact, some years ago—I am surprised Dora Schary didn't mention that—M-G-M led the way in a series of crime shorts—some of you may recall—called Crime Doesn't Pay, which was very, very effective.

Chairman KEFAUVER. He did mention that.

Mr. GREENSPAN. Did he? I didn't remember that.

Chairman KEFAUVER. He talked about the shorts, about the ones he had the G-men in, which were the "crime doesn't pay" shows.

Mr. GREENSPAN. I see. He didn't mention it by name. From time to time efforts are made to take recognition of this problem. I can recall during the 1930's, when the so-called gangster pictures were being made, it had reached quite a pitch at one time, especially where heroes were created, such as Jimmy Cagney and Eddie Robinson, and kids were going around imitating them and emulating them.

I recall one picture in that time called Angels With Dirty Faces in which a specific ending was arranged for that picture, in which Jimmy Cagney, the star, is led to the electric chair. He was shown as a cringing, cowardly, hysterical character, in order to cause the children and the little kids who had made him an idol previously, to change their minds about him.

Mr. BOBO. Mr. Greenspan, I have been interested in quite a bit of the testimony here, where the good things, such as showing Jimmy Cagney as a cringing person, would have an effect of teaching children there that the good man in the movies would teach the children this.

I wonder if the same thing is not true, when we show these particular scenes and teach children, and when we show the other scenes of brutality, of crimes, of horrible fights, of an absence of respect for law and order, aren't we teaching children at the same time, a great number of children, these things are condoned by the public, realizing there are a great many good movies and also in many of these movies are bad scenes that might also be teaching them?

Mr. GREENSPAN. I don't happen to be one who believes that you can change a child's mind or his personality or his character to that extent.

I believe that if a boy is wrong, or even a girl, he comes in wrong to see that movie. I don't think that any movie can that much change any child.

I know I was raised in a very tough town, among very tough people in Chicago, and I know others who have been, and yet they have grown up to be wonderful citizens and good Americans, and nothing has affected them. On the contrary, it served as an example.

Sometimes it is more important to see and know what not to do than to know what to do. By seeing what you shouldn't do you learn a great deal more along the line of what you should do. I just don't happen to believe that, I don't believe that movies are the cause at all of the juvenile delinquency. I am not one who subscribes to that.

Mr. BOBO. Do you believe that movies contribute at all to society, for good or for bad?

Mr. GREENSPAN. As an influence?

Mr. BOBO. Yes.

Mr. GREENSPAN. Yes. Yes, when you say, "Do they contribute to good or bad," generally speaking, not specifying juveniles or adults, I will agree with you.

It does have a definite influence for good or bad. There is such a thing as good taste, and I will put in with you on that. I am a great believer in good taste.

I think many times movies do often breach what is considered good taste, but then again that is, too, a relative termn, because what is considered good taste to one individual or group of people may be considered not good taste to another.

The same thing with morality. I know what is moral in one age is immoral in another. Who is going to decide that?

When Mr. Mooring spoke yesterday of a list of pictures and how terrible pictures are and the content of them, and exposing children to them, what about the Bible? I would like to have asked Mr. Mooring about the Bible.

What about all the stories of crime and violence and passion and adultery you can find all through the Bible? I happen to be a biblical student, so it is naturally on my mind.

Does that mean we shouldn't let our children read the Bible? Does that mean that we should expunge from the Bible these chapters? I don't believe it.

Mr. BOBO. No one would, I think, suggest in any motion picture or any book or any novel we shouldn't have some reference to life as it is around us every day, with some violence, but I don't think in many of our books—and I think in the realm of taste—where an extremely brutal and sadistic fight might be shown, that in the realm of taste I don't think there can be much difference of opinion——

Mr. GREENSPAN. No difference of opinion whatever.

Mr. BOBO. In a coldblooded killing, where 3 or 4 or 5 take place in 1 movie. I don't think in that realm we would have an element of taste. Some places in the sexual showings of movies, we might have that.

Mr. GREENSPAN. I agree with you.

Mr. Bobo. With the combined effect of magazines, with the combined effect of television and radio and the movies as a contributing factor, what is your feeling as to whether or not we are becoming immune to human suffering, to the impact of crime and violence through all the media of communication?

Mr. Greenspan. If we are becoming immune to human suffering, crime, and violence, I wouldn't lay it at the door of the movies alone. I wouldn't lay it at the door of comic books alone. I wouldn't lay it at the door of television alone. I would lay it at the door of civilization.

I think we become immune because of the 3 wars we have gone through in the last 50 years, because a new generation of children has grown up who have become hardened. They have become immune to things because that has become a sort of way of life, a sort of an expectancy, that we are sitting on a powder keg waiting to be blown up. That in itself has created more emotional upsets and disturbances in children as they grow up than any other factor I know of.

Mr. Young. Mr. Senator.

Chairman Kefauver. Just a minute, Mr. Young.

Mr. Greenspan, I take it that your council does serve a very useful purpose in bringing together representatives of all segments of the industry for a general discussion of all aspects of——

Mr. Greenspan. Right.

Chairman Kefauver. Labor relations, the type of movies, the public relations?

Mr. Greenspan. Not labor relations, as such.

Chairman Kefauver. But I mean public relations.

Mr. Greenspan. Public relations as affects labor, yes.

Chairman Kefauver. The movie industry realizes, with the competition it has from television and with also the criticism from time to time of types of movies, it is incumbent upon all segments of the people in the industry——

Mr. Greenspan. To share that responsibility.

Chairman Kefauver. To not only have good movies, to improve the quality of some of the poorer ones, and to avoid mistakes.

Mr. Greenspan. I agree with that 100 percent, Senator.

Chairman Kefauver. I am certain your council does serve a good and useful purpose.

Mr. Greenspan. That is right.

Chairman Kefauver. We appreciate your coming in and telling us about it.

I don't think you read all of the statement you had there. I would like to have it put in the record.

Mr. Greenspan. You can have it put in the record.

Chairman Kefauver. That will be put in the record following your statement.

The document referred to was marked "Exhibit No. 7," and reads as follows:)

Exhibit No. 7

Investigator Says Youth Not Damaged by Movies

Most have heard a great deal about the damage certain types of motion pictures are supposed to do to the minds of children. Reformers assure us that the gangster pictures might well lead a child along the path of wrongdoing. However every once in awhile someone familiar with the ways of children rises up and says it isn't so.

The latest to voice this view is the field director of the United States National Child Welfare Association, who has just finished studying the reactions of hundreds of children to all types of movies during a 3-month period.

He took time, for instance, to investigate a number of cases in which juvenile delinquents were supposed to have been led astray by things they had seen in the movies. In every case, he said, hereditary environment conditions proved chiefly responsible for the child's delinquency; in many cases the child concerned had never even seen a film that was supposed to have caused his downfall.

Said the director: "Even when a young delinquent himself puts the blame on a film, it doesn't necessarily mean anything. Children have an almost remarkable capacity for saying what they believe adults want to hear * * * On being brought before some judge for committing some crime they began searching for an excuse—an impressive excuse. The motion picture provides just that."

Newspaper readers whose memories go back 50 or 60 years ago can remember when the dime novel, instead of moving pictures, was the scapegoat. It use to be said that children who read of the exploits of gunmen in dime novels would grow up to be gunmen themselves; the current charge against the movies is only an adaptation of that old complaint.

Well, most of us read dime novels, years ago; and somehow we managed to escape the pitfall that was laid for us. The chances are that the same thing is true of children today. They take their lurid movies just as we took those old dime novels—with a grain or two of salt. Children usually have a better balance in such matters than adults are willing to admit.

Chairman KEFAUVER. Mr. Young, what was it you wanted?

Mr. YOUNG. Mr. Senator, Mr. Greenspan made a reference to Angels With Dirty Faces, at the end where the gangster was led to the electric chair. Mr. Greenspan is well familiar with the picture called Public Enemy No. 1, which Warner Bros. produced, with Jimmy Cagney, where Jimmy Cagney in one sequence, scene, took a grapefruit and smashed it right into the lady's face at the table.

Now, at that time or right thereafter, children who had seen that picture, Public Enemy No. 1, of Jimmy Cagney's, this gangster, hoodlum, portrayed in this picture, took this grapefruit and smashed it into this lady's face, or sweetheart, or whatever—I don't recall who she was—and a boy around 10, sitting with his little sister at the table, did the very thing.

It seemed that the mother, when the little girl started to cry and explain, et cetera, that she had called the motion pictures organization at the time—and I am quoting the press—and complained of the incident.

If I remember correctly—I am not sure, and Mr. Greenspan is more familiar with that—I have known Mr. Greenspan for many years and he has me. Warner Bros. at that time, I believe, were not members of the motion picture producers' organization and would not adhere to any of their——

Chairman KEFAUVER. Their code?

Mr. YOUNG. Their code. I am not sure about that, but Mr. Greenspan is familiar with it. I am citing the fact. At that very time, when that grapefruit incident was a big issue——

Mr. GREENSPAN. I will answer that.

Chairman KEFAUVER. Mr. Young, I think Mr. Warner testified they were members of the code from the time it began.

Mr. GREENSPAN. Yes. But I will answer the grapefruit charge.

Chairman KEFAUVER. We don't want the record not to present the facts, as to their position.

Mr. YOUNG. I will ask, Senator, if Mr. Greenspan will explain that. Mr. Greenspan, do you want to answer that?

Mr. GREENSPAN. Yes, I will answer that.

In the first place, nobody—how did you put that grapefruit, what did you say he did? That he smashed it into her face?

Chairman KEFAUVER. He said into his little sister's face.

Mr. GREENSPAN. In the first place, he didn't do any smashing. He shoved it gently.

In the second place, you may recall an actor by the name of Clifton Webb in a picture called Sitting Pretty, where he, too, sort of shoved a whole bowl of mush into a child's face, and got the biggest laugh that I have heard in years. It is still being talked about. And anybody here who has seen this picture I am sure will agree with me.

So that dissipates your argument about shoving grapefruits into people's faces.

Chairman KEFAUVER. Well, Mr. Greenspan, we don't want to encourage shoving grapefruits into little children's faces.

Mr. GREENSPAN. No. Before I go, to keep this in the light mood it started out in, I would like to show how movies get blamed for for a lot of things.

I am reminded of the story of the alcoholic who was a great problem to his family, friends, and wife. Along came a picture which Paramount made, incidentally, with Ray Milland—an Academy Award picture—called Lost Weekend. I am sure several of you remember that, many of you do.

This man's friends advised his wife to take him to see this picture, that it would be a good influence over him. And she did.

He sat with rapt attention and looked at that picture, and never said a word. She was watching him. On their way out, he kept saying to her, "Never again. Never, never again."

She looked at him and said, "You mean you won't ever drink again?"

He said, "No, dear. I mean I will never go to a movie again."

Chairman KEFAUVER. All right. Thank you very much, Mr. Greenspan.

Mr. GREENSPAN. It has been a pleasure.

STATEMENT OF GORDON S. WHITE, DIRECTOR, ADVERTISING CODE ADMINISTRATION OF THE MOTION PICTURE ASSOCIATION OF AMERICA, NEW YORK, N. Y.

Chairman KEFAUVER. Mr. White, you are the director, advertising code administration of the Motion Picture Association of America, is that correct?

Mr. WHITE. That is right, sir.

Chairman KEFAUVER. Mr. Bobo.

Mr. BOBO. Mr. White, for how long have you been associated in your present capacity?

Mr. WHITE. For 10½ years.

Mr. BOBO. What is the responsibility of yours, as director of the production and how the advertising of the administration is handled?

Mr. WHITE. Our responsibility is to pass on advertising submitted to us by companies, both members of the association and nonmembers, and to either approve or disapprove it, under our judgment, as to whether it meets or does not meet the requirements of the advertising code.

Mr. BOBO. Prior to going with the Motion Picture Production Administration, what was your background, Mr. White?

Mr. WHITE. My first working experience was as a newspaperman, as reporter and copy editor. After that I was a publicity man and finally an advertising executive.

It might be of interest to you, possibly, to note that at the time the advertising code was written 25 years ago I was the director of advertising and publicity for one of the association's member companies, and as such became one of the original signatories of the advertising code. So I watched it in operation from both sides of the fence, so to speak, since its inception.

Mr. BOBO. You have a statement outlining the work of the advertising code administration?

Mr. WHITE. I do, sir.

Chairman KEFAUVER. Mr. White, you read the statement or tell us about it, whichever you wish.

Mr. WHITE. Well, could I ask permission before I read this—because of the peculiar circumstances—to make a few remarks aside from this statement?

Chairman KEFAUVER. Oh, yes; you can read the statement and make any other remarks, or you can make any other remarks and read the statement.

Mr. WHITE. I would like to make a few comments first, if I could.

Chairman KEFAUVER. All right, sir.

Mr. WHITE. I should see, I suppose, some special distinction in being the first witness here who has had a special set built for him, or, at least, I assume this display of advertising matter was arranged for my special attention.

Chairman KEFAUVER. You are wrong about that, Mr. White. It was gotten together so some of the producers could talk about the advertising that went along with their shows.

I suppose this is advertising that was passed on by you. I should think you would want to have it to make any explanation in connection with it.

Mr. WHITE. I had hoped I might make a few comments, because I think possibly my statement might have more significance if I may do so.

First of all, a technical correction. This material was referred to several times yesterday as posters. These are not posters.

A poster is a large display item, advertising item, usually lithographed. They are prepared generally in certain established patterns, beginning with what is known as a 1-sheet, which is a key size of a poster, which is 28 by 42 inches. There are 3-sheets and 6-sheets, in corresponding sizes, that is, you multiply that by 3 and 6. And finally the largest of the established poster, which is 24-sheet. I think that runs about 8 feet 9 inches by 19 feet 6 inches.

It is not, as it was suggested yesterday, a thing that would cover this whole end wall, but it is a thing that would probably cover two-thirds of this panel of the wall here [indicating]. Those are posters.

These items here, most of them—I could make an exact count of them by going around looking at them—but most of them, Senator, are the covers of press books.

Now, a press book is a campaign book. It is put out by the producer or distributor of the picture, to present the entire promotional campaign on a particular picture, including the advertising, the prepared publicity, the special exploitation ideas, illustrations of the posters in lobby displays, and so forth.

Chairman KEFAUVER. Do you have one of the press books there with you, Mr. White?

Mr. WHITE. Yes, I do have several press books here. Those are some press books which I hope might enter into the committee's record.

Chairman KEFAUVER. Well, if we may do so, we will file these as exhibits and they will be studied by the subcommittee.

Mr. WHITE. In connection with those, I recall Mr. Schary's hope and Mr. Bobo's indication that it would be true, that in the full study of the advertising of this industry, that such films as Marty, A Country Girl, The Man Called Peter, that those things also might be taken into consideration. But, anyway, most of these items appear on the covers of these press books, which were never designed to go to the public. They were designed to go to the theaters, the theaterman.

Much of the material included in the panels inside of those covers, of course, is designed for public use. But these covers, as they stand here now, were never intended for distribution to the public. They are selling and service items, going to the theaters.

Chairman KEFAUVER. Let me get this, now. Let me see if I understand this. Of course, the large 9 by 19, or 8 by 19 foot posters I have seen. I didn't know how big they were. But aren't most of them replicas, or just larger editions of what we see here?

Mr. WHITE. Some of the units of art work in these would be included in some of the posters, of course.

Chairman KEFAUVER. Do you mean to say that this press material or press book is more unsavory than the larger posters? Is that the point you are making?

Mr. WHITE. No, sir. I was merely giving you a point of technical information, as to what these were.

Chairman KEFAUVER. It is your judgment these are fairly representative of the larger posters, the 8 by 19 foot posters that we see?

Mr. WHITE. Some items in here might be represented on those posters.

Chairman KEFAUVER. Are these worse or better than the actual posters?

Mr. WHITE. I don't know whether they are either worse or better, Senator.

Chairman KEFAUVER. Then you think they are about the same?

Mr. WHITE. Well, they might be.

Mr. YOUNG. Mr. Senator——

Chairman KEFAUVER. Mr. Young, let us go along a little while.

Mr. YOUNG. This is very important.

Chairman KEFAUVER. I know it is important. Every question is important.

Mr. YOUNG. Thank you.

Chairman KEFAUVER. We will carry on for a while. We will give everybody a chance.

This is a very nice poster, the last advertising, the Glass Slipper. We will put all of these in. We want to have a good cross section, so any others you have here, we can put in.

But your point is these are the front pages, apparently, or come from the press releases?

Mr. WHITE. From the press books; yes, sir.

Chairman KEFAUVER. Actually, the larger posters are just blown-up editions of what we see her, in most cases, aren't they?

Mr. WHITE. Not necessarily. I would have to look at the press book on each one of these separately, to see what the poster was. I couldn't possibly remember what the poster is, of course, on each one. Some of the art work included in these, certainly, just be included in some of the posters also.

As you would find in the case of, for example, Marty and the Country Girl and Magnificent Obsession; the same thing would apply there.

Mr. BOBO. Does the particular theater have the option of choosing from quite a number of press releases or pictures, as to the posters he will put up?

Mr. WHITE. As to posters, he doesn't have very much choice. That is, I was trying, for your information, to make a distinction as to what a poster was.

As to posters, they are expensive and they are prepared usually in possibly two styles in each size, so that the exhibitor who wants to use a poster doesn't have a great deal of choice.

In the advertising going into the newspaper, he does have more choice. You will see in these press books there are usually a number of ads. There are usually 2 or 3 different types of ads on any particular campaign.

The exhibitor, of course, has that choice and then the exhibitor also has the right, where he has the equipment he has the right to prepare advertising of his own. That, of course, we have no control over.

The things we do pass upon are the items of advertising publicity and poster items that go into these press books, on pictures which carry our production code seal.

Chairman KEFAUVER. Very well, Mr. White, you go on with your statement.

Mr. WHITE. All right. The advertising code is an integral part of the motion-picture industry's voluntary adopted system of self-regulation, and as I said earlier, has been in effect since 1930.

As with the production code, all members of the association subscribe to the advertising code and its services are open alike to nonmembers and members. There is no discrimination between them. There is no differentiation. Any producer or distributor of a picture bearing the production code seal of approval voluntarily agrees to keep the film's advertising in line with the advertising code.

In conformity with the principles of the advertising code, it is the job of the advertising code administration to maintain good morale standards and decency in advertising copy submitted to it.

The administration has two offices. One is in New York, where I am located, and where much of the film advertising originates. The other is here in Hollywood, in charge of Mr. Simmon Levy, associate administrator.

While the production code administration and the advertising code administration have identical principles and purposes, there are important differences in operations that I would like to discuss with you.

The production code administration has to do with the content of the story, the substance of the story, with the whole substance of a story. Producing a motion picture is one thing but writing an ad to promote is quite another. Of necessity, in advertising a man can only highlight some idea or theme in the picture. It reflects, it represents, it treats symbolically of the picture. It is designed to attract attention and sell the product. To induce the potential patrons to got out of the house and down the street to the theater. In these days of competition, motion-picture advertising must be especially striking and effective and appealing. It must convince in a line, in a word, in an illustration, and it must convince quickly.

All these are perfectly understandable designs and ends, as I am sure this committee fully realizes. But they are also the root, I am afraid, of some of the misunderstanding about film advertising copy.

Motion-picture advertising naturally is not expected to tell the story of a film. There is not space, there is not time. And if there was it would still be an error to do this, because it would take half the fun out of seeing a picture, if you knew the whole story in advance. And the advertising would thus defeat its own purpose.

What it does seek to do and what it should do is to convey the spirit, the atmosphere, the feeling, the general impression of the photoplay. This is fair. This is proper. This is accepted advertising practice. It is neither misleading nor misrepresentative.

In another advertisement you might see a young lady touching her ear with a particular brand of perfume that is designed to entice her date to a marriage proposal. But we all know that this doesn't assure that the girl, by buying the perfume, will get the good-looking man in the ad.

Such comparisons are endless. I mention them in the hope that all persons will keep these things—these elemental factors of advertising—in mind in speaking about and in judging motion-picture advertising. I think it would lead to better mutual understanding all around.

Now, let me get back to the direct operations of the advertising code administration. We handle a steady flow of all kinds of advertising material. Only a relatively small proportion of this ever causes us any real difficulty.

The greatest part of the copy is readily passable. At the other end of the scale is a small number of items, which are readily unpassable. This too creates no great problem in reaching a decision.

In between is a sort of a gray zone. It is copy that is not so very large in volume, that is on the line between acceptable and nonacceptable, under the code. Some of the copy in this area can be satisfactorily revised with minor changes, and can be passed on resubmission.

In deciding on this material in the gray zone, it is a matter of my judgment, as my responsibility as the director of the code administration.

I have to make decisions that are sometimes not easy. I have to interpret the rules as I believe them to apply to the specific advertisement. You can see that I am like the umpire in baseball. He may not be the most popular fellow in the world but the game couldn't be played without him.

I believe the production code and the advertising code have immeasurably aided the American motion picture in reaching its present high state. This is true, because the industry's long-established system of self-regulation fulfills ethical and moral principles and aspirations that reasonable men everywhere welcome and support.

In concluding, I am convinced that, in selling the product, motion-picture advertising approved by the code administration, by and

large over the years, well meets this sound test of general acceptability.

Chairman KEFAUVER. Mr. White, you didn't tell us how many advertising items are passed. You have something in your statement
about it.

Mr. WHITE. What we call an item, Senator, would be anything.
It could be a line of typewritten copy suggested for advertising use.
It might be a still photograph. It might be a poster displayed; it
might be anything.

We handle material that varies in volume, oh, maybe anywhere
from 120,000 to 140,000 pieces a year. Last year we handled approximately 130,000 pieces of material in the New York office and the
Hollywood office combined.

Chairman KEFAUVER. Now, does the code apply to shorts, trailers?

Mr. WHITE. Trailers, yes, sir. Trailers, we include a trailer as
one item in keeping our quantity records.

Chairman KEFAUVER. May they be passed upon either in Hollywood or in New York, according to where they are submitted?

Mr. WHITE. Yes, sir, they may.

Chairman KEFAUVER. If submitted here, and you living in New
York, who passes them?

Mr. WHITE. Mr. Simon Levy passes on them here.

Chairman KEFAUVER. Is there communication between you and
him with reference to passing?

Mr. WHITE. We are in frequent communication, yes, sir.

Chairman KEFAUVER. Some of these producers have their own advertising organizations, and others have outside, separate, distinct
organizations, do they not?

Mr. WHITE. All of the large producing and distributing organizations, the bigger companies, all have their own advertising departments. And many of them, in addition, employ outside agencies to do
some work for them, yes, sir. We get material both from the advertising departments and from agencies.

Chairman KEFAUVER. Does all the industry work through your
code, all the producers and distributors?

Mr. WHITE. All of the producers are supposed to send in their
material if they carry a production code seal of approval on their
pictures.

Chairman KEFAUVER. What percentage carry a code approval?

Mr. WHITE. I don't know what the exact figure is. It is a very,
very high figure, in the high 90 percent of American-made pictures.
A great many of the foreign pictures don't carry our seal, don't
ask for it.

Chairman KEFAUVER. What American-made pictures do not carry
the code seal?

Mr. WHITE. Only a few of the—maybe the imitation burlesque type
of picture which, fortunately, perhaps, does not have usual major
distribution or all the major play dates.

There is a small fringe of pictures that are made and played to a
limited distribution that don't carry our seal, but they are very few
in number. The proportion of foreign-made pictures that do not
carry our seal is very much larger.

Chairman KEFAUVER. Is it possible for foreign-made pictures to
operate through your organization and obtain your seal?

Mr. WHITE. It is possible for anybody who makes a picture anywhere in the world to submit his picture to the production code authority. If it is judged to be in keeping with the production code, he may have a seal on it under exactly the same terms as Metro, Paramount, or anybody else.

Chairman KEFAUVER. How is your organization financed? By the industry itself, of course. Is it by the number of items of advertising submitted?

Mr. WHITE. Mr. Shurlock will undoubtedly go into detail on the handling of that. The production code is financed by each producer or distributor paying a fee on his picture, whether he is a member or not a member of the association. The advertising code administration is financed by the dues of the association.

Chairman KEFAUVER. No particular fees?

Mr. WHITE. There are no fees on advertising or on our title registration bureau service.

Chairman KEFAUVER. How large an organization do you have, Mr. White?

Mr. WHITE. We have the two men, I mean Mr. Levy and myself in New York, and our clerical staff.

Chairman KEFAUVER. Well, do you have professionals to look at all this material or do you try to do it all yourself?

Mr. WHITE. The final judgment is mine in all cases, or is Mr. Levy's if the material is handled out here, just the same as the final decision on production work is Mr. Shurlock's. There are people in our office, of course, with whom I consult on this material.

Chairman KEFAUVER. In what form is it submitted to you, by the producer or by the advertising agent of the producer?

Mr. WHITE. In any form at all. We will get a piece of typewritten copy.

Chairman KEFAUVER. Here is MGM press book on Interrupted Melody. Will they submit something like that and you pass on it?

Mr. WHITE. Each piece of advertising there, Senator, was submitted in advance, and so with the page proofs showing the publicity stories and the exploitation ideas; they were all submitted in advance, before the press book was printed.

Chairman KEFAUVER. There is on the front of it, "Approved, Advertising Code Administration, New York."

Mr. WHITE. That was our file copy.

Chairman KEFAUVER. After approval by you, anything in here can be blown up, enlarged or used?

Mr. WHITE. They are already prepared when this press book is printed, Senator. The only thing that shows larger in actual use than it is indicated in there would be the posters and the lobby display cards. Those are merely illustrations, to show the exhibitor what he can expect to get when he orders, say, a six-sheet poster. There is an illustration there showing what he would get when he orders that.

Chairman KEFAUVER. Mr. Bobo.

Mr. BOBO. Mr. White, in your own office, in dealing with the code, your judgment is the final judgment on what constitutes good taste or good morals in advertising?

Mr. WHITE. My judgment is the final judgment as to whether each piece coming through separately does, in my opinion, reasonably meet the requirements of the code, yes, sir.

Mr. BOBO. It is set forth under the code at No. 11, for instance:

Nudity with meretricious purposes and salacious postures shall not be used; and clothed figures shall not be represented in such manner as to be offensive or contrary to good taste or morals.

Recently has there been an increase in the amount of sex-type advertising, which has been received by the code arministration?

Mr. WHITE. I have no figures. I don't think there has been any material increase. There may possibly have been a few more pictures in that category.

There certainly have been a few more pictures in the crime and violence category, of course, the advertising reflects it. I see a great many of these displays on pictures which would be called crime and violence stories [indicating].

Mr. BOBO. Mr. White, in the event you should disapprove of a certain piece of advertising, is it taken back and resubmitted to you for final approval?

Mr. WHITE. That is what we always hope will be done. Very, very rarely there will be something come through which we feel is irrevocably unacceptable. That is a very, very minute fraction of 1 percent. Most of the material is corrected and resubmitted and approved.

Chairman KEFAUVER. You said you hoped that would be done. That seems to express some idea it is not done occasionally.

Mr. WHITE. Well, sir, this is a human endeavor. It is a very difficult thing. We do not operate an arbitrary, complete authority where we can be dictators. We counsel, we advise.

Once in a while someone doesn't want to take our advice.

Chairman KEFAUVER. If they don't take your advice, what happens, do they go on and put their advertising out anyway?

Mr. WHITE. Very, very rarely. I was sort of smiling at that. I didn't want to make a 100 percent statement. Because it came up yesterday, I would like to tell you, if I may, about the ad over here on Hell's Island, which was criticized. The vice president in charge of the studio out here said he didn't like it.

I don't know what he objected to particularly. There are two pieces of art work there. There is a reclining figure in which the girl is covered, and also a figure of a girl in a bathing suit.

Now, this girl in the bathing suit is wearing a costume much more modest than a great amount of the material we see in magazine and newspaper illustrations, of bathing suits.

I didn't like the way they approached this campaign. I objected to it. And I was called over to the Paramount office in a conference with the advertising manager, the director of advertising publicity, who was a vice president, and the executive vice president of the company.

They felt and insisted that what they were doing was perfectly all right. My judgment can be wrong in one direction as well as another. I made the comparison with being an umpire. You try to call balls and strikes and you can be wrong either way. I suppose I am wrong as often in my judgment as any other human being is.

I didn't like this, but they insisted upon using it and I finally allowed myself in this case to be persuaded——

Chairman KEFAUVER. You didn't like it; Mr. Freeman said he didn't like it.

Mr. WHITE. The executive vice president in New York thought it was wonderful. Adherence to the code is a joint responsibility. I wish to give no one the slightest impression that I am not willing and eager to accept responsibility for my judgment. But it is a joint activity. After all, the companies are pledged to this and they are as much responsible for applying the code, of course, as we are. I simply give it to you as an example, to show you what could happen.

Senator KEFAUVER. I thought Mr. Freeman was the big boss in Paramount. He said he was. Apparently, the executive vice president in New York overruled you and him both.

Mr. WHITE. Mr. Freeman is the big boss out here in the studio in charge of Hollywood operations. I have to deal with the executive vice president in New York in charge of advertising.

You asked what would happen. I gave you an example of what might happen. Possibly I was persuaded, let us say, to make a judgment which afterwards, as a Monday morning quarterback, I might regret.

In turning out this volume of material, of course, that is possible. I say it is a joint responsibility, and since this particular ad was discussed yesterday, I thought you might like to have the facts.

I would like to ask two things, if I may. I would like to ask for a transcript of this part of the testimony, questions and answers, which included this reference yesterday. I would like to send that to Mr. Raiburn in New York.

I would like also, when we get through here——

Chairman KEFAUVER. We will send you that transcript, Mr. White.

Mr. WHITE. Thank you. I was hoping maybe I could pick it up here, because I wanted to send it to New York in a hurry, while it was hot.

Chairman KEFAUVER. Well, if this young lady can get it out for you, you can have it.

Mr. WHITE. Wonderful. The other thing I would like to suggest is that you lend me this display [indicating], the entire display. I would like to display it for the benefit of the advertising publicity directors here in Hollywood as soon as I can, after this session is over. And then I would like to take it back to New York with me and display it to the top advertising and publicity executives back there.

I wish you would let me say this one thing about it. I don't want you to think I want to defend any piece of copy, any particular piece of copy. I have no such desire.

I do desire to say, though, that it is impossible to make a collection of materials, such as this, and put them all in one mass display together, without their looking—even if they were good they wouldn't look good in a display of this kind, where they are all massed together.

We handle all of this material, of course, as units. We can go through this and discuss it, the material, piece by piece, and we would wind up probably as we did last summer in our office in New York when I took every item of criticism which had come in over a period of 6 months or so, and I listed every subject that had been mentioned in this criticism, even only once in an individual letter.

I had 12 picture titles. We got out advertising on these 12 titles. We analyzed the advertising on each one of them, and we wound up feeling that some of them might have involved a question of dispute over good taste, some of them were perfectly all right and we would pass them again. At the end there were two or three of them, looking at them as Monday morning quarterbacks again, that we would have just been as happy if they hadn't passed. I imagine that the same thing would happen if we went through this display.

I notice over there, starting at the upper lefthand corner, we read a display on a picture titled "Cell 2445, Death Row." I looked at it in amazement, trying to figure out what could possibly be wrong with it. It is a simple illustration of a man behind bars, surrounded by a one-color drab frame. The other extreme perhaps is a thing of this sort [indicating].

I make no attempt to argue about any piece of it. The basic responsibility is mine, but the joint responsibility is mine and the producers of the material, that is, the advertising men who create it.

Mr. Bobo. The advertising code, does it provide any type of penalty or fine for violation of the code?

Mr. White. Yes, itdoes provide penalty.

Mr. Bobo. In your history with the advertising code, has any producer or advertiser been fined?

Mr. White. Yes, once. There was a case when an ad was turned down. The advertising manager announced emphatically he was going to use it anyway, and he did use it, and the board of directors did assess a penalty against that company, and I believe the company took about half of it out of the man's salary.

Mr. Bobo. In the event of a picture, such as Hell's Island, where one person in the studio will overrule your opinion and overrule others' opinions, is there not a provision there where you can be more forceful with the penalty?

Mr. White. I don't want to leave the wrong impression. He did not overrule my opinion. He persuaded me to arrive at a decision that I originally didn't want to make.

That is a human process, I suppose, of argument and persuasion. That is what we are doing all the time, we are persuading all the time.

Mr. Bobo. Do you find among some of the producers that they are a little overeager in trying to push certain advertising, sexy ads or violent ads through the advertising code?

Mr. White. These men are always under great economic compulsion, Mr. Bobo, to sell their pictures. I believe it was Mr. Schary who said yesterday that the man at the head of a studio, if he made too many mistakes, wouldn't have a job long. The same thing applies equally, of course, to the men who write these ads. If they don't do a good job in selling a picture, they won't have their jobs very long.

They are constantly working under great pressure of deadlines, too. This is a pressure business. They are under economic pressure to sell the picture, once the great investment has been made. And they are under all sorts of working pressures. We work with them under those pressures.

Mr. Bobo. In the New York office where, I believe, the predominance of the advertising comes from, there is yourself and your clerical staff.

Mr. White. That is correct, sir. And other members of the staff with whom I consult.

As I tried to bring out in this statement, the quantity we work on sounds possibly more important and impressive than it really is. In fact, the handling of most of it is routine.

On a picture like Marty or a picture like Interrupted Melody, we have no problem. We have to look at each piece of material as it comes through, but if you look at that layout on Marty you will see it warms your heart as you read it. It is elevating, it is inspiring, it is no problem. We go through that material with the greatest of ease.

It is only when we come to approximately the last 2 percent that it begins to be difficult. As I say, there is this gray area in which is found unacceptable advertising copy at times. We have no difficulty saying "No" on that. And the ad which is like a Marty ad, of course, that is simple. In this gray area, there are pieces of material on which it is very difficult, often, to make a decision. We look at a thing this big and it is going to, you know, be 19 feet 6 inches long when it comes out in 24 sheets.

Mr. Bobo. You speak of "we" and the staff with whom you consult. How many members of that staff are there that do reviewing of the motion-picture advertising.

Mr. White. They don't review officially. They only consult with me when I go to them for the benefit of their judgment.

Mr. Bobo. Are they employed by the advertising code?

Mr. White. They are not employed directly in the advertising code, but they are employed by the association and they work in the same office with us.

Mr. Bobo. In fact, you are the only one, so far as the advertising code administration is concerned, that has any authority to review ads?

Mr. White. Who has any authority to review them officially and decide on them; that is right.

Mr. Bobo. Every case of advertising must be followed from the beginning to the end through with you for the advertising code administration?

Mr. White. That is right, or Mr. Levy in the office here.

Mr. Bobo. These others with whom you consult are employed by the industry in an advertising capacity?

Mr. White. Employed by the association, but not directly in an advertising capacity. There are, let's say, 3 or 4 with whom I consult most regularly. One of them is a man who has been with the association twenty-odd years, since shortly after the First World War. He has been a public relations man. He is head of the association's community relations department, which is the department that deals with the leaders of groups and public thought all over the country, that is, the PTA groups, women's club groups, women's club groups, and so forth. We call that the public relations department.

That man has a great mass of experience, including a great deal of work which he has done officially on both production code and advertising code types in the past. Another of my consultants is a man who was an advertising agency account executive for a great many years and has been in governmental work and public relations work and is now of our association staff. It is people of that kind with whom I consult and advise on copy.

Mr. Bobo. When you review the advertising of the picture, do you have before you a synopsis of what the picture is about?

Mr. WHITE. Not always. As a matter of fact, here is one of the things that makes the job a rather difficult job at times: This advertising is largely written or started while the picture is still in production out here, in a great many cases. Often not only do I not see the picture at the time we pass upon the advertising, but maybe the advertising man working on it doesn't see it. They work, of course, on the basis of complete information from their unit men in the studios out here.

We work generally on the basis of deciding whether the material is per se acceptable or not. When something comes along that raises a question as to what is in the picture, then we call for whatever information we want to call for. We may ask for a script and hold up the advertising and not give them a decision until we have received the script and read it. That I do constantly.

We may be satisfied with an adequate synopsis, or in a few cases the picture may be in and finished and we will go and look at the picture.

But as a general rule we don't wait for the picture or for reading the script, but we pass on the material on the basis of its per se acceptability or unacceptability.

Mr. BOBO. The advertising code doesn't know whether the advertising of a picture, in the majority of instances, illustrates the text and that the advertising faithfully represents the picture?

Mr. WHITE. Technically, you might say that. That is probably the hardest part of the code to administer.

That was the question that arose in the case of our discussion on Hell's Island. But, as a general rule, on pictures of the Marty type and the Interrupted-Melody type, we know enough about the story and the picture based on our files. I think you are acquainted with our files. We have files in the New York office to show what negotiations the Production Code Administration has had with the producer, and we have those accessible to us at all times, so if there is any question at all, we refer first to those files. We usually, therefore, know in a general way what the story or the picture is about.

Mr. BOBO. In the ad East of Eden, that drawing in the center of it, was a script of that picture. Does that truly represent the scenes as depicted in that picture?

Mr. WHITE. I would like to show you a photograph. These photographs are actual reproductions of frames from the motion picture. This is a Cinemascope print, so this is a squeezed print so it may be a little difficult to try to analyze, but if you look at it closely you can see there is the boy and girl and the tree.

(The photograph referred to was marked "Exhibit No. 8," and is on file with the subcommittee.)

Mr. WHITE. Now, these photographs, of course, obviously, are not of sufficient clarity to be used for reproduction, so they made a sketch of it and submitted the sketch.

Mr. BOBO. Was there some discussion between the advertising people and yourself over this ad in East of Eden?

Mr. WHITE. They sent over a photograph and said they wanted to work from that.

As I say, it was obvious to me it was not suitable for reproduction. I returned the shots and told them that in my judgment it was all right, and they made a sketch and submitted it, and I told them in my judgment that was acceptable.

Mr. Bobo. What is your opinion, Mr. White, of the representation East of Eden had?

Mr. White. My opinion of it at the time it was submitted was that it was thoroughly acceptable. It has created some criticism. I am still of the opinion it does not represent the worst that I have heard people interpret into it.

Again, it is easier to be a Monday morning quarterback and make these decisions than it is to make the decision while a man is trying to slide for second. This picture came to me in a small sketch. I approved it and I still think that it is acceptable and certainly I did not see in it what some people have thought it was.

Mr. Bobo. In the motion picture advertising code, on a number of pictures dealing with crime and police officers, the story of a brutal cop and the story of a cop that killed for money, stressing the fact of the indecent type of policeman, are these ads approved with the seal of the code?

Mr. White. Yes. I suppose you are referring particularly to Rogue Cop, the story of the film, I think the advertisement was a fair representation of the story of the film and I so approved it.

As another example of group villainy, there is the picture, New York Confidential, which I see displayed up there.

Rogue Cop is the story of one individual. It doesn't say the police department is wrong. It said one individual in the police department was wrong.

New York Confidential is a gangster story, and there are a number of killings in it. The police play a secondary part in it. The ads for it are a result of long and serious negotiations between Warners and myself.

You will find that, I think, every single piece of advertising copy displayed here points up the fact that this gangster activity brought about a great police crackdown, so that the forces of law and order are credited with being in there and being in at the end.

Mr. Bobo. Without seeing the picture, a person would never know that.

I was wondering about No. 8:

Pictorial and copy treatment of officers of the law shall not be of such a nature as to undermine their authority.

Mr. White. That is right. And I don't believe they are.

Mr. Bobo. If it is portrayed in the picture as that, it would be all right for the officer to be portrayed in the advertisement in that respect, and vice versa?

Mr. White. Yes, I believe an individual officer can be a villain, just as an individual councilman in a city council or an individual judge, even, possibly.

The codes are quite definite in their recognition of the fact that we do not wish to present the forces of law and order or the judiciary in such a way as to break down respect for them. But I do not believe that enjoins the industry from making a picture or presenting an ad showing one man in any one of these categories, who is a villain or a crook.

Mr. Bobo. The Blackboard Jungle copy ad there, do you think those scenes depicted in that one particular drawing there clearly represents the story of that picture?

Mr. White. I think they are fairly representative of the story of that picture. The illustration at the top has been criticized. I think I have heard three criticisms of it, specific criticisms of that particular ad. That is a stylized drawing of a scene which admittedly is only a short scene in the picture. But it is a drawing which typifies, which illustrates the general situation of these boys in this school, their attitude, their character and, in my judgment, and I still say in my judgment today, as well as my judgment when I passed on it, I think it is permissible and should be permitted if the picture is permitted. I would pass it again today, yes, sir.

Mr. Bobo. And the rape scene in the movie shown in every ad of the Blackboard Jungle scene?

Mr. White. Not every ad, but most of them.

Mr. Bobo. I would say a great proportion of the ads of the Blackboard Jungle. Do you think the emphasis on the sexual angle, the illicit, the illegal sex, and the rape scene is a justified advertisement for a picture which is supposed to portray the school system of the United States?

Mr. White. There are several things I could say about it. I am not sure the uninformed person, looking at this picture, would know it was a rape or attack of any kind, a murder or robbery, or anything else.

Which reminds me of the mention made yesterday of the picture of Johnny Belinda of several years ago. That was a classic example in our office.

That was a story of a rape attack on a girl. The illustration which became the basis of most of the advertising was a picture in which a man was approaching this girl in a menacing way, somewhat along this order. He wasn't touching her. His hands were grasping for her throat.

I wrote back a letter of congratulations to the company on the way they handled it, because they had an illustration which was suitable to the picture, and yet they didn't specify it was a rape. It was an attack of some kind coming upon this woman. It was adequate, it was dramatic, but it was not specific to the point of being offensive.

This ad, I think, has a little of that quality. I submit no one who doesn't know the story of Blackboard Jungle would know that this is a rape. They wouldn't know what it is.

Suppose it is rape? That scene in the picture was a scene which, in my judgment, motivated much of the action which followed. So, in my judgment, it was one of the key scenes of the picture. So whether we passed on it or not simply got itself down to a question of whether the presentation itself of the illustration was acceptable or whether it was offensive. If we had considered it offensive, we would have said, "No."

Mr. Bobo. In the Prodigal ad, which is admittedly the front cover, but which portrays some of the black and white ads we have seen——

Mr. White. As to color, I don't wish to leave any misleading impression. This illustration will be seen in a number of items, but not exactly that way, and that is the principal cover but the illustration will appear.

Mr. Bobo. Do you have any opinion as to the impression of sex within that ad?

Mr. White. I think it is probably an extreme case we have here. That is a retouched picture, to start with. The costume, as it showed in the stills when submitted to us, had nothing over the girl's hips, except beads. We required them at least to put some panties on the girl. I think that probably that is a borderline case, subject to argument. I don't wish to make any special show of defending it.

Mr. Bobo. In the retouching of that particular ad, do you notice that the costume varies on the two different legs of the girl there?

Mr. White. Yes, I do notice that.

Mr. Bobo. Did that come to your attention at the time the ad was submitted? Is it not in your opinion that offers much more of a suggestive pose?

Mr. White. Possibly; I don't know.

Mr. Bobo. Well, what would be your opinion of that at this time, Mr. White, as to whether it would be approved or disapproved by the advertising code as of this time?

Mr. White. Again I am being a Monday morning quarterback. If I had it come through now, I would insist, in the light of our experience and discussion of it, I would insist, at least, on having the same costume to be carried across it.

Mr. Bobo. Would it be your opinion now that borders slightly on the point of pornography?

Mr. White. No, I don't think that is pornographic. I am not defending it, Mr. Bobo.

I thoroughly acquiesce in your right to question and criticize. But I don't think there is anything in a motion picture bearing our seal or any ad running that has our approval that approaches pornography, as I understand pornography.

Mr. Bobo. I agree with you in most cases. That was one ad that was of particular interest to me, and I am sure at the time it went through that you didn't realize that one person would see it in one light and another person would see it in another light.

Mr. White. May I add this suggestion in the record, Mr. Bobo. We heard a great deal of discussion of the picture Blackboard Jungle. I understand that the principal criticism of that picture has come from people in the educational field. I think it is obvious that any one of the individual action scenes might have taken place somewhere in the United States in some school at some time, but what raises criticism is the fact that in the picture these actions are all packed into an hour and a half. It all happens in 1 school in 1 location in 1 season and, in the opinion of some critics, this makes it highly questionable and certainly overbearing.

That is what we have here right now. We have what might be called the worst possible examples, picked out, as I did last summer in our office, the worst possible examples, put up into one display. Even if they were good, they would look bad in this display.

Mr. Bobo. Most of these examples, Mr. White, we have scattered around, are pictures of recent releases. They are all combined in a group of pictures practically now in release and are showing in all the newspapers, practically, over the country.

Mr. White. Might I call your attention to this: I left New York last Thursday morning. As I left, I picked up the New York Times.

As I left Washington that night I picked up the Washington Post. And as I went through Chicago I picked up the Daily News and an early edition of the Chicago Daily Tribune.

And as I went through a town in Colorado, I picked up the Denver Rocky Mountain News.

And here are the advertising pages from those papers. There is no selection. I just picked up the latest papers as I went through the towns.

I submit there isn't one ad in any one of those papers to which any reasonable person would object. That is what I call a cross section.

Those are what I call more truly representative of our work than are these, most of them [indicating]. And I would like, if I might——

Chairman KEFAUVER. These will be filed as exhibits, and I think the advertising code, we will have that printed into the record and made a part of it.

(The documents referred to were introduced as exhibit No. 9 and are on file with the subcommittee.)

(The document referred to was marked "Exhibit No. 10," and reads as follows:)

EXHIBIT No. 10

AN ADVERTISING CODE FOR MOTION PICTURES AND REGULATIONS FOR ITS ADMINISTRATION

AN ADVERTISING CODE FOR MOTION PICTURES

(The advertising code was adopted by the board of directors of the Motion Picture Producers and Distributors of America, Inc. (now the Motion Picture Association of America, Inc.) June 10, 1930. It was amended and reaffirmed by the board of directors of the Motion Picture Association of America, Inc., July 30, 1947, and further amended December 3, 1947, and June 21, 1950.)

Preamble

The purpose of the advertising code is to apply to motion picture advertising, publicity, and exploitation, within their range, the high principles which the production code applies to the content of motion pictures.

The provisions of the advertising code shall apply to press books, newspaper, magazine and trade-paper advertising, publicity material, trailers, posters, lobby displays and all other outdoor displays, novelty distribution, radio copy, and every form of motion picture exploitation.

We urge all motion picture producers, distributors and exhibitors, and their advertising agents, whether affiliated with the undersigned or not, to adhere to these principles; and, for ourselves, we pledge compliance with these principles without reservation.

The Code

1. We subscribe to a code of ethics based upon truth, honesty and integrity. All motion picture advertising shall—

    (*a*) Conform to fact.

    (*b*) Scrupulously avoid all misrepresentation.

2. Good taste shall be the guiding rule of motion picture advertising.

3. Illustrations and text in advertising shall faithfully represent the pictures themselves.

4. No false or misleading statements shall be used directly, or implied by type arrangements or by distorted quotations.

5. No text or illustration shall ridicule or tend to ridicule any race, religion or religious faith; no illustration of a character in clerical garb shall be shown in any but a respectful manner.

6. The history, institutions, and nationals of all countries shall be represented with fairness.

7. Profanity and vulgarity shall be avoided.

8. Pictorial and copy treatment of officers of the law shall not be of such a nature as to undermine their authority.

9. Specific details of crime, inciting imitation, shall not be used.

10. Motion picture advertisers shall be guided by the provision of the production code that the use of liquor in American life shall be restricted to the necessities of characterization and plot.

11. Nudity with meretricious purpose and salacious postures shall not be used; and clothed figures shall not be represented in such manner as to be offensive or contrary to good taste or morals.

12. Court actions relating to censoring of pictures, or other censorship disputes, are not to be capitalized in advertising or publicity.

13. Titles of source materials or occupations or names of characters on which motion pictures may be based, should not be exploited in advertising or upon the screen if such titles or names are in conflict with the provisions of the production code affecting titles.

14. No text or illustration shall be used which capitalizes, directly or by implication, upon misconduct of a person connected with a motion picture thus advertised.

REGULATIONS FOR THE ADMINISTRATION OF THE ADVERTISING CODE

(The following regulations were adopted by the board of directors of the Motion Picture Association of America, Inc., April 22, 1948, and amended June 21, 1950.)

1. These regulations are applicable to all members of the Motion Picture Association of America, Inc. (hereinafter referred to as the "association"), subsidiaries of a member producing or distributing motion pictures, and to all producers and distributors of motion pictures with respect to each picture for which the association has granted its certificate of approval, pursuant to an application therefor.

2. The term "advertising" as used herein shall be deemed to mean all forms of motion picture advertising and exploitation, and ideas therefor, including, among other things, but without limitation thereto, the following: press books; still photographs; newspaper, magazine and trade paper advertising; publicity copy and art intended for use in press books or otherwise intended for use in press books or otherwise intended for general distribution in printed form or for theater use; trailers; posters, lobby displays and other outdoor.displays; advertising accessories, including heralds, throwaways, etc.; novelties; copy for exploitation tie-ups; radio and television copy.

The term "company" as used herein shall be deemed to mean any person, firm or corporation.

3. All advertising shall be submitted to the advertising code administration of the association for approval before use, and shall not be used in any way until so submitted and approved as hereinafter set forth. All advertising shall be submitted in duplicate with the exception of press books, which shall be submitted in triplicate.

4. The advertising code administration shall proceed as promptly as it finds feasible to approve or disapprove the advertising submitted on the basis of whether it complies with the advertising code.

The advertising code administration shall stamp its approval on one copy of all advertising approved and return such stamped copy to the company submitting the same. If the advertising code administration disapproves of any advertising, there shall be stamped the word "disapproved" on one copy thereof, which shall be returned to the company submitting the same; or, if the advertising code administration so desires, it may return the same with suggestions for such changes or corrections in the advertising as will cause it to be approved.

5. After advertising (as defined in sec. 2 above) for a motion picture shall have been approved by the advertising code administration, if circumstances arise, either before or after the picture's release, which in the judgment of the administrator seem to require the withdrawal of all, or any portion of such previously approved advertising, then, after consultation with the advertising advisory council, he shall immediately file a written report with the president and secretary of the association (a) setting forth the situation existing at the time such prior approval was granted for such advertising, (b) reciting the intervening circumstances with resultant changes in the situation, (c) listing the reasons why in the opinion of the administrator all or a designated portion of the advertising previously approved should be withdrawn and (d) certifying that if such advertising were then being presented to him for the first time, it would not be approved by him under the advertising code for stated reasons.

If the president of the association (or a vice president of the association in the absence of the president), upon receipt of such report from the advertising code administration, is of the opinion that the situation presented is sufficiently serious to justify consideration by the board of directors, the secretary of the association shall be instructed to call immediately an emergency meeting of the board, at which meeting the board shall sit as a board of appeal with adequate opportunity for the producer and/or distributor of the motion picture to appear in person or through a duly authorized representative and present reasons orally or in writing, or both, as to why the prior approval of the advertising should be affirmed, and with adequate opportunity for the administrator of the advertising code to appear and present reasons, either orally or in writing, or both, as to why in his judgment all or a designated portion of such previously approved advertising should be withdrawn.

Thereafter, the board, meeting in executive session with the producer and/or distributor of the picture not voting, shall determine by vote of a majority of the directors present and voting, whether all or any portion of the previously approved advertising shall be withheld from use and/or withdrawn, and such action of the board of directors shall be final and binding upon the producer and/or distributor of said film.

When any previously approved advertising for a motion picture is withdrawn pursuant to action of the board hereunder, the company withdrawing same shall be reimbursed the unrecoverable portion of its out-of-pocket expenditures for such advertising to the exent deemed equitable and proper under all the circumstances by the board. The amount of such reimbursement shall be prorated among all members of the association including the company affected on the same basis as dues to the association are currently paid.

If neither the producer nor the distributor of said film is a member of the association, then the nonmember withdrawing such advertising shall be reimbursed the unrecoverable portion of its out-of-pocket expenditures for such advertising by the members of the association to the exent deemed equitable and proper under all the circumstances by the board.

6. Appeals. Any company whose advertising has been disapproved may appeal from the decision of the advertising code administration, as follows:

Within 10 days after its advertising has been disapproved, it shall serve notice of such appeal in writing on the director of the advertising code administration and on the secretary of the association. Said notice of appeal shall set forth the grounds upon which the appeal is taken. Within a reasonable time after the receipt of such notice by the director of the advertising code administration and the secretary of the association, the president or, in the event of his absence from the country or his inability to act, a board consisting of three members of the executive committee of the board of directors of the association appointed by him, shall hold a hearing to pass upon the appeal. Oral and written evidence may be introduced by the company and the advertising code administration. Oral argument shall be had at the hearing and written memoranda or briefs may be submitted by the company and the advertising code administration. The president or said board, as the case may be, may admit such evidence as is deemed relevant, material and competent, and may determine the nature and length of the oral argument and of the written memoranda or briefs to be submitted. The president or said board, as the case may be, shall decide the appeal as expeditiously as possible and shall notify the company and the director of the advertising code administration in writing of the decision. Such decision shall be final.

A company appealing from a decision of the advertising code administration under section 14 of the advertising code shall have the right, by written notice to the secretary of the association, to appeal directly to the board of directors of the association, whose decision shall be final. The provisions relating to evidence, argument and written memoranda or briefs, set forth in these regulations, shall apply to such appeals.

7. Any company to which these regulations are applicable, which publishes, or makes available for sale or lease, or which in any way uses advertising without prior approval as hereinabove provided, may be brought up on charges before the board of directors by the director of the advertising code administration, or by any of the following officers of the association, viz: the president, a vice president, the secretary or the treasurer. The company shall be entitled to receive a written statement of the charges and to a hearing before the board of directors. Within a reasonable time after the receipt of said statement of charges by the company, the board of directors of the association shall meet in a special meet-

ing to hear and pass upon such charges. Oral and written evidence may be introduced by the company and by the advertising code administration. Oral argument shall be had and written memoranda or briefs may be submitted by the company and by the advertising code administration. The board of directors may admit such evidence as it deems relevant, material and competent, and may determine the nature and length of the oral argument and of the written memoranda or briefs to be submitted. The board of directors, by a majority vote of those present, shall decide the matter as expeditiously as possible.

If the board of directors finds that the company has published, or made available for sale or lease or in any way used advertising without prior approval as hereinabove set forth, the board may take one or more of the following actions:

(a) Direct the production code administration to void and revoke the certificate of approval granted by the association for the picture so advertised and require the removal of the association's seal from all prints of said picture, and the production code administration shall thereupon do so;

(b) Require the company, if a member of the association, to pay to the association as and for liquidated damages, not more than $100 for each publication, lease, sale, or use of an unapproved item of advertising which has been published, made available for lease or sale or used, provided, however, that the total sum assessed for advertising relative to one motion picture may not exceed the sum of $25,000. The amount so assessed and collected shall be used by the association for expenses incurred in the administration of the advertising code. It is recognized that any violation of the advertising code will disrupt the stability of the industry and cause serious damage to the association and its members which cannot be definitively computed.

The decision of the board of directors shall be final.

8. Each company shall assume responsibility for seeing that all its employees and agents comply with these regulations.

Chairman KEFAUVER. Anything else, Mr. Bobo?

Mr. BOBO. No.

Chairman KEFAUVER. Mr. White, what percentage of the display pictures are actual scenes in the picture and what percentage of them are pictures especially made and not taken from the actual scenes?

Mr. WHITE. I couldn't give you an accurate percentage. The majority of pieces of artwork that go into these displays are scenes or they are approximate reproductions of scenes in the picture.

Chairman KEFAUVER. Maybe it is what somebody thinks the scene is eventually going to be.

Mr. WHITE. No; because the stills are made on the set.

Chairman KEFAUVER. I thought you said the advertising is frequently started before the picture is anywhere near completed.

Mr. WHITE. I said while it is in production and hasn't been finally completed. The stills are made beginning with the day the picture goes into production. There is usually a still man around, making pictures, every day. As a mater of fact, there has been a great growth in the last few years of the use of the high speed, small size camera, where a cameraman can simply stand on the set and shoot while a scene is taking place, while it is being acted. Those stills are printed up and they go through the process of the advertising code operations, usually submited out here, and then they come back to New York and they begin to go to work on them. A picture will not be finished, completed and available for seeing until some time after the last day's shooting on it. There might be a gap of anything you want to guess, a month or 2 months between the day of the last day of the shooting and the time you see a picture in New York.

Chairman KEFAUVER. You said frequently, when they presented their pictures or their ad sheets for final approval, that the large billboards had already been prepared, is that so?

Mr. WHITE. It varies. Sometimes when the press books are presented, the big posters may already have been lithographed.

Chairman KEFAUVER. My question is then: The economic force for approval would be pretty great, because they would already have a whole lot of money in——

Mr. WHITE. I tried to explain that each item in that press book is supposed to have been submitted to us before the press book goes to press. We are supposed to see those as they are in operation.

We see a layout, we see the artwork, we see a photostat of the artwork, we see a photograph of it, and we are supposed to see it before it goes into printing.

Once in a great while there is a fluke and if there is trouble in the thing we have that pressure, yes, but that is a rarity.

Chairman KEFAUVER. On page 3 of your statement, Mr. White, the middle paragraph:

> What it does seek to do and what it should do is to convey the spirit, the atmosphere, the feeling, the general impression of the photoplay. This is fair, this is proper, this is accepted advertising practice. It is neither misleading nor misrepresentative.

I think that is a fine statement of a principle that advertising ought to follow.

A fair presentation of what the product is going to be. And these producers have told us that in all of the pictures, horror and crime and sex pictures, there is some moral they are trying to prove. I just wonder if you get the moral in this advertising up here. There is a "Kiss Me Deadly. White Hot Thrills. Blood Red Kisses." That is all it says about it. What is moral?

Mr. WHITE. I don't like that any more than you do, Senator.

Chairman KEFAUVER. What is the moral in "The Prodigal"?

Mr. WHITE. I don't think it is a moral. I think it is merely entertainment. This ad is designed to sell this. I said awhile ago that making the picture and telling a story of a picture is one thing. Writing an ad to sell it is another. The first part is art. The second part is industry, business.

An ad has to do three things, as the late Mr. Brisbane used to say. I has, one, to attract attention. It has, two, to have interest in the form of getting you to read it, and, three, it has to convince you to the point of buying the product. Otherwise, it is not successful. If these do not attract, then, of course, they cannot possibly achieve points Nos. 2 and 3.

Chairman KEFAUVER. Mr. White, my point is your statement is a very good one, that what it should do is convey the spirit.

Mr. WHITE. I think that contains the spirit.

Chairman KEFAUVER. Do you think these ads convey the spirit?

Mr. WHITE. In most cases, particularly in the crime things over here [indicating].

Here is a point that might have been of interest: This is a business of cycles. Pictures are made in cycles. There has been a cycle that involved a large number of these crime or violent pictures. I think, if you will take each one of those ads separately and analyze them separately, you might object to them, but if they did not present this picture as a picture of violence, as a picture of crime, they would not be honest advertising. They would not be fair to the mothers who don't want their youngsters to go to see this crime picture.

So I think they have a very definite point of honesty. If they do not go overboard in their gruesomeness, which the advertising code provides against and which we try to avoid, but still tell the story, e. g., it is a picture of crime and violence, the ads are the fairest possible representation we can give to the picture. If the mothers do not want their youngsters to see these crime pictures, they are warned and we have given them fair and honest warning.

Chairman KEFAUVER. The purpose of advertising is to get the people into the theater.

Mr. WHITE. Into the theater; yes, sir.

Chairman KEFAUVER. Mr. Freeman was talking about the moral a great deal in Hell's Island. I can't see all the writing there.

Mr. WHITE. I thought he was talking about a moral in the Hell's Island, the picture. I don't think he was talking about a moral in the ad.

Chairman KEFAUVER. What is the moral in that ad?

Mr. WHITE. I am not offering any moral in the ad.

Chairman KEFAUVER. What you say here that you did was "to convey the spirit, the atmosphere, the feeling, the general impression of the photoplay."

Mr. WHITE. And the argument that was given to me and the argument to which I finally yielded in this case was this was a fair representation of the principal girl character in this picture.

Chairman KEFAUVER. Did you read the scenario before you passed it?

Mr. WHITE. I saw the picture in this case, Senator. That was one of the cases in which, as I said, occasionally we even go to the point of seeing the picture. The picture was finished in that case, and we saw it.

Chairman KEFAUVER. What is the moral in "Girl Confesses Life With Big Combo Boss"?

Mr. WHITE. I insist again I am not trying to offer a moral in these ads.

Chairman KEFAUVER. What you are telling us then, Mr. White is that "this is fair, this is proper, this is accepted advertising practice. It is neither misleading nor misrepresentative."

Now, these producers tell us that all these pictures have morals. I think a great many of them do have morals, some good morals and very helpful. But I haven't seen a moral in any one of these, these posters you have up here.

Mr. WHITE. The fact that in a picture that may run an hour and a half you may be able to develop a moral, I don't think can necessarily be carried over into an ad you see in a flash. And I have never heard of anyone requiring, as a requirement of advertising, that each piece of advertising produce a moral.

This came up in the case of Blackboard Jungle, Senator. Some criticism came in on one or two pieces of this material, and I went to the advertising manager at M-G-M and I showed him the criticism for his information.

And he said this, "Our job is to sell this picture. The people who come to see this picture, by and large, go out liking it."

Now, if they are induced to come in to see the picture and they get the moral out of seeing the picture, I would think that is enough. I don't know how we can require them to tell a moral in an ad.

Chairman KEFAUVER. I am just comparing what you have done here with what you say you are doing, and I don't mean to argue with you about it.

Mr. WHITE. I don't, either, Senator.

Chairman KEFAUVER. In your statement you would give the impression that your advertisements give the spirit and portray what the picture is. If they portray what the picture is, then Kiss Me Deadly would all be one thing, apparently.

Mr. WHITE. Possibly it is. Have you seen it?

Chairman KEFAUVER. No; I haven't seen it. But here is your statement, sir:

> What it does seek to do and what it should do is to convey the spirit, the atmosphere, the feeling, the general impression of the photoplay. This is fair, this is proper, this is accepted advertising practice. It is neither misleading nor misrepresentative.

So I would think by that, if there is a moral in these things, that you have completely overlooked in these pictures the——

Mr. WHITE. I am sorry, Senator, but I just don't get the connection between producing a moral in a picture that runs for 2 hours, and trying to illustrate or produce a moral in a small ad layout, which you read in half a minute.

What I say in the statement is that we should represent the spirit of the picture, sir, yes; we should represent the theme of the picture.

Chairman KEFAUVER. Then, according to your analysis, if you represent the theme of the picture, the theme of the picture is not any moral, because you say you represent the theme and general impression, but none of these show any moral.

Mr. WHITE. I think in most cases these ads do represent the theme of the picture.

Chairman KEFAUVER. Very well. I know your problem is difficult, Mr. White.

Mr. WHITE. It is a very difficult one.

Chairman KEFAUVER. We appreciate that fact. We will be glad for you to have these exhibits when we get through with them here today. Keep them intact and send them back to us.

Mr. WHITE. I will keep them intact.

Chairman KEFAUVER. I think it is fair to say that the correspondence and complaints we have, that we literally have hundreds and hundreds of letters from people and organizations, sending samples of protests, a whole lot more about the advertising form of these than we have on the movies themselves.

There is a rising tide of public resentment against some of these ads that you have passed. We will be glad to show you a lot of our letters if that will help in your battles with the advertising agencies. We want to cooperate with you. We know your task is hard, it is difficult.

You show something to get people into the house. But this isn't a healthy thing, to have criticism by so many organizations, by people, as to the ads for some of these movies.

We will go over all of these with you, and we want to help you with your problem, if there is any way we can do it.

Mr. WHITE. As a starter, as I said, I would like to display this material to a meeting of the advertising directors here, and take it back to New York with me and have another meeting with the heads of the departments there. It will certainly convey to them your expressions, Senator.

Chairman KEFAUVER. We don't want to be unfair in our criticism. We just want to let you know what has been coming to us. That doesn't mean that a great amount of people are not entirely satisfied with the advertisements. It does mean, though, that out of the few mistakes, or a few that go too far, cause criticism of the whole mass of them, as you know.

Mr. WHITE. Of course, they do. I know that better than any of you could possibly. Criticism of 2 or 3 ads usually winds up in a blanket criticism, that they are all wrong. And there is the proof in the six newspapers that they aren't all wrong.

Chairman KEFAUVER. That is right. All right! Thank you very much, Mr. White.

Mr. YOUNG. I wonder if I may speak to you about Mr. White's statement. It is very important to the Senate and the public, as well.

Chairman KEFAUVER. Let's see what Mr. Young has. Make it short and to the point, Mr. Young.

Mr. YOUNG. I will make it very brief. As to the advertising that Mr. White refers to——

Chairman KEFAUVER. You address your remarks to me, if you have any.

Mr. YOUNG. I do, Mr. Senator, I do, sir, and the committee.

As to the advertising that Mr. White refers to, which I am familiar with, as I stated before, having been associated with motion-picture studios, these display advertisiments that are taken from still pictures and then exaggerated to excite the emotions by an artist using what we term the 1-sheet and the 24-sheet, I want to call your attention, Mr. Senator—when Mr. White made a statement as to viewing and approving the code of advertisements—a publication known as Bold— B-o-l-d—Bold, one of these promiscuous publications sold on the newsstands, in the various drugstores, or magazines that you see young boys and your children sit there and look at them, sit and look at them, of July 15, on page 60—6-0—where one of the featured players or leading ladies, by the name of Jan Sterling, is publicized in that type of a picture.

Mr. Senator, I ask if the Senator would please ask Mr. White whether he saw that picture before it was sent out, whether he approved of that.

I also call attention to a publication known as the Variety and that Variety is read by everyone—when I say everyone I mean the motion-picture industry and show people, but is displayed and sold on newsstands, and also on the magazine stands—of June 16 which was yesterday, Thursday, the back cover.

Chairman KEFAUVER. Mr. Young, we want to be democratic in this meeting. If anybody has any observations they want to make, all right, but you will have to get to the point.

Mr. YOUNG. Yes. This particular picture sent out and publicized on the back cover of Variety of yesterday, June 16——

Chairman KEFAUVER. Do you have a copy of it there?

Mr. YOUNG. I have, yes.

Chairman KEFAUVER. Let's see it.

Mr. YOUNG. I wanted to ask, Mr. Senator, whether Mr. White saw that picture on the back cover, which is sent way in advance, and not as a deadline, because they have to reserve that space.

Chairman KEFAUVER. Well, Mr. White——

Mr. YOUNG. I think I left that at home. I am sorry. But that cover is very important to the committee and the public at large, as to what is permitted to go in publications that adolescents and children see.

As to these pictures, if I may make the statement, when that is exhibited in the lobby of the theaters and on our streets—on Fairfax, with thousands of cars and thousands of pedestrians walking by—showing that very 24 sheet. And also the adolescents and children see these pictures in our theaters, first-rate theaters, let's say, on a Saturday afternoon or in the evening——

Chairman KEFAUVER. Mr. Young, I want to be patient with you, but don't make a speech. State any facts you want to state.

Mr. YOUNG. When adolescents see this picture in the lobby and enter the theater and see the picture on the screen, as he approaches that particular scene, isn't it true that the adolescents whistle at that very attempt that is about to be made or is made?

Let him answer that, if that isn't so. That it is made to excite the emotions of children and adolescents in our audiences, in our theaters and in our displays in the lobbies, and on the streets. Thank you, Mr. Senator.

Chairman KEFAUVER. I take it that Mr. White doesn't have anything to do with what happens inside. I know there is a lot of whistling and whatnot.

Mr. YOUNG. Mr. Senator, Mr. White did state he approves these pictures—rather, he passes on them. And if he does pass on them, that is the very thing that the Senator called attention to, whether he approved of these very things. And they are distributed by the thousands throughout the country, sent throughout the country, to the various magazines.

And when he shows you a newspaper advertisement, that they are not as bad as the ones that they exhibit, there may be a possibility that different cities and different States do not print that type of thing. They do send them there.

They send all those pictures there as fast as they can send them, by airmail, to these various publications, and so forth, so they can use them, what they believe to be good copy, and draw them into the box office.

Chairman KEFAUVER. All right, Mr. Young, you get a copy of that Variety and send it in.

Mr. YOUNG. I will do that, sir. Thank you.

Chairman KEFAUVER. Mr. White, a question has been brought up about some picture on Variety. Do you know what the matter is?

Mr. WHITE. I never heard of it. As far as the other magazine is concerned, I never heard of it.

If you want a serious comment on the matter of publicity pictures in publications, they include, it should be remembered, not only approved still material but perhaps to a much greater extent pictures over which I could possibly have no control at all. There are millions and millions of photographs that go into circulation for release by publications of all kinds, all over the country. Heaven knows I don't want——

Chairman KEFAUVER. Of course, we know about the other material. We are only talking about the material that advertises movies.

Mr. WHITE. This gentleman was talking about something that appeared in a magazine called Bold or something.

Chairman KEFAUVER. Mr. Young, is what you are talking about in the magazine Bold, does it have anything to do with movies?

Mr. YOUNG. Yes. It is one of the pictures that is made——

Chairman KEFAUVER. Do you have a copy of that?

Mr. YOUNG. The Bold magazine?

Chairman KEFAUVER. Yes. With you?

Mr. YOUNG. No, I have not. I don't like to carry those things on my person.

Chairman KEFAUVER. Well, we can't tell whether what you are talking about has anything to do with pictures or not. It would be better it you submit it. We don't know exactly what the pictures are.

Mr. YOUNG. Mr. White can if he thinks so much will come out of— let Mr. White submit it and see whether it is one of those he approved of.

Chairman KEFAUVER. Very well, Mr. Young. Sit down. We don't know what the pictures were and you don't know anything about them?

Mr. WHITE. No.

Chairman KEFAUVER. The Bold magazine.

Mr. WHITE. No.

Chairman KEFAUVER. All right. Thank you very much, Mr. White. We will have a short recess at this time.

(Short recess taken.)

Chairman KEFAUVER. Unfortunately, we are getting a little behind with our time schedule.

The chairman is glad to see an old colleague in Congress, a former Congresswoman, former Congresswoman Bosone from Utah, who is a very distinguished juvenile judge in Salt Lake City, and has been for a number of years. Mrs. Reva Beck Bosone is here somewhere. We will be glad to have her come up and sit with us.

She has done a great deal of juvenile work and sponsored a number of bills for the welfare of young people when she was a Member of Congress.

Also Stanley Long, a former assistant supervisor, is with us.

And we are also glad to have with us State Senator Dick Richards, who has been interested in legislation in the general assembly or legislature of California. He is one of our fine leaders in the California Legislature.

It is good to have you here, Dick. Would you like to have anything to say?

Mr. RICHARDS. I would like to just make one statement, if I may.

Chairman KEFAUVER. All right, sir.

STATEMENT OF RICHARD RICHARDS, CALIFORNIA STATE SENATOR, LOS ANGELES, CALIF.

Mr. RICHARDS. Having just gotten back from the State legislature, I want to extend a welcome, which is belated for the reason I wasn't able to extend it before, on behalf of the State senate of the State of

California, welcoming you to our State, and on behalf of the people of the county of Los Angeles, whom I am privileged to represent in the senate.

We are all vitally interested in what you are doing and appreciative of the efforts you are extending here in our area. I am aware as an individual that that which you are doing is seeking objectives, which I think the majority of the public would like to have sought. I am convinced, so far as the motion-picture industry is concerned, that they and the advertising industry connected therewith, are as anxious as are you and all of us to bring improvements into the picture which you are seeking.

I might only comment, in passing, very briefly, that we in the State legislature have recently faced similar problems, have not been analyzing exactly the same field, but those problems with which I am certain you are familiar. The problem of the crime comic book, upon which and around which there is a great deal of public interest in the course of the last session of the State legislature.

Frank Bonelli authored in the assembly and I was privileged to carry in the senate, assembly bill No. 183, which, after the rejection of many other bills, aimed in the direction of trying to curb or eliminate the real evil that does exist in crime and horror comic books. This particular bill was passed. It will now be put to a test. And I feel it will be a step in the direction of improvement along the same lines that you are, of course, seeking in the broader field you are now investigating.

I am sure that you are as acutely aware as we were in the State legislature, in analyzing of communications, of the problems of differentiation, of the problems of censorship, which are very real problems and which we have to avoid, whenever and however we can, while we still seek the objectives that the public wants us to reach, and that is general improvement in the communications field and the elimination of the abridgment and the violations of the privileges which exist in those fields.

I would merely like to say, congratulations on the work you are doing now, senator, and it was a pleasure to be able to sit with you briefly this morning, listening to the testimony of Mr. White and the others.

Chairman KEFAUVER. Thank you very much, Senator Richards. We appreciate your welcome and we appreciate your interest as a member of the State senate in this general problem.

We do not have a copy of the act passed by the legislature. Do you have a copy?

Mr. RICHARDS. I do happen to have one with me.

Chairman KEFAUVER. Good. You are right on the job.

For the information of other States considering this, who will read our hearings, we will have this printed in the record, so it will be in our Senate hearings.

Thank you very much, and you stay with us as much as you can.

Mr. RICHARDS. Thank you.

Chairman KEFAUVER. During Mr. White's testimony Mr. Young indicated that he had seen on the back page of Variety of June 16 a large picture of a woman mostly nude. We have gotten a copy of the Variety of that day, and what Mr. Young said about it is correct.

Also, on Friday, June 17, a picture explaining what was on the back cover of the preceding day's Variety, but the inference may have been this was in connection with a motion-picture advertisement which Mr. White had some jurisdiction over. That is not the case.

It is an advertisement of a young lady who is going to appear in a night-club show and has nothing to do with the movies. I don't want the record to have any inference Mr. White had anything to do with it.

We realize the difficult position Mr. White has, and he seems to be a sincere man. I know he is trying. I hope we can be of some assistance to one another.

I think in the number of people who have spoken to me about wanting to ask questions, or what not, that if we had a lot of time I would give everybody who wanted to ask a question a chance to stand up and say something about it or make a statement. I think, though, as a rule, in view of the shortage of time, that anyone who has a question, if they would write it out and submit it to me, I will go over them and if they wish to make a statement, if they will write it down and give a summary or indication of what they want to talk about, we would probably save time.

Our next witness will be Mr. Max Gilford, of the Independent Motion Picture Producers and Independent Motion Picture Producers for Television.

(Assembly bill No. 183 was marked "Exhibit No. 11" and reads as follows:)

EXHIBIT No. 11

Amended in Assembly May 27, 1955

CALIFORNIA LEGISLATURE—1955 REGULAR SESSION

ASSEMBLY BILL NO. 183

Introduced by Mr. Bonelli, January 6, 1955. Referred to Committee on Judiciary

An act to add Section 299 to the Penal Code, relating to comic books and magazines

The people of the State of California do enact as follows:

SECTION 1. Section 299 is added to the Penal Code, to read:

299. Every person, firm or corporation is guilty of a misdemeanor who sells, gives away or in any way furnishes to any person under the age of 18 years any illustrated crime comic book or magazine in which there is prominently featured an account of crime and which depicts, by the use of drawings or photographs the commission or attempted commission of the crimes of arson, assault with caustic chemicals, assault with a deadly weapon, burglary, kidnapping, mayhem, murder, rape, robbery, theft, or voluntary manslaughter.

299. *Every person who sells, gives away, or otherwise furnishes to any minor, or who has in his possession with intent to sell, give away, or otherwise furnish to such a minor, any illustrated crime comic book or magazine devoted to the publication and exploitation of real or fictional deeds of violent bloodshed, lust, or immorality, or of horror, so massed as reasonably to tend to incite minors to violence, or depraved or immoral acts against the person, or any book, pamphlet, magazine or other printed matter, specifically including comic books, devoted to the publication and exploitation of sex or of matter of an indecent character, which, for a minor, is obscene, lewd, lascivious, filthy, indecent, or disgusting, is guilty of a misdemeanor.*

As used in this section "illustrated crime comic book or magazine" means any book, magazine, or pamphlet in which an account of crime is set forth by means of a series of five or more drawings or photographs in sequence, which are accompanied by either narrative writing or words represented as spoken by a pictured character, whether such narrative words appear in balloons, captions or on or immediately adjacent to the photograph drawing.

This section shall not apply to those accounts of crime ~~which are a part of the general dissemination of news nor to drawings and photographs used to illustrate such accounts.~~ *which appear in a newspaper of general circulation or to those accounts of crime which delineate actual historical events, or to those accounts of crime which delineate occurrences actually set forth in the sacred scriptures of any religion.*

SEC. 2. In adding Section 299 to the Penal Code by this act, the Legislature finds that there is a great increase in the number and variety of illustrated crime comic books and magazines being offered for sale in this State which deal in substantial part with crimes of force, violence and bloodshed and that many of such books and magazines are designed to resemble closely those devoted to matters of humor and adventure and published primarily for sale to children and are often placed for sale side by side with such humor and adventure magazines. The Legislature also finds that children below the age of 18 years are of a susceptible and impressionable character and are often stimulated by collections of pictures and stories of criminal acts, and do in fact often commit such crimes partly because incited to do so by such publications and the possibility of harm by restricting free utterance through harmless publications is too remote and too negligible a consequence of dealing with the evil of the publication herein described, when in the hands of children. The Legislature also finds that many public organizations including local governing bodies, fraternal groups, service clubs and the like have publicly urged that a statute be adopted which would prohibit the dissemination of illustrated crime comic books and magazines to the extent that it is possible to do so without interfering with the freedom of the press.

Amended in Senate June 3, 1955

Amended in Assembly May 27, 1955

CAIFORNIA LEGISLATURE—1955 REGULAR SESSION

ASSEMBLY BILL NO. 183

Introduced by Mr. Bonelli, January 6, 1955. Referred to Committee on Judiciary

AN ACT To add section 299 to the Penal Code, relating to comic books and magazines

The people of the State of California do enact as follows:

SECTION 1. Section 299 is added to the Penal Code, to read :

299. Every person who sells, gives away, or otherwise furnishes to any minor, or who has in his possession with intent to sell, give away, or otherwise furnish to such a minor, any illustrated crime comic book or magazine devoted to the publication and exploitation of real or fictional deeds of violent bloodshed, lust, or immorality, or of horror, so massed as reasonably to tend to incite minors to violence or depraved or immoral acts against the person, or any book, pamphlet, magazine or other printed matter, specifically including comic books, devoted to the publication and exploitation of sex or of matter of an indecent character, which, for a minor, is obscene, lewd, lascivious, filthy, indecent, or disgusting, is guilty of a misdemeanor.

As used in this section "illustrated crime comic book or magazine" means any book, magazine, or pamphlet in which an account of crime is set forth by means of a series of ~~five or more~~ drawings or photographs in sequence, which are accompanied by either narrative writing or words represented as spoken by a pictured character, whether such narrative words appear in balloons, captions or on or immediately adjacent to the photograph drawing.

This section shall not apply to those accounts of crime which appear in a newspaper of general circulation or to those accounts of crime which delineate actual historical events, or to those accounts of crime which delineate occurrences actually set forth in the sacred scriptures of any religion.

SEC. 2. In adding Section 299 to the Penal Code by this act, the Legislature finds that there is a great increase in the number and variety of illustrated crime comic books and magazines being offered for sale in this State which deal in substantial part with crimes of force, violence and bloodshed and that many of such books and magazines are designed to resemble closely those devoted to matters of humor and adventure and published primarily for sale to children and are often placed for sale side by side with such humor and adventure magazines. The Legislature also finds that children below the age of 18 years are of a susceptible and impressionable character and are often stimulated by collections of pictures and stories of criminal acts, and do in fact often commit such crimes partly because incited to do so by such publications and the possibility of harm by restricting free utterance through harmless publications is too remote and too negligible a consequence of dealing with the evil of the publication herein described, when in the hands of children. The Legislature also finds that many public organizations including local governing bodies, fraternal groups, service clubs and the like have publicly urged that a statute be adopted which would prohibit the dissemination of illustrated crime comic books and magazines to the extent that it is possible to do so without interfering with the freedom of the press.

STATEMENT OF MAX M. GILFORD, GENERAL COUNSEL, NATIONAL SOCIETY OF TELEVISION PRODUCERS, LOS ANGELES, CALIF.

Chairman KEFAUVER. We are calling Mr. Gilford a little out of turn. His statement is brief and we will have to recess for lunch shortly.

Mr. GILFORD. Could I say, Senator, I am Max Gilford. I am general counsel for the National Society of Television Producers and also an attorney here for 26 years. I didn't happen to bring a biographical sketch or anything like that, so that is why I mentioned that.

I have also been a feature motion picture and television producer myself.

Before I read this statement, I wonder if I could call to your attention that I have arranged for half of the television producing industry, on a 2-day notice, to attend a meeting for you, at the Bitter-Sweet Restaurant, and it is slated to start at 12:20. I have a police car downstairs for you and have arranged to bring you out there expeditiously and to return here for your 2 o'clock meeting on time, so that that meeting could terminate at 1:30.

Could I be excused and be asked to appear before you at 2 o'clock, and could we discontinue at the present time so we could meet with these producers, who would like to hear you. The press, I think, is there and everybody wants to know your attitude and some of the things that have been uncovered. I have arranged this under about 2-day notice. I think some of your staff are aware of this.

Chairman KEFAUVER. Well, you would rather testify when we come back at 2 o'clock?

Mr. GILFORD. Yes.

Chairman KEFAUVER. Mr. Bobo, how many more witnesses do we have on the motion picture matter?

Mr. BOBO. We will have two more.

Chairman KEFAUVER. All right, Mr. Gilford.

Mr. GILFORD. Thank you.

Chairman KEFAUVER. Well, under the circumstances, we will stand in recess until 2 o'clock this afternoon.

(Whereupon, at 12:05 p. m., a recess was taken until 2 p. m. of the same day.)

AFTERNOON SESSION

Chairman KEFAUVER. We had matter of Mr. Whitfield scheduled the other day and we got mixed up on the time. Mr. Whitfield has been here 2 or 3 times and is ready to testify about the work he is doing with young people, and he is a fine example of a good American, young athlete.

STATEMENT OF M. G. WHITFIELD, COUNTY PARKS RECREATIONAL FACILITIES FOR THE COUNTY OF LOS ANGELES, LOS ANGELES, CALIF.

Mr. Whitfield good afternoon. We are glad to see you. We are glad to have you with us. Mr. Bobo, you take over.

Mr. BOBO. Mr. Whitfield, what type of work and in what activities are you engaged that envolve you?

Mr. WHITFIELD. I am commissioner of the county parks recreational facilities for the county of Los Angeles. I am also in business.

Chairman KEFAUVER. You are a great Olympic champion. Speak a little louder.

Mr. WHITFIELD. Yes, sir. I was a member of the 1948 Olympic team and in 1952 I won three gold medals in the Olympics.

Chairman KEFAUVER. You did the half mile, didn't you?

Mr. WHITFIELD. That's right, 800 meter.

Chairman KEFAUVER. What did you do that in?

Mr. WHITFIELD. I set both the 1948 and 1952 Olympic world's record, 1 minute, 49.2 seconds.

Chairman KEFAUVER. You still hold the record, don't you?

Mr. WHITFIELD. That is correct, sir.

Chairman KEFAUVER. I used to be a track man myself. I was a discus thrower. [Laughter.]

Well, we pay tribute to your accomplishments as an Olympic champion. I don't know of many who have won the record twice in succession, and you are a fine influence among your people. You have been recently appointed to this position by the board of supervisors?

Mr. WHITFIELD. Yes, by Kenneth Hahn, Supervisor Kenneth Hahn.

Chairman KEFAUVER. Tell us your recommendations and something about your work and what you think this subcommittee or the people can do to help with our problem of juvenile delinquency.

Mr. WHITFIELD. Thank you very much. Recently I returned from a 5-months tour with the Department of State as Ambassador of Good Will through the field of sports, and of course the State Department is using sports more than ever before to try and help foster good will between our country and countries abroad, and of course the problem, the tour was a success, and I was very happy to take part in it. Of course I felt it was very effective and most educational to me. From the program I learned that the people of the world think that America is the father country, and they feel they would look to pattern their country after America and their way of life, but I find some of things we have done in the past that these people have found out about, such as the gangsterism in Chicago and several other places, and making pictures showing these many things, they have come to criticize the American way of life, and they feel that a child, learning and seeing these things, develops the same attitude of what he sees in the picture, that that is not going to do the child too much good. They have criticized our way of life here in letting the youngsters find out too much about the way of life here, such as what older people are doing.

Also I think from my experiences that I have found that working with groups, families, mothers and fathers have really not done their job like they should. In other words, teaching a youngster the correct way to be a good citizen at the early stages of his learning, the age of 6 to 10, not waiting until he reaches the age of 16 and trying to correct them then. I feel if they start early enough that we won't have too many problems in America.

With respect to the churches, of course many of the churces have been visited by me in the past. Religion has not played such an important part. In some countries it does. In America we are free to worship under the type of religion we desire. Of course, I find my experience in working with groups that the churches are not working together enough. In other words, the Catholics and Protestants should get together more and organize programs which will develop better citizens in the community rather than working separately in their own groups.

I feel that documentary films should be made more and used in the schools in the early stages of learning, teaching the boy, for instance, the fundamental methods of being coordinated in mind and body, whether in athletics or everyday society, and not waiting until the boy has reached 16 or 17 years of age.

Also I think that factories and firms and companies should get together and sponsor more activities for the youngster, in other words, not trying in all of the effort of the company just to become rich. I think they should put back into the group the wonderful things they have received from the group in order to help elevate it, in other words, sponsoring boys and girls through community centers, having more of them. Now in this part of the world, California, it is growing so rapidly that I think we should expand more and faster.

Of course the elder people are responsible, those who are qualified to help give aid to the youngsters in order to prevent juvenile delinquency.

From what I have experienced in my travels and as ambassador of good will in the field of sports, I feel that this should be a national organization rather than brought forth by each State because there is not enough finances to support this wonderful thing to help combat juvenile delinquency, and of course I feel that if it was on a national basis and brought before the Senate or the committee members, then of course people in those areas in the different States would be able to benefit in committee organizations, and I think they would be able to stamp out or knock out some of the unfortunate things which have happened in the past.

Chairman KEFAUVER. Tell us about what you are doing in the city of Los Angeles.

Mr. WHITFIELD. Well, the city of Los Angeles, for instance, along with many other groups, this summer I am sponsoring four basketball teams of youngsters of all nationalities throughout the city. I am in the cleaning business, and of course I have set aside funds to sponsor this basketball team to keep the boys active and to send them to camp to keep them busy so that they will not be able to think about things which will destroy our society and also working with the county where we organize programs to help develop better citizens in our city, and of course trying to keep these youngsters as busy as possible so that they will not have any time to think of things which would destroy our State or our city.

Chairman KEFAUVER. Do you have any program for part-time youth employment for kids in the summertime?

Mr. WHITFIELD. Only camps, and of course we don't have enough community centers to finance or to promote such.

Chairman KEFAUVER. But you do organize a number of camps and have a number of camps where boys can go?

Mr. WHITFIELD. That is correct, sir.

Chairman KEFAUVER. You have them for kids that can't afford to pay their own way?

Mr. WHITFIELD. Yes, sir. They are sponsored by groups, breakfast clubs and various groups and social groups throughout the city of Los Angeles.

Chairman KEFAUVER. Well, we thank you very much for coming and being with us, and good luck to you. We will see you again. [Applause.]

I wish to make an announcement before we call our next witness. We had anticipated this to be a 3-day hearing. We had general subject matter and the movie industry and also we are going to go into pornographic literature and some crime and comic books testimony. We have gotten badly behind with our witness schedule, so that we have made arrangements to stay over and have a short hearing tomorrow in order to finish up. This afternoon will finish up the witnesses in connection with the movies. All of the witnesses who have been summoned to come and testify about other matters, pornographic literature and other things, will come back please at 9:30 in the morning. I regret that a Saturday session disrupts perhaps some who have planned to get away, but it is unavoidable. We have changed some of our engagements in Washington ourselves to have the hearing tomorrow. We thought that while we are out here that we should try to hear everyone who has been called.

All right, Mr. Bobo.

Mr. BOBO. Mr. Geoffrey Shurlock.

Chairman KEFAUVER. Mr. Shurlock, will you come around, sir?

STATEMENT OF GEOFFREY SHURLOCK, DIRECTOR OF PRODUCTION CODE ADMINISTRATION OF THE MOTION PICTURE ASSOCIATION OF AMERICA, LOS ANGELES, CALIF.

Chairman KEFAUVER. We are glad to see you, Mr. Shurlock. Are you the director of the production code administration of the Motion Picture Association of America?

Mr. SHURLOCK. Yes, sir.

Chairman KEFAUVER. All right, Mr. Bobo.

Mr. BOBO. Mr. Shurlock, for how many years have you been director of the production code administration of the Motion Picture Association of America?

Mr. SHURLOCK. I have been connected with it for 23 years but have only been director since last October.

Mr. BOBO. In your position as director, the duties of this office are what?

Mr. SHURLOCK. To pass upon all scripts and all finished pictures to make certain that they meet the requirements of the industry's voluntary production code.

Mr. BOBO. What have been your positions prior to being associated with the production code administration?

Mr. SHURLOCK. I was connected with Paramount Studios for 6 years prior to that, beginning in 1926.

Mr. BOBO. Mr. Shurlock, what is the composition of the staff in the office of the motion picture production code?

Mr. SHURLOCK. The Production Code's staff consists of a director and seven members.

Mr. BOBO. And is it the duty of these seven members to review and pass on all motion pictures produced in America?

Mr. SHURLOCK. It is the duty of the staff to review and pass on all pictures produced by the members of the motion-picture associations who are signatory to the code, and also on any and all other scripts or pictures which independents may wish voluntarily to submit to us. I want to say that that includes probably 99 percent of the pictures produced in the United States for theatrical entertainment.

Mr. BOBO. In addition to the seven staff members and the director, is there any type of advisory board composed of professional persons in psychiatry of psychology or criminalogy connected with the motion picture code?

Mr. SHURLOCK. No, sir; there is not. We are bound in our duties under our own code and not authorized to go very far outside of that.

Mr. BOBO. Mr. Shurlock, the funds for the operation of the motion picture production code are secured from what source?

Mr. SHURLOCK. Each producer submitting a picture pays a fee based on the negative cost of the picture.

Mr. BOBO. You have a statement, Mr. Shurlock. Would you like to give it?

Mr. SHURLOCK. Yes, sir, if I may.

Chairman KEFAUVER. All right, Mr. Shurlock. You have a brief statement here which goes to the point, so suppose you read your statement.

Mr. SHURLOCK. My name is Geoffrey Shurlock. My home is here in Los Angeles. I have worked for the Motion Picture Association of America since 1932, and have been on the staff of the production code administration since its formation in June 1934, under its first director, Joseph I. Breen. Upon Mr. Breen's retirement in October 1954, I became the director.

This year is the 25th anniversary of the voluntary adoption by the industry of the Motion Picture Production Code. The code, as this committee of course knows, sets forth principles to assure good moral standards and decency in motion-picture entertainment.

Looking back over this quarter of a century I think it must in right and justice be said that the code truly marks the embodiment and acceptance of moral responsibility on the part of the industry to the vast worldwide public that it serves.

Our industry was the first among the media of communications in the United States to adopt a system of self-regulation. Other media have since paid us the sincerest form of flattery by imitating our code. We are pleased that this has been so. For example, the Television Code, adopted not long ago, was patterned upon our code, and indeed, contains much the same language.

But our system goes much further. It provides efficient machinery for supervision during production and for enforcement before a picture is seen by the public. We are still alone among the mass media in having machinery of this kind.

The production code administration, charged with enforcement of the code, consists of eight members, with headquarters in Hollywood. As an autonomous unit, it is responsible for its own decisions. Any producer who disagrees has the right to appeal to the board of directors of the Motion Picture Association of America, in New York. Appeals have been few over the years.

The services of the administration are open to all producers of motion pictures, members as well as nonmembers of the association, foreign as well as domestic. In actual practice all but a very few of the films were made in Hollywood are submitted to the production code administration for its approval.

Last year the code administration approved 303 feature-length pictures. Of these, 228 were submitted by member companies and 75 by nonmembers.

I might inject here some further figures. Since June of 1934, at its inception, the production code has given its seal of approval to 10,401 feature pictures and to 12,243 shorts.

Members of the association, having voluntarily subscribed to the code, are required to submit their films to the code administration before releasing them for public exhibition. Nonmembers are not required to do so, but I want here to say to the everlasting credit of nonmember producers that practically all of them do voluntarily submit their pictures and do abide by the principles of the code. In all my years in Hollywood I have yet to meet a responsible producer who would wish to abolish the sytem of self-regulation.

I can confidently say that the code is as strongly supported and as warmly approved in Hollywood today as it has ever been. There are no signs of weakness or wavering.

In the early days, there were those who feared that the code would rob films of integrity or reality, that it would impede advancement and development. These fears have proved groundless.

In the early days, too, there were those who felt that the code might be observed more in the breach than the performance. Like the other doubters, they have been proved wrong, too. The code's accomplishments, the industry's steady adherence to it, have been convincing rebuttals of these misgivings.

Now I don't mean to tell you that the code is perfect, or that its enforcement is perfect. It is, after all, a human document, and it is administered by human beings, who assuredly lay no claim to being always right and who are always infallible.

We have made mistakes, of course. I have made mistakes. But whatever mistakes we have made have been errors of judgment, and nothing else. We call 'em as we see 'em within the framework of the code—and I'd like to brag just for a moment about my staff. I know of no more conscientious group of men anywhere. The success the code enjoys is due in the largest measure to their able and ceaseless efforts to make it work.

Sometimes we are criticized as severely, or more so, for alleged mistakes of omission as for reputed mistakes of commission. Senators doubtless understand that. As is perhaps similar in political affairs, we sometimes find, when we run down complaints, that the critics are familiar neither with the picture assailed nor with the code. And we sometimes find that critics judge us not by the standards of the code, which are the only fair criteria, but by their likes or dislikes, by their own particular set of principles or beliefs, even by their prejudices.

We are far from impervious to the public's attitude, I assure you, but I must also add that we would be serving neither the audience nor the industry well if we were to sway and bow before every breeze of criticism that comes along. That would certainly not be good or reliable self-regulation. Our job, as I view it, is always to maintain the code's honesty and forthrightness and integrity.

Now, Mr. Chairman, to sum up:

Our industry a long time ago, a quarter of a century ago, recognized its public responsibility by adopting voluntarily a system of self-regulation. This system has made positive and constructive contributions to the welfare of the public by assuring good moral standards and decency in motion picture entertainment.

Under this system American motion pictures have achieved the highest artistic and dramatic stature and are universally welcomed the world over. Under this system the American motion picture has achieved the universal distinction of being the most popular form of family entertainment that there is.

And, finally, this system assures that the American motion picture will always remain moral and decent entertainment.

Thank you very much for listening to me.

Mr. Bobo. Mr. Shurlock, in receiving the motion picture code seal, do the theaters around the country require that they have the seal before they show the picture?

Mr. Shurlock. No, sir; not now.

Mr. Bobo. Have you been aware, Mr. Shurlock, during the last year or the last few years of the criticisms of motion picture context which contains excessive brutality and violence, both in this country and abroad?

Mr. Shurlock. Yes, sir. Recently there has been some.

Mr. Bobo. Have you given this information that you have received on this or brought it to the attention of the producers about the increasing amount of violence in the films?

Mr. Shurlock. Yes, sir. About last November, shortly after I took over, I went back to New York and discussed the matter with the president of the association, Eric Johnston. I then came back and started a very definite campaign to warn producers that there seemed to be an increasing resistance on the part of the public to being entertained or amused by seeing violence or brutality in pictures or pictures that seemed to be of a violent nature.

I may explain here that this thought of mass criticism has occurred before in the course of the 20 years we have been applying the code. In the early thirties, 1936 perhaps, 1937, there was quite an outcry against the industry because of the fact that there seemed to be an excessive number of what were then known definitely known as gangster pictures. I mean definite gangster pictures in the sense that they dealt with the gangs of the prohibition era. The industry took notice of this fact. In fact at that time they actually staggered the release of this accumulation of this type of picture and stopped making them, at least in mass. Later on, about 1940, there was some complaint of the fact that there was an unusual number of what we call horror pictures in circulation—Dracula, the Wolfman, Frankenstein, the Son of Frankenstein, Daughter of Frankenstein, and so forth. When the industry found out that these were no longer being liked, and we live by pleasing the public, they stopped making them.

About 4 years ago we seemed to be getting a great number of complaints about drinking in pictures. We took this up with the producers, and they decided they would take care of the complaints, which they did rather successfully. I think it would be interesting to explain what they did. The complaint seemed to be over the fact that there was too much drinking portrayed in the American home. I don't think actually we were portraying more drinking than exists in the American home, but if the public didn't like it, it was a matter which we took under advisement. So the producers pretty well agreed that from that time on they would confine drinking to such places as night clubs and bars, and keep the display of liquor as much as possible out of the average American home.

This worked so successfully that we have corresponded with the Methodist Board of Temperance in which they acknowledge greatly the cooperation of the industry in reducing the emphasis on drinking.

Now, we have these complaints against violence, and as I say, we started as recently as last November to urge producers to tone down these scenes. It will be a little time before the effect of this campaign will show up. I think Mr. Freeman yesterday indicated that it sometimes takes him 18 months to get a picture finished after the initial idea is set in motion. So it will take at least until the end of this year before the improvement which we feel is coming will be apparent on the screen.

Mr. BOBO. Mr. Shurlock, if the Production Code Administration feels that in certain movies there is an excessive amount of violence, an excessive amount of brutality, or a low tone of morals shown in the picture, would it be possible for them to withhold their seal if there was a signatory member of the association?

Mr. SHURLOCK. It would be possible for us to hold our seal under any circumstances.

Mr. BOBO. How many pictures since the office has been inaugurated has the seal been withheld on?

Mr. SHURLOCK. I don't really know. I would have to go through our records. Maybe I should amplify that. Of the major companies——

Mr. BOBO. About how many, just approximately; do you know?

Mr. SHURLOCK. Well, I want to give you a reasonably correct answer In the early days, we had to withhold quite a few because all pictures—because a great many unsatisfactory pictures were being presented.

Let me say this: Of the major companies in the last 10 or 15 years, I only know of two. There have been a number of foreign films also submitted to us which we had to refuse the seal, and I cannot count them up in my mind at this moment.

Mr. BOBO. What were these pictures, Mr. Shurlock?

Mr. SHURLOCK. One was an independently produced picture called The Moon is Blue and one was a picture produced by one of our studios called the French Line. I must hasten to add that that picture has since been reedited and it now has the code seal.

Mr. BOBO. In the event that a producer that is a signatory member or has submitted a film to you for approval, is the only recourse that you have to withhold the seal?

Mr. SHURLOCK. If we cannot come to an agrement on how the picture should be satisfactorily reedited.

Mr. BOBO. If he goes ahead and releases the picture there is no system of fine or regulation within the association itself?

Mr. SHURLOCK. Yes, there is a fine of $25,000 for the release of any picture not bearing our seal by a member company.

Mr. BOBO. The pictures you mentioned that were released without the seal, were the producers of these pictures fined by the association?

Mr. SHURLOCK. Neither the producer nor the distributing company was then a member of the association, so they were not subject to the fine. In the case of the French Line, the fine was never assessed, I understand, and of course now, since the picture has been brought in line with the code, I suppose the matter has been dropped. That I know nothing about. That is a matter that would be handled by the board of directors in New York.

Mr. BOBO. Mr. Shurlock, you state that you have brought this to the attention of the producers, the excessive crime and violence. What has been the reaction of them to this criticism?

Mr. SHURLOCK. As in the former cases, they agreed that if there is a public reaction against any element in the picture to the point where the pictures are not being enjoyed, they will change their type of production and their approach.

Mr. BOBO. Do you think that this particular type of approach to crime and violence has materially changed within the last 6 months?

Mr. SHURLOCK. I think it is definitely beginning to change. I think that there will be an improvement visible in the pictures released this fall, or certainly this winter.

Mr. BOBO. Do you have opinion, Mr. Shurlock, as to what might be the cause of this constantly increasing violence in movies?

Mr. SHURLOCK. I think the following: I think first of all that the type of violence that is being objected to—I should say that the reason that some of this violence is being objected to is that it no longer appears in the old type western picture, but has been brought up to date into a type of picture in which the characters are more readily recognizable and identifiable.

In the standard weapons there is an area of the fairy tale about the portrayal that does not bring an audience into direct identification. I think when that type of story is told in modern setting, the violence and the brutality affect the public more strongly.

I also think the following, that there is on the part of the public a greater resentment against violence because unfortunately there have been recently fewer of the old style family type of picture. I don't think we are making many more than we did previously. I think perhaps we have been making fewer of the domestic comedies and pictures completely divorced from violence, so that when the family goes to the movies they see during the course of the year a greater proportion of violent pictures than they may have done previously, and I also have a feeling—it is my personal guess—that a family which has sat through a television play between 5 and 6:30 of good standard western violence, and then they put the children to bed and go out to the theater, sit through a double bill consisting of Crashout and that type of thing, they simply feel that they have had too much violence for the day. I think they take out their resentment on the movies which are not necessarily any more violent than the previous shows because they had to pay for the movies.

Mr. Bobo. Do you think it would be possible, Mr. Shurlock, that the children that they put to bed might also see the twin bill and have a tremendous amount of violence thrust at them in one evening's entertainment?

Mr. Shurlock. Yes, it is possible.

Mr. Bobo. Do you feel that the ads that we have displayed around the room today, do you think that they accurately reflect the type of picture which they are supposed to sell—the Prodigal, Womens' Prison, Blackboard Jungle, or Kiss Me Deadly?

Mr. Shurlock. I know very little about advertising, I will admit. It has always been a mystery to me. None of these ads would get me anywhere near a picture, I admit. But I suppose the advertising people in New York know what they are doing or are kept on the payroll on the basis that they know what they are doing.

Mr. Gordon White, who is head of the advertising in the code administration, I thought explained the matter as thoroughly as it could be done. He is an advertising expert. I am not.

Mr. Bobo. I was asking that question in line with the regulations as set forth in the code that subjects would be treated with care and within the limits of good taste would be brutality, the sale of women or a woman selling her virtue, things such as that. In the Big Combo, for example, would that be the theme of the picture which a person would see?

Mr. Shurlock. I didn't see the picture. I doubt very much in the Combo whether it is about a girl who gives herself to the boss, I think there is more about the boss than the combo, whatever that is.

Mr. Bobo. Mr. Shurlock, you were here and heard the testimony the other morning of Mr. Mooring in which he introduced a number of pictures and gave an opinion on them, one of them being Black Tuesday. The description of that picture has been brutal killings, a new and unique trick for concealing a gun, a perfect pattern for crime, escape from the just process of law, and excessive brutality, all of which are expressly forbidden by the code. Were you familiar with that particular picture? Does that adequately describe the type of picture that it was?

Mr. Shurlock. Here is where I think I fall on my face. I never saw the picture.

Mr. Bobo. Did you receive a report of the picture from a member of your staff or pass on it for the approval of the code?

Mr. Shurlock. I don't believe so. I think it was probably passed in the usual routine of our office. Two staff members must have read the script and reviewed the picture, and I do not recall that they called me or anybody in for a review, a real review of the picture or any part of it. Apparently the question was not raised.

Mr. Bobo. The Big House dealt with the kidnaping of a child which became the main theme, despite even efforts to cover the fact by introducing prison breaks as a secondary theme. I am quoting the words of Mr. Mooring. It has also introduced excessive brutality and gave details of the crime of kidnaping which is also in violation of the Production Code.

Mr. SHURLOCK. I know something about that picture, although I did not see it all. I reviewed some sections of it which seemed to be excessively brutal and we agreed with the producer that there would be some eliminations made. I do not know about the discussions at the script level on the basic story. As far as we in our interpretation of the code are concerned, Mr. Mooring is in error. There is no kidnaping in the story. Now, I speak without having seen the picture, but this is what we agreed with the producer would be permissible. The child is not kidnaped. The criminal, having broken out of jail, hiding out in the hills, the child stumbles in on them. They had no kidnaping plans at all. They tried to hold him for ransom which was never paid. In fact, the child was killed unfortunately in the course of their operations. This is one episode in the story, which is by no means the basic story, so it did not violate the rather involved regulations in the code on kidnaping.

Mr. BOBO. Actually, in the script, he was originally a kidnaper and as the picture finally came out the child was held as a hostage rather than being kidnaped.

Mr. SHURLOCK. That is correct. The original story which was rejected by us had the leading criminal a kidnaper. We told the producer this is in violation of the code. He thereupon came back some days or weeks later with his revised treatment which did not in our estimation violate the kidnaping provisions of the code.

Mr. BOBO. And in the picture the child was thrown over a cliff and brutally killed.

Mr. SHURLOCK. I think it was. I did not see that episode.

Mr. BOBO. In Cell 2455 Death Row, it dealt with the life of a notorious criminal of current times, and identified him in the screen title, thus while sidestepping the rule against the use of the crimnal's name in the film, it violated the expressed purpose of the rule. It also contained intimate reference to sexual behavior, detailed partly by pictorial means, then confirmed by sound effects.

Mr. SHURLOCK. I don't quite know what the second charge means. The first charge I will answer as follows: When the regulation about criminals, notorious criminals, was written into the code, I don't think that anybody thought that one of these criminals would be literary enough to write a book. Chapman did write a book and the studio bought his book. Now, I have not gone into this phase of the matter, but I think that the reason his name appeared on the main title probably comes from the fact that the Authors League insists that when a property is purchased for the screen the author of the book will be given proper credit on the main title. The studio endeavored, and I think successfully, to sidestep this legal inconvenience. In the whole body of the story the name was never used.

Mr. BOBO. In the scenes he is referring to of a sexual nature, Mr. Shurlock, would it be proper for the motion picture to lead up to an actual scene and then drift off into a background of music; would that meet with the requirements of the code without showing the actual act?

Mr. SHURLOCK. We would not approve any scene at all unless it had first of all a real moral basis in the picture. We would probably insist that they cut the scene short, very short, of any actual preparation for seduction or adultery. We also would insist that the scene end very abruptly and avoid any of this lingering music which suggests that intimacies are being indulged in while the music plays or the cameras fan through the trees or the moon or whatever it is. We have been for years cutting out those scenes and insisting that the scene end after the embrace.

Mr. Bobo. Well, is it true that in a very brutal or sadistic type of fight that it teaches a moral lesson within the picture, that it could then be approved by the code?

Mr. Shurlock. No, not if it got into the area of excessive brutality which the code forbids. "Excessive," of course, is a matter of opinion. The producer has the one idea of what is excessive, as do we, and very often the public changes its mind as to what is excessive. I'd like to bring up a picture which has now become a classic. It was Shane. There was one of the longest and bloodiest fights I ever saw in my life in Technicolor. I never heard a complaint about it. If Shane were released today, I think, there would be complaints about the length of that fight. Within the industry, in the first version we thought the fight went on too long and after some discussion with the studio, we got I think about a third of it trimmed down, so even then we were concerned, as we should have been with excessive brutality, and that picture seemed to have satisfied the public.

Mr. Bobo. In the picture Son of Sinbad, it exploits nudity which the code forbids, coming under the heading of immoral actions. It also presents dancers identified with sexual actions, and after the fashion of burlesque, and is intended to excite emotional reaction of an audience through exposure and movement.

Mr. Shurlock. Yes, I understand that. I was just thinking how to answer that. I would like to tell something of the story of the Son of Sinbad. That picture was submitted to us at least 16 months ago. We refused to approve it in its then form. It lay on the shelf until I think last February when the company had a change of heart evidently and came to us and said, "Look we will do whatever we can within reason to reedit this picture so that it will be given a seal and put in circulation." We did the best we could with a picture which was in its first form quite unacceptable. We took anywhere between 40 and 60 percent of the footage out of the dances. One particular dance which was originally 247 feet long ended up 80 feet long, and that isn't all dance. It includes other scenes of cutting away to the people watching. We cut out as much of the questionable costuming as we could.

Now, we have been criticized for not having cut enough. That is possibly an error in judgment. I was worried about the possible reaction to this film. I would like to say that I went down to a theater here Tuesday and Saturday night deliberately. I caught the 8 o'clock showing and would like the committee to believe me when I say I listened most carefully and I heard not one single whistle, wolf call, laugh, or wisecrack at any of the dances. The audience apparently accepted it as just another Arabian Nights fantasy. We make 2 or 3 of them every year. There was considerable laughter but it was all at legitimate jokes in the picture, and I was much encouraged by this public reception of the picture which seemed, inasmuch as I could see of the picture that evening, to sustain our judgment that we had done a reasonably good job on the reediting.

Mr. Bobo. Mr. Shurlock, it seems that if we do, and we do get reactions such as we got from Mr. Mooring and from others, that what has come out after you have approved and put a seal on it, that the version of the picture which you see must be a mighty terrific version of the picture in its brutality or its sex scenes. Is there quite a bit of cutting and editing done by your organization on this type of picture?

Mr Shurlock. No. I want to be fair to the industry. If I may, I will except Son of Sinbad which was a bit of an exception. Most of the pictures are in reasonable shape when they come to us. We do get into an argument with them on degrees of brutality, as to the length of these scenes. We have just had an argument in 1 studio, cutting down a fight which ran I think 4 minutes, a western, a standard western barroom brawl which had been acceptable for 40 years, I suppose. We thought this one went too long in the first place. We further adduced the fact that there had been some complaints about the length and the violence of this type of fight. We got the studio to cut it down, I think—well, just a little over 2 minutes.

Now, most of the scenes, however, are rather short scenes and are much more easily susceptible to filming. For about 4 years we have steadily insisted, vigorously insisted, that all excessively and unusually brutal acts such as specifically, kicking or kneeing or eye gouging should be omitted entirely. Occasionally on the set a couple of these stunt men, mixing up and putting on one of these phony movie fights get a little overenthusiastic and put in a couple of imaginary kicks. We then insist that they be cut out. I think if you will look at the picture, you will see that there is occasionally an indication that a man has been kicked out of play. That was because he got into the fight when he shouldn't have, but the studio eventually trims it out and most of these fights are just straight fist fights and avoid the excessive details, the brutality of kicking and kneeing and gouging that we sometimes see in some other media.

Mr. Bobo. In the picture Fort Yuma I think the Motion Picture Production Code office reduced 24 personalized killings in that picture to the number of 10. The other night I saw the picture 10 Wanted Men and there were 17 killed within that picture. What is the criteria that you use as to the number of people that will be killed in any 1 picture?

Mr. Shurlock. There is no very definite criteria. Each story, of course, is pretty much sui generis and has to be judged by its own merits.

We took cognizance of the fact in reediting Fort Yuma that there were complaints about the number of killings, and the producer agreed that this was not good entertainment now even if it had been 6 months ago, and being a sensible man he concurred in our suggestion to reduce it. We did not evidently take that action with Ten Wanted Men, a picture which I have also not seen. Maybe we should have, I don't know. I would have to see the picture. But anyhow, the Fort Yuma episode, I think, will indicate to the committee that the industry is definitely out to reduce and eventually perhaps stop a great deal of this excessive violence.

Mr. Bobo. I notice in one of the pictures that we have that the picture is advertised as the story of a perfect crime, the picture being Five Against the House, which presents a pattern of crime conceived by four young college men. These are Mr. Mooring's statements here. One of them, a popular TV film hero. It was executed by methods most calculated to inspire others with the desire for imitation, which is contrary to the Motion Picture Production Code which says methods of crime should not be explicitly presented.

Mr. SHURLOCK. Mr. Mooring is a little in error. The crime is not perfect. It does not come out. In our interpretation of the code—and I might explain that we have been guided since about 1936 by a very interesting interview we had with a crime expert named August Balmer who was at that time, I think, professor of criminology at Berkeley. We had him down for a day, and we threw all kinds of crime situations out of scripts before him and asked him for his advice. His advice boiled down to something rather simple as a rule of thumb. He said—

The more involved the crime, the more easy it is for the police to come upon a clue and for the criminal to make a slip.

He encouraged us to believe that rather involved crimes would not cause any serious social damage. He says the thing to watch out for is a simple way of committing a crime.

Now, in this particular picture, the crime, not perfect, was so involved by—if I were to tell it to you, I would tell you very simply that it consisted of putting a tape recording machine inside one of those wagons in Harold's Club in Reno where they pick up the money and carry it from the tables to the safe. This tape machine made a speech which suggested that there was a dwarf inside this little trolley with a gun, and if the man didn't drop the money, he would shoot him. This seemed to be so fantastic that anyone who really tried to do it would be rather simple minded. Of course it did not work in the picture.

Mr. Mooring gives a little unfair portrayal also of the college graduate. They do plan the perfect crime, and then they decide they will not go through with it, but one of them because of a wound has got some psychopathic features in his character suddenly changes his mind and at the point of a gun he forces the rest of them to go through with the attempt after they had said, "Well, fellows, let's call this whole thing off. This is silly."

Mr. BOBO. Well, then, the advertisement would mislead you if you were to go to see the story of The Perfect Crime.

Mr. SHURLOCK. Yes.

Mr. BOBO. Well, in the picture Violent Saturday, again dealing with violent crime and methods of committing criminal acts, it expressly details the methods of a bank robbery crime.

Mr. SHURLOCK. I did not see the picture, but I checked that accusation with the members of the staff who had seen the picture. They said that it was no more explicit than walking into the bank and saying, "Give over the money," and by the way, the crime there is frustrated too. There were no interesting or conceivably successful plans that would excite anybody's interest anymore than he might learn from a weekly perusal of the newspapers.

Mr. BOBO. In the picture, Kiss Me Deadly over here, which is white hot thrills, blood red kisses, and Mickey Spillane's latest H bomb, is the tone of that picture of an acceptable nature as far as violence and brutality and dealings with the opposite sex?

Mr. SHURLOCK. Well, fairly. This is a rather low-tone type of literature to bring to the screen. There is no use denying that. It must be said, however, in its defense, that it is a story of Mickey Spillane trying to solve a crime, not to commit one. He undertakes unconventional methods of doing this. There is a very good representation of the police department who denounce Mickey Spillane, who call him a cheap divorce lawyer who is trying to horn in on their territory. They speak very severely to him. They blame him for confusing their own work. It is true that at the end, as in so many of these private-eye stories, he does solve the problem, but his unconventional methods are put in their proper light by a very well presented police officer.

The sex situations were very mild in as much as it is one of the characteristics of Mickey Spillane that while the girls are crazy about him, he pays very little attention to them. So at no time is there any getting together on that score, though a lot of the girls made passes at him.

Mr. BOBO. Was there at one time a discussion as to whether the seal would be withheld from this picture, or the picture approved?

Mr. SHURLOCK. I don't think so.

Mr. BOBO. Mr. Shurlock, in your feeling of the presentation of crime and violence and the presentation of crimes, is it your reaction that because of the revulsion of the public to these particular scenes is the reason they should be trimmed or do you have an opinion on what adverse effect it might have on the personality development or the emotional development of our juvenile population?

Mr. SHURLOCK. That is an area about which I do not know too much, frankly. I have confined my activities and thoughts almost entirely to the code. We would be very happy to accept any authoritative judgment in the matter, but heretofore the literature that has come our way has seemed to suggest that pictures have not been having too serious an effect on the youth. I have some pamphlets in my office based on a study by some organization in England. Now, the British have always been the most sensitive of the foreign markets about our violence. They were the ones who were the most sensitive about the horror pictures back in 1940 to which I adverted. In fact, they put a special category on what they called a horror picture— H pictures. They classify pictures over there and the picture in the H category meant that no child under 16 could go in to see it even if accompanied by a parent. They also have been very much concerned about violence and brutality, but this study coming from them states rather categorically that they do not believe that the movies have any seriously deleterious effect upon the youth or upon children, perhaps.

Mr. BOBO. Thank you, Mr. Shurlock.

Mr. STEWART. May I present just a thought to Mr. Shurlock, Mr. Chairman, which I think is fundamental and pertains to his organization?

Chairman KEFAUVER. Just a minute. I had suggested that people write out any questions that they want to ask and send them up here. What is your name?

Mr. STEWART. Mr. Stewart. Ted Stewart. I am a retired police officer, and I am very much interested in juvenile work.

Chairman KEFAUVER. What is your observation, Mr. Stewart?

Mr. STEWART. My observation is this: In view of the fact that his organization Q. K.'s 99 percent of our movies, and in view of the fact that they have O. K.'d possibly ten or twelve thousand of them over a period of time and in view of the fact that he and his committee are not able to see all of those at one time, and also in view of the fact that I am the subject matter to which his propaganda is subject, I think it would be wise—or maybe it would be—I would like to offer the suggestion that over a period of time his organization consider the use of maybe 5 or 10 psychiatrists in different parts of the country as an advisory committee to find out just what the audience reactions are in the various parts of the country, because it might help them to present better picures.

Chairman KEFAUVER. What do you think about that, Mr. Shurlock?

Mr. SHURLOCK. That is not exactly in my area. That is a public relations job, and I would not want to speak with any apparent authority.

Chairman KEFAUVER. In other words, his idea, I take it, is that you or the member of your staff that reviews the picture might think it is all right, that the subtlety of it or something that you might not see in it might have a different effect, and that psychiatrists or someone specially trained in the reaction of children, there might be something in the picture that would be helpful to you in passing upon it that you might miss. I understood from Mr. Johnston with whom I talked at length that you did have psychiatrists, that you used from time to time with these pictures.

Mr. SHURLOCK. I would like to say this: If such a plan were to be adopted, it would be essential that the psychiatrist or the counselor get to work on the script before the picture is finished. Whether we would have a psychiatrist read every script that comes in, I don't know. In pictures dealing with psychiatry I am quite certain that the studios get technical advice. In a good many of the pictures dealing with the police, they get police advice. In the case of Blackboard Jungle I believe Mr. Schary testified yesterday they had considerable advice before proceeding and releasing the picture. I think the companies themselves would prefer to handle the question of getting this kind of advice in their own way and with their own staffs, and leave us to be concerned with the morals code. The technical points of psychiatry or such fields I think, should be handled in the case of an individual picture by the company producing it.

Chairman KEFAUVER. I don't wish to press the matter, but I do think that the gentleman has a suggestion which is worth considering.

Mr. SHURLOCK. Thank you, Senator, I will pass it on.

Chairman KEFAUVER. Now, Mr. Shurlock, your administration is part of the motion picture general overall association of which Mr. Johnston, Eric Johnston, is the chairman or president; is that right?

Mr. SHURLOCK. The president; yes, sir.

Chairman KEFAUVER. And does the advertising part of the industry come under Mr. Eric Johnston as well as the production?

Mr. SHURLOCK. Well, inasmuch as Mr. Johnston is the president of the association, all of the activities eventually come under him.

Chairman KEFAUVER. Mr. Johnston has been quite cooperative in helping us to get information for this hearing. I have had a good deal of admiration for Mr. Johnston, and I am glad to report that he too has told us when we went into this hearing that they were concerned—that he was concerned about amounts of violence and brutality, and in some cases sex, that he thought in overly large amounts, had been getting into recent pictures. So I think that it is a healthy sign that you indicate, and I am glad that you are taking some cognizance of it as are the motion pictures people themselves.

On the bottom of page 2 of your statement:

> In actual practice all but a few films made in Hollywood are submitted to the production department code administration for its approval.

There are some made in Hollywood that are not submitted?

Mr. SHURLOCK. Well, in the past there have been occasional films made there that were of the type that, of course, we wouldn't even begin to think of approving. There are very few. Now that statement is merely a generalized statement to indicate that there may be 1 or 2 a year.

Chairman KEFAUVER. Are there some particular companies, production companies, that don't submit their pictures to you?

Mr. SHURLOCK. No, sir. These are entirely fly-by-night producers. They verge on the type of sex exploitation picture and they know that they cannot conceivable get the production code seal of approval.

Chairman KEFAUVER. Is there any significance to the word, "Hollywood"? How about pictures made—of course some of them are made here, but some are not made here.

Mr. SHURLOCK. Yes; that is correct. It would be better if I had said in the United States. Some are produced in New York.

Chairman KEFAUVER. And then, sir, what is your connection with foreign companies with reference to the operation of your code?

Mr. SHURLOCK. Occasionally a foreign producer would like to get his picture released in the United States. There is nothing to prevent him from releasing the picture without our seal. Sometimes, however, he would like to obtain the services of one of our major releasing companies who require our seal before they will handle the picture. In that case he sends or brings the picture to us and asks us to review it and report whether or not it conforms with the code and we grant it our seal, which would enable him to then ask a major releasing company to handle the picture. I suppose in this way he would possibly get a larger circulation.

Chairman KEFAUVER. Mr. Shurlock, what is the relationship between your association and the actual showhouses, the theater owners, themselves? Do the theater owners through their organization, Theater Owners of America, require the seal of approval as a prerequisite for the showing of pictures in their particular houses?

Mr. SHURLOCK. No, sir. Since divorcement, brought about by Government decree in which the producing and distributing companies were ordered to sell all of their theaters, the members of the Motion Picture Association of America, own no more theaters.

Chairman KEFAUVER. And so there is no working agreement as to requiring a seal of approval on the part of the theater owners at the present time.

Mr. SHURLOCK. As far as I know, none at all.

Chairman Kefauver. Now, in your work of course you read the script and study it. Do you always actually see the picture itself, either you or some of your men?

Mr. Shurlock. It is mandatory upon the producer to submit the finished picture to us before we give it the seal, and as a matter of fact, whenever we write them a letter on the script, we always add a final paragraph saying, "You understand, of course, our final opinion will be based upon the finished picture."

Chairman Kefauver. Now, will you explain again how your association—of course, you are just a part of the overall association, and I suppose the assessments or the dues are paid to the Motion Picture Association and they in turn finance your part of the work.

Mr. Shurlock. No, sir.

Chairman Kefauver. Is there a fee for the passing upon a picture?

Mr. Shurlock. We are financed autonomously by the fees. We do not get any money from the parent association. The fees are made out to the Production Code Administration. We have our own accounting system, all of this under the control of an auditor in New York. That was done originally because a great many of the people submitting their pictures were not members of the association, and it was thought better that we operate entirely as an autonomous association, not financed by the major companies. In that way the independent might think that he was dealing with a company which was not controlled by the majors. This was set up in the early days. It has become less important in the last 10 years, perhaps, but the system still persists.

Mr. Young. Mr. Senator——

Chairman Kefauver. Just a minute, Mr. Young. This organization started, your part of it, in 1932——

Mr. Shurlock. 1934.

Chairman Kefauver. 1934. It was the public opinion at that time that the major picture industry felt it has to regulate and control itself. That was at the time that Mr. Hays was appointed; is that right?

Mr. Shurlock. No, sir. That is not quite the sequence of events. Mr. Hays had been president of the association since 1922. The production code was written and adopted in 1930. It, however, was not until 1934 that the successful method of implementing the code was worked out. That method is the granting of the certificate of approval and an agreement on the part of the producers and distributors not to handle a picture that did not bear the certificate of approval. Up to that time there had been no such definite sanction, and this is what made it work, of course.

Chairman Kefauver. Anything else, Mr. Bobo?

Mr. Bobo. No.

Chairman Kefauver. This is the latest code that I have here?

Mr. Shurlock. Yes.

Chairman Kefauver. I will order this to be printed in the appendix of the record, or as a part of the appendix of the hearings, as part of our record. Is this code altered from time to time?

(The document referred to was marked "Exhibit No. 12," and reads as follows:)

EXHIBIT No. 12

A CODE TO GOVERN THE MAKING OF MOTION PICTURES, THE REASONS SUPPORTING
IT, AND THE RESOLUTION FOR UNIFORM INTERPRETATION

(Motion Picture Association of America, Inc., 1930–55)

PREAMBLE

The Motion Picture Production Code was formulated and formally adopted by
the Association of Motion Picture Producers, Inc. (California), and the Motion
Picture Association of America, Inc.[1] (New York), in March 1930.[2]

Motion picture producers recognize the high trust and confidence which have
been placed in them by the people of the world and which have made motion
pictures a universal form of entertainment.

They recognize their responsibility to the public because of this trust and
because entertainment and art are important influences in the life of a nation.

Hence, though regarding motion pictures primarily as entertainment without
any explicit purpose of teaching or propaganda, they know that the motion
picture within its own field of entertainment may be directly responsible for
spiritual or moral progress, for higher types of social life, and for much correct
thinking.

During the rapid transition from silent to talking pictures they realized the
necessity and the opportunity of subscribing to a code to govern the production of talking pictures and of reacknowledging this responsibility.

On their part, they ask from the public and from public leaders a sympathetic
understanding of their purposes and problems and a spirit of cooperation that
will allow them the freedom and opportunity necessary to bring the motion
picture to a still higher level of wholesome entertainment for all the people.

THE PRODUCTION CODE

General principles

1. No picture shall be produced which will lower the moral standards of those
who see it. Hence the sympathy of the audience shall never be thrown to the
side of crime, wrongdoing, evil or sin.

2. Correct standards of life, subject only to the requirements of drama and
entertainment, shall be presented.

3. Law, natural or human, shall not be ridiculed, nor shall sympathy be
created for its violation.

Particular applications

I. Crimes against the law.[3]—These shall never be presented in such a way as
to throw sympathy with the crime as against law and justice or to inspire others
with a desire for imitation.

1. Murder:

(a) The technique of murder must be presented in a way that will not
inspire imitation.

(b) Brutal killings are not to be presented in detail.

(c) Revenge in modern times shall not be justified.

2. Methods of crime should not be explicitly presented.

(a) Theft, robbery, safecracking, and dynamiting of trains, mines, buildings,
etc., should not be detailed in method.

(b) Arson must be subject to the same safeguards.

(c) The use of firearms should be restricted to essentials.

3. The illegal drug traffic, and drug addiction, must never be presented.

II. Sex.—The sanctity of the institution of marriage and the home shall be
upheld. Pictures shall not infer that low forms of sex relationship are the
accepted or common thing.

1. Adultery and illicit sex, sometimes necessary plot material, must not be
explicitly treated or justified, or presented attractively.

2. Scenes of passion:

(a) They should not be introduced except where they are definitely essential
to the plot.

---

[1] Until December 14, 1945, the Motion Picture Producers and Distributors of America, Inc.
[2] The code as presented in this edition contains all revisions and amendments through
1954.
[3] See also Special Regulations on Crime in Motion Pictures.

(*b*) Excessive and lustful kissing, lustful embraces, suggestive postures, and gestures are not to be shown.

(*c*) In general, passion should be treated in such manner as not to stimulate the lower and baser emotions.

3. Seduction or rape:

(*a*) These should never be more than suggested, and then only when essential for the plot. They must never be shown by explicit method.

(*b*) They are never the proper subject for comedy.

4. Sex perversion or any inference of it is forbidden.

5. White slavery shall not be treated.

6. Abortion, sex hygiene, and venereal diseases are not proper subjects for theatrical motion pictures.

7. Scenes of actual child birth, in fact or in silhouette, are never to be presented.

8. Children's sex organs are never to be exposed.

III. Vulgarity.—The treatment of low, disgusting, unpleasant, though not necessarily evil, subjects should be guided always by the dictates of good taste and a proper regard for the sensibilities of the audience.

IV. Obscenity.—Obscenity in word, gesture, reference, song, joke, or by suggestion (even when likely to be understood only by part of the audience) is forbidden.

V. Profanity.—Pointed profanity and every other profane or vulgar expression, however used, are forbidden.

No approval by the Production Code Administration shall be given to the use of words and phrases in motion pictures including, but not limited to, the following: Bronx cheer (the sound) ; chippie; God, Lord, Jesus, Christ (unless used reverently) ; cripes; fairy (in a vulgar sense) ; finger (the) ; fire, cries of; Gawd; goose (in a vulgar sense) ; hot (applied to a woman) ; "in your hat"; madam (relating to prostitution) ; nance; nuts (except when meaning crazy) ; pansy; razzberry (the sound) ; S. O. B. ; son-of-a ; tart; toilet gags; whore.

In the administration of section V of the production code, the Production Code Administration may take cognizance of the fact that the following words and phrases are obviously offensive to the patrons of motion pictures in the United States and more particularly to the patrons of motion pictures in foreign countries: chink, dago, frog, greaser, hunkie, kike, nigger, spig, wop, yid.

It should also be noted that the words "hell" and "damn," if used without moderation, will be considered offensive by many members of the audience. Their use, therefore, should be governed by the discretion and the prudent advice of the Code Administration.

VI. Costumes.[4]—1. Complete nudity is never permitted. This includes nudity in fact or in silhouette, or any licentious notice thereof by other characters in the pictures.

2. Undressing scenes should be avoided, and never used save where essential to the plot.

3. Indecent or undue exposure is forbidden.

4. Dancing costumes intended to permit undue exposure or indecent movements in the dance are forbidden.

VII. Dances.—1. Dances suggesting or representing sexual actions or indecent passion are forbidden.

2. Dances which emphasize indecent movements are to be regarded as obscene.

VIII. Religion.—1. No film or episode may throw ridicule on any religious faith.

2. Ministers of religion in their character as ministers of religion should not be used as comic characters or as villains.

3. Ceremonies of any definite religion should be carefully and respectfully handled.

IX. Locations.—The treatment of bedrooms must be governed by good taste and delicacy.

X. National feelings.—1. The use of the flag shall be consistently respectful.

2. The history, institutions, prominent people, and citizenry of all nations shall be represented fairly.

XI. Titles.—The following titles shall not be used :

1. Titles which are salacious, indecent, obscene, profane, or vulgar.

---

[4] See also special resolution on costumes.

2. Titles which suggest or are currently associated in the public mind with material, characters, or occupations unsuitable for the screen.

3. Titles which are otherwise objectionable.

XII. Special subjects.—The following subjects must be treated within the careful limits of good taste:

1. Actual hangings or electrocutions as legal punishments for crime.
2. Third degree methods.
3. Brutality and possible gruesomeness.
4. The sale of women, or a woman selling her virtue.
5. Surgical operations.
6. Miscegenation.
7. Liquor and drinking.

SPECIAL REGULATIONS ON CRIME IN MOTION PICTURES

Resolved (December 20, 1938), That the board of directors of the Motion Picture Association of America, Inc., hereby ratifies, approves, and confirms the interpretations of the production code, the practices thereunder, and the resolutions indicating and confirming such interpretations heretofore adopted by the Association of Motion Picture Producers, Inc., all effectuating regulations relative to the treatment of crime in motion pictures, as follows:

1. Details of crime must never be shown and care should be exercised at all times in discussing such details.

2. Action suggestive of wholesale slaughter of human beings, either by criminals in conflict with police, or as between warring factions of criminals, or in public disorder of any kind, will not be allowed.

3. There must be no suggestion, at any time, of excessive brutality.

4. Because of the increase in the number of films in which murder is frequently committed, action showing the taking of human life, even in the mystery stories, is to be cut to the minimum. These frequent presentations of murder tend to lessen regard for the sacredness of life.

5. Suicide, as a solution of problems occurring in the development of screen drama, is to be discouraged as morally questionable and as bad theater—unless absolutely necessary for the development of the plot. It should never be justified or glorified, or used to defeat the due processes of law.

6. There must be no display, at any time, of machine guns, submachine guns, or other weapons generally classified as illegal weapons in the hands of gangsters, or other criminals, and there are to be no off-stage sounds of the repercussions of these guns.

7. There must be no new, unique, or trick methods shown for concealing guns.

8. The flaunting of weapons by gangsters, or other criminals, will not be allowed.

9. All discussions and dialogue on the part of gangsters regarding guns should be cut to the minimum.

10. There must be no scenes, at any time, showing law-enforcing officers dying at the hands of criminals, unless such scenes are absolutely necessary to the development of the plot. This includes private detectives and guards for banks, motortrucks, etc.

11. With special reference to the crime of kidnaping—or illegal abduction—such stories are acceptable under the code only when (a) the kidnaping or abduction is not the main theme of the story; (b) the person kidnaped is not a child; (c) there are no details of the crime of kidnaping; (d) no profit accrues to the abductors or kidnapers; and (e) where the kidnapers are punished.

It is understood, and agreed, that the word "kidnaping," as used in paragraph 11 of these regulations, is intended to mean abduction, or illegal detention, in modern times, by criminals for ransom.

12. Pictures dealing with criminal activities, in which minors participate, or to which minors are related, shall not be approved if they incite demoralizing imitation on the part of youth.

13. No picture shall be approved dealing with the life of a notorious criminal of current or recent times which uses the name, nickname, or alias of such notorious criminal in the film, nor shall a picture be approved if based upon the life of such a notorious criminal unless the character shown in the film be punished for crimes shown in the film as committed by him.

SPECIAL RESOLUTION ON COSTUMES

On October 25, 1939, the board of directors of the Motion Picture Association of America, Inc., adopted the following resolution:

"*Resolved*, That the provisions of paragraphs 1, 3, and 4 of subdivision VI of the production code, in their application to costumes, nudity, indecent, or undue exposure and dancing costumes, shall not be interpreted to exclude authentically photographed scenes photographed in a foreign land, of natives of such foreign land, showing native life, if such scenes are a necessary and integral part of a motion picture depicting exclusively such land and native life, provided that no such scenes shall be intrinsically objectionable nor made a part of any motion picture produced in any studio; and provided further that no emphasis shall be made in any scenes of the customs or garb of such natives or in the exploitation thereof."

SPECIAL REGULATIONS ON CRUELTY TO ANIMALS

On December 27, 1940, the board of directors of the Motion Picture Association of America, Inc., approved a resolution adopted by the Association of Motion Picture Producers, Inc., reaffirming previous resolutions of the California association concerning brutality and possible gruesomeness, and apparent cruelty to animals:

"*Resolved, by the board of directors of the Association of Motion Picture Producers, Inc.*, That

"1. Hereafter, in the production of motion pictures there shall be no use by the members of the association of the contrivance or apparatus in connection with animals which is known as the running W, nor shall any picture submitted to the production code administration be approved if reasonable grounds exist for believing that use of any similar device by the producer of such picture resulted in apparent cruelty to animals; and

"2. Hereafter, in the production of motion pictures by the members of the association, such members shall, as to any picture involving the use of animals, invite on the lot during such shooting and consult with the authorized representative of the American Humane Association; and

"3. Steps shall be taken immediately by the members of the association and by the production code administration to require compliance with these resolutions, which shall bear the same relationship to the sections of the Production Code quoted herein as the association's special regulations re crime in motion pictures bear to the sections of the production code dealing therewith; and it is further

"*Resolved*, That the resolutions of February 19, 1925, and all other resolutions of this board establishing its policy to prevent all cruelty to animals in the production of motion pictures and reflecting its determination to prevent any such cruelty, be and the same hereby are in all respect reaffirmed."

REASONS SUPPORTING PREAMBLE OF CODE

I. Theatrical motion pictures, that is, pictures intended for the theater as distinct from pictures intended for churches, schools, lecture halls, educational movements, social reform movements, etc., are primarily to be regarded as entertainment.

Mankind has always recognized the importance of entertainment and its value in rebuilding the bodies and souls of human beings.

But it has always recognized that entertainment can be of a character either helpful or harmful to the human race, and in consequence has clearly distinguished between:

(*a*) Entertainment which tends to improve the race, or at least to re-create and rebuild human beings exhausted with the realities of life; and

(*b*) Entertainment which tends to degrade human beings, or to lower their standards of life and living.

Hence the moral importance of entertainment is something which has been universally recognized. It enters intimately into the lives of men and women and affects them closely; it occupies their minds and affections during leisure hours; and ultimately touches the whole of their lives. A man may be judged by his standard of entertainment as easily as by the standard of his work.

So correct entertainment raises the whole standard of a nation.

Wrong entertainment lowers the whole living conditions and moral ideals of a race.

Note, for example, the healthy reactions to healthful sports, like baseball, golf; the unhealthy reactions to sports like cockfighting, bullfighting, bear baiting, etc.

Note, too, the effect on ancient nations of gladiatorial combats, the obscene plays of Roman times, etc.

II. Motion pictures are very important as art.

Though a new art, possibly a combination art, it has the same object as the other arts, the presentation of human thought, emotion, and experience, in terms of an appeal to the soul through the senses.

Here, as in entertainment—

Art enters intimately into the lives of human beings.

Art can be morally good, lifting men to higher levels. This has been done through good music, great painting, authentic fiction, poetry, drama. Art can be morally evil in its effects. This is the case clearly enough with unclean art, indecent books, suggestive drama. The effect on the lives of men and women is obvious.

Note: It has often been argued that art in itself is unmoral, neither good nor bad. This is perhaps true of the thing which is music, painting, poetry, etc. But the thing is the product of some person's mind, and the intention of that mind was either good or bad morally when it produced the thing. Besides, the thing has its effect upon those who come into contact with it. In both these ways, that is, as a product of a mind and as the cause of definite effects, it has a deep moral significance and an unmistakable moral quality.

Hence: The motion pictures, which are the most popular of modern arts for the masses, have their moral quality from the intention of the minds which produce them and from their effects on the moral lives and reactions of their audiences. This gives them a most important morality.

1. They reproduce the morality of the men who use the pictures as a medium for the expression of their ideas and ideals.

2. They affect the moral standards of those who, through the screen, take in these ideas and ideals.

In the case of the motion pictures, this effect may be particularly emphasized because no art has so quick and so widespread an appeal to the masses. It has become in an incredibly short period the art of the multitudes.

III. The motion picture, because of its importance as entertainment and because of the trust placed in it by the peoples of the world, has special moral obligations.

A. Most arts appeal to the mature. This art appeals at once to every class, mature, immature, developed, undeveloped, law abiding, criminal. Music has its grades for different classes; so have literature and drama. This art of the motion picture, combining as it does the two fundamental appeals of looking at a picture and listening to a story, at once reaches every class of society.

B. By reason of the mobility of a film and the ease of picture distribution, and because of the possibility of duplicating positives in large quantities, this art reaches places unpenetrated by other forms of art.

C. Because of these two facts, it is difficult to produce films intended for only certain classes of people. The exhibitors' theaters are built for the masses, for the cultivated and the rude, the mature and the immature, the self-respecting and the criminal. Films, unlike books and music, can with difficulty be confined to certain selected groups.

D. The latitude given to film material cannot, in consequence, be as wide as the latitude given to book material. In addition:

(a) A book describes; a film vividly presents. One presents on a cold page; the other by apparently living people.

(b) A book reaches the mind through words merely; a film reaches the eyes and ears through the reproduction of actual events.

(c) The reaction of a reader to a book depends largely on the keenness of the reader's imagination, the reaction to a film depends of the vividness of presentation.

Hence many things which might be described or suggested in a book could not possibly be presented in a film.

E. This is also true when comparing the film with the newspaper.

(a) Newspapers present by description, films by actual presentation.

(b) Newspapers are after the fact and present things as having taken place; the film gives the events in the process of enactment and with the apparent reality of life.

F. Everything possible in a play is not possible in a film:

(a) Because of the larger audience of the film, and its consequential mixed character. Psychologically, the larger the audience, the lower the moral mass resistance to suggestion.

(b) Because through light, enlargement of character, presentation, scenic emphasis, etc., the screen story is brought closer to the audience than the play.

(c) The enthusiasm for and interest in the film actors and actresses, developed beyond anything of the sort in history, makes the audience largely sympathetic toward the characters they portray and the stories in which they figure. Hence the audience is more ready to confuse actor and actress and the characters they portray, and it is most receptive of the emotions and ideals presented by their favorite stars.

G. Small communities, remote from sophistication and from the hardening process which often takes place in the ethical and moral standards of groups in larger cities, are easily and readily reached by any sort of film.

H. The grandeur of mass settings, large action, spectacular features, etc., affects and arouses more intensely the emotional side of the audience.

In general, the mobility, popularity, accessibility, emotional appeal, vividness, straightforward presentation of facts in the film make for more intimate contact with a larger audience and for greater emotional appeal.

Hence the larger moral responsibilities of the motion pictures.

REASONS UNDERLYING THE GENERAL PRINCIPLES

I. No picture shall be produced which will lower the moral standards of those who see it. Hence the sympathy of the audience should never be thrown to the side of crime, wrong-doing, evil, or sin.

This is done—

1. When evil is made to appear attractive or alluring, and good is made to appear unattractive.

2. When the sympathy of the audience is thrown on the side of crime, wrong-doing, evil, sin. The same thing is true of a film that would throw smypathy against goodness, honor, innocence, purity, or honesty.

Note: Sympathy with a person who sins is not the same as sympathy with the sin or crime of which he is guilty. We may feel sorry for the plight of the murderer or even understand the circumstances which led him to his crime. We may not feel sympathy with the wrong which he has done.

The presentation of evil is often essential for art or fiction or drama.

This in itself is not wrong provided:

(a) That evil is not presented alluringly. Even if later in the film the evil is condemned or punished, it must not be allowed to appear so attractive that the audience's emotions are drawn to desire or approve so strongly that later the condemnation is forgotten and only the apparent joy of the sin remembered.

(b) That throughout, the audience feels sure that evil is wrong and good is right.

II. Correct standards of life shall, as far as possible, be presented.

A wide knowledge of life and of living is made possible through the film. When right standards are consistently presented, the motion picture exercises the most powerful influences. It builds character, develops right ideals, inculcates correct principles, and all this in attractive story form. If motion pictures consistently hold up for admiration high types of characters and present stories that will affect lives for the better, they can become the most powerful natural force for the improvement of mankind.

III. Law, natural or human, shall not be ridiculed, nor shall sympathy be created for its violation.

By natural law is understood the law which is written in the hearts of all mankind, the great underlying principles of right and justice dictated by conscience.

By human law is understood the law written by civilized nations.

1. The presentation of crimes against the law is often necessary for the carrying out of the plot. But the presentation must not throw sympathy with the crime as against the law nor with the criminal as against those who punish him.

2. The courts of the land should not be presented as unjust. This does not mean that a single court may not be represented as unjust, much less that a single court official must not be presented this way. But the court system of the country must not suffer as a result of this presentation.

I. Sin and evil enter into the story of human beings and hence in themselves are valid dramatic material.

II. In the use of this material, it must be distinguished between sins which repel by their very nature, and sins which often attract.

(a) In the first class come murder, most theft, many legal crimes, lying hypocrisy, cruelty, etc.

(b) In the second class come sex sins, sins and crimes of apparent heroism, such as banditry, daring thefts, leadership in evil, organized crime, revenge, etc.

The first class needs less care in treatment, as sins and crimes of this class are naturally unattractive. The audience instinctively condemns all such and is repelled.

Hence the important objective must be to avoid the hardening of the audience, especially of those who are young and impressionable, to the thought and fact of crime. People can become accustomed even to murder, cruelty, brutality, and repellent crimes, if these are too frequently repeated.

The second class needs great care in handling, as the response of human nature to their appeal is obvious. This is treated more fully below.

III. A careful distinction can be made between films intended for general distribution, and films intended for use in theaters restricted to a limited audience. Themes and plots quite appropriate for the latter would be altogether out of place and dangerous to the former.

Note: The practice of using a general theater and limiting its patronage during the showing of a certain film to "Adults Only' 'is not completely satisfactory and is only partially effective.

However, maturer minds may easily understand and accept without harm subject matter in plots which do younger people positive harm.

Hence: If there should be created a special type of theater, catering exclusively to an adult audience, for plays of this character (plays with problem themes, difficult discussions and maturer treatment) it would seem to afford an outlet, which does not now exist, for pictures unsuitable for general distribution but permissible for exhibitions to a restricted audience.

I. Crimes against the law

The treatment of crimes against the law must not—

1. Teach methods of crime.
2. Inspire potential criminals with a desire for imitation.
3. Make criminals seem heroic and justified.

Revenge in modern times shall not be justified. In lands and ages of less developed civilization and moral principles, revenge may sometimes be presented. This would be the case especially in places where no law exists to cover the crime because of which revenge is committed.

Because of its evil consequence, the drug traffic should not be presented in any form. The existence of the trade should not be brought to the attention of audiences.

II. Sex

Out of regard for the sanctity of marriage and the home, the triangle, that is, the love of a third party for one already married, needs careful handling. The treatment should not throw sympathy against marriage as an institution.

Scenes of passion must be treated with an honest acknowledgment of human nature and its normal reactions. Many scenes cannot be presented without arousing dangerous emotions on the part of the immature, the young or the criminal classes.

Even within the limits of pure love, certain facts have been universally regarded by lawmakers as outside the limits of safe presentation.

In the case of impure love, the love which society has always regarded as wrong and which has been banned by divine law, the following are important:

1. Impure love must not be presented as attractive and beautiful.
2. It must not be the subject of comedy or farce, or treated as material for laughter.
3. It must not be presented in such a way as to arouse passion or morbid curiosity on the part of the audience.
4. It must not be made to seem right and permissible.
5. In general, it must not be detailed in method and manner.

III. Vulgarity; IV. Obscenity; V. Profanity

Hardly need further explanation than is contained in the code.

VI. Costumes

General principles.—1. The effect of nudity or seminudity upon the normal man or woman, and much more upon the young and upon immature persons, has been honestly recognized by all lawmakers and moralists.

2. Hence the fact that the nude or seminude body may be beautiful does not make its use in the films moral. For, in addition to its beauty, the effect of the nude or seminude body on the normal individual must be taken into consideration.

3. Nudity or seminudity used simply to put a "punch" into a picture comes under the head of immoral actions. It is immoral in its effect on the average audience.

4. Nudity can never be permitted as being necessary for the plot. Seminudity must not result in undue or indecent exposures.

5. Transparent or translucent materials and silhouette are frequently more suggestive than actual exposure.

VII. Dances

Dancing in general is recognized as an art and as a beautiful form of expressing human emotions.

But dances which suggest or represent sexual actions, whether performed solo or with two or more; dances intended to excite the emotional reaction of an audience; dances with movement of the breasts, excessive body movements while the feet are stationary, violate decency and are wrong.

VIII. Religion

The reason why ministers of religion may not be comic characters or villains is simply because the attitude taken toward them may easily become the attitude taken toward religion in general. Religion is lowered in the minds of the audience because of the lowering of the audience's respect for a minister.

IX. Locations

Certain places are so closely and thoroughly associated with sexual life or with sexual sin that their use must be carefully limited.

X. National feelings

The just rights, history, and feelings of any nation are entitled to most careful consideration and respectful treatment.

XI. Titles

As the title of a picture is the brand on that particular type of goods, it must conform to the ethical practices of all such honest business.

XII. Special subjects

Such subjects are occasionally necessary for the plot. Their treatment must never offend good taste nor injure the sensibilities of an audience.

The use of liquor should never be excessively presented. In scenes from American life, the necessities of plot and proper characterization alone justify its use. And in this case, it should be shown with moderation.

RESOLUTION FOR UNIFORM INTERPRETATION

As amended June 13, 1934

1. When requested by production managers, the Motion Picture Association of America, Inc., shall secure any facts, information or suggestions concerning the probable reception of stories or the manner in which in its opinion they may best be treated.

2. Each production manager shall submit in confidence a copy of each or any script to the production code administration of the Motion Picture Association of America, Inc. (and of the Association of Motion Picture Producers, Inc., California). The production code administration will give the production manager for his guidance such confidential advice and suggestions as experience, research, and information indicate, designating wherein in its judgment the script departs from the provisions of the code, or wherein from experience or knowledge it is believed that exception will be taken to the story or treatment.

3. Each production manager of a company belonging to the Motion Picture Association of America, Inc., and any producer proposing to distribute and/or distributing his picture through the facilities of any member of the Motion Picture Association of America, Inc., shall submit to such production code administration every picture he produces before the negative goes to the laboratory for printing. Said production code administration, having seen the picture, shall inform the production manager in writing whether in its opinion the picture conforms or does not conform to the code, stating specifically wherein either by theme, treatment or incident, the picture violates the provisions of the code. In such latter event, the picture shall not be released until the changes indicated by the production code administration have been made; provided, however, that the production manager may appeal from such opinion of said production code administration, so indicated in writing, to the board of directors of the Motion Picture Association of America, Inc., whose finding shall be final, and such production manager and company shall be governed accordingly.

Mr. SHURLOCK. Yes, whenever the industry generally and the board of directors in particular feel that certain amendments are advisable, the get the board of directors together and approve such amendments, which are then put into the code.

Chairman KEFAUVER. Anything else, Mr. Shurlock?

Mr. SHURLOCK. May I make one additional observation inasmuch as Mr. Mooring's statement has been referred to of this afternoon? I would like to say a few words in that respect. Mr. Mooring was very gracious about me personally yesterday, and I would like to be equally gracious about him. He is a very intelligent reviewer of pictures, and he is a very sincere and honest man whom we know personally and whom we admire. I'd like to say first of all that inasmuch as Mr. Mooring stated categorically that the Production Code Administration has been lax in its operations recently, I want to categorically deny that. Mr. Mooring cited a number of pictures as being code violations in his opinion. If I may, I would like to explain how impossible it is and how dangerous it is for an outsider to pass judgment on the code operations, and our reasons for approving a picture. Now, Mr. Mooring spoke twice about the picture Not as a Stranger. He evidently was very much concerned about a certain scene in which an act of adultery was indicated, by a cross-cut to some horses pawing the ground. The producer insisted this particular element was vitally important to the proper moral understanding of the point he was making. Adultery of course, is a sin, and the producer says, "I want to suggest that people about to commit adultery are, to use the standard phrase we always use, giving in to their animal passions. That is why I want this counterpoint of the animals." He wanted to completely deglamorize adultery, the very point we try to make in code operations. Movies are often accused of glamorizing illicit sex. It is rather ironical that in a case in which a producer sets out to deglamorize the act and to pass a moral judgment on it, a moral condemnation on it by associating it with animal passion, that we are accused of violating our own code.

I want to say again that we are still as careful and as conscientious as we ever have been in the application of this code.

Chairman KEFAUVER. Well, Mr. Shurlock, I think I should say frankly to you that Mr. Mooring's criticisms, whether you agree with them or not, he is intelligent and sincere and it represents a fairly good cross-section, what he had to say of hundreds of letters and things that we are getting through our subcommittee. I mean a lot of people are thinking along the same lines. I am sure you are aware of that, that doesn't indicate that the movies generally are not good, but there has been a rising amount of criticism right along the line.

Mr. SHURLOCK. Yes, sir.

Chairman KEFAUVER. And frequently, of intelligent, thoughtful people. All right, thank you very much, Mr. Shurlock.

Mr. BOBO. Mr. Roger Allbright. Will you come around here, please?

Mr. YOUNG. Senator Kefauver, I wanted to answer one point.

Chairman KEFAUVER. Mr. Young, I have suggested that you write down any questions that you want asked and send them up.

Mr. YOUNG. I wanted to answer one point as to Mr. Shurlock. If I may speak for a minute, then I will leave. When they say the seal of approval is based on the picture, isn't it a fact that the complaints that come into the investigating committee and Mr. Mooring are because these pictures are viewed not with a seal in the theaters that they pay the admission to, that thereafter the seal has been given and approval given and certainly it is not a true statement as to the elimination of scenes, because after the picture goes out they are not empowered to eliminate these scenes, because they go all through the country.

Chairman KEFAUVER. I think, Mr. Young, in fairness, and if there is any misunderstanding on the record, I think the seal must be placed on them before they go out to the theaters. Mr. Shurlock, is that right?

Mr. YOUNG. That's right. That's right. I agree that they are, but the complaints come in from the viewers, from the public, from these mothers of children that see these pictures in the theaters.

Chairman KEFAUVER. Your point is that Mr. Shurlock's office should reconsider the matter then.

Mr. YOUNG. If they approve the picture, it goes out and the public goes to see it, and the adolescents go to see it, and these children see it on Saturday afternoon, like "The Moon is Blue," which is considered one of the most risqué plays in the country.

Chairman KEFAUVER. Well, I don't believe "The Moon is Blue" got the code.

Mr. YOUNG. And this play is put on in the major theaters—United Artists Theaters which is a member of the code—and that is not a true statement, Your Honor—Mr. Senator.

Now, the "Moon Is Blue" is of a risqué quality and it has been stopped in some cities and States.

Chairman KEFAUVER. Well, I think one weakness that there may be here in one part of the situation is that there is no relationship in the theater owners. Apparently some will show pictures whether they have a seal or not. That is not the matter we are investigating here now. We are not investigating the theater owners.

Mr. YOUNG. I will grant you that. But your complaints, Mr. Senator and the committee, come from the mothers and the public who see these pictures.

Chairman KEFAUVER. We know that. Well, thank you, Mr. Young, very much.

Mr. YOUNG. I shall write that.

Chairman KEFAUVER. Yes, all right. We will look for you. I want to state that I appreciate Mr. Young's questions and suggestions from anyone else. I think it is a good thing to get public reaction.

Some people in the audience have good ideas and good thoughts. I have had 2 or 3 questions sent up here which are very, very good ones. If anyone else in the audience thinks they have something worthwhile to contribute, I would rather prefer that they write me a little note about it because we want to get along, but if they don't feel they can write, just let me know, and I will give them a chance.

STATEMENT OF ROGER ALBRIGHT, DIRECTOR, DEPARTMENT OF EDUCATIONAL SERVICE, MOTION PICTURE ASSOCIATION OF AMERICA, LOS ANGELES, CALIF.

Mr. Albright, you are the director of the Department of Educational Services of the Motion Picture Association of America, and this is another branch of the overall organization headed up by Mr. Eric Johnston.

Mr. ALBRIGHT. That is right, sir.

Chairman KEFAUVER. And how long have you been head of the educational services?

Mr. ALBRIGHT. For 8 years, sir, and prior to that I was with the association as assistant to the director of community service. This was a type of program which has a similar function in the overall setup of our association.

Chairman KEFAUVER. Mr. Bobo, do you want to bring anything out about the size of the staff he has before he reads or tells us about his statement?

Mr. BOBO. Your statement sets forth the size of your staff?

Mr. ALBRIGHT. It doesn't happen to, and I shall be glad to describe that. I have my offices in Washington where there are three of us, myself, and assistant and secretary and then in addition to that we have in New York City an office where there are 9 people, 4 of whom are professional staff and 5 of them are secretarial staff in New York.

Mr. BOBO. Mr. Albright, I think you have a statement which explains the work which you do there. Do you wish to read your statement?

Mr. ALBRIGHT. Yes, thank you, Mr. Bobo.

So far our discussion has been in the area of what some people may think a motion picture has, contributes to juvenile delinquency. There has been for many years a program through which the industry has consciously been trying to exert an influence in the other direction. It takes a long time to tell it, and I thought it would be better to reduce it to writing.

Chairman KEFAUVER. All right, Mr. Albright, you proceed in your own way. Just talk so that everybody can hear you.

Mr. ALBRIGHT. Mr. Chairman, my name is Roger Albright. My business address is 1600 Eye Street, Washington, D. C. I am director of the department of educational services of the Motion Picture Association of America, an organization of the 10 principal producers and distributors of motion pictures in the United States.

For the record, these 10 companies are Allied Artists Pictures Corp., Columbia Pictures Corp., Loew's, Inc., Paramount Pictures Corp., RKO Radio Pictures, Inc., Republic Pictures Corp., Twentieth Century-Fox Film Corp., United Artists Corp., Universal Pictures Co., Inc., and Warner Bros. Pictures, Inc.

Here on the west coast, where motion-picture production is concentrated, there is a companion but separate organization known as the Association of Motion Picture Producers. Nine of the ten companies are also members of this producers group. United Artists, which is engaged solely in picture distribution, is therefore not a member of the producers organization.

I appear here as a representative of the Motion Picture Association, with which I have been actively identified for 20 years. I will endeavor to present to your committee a comprehensive summary of the affirmative policies and programs of an industry which voluntarily initiated a quarter of a century ago the first self-imposed code of public responsibility ever undertaken by an industry in this country or in the world. We are proud of that and of how it has worked because we think it is the best evidence of our awareness of the obligation we have to millions of people who see and enjoy our product each week throughout the world.

First, however, as one who has been rather intimately associated with educational and community problems for nearly a quarter of a century, I would like to take the opportunity to commend this committee for undertaking its study of juvenile delinquency.

I use the word "study" advisedly since I am sure the committee and its competent staff know that there are no pat answers, no magic formulas, no quick and easy solutions to this question. It is a continuing issue, shifting both in degree and character with changing world and national conditions.

But because it is a subject that requires patience and an alerting of national attention, this Senate committee is doing a praiseworthy job with its hearings in dramatizing the situation and examining what appear to be contributing causes of juvenile delinquency.

In a different way, we in the American motion picture industry have sought to take strong affirmative steps in coping with the problem. As we look back we know we have made substantial progress. We look forward confident that we are on the right track, we welcome advice, suggestions, and counsel from every responsible source, and in fact much of our program is based on the help of the representatives of literally millions of members of public spirited organizations and groups who for years have been an integral part of our policy of providing decent, moral family entertainment.

This policy is actively expressed through and is constantly enforced, enhanced, and bulwarked by five basic activities, which I shall deal with in some greater detail hereafter. Briefly described, they are:

1. The quarter-century old self-enforced production and advertising codes through which the companies conform to acceptable moral and social standards in both content of pictures and type and kind of advertising.

2. The classification of our pictures by outside, wholly independent viewing groups into what they regard as suitable for different age groups.

3. The selection by outstanding educational leaders of pictures of social, cultural and patriotic values for use in the classroom for further emphasis of discussion.

4. The development of local community programs throughout the Nation which under the auspices of many national organizations

regularly use pictures with special significance for children adolescents.

5. The production by our individual companies of hundreds of pictures specially intended to stress high moral values with the purpose of making the screen a force for education and good living as well as entertainment.

The first four activities are the day-by-day concern of our association. We have departments staffed with employees who devote their full time to these activities. In further answer to your question, Mr. Bobo, I counted up on my fingers last night and found the various departments which are concerned with these activities, and they sum total 19. They are under the supervision of the production code administration here in Hollywood, the advertising code administration in New York and Hollywood, the title registration bureau in New York, the community service department in New York, and the educational services department in Washington. The operations of these departments of the association involve the cooperation of and close liaison with scores of national organizations, and the fulfillment of thousands of requests from those who want the help which motion pictures can give to their particular needs and programs.

Now, to discuss the specific activities:

1–2. THE PRODUCTION AND ADVERTISING CODES

Mr. Geoffrey Shurlock who is responsible for the administration of the production code, and Mr. Gordon White who is responsible for the administration of the advertising code, have already described to you in detail the procedures by which these codes are applied to motion picture production and advertising.

3. THE FILM ESTIMATE BOARD OF NATIONAL ORGANIZATIONS

In addition to the production and advertising code operations, there exists a national motion picture previewing group made up of and controlled and operated by the representatives of 13 universally respected nationwide organizations with a national membership of many millions. They are: American Association of University Women, American Jewish Committee, American Library Association, Children's Film Library Committee, National Society Daughters of the American Revolution, National Federation of Music Clubs, National Federation of Women's Clubs, Girl Scouts of the U. S. A., National Council of Women of the U. S. A., Protestant Motion Picture Council, National Congress of Parents and Teachers, Schools Motion Picture Committee, and the United Church Women.

I think the committee may be interested in just how these organizations screen and classify motion pictures. Each has its own national previewing chairman who appoints a motion picture previewing committee. This results in the establishment of 13 previewing groups with a large combined membership. Then the combined membership is divided into numerous subcommittees each having a complete cross-section representation of all 13 participating organizations. The subcommittes screen, judge, and rate pictures in the following categories: A for adults over 18 years; F for family all ages; YP for young people over 12 years; MYP for mature young people; CPR for children's program recommended 8 to 12 years; CPA for children's programs acceptable 8 to 12 years; and FR for family recommended.

Before pictures are released to theaters, prints of all films are made available by each of our producing companies for screening by these subcommittees. Our people cooperate carefully to maintain convenient schedules for the viewing groups to insure that every film is seen and appraised.

Each member of the viewing committee makes an individual report and these are then assembled and referred to a joint editorial committee which prepares the final joint estimate. When there are appreciable variances among those who evaluate a picture, these variances are included in the published appraisal.

The final estimate, widely known throughout the United States as the Green Sheet is now ready for publication and distribution. Throughout the Nation this advance information on forthcoming motion pictures becomes available to thousands of parents, teachers, clergymen, and community leaders of all kinds. Most of the participating national organizations also print the Green Sheet estimates in their national publications. Libraries and schools and churches regularly display them. The Parent-Teacher magazine, for example, carries in every issue two pages of these motion-picture estimates. These estimates are available to the parents and the teachers and to the people who are directing the thinking of juveniles throughout the country. We are very regretful they are not more widely used even than they are.

I have taken the committee's time to explain the operation of the Green Sheet because I think it merits special consideration. It is not censorship. It is a kind of an independent audit of our product by a representative cross section of the American people. It is a critical analysis intended primarily as a guide, for parents and teachers who have a specific responsibility to juveniles. But it is helpful to us, too. You can be sure that we read the Green Sheet appraisals with great care and reflection.

Operating apart from the 13 national groups which prepare and edit the Green Sheet is another large national organization, the Catholic Legion of Decency. It too views our films and publishes its ratings. It appraisals, an important and persuasive guide to millions of theater patrons, are expressed in these categories: Class A, section I—Morally unobjectionable for general patronage; Class A, section II—morally unobjectionable for adults; Class B—Morally objectionable in part for all; and Class C—Condemned.

4. SCHOOL AND EDUCATIONAL USE OF MOTION PICTURES

I come now to the fourth activity of the industry, that of making films available for schoolroom and general educational use. This is a program now in its 16th year, during which more than 900 motion pictures have been selected by committees of educators in almost every field of teaching for classroom use.

It is a program administered by Teaching Film Custodians, a nonprofit affiliate of the Motion Picture Association. Nine of America's distinguished educators are its board of directors and nine leaders from the motion-picture industry work hand in hand with them. Our producing companies, without a penny of financial return to them, set up previewing facilities for committees of educators, make 16-millimeter prints of the pictures selected, and then distribute the prints to the 1,100 16-millimeter film libraries maintained throughout the country. Some idea of the extent of this program is evidenced when it is realized that about 70,000 different prints of these films have been prepared and distributed.

I think the full significance of this program of classroom use of so many of our pictures lies in the fact that impartial, competent authorities have felt that such a large amount of our product has affirmative, positive, cultural value. It is committees of teachers in the fields of literature, music, history, science, sociology, and family life problems that have initiated the program and selected the pictures.

They come from 7 national teacher organizations with a membership of more than 120,000. They work with Teaching Film Custodians to develop motion-picture programs in their special fields of study. They represent the American Association for Health, Physical Education, and Recreation; Home Economics Department of the National Education Association; American Home Economics Association; Music Educators National Conference; National Council for the Social Studies; National Council of Teachers of English; National Science Teachers Association; and American Vocational Educational Association.

These committees are continuously enthusiastic about the contributions which these many subjects make to the development of desirable viewpoint of the growing generation. It would be difficult to describe with certainty all of the educational values with accrue from this program. For thousands of students the steady stream of excellent entertainment pictures which are seen in the school creates a wholesome appetite to see excellent pictures in the theater. The classroom discussions of these selected pictures tends to fix attitudes and create behaviour which is socially desirable. The great men of the past, the great events of the past, the great literature of the past, are made attractive and understandable, and the total impact in the view of educators is enormous. They frequently express themselves as being impressed with the fact that so many motion pictures with such great constructive value have been shown to the American people in the theater, thus bringing to this great public these same values which are now being selected for special emphasis to the adolescents in the high school.

In addition to this Motion Picture Association program, which all of the companies support, several of the companies—Twentieth-Century Fox, Warner Bros., Columbia, Universal, RKO Radio—have their individual, nontheatrical programs which their companies' motion-picture product is similarly made available to schools.

The total volume of school use of films which have been intelligently selected by teachers and education supervisors far outbalances the relatively exceptional pictures which some seem inclined to criticize.

Finally, Senator, there are the things which have been done in cooperation with other community agencies outside the educational field.

More than 20 years ago the Committee on Social Values in Motion Pictures came to the motion-picture industry for help in the development of a series of character education subjects. The committee was headed by Dr. Howard M. Le Sourd, then dean of Boston University, and included criminologists like Dr. Miriam Van Waters, of Massachusetts, and Dr. Phyllis Blanchard, of Philadelphia. Our member companies were glad to help and a series of films was made by excerpting footage from feature films. We paid the cost. The films were given free distribution to schools throughout the country and were used to discuss behavior problems with elementary and high school groups. It was discovered that the students were willing to discuss frankly the conduct situations which were thrown on the screen even though they might not have been willing to discuss similar situations present in their own lives.

Subsequently this series of films was transferred to a larger group known as the Commission of Human Relations of which Dr. Alice V. Keliher, now professor of education at New York University, was the directing head. The film series was expanded to 55 subjects, again with our aid and without cost. These pictures are still in distribution and use.

Another worthwhile project was developed at the request of the National Council of Teachers of English. This group felt that there would be decided advantage in having student study guides made on about 100 motion pictures based on such classics of literature as David Copperfield, Treasure Island, Les Miserables, and others. The National Council of Teachers of English, through a specially appointed committee, authored the study guides, and each member company which had produced the classic prepared research information and other data and financed the printing of the guides. These were then distributed to local high schools through the theaters.

In 1936 the public libraries wanted materials which would stimulate the reading of books from which motion pictures had been made and requested research display charts to be placed in public library lobbies.

The first such exhibit, developed experimentally, was on Romeo and Juliet. This activity was carried on with the cooperation of the American Library Association, and at its peak more than 2,600 libraries were using these materials.

Eight years ago the Children's Film Library Committee requested the cooperation of the industry in selecting subjects for juvenile entertainment. These films would be used in special children's matinees on Saturday mornings in theaters throughout the country. Some 53 pictures were selected and the producing companies had sufficient numbers of prints made so that they would be promptly and easily available to theaters wherever interested community groups sponsored the project. Nearly 5,000 theaters have participated in these weekly programs.

Another cooperative project with the American Library Association is the motion-picture industry's participation in their American Heritage program. This is a program in which public libraries throughout the Nation show an appropriate patriotic or historical film as the basis for a film forum in which are discussed the basic elements of the American heritage.

One of the most valuable programs is the production by all of our member companies, without regard to their general box-office appeal, of films of significant constructive value to America's young people. I would like to list a few.

1. CRIME PREVENTION—CRIME DOES NOT PAY

Beginning more than 15 years ago, Metro-Goldwyn-Mayer produced a series of dramatized incidents proving that crime doesn't pay. Some of these incidents relate to serious crimes like arson, armed robbery, and murder; some have to do with racketeering which milks the public, such as dishonest loan. agencies, dishonest employment agencies, and dishonest charity solicitations; and some deal with such civilian practices as smuggling. These pictures have had very wide distribution in the theaters throughout the years. The crime prevention bureaus of several States have availed themselves of these pictures in 16 mm. film for use in juvenile courts and elsewhere after the theatrical distribution has been completed.

2. CITIZENSHIP AND PATRIOTISM

(a) *The Washington Parade series*

Those of us who live in Washington realize how many thousands or high-school students come to Washington to see the Nation's Capital and the shrines which are associated with it. These, however, are but a small fraction of the millions of young people who should have this inspiring experience.

With this in mind, Columbia Pictures made a series of pictures called the Washington Parade with separate subjects on the Capitol, the White House, the Treasury, the Library of Congress, the FBI, the social security program, and others.

These were made with the close collaboration and advice of the Government departments, and the pictures were distributed in theaters throughout the country. Each subject reached many millions of people.

Following theatrical distribution, they were then made available to the schools of the United States, with no profit to the company, and are still being seen and enjoyed by the many who don't have the opportunity to visit Washington in person.

(b) *Epics of American history*

For a number of years, Paramount Pictures has dramatized expansion movements which have made the United States the great Nation it is. The list is too large to detail here in its entirely, but included are such motion pictures as The Plainsmen, Union Pacific, Maid of Salem, Wells Fargo, and High, Wide and Handsome, which is the story of the discovery and development of oil.

(c) *This is America series*

RKO Radio Pictures has produced and distributed a series which interprets various phases of American life and thinking. The series is called This is America. In this way, the movements and mores of America have been interpreted not only to our own people, but in showing the rest of the world some of the things that make America great.

(d) *The Warner patriotic series*

Another project is the series of 12 patriotic short subjects produced by Warner Bros. as a tribute by its president, Mr. Harry M. Warner, to what he called the only country in the world where I could have realized my achievements.

These short subjects, widely known both because of their theatrical and nontheatrical use, dramatize the contributions of our Founding Fathers and clarify the basic principles of freedom on which our Republic was founded, and through which it has developed. Some of the titles of these short subjects are The Declaration of Independence, the Bill of Rights, Give Me Liberty, The Romance of Louisiana, Man Without a Country, the Monroe Doctrine. Currently, these pictures form basic curriculum materials in thousands of American history classes in the high schools of the United States.

3. BIOGRAPHIES OF GREAT MEN

(a) *The Passing Parade series*

Metro-Goldwyn-Mayer has produced a Passing Parade series which gives recognition through biographical dramatization of more than 30 outstanding heroes of peace. About half of these are Americans.

(b) *Dramatized biographies*

Twentieth Century-Fox has produced dramatized biographies of some of America's great men—Alexander Graham Bell, Brigham Young, Woodrow Wilson, Rev. Peter Marshall, to name only a few.

4. INTERNATIONAL UNDERSTANDING—THE WORLD AND ITS PEOPLES

Universal Pictures has financed the sending of five camera crews into all parts of the world to film motion picture studies of how people live. These 36 films will contribute to better world understanding, and we in America will know our world neighbors better because of them.

This summary of some of the activities of our member companies and the association in the public-service field reflects, I think, the basic policy that has guided our industry for many years.

We are conscious always of our responsibility as producers and distributors of a medium which has, perhaps, greater worldwide appeal than any other thing made in America. And in producing and marketing our pictures we are conscious too of the likes and dislikes of the more than 250 million people who each week all over the world are our customers. The American motion picture industry, the only free, unsubsidized motion picture industry in the world, would shrivel away if it did not keep up with the changing times, if it did not produce what the overwhelming majority of the people want and like.

This brings into sharp focus the constantly changing human behavior pattern, the plain simple fact that customs, social views, and ideas have undergone substantial shifts in 20 years. These are facts which we in our industry must deal with in our day-to-day operations. What I am talking about is the moral climate in which those of us who are primarily concerned with the problems of younger people live and must work.

The most striking outward evidence of changed public attitudes is public acceptance and even approval of the frankness and the casualness with which the facets of human behavior, notably those dealing with sex matters, are discussed and written about. Best-selling books, stage plays, paintings, even national magazines and daily newspapers are the best evidence of this trend.

Not more than 2 or 3 generations ago, Nathaniel Hawthorne's Scarlet Letter was regarded by many educators and most parents as questionable reading for young people. This generation is confronted daily with sordid stories of rapes, abortions, and heinous sex crimes in the news columns of daily newspapers. Best-selling novels concern themselves with themes of sexual aberrations and revolting brutality. Hit plays on Broadway deal openly and frankly with plots and situations which would have been regarded as licentious 20 years ago.

Widely read and reputable magazines carry articles on sexual and social behaviour patterns among adolescents in Sweden and France which are at great variance with acceptable practices in this country. Publications of tremendous circulation with these and similar articles in the medical and scientific field are part of the every-day reading habit of millions of our people.

I want to say as emphatically as I can that the motion-picture industry has strongly resisted this trend. We are not at the head of this parade, nor indeed in the middle of it. We are, in fact, far behind and are rather proud that we are. Our people, our producers, our writers, our directors, and our executives have been lambasted by some critics for being namby-pamby, for being pollyannish, and for failing to produce mature entertainment.

Our production companies through the production code and the advertising code, have placed upon themselves definite restrictions of morality and decency. We have over the years adhered to these self-imposed restrictions, and have thus eliminated from motion pictures many types of material which are openly treated in other mass media and entertainment forms. Moreover, I repeat, this was the first industry to impose on itself these standards of decency and we remain as the only non-Government regulated enterprise to continue this practice.

From all of these things two facts must be apparent. The leaders of the motion-picture industry have shown their desire to make this medium a constructive social force in the United States with particular emphasis on its impact for good on the young people of America. The second fact, perhaps more significant, is that the reaction of public leaders and national organizations to the motion-picture industry's product and their use of it is the best evidence that our contribution has been fruitful.

So long as creative works are produced by human beings, there will, of course, be unevenness of quality and value. Not all books were written by high-minded authors; not all Elizabethan plays were written by Shakespeare; not all religious leaders have necessarily always pointed to the higher life.

We must expect that our young people will be confronted with some nonconstructive experiences which must be offset with many other experiences which will overcome with good effect those influences which have had bad conotations.

I was very much interested Wednesday afternoon, Senator, when Mr. Sanders, Mr. Lindquist, Mr. Johnson, and Mr. Wyley stressed over and over again that the thing that they felt was important was that those who are socially impaired or socially maladjusted shall have many many experiences of a constructive kind that will be offsetting influences.

For many years, the motion-picture industry has been providing a wide variety of those wholesome offsetting experiences. They have doubtless counterbalanced much that has been less good. Through the operation of our code, through the sincerity of our leadership, and through the cooperation of thousands of community leaders, our industry is producing a great volume of motion pictures which resist trends that are destructive to the morals, ideals, and behavior of our young people.

I am sorry I have taken so much of the committee's time. Thank you for hearing me out.

Chairman KEFAUVER. Well, thank you, Mr. Albright, for a very comprehensive and good statement in explaining the work of the educational services of your association. It shows a great many fine accomplishments have been made.

Mrs. FOSTER. Mr. Chairman, pardon me, but while these members of the hirelings of the movie industry are here, how about those kind of pictures for our children? Is that what you call constructive Mr. Chairman? I'd like to know if those things are constructive, that's all I'd like to know.

Chairman KEFAUVER. Thank you Mrs. Foster. I don't think Mr. Albright would approve or would think very well of these posters back here.

Mr. ALBRIGHT. I think you have come to a very worthwhile conclusion in that matter.

Chairman KEFAUVER. That is a part of the industry, of course Mr. Albright. But what Mrs. Foster said is what a lot of people are thinking.

Any questions, Mr. Bobo?

Mr. BOBO. No questions.

Chairman KEFAUVER. Well, Mr. Albright, we think that you have given us a good statement, and undoubtedly the pictures that you have talked about here are great educational efforts, and in the schools they have played a very important part. I think lot of good and a tremendous amount of real education will be derived from what they see in these pictures in the schools. I know the sincerity with which you carry on your part of this work, and I want to compliment you and to congratulate you.

Mr. ALBRIGHT. Thank you.

Chairman KEFAUVER. I hope that the criticisms that have been brought out here will be considered by all of you in carrying out your program in the future, and our criticisms have not been directed to the pictures going into the schools. I think they have been very well considered. We have very few letters of criticism about them. Thank you very much.

Mr. ALBRIGHT. Thank you.

Mr. Irving BENESCH. I would like to ask the chairman a question. I will have to read part of Mr. Albright's statement in order to ask the question.

Chairman KEFAUVER. What is your name, sir?

Mr. BENESCH. Irving Benesch.

Chairman KEFAUVER. Tell us where it is.

Mr. BENESCH. Page 3, under "This policy" under paragraph No. 1:

The quarter century old self-enforced production and advertising codes through which the companies conform to acceptable moral and social standards in both content of pictures and type and kind of advertising.

Now, mark this well, "and type of kind of advertising." This sort of underlines the question you just asked, Senator. This is Mr. Albright's statement. Shall we believe the first part of it or the last part it?

Chairman KEFAUVER. Well, he doesn't say that particularly that he approves of what is being done in the advertising part of the code.

Mr. BENESCH. This is the statement.

Chairman KEFAUVER. He says:

The quarter century old self-enforced production and advertising codes through which the companies conformed to acceptable to moral and social standards * * *

Mr. BENESCH. I maintain they do not conform.

Chairman KEFAUVER. I take it, Mr. Albright, that you would amend your statement on page 3 where you say—

to acceptable moral and social standards in both content of pictures and type and kind of advertising * * *

that you don't mean to approve of all of the pictures or all of the advertising.

Mr. ALBRIGHT. I certainly would limit that statement to development of the code. You have been discussing today with Mr. White and Mr. Shurlock the application of that code to the material, and I think we have had a rather thorough sifting of that.

Chairman KEFAUVER. I took it that what you meant there was that this is what your conception of what the code was designed to do, and so far as the application of the code, that is not your matter.

Mr. ALBRIGHT. It doesn't happen to be my bailiwick.

Chairman KEFAUVER. Does that answer your question?

(Mr. Albright's statement reads as follows:)

STATEMENT OF ROGER ALBRIGHT, DIRECTOR, DEPARTMENT OF EDUCATIONAL SERVICES OF THE MOTION PICTURE ASSOCIATION OF AMERICA

Mr. Chairman, my name is Roger Albright. My business address is 1600 I Street, Washington, D. C. I am director of the Department of Educational Services of the Motion Picture Association of America, an organization of the 10 principal producers and distributors of motion pictures in the United States. For the record, these 10 companies are Allied Artists Pictures Corp., Columbia Pictures Corp., Loew's, Inc., Paramount Pictures Corp., RKO Radio Pictures, Inc., Republic Pictures Corp., Twentieth Century-Fox Film Corp., United Artists Corp., Universal Pictures Co., Inc., and Warner Bros. Pictures, Inc.

Here on the west coast, where motion picture production is concentrated, there is a companion but separate organization known as the Association of Motion Picture Producers. Nine of the ten companies are also members of this producers group. United Artists, which is engaged solely in picture distribution, is therefore not a member of the producers organization.

I appear here as a representative of the Motion Picture Association, with which I have been actively identified for 20 years. My associates and I will endeavor to present to your committee a comprehensive summary of the affirmative policies and programs of an industry which voluntarily initiated a quarter of a century ago the first self-imposed code of public responsibility ever undertaken by an industry in this country or in the world. We are proud of that and of how it has worked because we think it is the best evidence of our awareness of the obligation we have to millions of people who see and enjoy our product each week throughout the world.

First, however, as one who has been rather intimately associated with educational and community problems for nearly a quarter of a century, I would like to take the opportunity to commend this committee for undertaking its study of juvenile delinquency.

I use the word "study" advisedly since I am sure the committee and its competent staff know that there are no pat answers, no magic formulas, no quick and easy solutions to this question. It is a continuing issue, shifting both in degree and character with changing world and national conditions.

But because it is a subject that requires patience and an alerting of national attention, this Senate committee is doing a praiseworthy job with its hearings in dramatizing the situation and examining what appear to be contributing causes of juvenile delinquency.

In a different way, we in the American motion picture industry have sought to take strong affirmative steps in coping with the problem. As we look back we know we have made substantial progress. We look forward confident that we are on the right track. We welcome advice, suggestions, and counsel from every responsible source, and in fact much of our program is based on the help of the representatives of literally millions of members of public-spirited organizations and groups who for years have been an integral part of our policy of providing decent, moral family entertainment.

This policy is actively expressed through, and is constantly enforced, enhanced, and bulwarked by, five basic activities, which I shall deal with in some greater detail hereafter. Briefly described, they are:

1. The quarter-century-old self-enforced production and advertising codes through which the companies conform to acceptable moral and social standards in both content of pictures and type and kind of advertising.

2. The classification of our pictures by outside, wholly independent viewing groups into what they regard as suitable for different age groups.

3. The selection by outstanding educational leaders of pictures of social, cultural, and patriotic values for use in the classroom as an educational medium.

4. The development of local community programs throughout the Nation under the auspices of many national organizations which regularly use pictures with special significance for children and adolescents.

5. The production by our individual companies of hundreds of pictures specifically intended to stress high moral values with the purpose of making the screen a force for education and good living as well as entertainment.

The first four activities are the day-by-day concern of our association. We have departments staffed with employees who devote their full time to these activities. They are under the supervision of the production code administration here in Hollywood, the advertising code administration in New York and Hollywood, the title registration bureau in New York, the community service department in New York, and the educational services department in Washington. The operations of these departments of the association involve the cooperation of and close liaison with scores of national organizations, and the fulfillment of thousands of requests from those who want the help which motion pictures can give to their particular needs and programs.

Now, to discuss the specific activities:

1–2, THE PRODUCTION AND ADVERTISING CODES

Mr. Geoffrey Shurlock, who is responsible for the administration of the production code, and Mr. Gordon White, who is responsible for the administration of the advertising code, will describe to you in detail the procedures by which these codes are applied to motion picture production and advertising

3. THE FILM ESTIMATE BOARD OF NATIONAL ORGANIZATIONS

In addition to the production and advertising code operations, there exists a national motion picture previewing group made up of and controlled and operated by the representatives of 13 universally respected nationwide organizations with a national membership of many millions. They are: American Association of University Women, American Jewish Committee, American Library Association, Children's Film Library Committee, National Society Daughters of the American Revolution, National Federation of Music Clubs, National Federation of Women's Clubs, Girl Scouts of the USA, National Council of Women of the U.S., Protestant Motion Picture Council, National Congress of Parents and Teachers, Schools Motion Picture Committee, and the United Church Women.

I think the committee may be interested in just how these organizations screen and classify motion pictures. Each has its own national previewing chairman who appoints a motion picture previewing committee. This results in the establishment of 13 previewing groups with a large combined membership. Then the combined membership is divided into numerous subcommittees each having a complete cross-section representation of all 13 participating organizations. The subcommittees screen, judge, and rate pictures in the following categories: A for adults over 18 years; F for family all ages; YP for young people over 12 years; MYP for mature young people; CPR for children's programs recommended 8 to 12 years; CPA for children's programs acceptable 8 to 12 years; and FR for family recommended.

Before pictures are released to theaters, prints of all films are made available by each of our producing companies for screening by these subcommittees. Our people cooperate carefully to maintain convenient schedules for the viewing groups to insure that every film is seen and appraised.

Each member of the viewing committee makes an individual report and these are then assembled and referred to a joint editorial committee which prepares the final joint estimate. When there are appreciable variances among those who evaluate a picture, the variances are included in the published appraisal.

The final estimate, widely known throughout the United States as the green sheet, is now ready for publication and distribution. It is printed every 2 weeks and 20,000 copies are distributed. Throughout the Nation this advance information on forthcoming motion pictures becomes available to thousands of parents, teachers, clergymen, and community leaders of all kinds. Most of the participating natonal organizations also print the green sheet estimates in their national publications. Libraries and schools and churches regularly display them. The Parent-Teacher Magazine, for example, carries in every issue two pages of these motion picture estimates.

I have taken the committee's time to explain the operation of the green sheet because I think it merits special consideration. It is not censorship. It is a kind of independent audit of our product by a representative cross-section of the American people. It is a critical analysis, intended primarily as a guide for parents and teachers who have a specific responsibility to juveniles. But it is helpful to us, too. You can be sure that we read the green sheet appraisals with care and reflection.

Operating apart from the 13 national groups which prepare and edit the green sheet is another large national organization, the Catholic Legion of Decency. It too views our films and publishes its ratings. Its appraisals, an important and persuasive guide to millions of theater patrons, are expressed in these categories: Class A, section I—Morally unobjectionable for general patronage; class A, section II—Morally unobjectionable for adults; class B—Morally objectionable in part for all; and class C—Condemned.

4. SCHOOL AND EDUCATIONAL USE OF MOTION PICTURES

I come now to the fourth activity of the industry, that of making films available for schoolroom and general educational use. This is a program now in its 16th year, during which more than 900 motion pictures have been selected by committees of educators in almost every field of teaching for classroom use.

It is a program administered by Teaching Film Custodians, a nonprofit affiliate of the Motion Picture Association. Nine of America's distinguished educators are its board of directors and nine leaders from the motion picture industry work hand in hand with them. Our producing companies, without a penny of financial return to them, set up previewing facilities for committees of educators, make 16-millimeter prints of the pictures selected, and then distribute the prints to the 1,100 16-millimeter film libraries maintained throughout the country. Some idea of the extent of this program is evident when it is realized that about 70,000 different prints have been prepared and distributed.

I think the full significance of this program of classroom use of so many of our pictures lies in the fact that impartial, competent authorities have felt that such a large amount of our product has affirmative, positive, cultural value. It is committees of teachers in the fields of literature, music, history, science, sociology, and family life problems that have initiated the program and selected the picture.

They come from 7 national teacher organizations with a membership of more than 120,000. They work with Teaching Film Custodians to develop motion picture programs in their special fields of study. They represent the American Association for Health, Physical Education, and Recreation; Home Economics Department of the National Education Association; American Home Economics Association; Music Educators National Conference; National Council for the Social Studies; National Council of Teachers of English; National Science Teachers Association; and American Vocational Education Association.

Of course, neither this program nor that of the classification and rating activities could be effective without our industry's warm and friendly cooperation. There are costs entailed in both programs which we cheerfully bear as a worthwhile contribution to a better society of free people.

There are, of course, other programs and projects in which our industry through the association has played an important part.

More than 20 years ago the Committee on Social Values in Motion Pictures came to the motion picture industry for help in the development of a series of character education subjects. The committee was headed by Dr. Howard M. Le Sourd, then dean of Boston University, and included criminologists like Dr. Miriam Van Waters of Massachusetts, and Dr. Phyllis Blanchard of Philadelphia. Our member companies were glad to help and a series of films was made by excerpting footage from feature films. We paid the cost. The films were given free distribution to schools throughout the country, and were used to discuss behavior problems with elementary and high school groups. It was discovered that the students were willing to discuss frankly the conduct situations which were thrown on the screen even though they might not have been willing to discuss similar situations present in their own lives.

Subsequently, this series of films was transferred to a larger group known as the Commission of Human Relations of which Dr. Alice V. Keliher, now professor of education at New York University, was the directing head. The film series was expanded to 55 subjects, again with our aid and without cost. These pictures are still in distribution and use.

Another worthwhile project was developed at the request of the National Council of Teachers of English. This group felt there would be decided advantage in having student study guides made on about 100 motion pictures based on such classics of literature as David Copperfield, Treasure Island, Les Miserables, and others. The National Council of Teachers of English, through a specially appointed committee, authored the study guides, and each member company which had produced the classic prepared research information and other data, and financed the printing of the guides. These were then distributed to local high schools through the theaters.

In 1936, the public libraries wanted materials which would stimulate the reading of books from which motion pictures had been made, and requested research display charts to be placed in public library lobbies.

The first such exhibit, developed experimentally, was on Romeo and Juliet. This activity was carried on with the cooperation of the American Library Association, and at its peak more than 2,600 libraries were using these materials.

Eight years ago, the Children's Film Library Committee requested the cooperation of the industry in selecting subjects for juvenile entertainment. These films would be used in special children's matinees on Saturday mornings in theaters throughout the country. Some 53 pictures were selected, and the producing companies had sufficient numbers of prints made so that they would be promptly and easily available to theaters wherever interested community groups sponsored the project. Nearly 5,000 theaters have participated in these weekly programs.

Another cooperative project with the American Library Association is the motion picture industry's participation in their American heritage program. This is a program in which public libraries throughout the Nation show an appropriate patriotic or historical film as the basis for a film forum in which are discussed the basic elements of the American heritage.

One of the most valuable programs is the production by all of our member companies, without regard to their general box-office appeal, of films of significant constructive value to America's young people. I would like to list a few.

Crime prevention—Crime Does Not Pay series

Beginning more than 15 years ago, Metro-Goldwyn-Mayer produced a series of dramatized incidents proving that crime doesn't pay. Some of these incidents relate to serious crimes like arson, armed robbery, and murder; some have to do with racketeering which milks the public, such as dishonest loan agencies, dishonest employment agencies, and dishonest charity solicitations, and some deal with such civilian practices as smuggling. These pictures have had very wide distribution in the theaters throughout the years. The crime prevention bureaus of several States have availed themselves of these pictures on 16-millimeter film for use in juvenile courts and elsewhere after the theatrical distribution has been completed.

Citizenship and patriotism

(a) *The Washington Parade series.*—Those of us who live in Washington realize how many thousands of high school students come to Washington to see the Nation's Capital and the shrines which are associated with it. These, however, are but a small fraction of the millions of young people who should have this inspiring experience.

With this in mind, Columbia Pictures made a series of pictures called the Washington Parade with separate subjects on the Capitol, the White House, the Treasury, the Library of Congress, the FBI, the social-security program, and others.

These were made with the close collaboration and advice of the Government departments, and the pictures were distributed in theaters throughout tne country. Each subject reached many millions of people.

Following theatrical distribution, they were then made available to tne schools of the United States, with no profit to the company, and are still being seen and enjoyed by the many who don't have the opportunity to visit Washington in person.

(b) *Epics of American history.*—For a number of years, Paramount Pictures has dramatized expansion movements which have made the United States the great Nation it is. The list is too large to detail here in its entirety, but included are such motion pictures as The Plainsman, Union Pacific, Maid of Salem, Wells Fargo, and High, Wide and Handsome, which is the story of the discovery and development of oil.

(c) *This Is America series.*—RKO Radio Pictures has produced and distributed a series which interprets various phases of American life and thinking. The series is called This Is America. In this way, the movements and mores of America have been interpreted not only to our own people, but in showing the rest of the world some of the things that make America great.

(d) *The Warner Patriotic series.*—Another project is the series of 12 patriotic short subjects produced by Warner Bros. as a tribute by its president, Mr. Harry M. Warner, to what he called "the only country in the world where I could have realized my achievements."

These short subjects, widely known both because of their theatrical and nontheatrical use, dramatize the contributions of our Founding Fathers and clarify the basic principles of freedom on which our Republic was founded and through which it has developed. Some of the titles of these short subjects are The Declaration of Independence, The Bill of Rights, Give Me Liberty, The Romance of Louisiana, Man Without a Country, The Monroe Doctrine. Currently, these pictures form basic curriculum materials in thousands of American history classes in the high schools of the United States.

Biographies of great men

(a) *The Passing Parade series.*—Metro-Goldwyn-Mayer has produced a Passing Parade series which gives recognition through biographical dramatization of more than 30 outstanding heroes of peace. About half of these are Americans.

(b) *Dramatized biographies.*—Twentieth Century-Fox has produced dramatized biographies of some of America's great men—Alexander Graham Bell, Brigham Young, Woodrow Wilson, Rev. Peter Marshall, to name only a few.

International understanding—The world and its peoples

Universal Pictures has financed the sending of five camera crews into all parts of the world to film motion picture studies of how people live. These 36 films will contribute to better world understanding, and we in America will know our world neighbors better because of them.

This summary of some of the activities of our member companies and the association in the public service field reflects, I think, the basic policy that has guided our industry for many years.

We are conscious always of our responsibility as producers and distributors of a medium which has, perhaps, greater worldwide appeal than any other thing made in America.

And in producing and marketing our pictures we are conscious, too, of the likes and dislikes of the more than 250 million people who each week all over the world are our customers. The American motion picture industry, the only free, unsubsidized motion picture industry in the world, would shrivel away if it did not keep up with the changing times, if it did not produce what the overwhelming majority of the people want and like.

This brings into sharp focus the constantly changing human behavior pattern, the plain simple fact that customs, social views, and ideas have undergone substantial shifts in 20 years. These are facts which we in our industry must deal with in our day-to-day operations. What I am talking about is the moral climate in which those of us who are primarily concerned with the problems of younger people live and must work.

The most striking outward evidence of changed public attitudes is public acceptance and even approval of the frankness and the casualness with which the facets of human behavior, notably those dealing with sex matters, are discussed and written about. Best-selling books, stage plays, paintings, sculpture, even national magazine and daily newspapers are the best evidence of this trend.

Not more than 2 or 3 generations ago, Nathaniel Hawthorne's Scarlet Letter was regarded by many educators and most parents as questionable reading for young people. This generation is confronted daily with sordid stories of rapes, abortions, and heinous sex crimes in the news columns of daily newspapers. Best-selling novels concern themselves with themes of lesbianism and revolting brutality. Many modern paintings and sculptures are frankly perverted in theme. And some recognized and widely applauded writers and artists are openly and notoriously psychotics in the Krafft-Ebing pattern. Hit plays on Broadway deal openly and frankly with plots and situations which would have been regarded as pornographic and licentious 20 years ago.

And abroad, in some countries, there is even greater liberty and license.

Widely read and reputable magazines carry articles on sexual and social behavior patterns among adolescents in Sweden and France which are at great variance with acceptable practices in this country. Publications of tremendous circulation with these and similar articles in the medical and scientific field are part of the everyday reading habit of millions of our people.

I want to say as emphatically as I can that the motion-picture industry has strongly resisted this trend. We are not at the head of this parade, nor indeed in the middle of it. We are, in fact, far behind and are rather proud that we are.

Our people, our producers, our writers, our directors, and our executives have been lambasted by critics for being namby-pamby, for being pollyannish, and for failing to produce mature entertainment.

Our production companies, through the production code and the advertising code, have placed upon themselves definite restrictions of morality and decency. We have over the years adhered to these self-imposed restrictions, and have thus eliminated from motion pictures many types of material which are openly treated in other mass media and entertainment forms. Moreover, I repeat, this was the first industry to impose on itself these standards of decency and we remain as the only non-Government-regulated enterprise to continue this practice.

So long as creative works are produced by human beings, there will, of course, be unevenness of quality and value. Not all books were written by high-minded authors; not all Elizabethan plays were written by Shakespeare; not all religious leaders have necessarily always pointed to the higher life.

And so long as human beings are the judges of what is desirable and undesirable, there will be honest differences of opinion about the effect on the reader, listener, or viewer. Criticism is a subjective thing, a product of man's mind conditioned by his training and experience.

We in the motion-picture industry are not perfect. We have made mistakes and I assume that we will make them in the future. But I want to emphasize that the men and women who produce our pictures and the men and women who administer our codes are decent, high-minded people who adhere conscientiously to the standards which the industry has imposed upon itself.

We believe that any fairminded analysis of our overall operations will disclose that we do a remarkable job—a job deserving of commendation.

I want to thank the committee and its staff for this opportunity to appear and for its uniform courtesy and fairness in its study of a problem which deserves the most earnest consideration of all our people.

STATEMENT OF PAUL JACOBS, CHAIRMAN, CIVIL LIBERTIES UNION, LOS ANGELES, CALIF.

Chairman KEFAUVER. Mr. Paul Jacobs, chairman of the Civil Liberties Union, has asked for permission to testify for a few minutes. All right, Mr. Bobo.

Mr. BOBO. Mr. Jacobs, will you identify yourself and your connection?

Mr. JACOBS. My name is Paul Jacobs, and I am the chairman of the censorship committee of the American Civil Liberties Union in southern California.

Chairman KEFAUVER. Are you a lawyer?

Mr. JACOBS. No, I am a writer by trade, by profession.

Chairman KEFAUVER. You are chairman of the censorship committee of the Civil Liberties Union.

Mr. JACOBS. Yes. The Civil Liberties Union has a censorship committee whose function it is to investigate cases of alleged censorship, illegal censorship. We are concerned with censorship of books in school libraries. We are concerned with the censorship of films. We are concerned with the censorship of comic books, and we are concerned with the relationship between all of these and juvenile delinquency.

I should like to state the Civil Liberties Union doesn't profess to be a group of sociologists or experts in juvenile delinquency. Our concern, our interest, and our knowledge is restricted to civil liberties, but we are rather deeply concerned over the professed relationship between films and comic books and juvenile delinquency. The Civil Liberties Union isn't prepared to accept the concept of censorship for these media based on what we believe to be as yet rather uncertain knowledge of the real effect of comic books or films, even of the kind described here, upon juvenile delinquency. It seems to us that there are at least three points of view.

Chairman KEFAUVER. Well, Mr. Jacobs, I thought you said you didn't know anything about the sociological or the psychiatric effects of these things upon juveniles.

Mr. JACOBS. No, I don't profess to, but I am willing to concede——

Chairman KEFAUVER. If you don't profess to, how do you get into the field of being willing to—you say it hasn't been shown to you—if you don't pretend to know anything about it?

Mr. JACOBS. Well, because the Civil Liberties Union and I have made some study of the varying statements in this field. There are eminent sociologists and psychologists who believe that there is a relationship between juvenile delinquency and comic books. There are equally eminent sociologists and psychologists who believe that no such relationship exists.

Chairman KEFAUVER. Who are those?

Mr. JACOBS. Well, I'll be glad to give you some names. In the first group, the group who believe that there is a relationship——

Chairman KEFAUVER. We know all of them.

Mr. JACOBS. In the second group there are a group of people who take the position that there is some relationship but not a very significant relationship between the reading of comic books and——

Chairman KEFAUVER. Who are the ones who say there is no relationship?

Mr. JACOBS. Those who say there is no relationship are Filip Ochard, a French sociologist, who published a book called The Child's Voice. There is Charles Glock who is director of the Bureau of Applied Research at Columbia University. There is Eric Ericson who is senior staff member of the Austin Riggs Center, which is a center dealing with juvenile delinquency. There is Eldon Winston of the North Carolina State Board of Public Welfare. There is Wallace

Curalt, superintendent of the Department of Public Welfare in North Carolina. There is John Doyle who is the probation officer in Minnesota. There is Mr. E. W. Brewer who is the case work supervisor of the Superior Court, Kings County. There is a Joseph Homer, probation officer in the Juvenile Court of Allegheny County in Pittsburgh.

Now, we don't pretend that we are experts ourselves——

Chairman KEFAUVER. Well, Mr. Jacobs, I don't know what all of these men have said, but I have read the writings of some of them, and you don't quite correctly represent the writings of some of them in saying that they say there is no relationship. They say that they don't think it is particularly important or not primary or not a leading relationship, but some of them do give some significance to pornographic literature and horror and crime comics.

Mr. JACOBS. Well, Senator, Mr. Glock, for example, states:

On close examination the evidence which has been accumulated in the report is not conclusive. We are still groping to learn just what effects exposure to the mass media do have on our children.

Chairman KEFAUVER. Well, but you said that he said there wasn't anything to it. He says he doesn't know.

Mr. JACOBS. No, as a matter of fact, he says there isn't; he doesn't have any evidence to indicate that there is any relationship.

Chairman KEFAUVER. I don't want to argue the point, except I feel like several of those who say they just don't know yet; they haven't made up their minds. That's inconsequential. What is your point here?

Mr. JACOBS. Well, the point is that since we don't know whether there is any direct linkage between juvenile delinquency and the effect of comic books or the effect of films, it seems to us that to blame comic books or films for juvenile delinquency, that that is stretching it, with all good intentions, too far, because the effects of such blame will be perhaps to lead to censorship of either films or of comic books. I think the thing that troubles many a great deal, is that this implies almost a total breakdown of the home relationship and of the church and of society. If our children are unable to stand up to the impact of comic books or films without becoming prone to supposedly obscene acts that would be related to this, this would seem to indicate that all of the influence of the home and the church and the school has gone for naught. We like to think that the children in our society are able to withstand any of this.

Chairman KEFAUVER. Mr. Jacobs, apparently you haven't followed the work of this subcommittee very closely. Personally, censorship is repugnant to me, governmental censorship. I hope that in all phases of mass media communication and information that there will always be such a restraint and such a handling of their responsibility that there will never be Government censorship. I would certainly hate to see Government censorship of movies, even of comic books. I am not in favor of it. I would hate to see Government censorship of anything. But the point is, actually what we are doing is helping to prevent censorship. We are not advocating censorship, but censorship will come in a lot of these things eventually unless the industry and the people who are responsible do something about it themselves. So if you are interested in censorship, I think you ought to join with us in trying to expose and ferret out and get these people to stop doing a lot of things they are doing.

Mr. JACOBS. Well, Senator, we would be opposed to even industry codes such as were discussed here this afternoon. We would think that this is a form of censorship. You say self-imposed censorship. It seems to us that the good taste and intelligence of the American people is a forceful guide and a sufficient guide to a mass media as to what goes on the screen. We don't think that anybody has the right to determine for anybody else what they ought to see on the screen or what they ought to read within the limits of what you indicate yourself, that is of salacious material. But salacious material can be handled by coast pu.Jication, trial if necessary. If somebody publishes an obscene book, he could be tried. While prior censorship of this means that some group of individuals, in this case in the movie industry, happens to determine what all of us shall see on the screen. Now, perhaps we might agree with that. But on the other hand, it sets a kind of uniformity and a kind of conformity of the pattern of all the movies that we see, and I'm not sure that we think that that is a desirable thing. We would rather when people complain, and that I am sure they do, and I am sure that their complaint is quite legitimate about what they see in the movies or what they see on television or what they read. It seems to us that the simplest solution is for them not to look at these things. It's a very simple matter to shut the television set off. It's a simple matter not to go to a movie if one thinks it is a bad film, and certainly children ought to be directed by their parents. We subscribe to this completely. If a parent thinks a film is a bad film, he ought not to allow his child to see that film. But for adults— and it's extremely difficult to censorship something for children without ending up censoring it for adults—it seems to us that the whole concept of democracy is based on a man's individual right to choose for himself what he wants. And there are lots of people who would think James Joyce Ulysses is an obscene book. I don't happen to think so. I wouldn't force them to read the book. On the other hand, I wouldn't like the book publishers to say to me that I can't read it.

Chairman KEFAUVER. Mr. Jacobs, of course in the movie code and the other codes that we have, I think it should be pointed out that a producer doesn't have to work with the code authorities unless he wants to. He can go on and write his plays and then get them produced and get pictures to show it. It is just a voluntary method of trying to meet certain standards that they have imposed on themselves. I can appreciate that in a highly technical, legalistic sense that you do have a point. On the other hand, we all censor ourselves a certain amount even in our own person. We say we have freedom of speech. That doesn't give us freedom to go out on the street and curse and take the Lord's name in vain and call people bad names, to expose ourselves.

Mr. Norman Thomas for whom I know you have great respect wrote us a letter in New York when we were there and asked for permission to testify. We didn't call him; he came himself. The burden of his testimony was that while he has been the greatest defender of civil liberties always, he was in favor of outright censorship of the pornographic material. You remember his testimony.

Mr. JACOBS. Yes; I do.

Chairman KEFAUVER. I didn't agree with him. He went further than I would go. But his statement was that freedom of the press or freedom of speech doesn't give the right or license for indecency, and if it is used as a license for indecency, sooner or later you would lose your freedom, as he says, of the press and your freedom of speech.

Mr. JACOBS. You know, Senator, I would like to direct your attention to this code that you spoke of in the motion picture industry. There is indeed an economic faction attached to nonconformity with that code, and this is what troubles us. If a producer makes a picture which doesn't get a seal, that picture will have great difficulty in being shown, and this thing is some kind of economic restraint upon the individual producer.

I would agree that in general my standards, and I am sure your standards, would be probably close to that of the code. Nevertheless, I don't want to impose my standards upon anybody. I think these things are in bad taste to me. They are in bad taste to me. But I think that the movie industry ought not to be specially singled out. I don't think it has any more effect upon anybody, and I think that in many cases, this voluntary code, goes much much further, and that is one of the great difficulties. We start out with a code to eliminate references to sex, to eliminate references to violence, and we end up in a code which tends to be all-inclusive, which you must have seen in looking at that code; there are many things in the motion picture code which have nothing whatsoever to do with either violence or sex, and yet there is part of the burden which any motion picture producer carries with him. I think it would be pretty dreadful if the book publishers got together and set up a code and set their standards. They might not agree with your standards or my standards as to what or what not to be published.

Chairman KEFAUVER. Well, Mr. Jacobs, I think one trouble with codes is that people sometimes get to feel that anything approved by a code authority like the crime book code, anything approved by them is going to be all right; whereas they may pass many things that people will accept as all right that really are not so good. So I think in the case of movies and television and crime books and what-not, while we might do some things to stop the circulation of the bad ones, in the final analysis it is the interests and the attitudes of the people at the local level that will be the deterrent.

Mr. JACOBS. We would like to suggest that the one thing that certainly be done in which your joint committee would be extremely helpful in recommending that research be done into the relationship between delinquency and mass media, because this really is an area in which there are sharp and divergent opinions by all sincere people.

Senator KEFAUVER. Well, as far as I am concerned, we have had a lot of testimony by very eminent authorities on that subject, and I don't think that—the more I get into this juvenile delinquency problem, the more convinced I am that there are so many, many reasons. What might be a reason in one case would not be a reason in another. Different environment would affect different people in different ways. But certainly certain types of pornographic literature, certain crime and horror comics, according to the great weight of the evidence, some violence and brutality on television, some suggestive brutality in some movies, maybe don't cause delinquency but maybe in an unstable kid they give him a little push along the road. It might be the trigger.

We have had an awful lot of evidence on it, and I hope you will get our hearings and read them. Thank you for your statement.

Mr. JACOBS. Thank you.

Chairman KEFAUVER. We are going to adjourn shortly, but before I do, I had a letter a little while ago from Mrs. Alice Good. It says:

MR. SENATOR. In the interest of good citizenship, will you please ask the audience if they would join me in an informal meeting or two to determine if we can form a permanent group which will continue to explore delinquency. Our purpose will be to try to formulate some constructive ideas which will benefit the community and channel these ideas through existing organizations.

It is signed, "Mrs. Alice Good."

We are glad to have people who are interested in calling the citizens meetings for purposes of that sort. I understand Mrs. Good is a highly respected lady, and if any one would like to stay here and meet with her after we adjourn, the custodian of the building and the officers have been so kind about it, I am sure they will cooperate with you.

Mrs. Good, will you stand up and tell us your name, I mean who you are?

Mrs. ALICE GOOD. Well, I am really a very ordinary person. I am not anybody of great importance, and I am sorry to say that I haven't given these things much attention in most of my life. I happened to have been brought up in an environment where the political situation was pretty rank, and I turned my back on all types of political interests and I have just made myself happy with my own interests, but of recent years I couldn't help but be attracted by conditions and the circumstances of our living, and in fact, any ordinarily intelligent person couldn't help being attracted to it.

Chairman KEFAUVER. Well, Mrs. Good you are just a good housewife and citizen who wants to generate some activity and interest in helping out children with a lot of their problems and create an interest in it, and I think that is a very noble purpose, and I hope that some of these good people will stay and meet with you.

Mr. ROBERT L. LOUCKS. Did I understand you are going to adjourn?

Chairman KEFAUVER. Yes, we are about to adjourn.

Mr. LOUCKS. I would like to be heard. I have been trying to get in contact for about 10 days.

Chairman KEFAUVER. Well, I have considered the matter you want to talk about and I don't exactly see the relation to this subject matter here. It is a pretty general subject matter you have, Mr. Loucks.

Mr. LOUCKS. It is the point on that relationship.

Chairman KEFAUVER. Well, if you want to call a meeting of your own——

Mr. LOUCKS. If I want to what?

Chairman KEFAUVER. Well, all right. We will give you about 2 minutes. What is it you want to say?

Mr. LOUCKS. Two minutes? Can an American citizen present his opinion in 2 minutes?

Chairman KEFAUVER. But we are talking about juvenile delinquency.

Mr. LOUCKS. I am talking about juvenile delinquency and what is back of it. I am talking about that relationship.

Chairman KEFAUVER. I understood you had some constitutional amendments.

Mr. Loucks. I have some amendments, and I have the ways and means. I have charts and compasses that will assist your committee on the one hand, and for an understanding that will help the industry on the other. It will harmonize the whole thing in accordance with teh United States Constitution construction, and I happen to be a lawyer and retired attorney and student of fraternal law all my life. I'd like to present some of those laws that I have found in the Constitution of the United States, in our Bill of Rights.

Chairman Kefauver. Well, now, what is the law that you want to present? You are Mr. Robert G. L. Loucks, L-o-u-c-k-s.

Mr. Loucks. Yes.

Chairman Kefauver. I have asked you to explain all of this to one of our counsel, and he didn't think it related to juvenile delinquency.

Mr. Loucks. I just gave him a summary. I didn't explain all of it. I didn't get started with your counsel.

Chairman Kefauver. Well, if you couldn't explain it to our counsel, I don't know how you could here, I mean how we are going to be able to give you time to explain it here.

Mr. Loucks. I'd like to get acquainted with you first to find out the scope of what I am trying to give you. I'm trying to present some constitutional points that will help you on juvenile delinquency and like to present some of those laws that I have found in the Constitution and the Bill of Rights doesn't mean that it is going to interfere with the problem of juvenile delinquency or the solution of it. It is a solution to the problem of building character and manhood under the Constitution. It's a process, a ways and means that will help you. It will help the United States Supreme Court in getting these ways and means and the procedure started, and to give us more light and enlightment.

Chairman Kefauver. Well, I'll tell you, Mr. Loucks, ordinarily I have our counsel or associates talk with witnesses who want to present some viewpoint, but you are so sincere and you have been so patient, after we adjourn this afternoon you go with me back to a little office, and I'll look over what you have got to present.

Mr. Loucks. I have been wanting to meet you, Senator, for a long time.

Chairman Kefauver. All right, sir.

Mr. Loucks. But I'd like to get it in the record. I want a petition to the United States Congress in the three departments. I want to make a motion in accordance with a recent decision in the United States Supreme Court in the Negro segregation cases presenting these problems back to local government and recognizing them as important, because that is the place of the origin, the place where the trouble started, where the trouble is. It is right here, and they say that the United States district court has prescribed rules and regulations and procedures to carry out the instruction, instead of having all of these run arounds, and these meetings; let the Congress of the United States, the three departments jointly and severally do it. I'll give you this to start with: They are obligated to uphold and protect the Constitution of the United States. All right, let those three departments get together jointly and severally and adopt the rules and regulations and the procedures.

Chairman KEFAUVER. Yes, sir. Well, now, Mr. Loucks——

Mr. LOUCKS. Not one department.

Chairman KEFAUVER. Just a minute, sir.

Mr. LOUCKS. Now, how about that?

Chairman KEFAUVER. Well, you are getting on to something that doesn't pertain immediately to juvenile delinquency and that is the subject matter of our hearing here. But you have a seat, and when we get through——

Mr. LOUCKS. That goes right to the protecting of the American home.

Chairman KEFAUVER. I don't want to interrupt you, but if you will have a seat, I will go over it with you——

Mr. LOUCKS. You don't give me a chance to be heard, and I have been trying for 10 days to get to you, Senator. You don't understand me.

Chairman KEFAUVER. Yes, Mr. Loucks, but I don't find that what you have to present pertains to the subject matter of our hearing, but when we adjourn here, I will go into it with you personally.

Mr. LOUCKS. Well, listen——

Chairman KEFAUVER. I will ask you to take your seat now.

Mr. LOUCKS. One sentence more.

Chairman KEFAUVER. No, sir. No, Mr. Loucks——

Mr. LOUCKS. Under the Constitution, I am asking for that insurance and that security.

Chairman KEFAUVER. I will ask you to take your seat now, Mr. Loucks——

Mr. LOUCKS. For domestic tranquillity.

Chairman KEFAUVER. You take your seat.

Mr. LOUCKS. I have got the insurance and the security record when you want it.

Chairman KEFAUVER. I asked you to take your seat, Mr. Loucks.

Mr. LOUCKS. We have been shut off now for——

Chairman KEFAUVER. Mr. Loucks, we are going——

Mr. LOUCKS. We have been shut off here for 50 years. I'm anxious about this, that's all. I am an American citizen, and I want the constitution enforced for security and security insurance for domestic tranquillity, and if they perform their duty in Washington, with proper procedures we will have an American home.

Chairman KEFAUVER. I am the chairman of this subcommittee, and I have asked you to take your seat.

I would like to insert into the record at this point two communications received by the subcommittee in answer to a letter of inquiry regarding the movie investigation. One is from the Joint Estimate of Current Entertainment Films and the other is from the National Legion of Decency.

(The documents referred to were marked "Exhibits Nos. 13 and 14," and read as follows:)

EXHIBIT No. 13

JOINT ESTIMATES OF CURRENT ENTERTAINMENT FILMS,
New York, N. Y., June 10, 1955.

Senator ESTES KEFAUVER,
United States Senate, Juvenile Delinquency Committee,
Los Angeles, Calif.

GENTLEMEN : In response to your inquiry of June 2, 1955, we are unable to volunteer as witnesses before your committee because of the travel involved.

This board, composed of representatives of 13 national organizations whose combined membership totals 40 million Americans, reviews those 35-millimeter feature-length entertainment films intended for widespread distribution in the United States. This voluntary work consists of screening, appraising, and classifying each film as to audience suitability. The frank and unbiased reviews are distributed gratis, upon request, to schools, colleges, libraries, churches, club groups, local newspapers, radio stations, and motion-picture exhibitors.

Over the past several years, this board has been well aware of the alarming rise in the incidence of juvenile delinquency. We are also aware of the pervasive and worldwide climate of violence which has found increasing expression in contemporary novels, plays, motion pictures, comic books, radio, and TV, and in the public press. Regarding the possible influence of any one medium or another on present or potential juvenile delinquents, we are in accord with the findings of Secretary Hobby's Special Conference on Juvenile Delinquency, June 1954, which stressed the home and the child's individual environment as the real roots of such delinquency. We also believe that in the maladjusted child any item of his or her experience, either real or vicarious, may suggest antisocial or illegal actions.

With regard to your specific question concerning the presentation of illicit sex in motion pictures, we have found that such situations are implied rather than shown or verbalized ; we believe that they would not necessarily affect adolescents. However, we have been concerned with the increase of sex suggestiveness in recent films.

During the last year there has been a definite increase in the number of crime films as well as films with specific instances of unnecessary violence. We fully realize and accept the fact that in action, war, adventure, or historical films, violence is an inevitable ingredient. We must see the enemies biting the dust, the villains coming to a bad end ; these are obligatory scenes. But now, in such films, we have not 1 or 2 villains, but a whole score, all of whom come to bad ends, so that the amount of footage devoted to violence has increased.

Secondly, the kind of violence shown has assumed many new forms. Instead of a swift bullet disposing of the malefactor, he meets his end in a variety of fashions, either shown or implied. Similarly, almost all heroes are now required to prove their courage and stamina by prolonged brutal fights or semilethal exhibitions of jujitsu. Although each single episode of violence may conform to the restrictions of the Production Code, we feel that the cumulative effect is often an overdose of mayhem.

Finally, we feel that present-day scenes of violence exercise enormously increased audience impact because of the technical advances in photography and projection. Vividly lifelike color, giant screens, and stereophonic sound accentuate such scenes so that they frequently become overpowering. Since January 1955, this committee has been cooperating with Mr. Shurlock, director of the Production Code, at his request, in advising him of specific scenes in specific pictures, which, in our opinion, contain excessive brutality or unnecessary violence.

At this point, we wish to go on record once again as opposing censorship of any of the mass media whether by Federal, State, or local ordinance, as being thoroughly undemocratic. On the other hand, we feel that the mass media of communication must not confuse freedom with license ; they must exercise due responsibility for the type of material which they present to the public.

While affirming our support of the principle of self-regulation, we do, however, urge that the motion-picture companies uphold the spirit as well as the letter of the Production Code so that motion pictures may accurately reflect and reenforce our traditional American culture.

Very truly yours,

Film Estimate Board of National Organizations: Ada Comerford, American Association of University Women; Rose Marie Alexander, American Jewish Committee; Marilla Waite Freeman, American Library Association; Lillian A. Lilly, Children's Film Library; Dorothy Grover Cooper, Daughters of the American Revolution; Sigmund Spaeth, National Federation of Music Clubs; Charlotte Baruth, General Federation of Women's Clubs; Alvina E. Murphy, Girl Scouts of the U. S. A.; Louise S. Walker, National Congress of Parents and Teachers; Golda E. Bader, Protestant Motion Picture Council, United Church Women; Clara Edwards, National Council of Women of the U. S. A.; Marie Hamilton, Schools Motion Picture Committee.

EXHIBIT No. 14

NATIONAL LEGION OF DECENCY,
New York, N. Y., June 7, 1955.

Hon. ESTES KEFAUVER,
Chairman, Committee on the Judiciary,
Subcommittee To Investigate Juvenile Delinquency,
Los Angeles, Calif.

DEAR SENATOR KEFAUVER: Pursuant to your recent correspondence, we are enclosing a breakdown, statistically, of those pictures found either objectionable in part or completely objectionable from October 1953 to October 1954 and from October 1954 to June 1955.

We are also forwarding, Your Honor, the comparative statistics on feature pictures reviewed and classified by the Legion of Decency since 1938.

I trust that Your Honor will find this breakdown sufficiently self-explanatory to answer the questions which you have posed in your recent letter.

With best personal wishes, I remain,

Sincerely yours,

REV. THOMAS F. LITTLE,
Executive Secretary.

Comparative statistics on feature pictures reviewed and classified

	Class A–I		Class A–II		Class B		Class C		Total
	Number	Percent	Number	Percent	Number	Percent	Number	Percent	
(1)_____	780	61	380	30	98	8	13	1	1, 271
1938_____	332	62	164	31	32	6	5	1	535
1939_____	312	54	200	35	50	9	9	1. 67	573
1940_____	271	50	210	39	47	9	10	2	539
1941_____	267	51. 25	197	37. 81	50	9. 6	7	1. 34	521
1942_____	271	51. 13	202	38. 11	51	9. 62	5	. 95	530
1943_____	229	52. 16	151	34. 40	55	12. 53	4	. 91	439
1944_____	191	44. 52	184	42. 89	51	11. 89	3	. 70	429
1945_____	143	38. 1	189	50. 4	43	11. 5	0	0	375
1946_____	155	39. 64	176	45. 01	60	15. 35	0	0	391
1947_____	195	44. 32	172	39. 09	70	15. 91	3	. 68	440
1948_____	174	38. 58	188	41. 69	82	18. 18	7	1. 55	451
1949_____	193	41. 33	165	35. 33	96	20. 56	13	2. 78	467
1950_____	179	39	169	36. 82	103	22. 44	8	1. 74	459
1951 ²____	148	33. 49	195	44. 12	85	19. 23	14	3. 16	442
1952 ³____	182	40. 81	172	38. 56	78	17. 49	14	3. 14	446
1953_____	148	38. 6	142	37. 1	89	23. 2	4	1. 1	383
1954_____	138	39. 20	127	36. 08	78	22. 16	9	2. 56	352

¹ The comparative statistics of the Legion of Decency date from February 1936. 1st period covers films reviewed from February 1936 to November 1937. From 1938 through 1950 periods are based on films reviewed from November to November.
² This period covers films reviewed from November 1950 to October 1951.
³ As of 1952 periods run from October to October.

Comparative statistics on domestic and foreign feature pictures

DOMESTIC

	Class A–I		Class A–II		Class B		Class C		Total
	Number	Percent	Number	Percent	Number	Percent	Number	Percent	
1948	162	44.14	152	41.42	52	14.17	1	0.27	367
1949	177	45.62	139	35.82	69	17.78	3	.78	388
1950	171	42.54	150	37.31	79	19.65	2	.50	402
1951	136	37.26	162	44.38	66	18.08	1	.27	365
1952	164	44.33	141	38.11	64	17.29	1	.27	370
1953	140	41.67	124	36.90	71	21.13	1	.30	336
1954	120	43.01	101	36.13	56	20.07	2	.72	279

FOREIGN

	Class A–I		Class A–II		Class B		Class C		Total
1948	12	14.29	36	42.86	30	35.71	6	7.14	84
1949	16	20.25	26	32.91	27	34.18	10	12.66	79
1950	8	14.03	19	33.33	24	42.11	6	10.53	57
1951	12	15.58	33	42.86	19	24.68	13	16.88	77
1952	18	23.68	31	40.79	14	18.42	13	17.11	76
1953	8	17.02	18	38.30	18	38.30	3	6.38	47
1954	18	24.66	26	35.62	22	30.14	7	9.59	73

In appraising the moral status and trend of motion pictures, statistics alone do not provide adequate and reliable measurement. Statistics should be considered in conjunction with other factors such as the kind and amount of objectionableness in a film rated in any given objectionable or condemned category. The evaluation of the situation must be based on qualitative and quantitative consideration as well as the popularity potentiality of the subject, together with its thematic character.

Tabulation of films according to distributor

Distributor	A–I	A–II	B	C
Miscellaneous	9	8	9	4
Allied Artists	16	11	0	0
Columbia	8	18	8	0
Disney	7	0	0	0
Mayer-Kingsley	5	3	0	1
IFE Releasing Corp	1	13	11	3
MGM	12	8	6	0
Paramount	4	8	7	0
Republic	8	6	2	0
RKO	5	1	7	1
20th Century-Fox	9	9	7	0
United Artists	25	21	11	0
Universal-International	17	12	6	0
Warners	12	9	4	0

Period of time	AI	AII	B	C	Total
October 1953–October 1954	138	127	78	9	352
October 1954–June 1955	67	73	79	9	228

Objections for B pictures

DOMESTIC

	October 1953–54	October 1954–June 1955
Suggestiveness in—		
Song	2	0
Situations [1]	23	25
Situation [2]	0	1
Dances	5	8
Costuming	19	30
Sequence [2]	11	10
Sequences [1]	0	11
Dialogue	10	15
Tends to degrade dignity of marriage	0	1
Light treatment of marriage	9	5
Reflects the acceptability of divorce	7	6
Tends to condone immoral, illicit actions	7	8
Suicide in plot solution or sympathetically portrayed	2	2
Material seriously offends Christian and traditional standards of morality and decency	1	0
Methods of crime too minutely detailed	1	2
Excessive brutality	7	17
Low moral tone	12	13
Tends to arouse sympathy for wrongdoing	3	1
Insufficient moral compensation	2	0
Objectionable sequence	1	0
Misrepresents or ridicules religion	0	2
Tends to glorify crime and criminals	0	1
Undue sympathy for immoral actions	0	3
Tends to arouse disrespect for law and order	0	4
Taking the law into one's own hands	0	1
Light treatment of the virtue of purity	0	2

[1] Multiple offense.
[2] Single offense.

Objections for C pictures

FOREIGN

	October 1953–54	October 1954–June 1955
Suggestiveness in—		
Situations	3	2
Costuming	3	2
Sequence	2	0
Dialogue	1	2
Tends to condone immoral, illicit actions	3	3
Contains material offensive to religion	2	0
Suicide in plot solution or sympathetically portrayed	1	0
Material morally unsuitable for entertainment motion-picture theaters or audiences	4	0
Offends Christian and traditional standards of morality and decency	4	4
Disrespect for the virtue of purity	0	1
Sympathetic treatment of divorce	0	1

DOMESTIC

	October 1953–54	October 1954–June 1955
Suggestiveness in—		
Dances	0	1
Costuming	1	1
Dialogue	1	0
Situations	0	0
Offensive to Christian and traditional standards of morality and decency	2	4
Contains grossly obscene and indecent action	1	0
Contains material capable of grave evil influence	1	0
Material morally unsuitable for entertainment motion-picture theaters or audiences	1	3
Disrespect for the virtue of purity	0	2

EXPLANATION OF LEGION CLASSIFICATIONS

A–I: Morally unobjectionably for general patronage.—These films are considered to contain no material which would be morally dangerous to the average motion-picture audience, adults and children alike.

A–II: Morally unobjectionable for adults.—These are films which in themselves are morally harmless but which, because of subject matter or treatment, require maturity and experience if one is to witness them without danger of moral harm. While no definite age limit can be established for this group, the judgement of parents, pastors and teachers would be helpful in determining the decision in individual cases.

B: Morally objectionable in part for all.—Films in this category are considered to contain elements dangerous to Christian morals or moral standards.

C: Condemned.—Condemned films are considered to be those which because of theme or treatment are what has been described by the Holy Father as "positively bad."

Separate classifiication.—A separate classification is given to certain films which, while not morally offensive, require some analysis and explanation as a protection to the uninformed against wrong interpretations and false conclusions.

Chairman KEFAUVER. We will recess until 9:30 in the morning. We hope to get through about 12:30.

(Whereupon at 5 p. m., Friday, June 17, 1955, the subcommittee recessed to reconvene at open session at 9:30 a. m., Saturday, June 18, 1955.)

JUVENILE DELINQUENCY
(Motion Pictures)

SATURDAY, JUNE 18, 1955

United States Senate,
Subcommittee of the Committee on the Judiciary
To Investigate Juvenile Delinquency,
Los Angeles, Calif.

The subcommitee met, pursuant to recess, at 9 : 40 a. m., at room 518, United States Postoffice and Courthouse Building, Los Angeles, Calif., Senator Estes Kefauver presiding.

Present: Senator Kefauver.

Also present: James H. Bobo, counsel; and William Haddad and Carl Perian, consultants.

Chairman Kefauver. Before we proceed with the chief matter of obscene and pornographic materials this morning, Mr. Max Gilford was to have appeared yesterday, and we excused him until this morning.

Mr. Gilford, you come around. I am glad to see you again this morning.

Mr. Gilford. Thank you, Senator. Good morning.

STATEMENT OF MAX M. GILFORD, GENERAL COUNSEL, NATIONAL SOCIETY OF TELEVISION PRODUCERS, LOS ANGELES, CALIF.

Chairman Kefauver. Mr. Gilford, you have a statement written out. Suppose you file your statement. We will treat it as read, and you summarize briefly just the points that—let me have a copy.

Mr. Gilford. Yes.

Chairman Kefauver. Oh, here it is.

Mr. Gilford, first will you identify yourself? You are the attorney for the National Society of Television Producers?

Mr. Gilford. That is correct. I am general counsel for the National Society of Television Producers; and, as I stated, I have been an attorney for 26 years and in the motion picture industry for about 20, and have also acted as a feature motion picture producer and television producer.

I appreciate the opportunity of presenting the viewpoint of the independent television producer so that the television industry will have some representation before this committee, and so that the committee can get the viewpoint of the independent television producer. I have filed a statement with Mr. Bobo which contains the viewpoints that I feel most of the television producers will believe and follow in. The statement, unfortunately, we didn't have time to have confirmed by the board of directors of the National Society of Television Producers or the Alliance of Television Producers. I might summarize and say that we feel that we have done everything possible in the television field to keep the television pictures in accordance with the code. The National Society of Television Producers has a code and, of course, you know that the Motion Picture Producers Association has a code. Even though the television producers do not have an enforcement organization to enforce any code provisions, I believe that between the producers, the advertising agency, the directors, and those connected with the technical phases, in every way and at all times attempt is made to follow the code provisions and see to it that television motion pictures keep up a very high moral standard.

I do think that some of the complaints that you have received regarding television pictures probably are the western type of picture, wherein and whereby in the pictures there are some shootings and the heavy, as we call him, is done away with. Now, I don't think that that has affected juvenile delinquency in any way, because that can be shown by the merchandisers. The merchandisers will tell you that children buy the suits or replicas or assemblies of the hero, and that is true from the days of Hopalong Cassidy to Davy Crockett. They don't try to emulate the heavy or the evil men.

I also believe that most of your complaints that have arisen in television are because of the fact that in television in the past, in order to use up the time and in order to take care of the time that was available, many of the exhibitors, distributors, networks, and independent stations have purchased films, theatrical films, for release over television. It is to be noted that these films were made at a time when television was never thought of nor was it ever thought that these pictures would be telecasted over a television station. Therefore, they do not have the view point of television production. Consequently, in those films probably they have violence and things of that nature, which when shown over television—and the impact is therefore much greater than in motion pictures—much complaint has arisen and has come to the attention of this committee.

Now, in conclusion, as you will find in the statements, we have attempted to distribute our code to most of the television producers. We have asked them to conduct themselves on a voluntary basis; and as it has been said here before, I think the sponsor is a terrific administrator of a voluntary code himself and doesn't want anything disseminated over television wherein and whereby the show might reflect upon his product. We have done, because of all of those things, a pretty good job; but I say in the end that if for any reason this committee, after its thorough investigation, finds that the voluntary code conduct on the part of the television producers is inadequate, then I would say that—and if you feel that the code should be operated by the television producers on more of a compulsory basis, somewhat similar to the motion picture producers association code and that we should follow through by the seal method, granting seals; then I call to your attention a very important item in television. If 50 percent of the television that is telecasted is on film 12 hours a day, 7 days a week, and motion pictures for television are generally sold on a 39-week cycle, and breakdowns of 13 weeks for each group of films on a particular subject; you would have almost 294 hours of film a week that would have to be reviewed. That is, the teleplays would have to be reviewed by a code administration committee. You can see that the job there to do that would be almost 20 times greater than the job in supervising the motion picture film by the Motion Picture Production Code Administration Committee. So because of that terrific job it would be a very voluminous and very costly one, and I would suggest that the Government, the Federal Government, subsidize for a period of time the organizations of television production code administration until by the voluntary cooperation of the producers they could between themselves accumulate sufficient funds and operate on a pay-as-you-go basis.

Chairman KEFAUVER. Well, Mr. Gilford, you do feel that some of these shows that were made a long time ago before television was thought of were not intended primarily for juvenile——

Mr. GILFORD. Consumption.

Chairman KEFAUVER. Consumption and audiences; but that since television came along they are being shown late in the afternoon at a time the kids, particularly, view television; and you do feel that there is too much crime and too much shooting and violence in some of those pictures that they have been seeing that were made a long time ago?

Mr. GILFORD. Yes; I agree with you, Senator, that that is very possible; and you realize that as time goes on—I should say here, though, that the major motion picture producers have not let any of their films loose for distribution on television, and you can understand why that is. That is because of the fact that they have to feed their films to motion-picture exhibitors and theaters. Consequently, the accumulation of film that the exhibitors and distributors for television could get were only these old films that were made by independents and were not tied up in the vaults of the major producing companies. Consequently, I think we have something that is also in the future that may help this situation, and that is that eventually television producing companies will make feature-length films for television of an hour length or so, and also the pay-as-you-go plan that is now being investigated by the Federal Communications Commission may be the thing; because I personally believe that if a man wants to buy something, he is entitled to have that privilege. I think eventually that may come about and be a solution, too.

Chairman KEFAUVER. Then, as I understand, your second point is that if you were to have inspection or going over of all the television programs, it would be too big a job for the industry itself and there would have to be some Government subsidy?

Mr. GILFORD. Yes; I think they would need assistance. Censorship is not the answer. Self-regulation has proven to be the best means, and if the television industry could get help in that connection, I think then your problem would be completely solved or pretty well solved.

Chairman KEFAUVER. Well, I want to say this personally, speaking in that connection: That I am highly in favor of self-regulation; but I hope that we never get to the point where it becomes a province of the Government to review and quasi-censor television programs. I think the Government's only province, and the only one I would suggest in that connection, would be a consideration of the type of programs when the application for renewal of the license comes before the Federal Communications Commission. I hope the industry doesn't get the idea that the Government is going to take over any responsibility in connection with viewing, and with its self-regulation. Of course, I don't think that is really our province.

Mr. GILFORD. I am certainly glad to hear you say that, Senator. I think you will find that every effort is being made by the Motion Picture Producers Association code administration committee to keep the motion pictures under hand, and I think that if the television producers are given a similar opportunity, you will find that they will cooperate in the same respect. The National Association of Radio and Television Broadcasters Code is doing a fine job. That is the code that the television broadcasters and the networks are affiliated with, and all shows that are played by the networks or are made for the networks by contracted producers make every effort to abide by that particular code. That code is also similar to the Motion Picture Producers Association; so I agree with you, and I know that the television is very pleased to hear you say that self-regulation is the answer and not censorship.

Chairman KEFAUVER. That is the way I feel about it; but I must say, frankly, also I think the television industry has a long way to go, in the first place, to get all of the industry into the self-regulation association; and then we are not actually satisfied with the compliance with the code on the part of some parts of the industry in connection with some of the programs that have been produced. We think that some of them are definitely deleterious to our young people, but we hope that there are signs of headway being made and we hope that progress continues.

Mr. GILFORD. I think you will find it that way. I appreciate the opportunity of presenting the television viewpoint.

Chairman KEFAUVER. Thank you very much, Mr. Gilford.

Mr. GILFORD. All right. Goodby.

(The subcommittee concluded its hearing on the subject of obscene and pornographic materials.)

JUVENILE DELINQUENCY
(OBSCENE AND PORNOGRAPHIC MATERIALS)

HEARINGS

BEFORE THE

SUBCOMMITTEE TO INVESTIGATE
JUVENILE DELINQUENCY

OF THE

COMMITTEE ON THE JUDICIARY
UNITED STATES SENATE

EIGHTY-FOURTH CONGRESS

FIRST SESSION

PURSUANT TO

S. Res. 62

INVESTIGATION OF JUVENILE DELINQUENCY
IN THE UNITED STATES

MAY 24, 26, 31, JUNE 9 AND 18, 1955

Printed for the use of the Committee on the Judiciary

COMMITTEE ON THE JUDICIARY

HARLEY M. KILGORE, West Virginia, *Chairman*

JAMES O. EASTLAND, Mississippi
ESTES KEFAUVER, Tennessee
OLIN D. JOHNSTON, South Carolina
THOMAS C. HENNINGS, JR., Missouri
JOHN L. McCLELLAN, Arkansas
PRICE DANIEL, Texas
JOSEPH C. O'MAHONEY, Wyoming

ALEXANDER WILEY, Wisconsin
WILLIAM LANGER, North Dakota
WILLIAM E. JENNER, Indiana
ARTHUR V. WATKINS, Utah
EVERETT McKINLEY DIRKSEN, Illinois
HERMAN WELKER, Idaho
JOHN MARSHALL BUTLER, Maryland

SUBCOMMITTEE TO INVESTIGATE JUVENILE DELINQUENCY IN THE UNITED STATES

ESTES KEFAUVER, Tennessee, *Chairman*

THOMAS C. HENNINGS, JR., Missouri
PRICE DANIEL, Texas

WILLIAM LANGER, North Dakota
ALEXANDER WILEY, Wisconsin

JAMES H. BOBO, *General Counsel*

II

CONTENTS

Statement of—   **Page**
  Burgum, Leslie R., attorney general, State of North Dakota, Bismarck, N. Dak_____ 299
  Egan, Father Daniel, Franciscan priest, Graymoor, Garrison, N. Y___ 70
  Karpman, Dr. Benjamin, chief psychotherapist, St. Elizabeths Hospital, Washington, D. C_____ 80
  Thomas, Norman, New York, N. Y_____ 217
Testimony of—
  Alberts, David S., accompanied by counsel, Stanley Fleishman, Los Angeles, Calif_____ 387
  Alberts, Mrs. Violet Evelyn Stanard, Los Angeles, Calif_____ 390
  Bair, Robert R., assistant United States attorney, district of Maryland_____ 141
  Barnes, Phillip I., police officer, administrative vice squad, pornographic detail, Los Angeles Police Department, Los Angeles, Calif__ 374
  Blick, Inspector Roy, head of vice squad, Police Department, Washington, D. C_____ 103, 272
  Brown, Sergeant Joseph E., Detroit Police Department, Detroit, Mich_____ 134
  Butler, Lieutenant George, Dallas Police Department, Dallas, Tex., investigator for the Subcommittee_____ 255
  Caidin, Stanley R., attorney at law, Beverly Hills, Calif_____ 339
  Cavanaugh, Eugene O., chief, youth squad, New York City Board of Education, New York, N. Y_____ 93
  Chumbris, Peter N., associate counsel, United States Senate Subcommittee To Investigate Juvenile Delinquency_____ 46
  Deerson, William, dean of discipline, Haaren High School, New York, N. Y_____ 76
  Fishman, Irving, Deputy Collector of Customs, New York, N. Y____ 249
  Fodor, George, St. Petersburg, Fla_____ 154
  Gillman, Morris, New York, N. Y_____ 245
  Grimm, Clarence, Coral Gables, Fla_____ 223
  Henry, Dr. George W., professor of clinical psychiatry, Cornell University, college of medicine, Ithaca, N. Y_____ 210
  Klaw, Irving, accompanied by counsel, Coleman Gangel, New York, N. Y_____ 229
  Maletta, Eugene, accompanied by counsel, Leon D. Lazer, Richmond Hill, N. Y_____ 175
  Miller, William J., Hollywood, Calif_____ 397
  Mishkin, Eddie, accompanied by counsel, Daniel Weiss, Yonkers, N. Y_____ 158, 239
  Nelson, James F., deputy district attorney, Los Angeles County, Calif_____ 413
  O'Brien, William C., Assistant Solicitor, Post Office Department, accompanied by Harry J. Simon, inspector, Post Office Department, Washington, D. C_____ 283, 306
  Roth, Samuel, New York, N. Y_____ 187
  Rotto, Abe, accompanied by counsel, H. Robert Levine, Brooklyn, N. Y_____ 172
  Rubin, Abraham, accompanied by counsel, Daniel Weiss, Brooklyn, N. Y_____ 149, 243, 260
  Sheehan, Lt. Ignatius, morals squad, Chicago Police Department, Chicago, Ill_____ 124

Testimony of—Continued   Page
    Shomer, Louis, accompanied by counsel, Jacob Rachstein, Brooklyn,
        N. Y_____ 178, 265
    Sobel, Arthur Herman, accompanied by counsel, Morris D. Hohrar,
        New York, N. Y_____ 161
    Stapenhorst, Ralph E., postal inspector, Glendale, Calif_____ 355
    Sullivan, Lt. Walter J., investigator for the District Attorney, Los
        Angeles County, Calif_____ 392
    Tager, Mary Dorothy, Balboa, Calif_____ 315
    Thoms, Mr. and Mrs. Robert, Rutherford, N. J_____   96
    Whipple, Lawrence A., director of public safety, Jersey City, N. J.,
        accompanied by Sgt. Alfred Jago and Detective John Higgins,
        Jersey City Police Department, Jersey City, N. J_____ 114

EXHIBITS

Number and summary of exhibit
 1. Copy of Perspectives On Delinquency Prevention, a report by Henry
    Epstein, deputy mayor to Robert F. Wagner, mayor of the city of
    New York_____   ² 2
 2. Copies of Senate Resolution 89, 83d Congress, 1st session; Senate
    Resolution 190, 83d Congress, 2d session; Senate Resolution 62,
    84th Congress, 1st session; and resolutions dated May 20, 1955, au-
    thorizing Senator Estes Kefauver to hold hearings_____   ² 44
 3. Copies of Federal Statutes Nos. 1461, 1462, 1463, and 1464_____   ² 48
 4. Summary of State laws pertaining to obscene and pornographic ma-
    terials_____   ² 49
 5. Copy of the subcommittee letter sent to various police officials through-
    out the country_____   ² 53
 6. Copy of letter dated February 3, 1953, from Louis Stevens Saxton
    addressed to Clarence Meade Barnes, and related material_____   ² 62
 7. Copy of subpena dated May 19, 1955, addressed to Irving Klaw_____   ² 89
 8. Copy of a doctor's certificate concerned with the health of Louis
    Finkelstein_____   ² 91
 9. Information of Eugene Cavanagh outlining the activities of the youth
    squad from April 1, 1954, to March 31, 1955_____   ¹ 94
10. Copy of an admission ticket to Colossal Good Time Night, March 29,
    1953_____   ¹ 105
11. Copy of a receipt from Anderson Film Rental Service, Elgin, Ill____   ² 130
12. Copy of the police record of Al Stone, alias Abraham Rubin, from the
    Detroit Police Department, Detroit, Mich_____   ¹ 135
13. Copy of income tax and bank statement information, 1950 through
    1954, of Al Stone, alias Abraham Rubin_____   ² 152
14. Copy of the stenographer's minutes of the case *United States of
    America* v. *Harold Kantor*, heard in the United States District
    Court, Southern District of New York_____   ¹ 164
15. Stock Theft "Fence" Given Prison Term, article appearing in the
    October 26, 1937 issue of the New Haven Evening Register, New
    Haven, Conn_____   ² 167
16. List of pornographic material found in the possession of Abe Rotto on
    July 29, 1954_____   ² 173
17. Copy of an advertisement of the Atine Co., New York City, received
    by a juvenile_____   ¹ 183
18. Advertisement and letter of transmittal concerned with obscene litera-
    ture received through the mails_____   ² 191
19. Additional advertisements and letters of transmittal concerned with
    obscene literature received through the mails by several individuals__   ² 193
20. Newspaper clippings from several Florida papers_____   ¹ 228
21. Copy of the 97th edition of Cartoon and Model Parade, published by
    Irving Klaw_____   ¹ 233
22. Photographs submitted by Irving Fishman_____   ¹ 254

CONTENTS   V

                                                                  Page
23. Samples of pornography submitted by Lieutenant Butler_____ [1] 259
24. Road map of the Northeastern United States with numerous cities
    circled alleged to have been taken from the possession of Abraham
    Rubin, alias Al Stone, by the Detroit Police Department_____ [1] 263
25. Name and address book belonging to Abraham Rubin, alias Al Stone__ [1] 265
26. Copy of a subpena dated May 19, 1955, addressed to Aaron Moses
    Shapiro_____ [2] 267
27. Copy of a subpena dated May 19, 1955, addressed to Joseph Piccarellie_ [2] 268
28. Photograph of pornographic materials_____ [1] 282
29. List of film titles in the possession of Simon Simring_____ [1] 282
30. Three photos of indecent acts by children 4, 6, and 10 years old_____ [1] 283
31. Letter dated June 8, 1955, from Congressman John A. Blatnik of
    Minnesota, addressed to Mr. Peter Chumbris, associate counsel,
    United States Senate Subcommittee To Investigate Juvenile Delin-
    quency_____ [2] 291
32. Copy of House bill No. 825, 34th North Dakota Legislative Assembly,
    prohibiting the sale, distribution, or exhibition of lewd and obscene
    matter to persons under 21 years of age_____ [2] 301
33. Samples of literature sent to customers by Mrs. Dorothy Tager_____ [1] 324
34. Copy of a check in the amount of $1,329.95 made payable to Stanley
    Caiden, from Mrs. Louis Tager's account at the California Bank,
    Los Angeles, Calif_____ [2] 342
35. Reporter's transcript of partial proceedings in the case of *United
    States* v. *Roy J. Ross* of the United States District Court, Southern
    District of California, March 23, 1954_____ [2] 357
36. Copy of an advertisement from Male Merchandise Mart, Hollywood,
    Calif_____ [1] 368
37. Copy of an accompanying folder to the advertisement from Male
    Merchandise Mart, Hollywood, Calif_____ [1] 368
38. Copy of advertisement received by the subcommittee from Male
    Merchandise Mart, Hollywood, Calif_____ [1] 369
39. Clean-Up-The-Mails Campaign, article appearing in the March 17,
    1955, issue of the Postal Bulletin, United States Post Office Depart-
    ment_____ [2] 373
    photography_____ [2] 381
    photography _____
41. Copy of a subpena dated June 10, 1955, addressed to David S. Alberts__ [2] 389
42. Copy of the police record of William Miller_____ [2] 408

[1] On file with the subcommittee.
[2] Printed in the record.

JUVENILE DELINQUENCY
(Obscene and Pornographic Materials)

TUESDAY, MAY 24, 1955

United States Senate,
Subcommittee of the Committee on the Judiciary
To Investigate Juvenile Delinquency,
New York, N. Y.

The subcommittee met, pursuant to notice, at 9 a. m., in room 104, United States Court House, Foley Square, New York City, N. Y., Senator Estes Kefauver, chairman, presiding.

Present: Senator Estes Kefauver, Senator William Langer.

Also present: James H. Bobo, general counsel; Peter N. Chumbris, associate counsel; Vincent Gaughan, special counsel; Edward Lee McLean, editorial director; George Martin and George Butler, consultants to the subcommittee.

Chairman KEFAUVER. The subcommittee will come to order.

This is a subcommittee of the Senate Committee on the Judiciary, established by order of the Senate. The members of the subcommittee are the distinguished Senator from North Dakota, Senator Langer, who is with us today, and who has taken a great deal of interest in the work of the subcommittee, and was former chairman of the full Committee on the Judiciary; Senator Wiley, of Wisconsin; and Senator Hennings, of Missouri.

The subcommittee wishes to first express its appreciation to Mr. Mike Lordan, superintendent of the building, and the others who have been so cooperative in arranging for this courtroom; Judge Hart and members of the court.

We are glad to again be in the great city of New York. The problem of juvenile delinquency which brings us here at this time deserves and requires the best attention and the best effort of every American citizen. The future of this country is irrevocably tied with our young people. If this is a great generation we are rearing, and I am firmly convinced it is, then the future of our democracy is secure. Yet we must face up to the problems besetting our young people.

These 3 days of hearings will be devoted to pornographic material, a specialized subject within the general field of juvenile delinquency. This is a nationwide hearing. Later our subcommittee will return to New York to hold additional hearings on the broad aspects of juvenile delinquency; but at this time I do want to commend the many fine efforts being made to remedy the problems of juvenile delinquency here in the Nation's largest city by public officials, churches, schools, and individuals.

I have been particularly impressed by the report of Deputy Mayor Henry Epstein concerning all phases of juvenile delinquency here and

1

his recommendations designed to correct the problems inherent in juvenile delinquency.

Now I want to order Mr. Epstein's report to be printed in the record at this time.

(The report above referred to, entitled "Perspectives on Delinquency Prevention," was marked "Exhibit No. 1," and is as follows:)

EXHIBIT NO. 1

PERSPECTIVES ON DELINQUENCY PREVENTION

(City of New York, 1955. Robert F. Wagner, mayor)

"* * * if we would guide by the light of reason, we must let our minds be bold."—LOUIS D. BRANDEIS.

CITY OF NEW YORK,
OFFICE OF THE MAYOR,
New York, N. Y., May 6, 1955.

Hon. ROBERT F. WAGNER,
    Mayor, City of New York,
        City Hall, New York, N. Y.

DEAR MAYOR WAGNER: Attached is a brief report on the coordination of new and improved programs to cope with the problem of juvenile delinquency in our city.

It has only been possible to undertake a relatively brief study in this field to which so many have devoted a lifetime. I am, however, making a number of suggestions in specific areas and have indicated particular problems which merit special consideration in the near future. I hope, for example, to treat the whole matter of the courts and correctional institutions at some length in another report.

The only expenditures to date from the $25,000 budgeted for this study have been 4½ months' salary for my consultant and his secretary, plus less than $100 for technical literature, supplies, etc. After our printer's bill is paid, I believe enough money will remain to complete the report mentioned above as well as one on services for infants and preschool children.

John J. Horwitz, who served as consultant on this project, was responsible for most of the research and field contacts. He also is to be commended for writing the draft of this report, laying it out and seeing it through the press. I wish to pay particular tribute to the rich background Mr. Horwitz brought to the planning of this project. His broad social science skills and his rich experience as settlement house director, psychiatric caseworker, and community organization specialist all contributed materially to the coherent overview so essential in a study of this sort.

I feel deeply indebted to former deputy city administrator John V. Connorton for his invaluable assistance in coordinating the committee consultations with private social agencies.

Dr. Luther Gulick, the city administrator, offered my staff office space and all conceivable cooperation. His friendly interest advanced the work materially.

Especial thanks are due my colleagues heading up various city departments and agencies, welfare and civic leaders, and the many experts on various aspects of the delinquency problem who have given me and my staff the benefit of their counsel. Many helpful suggestions have also been received from scores of private citizens who have passed along to us their suggestions as to the causes of juvenile delinquency or measures which might be undertaken to cope with our problem. The cooperative zeal so many people have brought to this effort has been a gratifying sign of the vitality of civic spirit in our city. The fine resolution of Council President Abe Stark, for example, is supported in the expanded youth board projects of private agencies. I might add that the tenor of a number of letters received from young people themselves has been a great source of encouragement.

May I emphasize in recommending the programs listed below that none are intended to substitute for ongoing operations in the same fields, nor should services be taken out of one neighborhood to provide for another.

Very sincerely yours,

HENRY EPSTEIN, *Deputy Mayor.*

INTRODUCTION

At the request of the mayor, I have during the past 8 months made a fairly extensive review of the scientific literature in the juvenile delinquency field, and have endeavored to inform myself on current developments of interest in other communities, and even in foreign countries.

Herewith are presented certain findings of fact as to the nature of the challenge and programs which we may undertake in order to meet it. This report is designed to help speed planning, and to inform the public about some of the problems we face. In addition, in appendix V, I have listed some important ways each and every citizen can help fight juvenile delinquency.

We can record many real achievements through services to children. But New York is a city which never has been afraid to face up to its shortcomings. I have not endeavored to produce a piece of promotion material; attention in this report is focused upon many areas where our performance is less than perfect, sometimes less than adequate.

We cannot feel satisfied with less than the best, especially where our children are concerned. In those existing programs where something vital may be wanting, no lack of conscientiousness or capacity on the part of personnel involved should be inferred. Over the years, there may have been many reasons why some strategic area has been neglected. In a city as large as ours, it may also happen that a service eminently worthwhile in years past, today needs to be reconsidered and replanned.

Our task is one to be accomplished only over a period of time. Deliberations today build upon work that has gone before. This report is related to earlier studies: and a number of important matters are only touched upon here, as they will be covered at greater length in other reports.

My emphasis throughout, has been upon employment of public funds through programs in public agencies. However, there are areas where private and sectarian agencies have clearly demonstrated an ability to provide valuable services of a supplementary character, when public moneys are placed at their disposal. I recommend continuance of this pattern, along already well established lines, through the youth board contract program (see appendix II). Nongovernmental bodies have a most important part to play in any community program. It is to be hoped that the fund-raising efforts of responsible private and sectarian agencies this year will permit the ambitious and highly laudable program expansions they projected in our joint discussions.

A joint policy statement of private and sectarian agencies appears here as appendix IV.

Certain highly important projects (which have come to my attention from various sources) do not seem appropriate or possible enterprises for the city government to undertake. These I have listed in appendix III. Should civic groups, service organizations, individual philanthropists, or foundations be interested in details on any of these undertakings, my staff have prepared brief outlines of possible first steps on each of them.

I do wish, however, to present for immediate consideration 10 programs I believe should be acted upon without delay. You will find here, and throughout my report, two equally important emphases: services for more children and more effective service to the children we do reach. A sound approach must be rooted in these foundations.

TEN PRIORITY PROGRAMS

Provision of competent staff for recreational facilities already available in 27 public-housing projects (for residents of projects and their neighbors); planning for staff in all the other projects not presently served.

Expansion of the remedial reading program in our schools to enable children to get 100-cent value on the education dollar.

Police services affecting juvenile delinquency.

Expansion of the youth board street club project and its services to families and children.

Provision of programs under youth board contract to the three areas in Manhattan, Staten Island, and Queens where delinquency rates have increased alarmingly; contracts for casework, group work and recreation services from private as well as public agencies.

Reexamination of teacher rotation policies, in an effort to assure placement of a larger proportion of our more highly experienced teachers in "difficult" schools.

Parent education programs centered around informal discussion groups.

Expansion of the co-op program which provides students an opportunity to complete their high school education while working half time in private industry at prevailing wages; more guidance services.

Inauguration of training services through the youth board to equip its own personnel to do an even more effective job, and to serve other departments which have approached the youth board for this kind of help; a fellowship study program for adding to the professional skills of workers on key projects in various city youth-serving agencies.

Provision for small, top-caliber units to do overall planning and to be responsible for assessment.

Before detailing the value of the 10 programs mentioned above, it is important that some general considerations be clarified.

May I remark at the outset that juvenile delinquency is neither a new problem nor one we can expect to meet with temporary expedients.

With so much talk of juvenile delinquency in the air and scare headlines all too frequently in the press, we are apt to forget the 97 juveniles in 100 who do not come in conflict with the law.

When the word "teen-ager" comes up, how often do we think of the nation-wide science talent search, in which our students, less than 4 percent of the Nation's high school population, regularly walk off with 20 percent or more of the awards.

How loud did the sirens blow when a teenager in or town a year ago won first prize for school-or-community life photographs in the national contest with 27,000 entries? And how many people have heard about the youth group here that volunteers regular work sessions adding to a library for the blind which houses the Nation's largest collection of hand-transcribed books?

Here are a few headlines which will seem more familiar: "Eleven-Year-Old Steals Teacher's Purse," "Boys Bind and Rob Playmates," "Schoolgirls Sweethearts, 16 and 17, Fight a Duel." These are the sort that have always made news. But here's one from the month before: "Legislator Aids Boy"—the story is about Assemblyman Robert F. Wagner, who volunteered his services to defend a 17-year-old he believed wrongly accused of shooting his employer. The year, for all those stories, 1905, exactly 50 years ago.

It seems to me we would do well to ponder awhile on the manner in which public opinion today may affect law enforcement as respects juveniles. It would come as a real shock to hear the casual suggestion that three men standing on the corner talking ought not to be on the street, but change the men to 17-year-olds and it would almost seem they had lost their rights as citizens. Or think of a driver who has run through a red light; when he receives his ticket, we think of him as a traffic violator, not a criminal. Let the driver be a youth, however, and there's a buzz of voices immediately against the "juvenile delinquent."

This may seem a trival consideration, but it is not trival to one who feels a door has been slammed in his face. New York has always taken pride in its young people; we have always felt this was the city, of all cities, that opened wide the door to citizenship. Yet today it almost seems as though no one is a citizen until he has attained the magical age of 21; and all the unfortunates who must wait the years until they attain that enviable distinction are high handedly placed on continuous probation.

We cannot have it both ways: Either our young people are a welcome part of the New York community, or they are some curious alien breed, shut out, marking time till their 21st birthday.

We in the city administration share a common concern with the community's religious leaders. There is a need for reawakening our young people's appreciation for higher values. We must labor, each in his own fashion, to open wide a door to the world of satisfaction through social responsibility.

As adults we would do well to reflect upon our own behavior when we warn youth against false values. And we would do well to think about the ways we can demonstrate, on a day-to-day basis, that the good life is really a rewarding one.

Much has been made of the unfortunate impact a particular type of publication is making upon our children and young people. It seems to me that it is unjust to focus criticism upon a single influence of this sort.

We live in times of world conflict and the threat of war. Wherever the child turns there is violence and talks of violence. To a stranger crime and sex might almost seem the sinister preoccupations of our people. The child grows up in a world of tension, not of his making. Yet 97 children in 100—even more if we confine our attention to the delinquents who are brought to court—make a "go" of it in a world that seems pretty confusing even to sophisticated adults.

The example we set is not always the best. There have been reports in these past months of a tax authority who committed suicide while under indictment for income-tax evasion; three different schoolteachers (not of this city) who sought special consideration when arrested for driving past a halted school bus; the reader can add examples of his own. We have our Schweitzers and our Einsteins, our Helen Kellers, and our Marion Andersons, true. But it is well to dwell a moment upon the observation of the director of one of our better juvenile institutions "adults deceive each other and children deceive the adults."

Our Nation takes pride in the fact that our press, films, radio, television, etc., are not under Government control. Private initiative in the great media of information has demonstrated time and again that it can make a responsible social contribution in periods of crisis. These times cryingly demand imagination and leadership from those entrusted with the media. I believe there are many who have already perceived the challenge and are moving forward as responsible citizens. The task of glamorizing socially constructive activities—of better informing the public as to the nature of juvenile delinquency—is a great one. To reach beyond the glorification of crime and the confusion of moral values must be more than an aspiration—we look to the industry for positive contributions.

HOME, FAMILY, COMMUNITY

In reviewing studies of the juvenile delinquency problem, probably the clearest picture that emerges is the difficulties commonly inherent in the home situation. Now in commenting upon juvenile delinquency, it must be remembered that our information pertains almost exclusively to youngsters who have been apprehended and appear for disposition before public authority. Furthermore, in pointing up the shortcomings of the family setting in which so many of these young offenders have been reared, we are often uninformed as to the number of children who, confronted by identical handicaps, have made "go" of social living.

Withal, there appears to be a consistent pattern of deprivation, which I believe any fair-minded person would agree creates a real hazard to the growing child.

There are social handicaps which exert a real pressure upon youngsters from underprivileged neighborhoods; overcrowded, unhealthy tenement living, discrimination, grinding poverty, lack of recreation facilities, an atmosphere of crime in the very air they breathe. But as Prof. Gordon Allport, of Harvard University, has observed (175, introduction), it is the emotional tone of the home, not the plumbing, that is likely to prove a decisive determinant of juvenile delinquency.

We may be on the threshold of a greater understanding of the nature of this disorder. Prof. Sheldon Glueck and Dr. Eleanor Glueck believe they have developed a technique for recognizing, by the characteristics of family psychology, just which children are growing up in the most hazardous surroundings. If their predictive measures prove reliable, we could ascertain in advance precisely which children (and which families) are in need of preventive services—before serious trouble ever develops.

Many delinquent children have parents who can truly be said to poison the atmosphere of the home. Marital conflict between the parents is common, indeed one authority suggests that tensions in a home where the parents are deeply dissatisfied with one another are more injurious to children than a broken home would be (28). But studies of comparable groups of children have shown there are close to twice as many from broken homes in the delinquent as in the nondelinquent group (28). The Gluecks' recent research found I delinquent in 4 came from families where self-interest exceeded group interest; this was true of less than 1 in 100 children in their nondelinquent control group (67).

Children who turn up as delinquents are also more likely to have been set a criminal example at home. The study mentioned above, showed delinquents twice as likely as nondelinquents to have had a father, brother, or sister already in conflict with the law—and three times as likely to have had a mother with a criminal record (67). Another researcher reporting on youths discharged from a truant school but subsequently charged with felonies, found 4 out of 5 were reared in families in which another member had a criminal record (28).

Parents' attitudes toward children, and children's conceptions of their parents differ significantly in comparable groups of delinquents and nondelinquents.

The Gluecks report 60 percent of their delinquents felt their fathers were indifferent or hostile; this was true of only 1 in 5 among the nondelinquents (226).

Delinquents felt their mothers were not deeply concerned about their welfare in 8 cases out of 10; only 3 mothers out of 10 among the nondelinquents (226). Of the groups studied, one-fifth of the mothers worked, mothers of delinquents as well as mothers of nondelinquents. Nevertheless while 7 mothers of delinquents in 10 were found giving "wholly unsuitable" supervision to their sons, among the nonedlinquent boys,[2] only 1 mother in 10 failed in this respect (226).

I do not wish to bog down in statistics, but mention ought to be made of one more highly illuminating inquiry. Close to 20 years ago a volume was published examining the differences between delinquents and nondelinquent youngsters reared in the same houses and families. Healy and Bronner (86) reported that the nondelinquents found home relationships more satisfying than delinquents in the same family did. And seven times as many delinquent children were found to have had emotional disturbances in their relations with others, mostly in the home. The delinquents were unhappy, discontented youngsters, shortchanged in some fashion as compared with their own non-delinquent brothers and sisters.

The same story is repeated by child-guidance workers, police, probation officers, social workers, teachers, pastors. The child who becomes a delinquent is more likely than not to come from a home where he is neglected, rejected, or subject to harsh and even unjust punishment. In a large proportion of cases, one parent is missing; and when both parents are in the home, in case after case it has been found the child is suffering because of continual bickering or open violence between father and mother.

In situations such as these, and where parental discipline is irregular or completely neglected, the child will tend to strike out for himself. And there is every likelihood he will strike out in the wrong direction.

It is only with the very greatest rarity that a thorough examination of the life history of a detected delinquent will fail to uncover pressures (psychological or social) which may reasonably be regarded as the roots of maladjustment.

In our understanding of particular situations, there is undoubtedly a certain gap between the commonly accepted causative factors and delinquent acts on the part of an individual. Nonetheless, certain social situations can with considerable assurance be said to constitute fertile soil for delinquency.

To recapitulate, these are: rejection, tyranny, abuse, frustration, failure, limitation of opportunity, conflict of cultures.

A child can grow into a socially integrated adult even in a home where a brother or sister is shown preference. A child can grow into a socially integrated adult even though deprived of a parent's love. A child can grow into a socially integrated adult despite discrimination by reason of race. A child can grow into a socially integrated adult despite slum environment with all its deprivations. Even a child who is brutally abused, or punished unjustly can grow into a socially integrated adult.

It is most important that these facts not be ignored. But we do know that a cumulation of deprivation and destructive experiences leaves a mark. The child reared under such conditions is in hazard; where the negative forces multiply, the hazard is increased.

Frequent mention will be made in this report of the situation of children and youth in deteriorated or deteriorating neighborhoods. Let it be clearly understood at the outset that delinquents are found in families more fortunately circumstanced as well.

It is a fact that the larger part of our juvenile court cases come from among the poorest segment of the city's population. It seems most likely that this is due to lack of home and neighborhood advantages (material, social, and phychological). But another consideration is fashions in delinquent behavior, which may have the outcome of more crimes of a violent character, say, in one sort of neighborhood and more crimes of stealth in another. Finally, there are the very important differentials in financial ability of parents to make private arrangements for the care and treatment of problem youngsters.

Ours is a Nation dedicated to the proposition that all people should be accorded an equal opportunity to make their way in the world, that a man should be judged on his merits. Reflect upon the measure of our failure if I report that an out-

---

[2] Juvenile court records list 3 or 4 times as many boys as girls, however girls' social histories reflect similar problems. In my own report, "boys," in most instances may also be read "children."

standing scholar in the field contends that "the permanent factor which perhaps contributes more than any other to the creation of delinquency (is) bad housing." As it happens, our achievements in this field and the nature of the road ahead lie beyond the province of this report. But I would like to add one more homely example of the kind of environmental pressures affecting children in New York, 1955. A well-informed official [3] estimates on the basis of reported cases that in our city some 25,000 human beings—mostly babies—are bitten by rats every year. It is hardly necessary to ask oneself how such an occurrence affects the outlook on life of the victim—and his family.

Perhaps one final note on environmental deprivations will suffice. This story is told by a social worker who has a most distinguished record of service over the decades in some of our more underprivileged neighborhoods:

"(There are neighborhoods characterized by) acceptance of the inevitability of adult crime, juvenile delinquency * * * racial tensions, gang warfare * * *. In such a neighborhood I was told by a 15-year-old boy who had just stabbed another boy with a penknife, that 'you could get a good paid job sticking people if you got good at it.' That was 25 years ago, and that neighborhood is worse today, not better. The bootleggers of prohibition have given way to the narcotics pushers."

PUNISHMENT AND REFORM

In devising programs to meet the challenge of juvenile delinquency, we are confronted with a major dilemma of approach at the outset. Many would subscribe to the philosophy of a social agency which has been notably successful in its work with every sort of delinquent over a period of more than 50 years:

"The delinquent (is) primarily a products of social forces, of disorganized homes and unhealthy neighborhood conditions. He is in the main a deprived youngster whose emotional needs have been insufficiently satisfied. His behavior is a reaction to his life experience."

Others contend that a crime is a crime and that anyone not a mental incompetent should be made to answer for his actions. They contend that a "sentimental" approach is interpreted as weakness on the part of society, that punishment is the sure deterrent.

But the facts simply do not support this latter view.

"* * * in all the reliable 20th century studies on the causation of delinquency and crime, it is almost impossible to find a reference to leniency of punishment as a cause. * * * The history of punishment shows that there is no necessary correlation between the severity of punishment and the incidence of crime. * * *"

There would seem to be a need to steer a sure course between what most thoughtful citizens might characterize as the "sentimental" and the "revenge" approaches to this question. Mr. Justice Cardozo many years ago observed that the justice due the offender is due the community as well. Law is the adhesive that binds our society together; it is not to be violated lightly.

Actually, the most "moderate" of the experts in the field seem to feel that punishment can play a constructive role in rehabilitation, if it is applied planfully and for helpful rather than vengeful purposes. Unfortunately, many people believe that juvenile delinquency is the evil fruit of a "spare the rod" philosophy. There certainly can be no doubt that there are children who, as a result of having been spoiled, are completely regardless of the rights of others. A larger group of juvenile delinquents, however, and a group more typical of these problem youngsters by and large, have experienced punishment—and corporal punishment at that. They have probably had too much such treatment, rather than too little.

Recent studies show that one-fifth to one-third of all our nondelinquent children and young people experience physical punishment at home. A study of delinquent children on the other hand, shows twice as many receiving physical punishment. The superintendent of a midwestern reform school remarked to a visiting journalist that he used the paddle because 90 percent of his boys reported they'd been whipped at home. And the reporter [4] very acutely observed that "apparently whipping failed to act as a deterrent for 90 percent of the boys who ended up in this institution. It seems to me that there is a lesson here to reflect upon as we proceed with our planning.

---

[3] Charles Abrams.
[4] Albert Deutsch.

In my own thinking, I would be inclined to go along with the joint public-private service bureau which operates in the offices of our district attorneys. This organization contends that even youthful offenders should not be regarded as completely helpless victims of social forces. The offender has played an important part in whatever train of events has culminated in his conflict with the law. And he has a part to play—in a very real sense, an independent part—in the process of finding a constructive place for himself in the world.

"Nobody can mold anybody else's character because a human is not a lump of putty. He is a living being—he grows * * *. The impulses which may have taken a vicious form and brought boys into conflict with authority are basically the energies of life. It is within the realm of the possible to redirect these energies so that they will no longer destroy but instead serve the better interests of (young people) and of society * * *. (This redirection) is an achievement of the youth himself. His counsellors help by making his problem clearer to him, by encouragement and suggestion. But when the change takes place, it is the individual concerned who makes the effort."

Before proceeding to discussion of the particular programs I have suggested for high-priority consideration, a few more general observations may not be out of order.

RECIDIVISM

While I shall not discuss the matter at length in this report, the problem of repeated delinquency, unreformed offenders, is a crucial one. When a wrong-doer is caught, society has an opportunity—in cases where he is not executed or imprisoned for life—to set him on the right path. The ultimate test of correctionel institutions is the recidivism rate; do offenders reform, or does the correctional treatment leave them uncorrected.

There is beginning to be a highly illuminating body of literature in answer to that question. And some people may be surprised to learn that in study after study of juvenile delinquents, it is the institutions with the social workers, the psychologists, the special teachers—the institutions that talk about "trying to understand and help each boy"—it is these institutions that prove to have the smaller proportion of children reappearing in our courts and police stations.

Nationwide studies, studies in Chicago and in Boston, show that 6 delinquents in 10 (in some places more), turn up again, following institutionalization. But 2 really treatment-oriented centers here in New York report less than 3 in 10 of their boys turn up in court after being released. Dr. Frank Curran (who served the New York City children's courts as a psychiatrist at Bellevue Hospital) reports that of his first 300 juvenile cases there,[5] only 1 in 10 had reappeared in the courts for antisocial acts, 1½ to 2 years later.

In the case of those who have to be removed from circulation for a period, the case seems clear. Our interest is cutting down on delinquent behavior for the sake of the community, and with an eye to a useful, satisfying, socially accepted life for the adjudged delinquent. If our interest in short is rehabilitation rather than vengeance we are now in a position to say that reeducation must go on alongside the temporary loss of liberty that the offender must not merely be punished but counseled and helped. Of "correction" and correctional institutions it is truly possible to say "by their fruits ye shall know them."

A "HARD CORE" OF JUVENILE DELINQUENCY?

Our city is growing; there is an ever larger crop of youngsters entering the delinquency-hazard age bracket, 5–20 years.[6]

In 1950 one-fifth of our population fell into this age group. But by 1960, with the war babies and the postwar babies growing up, 1 New Yorker in every 4 will be between 5 and 20.[7]

If juvenile delinquency is a problem now, we really have something to insure against, with regard to the future. For if the delinquency rate were to stop rising, if we could merely hold our own, the number of delinquents in the larger youth population—at the present delinquency rate (roughly 2½ percent)—would by 1960 stand 9,000 higher than the present figure.

---

[5] In 85 percent of which, the courts concurred with psychiatric counsel.
[6] If 5 seems a tender age to list as the lower limit, I might mention the fact that in the Gluecks research, more than 44 percent of their 500 delinquents displayed clear signs of antisocial behavior between the ages of 5 and 7.
[7] City Planning Commission estimates.

A possibly fruitful line of inquiry in determining just where preventive services might most suitably be directed, is suggested by two recent studies in St. Paul, Minn. and in San Mateo County (around San Francisco). This research concentrated on the proportion of social problems presented by a relatively small number of families in each community. The San Mateo report, for example, reported that 1,267 families, only 1½ percent of the total number, accounted for every (detected and reported) case of juvenile misbehavior as well as about half of the petty crimes and misdemeanors in the whole community. Findings along the same lines are reported by parallel welfare research projects in Maryland and Minnesota.

If our own youth-board data are analyzed along roughly the same lines, focussing upon the relatively small number of delinquents who appear on the register more than once, a figure for New York of the same order of magnitude is suggested. The hard core of the juvenile delinquency problem may well be found in just a few thousand families here, out of a total of close to a million families with children aged 5 to 20.

A study of the actual dimensions of this small but crucial aspect of the problem may open the way to new approaches to the challenge of delinquency. The idea certainly seems worthy of the most serious consideration in our overall planning. But it must be well understood that working with the segment of the population considered here means working with those presenting the thorniest problems: people often demoralized, hopeless, long and deeply entangled in a multitude of social problems, people often suspicious and hostile toward both officials and social agencies. These are the uncooperative, the unresponsive, the cases with poor prospects. But they are people who badly need help, and people who present a formidable problem to the community at large, draining resources from a variety of channels both as criminals and as chronic dependents. The particular group to which I refer includes families known at one time or another to a very large number of welfare agencies. It cannot in any sense be regarded as identical with the welfare department caseload, the overwhelming majority of whom are good citizens dependent through no fault of their own.

CONSERVING PUBLIC FUNDS

In considering which programs we should underwrite, there is an important word to be said about conserving public funds. For one thing, our endeavor should be to channel what money we do have into programs where the largest possible proportion of it gets to the firing line.

We should, however, be prepared to reexamine operations that seem promising, after a time has passed. Careful assessment and factfinding programs should be built into our various activities in this area, as we embark upon them.[8] This is a task calling for scientific know-how, it cannot be adequately handled by mere administrative procedure. I am therefore recommending an overall coordinated study project in addition to factfinding in particular agencies.

To undertake a course of action without a positive knowledge that it will succeed is unfortunately a not-uncommon necessity. In our present situation we cannot mark time. But to muddle along indefinitely without even trying to ascertain whether we were moving in the direction of a solution, would be unpardonable. "Practice cannot and should not wait upon research, nor should research be delayed until practice is well established. We shall be most likely to discover how to prevent delinquency if research is undertaken coordinately with the development of new measures and the refinement of old ones, if research and practice are conceived as inseparable parts of a single process."

PRIORITY PROGRAMS

A thorough-going preventive program that would attack juvenile delinquency at the most basic level might include operations having to do with housing, employment, family living standards, social discrimination. And even the most ambitious program, we must realize, can be expected rather to diminish delinquency than to abolish it. We are no more likely completely to prevent delinquency than we are to abolish adult crime.

---

[8] Note in this connection the youth board's research project to find out whether we can spot delinquents before they get into trouble, and how effective our help proves to be. This is a follow-up on the Gluecks' study mentioned above.

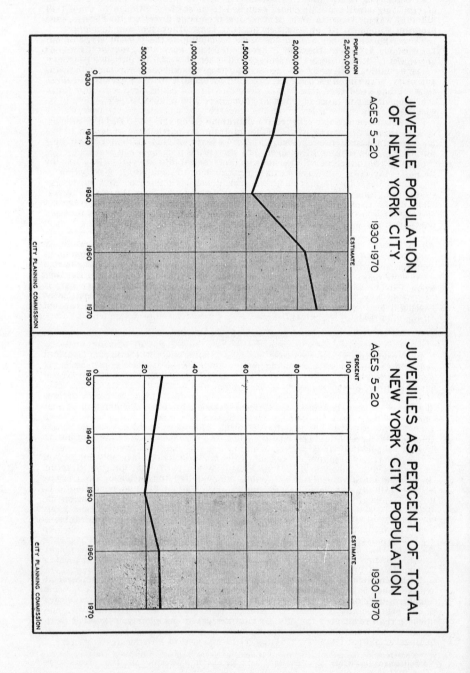

JUVENILE POPULATION
OF NEW YORK CITY

AGES 5-20   1930-1970

JUVENILES AS PERCENT OF TOTAL
NEW YORK CITY POPULATION

AGES 5-20   1930-1970

In presenting these priority programs, then, I am proposing merely a number of relatively small-scale projects, designed to meet the challenge in some very different ways. All seem to be pointed in a promising direction; in a sense, each program stands on its own, but in another sense, they are complementary. These approaches are among the more promising at the present stage of our knowledge. I present them in a firm belief they have the greatest likelihood of success. But even those that seem the most sensible offer no gilt-edge guaranty.

For example, I am endorsing recreation programs through our public housing authority, in the public scools, through the youth board (private agency contracts, etc.). I have endorsed these three programs in the belief they will offer indispensible services to large numbers of youngsters who might otherwise have to do without.

But we cannot depend upon recreation alone to do the job. Despite our best wishes, there are complications: (1) Children can participate at length in the the best of recreation programs, yet have plenty of time in odd hours to get into mischief, if they're so inclined; (2) recreation programs can reach half the children, three-quarters of the children in a neighborhood, yet fail to include precisely the ones who are headed for trouble. I can recall one authority remarking upon the fact that he never had known a member of a particular youth organization to have turned up as a delinquent. Now, he meant to call attention to the value of the organization in preventing delinquency, but he may actually have only pointed out that the organization simply failed to reach the kind of boy who got into trouble.

I have digressed to point out the possible weaknesses of a kind of program in which I really have great faith. My intention was not a confuse the issue but to bring to the reader's attention the very imprecise state of our knowledge as to what may really serve to cut down on delinquency. Every one of the 10 priority programs detailed in the following pages has already been well tried in the field and seems to be meeting a vital need. I am convinced that neither parent education, nor club work, nor school programs, nor youth police alone can solve our problem. Together, however, they piece our a fairly inclusive pattern of attack upon the variety of anti-social acts we call juvenile delinquency.

Recreation and community programs in public housing

Some 78,000 child live in only 27 of New York's public housing projects. In order to provide for full utilization of existing community recreation facilities in these buildings, I have recommended adoption of a $203,513 per annum staffing program developed with the collaboration of Chairman Philip Cruise of the housing authority. This, I am happy to say, was appropriated March 25, 1955.

Six facilities will be operated as extensions of settlement house programs, two by the authority itself, 19 by the bureau of community education of our public schools.

Asked for his reaction to this proposal, Professor Sheldon Glueck of the Harvard Law School, regarded my many as probably the foremost authority on juvenile delinquency wrote:

"I think you are definitely working in the right direction. My only suggestion as to the budget request is that perhaps it would point out that the proposed community facilities could be of value not only for the children, but for the parents. One of the basic differences between delinquents and nondelinquents is the relative infrequency with which the families of the former engage in group recreation. The provision of leadership for the proposed community centers should stimulate the restoration of a long lost and highly social value—family-group recreational activities both in and out of the centers.

Another suggestion that might strengthen the appeal of the budget requests would be that the proposed community centers might also be used as places where troubled parents could go for consultations and guidance regarding the emotional and behavioral problems of children. It could be provided, in collaboration with child guidance clinics, to have such consultation services supplied once or twice a week at the centers."

These additional facilities will be made available as fast as this program can be put into operation. It should be noted that the cost of year-round program in these centers all over the city, serving 191,400 of our citizens (78,000 of them children) [9] is relatively insignificant, in view of the kind of job we know can be done by skilled leaders. These services (housed in already available plant)

---

[9] To these should be added those served in the surrounding neighborhood.

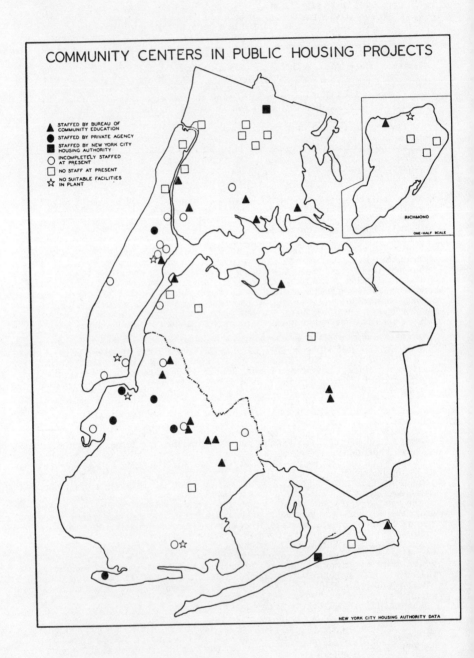

COMMUNITY CENTERS IN PUBLIC HOUSING PROJECTS

▲ STAFFED BY BUREAU OF
   COMMUNITY EDUCATION
● STAFFED BY PRIVATE AGENCY
■ STAFFED BY NEW YORK CITY
   HOUSING AUTHORITY
○ INCOMPLETELY STAFFED
   AT PRESENT
□ NO STAFF AT PRESENT
☆ NO SUITABLE FACILITIES
   IN PLANT

RICHMOND
ONE-HALF SCALE

NEW YORK CITY HOUSING AUTHORITY DATA

will cost the city no more than the operating expense of a single large-scale facility which would hardly be in a position to provide for so large a number.

This program, a beginning, should be followed by like programs in other public housing projects on a selective neighborhood need basis. Provision of staffs for middle-income projects, for example, is presently under consideration.

Remedial reading

Reading retardation is one of the special handicaps often associated with juvenile delinquency. The retarded reader is unable to meet other children on equal terms since he is materially handicapped in the area of activity that consumes the largest single block of his waking hours. As he moves into the higher grades ability to read becomes essential to any other kind of learning—textbooks and other printed material become the major tool.

The child who can't make a "go" of things in school gets more and more into a rut of failure and frustration. He becomes insecure, hostile, rebellious. A midwestern school official writes:

"As to the question of relationship between reading disability and what is called juvenile delinquency, there is no question in my mind. When children are required to perform with textbooks for 5 hours of the day, they have to be at least moderately successful. When they are not, the tension and strain of fruitless effort, aggravated by the censure of the school, becomes intolerable and the kids will compensate. They may do so by heaving rocks through windows or punching other kids, but when these outlets pale they have to move on to more spectacular and undesirable behavior * * * Problem children who have been given reading skills generally cease to be behavior problems when they are released from the clinics."

The bureau of child guidance in our own public-school system estimates that:

"Two-thirds of the children referred (for problems of various sorts) show some degree of retardation in reading * * * fully one-fifth show a severe reading handicap * * * It is highly probable that the proportion of children with reading handicaps among * * * truants and delinquents would prove to be higher than 20 percent * * * systematized individual and small-group instruction for these children often overcomes this handicap and reestablishes a degree of confidence in themselves which can do much to facilitate their readjustment."

The board of education personnel who know this field agree that: "failure in reading accounts more than any other single factor for behavior problems, truancy, and general school failure."

Chief Justice John Warren Hill of our children's court contends: "It has been shown conclusively that there is a definite link between * * * reading-retardation and delinquency." Reading difficulties were reported for 75 percent of the delinquents in the nonschool part of children's court; of the boys in detention at Youth House, 85 percent are handicapped by being unable to read books appropriate to their grade in school.[10]

This is no small scale challenge. As of 4 years ago, 35 percent of our students entering academic high schools and 80 percent of those entering vocational high schools were a year or more retarded in reading (joint State-city study).

In June 1954, 20,000 New York City children, from the fourth to the sixth grade alone, showed a reading retardation of 2 years or more.

More than half of 55,000 New York City eighth graders examined a few years ago were below grade in reading ability, and 1 in 5 failed even to score at sixth grade level.

Our public schools are presently providing "remedial reading teachers" for less than 20 percent of the children who are handicapped by major reading disabilities. Four children in five have to "make do" with regular classroom resources.

Only 117 of 553 grade schools have a "remedial reading teacher." There is no developed program, centrally staffed for the junior high schools. Any remedial reading work in the high school is strictly on the initiative of the individual principal.

In grade schools the "remedial reading teachers" (who have helped many children and are a source of valuable counsel to other teachers) are almost all regular classroom personnel who have had 2 weeks of in-service training.[11]

---

[10] This compares with Traxler's study indicating only 10 percent of the Nation's school population requires special help because of retardation in reading.
[11] It should be recognized that many have gone on to secure certain training beyond the minimum.

Authorities outside our school system feel that it takes a year's or 2 years' training to acquire real competence in coping with the variety of problems presented by retarded readers.

Although reading retardation is commonly associated with emotional problems, it is the rare case served by remedial reading staff in which the bureau of child guidance is also involved.

There is an urgent need for expansion of the volume of remedial teaching available in our schools.[12] And there is a need, too, for adding a number of fully qualified specialists to provide intensive services for children with major conflicts in their approach to school work. The coaching job that present staff contributes is a creditable one, but there are many cases where coaching is not enough.

Reading disability is most commonly associated with boredom with school and general maladjustment. While native intelligence is about the same for both boys and girls, reading retardation (like delinquent behavior) is found far more commonly in boys. Since there is good reason to presume that emotional rather than purely intellectual obstacles are involved, service in this field cannot be carried on single-handed by classroom teachers, no matter what in-service helps are made available to them. Wherever a remedial reading operation is offered, it realistically must provide for adequate social work and psychological services on a "built-in" basis. Employment of such personnel should not be at the expense of bureau of child guidance services.

To place on remedial reading teacher in every school having 30 or more eligible children would require at least 100 additional positions. If fully qualified specialists are not recruited for this work, there should at least be a psychologist and a social worker as consultants to the reading teachers; 1 such team with each of the 24 assistant superintendents.[13]

Superintendent of Schools Jansen is agreed on the importance of focusing efforts upon reading. As a matter of fact, an attack upon reading problems has been chosen by the school authorities as a No. 1 objective for the next academic year.

The board of education budgeted expansion centers about an imaginative summer program (integrating coaching in reading with a recreation approach) and "reading clinics" so small as to be of a demonstration character. The two undertakings combined were budgeted at $48,000, scarcely more than one one-hundredth of 1 percent of next year's school expenditures. A larger commitment would seem desirable. I would in fact go beyond the board of education's modest request. So vital do I consider this activity that I would strongly urge at least 150 added reading teachers and specialists, and combined summer reading and recreation programs on a substantial scale. A start should be made promptly.[14]

Police services and juvenile delinquency

I have reviewed with Police Commissioner Adams the role of the police in meeting the challenge of juvenile delinquency. We see eye to eye on the importance of adequate provisions for law enforcement. Our city must dedicate itself to a reign of law and order, and youth who think they are outside limitations which the rest of society accepts have got to learn the facts of life.

But the law does not survive by force alone. And the police have a real contribution to make beyond deterrence, enforcement, apprehension, detection. We are returning to the good days of "the officer on the beat," and the police officer on the beat is as likely a man as any to know just which kids are headed for trouble. There are situations where a friendly interest will "turn the trick," others where a judicious word to parents will help set a youngster straight.

In some situations, however, a good deal more than incidental interest or a few well-chosen words are called for. And while force may clamp down the lid for a while, I am convinced it can never solve problems in the long run. There are boys, and girls, too, who can be set straight even after the first transgression. But setting them straight may take more time than an officer on street patrol can give, and oftentimes a little highly specialized understanding is needed as well. This is, I believe, where a police unit such as the juvenile aid bureau could come into the picture.

---

[12] At present, despite an increase in the number of pupils, the number of "remedial reading teachers" is one-fifth lower than it was in 1947.
[13] At present there are no such personnel at all assigned to this program.
[14] The cost of the program outlined above would be about $750,000 per annum. This, however, does not provide more than one teacher for schools having large numbers of retarded readers.

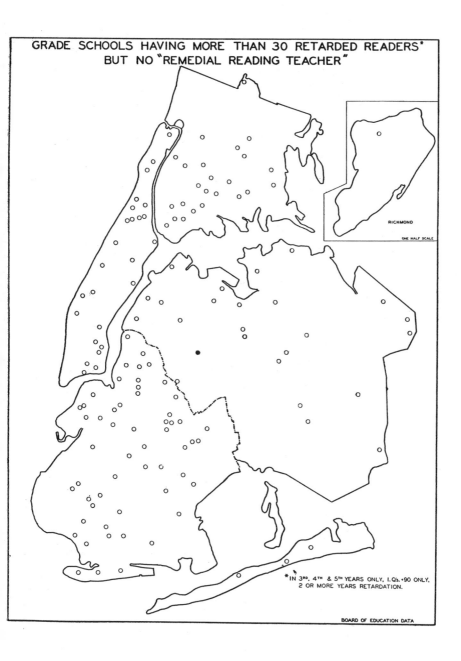

GRADE SCHOOLS HAVING MORE THAN 30 RETARDED READERS*
BUT NO "REMEDIAL READING TEACHER"

RICHMOND

ONE HALF SCALE

*IN 3ᴿᴰ, 4ᵀᴴ & 5ᵀᴴ YEARS ONLY, I.Q's. -90 ONLY,
2 OR MORE YEARS RETARDATION.

BOARD OF EDUCATION DATA

Replying to an inquiry in 1952, of members of the International Association of Chiefs of Police, every one of the 20 reporting for American cities of over 500,000 population had officers of whom special qualifications were required, assigned to work with juveniles. These are policemen who can make social investigations of sorts, as well as criminal investigations. All our great cities have special policemen and policewomen who understand young people, who can be friendly and who can be firm—police who bring to their assignment a groundwork in psychology—officers who know which agencies in the community are best in a position to help a youngster headed for trouble, before catastrophe engulfs him.[15] This mission involves something more than surveillance of bars and dancehalls.

Our own juvenile aid bureau personnel must all have served at least a year in the precincts; almost all of them have had special schooling in the social sciences. This arm of the force has a vital job to do in explaining the law and the police to young troublemakers. JAB patrolmen are in a position to make immeasurably easier the job of the pastor, the settlement club leader, the school-teacher—yes, and the parent.[16]

JAB followups on juveniles not arrested (probably the major service JAB renders the rest of the force) were up by 19 percent last year. But during the same period, personnel available for service in the field dropped by 2 percent.

JAB at present is without units in almost half the divisions in the city.[17] From sunset to dawn the Bureau is such a skeleton that there is practically no JAB. If we were to staff our JAB to a level where half the cities in the country were ahead of us in number of juvenile officers per 100,000 population, JAB strength would be 280. I hope New York eventually will be above average.

Commissioner Adams recognizes the valuable work done by JAB officers. The accompanying map, showing incidence of youth offenses in the city of New York, is based upon data supplied by JAB from its records and knowledge of conditions.[18] But the commissioner and top level police department staff do not feel that they have sufficient adequate and reliable data on the work of JAB and youth patrolmen to warrant a present citywide expansion of such forces. Where adult crime has dropped sharply as a result of the experiment in providing a larger number of officers to particular precincts, a corresponding result has, at least outwardly, been evident in juvenile offenses in the same areas. The commissioner is convinced that he must, in justice to his duty to the city, concentrate on basic police protection problems. Yet he is sufficiently convinced of the inseparable interrelationship of youthful offenses and criminal activities generally, not to abandon the work of the JAB and youth patrolmen at this time.

Commissioner Adams and I have agreed that the work of the JAB[19] should be put to an intensive test and study in, say, 4 areas in which the incidence of juvenile offenses is greatest. Controlled observation of results is planned over a period of 5 years (a maximum figure). The roles of both JAB and youth patrolmen in the police department are presently undergoing review and appraisal. This control period will permit an evaluation on which to base conclusions for citywide expansion, or a transfer of this phase of community work to some other agency. Such experimentation and close observation will cost less than an overall program in this field for the entire city.

I believe that while Commissioner Adams' experiment is in progress, provision should be made for enlisting the services of civilian specialists to make available to the Department useful approaches from related fields. Mr. Adams is, of course, interested in evaluating the effectiveness of a youth-police operation that is no "strawman." I know that he will cooperate in every way with the professors on the overall assessment unit which will integrate factfinding with reference to operations of all agencies working in the juvenile deliquency field.

---

[15] Every one of the units in cities of over 500,000 population is affiliated with at least one community planning or coordinating agency (such as welfare and health council).

[16] I believe that specially trained police personnel can make a unique contribution in working directly with parents, perhaps on a block-by-block basis. But a program along such lines may have to be deferred pending completion of the study process mentioned below.

[17] Juvenile aid bureau units are assigned responsibilities which cover the entire city. However, as JAB is not organized on a divisional basis, most units must serve two or more divisions, regardless of the division in which they are located.

[18] Comparisons are in terms of the number of actions per precinct. These figures are not adjusted for differences in the size of youth population, which varies from precinct to precinct; delinquency statistics computed "per 1,000 youth" are presented on the map showing youth board data.

[19] With which should, I believe, be combined that of the youth patrolmen.

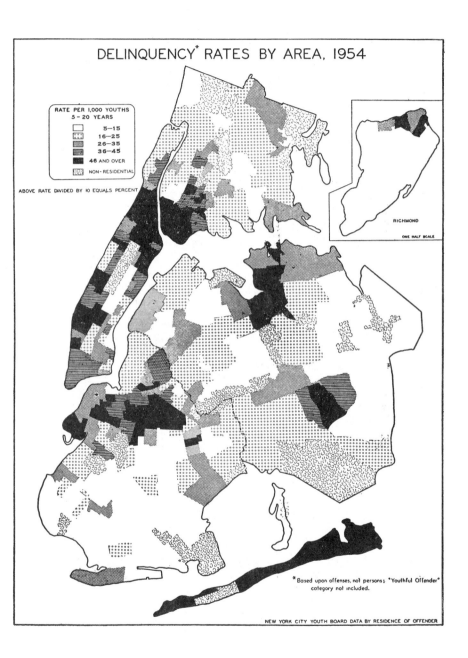

DELINQUENCY* RATES BY AREA, 1954

RATE PER 1,000 YOUTHS
5 - 20 YEARS

5—15
16—25
26—35
36—45
46 AND OVER
NON-RESIDENTIAL

ABOVE RATE DIVIDED BY 10 EQUALS PERCENT

RICHMOND
ONE HALF SCALE

* Based upon offenses, not persons; "Youthful Offender"
category not included.

NEW YORK CITY YOUTH BOARD DATA BY RESIDENCE OF OFFENDER

Narcotics

I regret to report that while drug addicts have disappeared (or have been pretty well driven underground) in our schools, there is every reason to believe that narcotics still represent a major problem in the juvenile field and addiction is on the increase.[20] A large majority of our youthful drug users come from neighborhoods where narcotics are more readily available and represent the poorest educated youths. Interestingly enough, it appears that although most of the addicts are found in high delinquency areas, there are certain areas of equally high delinquency where drug use has not spread to any great extent.

Researchers report taht while there are more delinquencies for profit in high drug use areas, the increase in delinquency as a whole (and in felonies) has been no greater in high drug use than in low use areas. Indications are that gang membership (as such) by and large does not lead to addiction. Furthermore, education regarding the effects of drugs has proved effective in the cases of children reached before the critical age; by the time a boy is 16, it may already be too late. There is every reason to believe that such factual information serves an especially useful purpose when provided to youth in the areas where drugs are in any case more readily available.

The board of education a couple of years ago provided the schools with curriculum materials on drugs for grades 7-12. Consideration might well be given to doing some of this teaching in the 6th grade as well, to reach more children approaching their 14th year.

There appear to be no particular measures indicated at this time which are not already being applied. Research still in progress, however, may point to new programs. We have a demonstration program at Riverside Hospital to provide special treatment and followup care to teen-age addicts. An evaluative study of this project will be undertaken very shortly, to report to the community on what has been learned there and what is being accomplished.

Youth board street clubs and casework services

The New York City Youth Board has been doing a notable job with predelinquent and delinquent youth who seemed too tough for any other agency to handle. Developing from a pilot project sponsored by welfare council, the council of street clubs, now provides a corps of specially trained, highly skilled group workers who maintain a continuing contact with some 22 teen-age gangs.

As a result of the patient efforts of the social group workers, youths who were prone to street fighting and even more serious crime are now moving in the direction of running successful social affairs and building their reputation in a more socially acceptable fashion.

Make no mistake, this work is difficult and sometimes disappointing. Boys who have been embittered by school failure, poverty, and social discrimination, who have acquired their learning from hard tutors in the streets, do not become little gentlemen overnight. It is just as well we recognize this so that no impossible demands for window dressing "progress" reports confront this staff. They are walking a tortuous road, but there have been some notable achievements.

Among the groups reached by this work, "gang wars" are virtually ancient history. But the same cannot be said of other clubs in the same or other neighborhoods, for whom we have not provided helpful leaders. To "pal around" with the boys, to help arrange activities, to smooth school relations, more leaders are needed.

The youth board proposes doubling the number of street clubs served in the present project areas; extension of service to other neighborhoods in equal volume is also suggested. I strongly recommend that every cent requested for this work be appropriated without delay.

There are precious few private agencies willing to undertake the difficult area the youth board has cut out for itself. There is no agency in a position to carry this work through on the scale of the youth board operation. Their leaders have the spirit, the will, and the know-how; money is needed to quadruple staff on this operation. It means reaching directly a pretty obstreperous sector of youth, some of them before they get into serious trouble.

The street clubs project needs an increase of $508,000 by 1957-58. The youth board can indicate by how much it is in a position to expand operations this next year.

---

[20] Juvenile drug arrests were up 30 percent in 1954. However, this may in some degree reflect the availability of a larger number of enforcement personnel. Commissioner Adams has been adding to the drug squad for some time and three times as many men are now on the job as compared with 1951. New York owes its welfare council a salute for sounding a danger signal several years ago.

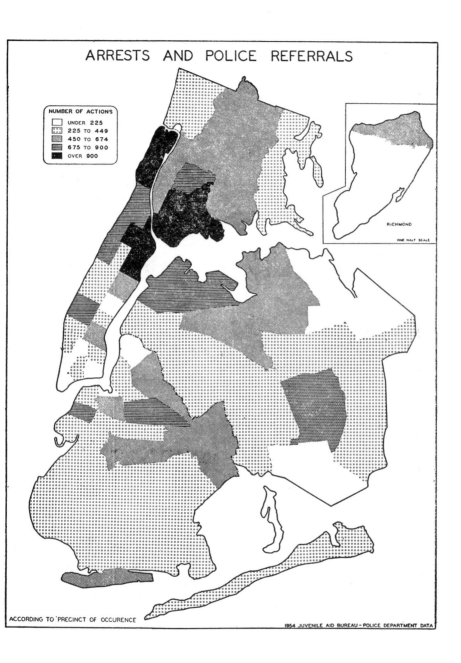

ARRESTS AND POLICE REFERRALS

NUMBER OF ACTIONS

☐ UNDER 225
▦ 225 TO 449
▧ 450 TO 674
▨ 675 TO 900
■ OVER 900

RICHMOND

ONE HALF SCALE

ACCORDING TO PRECINCT OF OCCURENCE

1954 JUVENILE AID BUREAU - POLICE DEPARTMENT DATA

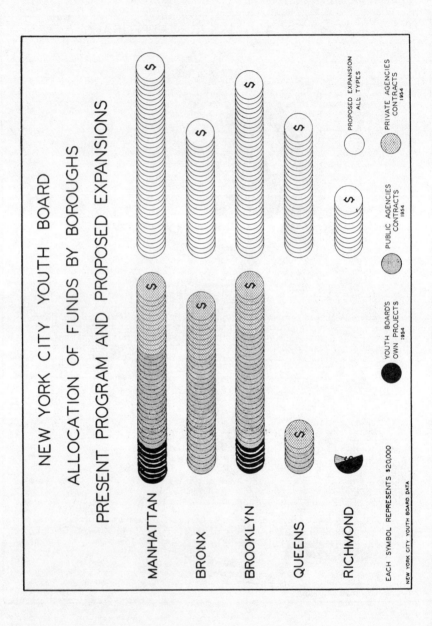

NEW YORK CITY YOUTH BOARD

ALLOCATION OF FUNDS BY BOROUGHS

PRESENT PROGRAM AND PROPOSED EXPANSIONS

MANHATTAN

BRONX

BROOKLYN

QUEENS

RICHMOND

YOUTH BOARD'S OWN PROJECTS 1954

PUBLIC AGENCIES CONTRACTS 1954

PRIVATE AGENCIES CONTRACTS 1954

PROPOSED EXPANSION ALL TYPES

EACH SYMBOL REPRESENTS $20,000

NEW YORK CITY YOUTH BOARD DATA

To back up the street club workers, the youth board is ready to recruit social caseworkers and even psychiatrists who are prepared to work on the street, in poolrooms, in the back of a store, where these youth are to be found. Many have problems of adjustment, employment problems, other needs beyond the skills of their group leaders. In some instances, a good counselor can be of real help not only to the boy but in straightening out a difficult family situation as well.

There is a crying need in this city for a corps of specialists in personal and family problems who are willing and able to go out to people who need help instead of sitting in an office waiting for clients. The youth board services to families and children has demonstrated over a period of time that it is up to this job and has the will to carry it through.

An increase of $270,000 by 1957–58 has been requested. Here, too, there is virtually no other agency to provide the service.

I strongly recommend that these funds be granted. However, I suggest that a clear statement be obtained from the youth board as to what proportion of this program will be earmarked for services to adolescents and their families. This work to date has been focused around 9-year olds, and while that service sector should unquestionably be supported and extended, there is a crying need for work with the older group as well.

I think our city can take real pride in the pioneer job the street-club project and the services for families and children are doing. I have seen the letters of inquiry the youth board has received from other cities contemplating similar programs, the letters from overseas, as well. We are charting a new path of service to those who need it most; this is an approach to some of the very thorniest problems in the whole welfare field. And it is an approach that seems to pay off.

Providing comprehensive youth board services in three additional areas

The youth board's comprehensive juvenile delinquency index, which includes all police and court reports,[21] shows that in addition to the 11 neighborhoods in which program is presently concentrated, 3 new areas have passed the critical point. Funds should be allocated without delay for putting into Chelsea, part of Long Island City and northern Staten Island the full battery of case work, group work, and recreation services which already are contributing so largely to stemming of the tide of delinquency in other high-hazard neighborhoods.

Right now, in Chelsea, for example, the private agencies are making a real effort to cope with an increase in delinquency, but the problem is simply beyond their resources. There are large numbers of teen-agers drifting about the streets, loath to participate in established recreation programs, looking for a little excitement. We should be imaginative enough to throw something substantial into the gap right now, before trouble breaks out.

This is a tough neighborhood, but it has good citizens who have organized to try to get some action on their problems. Newcomers, who have moved in of recent years, are finding a place in the life of the community but they need help; so do the people who have lived on the lower West Side all their lives.

It is regrettable that shortage of funds impels us to wait until the 11th hour to provide opportunities that should have been made available all along. But it is the 11th hour now. I have examined the shifting pattern of delinquency rates. To wait any longer would be disastrous.

To serve three new areas, youth board estimates the increase in cost as of 1957–58 would total $1,314,500.

That is a lot of money, but the youth board is prepared to show how many would be reached in recreation programs, in club work, through case-work treatment and counseling.[22] Included in the total also are funds for referral units; special groups of social workers to talk with problem youngsters right in the school and take steps to insure proper followup.

In connection with the referral units, however, I would recommend that the youth board be urged not to confine them to grade schools alone, as has been pretty much the practice to date. More of an attempt should be made to reach teenagers. This means consideration not only of junior highs, but of high schools as possible locations for referral units.

---

[21] Except for confidential "youthful offender" data.
[22] An important aspect of the youth board's program is the fact that it centers around services available, for the most part, in the neighborhoods. Patience and persistence are called for in promoting the use of neighborhood resources. The tendency of certain agencies, even those receiving public funds on contract, to shift operations to a few central locations is deplorable.

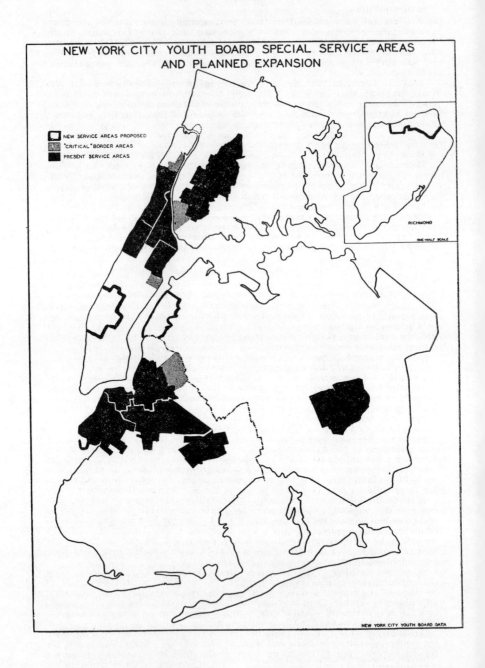

NEW YORK CITY YOUTH BOARD SPECIAL SERVICE AREAS
AND PLANNED EXPANSION

☐ NEW SERVICE AREAS PROPOSED
▨ "CRITICAL" BORDER AREAS
■ PRESENT SERVICE AREAS

RICHMOND

ONE-HALF SCALE

NEW YORK CITY YOUTH BOARD DATA

Teacher rotation

It is generally recognized that there are a number of regular schools in our public system which present teachers with especially demanding requirements. I refer to problems in the encouragement of learning and in the discipline area. In order to assure the students in these schools equal educational opportunities, a real effort to provide teachers of perhaps above average competence is indicated.

There is a substantial body of opinion in informed quarters contending that while many highly effective and dedicated teachers are to be found in such settings, there may be a disproportionate number of teachers who, for one or another reason, simply are not equal to the special demands of the situation. Dr. Jansen has informed me that a systematic review of one aspect of this problem is underway, with an eye to assuring the students in "difficult" schools a group of teachers not including an inordinate proportion of substitutes or newcomers to the system.

Delinquency rates vary markedly from school to school. Every effort should be made to assure assignment of our most capable teaching personnel to children growing up in high hazard environments. This is a top priority question. There is a real need for reevaluation of our teacher rotation policies.

Steps have already been taken to offer special incentives to experienced teachers contemplating transfer. Class size in these schools has been cut down and extra teachers and other teaching personnel have been added. The question of incentives merits further consideration. Professional people, who do not labor for bread alone, may appreciate some recognition of unusual service.

Parent education

There is no denying the fact that the one most important influence upon the growing child is that of his parents. It seems to me, however, that much of the criticism attributing to parents responsibility for juvenile delinquency is essentially uncharitable. Now we have on the statute books laws making adults, and parents in particular, answerable for offenses of minors in cases where the part played by the adult is clearly demonstrable. What is to be said, however, of the extent of general responsibility on the part of people who were themselves reared under the most bitter conditions: who as children, and subsequently as adults, have found themselves alone in what has seemed an essentially indifferent, even hostile and exploitative world. How sharply and righteously have we a right to criticize parents who were themselves beaten unjustly, parents who have known at first hand what is means to feel shut out and alone. Some will respond to such deprivations with special efforts to assure a richer life, a warmer world for their children; some will take it out on a child if he's the only helpless person at hand; and some will feel that their children by hook or crook will achieve adulthood after all, as they themselves have done.

Perhaps these obervations seem far afield from the traditional parent education references to toilet training and the size of a child's allowance, and the age at which a girl should be given the money for her first "formal." But perhaps, instead, they point to some new directions in parent education—to parents who are still "learning the ropes" of metropolitan living, parents whose aspirations for their children may be no less poignant for all their inarticulateness.

Perhaps, there has been much talk of parental incompetence and neglect. Our city over the decades has known many who have failed their children not out of malice or indifference but because they did not know the new ways—or were too troubled getting acquainted with a new land and a new way of life. Today, we can make the getting acquainted easier, and today, for the old-timers, too, we can open the door to help. To seek counsel, especially the counsel of one's own neighbors, need imply no confession of failure.

Sometimes I think public attitudes toward juvenile deliquency today have that embarrassed quality that characterized the approach to tuberculosis at the turn of the century. Juvenile deliquency, like scarlet fever, is a disorder of children—whether there will be complications depends to a fair extent on how the case is treated. And attitudes in the homes are decisive in making the vital decisions as to handling.[23]

Our board of education has projected a little demonstration through the evening centers operating in more and more of our schools. Their plan is not for formal lectures, but rather along lines of the friendly discussion group. I

---

[23] The foregoing by no means is intended to neglect the problems raised by a certain number of truly irresponsible individuals who have simply ignored their children.

haven't asked, but perhaps members will chip in so there'll be coffee, too. I suggest also, that experience has demonstrated that some parents who shy away from "a discussion group" will feel more free to chat in a sewing class or furniture repair project. As these are oftentimes precisely those we are most anxious to reach, I trust that those responsible for the program will plan imaginatively with this in mind.

This type of enterprise is deserving of the most highly qualified leadership. Dr. Jansen assures me that while funds will not permit overly attractive payment for such service, the schools will welcome capable and experienced people in our city, not presently on the teaching staff, who would be qualified for part-time employment on this project.

The board of education's budget request for parent education was $19,000. This sum was a mere 1½ percent of the total community and recreation centers budget request. Salaries to leaders in the sports program were budgeted at a sum 27 times as large.

The fact that this type of parent education is a new program in the schools need not, I believe, necessitate such a creakingly slow start. Parent discussion groups may be an experiment for the bureau of community education, but work along these lines has been carried on successfully elsewhere for many years. There is a real reservoir of experience to draw upon.[24]

I therefore recommend as a minimum that a worker with parents be added to the staff of every single one of the 87 evening community and recreation centers in areas designated by the youth board as high delinquency neighborhoods. These people should be retained for a sufficient number of sessions per week to allow them adequate time to plan their material and to make occasional necessary visits to homes and community agencies. And the emphasis should be on continuity of service and specialist personnel; this will probably necessitate recruitment of the larger proportion of these discussion leaders from outside the schools, according to procedures already in effect.

If such personnel were added to the program of the centers in the 14 youth board special service neighborhoods only, no more than 87 people would be needed. To employ 268 parent education teachers on the same basis in every such center in the city, would cost approximately $195,000.

I recommend that this program be financed by a special appropriation to the youth board, but be operated by the bureau of community education. Following already tested operating practices, the youth board would develop personnel specifications as a guide to the bureau of community education in the recruitment of personnel.

I further recommend providing adequate consultant-supervisor-trainer personnel for the professional leaders of the parent groups. Even skilled people are going to need counsel themselves in carrying out any program that really gets into basic problems of parents. I believe that we should make it possible for such a coordinator to have a conference once a month with each one of the parent group workers. Two full-time coordinators ($13,900 per annum total) might provide sufficient consultation service for 87 group workers if only the schools in youth board service areas where served; to provide adequate consultation services for leaders of groups in all the schools involved would require about six more full-time coordinators. It is absolutely essential that we provide for supervisors specifically detailed to this project.

The expanded operation projected here would in no wise affect the parent education experiment in the amount of $19,000 per annum proposed by the board of education as part of the regular program of the Bureau of Community Education.

In connection with the well-baby clinic program of the health department, our city has obtained the services of an internationally recognized authority on children's behavior.[25] This gifted physician, sitting in with regular clinic staff, talks over everyday problems with mothers and children, making a real contribution in forestalling habit problems, tension, and anxiety at an early age.

In training pediatricians to serve along these lines, we are erecting a first line of defense against delinquency, as well as against personal maladjustment and unhappiness. Services to a cross-section population of normal babies and their mothers now, may save untold thousands in services to the abnormal a few years hence.

I am therefore recommending that $17,000 be allotted the health department to institute service along these lines as part of its program in two additional

---

[24] This would include, of course, the rich experience of our parent-teacher associations.
[25] Dr. David Levy.

neighborhoods. The districts served will both lie within youth board service areas and the population served will be a real cross section of our youngest children's parents, getting advice when it can do the most good—before delinquency becomes a problem. I hope that our mental health board will give further expansion of this project top priority among those to be considered in its plans later this year.

Already underway, also in our heath department, is a parent education program, employing informal discussion groups. Especially trained personnel lead the sessions, and parents have an opportunity to reconsider their own problems in the friendly light of neighbors' shared experience.

I believe that this work should be expanded, with the understanding that the discussion group leaders be qualified to plan programs covering all aspects of the child-rearing process. All parents can profit by this counsel; all children are entitled to the benefits of this service. Through the health department, we are in a position to extend this help to parents who are already coming periodically for other services. I therefore recommend that the youth board be granted $20,000 enabling the health department to extend this service in those youth board service areas where it is not presently operating. (I might add that a number of the community's social work agencies have projects along similar lines, which they will wish to expand as private benefactors make funds available.)

The co-op program and guidance in the schools

A major problem related to juvenile delinquency centers about the compulsory education law, and the school-leaving age. Some have suggested that boys who seem uninterested in school and are always getting into trouble there "get out and get a job." [26]

It seems to me that we have a long way to go in making adequate provision for such difficult students within the school before we write them off as a bad lot. The school authorities have a real problem in maintaining discipline so that teaching can go on. The number of troublemakers is not large and our teachers have every right to expect community support in dealing with them. About this, let there be no mistake. We must recognize that not only law and order, but the rights of the great majority of students—those who can get along—are at stake here.

Those who feel that delinquents and potential delinquents in our schools should be turned out on the street "to find a job" may be interested in the facts to date. A large statewide study in California disclosed that four times as many dropouts as graduates were still looking for work. The same study showed 6 out of 10 of school dropouts were children of unskilled or semiskilled laborers; yet workers in these categories make up nowhere near that large a proportion of the population. The problem is clear: it is a basic American principle that children have an equal chance at education, regardless of their parents' circumstances. Yet it seems that there is a differential when we look to see for whom the schools have made themselves attractive. (It should be noted here that there is real question as to ineducability being a substantial consideration for any large proportion of these dropouts).

It should be noted also that children leave school because they're "fed up" or feel they'd enjoy working more. In the majority of cases, the reasons for leaving school are not financial. Follow up studies show that dropouts very rarely get any schooling subsequently, and that more find themselves in "deadend" jobs. In the Glueck's recent delinquency study, it was found that while a good majority of both the delinquents and nondelinquents worked, three times as many nondelinquents were employed on supervised jobs or in factories. And more of the delinquents were working (unsupervised, of course) in street trades.

I wonder how many who advocate getting the older, slower student out of school have thought about where he would land afterward, about placement on the right kind of job, or the contrast between supervision (of sorts at least) in school and the possibility of no supervision at all on the outside.

Are we to retreat from the ground the British can only now contemplate achieving? D. Archibald, writing from London declares "one of the best methods of preventing delinquency is to keep children within the framework of a good educational system during the most restless adolescent years"—to 16.

We have a responsibility to try to help the youngster who seems bent on throwing away his right to an education. He is still a juvenile; we cannot say

---

[26] There may be some point to amending the provisions of the statute setting up continuation schools, to allow greater flexibility in the planning of extended school services for young workers. But the schools must continue their guidance role.

to him, "If you choose to neglect your education, it is no one's concern but your own." Consideration must be given to the vitality of the curriculum offered, and to teacher attitudes toward the slow learner. I know these are areas where my concern is shared by the administrators of our school system, and many who are classroom teachers. Until we have made the broadest guidance programs and real flexibility of curriculum available to "misfits" there would seem to be no call for basically revising our compulsory attendance law. I have yet to be persuaded that the children who would in consequence be beyond the reach of school services would find themselves on the road to better citizenship.

Over a period of years, a program has been developed within our high schools to provide an opportunity for selected students to complete their studies [27] while employed in private industry halftime, at prevailing wages. Last year 4,000 students were enrolled in this co-op program in 33 high schools; they worked at beauty culture, as salesmen, as typists, in machine shops, in offices, and in stores. It is time to move this experiment out of the experimental class; 40 years have demonstrated its worth.[28] The time has come to extend this curriculum to more students; perhaps the selection process has been just a little too fine.

Counseling in the schools.—A common observation by delinquency researchers is the need for more effective counseling, especially vocational counseling, for young people. Youths graduating or dropping out of high school are too often vague as to their employment plans and frequently seem to bring little to a prospective employer. If the co-op program is to be expanded, there must be a more thorough going guidance operation, as well.

There are today 1,765 teachers doing guidance work in the schools; of these, only 82 are licensed counselors. The 82 put in full time on the guidance job; 63 other teachers with a varied background of experience are also detailed to guidance full time. Thus, over 90 percent of the personnel engaged in guidance have to fit it into a program which makes other demands on their time—most of them put in the equivalent of 1 day a week in this work. It has been estimated that the amount of time available for counseling averages out to less than 5 minutes per student per school year in the high schools.

It is to be hoped that ways will be found to add a larger number of specially qualified full-time people to help with this vital responsibility.

Youth board in-service training

The youth board is again appealing for a pitifully small grant so that it can set up a thoroughgoing training program, not only for its own staff but also for other city departments which have requested help for their workers in the areas where youth board is expert. Every dollar spent for training, it is clear, multiplies itself by making it possible to do more of a job with the same number of people.

The kind of work the youth board is carrying on requires the best. To assign it a task and then hold back on the wherewithal for performing the task effectively is false economy.

The in-service training-program request is for $38,000. That hardly seems like much of a training program for so large a staff, but that is the youth board's best judgment. Whatever objections there may have been to this enterprise in the past, I can see no point in niggardliness today. I heartily endorse this request as a top-priority program.

Fellowship study program: Some provision must be made to support the efforts of workers in certain strategic programs to obtain the special professional training needed for most effective preformance on their jobs.[29]

This problem is especially acute in the case of positions where social work skills are involved, as the training program in that field, as in medicine, makes a period of full-time field experience mandatory. The schools of social work have shown some willingness to credit adequately supervised paid experience with the city in lieu of the customary field work, but these plans need further development.

In any event, it must be recognized that there are city workers who need special training involving something more than an evening or two a week of their own time. They are deserving of public support. Our educational leave policy is in

---

[27] Only 1 percent of co-op students drop out.
[28] Some additions to central office staff, and sufficient funds to permit co-op supervisors in the various high schools to devote full time to this work would add some $90,000 to the cost of the program.
[29] We now allow welfare about one-sixth the training period budgeted for police.

crying need of review; every possible help must be provided career people seeking special training in order to do a better job. The obstacles in the way of a liberalized educational leave program must be swept aside, in the interest of better services to children in trouble.[30]

Planning and coordination

Planning and coordination of programs in the juvenile delinquency field involves close operating relationships with many city departments and a multitude of private agencies. The New York City Youth Board has for some years now been charged with this responsibility. There is every reason for continuing to lodge the function with that body.

However, I believe the youth board might well give consideration to placing greater emphasis upon its role in planning. To date a very large proportion of its energies has gone into program development and liaison with contract agencies.

Someone has got to be given the time to step back and take the long view. Progress in this direction has been pretty well limited to some examination of the youth board's own programs. Much more of a commitment to this work area is urgently needed. Head counting is important, but more is needed for planning than merely data on fluctuations in the volume of delinquency.

The makeup of the youth board itself should exemplify the breadth to be encompassed in the coordination of operations. Workers in the field can become better acquainted, and leadership in all departments can reach beyond particularized interests to a common understanding of the integration of services we need. Despite some years' endeavor, there are problems still to be grappled with. Given good will, cool heads, and deployment of enough critical brainpower at the center, there is a good chance of a well-rounded, effective battery of programs.

In addition to a broadened research perspective, I therefore believe the youth board needs a small unit of full-time experts who can bring various special skills to the problems of coordination and long-range planning. This team would be responsible for smoothing working relationships with other agencies and for the development of overall operations plans with the youth board members and executive director. It would be well to involve in planning the chiefs of the board's operating divisions, and perhaps private agency representatives as well. But the pressing need is for additional personnel who can look beyond day-to-day problems and have no direct responsibility for operations, no commitment to a particular aspect of today's problem.

The planning unit, including a director, and senior analysts who would rank with the present casework, recreation and group work, and research chiefs, should report quarterly directly to the board. Its responsibilities should center about the need for communitywide coordination of service programs; operations being carried on by the youth board directly should not be its primary concern.[31]

Evaluation.—Reasonable assumptions rather than established facts must provide the justification for most of our programs in this field today. But for long-range planning, reasonable assumptions simply will not suffice. A scientific fact-finding and assessment program is called for.

Operations costing in the neighborhod of $25 million are in a pretty expensive neighborhood. We want to know, as we move ahead, which ones work and which do not. And we want to know which programs are the more effective among those which really do work.

For all this, we need a factfinding group not attached to any particular program but in a position to work freely with all.

I believe the most suitable location for this assessment operation is not only outside the field agencies but outside the city government itself. The research people should be free to carry through scientific studies of our best efforts, without any possibility of political interference. The place for such a project is in an institution of learning and President Gallagher, of the City College, has indi-

---

[30] The cost of this program will depend upon whether salary is granted workers away on educational leave. Perhaps $30,000 would suffice for a year's demonstration. Note that new State legislation will provide help to probation officers. Money is still neded, however, in other fields.

[31] The cost of a unit comprised of 7 professionals and 3 secretaries would be about $82,000 per annum. With youth board budget projections at levels of $4 to $5 million, this hardly seems a great sum to put into planning. It must also be remembered that the planning will be with reference to programs in the entire community, not merely in the youth board.

cated a willingness to provide a home for the evaluation team; this is in line with the interest this college has already demonstrated through action projects in our field. Among these, I might mention the college's community service division.

To carry through the task effectively will require the services of a person with rank equivalent to a full professor as director; proper staffing would probably call for an associate professor, 2 assistant professors, and 10 research associates—plus clerical personnel. The assessment unit would not need to be fully staffed until perhaps a year after it got underway, but the key people in particular should be recruited at the outset, and for a period of time long enough to assure a coherent operation. The project should be clearly understood as of a temporary character. It seems to me we should plan on a 5-year basis, and should allow flexibility so that certain personnel could be retained for special studies, even of a relatively brief sort.

The entire factfinding operation will be carried out by specially trained and experienced people who have no special axe to grind and are beholden to no particular agency. They should have the freest access to any city project which affects juvenile delinquency.[32] I believe that private agencies, too, will respond positively to an invitation to cooperate.

Welfare and civic leaders, as well as certain strategically situated civil servants can play an important role in helping orient this work. A group of such people is well-nigh indispensable in helping prepare the ground for the action-research team. But we would want to have a clear understanding from the outset, that the researchers would be free from any outside control.

The senior personnel for this work will be sought in a nationwide canvass of the most promising prospects. Dr. Gallagher believes he could be in a position at an early date to submit names to the mayor for endorsement. This would enable us to get underway without losing a whole academic year because of key personnel having made other commitments.

It should be emphasized that what will be sought is topnotch scholars who have already demonstrated a capacity to carry out action research. This cannot be a center for theoretical or basic studies.

Without committing the college in advance to any particular design in balancing the research team, I believe we would do well to bear in mind that the problem we are attemping to solve is in its largest aspects a social, not a purely clinical problem. The techniques we employ in the prevention and treatment of juvenile delinquency certainly include clinical techniques. But the problem in evaluating a proper balance among programs is a problem calling primarily for a social scientist with a strong research background. In addition to personnel with sociological skills, experts with capacities along psychiatric, psychological, social work, and statistical lines (for example) are all indispensable. I believe it should be possible, in every instance, to find for this work people who have skills and a deep appreciation of more than a single one of these fields. This job is a tough one, and not for the narrow specialist; the team approach has got to be an agreed-upon foundation before we can even think of getting started.

I believe that an effective factfinding program will save us hundreds of thousands of dollars yearly, by making clear just which programs in the delinquency field are actually carrying out fruitful operations. A centralized assessment project will make valid comparisons possible and enable us to plan tieing together the impact of programs under diversified auspices. A centralized research operation should also prove more economical in meeting the need for new information as indicated above.[33]

The $95,000 per annum this research program would cost when it got fully underway is a small amount indeed, if we bear in mind the magnitude of the sums (perhaps $25 million) expended upon all our operational programs. Any well-run enterprise in the business field would consider this small allocation for factfinding and quality control, a very minimum level, indeed.

In addition to the 10 priority programs which I have recommended for immediate attention, there are a number of others meriting the most serious consideration. Some touch upon operations on which I wish to inform myself more fully; I, therefore, merely make mention of them at this time, by way of preface to future reports.

---

[32] This might be promoted by providing for some continuity in the research personnel assigned to this or that operating program.

[33] There will still be a need for the research work presently going on in the New York City Youth Board, for example.

In this section, also, I am touching briefly upon a few projects to which I wish to lend a hearty endorsement as proper areas for the initiative of private individuals and agencies. The city, in the last analysis, can carry only so much of the load. Private social agencies, service clubs, philanthropists, foundations, individual citizens have all played an historic role in coping with the community's welfare problems. To meet the challenge of juvenile delinquency will require the mobilization of all of our resources. The good work already being carried on must be extended even further. This is a challenge to every New Yorker, according to his personal resources of skill and of money. In addition to the small number of areas I enlarge upon briefly here, appendix III lists some two dozen projects, large and small, which should prove of interest.

To these I wish to add the great contribution employers can make in planning for part-time employment by youth in commerce and industry. Many of the largest department stores, offices, and factories in our city are partners in the board of education's co-op program, but more job opportunities are needed. In addition, the law permits work on the widest variety of jobs on a part-time basis even by students not reached by the co-op program. I cannot place too great an emphasis upon the value of socially useful, properly paid work under conditions not detrimental to juvenile health and morals. This is an area where concern about delinquency can be translated into action—to the mutual advantage of the youth, the employer, the school, and the community at large.

RECOMMENDED PROGRAMS AND PROJECTS FOR FUTURE STUDY

Neighborhood civic organization

In a number of cities experiments in the development of grassroots civic development associations are pointing a way to real progress toward meeting the challenge of juvenile delinquency, along with a number of other long-standing social problems. This is a job to be carried on, in the last analysis, by the neighbors themselves, although outside help can play a constructive role.

In his first annual report, our mayor pointed out that in "any given area of the city the number of oldtime families who have struck deep roots in the neighborhood is relatively small. It is for that reason that special efforts must be exerted to develop citizen participation in the various neighborhoods throughout the city."

It is simply not possible to put too much emphasis upon the potentials of activity along these lines. In high-delinquency areas in particular such civic groups have an invaluable part to play in overall welfare planning and in encouraging constructive social action on the part of youth. A constructive social action on the part of adults, by the way, would be seeking employment in the police department's expanded street-crossing guard program. This work is something that any reasonably intelligent and responsible person might undertake, and I know Mr. Adams would welcome inquiries from neighborhood people desiring to qualify for this part-time employment.

It is my opinion that community organization projects are most appropriately developed under independent auspices; city officials and workers in a number of departments may quite appropriately be involved in auxiliary capacities, or in their own right, personally, as citizens. But the type of citizen effort the mayor and other forward-looking community leaders envision should be completely free of any hazard of official domination.

Neighborhood civic associations planned as membership organizations would play a role essentially different from that undertaken by the mayor's community advisory boards, whose members serve by appointment. Civic associations serve a complementary purpose.

As people in our several neighborhoods evolve organizational forms appropriate to their own needs, and bring forward articulate, dedicated, responsible leadership, the whole city will be the gainer. And our own job in planning common services will be facilitated immeasurably.

I am sure that as this initiative develops, a multitude of opportunities will be presented for city agencies to prove helpful. This is a fine prospect to look ahead to. And for the time being, a great challenge to New Yorkers to work with New Yorkers—and, perhaps, for those who have funds or know-how to lend a hand to those who may just now be making a beginning.

Time-honored procedures and regulations are reexamined in times of crises. Enlightened self-interest can be nicely blended with a sense of responsibility to the larger community. It is to be hoped that New Yorkers are moving toward the sharing of facilities jealously guarded for good reason over the years.

Columbia University, for example, last year for the first time opened Baker Field to an outside group. Their generosity made possible the development of a teen-age baseball league in this neighborhood, where there is a high hazard of youngsters becoming delinquent.

Our public schools are doing a fine job in opening their doors for a wide variety of projects. In the coming year, this will be the case more than ever before. Doubtles there are other buildings in our neighborhoods which may be put at the disposal of the community at large during idle hours. Perhaps there will be those among our church and synagogue leaders who will come forward at this time to offer facilities on a nondenominational basis for communal enterprises. A number of fine examples have been set already.

Those charged with pastoral responsibilities can render a real service to the entire community by making space for wholesome, nonsectarian recreation programs available to all youth, as well as those they number in their own flock. Surely there is no nobler proof of a belief that all men are brothers, than this practical sort of fellowship.   There are many who fee forsaken, many lolling on stoops or crowded on a bleak corner under the lamppost who would respond to an opportunity to participate in a vital leisure-time program under imaginative leadership.

Role of the school

The schools can make significant contributions to the solution of the delinquency problem in a variety of ways. I have discussed a number of special programs at various points in this report. But most important is the opportunity afforded the day-to-day classroom teacher.

The challenge is not to be a substitute parent, a substitute psychiatrist or a substitute policeman. The challenge is to motivate learning, never to cease trying to capture the elusive imagination of the growing child. This is what we mean by "helping open the doors of the world." The challenge to the teacher is to teach—hopefully, to teach from a loving heart; but, in any event, really to teach.

"Many learnings occur simultaneously * * * The teacher who knows the children under his care can do much by using the total learning situation to help the child with disturbed conditions of life. The attainment of this end requires no abstruse knowledge or newly discovered techniques; the teacher who is fair-minded, sympathetic, emotionally reliable, who has concern for the development of healthy personality in his pupils, and who is skilled in teaching, helps to diminish the dissatisfactions that lead to maladjustment. Nothing is gained by describing his work as group therapy."

Of recent years, there have been a growing number of indications of lowered morale among teachers in our public schools. The reasons for discontent are varied, and it may be that some of the teachers' wishes cannot be met.

A crucial problem was raised by Superintendent Jansen at the time of the school budget hearings. "The teenager in our present high-tension world is in great need for closer contact with his teachers that can only come when the class size is considerably reduced." This, of course, is equally true of the needs of preteens. I shall have to refrain from making any specific recommendations here, because the magnitude of the sums involved puts this program outside the budgetary limitations of the present enterprise.

After the parent, no one, probably, has a greater influence upon the growing child than his teachers. To the child maturing in a setting replete with delinquency hazard, the teacher is in an especially strategic position to be of help.

The board of education has provided real leadership through such special programs as those in the all day neighborhood schools, the play schools, and the bureau of community education. Much that is helpful proceeds from 110 Livingston Street, by way of curriculum materials and other publications.

But to some, the very size of the public school system seems to militate against the free flow of ideas from the classroom teacher back to the administration. There is real need for experimentation with devices to bring classroom opinion more directly to bear upon central planning. Just what methods will prove most effective in attaining that end, I leave, at this time, to the schoolmen.[34]

---

[34] The informal weekly conferences board of education President Charles H. Silver has been holding with groups of principals, certainly seem a positive contribution. An extension of this program to include groups composed exclusively of classroom teachers has been reported under consideration.   I am sure such discussions would prove worthwhile for all concerned.

The spark of interest, the warm flame of dedication, are an indispensable part of teaching. Children who spend their days with teachers who are serving time, are quick to sense that fact. Disillusionment with school is generally recognized as playing an important part in the development of delinquent patterns. Any contribution the administration can make to reviving a flagging teacher morale, will prove a real blow against juvenile delinquency. And the community at large can do more to demonstrate the high regard in which it holds those who have dedicated a lifetime of service to this honored calling.

Truancy

Unexcused absence from school is far and away the most frequent of all delinquencies. And truancy not uncommonly proves to have been the first important misstep if we examine the personal history of a hardened criminal.

If it were possible to do something for children who have not yet come in major conflict with the law at the time they first start to truant, many delinquent careers might be nipped in the bud. The bureau of attendance of our school system has a large staff engaged, among other things, in investigating all unexplained absences of more than a few days. As it happens, in 7 investigations out of 10, the absence proves to have been "lawful;" only 21 percent of the investigated absences turn out to be "trunacies." [35] Focussing upon making a very large number of investigations means that it is only possible to spend a limited amount of time looking into any particular case; I believe there is a real need for deployment of personnel under revised procedures more likely to result in intensive work-up of the small proportion of cases needing long-term service. [36]

Our attendance officers should have a real opportunity to help children who are drifting—before they drift too far and in the wrong direction. "By definition, truancy implies that school is an unsatisfactory experience." To what extent are our attendance officers in a position to help children achieve a more satisfactory experience in the schools? Is there opportunity for intensive followup with the child, his parents, his classroom teacher—in that crucial fraction of cases where the pattern is not yet set? Is it possible, for example, to give special attention to the relatively small proportion of truants in the second and third grades, say, who may be just commencing to experiment in delinquency? Or is the emphasis upon maintaining a certain volume of completed investigations for accounting purposes in connection with State aid? [37]

"The normal truant belongs in the group of those who resist school because of boredom. Perhaps at one time or another it has included all of us, for it is in the nature of living to resist conformity, routine, rigid rules, and to seek variety and creativity, using freedom to explore at the unfettered dictates of the will.

"When rules are avoided by a few, control over the group is threatened. These children challenge the imagination of teachers and school administrators. Giving them enriched programs and understanding and wise counsel is usually the best answer. Labeling them "truants" or "delinquents" is as fruitless as it is dangerous. Individual treatment is best for them as well as for the morale of the school."

The attendance officer can be a key man in the team approach to delinquency.

The "600" schools

A few years ago an experiment was undertaken by the board of education to provide special opportunities for grade-school students presenting disciplinary problems in the regular school. Teachers in the special schools are paid additional salary, but on the whole cannot be regarded as specialist personnel. The selection process is designed to secure experienced teachers who have demonstrated a capacity to work with problem youngsters. But the additional training demanded is essentially minimal, and questions have been raised as to the real value of this isolation program, which now costs more than $1 million per annum for salaries alone.

A thoroughgoing assessment of the operation has yet to be undertaken, and while there are unquestionably positive aspects, the public is entitled to some real facts as to the value of the program as reflected in the subsequent careers of graduates. I feel that plans for high schools of the same sort, as well as similar schools for girls, should be held in abeyance. Some concerted fact-

---

[35] Most of the remainder are children unlawfully detained by parents or guardians together with a scattering of children unlawfully employed.

[36] Last year there were no less than 376,000 separate investigations.

[37] My concern is that a maximum of attention be turned to counselling. I am not suggesting that investigation of absences, as required by law, be abandoned.

finding is in order, and it is my hope that a study committee Superintendent Jansen will soon appoint will include not only board of education personnel but experts from outside the school system and consultants suggested by interested civic groups, as well.

The Bureau of Child Guidance

This essential service in our schools is being enlarged during the coming year, as additional psychiatrist-psychologist-socialworker teams are activated. Dr. Jansen is presently working on plans for certain improvements in the operation, in the light of an extensive study only recently completed. This ambitious survey (made posible by the joint effort of our board of education, the Field Foundation, the New York Fund for Children, and the New York Foundation) offers a real point of departure for enlightened planning. I shall put off making any recommendations about this bureau while the survey report is till being studied.

Recreation programs

The bureau of community education in our public schools, under the able leadership of Mark McCloskey (who now heads the New York State Youth Commission) has done a notable job in providing extended recreation services in some 288 schools. The bureau in recent years has been able to employ full-time center directors, thanks to grants from the New York City Youth Board, and, for the first time, professionally trained group workers as well.

The increase in budget recommended for this operation in the new year should make possible a major extension of operations. I trust that these funds will include provisions for a larger staff at the citywide level. There also is need for a pool of supervisory personnel who will be at the disposition of the acting head of the bureau, so that manpower can be deployed from one school district to another with a minimum of redtape. I believe, too, that consideration ought to be given the possibility of putting two-man teams into schools which have on their own initiative already developed community programs. These activities should not be confined to plants which have full-scale comprehensive programs only.

Our school buildings, meeting rooms, swimming pools, auditoriums, gyms, and playgrounds should increasingly be made available on a 7-day-per-week basis, with a larger volume of evening operations, as well. This is a tried-and-tested program meriting all possible expansion, substantially along present lines.

The special contribution of group work.—In all our recreation programs, including those in the schools, I should like to call attention to the importance of including group work as well as the customary crafts, dramatics, and sports. There are real benefits by way of personal growth and guidance which are likely to be achieved only in the club setting, among groups of perhaps only 12 to 20 people. Group workers who have special skills in the field of interpersonal relations are as indispensable to a balanced leisure-time program as athletic coaches or activity instructors. In recruitment of personnel, an effort, I believe, should be made to reach leaders who have demonstrated interest, understanding, and ability in the family and the neighborhood approaches to this work.[38]

School-building design.—In planning school buildings for the future, we should continue to incorporate in the design opportunities for extended community service programs. Plants should provide facilities suitable for crafts shops and club meeting rooms. Auditorium, etc., are already being designed so that access is possible without an entire school building's being thrown open. These details are simple, but crucial. There is not reason why the city should invest millions in special plant for recreation while facilities are at hand or could be at hand in the schools.

Weekend, holiday programing.—The city is taking positive measures to insure its various youth programs remaining in operation 7 days a week to an increasing degree. Where overtime costs have to be met, they are being budgeted. Private agencies naturally determine their own operating policies, but in view of an impressive weight of expert opinion, I would hope they would consider seriously the provision of more weekend and holiday programs.[39]

---

[38] Those activities staffed with 1 leader for every 12 to 20 people are obviously more expensive (on a per capita basis) than those in which a single leader works with 100 people. A well-balanced program will include both clubs and square dancing, say. There is an important place for both kinds of leaders.

[39] Agencies in the case work and guidance fields might also give the most serious consideration to the need for scheduling standby staff and instituting a greater volume of service during hours when prospective clients are likeliest to be away from their jobs or household duties.

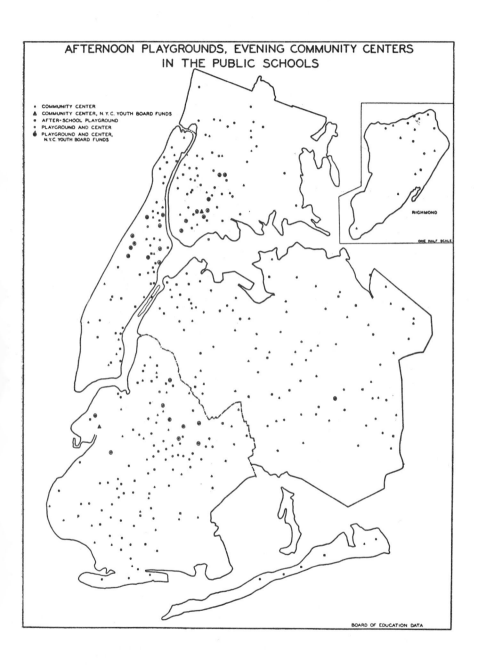

AFTERNOON PLAYGROUNDS, EVENING COMMUNITY CENTERS
IN THE PUBLIC SCHOOLS

• COMMUNITY CENTER
▲ COMMUNITY CENTER, N.Y.C. YOUTH BOARD FUNDS
• AFTER-SCHOOL PLAYGROUND
• PLAYGROUND AND CENTER
◉ PLAYGROUND AND CENTER,
   N.Y.C. YOUTH BOARD FUNDS

RICHMOND

ONE HALF SCALE

BOARD OF EDUCATION DATA

Adventure playgrounds

In recent years, there has been a growing body of opinion in the recreation field calling for a new approach to playgrounds and playground programs. In virtually empty lots, practically devoid of apparatus, highly successful programs have been developed in Copenhagen, Denmark, in London, in Kensington, in Crawley, England, and in Minneapolis, for example, in our own country. It appears that children welcome the opportunity to use tools to construct their own playhouses—that attendance at such playgrounds is continuous and high. And it is reported the police find a marked decline in so-called delinquency; playground personnel report fewer accidents (115).

I believe that serious consideration should be given both to the "junk playground" and to playgrounds employing apparatus of a new type. These latter are designed to provide more opportunities for free and dramatic play, new opportunities for group play of a highly informal character. This is not to say that the free-for-all is an ideal recreation program, but experience has shown that, given the chance, children can work out games of their own which may prove even more enjoyable than the traditional swings or ball diamonds. And in Philadelphia, for example, children who otherwise stay away, seem drawn to projects of this type. While the new kinds of apparatus have, in some cases, proved more expensive, increased attendance has more than justified the expenditure.

New Yorkers will soon have an opportunity to get an idea of the sort of advantages enjoyed by children in Oakland, Calif., Boiceville N. Y., and in Fort Wayne, Ind. When it opens, public school 130 in the Bronx will have as part of its playground plant the first and third prize items from last year's national competition for new designs in play sculpture; officials of the National Recreation Association and the Museum of Modern Art were among the judges.

Certain illegal activities, like hitching a ride on the back of a bus, seem to provide an excitement with which playgrounds and recreation programs of a cut and dried character don't seem to be able to compete. There is a kind of thrill, I suppose, in breaking the law; that is a thrill we cannot permit. But surely we have an obligation seriously to consider every sort of project and program that bears promise of meeting that very human desire for a safe scare, a limited habard. After all, not every child who may want to gets the chance to spend a day at Coney Island.

Problems of preschool-age children

At a later date I wish to report on the importance of some recent researches dealing with healthy infants confined in institutions or hospitals away from their parents for long periods while still of very tender age. It seems that a child who misses out on some really close and personalized affection in his first year or two is pretty likely to turn out to be an emotional cripple. This extremely small segment of our population has produced a disproportionately large number of criminals and maladjusted individuals. Certainly, we already know enough to endorse most vigorously the endeavors of welfare workers seeking foster care in private homes for all homeless well infants.

Both the health department and the hospitals department have called my attention to the fact that considerable sums are being expended to maintain completely healthy but homeless babies in our hospitals because of lack of facilities for foster home care.[40] It is nothing short of fantastic to contemplate the prospect of helpless infants being institutionalized for lengthy periods simply because we have been lax in making adequate appropriations for personnel who could arrange for care in homes. Yet the latter course would not only be the more humane, but would cost the city far less money.

An important welfare department program which will be discussed in the above mentioned report provides for 1,000 dependent children who cannot be cared for in their own homes. The problem is especially pressing in the case of children from certain minority groups—doubly so for older children, whom prospective foster parents often feel are "less attractive." The Children's Shelter is dangerously overcrowded, yet the bottleneck in the foster home field has still to be broken; capable professionals are needed for a home-finding program. Of all this, more at another time.

---

[40] In addition there are children who could be returned to their own homes if certain special services (more part-time "homemakers" for example) were available.

Welfare Department

The staff of our welfare department come in contact with numbers of families whose children are in high hazard of becoming delinquents. While such families represent only a small fraction of the total number of children who receive service from the department, it is important that every effort be made to use the regular contacts to advantage. The city funds expended for DW staff who work with families must be sufficient to employ workers with skill to recognize the danger signals of strain and maladjustment in children and in families which require treatment and to take the necessary steps to help these families. These workers must also have the ability to recognize which problems can be treated by the department and those which require the help of other public and private social agencies within the community.

The special program this department has been operating jointly with the youth board has provided a real idea of what can be done by competent social workers, assigned caseloads of reasonable size. Inasmuch as the services for families and children is in the process of reorganization, I am at this time deferring specific recommendations with reference to the welfare department's role

The pilot study recently initiated by this department which provides preventive service on an intensive basis to certain children in public-assistance families has also demonstrated what can be accomplished by competent child-welfare workers.

In concluding this section, mention should be made of an important welfare demonstration just a few years ago. An attempt was made to bring together, under one roof, a staff that included health, counseling, employment, housing, relief, legal, and recreation specialists. A neighbor in need could come to this center and employ the skills of a whole battery of experts working together in rooms just across the hall from one another. The person in trouble didn't find himself shuttling all over town and spending a couple of weeks getting help from half a dozen different organizations.

The experiment to which I have referred was not a project of the welfare department; the department merely was one of the participating agencies. But I know how enthusiastically Welfare Commissioner McCarthy responded to this opportunity. I believe that a program along the indicated lines can be a sound one; we should muster the necessary forces once again.

Service opportunities for youth

There is good reason to believe that contributory to juvenile delinquency in many cases are feelings of fear and hatred toward adults, a sense of being divorced from society (or at least from the adult community), and a pervasive personal insecurity in many vital aspects of the life of a youth. Programs oriented to the changing of these attitudes would seem likely to make significant contributions.

Youth-serving organizations have for some time been concerned about providing young people with service opportunities. Meaningful work, in units that permit a person a sense of achievement, has long been recognized as contributing to an individual's self-respect. Yet there are only slim chances of young people being involved in projects of a service character that are truly appealing to youth themselves. Many adult-conceived enterprises reportedly have the look of made work to young people, or are intended to serve ends which the adult may appreciate but which may remain obscure to youth.

Giving youth a chance to help implies work we ourselves regard as of vital importance, not some incidental tidying-up operation. Giving youth a chance to help means accepting the possibility they will make mistakes on the job now and again—and it means being willing to accept the mistakes. Giving youth a chance to help means designing projects with an eye to youth participation in leadership and control, not service time and again as handmaiden only.

Perhaps city departments will have youth service projects of their own to suggest. But a variety of statutory limitations upon the city make this area of operation one probably more feasible for private organization. I know from our discussions with them that a number of social agencies would be most interested in reviewing with any interested donor a number of service programs presently awaiting sponsorship.

A kind of service project which might also be more largely developed under private auspices is self-service—by youth for youth. There have been occasions in the history of the youth board's street clubs project, when a group which, perhaps, had been hanging out in candy stores or on the curb, got together and set up their own clubhouse in a vacant store front. Neighborhood merchants sometimes provided paint and the brushes with which the boys worked. Some undertakings along these lines were eminently successful; upon occasion, the outcome left something to be desired. In principle, however, an opportunity for youth to operate directly upon their own concerns would seem to be worth the planning. Certainly there is a tremendous range of possibilities in the schools. if adult advisors can accord youth any sizable area of free operation.

The most ambitious efforts in the service area are work camps. Under private auspices, mostly by denominational service committees, important projects have been undertaken by small work crews in resident settings. And some years ago, under public auspices, there were the resident work centers of the National Youth Administration, and the forestry camps of the Civilian Conservation Corps. People who have spent many years at youth work feel very strongly that a broadened conception of one's place in the world is provided by projects along these lines, perhaps more effectively than in any other way.

To live among one's peers; to be continuously in the company of a few friendly, helpful, genuinely interested adults; to have an opportunity both to work and to learn; to be working at something both interesting and important (like building new cabins in a children's camp); to have some fun in a place in some sense one's own; these are the attraction work camps offer youth.

While the city cannot undertake any major program along these lines in the forseeable future, several private agencies have indicated an interest in this sort of project, if they had the money. This is one of a number of projects I feel should be brought to the attention of the people of New York, in the event new resources could be made available to the interested private agencies.

JOINT PLANNING

I have not discussed the financing of various programs in detail. Most will be found to come under formulas for State reimbursement. A number relate to areas which may be covered by Federal programs presently under discussion, especially the Kefauver bill (S. 728) which not only provides for subsidizing programs but details adequate administrative procedures as well.[41]

That we will cooperate with the Govnernor's juvenile delinquency study committee goes without saying. But there are even now 1 or 2 matters of special interest.

The New York City Youth Board, for example (which is the hub about which our whole program revolves) carries on from year to year as a temporary agency because of the terms of pertinent legislation at the State level. As a result the city departments operating programs under youth board subvention—and the private agencies, to an even greater extent, are left continually uncertain in the projection of any even moderately long-range plans.

One specific project which might be undertaken in a State agency would be the inauguration of special units in the public employment service to provide personnel in a position to find jobs and carry on the necessary follow-up on the employment problems of maladjusted youth. A few private services are doing a notable job in this field, but their resources are pitifully small. Those who know the field assure me there are young people ready and able to go to work who are getting into trouble simply because we have no really effective, thoughtful, patient placement program to help them.

The New York City Mental Health Board will play an important part in the development of programs for maladjusted youth.

For example, there are virtually no treatment programs for older boys with emotional disorders leading to violent behavior—yet many youths who fall into this category could be taken care of without being sent to an institution. There is a similar lack of facilities for boys who could make a decent adjust to society if there was a club of some sort where they could live and have some counseling help, while continuing on their jobs or at school. Their families have failed them, and in this small but significant number of cases, their homes seem simply out of the question for the boys involved.

Still another need is for large-scale professional training programs over relatively long periods; the youth board institutes I have recommended are not designed to take college students and make psychiatrists, caseworkers, and the

---

[41] It would be well to bear in mind, however, that only $5 million would be made available for all 48 States together, if the bill were passed.

SPENDING MONEY ^OR
SAVING MONEY ?

WHAT $2500 A YEAR WILL PAY FOR:

 ONE BOY IN A CORRECTIONAL
INSTITUTION

——————————— OR ———————————

 INTENSIVE CASEWORK WITH
12 FAMILIES

OR

 RECREATION & CLUB PROGRAMS
FOR 85 KIDS

OR

 A TRAINED YOUTH LEADER FOR
25 TEEN-AGERS IN A STREET CLUB

OR

 A "REMEDIAL READING TEACHER"
FOR 15 CHILDREN

OR

 TRAINING INSTITUTES FOR
330 YOUTH WORKERS

 OR

 JUVENILE AID BUREAU
PATROLMAN; 165 CASES

like out of them.[42] They may not even be in a position to provide the major retraining which many professionals seem to need in order to work with some more violent youths.

We have profited in this study by consultation with Dr. Lemkau, and I have mentioned specific areas here more by way of example than as specific recommendations to the mental health board. As its own studies proceed, I am sure it will move in on a whole series of problems in our common effort to provide better services for delinquent and predelinquent youth.

THE ROAD AHEAD

We use the term "juvenile delinquent" to apply to children and youths guilty of a wide range of misbehavior. Most of these young people fall within the normal intelligence range. Their delinquency, in the overwhelming majority of cases, is not the outcome of any physical or hereditary defect. Most of the attitudes we deplore are not in any sense a reflection of brain disorders.

"Most juvenile delinquents are * * * potentially normal persons whose background is lacking in stabilizing influences both culturally and economically."

We would do well to bear in mind the words of a distinguished psychologist [43] from the National Institute of Mental Health, "Delinquency is as general a term as bellyache." It is important in approaching this problem that we bear in mind that the same delinquency may mean different things in the lives of different boys. Stealing, for example, may be the compulsive act of a habitual neurotic; or it may be the impulsive satisfying of a whim, a purely transitory phenomenon. It may represent a response to what a youngster conceives to be a challenge to his ingenuity; or it may be a hostile gesture against an unfriendly adult; or it may be the irresponsible "borrowing" of someone else's auto for an evening's joyride.

A crime is a crime and the wrongdoer must be made to answer for it. Yet in a very real sense, "circumstances alter cases" and the approach to rehabilitation for one offender may prove fantastically inappropriate in the case of another.

In considering remedial measures we will do well to proceed planfully, not acting on impulse, or going overboard for some precious scheme which is designed to wrap up the whole juvenile delinquency problem in one neat package. We will really start off on the wrong foot if we presume that there is a single appropriate approach to this riddle.

There are hard facts to be faced. Probably the most authoritative review of work in progress in this field, prepared by the United States Children's Bureau points out that:

"The causes of delinquency are numerous both in toto and within the individual case. This makes it unlikely that any program will achieve spectacular results. Most programs are single-focused. They aim at the elimination or amelioration of some condition that the backers regard as especially important in delinquency causation. Since, however, these conditions do not operate in isolation—either in the community or within the individual child and family—it is not to be expected that any single approach to delinquency prevention will be strikingly successful."

Helping rehabilitate delinquents, preventing youth in hazard from taking the delinquent path, requires focusing of skills from a number of fields. The teacher's knowledge in encouraging the acquisition of essential skills for living; the social worker's understanding of the interplay of emotion and action; the psychiatrist's insight into the deeper motives of behavior; the psychologist's skill in evaluating mental processes—no one alone suffices.

Programs to cope with delinquency may stand or fall depending upon the breadth of vision of professionals in those and other fields. Children will be receiving something less than the best we can offer, unless these specialists (along with religious leaders, guidance counselors, police and court officers) are, as people, big enough to pull together on a team, to share one another's skills.

Services to delinquent and pre-delinquent youth have crucial implications for the future of our city:

"Lest the generations of these maimed in childhood, each making the next in its own image, create upon the darkness, like mirrors locked face to face, an infinite corridor of despair."

---

[42] Our projected school of social work at Hunter College will not be in position to even start meeting this need for at least 18 months.

[43] Fritz Redl.

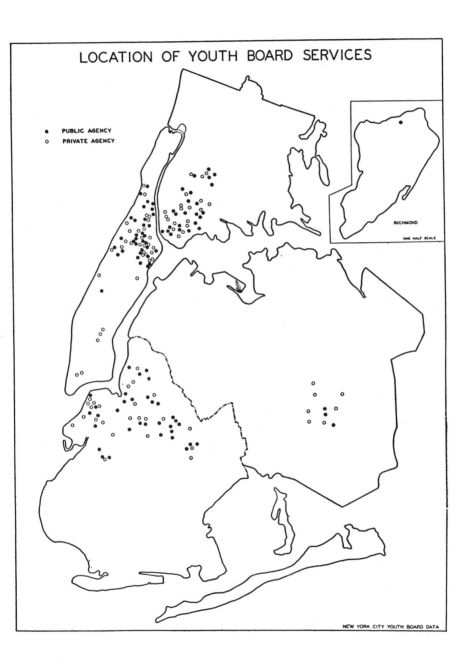

LOCATION OF YOUTH BOARD SERVICES

● PUBLIC AGENCY
○ PRIVATE AGENCY

RICHMOND

ONE HALF SCALE

NEW YORK CITY YOUTH BOARD DATA

Chairman KEFAUVER. I am cognizant of the fact that the New York Legislature did unusually fine work in the area of crime and horror comic books and pornographic literature earlier in the year. Assemblyman James Fitzpatrick's committee of the State legislature did a great deal of serious, conscientious work in this field.

We have come here with no intention of criticizing New York or any other one city or area; rather, we are here to show a nationwide picture. We seek and we feel we are entitled to receive the full cooperation of all public officials and thoughtful citizens throughout the Nation in this effort. Juvenile delinquency in general and pornographic literature in particular are problems facing every section. No one area should be singled out for censure. We must work together on a cooperative basis to solve this perplexing problem.

I would like to say at this time that no Senator has given more thoughtful attention to juvenile delinquency than my distinguished colleague, Senator William Langer, of North Dakota, who is here with us today. Senator Langer has personally conducted many hearings into this problem in all parts of the country. He has spent many hours conferring with those who have worked in this field and has conscientiously prepared valuable reports on this subject.

Since assuming the chairmanship of the Senate Subcommittee To Investigate Juvenile Delinquency in February of this year I have become increasingly concerned during each passing week with the effect pornographic material has on American adolescents and juveniles, and with the widespread distribution of this insidious filth. Therefore, some 2 months ago we directed the subcommittee staff—and I think we have a very excellent staff; several of the members being here, our chief counsel, Mr. James Bobo, on my left—to make an intensive investigation in this field.

Those of us on the subcommittee first became acutely aware of this problem while doing the preparatory work for the hearings on crime and horror comic books. In the course of our investigation on pornography the subcommittee has sent out more than 200 questionnaires to police chiefs in cities with a large population, and to more than 250 chiefs in small cities, rural areas, and university communities. An unusually high percentage of this group is cooperating.

I say without hesitation that I have been shocked and deeply disturbed personally by their findings.

The entire problem was pointed up by Mr. J. Edgar Hoover, Director of the Federal Bureau of Investigation, when he said:

The publication and distribution of salacious material is a peculiarly vicious evil; the destruction of moral character caused by it among young people cannot be overestimated. The circulation of periodicals containing such material plays an important part in the development of crime among the youth of our country.

Many people are under the impression that pornographic movies, so-called party records, pictures showing unnatural sexual activities, and other material of this sort is produced primarily for stag parties and men's smokers. The effect of this material on adults is undoubtedly degrading, but the long-range impact on juveniles is far more serious; and that is what we are considering here today.

We shall show by these hearings that a large portion of the market for this material is with the inquisitive and impressionable teenagers. This means that after young people have been exposed to these pornographic pictures and movies showing all types of perversion, they may tend to regard these things as normal. Indeed the influence is to lead them to embrace the abnormal and thus mar youthful lives.

We are calling witnesses who can testify to the effect this material has on the thinking and the habits of youngsters. I think it is time that this whole sordid business in insidious filth be brought into the open. The traffic in pornography has been growing by hundreds of thousands of dollars annually since the war.

While this traffic has been growing, sex crimes have increased with almost unbelievable rapidity. The statistics speak for themselves. A survey by the Federal Bureau of Investigation recently showed that during 1953 a sex criminal was arrested somewhere in our Nation every 6.7 minutes, day and night. Rape cases have increased 110 percent since 1937. More rapes are now being committed by 18- and 19-year-old boys than by males in any other age group, and the percenage of rapists under 20 has approximately doubled since 1940. The impulses which spur people to sex crimes unquestionably are intensified by reading and seeing filthy material. Certainly something must be done about this filth.

The control of pornography rests with three distinct yet interconnecting groups. They are: (1) The Federal Government; (2) States and local communities; and (3) the individual. Generally, none have shown sufficient awareness of this acute situation.

In this respect I believe that the Federal Government has been the chief offender. On the Federal level we can stop the importation of this salacious material by adequate legislation and increased enforcement. The Federal Government must also be concerned about the distribution of pornographic material through the mails and its transportation by private automobile in interstate commerce.

Basically, however, it is the responsibility of the Federal Government to provide leadership in the overall effort to combat the distribution of pornographic material.

On the State level, there is desperate need for improved State statutes. Several States are showing the way in this respect, and the signs are becoming more hopeful in many others.

Local law enforcement and the public interest in this problem still tends to be spasmodic and insufficient. This subcommittee means to do its best to insure that the Federal Government assumes its responsibility. I have great confidence that when the facts are known others will be willing and anxious to do their part.

It is my strong feeling and the feeling of my colleagues on the subcommittee that the most plausible solution is Federal legislation which will stamp out the traffic. We already have several possible bills in mind designed to plug the gaping loopholes in existing legislation. This subcommittee has already reported 2 bills—Senate bills 599 and 600—which are aimed at tightening Federal control of pornographic materials in interstate commerce. These bills were passed by the Senate and now await action of the House of Representatives.

We have come to New York City to hold these hearings because of the national and international character of this racket. While it is true that New York City has a great deal of difficulty with the distribution of pornographic material, this is also true in a great many other cities in the Nation. This problem is both local and national. Since New York is the most important port of entry, the subcommittee felt the national effort would be best helped by holding these hearings here. Several parts of the country, including the area around New York, are used as distribution points to channel the flow of smut into villages and hamlets across our great land. The Federal Government is responsible for stopping the influx of this material through the ports of entry and for its movement in interstate commerce.

We intend later to hold additional hearings on pornography in other parts of the Nation.

At the very outset let me make clear that the term "pornography" as it will be used in these hearings does not refer to legitimate magazines and books, although many of these border on the pornographic. This hearing will not even deal with the so-called art and health books, though some of them appear to be nothing more than a shrewd cover for pornography. Certainly we have no thought of censorship of any sort in mind. No one is more interested in the fullest freedom of the press than Senator Langer and me, but freedom of the press does not mean a license for indecency. Rather, we are concerned with publications and movies which everyone will agree portray and describe the basest sexual acts of perversions.

I have been greatly disturbed as I have looked through examples of material confiscated throughout the Nation in police raids. I cannot commend highly enough the many police chiefs who have cooperated so splendidly with our subcommittee and with our staff. Most are acutely aware of the seriousness of the situation. When I realize that much of the pornographic material is actually designed for the impressionable juvenile mind, it is certainly obvious that these materials could do incalculable damage to the moral and phychological fabric of our society through their effect on youngsters.

A large mail-order business in pornography is flourishing in every section of our land. We have received from many irate parents examples of advertisements sent through the mail trying to sell all sorts of filth to the very young. From our own State of Tennessee have come numerous advertisements of this material mailed orginally to teen-agers.

Not only do children see movies made by the pornographers, but we have examples of the obvious use of children ranging from 14 to 18 years of age participating in the making of the poronographic films. Youngsters are used a great deal to peddle the filth to other children.

Pornography is only one of the subjects with which this subcommittee is dealing. We have held extensive hearings on youth employment, the effect of television on young minds, runaway children, juvenile courts, problems among Indian children, public and private social and welfare agencies, and other subjects. The subcommittee also has dealt with the overall problem in some 20 communities; but certainly pornography is an important phase.

In summary, let me say that in our hearings on pornography here and elsewhere we shall explore principally these five fields:

First, the magnitude of the traffic in obscene and lewd publications, pictures, records, and movies.

Second, the international and interstate ramifications of pornography, its production, distribution, and sale.

Third, the impact of this material on juveniles and the use of juveniles in this traffic.

Fourth, expanded Federal legislation designed to eliminate this cancerous growth on our social fabric.

Fifth, advising law-enforcement officials, parents, and others of the situation because on them eventual success will rest.

This, I am sure all of you realize, is a delicate subject with which we are dealing. I feel confident that the press, the witnesses and all others will handle this problem according to the highest tenets of good taste. I do not want to arouse any curiosity among those groups which have not seen this sort of literature. On the other hand, I do not want to be like the proverbial ostrich and hide our heads in the sand to avoid the perplexing problem.

At one time there were those who said narcotics as a problem should be avoided. That is, publicity about it. Others have proposed closing their eyes to the existence of venereal disease. Experience and the tests of time have shown that only by facing up to these problems can they be solved. Intensive educational campaigns have reduced the incidence of venereal disease. A public awareness of all that is involved in narcotics addiction has been proved to be a vast help in this field.

This subcommittee proposes to handle pornography in an adult, enlightened, and restrained fashion. No evil can be cured by being ignored. I believe that the healthful sunshine of public opinion is the best cure for this problem or any other. We are determined to arrive at some substantial results from these hearings.

Let me say in the begining that because of the rules of the building we cannot have smoking in the courtroom. That is difficult for some, including the chairman.

Also, some names will necessarily be used by witnesses. For that purpose, for that reason we will swear the witnesses, place them under oath, and they will testify. Anyone whose name is brought out, if he feels that his position has not been properly presented, if he will let the staff of the committee know we will immediately give him an opportunity of being heard.

Our staff has scanned the evidence, gone over it as fairly as possible. We don't want to do anyone an injustice. If anyone feels that their position has not been properly presented, they will be allowed to testify immediately.

We are honored to have the movie cameras and the TV here with us. To the extent that it is feasible and possible, we want all media of publication to participate; but any witness who feels that he or she would be embarrassed or discommoded by the lights or by television and the movie cameras, if they will let the staff or the subcommittee know, they will not be asked to testify for television.

Also, some of these lights are pretty warm at times.

Senator Langer, do you wish to may any comments before we start?

Senator LANGER. No, Mr. Chairman.

Chairman KEFAUVER. I think I would probably better swear you reporters.

(At this point Chairman Kefauver swore Maxwell S. Lipton and H. Schneider to duly report the hearings of the subcommittee.)

Chairman KEFAUVER. Mr. Bobo, do you have any comments about the hearings before we start?

I might say that our hearing today will have to be cut short at about 12:30 because Senator Langer and I have to return to the Senate to be counted for a vote, which will be held at about 3 o'clock. We will have to recess here about 12:30. We will have a break at about 11, and then we will resume and carry on through until 12:30.

Tomorrow we have, unfortunately, the same situation. We will begin at 9 and will carry on, have a short lunch period and carry on until about 3; then we have to return to Washington for another vote. We will be back for the hearings to start at 9 o'clock Thursday.

Mr. Bobo, do you have a certain resolution that you want to read into the record?

Mr. BOBO. Yes; I have.

Resolved by the subcommittee of the Committee on the Judiciary——

Chairman KEFAUVER. Just state what it is.

Mr. BOBO. This is a resolution authorizing the sitting of this subcommittee in New York, with Senator Estes Kefauver and such other members as are present and are authorized to take sworn testimony, a copy of which is here agreed to by the full membership of the subcommittee.

Chairman KEFAUVER. Also let a copy of the resolution creating the subcommittee and the appointment of the subcommittee members be made a part of the record at this point.

(The documents referred to were marked "Exhibit No. 2," and read as follows:)

EXHIBIT No. 2

[S. Res. 89, 83d Cong., 1st sess.]

[Omit the part struck through and insert the part printed in italic]

RESOLUTION

Resolved, That the Committee on the Judiciary, or any duly authorized subcommittee thereof, is authorized and directed to conduct a full and complete study of juvenile delinquency in the United States. In the conduct of such investigation special attention shall be given to (1) determining the extent and character of juvenile delinquency in the United States and its causes and contributing factors, (2) the adequacy of existing provisions of law, including chapters 402 and 403 of title 18 of the United States Code, in dealing with youthful offenders of Federal laws, (3) sentences imposed on, or other correctional action taken with respect to, youthful offender by Federal courts, and (4) the extent to which juveniles are violating laws relating to the sale or use of narcotics.

SEC. 2. The committee, or any duly authorized subcommittee thereof, is authorized to sit and act at such places and times during the sessions, recesses, and adjourned periods of the Senate, to hold such hearings, to require by subpenas or otherwise the attendance of such witnesses and the production of such books, papers, and documents, to administer such oaths, to take such testimony. to procure such printing and binding, and, within the amount appropriated therefor, to make such expenditures as it deems advisable. The cost of stenographic services to report hearings of the committee or subcommittee shall not be in excess of 40 cents per hundred words. Subpenas shall be issued by the chairman of the committee or the subcommittee, and may be served by any person designated by such chairman.

A majority of the members of the committee, or duly authorized subcommittee thereof, shall constitute a quorum for the transaction of business, except that a lesser number to be fixed by the committee or by such subcommittee, shall constitute a quorum for the purpose of administering oaths and taking sworn testimony.

SEC. 2 *3.* The Committee shall report its findings, together with its recommendations for such legislation as it deems advisable, to the Senate at the earliest date practicable but not later than March 1, 1954.

SEC. 3 *4.* For the purposes of this resolution, the Committee, or any duly authorized subcommittee thereof, is authorized to employ upon a temporary basis such technical, clerical, and other assistants as it deems advisable. The expenses of the Committee under this resolution, which shall not exceed $50,000, shall be paid from the contingent fund of the Senate upon vouchers approved by the Chairman of the Committee.

[S. Res. 190, 83d Cong., 2d sess.]

RESOLUTION

Resolved, That section 3 of S. Res. 89, Eighty-third Congress, agreed to June 1, 1953 (authorizing the Committee on the Judiciary to make a study of juvenile delinquency in the United States), is amended to read as follows:

"SEC. 3. The committee shall make a preliminary report of its findings, together with its recommendations for such legislation as it deems advisable, to the Senate not later than February 28, 1954, and shall make a final report of such findings and recommendations to the Senate at the earliest date practicable but not later than January 31, 1955."

SEC. 2. The limitation of expenditures under such S. Res. 89 is increased by $175,000, and such sum together with any unexpended balance of the sum previously authorized to be expended under such resolution shall be paid from the contingent fund of the Senate upon vouchers approved by the chairman of the committee.

[S. Res. 62, 84th Cong., 1st sess.]

RESOLUTION

Resolved, That in holding hearings, reporting such hearings, and making investigations as authorized by section 134 of the Legislative Reorganization Act of 1946, and in accordance with its jurisdictions specified by rule XXV of the Standing Rules of the Senate insofar as they relate to the authority of the Committee on the Judiciary to conduct a full and complete study of juvenile delinquency in the United States, and including (a) the extent and character of juvenile delinquency in the United States and its causes and contributing factors, (b) the adequacy of existing provisions of law, including chapters 402 and 403 of title 18 of the United States Code, in dealing with youthful offenders of Federal laws, (c) sentences imposed on, or other correctional action taken with respect to, youthful offenders by Federal courts, and (d) the extent to which juveniles are violating Federal laws relating to the sale or use of narcotics, the Committee on the Judiciary, or any subcommittee thereof, is authorized from March 1, 1955, through July 31, 1955, (1) to make such expenditures as it deems advisable including no more than $2,000 for obligations outstanding and incurred pursuant to S. Res. 49, agreed to February 4, 1955; (2) to employ on a temporary basis such technical, clerical, and other assistants and consultants as it deems advisable; and (3) with the consent of the heads of the department or agency concerned, to utilize the reimbursable services, information, facilities, and personnel of any of the departments or agencies of the Government.

SEC. 2. The expenses of the committee under this resolution, which shall not exceed $125,000, shall be paid from the contingent fund of the Senate by vouchers approved by the chairman of the committee.

SEC. 3. This resolution shall be effective as of March 1, 1955.

RESOLUTION

Resolved by the subcommittee of the Committee on the Judiciary to Study Juvenile Delinquency in the United States, That pursuant to subsection (3) of rule XXV, as amended, of the Standing Rules of the Senate (S. Res. 180, 81st Cong., 2d sess., agreed to February 1, 1950) and committee resolutions of the Committee on the Judiciary adopted January 20, 1955, that Senator Estes Kefauver (Democrat, Tennessee), and such other members as are present, are authorized to hold hearings of this subcommittee in New York, N. Y., on May 23, 24, 25, and 26, and such other days as may be required to complete these hearings, and to take sworn testimony from witnesses.

Agreed to this 20th day of May 1955.

THOMAS C. HENNINGS, Jr.,
WILLIAM LANGER,
ALEXANDER WILEY,
Members of Subcommittee to Study Juvenile Delinquency.

Chairman KEFAUVER. Anything else, Mr. Bobo?

Mr. BOBO. That is all.

Chairman KEFAUVER. Our first witness.

Mr. BOBO. Mr. Peter N. Chumbris.

TESTIMONY OF PETER N. CHUMBRIS, ASSOCIATE COUNSEL, UNITED STATES SENATE SUBCOMMITTEE TO INVESTIGATE JUVENILE DELINQUENCY, OF THE COMMITTEE ON THE JUDICIARY

(Mr. Chumbris was sworn by Chairman Kefauver.)

Chairman KEFAUVER. We have a lot of witnesses. We want to get to the important points.

All right, Mr. Bobo, will you proceed?

Mr. BOBO. Mr. Chumbris, you have a statement there outlining the investigation which you have made as a member of the staff, showing the data that has been gathered by the subcommittee. I will ask you to proceed with your statement.

Chairman KEFAUVER. Mr. Chumbris is our associate counsel of our subcommittee, a very capable lawyer from Washington, D. C., who has been with the subcommittee for some time, and is a competent and fair attorney; and his investigation in this field has been very substantial.

Mr. CHUMBRIS. Thank you, Mr. Chairman.

Realizing the great impact that such lewd and obscene pornographic matter would have on youth, the subcommittee assigned to several members of the staff the investigation to be made of the nature and extent of the pornographic traffic in the United States and to determine if said traffic were of interstate character.

During the course of the investigation, I made it a practice to visit the police departments of the respective cities and counties or the prosecuting attorneys that I visited during the course of the investigations and hearings, as well as making special visits to these cities. We examined the exhibits that the departments had in their files that were taken from the violators of pornography.

In discussing the matter we obtained much information as to who the leading producers and distributors and small stores were that were selling this pornography, not only to adults but to many of the juveniles. We obtained their criminal records, their methods of operation and the territories which they covered.

Throughout this procedure the subcommittee showed that the traffic in pornography is interstate in nature and that it is fanned out across the four corners of our Nation.

If you will look at the map on my right here [exhibiting], each one of these dots represents various activities as is indicated at the top.

The related dots represent actual reports that we have received from the chiefs of police that pornography is being sold to juveniles. The blue dots indicate the cities that one distributor alone in Houston, Tex., fans out his operations in all of those cities.

Chairman KEFAUVER. Mr. Chumbris, it is hard to see just what the cities listed in the files of the Southwest distribution is. I cannot see what colors they are. Generally where does one man out of Houston operate?

Mr. Chumbris. The one man out of Houston, for instance, are these black dots [indicating], and you can see them all along in here. They go up into Kansas, Oklahoma, Arkansas, into Louisiana, Mississippi, Alabama, Georgia, Florida, part in Tennessee, Missouri. They go into Colorado, into two towns in New Mexico, and into Los Angeles, San Francisco, Sacramento, on north. They even reach up to Tacoma, Wash.; and that is one distributor from Houston, Tex.

Incidentally, the subcommittee worked with the police department of Houston, Tex., in apprehending this person who had that great traffic in distributing pornographic materials.

Chairman Kefauver. Is there any reason why you cannot tell us who he is?

Mr. Chumbris. That will be brought out later, Senator, during the course of these hearings.

Mr. Bobo. The man you are referring to, is that Ed Florance, of Houston, Tex.?

Mr. Chumbris. That's correct. And it was approximately about a week ago that this raid took place and this great haul was made by the police department of Houston.

Mr. Bobo. It is true this man's operations extended into Canada, South America, and Mexico?

Mr. Chumbris. That is correct, Mr. Bobo. Some of the cities and States——

Chairman Kefauver. Just a minute. Whenever you want to take any pictures, turn these lights on; but it is awfully hot. I don't know how we can arrange that. If you cannot, just say so.

Mr. Chumbris. Some of the cities and States from which information was received from the police departments and other city and State officials were: Philadelphia, Pa.; New York City, N. Y.; Pittsburgh, Pa.; Chicago, Ill.; Detroit, Mich.; Milwaukee, Wis.; Cleveland, Ohio; Miami, Fla.; St. Louis and Kansas City, Mo.; New Orleans, La.; Los Angeles, Calif.; Connecticut; and various cities in such States as Connecticut, Rhode Island, Massachusetts, North Carolina, the State of Washington, and several others.

From these personal interviews and in corresponding with these officials, the subcommittee was able to determine that certain individuals were known in many of these cities and States, and were known to be large distributors of pornographic matter in many parts of the country.

Several key witnesses will present testimony of the extent and nature of the interstate character of the filthy pornographic traffic; most of them are representatives of the police departments of these various cities.

Now, at the outset it would be interesting to note that with the changing of the times has also come a change in pornographic matter. Back in 1900 many States had inaugurated statutes to stop the traffic of pornography, but in those days they were little 2-by-4's known as "Maggie and Jiggs" books, little pamphlets, a few pictures. But today the business has become highly specialized. We have film, we have film in color, we have film with sound, we have wire recordings, tape recordings, records, playing records; we have booklets in color, and the usual type to which I have already referred.

Many of these statutes have been unaltered throughout the years, and because of this new influx of the type of pornographic material we have received from the various officials of the various States the complaint that the statutes need to be changed to meet this new problem that now confronts them.

Chairman KEFAUVER. That is true of the States' statutes, but it is especially true of our Federal statutes.

Mr. CHUMBRIS. That is correct. Federal statutes 1461, 1462, 1463, and 1464, a copy of which I have here and which I would like to introduce into evidence——

Chairman KEFAUVER. Let them be printed in the record.

(The documents referred to above were marked "Exhibit No. 3," and are as follows:)

EXHIBIT NO. 3

SEC. 1461. MAILING OBSCENE OR CRIME-INCITING MATTER

Every obscene, lewd, lascivious, or filthy book, pamphlet, picture, paper, letter, writing, print, or other publication of an indecent character; and

Every article or thing designed, adapted, or intended for preventing conception or producing abortion, or for any indecent or immoral use; and

Every article, instrument, substance, drug, medicine, or thing which is advertised or described in a manner calculated to lead another to use or apply it for preventing conception or producing abortion, or for any indecent or immoral purpose; and

Every written or printed card, letter, circular, book, pamphlet, advertisement, or notice of any kind giving information, directly or indirectly, where, or how, or from whom, or by what means any of such mentioned matters, articles, or things may be obtained or made, or where or by whom any act or operation of any kind for the procuring or producing of abortion will be done or performed, or how or by what means conception may be prevented or abortion produced, whether sealed or unsealed; and

Every letter, packet, or package, or other mail matter containing any filthy, vile, or indecent thing, device, or substance; and

Every paper, writing, advertisement, or representation that any article, instrument, substance, drug, medicine, or thing may, or can, be used or applied for preventing conception or producing abortion, or for any indecent or immoral purpose; and

Every description calculated to induce or incite a person to so use or apply any such article, instrument, substance, drug, medicine, or thing—

Is declared to be nonmailable matter and shall not be conveyed in the mails or delivered from any post office or by any letter carrier.

Whoever knowingly deposits for mailing or delivery, anything declared by this section to be nonmailable, or knowingly takes the same from the mails for the purpose of circulating or disposing thereof, or of aiding in the circulation or disposition thereof, shall be fined not more than $5,000 or imprisoned not more than five years, or both.

The term "indecent," as used in this section includes matter of a character tending to incite arson, murder, or assassination. (June 25, 1948, ch. 645, sec. 1, 62 Stat. 768, eff. Sept. 1, 1948.)

SEC. 1462. IMPORTATION OR TRANSPORTATION OF OBSCENE LITERATURE

Whoever brings into the United States, or any place subject to the jurisdiction thereof, or knowingly deposits with any express company or other common carrier, for carriage in interstate or foreign commerce any obscene, lewd, lascivious, or filthy book, pamphlet, picture, motion-picture film, paper, letter, writing, print, or other matter of indecent character, or any drug, medicine, article, or thing designed, adapted, or intended for preventing conception, or producing abortion, or for any indecent or immoral use; or any written or printed card, letter, circular, book, pamphlet, advertisement, or notice of any kind giving information, directly or indirectly, where, how or of whom, or by what means any of such mentioned articles, matters, or things may be obtained or made; or

Whoever knowingly takes from such express company or other common carrier any matter or thing the depositing of which for carriage is herein made unlawful——

Shall be fined not more than $5,000 or imprisoned not more than five years, or both. (June 25, 1948, ch. 645, sec. 1, 62 Stat. 768, eff. Sept. 1, 1948.)

Sec. 1463. Mailing Indecent Matter on Wrappers or Envelopes

All matter otherwise mailable by law, upon the envelope or outside cover or wrapper of which, and all postal cards upon which, any delineations, epithets, terms, or language of an indecent, lewd, lascivious, or obscene character are written or printed or otherwise impressed or apparent, are nonmailable matter, and shall not be conveyed in the mails nor delivered from any post office nor by any letter carrier, and shall be withdrawn from the mails under such regulations as the Postmaster General shall prescribe.

Whoever knowingly deposits for mailing or delivery, anything declared by this section to be nonmailable matter, or knowingly takes the same from the mails for the purpose of circulating or disposing of or aiding in the circulation or disposition of the same, shall be fined not more than $5,000 or imprisoned not more than five years, or both. (June 25, 1948, ch. 645, sec. 1, 62 Stat. 769, eff. Sept. 1, 1948.)

Sec. 1464. Broadcasting Obscene Language

Whoever utters any obscene, indecent, or profane language by means of radio communication shall be fined not more than $10,000 or imprisoned not more than two years, or both. (June 25, 1948, ch. 645, sec. 1, 62 Stat. 769, eff. Sept. 1, 1948.)

Mr. Chumbris. Of statutes prohibiting obscene, pornographic, lewd matter from being mailed or transported across State lines, or being brought into the United States.

Now, we also go into the State laws, and, Mr. Chairman, I also have here a summary of the State laws of the 48 States that I would like to have presented here this morning.

Chairman Kefauver. That will be printed in the Record as an exhibit in your testimony.

(The document referred to above was marked "Exhibit No. 4," and is as follows:)

Exhibit No. 4

The Library of Congress,
Legislative Reference Service,
Washington 25, D. C., May 19, 1955.
To: Senate Subcommittee on Juvenile Delinquency.
Attention: Mr. Schonberger.
From: American Law Division.
Subject: Minimum and maximum penalties imposed for violations of State laws pertaining to obscene and pornographic materials.

Alabama

Posting or leaving obscene picture or printed matter near a church, school, highway, etc.—Fine of $10 to $500, or punishment at hard labor by the county up to 12 months.
Introducing, advertising, or selling obscene material.—Fine of $50 to $1,000.
Display of nude pictures in public places, except galleries.—Fine of $50 to $500.
Code (1940) Lit. 14 §§ 372–374.

Arizona

Preparation, advertisement, distribution, sale or exhibition of obscene materials.—Imprisonment in county jail up to 6 months, or fine up to $300, or both.
Code Ann. (1939) §§ 43–110; 43–3002.

Arkansas

Circulation, offer for sale, and sale of obscene materials.—Fine of $100 to $300 for first offense; $500 to $1,000 for second offense.
Selling, offering for sale, or possessing any materials, the shipment of which has been rejected by the United States mails, or which the Federal Government will not permit to be shipped or handled. Fine of $50 to $100; each day of violation being a separate offense.
Stat. Ann. (1947) §§ 41–2704, 41–2706 to 41–2708.

California

Imprisonment in county jail up to six months or fine up to $500, or both, for the first offense; or imprisonment in state prison for not less than one year for subsequent offenses.—Penal Code (Deering, 1949) §§ 19, 311.

Colorado

Fine of $100 to $2,000 with costs, and imprisonment in the county jail up to one year.
Rev. Stat. (1953) § 40–9–17.

Connecticut

Imprisonment up to two years, or fine up to $1,000, or both.
Gen. Stat. (1949) § 8567.

Delaware

Fine of $250 to $2,500, or imprisonment for 30 days to three years, or both; and fine of $500 to $5,000, or imprisonment for six months to five years, or both, for subsequent offenses.
Code Ann. (West, 1953) ch. 11 §§ 711–712.

Florida

Imprisonment in state prison up to five years, in the county jail not exceeding one year, or fine up to $100.
Stat. Ann. (1944) § 847.01.

Georgia

Imprisonment for one to five years; or, on jury's recommendation, a fine not to exceed $1,000 or imprisonment up to six months at work on the public roads, or on other public works, not to exceed 12 months, or or more of these penalties.
Code Ann. (1953) §§ 26–6301; 27–2506.

Idaho

Imprisonment in county jail up to six months; or fine not exceeding $300, or both.
Code Ann. (1948) §§ 18–113, 18–4101.

Illinois

Imprisonment in county jail up to six months, or fine of $100 to $1,000.
Ann. Stat. (Smith-Hurd, 1935) ch. 38 § 468.

Indiana

Fine of $10 to $200, to which may be added imprisonment up to 90 days.
Stat. Ann. (Burns, Supp. 1953) § 10–2805.

Iowa

Imprisonment up to one year, or fine up to $1,000.
Code Ann. (West, 1950) § 725.4.

Kansas

Fine of $5 to $300, or imprisonment up to 30 days, or both, for dealing in obscene literature; fine of $50 to $1,000, or imprisonment from 30 to six months, or both, for publishing such literature.
Gen. Stat. Ann. (Corrick, 1949) §§ 21–1101 to 21–1102.

Kentucky

Fine of $50 to $1,000, or imprisonment from 10 days to one year, or both.
Rev. Stat. (1953) § 436.100.

Louisiana

Fine up to $500, or imprisonment up to two years, or both.
Rev. Stat. Ann. (West, 1951) Tit. 14 § 106.

Maine

Fine of $100 to $1,000, and imprisonment up to five years for publishing and circulating obscene materials. Fine of $25 to $100, or imprisonment up to six months, or both, for circulating such materials among minors.
Rev. Stat. (1954) ch. 134 § § 24, 27.

Maryland

Fine up to $200, or imprisonment up to one year, or both.
Code Ann. (Flack, 1951) art. 27 § 515.

Massachusetts

Imprisonment up to two years, or fine of $100 to $1,000, or both, for first offense; imprisonment of six months to two and one-half years, or fine of $200 to $2,000, or both, for subsequent offenses. These penalties apply to sales or distribution of obscene literature to persons under 18.

Imprisonment up to two years, or fine of $100 to $1,000, or both, for sale or distribution of obscene pamphlets, records and pictures, and books.

Ann. Laws (Supp. 1954) ch. 272 § § 27–28B.

Michigan

Imprisonment in county jail up to 90 days, or fine up to $100, or both, for first offense; imprisonment up to one year, or fine up to $500 for second offense; imprisonment up to four years, or fine up to $2,000, or both, for third and subsequent offenses.

Stat. Ann. (1938) § § 28.575–28.577, 28.577 (1), 28.771–28.772.

Minnesota

Imprisonment of 90 days to one year in county jail, or fine of $100 to $500, or both.

Stat. Ann. (West, 1947) § 617.24.

Mississippi

Fine up to $500, or imprisonment in county jail up to six months, or both.

Code Ann. (1942) § 2288.

Missouri

Fine of $50 to $1,000, or imprisonment in county jail up to 1 year, or both.

Ann. Stat. (Vernon, 1953) § 563.280.

Montana

Imprisonment in county jail up to 6 months, or fine up to $500, or both.

Rev. Code (1947) § § 94–116, 94–3601 to 94–3603.

Nebraska

Fine of $50 to $1,000, or imprisonment in county jail up to 1 year, or both.

Rev. Stat. (1943) § 28–921.

Nevada

Fine of $500 to $1,000, or imprisonment in county jail from 6 months to 1 year, or both.

Comp. Laws (Hillyer, 1929) § § 9968, 10144.

New Hampshire

Fine up to $500, or imprisonment up to 6 months, or both.

Rev. Laws (1942) ch. 441 § § 14–17; am. Laws 1947 ch. 73; 1953 ch. 233.

New Jersey

Fine up to $1,000, or imprisonment up to 3 years, or both.

Stat. Ann. (West, 1953) § § 2A : 85–7, 2A : 115–2.

New York

Imprisonment from 10 days to 1 year, or fine of $150 to $1,000, or both, for each offense.

Penal Law (McKinney, Supp. 1954) § 1141.

North Carolina

Common law penalty for misdemeanors; presumably by imprisonment in county jail up to 1 year, or fine in the discretion of the court, or both.

Gen. Stat. Ann. (Michie, 1944) § § 14–1 to 14–3, 14–189.

North Dakota

Fine of $5 to $100; or imprisonment in county jail up to 30 days, or both.

Rev. Code (1943) § 12–2109.

Ohio

Fine of $200 to $2,000, or imprisonment up to 7 years, or both.

Rev. Code (Page, 1954) § 2905.34.

Oklahoma

Fine of $10 to $1,000, or imprisonment from 30 days to 10 years, or both.

Stat. Ann. (West, Supp. 1954) Tit. 21 § 1021.

Oregon
  Imprisonment in county jail up to 6 months, or fine up to $500, or both.
  Rev. Stat. (1953) § 167.150.

Pennsylvania
  Fine up to $500, or imprisonment up to 1 year, or both.
  Stat. Ann. (Purdon, 1945) Tit. 18 § 4524.

Rhode Island
  Fine of $100 to $1,000, or imprisonment up to 2 years.
  Gen. Laws (1938) ch. 610 § 13.

South Carolina
  Fine up to $1,000, or imprisonment up to 2 years, or both.
  Code Ann. (1952) § 16–414.

South Dakota
  Fine up to $500, or imprisonment in county jail up to 1 year, or both.
  Code (1939) §§ 13.0607, 13.1722.

Tennessee
  Fine up to $1,000, or imprisonment in county jail up to 1 year, or both.
  Code Ann. (Williams, 1934) §§ 10756, 11190.

Texas
  Fine, up to $100.
  Penal Code Ann. (Vernon, 1952) art. 526.

Utah
  Fine up to $300, or imprisonment in county jail up to 6 months, or both.   Corporations may be fined up to $1,000.
  Code Ann. (1953) §§ 76–1–16, 73–39–1.

Vermont
  Fine up to $200, or imprisonment up to 1 year.
  Stat. (1947) § 8490.

Virginia
  Fine up to $500, or imprisonment up to 1 year, or both.
  Code Ann. (Michie, 1950) § 19–265; (Supp. 1952) § 18–113.

Washington
  Publishing detailed accounts of adultery, sexual crime, or of evidence of immoral acts offered in court: Fine up to $1,000, or imprisonment in county jail up to 1 year, or both.
  Sale, possession, distribution, or exhibition of obscene material: Fine up to $250, or imprisonment in county jail up to 90 days.
  R. C. W. (1951) §§ 9.68,010, 9.68.020, 9.92.020, 9.92.030.

West Virginia
  Fine up to $1,000, and imprisonment up to 1 year.
  Code Ann. (1949) § 6066.

Wisconsin
  Imprisonment in county jail from 3 months to 1 year, or imprisonment in State prison from 1 year to 5 years, or fine of $100 to $5,000.
  Stat. (1951) § 351.38.

Wyoming
  Fine up to $100, to which may be added imprisonment in county jail up to 6 months.
  Comp. Stat. (1945) § 9–513.

NORMAN G. SMALL.

Chairman KEFAUVER. Incidentally, in that connection, a New York law has been amended, an admirable effort to do something about this problem, in the last legislature.

Mr. CHUMBRIS. That is correct, Senator. And I will point out that there are several other States that have seen the light in view of the

CITIES WHERE THE SALE, DISTRIBUTION, OR POSSESSION OF PORNOGRAPHIC LITERATURE
HAS BEEN ESTABLISHED ON THE BASIS OF 20% RETURNS OF 500 SUBCOMMITTEE
QUESTIONAIRES

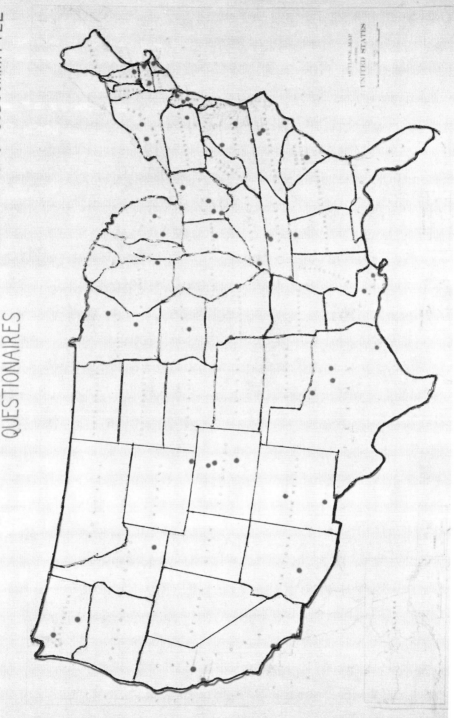

OUTLINE MAP
UNITED STATES

[Face p. 52]

mounting complaints by police officials, by the courts themselves, and by the legislators themselves. We have had several statutes that have been amended to make it more stringent, and also to take in pornographic matter that was not previously covered by the laws.

For example, here are some of the quotations that we have received from chiefs of police and other officials.

City of St. Paul, Minn.——

Chairman KEFAUVER. Mr. Chumbris, will you make it clear the number of inquiries sent out to the chiefs of police?

Mr. CHUMBRIS. Yes, sir. As you stated in the opening statement, Senator, we sent out questionnaires to all cities in the United States with a population of 100,000 or more. Besides that, we sent them to the State capitols of the States in which the population does not quite reach 100,000, and also to the larger cities in some States which do not quite reach 100,000 population. (See map.)

We also sent them to the towns where there are colleges or other large concentrations of youth, to see if there is any specific traffic going into prep school areas and colleges, and Army camps, and so forth.

From the returns that we have received, which are still incomplete returns, I have these following quotations which will point out the problem that the States have in dealing with this pornographic material.

In St. Paul, Minn.:

> I believe that penalties for the manufacture of such materials should be so strong as to discourage any repeating by violators. The State legislature is now in the process of passing new laws tightening restrictions on this matter.

The State legislature of Wisconsin at the present time has under consideration more stringent bills for violation of the obscenity laws of the State.

In Minnesota, the police department of the city of Minneapolis states:

> In some cases, we do not feel that our laws, either State or local, are adequate to cope with the so-called art magazines and photos. Without any question, certain of these magazines would be detrimental to the minds of juveniles.

The police department of city of Worcester, Mass.: "Penalties are not sufficient," is their answer to the question propounded:

> In your opinion, are penalties rendered for these offenses sufficient to act as a deterrent to committing the offense?

At this time, Mr. Chairman, I would also like to present a copy of the questions that we sent out to these various police officials throughout the country.

Chairman KEFAUVER. Let it be printed in the record.

(The document referred to was marked "Exhibit No. 5," and is as follows:)

EXHIBIT No. 5

APRIL 12, 1955.

Mr. ----------------------
      Chief of Police
Address ----------------------
DEAR MR. ----------------------

This subcommittee, in investigating the overall problem of juvenile delinquency, has become concerned with certain special problems. One of these is the manufacture, distribution, sale, and possession of pornographic materials. A preliminary survey of the problem revealed valuable information and secured leads to persons connected with the traffic in this insidious filth.

Another special problem which has an impact on youth is the so-called white-slave racket, of which the subcommittee is seeking further information.

In order to determine the nature, extent, and national scope of these operations, answers to the following questions will prove most beneficial to the subcommittee. Staff investigators will be available to follow up leads furnished by you.

1. Please list the names (with aliases) and addresses of all persons arrested and/or convicted in the past 2 years in your jurisdiction of the production or distribution of pornographic literature of any kind.

2. Will you make any photos, criminal records, or other information of the above available to the subcommittee?

3. Please furnish names and addresses of accomplices of the above, even though not arrested or charged with violation of the obscene-literature statutes or ordinances.

4. Please give the names and addresses of owners of buildings where pornographic literature was produced, stored, or sold.

5. Please furnish names and addresses of persons, other than above, known to be engaged in manufacture or sale of pornography.

6. In your opinion, is traffic in pornographic material in your jurisdiction extensive, medium, or light? Is it directed to adult or children?

7. In your opinion, are penalties rendered for these offenses sufficient to act as a deterrent to committing the offenses?

8. In your opinion, are State and local laws adequate to cope with the problem?

9. Do you have samples of pornographic materials? If so, will you make them available for subcommittee staff inspection?

10. Do you have evidence or reason to believe that persons dealing in pornographic materials are connected with a ring or other criminal activity such as narcotics or white slavery?

11. Please furnish copies of any lists of customers you may have confiscated from persons dealing in such materials.

12. Please furnish names and addresses of all persons arrested in the past 2 years in your jurisdiction on charges of white slavery.

Any suggestions you might care to make on measures designed to curb the traffic in pornography and/or white slavery will be greatly appreciated and will be given serious consideration. The above questions are posed with the idea that they will be a guide in submitting the information the subcommittee desires.

With kindest personal regards, I am,
Sincerely,

ESTES KEFAUVER, *Chairman.*

Mr. CHUMBRIS. The chief of police from Gary, Ind.:

In our poinion, the sentences should be greater, especially where juveniles are the purchasers.

Chief of police of Durham, N. C.:

In my opinion, the penalties rendered in these cases should be more severe— and, further—

I believe that the State and local laws should be made stronger with respect to obsence literature.

Chief of police, city of Norfolk, Va.:

In my opinion, State and local laws are adequate to cope with the problem, however, I feel that the punishment should be more severe.

Chief of police of Dallas, Tex., states:

In my opinion, State and local laws are not adequate to cope with the problem. Under Texas laws, violations of this type are claimed as misdemeanors.

And we find that to be the case in many States, that they are misdemeanors and not felonies.

The city of Los Angeles has an interesting statement:

Under our present laws, it is sometimes difficult to obtain convictions that discourage future participation by the defendant, because the sentence imposed is quite often negligible. It is generally felt that if such a conviction would require registration as a sex offender, the frequency of repeaters would drop noticeably. Uniformity of the laws pertaining to pornography would be of great value insofar as the liaison between police agencies is concerned. Many acts constituting a violation of the Los Angeles municipal code sections are not illegal acts in other States and cities.

As to our questionnaires, we also received some very pertinent information as to how the traffic reaches individual juveniles.
Rochester, N. Y.:

Violator was charged with possessing indecent pictures. Officer found subject showing indecent pictures and books to a group of 13-year-old girls in front of No. 14 School on University Avenue. Subject pleaded guilty.

This was in 1954, in March.
Columbus, Ohio:

Subject now in Ohio State Penitentiary—used juvenile girls for models to lewd photographs.

I might point out that the State of Ohio has one of the stiffest penalties for pornography. It is up to 7 years in the penitentiary, and $2,000 fine.

I would also like to point out that the subcommittee, in official business in North Dakota, conferred with the judiciary committee of the house, in which the opinion of the subcommittee was asked, and they accepted the recommendations of the subcommittee, and they now have one of the most stringent laws, most up-to-date laws, dealing with pornography.

They even provide for the confiscation of the equipment, so that the man cannot go back in business. I understand that that is one of the few States in the United States that does have that law in effect.

Chairman KEFAUVER. By "equipment" you mean not just films, you would mean the projector and the others?

Mr. CHUMBRIS. The projector, the automobile that transports the pornography into other States, any type of equipment they may have. Because we have found instances where the city police say:

We throw up our hands; we grab a man with $50,000 worth of pornography, and his equipment, his car, and they burn up the pictures and so forth; they give him back his car, they give him back his equipment, and right away he is setting up business again in another town after he gets out of the jurisdiction of that particular court.

Seattle, Wash., going back to places where juveniles are purchasing or are being confronted with pornographic matter:

That where there is pornographic material, it is somewhat difficult to determine what is directed specifically to adults or to children. As long as it is in a community, it appears to us that it is available to either.

Trenton, N. J.:

Subject sold indecent and obscene literature and pictures to juveniles. Convicted of violation of the crimes act, sentenced to 18 months.

Senator LANGER. Mr. Chumbris, would you say that the North Dakota law would be a model for other States to follow?

Mr. CHUMBRIS. I think so, Senator. I think it would be an excellent law, especially the provision of confiscation of the equipment. Our subcommittee last year introduced such a bill in the Congress of the United States covering the District of Columbia, where we do now have jurisdiction, and that bill did not pass; but it will be considered again by this Congress.

Chairman KEFAUVER. As a result of our hearings in North Dakota, and Senator Langer, that the legislature out there did change the law in North Dakota; is that correct?

Mr. CHUMBRIS. That is correct. We appeared before the judiciary committee, and they followed our suggestions. They asked us for our suggestions, and they followed them to the letter.

Chairman KEFAUVER. All right.

Mr. CHUMBRIS. Los Cruces, N. Mex. In answer to a question of how much of the pornographic matter reaches minors, the chief of police answered:

Approximately 75 percent of the pornographic material reaches minors.

Des Moines, Iowa:

As mentioned previously, some of these pornographic books were found in one of our schools by a teacher who chanced to notice a group of boys looking at them, they notified police and more of the booklets were found in subject's store, hidden in the back counter. The boy who obtained the books had worked at the store after school hours. Subject was arrested a second time for possession of pornographic booklets.

In this instance some of the materials were found on children in elementary schools, not junior high or high school, but elementary schools.

On a complaint from a father who claimed a photograph dropped from his daughter's school book, the subject was arrested and found to have 600 pornographic pictures and 7 reels of film depicting lewdness at its worst. The subject stated that the salesman was driving a car with New York plates.

Yakima, Wash.——

Chairman KEFAUVER. Just a minute. You spoke of a pornographic material being found among kids in elementary school. Does it indicate what age group that is?

Mr. CHUMBRIS. In this report it did not. This was taken from the questionnaire that the chief of police sent us. But children of elementary school——

Chairman KEFAUVER. That would be 12 or under, 13 or under?

Mr. CHUMBRIS. That's right. From 6 to 12, 13 would be the highest age of the children in elementary school, I would assume.

Yakima, Wash.:

In December, 1954, it came to the attention of the police department that a number of juveniles in one of the junior high schools had in their possession some lewd pictures. Subject was arrested and charged with possession of obscene photographs and fined $50 and given a 30-day jail sentence. Subject, an amateur photographer, stated he borrowed the pictures and made a set of negatives. He admitted printing over 400 of these pictures.

South Hadley, Mass.:

Pornographic material of lewd playing cards and pictures were strewn about a pond that is frequented by children in the neighborhood. The ages of the children were of school age—8 to 10 years of age—and pupils of Woodlawn School here in town. In all, I would say about 25 to 30 pictures were turned over to the police department.

Minneapolis, Minn.:

This letter was from a criminologist: "I gather that the use of pornographic movies is extensive among university and high school students in Minneapolis. Matteson, in the State bureau of apprehension, says that he doubts whether any college student goes through 4 years without being exposed at least once to a pornographic movie. Recent graduates of the University of Minnesota confirmed this. If so, there is extensive distribution of which the police are unaware or in which they are impotent."

Paducah, Ky.:

In answer to our question of estimate of pornographic material getting to minors, the answer is, "about 75 percent."

Manchester, N. H.:

Subject, aged 18, was arrested for giving obscene books away and for showing obscene books. He pleaded nolo contendere to both counts and was placed on probation for 6 months.

Raleigh, N. C.:

Subject was convicted of selling sexy comic books to high school students and was given 12 months sentence. It seems to me that this could be more effectively attacked on a nationwide basis, because that is the only basis whereby the sources can be controlled.

This is still the quotation from the chief of police:

If this department may be of further service to you or your committee, 1 assure you that we shall endeavor to do so to the best of our ability.

Harrisonburg, Va.:

Recently we received a complaint of a subject selling these materials, and subject had been selling this material to high school students.

Wilmington, N. C.:

During the entire investigation of obscene literature we received information that this literature had filtrated throughout the schools of the county and that it could be purchased by anyone who applied for it from the Piner or the Carolina Camera Shops.

West Allis, Wis.:

Subject had 22 obscene films in his possession. He was showing them in his basement, and 12 juveniles came to our attention who had viewed these films.

Boy 12 years old picked up with a telescope that had a picture of a nude woman in it. This boy took this from the bureau of his older brother, who had purchased it from an unknown man in a tavern.

Boy 17 with two obscene pictures, origin unknown. Boy was picked up as a prowler, was referred to juvenile authorities.

St. Louis, Mo.:

The pornographic material has been known to find its way into schools, as was true in the case of three individuals who were charged with sale and distribution of pornographic literature.

Eddyville, Ky.:

Pornographic literature is being sold to minors at numerous gasoline filling stations in this area.

Burlington, N. J.:

Pornographic literature is being sold at quite a number of the newsstands. Nine minors have committed illegal sexual acts as a result of reading this material.

New York, N. Y.:

Pornographic literature is being sold at several bookstores in New York City.

Philadelphia, Pa.:

Pornographic literature has stirred up male youth, who consequently go out and commit "gang rape." This mass rape is an integral part of the juvenile gang warfare system. Its frequency is underestimated, and that is because many of the victims are afraid to report these crimes to the authorities.

Boulder, Colo.:

What percentage of this traffic would you estimate reaches minors?

The answer:

If any traffic, would suppose that most of it is among schoolchildren.

City of Long Beach, Calif.:

Traffic in pornographic material is light in this jurisdiction, and it is mainly directed to adults—

meaning that still some of it goes to juveniles.

Buffalo, N. Y.:

Our last referral to the youth bureau of the Buffalo Police Department was in connection with the distribution of pornographic literature and obscene comics among schoolchildren in the local area.

Boston, Mass.:

Subject was found guilty of rape of a 16-year-old girl, and investigation of premises revealed 50 photos of pornographic nature. There are other instances of individuals being charged with sex offenses and exhibiting obscene material to 9- and 10-year-old girls.

Cleveland, Ohio:

Nude sequence photographs found in subject's house, with girls in photos obviously juveniles.

Baton Rouge, La.:

Examination of case records (three such cases) tend to show, as does past experience in our department, that the nature of this pornographic literature is reaching students and children of junior high and high school age brackets.

Denver, Colo.:

Subject charged with attempting to molest two teen-age girls, was found to have six small pulp magazines of pornographic nature in the glove compartment of his car.

This bears out, Mr. Chairman, the opening statement where J. Edgar Hoover states that the growing sex crimes committed by 17- and 18-year-old boys—they read the stuff, and they go out and molest these young girls.

Several cities, such as the city of Roanoke, Va., state that they are unable to say what percentage of the pornographic traffic would reach minors, indicating there that it is there, but they cannot break it down as to how much goes to adults and how much goes to minors.

Phoenix, Ariz.:

In answer to our question of whether traffic is directed to adults or children, the answer was directed to juveniles.

The police further state:

It is our suggestion that parents of juveniles be impressed with the necessity of training their children to report any display of or attempt to sell them pornographic literature.

I think that is a sentence that can be well borne in mind by the parents of America.

Now we come to advertisements by mail. We are going to have witnesses from the Post Office Department who will give us their problems and the full picture; but I would like to point out that in this mailing of pornographic material, first they have these name lists where the companies, A, B, C, for instance, at a certain address, will send out these circulars. The circulars are very, very suggestive. The question is, How to stop that advertising from getting to these minors, because we are receiving many complaints.

Name lists is a big business. Some of them are very, very legitimate; they are very legitimate name lists of juveniles used by baby-clothing stores and baby-food operators, and so forth; but somehow or other these certain individuals will obtain these name lists from legitimate sources, by hook or crook, and then take and turn around and sell these name lists and make a terrific amount of money.

In one of the cases that we will present during the course of these hearings I personally examined the material that was confiscated by the police department, and they had a file case that is almost as big as some of our governmental agencies, full of name lists that this man had at his command, over 100,000 names of different persons, and he concentrated as much as possible, as much as he could, on juveniles. I mean, that seemed to be the big business to them.

In order to see how that operation went into effect, the subcommittee used a procedure used by the Post Office Department. A definite name and address was taken, a letter was written to those people who advertised in these magazines of these type of photos and films that are supposed to be of a shady nature. It was written in the handwriting of a juvenile, on high-school stationery, sent to these advertisers. None of the advertisers attempted to find out whether the letter which was written on high-school stationery in juvenile handwriting was a person underage or overage. He immediately sent the order that was requested.

That type of advertising is a headache to the Post Office Department, and I am sure they will bring it out in full during the course of these hearings.

That name-list business is big business, and it has stumped the law-enforcement agencies as to how best treat it.

Chairman KEFAUVER. Tell us in a little more detail how the name list works. These pornographic outfits get the name lists and they send something not only suggestive literature, but they don't exactly describe what it is?

Mr. CHUMBRIS. That's right. They give you an idea that it is of the lewdest type, and the person answer, and the first time they will send you back something that will be, let's say, a nude picture which they think that they can get by without prosecution from the law.

Then what they hope to do is establish a relationship, and the next order will be for more of the pornographic, until finally, we believe and we do hope that we will be able to establish that before we complete our investigation on pornography, that the first orders are come-ons, and finally they go into the lewd filthy, pornographic material. And this goes to juveniles.

Chairman KEFAUVER. A big part of it is with juveniles?

Mr. CHUMBRIS. A great amount of it is with juveniles.

As a matter of fact, one of the pictures that we received was of a boy in the nude, part of it was blacked out, but that boy couldn't have been more than 15 years old, from his appearance.

Chairman KEFAUVER. All right, sir, will you proceed.

Mr. CHUMBRIS. The other map that you see there [indicating] on the board, the smaller map is the one dealing with returns that we have received from police officers showing traffic to juveniles alone; I mean traffic to juveniles. So you can see how well it is spread out throughout the country, and that is only a 20-percent return on the questionnaries that we have received.

I have just one more topic to discuss, Mr. Chairman, and that is a specific case that I am going to present here this morning, one in which the police officers of that city are not here to testify, and since I personally made the investigation and know, examined the court records and talked with the police officers, I know of it personally of my own knowledge, and I would like to explain that case to you now.

Mr. Bobo. Mr. Chumbris, on this mail-order business which you have been discussing, I think also you are involved in that business are a number of dildoes, d-i-l-d-o-e-s, as they are referred to in the trade, of a sexual nature, that have been going out in the mails to youngsters as young as 12 and 13, of which I believe we have evidence in our files.

I think also you have within your information, it could be within your possession this morning, a number of letters advertising these books, the messages from the parents, showing the widespread operation of it, concerning Gallatin, Tenn., which deals in this material; concerns New York and Los Angeles, and various other cities around the country.

Do you have any more information on the mailing lists? I know that you referred to baby foods and diaper shops. I don't think that the mailing list would be obtained from baby foods and diaper shops for the mailing of this material.

Mr. Chumbris. That's one of the leads. The baby foods and diaper shops have legitimate name lists. Somehow or other these people who operate in mailing lists will get some of these names from that list.

For example, in these sample letters that we sent out they were sent to certain, let's say, three different companies. Then a month or so later 4 or 5 companies with whom no correspondence was had suddenly got hold of the names, which indicates that there is a method of transferring names, exchanging names, or in some instances it might be—well, I couldn't exactly explain what their method of procedure is, and that is one of the problems that we would like to explore.

Mr. Bobo. In your investigation with this subcommittee, is it not true that we have uncovered instance after instance where children would answer a magazine ad, in either a comic book or a legitimate trade magazine, and at a later date he would receive through the mail advertisements for material of a pornographic nature?

Mr. Chumbris. That's correct.

Mr. Bobo. That might be mailable, and then at a later time the more lewd stuff would be presented to him?

Mr. Chumbris. That's right. And how they would get those names we have not definitely established that; but it is being done.

Mr. Bobo. Presumably a mailing list from answers to advertisements.

Mr. Chumbris. Yes.

Mr. Bobo. All right. Suppose you continue.

Mr. Chumbris. In this case, the Saxton case, which was in Pittsburgh, Pa., one Louis Stevens Saxton, of 4204 Verona Boulevard, Pittsburgh, Pa., was arrested on October 25 of 1951 and charged with the manufacture and statewide distribution and sale of obscene literature——

Mr. Bobo. Mr. Chumbris, is this the case that you are speaking of now, the man who was operating from the jail cell?

Mr. Chumbris. That's correct. Then after he was convicted?

Chairman Kefauver. Let's get his name again now.

Mr. Chumbris. His name is Louis Stevens Saxton.

Chairman Kefauver. You have his criminal record; you have the official records?

Mr. Chumbris. Yes. We have his record; we have his mug; everything was furnished to us by the police department.

He was convicted and was serving time. While he was in jail he contacted an accomplice known as Clarence Meade Barnes, who was on the outside. Clarence Meade Barnes continued the operations on the outside while Saxton masterminded from the jail. He was also indicted with Barnes on that particular offense and was also sentenced.

Chairman Kefauver. Was that a big operation?

Mr. Chumbris. Yes; it was quite a big operation. The interesting part of the operation was that besides manufacturing the pornographic material they actually acted as distributors; they were known distributors in the East who would make big drops of this particular material in the Pittsburgh area, and Saxton would be the person who would handle it.

For instance, in a letter from Saxton to Barnes, which was written in code and then later Barnes explained to——

Mr. Bobo. Mr. Chumbris, do you have a copy of that letter in your files?

Mr. Chumbris. That's up in the files of the subcommittee.

Barnes, in finally revealing the full statement to Lieutenant Carnahan of the police department of Pittsburgh, stated that the letter was in code. For instance, they would use the word "jewelry." Every time they used the word "jewelry" it referred to pornography. If it said "$50 worth of jewelry," it meant that it was $50 worth of pornography. If it mentioned "John owes $50 for jewelry," it meant that John owed $50 for pornography, "Will you go by and pick up the checks," and so forth.

In it the actual operations were explained by Barnes to the police officer, how Saxton had him go ahead and print these "Maggie and Jiggs" books, and Barnes went ahead and did it. He admitted that he went ahead and produced it.

Mr. Bobo. When you speak of "Maggie and Jiggs" books, Mr. Chumbris, I think you should explain what a "Maggie and Jiggs" book is.

Mr. Chumbris. Yes. I mentioned earlier, when I was explaining the different types of pornography, the "Maggie and Jiggs" books are two-by-fours, they are books 2 inches by 4 inches; they are also known as 8 pages, because it contained 8 thin pages. They are caricatures, they are cartoons. They usually take people from the comic strips, or famous movie stars, and they portray them in very lewd, perverted acts.

Chairman Kefauver. You are not getting us mixed up with Bud Fisher?

Mr. Chumbris. No. That is very legitimate operation. Not only Maggie and Jiggs, but almost every known legal comic strip in the business, their characters are being stolen and placed into these filthy, lewd books.

Chairman KEFAUVER. Plagiarized, is that what you call it?

Mr. CHUMBRIS. That's right.

Chairman KEFAUVER. I think it would be well to get this letter and put it in the record, and let the press see it.

Mr. CHUMBRIS. Do you have any further questions on the Saxton case?

Chairman KEFAUVER. How long is this letter that you have?

Mr. CHUMBRIS. Well, the first letter is about a page long, and the questions and answers are approximately three pages long.

Chairman KEFAUVER. What are the questions and answers?

Mr. CHUMBRIS. That was the interview.

For instance, he says, "What is your full name?" This is the interrogation of the witness. And then he explained the full operation.

For instance—I may read part of it——

Mr. BOBO. Would you read the letter into the record?

Mr. CHUMBRIS. Yes. [Reading:]

DEAR BUD: Sorry you were not able to get over to the hospital before I left. Alice said that you and Margaret were over, and that you called last week. Do hope you and the family are all well. No doubt, I will have to return to the hospital and have my leg amputated; it is much worse, and nothing can be done here; it is a tough decision to have to make.

And I do believe that that means that he would like to get back into the business, when he is referring to a statement of that type.

Did want to ask you a few questions. You do not have to write and answer them, but I remember a few things that may help out in a business way. Did you ever get the color formula from Mr. Wilner? Believe he has to have it in a week or so, for you. How is your friend in Kinsman? You said you talked with him, and he wanted to get 4 of your $8 size watches.

Mr. MARTIN (consultant to subcommittee). Mr. Chumbris, will you show the relationship between the reference to the $8 watch and the corresponding information from his accomplice which established what he means?

Mr. CHUMBRIS. Yes. He says here, for instance, the next statement that he has—

How is your friend in Kinsman? You said you talked with him and he wanted to get 4 of your $8 size watches. No doubt they will cost him $30 each, but they are worth it.

Now, who is Kinsman, and what does he mean by "these watches" and the price? Kinsman is a man from Ohio, and as far as the watches, it means 8-millimeter film, movies, and the price is $30 each. That's the way they go all the way through the letter.

Chairman KEFAUVER. Put the letter and the questions and answers into the record; let them be printed in the appendix and made part of the record. The letter is received.

(The information referred to was marked "Exhibit No. 6," and is as follows:)

FEBRUARY 3, 1953.

To: Mr. C. M. Barnes, 514 Cato Street, Pittsburgh, Pa.

DEAR BUD: Sorry you were not able to get over to the hospital before I left. Alice said that you and Margaret were over, and that you called last week. Do hope you and the family are all well. No doubt, I will have to return to the hospital and have my leg amputated; it is much worse, and nothing can be done here; it is a tough decision to have to make. Did want to ask you a few questions. You do not have to write and answer them, but I remembered a few things that may help out in a business way. Did you ever get the color formula from Mr. Wilner? Believe he was to have it in a week or so for you. How is your friend in Kinsman? You said you talked with him, and he wanted to get 4 of your $8-size watches. No doubt they will cost him $30 each, but they are worth it. Did Ben ever drop around? Oh, I owe Nick $17.50 in case he wants any jewelry. Have you seen Whitey lately? You should see him some evening when you go bowling. Papy, no doubt, has not seen the advertising match display, or has he? Wish you would call Jonney, the bakery salesman, up, or Margaret could call. The best time is on a Saturday morning between 10:30 and 11. The name you have. He can use those five $16 watches at $30 plus the 2 special ones you have in the same size. He said he would need them. The specials I told him you wanted $70 for the 2. Did your other friend collect that $50 for the check that was returned? Should Margaret call Jonney this Saturday, have her tell him to give Alice the $50 he owes me for perfume, as I need it for insurance payments; and he should pay Margaret for the watches he takes. Did your friend finish all the advertising matches, less what he spoiled? You should keep count of what you receive. You could pay him what is due when Jonney pays for the jewelry. Give Alice any balance due. By the way, I know that George, your pal in Murrysville, was asking about you. I told him I would tell you. Would you write a letter to Mrs. Sofie Levy, 2992 Tinker Drive, Oceanside, N. Y., and explain to her that I did not know about the insurance check until you advised me? Tell her that as soon as possible the amount will be sent you for the balance due on the fur coat. Also tell her it would not be advisable to come to Pittsburgh during the bad weather, but you will let her know. Hope you get to see your pal from Kinsman. Of course you could call him up. Keep Alice advised, but be sure and have Jonney leave the $50 with her; and his 'phone number I believe you have. Should you be going out past Whitey's, tell Alice to give you two bottles of perfume to give to his wife. Say hello for me. Hope you understand everything. The fireworks display business should begin to book their orders soon. Sure could use a good year. Best wishes and regards to all of you, and get your match advertising finished and pay it off. Did you pay the bill at Shield's Rubber Co.. How's the car doing? You could look at the thermostat in Alice's car. It does not work. Also, the trunk door lock. Write me when you can.

Yours always,

LEW.

P. S.—Those 2 special watches I told him were $70.

This is the statement of Clarence Meade Barnes, white, aged 42, of 514 Cato Street, Pittsburgh, Pa. It is taken in the office of Assistant Superintendent of Police Adam A. Geisler under the direct examination of Acting Lt. Allen Carnahan, the interrogator and James Patton, city detectives, Narcotic Squad. Also present in the room while the statement is being typed is Margaret Barnes, wife of Clarence Barnes. J. H. Gamble is the typist. Statement is begun at 4:05 p. m., February 23, 1953.

Q. What is your full name?—A. Clarence Meade Barnes.

Q. How old are you?—A. 42.

Q. Where do you live?—A. 514 Cato Street, Pittsburgh, Pa.

Q. Are you married or single?—A. Married.

Q. Are you employed?—A. Yes.

Q. Where?—A. Westinghouse Electric Corp., East Pittsburgh, Pa.

Q. Now, Clarence, do you understand that you are under arrest by this department charged with the manufacture, possession, and sale of obscene literature, pornographic pictures, obscene movies and books?—A. I know I'm here because I had that "junk."

Q. We are going to ask you to give us a statement concerning this charge against you. Before you give us this statement in your own words in answer to our questions, we wish to advise you of your rights. You will not be forced to say anything here, but what you do say may be used against you or for you at the time of your trial in a court of law. Do you understand this?—A. All right.

Q. We also wish to advise you that you have the right to secure legal counsel, an attorney, if you so desire. Do you understand this?—A. Yeah.

Q. And now that you understand what we are doing here and your rights have been explained to you, are you still willing to go along with us and to answer the questions in your own language that we may ask you?—A. That's right, I'm willing.

Q. Clarence, this obscene material that we confiscated from your home on Saturday, February 21, 1953; do you own that?—A. No.

Q. Who owns it?—A. Lew Saxton.

Q. I am going to show you Pittsburgh police photograph No. 12979 and ask you if you can identify that picture?—A. Yeah, that's Lew Saxton.

Q. How long have you known Saxton?—A. About 3 years, I think. I transacted business with him before he went to the vet's hospital at Aspinwall.

Q. How long have you had this obscene merchandise in your home?—A. Since about a week before Christmas of 1952.

Q. Explain in your own words how he contacted you.—A. By telephone from the vet's hospital to my home.

Q. Then did you go to the veteran's hospital to see him?—A. Twice.

Q. Explain your conversation there, and what he asked you to do in regards to this material.—A. He asked me to take it into my home and keep it there until he was released by the police. Also, to manufacture novelty named "Maggie and Jiggs" with no price given on manufacture. He said he would take care of me. That was the first visit, and on the second visit, he wanted me to manufacture of French Ticklers, still no price given.

Q. Did you agree to do this?—A. Yeah.

Q. When were these two visits that you made to the hospital?—A. Thanksgiving Day, and one, 2 weeks later.

Q. Did he give you any of the material at that time?—A. No.

Q. When was this material delivered to your home?—A. Johnny, the baker, brought it on a Saturday, the first part of December.

Q. He brought all of the stuff, Johnny, the baker brought all of the merchandise?—A. No; he didn't bring all of the stuff, he brought the stuff for the French Ticklers, the rubbers; for the rubbers.

Q. Who is this Johnny, the baker, and do you know what his telephone number is?—A. No; I don't know his last name, all I know him by is Johnny.

Q. Do you know where Johnny got this rubber for the French Ticklers that he brought to you?—A. From Lew Saxton at the vet's hospital.

Q. Was this cut up in small pieces?—A. All ready cut; ready to assemble.

Q. Who else brought obscene material to your home?—A. His first name is Jack; that's all I know him by.

Q. Anyone else that you can name that brought this type of material into your home?—A. Just that Mr. Levy.

Q. Do you know where he lives?—A. Yes.

Q. Where?—A. Oceanside, N. Y.

Q. What did he bring to your home?—A. Cartoons, movies, cards, French Ticklers, obscene pictures.

Q. Did you pay for any of this material?—A. No.

Q. Did Saxton tell you what you were to do with it?—A. Hold it, and he would call me when somebody was to pick up.

Q. Did you ever collect any money for any of this material?—A. $12, I think it was.

Q. From who?—A. I don't remember.

Q. Did anybody pick any of this stuff up at your home?—A. Yes, Johnny, the baker salesman.

Q. Did you receive a letter from Lew Saxton from the Allegheny County Workhouse dated February 3, 1953?—A. Yes.

Q. I am going to ask you some questions about this letter; first one thing (is this a copy of that letter you received)?—A. Yes.

Q. Clarence, in one statement in this letter it says, "Did you ever get the color formula from Mr. Wilner, believe he was to have it in a week or so for you"; what did Saxton mean by "color formula"?—A. When ticklers are finished, they are dipped into a color so that the end of the tickler is whatever color you want it. That was what he meant.

Q. The next statement that he has he says, "How is your friend Kinsman, you said you talked with him, and he wanted to get 4 of your $8 size watches, no doubt they will cost him $30 each, but they are worth it." Now, who is Kinsman, and what does he mean by these watches and the price?—A. Kinsman is a man from Ohio; as for watches, it means 8-mm movies (millimeter). The price is $30 each.

Q. Are these obscene movies?—A. Yes.

Q. Did Kinsman get these movies?—A. No.

Q. The next sentence in the letter, Saxton asks, "Did Ben ever drop around?"; who is Ben, and did he ever drop around; did you ever sell him anything?—A. He's the individual who delivered rubbers to be manufactured into ticklers to my home. He never dropped around! I never sold him anything.

Q. Do you know Ben's last name?—A. No.

Q. The next statement, "Oh, I owe Nick $17.50, in case he wants any jewelry"; who is Nick?—A. I don't know the last name; he lives in the Turtle Creek Valley; I have his telephone number at home.

Q. What does Saxton mean that he "owes Nick $17.50 in case he wants any jewelry"?—A. Referring to jewelry means merchandise of obscene material.

Q. Did you give Nick any obscene pictures?—A. Yeah.

Q. Approximately when?—A. February 3, 1953.

Q. How much merchandise did he receive from you?—A. About $17.50 plus about $6.50 more which he said he would pay later.

Q. Did you do any business with a man named Whitey that Saxton mentions in his letter?—A. I went to see him at the gasoline station on Route 22; it's called Gravity Fill; about 6 miles past Wilkinsburg, past the Turnway Inn.

Q. Did you sell Whitey any merchandise?—A. Cards and matches——

Q. By matches, you mean obscene matches?—A. Obscene matches, the same with the cards.

Q. The next statement in Saxton's letter says, "Papy, no doubt, has not seen the advertising match display, or has he?"; who is Papy, and where does he live?—A. I think he owns a bar in East Pittsburgh.

Q. What does Saxton mean by the "advertising match display"?—A. He means matches with obscene pictures on them.

Q. Where did you get these matches?—A. Were delivered to my home by a fellow named Jack.

Q. Did you collect any money from Whitey for matches?—A. Yes; about $20; was used to pay Jack for matches.

Q. Did you order these matches made up, or did Saxton?—A. Saxton.

Q. The next statement in Saxton's letter states: "wish you would call Johnny the bakery salesman up, the best time is in the morning between 10 : 30 and 11 : 00; the name you have he can use those five $16 watches at $30 plus the 2 special ones you have in the same size"; will you explain that statement in your own words?—A. Did not contact Johnny. In regards to five $16 watches means, 16-mm. movies; that's obscene movies; 2 specials is the same thing.

Q. Next Saxton says: "Did your other friend collect that $50 for the check that was returned," what does he mean by this in this statement?—The $50 was for merchandise received; the check bounced, but he finally made it good.

Q. Who was the check from; who signed the check?—A. I don't know his name.

Q. The next statement in the letter says: "Should Margaret call Johnny this Saturday, have her tell him to give Alice the $50 he owes me for perfume as I need it for insurance payments, and he should pay Margaret for the watches he takes"; what does he mean by this statement?—A. In the first place, Margaret didn't make any contact with him. $50 means price of merchandise received from Mr. Saxton.

Q. Next he says: "Did your friend finish all the advertising matches less what he spoiled, you should keep count of what you receive, you could pay him what is due when Johnny pays for the jewelry, give Alice any balance due"; Clarence explain that statement?—A. The advertising matches are not finished; in the second place, Johnny did not buy.

Q. Who is Alice, and where does she live?—A. Alice is Lew Saxton's girl friend; lives on Homewood Avenue.

Q. Does she handle any obscene material?—A. No.

Q. The next statement: "I know that your pal George in Murrysville was asking about you. I told him I would tell you"; who is George, and what is his connection with this ring?—A. George was a possible buyer but did not buy any merchandise.

Q. Did you try to sell him some merchandise?—A. Yeah, Lew sent me out there.

Q. Now the next statement: "Would write a letter to Mrs. Sofie Levy, 2992 Tincker Drive, Oceanside, N. Y., and explain to her what I did not know about the insurance check until you advised me; tell her that as soon as possible, the amount will be sent you for the balance due on the fur coat"; Clarence, will you explain what Saxton means by this statement?—A. I wrote a letter explaining that Lew did not know the insurance check was no good; that he would pay the amount as soon as possible plus the balance.

Q. What does he mean by the fur coat?—A. Obscene merchandise.

Q. He further states in the letter to "tell Mrs. Levy it would not be advisable to come to Pittsburgh during the bad weather, but you will let her know"; what does Saxton mean by that?—A. He (Lew Saxton) could not contact Levy here in Pittsburgh.

Q. He next says: "should you be going out past Whitey's, tell Alice to give you two bottle of perfume to give to his wife"; what does he mean by this statement?—A. I suppose he actually means perfume there; I didn't stop at Alice's at all.

Q. Have you ever taken any money to Lew Saxton?—A. No.

Q. Is there anything that you can add to this statement?—A. [None.]

Q. Clarence, after you and your wife have had an opportunity to read this statement over, and if you find that it is true to the best of your knowledge, are you willing to sign it and to swear that you have told the truth?—A. Yeah.

Q. Have you been treated properly by Superintendent Geisler and the officers in the detective division of the Pittsburgh Police Department?—A. –Very true.

Q. And the answers to the questions have been typed just as you have given them and are your own words, is that right?—A. Right, it is correct.

(Signed)   CLARENCE M. BARNES, Jr.

This statement has been read by the deponent, Clarence Meade Barnes, after which, it was sworn and subscribed to before me, the undersigned authority on this 23d day of February, 1953.

> HECTOR R. MARIANI,
> *Notary Public.*
> ALLEN CARNAHAN,
> *Witness.*
> JAMES PATTON,
> *Witness.*
> MRS. C. M. BARNES, JR.,
> *Witness.*

ADDED INFORMATION, 6:03 P. M., FEBRUARY 23, 1953, VOLUNTEERED BY BARNES

On Thanksgiving Day, received $40. and some odd cents from Lew Saxton to pay for a punch press for assembling "Maggie & Jiggs." Press purchased from Star Stapling & Products Company, 929 Fifth Avenue, Pittsburgh. There was also 2,000 eyelets on the order received for the above amount. Press ordered by Lew Saxton, picked up be me.

(This additional information typed hereon by J. H. Gamble, Stenographer.)

> (Signed)   J. H. GAMBLE.

[SEAL]

> H. R. MARIANA.
> (Signed)   J. H. GAMBLE,
> *Stenographer.*

Chairman KEFAUVER. Go ahead, Mr. Chumbris.

Mr. CHUMBRIS. In conclusion, I would like to summarize, since the subcommittee has started its investigations and has had a certain amount of pornographic discussion at some of the community hearings throughout the country, we have been able to accomplish certain, what I think, are successful results.

For instance, as I explained earlier, in working with the Houston police, that big raid of the Southwest distributor was made. As I mentioned earlier, the North Dakota statute was changed to give it one of the most——

Mr. BOBO. Will you let me ask you there. Are you speaking of the Police Department of Houston, Tex., or the Sheriff's Department of Houston County, Tex.?

Mr. CHUMBRIS. It was the Sheriff's Department of Houston County, Tex.

And the North Dakota statute was changed as I stated.

Further, on one of the trips that I was making on this pornographic investigation, in Michigan a grand jury went into the question of pornographic literature. I went over and talked to the district attorney and to the district judge there, explained to him what we were trying to do. They gave us all of the cooperation that we could possibly expect. They gave us a full report of their findings.

In many areas, civic and religious organizations united to conduct cleanup campaigns, to clean up this pornographic mess that has been sweeping throughout the country, not only the dirty, lewd pornography that we are talking about today, but they are also attacking the borderline pornography, and some of the pinup magazines that are found on the newsstands, especially those around the schools and the churches.

Chairman KEFAUVER. Mr. Chumbris, two questions.

In your survey and the returns you have gotten from the police chiefs is there any question about that pornography among juveniles—and that is what we are concerned with here—that it does have a degrading effect, leading to the marring of the lives of many of our young people, and also increasing the amount of juvenile and criminal activity among children?

Mr. CHUMBRIS. There is no question about it. I think that practically——

Chairman KEFAUVER. Is that the concensus of all the police chiefs?

Mr. CHUMBRIS. Every one of them. They even went so far as to say that this is one filthy mess that has got to be cleaned up, and that's why they are so anxious about more stringent laws and more severe punishment, because most of them will say, "I don't want my children to run into any of this."

Chairman KEFAUVER. Is it also the result of your inquiries to show that as the extent of the distribution of pornography among the juveniles increases in a given section, you have a corresponding increase in deliquency and sex crimes?

Mr. CHUMBRIS. That's correct; absolutely.

Chairman KEFAUVER. Along the same line as set forth by Mr. Hoover on a national scale?

Mr. CHUMBRIS. That's correct.

Chairman KEFAUVER. Now, sir, can you give us any estimate—before that. Does your investigation show that over the last few years the publication and the distribution of pornography among children, teen-agers, has been substantially on the increase?

Mr. CHUMBRIS. From the information that I have received there is a definite increase of pornography going to children, and there is a definite increase of pornography that is being distributed throughout the United States. And they are bringing in a new type of pornography.

Some people are remarking about the number of pornographic records, pornographic phonograph records spreading out throughout the country.

Chairman KEFAUVER. And this is in all parts of the United States, even Tennessee I believe you said?

Mr. CHUMBRIS. That's correct. I believe we have another chart there, the Baltimore, the Houston, and the one from the South.

Chairman KEFAUVER. Finally, sir, can you give any estimate of the size of this business?

Mr. CHUMBRIS. Well, the one in Baltimore—this will portray the size. If I may mention it from here [indicating], this is a point where it started. One shipment——

Chairman KEFAUVER. That is Baltimore?

Mr. CHUMBRIS. That's right. And all of these big blocks indicate where this shipment went by railway express. The total value of just one shipment was $30,000 declared value, with an estimated retail value of $250,000. Mind you, that's just one shipment that that man made.

Mr. Bobo. Isn't that 291 railway express shipments, Mr. Chumbris?

Mr. Chumbris. Yes.

Mr. Martin. I think, Mr. Chumbris, what you want to say is that these are shipments from just one source.

Mr. Chumbris. That's correct. From the Baltimore source.

Chairman Kefauver. This fellow got convicted the other day, did he not?

Mr. Chumbris. He was convicted in Federal court in Baltimore.

Chairman Kefauver. What is his name? I think this is an interesting case; we ought to have some description of it later on. Are you, or will somebody else describe what happened in this Baltimore case?

Mr. Chumbris. Yes. Well, we will have the assistant United States attorney who will be here; and we have policemen, the inspector from Washington, and Sergeant Brown from the Detroit Police Department, who will give specific cities and the operations from those cities.

This [exhibiting] is a picture as it was taken of these packages as they were impounded, with the addresses where they are going. And the different value is illustrated that was declared for the various shipments.

Mr. Martin. Mr. Chumbris, this photograph, as I understand it, represents one of the 291 shipments?

Mr. Chumbris. That's correct.

Chairman Kefauver. And one of the 291 shipments apparently has 87,960 pieces of pornography.

Mr. Chumbris. That's right.

Photograph of seizures by the United States Government of 87,960 pieces of pornography——

Chairman Kefauver. These pictures and charts will all be made exhibits in the record.

Go ahead, sir.

Mr. Bobo. Mr. Chumbris, have you received any information as to the size or the volume, dollarwise, outside of this one case here, as to what this traffic might be throughout the United States?

Mr. Chumbris. Well, I have asked that question and because of the fact that—let me answer it first with one illustration.

We asked the customs officials——

Chairman Kefauver. They will be here to testify?

Mr. Chumbris. Yes, sir. We asked them a question, how much comes into the United States? And they said that, "We are only able to ascertain or get hold of 5 percent of the traffic." So 95 percent gets by them.

The same thing can be applied to the various police departments. They can't possibly estimate at this particular time, I don't think a complete survey has been made or might not be able to be made because of the fact that it is just getting so gigantic, and every day we are running into distributors like Soloday, for instance, who has a $250,000 retail value from just that one outlet.

Chairman Kefauver. Now, will some witness other than you describe the fact that from the United States is shipped a lot of pornog-

PHOTOGRAPH OF SEIZURES BY U.S. GOVERNMENT OF 87,960 PIECES OF PORNOGRAPHY. NUDES AND BONDAGE PHOTOS OF WOMEN. SHIPMENTS WERE MADE TWICE A WEEK FROM BALTIMORE TO 45 OR MORE OUTLETS IN THE U.S. BY "SOLODAY", BALTIMORE, MD. RETAIL TRAFFIC OF "SOLODAY" SENT BY AMERICAN EXPRESS C.O.D. AMOUNTED TO APPROXIMATELY A QUARTER OF A MILLION DOLLARS A YEAR. "SOLODAY" IS NOT THE LARGEST DISTRIBUTOR.

raphy to other countries, and from other countries a lot is shipped to us?

Mr. CHUMBRIS. Yes. That will be taken care of by one of our other witnesses.

Chairman KEFAUVER. Very well. Is there anything else? Senator Langer, do you have any questions to ask Mr. Chambris?

Senator LANGER. Mr. Witness, what is a bondage photo?

Mr. CHUMBRIS. A bondage photo are these photos where the girl wears very little clothing, practically nude, and usually their hands and their legs are bound together either by chain or by rope, and they are known as bondage photos.

Senator LANGER. I inquired because you say "nudes and bondage photos." I never heard that term used before. I thank you. That's all, Mr. Chairman.

Chairman KEFAUVER. Thank you, Mr. Chumbris.

Our next witness, Mr. Bobo.

Mr. BOBO. Father Daniel Egan.

STATEMENT OF FATHER DANIEL EGAN, FRANCISCAN PRIEST, GRAYMOOR, GARRISON, N. Y.

Chairman KEFAUVER. No one can ever question your veracity, but if you mention any names I think I should place you under oath.

Father EGAN. I won't mention any names.

Chairman KEFAUVER. Very well.

Father Egan, it is a pleasure for the chairman to see you again. I know over the course of a long time your interest in the young boys and young people, especially with the problem with which we are dealing here today. We are grateful to you for coming here and giving us the benefit of your experience and findings on this important problem affecting our children.

Mr. Bobo, do you want to ask Father Egan any preliminary questions?

Mr. BOBO. Yes. I would like to ask Father Egan briefly some questions, describing your work, Father, that you had and the contact you have with the young people.

Father EGAN. I am a priest, ordained just 10 years. In the past 10 years I have been specializing in high school and teen-age missions.

During the course of a year I might travel from Louisville to Cincinnati, to Cleveland, to Detroit, to Rochester, to Boston, to Brooklyn, to the South, to city after city. Today I go to Boston.

Chairman KEFAUVER. Before you tell your experiences, Mr. Bobo, for the record, because we can always see the Father, but the record must be presented. Let's get how old he is, who he is, how long he has been a Father, what his assignment is.

Father EGAN. I will be 41 this year. I am ordained 10½ years.

Mr. BOBO. In what order are you ordained?

Father EGAN. I am a Franciscan, from a monastery at Graymoor, Garrison, N. Y.

Mr. BOBO. And how long have you been ordained?

Father EGAN. 10½ years.

I am on what we call a mission bend, and we go from city to city giving missions; some of our Fathers go to the foreign missions.

Mr. BOBO. And your full name?

Father EGAN. Father Daniel Egan.

Mr. BOBO. Now, Father Egan, would you tell us some of the things of which——

Chairman KEFAUVER. Is this a special work that you are designated to do, Father Egan? Will you give us the background of your assignment and what you have undertaken?

Father EGAN. I received requests from various cities to conduct high school retreats in Catholic schools, and also to go to cities that do not have Catholic high schools and conduct teen-age missions in the evening for Catholic students who go to public schools, and many Protestants and Jewish children, and teen-agers attend as well; they are all mixed up.

So I, well I get the kids in the church for an hour and 10 minutes every evening, and I talk to them about their problems. During the course of the week's mission their problem does come up. In talking to me on the streets, or on the corners, the problem of the pornographic literature is increasing.

Mr. BOBO. Father Egan, would you tell us where you have been, in what cities you have been, and how many years you have been doing this?

Father EGAN. I have been in teen-age missions in Louisville, Cincinnati, Cleveland, Rochester, Boston, Washington, Brooklyn—well, too numerous to mention in 10 years.

Since February I have been in Cleveland, Washington, Boston, Jersey, up in Cornell University—well, cities like this.

Mr. BOBO. And in the cities do you hold youth meetings?

Father EGAN. Throw-aways are given out in the public high schools a week or two beforehand announcing a teen-age mission.

All your problems are frankly discussed. God's point of view with regard to your troubles.

Then the kids come sometimes; in Springfield last year we had 1,200 kids every night; the following week 1,600 kids every night. And these were by and large 75, 85 percent of them public high school kids.

Chairman KEFAUVER. I did not understand how many you said you would have every night.

Father EGAN. It would vary with the city, Senator. In Springfield we had 1,200 every night. In the following week in Holyoke we had 1,600 every night.

Starting tonight up in Gardiner, Mass., there will be a series of teen talks. I don't know how many to expect.

Mr. BOBO. After you have had these talks with them, and you have talked to them, do they then come to you for counseling?

Father EGAN. Yes. So naturally from here on in, if you ask me any questions, since I am a professional man, I will say that I have encountered this literature in a Midwest city, in a Northern city, or in a Southern city, unless you demand that I specify the city. Would it do any good if I mentioned the name of the city?

Chairman KEFAUVER. Sure. Tell where you found it.

Mr. BOBO. I think if you would tell us the city where you found it, it would show the interstate traffic in this material, Father.

Father EGAN. Since February I have seen this pornographic literature in Cleveland, Washington, and in New York City. I have seen it, looked at it. The kids brought it to me.

Mr. Bobo. You speak of pornographic literature. Of what type are you speaking now, Father?

Father Egan. I do not mean the magazines that are very lurid and filthy and sexy that can be bought on newsstands. I rather mean the type of literature that might be printed as this [indicating], and then circulated through high schools, sold to a kid on the corner, or just sold to them any place.

Mr. Bobo. You mentioned that you have seen this in this city. Have you seen it in the hands of teen-agers or younger?

Father Egan. Yes. In one city I was conducting, I usually conduct a parent night to arouse a public indignation against this condition, to get the parents aware of it. Most of them are not aware of it. So, in this particular city, I asked 2 of the boys, 15 years of age, would they go out and buy me some real filthy literature. They said, "What kind do you want?"

I said, "Real filthy."

They said, "How much money do you want to spend?"

I had a $5 bill with me. I gave it to them. Inside of an hour they brought back some of the material I sent back to your office.

Mr. Bobo. In the city of Washington, was that where this particular thing happened?

Father Egan. No; this was in Cleveland.

I mean now by pornographic literature, the specific kind that shows in a degrading way, and in unnatural ways the act of sex relations.

Mr. Bobo. Father, in traveling around the country you have become acquainted with college campuses. Have you known on these campuses of the showing of pornographic stag party films?

Father Egan. At fraternity houses, I know that they are shown to just stag parties.

Mr. Bobo. Would you say this was very widespread among the high schools and colleges? I am speaking now of the films.

Father Egan. I am not in a position to say; I do not work too frequently on the college level.

Mr. Bobo. Among high-school children, has it ever come to your attention that they have viewed these?

Father Egan. I have heard it on many occasions when a teenager will go baby sitting, that while there they will be shown or they will see some of this pornographic film material that you speak about.

Mr. Bobo. Could you give us, Father Egan, in your opinion, what the effect of this pornographic material is upon a young mind?

Father Egan. We speak a great deal at the present moment about the blackboard jungles. Emotional problems in high school. And yet there are some people that would like to tell us that there is nothing wrong with stealing. The God-given pleasures of sex, outside of marriage. Still, when a kid does do it, he does experience—and this is something God is responsible for—they do experience a guilt complex. This guilt complex, I am certain, is reflected in the emotional problems they reveal in the classroom. These pornographic materials are bound to produce in the lives of the teen-agers acts of masturbation, acts of self-abuse, acts of unnatural things between fellows and girls, and this is shown up, then, in the sense of guilt, and that reveals itself in emotional problems in the classrooms.

The teachers in the public high schools, God bless them, they are doing a wonderful job with the problems that they have, but they are treating a symptom over here, and the real cause is over here.

You were speaking a short while ago about the penalties for this——

Mr. Bobo. May I ask you this: When you are speaking of a symptom over here and a cause over there, to what are you referring?

Father Egan. They are treating the emotional symptoms of filthy language on the walls and on the toilets, and they are treating the emotional problems of disbehavior, or fighting and gang instincts in the schools, but this may be a mere symptom of something deeper away over here, that when a boy or a girl is possessed with a sense of guilt, that they are committing acts of impurity alone or with others, it is revealed then in these other things, and they are creating this thing, but the real cause is over here.

This deluge of filth is sweeping over the country and is having its effect in other things. I am convinced of this.

No normal teen-ager today could look at this unless he has ice water in his veins. If he has real blood he couldn't possibly look at this without showing some effect in other ways.

Mr. Bobo. You think of the normal teen-ager only the emotional disturbed teen-ager; do you think it would be possible by looking at some of the material which has come into your hands that he might thereby be stirred up to go out and commit a sex crime against a fellow playmate, boy or girl?

Father Egan. I am certain of it. A boy looks at this, shows it to his girl friend. They go to a show together, a movie, and things are bound to happen.

Mr. Bobo. Do you think that among the sexually uneducated children who are inquisitive, as most of them are about sex, that this might tend to make him think this is normal sex, pictures of which we have here, if he had no other outside instruction from either the home, school, or church?

Father Egan. I agree with you very much, that if he is sexually uneducated, if he has not been taught to see the sanctity and the dignity and the holiness of sex from God's point of view, if they see this early in life, they do think it is a normal thing.

Chairman Kefauver. Father Egan, you have now been 10 years in all these cities doing this wonderful work, giving youth guidances. This filth that is flooding the country now, all over the country, is it on the increase among children?

Father Egan. The mere fact that I have encountered in the last 3 months what I have not encountered before would prove to me that it is definitely on the increase in many various forms.

A little kid showed me recently a magazine you can buy at the corner now, and inserted in the top of it are these colored glasses that you can look at a picture and you see a picture now in triple dimensions. Like when you go to the movies—I haven't been to a movie in a couple of years—but you go to some movies, I understand, you look through some glasses, I understand, and you see the thing in triple dimensions. Now they sell them at the corner, so that you look at the art magazines, and with these glasses you can see them in triple dimensions.

Kids, I know, numerous cases of some of the modern magazines that you can't class legally as pornographic material, and yet while the man is mixing a coke, they can rip out these nude pictures in magazines like, here I will mention—well, under some of the magazines they can rip it out and circulate it through a school, and that one picture can be responsible for more emotional problems that way than anything else.

Mr. Bobo. You are speaking now of magazines that are sold upon the newsstand, and the effect that they might have but not of—previous to this you were speaking of pornography?

Father Egan. I was speaking of pornography; yes.

Mr. Kefauver, I don't think that the average person is aware of this 1 fact, that whereas if a man were to sell 1 teen-ager 1 marihuana, that marihuana will affect this 1 teen-ager. We can see the effects of that in his life. But 1 piece of this pornographic material allowed to circulate through 1 classroom or 1 school can do harm that we can't estimate. And I speak under correction, but I understand there is some suggestion of making it life imprisonment for anyone who is importing heroin or marijuana as in vast numbers. Why couldn't you make it even more severe, 7 years, for a man who is importing and producing this, he is corrupting, he is rotting at the very roots of our Nation. Communism will never defeat America; it is something within the Nation that is going to rot and corrupt it; and there should be a more stringent law than just 2 or 3 years, or 7 years.

Chairman Kefauver. You think that this pornographic literature is having a substantial effect upon that degrading process?

Father Egan. Positively, Senator.

Chairman Kefauver. I was amazed, Father Egan, one day you came to my office, and I will always remember. You said you had just been around on the streets of Washington and you picked up a whole bundle of this, not art magazines but pure filth, in the Nation's Capital, and you brought it in and gave it to me.

Father Egan. Yes.

Chairman Kefauver. That is the kind of thing we are finding in increasing amounts all over the country.

Father Egan. Yes.

Chairman Kefauver. Senator Langer?

Senator Langer. No questions. Thank you.

Chairman Kefauver. Mr. Bobo, anything else?

Mr. Bobo. Father Egan, does this make generally the entire social ground, I mean from the low social, economic group up to the very highest? Where would you say it was most prevalent?

Father Egan. I don't work very often with the higher social strata.

Mr. Bobo. So your working is within the great middle group where this stuff is striking?

Father Egan. I talked to numerous girls who have posed for these pictures.

Chairman Kefauver. Teenagers, kids?

Father Egan. Kids who would be playing to and from school. They might be down at the corner having a coke, or they might be at a show, and someone will glide up to them and convince them that they are photogenic, or they would look pretty in a picture, and give them $5 or $10, and from that one negative they will produce many others.

Chairman Kefauver. What did you start to say, sir?

Father Egan. I will finish this, Senator, by saying that it is my convinced opinion that if we are going to do anything about this, it is something far deeper, and even though we increase the number of playgrounds, even though we increase the number of policemen, even though we increase everything else, this will never remove the danger of this, unless we find the cause of it all.

Today, if you were to release in the classroom some cold germs, teenagers who are physically weak will be more susceptible to the germs; strong, healthy kids will not be contaminated by the cold germs.

Today teenagers are becoming susceptible to all this filth, not because there is really more of it, I don't think—maybe it is on the increase, I am not prepared to say that definitely—but the kids today are so spiritually sick, they don't know the laws of God, they don't know why they should be good, they don't know the sanctity of sex, and because of this they are susceptible to all these germs.

If we are going to do anything about it, it won't be just sufficient to clear this up. I have seen this when I—I went to public high school in New York, and this stuff has no effect on some kids. Because they knew about God, they knew about the Ten Commandments, which are common to every kid, and unless they know this, unless they know the Commandments, unless they know why they should be good, then there is no sense just clearing up the newsstands or increasing the police force.

Chairman Kefauver. Father Egan, in your testimony you have mentioned some specific cities where you found this material. I wouldn't want your testimony, or your reference to those particular cities to make it appear that they are different or any worse than many, many others. The fact is, some of them may be better.

I mentioned the fact that you have found some material in the Nation's Capital. I think you may also be aware of the tremendous effort that is being made by the Washington police force, and many groups in Washington, and they have been quite effective in the recent months and in the recent years in cleaning up this pornography and filth for which we commend them.

So that I don't want, I know you don't want your testimony to be singling out one place as a bad example.

Father Egan. Certainly not, Senator.

Chairman Kefauver. And I don't want to do that either. I do want to commend some of these places where you have mentioned. Here in New York there have been some good efforts made. There have been some fine efforts made in Washington. They are still on the alert. I hope that we can all do better with the problem, however.

All right, Father Egan, thank you very much. Our best wishes in your continued work with the young people of our Nation.

Father Egan. Thank you, Senator.

Chairman Kefauver. We will have a 5-minute recess.

(Short recess taken.)

Chairman Kefauver. The subcommittee will come to order. Everybody have a seat, please.

The subcommittee is glad to have James A. Fitzpatrick, a member of the assembly. He has made an investigation of this problem, and has sponsored some legislation in connection with it.

For the benefit of any witnesses who were not here when we started, anyone who is called and feels that the lights and movie cameras and television discommodes them, or they would be embarrassed, will not be required to testify before TV or the cameras, if they will let the staff of the subcomittee know. We appreciate the cooperation of the television and movie people in this connection.

Mr. Bobo, who is our next witness?

Mr. Bobo. We have subpenaed a number of witnesses to appear before this subcommittee either today, tomorrow or the following day; and we have asked for the books and records of these individuals to be produced today.

I will ask Mr. Martin now to call the names of these individuals.

Chairman KEFAUVER. Mr. Bobo, it is apparent we are not going to get all these witnesses today; and if you could tell the witnesses when to come back, we might save them some time.

All right, Mr. Martin.

Mr. MARTIN. Abraham Rubenstein.

Chairman KEFAUVER. Is Mr. Rubenstein here? The fact any witness' name has been called doesn't mean he is in the pornographic business. We have some witnesses who will testify as experts.

We have had some charts made. As Mr. Chumbris said, we are happy to state this has been exposed. Prosecutions have been brought, and the operation shown on that chart no longer exists by virtue of the police department and public officials of Baltimore.

Mr. Deerson is our next witness. Mr. Deerson, will you come around? Mr. Deerson, no one questions your veracity, but it is possible that you might mention someone's name, so if you have no objection I would like to swear you.

TESTIMONY OF WILLIAM DEERSON, DEAN OF DISCIPLINE, HAAREN HIGH SCHOOL, NEW YORK, N. Y.

(William Deerson was duly sworn.)

Chairman KEFAUVER. Mr. Bobo, let us qualify Mr. Deerson—who he is.

Mr. Bobo. Will you state your full name and address for the record?

Mr. Deerson. My name is William Deerson. I am the dean of a New York city high school.

Mr. Bobo. What high school is that?

Mr. Deerson. Haaren High School, New York City.

Mr. Bobo. And the address of that?

Mr. Deerson. Eight hundred and ninety-nine 10th Avenue. I am also employed as the director of recreational activities at the Jewish Settlement House, at 128 Stanton Street, New York City.

Mr. Bobo. For how many years have you been dean of discipline at the Haaren High School?

Mr. Deerson. One year.

Mr. Bobo. Previous to that time what was your position?

Mr. Deerson. Teacher of health education in that particular school.

Mr. Bobo. For how long were you teacher of health education in that school?

Mr. Deerson. For 12 years.

Mr. Bobo. And your local address is what?

Mr. Deerson. 2555 Bainbridge Avenue, Bronx, N. Y.

Mr. Bobo. For how long have you been a school teacher?

Mr. Deerson. Since 1934.

Mr. Bobo. Has all that time been in the city of New York?

Mr. Deerson. Yes, sir.

Chairman Kefauver. You are also employed by the Jewish Settlement House on the East Side, located at 128 Stanton Street; is that correct?

Mr. Deerson. That is correct.

Chairman Kefauver. You are employed there in what capacity?

Mr. Deerson. Director of recreational activities and physical activities.

Chairman Kefauver. How long have you been so employed?

Mr. Deerson. 12 years.

Chairman Kefauver. In your two positions do you come in contact with a very large number of school children?

Mr. Deerson. Yes, I do.

Chairman Kefauver. And you have a chance to observe them, and talk with them, and see what influences them for the good or the bad?

Mr. Deerson. Yes, sir.

Chairman Kefauver. See what they are reading, and what is influencing their minds?

Mr. Deerson. That is right.

Chairman Kefauver. Very well, proceed, Mr. Bobo.

Mr. Bobo. How many students are at Haaren High School?

Mr. Deerson. About 2,000 boys.

Mr. Bobo. As dean of discipline is it your position to deal with wayward acts and delinquent acts of children in the school?

Mr. Deerson. That is correct.

Mr. Bobo. Misbehavior problems within the school?

Mr. Deerson. That is correct.

Mr. Bobo. Has it come to your attention, Mr. Deerson, that any of the students of the high school, Haaren High School, have come in contact with or had in their possession any pornographic materials of any types?

Mr. Deerson. Yes, they have.

Mr. Bobo. Would you say to what extent?

Mr. Deerson. Well, recently I noticed that quite a few boys have been passing theses booklets around among the other boys. Some have been selling them. It seems that some boys purchase a booklet, and after they have seen it and passed it around they may sell it to another boy at a profit.

Mr. Bobo. Would you describe what these booklets are that you are speaking of?

Mr. Deerson. The booklets are the severe filthy type of pornographic material, unnatural perverted types of sex acts.

Chairman Kefauver. You are not talking about art magazines?

Mr. Deerson. No, I am not.

Mr. Bobo. You are speaking of what is commonly referred to as the 2-by-4 book and 4-by-5-type book that is sold—photographic pictures along with a printed story?

Mr. Deerson. That type and others.

Mr. Bobo. In the questioning of some of the boys who have had it in their possession, and those who have sold it, what is the price these books usually sell for in the school?

Mr. DEERSON. Usually the postal-card type is sold for about 25 cents. The Maggie and Jiggs type may be sold anywhere from 25 cents to half a dollar. The card-playing type, where a deck of cards is purchased, let us say, for $5 on the outside, they are resold for anywhere from 15 to 25 cents per card.

Mr. BOBO. Do you have the figures as to the number of boys that have been known to sell pornographic literature within the high school?

Mr. DEERSON. I have discovered three boys this term.

Mr. BOBO. Three boys selling?

Mr. DEERSON. Yes.

Mr. BOBO. Do you have any figures as to the number who have had it in their possession?

Mr. DEERSON. No; I have not.

Mr. BOBO. Do you have any knowledge as to the extent that this traffic might reach where one boy would buy it, and to how many it would be passed around?

Mr. DEERSON. I have only discovered about five boys selling the material this term. There may be others. I don't know.

Mr. BOBO. Have you found out from the three boys who have been selling it where they might have obtained the material themselves to sell it?

Mr. DEERSON. Yes; they have told me they purchase it from men around New York City. They purchase it on the Bowery. Some have said they have purchased it on 42d Street, Sixth Avenue, the lower East Side, and especially among the men who sell old hats, razor blades. They sell old watches.

Mr. BOBO. A typical street peddler?

Mr. DEERSON. Street peddlers; and among their items will be pornographic material.

Mr. BOBO. Have you found, Mr. Deerson, that this is usually a surreptitious operation, not open and aboveboard among the boys, or among the street peddlers; that it is carried under the counter or under other goods which they have?

Mr. DEERSON. The material is in the man's pockets; and in passing by a man will approach a young teen-ager and ask him to purchase it.

Mr. BOBO. As dean of discipline in this particular high school, have you found that there is a certain inquisitiveness among the students there to read this particular type of literature?

Mr. DEERSON. Definitely.

Mr. BOBO. Would you think that this particular type of literature would cause any increase in sexual activities among the students at Haaren High School?

Mr. DEERSON. I believe so.

Mr. BOBO. Is this a coeducational school?

Mr. DEERSON. No; it is all boys.

Mr. BOBO. Would you think this particular material and the reading of this material would in any way affect the juvenile-delinquency rate of the students in this particular high school?

Mr. DEERSON. I believe there is some relationship. There is definitely a connection between the juvenile-delinquency rate and the reading of this material.

I feel that the material when read excites the young man; it stimulates him and may lead to some overt act.

Mr. Bobo. From your contacts with the other teaching staffs of the public schools in New York, and also in the parochial schools, and in other cities outside of the city of New York, has it come to your attention that they suffer from a similar problem which you face in your school?

Mr. Deerson. I believe so.

Mr. Bobo. Have you ever discussed it with any of them?

Mr. Deerson. No; I have never discussed it with anybody from anywhere else.

Mr. Bobo. I believe I asked you the question. Was this a coeducational high school?

Mr. Deerson. No; it is a boys' school.

Mr. Bobo. Altogether a boys' school?

Mr. Deerson. All boys.

Mr. Martin. I notice you have an envelope there. Would that be some of the material that has been confiscated?

Mr. Deerson. Yes. I have a variety of the various pornographic material in this envelope.

Mr. Martin. Would you object to turning it over to the committee?

Mr. Deerson. I don't object at all.

Chairman Kefauver. That is typical of what you have been finding among these boys?

Mr. Deerson. That is correct.

Chairman Kefauver. Give it to Mr. Butler.

Mr. Deerson. I will be glad to.

Chairman Kefauver. How old are these boys?

Mr. Deerson. From 14 to 18.

Chairman Kefauver. Do you find the same sort of thing at the Jewish Settlement?

Mr. Deerson. Yes. Only there it might be younger than 14.

Chairman Kefauver. How old are they?

Mr. Deerson. They range anywhere from 11 to 20.

Chairman Kefauver. And you find that some of these people sell them pornographic literature, and they in turn distribute it and sell it to other kids?

Mr. Deerson. In the settlement house it is not sold.

Chairman Kefauver. But among the boys that you see at the settlement house?

Mr. Deerson. Yes; some of them do sell some of the pictures, especially the playing-card type.

Chairman Kefauver. Go ahead, Mr. Bobo.

Mr. Bobo. Do you have any knowledge as to what the extent of this traffic might be among the teen-agers in New York City?

Mr. Deerson. I have noticed an increase in the amount of booklets being passed around. By booklets, I mean pornographic story type with pictures. I understand from one boy that there is a series of 10 of a similar size, approximately 4 by 6. In the exhibit that I just brought in I have two samples of that type.

Of course, as Father Egan said, it is not the number of booklets; it is the passage of one from one boy to another that causes a greater damage.

Mr. Bobo. Is that a new problem at the school? Have you noticed a steady increase, or is it a recent problem?

Mr. DEERSON. I have noticed a steady increase, especially the passing from one stage to another.

The art books sold on the newsstands, I believe, tend to stimulate these boys to seek a stronger type of material.

Chairman KEFAUVER. Senator Langer, do you have any questions?

Senator LANGER. No.

Chairman KEFAUVER. Mr. Deerson, do you feel that this influence is one of the influences that is contributing to juvenile delinquency?

Mr. DEERSON. I definitely believe so.

Chairman KEFAUVER. And it is on the increase?

Mr. DEERSON. I believe so.

Chairman KEFAUVER. What you have in your school, of course, is just a typical situation not only of other high schools but high schools all throughout the Nation? Your high school is just about like any other boys' school?

Mr. DEERSON. That is right. I believe it is a typical school.

Chairman KEFAUVER. I wanted it clear that we asked you to come here, not in an effort to criticize your school, but to show that happens in a typical school like you have.

Mr. DEERSON. That is correct.

Chairman KEFAUVER. Thank you very much, sir.

Dr. Benjamin Karpman.

STATEMENT OF DR. BENJAMIN KARPMAN, CHIEF PSYCHOTHERAPIST, ST. ELIZABETHS HOSPITAL, WASHINGTON, D. C.

Dr. Karpman, are you going to talk about names of people, and whatnot, in your testimony?

Dr. KARPMAN. Professional people don't mention names.

Chairman KEFAUVER. Very well. If these lights bother you, you can say so.

Dr. KARPMAN. It is all right.

Chairman KEFAUVER. Dr. Karpman, it is good to have you with us. You are Dr. Benjamin Karpman, chief psychotherapist of St. Elizabeths Hospital in Washington, D. C.?

Dr. KARPMAN. Yes, sir.

Chairman KEFAUVER. The St. Elizabeths Hospital is one of the largest and best known and best operated of our mental institutions for the treatment of mental disturbances; is that correct?

Dr. KARPMAN. Yes, sir.

Chairman KEFAUVER. You have been connected with St. Elizabeths Hospital for how long?

Dr. KARPMAN. 35 years.

Chairman KEFAUVER. Since 1919?

Dr. KARPMAN. That is right.

Chairman KEFAUVER. What is your educational qualifications and background, Dr. Karpman?

Dr. KARPMAN. I have a degree in chemistry and pharmacy from Columbia; a bachelors degree from the University of North Dakota; a bachelor of medicine degree from the University of Minnesota; and I also have a diploma from the University of Vienna, postgraduate work.

Chairman KEFAUVER. The study of criminology is your life's work?

Dr. KARPMAN. That is right.

Chairman KEFAUVER. I think I can say that Dr. Karpman is one of the most eminently and highly respected and knowledgeable criminologists in the world.

Dr. Karpman, we feel you are unusually well qualified to tell us ·in some detail of the matters that we are discussing here today as it relates to juvenile delinquency.

Mr. Bobo, will you carry on.

Mr. BOBO. Dr. Karpman, would you describe for us in professional terms the meaning of pornographic literature—what you interpret pornographic literature to be?

Dr. KARPMAN. Every community employs certain restrictions on its citizens, and one of the restrictions is verbal communication of certain private matters which can be discussed very privately among some people, but cannot be discussed in public. Among this is included certain material dealing with the private sex lives of individuals.

The intimate relations that are established between people in private relations—however, there are some people who seem to take satisfaction in spreading this type of material abroad; and these are the people who indulge in pornographic material.

There are two aspects to this pornographic material. There is the doer, the one that secures pornographic material for distribution; and then there is the victim who is exposed to that by the material of the other doer.

For this reason in order to develop pornographic literature you have got to have people who make a speciality of this pornographic literature. They go to the trouble of engaging people to pose for them in various unmentionable poses, and then after they get the material they get victims who pay certain amounts of money for the purpose of being able to see this material.

This material deals with sexual matters, with sexual relations, but not with the normal so-called average type of sexual relations. There is no interest in that, but usually with the type of sex material that ordinarily is prohibited or at least is unmentionable.

For instance, homosexuality and perversions. In homosexuals we often get pictures of people engaged in homosexual relations of a great variety. There are differences in homosexual relations in men, and there are differences in homosexual relations in women. This is pure homosexuality; but between homosexuality on the one hand, and so-called heterosexuality, on the other hand, there are a large group of people and activities which are called perversions.

Perversions may occur between couples, men and women, but in entirely abnormal and pathological ways—for instance, different positions, different matters of acting.

This is what is the purpose of pornographic men, and people pay money for that.

There would be no problem in pornographic literature if this was exposed to people who are normally developed and have been able to develop normal inhibitions, repressions and control.

Unfortunately it is often given to people of adolescent ages, which from our point of view is a very unstable period of life. Anything may happen during adolescence. You can take a perfectly healthy boy or girl and by exposing them to abnormalities you can virtually crystallize and settle their lives for the rest of their lives.

If they are not exposed to that they may develop to perfectly healthy, normal citizens. It is here that objection comes upon pornographic literature.

Mr. BOBO. You mean a perfectly normal, healthy boy or girl, 12 or 13 years of age, if exposed to pornographic literature, could thereby develop into a homosexual?

Dr. KARPMAN. That is right; because from our point of view—we are not all normally, what we call heterosexual. We don't belong to one sex. All of us are bisexual. Every man has some element of a woman in him, because he has inherited that from his mother. In other words, every man has, from our point of view, a feminine component. Every women has, from our point of view, a masculine component, which she has inherited from her father.

The proportion of this varies, but usually the masculine component in a man is large, let us say, 85 percent, whereas the feminine component in a man is very small, let us say, 10 to 15 percent; but because adolescence is a very unstable stage of development, if you expose a boy to an abnormal behavior it will play upon the undeveloped feminine component, and he might become homosexual.

Mr. BOBO. Do you think the reading of pornographic literature in addition to maybe changing his sex habits in life might also have an effect upon him more of a tendency to become a juvenile delinquent?

Dr. KARPMAN. I believe there is a definite relationship between juvenile delinquency and sex life. We started from this point of view. Our life from our point of view is guided by our instincts. We have two main instincts—the self-preservative instinct, and the race-preservative instinct, commonly known as the hunger and sex instincts.

Instincts that spread by tension—you and I will never know that we are hungry unless there would develop in the stomach some sort of tension which sends a message to the brain and tells us that we are hungry. In other words, we know of our sex life and of our personal life, of hunger life, only through the medium of tension developing.

Tension is tension. When a young boy and girl, for instance—you take a young boy who is reaching adolescence, and he is hungry for information on sex, but for some reason or another doesn't get it at home because the mother and father are too tired to talk to them about four-letter words and other nasty things.

Where is the boy going to find it? He cannot find it at home. He doesn't always find it in school. Very few schools have developed to the point of giving lectures on the subjects of the facts of life. He looks for it in the gutter, and there he comes across pornographic material and literature, and that draws him into all sorts of gang life, which later discharges itself as juvenile delinquency.

In other words, here is a boy who is under a great deal of sexual tension. The home environment will not permit him to discharge the sexual tension in normal sex relations. Society doesn't permit that in a premarital way. Tension is tension. It must break through. If he cannot discharge it in a sexual way, he discharges it in a criminal antisocial way.

Mr. BOBO. Thereby causing him to engage in gang activities?

Dr. KARPMAN. That is right. There is a very direct relationship between juvenile delinquency, sex life, and pornographic literature.

Mr. Bobo. Would it be your opinion that a young boy in reading pornographic literature would be inclined to commit some of the various sex crimes of rape, or many other variations?

Dr. Karpman. Some; not all. It all depends on the original make-up of the boy. There are some boys who have developed from early childhood interest in dirty matters. For instance. I have known boys only 5 or 6 years old, who every time they would go to the bathroom to move their bowels would always look at the stool. They would even take the stool and press it and squeeze it, showing a certain curiosity about it.

This type of boy who from early childhood has shown interest in those matters is the type of boy when confronted with pornographic literature will just fall for it hard.

There are, however, other boys who are brought up in a very severe puritanical environment, and that boy may shy away from pornographic literature. There is no set rule about it.

Mr. Bobo. Have you noticed coming to your attention more children that have had contact with pornographic literature?

Dr. Karpman. I wouldn't say that I have come in contact with more. I am not able to give you any statistics. I know that I have been testifying very often for the Post Office Department. They come in contact with a larger amount of pornographic literature. This has been a problem of the Post Office Department all the time.

For instance, there are a group of people that we call perverts, who specialize in spanking. They derive satisfaction, sexual satisfaction, out of spanking others and being spanked.

You sometimes get pictures of people, naked, nude, one after the other, each one in front spanking the other one. They even published a journal called Bareback, and that is how the Post Office Department got it, because they were sending obscene literature through the mail. They arrested them. That doesn't make any difference. You can arrest today all the people of this type that you can. Tomorrow morning you have another group, because the conditions which produce them remain constant.

Mr. Bobo. In these spanking photos—and I presume that you would include the chain photos—the ones where the women wear the long black highheel boots?

Dr. Karpman. That is right.

Mr. Bobo. Do you think it is possible this particular type of literature, even though it doesn't show a complete nude body, might also have an effect upon juveniles and their sex life?

Dr. Karpman. Yes; indeed. What they do not see, the imagination supplies the rest. In other words, you only have to expose, we will say, one bare leg of a woman, and her thigh, and then the imagination will supply the rest.

Mr. Bobo. So that the fact that under your definition, these bondage and spanking and whipping photos are pornographic in nature?

Dr. Karpman. Absolutely; they are pornographic in the sense that they stimulate the mind to abnormal sexual practices.

What you speak of is what we psychiatrists know as sadism, masochism, fetishism, and so on. These are abnormal sexual practices—men who are sadists and masochists usually get together. One is a sadist and one is a masochist. The couple need not be only men or only women. Sometimes it is a man and a woman.

Oddly enough, it is the woman who is the sadist, and it is a big strong husky man that is the masochist. The woman gets a hold of a whip, and it is amazing how they can use a whip on a big strong husky man, and he takes all she can give him, and out of that both derive a certain amount of what we call physical satisfaction.

These things are sometimes enlarged in people, in children brought up at the age of 3, 4, 5 years old. If pornographic literature would not come along it would remain within certain confines—not normal, because only psychoanalysis can cure that.

The pornographic literature casts it broadly and widely, and attracts people who would otherwise remain entirely innocent.

Mr. Bobo. Pornographic literature, as I understand you, doesn't affect only teen-agers, but can go down to the age of 5 or 6?

Dr. Karpman. Yes, absolutely; if it falls on proper soil. You take, for instance, a person who has developed normally. If you take that kind of a person and expose them to literature when they were 5 years old, he wouldn't know what it means. He may have been brought up in a very good home which was probably severely puritanical, but he went to church and controlled himself, and so on. That boy is not likely to be influenced by the exposure; but you take a boy who has developed from early childhood, from our point of view, developed from early childhood sadistic, masochistic, fetishistic, or cannibalistic tendencies, and there you have something from which he can go.

Chairman Kefauver. Would you say that among the juvenile population of today that sexual perversion is on the increase?

Dr. Karpman. I would have to cite statistics, and it is impossible under these circumstances to cite statistics. You cannot, because they will deny it. I believe it is on the increase, and I will give you one proof; the world war.

As a result of war certain changes have taken place in our sex life. Women were committing adultery because they were left without men. That is one change. That disturbs the basic living of our communities.

Some women have taken other women as partners to take the place of the husband, because they did not want to commit adultery, and so they thought they were remaining within the levels of normality; but two women would get together and play with each other, and some, even harmless.

Men coming from war over and over again would become changed in their sex lives. That was demonstrated very well by the popular song during World War I—My Buddy. It is a typical homosexual song which glorified the companionship of men with men.

Then during the war there were also magazine articles—Men Without Women—which also emphasizes the problem of homosexuality.

There have been many divorces as a result of the war. There have been many murders. A man stayed away during the war for 2 or 3 years, came back, and regardless of how faithful the wife might have been to him, there was always a suspicion of jeolousy in them, and many of them committed murder. I had a number of them among my patients.

Mr. Bobo. In addition to creating certain perversions among children, when an older person shows to a child pornographic literature, what is the effect of that? Is he attempting to get him to engage in perversion acts?

Dr. KARPMAN. Men somehow or another do not realize they cannot be as competent sexually at 65 as they were at 25, and they still expect at 65 to be perfectly healthy and normal and be able to satisfy a woman. A time comes when they are not able to satisfy a woman. A time comes when they are able to satisfy only in a moderate degree, but not the way they were able to satisfy them before.

Very often it happen that men, as·time goes on, become less and less and less competent sexually, but they don't want to admit it. Then they suffer what we call regression. They begin to go down to the level of childhood, and the man becomes almost like a child, and being a child he thinks like a child. He feels like a child, and therefore tries to play with children.

Mr. BOBO. Do you think also that among the young people, especially of high-school age, that rather than involve the danger of possible conception, that pornography has given them the idea in other forms of sexual satisfaction?

Dr. KARPMAN. Pornography may not have given them the idea, but it may have supported it. One homosexual woman that I had under observation told a young girl who was perfectly normal—but it was during the war, and men were scarce—and she came to her and said, "What do you want to bother with men for anyway? There is always the possibility of disease; there is always the possibility of pregnancy. There would be no chance of pregnancy if you went out with me. What is there a man can do that I cannot do?"

She dresses herself up in male clothes, and looks like a man and acts like a man, and she tries to simulate the activities of men; and that is how women homosexuals often develop.

Chairman KEFAUVER. Senator Langer, do you have any questions?

Senator LANGER. How long have you been at the hospital in Washington?

Dr. KARPMAN. 35 years, with the exception of a year and a half when I was in Europe studying and doing postgraduate work.

Senator LANGER. Thank you.

Chairman KEFAUVER. You were born in North Dakota?

Dr. KARPMAN. No.

Chairman KEFAUVER. You lived in North Dakota?

Dr. KARPMAN. Yes. I was at Columbia; I was at Michigan, and I was always looking for a smaller school, and I found it in North Dakota. Everybody knows everybody else. You are just like friends. You have no such thing like that in a large city like this, where everybody is everybody else's enemy. In North Dakota everybody is everybody's friend, just like in Tennessee.

Chairman KEFAUVER. Dr. Karpman, we do certainly thank you for the valuable information you have given to this committee.

Dr. KARPMAN. Thank you very much.

Chairman KEFAUVER. We appreciate your coming up to New York.

Mr. BOBO. I am going to ask Mr. Martin to call the names of the witnesses who have been subpenaed to appear here today and to present their books and records—and will you come forward at the time in which he calls your name?

Mr. MARTIN. Abraham Rubenstein. Abraham Ruben.

Chairman KEFAUVER. What is your name?

Mr. WEISS. Daniel S. Weiss, 15 East 40th Street.

Chairman KEFAUVER. You represent Mr. Ruben?

Mr. WEISS. Yes.

Chairman KEFAUVER. Let us make it the first thing in the afternoon. Let us say 1 : 30.

Mr. WEISS. Very good.

Mr. MARTIN. Has Mr. Ruben brought his books with him?

Mr. WEISS. What books are you interested in?

Mr. MARTIN. He has been asked to produce his State and Federal income-tax returns for the years 1950 to 1954.

Mr. WEISS. We have that.

Mr. MARTIN. The records of his business, bankbooks, bank statements, checkbooks, check stubs.

Chairman KEFAUVER. Mr. Weiss, we will take care of those things and see that they are returned intact. Mark them and catalog them carefully.

Mr. WEISS. That will be tomorrow at 1 : 30?

Chairman KEFAUVER. We will recess for lunch and come back at 1 : 30 or 2 o'clock. Let us say 1 : 30 to be sure.

Mr. WEISS. Thank you very much.

Mr. MARTIN. Mr. Herman Sobel.

Mr. BOHRAR. I am the attorney for Mr. Sobel.

Chairman KEFAUVER. We will be glad to have you with us, Mr. Bohrar. You are the attorney for Mr. Sobel?

Mr. BOHRAR. I am.

Chairman KEFAUVER. When did you want to have Mr. Sobel come to testify? Would it be convenient to come back at 2 : 30 tomorrow?

Mr. BOHRAR That will be perfectly all right. We have some records here.

Mr. MARTIN. I wonder if Mr. Bohrar would care to define what records you have produced?

Mr. BOHRAR. Canceled checks.

Mr. MARTIN. How about the State and Federal income-tax returns?

Mr. BOHRAR. He hasn't got any. He hasn't kept any records. He has filed reports, but he hasn't kept copies of them.

Mr. MARTIN. Don't you know under the law he is required to keep records of his business?

Mr. BOHRAR. I understand that, but he hasn't got them.

Chairman KEFAUVER. Is Mr. Sobel the head of a corporation?

Mr. BOHRAR. He is an individual.

Chairman KEFAUVER. What kind of books did you keep, sir?

Mr. BOHRAR. He doesn't keep any books.

Chairman KEFAUVER. Just keeps them in his head?

Mr. BOHRAR. Keeps them in his head. He tells me there are a great number of judgments against him, and he cannot keep records for that reason. He doesn't keep any money in the bank because he hasn't got any money.

Chairman KEFAUVER. He is in bad shape?

Mr. BOHRAR. He puts a certain amount of money in the bank just to make good the checks.

Mr. MARTIN. He was subpenaed to produce checkbooks, and check stubs. Where are they—the canceled checks?

Mr. BOHRAR. That is all he has.

Chairman KEFAUVER. I suggest you look again and see if you cannot find more records and books of your business.

Mr. Butler, will you mark those? We will keep them and return them to you, Mr. Bohrar.

Mr. MARTIN. Mr. Abe Rotto.

Mr. ROTTO. I was subpenaed for this morning. I am waiting for my attorney.

Chairman KEFAUVER. How about 11 o'clock tomorrow morning?

Mr. ROTTO. That will be all right.

Chairman KEFAUVER. You have some books and records, Mr. Rotto?

Mr. ROTTO. What I was asked to bring along—the income-tax reports. I haven't kept any books.

Mr. MARTIN. Do you have any books?

Mr. ROTTO. I haven't kept any books. I am just a free-lance salesman.

Mr. MARTIN. How about your bank accounts?

Mr. ROTTO. I have one of those 10-cent checking accounts.

Mr. MARTIN. Do you have the canceled checks?

Mr. ROTTO. Only for the last month or so. I get my statement, check it off, and throw it away. I never have more than 50 or 60 dollars in the bank.

Mr. MARTIN. Do you own any property?

Mr. ROTTO. No, sir.

Mr. MARTIN. No automobile; or anything?

Mr. ROTTO. I have an automobile; yes, sir.

Mr. BOBO. Do you have your income-tax returns for the years requested?

Mr. ROTTO. Yes, sir.

Chairman KEFAUVER. We will take care of what records you have. Turn them over, and at the end of the hearing they will be returned to you.

Mr. ROTTO. Thank you.

Chairman KEFAUVER. Catalog carefully what he gives you.

Mr. ROTTO. Eleven o'clock tomorrow morning?

Chairman KEFAUVER. Eleven o'clock in the morning.

Mr. MARTIN. Louis Shomer.

Chairman KEFAUVER. You are Mr. Shomer?

Mr. SHOMER. Yes.

Chairman KEFAUVER. You are——

Mr. RACHSTEIN. Mr. Rachstein.

Chairman KEFAUVER. You are Mr. Shomer's attorney?

Mr. RACHSTEIN. Yes, sir.

Chairman KEFAUVER. What is your first name, Mr. Rachstein?

Mr. RACHSTEIN. Jacob; 280 Broadway, New York.

Chairman KEFAUVER. We will be glad to work out Mr. Shomer's appearance at a time that is convenient with you.

Mr. RACHSTEIN. I was going to trial tomorrow, but if we are going to have a hearing tomorrow, any time will do. I will just adjourn the case. Is it planned to hear Mr. Shomer tomorrow?

Chairman KEFAUVER. Will 1:30 be all right?

Mr. RACHSTEIN. Yes; Your Honor.

Chairman KEFAUVER. We will look for you at 1:30.

Mr. MARTIN. Has Mr. Shomer produced the records?

Mr. RACHSTEIN. He brought his checkbooks and stubs. He is unable to produce his tax returns because they are in the possession of his accountant. He was served last night at 9 p. m. He has had no opportunity before coming here this morning to see his accountant.

Mr. MARTIN. Can he get them?

Mr. RACHSTEIN. He will have them here at 1 : 30.

Chairman KEFAUVER. If necessary, bring your accountant with you. Turn over what you have now.

Mr. RACHSTEIN. Thank you.

Mr. MARTIN. Roy Ald.

(No response.)

Mr. MARTIN. Irving Klaw.

Chairman KEFAUVER. You are Mr. Klaw?

Mr. KLAW. Yes.

Chairman KEFAUVER. Irving Klaw?

Mr. KLAW. Yes.

Chairman KEFAUVER. You are Mr. Gangel?

Mr. GANGEL. Yes.

Chairman KEFAUVER. What is your address?

Mr. GANGEL. 165 Broadway, New York City.

Chairman KEFAUVER. You are the attorney for Mr. Klaw?

Mr. GANGEL. I am his attorney, but his regular attorney is in the hospital, and I have filed a written motion for an extension of the return date of this subpena. Mr. Joseph E. Brill is Mr. Klaw's attorney. He is confined to the Beth Israel Hospital, and so I have asked that the return date be extended, and if necessary we would appear before the committee in another city if the date were extended, when Mr. Brill is available.

Chairman KEFAUVER. Have you represented Mr. Klaw in other matters?

Mr. GANGEL. Our firm has. Mr. Brill has been in charge of it.

Chairman KEFAUVER. Mr. Brill is a partner in your firm?

Mr. GANGEL. That is correct.

Chairman KEFAUVER. How many members are there in the firm?

Mr. GANGEL. Two members.

Chairman KEFAUVER. And the firm has handled Mr. Klaw's matters?

Mr. GANGEL. Yes; but exclusively by Mr. Brill.

Chairman KEFAUVER. Mr. Gangel, I think we will get along all right. All we want to get are some facts. We won't get into any involved legal complications, I wouldn't think. We would like to get as much of this hearing over with during these 3 days as possible.

Mr. GANGEL. I will cooperate as much as possible, but I am not sure there won't be any legal problems, and that is the reason I wanted the client to have the benefit of Mr. Brill's advice and counsel, but I will, of course, abide by the chairman's ruling.

Chairman KEFAUVER. I think we will get along all right.

Mr. GANGEL. Thank you.

Chairman KEFAUVER. When would it be convenient for Mr. Klaw to come? Would 1 o'clock Thursday afternoon be convenient?

Mr. GANGEL. I don't have my diary here, but we will be here whatever time the committee fixes.

Chairman KEFAUVER. One o'clock Thursday afternoon.

Mr. Klaw, were you requested to bring any records or books?

Mr. KLAW. Yes.

Chairman KEFAUVER. Do you have them, sir?

Mr. KLAW. I decline to make them available under the fifth amendment of the Constitution; that they may tend to degrade or incriminate me; and under the fourth amendment of the Constitution, that the subpena is vague and illegal.

Chairman KEFAUVER. Well, sir, as to the second point, vagueness and illegality of the subpena—the subpena should be copied in the record at this point. Let it be exhibit 7.

(The subpena was marked "Exhibit 7," and is as follows:)

EXHIBIT NO. 7

UNITED STATES OF AMERICA

CONGRESS OF THE UNITED STATES

To IRVING KLAW, 212 East 14th Street, New York City, Greeting:

Pursuant to lawful authority, you are hereby commanded to appear before the Subcommittee To Investigate Juvenile Delinquency of the Senate of the United States, on May 24, 1955, at 10 o'clock a. m., at their committee room 104, United States Court House, Foley Square, New York, N. Y., then and there to testify what you may know relative to the subject matters under consideration by said committee, and bring with you copies of your State and Federal income-tax returns for the years 1950 to 1954, inclusive; records of your business, including bankbooks, bank statements, checkbooks and check stubs, profit and loss statements, statements of assets and liabilities, and all documents reflecting your interest in property, real, personal, or mixed.

Hereof fail not, as you will answer your default under the pains and penalties in such cases made and provided.

To United States Marshall, southern district of New York to serve and return.

Given under my hand, by order of the committee, this 19th day of May, in the year of our Lord one thousand nine hundred and fifty-five.

ESTES KEFAUVER,
Chairman, Subcommittee To Investigate Juvenile Delinquency.

Chairman KEFAUVER. As to the second point, you, of course, are entitled to rely upon the fifth amendment. Do you wish to make any statement as to why you think producing any books or records called for here, might tend to incriminate you?

Mr. KLAW. I decline to answer under the fifth amendment of the Constitution; that an anwer to that may tend to incriminate me.

Mr. GANGEL. According to your suggestion, we don't want any pictures.

Chairman KEFAUVER. Mr. Klaw said he didn't want any lights or pictures.

Mr. GANGEL. There is just one aside from the question you have just addressed to this witness. If you would fix our appearance for Thursday morning instead of Thursday afternoon, I would very much appreciate it, because I have to conduct a hearing at 2 o'clock on Thursday, and I am afraid this would interfere. If it could be arranged, I would appreciate it.

Chairman KEFAUVER. Nine o'clock Thursday morning.

Mr. GANGEL. All right, sir.

Chairman KEFAUVER. Mr. Klaw, you have refused to comply with the subpena and bring in certain books. You have a copy of the subpena, do you not?

Mr. GANGEL. We have a copy of the subpena. Mr. Klaw had it and turned it over to me.

Chairman KEFAUVER. It was duly served on Mr. Klaw.

Mr. Klaw, the subcommittee will order and direct you to bring the books and records specified in this subpena when you come Thursday morning. You will remain under continuing subpena to appear here at 9 o'clock Thursday morning with the books and records described in this subpena. Is that clear?

Mr. GANGEL. We understand, sir.

Chairman KEFAUVER. Thank you, sir.

Mr. MARTIN. Aaron Moses Shapiro.

Chairman KEFAUVER. Is Mr. Shapiro not here?

Mr. BOBO. Mr. Shapiro hasn't made an appearance.

Chairman KEFAUVER. Let us ask the assistants of the marshal to locate him.

Mr. BOBO. Is the marshal present?

The MARSHAL. Mr. Shapiro is not in the back room.

Mr. MARTIN. Martin Goodman.

Mr. FROLICH. Mr. Goodman's counsel was out of town. I believe he got in touch with the committee.

Mr. MARTIN. Edward Mishikin.

Chairman KEFAUVER. You are Mr. Mishikin?

Mr. MISHIKIN. That is correct.

Chairman KEFAUVER. You appear for Mr. Mishikin?

Mr. WEISS. Yes, sir.

Chairman KEFAUVER. He will continue under subpena and come back at 1 : 30 tomorrow.

Mr. WEISS. Fine.

Chairman KEFAUVER. Do you have some books and records?

Mr. WEISS. He has.

Chairman KEFAUVER. Have you?

Mr. MARTIN. Aren't there more records than what he has in his hands?

Mr. WEISS. Most of those records with respect to income tax are now in the possession of the Internal Revenue Department. He is under investigation there.

Chairman KEFAUVER. Will you take charge and catalog the records? They will be returned to him.

Have him look again and see if he finds any other records.

Mr. WEISS. All the records he has in his possession have now been turned over.

Mr. MARTIN. Do we have the documents reflecting his interest in property, real, personal, and mixed?

Mr. WEISS. Yes.

Mr. MARTIN. Do we have a statement of his assets and liabilities?

Mr. WEISS. All of those records are with the Internal Revenue Department.

Mr. MARTIN. All of them?

Mr. WEISS. Yes; I imagine all of them.

Mr. MARTIN. For 1954, too?

Mr. WEISS. They are either in the possession of the Internal Revenue Department or his tax representatives who is presently negotiating with the Internal Revenue Department.

Chairman KEFAUVER. Your client must have copies of these reports, or must be able to get in touch with his tax representative.

Mr. WEISS. I will try to do that myself if it is possible.

Mr. MARTIN. How about his profit and loss statement?

Mr. WEISS. All of those are in, I believe.

Mr. MARTIN. His bank statements?

Mr. WEISS. The bank books have been turned over. There are no checking accounts, and there haven't been any.

Mr. MARTIN. Mr. Weiss, it isn't customary for the Internal Revenue Department to be that much on the ball that they will be investigating a man's 1954 income tax in 1955.

Mr. WEISS. It is more or less of a continuation of an original investigation. I think there has been an extension on it to cover other years. Frankly, I am not too familiar with that, but I know all the records he has, he has turned over either to the Internal Revenue Department or to the tax consultant who is handling the matter with the Internal Revenue Department.

Mr. MARTIN. You will take it up with the tax consultant?

Mr. WEISS. I will definitely call him. Is it 1:30 or 2 o'clock tomorrow?

Chairman KEFAUVER. Yes. If you will advise a member of the staff in the morning as to what the tax consultant says—whether you have gotten those records or not, that will be all right.

Mr. WEISS. Yes; of course.

Mr. MARTIN. Do you have any other clients, while you are here?

Mr. WEISS. I have one who is ill, and I have turned in a doctor's certificate with respect to him. That is Louis Finkelstein.

Mr. MARTIN. Mr. Finkelstein?

Mr. WEISS. That is correct.

Mr. MARTIN. The day the marshal made service, I believe Mr. Finkelstein was at the doctor's office in Brooklyn.

Mr. WEISS. I believe the marshal spoke to the doctor.

Mr. MARTIN. Mr. Finkelstein was able to drive his own car to Brooklyn.

Mr. WEISS. I don't know that to be the fact, nor can I dispute it.

Chairman KEFAUVER. 139 Winthrop Road, Teaneck, N. J.?

Mr. WEISS. That is correct.

Chairman KEFAUVER. Will you contact him and see if in the 3 days we are here it won't be possible for him to come in? It doesn't indicate there is anything seriously wrong with him.

Mr. WEISS. I believe he did have one stethoscopic test of some sort, and I understood he was either going into the hospital today or the next day for another one. I don't know. That is the information that I received.

Chairman KEFAUVER. Make inquiry and let our staff know.

Let the doctor's certificate be made part of the record.

(The doctor's certificate was marked "Exhibit No. 8," and is as follows:)

EXHIBIT No. 8

BROOKLYN, N. Y., *May 21, 1955.*

Name: Louis Finkelstein. Age 42.
Address: 379 Winthrop Road, Teaneck, N. J.

To Whom It May Concern:

This is to certify that Louis Finkelstein is ill and has been under my and Dr. Harold Berlowitz's (urologist) care for the past month. He is suffering from a kidney and urinary bladder ailment, and is in need of additional cystoscopic, urinary, and X-ray observation, tests, and treatment.

Yours truly,

SAMUEL L. MAILMAN, M. D.

Mr. MARTIN. Eugene Mulletta.

Chairman KEFAUVER. You are Mr. Mulletta?

Mr. MULLETTA. Yes.

Chairman KEFAUVER. What is your name?

Mr. LAZER. Leon D. Lazar.

Chairman KEFAUVER. You are attorney for Mr. Mulletta?

Mr. LAZER. That is right.

Chairman KEFAUVER. What is your address?

Mr. LAZER. 120–09 Liberty Avenue, Richmond Hill, N. Y.

Chairman KEFAUVER. Your phone number there?

Mr. LAZER. MIchigan 1–1515.

Chairman KEFAUVER. When is Mr. Mulletta scheduled to appear? Would 10 o'clock Thursday morning be satisfactory?

Mr. LAZER. That will be satisfactory.

Chairman KEFAUVER. Mr. Mulleta, were you requested to bring any books and records?

Mr. MULLETTA. I have them in the car. I have two large cartons. It would be impossible for me to carry them.

Chairman KEFAUVER. Mr. Butler, will some of you make arrangements to see what is in the car.

Mr. MULLETTA. The 1954 accounts receivable, and my bills. I am under charges in special sessions in Long Island City on some accounts. I feel that they would tend to incriminate me if they were shown to the wrong people.

Chairman KEFAUVER. Why don't you separate what you think would tend to incriminate you. We will argue about that later.

Mr. LAZER. We are willing to give you all the records up to 1954. Since my client is under indictment under a charge which may be in some way related to the purpose of the investigation here, I feel the production of those records at this time would tend to incriminate him. He feels that way himself.

Chairman KEFAUVER. I would be inclined to agree with you; but you bring them in.

Mr. LAZER. We will bring the records. They are downstairs in his car, and we will bring them right up.

The proceeding is in the general sessions court. It is a State court.

Chairman KEFAUVER. Ordinarily an incrimination matter doesn't relate from a State jurisdiction to a Federal jurisdiction, or vice versa. Bring them all in and let us talk about it when you appear.

Mr. LAZER. We will do that, sir.

Chairman KEFAUVER. Thank you very much, sir.

Mr. MARTIN. John Cassel.

Chairman KEFAUVER. You are Mr. Cassel?

Mr. CASSEL. Yes.

Mr. MARTIN. Do you have any books and records?

Mr. CASSEL. Not books, just the records—income tax.

Mr. MARTIN. Bankbooks, bank statements?

Mr. CASSEL. Just one bankbook.

Chairman KEFAUVER. You were told to bring in a whole lot of other things.

Mr. CASSEL. That is all I have.

Chairman KEFAUVER. Where do you keep the books of your business?

Mr. CASSEL. I have no business. I work as a shipping clerk.

Chairman KEFAUVER. Mr. Butler, will you catalog what Mr. Cassel has there?

Mr. Cassel, can you come back at 10 o'clock in the morning?
Mr. CASSEL. Could I come on Thursday, please?
Chairman KEFAUVER. Tomorrow morning.
Mr. CASSEL. Thank you, sir.
Mr. MARTIN. Roy Ald.
(No response.)
Mr. MARTIN. William Landsman.
Chairman KEFAUVER. You are Mr. Landsman?
Mr. LANDSMAN. I am.
Chairman KEFAUVER. Will 10 o'clock in the morning be satisfactory
to you, Mr. Landsman?
Mr. LANDSMAN. Yes.
Chairman KEFAUVER. Do you have any books and records?
Mr. LANDSMAN. I am not in the capacity of having books and
records.
Chairman KEFAUVER. You don't have any at all?
Mr. LANDSMAN. No, sir.
Chairman KEFAUVER. Do you have a copy of your income-tax re-
turns?
Mr. LANDSMAN. No, sir. I am on social security.
Chairman KEFAUVER. You have no books of any kind?
Mr. LANDSMAN. No, sir.
Chairman KEFAUVER. No checking account?
Mr. LANDSMAN. No, sir.
Chairman KEFAUVER. All right, we will see you in the morning at
10 o'clock.
Mr. MARTIN. Frank Adler.
Chairman KEFAUVER. Mr. Adler doesn't seem to be here.
Call the next witness, Mr. Bobo.
Mr. BOBO. Eugene O. Cavanaugh.
Chairman KEFAUVER. Mr. Cavanaugh, we are glad to have you with
us.

TESTIMONY OF EUGENE O. CAVANAUGH, CHIEF OF THE YOUTH SQUAD, NEW YORK CITY BOARD OF EDUCATION

(Eugene O. Cavanaugh was sworn.)
Chairman KEFAUVER. Mr. Bobo, will you take over.
Mr. BOBO. Would you state your full name.
Mr. CAVANAUGH. Eugene O. Cavanaugh.
Mr. BOBO. You are employed on the youth squad of the board of
education?
Mr. CAVANAUGH. The chief attendance officer, board of education,
city of New York.
Mr. BOBO. What is the address?
Mr. CAVANAUGH. 110 Livingston Street, Brooklyn, N. Y.
Mr. BOBO. How long have you worked in that capacity?
Mr. CAVANAUGH. As chief attendance officer, 4 years; in the attend-
ance field, 27 years.
Mr. BOBO. What is your duty in the attendance field and in the
youth squad of the board of education?
Mr. CAVANAUGH. My duties are to supervise the attendance staff,
that is, including the supervisory staff and the attendance officers in

the field, of which we have 32; 42 supervisory members, and 340 attendance officers.

Chairman KEFAUVER. State those figures again.

Mr. CAVANAUGH. We have 42 supervisory members of our staff, and 340 attendance officers. I personally supervise the youth squad that goes about the city apprehending children on the streets during school hours.

Mr. BOBO. Your squad has no police powers?

Mr. CAVANAUGH. They have police powers. They may arrest truants on the streets during school hours.

Mr. BOBO. What have you found to be the major activities of truants from school?

Mr. CAVANAUGH. The major activity is to find some place that they can be entertained during school hours rather than attend school. Moving picture houses used to be a favorite hangout of children until the moving picture theater owners cooperated with us, and we have very little difficulty on that score now.

Candy stores are a source——

Chairman KEFAUVER. You say moving picture houses used to be a favorite hangout, but the moving picture theater owners have cooperated with you and it is no longer true?

Mr. CAVANAUGH. It is no longer true.

Chairman KEFAUVER. That is something that I think ought to be noted.

Mr. BOBO. Have you come in contact with any pornographic material through your organization or through your own personal contacts?

Mr. CAVANAUGH. Well, over the years it has been an occasional problem. We have had pornographic material come into the possession of children. It hasn't been on the increase of late, but it still is with us.

Mr. BOBO. Has there been any increase in the number of sex offenses among students at school?

Mr. CAVANAUGH. Not that we know of; no.

Mr. BOBO. Not among the truants with whom you deal?

Mr. CAVANAUGH. No.

Mr. BOBO. I believe that some time ago you submitted a report dated April 12, 1955, that spoke of some of the activities that the youth squad has come in contact with in New York City.

Do you have any objection, Mr. Cavanaugh, if we should make this part of the record of the hearings of this subcommittee?

Mr. CAVANAUGH. I will be glad to.

Mr. BOBO. Are there any special sections——

Chairman KEFAUVER. You said it would be all right?

Mr. CAVANAUGH. Yes, sir.

Mr. BOBO. I ask it to be appended in the record.

Chairman KEFAUVER. It will be so ordered.

(The information was marked "Exhibit No. 9," and is on file with the subcommittee.)

Mr. BOBO. In addition to speaking of truants, and so forth, I notice in this report:

We know that this condition contributes to juvenile delinquency. Pupils have informed us that they have been offered alcoholic beverages, obscene literature has been circulated, and youth in the 17 to 20 years age group are constantly soliciting teen-age girls to accompany them on dates and automobile rides in most of these premises.

Would you say that is an increase in activity?

Mr. CAVANAUGH. Yes; that is an increased activity. Our difficulty today is in the local candy store where the 17-year-olds hang out, and invite girls in, or younger children into the store; and they are known to hang out there; and it is an attraction to these teen-age girls to go to the store for whatever amusement is there. It may be for just hanging out in the store. It may be to look at these pornographic pictures, or it may be to drink beer, or whatever it may be.

Mr. BOBO. Have any street peddlers or the candy stores come to your attention insofar as that they are selling or peddling pornographic literature?

Mr. CAVANAUGH. No.

Mr. BOBO. None have come to the attention of your department at all?

Mr. CAVANAUGH. No, sir.

Mr. BOBO. Would you say that pornographic literature has had any effect upon truancy or delinquency among the schools of New York?

Mr. CAVANAUGH. There is no doubt in my mind that pornographic literature does have an effect upon the child.

As Father Egan pointed out, some children are able to throw it off. Some children, it whets the appetite, and they look for more. It creates a problem. There is no doubt that it adds to the juvenile delinquency that we are now faced with.

Chairman KEFAUVER. Senator Langer, do you have any questions?

Senator LANGER. No.

Chairman KEFAUVER. Mr. Cavanaugh, we thank you very much for coming. We wish you success in your effort, which we know is a very difficult one.

Mr. CAVANAUGH. Thank you, sir.

Senator LANGER. How many boys have you dealt with in connection with your work?

Mr. CAVANAUGH. In 27 years?

Senator LANGER. Yes.

Mr. CAVANAUGH. I would say offhand probably there came into my own hands—that I had personal contact with?

Senator LANGER. Yes.

Mr. CAVANAUGH. I would say about 50,000 children that I had personal contact with.

Senator LANGER. What would be their ages?

Mr. CAVANAUGH. The ages run from 7 to 17.

Senator LANGER. Thank you very much.

Chairman KEFAUVER. We would appreciate hearing from you.

Mr. CAVANAUGH. We would be glad to write to you.

Chairman KEFAUVER. Our next witness.

Mr. BOBO. Mr. and Mrs. Robert Thoms.

(Mr. and Mrs. Robert Thoms were sworn by the chairman.)

Chairman KEFAUVER. Mr. Bobo, will you take over. I don't know how you are going to testify together, but we will work it out some way.

Mr. BOBO. Do you have any preference as to which one will testify first?

Chairman KEFAUVER. Let Mrs. Thoms tell her story.

Mr. BOBO. Mrs. Thoms, would you state your name for us.

TESTIMONY OF MR. AND MRS. ROBERT THOMS, RUTHERFORD, N. J.

Mrs. THOMS. Mrs. Helen C. Thoms.

Mr. BOBO. Your address where you live now?

Mrs. THOMS. Seventy-three Barrows Avenue, Rutherford, N. J.

Mr. BOBO. Are you a parent?

Mr. THOMS. Yes.

Mr. BOBO. How many children do you have?

Mrs. THOMS. Five.

Mr. BOBO. Five children?

Mrs. THOMS. Yes.

Mr. BOBO. Mrs. Thoms, I believe you formerly lived in Fairlawn, N. J., and you had an experience with pornographic literature?

Mrs. THOMS. Yes.

Mr. BOBO. And it involved your children?

Mrs. THOMS. Yes.

Mr. BOBO. Will you tell us about that?

Mrs. THOMS. Last May my sons came in——

Chairman KEFAUVER. Last May—1954?

Mrs. THOMS. Yes. My sons came in at dinner time, and they were taking their baths, and I was taking the laundry down; and as usual I was emptying the pockets of the dungarees, and I came across——

Chairman KEFAUVER. How many sons are they?

Mrs. THOMS. Just one pair of dungarees had the books in them. He was 13 years old—my son Vincent.

Chairman KEFAUVER. Go on and tell us all about it in your own words.

Mrs. THOMS. At first I picked the two books out of his pocket and I thought they were just children's book, and I didn't know whether to throw it away or not. I looked inside of it, and I was so surprised.

When I asked him where he got them he said some boy had given it to him, and he was going to throw them away.

Mr. BOBO. You say that you were surprised. They weren't the type of books you thought they were—children's books? They were the pornographic type of books showing nude and obscene pictures?

Mrs. THOMS. No; I never had experience with anything near like it.

Chairman KEFAUVER. What kind of books are we talking about now?

Mr. BOBO. Is this the type of book you are talking about which was in the hand of your child?

Mrs. THOMS. Yes.

Mr. BOBO. Entitled "Jiggs"?

Mrs. THOMS. Yes.

Mr. BOBO. And "Ella Cinders"?

Mrs. THOMS. Yes, sir.

Chairman KEFAUVER. Let us make it clear that some of these pornographers have plagiarized the names of very fine comic strips, like Maggie and Jiggs, and Ella Cinders. That was a despicable thing to do.

Go ahead, Mr. Bobo.

Mr. BOBO. You found these in the pocket of your 13-year-old son?

Mrs. THOMS. Yes. I asked him why didn't he show them to me. He said he had just got them. It was at 5 o'clock. He came in the house. It was a few minutes before 5 when he said he got them. I said, "From who?"

He said, "A certain boy."

I went to the certain boy's house. He said he found them on the school grounds. I took him to the police department and left one copy.

Mr. BOBO. Did the boy who had given them to your son go to the same school, and did he find them at the school ground in Fairlawn?

Mrs. THOMS. No. He said he found them on the school grounds across the street from my house, but that is not where they came from. They were being sold in the schoolyard of a school a mile away from us.

Mr. BOBO. Will you tell us how your son came into contact with these books. Where did he get them?

Mrs. THOMS. Would you ask me the questions more directly?

Mr. BOBO. Where did you say your son got these books?

Mrs. THOMS. He said that this boy gave them to him.

Mr. BOBO. Did you make a further investigation to determine where the boy who gave them to your son got them?

Mrs. THOMS. Well, he denied it. He said he just found them on the school ground, but later that evening my 10-year-old boy—I have 3 boys—the youngest boy said, "They sell those in the schoolyard."

Mr. BOBO. Was he talking about the school where he went to school?

Mrs. THOMS. Yes.

Mr. BOBO. And then did you make a further investigation to determine if they were being sold in the schoolyard where your son was at school?

Mrs. THOMS. Yes.

Mr. BOBO. Did you find that they were?

Mrs. THOMS. Yes.

Mr. BOBO. Did you find out the number of boys that were selling them in that particular school?

Mrs. THOMS. Well, I knew of two definitely that were selling them.

Mr. BOBO. Did you go to the school authorities and ask them to help you with the investigation?

Mrs. THOMS. Yes.

Mr. BOBO. Were they cooperative?

Mrs. THOMS. They were expelled boys. They have over 1,500 children. They said they would expel them immediately rather than keep them there and make any question about it.

Mr. BOBO. Did they give you any idea as to the extent of the traffic in this particular school of these types of books?

Mrs. THOMS. Yes. The teacher said they had confiscated a few in the fifth, sixth, and seventh grades—a couple of boys once in a while would be caught with them, and the teachers would take them away from them.

Mr. BOBO. Did you make a report to the police department about that?

Mrs. THOMS. Yes.

Mr. BOBO. Did you receive the cooperation of the police department in tracking down where the books had come from?

Mrs. THOMS. Well, I don't know whether you would call it cooperation or not. You will have to ask me more specifically. I was told not to do anything further about it. I was told to forget about it and not to talk about it, and let them take care of it.

Chairman KEFAUVER. Who told you that?

Mrs. THOMS. Police Captain Reisacker and Mr. LaGrossa, in charge of the juvenile police. They said they will take care of it and for me to be quiet and not do any more about it.

Mr. BOBO. Did they give you any reason for you being quiet?

Mrs. THOMS. Yes. They said, "You will only muff things. You will do things wrong. Let us handle it, and you be quiet about it."

Mr. BOBO. Did you go back to see them later to determine what investigation has been made?

Mrs. THOMS. Well, Mr. LaGrossa had come to my house, and he said, "This is hopeless, because you are going to have to show us evidence where a boy goes in a store and buys these books, and we will have to see them."

I got one of the boys who sells these books——

Mr. BOBO. How old a boy was this that was selling them?

Mrs. THOMS. He was 13. He said, "I will go in and buy them;" and on the way down he said, "Yes; I handle the post cards, and I have handled about 50 of these books. I buy them from this store-keeper and sell them on the school grounds at a profit."

Mr. BOBO. Did he tell you how much he bought them for, and how much he sold them for?

Mrs. THOMS. He said he bought them for 20 cents, and sold them for a quarter up to 40 cents—whatever he could get from the kids.

I then called Mr. LaGrossa and told him, "This afternoon at 3 o'clock this boy is going to buy this book."

Mr. BOBO. Mr. LaGrossa of the police department?

Mrs. THOMS. Yes. I said, "This boy is going to buy the books. You be there to witness it."

When I got there he was right there in front of the store. I noticed later there were police cars parked on the block; and the boy immediately got nervous and said that this man in the store was his friend. He said, "I am not going to get him in trouble."

He immediately backed out. I said to Mr. LaGrossa that he told me he got them from that man.

Mr. BOBO. Do you know what the man's name and the store was, and the store name?

Mrs. THOMS. No; just the name of their store is Jean and Al.

Mr. BOBO. Where is that located?

Mrs. THOMS. On Broadway in Fairlawn. It is right next to a bicycle store that all the boys patronize. The man that owns the store is very friendly, and his wife is there. I usually drive over. It was a nice store; but right next door was the candy store where on a hot day they would go in for a coke. My son went in for a coke this day, and the owner said, "Would you like to buy some funny books," so they said, "Sure."

The man gave them these two books. He said he destroyed them immediately when he saw what was in them, but that proved where they came from; and they said they know the boys would go in there and buy these books and sell them on the school grounds.

Mr. BOBO. Did you question the man as to whether or not he sold the books?

Mrs. Thoms. That day Mr. LaGrossa called the owner outside and said, "Did you sell this boy obscene books?" and he said, "Of course not."

He said to the boy, "Did this man give you the books"; and he said, "No."

He said, "You go back in the store."

As soon as he went in the store the boy said, "Of course he did; I have 50 of them, and post cards too, but I don't want to get them in trouble." He said that to Mr. LaGrossa.

I said, "Isn't that enough evidence?" His mother was there witnessing it, too. I said, "Why should this boy lie?"

Mr. Bobo. Mr. Thoms, did you go down and question this man at any time?

Mr. Thoms. Yes.

Mr. Bobo. Did he admit to you he was selling them?

Mr. Thoms. No.

Mr. Bobo. He never admitted it?

Mr. Thoms. No.

Mr. Bobo. You never knew except what the students told you?

Mr. Thoms. He merely told me when he took the business over that the books were in the store, and upon seeing them he destroyed them; and he claimed they were in a cigarbox under the counter; and, of course, the boys' remarks were it was a cigarbox when they were purchased by the children in town even after he took the store over.

Chairman Kefauver. Thank you very much, Mr. and Mrs. Thoms.

Mr. Martin. Mr. Ben Himmell.

Chairman Kefauver. Mr. Himmell, do you object to these lights?

Mr. Himmell. Yes; I do.

Chairman Kefauver. You have been subpenaed to appear here. Will you be here in the morning at 10 o'clock?

Mr. Himmell. What is this about?

Mr. Bobo. We asked you to bring in your books and records as to your business dealings and the type of work which you are doing.

Mr. Himmell. In other words, you want my business books?

Mr. Bobo. Yes, sir; according to the directions that were given on the subpena.

Mr. Himmell. I received that subpena at 8 o'clock this morning.

Mr. Bobo. Could you have those books and records here by 10 o'clock in the morning?

Mr. Himmell. I will call my accountant and find out.

Chairman Kefauver. You do the best you can to get them here by 10 o'clock in the morning.

I regret we cannot carry on this afternoon, but Senator Langer and I have to go back for a vote this afternoon, so we will stand in recess at this time until 9 o'clock in the morning.

Any witnesses under subpena who haven't been told a special time to come back will report in the morning, and we will hear them then.

(Whereupon, at 12:30 p. m., May 24, 1955, the subcommittee recessed until 9 a. m., May 25, 1955.)

JUVENILE DELINQUENCY

(Obscene and Pornographic Materials)

THURSDAY, MAY 26, 1955

United States Senate,
Subcommittee of the Committee on the Judiciary,
To Investigate Juvenile Delinquency,
New York, N. Y.

The subcommittee met, pursuant to notice, at 9 a. m., in room 1705, United States Courthouse, Foley Square, New York, N. Y., Senator Estes Kefauver, chairman, presiding.

Present: Senator Estes Kefauver.

Also present: James H. Bobo, chief counsel; Peter N. Chumbris, associate counsel; Vincent Gaughan, special counsel; Edward Lee McLean, editorial director; George Butler and George Martin, consultants to the subcommittee.

Chairman KEFAUVER. The subcommittee will come to order.

I regret exceedingly the situation we were confronted with yesterday in not being able to continue our hearing; but we had a very important piece of legislation in the Senate which I thought would be voted on Friday of this week, but it was decided to vote on it yesterday.

I am sorry we inconvenienced some witnesses.

We hope that Senator Langer will be with us later today, but we will have to carry on. I dislike very much having a one-Senator hearing, but, under the circumstances, we will have to proceed as best we can.

Again I want the witnesses and the public, or anyone, to know, if anyone's name is used adversely, and they want to make any explanation, they are invited to appear immediately, and the subcommittee will give them a chance to testify and make any explanation.

Before hearing our first witness today, I want to take this opportunity to comment on our hearings thus far, and to say what it is that we hope to achieve as a result of these hearings.

In my view a congressional committee, given a specific problem, has as its first and primary responsibility the production of legislation designed to remedy the situation which produces the problem. That is the purpose of the Juvenile Delinquency Subcommittee under my chairmanship.

However, we cannot legislate intelligently in a vacuum. We must know the facts. We find these facts by investigation and in public hearings such as this one. At the same time, because these hearings are open to coverage by all the media, we inform the public of the

101

conditions we have discovered; and in my view no problem is ever solved without public awareness and interest.

In our hearings here Tuesday we established the relationship between pornography and juvenile delinquency. We did this through the expert testimony of Dr. Benjamin Karpman, the famous criminologist and psychiatrist of St. Elizabeths Hospital in Washington; by the testimony of the Rev. Daniel Egan, who has done so much work with youth for the Catholic Church; Mr. William Deerson, director of discipline at Haaren High School, New York; and Mr. Eugene O. Cavanaugh, head of the youth squad of the New York Board of Education.

We established the nationwide aspects of pornography through the testimony of Mr. Peter N. Chumbris, associate counsel of this subcommittee, and I am informed by counsel that we shall further show the nationwide aspects in testimony of police and public officials of different cities today. This interstate aspect will also be shown by documentary exhibits which will be offered in evidence.

During the course of today's hearings we hope to learn through the testimony of subpenaed witnesses of certain information concerning the production and distribution of this material which we do not now have.

I want to reemphasize that the material we are talking about is not the art magazines, so-called—not the various girlie and gossip publications, which certainly border on the pornographic—but the undeniably lewd, lascivious, sadistic, and perverted publications; the kind which Dr. Karpman testified might very well upset the delicate sex balance of a juvenile in formative years, and which Father Egan testified could not help but affect any juvenile "who has blood in his veins."

This material, I am informed by counsel, goes into all 48 States.

I am convinced at this stage of the hearings that certain Federal legislation is needed. Our committee as a result of our preliminary investigations into these problems recommended and the Senate at its present session has adopted Senate bills 599 and 600.

These bills make it illegal to transport obscene literature across State lines in private conveyances. It is already illegal to transmit such literature through the mails. I intend to take the information gathered at these hearings and go before the House Judiciary Committee, where these bills are now pending. I hope with this additional information to be able to convince the House of the desirability of this legislation.

Several other proposals for legislation have occurred to me during these hearings, and we will develop further.

They are, to make it illegal to ship in interstate commerce any publications which do not include the name and address of the publisher, or, in the case of those published outside of the United States, the name and address of the distributor in this country.

The spelling out in legislation of a clearer and more definite definition of pornographic literature, which would include the various forms of perversion.

To strengthen Post Office regulations, permitting the impounding of obscene literature.

Increasing the penalties for publishing or peddling pornographic literature.

Strengthening the customs laws which we will have a good deal of testimony about during this hearing.

Before we start I have been advised by counsel that Father Egan wished one point of his testimony corrected. I think his testimony indicated that certain publications he had brought to me in my office at Washington had been purchased in Washington. I am advised that Father Egan says they were purchased elsewhere and brought to my office in Washington. I am glad to make that correction.

Mr. Bobo, are there any preliminary matters before we get started?

Mr. Bobo. I would like to call the names of the witnesses who will appear today. Inspector Roy Blick; Commissioner Lawrence A. Whipple; Sgt. Alfred Jago; Detective John Higgins; Al Stone, alias Abraham Rubinstein, Al Rubin, Abraham Rubin, Rubin Stone, and Stony Rubin White; Sgt. Joseph Brown; Lt. Ignatius Sheehan; Edward Mishkin; Arthur H. Sobel; Abe Rotto; Lou Shomer; William Landsman; and George Fodor. If there are any witnesses under subpena at present, I wish you would make yourselves known at this time.

Chairman KEFAUVER. Any witnesses from out of the city, I think we ought to try to have them today, because we have held them here for several days. Are there any others from out of the city?

Mr. GANGEL. What about Mr. Klaw?

Mr. Bobo. Due to the fact that we didn't have a hearing yesterday, we have scheduled Mr. Klaw to appear on Tuesday, so you will be excused today.

Mr. GANGEL. To return Tuesday?

Mr. Bobo. Tuesday at 9:30.

Chairman KEFAUVER. Let us say 10.

Mr. GANGEL. I would prefer 10, if the committee would permit that.

Chairman KEFAUVER. 10 o'clock. Is that convenient with you?

Mr. GANGEL. Yes. That would be June 1, I take it?

Chairman KEFAUVER. The day after Memorial Day.

Mr. Bobo. Inspector Roy Blick.

TESTIMONY OF INSPECTOR ROY BLICK, HEAD OF VICE SQUAD, POLICE DEPARTMENT, WASHINGTON, D. C.

(Roy Blick was duly sworn.)

Chairman KEFAUVER. Our first witness is Mr. Roy E. Blick, Inspector in Charge, Morals Division, Metropolitan Police Force, Washington, D. C.

I have known Mr. Blick a number of years. I think he is capable, hard-working, effective police officer. We appreciate the cooperation you have given our subcommittee, Mr. Blick. We are glad to have you here with us.

Mr. Bobo, will you proceed.

Mr. Bobo. Mr. Blick, you are an inspector of the Washington Metropolitan Police Department?

Mr. BLICK. I am.

Mr. Bobo. You are the head of what is known as the morals squad?

Mr. BLICK. I am.

Mr. Bobo. The vice squad?

Mr. BLICK. I am.

Mr. Bobo. How many years have you been employed with the Washington Police Department?

Mr. Blick. 24 years.

Mr. Bobo. And of that number of years, how many years have you been connected with the vice squad?

Mr. Blick. All except 3 weeks.

Mr. Bobo. For how long have you been head of the vice squad in Washington?

Mr. Blick. I would say around 18 years, 19 years.

Mr. Bob'o. Coming within the jurisdiction of the vice squad on the Police Department, is pornographic material within the jurisdiction of your squad?

Mr. Blick. It is.

Mr. Bobo. When I speak of pornographic material, would you describe what pornographic material comes within the jurisdiction of your squad?

Mr. Blick. Filth.

Mr. Bobo. Made up of books, pamphlets, film, phonograph records?

Mr. Blick. Yes, sir.

Mr. Bobo. Lewd and perverted character?

Mr. Blick. Obscene, indecent, and lascivious.

Mr. Bobo. Do you have any record of the number of arrests which you have made within the last 2 years of persons dealing, producing, or distributing pornographic material?

Mr. Blick. I have.

Mr. Bobo. What is the number of persons that have been arrested in Washington during the last 2 years for dealing in this type of material?

Mr. Blick. Approximately 34, to the best of my knowledge.

Mr. Bobo. Are all of those persons adults?

Mr. Blick. All except 2 or 3.

Mr. Bobo. What was the age of the 2 or 3 that were not adults?

Mr. Blick. One was 17, and the other one was 15 or 16, if I recall correctly.

Mr. Bobo. Among those selling pornographic material, adults and juveniles alike, have you had any occasion to notice whether or not pornographic material was sold or distributed to those of juvenile age?

Mr. Blick. Mr. Bobo, we have received complaints on juveniles receiving this pornographic material, and we go out to make an investigation. We find out that it is true that at times these kids do have, or that juveniles do have in their possession photographic material that is classified obscene and indecent.

Mr. Bobo. Do you have any record of where specifically pornographic material has been sold to juveniles, either sold or exhibited to juveniles?

Mr. Blick. Only by hearsay. This material is sold from under-the-counter. I could not under oath say that it was actually sold to the juveniles. We have found it in their possession. We have raided places within the bounds of the school area, and have found with a search warrant material that was obscene and indecent.

Mr. Bobo. Inspector, did your squad or did a member of the Washington Police Department—did he or did he not pick up a deck of 52 supposed playing cards showing 52 various forms of perversion from a youngster of the age of 13?

Mr. BLICK. We did.

Mr. BOBO. Did you receive any explanation from this youngster as to where he received this deck of cards?

Mr. BLICK. If I recall correctly, that he bought them from some other person, but he did not know who it was from.

Mr. BOBO. Are you familiar with this particular type of pornography—a deck of playing cards?

Mr. BLICK. I am.

Mr. BOBO. Do you find that this particular type of pornography is widespread in distribution?

Mr. BLICK. It is.

Mr. BOBO. Do you know the selling price of a deck of these pornographic playing cards?

Mr. BLICK. The cheapest set you can buy them for, the black and whites, are $5. They run from $5 to $8 a pack. The colored ones run from $8 to $12 a pack.

Mr. BOBO. In your experience in Washington with the morals squad or vice squad, have you had occasion to run across pornographic movie film?

Mr. BLICK. I have.

Mr. BOBO. Have you ever known of any case of pornographic movie film seing sold or exhibited to minors and teenagers?

Mr. BLICK. I have.

Mr. BOBO. Did your squad conduct a raid in the city of Washington, D. C., at the Don Pallini Dance Studio?

Mr. BLICK. They did.

Mr. BOBO. On what date was this?

Mr. BLICK. March 18, 1953.

Mr. BOBO. In conducting this raid what were the number of teen-agers and minors who were present at the Don Pallini Dance Studio?

Mr. BLICK. 197.

Mr. BOBO. Ranging in age from?

Mr. BLICK. Eleven years up.

Mr. BOBO. Did you confiscate a film from this particular studio?

Mr. BLICK. I did.

Mr. BOBO. What was the length of the roll of film which you confiscated, Inspector?

Mr. BLICK. Approximately 1,800 feet.

Mr. BOBO. Did you determine what the price to view this film for these adolescents and teen-agers was?

Mr. BLICK. The tickets were being sold for $5 per person.

Mr. BOBO. Did you confiscate any of these tickets?

Mr. BLICK. I did.

Mr. BOBO. Do you have any of them with you at the present time?

Mr. BLICK. I do not. I believe that I have a copy.

Chairman KEFAUVER. Here is one. It says:

Colossal good time tonight. Admit one. Entertainment, buffet style, movies, beverages.

We will file this for the subcommittee.

(The ticket was marked "Exhibit No. 10," and is on file with the subcommittee.)

Mr. BOBO. What was the nature of the 1,800 feet of film which was to be shown this evening?

Mr. BLICK. The first 150 or 200 feet of film was just a hula dancer, which is a great trait for these promoters, in case that someone should walk into these places before the film gets started, and they would walk out and say they are just having a good time.

The rest of the film was the filthiest that I have ever seen in my life.

I had Dr. Corning of the public schools, by permission of Mr. Rover, who is a United States district attorney, to invite ministers from the different churches, and the PTA and civic organizations to come down, and newspapermen, to view the pictures. There were quite a few of them who before the picture was completed were sick from the filth that was in the picture.

Mr. BOBO. Do you have the names of the people who were showing this film, or exhibiting it?

Mr. BLICK. I do.

Mr. BOBO. Did you make an arrest of these people at that time?

Mr. BLICK. I did.

Mr. BOBO. What were the names of these people, Inspector?

Mr. BLICK. Phil Stone and Fred Sanders.

Mr. BOBO. Where do they live?

Mr. BLICK. They live in Washington; one just outside of Washington.

Mr. BOBO. Do you know the city outside of Washington where he lives?

Mr. BLICK. In Prince Georges County.

Mr. BOBO. In Maryland.

Mr. BLICK. Yes.

Mr. BOBO. Was it College Park, Md.?

Mr. BLICK. Yes, sir.

Chairman KEFAUVER. Put in the record the address of each of those men so it will be part of the record.

(The addresses appear on p. 107.)

Mr. BOBO. Did you determine from these persons, Phil Stone and Fred Sanders, where they obtained this film.

Mr. BLICK. I tried to, but there was very little information from these people at first. Nobody knew the ownership of the film; no one knew anything about it.

When we came in we came in a little too early, and I was thankful that we did; that we prevented these kids from seeing such pictures.

They had cut off the lights, and we gave them about 10 minutes and we crashed the door and went up, and only the screen was up.

One of my men caught one of the men going across the roof of the rear with the film, and he chased him back into the place.

We questioned the older men that were up there, and they were the paters of the fraternity.

Chairman KEFAUVER. What does that mean?

Mr. BLICK. A pater that is supervising the children. When I seized the machine, and the man knew he was going to lose the machine, he then admitted that he was the one that was going to put the show on. That was Philip Stone.

Mr. BOBO. Do you mean by that "sponsor of the film"?

Mr. BLICK. No; the pater, as far as I can learn, is the overseer of the organization that these kids belonged to.

Mr. BOBO. This was a high-school fraternity?

Mr. BLICK. Yes, sir. There were three schools involved.

Mr. BOBO. Three high-school fraternities all belonging to the overall same group, except the chapters of them?

Mr. BLICK. That is right. The following day we got a warrant for Fred Sanders and Philip Stone. They had a hearing in the district attorney's office, and Fred Sanders stated that Antonelli, who was the father of one of the boys, had come to him to see whether he could get some pictures to show to the boys.

Sanders stated that he worked with Phil Stone, who had a motion picture machine, and that he made arrangements with Stone to show the pictures.

Stone admitted to it and plead guilty to the charge of possession and exhibiting obscene and indecent pictures.

Mr. BOBO. Phil Stone lives at 4314 Rowalt Drive, College Park, Md?

Mr. BLICK. Yes, sir.

Mr. BOBO. And Fred Sanders lives at 4921 4th Street NW., Washington, D. C.?

Mr. BLICK. Yes, sir.

Mr. BOBO. Did you receive any information from these men that they had received this film from one George Fodor?

Mr. BLICK. Later on I received information that Stone had received this film from George Fodor, from whom we made a purchase of about five-hundred-and-some-odd dollars of material in order to get into his house.

Mr. BOBO. When you speak of material, you are speaking of pornographic material?

Mr. BLICK. Yes, sir.

Mr. BOBO. Is that decks of cards, books, magazines, pictures?

Mr. BLICK. Cards, film, pictures, anything that was indecent or obscene.

Mr. BOBO. Did you discover whether or not Mr. Fodor had previous records of dealing in obscene and pornographic material?

Mr. BLICK. At that time, no, sir.

Mr. BOBO. Did you determine at a later time whether or not he has dealt in obscene and pornographic pictures?

Mr. BLICK. Mr. Fodor is from Tel Aviv, and Mr. Stone has a previous record.

Mr. BOBO. In what cities did Mr. Philip Stone operate?

Mr. BLICK. Canada, New York.

Mr. BOBO. Where in Canada?

Mr. BLICK. Ottawa, if I recall correctly.

Mr. BOBO. Ottawa, Canada?

Mr. BLICK. Yes, sir.

Mr. BOBO. Could it have been Toronto, Canada?

Mr. BLICK. It could have been; yes, sir. He stated that someone had put that in his trunk. He said that he was an innocent victim of that.

Mr. BOBO. Did you determine whether or not he had ever operated in Miami, Fla.?

Mr. BLICK. Yes, sir. He had four 16-millimeter sound machines in Miami; and he was confronted with that, and he stated he used these machines to go around to the different hotels to show old type movies.

Mr. Bobo. Do you know of any other cities in which Mr. Stone has operated, that your investigation showed, besides Toronto, Canada, and Miami, Fla., and Washington, D. C.?

Mr. Blick. Offhand, no.

Mr. Bobo. Do you know whether or not he ever operated in New York City?

Mr. Blick. He had connections. I know that he had connections here in New York. If you want me to give you the lifeline I will be glad to do so.

Mr. Bobo. What do you mean by the lifeline?

Mr. Blick. The connections.

Mr. Bobo. Yes; I wish you would give us that.

Chairman Kefauver. This is from your police records?

Mr. Blick. No; it is from my investigation.

Mr. Bobo. From your own knowledge would you give us the lifeline.

Mr. Blick. Mr. Stone received the film from George Fodor. George Fodor received the film from Ike Dorman, in Baltimore, Md.

Mr. Bobo. Do you have a record of Mr. Dorman?

Mr. Blick. I do not; no.

Mr. Bobo. Do you know whether or not Mr. Dorman is a known dealer in pornographic material?

Mr. Blick. I do.

Mr. Bobo. That he has a record of dealing in pornographic material?

Mr. Blick. It was just in the last 48 hours that I have the record, which has not been sent to me, that we have been working on constantly to locate Dorman.

Mr. Bobo. Will you make this record available to the committee when you receive it?

Mr. Blick. Yes, sir; I have asked for it to be sent to the committee.

Mr. Bobo. You were describing the lifeline of where the material came from.

Mr. Blick. George Fodor and Ike Dorman left Baltimore, came to New York, and they met a man named Lou Shomer, and another person by the name of——

Mr. Bobo. On each one of these would you spell out the name, and give us the address of them if you have them.

Mr. Blick. I do not have the address of Lou Shomer. The other man's name was Ben.

Mr. Bobo. Do you know his last name?

Mr. Blick. I do not.

Mr. Bobo. Where did he reside?

Mr. Blick. In New York.

Chairman Kefauver. Mr. Blick, any names that you have in your investigation or in your police records, get the names fully, and also the address and the city, so we can identify it in the record.

Mr. Blick. I think you have, if I may say so, Mr. Chairman, the person who I have reference to at the present time, that he has a subpena before this committee now, to appear before the committee.

Mr. Bobo. Who are you speaking of there?

Mr. Blick. Lou Shomer.

Mr. Bobo. Yes, sir; we have Mr. Shomer under subpena. He is from Brooklyn, N. Y.?

Mr. Blick. That is right.

Mr. Bobo. How were these materials transported from New York to Washington? Did your investigation reveal that?

Mr. Blick. My investigation revealed that the car was left, and someone picked the car up; they had drinks while the car had disappeared; when they came back the car was loaded, and they returned to Baltimore by private automobile.

Mr. Bobo. They described to you that they brought their automobile to New York City, left it? Did they tell you where they had left their automobile?

Mr. Blick. When you say "they," who are you talking about?

Mr. Bobo. George Fodor and Ike Dorman.

Mr. Blick. Neither one of them told me a thing. It was through my investigation, from confidential sources that I cannot reveal.

Mr. Bobo. Do you have any estimate, Inspector, as to the number or the value of seizures of pornographic material that you have confiscated in Washington within the past 2 years?

Mr. Blick. Conservatively I would say around $50,000.

Mr. Bobo. Inspector Blick, have you ever seized in the city of Washington any phonograph records which are pornographic in nature?

Mr. Blick. I have.

Mr. Bobo. Would you describe whether or not these phonograph records portrayed in voice various kinds of sexual activity and perversion?

Mr. Blick. They do.

Mr. Bobo. How many of these pornographic records have you seized?

Mr. Blick. A very large quantity of them.

Mr. Bobo. Could you put an approximate evaluation upon these phonograph records?

Mr. Blick. At the retail value, I would say between ten and fifteen thousand dollars.

Mr. Bobo. Is this a comparatively new innovation in the pornographic field, to your field?

Mr. Blick. No; it is becoming more popular, though.

Mr. Bobo. Do you know the source of these phonograph records?

Mr. Blick. I do not.

Mr. Bobo. Are these phonograph records marked with the manufacturers' names?

Mr. Blick. They are not.

Mr. Bobo. Are there any addresses shown?

Mr. Blick. No, sir.

Mr. Bobo. Did you bring some of these phonograph records with you to New York City?

Mr. Blick. I brought the tape recording in preference to the records, because the records could be very easily broken on the way to New York and return.

Mr. Bobo. You will make this tape recording available to the subcommittee?

Mr. Blick. I will; yes, sir.

Chairman Kefauver. Let it be filed as an exhibit.

Mr. Blick, I have been interested in some pictures here that I see. Apparently the place where this movie was being shown—here are some pictures with whisky bottles, and the place is torn up. It looks like a pretty rough party. How many boys did you say you found there?

Mr. BLICK. Approximately 197.

Chairman KEFAUVER. Will you identify these pictures and state whether they are the pictures made at that place—and file them in the record if they are.

Mr. BLICK. These pictures were taken by a police photographer.

Chairman KEFAUVER. What did you find in the room?

Mr. BLICK. This is the way the kids left the place. It was like a bunch of animals stampeding, trying to get out. After we had been there and called the juvenile squad, for about an hour and a half—one kid jumped out of the window.

Chairman KEFAUVER. Did it hurt him bad?

Mr. BLICK. We thought he was dead, but when he got up and had the doctor examine him, I said, "Why in the world did you jump out of that window?"

He made the remark, "Someone told me the police was coming in."

I said, "We have been in here for about an hour and a half or 2 hours, son."

He said, "I just got the information."

Chairman KEFAUVER. Some of these kids were 11 years old?

Mr. BLICK. Yes, sir.

Chairman KEFAUVER. All of them were under 21?

Mr. BLICK. All of the kids; yes, sir. As I said, some of the men that were there, that were the paters of the fraternity—they were there.

Chairman KEFAUVER. What else did you find in this room?

Mr. BLICK. Contraceptive material thrown against the wall, and on the floors that the boys had in their possession. Whiskey bottles, beer bottles. Up on the next floor they had crap tables—these portable tables, and card tables.

Chairman KEFAUVER. Mr. Blick, have you been getting information about similar parties of that kind that led you to raid this particular one?

Mr. BLICK. Whenever we get information of this type we work hard, and if we cannot get sufficient evidence to get a warrant to get in, I personally supervise the job to crash it so we can prevent these kids from seeing or having this kind of fun, if you want to call it fun.

Chairman KEFAUVER. There have been other instances of this kind that you have broken up?

Mr. BLICK. Yes, sir.

Chairman KEFAUVER. About how many in the last 2 years in Washington?

Mr. BLICK. Well, in the last 2 years I would say not over 2.

Chairman KEFAUVER. There have been some over a period of a longer time?

Mr. BLICK. Yes, sir. Most of these things are not carried on in public places. A smaller amount of boys, or a mixed crowd, will patronize them; and, of course, we do not get word of it.

Chairman KEFAUVER. Did you establish who owned this Don Pallini dance studio at 2625 Connecticut?

Mr. BLICK. A man by the name of Kurtz. Nick Scholnick was running the place; also known as Nick Martin.

Chairman KEFAUVER. Does he have a police record?

Mr. BLICK. We could not fingerprint him because the District Attorney would not give us papers against him.

Chairman KEFAUVER. Proceed, Mr. Bobo.

Mr. BOBO. At one time you arrested, on February 29, 1952, a Mr. Vincent Chucoski, 607 Fourth Street NW., Washington, D. C.?

Mr. BLICK. I did.

Mr. BOBO. For what was he arrested, and what did he have in his possession, Inspector?

Mr. BLICK. Vincent Chucoski at the time of his arrest at 607 Fourth Street NW, apartment 1, had 14 boxes containing obscene and indecent pictures, assorted photograph supplies, slides with obscene pictures on them, obscene books, and obscene pamphlets, two movie projectors, screens, pictures, dryers, enlargers, slide projectors, 2 rewinders, 10 albums of assorted sizes containing indecent, obscene pictures.

Mr. BOBO. Did you place a value upon this material, Inspector?

Mr. BLICK. You mean a commercial value or what I would value it at?

Mr. BOBO. A commercial value and what you would value it at.

Mr. BLICK. The commercial value of this would run around from one thousand to two thousand dollars. My value of it would be trash.

Mr. BOBO. Did you seize a card file of 500 negatives of pornographic photographs?

Mr. BLICK. I did.

Mr. BOBO. Was this card file indexed according to the type of perversion it represented?

Mr. BLICK. Yes.

Mr. BOBO. Did you determine from this person where the negatives were developed?

Mr. BLICK. They tell you nothing. He developed his own pictures.

Mr. BOBO. Did you determine from this person the extent of the traffic in which he was engaged?

Mr. BLICK. He told us nothing.

Mr. BOBO. Was this person convicted?

Mr. BLICK. He was.

Mr. BOBO. What sentence did he receive?

Mr. BLICK. Sixty days and $200.

Mr. BOBO. Among these negatives, were there any pictures of juveniles?

Mr. BLICK. There were.

Mr. BOBO. Have you found in pornographic material, both film and pictures, that there is a frequency of juveniles being used as models and to act out these scenes?

Mr. BLICK. I have.

Mr. BOBO. What is the age of the youngest person you have seen posed in these pictures?

Mr. BLICK. About 3½, 4 years old.

Mr. BOBO. Do you find that a number of 14- and 15-year-old boys and girls are portrayed in acts of perversion in these films and pictures?

Mr. BLICK. Not the boys as much as the young ladies.

Chairman KEFAUVER. Don't use any names, but you mentioned a 3½-year-old. Do you want to elaborate on that, Mr. Blick?

Mr. BLICK. Mr. Chairman, my undercover men went to a residence to make a purchase of merchandise of obscene and indecent pictures, and in his report he reported back that the man at the time was taking a picture of his three children and his wife, all nude. The children were looking at the wife's person.

Chairman KEFAUVER. You have run across a good deal of these very young children being used in that way?

Mr. BLICK. Not as young as that; no, sir; but in adolescents I would say "Yes."

Chairman KEFAUVER. All right.

Mr. BOBO. Inspector Blick, were you familiar with the investigation made by an investigator of this subcommittee involving a person by the name of Joe or Jake?

Mr. BLICK. I have.

Mr. BOBO. The investigator purchased a quantity of obscene material from Jake, who was a street peddler in Washington?

Mr. BLICK. That is right.

Mr. BOBO. Do you have the full name of this person?

Mr. BLICK. James Hammon.

Chairman KEFAUVER. Do you know his address?

Mr. BLICK. Lorton, Va.

Chairman KEFAUVER. That is a penal institution?

Mr. BLICK. Yes, sir. He is serving 2 years.

Mr. BOBO. Do you have his record—the number of times of his arrest?

Mr. BLICK. I do not.

Mr. BOBO. He has been arrested numerous times?

Mr. BLICK. He was arrested so many times, the judge finally said, "I am going to put you away this time to be sure to keep you off the streets."

Chairman KEFAUVER. Tell us in your own experience what can be done to help stamp out this business. In the District of Columbia it is all on a Federal level.

Mr. BLICK. Mr. Chairman, I have personally asked, myself, laws that would help us, because we come under the jurisdiction of the Federal Government. Transportation, regardless of how the transportation might be involved, would be a Federal act.

Chairman KEFAUVER. As it is now it is unlawful to send this stuff through the mails, but the mail statute is vague and indefinite. It is very questionable whether it covers film and phonograph records.

Mr. BLICK. It covers that—anything obscene, indecent, or lascivious, it covers.

Chairman KEFAUVER. There is some question about it, though; but the trouble is that they carry it in trunks in automobiles, and they may not use the mails.

Mr. BLICK. That is right. The Federal law of the ICC—that is interstate transportation—I may carry this suitcase on the train as long as a porter on the train does not touch this suitcase, and you cannot charge me with interstate transportation.

Chairman KEFAUVER. That is the way a lot of it is transported.

Mr. BLICK. That I cannot say, but it is transported. That is the only thing I can say.

Chairman KEVAUVER. How about the stiffness of sentences? Looking over the police records—this is your official record—$250 or 90 days; $100 or 60 days; nolle prossed, nolle prossed, nolle prossed, not guilty, nolle prossed, $100 or 90 days. It looks like the big majority of them either don't get convicted, or nolle prossed, or have a fine of $100 or 60 days. Do you think that is sufficient?

Mr. BLICK. I do not.

Chairman KEFAUVER. So you would recommend something more than a misdemeanor?

Mr. BLICK. I certainly do. This is more dangerous than narcotics, because you inject narcotics to an individual and it is over with. These pamphlets, these booklets, can be passed from one to another.

It is the same as a prostitute that can infect an army of men if she is permitted to hang around the camp. It is the same as this pornography that is being passed around. It can be passed from one hand to another, and it is causing a lot of headaches in the country. It is causing kids who are just at the age that they should know right from wrong to become perverts and homosexuals.

Chairman KEFAUVER. Is there any doubt in your mind that a lot of sex crimes that we have had—that is, criminal assault, rape, and other kinds of sex crimes, are the direct result of this pornographic literature that is being distributed?

Mr. BLICK. That would be only my personal opinion.

Chairman KEFAUVER. What is your opinion?

Mr. BLICK. I would say yes, because you would incite the individual that would read such filth, and then he would go out to look for relief.

Chairman KEFAUVER. And there is an increasing percentage of sex crimes, particularly among young people these days.

Mr. BLICK. According to the newspapers; yes, sir.

Chairman KEFAUVER. Mr. Blick, I hand you here what is marked as "Exhibit A." Is that the list of court records of people charged and brought to trial, and what happened to them in the last 2 years?

Mr. BLICK. It is.

Chairman KEFAUVER. Showing what the extent of the sentence was.

Mr. BLICK. Yes, sir.

Chairman KEFAUVER. Let that be filed as an exhibit in your testimony.

Mr. Blick, we appreciate your cooperation and that of Chief Murray, and I want to personally express my thanks for the vigor that you and Chief Murray and your department has been going after this sort of filth in Washington during recent times.

Mr. BLICK. Thank you, Mr. Chairman. You can rest assured that we will continue to do so.

Chairman KEFAUVER. We hope you will continue even more vigorously, if possible.

Mr. BLICK. Thank you, sir.

Mr. CHUMBRIS. Mr. Blick, have you also been interested in legislation—confiscating the equipment, the automobiles that pornographers use in their trade?

Mr. BLICK. I have. I think that the law should be passed that where these seizures are taken from an automobile, or a bookstore, that everything—the automobile or the bookstore, or any other store that the buy is made in—should be confiscated. The merchant, or whoever he might be, should forfeit his rights to all of his property within the jurisdiction where the buy was made.

Chairman KEFAUVER. That is the law at present as to narcotics. Also, when any alcoholic beverage—during the time of prohibition— and I suppose now where it doesn't have a Federal stamp on it—it is not only subject to confiscation, but the vehicle of conveyance is also subject to confiscation.

Mr. BLICK. Yes, sir.

Chairman KEFAUVER. You would have the same thing apply to this pornographic literature.

Mr. BLICK. If we could get the search and seizure from the narcotics section of the narcotics law to apply to pornography, it would be a great help to us.

Chairman KEFAUVER. Thank you, Mr. Blick.

Mr. BOBO. Mr. Lawrence A. Whipple.

Chairman KEFAUVER. You have somebody with you?

Mr. WHIPPLE. I have two men with me.

Chairman KEFAUVER. Commissioner Whipple, you have with you Sgt. Alfred Jago and Detective John Higgins?

Mr. WHIPPLE. Yes.

(Lawrence A. Whipple, director of public safety of Jersey City, N. J., and Sgt. Alfred Jago and Detective John Higgins, of the Jersey City Police Department, were duly sworn by the chairman.)

TESTIMONY OF LAWRENCE A. WHIPPLE, DIRECTOR OF PUBLIC SAFETY, JERSEY CITY, N. J., AND SGT. ALFRED JAGO AND DETECTIVE JOHN HIGGINS, JERSEY CITY POLICE DEPARTMENT, JERSEY CITY, N. J.

Chairman KEFAUVER. I have been told by the members of our staff of the outstanding effort that you, Mr. Whipple, as commissioner, and your associates in Jersey City, have been making—the special drive against pornographic literature, and of the wonderful cooperation you have given. I want to take this opportunity of personally thanking you for helping us, and commending you on your work.

Proceed, Mr. Bobo.

Mr. BOBO. You are Commissioner Lawrence A. Whipple?

Mr. WHIPPLE. Yes, sir.

Mr. BOBO. Director of public safety of Jersey City, N. J.?

Mr. WHIPPLE. That is correct, sir.

Mr. BOBO. Your address is what?

Mr. WHIPPLE. My home address is 92 Bentley Avenue, Jersey City.

Mr. BOBO. For how many years have you been director of public safety?

Mr. WHIPPLE. Since December 15, 1953.

Mr. BOBO. Were you connected with police work prior to that in any capacity?

Mr. WHIPPLE. No, sir; but I was with the Office of Price Stabilization a little over 2 years in the city of New York, as the chief law enforcement officer there, special assistant attorney general under Attorney General Richmond in Newark for approximately a year.

Mr. BOBO. In Jersey City there has been quite a campaign waged by your division and by the police department and by the city against pornographic literature?

Mr. WHIPPLE. That is correct.

Mr. BOBO. Would you tell us about this campaign which you all have waged there?

Chairman KEFAUVER. Tell us in your own words, and if you want to call on Mr. Higgins or Mr. Jago to supplement anything you say, you call on them.

Mr. WHIPPLE. Briefly, I would like to explain it from an administrative viewpoint, and then for the details follow Senator Kefauver's suggestion and let the two policemen carry on from there.

A short time after I went into office I was frankly very concerned with newspaper reports and magazine articles I had read concerning the distribution of this so-called pornographic salacious literature.

I had these two men dispatched to my office to work in what might be called a confidential squad, checking newsstands and certain sources of what we considered might be distribution points for this so-called literature.

I instructed these men to follow any and all leads regardless of whether they considered them crank letters or any letters of any kind from citizens or anybody in any capacity in the city that reported the seeing or finding of this literature on stands.

Together with this one of the denominations in the city—I don't want to mention it unless you give me permission to—started a concentrated campaign in their parish, and a certain clergyman was put in charge.

Chairman KEFAUVER. Anything worthwhile like that, mention the names.

Mr. WHIPPLE. St. Adens Roman Catholic Church. Father Van Wie happens to be in charge. He and Father Belger, also from St. Nicholas Roman Catholic Church—they formed committees in their parish, comprised primarily of women who went out and visited all the newstands, stationery stores, cigarstores or candy stores where this literature might be found.

They called weekly and biweekly meetings. The women would go out like a vanguard or a vigilante committee, if you might call it such. They would come back and report the locations of where these periodicals were being sold.

The priests would send somebody from the police department, or one of these women, or both, to this man; talk to him about the effect that the sale and distribution of these periodicals would have upon the juveniles, particularly in the locality, and ask him to cooperate with the drive; to clear the stands of this literature.

I would say that in more than half the instances the dealers cooperated. They in turn would receive an emblem or a shield which would be pasted on the window of their stores or establishments, where they were selling their merchandise, with wording something like "Approved." It was a little short gold emblem.

In some instances we met resistance. I can recall 2 instances where I happen to know counsel who represented 2 of these people. I called them in together with one of the clergymen. We spoke to their counsel, who in turn spoke to his client, and they immediately cooperated and received a shield.

This has worked tremendously well in the city of Jersey City.

Statistics I don't have at my fingertips, but I tell you frankly and very honestly as far as this city is concerned, this is one problem that has not come to the surface as yet. I don't dare say it doesn't exist there, but if it does it is well hidden.

Chairman KEFAUVER. You mean you have got it under control?

Mr. WHIPPLE. Yes, sir.

Chairman KEFAUVER. And you have substantially eliminated it?

Mr. WHIPPLE. Yes, sir.

Chairman KEFAUVER. Are you keeping up this effort?

Mr. WHIPPLE. Yes, Senator. It is a day-to-day operation, and these men have instructions that is their primary job in the department of public safety, to stay on top of this problem and keep this filth off the newsstands in the city of Jersey City.

I have styled this program a community-counteraction program, and I don't want to leave the impression that only the Catholic Church is doing something about this; because I firmly believe that whether it be Catholic, Protestant, or Jewish, any civic association or society, or religious society, could do the same thing or follow the same pattern.

It is my firm belief that this must start right at the community level with the cooperation of all civic, fraternal, and religious societies and associations, to rid society of what I consider to be a real menace today.

Chairman KEFAUVER. We have information that churches of all denominations are doing similar very worthwhile kinds of activities in different parts of the country, so that they are all interested.

Tell us what condition you found when you started out in this effort, or do you want to get one of your men to help out?

Mr. WHIPPLE. Perhaps one of the policemen should answer that.

Sergeant JAGO. When we were given this assignment we made checks at different times of the day in and around the school areas, stationery stores, where most of the juveniles would congregate during lunch hours and after school.

We checked most of these newsstands, and the ones we did find we confiscated—there might have been 6, 10, 12 books around. We made visits later on and we kept it down more or less to a pretty good minimum.

Mr. BOBO. Did you find this pornographic material the type of material which you are speaking about, among schoolchildren or children of young age?

Sergeant JAGO. No, we didn't find it among the children. It was just salacious books that were in the stores. That was primarily our investigation—to keep that down, because we did receive a few complaints from different parishes that there was some of it around; but up until the time that we—back in April—we didn't run into any of the pornographic material at all.

Mr. BOBO. You were aiming primarily at the comic book and paperbound book in the newstands at this time?

Sergeant JAGO. That is right.

Mr. BOBO. You say in April you ran into the pornographic literature trade?

Sergeant JAGO. That is correct.

Mr. BOBO. Did it come to your attention this was coming into the hands of juveniles?

Sergeant JAGO. At that time due to our efforts in going around we had in the course of our stopping different people and going into the different stores, we more or less created a good fellowship, and we received a call on April 23 that there was some strange thing going on in the basement of one of the houses in our city.

Chairman KEFAUVER. April 23 of last year?

Sergeant JAGO. This year, sir, 1955. Two officers were dispatched around there, and when they went in—two policemen went down into the basement.

Mr. BOBO. Would you give us the address of where you are talking about.

Sergeant JAGO. Five hundred and forty Ocean Avenue, in our city.

Mr. BOBO. Do you have the name of the occupant of that property?

Sergeant JAGO. It so happened that the boy—his parents were the owners of that property, and he lived about 3 or 4 streets away from there, but he did take these boys into that particular building, but he didn't reside there.

Mr. BOBO. His name was what?

Sergeant JAGO. Joseph Cinnelli.

Mr. BOBO. What is his address?

Sergeant JAGO. Forty-three Clerk Street, Jersey City.

Mr. BOBO. All right, sir.

Sergeant JAGO. Two officers went into the basement, and there were make-shift chairs or benches there, and there were six boys between the ages of 18 and 21, and were at the stage where they were going to witness Cinnelli showing these rolls of film. At that time he had six to be shown. He did not start his operation when the policemen arrived.

Mr. BOBO. Were these 16-millimeter, 8-millimeter——

Sergeant JAGO. He had six 8-millimeter at that time.

Mr. BOBO. Were they black and white, or colored?

Sergeant JAGO. They were black and white.

Chairman KEFAUVER. The chap whose name you gave, is he a juvenile?

Sergeant JAGO. He was 27 years of age.

Chairman KEFAUVER. How old were the kids arounds?

Sergeant JAGO. The boys were between the ages of 18 and 21. Two of them were in the service, in the Army, and four were leaving the following week to go into the service; and this was a little going-away party they were having at that time.

He was taken to the precinct and questioned, and after talking to him for a while he did admit that he had 4 more rolls of film at home; so the detectives went down to the house and came back with some more—all told he had 10.

Mr. BOBO. Did he tell you where he had received these films from?

Sergeant JAGO. At that time he did not. That was on Saturday night. Over the weekend he was confined to City Prison, and Monday morning we asked the magistrate to postpone the case for 24 hours to see if we could get the source of his supply. The judge granted our request.

We took him to a captain's office in the precinct where the court is also located, and we talked to him for practically 2 hours. He finally cooperated and gave us the name of the man who was supplying him, who on five different occasions he had bought film from.

Mr. BOBO. What was that man's name?

Sergeant JAGO. At that time he gave us the name of Smitty. He knew him as "Smitty," and all he had was a phone number.

Mr. BOBO. Did he give you the phone number at that time?

Sergeant JAGO. He did, sir.

Mr. BOBO. What was that phone number?

Sergeant Jago. At that time the phone number was Schuyler 4–1800.

Mr. Bobo. Was that in Jersey City, N. J.?

Sergeant Jago. No; that is in New York City. It is a hotel in New York City at 91st Street and Broadway.

Mr. Bobo. What is the name of that hotel?

Sergeant Jago. The Greystone Hotel.

Mr. Bobo. Did you check with that number to determine who Smitty was?

Sergeant Jago. We checked with that number, and made a call for Smitty, and we stayed by the phone because Smitty wasn't around; but we were told to stand by; that he would get in touch with us—by the operator in that hotel.

Maybe about half an hour later we received a call from the man known as Smitty. We spoke to him on the pretext that I was Cinelli. I asked him could he sell me some film.

He said, "Sure, I will be right over."

I said, "I don't want it now. How about tomorrow?"

Through our investigation knowing this man had never been in Jersey City, we made an appointment for Secaucus, which is adjacent to our city.

Mr. Bobo. Secaucus, N. J.?

Sergeant Jago. Yes, sir. The next morning we had made a date to meet him at 10:30, the next morning. Fortunately we were there at 9:30, and Smitty got off a bus, carrying a brown leather bag; and at that time we went over and apprehended him.

Mr. Bobo. What was the quantity of material that you seized from him?

Sergeant Jago. He had in that bag at that time, which was the 26th of April, he had thirteen 8-millimeter rolls of film, and one 16-millimeter. He had 216 still photographs, one rubber penis, three decks of obscene playing cards, 70 cartoon books, six magazines, and 50 French story books.

Mr. Bobo. We have here an envelope marked "Exhibit No. 5". Can you identify this envelope and say whether or not it contains material seized in that particular raid? Do you have the deck of 52 playing cards showing different pictures of various forms of perversion?

Sergeant Jago. Yes, sir.

Mr. Bobo. Between men and women?

Sergeant Jago. Yes, sir.

Mr. Bobo. Did you determine the selling price of those?

Chairman Kefauver. Can you identify that?

Sergeant Jago. Yes; that is the material that he had on his person when he was apprehended.

Chairman Kefauver. The committee staff will take possession of it.

Mr. Bobo. What was the value of the material?

Sergeant Jago. His estimate was about $500 at that time. He said it was worth about $500. He gave us information on the still photographs which he had 216 of. He said he would receive 50 cents apiece, but like all peddlers, he would take 40 cents or he would take 35 cents if that is all you had on your person.

Mr. Bobo. How much did he offer to sell it to you for. Did he determine the sale price to you?

Sergeant JAGO. Yes; he said 50 cents. Of course, he didn't stick right to the price. The decks of obscene playing cards, which were just displayed here, they were selling for $2 a deck. Magazines, he had six of them. They were $2.50 apiece. The French story books were anywhere from 2 to 3 dollars.

Mr. BOBO. Did you determine from him how many trips he made back and forth between New York City and into Jersey City?

Sergeant JAGO. Well, he had never been into Jersey City.

Mr. BOBO. Or into New Jersey?

Sergeant JAGO. He did give us information that he did come in around the docks of Hoboken, and also on one occasion he had made a sale to Cinelli in Secaucus.

Mr. BOBO. Did you get his police record?

Sergeant JAGO. We never received a police record on him because the arrest was made in Secaucus; but I don't believe he had a police record, because nothing ever came back; but I know with the cooperation we received from the Secaucus Police Department, if a record came back he would have sent it to us.

Chairman KEFAUVER. He distributed it around in several different places?

Sergeant JAGO. He did.

Chairman KEFAUVER. How did he come to you with that—in a suitcase?

Sergeant JAGO. He had this in a man's overnight bag. He had this material in there, and he came over on the bus from the Port of Authority Terminal into Secaucus. The buses run over through the Lincoln Tunnel, and out that way.

When he came to Hoboken he used to come over on the ferry—at Hoboken, around the docks, 14th Street, the Bethlehem Steel places.

Chairman KEFAUVER. Proceed.

Mr. BOBO. I have a picture here that I would like you to identify— a photograph of the bag this material came in.

Sergeant JAGO. Yes. In the photograph the bag is on the left, and the other material is stuff that was seized later on.

Mr. BOBO. What disposition was made of the case?

Sergeant JAGO. At a hearing in Secaucus, before Magistrate King, he was given a year on a disorderly person charge—a year in the county jail. He was held under $10,000 bail for the action of the grand jury of the possession of the obscene literature and the films.

Mr. BOBO. I don't believe you ever gave us for the record what his correct name was, other than the name of Smitty.

Sergeant JAGO. His correct name was Andy Bruckner.

Mr. BOBO. Is he at present confined in the county jail?

Sergeant JAGO. The information we received Tuesday night, after being here on Tuesday, was that he was released Tuesday evening on an appeal on the disorderly person charge.

Mr. BOBO. He is now under bond?

Sergeant JAGO. Yes; and a subpena by your committee was served on him.

Chairman KEFAUVER. He is the one we were trying to get out of jail to bring over here?

Sergeant JAGO. That is correct.

Chairman KEFAUVER. He is now under subpena?

Sergeant Jago. Yes.   A subpena was served on him as he left the jail on Tuesday evening.

Chairman Kefauver. All right, sir.

Mr. Bobo. Did you participate in the arrest of a person by the name of Selig Wildman?

Sergeant Jago. No; I did not participate in that arrest at that time. That is going back to 1951.

Mr. Bobo. In 1951 were you familiar, or do you have the record of that case with you?

Sergeant Jago. I have a report here from our police department. We knew about the case, but we were assigned to another precinct at the time, and it is only since Commissioner Whipple has become director that we were given this assignment insofar as lewd material. I have a record of that particular case going back to November 21, 1951.

Chairman Kefauver. Tell us about it.

Sergeant Jago. Well, it seems there was some information received at that time by Chief James L. McNamara concerning some material that was being sold in Ohio. There was a gentleman, a truck-driver, who was apprehended there, and he had some material; and he gave the police information in Ohio that he did buy it from a fellow in Jersey City, who does business around truck depots.

The chief assigned Lt. Mark Fallon at that time, who is now a captain, and Detective Carroll to see if he could apprehend this man as he was coming over our highways. He was arrested November 21, 1951, in a truck. I believe it was about a 2-ton panel delivery truck which he was using, which we have a picture of here, and I believe your committee has some photos, too. This is an enlargement of the one that we did originally give you.

Chairman Kefauver. That is a photo of what you found in the truck?

Sergeant Jago. That is the truck that he was using to transport the material.

Chairman Kefauver. Let these pictures be filed as exhibits.

Sergeant Jago. When they apprehended him with the truck they brought him to police headquarters, and at that time they found books, cards, pictures, pamphlets, and other obscene literature, and also in his truck he had men's work gloves and overalls, and stuff that he would sell at these depots, and while making a sale of this particular type he would also try to induce them to buy some of this obscene material, which he did sell to them; and if they went on the road to some other city they would dispose of it there or keep it for their own use.

Mr. Bobo. Did you investigate that truckdrivers bought this material and transported it to other cities?

Sergeant Jago. The original complaints came from Ohio, from the chief of police of one of the cities in Ohio, that a man arrested there gave information that he bought it from Wildman.

Mr. Bobo. He was the truckdriver that picked it up in Jersey City?

Sergeant Jago. That is correct.

Mr. Bobo. Was there any evaluation placed on the seizure?

Sergeant Jago. There was no evaluation, but it was given in tonnage. They did search his garage where he lived. He did reside at that time at 233 Union Street, in Jersey City; and they found in his garage about a ton of this particular type of material.

Chairman KEFAUVER. Since he has been arrested and has a record, will you give his full name and address.

Sergeant JAGO. His full name is Selig Wildman.

Chairman KEFAUVER. What is his address?

Sergeant JAGO. He is 66 years of age. He was then in 1951. He lived at 233 Union Street, Jersey City.

Mr. BOBO. Was he tried and convicted?

Sergeant JAGO. He was tried and convicted, and sentenced to 2 to 3 years in State prison.

Mr. BOBO. At the present time he is in the State prison?

Sergeant JAGO. No; he has been released. He has served his sentence.

Chairman KEFAUVER. This is the sign that you put in the stores that complied to get rid of all that material?

Mr. WHIPPLE. That is right.

Chairman KEFAUVER. Let that be filed for the record as an exhibit.

Mr. BOBO. Detective Higgins, did you have anything you wished to add to what Sergeant Jago has testified to?

Detective HIGGINS. Sergeant Jago covered it pretty well, but he didn't mention the seizure in New York. I was designated, together with a sergeant from Syracuse, and we came——

Mr. BOBO. What was his name?

Sergeant JAGO. I have it here, sir. Gustave Nicolia.

Detective HIGGINS. Sergeant Nicolia and I came to New York to make a seizure of some salacious literature and obscene books. Bruckner had given us the address of his hotel.

Mr. BOBO. The Bruckner you speak of is Andy Bruckner who was mentioned in previous testimony?

Detective HIGGINS. That is right, sir. He gave us permission to come over and get the rest of this material. We went to the 100th Street Station, and we picked up Detective Vincent Satriano. He was of the 24th squad.

Chairman KEFAUVER. The New York City Police?

Detective HIGGINS. New York City. We went to room 411 with the superintendent of the hotel, or the manager of the hotel.

Mr. BOBO. Room 411 of what hotel?

Detective HIGGINS. Greystone Hotel, 91st Street and Broadway. We seized 14 rolls of film and quite a quantity of other literature—magazines and story books. There were 3 steel suitcases containing 12 rolls of 8-millimeter film, and two 16-millimeter films; 6 cartons of material—the same type that was found in the bag he was carrying when he was arrested.

I think your committee has a photo of the material that was picked up in New York. It is right here in this picture. He valued it at about $600.

Mr. BOBO. Did you determine whether Mr. Bruckner ever operated in any States other than the States of New York and New Jersey?

Detective HIGGINS. He said that was about the area that he covered—New Jersey and New York.

Chairman KEFAUVER. Who is the New York policeman who cooperated with you?

Detective HIGGINS. Lieutenant Weiss was the desk officer in charge of the 24th squad, and Detective Vincent Satriano, shield No. 1646, 24th squad, New York City.

Chairman KEFAUVER. You had an authorization from Bruckner to come over and pick up the rest of this?

Detective HIGGINS. Yes, sir.

Chairman KEFAUVER. I wanted to have the record made clear that these officers worked with you.

This man Bruckner was what you call a foot peddler?

Detective HIGGINS. That is all.

Chairman KEFAUVER. Did you tell how much profit he was making every week?

Detective HIGGINS. About $300 a week would be his profit.

Chairman KEFAUVER. Is that what he said?

Detective HIGGINS. That is what he claimed. He was paying $115 for a room in the hotel.

Chairman KEFAUVER. $115 a week?

Detective HIGGINS. A month.

Chairman KEFAUVER. I assume the hotel didn't know what his business was?

Detective HIGGINS. I doubt very much whether they did.

Chairman KEFAUVER. I would like to give them the benefit of the doubt. He was paying for his room?

Detective HIGGINS. That is right, sir.

Chairman KEFAUVER. Did you think by looking at the way he lived that is probably the kind of money he was making?

Detective HIGGINS. I would say so.

Chairman KEFAUVER. Mr. Jago, do you have anything else to add?

Sergeant JAGO. From sitting in on these hearings, and during the questioning of Bruckner—I would like to say that he did mention, as the inspector from Washington mentioned before, this fellow Al Stone. We were trying to find out who were the big men. He mentioned Al Stone, and gave us names of local men which we turned over to Mr. Butler of your committee.

Chairman KEFAUVER. You have helped Mr. Butler a great deal. Mr. Butler is a lieutenant from the Dallas Police force, and he was with us during the crime investigations.

Sergeant JAGO. He did mention Morris Gillman. As far as his source of supply, it was Morris Gillman. About 41 years of age, 1415 Davidson Avenue, Bronx, N. Y. If he needed any material he called Tremont 2–7940 from the Greystone Hotel, and Mr. Gilman came down, met him outside, said hello, and then they went up into the room and did the business so far as transactions of material were concerned.

Chairman KEFAUVER. Let us get the telephone number correct.

Sergeant JAGO. TRemont 2–7940.

Chairman KEFAUVER. Anything else, Mr. Jago?

Mr. MARTIN. Is that the same Gillman the committee has under subpena now?

Sergeant JAGO. Yes.

Mr. CHUMBRIS. Do you know if the telephone number is still in use?

Sergeant JAGO. No; I wouldn't know whether it is still in use or not.

Mr. BOBO. Did this man make a statement he had ever bought material from Al Stone?

Sergeant JAGO. No. It was hearsay as far as he was concerned.

Chairman KEFAUVER. Anything else?

Sergeant JAGO. I am looking at our report. He did mention another phone number that he contacted in Brooklyn, who also supplied him with material. He called the number HYacinth 3–8636, and he would ask for Joe. Sometimes he would get Joe, or he would get Joe's mother, who would leave word with Joe to call Andy at the hotel. This number was traced through the telephone company, and it was listed to a John Robbins, residence 59 East 96th Street, Brooklyn, N. Y.

Mr. MARTIN. Was any effort ever made to identify this Joe?

Sergeant JAGO. In Brooklyn?

Mr. MARTIN. Yes.

Sergeant JAGO. No, sir.

Mr. MARTIN. Were you able to obtain any information as to the character of his operation?

Sergeant JAGO. Outside of Bruckner saying he was Mr. Big.

Mr. MARTIN. Did Bruckner also tell you about the character of the car he was driving, or anything of that character?

Sergeant JAGO. He did mention that he had a Nash car. I believe he said the color was green.

Chairman KEFAUVER. These numbers may be reassigned to someone else, and we don't want to cause any trouble. I will have to order these telephone numbers given be placed in executive session of the committee, and I will ask the cooperation of the press in not putting the numbers out. They may be asigned to someone else, and we don't want to embarrass anyone.

Is there anything else?

Sergeant JAGO. I believe that is all.

Chairman KEFAUVER. Mr. Higgins, did you have any observations to make?

Mr. HIGGINS. Jago did a good job. He didn't leave much for me.

Chairman KEFAUVER. Mr. Whipple.

Mr. WHIPPLE. I think that is all.

Chairman KEFAUVER. Tell us your thoughts of what the Federal Government can do to help this problem.

Mr. WHIPPLE. It is my considered opinion that without effective Federal legislation, dealing as you and I know with the interstate transportation of these articles, any effort at the community level or the State level, of course, would be helpful; but I think we need stringent Federal legislation with very severe penalties.

I am not too sure consideration shouldn't be given by the Congress to maybe install some sort of a plan like we have with the Department of Agriculture—having these sources of distribution checked, to see what kind of material is being printed and sent out to the various buyers of these materials.

I realize there might be constitutional prohibitions to something like that, but at any rate I think the Congress should go to work immediately and pass stringent legislation dealing with the interstate transportation of this pornographic material.

Chairman KEFAUVER. Well, newspapers and magazines that have a second-class mail permit have to give the name and address of the publisher. All of this stuff that you are talking about, I have observed that none of it has any name of where it is published, and no responsibility whatsoever as to where it came from. That would at least help trace it down; wouldn't it?

Mr. WHIPPLE. Yes, it would.

Chairman KEFAUVER. You have shown what can be done in a large city by community interest of church people. I think that is an excellent example that I hope will be heard all around the Nation.

Mr. WHIPPLE. Thank you, Senator.

Chairman KEFAUVER. I want again to compliment you, Mr. Commissioner, and Mr. Higgins and Mr. Jago, and those who have worked with you, on a job well done, which I have heard a good deal about; and also to point out what I am sure you know, that if you relax your efforts you will have the problem with you back again.

Mr. WHIPPLE. Thank you very much.

Chairman KEFAUVER. Thank you very much, gentlemen, for your cooperation.

We will have a 10-minute recess.

(A short recess was taken.)

Chairman KEFAUVER. I saw Mr. Younglove, a member of the New York Assembly, here a little while ago. He is also a member of Mr. Fitzpatrick's committee.

Mr. Younglove, would you come up and sit up here with us? We would be glad to have you.

(Mr. Younglove took a seat at the bench.)

Chairman KEFAUVER. Mr. Bobo, do you have some matter you wish to present at this time?

Mr. BOBO. Yes, Mr. Chairman.

I would like to correct an erroneous impression concerning Mr. Roy Ald, who was subpenaed by this subcommittee. He was called because he is a well-known writer, and supplied very valuable technical information to the subcommittee staff. He did not fail to answer his subpena but reported to the subcommittee's office and not in the courtroom.

Chairman KEFAUVER. We will be glad to have that correction made. Now, who is our next witness?

Mr. BOBO. Lt. Ignatius Sheehan, Chicago Police Department.

TESTIMONY OF LT. IGNATIUS SHEEHAN, CHICAGO POLICE DEPARTMENT, CHICAGO, ILL.

Mr. BOBO. Lieutenant Sheehan, your first name is spelled I–g–n–a–t–i–u–s?

Lieutenant SHEEHAN. That is correct, sir.

Mr. BOBO. And you are head of the censor squad of the Chicago Police Department; is that the name of it?

Lieutenant SHEEHAN. Yes, sir.

Mr. BOBO. How long have you been head of the censor squad of the Chicago Police Department?

Lieutenant SHEEHAN. Since 1952.

Mr. BOBO. For how many years have you been connected with the Chicago Police Department?

Lieutenant SHEEHAN. Thirty-three years.

Mr. BOBO. Has all of that time been devoted to so-called censor squad vice or moral squad?

Lieutenant SHEEHAN. No, sir. The last 4 years, the past 4 years.

Mr. BOBO. Is part of your duties as head of the censor squad the keeping up of traffic in pornographic literature as one of your prime responsibilities?

Lieutenant SHEEHAN. Yes, sir.

Mr. BOBO. Do you have any estimate as to the extent of what the traffic is in pornographic material in the city of Chicago?

Lieutenant SHEEHAN. Well, that would be hard to say. It is from the arrest of distributors that it would run into large figures.

Chairman KEFAUVER. Lieutenant Sheehan, that microphone is not for the room; it is just for the radio or television; so you speak up so that we can hear you.

Lieutenant SHEEHAN. Yes, sir.

Mr. BOBO. Most of this business—and you are familiar with the operations of those dealing in pornography—is a surreptitious business and an under-the-counter business; is that correct?

Lieutenant SHEEHAN. Yes, sir.

Mr. BOBO. Have you been able in your dealings with those selling pornographic material, to determine a source of supply for those you have arrested?

Lieutenant SHEEHAN. Yes, sir.

Chairman KEFAUVER. First, how big did you say the business was? I suppose Chicago is like most other cities, the same problem everywhere, even in rural sections. Is it big business in Chicago?

Lieutenant SHEEHAN. Yes, sir; that's right, Mr. Chairman.

Chairman KEFAUVER. A lot of it hard to keep your fingers on?

Lieutenant SHEEHAN. Yes; it is a tremendous business.

Mr. BOBO. The type of pornography with which you have come in contact, is it generally the type of pornography that has been described here this morning by the other police officers?

Lieutenant SHEEHAN. Yes, sir.

Mr. BOBO. Do you find a great number of movie film, 16-millimeter, 35-millimeter, and 8-millimeter movie film?

Lieutenant SHEEHAN. Mostly 16-millimeter and 8-millimeter, in the pornography.

Chairman KEFAUVER. Are these films that you are talking of movies too?

Lieutenant SHEEHAN. Some of them; yes, sir.

Mr. BOBO. Have you discovered them in color also?

Lieutenant SHEEHAN. In color also.

Mr. BOBO. Does the pornographic traffic in Chicago also include the deck of 52 playing cards, the 4-by-5 French novelty, the 2-by-4 comic-book type, plus the still photos in color and black and white pictures describing all acts of perversion?

Lieutenant SHEEHAN. Yes, sir.

Mr. BOBO. Has your investigation into dealers of pornographic material in Chicago shown that it is produced in that city?

Lieutenant SHEEHAN. No, sir.

Mr. BOBO. Has your investigation revealed where the pornographic literature reaching Chicago comes from?

Lieutenant SHEEHAN. Yes, sir.

Mr. BOBO. Lieutenant Sheehan, I believe you participated in the arrest of a person by the name of Frank Mustari, alias Frank Lano?

Lieutenant SHEEHAN. Yes, sir.

Mr. Bobo. On what date was Mr. Mustari, alias Lano, arrested?

Lieutenant Sheehan. In February of 1954.

Mr. Bobo. At that time what was his address?

Lieutenant Sheehan. 1356 North Parkside Avenue, Chicago, Ill.

Mr. Bobo. Is Mr. Lano presently living at this address or is he incarcerated?

Lieutenant Sheehan. No, sir; he is living at that address.

Mr. Bobo. When you arrested Mr. Lano in Chicago, what was the type of pornography which he had in his possession?

Lieutenant Sheehan. He was arrested by the Oak Park Police Department. They got something like $15,000 worth of different material.

Mr. Bobo. That included films, books, pictures, playing cards?

Lieutenant Sheehan. Yes, sir.

Mr. Bobo. Did Mr. Lano reveal to either you or—were you engaged in that case, Lieutenant?

Lieutenant Sheehan. Indirectly; yes, sir.

Mr. Bobo. You participated in that?

Lieutenant Sheehan. It came from our office.

Chairman Kefauver. You had no supervision over it; is that it?

Lieutenant Sheehan. Yes, sir.

Mr. Bobo. Did Mr. Lano, or did your investigation reveal where he had received this material from?

Lieutenant Sheehan. Through our investigation; yes. Not from Mr. Mustari, but another party.

Mr. Bobo. Your investigation revealed where it was from. Where was that, Lieutenant?

Lieutenant Sheehan. From New York City.

Mr. Bobo. Did your investigation reveal from whom he received it in the city of New York?

Lieutenant Sheehan. Yes, sir.

Mr. Bobo. Who is that person?

Lieutenant Sheehan. Al Stone, alias Abraham Rubinstein, alias Abraham Rubin, Ruben Stone, and Stoney, Ruben White. Those are his aliases. He was known to us as Al Stone.

Mr. Bobo. Known to the Chicago police as Al Stone?

Lieutenant Sheehan. Yes, sir.

Mr. Bobo. Did your investigation show how Mr. Lano received this material from Mr. Stone?

Lieutenant Sheehan. Yes, sir.

Mr. Bobo. And how did he receive this material from Mr. Stone?

Lieutenant Sheehan. Well, they will come to New York City and procure a hotel room. After putting their car in a designated garage——

Mr. Bobo. Do you have the name of that designated garage?

Lieutenant Sheehan. No, sir.

Mr. Bobo. Continue, please.

Lieutenant Sheehan. Then Lano would call Al Stone. In turn, Stone would pick up, or have Lano's car picked up.

Mr. Bobo. Do you have the number at which he would call Stone?

Lieutenant Sheehan. Yes, sir.

Chairman Kefauver. The number will be treated as in executive session.

Lieutenant Sheehan. Yes, sir.

Mr. Bobo. All right, sir. Continue.

Lieutenant Sheehan. Is it all right to read it?

Mr. Bobo. Don't read the number; no, sir.

Chairman Kefauver. Give the subcommittee the number.

Lieutenant Sheehan. Yes, sir.

Chairman Kefauver. Write it out and give it to the subcommittee.

Lieutenant Sheehan. I think the subcommittee has it.

Mr. Bobo. We already have it.

Chairman Kefauver. The staff will furnish the number. Go ahead. We will call it No. X.

Mr. Sheehan. Shall I continue?

Mr. Bobo. Yes, sir; go right ahead. He would call Mr. Stone——

Lieutenant Sheehan. And Stone would have his car picked up. He would buy about $2,000 worth of material from Stone. It would be put in his car and his car delivered back to the garage. Then he would pick it up and return to Chicago.

Mr. Bobo. Was there any value put on this $2,000 worth of material as it was delivered in Chicago, its resale value?

Lieutenant Sheehan. Yes, sir.

Mr. Bobo. What was the value of each carload?

Lieutenant Sheehan. Oh, about $5,000.

Mr. Bobo. Did Mr. Lano state how many trips he made between New York City and Chicago?

Lieutenant Sheehan. Well, our informant did, he made four trips a month.

Mr. Bobo. He would average approximately $12,000 a month, considering $3,000 profit each trip and 4 trips per month?

Lieutenant Sheehan. Yes, sir. At times he would stop off and drop off a load at Indianapolis on his way back.

Mr. Bobo. Indianapolis, Ind.?

Lieutenant Sheehan. Yes, sir.

Mr. Bobo. Did he state to whom he would drop this load off, or did your informant, or did your investigation reveal to whom he would deliver this material in Indianapolis?

Lieutenant Sheehan. No, sir; he did not give us the name.

Mr. Bobo. Lieutenant Sheehan, are you familiar with the Fuller Brush Man series of comics—and let me say that this a a plagiarized name from the Fuller Brush Co..

Lieutenant Sheehan. Yes, sir.

Mr. Bobo. Do you have any information as to who the originator and chief distributor of this particular type of pornographic comic was?

Lieutenant Sheehan. Al Stone was originally reported as the original printer and originator of this Fuller Brush Man pornographic type of literature.

Mr. Bobo. This particular type of series covered all types of sexual perversion?

Lieutenant Sheehan. Yes, sir.

Mr. Bobo. In a comic book drawing?

Lieutenant Sheehan. Drawing; yes, sir.

Mr. Bobo. From the sources of information available to you as head of the censor board of the Chicago Police Department, do you have any opinion as to the size of dealer in pornographic material that Mr. Al Stone is?

Lieutenant Sheehan. No, sir; I have not.

Mr. Bobo. Has his name come to your attention in any other case other than this one?

Lieutenant Sheehan. No, sir.

Mr. Bobo. Lieutenant, did you also take part, or are you familiar with the arrest of Mr. Clarence Anderson of Elgin, Ill.?

Lieutenant Sheehan. Yes, sir.

Mr. Bobo. Was that raid made in cooperation with the Illinois State Police?

Lieutenant Sheehan. Yes, sir.

Mr. Bobo. Did you determine during the course of this investigation the source of supply for this particular dealer?

Lieutenant Sheehan. Well, he was a printer—he was a printer and distributor himself.

Mr. Bobo. He was the printer and distributor and publisher?

Lieutenant Sheehan. Himself; sir.

Chairman Kefauver. That was one of the big sources of supply in that part of the country?

Lieutenant Sheehan. In the Middle West, yes.

Mr. Bobo. During the raid on this man Anderson, how much material, pornographic material, was confiscated?

Lieutenant Sheehan. Well, we valued it at, the police value, at about $25,000.

Mr. Bobo. Did it consist of two truckloads of material?

Lieutenant Sheehan. Yes, sir.

Mr. Bobo. What size trucks?

Lieutenant Sheehan. Well, big stake trucks, the regular large trucks; big trucks.

Mr. Bobo. In this particular seizure were there 1,000 rolls of pornographic film?

Lieutenant Sheehan. Yes, sir.

Mr. Bobo. Did Mr. Anderson process this film himself?

Lieutenant Sheehan. Yes, sir.

Mr. Bobo. Also included in this raid were there 1,500 rolls of pornographic film which had not yet been printed?

Lieutenant Sheehan. Well, that was the raw film that had not been—just the raw film.

Mr. Bobo. It had never been taken off?

Lieutenant Sheehan. I presume that was what he had it for.

Mr. Bobo. Did you determine during this investigation where the models or the actors in these pornographic films were obtained?

Lietenant Sheehan. Yes, sir.

Mr. Bobo. Where were these pictures taken?

Lieutenant Sheehan. One was taken at 746 Oakwood Boulevard. That's the Oakwood Hotel. On the South Side of Chicago. It was taken up in a hotel room.

Mr. Bobo. These people would just rent a hotel room and go in there with their equipment, without knowledge of the hotel?

Lieutenant Sheehan. Well, this man named Edgar Flagg.

Mr. Bobo. How do you spell that, F-l-a-g-g?

Lieutenant Sheehan. Yes, sir; F-l-a-g-g.

Mr. Bobo. What is his address; where does he live?

Lieutenant Sheehan. He lives at 746 Oakwood, and he was manager of the hotel.

Mr. Bobo. Was he aware of the fact that pornographic films were being taken in his hotel?

Lieutenant SHEEHAN. These girls said that he took the pictures, that Flagg took the pictures.

Mr. BOBO. He took the pictures and in turn he sold them to Anderson?

Lieutenant SHEEHAN. Either that or he sent them out there for processing. That is how we got them, from Anderson.

Mr. BOBO. And this 1,000 rolls of lewd film, were some of them of the same title or the same acting, or were each one of the 1,000 a different film?

Lieutenant SHEEHAN. They were different film, each one. They were the same type of acts of perversion.

Mr. BOBO. The same type of acting, but each one was a different subject and a different film?

Lieutenant SHEEHAN. Yes, sir.

Mr. BOBO. Did you have an opportunity to view any of this film, Lieutenant?

Lieutenant SHEEHAN. Yes, sir.

Mr. BOBO. Included among the actors, both among the men and the women, were there any apparent juveniles as actors in these films?

Lieutenant SHEEHAN. No, sir.

Mr. BOBO. Did the records at the time at which you raided Mr. Anderson show that Mr. Anderson had bought quantities of pornographic material from others, or did he produce all of them?

Lieutenant SHEEHAN. Well, I would say some of it was sent to him through—produced for him. They would take the original film and have him process it for them.

Mr. BOBO. Did any of his records indicate that he had purchased material from a person by the name of Morris and a person by the name of Eddie?

Lieutenant SHEEHAN. Yes, sir.

Mr. BOBO. Were there any other identifying marks concerning the men Morris and Eddie?

Lieutenant SHEEHAN. The only thing was Flint, Mich.

Mr. BOBO. The name of Morris and the name of Eddie would fit the Michigan notation?

Lieutenant SHEEHAN. Yes, sir.

Mr. BOBO. Did Mr. Anderson describe to you or identify to you who Morris and Eddie were?

Lieutenant SHEEHAN. Well, he said they were the same, one and the same person.

Mr. BOBO. Just going under different names?

Lieutenant SHEEHAN. Different names when they buy; and that they would buy from him, this one particular Eddie and Morris. Then Morris would distribute it all over the Middle West.

Mr. BOBO. Did Anderson give you any idea as to how distribution was made? Was it made through the mails, through Railway Express, or through private conveyance?

Lieutenant SHEEHAN. Mostly through private conveyance, automobile.

Mr. BOBO. When it was loaded on these stake-body trucks was it just in the process of being delivered some place, at a distance?

Lieutenant SHEEHAN. No. It was all loose in the back of his garage, in his garage.

Mr. Bobo. The trucks were in his garage loaded?

Lieutenant Sheehan. No, sir; it wasn't in—it was loose in his garage, and he loaded them into trucks.

Mr. Bobo. During this investigation did you determine what the wholesale price of 16-millimeter film was?

Lieutenant Sheehan. Yes, sir.

Mr. Bobo. And what price was what?

Lieutenant Sheehan. Well, anywhere from $25 to whatever the traffic would allow, and that he would charge. But that was the lowest.

Mr. Bobo. That is, the film after it had been made into a picture?

Lieutenant Sheehan. Yes, sir.

Mr. Bobo. And he would sell it for anything the traffic would bear, ranging from $25 up?

Lieutenant Sheehan. Yes, sir.

Mr. Chumbris. That was for each film?

Lieutenant Sheehan. For each film.

Mr. Bobo. Did there appear to be any type of connection between dealers and buyers in this film, such as trading in one roll of film at a reduced price for a new roll of film?

Lieutenant Sheehan. Yes, sir. I got a receipt here from Anderson's Film Rental Service, where Morris bought film and he owed $659. He traded in other film back to him of $360.

Mr. Bobo. That would more than balance the difference?

Lieutenant Sheehan. Yes.

Chairman Kefauver. Let that be made an exhibit, Mr. Anderson's firm name seems to be Anderson's Film Rental Service, 1047 Morton Avenue, Elgin, Ill. Is that it?

Lieutenant Sheehan. Yes, sir. He has a legitimate film store in the front. In the back in his garage is where he had all the obscene stuff.

(The receipt referred to was marked "Exhibit No. 11," and is as follows:)

Exhibit No. 11

Anderson's Film Rental Service
ELGIN, ILL.

Order No_____
Name: Morris.
Address: Flint, Mich.
Oct. 27, 1952:
    Bought goods_____ $410
                                                        9

                                                          419
    Paid _____ 100

    Balance_____ 319
Nov. 13, 1952:
    Goods _____ 340

                                                            659
    Films and cash ($275 in films)_____ 360

    Balance_____ 299
Dec. 18, 1952:
    Balance_____ 77
Paid in full.

Mr. Bobo. In addition to the arrest of Anderson in this case, were any other persons arrested?

Lieutenant Sheehan. Yes, sir. This Edgar Flagg, I spoke about, that took the pictures up in the hotel room. And a girl named Theresa Anderson, Gene Newton.

Mr. Bobo. Do you have the addresses of these persons?

Chairman Kefauver. Well, were they convicted?

Lieutenant Sheehan. No, sir. Flagg was convicted. The girls were all discharged.

Chairman Kefauver. They were all disciplined?

Lieutenant Sheehan. Yes, sir.

Chairman Kefauver. Did they plead guilty?

Lieutenant Sheehan. No; but they testified for the State.

Chairman Kefauver. They said that they were participants?

Lieutentant Sheehan. Yes, sir.

Chairman Kefauver. Suppose you leave their names out.

Lieutenant Sheehan. Yes, sir.

Mr. Bobo. In addition to the film, this confiscation also included 600 decks of pornographic playing cards?

Lieutenant Sheehan. Yes, sir.

Chairman Kefauver. Let me see if I understand. This 1,000 rolls of films, the pictures had been taken, were they all different pictures?

Lientenant Sheehan. Every one was a different subject. It was all on the same pornographic type.

Chairman Kefauver. The same type, but each one was a different——

Lieutenant Sheehan. Yes, sir.

Mr. Chumbris. Lieutenant, from those couldn't more be developed?

Lieutenant Sheehan. Oh, thousands.

Mr. Chumbris. As many as you wanted?

Lieutenant Sheehan. He could keep developing as many as he wanted.

Chairman Kefauver. All right, sir.

Mr. Bobo. What sentence did Clarence Anderson receive as a result of this raid?

Lieutenant Sheehan. He received 2 years probation.

Mr. Bobo. Two years probation?

Lieutenant Sheehan. Yes, sir.

Mr. Bobo. Has he come to your attention at any time since that?

Lieutenant Sheehan. Yes, sir.

Mr. Bobo. Was he again caught selling pornographic material in Walworth County, Wis.?

Lieutenant Sheehan. Yes, sir.

Mr. Bobo. What was the charge against him in Walworth County?

Lieutenant Sheehan. He was charged, he was arrested on February 14, 1954, charged with reckless driving, and possession of obscene film. He was fined $750 and costs, and the films were destroyed by the order of the court.

Chairman Kefauver. Let me see if I understand this correctly. You mean this first operation, with all this material about which you are talking, he was convicted after a trial in court and given 2 years and put on probation?

Lieutenant Sheehan. Yes, sir.

Chairman Kefauver. In what court was that?

Lieutenant SHEEHAN. That was the judge of the county court of the county of Geneva, Ill. It wasn't in our county where the arrest was made. We had to try the case in Geneva County.

Chairman KEFAUVER. You were down there during the trial?

Lieutenant SHEEHAN. Yes, sir.

Chairman KEFAUVER. All right.

Mr. BOBO. Lieutenant Sheehan, are you also familiar with a case involving a Mr. Sam Atlas, A-t-l-a-s?

Lieutenant SHEEHAN. Yes, sir.

Mr. BOBO. Do you have the address of Mr. Atlas?

Lieutenant SHEEHAN. 3401 Beach Street, Chicago, Ill.

Mr. BOBO. In this case, can you give me the approximate retail value of the material seized, pornographic material?

Lieutenant SHEEHAN. Yes. It would be about, around $20,000 in wholesale.

Mr. BOBO. What was involved in this, was it the same type of material?

Lieutenant SHEEHAN. Yes, sir; 16-millimeter motion-picture films, all motion picture-printer and developing tanks; 1,958 pages of paper-bound obscene books; 800 obscene photographs; 117 red carton decks of obscene playing cards; and then 35 of the black and white obscene playing cards; 11 reels of 8-millimeter movie film; 1 black plastic viewer with 15 obscene poses on 35 millimeter film.

Mr. BOBO. Prior to this time had the Chicago police department been aware of any large scale traffic in pornographic literature?

Lieutenant SHEEHAN. No, sir; not to any great extent.

Mr. BOBO. Is it your opinion that in the last 5 years the traffic in pornographic literature has greatly increased?

Lieutenant SHEEHAN. Yes, sir.

Mr. BOBO. How many men do you have assigned in the Chicago police department to pornography investigation?

Lieutenant SHEEHAN. We have four assigned that specialize in that.

Mr. BOBO. Do you have any information of pornography coming into the hands of children of school age or younger?

Lieutenant SHEEHAN. No, sir; I can't say that I do.

Mr. BOBO. No case has ever come to your attention where a child received pornographic literature or viewed pornographic literature in any manner?

Lieutenant SHEEHAN. We had one case where, I think he was a 12-year-old boy, came to school and he had 1 card of a 52-deck, obscene playing card deck. The principal called us and we found out he got it from his grandfather; that he lived with his grandfather and he got it out of his dresser drawer.

Mr. BOBO. Lieutenant Sheehan, you have been very active in the Illinois Legislature. Would you have any recommendations that you would make to make the traffic in pornography more difficult?

Mr. SHEEHAN. You mean from——

Mr. BOBO. From the Federal viewpoint.

Chairman KEFAUVER. Tell what he tried to do in the Legislature of Illinois this year.

Lieutenant SHEEHAN. We asked for a bill, which is now in the legislature, making it a violation to sell to minors, any boy or girl under 18 years of age.

Chairman KEFAUVER. Making it a felony?

Lieutenant SHEEHAN. No, sir; a misdemeanor—not on pornography, on girlie books and these pocket-sized books. That was what they were doing in Springfield. We got the law on——

Chairman KEFAUVER. You got the law passed?

Lieutenant SHEEHAN. No, sir. It is pending now in the legislature.

Chairman KEFAUVER. The legislature is still in session?

Lieutenant SHEEHAN. Yes, sir.

Chairman KEFAUVER. Do you have a copy of the bill you proposed?

Lieutenant SHEEHAN. Yes, sir.

Chairman KEFAUVER. Let it be filed as an exhibit.

Lieutenant SHEEHAN. I have a copy of my statement before the legislature.

Chairman KEFAUVER. All right, sir.

Mr. BOBO. Lieutenant Sheehan, in view of your experience in the Anderson case, where such a large quantity of this material was seized that had moved both intrastate and in interstate traffic, as a policeman would it not be helpful to you if the degree of the offense was not raised from a misdemeanor to a felony?

Lieutenant SHEEHAN. Oh, it would help us an awful lot. The best sentence we ever got was where a jail sentence was provided of 6 months in the county jail. You can either fine, or 6 months in the county jail. It is just a misdemeanor in the State of Illinois now.

Mr. BOBO. Usually it amounts to nothing more than a small fine, which is practically a license to operate?

Lieutenant SHEEHAN. Nine out of every 10 is a fine.

Chairman KEFAUVER. Lieutenant Sheehan, is there anything else that you want to tell that would be helpful to the committee?

Lieutenant SHEEHAN. I think I covered everything I recall.

Mr. MARTIN. I have a question, Senator, if I may.

Chairman KEFAUVER. Yes.

Mr. MARTIN. Lieutenant Sheehan, I notice in examining this Atlas inventory here, that included in the seizure was one .45 caliber automatic pistol, Army Colt, with clip and several rounds of ammunition. I wonder if you could shed any light on that?

Lieutenant SHEEHAN. No; I cannot. He was given the gun back by order of the court. He showed where he owned it and was entitled to it.

Mr. MARTIN. In connection with Sam Atlas, there is a record here, too, of a peddler who went to the house and obtained some material. One Walter Liepert, stuff that was confiscated from his car included three rifles.

Lieutenant SHEEHAN. Well, he claimed he was hunting; they were hunting rifles.

Mr. MARTIN. That is all.

Mr. CHUMBRIS. Lieutenant, Anderson was placed on probation in a court in Illinois; is that correct?

Lieutenant SHEEHAN. Yes, sir.

Mr. CHUMBRIS. Then after he was put on probation he went into Wisconsin; is that correct?

Lieutenant SHEEHAN. Yes, sir.

Mr. CHUMBRIS. And while in Wisconsin he was apprehended, arrested, convicted, and placed on probation again in Wisconsin?

Lieutenant SHEEHAN. Yes, sir.

Mr. CHUMBRIS. Do you have any information as to whether the Wisconsin court was advised of the probation in Illinois?

Lieutenant SHEEHAN. No, sir. Of course we knew about it when we wrote—I believe it was in the—we read it in our newspapers where he had been arrested and convicted up in Walworth, and we wrote to the sheriff up there, and he verified it.

Mr. CHUMBRIS. Do you have any information that the State's attorney in Illinois contacted the State's attorney in Wisconsin in this matter?

Lieutenant SHEEHAN. No, sir.

Chairman KEFAUVER. It would be a breach of parole would if not if he was caught the second time?

Lieutenant SHEEHAN. It would. Our State's attorney wrote the judge of Geneva, Ill., Geneva County, and told him about the arrest in Wisconsin, and how he violated his probation, but we never heard back.

Chairman KEFAUVER. Anderson is still out?

Lieutenant SHEEHAN. Yes, sir; he is still in business.

Chairman KEFAUVER. Thank you very much, Lieutenant Sheehan. We appreciate your cooperation with our subcommittee. Thank you for coming here to testify.

Who is our next witness, Mr. Bobo?

Mr. BOBO. Sgt. Joseph E. Brown.

TESTIMONY OF SGT. JOSEPH E. BROWN, OF THE DETROIT, MICH., POLICE DEPARTMENT

(Sergeant Brown was sworn by the chairman.)

Chairman KEFAUVER. You may proceed, Mr. Bobo.

Mr. BOBO. You are Sgt. Joseph E. Brown, of the Detroit Police Department?

Sergeant BROWN. Yes, sir.

Chairman KEFAUVER. Sergeant Brown, you are a great big man. Will you speak loudly so everybody can hear; will you, sir?

Sergeant BROWN. Yes, sir.

Mr. BOBO. How long have you been with the Detroit Police Department, sir?

Sergeant BROWN. Since October 15, 1945.

Mr. BOBO. At the present time what is your duty assignment?

Sergeant BROWN. I am the sergeant assigned to the censorship bureau of the police department.

Mr. BOBO. Included in that responsibility is books, magazines, movies, night clubs, and pornographic literature?

Sergeant BROWN. Yes, sir.

Mr. BOBO. Would one of the primary duties which you have be the enforcement of the laws regarding pornography?

Sergeant BROWN. Yes, sir. That is one of the most important functions of the bureau. The separation of obscene literature and the apprehension and conviction of the people that deal in it.

Mr. BOBO. Sergeant Brown, has it ever come to your attention in Detroit as to whether or not pornographic material is coming into the hands of juveniles?

Sergeant Brown. I can think of no specific instance where it has come into the hands of juveniles. If it has, it would be an isolated case.

Now I am speaking of out-and-out pornography, with which the subcommittee has been dealing, I presume.

Mr. Bobo. This is usually a very clandestine type of operation. You do not deal with the juvenile squad yourself, do you?

Sergeant Brown. No, sir. We have a youth bureau in the police department that has been in function about 3 or 4 years, established by the police commissioner. They deal primarily with juvenile problems in the city of Detroit.

Mr. Bobo. Sergeant Brown, on May 18, 1953, did you have an occasion to arrest a person by the name of Al Stone?

Sergeant Brown. I did.

Mr. Bobo. For what was his arrest?

Sergeant Brown. For possession of obscene movie film.

Mr. Bobo. Did you have the address of that man, Al Stone?

Sergeant Brown. The address that he gave at the time of his apprehension was 1639 41st Street, Brooklyn, N. Y. That was what the driver's license indicated was his address.

Mr. Bobo. Did he have other aliases?

Sergeant Brown. He was known as Al Stone. The operator's license was issued to Abraham Rubin.

Mr. Bobo. How do you spell it?

Sergeant Brown. R-u-b-i-n. Those are the two names that I know Mr. Stone by.

Mr. Bobo. Do you have his record that would indicate any other aliases?

Sergeant Brown. I have a record here from the Detroit Police Department, Al Stone, mug No. 109385, showing 10 arrests. At the time of these arrests, they were all Abraham Rubin.

Mr. Bobo. All going under the name of Abraham Rubin?

Sergeant Brown. Yes, sir.

Mr. Bobo. When he was arrested in Detroit on May 18, 1953, what did you say he had in his possession?

Chairman Kefauver. You have read from the police record. Is that the official document there?

Sergeant Brown. Yes, sir. That is the request for a warrant, Mr. Chairman, that was drawn up.

Chairman Kefauver. All these arrests, is that on your official record there?

Sergeant Brown. Yes, sir.

Chairman Kefauver. Will you file that so we can have that as a part of our record? You also have his photograph there?

Sergeant Brown. Yes, sir.

Chairman Kefauver. That will, then, be filed as exhibits.

Sergeant Brown. Yes, sir.

(The information was marked "Exhibit No. 12," and is on file with the subcommittee.)

Chairman Kefauver. Where were these arrests?

Sergeant Brown. The one arrest was in Detroit.

Chairman Kefauver. Where were these others on the record?

Sergeant Brown. Starting chronologically. In 1928, New York City. The charge was rape. He was discharged.

1930, New York City. Reckless driving. 30 days.

1932, in Poughkeepsie, N. Y. The charge was possession of obscene literature. Six months, suspended sentence.

In 1933, Darien, Conn. Possession of obscene pictures. Sentenced to a fine of $250 and costs, and 6 months in jail. The jail term, I believe, was SS. I think that indicates suspended sentence.

1933, in Buffalo, N. Y. There is a number here, I don't know what the number indicates. It is 1141–P. L., it is apparently a law number. He received 3 months in the Erie County Penitentiary, that's Erie County, N. Y.

Mr. Bobo. For the record, that 1141–P. L. is the Obscene Statute of the State of New York

Sergeant Brown. I was not aware of that. 1141–P. L. is the way it is indicated on the record.

And in 1939, Erie County—no; that's the same record, I am sorry. It refers to the above-mentioned arrest.

In 1934, in Albany, N. Y., possession of obscene pictures. Seventy-five dollar fine or 30 days in Albany County Jail.

1934, in Providence, R. I., possession of indecent literature. Thirty days in the Providence County Jail.

1934, in Howard, R. I., possession of obscene pictures. Sentenced to 30 days and costs. May 18, 1953, Detroit, Mich., possession of obscene literature, $100 fine and 90 days imprisonment in the Detroit House of Correction.

Mr. Bobo. When he was arrested in Detroit he had 558 rolls of obscene movies?

Sergeant Brown. That is right. Five fundred and fifty-eight rolls of motion-picture film, consisting of 501 8-millimeter, and 57 16-millimeter prints. Of these reels, they were pornography, per se, each and every one.

Mr. Bobo. Showing all types of sexual perversion?

Sergeant Brown. That is right.

Mr. Bobo. Did you also find on Mr. Stone, alias Rubin, an address book?

Sergeant Brown Yes, sir.

Mr. Bobo. Listed in this address book, who was listed in this address book, Sergeant?

Chairman Kefauver. Well, let's see about that, now.

Let the address book be in executive session, but you can tell where connections are made in the address book.

Sergeant Brown. New Orleans, La.; Utica, N. Y.; Philadelphia, Pa.; Syracuse, N. Y.; Utica, N. Y.; Brooklyn, N. Y.; Brooklyn, N. Y.; New York City; Philadelphia, Pa.; Chicago, Ill.; Chicago, Ill.; Chicago. Ill.; Bellaire, Ohio; Jacksonville, Fla.; St. Louis, Mo.; Pittsburgh, Pa.; Harrisburg, Pa.; New Orleans, La.; Chelsea, Mass.; Chicago, Ill.; Sheffield, Ala.; St. Louis, Mo; Columbus, Ohio; Lancaster, Ohio; Jacksonville, Fla.; Louisville, Ky.; Pittsburgh, Pa.; Gettysburg, Pa.; Scranton, Pa.; Washington, D. C.; Indianapolis, Ind.; Pittsburgh, Pa.; Marbury, Md.; Pittsburgh, Pa.; Chicago, Ill.; Detroit, Mich.; Louisville, Ky.; Indianapolis, Ind.; Birmingham, Ala.; Rome, Ga.; Birmingham, Ala.; Atlanta, Ga.; Linton, Ind.; Flint, Mich.; St. Louis, Mo.; New Orleans, La.; Baltimore, Md.; Reading, Pa.; Richmond, Va.; Salisbury, N. C.

Now, there are other names with those numbers indicated in those cities listed.

Mr. BOBO. Were any of the persons listed on that list known to you to be dealers in pornographic material?

Sergeant BROWN. Yes, sir. The Bizon Sales, 12th Street and Pingree in Detroit, Mich. The proprietor of that establishment has twice been convicted of the sale and possession of obscene literature in the city of Detroit. The first time he received a fine of either $90 or $100 under the misdemeanor. On the second offense we prosecuted this defendant under a statute that we have in Michigan, making the second offense a high misdemeanor, which is punishable by $500 fine or a year in the House of Correction. He was convicted of the second offense and was fined $100 or 1 year.

I might also add at this time, if I may, that in the State of Michigan under our statutes 753-43, under which we operate, the obscenity statute, the third offender, upon conviction, or the third offense is treated as a felony, and we have 1 defendant that was convicted about 3 or 4 weeks ago, or he was convicted about 3 or 4 months ago under the second offense of the act. He received 10 months probation.

One of the officers from our bureau made another purchase of obscene material about a month ago from this defendant. He was immediately ordered at a probation hearing to serve 10 months in the Detroit House of Correction, and he will then be tried in felony court as a third offender.

Mr. BOBO. Was there also taken from Mr. Stone at this time a road map showing the route that he had covered?

Chairman KEFAUVER. Just a minute, before you get to that.

Sergeant Brown, the names in the address book that you investigated turned out to be pornographic dealers; is that not so?

Sergeant BROWN. Yes, sir. This one name in particular, Mr. Chairman, was——

Chairman KEFAUVER. You have Mr. Chumbris who gave the story about Lou Saxton in Pittsburgh, who was a dealer, in his testimony the day before yesterday. Do you have Lou Saxton as one of the names, from Pittsburgh?

Sergeant BROWN. There was a name listed, Mr. Chairman, as Lou, Pittsburgh, Pa. No address showing and no last name showing.

Chairman KEFAUVER. Then do you have listed a Japloski who has been convicted in St. Louis? We have a record of him distributing lewd literature, but he resides in Jacksonville, Fla. Is his name listed?

Sergeant BROWN. What was the name again, Mr. Chairman?

Chairman KEFAUVER. Japloski.

Sergeatn BROWN. What was the first name?

Chairman KEFAUVER. Stanley Japloski.

Sergeant BROWN. Mr. Chairman, I have a Stanley listed, Jacksonville, Fla., no last name.

Mr. CHUMBRIS. Do you have his address?

Sergeant BROWN. No; there is a notation, numerals is all that is listed.

Now, should I read the numerals? There is no indication—it presumably is a phone number, although there is no exchange listed, it is merely numerals.

Mr. Chumbris. If you will look further on that list you will find another reference to Jacksonville, Fla., that might indicate that name.

Sergeant Brown (complying). Yes. On further observation I find a Stanley, no last name listed, in Jacksonville, Fla., on Washtonian Street. It is 3510 Washtonian Street.

Chairman Kefauver. Proceed, Mr. Bobo.

Mr. Bobo. Do you have any reference to Anderson in Elgin, Ill?

Chairman Kefauver. He did not read Elgin.

Mr. Bobo. Sergeant, while you are checking that also, would you see if you have one listed Eddie in New York City?

Sergeant Brown. Yes, sir.

Mr. Bobo. With no address given? It is on the part of the list, I think, Sergeant, that does not have the addresses, and so forth, the bottom part of the list.

Sergeant Brown. I see in the second group an Eddie listed just as that, no last name given.

Mr. Bobo. Is a telephone number given?

Just keep the telephone number in executive session.

Sergeant Brown. Yes, sir. I presume that that is a phone number.

Chairman Kefauver. Is that the same number we had here a little while ago?

Sergeant Brown. I don't recall the other number. You mean in my testimony, Mr. Chairman?

Chairman Kefauver. No; in somebody else's testimony.

Sergeant Brown. Not to my knowledge.

Mr. Bobo. Sergeant, do you have any suggestion or any comments you might want to make on pornographic literature?

You also confiscated from Mr. Stone at the time of his arrest a roadmap showing the route covered by him?

Sergeant Brown. Here is a roadmap that was taken by me from the automobile, or the glove compartment of his automobile at the time of his arrest [exhibiting].

Chairman Kefauver. Does he have his route marked where he had been going?

Sergeant Brown. Mr. Chairman, it has a route marked from the city of New York to Philadelphia, to Harrisburg, Pa.; Pittsburgh, Pa.; Akron, Ohio; Toledo, Ohio; Detroit, Mich.; Fort Wayne, Ind.; Indianapolis, Ind.; St. Louis, Mo.; Louisville, Ky.; Charleston, W. Va.; into Richmond, Va. It terminates at Richmond, Va., the markings on the map.

Mr. Bobo. Is this map over here [indicating], showing the interstate connections of Al Stone, alias Rubin, does that indicate the cities which you have marked there, some of the cities?

Sergeant Brown. I would say that it indicates a great many of them, from my observation from the chair here, counsellor.

Mr. Bobo. Is it also a composite of the cities listed in his address book?

Sergeant Brown. To a great extent; yes.

Mr. Bobo. Thank you, Sergeant. That is all.

Chairman Kefauver. Sergeant, you do have a big program in Detroit to stamp out this business, do you not?

Sergeant Brown. Yes, sir, Mr. Chairman. I would like to bring out a couple of the highlights of that program that we have in Detroit.

We have a great many active groups, PTA, the church, and fraternal organizations. We cooperate very closely with them, and they with us. We go out and make public speeches to these people. We try to keep in very close contact. We feel that in that way we get a firsthand viewpoint from the parents of what's going on.

Now, last Tuesday night, Mr. Chairman, I spoke to a PTA group in Detroit that consisted of 350 parents. They were aware that I had been subpenaed here by this committee to delve into some of the problems of the juvenile delinquency question, and the problems of obscene literature; and they are, I understand, anxiously awaiting a report of your findings and the corrections that can be made.

Now, we do feel in the State of Michigan that the statute covering obscenity is a very good, strong statute; it is 750, section 343. Under this statute, as I mentioned previously, Mr. Chairman, I would like to point out again, on the first arrest and conviction it is a misdemeanor. The second arrest is treated as a high misdemeanor.

Now, on an ordinary misdemeanor it is punishable by 90 days in the house of correction or $100 fine; the second offense is punishable by a year in the Detroit House of Correction or a $500 fine; and the third offense is treated as a felony, and it is punishable by State prison.

We have had very good success, we have had a great amount of cooperation from the prosecuting attorney's office, from all the judges in recorder's court. They are backing us 100 percent on this problem.

We had one judge there, I had 3 cases before him in the last 6 weeks, and that is first offenders.

Chairman KEFAUVER. Is that Judge George Edwards?

Sergeant BROWN. No. George Edwards is in the probate court of juvenile, and a very, very capable judge by the way, Mr. Chairman.

Chairman KEFAUVER. I know him.

Sergeant BROWN. Judge Shimansky has a standing policy there that, upon conviction, it is automatically 60 days in the house of correction and a year's probation.

We feel that that law has teeth in it, but we would also like to see——

Chairman KEFAUVER. When was that law passed?

Sergeant BROWN. That was amended in 19—it was passed, I believe, in 1935, and I believe it was amended in 1953, Mr. Chairman.

Chairman KEFAUVER. Has the traffic in Detroit gone down since you had that law amended and you have been enforcing it more vigorously?

Sergeant BROWN. We feel that the traffic has greatly decreased.

Chairman KEFAUVER. Tell us a little more about the splendid interest and activity of the PTA men and women and civic clubs and others in Detroit, Sergeant Brown.

Sergeant BROWN. Well, as I mentioned before, these——

Chairman KEFAUVER. How many people are participating?

Sergeant BROWN. Well, it would be hard to say, but it would be a very, very great number of organizations, Mr. Chairman.

Chairman KEFAUVER. Each in their own neighborhood?

Sergeant BROWN. Each in their own neighborhood.

They have a program—before I mention this, in answer to your question there, Mr. Chairman, I would like to mention that under this law in the State of Michigan—now, this is getting away from pornography just a little bit, but I think I would like to touch on it if it is permissible.

These pocket-sized and these cheesecake books, cheesecake and girlie magazines, when these books come into the city of Detroit, we have such cooperation from the two large distributors that they voluntarily submit each and every one of these pocket books to the censor bureau for screening. We have a staff of 13 men. They screen these books, and if they find obscene passages, or anything of a filthy nature, we immediately submit it to our legal counsel, the prosecuting attorney of the county. He gives us a legal opinion, and if it is a violation of the law he sends us a letter, 1 for our files and another 1 for the distributor, that if distribution is made on that book in the city of Detroit or in the county of Wayne, that prosecution will result.

Now, as a result of this action, we have withheld between four and five hundred separate titles of these pocket books in the city of Detroit in the last 5 years. Each one of these titles in the city of Detroit alone would enjoy a circulation of approximately five to ten thousand.

Chairman KEFAUVER. Each one of these what?

Sergeant BROWN. Each one of these books, each title, each separate title would enjoy a circulation of from five to ten thousand in the city of Detroit alone.

Chairman KEFAUVER. But they are not circulated?

Sergeant BROWN. No, sir.

When the prosecuting attorney rules that they are in violation of the law, the distributor is notified, there is no distribution made in the city.

Now, we had a test case just a year ago now on one of these pocket books in recorder's court, and we were sustained. There was a conviction obtained.

Now, it is my understanding at the present time that this case is being appealed to the Michigan State Supreme Court.

Chairman KEFAUVER. Sergeant Brown, then in our horror and crime comic-book hearing, we ran into a situation where some news dealers were forced to take a whole range of things in order to get the better magazines; they had to take some horror comics and they had to take some literature that is not so good, and that it was a pretty difficult position in which they were placed. They would lose their license if they did not take all those things, and yet they did not want to sell them on many occasions.

However, your news dealers are cooperating and just turning them back; is that it?

Sergeant BROWN. That is correct.

Chairman KEFAUVER. I think you call that tie-in sales?

Sergeant BROWN. I believe that would be the term.

Mr. CHUMBRIS. Sergeant, I believe you, or members of your staff, went to the city just northeast of Detroit last year and testified before a grand jury on some of these particular problems to clean up the——

Sergeant BROWN. The city of Port Huron. Inspector Case was up there in an advisory capacity.

Mr. CHUMBRIS. I understand they have quite a program up there to clean up these pin-up magazines, like Eye; is that correct?

Sergeant BROWN. I can't testify too much about that program; I am not too familiar with the Port Huron program.

Chairman KEFAUVER. Sergeant Brown, we thank you very much for coming here.

Sergeant BROWN. Mr. Chairman, one more point. I would like to tell you at this time that, speaking for myself and the police department of the city of Detroit, and the citizens of the city of Detroit, we would like to see some sort of Federal legislation passed that would put teeth in the law to keep this smut from being distributed by any means, whether it is in an automobile or carried across the State lines, or by any means. That's what we are all in hope of.

Chairman KEFAUVER. That is what all the people who are working with you on this want done?

Sergeant BROWN. That is what they want done.

Chairman KEFAUVER. You tell them that we appreciate their recommendation and their activity, and the report that we have from you.

Sergeant BROWN. Thank you very much.

Chairman KEFAUVER. Mr. Bair, we aren't going to get to finish you before noon, but come around and let us have your testimony. We are going to adjourn in about 10 minutes.

(Mr. Bair was sworn.)

TESTIMONY OF ROBERT R. BAIR, ASSISTANT UNITED STATES ATTORNEY FROM THE DISTRICT OF MARYLAND

Chairman KEFAUVER. Proceed, Mr. Bobo.

Mr. BOBO. Mr. Bair, you are Mr. Robert R. Bair, B-a-i-r?

Mr. BAIR. That is correct.

Mr. BOBO. You are assistant United States attorney from the district of Maryland?

Mr BAIR. That is right, sir.

Mr. BOBO. Baltimore, Md.? How long have you been with the United States attorney's office in Baltimore?

Mr. BAIR. Since September 1954.

Mr. BOBO. And your duties in that office are to prepare and present cases?

Mr. BAIR. That is correct, sir. Enforcing the laws of the Federal Government.

Mr. BOBO. Were you the person in the office of the United States attorney in Baltimore who prepared the case against Herman Solomon and Saul Norman Daymont?

Mr. BAIR. I am.

Mr. BOBO. Louis Passetti and Ruby Martin Tayfoia?

Mr. BAIR. Yes, sir.

Mr. BOBO. That was a case involving what, Mr. Bair?

Mr. BAIR. That was a case involving the depositing with the Railway Express Agency for shipment in interstate commerce of certain obscene, lewd, and lascivious photographs.

Chairman KEFAUVER. Mr. Bair, this map here on the left was made, I believe, from the evidence worked up and brought out by you in this case?

Mr. BAIR. That is correct. That evidence was available to us.

Chairman KEFAUVER. That is a so-called "Soloday" operation?

Mr. BAIR. Yes, sir.

Chairman KEFAUVER. I want to say just as we close, as we recess for lunch, that I know of the security in this case, and I think this is one of the most important 'decisions enabling enforcement agencies and the courts to get at this problem that we have ever had in the field of indecent and pornographic literature.

Many prosecutors all over the Nation are awaiting the outcome of the trial of this case that you have concluded, and it is a very important case. We want you to take some little time in describing the operations, just what was involved in the case.

You will continue with your testimony right after our recess for the lunch period.

The subcommittee will stand in recess until 1 : 30.

(Whereupon, at 12 noon, a luncheon recess was taken until 1 : 30 p. m.)

AFTERNOON SESSION

Chairman KEFAUVER. We will resume with the testimony of Mr. Bair. All right, Mr. Bobo, proceed.

Mr. BOBO. The operations which we were discussing before the recess was the operation "Soloday"?

Mr. BAIR. That is correct. The address was 3500 Harford Road, Baltimore, Md.

Mr. BOBO. When did this case originate?

Mr. BAIR. The FBI in Baltimore received an anonymous letter about August 4, 1953, and it was from somebody out in San Francisco who stated that there were two men who were shipping large shipments of lewd photographs from Baltimore, after having been convicted of the same offense out in Los Angeles.

After that letter the FBI investigated the case, and conducted surveillance of the premises at Harford Road, and looked into the men who were going in and out of that building.

Four persons were primarily involved. Herman Solomon, William Daymont, Louis D. Passetti, and Ruby Martin Tayfoia.

After a good deal of investigation in which the Railway Express Agency was cooperating with us, on December 14, 1953, the FBI was notified that a rather large shipment had been deposited with them, and agents went down there and initialed the packages contained in that shipment.

Mr. BOBO. This photograph over here, was that the shipment that had been deposited with Railway Express?

Mr. BAIR. That is correct; that is the shipment of the 14th of December. That shipment consisted of 21 cartons destined for 14 consignees in 7 cities all over the United States.

The shipment was permitted to go through, and agents in various cities to which these packages were consigned, later picked them up and returned them to Baltimore.

On the basis of that, evidence warrants were issued, and the four-named persons were arrested.

Then on January 5, 1954, the Federal grand jury at Baltimore returned an 11-count indictment against Herman Solomon, William Daymont, Louis D. Passetti, and on Ruby Tayfoia, the indictment was based on section 1462 of title 18 of the United States Code; and it charged them with knowingly depositing with the Railway Express Agency at Baltimore for shipment in interstate commerce lewd, lascivious, obscene, and filthy photographs.

This 11-count indictment concerned only 17 of the cartons which were addressed to 11 consignees in 6 cities.

The volume was rather large. It consisted of 7,330 sets of photographs, and there were 12 photographs to each set; thus in all there were 87,960 photographs.

These had a declared value with the Railway Express Agency of almost $2,400. They were being consigned at about 35 cents a set. That was the cost to the retailer.

The retail value, however, was about $10,200, because I had 2 men, 2 of the consignees come to testify at the trial, and they indicated that they received about $1.50 per set.

The testimony at the trial also revealed that these shipments were taking place on the average of about twice a week, and that the production was in the neighborhood of 3,000 sets per week. If you want to apply that on an annual basis, that would be 156,000 sets, or 1,872,-000 photographs a year.

On a weekly basis, assuming that they were able to manufacture and sell 3,000 sets a week, at 35 cents a set, the shipments out of Soloday would come to about $1,050 a week. It is difficult to ascertain how much of that $1,050 was profit to Soloday. They indicated that maybe 22 cents of the 35 cents was the cost of production. I am inclined to think that is a little high, and I would say that closer to about half of the $1,000 was profit to Soloday.

Turning to the market for these photographs, as you can see from the map, there were a great number of consignees located all over the United States—about 45 or 46 in number; but as to the consignees involved in the prosecution in Baltimore, there were 11—and if you wish me to, I will read those into the record.

Mr. Bobo. If you would, please.

Mr. Bair. Kay's Bookstore, 1374 East Ninth Street, Cleveland, Ohio, they received 500 sets of photographs.

City Hall News & Novelty, 133 Lyons Street NW., Grand Rapids, Mich., they received 320 sets.

The Gallery, 347 North Clark Street, Chicago, Ill., they received 160 sets.

Frank's Magic, at 1220 K Street, Sacramento, Calif., received 725 sets.

The Satisfactory Distributing Co., 501 M. & M. Building, Houston, Tex., received 3 cartons containing 1,700 sets.

Capital News, 1709 East Ninth Street, Cleveland, Ohio, received 1,070 sets.

William Shatsky, 330 South Olive Street, Los Angeles, Calif., received 925 sets.

Joyland Novelty Co., 421 South Main Street, Los Angeles, Calif., received 300 sets.

Tom Libman, 331 South Main Street, Los Angeles, Calif., received 180 sets.

The G. & U. Newstand, 516 South Main Street, Los Angeles, Calif., received 275 sets.

E. Smith, 536 South Main Street, Los Angeles, Calif., received 1,175 sets.

Mr. Bobo. These you have just read indicate only those in which you had in the 11-count indictment that were consigned against Soloday?

Mr. BAIR. Those were the names of the consignees, 11 to be exact, named in the 11-count indictment in this particular case.

Mr. BOBO. In this particular case there were additional consignees which you are not at liberty to reveal at the present time?

Mr. BAIR. That is correct.

Mr. BOBO. Numbering some 46 altogether?

Mr. BAIR. There are about 46 names that we have in our file to which these photographs or similar ones were consigned.

Mr. BOBO. In addition to these did you investigate and did the trial bring out the fact that Solomon or Daymont not only did a Railway Express business but also made frequent trips by automobile?

Mr. BAIR. That is true. There is no question but that a great part of this business was not done by Railway Express. If the figure of 3,000 photographs a week is a correct figure, and that was given to us by Louis D. Passetti, a much smaller number than 3,000 per week was sent by Railway Express. We know about 27,000 sets of photographs were sent by Railway Express during the 5 months period of July to November 1953. At the same time at the rate of 3,000 sets a week, you would have about 60,000 rather than 27,000 sets produced during that period.

Mr. BOBO. Did the trial bring out, or did the preliminary investigation, the amount of film used by this operation—raw film?

Mr. BAIR. Yes; it did.

Mr. BOBO. I think I should correct that—processing paper.

Mr. BAIR. Records which were obtained by a search warrant indicated that between July 10 and November 23, 1953, Soloday purchased over $2,000 of photographic paper from Rochester, N. Y., and over $7,600 worth of photographic paper from a company in New York City.

Mr. BOBO. Did any of the pictures confiscated portray any minors in these lewd photographs?

Mr. BAIR. No; they did not.

Mr. BOBO. When this material was shipped out was it deposited with the Railway Express Co., or did they go by Soloday and pick up the material?

Mr. BAIR. As regards this particular shipment, I believe it was brought to the Railway Express Agency by automobile.

Mr. BOBO. You mentioned the names of Herman Solomon and William Daymont. Was this a partnership operation?

Mr. BAIR. I might give you some background information about those two, as well as what we know about Passetti and Tayfoia.

Of those four people, Herman Solomon and William Daymont were primarily responsible for the business and the success of Soloday, which is obviously a combination of the two names, Solomon and Daymont.

Solomon was the photographer. He had an apartment in New York City at 224 West 49th Street, where he also had a studio. There he took photographs of various models.

He then delivered the negatives to William Daymont at 35 Harford Road, in Baltimore, where they were developed, and where the photographs were printed from the negatives.

Louis D. Passetti was employed by Solomon at about $65 a week to help in packaging the photographs.

Ruby Martin Tayfoia assisted William Daymont in Baltimore in the printing of the photographs. Because of her small connection with the matter, the indictment against her was dismissed, and only the three men were tried.

What we know about Solomon and Daymont, we know primarily from the mouths of Passetti and Tayfoia. Mr. Passetti met Solomon in San Francisco in 1949, and was employed by him that year to package photographs. While he was in the hospital out there he was advised that the police had raided the place of business in San Francisco, and that was the last time he saw Solomon until September 1953, when he again began working for Soloday.

Miss Tayfoia was about 17 years of age when she first met Solomon and Daymont in Hollywood, Calif., in about January of 1952. She went to work for them there as a model, and after a month or two of posing she worked for them as a printer of photographs.

Just a few months prior to that, in October of 1951, both Solomon and Daymont were arrested by the Los Angeles Police Department on a charge of lewd photographs, and Solomon received in all 60 days suspended sentence, and a total of $200 in fines.

Daymont at that time received 1 year's probation, and a total of $150 in fines.

In May of 1952, while within the probationary period of Daymont, the business of "Soloday" moved from Santa Monica, Calif., to the Harford Road address. We know at that time, from September of 1952 until they were arrested in December 1953, they operated that business in Baltimore.

Solomon would go to New York about 4 days a week. He would then drive to Baltimore and remain in Baltimore about 3 days a week, conducting this business.

Daymont, I believe, resided solely in Baltimore.

As to the question of obtaining models, they would obtain them from night clubs and burlesque houses, et cetera. They would offer them something like $10 for a couple of hours' work in posing; and as I say, a good bit of that was done in a photographic studio in New York by Solomon.

However, a number of their consignees over the country, one in Cleveland in particular—we know they offered to get them models, and Daymont and Solomon would go out to these various places and photograph other models in studios in these various cities.

Mr. BOBO. Do you know how those negatives would be forwarded into Baltimore?

Mr. BAIR. I have no way of knowing that; no sir.

Mr. BOBO. Go right ahead.

Mr. BAIR. Going to the trial which took place in Baltimore, Solomon, Daymont, and Passetti were tried on this 11-count indictment on April 25, 1955, before Judge W. Calvin Chestnut. The jury was an all-male jury. However, they returned a verdict of guilty; and Solomon was sentenced to 90 days in jail, and $1,000 fine.

Daymont was sentenced to 90 days in jail, and $1,000 fine.

Passetti was fined $500.

The issue of the depositing for interstate shipment was stipulated out of the case by counsel, so that the only issue at that trial was the issue of obscenity.

That brings me to the type of photographs involved in this case. It was not pornographic per se. It was more or less borderline photographs, borderlining between the art type of photograph, or the stripping nude type of photograph. There were three types in all.

They were in sets of 12 photographs each. The girls were posed in varying stages of undress in one type. You might call it a stripping nude, but it was not strictly that inasmuch as there was not a complete nude in the whole group. They were dressed very cleverly by using long stockings and garters and black lingerie, black gloves, and black boots, and so forth. I don't think you could strictly call it an artistic stripping nude.

Mr. BOBO. Most of these portrayed long black leather gloves, and long black boots and high heels?

Mr. BAIR. Yes; I would describe it as that. I wish to repeat that it was not pornographic. There were no suggestive poses involved.

There was another type which we might refer to as a whip or a flagellation type, in which a woman would have a fairly serious, stern look on her face, and she would be holding a whip.

There was a third type which we might refer to as a bondage picture in which the woman was posed with her hands and feet tied with ropes, and in many cases lying on a bed, with a very frightened look on her face.

The problem before me was to see whether these pictures fitted the tests of obscenity which had been laid down in prior Federal court decisions; and the tests that we had to go by were whether these photographs were calculated to corrupt the morals of those into whose hands they might fall, by exciting lewd thoughts or suggesting sensual desires.

There were two appraches to the problem. One you might call a negative approach, and the other a positive approach.

As a negative approach, I had an expert from the Museum of Art come in to testify that they had little, if any, artistic merit to them; that they did not constitute art, in that if any little artistic merit which they had was completely outweighed by emphasis on sex.

There were a number of aspects to the positive approach to the problem. One was, of course, the huge volume, the huge market for these photographs. The second was their sole purpose, which was a pandering to the lascivious curiosity in men—just a strict commercialization of sex, and sex alone. That was emphatically put across to the jury.

The third approach was to show the clever and skillful method to commercialize this kind of thing. They didn't just submit one photograph. They submitted 12 in a series; and I think you can safely say that the cumulative effect of the 12 photographs was greater than the sum of just looking at 12 photographs separately.

Another very clever method used by them is the use of partial clothing. There was not a complete nude in all the 87,000 photographs. There was always just a little bit of clothing in the form of garters or long stockings, or black lingerie. Havelock Ellis and many others are well agreed that actually nudity is more chaste than partial clothing, and partial clothing is a much easier way—the use of partial clothing is a much easier way to incite sensuality in man than a complete nude.

That represented a very clever observation upon the part of these men, and they utilized it extensively.

Another method was the use of fetishes. The use of long black gloves and long boots, or high heeled shoes, the use of stockings and garters, the use of whips and ropes.

Necessarily these things might not be prima facie evidence to a jury; and so I had to bring in a psychiatrist to explain some of the symbols. I brought in Dr. Jacob Harry Conn, of Utah Place, in Baltimore, and he testified that pictures such as these represented a very skillful invitation and solicitation to persons who are in need of a substitute for a sexual experience.

From the huge market in these photographs I think we can infer that there are quite a few people in such a need. It represents the need of people who through weakness of character, through age, and lack of maturity, or through social and moral inhibitions are unable to find a normal outlet for the sexual urges.

In some cases the need is a pathological need, and it is represented by perverts, by impotents, borderline homosexuals. The whipping pictures and the flagellations, the bondage pictures, they are all directed to that type of person.

At the same time Dr. Conn pointed out an analogy between the impotent type of person who had this need and the adolescent who was just approaching the awakening of that type of life when he was awakening to sexual needs. It was clear to him that such a photograph would represent an outlet for a vicarious sexual experience.

Mr. Bobo. In other words, actually what it would do, if it was a juvenile and an immature person, it is liable to cause him to take up this partciular fetish—whipping, bondage, as an outlet for sex?

Mr. Bair. That is what Dr. Conn testified to.

Mr. Bobo. Mr. Bair, what was the end result of the case?

Mr. Bair. As I said, the only issue was that of obscenity, and the jury brought back a verdict of guilt; and the three men were sentenced as I have stated previously.

Mr. Bobo. Would a clearer definition in the statute 1461, 1462, 1463, 1464 of what constitutes pornographic literature, have assisted in this case in obtaining a stronger conviction for these individuals?

Mr. Bair. I don't think so. I would hesitate to legislate further as to the definition of obscenity.

I believe the courts over a long period of time have established certain standards which I might say are flexible in that the present test is the standard of the community here now; and as you know, these standards do change.

If you look back to the Greco-Roman era, or the Victorian era, these standards do change.

The present test allows you to look at the standards of the community here and now, and to decide whether this material is calculated to corrupt the morals by exciting lewd thoughts and sensual desires; and I think the test at the present time is adequate. To legislate further on it may restrict courts too much in the future.

Mr. Bobo. Prosecution and investigation of this case required approximately what—2 years?

Mr. Bair. The investigation required almost 5 months.

Mr. Bobo. How long was it in the courts?

Mr. BAIR. Well, the trial lasted a little over a day.

Chairman KEFAUVER. Mr. Martin, do you have any questions?

Mr. MARTIN. Mr. Bair, I believe you told us the cost to Solomon was 22 cents. I believe 22 cents was the price spread between the cost and what he was selling for. Wasn't the cost 13 cents?

Mr. BAIR. Well, at the trial they maintained that the cost was 22 cents. However, there is evidence in their books and records that the cost was 13 cents. It is a little hard to ascertain exactly what it cost. I would estimate they made about one-half of the 35 cents as profit.

Chairman KEFAUVER. When was the final judgment rendered in this case?

Mr. BAIR. On April 26, 1955.

Chairman KEFAUVER. I think there have been some other indictments brought. A good many cases were waiting on the outcome of this one?

Mr. BAIR. That is correct, Mr. Chairman. All of these consignees are subject to prosecution under 1462, and a great many of the districts had been awaiting the outcome of this case prior to authorization of prosecution.

Chairman KEFAUVER. I was interested in what happened to this girl, Ruby Tayfoia. She was in California?

Mr. BAIR. That is where she first met Mr. Solomon, out in Hollywood.

Chairman KEFAUVER. At that time she was just a teen-ager?

Mr. BAIR. Just 17 years old.

Chairman KEFAUVER. And they brought her back to Baltimore in the business there?

Mr. BAIR. That is correct.

Chairman KEFAUVER. What did these fellows do before they got into this business—do you know?

Mr. BAIR. We have no way of knowing that, Senator.

Chairman KEFAUVER. Doesn't Solomon have some record?

Mr. BAIR. In 1951 he was convicted in Los Angeles on the same type of charge. At that time he received 60 days suspended sentence and $200 fine. We know that he was also printing these photographs as early as 1949, but what he was doing prior to that we don't know.

Chairman KEFAUVER. After leaving Los Angeles he came to Baltimore?

Mr. BAIR. Yes; he came to Baltimore in May of 1952.

Chairman KEFAUVER. Didn't some of the girls who posed as models make some claims about not knowing what they were doing?

Mr. BAIR. Well, there is a little indication in the investigation that while they were posing for supposedly art pictures, there were two cameras focused on them—one that they didn't know about.

Chairman KEFAUVER. And they claim they didn't sign the release for some of the pictures, but they were used notwithstanding, or they didn't know what they were signing when they signed the release?

Mr. BAIR. I do not know, sir.

Chairman KEFAUVER. Thank you very much, Mr. Bair.

We appreciate the hard work that you have put in on this case, and the fact that you have stayed with it so long, and finally won your case.

As I said before, I think it had a very salutory effect throughout the Nation.

We will have about a 3-minute recess.
(A short recess was taken.)
Chairman KEFAUVER. Proceed, Mr. Bobo.
Mr. BOBO. Mr. Rubin.
(Abraham Rubin was sworn.)
Chairman KEFAUVER. Proceed, Mr. Bobo.

TESTIMONY OF ABRAHAM RUBIN, BROOKLYN, N. Y.

Mr. BOBO. You have counsel here with you?
Mr. RUBIN. Yes, sir.
Mr. BOBO. Will you identify yourself?
Mr. WEISS. Daniel S. Weiss, 15 East 40th Street.
Mr. BOBO. Will you state your full name and present address?
Mr. RUBIN. Abraham Rubin, 1639 41st Street, Brooklyn.
Chairman KEFAUVER. I didn't understand that.
Mr. RUBIN. Abraham Rubin.
Mr. BOBO. Have you also at other times been known by a different name?
Mr. RUBIN. I refuse to answer under the immunity provision of the fifth amendment of the Constitution.
Chairman KEFAUVER. Just a minute now. Do you plead immunity under the fifth amendment?
Mr. RUBIN. Yes, sir.
Chairman KEFAUVER. As we go along I will pass on whether the witness should be ordered to answer the question. I will have to order you to answer that question, Mr. Rubin. If you refuse to answer, just say, "I refuse to answer."
Mr. RUBIN. Thank you, sir.
Chairman KEFAUVER. But under the rules and for the record, questions are asked, and if you refuse to answer under the fifth amendment, if I think it is a proper question I will have to ask you to answer. You either answer or refuse to answer.
Proceed, Mr. Bobo.
Mr. BOBO. Have you furnished this subcommittee all the available records which were requested in the subpena issued to you?
Mr. RUBIN. I refuse to answer under the immunity of the provision of the fifth amendment of the Constitution.
Chairman KEFAUVER. The chairman directs you to answer, Mr. Rubin.
Mr. RUBIN. I refuse to answer under the immunity provision of the fifth amendment of the Constitution.
Mr. BOBO. In 1950 you had a reported income of $7,796.82; in 1951, $8,635.35; in 1952, $8,688.76; in 1953, $8,099.94; in 1954, $7,919.44.
On what basis did you arrive at these figures without producing records to show your income for those years?
Mr. RUBIN. I refuse to answer under the immunity provision of the fifth amendment of the Constitution.
Chairman KEFAUVER. The chairman directs you to answer the question.
Mr. RUBIN. I refuse to answer under the immunity provisions of the fifth amendment of the Constitution.
Chairman KEFAUVER. Mr. Weiss, to save time and with full understanding, if in answer to a question if he wishes to plead the fifth

amendment, it will be understood and we let the record make that clear, that if he says "I refuse to answer," we will understand that that is on the basis of the immunity provisions of the fifth amendment.

Mr. WEISS. That will save time.

Chairman KEFAUVER. Shall we also let the record show that I have ordered him to answer after he says "I refuse," unless it is some question that I feel should not be asked him, in which event I will so designate, so that will save a lot of time.

Mr. WEISS. I agree with you.

Chairman KEFAUVER. Very well. Let me ask this question. Would the witness give us any statement, or does counsel wish to give us any statement just what offense, or what law, the prosecution of which the witness may be afraid that he would be subject to in the event he answered?

Mr. WEISS. His answer will be the same, Senator.

Chairman KEFAUVER. His answer will be the same?

Mr. WEISS. Yes.

Mr. MARTIN. Is it a State or Federal offense?

Mr. WEISS. His answer will be the same.

Chairman KEFAUVER. Mr. Bobo, ask such pertinent questions as you wish to bring out.

Mr. BOBO. What kind of business are you engaged in, Mr. Rubin?

Mr. RUBIN. I refuse to answer.

Mr. BOBO. I cannot understand you.

Chairman KEFAUVER. He said he refused to answer.

Mr. BOBO. Are you the same Abraham Rubin that was arrested in Detroit, Mich., in 1953?

Mr. RUBIN. I refuse to answer.

Mr. BOBO. Is that a photograph that was taken of you at that time?

Mr. RUBIN. I refuse to answer.

Chairman KEFAUVER. Let the photograph be filed as an exhibit.

Mr. BOBO. Were the charges against you at that time possession of obscene literature?

Mr. RUBIN. I refuse to answer.

Chairman KEFAUVER. Hand him his whole record here. There is no use going over each one. This is the record that has been introduced in evidence as an exhibit here.

The question is: Is the photograph on top of it, and is this your record of arrests, convictions, or acquittal?

Mr. RUBIN. I refuse to answer.

Chairman KEFAUVER. Let it be filed.

Mr. BOBO. Mr. Rubin, isn't is true you are considered one of the major suppliers of pornography in the United States?

Mr. RUBIN. I refuse to answer.

Mr. BOBO. In the business in which you are engaged in, in how many States do you operate?

Mr. RUBIN. I refuse to answer.

Chairman KEFAUVER. Let this chart be inserted here.

Mr. BOBO. In the business in which you are engaged in, have you ever operated in the State of New York, Pennsylvania, Ohio, Indiana, Missouri, Kentucky, West Virginia, Virginia, and New Jersey?

Mr. RUBIN. I refuse to answer.

Mr. BOBO. Have you ever had any contacts with any persons in any of those States?

Mr. Rubin. I refuse to answer.
Mr. Bobo. Have you ever been arrested before?
Mr. Rubin. I refuse to answer.
Mr. Bobo. How long have you been associated either directly or indirectly with Eddie Mishkin in the pornography traffic?
Mr. Rubin. I refuse to answer.
Chairman Kefauver. Does he know Mr. Miskin?
Mr. Bobo. Do you know Mr. Mishkin?
Mr. Rubin. I refuse to answer.
Chairman Kefauver. Where were you born?
Mr. Rubin. I refuse to answer.
Mr. Bobo. What is your citizenship, Mr. Rubin?
Mr. Rubin. I refuse to answer.
Chairman Kefauver. How many children do you have?
Mr. Rubin. I refuse to answer.
Mr. Bobo. What is your present home address?
Mr. Rubin. I already gave it to you.
Mr. Bobo. What is your present telephone number?
Mr. Rubin. I refuse to answer.
Chairman Kefauver. Is your refusal to answer upon fear of bodily harm or reprisal?
Mr. Rubin. I refuse to answer.
Mr. Bobo. Do you know Frank Lano, of Chicago, Ill.?
Mr. Rubin. I refuse to answer.
Mr. Bobo. Have you ever done business with Mr. Lano in Chicago, Ill., or in New York City?
Mr. Rubin. I refuse to answer.
Mr. Bobo. Mr. Rubin, is it true that your business in pornography amounts to approximately $100,000 a year?
Mr. Rubin. I refuse to answer.
Mr. Bobo. How long have you known Mr. Lou Shomer?
Mr. Rubin. I refuse to answer.
Mr. Bobo. Have you ever done business with Mr. Shomer?
Mr. Rubin. I refuse to answer.
Mr. Bobo. How long have you been doing business with Mr. Arthur Herman Sobel?
Mr. Rubin. I refuse to answer.
Chairman Kefauver. The proper question would be does he know Mr. Sobel, and does he do any business with him.
Mr. Bobo. Do you know Mr. Sobel?
Mr. Rubin. I refuse to answer.
Mr. Bobo. Do you know Mr. Rotto?
Mr. Rubin. I refuse to answer.
Mr. Bobo. Have you ever done any business with him?
Mr. Rubin. I refuse to answer.
Mr. Bobo. Do you know Mr. Stanley Jablonski?
Mr. Rubin. I refuse to answer.
Mr. Bobo. Have you ever done any business with Mr. Jablonski?
Mr. Rubin. I refuse to answer.
Mr. Bobo. Do you know Mr. Morris Lowenstein?
Mr. Rubin. I refuse to answer.
Mr. Bobo. Have you ever done any business with him in Flint, Mich.?
Mr. Rubin. I refuse to answer.

Mr. Bobo. Do you know Mr. Lou Saxton, of Pittsburgh, Pa.?
Mr. Rubin. I refuse to answer.
Mr. Bobo. How long have you known Mr. Saxton?
Mr. Rubin. I refuse to answer.
Mr. Bobo. Isn't it true that you have made numerous large deliveries of pornographic material to the Bizon Co., in Detroit, Mich.?
Mr. Rubin. I refuse to answer.
Mr. Bobo. Isn't it true that you were the original printer and distributor for the "Fuller Brush Man" series of obscene comics?
Mr. Rubin. I refuse to answer.
Mr. Bobo. For how many years did you publish these comics?
Mr. Rubin. I refuse to answer.
Mr. Bobo. Can you explain how it is that your name and telephone number has been found in the address books of large dealers arrested over the country—dealers of pornography throughout the United States?
Mr. Rubin. I refuse to answer.
Mr. Bobo. Do you know Mr. E. Red Florence of Houston, Tex.?
Mr. Rubin. I refuse to answer.
Mr. Bobo. How long have you done business with Mr. Florence?
Mr. Rubin. I refuse to answer.
Mr. Bobo. Do you know Mr. George Fodor, of Washington, D. C.?
Mr. Rubin. I refuse to answer.
Mr. Bobo. For how long have you done business with Mr. Fodor?
Mr. Rubin. I refuse to answer.
Chairman Kefauver. The witness refuses to answer.
Mr. Rubin, in the scant records which you gave to the subcommittee, is a copy of a statement of expenses and other things prepared by Mr. Marvin R. Fullmer.
My question is: Will you identify this, or are you willing to identify it?
Mr. Rubin. I refuse to answer.
Chairman Kefauver. We will let the record be put in evidence as going with the questions which you refuse to answer.
(The information was marked "Exhibit No. 13," and is as follows:)

REVIEW OF INCOME TAX AND BANK STATEMENTS, 1950 THROUGH 1954

(By Marvin R. Fullmer)

Name: Abe Rubin, alias Al Stone.
Occupation: Wholesale trade, jewelry salesman, commission merchant.

Income tax

	Earnings	Tax paid
1950	$9,796.82	$1,059.80
1951	8,635.35	1,473.08
1952	8,688.76	1,613.50
1953	8,099.94	1,483.14
1954	7,919.44	1,332.06

Business figures

	Total receipts	Cost of mdse
1951	$13, 663. 00	$3, 996
1952	16, 429. 25	5, 737
1953	16, 371. 00	6, 348
1954	16, 820. 00	6, 145

How are these figures derived?
Receipts?
Bill of sale, etc.?
What is your basis of these figures?

Savings accounts

Greater New York Savings Bank: Present balance, $8,314.40. Opened December 7, 1945, Mary Gordon, in trust for Abraham Rubin. Opening deposit, $500.
Bay Ridge Savings Bank: Present balance, $5,362.37. Opened May 23, 1950, Mary G. Rubin or Abraham Rubin. Opening deposit, $350.

Checking account

The Public National Bank and Trust Co. of New York. Opened account October 29, 1951, $1,500 deposit.

Total deposits

1951	$6, 748
1952	9, 012
1953	5, 275
1954	6, 175

1954 expenditures taken from canceled checks

Auto, 5 months at $75	$375
Auto, 5 months at $106	530
12 house payments at $50	600
Income tax	1, 500
Martin Harris (insurance)	800
Standard Oil (car expenses)	250
Net savings, deposits	4, 072
City tax, etc	[1] 175
Telephone	[1] 75
Consolidated Edison	[1] 120
Total	8, 494

[1] Approximate.

Reported income, $7,919.
July 28, 1954, $3,102.32 deposit by check (payor unknown) in savings account, Bay Ridge Savings Bank.
Safe-deposit box: The Public National Bank and Trust Company of New York, vault, No. 332. In whose name?
Any other boxes, etc.?

Chairman KEFAUVER. One part of it is that you have a safety-deposit box, No. 332, at the Public National Bank and Trust Co. of New York. Is that in your name, or not?

Mr. RUBIN. I refuse to answer.

Chairman KEFAUVER. Very well, Mr. Rubin. Mr. Rubin, I will have to ask you to remain under continuing subpena in the event we want to call you back. In that event, you or Mr. Weiss will be notified.

I believe that is all for the time being.
Call the next witness, gentlemen.

Mr. BOBO. Mr. Andy Bruckner.

Chairman KEFAUVER. Is Mr. Bruckner here?

(There was no response.)
Mr. Bobo. Mr. George Fodor.

TESTIMONY OF GEORGE FODOR, ST. PETERSBURG, FLA.

(George Fodor was sworn.)
Chairman KEFAUVER. All right, Mr. Bobo. Proceed.
Mr. Bobo. Mr. Fodor, will you give us your full name and address?
Mr. Fodor. George Fodor, 3710 39th Street North, St. Petersburg.
Mr. Bobo. Do you also maintain a residence in Washington, D. C.?
Mr. Fodor. No, sir.
Mr. Bobo. Have you lived in Washington, D. C.?
Mr. Fodor. Yes; I did.
Mr. Bobo. When did you leave that city?
Mr. Fodor. Three and a half months ago.
Mr. Bobo. How are you employed, Mr. Fodor?
Mr. Fodor. What?
Mr. Bobo. How are you employed, what is your job?
Mr. Fodor. Working in a little store.
Mr. Bobo. Where were you born, Mr. Fodor?
Mr. Fodor. Warshaw, Rumania.
Mr. Bobo. Are you presently a United States citizen?
Mr. Fodor. Yes, sir.
Mr. Bobo. When you lived in Washington, D. C., how were you employed, Mr. Fodor?
Mr. Fodor. In the beginning or the end, or when?
Chairman KEFAUVER. Mr. Fodor, I cannot quite hear you. You are a big man; speak up.
Mr. Fodor. I will try, sir. When I started working, I worked at the J. Warehouse in Washington, D. C.
Mr. Bobo. Mr. Fodor, have ever dealt in pornographic material?
Mr. Fodor. Yes; I did.
Mr. Bobo. For how long a period did you sell pornography?
Mr. Fodor. Around 5 or 6 months.
Mr. Bobo. And where was this sold?
Mr. Fodor. In Washington, D. C.
Chairman KEFAUVER. When was this, Mr. Fodor; when were you in the business in Washington?
Mr. Fodor. I try to figure it out. I am very weak with the numbers memory. I guess in 3 years ago, or 2½ years ago.
Mr. Bobo. Three years ago?
Mr. Fodor. Yes, sir.
Mr. Bobo. What were the types of pornographic material handled by you, Mr. Fodor?
Mr. Fodor. I had films, comic books, and pictures.
Mr. Bobo. And from whom did you receive this pornographic material?
Mr. Fodor. Most of it I received from Mr. Dorfman.
Chairman KEFAUVER. I couldn't understand that.
Mr. Fodor. Most of it received from Mr. Dorfman, from Baltimore.
Mr. Bobo. D-o-r-f-m-a-n?
Mr. Fodor. Yes.
Mr. Bobo. Where did Mr. Dorfman live?
Mr. Fodor. In Baltimore some place. I don't know the address.

Chairman KEFAUVER. What is his first name?

Mr. FODOR. Ike.

Chairman KEFAUVER. Ike Dorfman?

Mr. FODOR. Yes, sir.

Chairman KEFAUVER. Isadore Dorfman, is it not?

Mr. FODOR. I don't know the name. Only I know Ike.

Mr. BOBO. Is Mr. Dorfman the only contact you had for pornographic material?

Mr. FODOR. No, sir. I had from Jacksonville, too.

Mr. BOBO. You got it from whom?

Mr. FODOR. Jacksonville.

Mr. BOBO. Jacksonville, Fla.?

Mr. FODOR. Yes.

Mr. BOBO. From whom did you buy it there, Stanley Jablonski?

Mr. FODOR. I don't know the name, sir.

Mr. BOBO. How would you buy it from the person in Jacksonville, Fla.?

Mr. FODOR. They brought to me. I brought in only once.

Mr. BOBO. They brought it to you?

Mr. FODOR. Yes, sir.

Mr. BOBO. In Washington, D. C.?

Mr. FODOR. Right, sir.

Mr. BOBO. How was the delivery made?

Mr. FODOR. He brought me with his car.

Mr. BOBO. He brought you his card?

Mr. FODOR. His car, his car.

Mr. BOBO. Do you know Edward Mishkin, M-i-s-h-k-i-n?

Mr. FODOR. I don't recognize his name, sir.

Mr. BOBO. Do you know anyone that goes by the name of Eddie, E-d-d-i-e, of New York City?

Mr. FODOR. No; if I know. If I see, maybe I know. But I don't know.

Mr. BOBO. Did you know Mr. Al Stone, or Mr. Abraham Rubin, of New York City?

Mr. FODOR. I saw just now here. That's all I know.

Mr. BOBO. That is the first time you have ever seen him?

Mr. FODOR. Yes.

Mr. BOBO. Have you seen Mr. Eddie Mishkin in the room today?

Mr. FODOR. Who?

Mr. BOBO. Mr. Eddie Mishkin.

(Mr. Fodor shakes head in negative.)

Mr. BOBO. Did you say you could recognize him if you saw him?

Mr. FODOR. I will try (looking through courtroom).

Mr. MARTIN. Is Mr. Mishkin in the room?

Mr. WEISS. I am his attorney. He is not coming up.

Mr. MARTIN. He is supposed to be in the courtroom here.

Mr. WEISS. He is here.

Chairman KEFAUVER. Sit down, Mr. Fodor.

Mr. BOBO. Who were your customers for pornographic material, Mr. Fodor?

Mr. FODOR. I had Mr. Chucoski.

Mr. BOBO. Is he the only person to whom you ever sold?

Mr. Fodor. No. I will tell you. Mr. Chucoski, Mr. King, Mr. Bannister.

Mr. Bobo. Where did they live, in Washington, D. C.?

Mr. Fodor. Yes; all Washington, D. C. Mr. Dockett.

Mr. Bobo. Did you ever make any trips to New York to purchase pornographic material?

Mr. Fodor. No.

Mr. Bobo. Do you know a Mr. Lou Shomer, S-h-o-m-e-r?

Mr. Fodor. If I see him, maybe I know him.

Mr. Bobo. Did you ever buy any materials from this man?

Mr. Fodor. I don't think so I did. I don't remember.

Mr. Bobo. Where would you make your purchases from Mr. Ike Dorfman, of Baltimore, Md.?

Mr. Fodor. I did; sometime he brought to me in Washington, D. C.

Mr. Bobo. What was the price that you paid for the materials you bought from him.

Mr. Fodor. Six cents I paid for the comic book.

Mr. Bobo. Six cents you paid for the comic book?

Mr. Fodor. Yes, sir

Mr. Bobo. How much did you sell them for?

Mr. Fodor. Ten cents.

Mr. Bobo. Did you deal in any other type of materials?

Mr. Fodor. Yes; films.

Mr. Bobo. Did you ever know where the films came from which you handled?

Mr. Fodor. No; I don't.

Mr. Bobo. You never manufactured or made any films yourself?

Mr. Fodor. No, sir.

Mr. Bobo. Did you rent a film to Mr. Philip Stone of Washington, D. C.

Mr. Fodor. Who?

Mr. Bobo. Mr. Phil Stone, of Washington, D. C.?

Mr. Fodor. I don't think so I ever heard that name. I heard mention this morning, I never give it up. I never sold, I never sold this Mr. Stone.

Mr. Bobo. Was the film that was confiscated at the Don Pallini Dance Studio in Washington, D. C.——

Mr. Fodor. What?

Mr. Bobo. Was the film that was confiscated taken by Inspector Blick of Washington from the Don Pallini Dance Studio your film?

Mr. Fodor. No, sir.

Mr. Bobo. You had not operated that film?

Mr. Fodor. I have no idea where is this dance studio, and I have no idea what was there, and I have no idea who is this man.

Mr. Bobo. Did you have a route serving approximately 300 customers for pornographic material?

Mr. Fodor. No, sir. Four.

Mr. Bobo. Four customers?

Mr. Fodor. That's right.

Mr. Bobo. What other type of business were you engaged in while you were selling pornography?

Mr. Fodor. No other venture. I had three——

Mr. Bobo. Did you sell school supplies to schools and drugstores?

Mr. Fodor. That's right. That is where I have 300 customers where I sold this; that's right.

Chairman Kefauver. You had 300 customers for your school supplies?

Mr. Fodor. That's right, sir.

Chairman Kefauver. Who were your four customers for pornography?

Mr. Fodor. Four.

Chairman Kefauver. Who were they?

Mr. Fodor. I just told you. Mr. Dockett, Mr. King, Mr. Chucoski, and Mr. Bannister.

Chairman Kefauver. Do you know their addresses?

Mr. Fodor. I did know. At that time I told to the inspector, and also to the FBI.

Mr. Bobo. Did you not have $30,000 worth of school supplies in your basement at the time of your arrest?

Mr. Fodor. No, sir.

Mr. Bobo. What was the value you placed upon your stock?·

Mr. Fodor. Six or seven thousand.

Mr. Bobo. Six or seven—what?

Mr. Fodor. Thousand.

Mr. Bobo. Six or seven thousand dollars?

Mr. Fodor. Between six and seven; yes, sir.

Chairman Kefauver. Do you remember just when you were in business, Mr. Fodor?

Mr. Fodor. I guess three, three and a half years ago.

Chairman Kefauver. What are you doing in Jacksonville now?

Mr. Fodor. I never was in Jacksonville, sir.

Chairman Kefauver. I mean in St. Petersburg?

Mr. Fodor. I try to do the same business what I had in Washington, D. C.—school supplies and notions and toys.

Chairman Kefauver. Anything else, Mr. Bobo?

Mr. Bobo. Did you have a total sales of $50,613 in 1954?

Mr. Fodor. In this paper, the income tax; yes.

Mr. Bobo. Was all that derived from your business?

Mr. Fodor. Yes, sir.

Mr. Bobo. School supply salesman?

Mr. Fodor. Correct.

Mr. Bobo. Of your $50,000 business in 1954, how much tax did you pay to the Government?

Mr. Fodor. I don't remember. You have the paper there.

Mr. Bobo. How much of this $50,613 represented pornographic literature?

Mr. Fodor. Nothing.

Chairman Kefauver. Mr. Fodor, I believe those are all the questions we have. Stay in the court room for a while this afternoon?

Mr. Fodor. Yes, sir.

Mr. Bobo. Mr. Eddie Mishkin.

Chairman Kefauver. Mr. Mishkin, I don't think you have been sworn, have you?

Mr. Mishkin. No, sir.

TESTIMONY OF EDDIE MISHKIN, YONKERS, N. Y.

(Eddie Mishkin was sworn.)

Chairman KEFAUVER. Let us get Mr. Mishkin's full name and address.

Mr. BOBO. Will you give us your full name and address?

Mr. MISHKIN. Edward Mishkin, 53 Algonquin Road, Yonkers, N. Y.

Chairman KEFAUVER. I didn't understand the road.

Mr. MISHKIN. Algonquin Road.

Chairman KEFAUVER. All right, Mr. Bobo.

Mr. BOBO. What are your businesses, Mr. Mishkin?

Mr. MISHKIN. I refuse to answer under the immunity provisions of the fifth amendment to the Constitution.

Chairman KEFAUVER. The chairman directs you to answer.

Mr. MISHKIN. I refuse to answer under the immunity provisions of the fifth amendment of the Constitution.

Chairman KEFAUVER. Mr. Weiss, can we have an agreement that in his refusal to answer, when he says "I refuse to answer," that it will be understood that it is under the immunity provision of the fifth amendment?

Mr. WEISS. Certainly.

Chairman KEFAUVER. And that after having refused to answer, that he is then directed to answer by the chairman.

Mr. WEISS. Yes, sir.

Chairman KEFAUVER. Proceed to the pertinent questions, Mr. Bobo.

Mr. BOBO. Mr. Mishkin, is it not true that you own the Times Square Book Bazaar, the Little Book Exchange, and the Kingsley Book Store, located in the Times Square area of New York City?

Mr. MISHKIN. I refuse to answer.

Mr. BOBO. Is it not true that part of your income is derived from the sales of pornographic material?

Mr. MISHKIN. I refuse to answer.

Mr. BOBO. Is it not true that your business amounts to approximately $1,500,000 a year?

Mr. MISHKIN. I refuse to answer.

Mr. BOBO. Did you not formerly operate the Harmony Book Store of New York City?

Mr. MISHKIN. I refuse to answer.

Mr. BOBO. Wasn't the Harmony Book Store, or is it not true that the Harmony Book Store was raided by the northern district attorney and over $50,000 of pornographic material seized?

Mr. MISHKIN. I refuse to answer.

Mr. BOBO. From whom did you receive the material that was confiscated in this rade?

Mr. MISHKIN. I refuse to answer.

Mr. BOBO. Confiscated in this raid were 2,600 volumes of Nights of Horrow. From whom did you receive these books?

Mr. MISHKIN. I refuse to answer.

Chairman KEFAUVER. Mr. Mishkin, what business are you in?

Mr. MISHKIN. I refuse to answer.

Chairman KEFAUVER. Are you in any ligitimate business?

Mr. MISHKIN. I refuse to answer.

Chairman KEFAUVER. Where were you born?

Mr. MISHKIN. I refuse to answer.

Mr. Bobo. Is it not true that you employed one Eugene Maletta to print copies of Nights of Horrow for you?

Mr. Mishkin. I refuse to answer.

Mr. Bobo. Did you furnish the plates to Eugene Maletta?

Mr. Mishkin. I refuse to answer.

Mr. Bobo. Did you furnish the money to Mr. Maletta to set up his printing shop?

Mr. Mishkin. I refuse to answer.

Mr. Bobo. How long have you done business with Mr. Eugene Maletta?

Mr. Mishkin. I refuse to answer.

Mr. Bobo. Did you ever give Mr. Maletta a check in payment for the work he did for you?

Mr. Mishkin. I refuse to answer.

Mr. Bobo. Did you pay him in cash?

Mr. Mishkin. I refuse to answer.

Mr. Bobo. What is the value in dollars of the pornographic material you have imported from foreign sources?

Mr. Mishkin. I refuse to answer.

Mr. Bobo. Do you import any pornographic material from foreign sources?

Mr. Mishkin. I refuse to answer.

Mr. Bobo. Have you ever made any buys from sources in Europe?

Mr. Mishkin. I refuse to answer.

Mr. Bobo. How much obscene material have you sold to Joe Carroll and Mr. Pellegrino, of New York City, during the past 2 years?

Mr. Mishkin. I refuse to answer.

Mr. Bobo. What types of material did you sell?

Mr. Mishkin. I refuse to answer.

Mr. Bobo. Have you ever stolen any material from other pornography dealers, copied what you wanted from it, and reproduced it for your own use?

Mr. Mishkin. I refuse to answer.

Mr. Bobo. Do you have any police record?

Mr. Mishkin. I refuse to answer.

Mr. Bobo. Do you have a man working for you by the name of Harry Revo?

Mr. Mishkin. I refuse to answer.

Mr. Bobo. Is this same Harry Revo that was arrested in Birmingham, Ala., with a load of pornographic material?

Mr. Mishkin. I refuse to answer.

Mr. Bobo. Did you not furnish Mr. Harry Revo and Johnny Melvin with this load of pornographic material?

Mr. Mishkin. I refuse to answer.

Mr. Bobo. Do you know Mr. Arthur Herman Sobel?

Mr. Mishkin. I refuse to answer.

Mr. Bobo. How much pornographic material have you sold Mr. Sobel during the past 5 years?

Mr. Mishkin. I refuse to answer.

Mr. Bobo. Do you know Mr. Lou Saxton, of Philadelphia?

Mr. Mishkin. I refuse to answer.

Mr. Bobo. And Pittsburgh, Pa.?

How much business have you done with Mr. Saxton?

Mr. Mishkin. I refuse to answer.

Mr. Bobo. Do you know Mr. Al Stone, alias Abraham Rubin?

Mr. Mishkin. I refuse to answer.

Mr. Bobo. For how long have you known Mr. Stone, alias Mr. Rubin?

Mr. Mishkin. I refuse to answer.

Mr. Bobo. Have you ever sold any pornographic material to Mr. Stone, alias Rubin?

Mr. Mishkin. I refuse to answer.

Mr. Bobo. Do you know Mr. Morris Gillman?

Mr. Mishkin. I refuse to answer.

Mr. Bobo. Have you ever done any business of any type with Mr. Gillman?

Mr. Mishkin. I refuse to answer.

Mr. Bobo. Have you ever sold any pornographic material on credit?

Mr. Mishkin. I refuse to answer.

Mr. Bobo. Do you know Mr. Lou Shomer, S-h-o-m-e-r?

Mr. Mishkin. I refuse to answer.

Mr. Bobo. Have you ever dealt with or lent money to Mr. Shomer?

Mr. Mishkin. I refuse to answer.

Mr. Bobo. Do you have any interest in the Times Square Book Bazaar?

Mr. Mishkin. I refuse to answer.

Mr. Bobo. In the Little Book Exchange?

Mr. Mishkin. I refuse to answer.

Mr. Bobo. In the Kingsley Book Store?

Mr. Mishkin. I refuse to answer.

Mr. Bobo. Do you have any interest in any other business in New York City?

Mr. Mishkin. I refuse to answer.

Chairman Kefauver. Any other questions, Mr. Bobo? We are not getting anywhere here. How old are you, Mr. Mishkin?

Mr. Mishkin. I refuse to answer.

Chairman Kefauver. Are you married—do you have a family?

Mr. Mishkin. I refuse to answer.

Chairman Kefauver. Mr. Mishkin, I will direct that you remain under subpena subject to the further call by this committee upon notification of you or your attorney, Mr. Weiss.

That is all now.

Who is our next witness, Mr. Bobo?

Mr. Bobo. Mr. Arthur Herman Sobel.

Chairman Kefauver. Mr. Bohrar, you gave your address and what not yesterday, did you not?

Mr. Bohrar. I did.

Chairman Kefauver. That is B-o-h-r-e-r?

Mr. Bohrar. B-o-h-r-a-r.

Chairman Kefauver. Let the record show that Mr. Bohrar is accompanying Mr. Sobel and is his attorney.

Does Mr. Sobel object to having the television cameras on?

Mr. Bohrar. He does.

Chairman Kefauver. Gentlemen, I will ask your cooperation. This is Mr. Arthur Herman Sobel. Is that correct, Mr. Bobo?

Mr. Bobo. That is correct.

Chairman Kefauver. I have not sworn you, have I?

Mr. Bohrar. Not yet. Mr. Sobel doesn't hear very well.

Chairman KEFAUVER. Mr. Sobel, you have not been sworn, have you?

Mr. SOBEL. No, sir.

TESTIMONY OF ARTHUR HERMAN SOBEL, NEW YORK, N. Y.

(Arthur Herman Sobel was sworn.)

Chairman KEFAUVER. Mr. Bobo, ask him in a loud voice so he can hear.

Mr. BOBO. Your name is Arthur Herman Sobel?

Mr. SOBEL. Right.

Mr. BOBO. Where do you live, Mr. Sobel?

Mr. SOBEL. 319 West 48th Street, Manhattan.

Mr. BOBO. That is Manhattan, New York?

Mr. SOBEL. That's right.

Mr. BOBO. How old are you?

Mr. SOBEL. Sixty-four.

Mr. BOBO. Mr. Sobel, have you ever been arrested before?

(Mr. Sobel confers with Mr. Bohrar.)

Mr. BOBO. Have you ever been arrested, Mr. Sobel?

Mr. SOBEL. I refuse to answer on the ground of incrimination, under section, fifth amendment.

Mr. BOBO. Were you arrested May 8——

Chairman KEFAUVER. Just a minute. Mr. Bohrar, is Mr. Sobel going to answer any questions?

Mr. BOHRAR. I don't think he will. In fact, I don't believe he will.

Chairman KEFAUVER. But you don't know for sure?

Mr. BOHRAR. I am certain.

Chairman KEFAUVER. Can we, then, Mr. Bohrar, have an understanding that when he says "I refuse to answer," that we will understand he is refusing to answer under the fifth amendment.

Mr. BOHRAR. He is invoking the fifth amendment.

Chairman KEFAUVER. And that as to each question he will be specifically directed to answer by the chairman of the committee.

Mr. BOHRAR. I understand.

Chairman KEFAUVER. Without formally directing him to answer.

Mr. BOHRAR. That is correct.

Chairman KEFAUVER. Proceed, Mr. Bobo.

Mr. BOBO. Were you arrested May 8, 1954, at Lincoln, R. I.

Mr. SOBEL. I refuse to answer on the fifth amendment.

Mr. BOHRAR. Just say you refuse to answer.

Mr. BOBO. Is it not true that the car you were driving contained a large amount of obscene literature when you were arrested at Lincoln, R. I.?

Chairman KEFAUVER. You refuse to answer?

Mr. SOBEL. Just a moment, your Honor. I would like to go into every detail about this particular case.

When I was arrested for speeding, they stopped me and they broke, the police broke into the car, for the reason because I had no proper license. They were registered under a name, Harold Kantor, to whom this car belonged.

They broke the lock of the car. They asked me for the keys of the trunk, a little suitcase about 2 by 1½, just about the size of the suitcase. They asked me whether I have the keys to the suitcase. I told them I have not. They searched me all over, even internally, to look for the keys, but they could not find the key. I don't know what's in there. It does not belong to me.

They broke the suitcase open. In the suitcase they found various literature, probably 10 books, or 10 rolls, or some pictures.

All in all, after I spoke to Mr. Kantor when he gave me the car to deliver some merchandise to a store out in Worcester, he told me the whole thing amounts to about $200, the entire thing, and that was actually what to my knowledge it would be worth, 10 books, 10 rolls, and a few other little things in it.

They arrested me. First they kept me overnight and they put me under $1,500 bail the first time, and about an hour later they raised my bail and put in another charge for transportation.

I got an attorney recommended from the barracks, and this man told me that he was going to charge me $100, and he got me a bondsman. I paid him the hundred.

Finally he told me he wants $2,000 to try the case. I thought he was only out for money; I engaged another man, but the judge will not let the release for that attorney, get another attorney, unless I pay this man $200 additional money, which I did.

A hearing was held. The troopers admitted that they broke into the car, they broke the lock, and they had all the evidence which they had right in that car. They had nothing on me whatsoever. I delivered the merchandise in Worcester, which I asked the man to let me have the car.

This man pleaded guilty, the same man who loaned me the car pleaded guilty in Federal court on January 5 for mailing and transportation of lewd literature. I don't know what happened to the sentence.

Chairman KEFAUVER. February 5 of this year?

Mr. SOBEL. This is a copy of the——

Chairman KEFAUVER. May I see that?

Mr. SOBEL. This is a copy of the pleading [handing to Chairman Kefauver].

This car belonged to this man.

Chairman KEFAUVER. You have given me, Mr. Sobel, United States District Court of the Southern District of New York, *United States of America* v. *Harold Kantor*, before the Hon. Lawrence E. Walsh, district judge, stenographer's minutes.

These minutes are where he pleaded guilty?

Mr. SOBEL. He pleaded guilty. You see, in this particular time, the case was on for about a year and a half.

This car was registered under his mother's name, which I found out later. He is the one who let me use the car. It was a 1937 Buick, that he paid $75 for it, and he let me use it. I never knew what he had in the back of that car.

Chairman KEFAUVER. Let me see if I understand this.

You had Mr. Kantor's car and he had some—who is Mr. Kantor?

Mr. SOBEL. Who is he?

Chairman KEFAUVER. Yes.

Mr. SOBEL. Well, a fellow that I knew, that he used to be in the chemical business. I never knew that he handled any of that stuff.

He happened to come up to the place on a Friday. When I told him that I have an order to deliver to Worcester, and I don't know how to get there, he says, "Why don't you use my car?"

With that, he gave me the keys and he told me he had some stuff in back which I don't need, and he let me use the car.

With that I went with that car. I didn't know nothing about it, what was in that car. There was nothing on me in any shape or form.

Chairman KEFAUVER. What was it you delivered at Worcester?

Mr. SOBEL. In Worcester, I delivered a magazine called Sunshine and Health, that was a decision last week in the Supreme Court that is legal to use the mail and sell it.

Chairman KEFAUVER. And so you delivered some Sunshine and Health at Worcester?

Mr. SOBEL. I don't hear.

Chairman KEFAUVER. You delivered a magazine Sunshine and Health at Worcester?

Mr. SOBEL. I sold it to a store up there. And the man gave me a check, which they found in my possession, and he told them what I sold him.

Chairman KEFAUVER. Then you went on to Providence?

Mr. SOBEL. Then I went to Providence. I was going to go to a race track on a Saturday, but it was raining so bad that I decided to go back to New York, which I was turning, going to New York. I never stopped—they check everybody in the whole vicinity. They found a list in the car and they called everyone of them when they found that, whether they ever heard of me or saw me or they knew me. No one said that they knew me.

Chairman KEFAUVER. What happened in the case in Rhode Island?

Mr. SOBEL. Here is what happened to the case: Originally I got a certain man——

Chairman KEFAUVER. Did they let you out, or did they convict you?

Mr. SOBEL. I got an attorney who told me that he will—there is nothing to it, that he is going to the Supreme Court instead of the district court; they had no right to break into the car; they had no right to search me, the stuff does not belong to me.

After dragging the case for about a year and paying him all the money that was due him, $1,000 that I agreed, he came down and he started to send me wires I should send him more money, 500, 500, which I didn't. And he saw that he couldn't get any more money out of me, he says, "The best thing for you in this particular case is for you to plead, whether no pros, it is not a conviction, you are letting the court to decide whether the decision in the case, and I will get a suspended sentence."

After I pleaded to that he sent me a wire back, which I have in my possession, I should send $1,000 fine, otherwise they can't do it.

I told him why not withdraw the case and go to court with it. Well, he says, "The best thing to do, I can't withdraw my claim," and that's what happened. They gave me $1,000 fine.

In other words, I was forced under duress, right in court, I told them I would like to withdraw my case and try the case, because I never had anything to do with it.

Chairman KEFAUVER. Anyway, you paid $1,000?

Mr. SOBEL. I paid $1,000 fine, and costs.

Chairman KEFAUVER. Where is Mr. Kantor now?

Mr. SOBEL. Mr. Kantor, I don't know where he is, but he is in—whether he was sentenced or not, I don't know.

Chairman KEFAUVER. Is he living now?

Mr. SOBEL. I don't know.

Chairman KEFAUVER. This transcript which shows about the car, will be filed as an exhibit here and not copied in the record, but filed as an exhibit.

(The document above referred to was marked "Exhibit No. 14," and is on file with the subcommittee.)

Mr. SOBEL. As a matter of fact, the lawyer had a——

Chairman KEFAUVER. How long were you in business in this Sunshine and Health magazine, Mr. Sobel?

Mr. SOBEL. About a year ago, in April, Dr. Boone came to me, I told him that if I can sell those magazines, and with that he gave me about 3,000 of them.

I knew that you can't sell them in New York—no; for a fact I had them quite awhile, but I didn't care to sell them in New York, for the reason that it was illegal to sell them on the newsstands, and I didn't want to handle them.

But he came down to me with a decision from a district court judge, admitting, getting an injunction against the postmaster. The United States court went and appealed the case to the court of appeals, and they upheld the decision of the district court.

Then the case went to the Supreme Court, it was last week or 2 weeks ago, and they refused to review the case, claiming this is not nudist.

Chairman KEFAUVER. The magazine you are talking about is called Sun Bathing; is that right?

Mr. SOBEL. Sun Bathing and—they have about 3 or 4 different magazines, but they are all on the similar, they have been printing them for the last 35 years, as I understood.

Chaiman KEFAUVER. How long were you in the business of handling these magazines?

Mr. SOBEL. Well, probably since that time, since about March or February or April 1954.

Chairman KEFAUVER. Who is this Dr. Boone that you talk about?

Mr. SOBEL. Where is Dr. Boone?

Chairman KEFAUVER. Well, who is he and where is he?

Mr. SOBEL. Well, he is in Jersey, Mays Landing. Under the name Nudist magazine, or something in that effect.

Chairman KEFAUVER. What is Dr. Boone's first name, do you know?

Mr. SOBEL. I don't know. He is the president of the company.

Chairman KEFAUVER. You are right, the Supreme Court did in its decision make some ruling in connection with some of these, with the Nudist magazine and Sun Bathing. Are you still in that business?

Mr. SOBEL. No, sir.

Chairman KEFAUVER. What is your regular business, sir?

Mr. SOBEL. My occupation now?

Chairman KEFAUVER. Yes.

Mr. SOBEL. Well, I sell various items, like perfume, which I have my own registered name. And I also sell various other novelty stuff, and so on.

Chairman KEFAUVER. Do you have a store?

Mr. SOBEL. No. I had quite an office, but being the publicity that came along, I had to curtail all my activities. I took just a mailing address, which I still maintain at the same place.

Chairman KEFAUVER. Where is your place of business?

Mr. SOBEL. 1133 Broadway.

Chairman KEFAUVER. What is the name of your business?

Mr. SOBEL. The name of the firm?

Chairman KEFAUVER. Yes.

Mr. SOBEL. Loki Co.

Chairman KEFAUVER. Along with your business, have you ever been in the business of selling pornography, distributing it?

Mr. SOBEL. No, sir. I had a factory on 11th Avenue for 5 years where I employed 400 people until 1949.

Chairman KEFAUVER. You had a factory in the——

Mr. SOBEL. Where I manufactured dolls and doll carriages.

Chairman KEFAUVER. You have perfume here, Loki, Paris of New York.

Mr. SOBEL. I am selling to various stores in New York, and Boston, and as a matter of fact in various other places.

Chairman KEFAUVER. You never have been in this film business?

Mr. SOBEL. No, sir; never did.

Chairman KEFAUVER. I don't see why you came here prepared to answer questions, then.

Mr. SOBEL. I don't know.

Chairman KEFAUVER. You haven't anything to hide?

Mr. SOBEL. I am charged with having in my possession $50,000 worth of merchandise. Evidently I should be worth at least $25,000, but my records, I have been sick in 1950 and 1951, I was operated in the hospital for about 3, 4 weeks, and I couldn't work after that. And then things didn't move along fairly well.

I started a few things. As a matter of fact, last year, in 1954, I had a firm that put up $15,000 to go in business with them, they financed me the deal in the perfume business, which I was working at until this thing came along.

Chairman KEFAUVER. This trouble in Rhode Island, is that the only trouble you ever had?

Mr. SOBEL. No, sir, never been in Rhode Island.

Chairman KEFAUVER. In Providence.

Mr. SOBEL. Providence; no. Well, I was in Providence, probably I used to go to the races now and then. And then I would go out and try to buy some jobs in jewelry, but I don't think I was down there more than twice or three times during my lifetime.

Chairman KEFAUVER. I said, this time you got arrested and where you paid a fine when you had Mr. Kantor's car, is that the only time you have been in trouble with the law?

Mr. SOBEL. I have been in trouble before with the law. I have been in trouble for a few other times. I have been in trouble for not renewing a license for a gun, which I went to Boston, I stayed there for a couple of years. When I come down here I brought them back the license and they say to me, "Well, technically you are not guilty; morally you are guilty," and they gave me a fine—no, a suspended sentence. But I showed them I had a license in Boston.

At the time I brought the gun back to the station house, to take that gun and hold it, if I will renew my license or not, I don't know. He says, "Take that check with you, and if the license will not be renewed, then you will bring it back."

As it came out, there was a fight in the street. They searched me and picked up the gun. They brought me back to the station, and they verified on it.

Chairman KEFAUVER. That was in 1930, possession of a revolver. You got a suspended sentence; is that it?

Mr. SOBEL. That's right.

Chairman KEFAUVER. I see in February 1934 you were charged with forging sweepstake tickets.

Mr. SOBEL. They weren't forged. As a matter of fact, I worked for the Government, for the Irish Government, a man by the name of Frisco employed me. I was getting at the time salary and expenses to work for him, for 2 years.

Chairman KEFAUVER. So that was a mistake.

Then October 1934, you got 3 months for gambling; did you not?

Mr. SOBEL. For gambling?

Chairman KEFAUVER. Yes.

Mr. SOBEL. That was the same charge. This is the same charge, gambling and possession of lottery tickets. That's what they charged for, possession of lottery tickets.

Chairman KEFAUVER. One seems to have been in February 1934, and the other seems to have been in October 1934.

Mr. SOBEL. No; it's wrong on that.

Chairman KEFAUVER. Then in July 1937, conspiring to transport stolen securities. What was that?

Mr. SOBEL. That was another case that has to be fully explained.

Just a moment, you fellows are laughing, but I will show you how justice was meted out in a United States court, which I have a copy of 1937 papers, where the papers came out, "Unusual procedure took place in Federal court," in two newspapers.

I had an attorney who died 3 days before the trial. It tells you everything right here. He died before the trial, and I wanted to get an adjournment, and the judge says, "No adjournment."

Butler objected to the adjournment, go on trial. And I had an attorney I just brought in for the day, and he appeared for me and he told the judge that the attorney died, which they knew, and they wanted an adjournment just to get the papers that my man, that my attorney had in his possession, because everything is locked on account of his death. They refused to give an adjournment.

Have you ever heard of it, like it?

Chairman KEFAUVER. If you want to file something here, we will make that an exhibit.

Mr. SOBEL. It is very interesting, what was done [handing document to Chairman Kefauver]. They promised me, after I refused; finally they coaxed me and threatened me with all kinds of threats. If I don't plead guilty I will get 10 years, or so many years.

As a result I pleaded guilty. The district attorney promised me I will get 3 months. Before, when it came up before the judge it came a year and a day.

But they claim here through my efforts, they bought $12,000 worth of stolen stock in my office, but the people who have robbed the bank, the president of the bank, and a brewery man, for $250,000, they got a suspended sentence. It is all on records. You can have this and read it.

Chairman KEFAUVER. Is all of that in here?

Mr. SOBEL. No; it doesn't say about them, but I know it. The papers said it. They got a suspended sentence, after robbing the public for a quarter of a million dollars.

Chairman KEFAUVER. You have given me a New Haven paper dated Tuesday, October 26, 1937.

Mr. SOBEL. That's right.

Chairman KEFAUVER. And this is the front page. It says:

STOCK THEFT "FENCE" GIVEN PRISON TERM

Herman Sobol, 49, New York City, alleged "fence" who is reported to have sold stolen securities at $18,000 to George Brott, former cashier of the East Hampton Bank & Trust Company of East Hampton, was sentenced to 1 year and a day.

What is that fence; I didn't know what that meant.

Mr. SOBEL. What's that?

Chairman KEFAUVER. What does the word "fence" mean in this story?

Mr. SOBEL. A "fence" would mean a receiver.

Chairman KEFAUVER. So they charged you with receiving the securities?

Mr. SOBEL. No. They charged me with selling them, for conspiracy to sell them. But I never sold any, nor have I ever bought any of them.

Chairman KEFAUVER. Let this be inserted in the record.

(The information was marked "Exhibit No. 15," and is as follows:)

[From the New Haven (Conn.) Evening Register, October 26, 1937]

STOCK THEFT "FENCE" GIVEN PRISON TERM—NEW YORKER ALSO FINED $2,000 BY FEDERAL COURT IN EAST HAMPTON BANK FRAUD

Herman Sobol, 49, New York City, alleged fence who is reported to have sold stolen securities at $18,000 to George Brott, former cashier of the East Hampton Bank & Trust Co. of East Hampton, was sentenced to 1 year and a day in the Federal Penitentiary at Lewisburg, Pa., by Judge Carrol C. Hincks in the United States district court today after he had entered a plea of guilty to a charge of conspiracy to transport stolen securities.

In addition to the penitentiary term, Sobol was fined $2,000, this to be paid before he is released from his sentence.

United States attorney Robert P. Butler informed the court that Sobol was 1 of 6 persons involved in the affairs of the defunct East Hampton bank. He said that Sobol was a fence who obtained 300 shares of Noranda Mines, Ltd. common stock valued at $18,000 in 1936 and sold them to Brott and one Harry E. Price of Hartford, for $1,200. These securities were later used by Brott as collateral to secure fake loans in the East Hampton bank, it was charged.

Mr. Butler said that when the affairs of the East Hampton Bank became known in 1936 an investigation revealed the stolen securities which were left as collateral for notes signed by Brott as cashier of the bank.

NAME FORGED

The stocks, Mr. Butler said, were stolen from the desk of R. Thornberry, an officer of the Nova Scotia Bank in New York. How they got into the hand of Sobol he said he did not know. The shares are issued in the name of William E. Cunningham, whose name was forged to the certificates.

Mr. Butler said that the person who forged the securities was known, but has not yet been apprehended. He said the man would probably be apprehended later.

Sobol appeared at first on a not guilty plea. He was represented by J. Michael Sullivan of New York City, prominent criminal lawyer, who asked the court for an adjournment of the case today declaring that he was called in at the last minute to represent Sobol when previous counsel died, and therefore had no time to prepare his case.

PLEA REFUSED

Mr. Butler objected to any adjournment declaring that he had witnesses present and that Sobol, up to 2 weeks ago, had employed David Paley. Judge Hincks turned down the plea for an adjournment and ordered Mr. Sullivan to proceed with the case. However, Mr. Sullivan said that the defendant would stand mute rather than go to trial unprepared.

Judge Hincks then asked if the defense counsel would desire a recess to inspect the indictment, and it was allowed. It was during the recess that Sobol decided to change his plea.

Bank Commission Walter Perry was among the spectators in court.

Mr. SOBEL. That's what happened in cases where you have no money to fight the cases and you are broke.

Chairman KEFAUVER. That was up in Connecticut in 1937, was it not?

Mr. SOBEL. That's the one; that's the case.

Chairman KEFAUVER. Now here in 1937 they have you charged with transporting stolen securities out in Pennsylvania.

Mr. SOBEL. This is the same identical case that you are referring to now. It happened, it took place—I was in New York. I was never in Connecticut. But the transaction took place in Connecticut. They had him indicted. Then they held me as a conspirator for selling it.

Chairman KEFAUVER. Did they try you down in Pennsylvania later, too?

Mr. SOBEL. No, sir.

Chairman KEFAUVER. Didn't you get charged down in Pennsylvania?

Mr. SOBEL. With what?

Chairman KEFAUVER. Didn't they make a charge against you in Pennsylvania?

Mr. SOBEL. No, sir.

Chairman KEFAUVER. Never had any trouble in Pennsylvania?

Mr. SOBEL. No, sir.

Chairman KEFAUVER. What is this July 1937, National Stolen Property Act?

Mr. SOBEL. What's that? National what?

Chairman KEFAUVER. National Stolen Property Act, 1 year and 1 day, and a $2,000 fine.

Mr. SOBEL. This is the same thing, right here.

Chairman KEFAUVER. Then this other thing was May 8, 1954, transporting obscene literature. That is the one you are talking about at Lincoln, R. I.?

Mr. SOBEL. That's right.

Chairman KEFAUVER. Mr. Bobo, do you have any questions you want to ask?

Mr. BOBO. I have a few questions, Mr. Chairman.

Did you ever sell any pornographic film to Mr. Harold Kantor?

Mr. SOBEL. No, sir.

Mr. BOBO. Did you ever have any business dealings other than this one time with Mr. Kantor?

Mr. Sobel. No, sir. Except about 2 or 3 years back, it was the alcoholic business in Jersey, and I had some deal with him trying to get some perfume out of him.

Mr. Bobo. Do you know a Mr. Fred Berson?

Mr. Sobel. Who?

Mr. Bobo. Fred Berson, B-e-r-s-o-n?

Mr. Sobel. No.

Mr. Bobo. You never approached or talked or did any type of business with Mr. Berson?

Mr. Sobel. Don't know him.

Chairman Kefauver. Have you ever done any business in Brooklyn?

Mr. Sobel. No, sir.

Mr. Bohrar. Did you hear the question? Did you ever do any business in Brooklyn?

Mr. Sobel. What kind of business?

Mr. Bobo. Have you ever done any business in Brooklyn?

Mr. Sobel. Well, I sold some merchandise up there, but I didn't sell any—except perfume, probably, or some other materials, like household goods.

Chairman Kefauver. Do you have some business with Delaware Wired Music Co. in Wilmington, Del.?

Mr. Sobel. No, sir.

Chairman Kefauver. Do you know that company?

Mr. Sobel. No; never heard of them.

Chairman Kefauver. You never heard of them?

Mr. Sobel. No, sir.

Chairman Kefauver. Would you make phone calls to there?

Mr. Sobel. Today?

Chairman Kefauver. No; to this Delaware Wired Music Co.?

Mr. Sobel. In Wilmington?

Chairman Kefauver. Yes.

Mr. Sobel. There were phone calls made by a fellow—if this is the fellow—who gives out information on races, and I think I had a fellow that was in my office—I mean, he used to come up occasionally—and told me he wants to make a few long distance calls. And I think those calls were made to Wilmington to get results on races, or something to that effect.

The same thing happened in Baltimore.

Chairman Kefauver. That is the Armstrong Sports Service in Baltimore?

Mr. Sobel. That's right. If he made the calls, I don't know anything about it. Whatever calls he made, he paid me for them.

Chairman Kefauver. Was that in connection with any bookmaking business?

Mr. Sobel. I don't know if he was connected, but he was using the phone. Probably a couple of times a week for about a month or so.

Chairman Kefauver. We have a long list of calls that you have made, and made back and forth to you, either by you or to you, from a whole bunch of what appear to be book stores or fun shops, and things of that sort. Do you know about those? I could name them off here to you.

Mr. Sobel. If you will ask me the names I will probably recollect and recall.

Chairman Kefauver. I will just hand you this memorandum and let you see it. Here are three pages of them [handing to Mr. Sobel].

Mr. Sobel. George Magic Store, I did call them a few times. As a matter of fact, I sold him some picture magazines, the same thing that I—I also had some stuff from a film out in Chicago. As a matter of fact, they are suing me for 2,000 books that they sent to me.

Chairman Kefauver. What kind of books were those?

Mr. Sobel. Those are picture books, just models, you know, nothing else but models. They are selling them right along, they are sending them through the mails. I have the name, the Magic—they have about three different titles. I have the papers, because Dun & Bradstreet were trying to serve me with a summons.

Chairman Kefauver. He is trying to sue you for books that he claims you have not paid for?

Mr. Sobel. What?

Chairman Kefauver. Is he trying to sue you for books he claims you have not paid for?

Mr. Sobel. That's right.

When this case came up to Providence, of course they teletyped it to the different stations here in New York. And when I got back on a Sunday morning, Monday morning the police were in my hotel and the manager let them in to search my room. I found out only about it 3 weeks later, 3 months later.

When I got back to the office on a Monday morning there were also police down there searching the rooms, the place of business. And they went away. But they did find in there the magazine that I got from Chicago. They also found the magazines that were from the Sunshine and Health.

They were there, and then they sent over the inspector. The inspector came back and took two of those books with him.

About a week later the same officers came in; they says they got orders from the inspector to take those books out, although they were laying in a corner all tightly packed.

They took them out and they took them to the property clerk. I was arraigned in special sessions court, and the case was dismissed. And still in this day I couldn't get——

Chairman Kefauver. You were buying books from somebody in Chicago, and he is trying to sue you. Did you buy a lot of books from him?

Mr. Sobel. Did I what?

Chairman Kefauver. Did you buy a lot of books from him?

Mr. Sobel. I bought, yes. But I told him, if it weren't for the fact——

Chairman Kefauver. Where did you buy books from, Mr. Sobel? Chicago and anywhere else?

Mr. Sobel. And those people here.

Chairman Kefauver. What people here?

Mr. Sobel. The Sunshine and Health, in Mays Landing.

Chairman Kefauver. What would you do with the books?

Mr. Sobel. They took the books away, and I never got them back.

So I reported to the property clerk to claim the books over there. They took it out of my place. Never offered to sell them, right here or any other place, except out of town.

Chairman KEFAUVER. Your counsel has a list there of 2 or 3 pages of fun shops where you called back and forth. What would all that be about? I don't want to go into the details.

Mr. SOBEL. This probably would be the Wilmington number. Hoboken number I don't know. Long Beach, St. Louis—that is one of the men that was in my office, Schlesser, calling St. Louis. Boston is Jack Goldberg. I was selling him perfume.

Philadelphia, Stanton Bernstein; I don't know him.

Jack Goldberg again in Boston.

Stone in Boston: I sold him a lot of perfume for a firm that I represented at the time, and I was working on a commission basis, and I probably called him a few times.

Stone Bros., they are on Hanover Street, this is the right address. I spoke to him a number of times.

Now, Irving, this is a man that I sold him magazines; he is a bookstore there.

Chairman KEFAUVER. Hand me back the book, please.

(Document returned to Chairman Kefauver.)

Chairman KEFAUVER. So those do represent some kind of calls back and forth about something, do they?

Mr. SOBEL. That's right.

Chairman KEFAUVER. Do you know Al Stone?

Mr. SOBEL. No; I don't know him.

Chairman KEFAUVER. Never saw him before?

Mr. SOBEL. No.

Chairman KEFAUVER. How about Mr. Mishkin, do you know him?

Mr. SOBEL. No; I don't know him either.

Chairman KEFAUVER. You have not had any business with Mr. Mishkin at all?

Mr. SOBEL. No, sir.

Chairman KEFAUVER. Do you know Mr. Rubinstein, of Brooklyn?

Mr. SOBEL. No, sir.

Chairman KEFAUVER. Who is Francis J. Pelletier?

Mr. SOBEL. Who?

Chairman KEFAUVER. Do you know Mr. Pelletier?

Mr. SOBEL. No, sir.

Chairman KEFAUVER. Mr. Bobo, anything else?

Mr. BOBO. No, sir.

Chairman KEFAUVER. We thank you for answering the questions. I think we got along a whole lot better than if you refused to answer. Don't you think so, Mr. Bohrar?.

Mr. BOHRAR. I think so. He did just exactly what he told me he wouldn't do.

Mr. SOBEL. If you people came and checked a picture, I couldn't hold out any more but tell the truth. This is actually the truth. It could be verified through the court over there, with my payment of the money, and the refusal to withdraw my plea after I gave the man all that money we agreed to, and I refused to go to court, after he had all the minutes written up.

Chairman KEFAUVER. Your experience with lawyers has not been very good, has it?

Mr. SOBEL. That's when you go through life, it happens.

Chairman KEFAUVER. I hope you don't get mixed up with these things any more.

Thank you, Mr. Sobel.

We will have about a 5-minute recess.

(Whereupon, a five-minute recess was taken.)

Chairman KEFAUVER. The subcommittee is glad to have a visit from Dr. Herbert C. Mayer, who is a distinguished former college president, who has given the subcommittee many worthwhile suggestions and helped us on several problems. We are glad to have you with us, Doctor.

Mr. Bobo, who is our next witness?

Mr. BOBO. Mr. Abe Rotto.

Mr. ROTTO. I object to the television.

Chairman KEFAUVER. I ask the cooperation of the press.

TESTIMONY OF ABE ROTTO, BROOKLYN, N. Y.

(Abe Rotto was sworn.).

Mr. LEVINE. I am H. Robert Levine, 154 Nassau Street, New York City.

Chairman KEFAUVER. You are Mr. Rotto's attorney, sir?

Mr. LEVINE. Yes; I am.

Chairman KEFAUVER. Proceed, Mr. Bobo.

Mr. BOBO. Your full name is Abe Rotto, R-o-t-t-o?

Mr. ROTTO. Yes, sir.

Mr. BOBO. What is your address, Mr. Rotto?

Mr. ROTTO. 55 Linden Boulevard, Brooklyn 26.

Mr. BOBO. In what business are you engaged?

Mr. ROTTO. At the present time I am selling novelties, pens, imported lighters, gadgets, balloons, various things for candy stores and small drugstores.

Mr. BOBO. Would you speak up, Mr. Rotto?

Mr. ROTTO. Yes, sir.

Mr. BOBO. From where do you conduct your business?

Mr. ROTTO. From 55 Linden Boulevard.

Mr. BOBO. Mr. Rotto, are you acquainted with a Mr. William Landers?

Mr. ROTTO. I refuse to answer under the immunity provisions of the fifth amendment.

Chairman KEFAUVER. Mr. Levine, I will direct the witness to answer questions that I wish answered. Can we let the record show that where he refuses to answer that he is directed to answer?

Mr. LEVINE. Yes; and that he refuses.

Chairman KEFAUVER. And that when he says he refuses to answer, we will have it understood that that is under the fifth amendment.

Mr. LEVINE. That is correct.

Mr. BOBO. Were you engaged in partnership with Mr. William Landers in the Landers Novelty Co., 220 Fifth Avenue, New York?

Mr. ROTTO. I refuse to answer under the immunity provisions of the fifth amendment.

Chairman KEFAUVER. We will let the record show what provision of the Constitution you are refusing to answer under. That is understood.

Mr. LEVINE. Yes.

Mr. ROTTO. Thank you.

Mr. BOBO. Do you know Mr. Ely Goldsmith of 1321 Nostrand Avenue, Brooklyn?

Mr. ROTTO. I refuse to answer.

Mr. BOBO. Were you arrested with Mr. Goldsmith on February 12, 1954, for the possession and sale of indecent books, films, and photos?

Mr. ROTTO. I refuse to answer.

Mr. BOBO. Were you released on $250 bail after this arrest?

Mr. ROTTO. I refuse to answer.

Chairman KEFAUVER. Mr. Bobo, do you have the police record?

For the record, the report on which you base your questions may be put in the record.

Mr. BOBO. Were you arrested on July 29, 1954, at 197 Clarkson Street for having in your possession indecent films, books and photos?

Mr. ROTTO. I refuse to answer.

Mr. BOBO. I hand you here a list of films and pornographic material and ask you is this a list of the material that was found in your possession as of that date [handing to Mr. Rotto]?

Mr. ROTTO. I refuse to answer.

Chairman KEFAUVER. Let it be put in the record to show on what the question was based.

(The document above referred to was marked "Exhibit No. 16," and is as follows:)

EXHIBIT No. 16

JULY 29, 1954.

At 11 : 30 a. m., July 29, 1954, Patrolman John Hayes, No. 9404, B H. B. P. S., assisted by Patrolman Ray Lamas, No. 7709, B. H. B. P. S., arrested one Abe Rotto, male, white, 61 years, United States, address 55 Linden Boulevard. (Arrest No. 342, 71st precinct) Charge No. 1, violation of section 1141 P. L. (indecent films, books, and photos). Charge No. 2, violation of section 1142 P. L. (contraceptives, "French ticklers") having had in his possession with intent to sell and stored in premises a store (first floor) 197 Clarkson Street (4-story brick, stores, and dwelling), owned by E. Miller, 197 Clarkson Street, second floor.

Following removed and held as evidence:

Film:	Rolls
8-mm. film (indecent photos)	230
16-mm. film	84

Griswald film splicer, R2–R43662	1
Mansfield film splicer, Model No. 950	1

Books and booklets:	Copies
Indecent books, Boudoir Secret	227
Indecent booklets:	
Lazy Lovers	316
The Honeymoon	130
Books:	
Weekend at Nudist Camp (price, $10 per copy)	201
Playing With a Mistress	60
Booklets:	
Various	103
Midnight Intimacies	18
Books, Affairs of Troubadore (price $25)	37

Books and booklets—Continued   *Copies*

Booklets:

	Copies
London Stage	38
Jaws of Fate	26
Erratic Professor	21
Hollywood in June	63
Various	1,130
Wedding Bells and others	740
Wally and the King and others	956

Photos:

Sets inuecent photos (25 photos per set)	29
Sets lewd photographs	12½
Sets of lewd postcards	4
Lewd photos	300
Decks lewd playing cards	450
Package pornographic poses	1
Slides, immoral poses	9
Pieces obscene objects	49
Obscene novelty pins	202
Contraceptives "French ticklers" (violation Public Law 1142)	183
Small suggestive telescopes	160

(Portion of film shown in presence of defendant at 71st precinct, who admitted ownership.)

Also defendant's auto, 1949 Pontiac, 4-door, license No. 6Y–8066 seized and held as evidence. Found in auto: 1 roll 8-mm. film and 1 roll 16-mm. film and miscellaneous cards and salesbooks.

Following present at scene: D. C. I. Goldberg, D. I. Bradley, Capt. William Fleig, Patrolman Robert Kirschmeier, No. 14250; Arthur Long, No. 4644; Alex Greenwald, No. 6650; Patrolman Nolan, legal bureau; Assistant District Attorney Gaza.

Mr. Bobo. Is it not true that you have been in the business of selling pornography since 1935?

Mr. Rotto. I refuse to answer.

Mr. Bobo. Do you know Mr. Al Stone, alias Abraham Rubin?

Mr. Rotto. I refuse to answer.

Mr. Bobo. Is it not true that you have been purchasing and distributing pornography from Mr. Al Rubin, Mr. Al Stone, alias Abraham Rubin, since 1945?

Mr. Rotto. I refuse to answer.

Mr. Bobo. Is it not true that Mr. Al Stone sold pornographic materials to you when you were in a partnership with William Landers?

Mr. Rotto. I refuse to answer.

Mr. Bobo. Is it not true that he also supplied you with pornographic materials at 197 Clarkson Street, Brooklyn, N. Y.?

Mr. Rotto. I refuse to answer.

Mr. Bobo. Is it not true that you refused to divulge the names of your suppliers of pornographic material because you feared bodily harm?

Mr. Rotto. I refuse to answer.

Mr. Bobo. Mr. Rotto, you are——

Chairman Kefauver. Mr. Rotto, are you refusing to answer any of these questions because of fear of retaliation, what might be done to you?

(Mr. Rotto confers with Mr. Levine.)

Mr. Rotto. I stand on my refusal, sir.

Chairman Kefauver. I did not understand. Are you in a business about which you can tell us at the present time?

Mr. Rotto. I told the counsel what business I am in.

Chairman Kefauver. How big a business is that?

Mr. Rotto. Very small, sir.

Chairman Kefauver. Do you sell just in your shop or do you get out on the street?

Mr. Rotto. I have no shop; I go out soliciting the business.

Chairman Kefauver. You go out what?

Mr. Rotto. I go out selling these items.

Chairman Kefauver. You go out selling the items about which you are talking?

Mr. Rotto. Yes.

Chairman Kefauver. Where do you sell them?

Mr. Rotto. I just got started; I just got a few, just a handful of customers I called on.

Chairman Kefauver. Do you sell in Brooklyn?

Mr. Rotto. Yes, sir.

Chairman Kefauver. On what street do you work?

Mr. Rotto. Wherever I can land, sir. No street. I am not a street-corner hawker, sir. I walk into a store and I try to sell the items that I have.

Chairman Kefauver. All right, Mr. Bobo; anything else?

Mr. Bobo. Have you ever been employed as a salesman for the Times Square Corp.?

Mr. Rotto. I refuse to answer.

Mr. Bobo. Have you ever received any telephone calls from Mr. Al Stone, alias Abraham Rubinstein?

Mr. Rotto. I refuse to answer.

Mr. Bobo. Do you know Edgar Maynard Levy, of Washington, D. C.?

Mr. Rotto. I refuse to answer.

Mr. Bobo. Have you ever done any business with Mr. Levy?

Mr. Rotto. I refuse to answer.

Chairman Kefauver. Well, Mr. Rotto, we will keep you under continuing subpena subject to further call of the committee, upon notice to you or your counsel, Mr. Levine. That is all now.

Mr. Rotto. Thank you, sir.

Chairman Kefauver. Call our next witness.

Mr. Bobo. Mr. Eugene Maletta.

Mr. Lazer. My client will object to the use of television.

TESTIMONY OF EUGENE MALETTA, RICHMOND HILL, N. Y.

(Mr. Maletta was sworn by the chairman.)

Chairman Kefauver. Mr. Maletta—by the way, what is your name, sir?

Mr. Lazer. Leon D. Lazer, 120–09 Liberty Avenue, Richmond Hill, N. Y.

Chairman Kefauver. Richmond Hill, N. Y.?

Mr. Lazer. Richmond Hill; yes, sir.

Chairman Kefauver. Mr. Maletta, what is your address?

Mr. Maletta. 188–29 120th Avenue, St. Albans, N. Y.

Chairman Kefauver. All right, Mr. Bobo. You ask Mr. Maletta your questions.

How old are you, sir?

Mr. Maletta. Twenty-eight.

Chairman Kefauver. Let me ask one or two questions.

Mr. BOBO. Yes.

Chairman KEFAUVER. Were you born here in New York?

Mr. MALETTA. Yes, sir.

Chairman KEFAUVER. Where did you go to school?

Mr. MALETTA. I don't want to get it in the papers.

Mr. LAZER. You have got to answer the questions.

Mr. MALETTA. I went to P. S. 62, P. S. 108. Then I went to Stuyvesant High School, and then to City. I finished school after I came out of the Army in Jamaica High School on Long Island.

Chairman KEFAUVER. Do you want to tell us what business you are in?

Mr. MALETTA. I am in the printing business, sir.

Chairman KEFAUVER. What is the name of your company?

Mr. MALETTA. Pilgrim Press.

Chairman KEFAUVER. 103-43 Lefferts Boulevard, Richmond Hill?

Mr. MALETTA. Yes, sir.

Chairman KEFAUVER. You started in this about 1950?

Mr. MALETTA. Yes, sir.

Chairman KEFAUVER. Is that a corporation?

Mr. MALETTA. No, sir; it is sole ownership.

Chairman KEFAUVER. How large a press is this?

Mr. MALETTA. I have a fairly large place, Senator.

Chairman KEFAUVER. How many people do you employ?

Mr. MALETTA. I employ three, sir, plus my wife who helps me out.

Chairman KEFAUVER. What do you print at this press?

Mr. MALETTA. We print any printing job at all, Senator, any type of printing. We do business cards, any type of printing that is called for in the normal course of an office work, or anything such as that.

Chairman KEFAUVER. Did you print Nights of Horror?

Mr. MALETTA. I refuse to answer that question under the fifth amendment, that it may tend to incriminate me, Senator.

Chairman KEFAUVER. I will have to direct you to answer it.

Mr. MALETTA. I would still have to refuse, Senator under the fifth amendment.

Chairman KEFAUVER. Can we understand, then, Mr. Lazer, that when the questions are asked, Mr. Maletta will be directed to answer.

Mr. LAZER. Yes; that is agreed to, Senator.

Chairman KEFAUVER. And if he refuses to answer we will understand that that is under the fifth amendment.

Mr. LAZER. That is agreed to.

Chairman KEFAUVER. All right, Mr. Bobo.

Mr. BOBO. Mr. Maletta, did you ever have in your possession plates used for printing Nights of Horror?

Mr. MALETTA. I refuse to answer.

Mr. BOBO. Mr. Maletta, have you ever been arrested?

Mr. MALETTA. I refuse to answer.

Mr. BOBO. It is not true that you were arrested in New York for printing and having in your possession obscene literature under the title of Nights of Horror?

Mr. MALETTA. I refuse to answer.

Mr. BOBO. Is it not true that the plates which you had in your possession were furnished to you by Mr. Eddie Mishkin?

Mr. MALETTA. I refuse to answer.

Chairman KEFAUVER. Do you know Mr. Eddie Mishkin?

Mr. MALETTA. I refuse to answer, Senator.

Chairman KEFAUVER. How large is this business of yours; what is your gross business a year?

Mr. MALETTA. Well, I don't have my tax forms; they have it. But I think last year I did—I am not sure, Senator; I mean, every day I do business. But I think I did about between thirty-five and forty thousand dollars. I am not sure exactly, Senator.

Chairman KEFAUVER. I understand that the reports you have given here show forty-odd-thousand dollars.

Mr. MALETTA. I will tell you the truth, all I did was sign the form. My accountant comes every month, and he does it.

Chairman KEFAUVER. Is Mr. Levine your regular lawyer—I mean Mr. Lazer?

Mr. LAZER. May I make a statement, Your Honor?

Chairman KEFAUVER. Yes.

Mr. LAZER. Rather, Senator. I represent Mr. Maletta in some, matters, and I don't in some other matters.

I think you might describe me as one of his lawyers.

Chairman KEFAUVER. All right. Thank you, sir.

Continue, Mr. Bobo.

Mr. BOBO. Mr. Maletta, when did you first begin in the printing business?

Mr. MALETTA. I first began in the printing business working for someone else, sir, after I came out of the Army.

Mr. BOBO. When did you first establish the Pilgrim Press?

Mr. MALETTA. I think 1950. I think I am in it 5 years.

Mr. BOBO. At that time what was your net worth, Mr. Maletta?

Mr. MALETTA. To start my business I borrowed money, to be exact.

Mr. BOBO. From whom did you borrow this money?

Mr. MALETTA. I borrowed money from my mother, and later on from banks to help increase the business.

Mr. BOBO. Have you ever borrowed any money from Mr. Eddie Mishkin?

Mr. MALETTA. I refuse to answer under the fifth amendment.

Mr. BOBO. What is your net worth as of today, Mr. Maletta?

Mr. MALETTA. I will estimate. I could not say exactly. I have about $35,000 worth of equipment and fixtures, plus stock.

Mr. BOBO. In the past 4 years you have purchased most of this equipment valued at approximately $35,000?

Mr. MALETTA. Yes, sir.

Mr. BOBO. Was all the income you derived from printing, stationery, business cards, and items of that type?

Mr. MALETTA. I refuse to answer this.

Mr. BOBO. Did anyone furnish you the money to purchase the equipment which you are now using?

Mr. MALETTA. No; no one furnished me with any money, except the banks. I did borrow from various banks.

Mr. BOBO. Mr. Maletta, have you ever printed any memo pads entitled "Things To Do Today"?

Mr. MALETTA. I refuse to answer.

Mr. BOBO. Did you ever sell any of these memo pads to Mr. Eddie Mishkin, or the Kingsley Book Store?

Mr. MALETTA. I refuse to answer.

Mr. BOBO. Did you buy an offset press at the figure of $5,000?

Mr. MALETTA. Yes. I bought it from Craig & O'Kane Corp.

Mr. BOBO. Did you receive any of the funds for purchasing this press, Mr. Eddie Mishkin?

Mr. MALETTA. I refuse to answer that.

Mr. BOBO. Is an offset press the type of press that uses plates to present printed matter?

Mr. MALETTA. If I interpret you, in other words, it uses plates to reproduce; and that's it.

Mr. BOBO. Have you ever printed any books or magazines of any type?

Mr. MALETTA. I have printed various books and literature.

Chairman KEFAUVER. Is it the Nights of Horror—do you know this Cosmo Boy—do you know the book Nights of Horoor?

Mr. MALETTA. I refuse to answer that.

Chairman KEFAUVER. Very well. I guess that is all, Mr. Maletta. We may want to call you back again, sir.

Mr. LAZER. We will hold ourselves ready.

Chairman KEFAUVER. I should say that a number of these witnesses plead the fifth amendment, all of these matters will be studied by the staff of the committee and submitted to the whole committee for such action as may be indicated.

I must say that personally I don't see the justification for the plea in answer to many of the questions that have been asked by counsel. We have had before us some people who the records show are substantial people in this pornographic business, Mr. Mishkin particularly, whose name appears as one of the big operators, the kingpins in the business, in a good part of the country.

I cannot say what will be the action on some of these pleas, but they will be presented to the committee, and my personal recommendation will be to the committee that the pleas are not justified in answer to a good many questions by counsel.

Who is our next witness?

Mr. BOBO. Mr. Lou Shomer.

TESTIMONY OF LOUIS SHOMER, BROOKLYN, N. Y.

(Mr. Shomer was sworn by the Chairman.)

Chairman KEFAUVER. You are counsel?

Mr. RACHSTEIN. Yes, sir. Jacob Rachstein, R-a-c-h-s-t-e-i-n.

Chairman KEFAUVER. What is your address, Mr. Rachstein?

Mr. RACHSTEIN. 280 Broadway, New York.

Chairman KEFAUVER. You are counsel here for Mr. Shomer?

Mr. RACHSTEIN. Yes, sir.

Chairman KEFAUVER. All right, Mr. Bobo.

Mr. BOBO. Would you give us your full name?

Mr. SHOMER. Louis Shomer.

Mr. BOBO. What is your present address, Mr. Shomer?

Mr. SHOMER. 1541 East Fifth Street, Brooklyn.

Mr. BOBO. Is that Brooklyn, N. Y.?

Mr. SHOMER. Yes, sir.

Mr. BOBO. Mr. Shomer, in what business are you engaged?

Mr. SHOMER. In the real-estate business.

Mr. BOBO. Would you speak up so I can hear you?

Mr. SHOMER. I am in the real-estate business.

Mr. Bobo. Mr. Shomer, have you ever been engaged in handling pornographic materials?

Mr. Shomer. Yes, sir.

Mr. Bobo. In what type of pornographic materials have you dealt?

Mr. Shomer. I took photographs, improper photographs.

Mr. Bobo. You took improper photographs?

Mr. Shomer. Yes, sir.

Mr. Bobo. Showing obscene acts and perversion?

Mr. Shomer. Yes, sir.

Mr. Bobo. When were you engaged in this business?

Mr. Shomer. Before the war.

Mr. Bobo. What year was that?

Mr. Shomer. 1940, I believe.

Mr. Bobo. To whom did you sell these photographs which you took?

Mr. Shomer. I didn't sell any photographs. I just took the photographs. I was a photographer.

Mr. Bobo. I can't hear you, Mr. Shomer.

Mr. Shomer. I didn't sell these photographs; I just did the photography.

Mr. Bobo. For whom did you work?

Mr. Shomer. For Jack Brotman.

Chairman Kefauver. I did not understand you.

Mr. Shomer. Jack Brotman.

Chairman Kefauver. How do you spell the last name?

Mr. Shomer. B-r-o-t-m-a-n.

Chairman Kefauver. Where does he live; where is he?

Mr. Shomer. I don't know, sir.

Chairman Kefauver. You don't know?

Mr. Shomer. No, sir. I haven't seen him since then.

Mr. Bobo. Did that take place in New York City?

Mr. Shomer. Yes, sir.

Mr. Bobo. Mr. Shomer, have you ever been arrested?

Mr. Shomer. I was arrested then.

Mr. Bobo. What sentence did you receive?

Mr. Shomer. I was sentenced to the city prison.

Mr. Bobo. Have you ever been arrested since that time?

Mr. Shomer. Once.

Mr. Bobo. What were you arrested for then?

Mr. Shomer. I don't remember the charge, but it was possession of indecent or improper literature, possession, and transportation.

Mr. Bobo. Where did that arrest take place?

Mr. Shomer. In Portsmouth.

Mr. Bobo. Portsmouth, Maine?

Mr. Shomar. No. Portsmouth, Va.

Mr. Bobo. At that time what type of pornographic material did you have in your possession?

Mr. Shomer. I didn't have it in my possession. I was accompanying a friend, and he was riding down to Florida. He had some trouble with the car then, and he was arrested and I was with him.

Mr. Bobo. Do you know from whom your friend received the pornographic material he had in the car?

Mr. Shomer. No, sir.

Mr. BOBO. What is the name of your friend that was arrested with you?

Mr. SHOMER. Ben Riceburg.

Mr. BOBO. How do you spell that?

Mr. SHOMER. R-i-c-e-b-u-r-g.

Mr. BOBO. R-i-c-e-b-u-r-g?

Mr. SHOMER. I think so.

Mr. BOBO. Where does Mr. Riceburg live?

Mr. SHOMER. Somewhere in New York. I don't see him.

Mr. BOBO. You have not seen him since the time you were arrested?

Mr. SHOMER. No; I saw him once last year.

Mr. BOBO. What was his address at the time you were arrested?

Mr. SHOMER. I don't remember.

Mr. BOBO. Mr. Shomer, have you ever had any dealings, or do you know Mr. Ike or Isadore Dorfman, of Baltimore, Md.?

Mr. SHOMER. No, sir.

Mr. BOBO. Haven't you ever met, or didn't you in fact, in 1953, meet Mr. Dorfman and George Fodor in Washington, D. C.?

Mr. SHOMER. No, sir.

Mr. BOBO. Did you meet these two people in Brooklyn, N. Y.?

Mr. SHOMER. No, sir.

Mr. BOBO. Have you had any business dealings at all with Mr. Isadore Dorfman and Mr. George Fodor?

Mr. SHOMER. No, sir.

Mr. BOBO. Do you know where the Brooklyn Navy is?

Mr. SHOMER. Yes, sir.

Mr. BOBO. Did you not in 1953 meet with Mr. Ike Dorfman and Mr. George Fodor in the company of a man named Ben?

Mr. SHOMER. No, sir.

Mr. BOBO. Do you know Edgar Maynard Levy of Washington, D. C.?

Mr. SHOMER. No, sir.

Mr. BOBO. You have never had any business dealings with Edgar Maynard Levy?

Mr. SHOMER. No, sir.

Mr. CHUMBRIS. He formerly lived on Tinker Drive on Long Island. Chairman KEFAUVER. You don't know him?

Mr. SHOMER. No, sir.

Mr. BOBO. Do you know Mr. Eddie Mishkin?

Mr. SHOMER. No, sir.

Mr. BOBO. Have you ever had any business dealings at all with the Kingsley Book Store?

Mr. SHOMER. No, sir.

Mr. BOBO. Or the Times Square Corp.?

Mr. SHOMER. No, sir.

Mr. BOBO. Have you ever had any, or do you know Mr. Al Stone?

Mr. SHOMER. No, sir.

Mr. BOBO. Have you ever had any business dealings with Mr. Al Stone, alias Abe Rubin?

Mr. SHOMER. No, sir.

Mr. BOBO. Mr. Shomer, do you have the original records which were called for in your subpena?

Mr. SHOMER. Yes, sir, I have everything.

Mr. Bobo. Do you have those where they could be presented to the subcommittee?

Mr. Shomer. Yes, sir.

Mr. Bobo. What was your income for the year 1954?

Mr. Shomer. I have the records here, sir.

Chairman Kefauver. Well, about how much was it?

Mr. Shomer. About eight or nine thousand. It's a joint income, sir.

Mr. Bobo. Joint income of you and your wife?

Mr. Shomer. Yes, sir.

Mr. Bobo. In the business in which you are engaged, what was the gross business which you did?

Mr. Shomer. Which business do you mean, sir? The real estate business?

Mr. Bobo. The real estate business.

Mr. Shomer. I have just gone into it in the last 2 months.

Chairman Kefauver. You have gotten out of the other and gone into this; is that right?

Mr. Shomer. I have been out of business now since 1947. I had a publishing business, and my health failed, and I had to give it up. The business was on its way down.

Chairman Kefauver. Didn't you write some books and some articles?

Mr. Shomer. I used to write the Laugh Library at that time, publisher. It was distributed nationally on the newsstands.

Chairman Kefauver. When you would make these pictures, to whom did you sell them?

Mr. Shomer. I didn't sell them; I just did the photography for someone else.

Chairman Kefauver. Someone else would furnish you the models and the equipment and you would make the pictures?

Mr. Shomer. No. The party that I worked for subsequently was arrested, we all were arrested, and his conviction, because he opened up on everyone. I was just the employee.

Mr. Bobo. Do you know Mr. Harry Kunkelman?

Mr. Shomer. No, sir.

Mr. Bobo. Cleveland, Ohio?

Mr. Shomer. No, sir.

Mr. Bobo. Akron, Ohio?

Mr. Shomer. No, sir.

Mr. Bobo. You have never sold or dealt in any motion-picture film with Mr. Kunkelman?

Mr. Shomer. No, sir.

Mr. Bobo. Have you ever received any negatives from Mr. Kunkelman or transferred any negatives to him?

Mr. Shomer. No, sir.

Chairman Kefauver. Mr. Shomer, we don't want to get you in any trouble here, but we have a lengthy letter from the captain of detectives out at Akron, saying that they had Harry Kunkelman before them and he received a great deal of films, from their investigation, and that Mr. Kunkelman's statement was that one of the principal sources of this material was from you.

Mr. Shomer. That's not true, sir.

Chairman Kefauver. You don't think that is true?

Mr. Shomer. I know it is not.

Chairman KEFAUVER. You never shipped any out to Akron?

Mr. SHOMER. Never, sir.

Chairman KEFAUVER. You don't know Mr. Kunkelman?

Mr. SHOMER. No, sir.

Chairman KEFAUVER. You don't know this man Harry Kunkelman at all?

Mr. SHOMER. No, sir.

Chairman KEFAUVER. How much material of pornographic nature was in this automobile in which you were riding with your friend in Portsmouth, Va.?

Mr. SHOMER. There were several packages, but I don't know how much.

Chairman KEFAUVER. You mean several big packages?

Mr. SHOMER. I really don't know.

Chairman KEFAUVER. Where was he taking it, to Florida?

Mr. SHOMER. I really wouldn't know.

Chairman KEFAUVER. You were riding with him. To where did you start out?

Mr. SHOMER. We left from Brooklyn.

Chairman KEFAUVER. And where were you going to?

Mr. SHOMER. We were going to Florida.

Mr. CHUMBRIS. Where in Florida?

Mr. SHOMER. Miami.

Mr. CHUMBRIS. Who to in Miami?

Mr. SHOMER. I wouldn't know.

Mr. CHUMBRIS. Where did you finally end up?

Mr. SHOMER. Portsmouth. In jail.

Mr. BOBO. Did your friend make any stops between Newark and Portsmouth, Va., and drop off any pornographic literature or anything in his car?

Mr. SHOMER. No, sir.

Mr. BOBO. Neither you nor he stopped at any place?

Mr. SHOMER. No, sir.

Mr. BOBO. Have you ever been in Port Chester, N. Y., Mr. Shomer?

Mr. SHOMER. Where?

Mr. BOBO. Port Chester, N. Y.

Mr. SHOMER. No, sir.

Mr. BOBO. You never have met Mr. Edgar Maynard Levy in Port Chester, N. Y., and transferred to him large quantities of pornographic material?

Mr. SHOMER. Never.

Chairman KEFAUVER. All right, Mr. Shomer. If we want you again, we will get in touch with Mr. Rachstein.

Mr. BOBO. I have just one more question, Senator, if I may.

Chairman KEFAUVER. All right.

Mr. BOBO. During the past month, from April through May 15, you have deposited in the bank some $16,733.20.

Mr. SHOMER. Yes, sir.

Mr. BOBO. Was that all derived from what source?

Mr. SHOMER. When I sold the large book company I had about $25,000 or $30,000, and I got about $10,000 for the large book company. Then I sold my house, I got $11,000 out of that.

Mr. BOBO. When did you sell your book company?

Mr. SHOMER. I sold that to——

Mr. BOBO. When?

Mr. SHOMER. In 1947.

Mr. BOBO. This is April 4, 1955, we were speaking of, March 29, 1955, through April 2, 1955.

Mr. SHOMER. Yes, sir. Now may I have the question again, please?

Mr. BOBO. From what source did you derive the $16,733.20?

Mr. SHOMER. I have the money at my broker's. I ordered the money from my broker. I got a $10,000 check and a $2,000 check from my broker.

Mr. BOBO. Who is your broker?

Mr. SHOMER. Barron G. Helbig & Co.

Mr. BOBO. Do you know Mr. Gennaio Di Napoli and Mr. Ralph Ardolina?

Mr. SHOMER. Yes, sir.

Mr. BOBO. You paid them on March 31, 1955, $4,000?

Mr. SHOMER. That's right.

Mr. BOBO. What was that payment for, sir?

Mr. SHOMER. That's a contract on a house on East Second Street, 1714. The closing will be the end of July, July 28, I believe—June 28.

Mr. BOBO. And your average income, according to your bank deposits, is some $2,000 a week from March 29 to April 2?

Mr. SHOMER. Bank deposit?

Mr. BOBO. Yes.

Mr. SHOMER. I have no bank deposit.

Mr. BOBO. In the National City Bank of New York City.

Mr. SHOMER. It is a bank account I just opened up to do the real estate business. Whenever I need any money I get it from the broker. I didn't have any prior bank accounts. I would sell some stock and get what I need.

Mr. BOBO. March 29 to April 2, April 4, 6 days, you had transactions involving $16,733.20?

Mr. SHOMER. Yes, sir. I have the contracts here.

Chairman KEFAUVER. All right, Mr. Shomer. Thank you.

Mr. RACHSTEIN. Your Honor, is his checkbook available, by any chance?

Chairman KEFAUVER. Can we return it to him, Mr. Bobo?

Mr. BOBO. Yes [handing].

Mr. RACHSTEIN. Thank you very much, Your Honor.

Chairman KEFAUVER. Since being here we have received a good many letters from people expressing interest in the hearing. I am particularly interested to receive one letter today postmarked Brooklyn, May 25. It says:

DEAR SIR: This is an unsolicited advertisement received by a 16-year-old high-school boy.
Sincerely,

AN ANXIOUS MOTHER.

The advertisement apparently came in this envelope [exhibiting], Atine Co., 631 Third Avenue, New York City. The advertisement will speak for itself. I am going to put the advertisement soliciting, trying to sell movies, nude pictures, various and sundry kinds of things, in the record. This will be made part of the files.

(The matter above referred to was marked "Exhibit No. 17," and is on file with the subcommittee.)

Chairman KEFAUVER. Maybe some of the press would like to see what is being sent out through the mails.

The other witnesses that we have subpenaed, and some others, will be asked to come back next Tuesday, the 31st. Our hearing that morning will begin sharply at 10 o'clock.

We stand in recess until next Tuesday.

(Whereupon, at 4 : 30 p. m., the subcommittee recessed until 10 a. m., Tuesday, May 31, 1955.)

JUVENILE DELINQUENCY

(Obscene and Pornographic Materials)

TUESDAY, MAY 31, 1955

UNITED STATES SENATE,
SUBCOMMITTEE OF THE COMMITTEE ON THE JUDICIARY,
TO INVESTIGATE JUVENILE DELINQUENCY,
New York, N. Y.

The subcommittee met, pursuant to adjournment, at 10:20 a. m., in room 1703, United States Court House, Foley Square, New York City, N. Y., Senator Estes Kefauver, chairman, presiding.

Present: Senators Estes Kefauver and William Langer.

Also present: Peter N. Chumbris, associate counsel; Vincent Gaughan, special counsel; George Butler, investigator; George Martin, investigator; Pat Kiley, investigator, and William Haddad, consultant.

Chairman KEFAUVER. As chairman of the subcommittee, I want to apologize for being late this morning; although I left Washington in ample time, my plane had some difficulty in landing and also finding a place to put out the airport—the traffic was pretty bad, too.

We are awfully glad to have Senator Langer with us again this morning at this hearing.

Today the subcommittee is holding its third hearing on pornographic material and its tie-in to juvenile delinquency.

At our first meeting last Tuesday, several witnesses established the correlation between pornographic material and juvenile delinquency, which I think most of us understood, anyway.

Dr. Karpman, for instance, the famous criminologist, said that he was convinced that the distribution of these materials among youngsters in many cases led to unnatural sex practices and to juvenile delinquency.

Father Egan and others testified that they had noticed a definite increase in the use of these materials by youngsters.

On Thursday the pattern of sale and distribution of these materials was established. Pornography was shown to be "big business" with tentacles in almost every community in the Nation.

The members of the subcommittee were shocked to learn that children as young as 3 and 4 years old were being used in making pornographic films. Although this low age bracket is the singular case, it was established that boys and girls in their upper teens, not only see these films, but actually engage in their manufacture and sale. In most cases these children are being exploited by unscrupulous adults.

On Thursday several witnesses saw fit to avail themselves of the self-incriminations of the fifth amendment. I feel that all of these witnesses were unjustified in refusing to answer some of the ques-

185

tions and, as I stated at the time, my recommendation would be that they be proceeded against for contempt of the Senate.

Today we are recalling some of these witnesses for additional questions. Several portions of their testimony are in need of clarification. If they see fit, they can use this opportunity to cooperate with the committee, and that will be taken into consideration.

Senator LANGER. I say, Mr. Chairman, you have unanimous support in your attitude as to those pleading the fifth amendment.

Chairman KEFAUVER. Thank you, Senator Langer. I am certain that the other members of the committee will feel that they were unjustified in refusing to testify and answer some of the questions.

In our hearings last week we saw that the pornography business operates partially, at least, because of loopholes in the Federal law to curtail distribution of these materials.

In addition, widespread use of pornography exists because of inadequate local and State laws. I sincerely hope that every community will evaluate its own pornography laws and possibly revamp them in the light of information extracted at these hearings.

Any community that desires the help of the staff of the subcommittee or of the subcommittee need only to write and we will assist them in any way possible.

I am glad to say that there is a communication and a contact between the members of this staff and many legislators and enforcement officials throughout the country.

Of course, in the final analysis the attitude of the public will be what will determine whether this business is going to be stamped out or not.

We have had witnesses who have testified as to the seriousness of this problem, one, that they think this is more serious than communism; others think that it is more serious than narcotics. In any event, we do think the hearings have brought out that it is of more sinister influence than most people have thought.

Today we will hear from postal and customs officials about their problems in curtailing the distribution of pornography; we will also hear from subpenaed witnesses who are allegedly engaged in the sale, distribution, and manufacture of pornographic materials.

By cooperating with this subcommittee these witnesses can help wipe out this hideous business that preys like a vulture upon many of our innocent children.

Senator Langer, do you wish to make any statement before we call our first witness?

Senator LANGER. No, Mr. Chairman.

Chairman KEFAUVER. Mr. Chumbris, our associate counsel, will conduct the examinations today. Mr. Bobo had another assignment he had to begin this morning.

Mr. Chumbris, who is our first witness?

Mr. CHUMBRIS. Samuel Roth.

Chairman KEFAUVER. Mr. Roth, will you come around, sir?

Do you solemnly swear the testimony you will give this committee will be the whole truth, and nothing but the truth, so help you God?

Mr. ROTH. Yes, sir.

TESTIMONY OF SAMUEL ROTH, NEW YORK, N. Y.

Mr. CHUMBRIS. Mr. Roth, will you please state your name and address?

Mr. ROTH. My name is Samuel Roth. My address is 110 Lafayette Street, New York City.

Mr. CHUMBRIS. And what is your occupation?

Mr. ROTH. I both write and publish books.

Mr. CHUMBRIS. For how long a period of time have you been writing and publishing books?

Mr. ROTH. About 38 years.

Mr. CHUMBRIS. How long have you been at that location at 110 Lafayette Street?

Mr. ROTH. About 5 years.

Mr. CHUMBRIS. Would you please state the names of some of the books that you publish?

Mr. ROTH. Before I do I have two very short statements I wish to make to the committee that may save it a great deal of trouble and time. May I?

Chairman KEFAUVER. All right, Mr. Roth.

Mr. ROTH. Thank you.

Chairman KEFAUVER. Providing you will talk a little bit louder.

Mr. ROTH. During my brief appearance before this committee last year I read a statement written by my attorney, Mr. Nicholas Atlas.

Chairman KEFAUVER. What is his name?

Mr. ROTH. Nicholas Atlas.

Chairman KEFAUVER. All right.

Mr. ROTH. This statement apprised the committee that I was under indictment in two courts, and it cited a United States Supreme Court decision that in effect establishes the immunity of all evidence offered by a witness before a congressional committee from use in any action against him in any other court.

Upon my concluding the reading of the statement, Senator Hendrickson accused me of pleading the fifth amendment.

I want it to be established in the record that this is not so. I believe in the fifth amendment, but I know that it will be at least 50 years before an honest man will be able to plead it without being misunderstood.

It is my stand before this committee that I have a right to the protection granted me under the above-mentioned United States Supreme Court ruling, but that I will happily answer the questions of the committee if I am ordered to do so.

Chairman KEFAUVER. We are glad to have your statement, Mr. Roth.

Mr. ROTH. I have one more, and I wish to read that.

Chairman KEFAUVER. Very well, sir.

Mr. ROTH. If this committee is limited to an inquiry into the causes of juvenile delinquency in our midst, it is going far off its course in questioning me. With the single exception of a book of instruction for children, entitled "Tina and Jimmy Learn How They Were Born," written by my daughter for the instruction of her own children. I have never published or advertised a book an adolescent would bother to read. I have never offered books to juveniles, and refused to serve them whenever they were so identified in my mails.

Sensational as my advertising appears to the eye, it can hardly be of interest to any but people sophisticated enough to resist my verbal charm.

I don't think this committee has reached the heart of the problem of juvenile delinquency. Father Egan only suggested it when he testified before this committee on its first hearings that there is no more smut in circulation today than in previous periods; it is just that the juveniles of our time have no respect for the religion of their elders. This goes to high office as well as to the home.

Chairman KEFAUVER. Anything else, Mr. Roth?

Mr. ROTH. Nothing else. Thank you. I am now ready to answer questions.

Chairman KEFAUVER. We are glad to have you make your statements. They will, of course, be printed in the record with the rest of your testimony.

Mr. ROTH. Thank you.

Mr. CHUMBRIS. Mr. Roth, where were you born, and when?

Mr. ROTH. I was born on November 17, 1894, in what is now Poland.

Mr. CHUMBRIS. When did you come to this country?

Mr. ROTH. I came to this country in 1904.

Mr. CHUMBRIS. Where did you first reside in the United States?

Mr. ROTH. I don't remember that. It was on Broome Street, 273 Broome Street.

Mr. CHUMBRIS. New York City?

Mr. ROTH. New York City.

Mr. CHUMBRIS. I understand you stated that you have been in this business about 38 years?

Mr. ROTH. That's right.

Mr. CHUMBRIS. In the publishing business?

Mr. ROTH. That's right.

Mr. CHUMBRIS. You are connected with certain companies that published such books as Gargantuan Books; is that correct.

Mr. ROTH. That is not correct. Gargantuan Books is a trade name which I have used for distributing books for a period of 6 weeks.

Mr. CHUMBRIS. And are there any other such books that you have used as a trade name; would you please tell us?

Mr. ROTH. I can't remember them, but there are at least 15.

Mr. CHUMBRIS. And Seven Sirens Press; is that one?

Mr. ROTH. No. Seven Sirens Press is the mother corporation of all my activities.

Mr. CHUMBRIS. How about Gargoyle Books?

Mr. ROTH. That is a name.

Mr. CHUMBRIS. Book Gems?

Mr. ROTH. That is another name.

Mr. CHUMBRIS. Falstaff Books?

Mr. ROTH. That is another name.

Mr. CHUMBRIS. Paragon Books?

Mr. ROTH. That, too.

Mr. CHUMBRIS. Do you publish and edit Good Times?

Mr. ROTH. Yes, sir.

Mr. CHUMBRIS. The American Aphrodite?

Mr. ROTH. That's right.

Mr. CHUMBRIS. Beautiful Sinners of New York?

Mr. ROTH. Yes, that is a past publication.

Mr. CHUMBRIS. Lila and Colette and the Isles of Love?

Mr. ROTH. Yes.

Mr. CHUMBRIS. Do you distribute any nudist books?

Mr. ROTH. Yes.

Mr. CHUMBRIS. Would you please name those?

Mr. ROTH. They are books whose names are really numbers. Their general title is "N. U. S.," and they are very beautiful nudes which come through the Customhouse and are sanctioned by the custom censorship.

Mr. CHUMBRIS. Do you distribute "Nudist Colony"?

Mr. ROTH. Yes. That was one of the titles.

Mr. CHUMBRIS. Adult Companion?

Mr. ROTH. I don't—it is something that has to do with my business, but I do not remember whether it is a book or—oh, yes. Of course. It is a Treasury of Literature, edited by Tiffany Thayer.

Mr. CHUMBRIS. Bedside Treasure?

Mr. ROTH. That's another book exactly like that.

Mr. CHUMBRIS. Lady of the Sofa?

Mr. ROTH. That's by Crabyon. That's one of my books. It is a great French classic.

Mr. CHUMBRIS. Nudes?

Mr. ROTH. That comes under N. U. S. I have never had the book called Nudes, as I remember it.

Mr. CHUMBRIS. Loves of the Orient?

Mr. ROTH. Yes; that's a book.

Mr. CHUMBRIS. Fiery French Nudes?

Mr. ROTH. No. It is the way I would adertise the book of nudes, but it is not the title of a book.

Mr. CHUMBRIS. The Nude in the——

Chairman KEFAUVER. Let's just see. Did you advertise the book that way?

Mr. ROTH. That's right. I think I remember advertising a book that way.

Mr. CHUMBRIS. The Nude in the French Theatre?

Mr. ROTH. Yes.

Mr. CHUMBRIS. Strange——

Mr. ROTH. That I should call your attention to it. The introduction to it was by Anatole France, who was a Nobel prize winner.

Mr. CHUMBRIS. Strange Loves?

Mr. ROTH. Yes. That's a regular—it is a book published by one or the other of the big publishers which I bought as a remainder.

Mr. CHUMBRIS. Red Light Babe?

Mr. ROTH. There you have got me. I don't remember that.

Mr. CHUMBRIS. You don't remember that one?

Mr. ROTH. It sounds like a paper-covered book that I also bought as a remainder.

Chairman KEFAUVER. What do you mean "bought as a remainder," Mr. Roth?

Mr. ROTH. Most of my business is buying regular publishers' books that the publishers themselves—if publishers publish 5,000 books and sold only 4,000, he sells the remainder of the 1,000 to me as a remainder, and that makes it possible for me to make almost a publisher's profit.

Mr. CHUMBRIS. Her Candle Burns Hot?

Mr. ROTH. That's the title of a book? If you say so, it would be one of those paper-covered books, but it would be a very harmless book if I sold it.

Mr. CHUMBRIS. Carnival of Passion?

Mr. ROTH. Yes; that I remember.

Mr. CHUMBRIS. Women of Plentipunda?

Mr. ROTH. Yes. That's an adaptation of an old book.

Mr. CHUMBRIS. Now, referring to the Women of Plentipunda, is that the same book which you described in this advertising, in these words:

Since adolescence represents an age, psychiatrists tell us, during which a youngster's normal sexual curiosity reaches a high point—

Would it be fair to say that the kinds of materials you handle would be of particular interest in this age group?

Mr. ROTH. You begin by saying that you were reading something of mine; you wind up with something that doesn't sound like me. Is that a question you are asking me?

Mr. CHUMBRIS. This is one of your advertisements on these particular books—on this particular book The Women of Plentipunda.

Mr. ROTH. Did you read me my advertisement of it?

Mr. CHUMBRIS. Yes.

Mr. ROTH. I didn't recognize it. Would you please read it again?

Mr. CHUMBRIS. Is that the same book which you describe in this advertising in these words, and I quote:

Since adolescence represents an age, psychiatrists tell us, during which a youngster's normal sexual curiosity reaches a high point—

would it be fair to say that the kinds of materials you handle would be of particular interest in this age group?

Mr. ROTH. I would say not, because in the first place the expression "Plentipunda" is a purely Indian one—it belongs to the Indian, to the religion of the Hindus.

In the second place, if you have a page, any page of that book, as a matter of fact, it is a philosophically written book, a description of what might be considered a Utopia, a Utopia that people imagine for themselves, but which is hardly described in that book in any language that could even be of the faintest interest to children.

Besides that, I can't be appealing to children because we advertise only in the most adult magazines. In the first circular that we send people we ask them for their age, and that is how our list is made up.

The cheapest book we sell is $1.98, and that very rarely—usually it is $2.98, and we can't expect children to pay us any prices like that; and we wouldn't sell them these books under the circumstances.

We don't think that any—I don't think that any kind of a book written in adult fashion can possibly appeal to children. If there is anything there that you think would appeal to children, I would like to hear it.

Mr. CHUMBRIS. I will hereby show you some advertising material that reached the hands of a minor. This advertising material, one is on the French Pornographer, Good Times, and The American Aphrodite, which return address is Book Gems, 110 Lafayette Street, which you testified are concerns with which you are connected.

Will you please tell us, is this your type of advertising [handing to Mr. Roth]?

Mr. ROTH. Yes. I have already conceded that my type of advertising is very exciting, but anybody can see who has ever tried to read one of those books—you take for instance the book The French Pornographer, you would find an adult under 30 who has not had a college education would find it difficult to go beyond the third page, or even beyond the first page.

It is a very fine book; it is a translation from the French.

I deal almost exclusively in French classics. I could say that my exciting style of advertising is a net that I spread among people who have not had a chance for a very good education to get good books into their homes, and I am prepared to prove that almost every book, except those paper-covered books, which I do not consider harmful, are within the realm of either contemporary or modern classics, except those books, and most of the books that I advertise in my magazines are books more than 2,000 years old, books that have been classics for 20 centuries.

Now, do you want me to tell you about this?

Chairman KEFAUVER. Well, first, Mr. Roth——

Mr. ROTH. I don't want to take up too much time.

Chairman KEFAUVER. Is all of this material you have here, advertising which you have sent out?

Mr. ROTH. Yes.

Chairman KEFAUVER. Very well. Let it be made——

Mr. ROTH. Except for the sheet of written paper on top of it. The front there seems to be a letter sent to the committee by somebody.

Mr. CHUMBRIS. By the mother of a minor child.

Mr. ROTH. That was really what I should have answered first.

Chairman KEFAUVER. It will be made an exhibit here and part of the record.

(The information was marked "Exhibit No. 18." The advertisement is on file with the subcommittee. The letter accompanying the literature reads as follows:)

This enclosed filth was sent to a 15-year-old boy from Gargoyle Books, 110 Lafayette Street, New York 13, N. Y. I think it's time something should be done about this contribution to juvenile delinquency. I intend to follow this through.

ANONYMOUS.

Mr. ROTH. I believe it got here by accident.

Mr. CHUMBRIS. Mr. Roth, you stated previously in answer to my question that you made sure that you asked the ages of persons to whom you sent your advertising and material.

Mr. ROTH. That's right.

Mr. CHUMBRIS. That particular letter did get to a minor; is that correct?

Mr. ROTH. That's right.

Mr. CHUMBRIS. Mr. Roth, do you have name lists?

Mr. ROTH. Yes, sir.

Mr. CHUMBRIS. How many names would you say are on your name lists?

Mr. ROTH. At present they come to about 400,000.

Mr. CHUMBRIS. 400,000?

Mr. ROTH. Yes, sir.

Mr. CHUMBRIS. Where do you receive those name lists?

Mr. ROTH. Mainly from publications?

Senator LANGER. From what?

Mr. ROTH. Mainly from publications. I, for instance, advertise by sending out lists like these to lawyers, doctors, dentists, bankers, responsible business people. There is no way in which I can help it if a child would grab his father's mail and put down on it that he is 80 years old. How would I know?

Mr. CHUMBRIS. Now, Mr. Roth, when you acquire these name lists from these various publications, what inquiry do you make as to whether the person is a minor or an adult?

Mr. ROTH. Well, the first circular we send them we ask them to put down their age. I admit that they don't always do so; but we judge by the fact—in the first place, I wish to make this very, very emphatic—I don't believe this circular might excite the mind of an older person to want the book, which is what it is intended to do, would be of the fainest interest to a juvenile, because the words won't mean anything to him; they are not written in his language.

Senator LANGER. What about the pictures? Would they interest a juvenile?

Mr. ROTH. They might. But they are always very beautiful pictures and within the law—entirely within the law.

I believe I shall have to comment on that as the questions are asked me.

Chairman KEFAUVER. Mr. Roth, just out of some of our correspondence that we have received—and this is not all of it [exhibiting]—here is a letter from Mrs. Shuler in Davenport, Iowa, saying that this was received by her 8-year-old son—some of your advertising [handing to Mr. Roth].

Here is a letter from Schoharie, N. Y., from Catherine S. Rickard:

We received some objectionable literature, but from another company, Gargoyle Books.

It says:

I am enclosing the whole thing, and I was just fortunate to notice it before the children got a hold of it.

Apparently this was addressed to her son. This is marked "Personal."

Mr. ROTH. Is the original envelope there?

Chairman KEFAUVER. Yes; it seems to be there.

Mr. ROTH. May I see it?

Chairman KEFAUVER. Yes [handing to Mr. Roth].

Here is one to L. Mann, Lake Junaluska, N. C.:

We have reason to believe this letter contains literature which should not be allowed to go through the mails.

This was addressed to a child, age 17:

We do not know where she is so cannot forward this. Two years ago she left camp.

Anyway, it was sent to a young girl who was in camp [handing to Mr. Roth].

Here is one to a 15-year-old boy. Postmaster in Erie, Pa., sent this. This was sent to a 15-year-old boy, apparently.

Here is one from Burlington, Iowa, in which a mother says it was sent to a juvenile—it does not give his age [handing to Mr. Roth].

Here is one that seems to have gotten to Mr. J. Edgar Hoover in some way [handing to Mr. Roth].

Mrs. Garrett Wilson back in Ohio, who complained to her Congressman about her children getting this thing here [handing to Mr. Roth].

Here is one from the president of a college at Columbus, Ohio, saying literature like this came to him and to others at the college [handing to Mr. Roth].

Here is one forwarded by a college president to Mrs. Oveta Hobby. She, in turn, sent it to us [handing to Mr. Roth].

Mr. Roth, you say you make sure that none of your literature reaches the young people. What do you say about all of this?

Mr. ROTH. I would like to answer this.

Chairman KEFAUVER. You identify these as being literature that you sent out?

Mr. ROTH. Yes; these were all things that were sent out by my office, under my general direction.

Chairman KEFAUVER. By your various corporations or publications, or publishing companies?

Mr. ROTH. Yes, sir.

Chairman KEFAUVER. They will all be made exhibits, together with the accompanying letters, which speak for themselves.

(The information was marked "Exhibit No. 19." The advertisements are on file with the subcommittee. The letters accompanying the literature read as follows:)

We have reason to believe this letter contains literature which should not be allowed to go through the mails. Miss M. is a (age 17) young girl who attended our camp several years ago and we do not know where she is so cannot forward this. Two years ago after she left camp, similar mail came for her, unsealed, second class, which we did not forward when we found it contained obscene material. Please investigate.

_____

ANONYMOUS.

POSTMASTER GENERAL,   BURLINGTON, IOWA, *November 20, 1953.*
    Washington, D. C.:

Enclosed find literature that was mailed to my home. It was sent to my son who tore it up. Why are such vile pictures permitted to be sent through the mail? It is no wonder we have so many sex crimes and juvenile delinquency if this kind of literature can be had. I think it is a disgrace to all decency and I am very angry that my address is used for such a purpose. I think this firm should not be permitted to use the mail and that they should not be permitted to print such pictures. I hope that you can do something to stop them.

Sincerely yours,

_____

Mrs. E. B.

POSTMASTER GENERAL,   DAVENPORT, IOWA, *October 28, 1953.*
    Washington, D. C.

DEAR SIR: Enclosed please find an advertisement that was sent to my 18-year-old son. He is now in college and this was forwarded but it is evident that these are being sent to boys in preparatory schools.

We are always hearing that the Postal Department is run at a loss and rates should be raised. I resent very much paying taxes to pay my postman to deliver this type of thing. I have always understood that there was a law about the type of literature that could be sent through the mail.

I should appreciate a statement from you as to the legality of this publication.

Very truly yours,

Mrs. C. S., Jr.

SCHOHARIE, N. Y., *November 20, 1953.*

POST OFFICE INSPECTOR,
       Washington, D. C.

DEAR MR. SIMON: Again we received some objectionable literature, but from another company: Gargoyle Books, 110 Lafayette Street (8th floor), New York, N. Y. I'm enclosing the whole thing, and I was just fortunate to notice it before the children got a hold of it.

Is there any way we can find out where they obtain my husband's address? Could such a practice be abolished—especially for such obscene material?

Thank you very much for your previous investigation, and for anything you do this time.

Sincerely yours,

C. S. R.

CORVALLIS, OREG., *June 12, 1953.*

Mrs. OVETA CULP HOBBY:

It is, to the best of my knowledge, that you are in the position of doing what you can for the welfare of our country. This is a problem that I wish could be solved. I live in a college town and for years these obscene ads have been coming to our students. I feel it is one of the worst demoralizing influences we have to bring our Nation low.

I have no idea if or how anything can be done about it.

The envelopes are marked "Personal." The P.' O.'s are strewn with them. Students are curious and make good bait.

Thank you.

C. D.

COLUMBUS, OHIO, *October 9, 1953.*

Mr. J. EDGAR HOOVER,
       Director, FBI, Washington, D. C.

DEAR MR. HOOVER: Isn't there some way to stop such filth as the enclosed, from coming to decent people through the United States mail?

This is the worst that I have ever seen and one of our graduate students who is helping out in the office was so shocked at this awful stuff that she insisted I write you at once about it.

Very truly yours,

G. S. R.

Mr. ROTH. May I continue, please?

Chairman KEFAUVER. Yes; you may continue.

Mr. ROTH. Thank you.

You will notice that a few of these in which the original envelope is offered, the addresses are not on stencils. This one [indicating] is not on a stencil; this one is not on a stencil; and those are where the original envelope has not been received; they are probably names of people who were addressed through the telephone directories, which is why their first name is "Dr. So-and-So." That covers the letter which reached Mr. Hoover—J. Edgar Hoover—and it covers another letter that I heard you say had been sent in by a doctor.

Chairman KEFAUVER. Apparently these are written out and copies are made, and then the name and address is just cut off with a scissors and pasted on.

Mr. ROTH. Yes, I realize that. But I want to explain what this means, this little thing [exhibiting]. It means that these people on the list, which another company addressed for me, and in which I got the best assurance you can possibly get from people you do business with, that they were not going to minors; and these happened to be minors.

There is no point in my disputing that, when my real point is that if they reached minors they couldn't possibly have any bad influence on them, and they would disregard them. They would disregard them because the language which my circulars are written in may mean something to a Senator, may mean something to a mature adult, but cannot mean anything to a boy or a girl.

Mr. CHUMBRIS. Mr. Roth, do you mean to say that these pictures that are present on this folder [exhibiting] will not excite a minor if it gets into his hands? Won't you take a good look at those [handing to Mr. Roth]?

Mr. ROTH. When you put these pictures against the battery of females that any child sees on any morning in a ride through the subway, in a walk through a street, this is ridiculous as an argument against my business. These are——

Chairman KEFAUVER. Mr. Roth, just a minute.

Mr. ROTH. Forgive me, I shouldn't have said that at all. I am sorry.

Chairman KEFAUVER. You have a pamphlet there with nude females in various positions, and some of them with nude males, apparently. You are comparing those with what you see when you ride on a subway?

Mr. ROTH. Yes. It is not unusual to see a man with his arm around a woman who is naked up to here [indicating], and if the child wants to play around with that kind of an image it can very well imagine the rest of the body to be as naked as the upper part of it.

Chairman KEFAUVER. Mr. Roth, if this won't excite children——

Mr. ROTH. I don't think so.

Chairman KEFAUVER. Children are more easily excited than adults.

Mr. ROTH. Look at this. This is a cartoon, and it is a cartoon that can hardly give anybody pleasure in looking at it.

Mr. CHUMBRIS. Why do you spend so much money putting these photos on that advertisement if it does not excite the men that you hope to sell the books to?

Mr. ROTH. I beg your pardon; I didn't say that. I said that I do hope to excite the men into buying these good books.

Mr. CHUMBRIS. Why doesn't it excite the children then?

Mr. ROTH. Because children's minds are different. They are probably better than the minds of mature people in that respect. A child you have got to tell, to give a real image, or the child just disregards it.

Chairman KEFAUVER. You think men, then, are more susceptible to harm from pornography, or lewd pictures, than children.

Mr. ROTH. I don't consider these lewd pictures by any means.

Chairman KEFAUVER. Whatever they are, you think men are more susceptible to being affected by them than children are?

Mr. ROTH. I think that is a matter of course. Their business is— they have more business in the relations with women than children have. Children don't know anything about it as yet, mostly. There is nothing in these pictures that I would say was in any way lewd or indecent. And certainly nothing that would be new to children whose eyes are wide open wherever they walk.

Mr. CHUMBRIS. Mr. Roth, have you ever received a letter from a minor with a high-school address on it?

Mr. ROTH. I know that we received such mail. My orders to the people who—you know that I don't fill the orders, or open them; but my orders are strictly not to pay any attention to such an address. And when money is enclosed, we return it, either by cash or by check. I think usually by check.

Mr. CHUMBRIS. But you stated a while ago that you buy name lists from other groups; is that correct?

Mr. ROTH. No; I don't buy them; I rent them. I am not there when they are addressed.

Mr. CHUMBRIS. And the name lists that you buy or rent are sometimes on a name plate, just a small little plate; is that correct?

Mr. ROTH. I wouldn't say that that's always so. These happened to be, I believe these were on these gum paper labels.

Mr. CHUMBRIS. That's right. And others are on mineographed sheets; is that correct?

Mr. ROTH. They have every way of addressing them that I have.

Mr. CHUMBRIS. Then when you buy or rent those name lists you do not have the slightest idea whether the person from whom you purchased that name list has a list of minors or adults, do you?

Mr. ROTH. I have the assurance that they are only adults; because I do not like to spend postage on addressing children.

Mr. CHUMBRIS. How did all of these exhibits—and we are just giving you a portion of what came into our office—how did you get——

Mr. ROTH. Have you any idea of how much mail that represents? That probably represents 10 million pieces of mail, and you have got about 20 or 30 pieces here, culled over a great many years. Why do you think that is representative of my business?

Chairman KEFAUVER. Mr. Roth, I think as to your point, the staff tells me that we have literally a file cabinet full of your mail which has been sent in from all over the country. I do not believe I have shown you all of what we have here.

Here is another one sent to the Postmaster General. This was sent to a 15-year-old boy, Gargoyle Books.

Now I want to ask you, Mr. Roth, you said that you put on these things that they were not supposed to be sent back or ordered by minors. I have not been able to find that on any piece of this literature.

Mr. ROTH. I didn't get that last part.

Chairman KEFAUVER. You said that your instructions on these pieces of advertising made it plain that minors could not order it, that only adults would be permitted to order it from these pamphlets.

Mr. ROTH. That's right.

Chairman KEFAUVER. I have not been able to find that on any of these pieces of literature.

Mr. ROTH. Well, that's not something I know how to explain.

Chairman KEFAUVER. You are the boss of the business?

Mr. ROTH. That's right.

Chairman KEFAUVER. Why did you tell us a little while ago——

Mr. ROTH. They were not sent in, though.

Chairman KEFAUVER. But, Mr. Roth, I want to get this straight. You said in the beginning in one of your statements that this was not any business of this subcommittee, handling juvenile—what you were doing was no business of this subcommittee, because, in the first place, you did not send the advertisements to minors, and, in the second place, it was definite that they were required to give their age, and if it appeared that they were a minor, the orders would not be fulfilled.

Mr. ROTH. That's right.

Chairman KEFAUVER. Where on any of this literature do you ask anyone's age [handing to Mr. Roth]?

Mr. ROTH. The first circular which I send to a person who has sent in an order, say through a magazine or through the mails, probably has never been sent in.

I wish to remind you again that these pieces are the results of millions of pieces of mail that have gone out in the last few years.

Chairman KEFAUVER. Mr. Roth, we have, I think, a cross-section of all the kinds you have sent out, and my staff tells me they find no inquiry about the age on any of them.

Mr. ROTH. That is my point, that these are never sent in; these are sent in to us, and the complaints come on those that come later. That's the only way I can explain it. I am not making a perfect explanation, because there is no perfect explanation.

Chairman KEFAUVER. Mr. Roth, you have a briefcase there. Do you find any in your briefcase that inquire the age of the person?

Mr. ROTH. I have none here. I have brought nothing with me.

Chairman KEFAUVER. You have no copy with you?

Mr. ROTH. No. And I wish to say we are in the process of winding up our business. I don't know whether any of these circulars show it, but the last circular we sent out we announced that that was the third of the last six announcements we are making, and so we are not using those lists any more.

Mr. CHUMBRIS. Mr. Roth, the staff using Eastern High School stationery in Washington, D. C., sent out letters to persons dealing in publications such as yours, pictures, and not only did they receive a reply from those people to whom the letters were directed, but within a month, 5 or 6 companies dealing in the type of material in which you deal, and pictures, bondage pictures, and fetish pictures, and nudes, and so forth, reached our office although no letter was directed to those companies.

Now, how would you explain how your office got answers from people to whom letters were not directed?

Chairman KEFAUVER. Mr. Chumbris, you have not made clear what you are trying to get at.

Mr. CHUMBRIS. I have made a statement, and I want him to explain the statement.

Chairman KEFAUVER. What he means is that on high-school stationery inquiries have been sent to other companies. Shortly after they are sent to other companies, your companies write these people who made the inquiry, the children who made the inquiries.

Mr. ROTH. I can answer that fully and very briefly.

Chairman KEFAUVER. In other words, you exchange lists?

Mr. ROTH. We do not.

Chairman KEFAUVER. That puts you on notice that these inquiries were from children, but shortly after the inquiries are made of other companies, your companies get the list and send them literature.

Mr. ROTH. Oh, that happens; yes. That can happen.

In the first place, I want to say, when you talk about companies like mine, I want to correct that. There isn't a company like mine. My business is unique, there is nothing like it in the world, No. 1.

No. 2, we have consistently in all our experience refused to rent out our lists, except to legitimate enterprises, like insurance companies, Life, Esquire, Time, all the big magazines.

We have been offered as much as $30 a thousand, which is twice as much as the regular rate, for people, such as some of your other witnesses here, to use our lists. We have never, never, allowed anyone but a legitimate enterprise to use our lists, and that we have kept down to a certain number.

Mr. CHUMBRIS. Mr. Roth, you just stated that there is no other business in the country like yours.

Mr. ROTH. That's right.

Mr. CHUMBRIS. You stated a while ago that you are connected with Gargoyle Sales Corp.

Mr. ROTH. That's right.

Mr. CHUMBRIS. I hereby show you an exhibit of advertisement of girls being whipped, or what is known as fetish and bondage pictures, which is a type of photograph and material sent out by another company here in New York City. I would like for you to look at that [handing to witness].

Chairman KEFAUVER. Will you identify that as being some of the literature that your company has sent out?

Mr. ROTH. Oh, no. That's an entirely different company; it has nothing to do with me.

Mr. CHUMBRIS. You just stated that Gargoyle Sales——

Mr. ROTH. I had a company called Gargoyle Books. This is Gargoyle Sales Corp. It hasn't the remotest connection with me. And I would like to see all the others that you think are like my business [returning to Mr. Chumbris].

Mr. CHUMBRIS. I read you the name of Gargoyle Sales Corp., and you said it was your company.

Mr. ROTH. One thing to answer as honestly as I could, and hearing "Gargoyle," which is a part of the name—I never heard of this company.

Mr. CHUMBRIS. This particular company is not one of your companies?

Mr. ROTH. I never heard of the name before.

Mr. CHUMBRIS. But the others that we have shown you, Good Times, and so forth, The American——

Mr. ROTH. These are my circulars and my business. I stand for them, and I do not believe that anyone under 25 could possibly be influenced; and if they were influenced, it would be for the good.

Chairman KEFAUVER. You don't think anyone under 25 could be influenced for the bad from these?

Mr. ROTH. What would be bad? The worst they could do is buy the book, and the books are——

Chairman KEFAUVER. Let me get this again. What did you say about 25 , a minute ago, that you did not believe anyone under 25 or over 25 would be influenced for the bad?

Mr. ROTH. I believe that very few people—it's very difficult to talk in a generality like under 25, over 25—very few people who haven't had a certain amount of experience would be attracted by this sophisticated language with which we sell this.

We don't—I haven't, for instance, read that circular, I never saw it, and I never saw the name before, but I would be willing to bet that that would prove my case. This is how they sell, and this is how I sell.

I sell only fine books. The biggest seller on my list in the last 4 years has been a book called "My sister and I" by Frederick Weacher, and that is a philosophical book. I have been able to get that in almost 100,000 homes, and that is a triumph. I don't expect any medals for it, but I don't expect to be called a publisher of pornographic books.

Chairman KEFAUVER. Of course the thing is not the reading material on these things so much as the pictures that you have sent around.

Mr. ROTH. I disagree with you, Mr. Kefauver; I really do not agree with that.

Chairman KEFAUVER. If pictures do not make any difference, why do you put so many pictures on them?

Mr. ROTH. I am a salesman. I remember once going into a haberdashery shop and asking to buy a shirt I saw in the window, and what was shown me didn't look at all like it.

I said, "Is that the same shirt I saw in the window?"

The man said, "Yes, Mister, but I spend a lot of money on the lights in my window, and I can't expect an ordinary shirt to look like that."

If I do it with good books, I don't think that could be held against me.

Mr. CHUMBRIS. Mr. Roth, you have not yet fully explained your role in avoiding sending that particular type of advertisement to youth.

Mr. ROTH. To young people, you mean?

Mr. CHUMBRIS. In view of the fact that you buy, rent, exchange, or what have you, mailing lists with other concerns.

Mr. ROTH. But I have just told you that I don't.

Mr. CHUMBRIS. What is that?

Mr. ROTH. I have just told you that I do not rent my lists to anyone except people like Life, Time, Esquire; these people rent my lists 2 or 3 times a year because mine are adult buyers and can subscribe to a magazine.

Mr. CHUMBRIS. Don't you rent lists from a party in Brooklyn?

Mr. ROTH. "From," but not "to." That's the difference.

Mr. CHUMBRIS. That is what I am referring to. If you are renting from a party, and you do not make a clear and direct analysis of the ages of that name list, then your material could get to juveniles, could it not?

Mr. ROTH. I believe that in that respect my business could be reinforced a little bit by greater care. I admit that; but I am always given the assurance that the people who bought these things spent at least $1.98, and that they were mature people. That's the best I can do at present.

Chairman KEFAUVER. Well, now, how many lists do you buy, how many thousands of names on them?

Mr. ROTH. Well, now, a company in Brooklyn was mentioned from whom I bought approximately 180,000 names, which dwindled down to about 70,000.

Mr. CHUMBRIS. Would you like to give his name, please, for the record?

Mr. ROTH. I don't know whether I should. I don't know whether I shouldn't, because I was assured that these were names of people who bought pinups. Now, pinups, I do not consider them as obscene matter. I consider them a little like the things I myself use.

Chairman KEFAUVER. In other words, you have a pinup mailing list to send your literature?

Mr. ROTH. That's right; yes.

Chairman KEFAUVER. Mr. Chumbris, you know the name of the man in Brooklyn; you give it to us.

Mr. CHUMBRIS. Mr. Vallon; is that right?

Mr. ROTH. Yes.

Mr. CHUMBRIS. Will you give the full name and address?

Mr. ROTH. I have his full name and his address in my books, but I don't remember it. I think, if you have difficulty finding his name in the Brooklyn directory, his business goes under the name of Mapleton Books, Mapleton something-or-other.

Chairman KEFAUVER. Anyway, Mr. Vallon has a pinup list of about 180,000 names to which he sends pinup materials?

Mr. ROTH. That's right.

Chairman KEFAUVER. You rented his list to send out this literature?

Mr. ROTH. That list I bought. I didn't rent it. But we dwindled it down to about 70,000.

Chairman KEFAUVER. Suppose we question the other list that you bought?

Mr. ROTH. That's the only list that I have ever bought in my life.

Chairman KEFAUVER. What other lists have you rented?

Mr. ROTH. I have rented lists from a regular list house called Book Buyers Lists. That's what it is called. That's on 369 Broadway. They are a very legitimate and fine enterprise.

Chairman KEFAUVER. What do you do to get the names of the juveniles out of them? It would seem that when you see a high school and when you see the account down in North Carolina, you would know that that was a juvenile.

Mr. ROTH. We would know that. I would mention this, although I do not hold it against these people, because they have a very heavy business, but I do not mail out, they mail out for me. I pay for the postage—no, no, forgive me. I do mail that out, but it is very difficult to—if I make a mailing, say, of 10,000, it is very difficult to go through and try to catch that.

I should say that we are supported by the feeling that we are not selling them anything bad, that's all. But we have had an understanding in advance that we do not contain the names of juveniles.

Chairman KEFAUVER. Mr. Roth, do you think it would be bad and deleterious for the children for you to mail this stuff to the children?

Mr. ROTH. It would be very bad business for me, I can tell you.

Chairman KEFAUVER. I mean, it would be bad for them, too, would it not?

Mr. ROTH. I don't think they would pay any attention to it. I give you my word of honor.

I have brought up a family. I have grandchildren, and my grandchildren occasionally come to see me. They look at these things and they drop them.

I can't see—an adult would be interested—but I cannot see how children would be interested.

Chairman KEFAUVER. And you think an adult would pay more attention to them than children would?

Mr. ROTH. They do pay attention, or I wouldn't be in business.

Senator LANGER. Mr. Chairman, I call attention to the fact that a few moments ago the witness stated that he had sent out 10 million. It is curious where he got all the 10 million names.

Chairman KEFAUVER. Is that the number you sent out—in how long a period of time?

Mr. ROTH. No, I meant that these were culled from a long period of my business, and that in that period I have sent out over 10 million pieces.

That's a guess, by the way, the 10 million. It could be 20 million and it might be only 5. I think it would be around 10 million, because my instincts in such matters are good.

Chairman KEFAUVER. Let's follow Senator Langer's question. Where did you get a mailing list for 10 million?

Mr. ROTH. I haven't a mailing list for 10 million, but I have, say, a mailing list for only 10,000 in 10 years I could send it out 10 million times—I mean, I could send out to 10 million people. It wasn't intended to be a single mailing.

I don't think anybody in the United States since the Literary Digest died, has sent out as many as 10 million pieces of mail.

Senator LANGER. A moment ago you said you had 400,000 names, did you not, Mr. Witness?

Mr. ROTH. That's right. That's very far from 10 million.

Chairman KEFAUVER. What mailing permit do you have to send these through the mails?

Mr. ROTH. I have the regular Pitney Bowes machine permit.

Chairman KEFAUVER. Is that second-class?

Mr. ROTH. Yes.

Chairman KEFAUVER. Second-class permit?

Mr. ROTH. That's right.

May I mention one more thing?

Chairman KEFAUVER. Have you had any trouble with the Post Office Department?

Mr. ROTH. Oh, lots of trouble.

We have a sign in our door that has been there ever since I can remember, maybe 18 years. It has been on different doors, of course, and the sign says "No books sold on the premises." No book goes out which hasn't got on it the post office's permission to open it and examine it.

Mr. CHUMBRIS. A moment ago you said you had plenty of trouble with the Post Office Department, but you always worked it out. That is not exactly true, is it?

Mr. ROTH. Yes; the post office accuses me of having sent an obscene book through the mails, such as Beautiful Sinners of New York, and it is put before a jury, and the jury comes back a few minutes later and sees nothing wrong with it. I have straightened it out with the post office.

Mr. CHUMBRIS. Have you ever been convicted of a violation of a post office regulation?

Mr. ROTH. Yes; for selling Ulysses, by James Joyce, which is now must reading in all colleges and high schools. Not all of them, but enough of them.

Mr. CHUMBRIS. When was that?

Mr. ROTH. I think 1929.

Mr. CHUMBRIS. And then, in 1930, you were also convicted of violations?

Mr. ROTH. Whenever I was convicted of a violation of a book that I sent through the mails I believed it was safe to send it. There are differences of opinion on that, yes; usually I go to jail, and then the laws confirm my being right.

Mr. CHUMBRIS. In 1936, would you please explain whether you had any difficulty with the law?

Mr. ROTH. I had a great deal of difficulty. I went to prison that year.

Mr. CHUMBRIS. Explain it, please.

Mr. ROTH. It involved about seven books which the post office considered obscene.

Mr. CHUMBRIS. Did you go to prison for that?

Mr. ROTH. That's right; I just told you that.

Chairman KEFAUVER. How long did you serve?

Mr. ROTH. I served a 3-year sentence.

Mr. CHUMBRIS. In 1941, did you have any trouble with the law?

Mr. ROTH. Yes; you have the record there. You tell me.

Mr. CHUMBRIS. April 14, 1941, you were found guilty of violating probation, is that correct; and your probation was extended to December 16, 1946; is that correct?

Mr. ROTH. Yes. May I say something now? The district attorney in charge of that case opened the case against me—I was really not convicted there. The judge dismissed it. He opened the case by saying, "This defendant is not being accused of selling any book which cannot be found in any bookstore in the United States. We just don't like a man on parole to sell these books."

Mr. CHUMBRIS. Your statement that you had difficulty with the Post Office Department, but you always worked it out, wasn't exactly true, was it?

Mr. ROTH. Well, I worked it out even when I went to prison. You must try it sometime.

Mr. CHUMBRIS. That gives a different connotation than "working it out."

Mr. ROTH. I mean that eventually the laws almost always justified what I had done. For instance, there was a time when you could go to prison for just a picture like this. Now you find—I would like to read you a list of the magazines that publish nudes almost all the time.

Chairman KEFAUVER. Before you get to that list—you have quite a record here of arrests, and being in court, and you and your wife together, usually.

Mr. ROTH. That's right.

Chairman KEFAUVER. You have your wife in all of these matters?

Mr. ROTH. That's right.

Chairman KEFAUVER. She has been convicted, too; is that correct?

Mr.ROTH. The only thing I can tell you is that we were right.

Chairman KEFAUVER. Sit down, Mr. Roth.

On December 16, apparently you and your wife got convicted for 2 years, and she got a suspended sentence; is that right?

Mr. ROTH. That is correct.

Chairman KEFAUVER. Mr. Chumbris, you have this entire history here. Do you want to go over it, or do you want to show it to Mr. Roth?

Mr. CHUMBRIS. Mr. Roth, on February 27, 1928, you pleaded guilty to mailing obscene literature, and were fined $500 and given 6 months' suspended sentence; is that correct?

Mr. ROTH. That is correct. Would you like me to explain it?

Mr. CHUMBRIS. Let me go through this.

Chairman KEFAUVER. Give him a right to explain. You plead guilty?

Mr. ROTH. I plead guilty after a conference with Judge Knox. I pointed out the book was a Hindu classic, and it should be permitted to be sold at the price which I sold it for, which was $35 a copy.

Chairman KEFAUVER. What did you plead guilty for?

Mr. ROTH. On the advice of counsel—very bad advice.

Mr. CHUMBRIS. On October 19, 1928, sentenced to serve 3 months on Welfare Island for possessing and selling obscene books.

Mr. ROTH. That is correct. It was a book which I have since sold freely and through the post office for a great many years.

Mr. CHUMBRIS. Did you plead guilty, or were you convicted?

Mr. ROTH. I was convicted of that in special sessions.

Mr. CHUMBRIS. November 27, 1929, arrested for possession and sale of obscene literature; case dismissed. Was that correct?

Mr. ROTH. I don't see why I have to argue with that. Go on.

Mr. CHUMBRIS. January 28, 1930, sentenced to 6 months in Federal Detention House for violation of probation; is that correct?

Mr. ROTH. Yes; that is correct. I didn't consider it a violation of probation, and I think the judge who kept the case—Judge Knox—who kept the case running for 3 years, didn't either, except he finally decided it was better to let me serve a sentence. I didn't serve 6 months. He changed it to 2 months at the last minute.

Mr. CHUMBRIS. July 7, 1930, sentenced to serve 60 days for the sale and possession of obscene books. Where was that?

Mr. ROTH. I know where that was. That was Philadelphia, and that was for protecting Ulysses so my grandchildren and your grandchildren will be able to read that book.

Chairman KEFAUVER. Did you plead guilty?

Mr. ROTH. I did plead guilty. Mr. Kefauver, I was threatened by the man who ruled Philadelphia if I dared stand trial on that book, he would see that I got at least 3 years. I have witnesses to that.

Chairman KEFAUVER. You pled guilty?

Mr. ROTH. I had to plead guilty.

Mr. CHUMBRIS. December 16, 1936, sentenced to 3 years in Lewisburg Penitentiary for mailing obscene literature.

Mr. ROTH. You covered that.

Mr. CHUMBRIS. April 14, 1941, found guilty of violating probation; probation extended to December 16, 1946.

Mr. ROTH. I have already covered that.

Mr. CHUMBRIS. Then recently, last year, you had some difficulty with the State authorities on obscene literature; is that correct?

Mr. ROTH. That's right. Have you on the record what happened on that?

Mr. CHUMBRIS. Yes; I think last week the matter was thrown out of court for illegal search and seizure; is that correct?

Mr. ROTH. Not only that, but because they picked up 70,000 books on my premises and didn't find a single bad one there, and there were none, and they are all being returned to me.

Mr. Chumbris. Was there any official ruling to that effect?

Mr. Roth. No; but I have no doubt that the official ruling will be made some day, maybe today.

Mr. Chumbris. As a matter of fact, they didn't even go into the contents of the book; they only went into the question of whether the search was legal or illegal?

Mr. Roth. That is true, but I do know they went into the books.

Chairman Kefauver. The Post Office Department issued fraudulent orders against trade styles used by you back in 1942?

Mr. Roth. That's right.

Chairman Kefauver. What does that mean?

Mr. Roth. "Fraud" in the language of the post office means almost anything except fraud, but it meant in my case that I had described books as very sexy, which they didn't think sexy at all. That is the whole thing.

Chairman Kefauver. You overstated the sex angle in your books?

Mr. Roth. That is it. I admitted that, but I thought I had a right to since it got good books into the hands of people who otherwise wouldn't have gotten them.

Chairman Kefauver. I don't understand, Mr. Roth, why it is that you have a great number of corporations. I have never seen such a list. Did you operate through one at one time and another one at another time? Why is that?

Mr. Roth. It is for reasons that anyone in the publishing business can explain. I am not the only such publisher. I sell philosophical books—and for every kind I have, I have a different name.

Chairman Kefauver. For each book you have a different corporation?

Mr. Roth. Every kind of book.

Chairman Kefauver. Isn't the real idea that if one gets knocked off by the postal authorities, you can continue to operate your other corporations?

Mr. Roth. That's right. Not only that. If there is any implication in that that I do that to hide myself, that isn't true. I do not change my address, 110 Lafayette Street.

Chairman Kefauver. You have one corporation publishing 5 or 6 different types of books, and if one was found in violation of postal operations, they might stop your whole business?

Mr. Roth. That's right.

Chairman Kefauver. So you have all these various corporations?

Mr. Roth. Not only for that.

Chairman Kefauver. It enables you to send out literature in different names to prospective purchasers?

Mr. Roth. My prospective purchasers know when they come from the 8th floor at 110 Lafayette Street, that we are the people from whom they bought in the past.

Chairman Kefauver. Do you think the children know that?

Mr. Roth. I don't think the children care. I don't think it is part of that thing. I think you pay too much attention to that, and therefore, do not pay attention to things that are more vital.

Chairman Kefauver. That is what this committee is organized for—to see what the children are getting.

For some reason, Mr. Roth, there has been a very sharp increase, over 110 percent in the last 10 years of sex crimes among juveniles.

You see about it in the papers, and we had always been taught, at least we thought, that there was something to the fact that children the atmosphere, environment, and the kind of things they read affected them. Psychiatrists and parents have told us, and have written us that the smutty literature and pamphlets we see here that you are sending out, do not have a very wholesome effect on young people. Don't you think that is true?

Mr. ROTH. No. I don't believe any circulars like this.

Chairman KEFAUVER. Why is it you have been so careful—or rather you think you have been careful not to send this to young people?

Mr. ROTH. The only reason why I have been careful mostly, I do not believe this can possibly touch the psychology of a juvenile, but mostly I have been careful because it would be very bad business to send out circulars and get no returns. You can only get returns from mature people. I am quite candid in telling you that. I think that the idea that the present juvenile delinquency comes of pornographic literature, I think it slightly wrong. I was a child myself in the public schools of New York.

Chairman KEFAUVER. You think that is overrated?

Mr. ROTH. I think it is very much overrated.

Chairman KEFAUVER. You naturally think it is overrated since that is your business?

Mr. ROTH. Yes; I admit I could be prejudiced by that.

Chairman KEFAUVER. You would be reluctant to admit that your business was doing very much to adversely affect juveniles, but you are in the business.

Mr. ROTH. I am in the business, and occasionally circulars of mine might reach juveniles, but I do not think that I could have any possible effect on that, and I do not believe that the very worst kinds of these things can be avoided, because they are underground. They do not send out mail the way I do. They reach children the way they reach children when I was a child. They come to you in front of school, and offer you an obscene pamphlet.

Chairman KEFAUVER. I don't want to labor the point. You don't think it is too bad for children, your type of literature, although you claimed at first you have taken unusual precaution about young people getting it. You wouldn't put your judgment up against that of J. Edgar Hoover, would you?

Mr. ROTH. I don't know about that. If Mr. Hoover made a study of this, he would know more than I do.

Chairman KEFAUVER. If Mr. Hoover said that it was degrading and increased criminal tendencies, and was one of the real evil influences leading to juvenile delinquency, you would rather have his judgment than yours?

Mr. ROTH. Yes, but I don't believe he had these circulars in mind.

Chairman KEFAUVER. He talked about this kind of literature, too. I read his statement into the record the first day here.

Mr. CHUMBRIS. Mr. Roth, what is your gross income from your operations in these books that we are discussing here this morning?

Mr. ROTH. It is around $260,000, $270,000 a year.

Mr. CHUMBRIS. What is the net profit that you receive from that gross income?

Mr. ROTH. I can put it to you this way: I get a salary of $10,000 a year, my wife gets a salary of $3,000 a year, and at the end of the year, we have never yet had so much money left that I could withdraw and call it a profit. My books are open. We do, I think, very well, because our appetites are not too great.

Mr. CHUMBRIS. I didn't hear that last statement.

Mr. ROTH. I said we do pretty well, living as we do in our community, and I am satisfied with what I do.

Mr. CHUMBRIS. Of the $260,000 to $270,000 gross, you say that you receive $10,000 a year and your wife receive $3,000 salary?

Mr. ROTH. That's right.

Mr. CHUMBRIS. And you have very little to share as profit?

Mr. ROTH. At the end of the year, yes. We have never done it yet.

Mr. CHUMBRIS. How many people do you employ?

Mr. ROTH. I would say we employ an average of about 15 people.

Mr. CHUMBRIS. Fifteen people?

Mr. ROTH. Yes.

Mr. CHUMBRIS. At 110 Lafayette Street?

Mr. ROTH. That's right.

Mr. CHUMBRIS. What are their duties mostly?

Mr. ROTH. They are writers, they are file clerks, they are typists, they are editors. I believe that about covers it. Shipping clerks, of course.

Mr. CHUMBRIS. Do you have any persons who print any of these so-called 2-by-4 booklets?

Mr. ROTH. We have never printed any 2 by 4 booklets.

Mr. CHUMBRIS. Have you or any of your employees made any of the cartoons that go into these 2-by-4 booklets?

Mr. ROTH. No.

Chairman KEFAUVER. How much is your subscription to all your books and magazines each year—about $400,000?

Mr. ROTH. I have been asked the gross income. The gross income is around $260,000, $270,000.

Chairman KEFAUVER. Do you have agents out on the road?

Mr. ROTH. No.

Chairman KEFAUVER. Do you send all these books by mail?

Mr. ROTH. We solicit by mail and fill orders by them.

Chairman KEFAUVER. You don't send by mail?

Mr. ROTH. None.

Chairman KEFAUVER. Have you ever sent by car or Railway Express?

Mr. ROTH. Never.

Chairman KEFAUVER. Always by mail?

Mr. ROTH. Railway Express, we mail occasionally; when a man tells us he has no post office near him, but there is a Railway Express office, then we make him pay the extra cartage.

Chairman KEFAUVER. Anything else?

Mr. CHUMBRIS. Do you have a complete list of the names and addresses of your employees?

Mr. ROTH. Yes, sir.

Mr. CHUMBRIS. Would you please furnish them to the subcommittee?

Mr. ROTH. I will be very happy to.

Chairman KEFAUVER. For the record, when will you send that in, Mr. Roth?

Mr. ROTH. If you want, I will send that in this afternoon.

Chairman KEFAUVER. Anything else?

Mr. Roth, do you try to get contracts with people so you can have publishers write their life and experiences about them?

Mr. ROTH. No. We are asked to, and we do not have anything to do with that.

Chairman KEFAUVER. Were you president of Seven Sirens Press, Inc.?

Mr. ROTH. That's right.

Chairman KEFAUVER. Will you explain what this seems to be on the letterhead of your corporation?

Mr. ROTH. Yes; I will be very glad to. At the end of the first Jelke trial, I contacted the woman known as Pat Ward, and offered her this contract for a book. If you meant this kind of a contract, we offer it to people whose books might interest us. This contract was never signed by Miss Ward, or, I know, by anybody else.

Chairman KEFAUVER. If you are dealing in abstracts, and heroes over in Europe, and metaphysical characters, why do you want to get a contract with Pat Ward right after the first Jelke trial?

Mr. ROTH. I believe a very fine book can be made on that. By the way, there is one in the making anyway.

Chairman KEFAUVER. You didn't get the contract?

Mr. ROTH. No.

Chairman KEFAUVER. She turned you down?

Mr. ROTH. She wanted too much money.

Chairman KEFAUVER. What is that?

Mr. ROTH. She wanted too much money.

Chairman KEFAUVER. Any way, you tried to negotiate for a contract?

Mr. ROTH. Yes; the book was to have been written by a very fine writer and was to have been a very fine book.

Chairman KEFAUVER. Why would you like to have a book about a person who had just been in a notorious trial?

Mr. ROTH. I believe the New Testament rotates around just that kind of a woman.

Chairman KEFAUVER. In this contract, you were going to do the dictating, and she was going to attach the name of Sandra to the book?

Mr. ROTH. I don't remember that as a detail, but if you say so, that is true.

Chairman KEFAUVER. Do you propose contracts like this to other people who claim notoriety in these kinds of trials?

Mr. ROTH. I believe that if a book like that has been published by me, and it is possible, that it has usually been planned in my office, and if it hasn't, it has usually been brought to me, but whether it is planned or brought, or whether I write it or it is written by the person himself, or herself, it has to be a good book before I publish it.

Chairman KEFAUVER. Paragraph 6 forces her to accept anything you write under the contract you proposed to her.

Mr. ROTH. May I see that?

Chairman KEFAUVER. Yes; that is your contract. You can see it. That is what she balked at? She would not agree to use her name at anything you wrote?

Mr. ROTH. Forgive me now. I remember that was just as big a stumbling point as the money. It wasn't Pat Ward. It was her mother who objected violently to this paragraph. I asked her why. She said, "I don't want any book published in which my daughter is looked upon as a whore."

I said, "The emphasis has been made so heavily, I don't see how you can object."

If it was $5,000, it would have been all right.

Chairman KEFAUVER. You offered her $5,000?

Mr. ROTH. No.

Chairman KEFAUVER. You offered a big percentage?

Mr. ROTH. Yes. I had to do that to make sure it would be a good book.

Chairman KEFAUVER. The fact that she was a juvenile, would that have any effect?

Mr. ROTH. Yes, it had consideration. I believe a book should appear that would give her a chance for living properly. I believe a book like that is in ordeı now. I believe that the courts have completely——

Chairman KEFAUVER. You don't think that a book that you had in mind there would be interesting for children?

Mr. ROTH. I don't think so; no—not the kind of book we would publish.

Chairman KEFAUVER. You don't think that would offend high-school children?

Mr. ROTH. I don't think children were interested in the trial.

Chairman KEFAUVER. We will ask you to make this contract which you proposed a part of the record. Let it be filed as an exhibit.

Mr. ROTH. May I say something?

Chairman KEFAUVER. Sure.

Mr. ROTH. You have said this about several of the items that passed here. When one has a lawyer at one's side, the lawyer usually says he objects and gives reasons. I have no means of knowing anything. If you think this should be a part of the record, I have no reason why it shouldn't be.

Chairman KEFAUVER. Mr. Roth, I think so, because it shows the kind of contracts that you try to get, even with minors.

Mr. ROTH. May I point out for the record that the reason why paragraph 6 is there is that I had no means of knowing that Miss Ward would put things into that book that might be obscene, that might be considered objectionable, and since I have to sell through the mails, I have to make absolutely certain that it will be the kind of a book that I sponsor. I can only sponsor a book that goes through the mails.

Chairman KEFAUVER. How much did you offer, and how much did she want?

Mr. ROTH. I think I offered $1,000, and she wanted $5,000.

Chairman KEFAUVER. Plus the royalties?

Mr. ROTH. Yes, royalties would depend on sales. She would have been entitled to more money.

Chairman KEFAUVER. Are you a naturalized citizen?

Mr. ROTH. Yes, sir.

Chairman KEFAUVER. When were you naturalized?

Mr. ROTH. I am not a naturalized citizen. Forgive me. I became a citizen on my father's papers, and that must have been when my father became a citizen in 1915. On the other hand, in 1940, or 1939,

I went to the Immigration Department and demanded a certificate, certifying that I was a citizen on my father's papers, and I have that certificate.

Chairman KEFAUVER. You think you became a citizen on your father's papers in 1915, but in 1939 you applied for citizenship?

Mr. ROTH. Yes. Some question was raised about it while I was in prison.

Chairman KEFAUVER. And you were issued——

Mr. ROTH. A certificate of citizenship.

Chairman KEFAUVER. What year?

Mr. ROTH. Either 1939 or 1940—probably 1939.

Chairman KEFAUVER. In the district court in the Federal Building in New York?

Mr. ROTH. No, I was issued that on Columbus Avenue—the Immigration Building. I think it is 16th Street.

Chairman KEFAUVER. Did you list these sentences and the time you served on the application for citizenship?

Mr. ROTH. Yes; all these things were discussed.

Chairman KEFAUVER. Were they listed on your application?

Mr. ROTH. I listed on the application whatever the application asked for.

Chairman KEFAUVER. All of them?

Mr. ROTH. Yes. I don't know what it was that was asked then.

Chairman KEFAUVER. Anything else?

Senator LANGER. Does the staff have a copy of the application he signed?

Mr. CHUMBRIS. You made one comparison that I would like for you to explain. You said that a purchase of a shirt is comparable to beautiful nudes. What did you have in mind when you made that statement?

Mr. ROTH. I never made such a statement.

Chairman KEFAUVER. You said if you went to buy a shirt, you might not be interested in going into the store, but if you saw an attractive shirt out in the window, you might buy it, and that is the reason you put the pictures of the nudes on your advertising.

Mr. ROTH. That is self-explanatory. If I put pictures around a description of a book——

Chairman KEFAUVER. You don't want to compare a shirt to a nude, do you?

Mr. ROTH. As a means of attracting attention—it wasn't a shirt that was being discussed, it was the lights that lit up the shirt in the window. I believe a nude has the same function in my circular.

Chairman KEFAUVER. Mr. Roth, we appreciate your coming here and talking very freely. You have cooperated in answering our questions. I think I must say that I know of no one that we have been in touch with who doesn't feel that the kind of slime that you have been sending through the mails is highly deleterious to our young people, and damaging to their morals, and part of the whole picture that we have today of the breakdown among a percentage of our children; that is the opinion of most of the experts that we have had, and I think I should say to you, Mr. Roth, also, that of all the people engaged in this business, we have had many, many more complaints—letters from parents, people interested in the welfare of the children—criticizing what you have been doing, than we have of any other person who publishes and distributes this stuff. Personally, I think it is very reprehensible.

Thank you, Mr. Roth.

Mr. ROTH. May I say something?

Chairman KEFAUVER. Yes.

Senator LANGER. The subcommittee agrees entirely in what you have just said about this stuff.

Chairman KEFAUVER. It may be within the law, but it has been on the border of the law. Sometimes it has been legal and sometimes illegal, but that isn't entirely the question here.

You have something to say?

Mr. ROTH. I believe the people who have criticized me are wrong. I believe you are a great deal more wrong than they are, because you are sitting in judgment on me, and I believe that I will someday within the very near future convince you that you are wrong.

Chairman KEFAUVER. It will take a good deal of convincing.

Mr. ROTH. I will do it.

Chairman KEFAUVER. Thank you, Mr. Roth.

Dr. Henry.

TESTIMONY OF DR. GEORGE W. HENRY, PROFESSOR OF CLINICAL PSYCHIATRY, CORNELL UNIVERSITY COLLEGE OF MEDICINE

Chairman KEFAUVER. Dr. Henry, you are going to give expert testimony. You may mention names. Do you solemnly swear the testimony you will give will be the whole truth, so help you God?

Dr. HENRY. I do.

Chairman KEFAUVER. During the course of our investigation in this field, I have been shocked that there are people who engage in the business of teaching sex deviation to young people, and people who make a profit therefrom. Because of inadequacy of our present Federal rules, we are calling witnesses who will testify as to the cause and result of this menace.

Dr. Henry, do you live at 184 Eldridge Street, New York City, and you are a psychiatrist and nationally known expert in psychosexual maladjustments. We know of your reputation and your standing.

Mr. Vince Gaughan, who is a special counsel of our subcommittee, whose home is in Buffalo, has been helping us here, and doing a good job for the subcommittee in New York, will ask you some questions.

Mr. GAUGHAN. Doctor, will you please, for the record, give us your name and address?

Dr. HENRY. Dr. George W. Henry, and my home address is Greenwich, Conn.

Mr. GAUGHAN. And for the record, Doctor, would you state the profession in which you are engaged?

Dr. HENRY. I am a psychiatrist.

Mr. GAUGHAN. How long have you practiced psychiatry, Doctor?

Dr. HENRY. Since 1916.

Mr. GAUGHAN. Doctor, would you please give us your educational background?

Dr. HENRY. I was graduated from Johns Hopkins Medical School in 1916. I have been on the staff of the New York Hospital since 1917, and I am associate professor of clinical psychiatry at the Cornell University Medical College.

Mr. GAUGHAN. Doctor, are you presently engaged in the private practice of medicine and psychiatry?

Dr. HENRY. I am.

Mr. GAUGHAN. Are you also presently associated with any medical group?

Dr. HENRY. Yes. I am a fellow of the American Medical Association, a fellow of the American Psychiatric Association; I am past president of the New York Psychiatric Society, and I am a member of a number of other societies. I am a diplomate in psychiatry.

Mr. GAUGHAN. Doctor, could you tell us, is there a growing tendency today toward sex deviations?

Dr. HENRY. That is my impression.

Mr. GAUGHAN. From your experience can you tell us what age group is most susceptible to deviation?

Dr. HENRY. Adolescence.

Mr. GAUGHAN. Can such deviation from the normal manifest itself in a number of forms?

Dr. HENRY. Yes.

Mr. GAUGHAN. Would you elaborate on that— the forms that deviation can take?

Dr. HENRY. Well, that involves quite a big problem. I will try to state it briefly.

Chairman KEFAUVER. Doctor, just tell us—what we want to know about here is the problem of juvenile delinquency, and the effect of this material that we have been seeing here, as to whether it is harmful or not, and what the committee and public can do, and what you feel you are familiar with, to help this situation and problem, to give our young people a better chance.

Dr. HENRY. I have heard the testimony given this morning, and if you want a simple answer I would say that what I heard, what I learned from what is published, I would say it is harmful to adolescents.

Mr. GAUGHAN. Are people born with such perversions bred in them, or must be taught and educated along this line?

Dr. HENRY. I could scarely imagine that anyone was born with these tendencies. There may be certain potentialities that can be trained, but I don't believe anybody would arrive at these various deviations unless they had some training.

Mr. GAUGHAN. Doctor, would you tell us what is a fetish?

Dr. HENRY. A fetish is usually some object, material, or substance which becomes the chief source of sexual stimulus for a particular person.

Mr. GAUGHAN. In your medical textbook entitled "All the Sexes" you state in your chapter on fetishes that high heel fetish, and women's lingerie fetish are two of the more common types of fetishes.

Dr. HENRY. That is correct, but any kind of clothing, any part of the body might become attractive or might become a fetish for a particular person.

Mr. GAUGHAN. Used as a substitute for the normal sex?

Dr. HENRY. That is right. It can become and does become as exciting to them as any other part of the body, or the body, to what is called a normal person.

Mr. GAUGHAN. Doctor, is there such a thing as leather and rubber fetish?

Dr. HENRY. Yes; that is true.

Mr. GAUGHAN. Is there also a fetish known as bondage, in which people are trussed up?

Chairman KEFAUVER. What do you mean by leather and rubber fetish?

Dr. HENRY. There are various devices that are manufactured for enclosing parts of the body, and that are used for the purpose of exciting people sexually.

Mr. GAUGHAN. In other words, certain leather types of shoes and boots and so on can be used as a substitute for a sexual outlet by persons who are trained along that line, who so enjoy it?

Dr. HENRY. That is correct. Almost anything can become a fetish, even a violin.

Mr. GAUGHAN. Is there a type of sexual deviation that is known as bondage where a person is trussed up with ropes and chains?

Dr. HENRY. Yes; that is fairly common.

Chairman KEFAUVER. You say bondage is fairly common?

Dr. HENRY. Fairly common in this particular group, that is the group of sexual deviates.

Chairman KEFAUVER. Tell us more about that bondage being fairly common.

Dr. HENRY. Among those who are familiar with this variety of sexual deviation, it is a matter of common knowledge to them. It is not common knowledge to the general public.

Chairman KEFAUVER. You mean they like to see someone who is bound up?

Dr. HENRY. Yes; they do.

Chairman KEFAUVER. Pictures of them?

Dr. HENRY. Some of them do.

Mr. GAUGHAN. And some of them might be bound up by themselves?

Dr. HENRY. Yes.

Mr. GAUGHAN. Is the act of spanking a part of the flagellation technique?

Dr. HENRY. Yes; one of the milder forms.

Chairman KEFAUVER. You mean whipping?

Dr. HENRY. Yes; whipping in any form, even to the extent of drawing blood.

Chairman KEFAUVER. You say it is a minor form. What are the more violent forms?

Dr. HENRY. They use actual whips, straps, sticks.

Mr. GAUGHAN. Sometimes they use the hands, sometimes whips, sometimes chains, and hairbrushes?

Dr. HENRY. Yes.

Mr. GAUGHAN. Is there a sex deviation wherein two females are able to find an erotic satisfaction by inflicting pain and injury upon each other?

Dr. HENRY. Yes.

Mr. GAUGHAN. What form of deviation does that come under?

Dr. HENRY. Sadism and masochism.

Mr. GAUGHAN. Dr. Henry, I am going to come down by you, because my questions are of such a form that I have to ask you to identify a number of pictures that I am going to produce as an exhibit here today.

Dr. Henry, I show you a booklet entitled "Cartoons and Model Parade" published by one Irving Klaw, of 212 East 14th Street, in New York City. I specifically call your attention to the movie offered by said Klaw as advertised on page 3 of this publication, called "Negligee Fight." I note that the heading reads that this 16-millimeter movie shows the terrific battle that ensues when both girls claim a black negligee, and, Doctor, I ask you, is this a form of the sadism or masochistic type of perversion to which we were just referring when I asked you if two females can get erotic pleasure from such carrying on?

Dr. HENRY. That is true.

Mr. GAUGHAN. I also call to your attention page 3 of this same publication, to pictures entitled, "Chris Strips for Bed." The mention there is the fact that she wears—it specifically mentions she wears 6-inch high heel, patent leather shoes. It mentions how she goes through this sensuous art of disrobing, and along with that I direct your attention to page 6 of this same publication, and on page 6 we find "Lounging Around in Lingerie," in which the man who offers this publication says he will sell this particular movie for $8, and he notes particularly the fact that the models wear 6-inch high heel, patent leather shoes.

Doctor, I want you to note the various other pictures with this 6-inch shoe business being graphically brought out by the photographers and the author of this publication, and I ask you, Doctor, is it a fair statement to say that these are pictures—these pictures are put therein for the purpose of exciting people to take part in the fetish that is known as the high-heel fetish? Is that a fair statement?

Dr. HENRY. That could be true. Such heels are sexually exciting, but they are also part of a picture, any part of which or all of which is sexually exciting.

Mr. GAUGHAN. The whole picture you consider sexually exciting?

Dr. HENRY. That is right.

Mr. GAUGHAN. There are a number of things in the picture besides the fetish we are particularly concerned with here that you find sexually exciting?

Dr. HENRY. Yes.

Mr. GAUGHAN. On page 7 of this publication I direct your attention specifically to a series of photographs called, "New Specially Posed," in which it says there are 44—the heading says there are 44 different bound-and-gagged photos, 8 being spanked, offered to you at 40 cents apiece. It also mentions the fact that there are three other different types of spanking photographs at 40 cents apiece, and the owner of this organization says he also offers 71 different high-heel and lingerie photos of models wearing 6-inch high-heel shoes, bras, and panties, at 25 cents.

Would you look at those photographs and tell the chairman of the committee whether you, in your opinion, believe that is a form of bondage, the type of deviation wherein the people get a sexual thrill or pleasure of being bound up or binding somebody else up, and inflicting a form of torture through these ropes and chains that you see in all these pictures?

Dr. HENRY. The answer to all your questions is "Yes."

Mr. GAUGHAN. I now give you this book as a whole. I ask you to go through this booklet, Doctor, and I ask you specifically, can you see any purpose for this publication other than the one purpose to cause erotic stimuli by showing acts of sexual perversion? First, I asked Dr. Henry to leaf through the book, and then asked him to tell us, after perusing the contents of this book, to tell us whether he can find any other purpose than publishing such a booklet for erotic stimuli for the people who will read it, and dwell upon it and study it.

Is there any desirable reason other than for erotic stimuli?

Dr. HENRY. No, the sole purpose is to stimulate people erotically in an abnormal way.

Mr. GAUGHAN. That is the only purpose of this booklet, in your expert opinion, Doctor?

Dr. HENRY. That is correct.

Mr. GAUGHAN. Doctor, I ask you, could children be sexually perverted by looking at, by studying, and by dwelling upon photos of this nature and the contents of this book?

Dr. HENRY. Yes.

Chairman KEFAUVER. Doctor, is it a very unwholesome influence, this sort of thing?

Dr. HENRY. It is.

Chairman KEFAUVER. In your opinion the increase in sex crimes, deviations that we are having—does that increase result in part at least from the reading and looking at magazines and pictures of this kind by children?

Dr. HENRY. I would think that was an important factor in the increase.

Chairman KEFAUVER. You think it is an important factor?

Dr. HENRY. Yes.

Mr. GAUGHAN. Doctor, would violence and murder be a natural outgrowth of such perversions that we have discussed here this morning with you?

Dr. HENRY. It might be.

Chairman KEFAUVER. You mean this bondage and whipping, and things of that sort?

Dr. HENRY. Yes.

Mr. GAUGHAN. Would you say it is a fair statement, that suicide, murder, and psychosis is the end result of this type of trash?

Dr. HENRY. In some instances; yes.

Mr. GAUGHAN. Doctor, I show you some clippings mounted on a board from the Miami Daily News, dated Tuesday, August 31, 1954; the contents of these articles. Doctor, specifically note the fact that one 17-year-old boy, Kenneth Grimm, was found hanging in an inverted position from a stick or board suspended between the forks of two trees, and trussed up in a fashion whereby his legs and arms are tied behind him, and a rope is thrown around his neck so that he strangles himself. He strangles himself by the position in which he has been forced. Doctor, I ask you is it your opinion, from perusing this article, from looking at the picture, would you say that this is the end result of a sex crime? Does this impress you as the type of thing that can happen as the result of bondage—this fetish we have been discussing this morning?

Dr. HENRY. Yes; it is an end result, a kind of result.

Chairman KEFAUVER. Let the picture and plaque be made part of the record.

Mr. GAUGHAN. "Gables boy found hanged. Weird death baffles cops." It also states "Father discovers body in trees."

I would like to announce at this point, the father of this boy is with us this morning, and has been so kind as to consent to testify following Dr. Henry's testimony.

Chairman KEFAUVER. All right.

Mr. GAUGHAN. Doctor, do you have any further comment that you would like to make on the subject that we have been discussing here—the subject under examination—and do you have any recommendations that you, as an expert, a nationally renowned expert in the field, would like to make to the subcommittee?

Dr. HENRY. I think I should clarify this sex problem a little bit so that innocent people would not be involved in it.

For instance, there is a tendency to associate such acts of violence with a homosexual—what is called the homosexual. The facts are that the homosexual is no more prone to violence than the heterosexual or the normal. If we were to divide humans roughly into four groups, we would call them heterosexual, biosexual, homosexual, and Narcissistic, and the groups that we have been talking about this morning belong primarily to the Narcissistic, more specially to people whom we call exhibitionists, or peeping individuals. These publications cater to people who are psychosexually immature, emotionally immature, and who get their major satisfaction out of looking at such displays. It has little to do with other fields of psychopathology that is commonly associated with such acts.

The only other thing that occurs to me is that I firmly believe that the majority of people are so constituted and live in environments such that they will grow up to be reasonably normal in their sexual adjustment.

There is, however, quite a large proportion of the population who are susceptible to training, training such as may be obtained from these publications, and whether or not they arrive at a point of violence is perhaps an academic matter in view of the seriousness of the other problem that no one can tell ahead of time who is going to arrive at that goal once they have been exposed to these publications.

Furthermore, there are all degrees of sadism and masochism which enter into human relations, and which seldom get into the newspapers.

Chairman KEFAUVER. Dr. Henry, murder—even crimes involving theft, beatings, most all kinds of crimes, can, to some extent, result from maladjustments which children might get from the kind of literature and pictures and whatnot they see?

Dr. HENRY. That is correct. A good many of the sexually maladjusted are not primarily interested in sex relations, but in the thrill or the danger which is associated with the sexual act.

Chairman KEFAUVER. In other words, these pictures, these bondage pictures and things of that sort are important in this matter, too?

Dr. HENRY. They are important.

Chairman KEFAUVER. Will one of you show this gargoyle thing, 478 Madison Avenue, to Dr. Henry?

Is that typical of the bondage pictures you were talking about?

Dr. HENRY. Yes. There is more of the whipping in this. You can see the whip in several of the pictures. Whipping means just what it says. They actually whip these people, sometimes until they bleed.

There are individuals who are so impelled to abuse others that they will keep on until they kill them.

Chairman KEFAUVER. Until they kill them?

Dr. HENRY. Yes.

Chairman KEFAUVER. I think there are places in that picture that will show bondage pictures.

Dr. HENRY. Yes.

Chairman KEFAUVER. If that was sent through the mail, I am sure the inspectors would stop that.

Dr. HENRY. Sometimes the greatest thrill is experienced at the time that somebody is dying.

Chairman KEFAUVER. By the person dying or the person causing the death?

Dr. HENRY. The person causing the death. There are also people who get their greatest thrill by being severely beaten.

Chairman KEFAUVER. You mean being the recipients of the beating?

Dr. HENRY. Yes.

Chairman KEFAUVER. Doctor, you saw how these pictures that Mr. Roth had—you heard him express his expert opinion based upon many years in the business. What did you think of that? What do you think of his philosophy?

Dr. HENRY. I don't agree with it at all.

Chairman KEFAUVER. You think this stuff he is sending out, these pamphlets that you saw here, are a bad influence and degrading to even grownups, let alone young people?

Dr. HENRY. Yes. I think there is a confusion between children and adolescence in a good deal of the testimony. When they use the word "children" they often mean "adolescents," and everyone knows that the adolescent is most sexually excitable, and has the least legitimate opportunity to find an outlet for that sexual excitability. As a result of that they find every conceivable means of finding an outlet, including what was shown this morning.

It is an error also to assume that if you sell something to an adult that it doesn't get to an adolescent. A great many of these so-called adults are really still adolescents, and feel most at home with actual adolescents.

More than that, some of them are primarily interested in introducing adolescents into abnormal practices.

Chairman KEFAUVER. So that his idea that the effect of this kind of stuff on adults might be stimulating and what not, but it would not have any effect upon adolescents is just without medical foundation?

Dr. HENRY. I would think it would be just the opposite. It would be more exciting to the adolescent.

Chairman KEFAUVER. Anything else?

Mr. GAUGHAN. Doctor, I might ask you, as the father of five children, and as many parents around the Nation have wondered from time to time, if we have read about the senseless killing by teenagers during these past few years, would you say it is a fair statement that many of these killings are the direct result of some sort of an erotic stimuli that has been given to these teen-agers, these children, which result in their taking part in the gang warfare and death and violence and torture, and so on?

Dr. HENRY. Yes; I would expect that entered into a large proportion of such killings.

Mr. GAUGHAN. A large proportion?

Dr. HENRY. Yes. That is related to the fundamental principle that a person who engages in such killings is an insecure person, and a great deal of his insecurity comes from the fact that he is poorly adjusted, usually, as a male. In order to bolster up his ego, he has to do something bold to give him the feeling that he is a man. If, in addition, he has been trained to sadistic ways of bolstering his ego, so much the worse.

Mr. GAUGHAN. That is all I have.

Chairman KEFAUVER. Dr. Henry, we appreciate very much your testimony, and I want to say while, as just a layman, and I am sure I might speak for the press in this regard, too, we appreciate the fact that you are one of the most eminent and highly thought of, most experienced psychiatrist in the whole United States, or the world, and you have spoken to us in such plain language that we can all understand. It was a little bit unusual.

Thank you very much, sir.

Dr. HENRY. Well, I have had the opinion, after many years of experience, that if you can't tell something in plain English, you don't understand it yourself.

Chairman KEFAUVER. We appreciate having you with us.

Mr. Norman Thomas, we will be glad if you will come down.

STATEMENT OF NORMAN THOMAS, NEW YORK, N. Y.

Mr. Thomas, yesterday I was advised that you had written the subcommittee a letter expressing your interest in the hearing, and the staff of the subcommittee contacted you and asked if you were willing to come down and give your views and ideas to the subcommittee.

I am not familiar with your various points of view, but you are an eminent and great American, for whom the American people of all political faiths have esteem and respect.

Mr. THOMAS. Especially since I quit running for office.

Chairman KEFAUVER. So we are honored that you have taken out time to come and give us the benefit of your counsel, and through this subcommittee, speak to the American people on anything you have to say about the problem of juvenile delinquency or pornography, which we are considering here.

Senator Langer is an old friend of yours. I know he has something to say at this time.

Senator LANGER. I can only say that I do not know any man in this country whom I respect more highly.

Mr. THOMAS. I used to be willing to compromise for more votes and less respect.

Senator LANGER. We are very happy that you wrote the subcommittee, and we are happy you are here.

Mr. THOMAS. Thank you very much.

Chairman KEFAUVER. Tell us anything you want to.

Mr. THOMAS. While I appreciate an opportunity to come, I am a little embarrassed, because, at short notice, I had no expectation of appearing before the committee. I wrote the letter on only one subject and that subject was the only subject on which I have any right to speak.

I am not, like many of your witnesses, an expert as a psychiatrist or as a teacher, or someone who has come in close contact with these problems. But I have, for a good deal of my life, spent a good deal of my time on civil-liberties issues, and I am a pretty stanch supporter of the first amendment, which I think has suffered some damage by Congress and certain other agencies of Government.

I am, however, not at all impressed by the degree to which defenders of certain kinds of comic books, and even of pornography, pure and simple, want to press the first amendment. I do not think the first amendment gives any guaranty to men to seduce the innocent and to exploit the kind of unformed mind and unformed emotions of children and adolescents.

I think there is a great deal of dangerous nonsense in this appeal to the first amendment and to freedom of the press when one is dealing with the kind of thing which I have just heard testimony about from the preceding witness.

I do not believe that in order to protect the fundamental liberties of the press we have to turn our children, who are, in a sense, the ward of all our society, over to the kind of visual exploitation of base emotion, and the arousal of base emotion to which, of course, this literature, this pornographic literature, these films and cards and all the rest are directed.

I understand that the evil has grown greatly. A great many years ago I was a secretary of a local school board. It was here in East Harlem, in Manhattan, and I know we had a great deal of trouble with deliberate circulation for money of pornographic postal cards in those days.

The situation has become much worse, I understand. It is an outrage to freedom to say there is any guaranty of freedom for this kind of thing.

Parents have the first responsibility, certainly, for protecting their children, but even the most careful parent cannot protect his children against the floods of certain kinds of comic books and certain kinds of pornographic literature now circulated; and there are a good many parents who have neither the knowledge or capacity to protect them, and society has to step in.

I do not believe that society can advantageously, or perhaps constitutionally in the United States, step in by prepublication censorship. That, I think is open to doubt in the light of history as a method of dealing with any of these problems.

I will be perfectly frank and express considerable doubt of the usefulness of the voluntary censorship set up by the comic book publishers.

There is a certain danger in giving a parent's seal of approval to rather bad stuff, even if it is within the code, as if it had authoritative blessing.

I should go along with the people who are opposed to censorship. But it seems to me that it ought to be possible to find ways of outright prohibition of the circulation, by any device whatever, of the kind of pornographic stuff you have been discussing and the kind of comic books that Dr. Wertham discussed.

I suppose there are difficulties of definition, but I think the job can be done. I am not at all impressed by some of the arguments I have heard by spokesmen for the industry, and from honest defenders of civil liberty who, I think, in this case are misguided.

I am not impressed by the kinds of arguments I hear. I am not at all impressed with the notion that you should deal with pornography and a certain type of comic book as you might deal with the discussion of ideals which would lead to sedition. You are dealing with an entirely different realm of affairs.

An idea, even a wrong idea, a bad idea in economics, in politics, and so on, can be met in the market place by a true idea, and history, at least in America, bears out this statement—that, on the whole, a true idea wins a victory. I haven't won often enough to say it always does, but on the whole, I believe that error in this field is better counteracted by truth, than when error goes out—rather, than when truth calls on a policeman's club in the matter.

The appeal that is then suggested by an idea is wholly different from the kind of thing about which you have just had testimony. To the unformed life of a child, the perversion of what, in itself, is a life-giving sexual instinct is a terrible thing for society, and does not fall in the class of ideas which was defended as able to win their own victories.

I am not at all impressed by the argument that I have heard that it is time to wait until you have proved clear and immediate danger by absolute and precise proof that a particular crime or a particular bit of outrageous juvenile delinquency has been caused by a particular comic book or pornographic publication. This is absurd.

There is a good deal of talk to the effect that those of us who believe that something has to be done are alleging that all juvenile delinquency is due to these publications. I never hear that allegation made by anyone except by people who want to knock down a strawman. I don't think that is the main cause of juvenile delinquency, but so serious is this delinquency, everything is dangerous.

What we are concerned with is not primarily, or chiefly, as I see it, the stopping of particular crimes that reach police court. It is the whole effect upon the minds of the young who are going to shape the future, and that is not subject to these precise tests of clear and immediate danger that have been alleged.

I have heard some of the psychiatric testimony—not here, but elsewhere—which apologizes for this. I have not been too much impressed. But I do believe there is immense value in modern psychiatry and in its research. I doubt if right and wrong is determined solely by psychiatric majorities one way or another, and I doubt if the commonsense of the communities is altogether gainsaid by the testimony of men who tell me, as one man did tell me, that the most horrible comics, exalting sadism and teaching crime, have no effect at all. That I just do not believe.

I would like awfully well, as a rule, to know whether the men who thus testified have gotten any fees from any of the self-interested parties. They have a right to get such fees. Everybody has a right to hire help, but I confess, without wishing to get into any row with any tobacco companies, that I would not be as much impressed by a doctor who is hired by a great tobacco company to prove there was no danger of lung cancer as I would by a more disinterested witness.

I am very much interested to know who pays what in the matter of some of this testimony.

I have been very much impressed, and depressed, to listen to pretty good people who argue very hotly, mostly against censorship, to which I also am opposed, but apparently in some cases against any kind of legislative action.

They allege one of two things. They have to. Either that this—after all, these horror prints do not do any harm, or else that you cannot help it that they don't do enough harm to run a certain risk.

What troubles me is that in almost every case you get a confusion of two ideas. I have here what was given me. I think it is called "Facts Kit." It was given to me by the Comic Book Publishers Association. Right through their literature there runs confusion of ideas. On the one hand they boast they are now pure, having set up their own authority; and on the other hand they argue they didn't need to, because it did no harm, that psychiatrists said what they were doing was all right.

They cannot have it both ways; in this connection, I am very skeptical of what is revealed by the confusion.

I am also extraordinarily unsympathetic with a notion that our society is so dull and so bound by rather extreme logic, that there is no way to prevent this horror literature, these horror pictures, with all their effect, which may not be extended to censorship or prohibition of Mother Goose, or Shakespeare, or, in another field, "Crime and Punishment."

I imagine that some of the artists that you have been discussing could make Mother Goose a pretty bad business with certain kinds of drawings. But I think it is all nonsense to argue that because there is silence in Jack the Giant Killer, and because one of the heroes of the Mother Goose rhyme was going to throw a man downstairs for not saying his prayers, that therefore there is no way of restricting the horror and pornographic literature that comes flooding out to the immense profit of the publishers, without prohibiting Mother Goose, or something of the sort.

I think the common sense American knows the difference. I think the difference could be written into laws that could pass the test of constitutionality. I am not a psychiatrist or a lawyer and cannot help you in framing those laws. I think the job could be done. I think it is defeatist to say that you cannot do it.

I think, moreover, that the interpretation of law depends in part, as we know, by the development of public opinion. The Chief Justice of the United States, himself, held that changes in public opinion, in the way we think about things, made the doctrine of Separate but Equal not tenable now.

I think in these times, with this terrible increase of juvenile delinquency, with this immensely profitably flood of pornography, using techniques never before available to the seducers of the innocent, I think it is nonsense to say that we are so bound by a very extreme interpretation of the freedom of the press that we cannot act.

We have acted in other cases, as I know. I think the post office, in some cases, has been given too much power not to accept for mailing certain things—religious books and political books—that are said to involve dissension. If that is constitutional, certainly the kind of legislation that I think you could shape would be constitutional.

The very effort is itself educational. It will open the eyes of lots of people—parents. It will give them authority and help in enforcing the law.

I heard a defense of this sort of business, this pornography, in the following terms—that some authority, not named, had said that a diseased mind might be more adversely affected by the mere presence of a person of the opposite sex than by any of this literature. That is a most shocking argument to advance. We are not talking about already diseased minds so far gone that they might be ruined by that which is normal and proper in life. We are talking about people who have tendencies that can be led into disease. That is a very different matter.

In other words, gentlemen, I apologize for a not too carefully worked out speech. I did not know I was coming until I had no time to do any writing, but I do want to put myself on record, just because I have so diligently tried to serve civil liberty, as believing that it is not only possible for you to frame legislation that will curb the enormous evils without abridging any desirable liberty; but it is necessary, for freedom, itself, is besmirched, if freedom comes to the tune of $500 million a year, and society and government is utterly powerless.

Chairman KEFAUVER. We thank you very much for an enlightening, forcible statement. It will be very helpful to our subcommittee, and, I am sure, to everyone who reads and hears this. It was fine of you to write us a letter, and we would like to make your letter part of the record.

While we haven't discussed some remedies that have been suggested by you in any detail, everybody knows that no citizen has been more vigorous in the defense of civil liberties and freedom of the press and speech than you; and your concern about this problem of pornography and horror crime books, and how you think it should be dealt with, is certainly very valuable to us.

Mr. THOMAS. May I add that I have been, on a number of occasions, a member of a jury. I believe you can trust the American jury to deal with nonsense and justice. They would act in ways that would not create a danger of interference with the true freedom of speech or the press. I know it will take some doing, and I don't altogether envy you the task of doing it, but I think it can and must be done.

Senator LANGER. I know of no man who has had more experience in his personal life than has Norman Thomas. He is a real true American citizen, and I am certainly proud he came here and testified before this subcommittee. It is a great tribute to this subcommittee to have Norman Thomas come here and testify before it.

Mr. THOMAS. Thank you very much. I am not seeking any particular applause; I am terribly interested in it.

The first time I found out how serious it could be was a great many years ago, and I think it has grown worse.

Chairman KEFAUVER. Thank you very much.

Mr. THOMAS. Thank you.

(The letter dated May 23, 1955, from Norman Thomas and addressed to Senator Kefauver is as follows:)

NEW YORK, N. Y., *May 23, 1955.*

Hon. ESTES KEFAUVER,
    Senate Office Building, Washington 25, D. C.

DEAR SENATOR KEFAUVER: Like every good citizen, I am deeply concerned for the success of the hearings you are holding concerning juvenile delinquency and related matters like the effect of so-called comic books on the young.

I am no expert at all in the field in which you are making inquiry. I have, however, long been active in behalf of civil liberties and I want to put on record with you my belief—in contrast to some champions of civil liberties—that government has not only a right but a duty to consider legislative controls of the publication and circulation of comic books in order to prevent the "seduction of the innocent" by the terrible mixture of sex sensationalism, if not outright pornography, sadism, education in crime, and sheer horror to which certain comic books have treated us.

It is, of course, fantastic to argue in behalf of any doctrine of freedom of speech or the press, that men have an inalienable right to corrupt the young and to make themselves rich in the process. The argument for a do-nothing policy by the Federal Government can only be supported on one or both of two lines. First, that these vicious comic books do no real harm; and, second, that Government is so clumsy an instrument that it can find no way to protect children without running the risk of assuming dictatorial powers over the press. I think both arguments are erroneous.

The case against the horror comics is not merely or chiefly the degree they may contribute to juvenile delinquency. It is the effect of them on the minds of those for whose education as good citizens society has responsibility. I am aware that supposedly expert psychological and psychiatric testimony has been brought forward to support the contention that these comics have no bad effect. This is a position that cannot be taken logically unless one is willing to advance the extraordinary proposition that there is no case at all for moral education or the inculcating of a lot of good literature. It is the experience of the race that children's minds are very impressionable for good or evil, particularly by the picture method which makes so strong an appeal to them. Good and evil are not determined by majority votes of psychiatrists and I should question the value of the vote of the psychiatrist who appears or ever has appeared for a fee paid by the publishers of comic books. They have a right to hire psychiatrists and psychiatrists have a right to be hired. But I would not give full weight to the evidence offered under these circumstances any more than I should give full weight to the testimony of a doctor on cancer who was in the employ of one of the great tobacco companies. I think the preponderance of evidence is entirely on the side of those who believe that these books are a contributory, though by no means the sole cause of juvenile delinquency.

I do not, however, accept as valid the attempt of certain advocates of civil liberty to claim that the Government can only interfere if at all on the basis of proof of clear and immediate danger of specific contribution of a comic book to overt juvenile delinquency. The right of free speech on political and economic matters up to a point of clear and immediate danger is one thing. The right of free speech or free press to corrupt the young is another.

The principal argument of advocates of civil liberties has been directed against censorship. I myself would doubt the efficacy or possibly the constitutionality of a law providing for a governmental precensorship of comic books. I am not favorably impressed by the private censorship suddenly set up by the comic book publishers here in New York. For one thing, the seal of approval carries too much weight in the mind of the young for inferior stuff. I should, however, think it possible to deal fairly well with the evil by invoking the Government's right to protect children by setting up in law a prohibition of the circulation of horror comics, generally defined in the law, among children. The enforcement of the law, as now of law against pornography, should be left to district attorneys and juries. It should be hoped the district attorneys would act more vigilantly than sometimes in the case of pornographic postal cards circulated among school children. It is also, I think, important in any effort either to turn on the light for arousing public opinion or to help in the enforcement of law that each comic book should bear the name of the responsible publisher, and author or authors.

I am aware that the wording of a definition of the kind of horror comics the sale and circulation of which to children should be prohibited is not easy. But I refuse to believe that it is impossible to make such a definition which will not apply to the proper publication and circulation of serious books like Crime and Punishment, for instance. I do not believe that we cannot pass a law dealing with comic books that will not apply to Shakespeare and Mother Goose. I am rather irritated by the argument to the contrary.

In this whole field it is important to distinguish between the kind of truth in religious, economic, and social theories which can make its own way in the market place of ideas and the kind of decency which can make its own way in the minds of children against these horror books. Pornography and sadism bypass the area of intellectual discussion or conflict. This is particularly true when one is dealing with the impressionable minds of children. Milton's argument against censorship was never meant by him to operate in this field of pornography and sadism. One does not need to be a psychiatrist to recognize the force of the difference.

I am addressing this to you personally because you are in charge of the investigation but I should be very willing to have it put on the record if you are recording written statements as well as oral.

Sincerely yours,

NORMAN THOMAS.

Chairman KEFAUVER. We will stand in recess until 15 minutes to 2. (Whereupon, at 12:35 p. m., the hearing was recessed until 1:45 p. m.)

AFTERNOON SESSION

Chairman KEFAUVER. Mr. Clarence Grimm.
Mr. Grimm, will you come around, sir?
Mr. Grimm, will you solemnly swear the testimony you will give this subcommittee will be the whole truth, so help you God?
Mr. GRIMM. Yes.

TESTIMONY OF CLARENCE GRIMM, CORAL GABLES, FLA.

Chairman KEFAUVER. Mr. Grimm, before counsel, Mr. Gaughan, asks you some questions, I want you to say that as chairman of this subcommittee I know the embarrassment and the distaste that you have in coming here to talk again, or to have anything to say about the tragic happening to your son on August 20 of last year. I know that you would rather not say anything about it; however, in the judgment of this subcommittee your testimony may be of some benefit in bringing to the attention of the people and to law enforcement agencies and to legislative bodies the kind of situation that might be of some help in preventing some other father's son from having a similar tragic experience.

It is on that basis that we have asked you to come today to testify. We appreciate your cooperation. We know that you would like to do anything you could to try to see that the kind of mania of which your son was the victim is removed from our society.

We know that your son was an outstanding young man, but we feel that by your telling us about it, it may enable us to help get at the problem. So, we do appreciate your cooperation.

Mr. Gaughan, you may proceed.

Mr. GAUGHAN. Mr. Chairman, I would like at the outset to state that in our investigations of this terrible tragedy, I myself was singularly impressed by the type of young man that met this tragic end. He was an Eagle Scout of Coral Gables, Fla.; a B-plus student in his school work, and a model young man in every sense of the word.

So, Mr. Grimm, for the record, would you please state your name, your full name?

Mr. GRIMM. My name is Clarence Grimm.

Mr. GAUGHAN. And your address, sir?

Mr. GRIMM. 5028 Maggiore, Coral Gables, Fla.

Mr. GAUGHAN. How are you employed, Mr. Grimm?

Mr. GRIMM. I am self-employed. I am an electrical contractor.

Mr. GAUGHAN. Mr. Grimm, are you acquainted with the purposes of this investigation, of this subcommittee, into juvenile delinquency and pornography, specifically, at this hearing?

Mr. GRIMM. Yes, sir.

Mr. GAUGHAN. Mr. Grimm, I am going to hand you an exhibit which has already been introduced into evidence. With your permission I will come down closer to you.

Chairman KEFAUVER. Yes, come down closer and get the essential points over.

Mr. GAUGHAN. Sir, I hand you a group of clippings from the Miami Daily News, of Tuesday evening, August 31, 1954, and also some from the same paper for August 21, 1954 [handing to Mr. Grimm].

Sir, can you identify those clippings?

Mr. GRIMM. Yes, sir; I can.

Mr. GAUGHAN. With what are they concerned?

Mr. GRIMM. They are concerned with the tragic death of my son.

Mr. GAUGHAN. Can you, Mr. Grimm, tell the subcommittee how it was that your boy met his sudden end on the evening of August 20, 1954; can you tell us specifically? I realize it is an unsolved murder and that the details are—you are as mystified as the police authorities by it—but tell us what you know about it, starting with what occurred that evening when you came home to dinner and saw your boy for the last time.

Mr. GRIMM. Well, I don't know how to go about telling it. These articles are self-explanatory.

We missed him in the evening. He had worked all day for me. He got home from his work about 5 o'clock and had come home dirty and tired, in his work clothes.

He turned on the water faucet to fill the tub with water, then went out in the yard and fired off a couple of firecrackers which he had brought back from Georgia. He had been to a summer camp.

He attracted his mother's attention to it. She called out to him to come in and shut the water off.

He was away all evening, which is unusual. He never left the house without telling us. He had no errand that we knew of. In fact, he had planned to go to a civil defense meeting that evening, where he was a member of the Ground Observation Corps.

I found him the next morning in a very grotesque, weird situation that I have never been able to cope with or understand yet.

Mr. GAUGHAN. Would you, sir, for the subcommittee, tell us how your son was trussed up, and the position in which you found him when you found his body on the morning of August 21?

Mr. GRIMM. He was trussed up in a very unnatural position. It looked like it had been planned in some way. It wasn't anything that I had ever seen before, or anybody else had ever seen before, that I know of.

He wasn't hung like most people hang themselves by the neck from a rope. The fact that he didn't have any clothes on, and he was a modest boy, led me immediately to believe that there was some sex angle to it, some sex act in some way, either with the help of someone else or through retaliation on the part of someone else—I don't know what it is. It is still a mystery to me.

Mr. GAUGHAN. I show you a picture from the Miami Daily News, a sketch of the boy [handing to Mr. Grimm]. Would you say that is an accurate sketch of how the boy was found when you saw him?

Mr. GRIMM. Yes; very accurate.

Chairman KEFAUVER. Well, Mr. Gaughan, you just describe the picture for the record; tell us what it shows.

Mr. GAUGHAN. The picture at which I am looking shows 2 saplings, with forks, and a 1- by 2-inch board is suspended between the 2 forks of the tree. Hanging by his knees and, of course, in an inverted position, is Kenneth Grimm. He is trussed up with ropes, tied around his ankles, the same ropes reaching from his ankles to his arms, and looped around his neck, so that his body is pulled back in a very grotesque-looking position.

The caption underneath the picture reads:

An artist's sketch shows how Kenneth Grimm, 17, was found trussed and hanging from a wooden crossbar between two trees in bushes near his Coral Gables home at 5028 Maggiore Street. The boy's feet were bound by a rope, and he was hanging from his knees. The rope from his feet encircled his neck, bending his body in a sharp backward arc.

Chairman KEFAUVER. Let that be entered into the record.

Senator LANGER. May I see it, please?

Mr. GAUGHAN. Yes, sir [handing to Senator Langer].

Mr. Grimm, do you recognize, sir, this booklet which I hand you, entitled, "Cartoon and Model Parade," published by Irving Klaw, "the Pin-Up King?"

Mr. GRIMM. Yes.

Mr. GAUGHAN. Would you tell the subcommittee how you first came upon a copy of this book?

Mr. GRIMM. Through a mutual friend who was interested in the case, why, he brought my attention to an ad in one of these so-called girlie magazines, which publicized this book.

It took him quite a while to find the thing and bring it to me, and he finally did. My son-in-law sent off for the catalog.

As a result of that, I found very similar situations, or very similar acts of tying people up in that book that reminded me of my son's case, and that is one reason why I got hot on this angle at this end of it. I had never come across anything like that before, and I was looking for a clue.

I feel that there is some connection in some way. I don't know just what the connection is, indirectly or directly, through someone else that studied this and knew about it; I don't know what happened. I do feel that this is the hottest thing that I have gotten onto since the boy died; I believe that, as far as this clue to the incident is concerned.

Mr. GAUGHAN. Sir, I direct your attention specifically to page 3 of this publication showing a young lady trussed up, and ask you to look at that picture, with her arms tied behind her back, her mouth gagged, the only dissimiliarity is that she is in a sitting position here.

In other words, if we were to flip her backwards, she would be upside down.

Is that somewhat similar to the position, the way the ropes were arranged when you found your boy?

Mr. GRIMM. I can't say this is a similar position. There are some in here which are very similar.

Mr. GAUGHAN. Let me direct your attention to page 4.

Mr. GRIMM. Even these cartoons here [indicating], some of these probably, if you invert them, would probably be very similar.

I can't say that I ever studied these. I would probably be more like this.

Mr. GAUGHAN. On page 8?

Mr. GRIMM. Yes.

Chairman KEFAUVER. I saw one in there where they had a person hanging with the feet down.

Mr. GAUGHAN. Yes. There are so many different illustrations of this hanging business and trussing business that it is hard to point to any particular one.

Let me show you this one here, sir. This picture here illustrates a model known as Betty Page.

Does that accurately reflect about how your boy was found?

Mr. GRIMM. It is more or less the same. It is a very similar position; there is a resemblance to the way I found him.

Mr. GAUGHAN. In other words, when you went through this book by yourself you were immediately struck by the number of illustrations in that book that depicted the same fashion in which your boy died?

Mr. GRIMM. That's right.

Mr. GAUGHAN. And you, sir, came to what conclusion after looking at this magazine?

Mr. GRIMM. As I say, I have been looking for some clue to this thing. I haven't had the police into it. They let the case rest as some type of accident due to some impulse on the part of the boy. They don't know anything beyond that, and they haven't been of any help beyond that.

In trying to solve the thing, in trying to arrive at some more definite reason for this, why, that is the closest thing I have gotten to it. The way that was tied, it wasn't anything that any youngster like him, with his character—it wasn't anything that he could concoct himself. There wasn't any history of that; no similar action on his part. He led an outdoor life. He was active in the Boy Scouts from the time he was a little bit of a fellow. He had attended a boys' camp in Tennessee for 5 or 6 seasons. He had only been home 2 days from the camp when this happened. He was a counselor there this year, and I don't think they would have selected him and invited him to have become a counselor if there was anything questionable about his actions.

Therefore, I feel that he could not have worked himself into this position of his own making, or couldn't have thought of anything like that. It would have had to have been brought to his attention by either someone else showing him how, or he saw a picture of it—I don't know. I feel there is a definite connection between this sort of thing and his death.

I also feel there is definitely an evil to this, and I am bound and determined to do what I can to suppress it. It isn't good. It is an unhealthy situation. It is not wholesome. There is nothing cultural about it. It is just no damned good. That's all I can say about it.

Naturally, I feel more keenly about it since I was involved in something that I feel is a direct result of something like this, you see.

Mr. GAUGHAN. Your boy is gone, and you are trying to prevent anything like this happening in the future to any other parents?

Mr. GRIMM. That's right.

Mr. GAUGHAN. In other words, sir, you became interested in this thing known as bondage, this tying, after your boy's death, and it was something with which you were not acquainted prior to this incident?

Mr. GRIMM. That's right.

Mr. GAUGHAN. And you are now in your mind thoroughly convinced that he was a victim of this thing that we have been discussing this morning with Dr. Henry, called the bondage and fetish?

Mr. GRIMM. That's right. In some way; yes, sir.

Mr. GAUGHAN. Sir, I hand you a clipping from, I believe this is, the Miami Herald of January 7, 1955 [handing to Mr. Grimm].

Mr. GRIMM. Yes.

Mr. GAUGHAN. Headed "Murder Charged to Vet in Beach Strangling." Would you, sir, tell us the contents of that article, what it purports to show?

Mr. GRIMM. It concerns the case of a young fellow about 21 years old, a veteran of the Marine Corps, just out of the marines, who it seems was invited to the apartment of a male hairdresser about 27 years old, and they found the hairdresser trussed up in a very similar fashion to the way these pictures look there, and the way I found my son—the same type of thing. In fact, the newspapers made reference to both cases, the similarity of both cases.

As a result, this 27-year-old fellow died, and the veteran has been sentenced and convicted, or convicted and sentenced to a lifetime sentence in prison.

The only tieup it has with my son's case is that there was newspaper references to the two, and it seems to me it has to do with the same sort of thing which we are all here discussing now.

Mr. GAUGHAN. I understand, Mr. Grimm, that this young man who died on January 6 of this year was found trussed up in the same type of position except that he was laid on the floor instead of suspended.

Mr. GRIMM. Similar, yes; very similar position. The rope was behind his back, of course. It was unnatural. If it was just a case of tying somebody up to keep them from getting away, when you study this, as you and I have since we have become interested in this, you recognize it immediately as an unusual practice. It isn't anything that happens just in the——

Mr. GAUGHAN. Normal course of events?

Mr. GRIMM. That's right. Somebody just tying somebody up to keep them from getting away—there is some sex angle connected with this, and the police recognize it as such. It evidently has a tie-in with this bondage idea, about which I never knew before I started studying it recently.

Mr. GAUGHAN. This clipping, sir, and other similar clippings to it, at the time the newspapers in the area called attention to the similarity of your boy's death, this boy's death——

Mr. GRIMM. That's right.

Mr. GAUGHAN. And it was pointed out at the trial of the young man—I believe he was a 20-year-old young man who was convicted and who is now serving life in the Florida State prison—that it was a definite sex crime, and that he had committed an unnatural act upon the young man who was trussed up.

Mr. GRIMM. No, sir; it wasn't exactly like that.

I believe that the theory behind the thing is that it was a sex crime of this nature, also, but I don't believe that—there was some evidence of a sex act involved, but just who was involved, I don't know.

As a matter of record, I don't believe it involved the young man. He claims the other fellow propositioned him, and as a result he tied him up. That's his story.

Chairman KEFAUVER. Let this be filed as an exhibit.

(The newspaper clippings were marked "Exhibit No. 20," and are on file with the subcommittee.)

Mr. GAUGHAN. In other words, this is an end result, as we discussed with Dr. Henry this morning, of the unnatural fetishes, and another boy is dead.

Mr. GRIMM. That's right.

Mr. GAUGHAN. Mr. Chairman, I have no further questions. Is there any question you would like to ask?

Chairman KEFAUVER. Senator Langer, any questions?

Senator LANGER. No, sir.

Chairman KEFAUVER. Mr. Grimm, tell us again how it was you got this publication?

Mr. GRIMM. He had an ad in the girlie-type magazine—a full-page ad, in fact—describing a lot of this tying up business.

A friend, being interested in my case, thought it might throw some light on my son's case, so he brought me the magazine. As a result, my son-in-law sent for this magazine to see what there was to it, and sent it to me. That's how I came upon this catalog.

Chairman KEFAUVER. In this catalog which has been shown to you——

Mr. GRIMM. Incidentally, after listening to the testimony this morning, there is no question there, again, as to whether it was a minor or who was asking for this literature. It was just sent out without any strings attached at all.

Chairman KEFAUVER. In this catalog are small examples of what you will see in larger and more numerous types——

Mr. GRIMM. Probably so; yes, sir.

Chairman KEFAUVER. Folders. When you send in the money you get the whole thing.

Mr. GRIMM. That's right. Evidently, we didn't send in for them, because this was just more or less as far as we cared to go with it at the time.

Evidently they come in serial form. The one picture encourages you to buy more. I suppose that's the idea. We never went in for that; we didn't know. I presume that that's the idea behind it.

In other words, you get on the mailing list, and I suppose you are a subscriber then, if you care to be, and you can buy as much of it as you want.

Chairman KEFAUVER. It gives a little example of what it is you are going to see; and then it says that after being bound and blindfolded, "Joan is led away in an automobile driven by a bound and gagged chauffeurette, taken to a training school." The price is 50 cents, each chapter, size 8 by 10.

So that you order by number, and then you get a large picture and a series of the similar kind of picture here. That is what this catalog is.

Mr. GRIMM. That's right.

Chairman KEFAUVER. I think it is interesting to look at this. This seems to be the 97th edition. The catalog itself costs 50 cents.

Mr. GRIMM. Yes. Obviously, I believe you will agree with me— I am no expert on this sort of thing, but I have been around a little bit in my life, in the type of work that I do—it doesn't take an expert to recognize that as not a wholesome, cultural type of literature. It definitely was not displayed or sent through the mails for that reason at all, to add to the cultural uplift of the country at all. It is evil; it is no good.

Chairman KEFAUVER. Well, it speaks for itself.

Mr. GRIMM. That's right.

Chairman KEFAUVER. Well, sir, we thank you for your cooperation and for the help you have given us.

Mr. GRIMM. Yes, sir.

Chairman KEFAUVER. Who is our next witness?

Mr. CHUMBRIS. Mr. Irving Klaw.

Mr. KLAW. I would like to request no photographs, no lights, if you don't mind.

Chairman KEFAUVER. The photographers have a right to take your picture. As customary, after you start testifying, we will ask that the lights be turned off.

Have you been sworn, Mr. Klaw?

Mr. KLAW. No.

Chairman KEFAUVER. Do you solemnly swear the testimony you will give the subcommittee will be the whole truth, so help you God?

Mr. KLAW. I do.

TESTIMONY OF IRVING KLAW, NEW YORK, N. Y.

Chairman KEFAUVER. You had counsel with the other day?

Mr. KLAW. Yes, sir.

Chairman KEFAUVER. Is he with you?

Mr. KLAW. Yes, sir.

Chairman KEFAUVER. Mr. Counsel, won't you come up?

Mr. GANGEL. I am available in the room for consultation if he wants me.

Chairman KEFAUVER. If you want to sit with Mr. Klaw, you may.

Mr. GANGEL. Yes, sir.

Chairman KEFAUVER. Just as you wish. If you will just be available for consultation, that is all right.

Mr. GANGEL. I will be available to him.

Chairman KEFAUVER. If you wish to consult with Mr. Gangel at any time, you will let the subcommittee know and we will interrupt the proceedings for that purpose.

Let the record show that Senator Langer and the chairman are present.

Mr. Chumbris, will you proceed?

Mr. CHUMBRIS. Mr. Klaw, will you state your full name?

Mr. KLAW. Irving Klaw.

Mr. CHUMBRIS. And your address?

Mr. KLAW. 212 East 14th Street, New York City.

Mr. CHUMBRIS. Mr. Klaw, in what business are you engaged?

Mr. KLAW. I decline to answer under the fifth amendment of the Constitution of the United States, that to answer may tend to incriminate me.

Chairman KEFAUVER. Mr. Chumbris, I think it would be well for you to make a brief statement as to the nature of the testimony that you expect to elicit from Mr. Klaw by your questions so that we can determine whether the evidence that you would expect to secure comes within the jurisdiction of the inquiry of this subcommittee.

Mr. CHUMBRIS. Mr. Chairman, our investigation reveals that Mr. Klaw is one of the largest distributors of obscene, lewd, and fetish photographs throughout the country by mail.

We expect to show that he has had difficulties with the Post Office Department.

We have had testimony today, as well as last week from Dr. Karpman, and Dr. Henry today, showing the effect that these photographs have on juveniles and on youth.

We have had testimony today from Mr. Roth, and other testimony, which indicates that this material does get into the hands of youth, and our subcommittee has received complaints from many parents to the effect that advertisements of these particular photographs, as well as the photographs themselves, have gotten to the youth.

Chairman KEFAUVER. Do you expect to ask Mr. Klaw, and do you have as to the material that he is sending out, information that they are getting to the children and to the young people; is that part of the showing?

Mr. CHUMBRIS. That is right. That is part of the overall investigation that not only Mr. Klaw but others are producing the type of fetish photographs and lewd photographs that not only in some instances have used youth as models, but they do get into the hands of the youth.

We do believe that that has a direct bearing on our juvenile delinquency investigation.

Chairman KEFAUVER. Part of this record will also include the testimony of Dr. Henry, Mr. Grimm, and of the exhibits which have been put into the record, including Cartoon and Model Parade, published by Irving Klaw, the Pin-Up King, for artists, photography students, and collectors.

Mr. Chumbris, do you expect to prove that our subcommittee has complaints and correspondence from parents or children, law-enforcement officers, showing that Mr. Klaw's publication has anything to do of a deleterious nature affecting juvenile delinquency with young people?

Mr. CHUMBRIS. Yes, Mr. Chairman. The Post Office Department has turned over to us advertisements similar to the advertisements that we introduced into the record this morning that Mr. Roth has sent out. These advetisements have gotten to the youth.

We have this exhibit which shows the type of photos that do go out throughout the country.

We have a statement here which shows that 65 percent of the customers that Mr. Klaw has of movie stills are girls from 6 to 16, thereby creating a mailing list of a great many minors.

We have in our investigation determined information to that effect, that he has a mailing list——

Chairman KEFAUVER. You mean that he uses young people or minors in the pictures and the magazines that go out?

Mr. CHUMBRIS. No; that they are the ones who request of Mr. Klaw the movie stills.

He has a mailing list—65 percent of that mailing list, customer list of those stills, are girls from 6 to 16. I would like to ask him those particular questions.

Chairman KEFAUVER. Very well. In the opinion of the subcommittee the statement of what you expect to prove by Mr. Klaw has relevancy and is within the jurisdiction of this subcommittee to make inquiry.

Would the reporter repeat the question?

(The reporter read the question, as follows:)

Mr. Klaw, in what business are you engaged?

Chairman KEFAUVER. Mr. Klaw, the subcommittee will order you to answer that question.

Mr. KLAW. May I speak to my counsel, please?

Chairman KEFAUVER. You may speak to your counsed. We will have a brief recess.

(Mr. Klaw confers with Mr. Gangel.)

Mr. KLAW. I decline to answer under the fifth amendment of the Constitution, that to answer may tend to incriminate me.

Chairman KEFAUVER. Mr. Klaw, in fairness and in compliance with the requirements of the Supreme Court, I must warn you that this committee will cite you for contempt of the Senate if you decline to answer, and I will now give you a further chance to answer.

That is within the power that we have, we feel that you are in contempt of the Senate by refusing to answer. It will be our intention to go through the legal proceedings and the legislative proceeding necessary to have you cited for contempt.

Do you still refuse to answer?

Mr. KLAW. I decline to answer under the fifth amendment of the Constitution.

Would that be sufficient to state, that I decline under the fifth amendment, or should I say it all the way through, Mr. Kefauver?

Chairman KEFAUVER. We are not asking any quarter and we are not giving any quarter, Mr. Klaw.

Mr. Counsel, or Mr. Klaw, I don't know what offense that your client may have in mind. We have no desire for him to answer any question or to direct him to answer a question where he pleads the fifth amendment if there is really some justification, if he is in actual fear of prosecution under some Federal statute, or even if while it is not the law, some imminent State statute of the State of New York.

Will you, Mr. Klaw, or you, Mr. Gangel, wish to elaborate under what law he fears he might incriminate himself?

Mr. GANGEL. I can state, Mr. Chairman, that in my opinion the witness has a reasonable apprehension that answers would tend to incriminate him.

Chairman KEFAUVER. You do not wish to be more specific, Mr. Gangel.

Mr. GANGEL. I don't believe that I can at this time.

Chairman KEFAUVER. I am not demanding that you do; I just want to give you an opportunity.

Mr. GANGEL. I believe, Mr. Chairman, that we will rest upon the asserted privilege of the witness as he has stated it upon the record.

Chairman KEFAUVER. Does your client have fear of any violence, of any retaliation of any outside nature in case he might answer?

Mr. GANGEL. If he has, I don't know, sir.

Chairman KEFAUVER. If he does, does he wish to say anything about it one way or the other? Mr. Klaw?

Mr. KLAW. I decline to answer on the same grounds.

Chairman KEFAUVER. Very well. Ask the next question. Mr. Chumbris, please go to the next question.

Mr. CHUMBRIS. Mr. Klaw, our investigation reveals that from 1933 to 1937 you operated a business as a furrier. I wish you would tell us about that.

Mr. KLAW. May I speak to my counsel, please, for a second?

Chairman KEFAUVER. Yes, you may.

(Mr. Klaw confers with Mr. Gangel.)

Mr. KLAW. Yes. I was employed as a furrier during that period mentioned.

Mr. GANGEL. Excuse me, Mr. Chairman, do I understand that there are pictures being taken now? I understood you to state at the outset that at the request of the witness that would not prevail.

Chairman KEFAUVER. Yes; that is the rule. If you request that the television or movies not be taken any further, we will ask them to desist.

All right, next question.

Mr. CHUMBRIS. Mr. Klaw, our investigation reveals that since 1937 you have produced——

Chairman KEFAUVER. Excuse me just a minute. What was the time he operated as a furrier?

Mr. CHUMBRIS. From 1933 to 1937.

Chairman KEFAUVER. Thank you.

Mr. KLAW. Approximately that time. I don't know the exact dates.

Mr. CHUMBRIS. Our investigation reveals that since 1937 you have produced and distributed obscene, nude, and fetish photographs throughout the country by mail. I wish you would tell us about this.

Mr. KLAW. I decline to answer under the fifth amendment of the Constitution, that to answer might tend to incriminate me.

Chairman KEFAUVER. Mr. Klaw, you are directed by the subcommittee to answer.

I want to state that the committee, this subcommittee, will expect to endeavor to have you held in contempt by the Senate, and through such legal and legislative procedures as may be necessary.

Then, if held in contempt by the Senate, the matter then goes to the district court, where you will be tried for that, or presented to a grand jury.

If the grand jury returns a true bill, presumably you will be tried unless the matter is dismissed by the district attorney.

That will be the procedure we will endeavor to follow if you refuse to answer.

Do you wish to consult your counsel?

Mr. KLAW. Yes.

(Mr. Klaw confers with Mr. Gangel.)

Mr. KLAW. I decline to answer under the fifth amendment to the Constitution, that to answer may tend to incriminate me.

Chairman KEFAUVER. You say that you decline to answer under the fifth amendment, basing your grounds upon the fifth amendment to the Constitution.

Next question, Mr. Chumbris.

Mr. CHUMBRIS. Mr. Klaw, I have here a publication known as Cartoon and Model Parade, 97th edition, price 50 cents, published by Irving Klaw, and in quotes, "The Pin-Up King"—"For artists, photography students, and collectors."

I show you this magazine and I would like for you to look at it carefully [handing to Mr. Klaw].

Chairman KEFAUVER. Ask your question, Mr. Chumbris.

Mr. CHUMBRIS. Our investigation reveals that you have published that magazine and that you have distributed throughout the United States photographs that have been produced——

Chairman KEFAUVER. The magazine speaks for itself.

Mr. CHUMBRIS. That have been produced by you that have been reflected in this particular catalog.

Will you tell us about the pictures in that catalog and your production and distribution of those pictures throughout the United States?

Mr. KLAW. I decline to answer under the fifth amendment of the Constitution, on the grounds that to answer may tend to incriminate me.

Chairman KEFAUVER. Mr. Klaw, it is again my duty to direct you to answer under penalty of contempt of the Senate. Do you still refuse?

Mr. KLAW. I decline to answer under the fifth amendment of the Constitution.

Chairman KEFAUVER. Mr. Klaw, do you or any company with which you are connected print or publish the magazine that has been handed to you and which will now be identified an 'Exhibit A" to your testimony?

Mr. KLAW. I decline to answer under the fifth amendment to the Constitution, that to answer may tend to incriminate me.

Chairman KEFAUVER. You are ordered to answer, and if you do not answer this subcommittee will do everything possible to have you held in contempt of the Senate.

Do you still refuse to answer?

Mr. KLAW. I decline to answer under the fifth amendment to the Constitution.

Chairman KEFAUVER. Let it be marked and identified as an exhibit. Will you so mark it at the present time, Mr. Chumbris?

(The catalogue was marked "Exhibit No. 21" and is on file with the subcommittee.)

Mr. CHUMBRIS. Mr. Klaw, our investigation reveals——

Chairman KEFAUVER. We order that the magazine marked "Exhibit A" is made a part of the official record.

Proceed, Mr. Chumbris.

Mr. CHUMBRIS. Mr. Klaw, our investigation reveals that you are known as one of the largest distributors of obscene, nude, and fetish photographs. I wish you would tell the subcommittee about this.

Mr. KLAW. I decline to answer under the fifth amendment to the Constitution that to answer may tend to incriminate me.

Chairman KEFAUVER. Mr. Klaw, you are directed to answer by the subcommittee under penalty of contempt of the Senate.

Mr. KLAW. I decline to answer under the fifth amendment to the Constitution, that to answer may tend to incriminate me.

Chairman KEFAUVER. Mr. Chumbris, your first question was about his business. I should like to ask Mr. Klaw if he will tell us in what business he has been engaged since 1937.

Mr. KLAW. May I consult my counsel, please?

Chairman KEFAUVER. Very well.

(Mr. Klaw consults with Mr. Gangel.)

Mr. KLAW. I decline to answer under the fifth amendment to the Constitution, that to answer my tend to incriminate me.

Chairman KEFAUVER. The chairman orders you to answer under penalty of the Senate.

Mr. KLAW. I decline to answer under the fifth amendment to the Constitution, that to answer may tend to incriminate me.

Chairman KEFAUVER. Next question, Mr. Chumbris.

Mr. CHUMBRIS. Mr. Klaw, our investigation reveals that you have been investigated by the United States Post Office Department for alleged violations of title 18, sections 1461 and 1462, which pertain to obscene matter sent through the mails. I wish you would tell this subcommittee your difficulties with the Post Office Department.

Mr. KLAW. I would like to consult with my counsel.

Chairman KEFAUVER. Very well.

(Mr. Klaw consults with Mr. Gangel.)

Mr. KLAW. I decline to answer under the fifth amendment to the Constitution, that to answer may tend to incriminate me.

Chairman KEFAUVER. The chair directs you to answer under penalty of contempt of the Senate.

Mr. KLAW. I decline to answer under the fifth amendment that to answer may tend to incriminate me.

Senator LANGER. Mr. Chairman, I should like to have a recess of 5 minutes. There is an important telephone call for me.

Chairman KEFAUVER. We will stand in recess for 5 minutes.

(A recess was taken.)

Senator LANGER. Thank you very much, Mr. Chairman.

Chairman KEFAUVER. We were glad to have a recess. The recess is now terminated. The record will show that Senator Langer and the chairman are present.

Mr. Chumbris, will you ask your next question?

Mr. CHUMBRIS. Mr. Klaw, did you ever employ a teen-ager to pose for your fetish and nude photos that you have distributed throughout the United States by mail?

Mr. Klaw, I ask you to answer that, please.

Mr. KLAW. I decline to answer under the grounds—under the fifth amendment to the Constitution, that the answer may tend to incriminate me.

Chairman KEFAUVER. The chairman will order you to answer the question under penalty of contempt of the Senate.

Mr. KLAW. I decline to answer under the fifth amendment to the Constitution, that to answer may tend to incriminate me.

Chairman KEFAUVER. Let's ask this question:

Have you ever employed any teen-agers, young people under 21 years of age, to pose or participate in photographs, in the making of photographs?

Mr. KLAW. I decline to answer under the fifth amendment to the Constitution, that to answer may tend to incriminate me.

Chairman KEFAUVER. The chairman orders you to answer under penalty of contempt of the Senate.

Mr. KLAW. I decline to answer under the fifth amendment to the Constitution, that to answer may tend to incriminate me.

Chairman KEFAUVER. Do you have or have you ever had a mailing list for send out any catalogs or information which includes teen-agers?

Mr. KLAW. I would like to speak to my counsel for a second.

Chairman KEFAUVER. You may.

(Mr. Klaw confers with Mr. Gangel.)

Mr. KLAW. I decline to answer under the fifth amendment to the Constitution, that to answer may tend to incriminate me.

Chairman KEFAUVER. You are ordered and directed to answer under penalty of contempt of the Senate.

Mr. KLAW. I decline to answer under the fifth amendment to the Constitution, that to answer may tend to incriminate me.

Chairman KEFAUVER. Let the record show that he declines to answer. Go ahead, Mr. Chumbris.

Mr. CHUMBRIS. Mr. Klaw, our investigation reveals that 65 percent of your customers for movie stills are girls from 6 to 16, thereby creating a mailing list of a great many minors.

Do you wish to tell the subcommittee about that mailing list? Is that true?

Mr. KLAW. I decline to answer under the fifth amendment to the Constitution, that to answer may tend to incriminate me.

Chairman KEFAUVER. The chairman directs you to answer upon penalty of contempt of the Senate.

Mr. KLAW. I decline to answer under the fifth amendment, that to answer may tend to incriminate me.

Mr. CHUMBRIS. Mr. Klaw, our investigation reveals that some of the girls who modeled for your obscene, nude, and fetish pictures have also posed for obscene and lewd pictures for other photographers. Is this true or not?

Mr. KLAW. I want to consult my counsel for a minute.

(Mr. Klaw confers with Mr. Gangel.)

Mr. KLAW. I decline to answer under the fifth amendment to the Constitution, that to answer may tend to incriminate me.

Chairman KEFAUVER. Mr. Klaw, you are directed to answer under penalty of contempt of the Senate.

Mr. KLAW. I decline to answer under the fifth amendment to the Constitution.

Chairman KEFAUVER. Mr. Klaw, have you ever employed or do you employ any young people under 18 years of age in your business?

Mr. KLAW. I decline to answer under the fifth amendment to the Constitution, that to answer may tend to incriminate me.

Chairman KEFAUVER. You are ordered and directed to answer under penalty of contempt of the United States Senate.

Mr. KLAW. May I consult my attorney for a second?

Chairman KEFAUVER. Yes.

(Mr. Klaw confers with Mr. Gangel.)

Mr. KLAW. I decline to answer under the fifth amendment to the Constitution, that to answer may tend to incriminate me.

Chairman KEFAUVER. All right. Anything else, Mr. Chumbris?

Mr. CHUMBRIS. Yes, sir.

Mr. Klaw, our investigation reveals that some of your clients request fetish and other photographs made to order to satisfy your client's specific perversions, that you fulfill such requests. Is that true or not?

Mr. KLAW. I decline to answer under the fifth amendment to the Constitution, that to answer may tend to incriminate me.

Chairman KEFAUVER. We order you to answer under penalty of contempt of the Senate.

Mr. KLAW. I decline to answer under the fifth amendment to the Constitution, that to answer may tend to incriminate me.

Mr. CHUMBRIS. Mr. Klaw, our investigation reveals that you do a gross business of $1,500,000 a year in the production and distribution of nude and fetish pictures. Is that true or false?

Mr. KLAW. I decline to answer under the fifth amendment to the Constitution, that to answer may tend to incriminate me.

Chairman KEFAUVER. The chairman will direct you to answer under penalty of contempt of the Senate.

Mr. KLAW. I decline to answer under the fifth amendment to the Constitution, that to answer may tend to incriminate me.

Mr. CHUMBRIS. Mr. Klaw, do you go under the title of "King of photographs," "King of the Pin-up Photographs"?

Mr. KLAW. May I speak to my counsel for a minute?

(Mr. Klaw confers with Mr. Gangel.)

Mr. KLAW. I decline to answer under the fifth amendment to the Constitution, that to answer may tend to incriminate me.

Chairman KEFAUVER. You are directed to answer under penalty of contempt of the Senate.

Mr. KLAW. I decline to answer under the fifth amendment to the Constitution—that to answer may tend to incriminate me.

Mr. CHUMBRIS. Mr. Klaw, our investigation reveals that you have the largest collection of movie stills of any one person in the United States of America. Is that true or false?

Mr. KLAW. I would like to consult my counsel for a minute.

(Mr. Klaw confers with Mr. Gangel.)

Mr. KLAW. I decline to answer under the fifth amendment to the Constitution—that to answer may tend to incriminate me.

Chairman KEFAUVER. You are directed to answer under penalty of contempt of the Senate.

Mr. KLAW. I decline to answer under the fifth amendment to the Constitution—that to answer may tend to incriminate me.

Chairman KEFAUVER. I think that covers the field fairly well.

Mr. Klaw, you will remain under continuing subpena and report back when you or your counsel is notified.

Mr. Gangel, I think we have your address.

Mr. GANGEL. I stated it for the record last Tuesday, Mr. Chairman.

Chairman KEFAUVER. State it again. It is G-a-n-g-e-l?

Mr. GANGEL. That's right.

Chairman KEFAUVER. What is your first name?

Mr. GANGEL. Coleman, C-o-l-e-m-a-n.

Chairman KEFAUVER. And your address?

Mr. GANGEL. 165 Broadway.

Chairman KEFAUVER. Upon notice to you, Mr. Klaw, or you, Mr. Gangel?

As we leave, Mr. Klaw, I think I should advise you again that we expect to endeavor to have you held in contempt for refusal to answer some or all of these questions.

If you wish to reconsider and give us any information about the subject matter which we have asked you, I will give you an opportunity to do so at this time.

Mr. GANGEL. May I ask the chairman whether a transcript of the questions and answers would be available to the witness upon payment of the cost?

Chairman KEFAUVER. I will instruct the reporter to let the witness or his attorney have a copy of the transcript upon payment of the costs.

That is all.

Mr. GAUGHAN. Mr. Chairman, may I direct the attention of counsel, and the attention of Mr. Klaw, to the fact that after Mr. Klaw claimed the privilege, he later answered a question concerning his past associations and business life, and then went back behind the privilege again and refused to answer questions.

I think, Mr. Chairman, that that probably will be the position of this subcommittee that he relinquished his right to claim the privilege once he answered the question concerning his past business association.

Mr. GANGEL. Mr. Chairman, I think that points up the burden of counsel in advising the witness under the circumstances.

Chairman KEFAUVER. Yes. That is Mr. Gangel's——

Mr. GANGEL. Headache.

Chairman KEFAUVER. I appreciate the suggestion, Mr. Gaughan; but that is a matter for Mr. Klaw and his counsel.

Senator Langer?

Senator LANGER. Could I see that exhibit 21?

(Exhibit 21 was handed to Senator Langer.)

Senator LANGER. No questions.

Chairman KEFAUVER. Mr. Klaw, you appeared here on last Tuesday. At that time you were asked to bring in certain books and papers as described in the subpena which had been served upon you. You refused to do so, either under the fourth amendment or under the fifth amendment.

Have you brought those books and papers in as directed?

Mr. KLAW. I decline to answer under the fifth amendment to the Constitution, that to answer may tend to incriminate me.

And furthermore, under the fourth amendment to the Constitution, the subpena is vague and illegal.

Chairman KEFAUVER. You are ordered to answer the question under penalty of contempt of the United States Senate.

Mr. KLAW. I decline to answer under the fifth amendment to the Constitution, that to answer may tend to incriminate me.

Chairman KEFAUVER. You have not complied with the subpena, Mr. Klaw, and it is my duty to warn you that your not having complied with the subpena, unless you express a willingness now to comply with the subpena, that this subcommittee will do all within its power to have you cited for contempt by the Senate.

Do you wish to comply with the subpena?

Mr. KLAW. I would like to speak to my counsel for a second.

Chairman KEFAUVER. You will have that opportunity.

(Mr. Klaw confers with Mr. Gangel.)

Mr. KLAW. I wish to answer that I decline to answer under the fifth amendment to the Constitution, that to answer may tend to incriminate me.

And furthermore, that under the fourth amendment to the Constitution, that to make them available may tend to incriminate me.

Chairman KEFAUVER. Again, sir, you are ordered to answer penalty of contempt of the Senate.

Do you continue to decline to answer and to produce the books and records?

Mr. KLAW. I decline to answer under the fifth amendment, that to answer may tend to incriminate me.

Chairman KEFAUVER. Mr. Gangel, I believe that is all.

Mr. GANGEL. Thank you, sir.

Mr. CHUMBRIS. Mr. Mishkin.

Chairman KEFAUVER. Sit down, Mr. Mishkin.

Mr. Mishkin, you were here on last Thursday. At that time you were accompanied by Mr. Weiss.

We have a note from Mr. Weiss. He called, or somebody called, saying that he cannot come today because he is in a city council meeting, but he is sending Mishkin and Stone here. It would be good to introduce this item into the record and show that Mr. Weiss is the counsel man.

Do you wish to secure any counsel to advise you upon any matters here?

Mr. MISHKIN. At the present moment?

Chairman KEFAUVER. Yes.

Mr. MISHKIN. I don't know of any. No, sir.

Chairman KEFAUVER. You intend to handle it yourself?

Mr. MISHKIN. I have been advised by him what to say.

Chairman KEFAUVER. You have talked to your counsel and he has advised you what to say. You have it before you?

Mr. MISHKIN. Yes, sir.

Chairman KEFAUVER. You have your instructions written out on a piece of paper, I understand.

Let the record show that Senator Langer and the chairman are here. Mr. Mishkin has returned again pursuant to subpena.

Mr. Chumbris, I wish you would state very briefly what it is that you expect or hope to prove by Mr. Mishkin which brings your questions or the information that you are eliciting within the jurisdiction of this subcommittee.

Mr. CHUMBRIS. Mr. Chairman, our investigation reveals that Mr. Mishkin deals in pornographic material; that not only does he distribute and sell the material but he has also been known to finance other persons in the distribution and sale of pornographic material.

Chairman KEFAUVER. Does this pornographic material reach children?

Mr. CHUMBRIS. From the information that we have received, this pornographic material reaches children throughout the many areas of the United States. Known pornographers have received their particular pornographic material through Mr. Mishkin's sources.

Chairman KEFAUVER. Is there evidence that this material contributes or increases juvenile delinquency among the young people?

Mr. CHUMBRIS. Yes. I think the testimony not only here in New York but in other hearings is replete with testimony to the effect that pornography in the hands of juveniles has a terrific impact on them and leads them to delinquent acts.

Chairman KEFAUVER. Mr. Mishkin was asked a number of questions the other day. Do you have questions you wish to ask him at this time?

Mr. CHUMBRIS. Yes; I have, Mr. Chairman.

Chairman KEFAUVER. Will you proceed.

The Chair will rule, and it is the consensus of the subcommittee authorized to sit here, showing what counsel would expect to prove by this witness has a connection with juvenile delinquency, which is the subject matter we are studying here.

Mr. Chumbris, you go on with your questions.

TESTIMONY OF EDWARD MISHKIN, YONKERS, N. Y.—Resumed

Mr. CHUMBRIS. Mr. Mishkin, our investigation reveals that you are in the business of pornography and obscene literature, and have been for quite some period of time, at least 3 to 5 years. Is that true?

Mr. MISHKIN. I refuse to answer under the immunity provisions of the fifth amendment of the Constitution.

Chairman KEFAUVER. Mr. Mishkin, this question has been asked of you, as others were the other day. The chairman will have to order you to answer this question.

I must warn you now that your refusal to answer this question will force this subcommittee to consider you in contempt of the United States Senate, and will endeavor to take such action as is necessary to have it presented to the Senate which, in turn, will refer it to a district attorney here in this district of New York for presentment to a grand jury.

In other words, it will be our intention to make you pay the penalty for contempt of the Senate if you refuse to answer this and other questions which you are ordered to answer.

Do you understand that, sir?

Mr. MISHKIN. I refuse to answer under the immunity provisions of the fifth amendment of the Constitution.

Chairman KEFAUVER. You are ordered to answer, and you still refuse to answer; is that correct?

Mr. MISHKIN. I refuse to answer.

Chairman KEFAUVER. I would like to ask a question.

Mr. Mishkin, in what business are you presently engaged?

Mr. MISHKIN. I refuse to answer under the immunity provisions of the fifth amendment of the Constitution.

Chairman KEFAUVER. You are ordered to answer upon penalty of being in contempt of the Senate.

Mr. MISHKIN. I refuse to answer under the immunity provisions of the fifth amendment of the Constitution.

Chairman KEFAUVER. The record will show that he still refused to answer.

Go ahead, Mr. Chumbris.

Mr. CHUMBRIS. Mr. Mishkin, our investigation reveals that you have developed your obscene-material business to the point that you manufacture, you wholesale, you distribute, and you have large retail business of obscene material in your store; that you also finance people to get into the obscene-material business. Is that true?

Mr. MISHKIN. I refuse to answer under the immunity provisions of the fifth amendment of the Constitution.

Chairman KEFAUVER. The chairman directs you to answer under penalty of being in contempt of the Senate.

Mr. MISHKIN. I refuse to answer under the immunity provisions of the fifth amendment of the Constitution.

Chairman KEFAUVER. Mr. Mishkin, in whatever business you may be engaged do you employ children?

Mr. MISHKIN. I refuse to answer under the immunity provisions of the fifth amendment of the Constitution.

Chairman KEFAUVER. You are directed to answer under penalty of being in contempt of the Senate.

Mr. MISHKIN. I refuse to answer under the immunity provisions of the fifth amendment of the Constitution.

Chairman KEFAUVER. Next question, Mr. Chumbris.

Mr. CHUMBRIS. Mr. Mishkin, our investigation reveals that a Mr. Cobb borrowed $2,000 from you to get started in the obscene-picture business.

Mr. MISHKIN. What was that name?

Mr. CHUMBRIS. Mr. Cobb, C-o-b-b. He borrowed $2,000 from you to get started in the obscene-picture business. Is that true?

Mr. MISHKIN. I refuse to answer under the immunity provisions of the fifth amendment of the Constitution.

Chairman KEFAUVER. You are ordered to answer under penalty of being in contempt of the Senate.

Mr. MISHKIN. I refuse to answer under the immunity provisions of the fifth amendment of the Constitution.

Chairman KEFAUVER. Next question.

Mr. CHUMBRIS. Our investigation reveals that Mr. Cobb and you had a dispute and a falling out in your business relationship on the pornographic material. Is that true?

Mr. MISHKIN. I refuse to answer under the immunity provisions of the fifth amendment of the Constitution.

Chairman KEFAUVER. I don't think that I will order him to answer that question.

Mr. CHUMBRIS. Mr. Mishkin, our investigation reveals that you have known distributors in Florida, in New York City, in St. Louis, Mo., who have distributed pornographic material to juveniles and minors. Is that true?

Mr. MISHKIN. I refuse to answer under the immunity provisions of the fifth amendment of the Constitution.

Chairman KEFAUVER. You are ordered to answer under penalty of being in contempt of the Senate.

Mr. MISHKIN. I refuse to answer under the immunity provisions of the fifth amendment of the Constitution.

Chairman KEFAUVER. Next question.

Mr. CHUMBRIS. Do you know Mr. Al Stone, alias Abraham Rubinstein, alias Abraham Rubin?

Mr. MISHKIN. I refuse to answer under the immunity provisions of the fifth amendment of the Constitution.

Chairman KEFAUVER. You are ordered to answer under penalty of being in contempt of the Senate.

Mr. MISHKIN. I refuse to answer under the immunity provisions of the fifth amendment of the Constitution.

Chairman KEFAUVER. Next question.

Mr. CHUMBRIS. Our investigation reveals that you plagiarized material from one Irving Klaw, resulting in serious arguments with said Irving Klaw. Is that true or false?

Mr. MISHKIN. What was that question again?

Mr. CHUMBRIS. Our investigation reveals that you have plagiarized material——

Mr. MISHKIN. What did I do?

Mr. CHUMBRIS. You have stolen material that Mr. Klaw used—Mr. Irving Klaw, resulting in serious arguments with said Irving Klaw.

Chairman KEFAUVER. Plagiarized. Do you know what plagiarized means?

Mr. MISHKIN. I know what that means now; yes, sir.

Chairman KEFAUVER. Do you want to answer that question?

Mr. MISHKIN. I refuse to answer under the immunity provisions of the fifth amendment of the Constitution.

Chairman KEFAUVER. You are ordered to answer under penalty of being in contempt of the Senate.

Mr. MISHKIN. I refuse to answer under the immunity provisions of the fifth amendment of the Constitution.

Chairman KEFAUVER. Mr. Mishkin, we have some information here that has been brought to our attention, that allegedly you purchased the plates and financed Kingsley Book Store operated by a young man who was in here the other day, for the printing of the Nights of Horror. Is that true?

Mr. MISHKIN. I refuse to answer under the immunity provisions of the fifth amendment of the Constitution.

Chairman KEFAUVER. You are directed to answer under penalty of being in contempt of the Senate.

Mr. MISHKIN. I refuse to answer under the immunity provisions of the fifth amendment of the Constitution.

Chairman KEFAUVER. Proceed.

Mr. CHUMBRIS. Mr. Mishkin, do you own outright or with other persons the Times Square Book Bazaar in New York City, the Little Book Exchange in New York City, and/or the Kingsley Book Store in New York City, all stores near the Times Square area in New York City?

Mr. MISHKIN. I refuse to answer under the immunity provisions of the fifth amendment of the Constitution.

Chairman KEFAUVER. You are ordered and directed to answer.

Mr. MISHKIN. I refuse to answer under the immunity provisions of the fifth amendment of the Constitution.

Chairman KEFAUVER. Do you employ any minors, any teen-agers, in any business with which you are connected?

Mr. MISHKIN. I refuse to answer under the immunity provisions of the fifth amendment of the Constitution.

Chairman KEFAUVER. You will be ordered and directed to answer under penalty of being in contempt of the Senate.

Mr. MISHKIN. I refuse to answer under the immunity provisions of the fifth amendment of the Constitution.

Mr. CHUMBRIS. Mr. Mishkin, do you permit minors and juveniles to peruse and/or buy obscene material that you sell in one of the three stores that I just mentioned—the Times Square Book Bazaar, the Little Book Exchange, the Kingsley Book Store, or any one of those three?

Mr. MISHKIN. I refuse to answer under the immunity provisions of the fifth amendment of the Constitution.

Chairman KEFAUVER. You are ordered and directed to answer under penalty of being in contempt of the Senate.

Mr. MISHKIN. I refuse to answer under the immunity provisions of the fifth amendment of the Constitution.

Chairman KEFAUVER. Proceed.

Mr. CHUMBRIS. Mr. Mishkin, how long have you been in the pornographic material business?

Mr. MISHKIN. I refuse to answer under the immunity provisions of the fifth amendment of the Constitution.

Chairman KEFAUVER. You are directed to answer under penalty of being in contempt of the Senate.

Mr. MISHKIN. I refuse to answer under the immunity provisions of the fifth amendment of the Constitution.

Mr. CHUMBRIS. Do you understand what the term "fetish pictures" means?

Mr. MISHIN. I refuse to answer under the immunity provisions of the fifth amendment of the Constitution.

Chairman KEFAUVER. You are ordered to answer.

Mr. MISHKIN. I refuse to answer under the immunity provisions of the fifth amendment of the Constitution.

Mr. CHUMBRIS. Do you understand what "obscene pictures," or "obscene booklets," or "obscene paper writings" mean?

Mr. MISHKIN. I refuse to answer under the immunity provisions of the fifth amendment of the Constitution.

Chairman KEFAUVER. Very well.

Now, Mr. Mishkin, you refused to answer some questions on last Thursday.

Senator LANGER. May I ask a question?

Chairman KEFAUVER. Yes, Senator Langer.

Senator LANGER. Mr. Witness, did you print or have printed, or did you manufacture, or did you wholesale or did you distribute pictures showing a young boy about 15 having sexual intercourse with a girl of 14?

Mr. MISHKIN. I refuse to answer under the immunity provisions of the fifth amendment of the Constitution.

Chairman KEFAUVER. You are directed to answer under penalty of being in contempt of the Senate.

Mr. MISHKIN. I refuse to answer under the immunity provisions.

Chairman KEFAUVER. Senator Langer.

Senator LANGER. Mr. Witness, did you print or have printed, or did you wholesale, or did you distribute pictures showing a bulldog having sexual intercourse with a girl approximately 15 years of age?

Mr. MISHKIN. I refuse to answer under the immunity provisions of the fifth amendment of the Constitution.

Chairman KEFAUVER. You are ordered to answer under penalty of being in contempt of the Senate.

Mr. MISHKIN. I refuse to answer under the immunity provisions of the fifth amendment of the Constitution.

Chairman KEFAUVER. Mr. Mishkin, you refused to answer some questions the other day, and you refused to answer some today.

The law bends over backward, or is very lenient, in giving witnesses the protection of the fifth amendment if they are entitled to it. I feel I must notify you and warn you that it will be our endeavor to have you cited for contempt for refusal to answer the questions the other day and your refusal to answer questions today, and to give you a final chance of doing so if you wish to do so now.

If there are any of these questions that you want to answer, or if there is any explanation you want to give, we will be glad to hear you now.

Mr. MISHKIN. I refuse to answer under the immunity provisions of the fifth amendment of the Constitution.

Chairman KEFAUVER. Very well, Mr. Mishkin. You will remain under subpena, and it may be we will want to call you again. You are excused now.

Call our next witness.

Mr. CHUMBRIS. Mr. Shapiro, please. Mr. A. M. Shapiro.

Chairman KEFAUVER. Let us call another witness if he is not here.

Mr. CHUMBRIS. Is Mr.—Mr. Kaplain, Mr. Shomer received the subcommittee's telegram this morning. Mr. Rachstein, his counsel, was away for the weekend. They expect Mr. Rachstein back about 4 o'clock.

Chairman KEFAUVER. We will defer his appearance until later on.

Mr. CHUMBRIS. Mr. Rubin.

TESTIMONY OF ABRAHAM RUBIN, BROOKLYN, N. Y.—Resumed

Chairman KEFAUVER. Mr. Rubin, you were sworn the other day and testified here last Thursday, I believe; is that right?

Mr. RUBIN. Yes, sir.

Chairman KEFAUVER. You have been notified to come back today?

Mr. RUBIN. Yes, sir.

Chairman KEFAUVER. He objects to being televised. Gentlemen, I will ask your indulgence.

Mr. Rubin, you go by the name of Abraham Rubin and not Al Stone?

Mr. RUBIN. That is right.

Chairman KEFAUVER. Which is correct?

Mr. RUBIN. Abraham Rubin.

Chairman KEFAUVER. Or is it Al Stone?

Mr. RUBIN. Abraham Rubin.

Chairman KEFAUVER. Are you known as Al Stone sometimes?

Mr. RUBIN. No, sir.

Chairman KEFAUVER. You never have been?

Mr. Rubin. Abraham Rubin.

Chairman Kefauver. I don't know where we got Al Stone. Have you ever been known as Al Stone?

Mr. Rubin. My name is Abraham Rubin.

Chairman Kefauver. My question was, have you been known as Al Stone?

Mr. Rubin. I refuse to answer under the immunity provisions of the fifth amendment of the Constitution.

Chairman Kefauver. Mr. Rubin, you were here the other day with your counsel, Mr. Weiss. We got a message he had been attending a city council meeting. Have you conferred with him, and do you wish to have counsel at this time?

Mr. Rubin. I will go ahead.

Chairman Kefauver. Have you conferred with Mr. Weiss—and you have a little piece of paper there?

Mr. Rubin. Yes, sir.

Chairman Kefauver. What is on that piece of paper?

Mr. Rubin. I refuse to answer under the immunity provisions of the fifth amendment of the Constitution.

Chairman Kefauver. Are you refusing to tell me what is on the paper, or are you talking about what is on the paper?

Mr. Rubin. That is on the paper.

Chairman Kefauver. That is what Mr. Weiss gave you to read out every time you are asked a question?

Mr. Rubin. Yes, sir.

Chairman Kefauver. Did you say "Yes"?

Mr. Rubin. Yes, sir.

Chairman Kefauver. Then you don't need Mr. Weiss here?

Mr. Rubin. That is right.

Chairman Kefauver. But if you want to have an attorney to consult with, we want to give you an opportunity to do so. Do you understand that?

Mr. Rubin. Yes, sir.

Chairman Kefauver. Do you want to have an attorney to consult with?

Mr. Rubin. You can postpone it.

Chairman Kefauver. Can you get Mr. Weiss here this afternoon?

Mr. Rubin. No. He is at a council meeting.

Chairman Kefauver. Mr. Rubin, what do you understand your immunity privilege to be? Do you understand your immunity under the fifth amendment? What do you understand it to be?

Mr. Rubin. I would like to have my counsel here.

Chairman Kefauver. Do you want to wait until later on this afternoon?

Mr. Rubin. He won't be here today.

Chairman Kefauver. We have had no application by Mr. Weiss to put off any of your hearing on the ground he isn't here; but if you want to get him or somebody else, we will give you a while this afternoon to do so. Would you rather come back a little later on this afternoon? Mr. Rubin, see if you can get your counsel here by 4:30 or some other counsel. We will call you back at that time.

Mr. Rubin. I won't get anybody else but Mr. Weiss.

Chairman Kefauver. A council meeting doesn't last all afternoon.

Mr. Rubin. I will try to get him, sir.

Chairman KEFAUVER. You are excused until 4:30. We will call you back then.

Who is our next witness?

Mr. CHUMBRIS. Morris Gillman.

Chairman KEFAUVER. Mr. Gillman, you have been here before?

Mr. GILLMAN. No.

Mr. GOLD. Jacob Lewis Gold, 280 Broadway, Manhattan. Mr. Chairman, my client objects to the television and moving pictures paraphernalia.

Chairman KEFAUVER. All right. Mr. Gold objects on behalf of Mr. Gillman. I will have to ask your indulgence.

Mr. Gold, you are counsel for Mr. Gillman?

Mr. GOLD. Yes.

Chairman KEFAUVER. Mr. Gillman, I don't think you have been sworn. Do you solemnly swear the testimony you will give this committee will be the whole truth, so help you God?

Mr. GILLMAN. I do.

TESTIMONY OF MORRIS GILLMAN, NEW YORK, N. Y.

Mr. CHUMBRIS. Your name is Morris Gillman?

Mr. GILLMAN. That is right.

Mr. CHUMBRIS. Where do you reside?

Mr. GILLMAN. 1815 Davidson Avenue, Bronx.

Mr. CHUMBRIS. What is your occupation?

Mr. GILLMAN. I am not employed right now because I am sick.

Mr. CHUMBRIS. How long has that been?

Mr. GILLMAN. Quite a few years.

Mr. CHUMBRIS. Could you be specific? What year was it—1950, 1951, 1952?

Mr. GILLMAN. The last time I was employed was in 1952.

Mr. CHUMBRIS. 1952?

Mr. GILLMAN. That is right.

Mr. CHUMBRIS. What month?

Mr. GILLMAN. It was during the summer.

Mr. CHUMBRIS. What type of work were you doing then?

Mr. GILLMAN. It was in a dye house in New Jersey.

Mr. CHUMBRIS. What was the name of the company?

Mr. GILLMAN. Ranko Finishing Co.

Mr. CHUMBRIS. What type of work did you do?

Mr. GILLMAN. I was watching the goods when they were coming out of the machine.

Mr. CHUMBRIS. What salary did you make?

Mr. GILLMAN. It wasn't steady. It was a couple of days a week, and I couldn't handle it because it was too heavy. Sometimes you have to lift the machine to get the goods out.

Mr. CHUMBRIS. How long had you been working at the Ranko Finishing Co.?

Mr. GILLMAN. A couple of months.

Mr. CHUMBRIS. What did you do before that time?

Mr. GILLMAN. I wasn't doing anything. I was staying home, taking care of the house. I was sick.

Mr. CHUMBRIS. Let us see if I get this straight. You haven't been doing anything for the past couple of years?

Mr. GILLMAN. Right.

Mr. CHUMBRIS. The last job you had was with Ranko Finishing, and you held that job for 2 months?

Mr. GILLMAN. That is right; I couldn't do it.

Mr. CHUMBRIS. Previous to that time what work did you do—previous to your job at Ranko?

Mr. GILLMAN. I haven't been doing anything.

Mr. CHUMBRIS. For how many years back?

Mr. GILLMAN. Maybe 10; maybe 9 or 10 years.

Mr. CHUMBRIS. How have you been supporting yourself?

Mr. GILLMAN. The wife has been working and supporting me.

Mr. CHUMBRIS. Did you bring any of your records with you?

Mr. GILLMAN. Yes, sir.

Mr. CHUMBRIS. Do you have those with you at this time?

Mr. GILLMAN. Yes.

Chairman KEFAUVER. Let us get the records in. What records do we have to be identified? Catalog them so they can be turned back to Mr. Gillman or his attorney.

Mr. CHUMBRIS. Mr. Gillman, do you know Andy Bruckner?

Mr. GILLMAN. No, sir.

Mr. CHUMBRIS. You have never had any business dealings with a person named Andy Bruckner?

Mr. GILLMAN. Not that I know of. I never heard of that name before.

Chairman KEFAUVER. Andy Bruckner, who lives in New Jersey, who was convicted of selling filthy pictures and whatnot.

Mr. GILLMAN. I don't know the man. I never heard of the name.

Chairman KEFAUVER. Do you know anybody there who might have been him, or was in that business?

Mr. GILLMAN. I was never in that business in my life.

Mr. CHUMBRIS. Do you know Kenneth Eads?

Mr. GILLMAN. I never heard that name.

Chairman KEFAUVER. If we got the wrong information about you, I certainly want to apologize. The investigation had a connection between you and Bruckner. If you don't know him, that is something else.

Mr. CHUMBRIS. Mr. Gillman, do you own an automobile or did you own a 1950 green Ford sedan, registered in the name of Morris Gillman, 1815 Davidson Avenue, Bronx, New York?

Mr. GILLMAN. When my wife bought it, it may have been under my name. I don't remember.

Mr. CHUMBRIS. Do you know of your own knowledge whether you ever loaned that automobile to Kenneth Eads of 473 Second Avenue?

Mr. GILLMAN. I never loaned my car to anybody.

Chairman KEFAUVER. Did he get the car and have it around in some business?

Mr. GILLMAN. Nobody ever drove that car.

Chairman KEFAUVER. Did he get it from your wife?

Mr. GILLMAN. Nobody drove that car except myself and my wife.

Chairman KEFAUVER. Did he get it from your wife?

Mr. GILLMAN. I don't think so. I don't know of any such name.

Chairman KEFAUVER. If he had your car and got arrested with your car, would you know about that?

Mr. GILLMAN. That is something new to me.

Chairman KEFAUVER. Is your car 4U9975?

Mr. GILLMAN. No, sir.

Chairman KEFAUVER. A 1950 green Ford sedan?

Mr. GILLMAN. What year?

Chairman KEFAUVER. 1950.

Mr. GILLMAN. I know we had a 1950 Ford.

Mr. CHUMBRIS. A 1950 Ford; is that correct?

Mr. GILLMAN. Yes, but I don't recall the plate number.

Mr. CHUMBRIS. Let me make this statement, and you tell us whether it is true or false. On March 11, 1950, it was decided to keep Kenneth Eads, of 473 Second Avenue under observation. At about 1 p. m. on March 11, 1950, Eads left 473 Second Avenue, carrying a carton and a suitcase, entered car license No. 4U9975, New York, a 1950 green Ford sedan registered to Morris Gillman of 1815 Davidson, Bronx, N. Y.

Mr. GILLMAN. I don't know of such a name.

Mr. CHUMBRIS. Who had police department record E–1403. The car was driven by an unknown male who drove Eads to 313 West 27th, where Eads left the car and entered a furnished rooming house.

Chairman KEFAUVER. You say you don't know Mr. Eads?

Mr. GILLMAN. I don't know Mr. Eads.

Mr. CHUMBRIS. You have no recollection of being in the car with the person going to that address that I mentioned?

Mr. GILLMAN. No, sir.

Chairman KEFAUVER. What have you ever done, Mr. Gillman?

Mr. GILLMAN. Before I went into the service I used to peddle ties.

Chairman KEFAUVER. Peddle what?

Mr. GILLMAN. Ties.

Mr. CHUMBRIS. Do you have a police record, Mr. Gillman?

Mr. GILLMAN. I paid a $50 fine in Jersey City.

Mr. CHUMBRIS. What was that for?

Mr. GILLMAN. That was for peddling at that time. I will tell you how it happened. I went into the saloon to sell the ties, and while I was selling the ties there was a fellow in there selling pictures, so I bought about 7 or 8 pictures from him; and then when I walked out the detective stopped me for a license, but I don't have any, so they searched me and found the pictures on me; and they arrested me at that time. That was in 1942.

Chairman KEFAUVER. What kind of pictures were they?

Mr. GILLMAN. They were fellows and girls. I was young at that time. I bought them for myself.

Chairman KEFAUVER. All right, go ahead.

Mr. CHUMBRIS. Were you ever arrested in April of 1942, in Jersey City, charged with the sale and possession of obscene pictures—in 1942?

Mr. GILLMAN. I just explained to you how it happened.

Mr. CHUMBRIS. That was in 1942?

Mr. GILLMAN. That is correct.

Mr. CHUMBRIS. Was that the only time you were arrested?

Mr. GILLMAN. I was arrested a couple of times for shooting dice, besides that.

Mr. CHUMBRIS. Where was that?

Mr. GILLMAN. Once it was at Newark.

Mr. CHUMBRIS. What year?

Mr. GILLMAN. I don't recall exactly. It was in 1945.

Chairman KEFAUVER. Do you know where Nick's shoeshine parlor and novelty store, in Ashburton Avenue, Yonkers, is?

Mr. GILLMAN. We live right near Yonkers, and we do a lot of shopping around there, but I don't know anybody by the name of Nick.

Chairman KEFAUVER. Did you ever meet a fellow from New Jersey there in the pornographic-literature business?

Mr. GILLMAN. Never.

Chairman KEFAUVER. And you don't know Mr. Bruckner?

Mr. GILLMAN. No, sir.

Chairman KEFAUVER. Do you know a man named Joe, who is in that business?

Mr. GILLMAN. No, sir.

Chairman KEFAUVER. All right.

Mr. CHUMBRIS. In September of 1953, were you held by the Naturalization and Immigration Service?

Mr. GILLMAN. I don't know what they wanted me down there for.

Mr. GOLD. There was a hearing, Mr. Chairman.

Mr. CHUMBRIS. There was a hearing.

Chairman KEFAUVER. What was it about?

Mr. GOLD. A question of these convictions, 1 for obscene literature, possession, in 1942; and 2 convictions for gambling—shooting dice.

Chairman KEFAUVER. It was on the revocation of his emigration citizenship?

Mr. GOLD. That is correct.

Chairman KEFAUVER. Where were you born?

Mr. GILLMAN. Quebec.

Chairman KEFAUVER. You were naturalized when?

Mr. GOLD. He was naturalized in the United States District Court, right here, on August 5, 1948.

Chairman KEFAUVER. That was in connection with the possible revocation of your citizenship?

Mr. GOLD. That is correct.

Chairman KEFAUVER. Did they charge him with moral turpitude at that time?

Mr. GOLD. No, they did not. It was the question of the convictions—the one for possession, and two for gambling. At that time we called the attention of the inspector conducting the hearing to the fact that the witness had received a discharge under honorable circumstances from the United States Navy. At that time the hearing was closed under the provisions of the Emigration and Nationality Act of 1940 which permits a naturalization without question to an applicant discharged under honorable conditions from the Armed Forces.

Chairman KEFAUVER. Mr. Gold, Mr. Gillman was called in primarily in connection with a staff report he was associated with Mr. Bruckner, who has been dealing in pornographic literature extensively, and who was arrested and sentenced for it.

He says he is not the right person, and this other matter apparently has had some connection with it in times past; but that is not the primary matter he was called in here about.

Mr. GOLD. I might point out to the chairman that as evidence of good faith Mr. Gillman and myself requested a preliminary hearing before one of the counsel to the committee to ascertain what he was here for, and to make his denials. He at that time was requested to tell the committee under oath the same things he had told Mr. Gaughan, I think it was, and I think he has so done.

Chairman KEFAUVER. Unfortunately, lack of passing information from one to another—it didn't get to us. Anyway, that is all for the present time.

Mr. Fishman.

Mr. Fishman, you are a good public official, and you might have to talk about somebody, so I guess I had better swear you. Do you swear the testimony you are about to give will be the whole truth, so help you God?

Mr. FISHMAN. I do.

TESTIMONY OF IRVING FISHMAN, DEPUTY COLLECTOR OF CUSTOMS, NEW YORK, N. Y.

Chairman KEFAUVER. Let us get on with Mr. Fishman.

Mr. CHUMBRIS. Mr. Fishman, will you give your full name and address and official capacity for the record, please?

Mr. FISHMAN. Irving Fishman; I live at 2095 Kruger Avenue; deputy collector of customs at the port of New York.

Mr. CHUMBRIS. Mr. Fishman, you have testified previously before congressional committees on your duties and responsibilities as a customs official?

Mr. FISHMAN. I have.

Mr. CHUMBRIS. And their relationship to combatting the pornographic distribution?

Mr. FISHMAN. I have; that is right.

Mr. CHUMBRIS. Do you have a prepared statement?

Mr. FISHMAN. I have a prepared statement which I would like to refer to very briefly.

Chairman KEFAUVER. Do you want to file your statement?

Mr. FISHMAN. I have submitted to the committee a copy of this statement. I merely wanted to establish the relationship of customs to the particular problem in question.

Chairman KEFAUVER. Your statement will be appended in full to the record.

Mr. CHUMBRIS. Will you please explain under what act you operate, and what your responsibilities are?

Mr. FISHMAN. Well, the present provision of the Tariff Act under which we operate has appeared for the first time in the Tariff Act of 1942. The language hasn't changed very much. The specific portion of the section, section 305 of the Tariff Act, deals with the prohibition against the importation of materials considered obscene or immoral. Those two tests must be met before we can detain or hold or seize any material for violation of this provision of the law. The determination must be first made that a book, or photograph, or magazine, or motion-picture film, is either obscene or immoral.

The determination that we make is subject to review. The owner has the right to judicial review, and before we can forfeit the material a report of the facts and circumstances of seizure, and so on, is sent to the United States attorney in the district for which the seizure is made.

Mr. CHUMBRIS. How much of a personnel does your office have to cover the many ports of the United States to stop the traffic of pornography from getting into the country?

Mr. FISHMAN. There are 45 customs districts in the United States. The detention of material as possibly objectionable is made by the examiners. For example, at the port of New York there is a book examiner who specializes in examining printed materials; and then, of course, we have our customs inspectors who examine the effects of members of the crew, baggage of incoming passengers; and we also have a force of inspectors who examine mail, foreign mail, which is turned over to the customs service by the Post Office Department for examination. The purpose of this is for the collection of revenue.

In making the examination to determine the possible assessment of duties, these examiners will hold any material which they suspect may be obscene or immoral. That material is then sent to my office, where our group makes the final determination as to whether the material detained is actually violative of this section of the law.

Mr. CHUMBRIS. I understand that your staff has set up some new offices in New Orleans and San Francisco and in Chicago, or, at least, enlarged those offices. Elaborate on that, please.

Mr. FISHMAN. The purpose of these control units is primarily to assist in the enforcement of a Foreign Agents' Registration Act and deals specifically with Communist-type political propaganda.

In connection with the examination of imported material for this purpose, anything found violative of the Tariff Act would also be held and seized and subsequently forfeited.

Mr. CHUMBRIS. The testimony of one of the customs officials at one of our community hearings stated that they are unable to ascertain the amount of pornography that comes into the country, and if he were to estimate he would place it at about 5 percent of what actually comes in.

Would you like to comment on that?

Mr. FISHMAN. I don't know what reference he was making, but it seems to me he might have been talking about our current problem—not current, but it has been our problem for some time, due to lack of adequate personnel, lack of appropriation, and so on.

We examine, as I mentioned, such mail from abroad, such foreign mail, as is suspected of being dutiable. In 1953, for example, the Post Office Department submitted to the customs service, countrywide at these districts that I mentioned, approximately 28 million mailed parcels for examination.

With the force available, we can look at about 5 percent of that mail. Probably his reference to 5 percent may have been to the part that we can examine.

Mr. CHUMBRIS. Do you have jurisdiction over the ships that come in at different ports?

Mr. FISHMAN. Yes. We make a search of the quarters of the crews; the seizures that come up as a result of that are frequent. Of course, we make an examination of the effects of passengers coming into the United States.

Mr. CHUMRBIS. Then lack of personnel is one of the problems that your agency has?

Mr. FISHMAN. Yes.

Mr. CHUMBRIS. Could you recommend to this subcommittee any amending legislation, or the amount of increased appropriation, that might be needed to properly meet this problem?

Mr. FISHMAN. Any observation that I might have must, of course, be strictly my own. I am not authorized to speak for the Treasury Department. Actually, the Treasury Department, Bureau of Customs, did apply for an increase of appropriation for the purpose of coping with this mail examination problem.

It looks as though this next fiscal year we may have some additional help for that purpose.

That, of course, is only one problem. The other feature of it is the difficulty of administering some of the provisions of the existing law, due to the difficulty of reaching a conclusion as to what is obscene. The courts have not been very clear. We find it a little difficult to operate.

Then, of course, there is the natural apathy of the public. The job of detaining or examining merchandise to ascertain whether it is obscene is not a very popular type of thing. Anybody who acts in the capacity of a censor, or if the word "censorship" is used, you are using a dirty word. It is a little difficult to come up with a real definition of what constitutes obscenity.

We have a number of problems. One of them was referred to in prior testimony. It deals with this problem of what is a nudist magazine and what is a magazine which may be considered obscene.

Mr. CHUMBRIS. Do you have any exhibits there of seizures you have made through your various offices?

Mr. FISHMAN. We have some samples of some of the things that we have been doing a little discussion with. Some of these things have been found objectionable and some have not. I brought along a few samples of the type of imported art study publications that we are constantly battling with. These are printed abroad. There are plenty of them printed in this country. This type of thing is alleged to be used by photographers and students of art.

Then we have the group of sunbathing type magazines, which give us a lot of difficulty. And then, of course, we have the type of foreign publications which we have found objectionable, as being pornographic.

I have also brought along for examination by the committee some of the situations that we have been able to correct. For example, it was a popular thing, and still is for time to time, a piece of business to advertise in college publications, that you can send away and buy various types of photographs, and a sample of the type of photograph you can buy is sent along. You can order by number.

If you order and your money happens to get through to the foreign country, they will send you these photographs. Whenever we find a concerted move to buy this type of thing, we notify the Post Office Department, which issues a fraud order, and we stop the money from leaving the United States to these foreign countries.

One of the things we are alert to and try to keep under control is the importation of negatives. The importation of one negative can result in the production of a couple of thousand copies in this country.

Mr. CHUMBRIS. Do you have many negatives that you have been able——

Chairman KEFAUVER. They will be filed as exhibits; also the negatives. We will return them later, if you would like to have them.

Mr. FISHMAN. Some of them we would like to have back for our evidence. We have recently made some large seizures.

Chairman KEFAUVER. What do you call a large seizure?

Mr. FISHMAN. A couple of thousand negatives and prints, and so on, and so forth—various assortments. For example, this sort of thing. These are negatives and they are in series—complete series of photographs which are subsequently printed and made into a book. One set of these negatives can result in the production of a heck of a lot of books.

These, of course, are from a current seizure and we would like to get them back.

Chairman KEFAUVER. Are they mainly pornographic?

Mr. FISHMAN. Yes. Some of them are not only pornographic but they are filthy. I don't think we would have any difficulty proving these are obscene. I put these aside separately and I would like to get them back, if we could.

Chairman KEFAUVER. Where do most of these things come from, Mr. Fishman?

Mr. FISHMAN. Oh, the nudist-type magazine; they are generally shipped from France and Sweden. We get some from Finland, some from Germany. It is pretty difficult to pinpoint them; they come from all over.

Chairman KEFAUVER. Where do the films come from?

Mr. FISHMAN. We have difficulty with the commercial type of motion-picture film, but that is generally not as hard to handle. The real obscene type of film, we pick that sort of thing up infrequently. We have a little difficulty with that.

We had 1 seizure some time ago of about 3,000 feet of film on 1 reel, and about half of it was made up of Mickey Mouse movies, and if our inspector hadn't been persistent enough to run the entire thing about halfway into the reel, he would never have found any of the objectionable material. Obviously, that was prepared with a view of getting it by us. Our surveillance is pretty tight and they very seldom attempt to smuggle commercial obscene motion-picture film into the United States.

Chairman KEFAUVER. As I understand it, on letters and things of that sort, you have a staff that can only look at about 5 percent; is that right?

Mr. FISHMAN. That is correct. We make a segregation of it. Our people are pretty expert in determining from the size of the package and the shipper what it contains. They try to segregate anything which looks like it might be questionable, so that we do have a look at it. The fact remains that we can only reach about 5 percent of all of this imported mail.

Chairman KEFAUVER. Is there an effort made to send a great deal of this stuff into the United States?

Mr. FISHMAN. It ebbs and flows, depending on the situation in the country. Every time the courts are apt to become liberal in their interpretation of what is objectionable, there is an increase in this type of thing.

Chairman KEFAUVER. When the courts crack down, then there isn't much of it that comes in?

Mr. FISHMAN. That is right. As a result of some of the recent rulings on motion-picture film, there was an increase of foreign motion-picture film into the United States, which we ordinarily would hold up, which we did still hold up.

Chairman KEFAUVER. As a result of the Supreme Court decision, has there been an increase?

Mr. FISHMAN. That didn't help us very much, although we haven't changed our views as a result of the ruling.

Chairman KEFAUVER. You were not ruling out "just are," anyway, were you?

Mr. FISHMAN. No.

Chairman KEFAUVER. Whom are these consigned to when they come over here?

Mr. FISHMAN. There are a number of dealers in this area, and also in areas throughout the United States, who receive commercial lots of this type of magazine. They will continue to bring in the type that we will pass, and periodically will attempt to increase the number of new magazines that they will produce. Some of them have been held as strictly obscene, and those they stopped.

It is a constant cat and mouse situation. As we hold them up, they go on to new publications and new titles.

Chairman KEFAUVER. Do you have a list available of the most frequent consignees?

Mr. FISHMAN. We can make up such a list.

Chairman KEFAUVER. Make it up and we will make it an official part of the record. Also, describe the kind of material that is being consigned to them.

Where is it paid for? Is it paid for upon delivery—that is, the freight?

Mr. FISHMAN. It is usually shipped pursuant to a letter of credit so that the funds are turned over to the shipper as soon as the shipment leaves the foreign country.

Chairman KEFAUVER. After it reaches the port of New York and the port of Boston, and the port of New Orleans, then it is shipped on, or is it usually received in the port?

Mr. FISHMAN. I would assume, judging by the quantities, that it is distributed throughout the United States.

Chairman KEFAUVER. And then shipped further by truck or automobile?

Mr. FISHMAN. By truck or automobile—anything to avoid the Post Office Department.

Chairman KEFAUVER. They don't send this through the mails?

Mr. FISHMAN. Not so far as we know.

Chairman KEFAUVER. I take it if the same ruler were applied to material shipped in as is applied to what is sent through the mails, a lot of this wouldn't get by?

Mr. FISHMAN. That is right.

Chairman KEFAUVER. If you had the same definition under the customs statute that you have in the postal statute, you would be relieved of a whole lot of headaches?

Mr. FISHMAN. That is right.

Chairman KEFAUVER. Do you recommend that be done?

Mr. FISHMAN. I do.

Chairman KEFAUVER. I can't see the logic prohibiting something from going through the mail, and at the same time letting it come in.

Mr. FISHMAN. It has been a loophole for a long time, but while it has been called to the attention of many groups and committees up until now nothing has been done about it. We testified to much the same problem before another committee, and I think the Post Office Department and the Postmaster General will have lots to say on the same subject.

Chairman KEFAUVER. That would be legislation that would stop a lot of it, and help you with your troubles?

Mr. FISHMAN. That is correct.

Chairman KEFAUVER. I am looking here at some of the big seizures that you have made of 6,000 cases, or books or what.

Mr. FISHMAN. May I see the photograph?

Chairman KEFAUVER. I was looking at some of the figures. The importer and the size of the seizures you have made.

Mr. FISHMAN. Well——

Chairman KEFAUVER. There are about 15 or 18 of them, and all of them seem to have been released except 2 of them.

Mr. FISHMAN. They represent this so-called art type of magazine. The ones that we have indicated as being released.

Chairman KEFAUVER. Sun Reviews, and so forth?

Mr. FISHMAN. I brought along some of that type of publication.

Chairman KEFAUVER. Do we ship much of this stuff out of the United States to other nations?

Mr. FISHMAN. I am afraid I couldn't answer that question.

Chairman KEFAUVER. That doesn't come under your jurisdiction?

Mr. FISHMAN. We have some control over exports, but we don't look for that sort of thing.

Chairman KEFAUVER. These photographs show how it is received?

Mr. FISHMAN. That is correct.

Chairman KEFAUVER. Let them be identified and be put in as exhibits.

(The photographs were marked "Exhibit 22," and are on file with the subcommittee.)

Chairman KEFAUVER. You have a fine service, and you do your work and sometimes get a little cooperation and a little praise. I hope this subcommittee can help get this law in shape so that your enforcement problem will be easier.

Senator LANGER. The Senate last year passed a law prohibiting transportation by automobile and by plane. It didn't pass the House. I want the witness to know that it has had some consideration down there in Washington.

Chairman KEFAUVER. I think you will be interested in knowing as a result of the work of this subcommittee we have a bill through the Senate prohibiting the shipment in automobiles, strengthening our customs laws and postal laws, and it has been over in the House, and since the hearings started up here the House Judiciary Committee has brought out the bill favorably, so it looks like we may get some action in this session of Congress.

We want to encourage you in your work and we appreciate you telling us your problems.

We will keep these exhibits separate and return them to you.

Thank you very much.

Let's have about a 5-minute recess at this time.

(A short recess was taken.)

Chairman KEFAUVER. Who is the next witness?

Mr. CHUMBRIS. Mr. Shomer or Mr. A. M. Shapiro.

Chairman KEFAUVER. Mr. Shomer or Mr. Shapiro.

We will let the subpena be made part of the record and. Mr. Marshal, will you notify Mr. Shapiro if he is not here before the hearing closes this afternoon he will be held in contempt for failing to answer the subpena?

Mr. CHUMBRIS. Has Mr. Shomer come yet?

Joseph Piccarelli?

Chairman KEFAUVER. Mr. Chumbris, will you check which witnesses appeared and which ones are missing?

Mr. Butler, do you solemnly swear the testimony you give will be the whole truth, so help you God?

TESTIMONY OF LT. GEORGE BUTLER, DALLAS POLICE DEPARTMENT, DALLAS, TEX., INVESTIGATOR FOR THE SUBCOMMITTEE

Mr. CHUMBRIS. Give your full name and address, and your official title for the record, please.

Lieutenant BUTLER. George Butler, 6447 Velasco Street, Dallas, Tex., investigator for the committee.

Chairman KEFAUVER. Let the record show Lieutenant Butler is on loan from the Dallas Police Force, and he is one of the outstanding police officers in Dallas. We had him on loan for our Senate Crime Investigating Committee, where he did a very remarkable job, and we appreciate him being with us now.

Also, he has acted in the investigation of the waterfront problems here, some of which were presented by our committee, and most of which were brought out by the New York Crime Commission.

Proceed.

Mr. CHUMBRIS. Lieutenant Butler, you know one Simon Simring operating in the southern part of the United States?

Lieutenant BUTLER. Yes, sir.

Mr. CHUMBRIS. Did you investigate that particular matter?

Lieutenant BUTLER. Yes, sir.

Mr. CHUMBRIS. Is Simon Simring under subpena of this subcommittee?

Lieutenant BUTLER. Yes, sir.

Mr. CHUMBRIS. Would you please explain why he isn't here?

Lieutenant BUTLER. The United States marshal hasn't been able to locate him.

Mr. CHUMBRIS. Have you personally investigated the Simring matter?

Lieutenant BUTLER. Yes, sir.

Mr. CHUMBRIS. Will you please tell us now in your own words the result of the investigation?

Lieutenant BUTLER. Well, to condense the investigation, I have drawn up a little brief on it. If it is permissible, I would like to read it into the record.

Chairman KEFAUVER. All right, Lieutenant Butler. These facts you know of your own knowledge from your official investigation?

Lieutenant BUTLER. Yes, sir.

Chairman KEFAUVER. Go ahead and read the report.

Lieutenant BUTLER (reading):

This man is regarded as one of the largest dealers in pornography in the southeastern section of the Nation. While no complete rundown on this subject is available at this time, it is known that he was arrested in St. Petersburg,

Fla., on April 23, 1952, for possession of obscene literature, film, and other material.

At that time he gave his address as 540 Northwest 39th Street, Miami, Fla. While out on bond in this case Simring was arrested on July 19, 1953, in Johnson City, Tenn., on a similar charge. Apparently he forfeited the $54.50 cash bond in this case. No disposition is shown.

On February 11, 1953, he was arrested with another large load of lewd and obscene material in Atlanta, Ga.

On April 23, 1953, he was charged on four counts in connection with this case. He was fined $1,000 and given 12 months on each count, all sentences being suspended. Still another charge resulting from this arrest was nolle prossed on December 16, 1953 (Exhibit 1—Police Record from Atlanta, Ga.).

Simring went to trial in the St. Petersburg court on June 24, 1953. He was sentenced to 4 years in Judge Bird's court. This trial was a result of charges filed against him on the arrest and seizure in that city on April 23, 1952. He appealed his case and was released on bond (letter from J. R. Reichert, chief of police in St. Petersburg, Fla., entered as exhibit 2 with police mug of Simring).

While out on bond in the St. Petersburg case, and under suspended sentences in 3 counts in Atlanta, Ga., Simring was arrested on April 30, 1955, in Orangeburg, S. C. A very large seizure of pornography material was made by the Orangeburg police department, and an outstanding investigation of Simring was made by Police Chief T. E. Salley. This investigation is still in progress.

In this seizure were 134 rolls of obscene film, 8-millimeter and 16-millimeter; 1,276 folders of lewd and obscene photographs, 12 in a folder; 512 folders of obscene photographs, 20 in a folder; 663 stereo slides of obscene nature; 1,900 color slides of nudes and suggestive poses; 61 books of printed material and pictures, "Permanent Virgin" and "Switch"; 330 books of very lewd printed material with illustrations titled "Alcohol," "Search," "Dark Paths," and "Nora's Sister"; 120 envelopes containing 10 each very lewd pictures; 567 various rubber novelties (inventory's exhibit 3).

A large roadmap of the southeastern section of the United States was found in possession of Simring—175 cities and towns were circled on this map (see exhibit 4 with page listing cities).

Simring was also in possession of customer list with 243 names listed. He had a card index file reflecting customer and contacts in 21 States and Washington, D. C. The index file carried 1,194 names. It is interesting to note that the list contained names and addresses of well-known dealers in the pornography racket, including:

Stanley Jablonski, 3510 Washington Avenue, Jacksonville, Fla.
Louis Shomar, 1541 East Fifth Street, Brooklyn, N. Y.
Harvey Brill, Baltimore, Md.
Red Florence, care of ABC Film Co., Houston, Tex.
Ike Dorfman, Baltimore, Md.
Frank Adler, 368 West 57th Street, New York City.

It will be interesting to note, at this point, that a lead furnished by this subcommittee out of Simring's address book resulted in a large pornography raid on E. "Red" Florence, 9362 Friendly Road, in Houston, Tex., by Sheriff C. V. Buster Kerns and Chief Deputy Lloyd Frazier. The outstanding work and cooperation of Sheriff Kerns and his staff is to be commended.

A comparison of the material seized from Simring shows it to be the same type handled by Lewis C. Allen, arrested in Memphis, Tenn.; Eddie Levy, arrested in Connecticut; Abraham Rubin and Al Stone, arrested in Detroit, Mich; Arthur Herman Sobel, arrested in Rhode Island; Wyman Parr, arrested in Atlanta, Ga.; Abe Rotto, arrested in Brooklyn, N. Y.; Casimer Wargula, arrested in Buffalo N. Y.; and Eddie Mishkin, arrested in the New York area.

Simring is out now on a 30-day leave, his sentence, and it was during this period we tried to get a hold of him but were unable to do so.

Chairman KEFAUVER. I understand, Mr. Butler, he has been under probation in Atlanta, and was found doing business and arrested in Johnson City and somewhere else?

Lieutenant BUTLER. Yes, sir. From the time he was arrested in St. Petersburg, Fla., he was arrested in Tennessee, Atlanta, Ga., and Orangeburg, S. C. He was out on bond in the St. Petersburg case.

Chairman KEFAUVER. Let these charts concerning Simring's operations be inserted here.

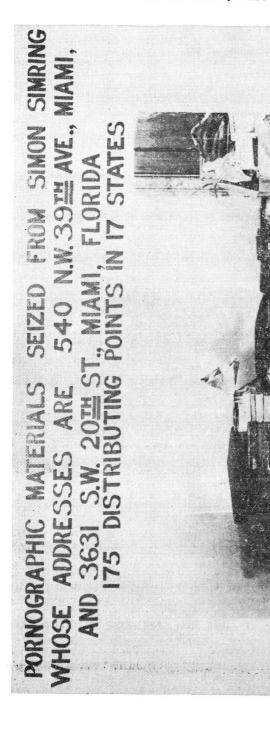

PORNOGRAPHIC MATERIALS SEIZED FROM SIMON SIMRING WHOSE ADDRESSES ARE 540 N.W. 39TH AVE., MIAMI, AND 3631 S.W. 20TH ST., MIAMI, FLORIDA 175 DISTRIBUTING POINTS IN 17 STATES

Chairman KEFAUVER. Anything else, Mr. Chumbris?

Your investigation showed him to be one of the largest ones operating in the southern part of the country?

Lieutenant BUTLER. Yes. These people seemed to have a definite territory that they operate in. It is more or less like a traveling salesman in any other business. They have a regular route that they cover.

Chairman KEFAUVER. This Houston, Tex., gang that was busted up as a result of this lead, was that a substantial one?

Lieutenant BUTLER. Yes, sir; that was a large seizure.

Chairman KEFAUVER. Who was the man that ran that?

Lieutenant BUTLER. E. Red Florence.

Chairman KEFAUVER. He has recently been convicted?

Lieutenant BUTLER. No; he was recently arrested. He is under charges in Houston, Tex., as of now.

Chairman KEFAUVER. Senator Langer, any questions?

Senator LANGER. They divided up the territory?

Lieutenant BUTLER. Yes, sir. They seemed to operate in various territories like that, and they get to be known; they are shipped around to some territory where their faces are not known.

Senator LANGER. Could you furnish the subcommittee with a map to show how it is divided and who is boss in each district?

Lieutenant BUTLER. I don't have that information yet. Here is a man operating in a southern section; here is a man operating more to the Midwest. This shows in effect the places that were covered by the raid in Houston, Tex. Up here is shown the same cities were marked where pornography was sold to juveniles, in the cities in the black here—the Southwest distributorship here.

Over here, in this Baltimore deal, the stuff coming to New York, and is being parceled out all over the United States.

Chairman KEFAUVER. That is from Baltimore?

Lieutenant BUTLER. Yes, sir. The stuff is sent to these distributors, which would be called a wholesaler, and it is our understanding that each one of these people sell material in that area that they work.

Senator LANGER. Would you go so far that a few men have a monopoly on this business?

Lieutenant BUTLER. They are trying to get it.

Senator LANGER. Senator Kefauver would be very interested in that. Have you got considerable evidence that it is divided up in territories?

Lieutenant BUTLER. Yes, sir. They seem to work a vast territory like this. Each man has a different locality. They don't seem to encroach on each other's territory.

Chairman KEFAUVER. We will go further into this in our Los Angeles hearings. We have some information already as to operations in the western part of the country. After those hearings have been completed, I think we will be able to get a nationwide picture of operations, some of which we do not have established in our testimony as yet.

Mr. CHUMBRIS. Lieutenant, have you examined any of the films and pictures that have been confiscated from Simring?

Lieutenant BUTLER. Yes, sir.

Mr. CHUMBRIS. Have you observed the age of some of the actors in those films and pictures?

Lieutenant BUTLER. In Simring's seizure, I don't recall any juveniles. There is evidence that the same type of material distributed by Simring has been picked up on various school grounds in the section that he operated in.

Mr. CHUMBRIS. Then his material has gotten to the juveniles in those areas?

Lieutenant BUTLER. The same type of material; yes, sir.

Chairman KEFAUVER. Do you have some of the samples that you can make exhibits here?

Lieutenant BUTLER. Yes, sir.

Chairman KEFAUVER. Let them be marked as exhibits.

They will be part of the record here.

Lieutenant BUTLER. The film that he had——

Chairman KEFAUVER. Make them exhibits, too.

(Samples of pornography were marked "Exhibit No. 23," and are on file with the subcommittee.)

Mr. CHUMBRIS. Do you know of your own knowledge that some more film that has been picked up from Simring had been sent to the subcommittee in Washington?

Lieutenant BUTLER. Yes, sir.

Mr. CHUMBRIS. And you don't know of your own knowledge whether there were any minors being participants in those films?

Lieutenant BUTLER. No, sir; I haven't seen them.

Chairman KEFAUVER. Any questions, Senator Langer?

Senator LANGER. Do you have any evidence at all that women are mixed up in this business?

Lieutenant BUTLER. Yes, sir. They play an important part in the posing of these pictures. You mean in the distribution of it, Senator?

Senator LANGER. What I want to know is whether there were any women mixed up in the manufacturing, printing, mailing it, distributing it?

Lieutenant BUTLER. No, the only women we know of so far are the women that posed for the pictures.

Chairman KEFAUVER. Thank you, Lieutenant Butler, very much. We appreciate your good work in this other field.

Mr. CHUMBRIS. Has Mr. Weiss come in yet, the attorney for Mr. Rubin?

Chairman KEFAUVER. Mr. Rubin, you come back around here.

You have been in touch with your counsel?

Mr. RUBIN. I have tried to get in touch with him, but he wasn't in.

Chairman KEFAUVER. He hasn't called to ask for any delay or extension of the hearing?

Mr. RUBIN. He told me to ask you, but if it is all right with you, I want to go ahead with it.

Chairman KEFAUVER. Are you ready to go ahead?

Mr. RUBIN. Yes.

Chairman KEFAUVER. You have got it written out there?

Mr. RUBIN. Yes.

Chairman KEFAUVER. You have got your counsel's advice on a piece of paper; is that right?

Mr. RUBIN. Yes, sir.

Chairman KEFAUVER. Mr. Chumbris, will you make a brief statement about the nature of your questions, and what you expect to bring out by the testimony of Mr. Rubin, or have you done that?

Mr. CHUMBRIS. Our investigation reveals that Mr. Abraham Rubin, alias Al Rubin, alias Abraham Rubinstein, alias Stoney Rubin White, alias Al Stone, is one of the large distributors of pornography throughout the United States, that he has contacts in many of the cities such as Chicago, St. Louis, New York City, Washington, D. C., Jacksonville, Fla.; he has been connected with E. Red Florence, of Houston, Tex., and Simon Simring, of Miami, Fla., as well as Eddie Mishkin, who was here this afternoon.

We have information that this pornographic material is distributed and gets into the hands of juveniles and definitely has an impact on youth and juvenile delinquency.

Chairman KEFAUVER. Is it distributed across State lines?

Mr. CHUMBRIS. It is distributed across many State lines. At least 20 States have been listed in areas where Al Stone distributes this pornographic material. The police chiefs of Detroit and Chicago were here and testified, and they definitely know of the operations of Al Stone, alias Abraham Rubin, as well as Inspector Blick, who also testified during the course of these hearings.

Chairman KEFAUVER. Their testimony is in the record and if necessary it will be made part of any special record.

You ask Mr. Stone any questions you have to ask him.

TESTIMONY OF ABRAHAM RUBIN, BROOKLYN, N. Y.—Resumed

Mr. CHUMBRIS. Will you please give your full name and address for the record again, please?

Mr. RUBIN. Abraham Rubin, 1639 41st Street, Brooklyn.

Mr. CHUMBRIS. Are you also known as Al Stone?

Mr. RUBIN. I refuse to answer under the immunity provisions of the fifth amendment of the Constitution.

Chairman KEFAUVER. Mr. Rubin, you have been here in the hearing room when we have had other witnesses who have taken the fifth amendment. We don't want to deny it to you or to any other witness whose testimony would, indeed, tend to incriminate you. It seems to me this is a proper question. The purpose of this subcommittee will be to ask that the full committee cite you for contempt if you refuse to answer this question. It will then be sent to the district atorney, who will present it to the grand jury, if he wishes to, and there will be a trial if a true bill is found.

I feel that I must warn you of the intention of this subcommittee, and also order you to answer that question.

Mr. RUBIN. I refuse to answer under the immunity provisions of the fifth amendment of the Constitution.

Chairman KEFAUVER. Let the record show that Mr. Rubin has a piece of paper that he is reading from.

Ask him the next question.

Mr. CHUMBRIS. Mr. Rubin, alias Mr. Stone——

Chairman KEFAUVER. Just say Mr. Rubin.

Mr. CHUMBRIS. Mr. Rubin, do you know Frank Leno, alias Frank Uderri, of Chicago, Ill.?

Mr. RUBIN. I refuse to answer under the immunity provisions of the fifth amendment of the Constitution.

Chairman KEFAUVER. The chairman orders you to answer under penalty——

Mr. RUBIN. I refuse to answer under the immunity provisions of the fifth amendment of the Constitution.

Mr. CHUMBRIS. Do you know Stanley Jablonski, of Jacksonville, Fla.?

Mr. RUBIN. I refuse to answer under the immunity provisions of the fifth amendment of the Constitution.

Chairman KEFAUVER. Let's ask the question in a different way. Do you know Stanley Jablonsky, who is purported to have some connection with pornographic literature, in Jacksonville, Fla.?

Mr. RUBIN. I refuse to answer under the immunity provisions of the fifth amendment of the Constitution.

Chairman KEFAUVER. You are ordered and directed to answer under the penalty of being in contempt of the United States Senate.

Mr. RUBIN. I refuse to answer under the immunity provisions of the fifth amendment of the Constitution.

Chairman KEFAUVER. What business are you in?

Mr. RUBIN. I refuse to answer under the immunity provisions of the fifth amendment of the Constitution.

Chairman KEFAUVER. You are ordered to answer.

Mr. RUBIN. I refuse to answer under the immunity provisions of the fifth amendment of the Constitution.

Chairman KEFAUVER. In any business that you might be in, do you employ children or teen-agers?

Mr. RUBIN. I refuse to answer under the immunity provisions of the fifth amendment of the Constitution.

Chairman KEFAUVER. You are ordered and directed to answer under penalty of being in contempt of the Senate.

Mr. RUBIN. I refuse to answer under the immunity provisions of the fifth amendment of the Constitution.

Chairman KEFAUVER. You know what the immunity provision is?

Mr. RUBIN. My rights of the fifth amendment of the Constitution.

Chairman KEFAUVER. You are fully apprised of your rights and the penalties that go with the refusal to answer?

Mr. RUBIN. I refuse to answer under the immunity provisions of the fifth amendment of the Constitution.

Chairman KEFAUVER. Will you tell us, Mr. Rubin, what information you have about what the fifth amendment is?

Mr. RUBIN. Constitutional rights.

Chairman KEFAUVER. Did you talk with your lawyer about it?

Mr. RUBIN. Yes, sir.

Chairman KEFAUVER. Who wrote out this piece of paper where you have that?

Mr. RUBIN. My lawyer.

Chairman KEFAUVER. Did the lawyer just tell you to read that whenever you were asked a question?

Mr. RUBIN. That is right.

Chairman KEFAUVER. Is that right?

Mr. RUBIN. That is right.

Chairman KEFAUVER. You are answering some questions. Did he say to you "Use your own judgment"?

Mr. RUBIN. I refuse to answer under the immunity provisions of the fifth amendment of the Constitution.

Senator LANGER. Do you know who is the President of the United States?

Mr. RUBIN. I refuse to answer under the immunity provisions of the fifth amendment of the Constitution.

Senator LANGER. Did you ever hear of Abraham Lincoln?

Mr. RUBIN. I refuse to answer under the immunity provisions of the fifth amendment of the Constitution.

Chairman KEFAUVER. We will order to direct you to answer that question under penalty of being in contempt of the Senate.

Mr. RUBIN. I refuse to answer under the immunity provisions of the fifth amendment of the Constitution.

Mr. CHUMBRIS. Mr. Rubin, I hand you an exhibit, which contains a front-face photograph and side-view photograph with "Department of Police, Detroit, No. 109385, FBI No. 608419, in the name of Abraham Rubin," and I show it to you, and ask you if you can identify that? Do you have any knowledge of that photograph?

Mr. RUBIN. I refuse to answer under the immunity provisions of the fifth amendment of the Constitution.

Chairman KEFAUVER. The Chairman orders you to answer under penalty of being in contempt of the Senate.

Mr. RUBIN. I refuse to answer under the immunity provisions of the fifth amendment of the Constitution.

Chairman KEFAUVER. This has been made part of the record, and will be filed as an exhibit.

Mr. Rubin, I think you ought to understand that the fifth amendment is for the real protection of people when they are called upon to testify. It is not a provision that is to be used just for coving up or to prevent a Senate committee from securing facts that it is entitled to have. Our purpose here is to get information. I think you ought to think seriously about what you are doing here today.

Is there anything that you will tell us about your business, Mr. Rubin?

Mr. RUBIN. I refuse to answer under the immunity provisions of the fifth amendment of the Constitution.

Chairman KEFAUVER. You are directed and ordered to and under penalty of being held in contempt of the Senate.

Mr. RUBIN. I refuse to answer under the immunity provisions of the fifth amendment of the Constitution.

Mr. CHUMBRIS. Mr. Rubin, I show you a record of the Detroit Police Department, No. 109385, in the name of Abraham Rubin, FBI No. 608419, and attached thereto is a photo, one is a side view, one is a front view, the front-view picture contains a notation "Detroit Police, 5-19-53," with the number of 109385, which is consistent with the number that I just read, of the Detroit Police Department. I show it to you and ask you if you can identify it, and if that is your picture?

Mr. RUBIN. I refuse to answer under the immunity provisions of the fifth amendment of the Constitution.

Chairman KEFAUVER. Let the exhibit which counsel asked about, be marked so that we can see what it is.

You are ordered and directed to answer the question under penalty of being in contempt of the Senate.

Mr. RUBIN. I refuse to answer under the immunity provisions of the fifth amendment of the Constitution.

Mr. CHUMBRIS. May I introduce into the record a road map of the Northeastern part of the United States?

Chairman KEFAUVER. That will be introduced into the record today.

Mr. CHUMBRIS. Mr. Rubin, I have here an AAA road map, American Automobile Association, covering the Northern States, and in this map it shows circles in a reddish purple color, with circles marked around the cities of New York, Richmond, Va; Louisville, Ky.; St. Louis, Mo.; Indianapolis, Ind.; Fort Wayne, Ind., an area covering the cities of Michigan City, New Buffalo, Michigan City being in Indiana, and New Buffalo being in Michigan; Detroit, Mich., and in the same map there is a green road identification covering those same cities which indicates a route map prepared by the AAA for those States.

Have you ever seen this particular map before, and was it not taken from your possession by the Detroit police department?

Chairman KEFAUVER. Ask the first question.

Mr. CHUMBRIS. Have you seen this map before?

Mr. RUBIN. I refuse to answer under the immunity provisions of the fifth amendment of the Constitution.

Chairman KEFAUVER. You are ordered to answer under the penalty of being in contempt of the Senate.

Mr. RUBIN. I refuse to answer under the immunity provisions of the fifth amendment of the Constitution.

Chairman KEFAUVER. Let it be Exhibit 24.

(The map was marked "Exhibit No. 24," and is on file with the subcommittee.)

I think you said it was found in his car, and other evidence shows that Mr. Rubin was in these towns set forth on the map.

Mr. CHUMBRIS. That is correct.

Chairman KEFAUVER. All right.

Mr. CHUMBRIS. I again show you this particular map, and wasn't this map, marked "Exhibit No. 24," covering the cities heretofore mentioned, the same map that was taken from your car, in your possession, on or about the 19th day of May 1953 by the Detroit, Mich., police department?

Mr. RUBIN. I refuse to answer under the immunity provisions of the fifth amendment of the Constitution.

Chairman KEFAUVER. You are directed to answer under penalty of contempt.

Mr. RUBIN. I refuse to answer under the immunity provisions of the fifth amendment of the Constitution.

Senator LANGER. Mr. Chairman, I note that Mr. Abraham Rubin got 6 months suspended sentence in Poughkeepsie for possessing obscene literature, in 1932, on November 23.

On the 24th of February, 1923, he was fined $250 and costs, and a suspended sentence of 6 months in jail, at Darien, Connecticut.

On the 4th day of May, 1933, he was sentenced to 3 months in Erie County Penitentiary, in Buffalo, N. Y.

On the 5th day of April, 1933, for violating section 1141 of the United States Code, he got 3 months.

I find, on the 14th day of February, 1934, according to the Detroit police record, for possessing obscene literature, he got a $75 fine or 30 days in the county jail in New York.

In 1934, for possessing obscene literature, he got 30 days in Providence, R. I.

On the 4th day of July, 1934, for possessing obscene literature, he got 30 days and costs.

On the 18th day of May, 1953, for possessing obscene literature in Detroit, Mich., he got $100 and 90 days in jail.

It seems to me that if that be the record, we should draw up legislation that would provide for a second and third and fourth offense that the penalty be more stringent. If this record is correct—and there is no reason to believe that it is not, we find here after the sixth offense for possessing obscene literature, Mr. Rubin received a $100 fine or 90 days in jail.

In New York we have the Sullivan law—we have a law which provides for four felonies a man gets life. Yet we have the absurd situation where, for a sixth offense, a man pays a $100 fine.

Chairman KEFAUVER. Your comments and suggestions are good, Senator Langer, and I agree with you that a man with this long record, still showing no heavy penalties, is not very effective law enforcement.

It may be that these different places did not know about his previous record, but certainly as to Federal convictions, to the extent that it comes under the Federal law, will, in the future—I will ask the staff to consider and make a study of just what we can do to have some more severe penalties as time goes on.

Senator LANGER. I will be happy to be a cosponsor.

Chairman KEFAUVER. Thank you. We will cosponsor it together.

Mr. Rubin, let me see if I can get clear again just what your lawyer told you with reference to pleading this fifth amendment.

Mr. RUBIN. I refuse to answer under the immunity provisions of the fifth amendment of the Constitution.

Senator LANGER. Did I hear you say your lawyer was a member of the city council of the city of New York?

Mr. RUBIN. I refuse to answer under the immunity provisions of the fifth amendment of the Constitution.

Chairman KEFAUVER. Did the attorney advise you to invoke your privilege on every question that was asked?

Mr. RUBIN. I refuse to answer under the immunity provisions of the fifth amendment of the Constitution.

Chairman KEFAUVER. Do you mean that the advice your attorney gave you might incriminate you if related to this committee?

Mr. RUBIN. I refuse to answer under the immunity provisions of the fifth amendment of the Constitution.

Chairman KEFAUVER. What did your lawyer say to you in his office at that time when you went to him for counsel?

Mr. RUBIN. I refuse to answer under the immunity provisions of the fifth amendment of the Constitution.

Chairman KEFAUVER. You mean again to say that any advice you may have gotten would cause you any trouble if related here, that it might incriminate you?

Mr. RUBIN. I refuse to answer under the immunity provisions of the fifth amendment of the Constitution.

Chairman KEFAUVER. Any other questions?

Mr. CHUMBRIS. I have just one more exhibit.

Chairman KEFAUVER. All right.

Mr. CHUMBRIS. Mr. Rubin, I have here a photostatic copy of a name and address book of Al Stone, also known as Abraham Rubin, which address list has in it numerous names, one of which is Abe

Rotto, New York City; another, Eddie, telephone number, SP 9–3384——

Chairman KEFAUVER. Let it be filed as an exhibit—and ask him about it.

(The address book was marked "Exhibit No. 25," and is on file with the subcommittee.)

Chairman KEFAUVER. Do you know anything about that list?

Mr. RUBIN. I refuse to answer under the immunity provisions of the fifth amendment of the Constitution.

Chairman KEFAUVER. You are ordered and directed to answer under penalty of being in contempt of the Senate.

Mr. RUBIN. I refuse to answer under the immunity provisions of the fifth amendment of the Constitution.

Chairman KEFAUVER. Let the purported address book be made an exhibit.

Mr. Rubin, I want you to understand again that the members of this subcommittee do not intend to let you get by with your refusal to answer questions propounded to you here. Complaints have come to us, in correspondence, that you are one of the biggest operators in this despicable pornography field in the whole United States; that you have connections with people all over the country; that you have been in this business a long time. You seem not to have learned any lesson from this long list of arrests and convictions. It is unfortunate that you do not appreciate the damage that your kind of business is doing to the young people in this country.

I want to tell you again that we expect to do everything in our power to secure a contempt proceeding against you, unless you, at this time, want to answer questions and tell us what the subcommittee has a right to know—in other words, purge yourself of any possible contempt.

Do you have anything further you want to say?

Mr. RUBIN. I refuse to answer under the immunity provisions of the fifth amendment of the Constitution.

Chairman KEFAUVER. You remain under subpena, and you will be hearing from this committee and other officials later on.

Mr. Shomer, will you come around?

TESTIMONY OF LOU SHOMER, BROOKLYN, N. Y.—Resumed

Mr. Shomer has been here. Mr. Chumbris, do you have anything else you want to ask him?

Mr. CHUMBRIS. Since you were on the stand the other day——

Chairman KEFAUVER. That was last Thursday.

Mr. CHUMBRIS. Last Thursday, to be exact, we have received some additional information that we would like to have your comment on. I believe you testified that you are in the real estate business at this time?

Mr. SHOMER. Yes, sir.

Mr. CHUMBRIS. How long have you been in the real estate business?

Mr. SHOMER. About 2 months.

Mr. CHUMBRIS. I believe you testified that you have no further interest in pornographic matters; is that correct?

Mr. SHOMER. Repeat the question.

Chairman KEFAUVER. He wants to know if you have any further connection with any pornographic literature business.

Mr. SHOMER. No, sir.

Chairman KEFAUVER. Is your answer "No"?

Mr. SHOMER. No, sir.

Chairman KEFAUVER. Are you answering the question?

Mr. SHOMER. I am answering "No."

Mr. CHUMBRIS. Mr. Shomer, from our investigation, it reveals that last year you traveled by automobile to the State of New York, Port Chester, to be exact, and at Port Chester, at a Safeway store, at the parking lot, transferred some pornographic material in large quantities to another person.

Is that true or false?

Mr. SHOMER. That is false. I have never been to Port Chester. I don't even know where it is.

Mr. CHUMBRIS. That statement that I just made, then, in your opinion, is false; is that correct?

Mr. SHOMER. I have never been in Port Chester.

Chairman KEFAUVER. Or any place around there?

Mr. SHOMER. I don't know the area.

Mr. CHUMBRIS. Mr. Shomer, did you ever make any transfer of pornographic material in any parking lot of a grocery store or a drug store?

Mr. SHOMER. No, sir.

Mr. CHUMBRIS. And any information that you have done such is false; is that your statement?

Mr. SHOMER. Yes, sir.

Mr. CHUMBRIS. Mr. Shomer, do you know Edgar Maynard Levy?

Mr. SHOMER. No, sir.

Mr. CHUMBRIS. You do not?

Mr. SHOMER. No, sir.

Mr. CHUMBRIS. Do you know of one Edgar Maynard Levy, who lives on Tinker Drive, Long Island, now living in Washington, D. C.?

Mr. SHOMER. No, sir.

Mr. CHUMBRIS. Do you know anyone on Tinker Drive in Long Island?

Mr. SHOMER. No, sir.

Mr. CHUMBRIS. Mr. Shomer, have you ever done any business with Eddie Mishkin?

Mr. SHOMER. No, sir.

Mr. CHUMBRIS. Have you ever done any business with Al. Stone?

Mr. SHOMER. No, sir.

Mr. CHUMBRIS. Alias Abraham Rubin?

Mr. SHOMER. No, sir.

Mr. CHUMBRIS. Were you here when the witness prior to you testified?

Mr. SHOMER. Yes, sir.

Mr. CHUMBRIS. Do you know that person?

Mr. SHOMER. No, sir.

Mr. CHUMBRIS. You have never seen him before?

Mr. SHOMER. No, sir.

Mr. CHUMBRIS. Let the record indicate that the witness previous to Mr. Shomer was Al. Stone, alias Abraham Rubin.

Mr. Shomer, do you know George Fodor, of Washington, D. C., and St. Petersburg, Fla.?

Mr. SHOMER. No, sir.

Mr. CHUMBRIS. Were you present last Thursday when Mr. George Fodor was here on the witness stand?

Mr. SHOMER. No, sir.

Mr. CHUMBRIS. You were not present?

Mr. SHOMER. No, sir.

Mr. CHUMBRIS. Do you know Mr. Ike Dorman, of Baltimore, Md.?

Mr. SHOMER. No, sir.

Mr. CHUMBRIS. Do you have any knowledge of George Fodor and Ike Dorman coming from Baltimore to New York City?

Chairman KEFAUVER. Anything else, Mr. Chumbris?

Mr. CHUMBRIS. Mr. A. M. Shapiro. Has Mr. A. M. Shapiro come in?

(There was no response.)

Chairman KEFAUVER. Mr. Shapiro has not turned up. We will recommend that he be held in contempt for not obeying the subpena of the subcommittee.

Senator LANGER. I so move, Mr. Chairman.

Chairman KEFAUVER. Without objection, it is so ordered and that will be the recommendation of the whole subcommittee.

I think I have already ordered the subpena and the return to be made a part of the record as an exhibit.

(The subpena and the return were marked "Exhibit No. 26," and are as follows:)

UNITED STATES OF AMERICA

CONGRESS OF THE UNITED STATES

To AARON MOSES SHAPIRO,
40 East 23d Street, New York City, Greeting:

Pursuant to lawful authority, you are hereby commanded to appear before the Subcommittee To Investigate Juvenile Delinquency of the Senate of the United States, on May 24, 1955, at 10 o'clock a. m., at their committee room 104, United States Court House, Foley Square, New York, N. Y., then and there to testify what you may know relative to the subject matters under consideration by said committee, and bring with you copies of your State and Federal income tax returns for the years 1950 to 1954, inclusive; records of your business, including bank books, bank statements, check books and check stubs, profit and loss statements, statements of assets and liabilities, and all documents reflecting your interest in property, real, personal or mixed.

Hereof fail not, as you will answer your default under the pains and penalties in such cases made and provided.

To U. S. Marshal, Southern District of New York, to serve and return.

Given under my hand, by order of the committee, this 19th day of May, in the year of our Lord one thousand nine hundred and fifty-five.

ESTES KEFAUVER,
Chairman, Subcommittee To Investigate Juvenile Delinquency.

Received this writ at New York, N. Y., on May 19, 1955, and on May 19, 1955, at 40 East 23d Street, New York, N. Y., I served it on the within-named Aaron Moses Shapiro by leaving a copy thereof or a subpena ticket with him.

THOMAS J. LUNNEY,
United States Marshal, Southern District of New York.
BY JAMES GUPP,
Deputy United States Marshal, Southern District of New York.

Chairman KEFAUVER. I may say as to Mr. Shapiro that there is a possibility there has been some mixup in the notice getting to his lawyer, but he will either testify or we will have contempt proceeding brought against him. If there is a mixup, he will be given a chance to testify later.

Is there anybody else?

Mr. CHUMBRIS. Joseph Piccarelli.

(There was no response.)

Chairman KEFAUVER. Let the subpena be put in the record. We will ask that he be held in contempt for failure to appear.

Senator LANGER. I so move, Mr. Chairman.

Chairman KEFAUVER. Without objection, it is so ordered.

(The subpena was marked "Exhibit No. 27," and is as follows:)

UNITED STATES OF AMERICA

CONGRESS OF THE UNITED STATES

To JOSEPH PICCARELLIE,
     119–18 178 Place, St. Albans, N. Y., Greetings:

Pursuant to lawful authority, you are hereby commanded to appear before the Subcommittee To Investigate Juvenile Delinquency of the Senate of the United States, on May 23, 1955, at 10 o'clock a. m., at their committee room 104, United States Courthouse, Foley Square, New York, N. Y., then and there to testify what you may know relative to the subject matters under consideration by said committee.

Hereof fail not, as you will answer your default under the pains and penalties in such cases made and provided.

To United States marshal, Eastern District of New York, to serve and return.

Given under my hand, by order of the committee, this 19th day of May, in the year of our Lord one thousand nine hundred and fifty-five.

ESTES KEFAUVER,
Chairman, Subcommittee To Investigate Juvenile Delinquency.

Chairman KEFAUVER. Senator Langer, do you have any comments you wish to make before we bring our hearings to a conclusion?

Senator LANGER. I have nothing to say, Mr. Chairman.

Chairman KEFAUVER. I want to state briefly for the record a few observations.

The subcommittee last year held some hearings into the operation, publishing, and distribution of pornographic literature, films—things of that sort.

This year we have received a great many complaints from parents and from young people themselves, police officers, of the increased amount of pornography that is being distributed around, getting into the hands of young people, teen-agers, many of whom are in school. These letters indicate the damaging effect and the degrading effect that they have.

We have talked with a number of experts in the field; they have confirmed the fact that it is a contributing factor, and a substantial one, in the increase of the number of sex crimes and the increase of juvenile delinquency.

So that the staff has made this investigation, and I think they have done a very fine job in getting such information as they could.

We came here to New York not because New York is any worse than any other city. As a matter of fact, many public officials here and private people have done much to eliminate the extent of pornography in New York, for which they deserve commendation.

Some of these groups, as the evidence shows, do do business here. This is a port of entry, and the place for bringing all of our witnesses together in one place, and we thought this would be the proper place for this hearing.

The hearings showed, first, the effect of all this material on the young people by a psychiatrist, a criminologist, and by people who are familiar with dealing with young people.

The public generally does not understand the extent of this business. I think the hearings have shown that it is big business—our investigation does—that the operation in it is extensive.

We have not in this hearing gone into the fringe cases, to any extent, of literature which many people claim is also damaging, because we have not wanted to get into any dispute about censorship.

We have found that while the use of the mails is prohibited, even the mail statute is insufficient; that it is carried in automobiles and other methods of conveyance in interstate commerce, and there is a definite loophole here that should be plugged. Also the customs laws, as we have found, are inadequate, and we hope to strengthen them to prevent this stuff from being imported from other countries.

We will take into consideration other recommendations such as those made by Mr. Norman Thomas in his appearance here—the recommendations for the confiscation of the vehicle in which the material may be transported and other material in connection with it, such as the projectors and the cameras, where films are used.

Unquestionably, pornography is one of the contributing factors to the increase in juvenile delinquency and sex crimes in the United States. We have been derelict at all levels of government in our vigor in dealing with them. Local communities have done much; they could do more. States have started to improve their enforcement and their statutes. I think the Federal Government has perhaps been more derelict than any other level of government in not bringing our laws up to date.

We mean this subcommittee to try to see to it that the Federal Government does its part. That is why we have had these hearings, and we think they have been very important hearings.

We hope that law-enforcement agencies and all other levels of government will do their part.

We have information which will be helpful, which has been brought out in this hearing, to law-enforcement officers and other sections. Our staff and our subcommittee are ready to cooperate with them.

We are glad to see some healthy developments in better enforcement at the State level. We hope that they will more adequately do their part.

I am impressed, though, in the final analysis, that citizen and parent interest, public interest in the problem, is the surest way of eliminating this evil. Public interest not only will bring about law enforcement and remedial legislation, but it will bring about affirmative action at the community level. In communities where they have banded together, like Jersey City and Boston, many other places, they have been able to stop this filth from circulating.

I feel and I hope that this will be coming about; that in communities throughout the United States—partly, at least as a result of these hearings—we are going to see a lot of activity at the local level.

I want to again thank the judges, Judge Clarke and Judge Bondy, and the wonderful superintendent and staff of the Federal courthouse, Mr. Carmichael from the district attorney's office, who has been sitting in, and many others, for their cooperation and assistance to us.

Our hearings have been a little bit disrupted from time to time, and the press has been very patient and has stayed with us.

We will write letters to the Department of Justice, the Attorney General, commending the many marshals who have helped us, who have served the subpenas, and who have looked after the courtroom.

I think I should announce that the subcommittee will have a further hearing later on in New York, at which time some of the fine efforts being made by the public officials and the people, churches, schools, and commissions and groups to combat juvenile delinquency, to give our children a better opportunity, to make parents more aware of their responsibility will be gone into.

There will be other problems that will be brought out in the hearings which we will hold later on in New York.

Mr. Gaughan, our assistant counsel, has been arranging for these hearings, and he will be the acting counsel to present them.

I don't know the exact time we will have our hearings; that will be announced later on.

Other hearings in connection with pornographic material—or other evidence in connection with it—will be brought out in hearings in other parts of the country, particularly in our Los Angeles hearings— not operations in Los Angeles, because they have been quite diligent there, but Los Angeles will be the center of our hearings in the West just as New York has been here.

The district attorney here will be furnished a copy of the record for any possible perjury, and we will be calling upon the district attorney, we hope, for cooperation in connection with these contempt cases.

I have already indicated the ones that Senator Langer and I will recommend to the Senate to be held for contempt.

With that, this hearing will now be recessed subject to further call of the chairman.

(Whereupon, at 5:20 p. m. the hearing recessed, subject to the further call of the chairman.)

JUVENILE DELINQUENCY

(Obscene and Pornographic Materials)

THURSDAY, JUNE 9, 1955

United States Senate,
Subcommittee of the Committee on the Judiciary
To Investigate Juvenile Delinquency,
Washington, D. C.

The subcommittee met, pursuant to notice, at 1:30 p. m., in room 457, Senate Office Building, Senator William Langer presiding.

Present: Senator Langer (presiding).

Also present: James H. Bobo, chief counsel; Peter N. Chumbris, associate counsel; Vincent Gaughan, special counsel; and Edward Lee McLean, editorial director.

Senator Langer. The meeting will come to order.

This is a continuation of the Subcommittee on Juvenile Delinquency, dealing with pornographic literature and any other matters that may involve juvenile delinquency.

Will you proceed, Mr. Chumbris?

Mr. Chumbris. I have an opening statement, Senator.

Senator Langer. Read it.

Mr. Chumbris. This afternoon the United States Senate Subcommittee To Investigate Juvenile Delinquency is holding its fourth public hearing on obscene, lewd, and pornographic materials and its impact on youth and juvenile delinquency.

The public hearings in New York City established the following: (1) The nationwide traffic in the manufacture, distribution, and sale of obscene, lewd, and pornographic material; (2) that obscene and pornographic material reaches the youth and children of our Nation; (3) that juveniles are induced to pose as models in such insidious filth; (4) that juveniles are induced to sell and distribute such filth to their friends and classmates; (5) that obscene and pornographic material has a direct impact on juvenile delinquency; (6) that psychiatric testimony established the types of delinquencies and perverted activities that obscene, lewd, and pornographic material can lead juveniles into; (7) that the traffic in pornography is a multimillion-dollar business; and (8) that there is a need for corrective legislation on the Federal, State, and local level to prohibit the distribution of pornographic material by mail, by common carrier, and by private conveyance. The first two methods of distribution are now violative of Federal law; however, amendments to those laws are necessary to close the loopholes.

The Senate Juvenile Delinquency Subcommittee has reported out Senate bill 599, which prohibits the transportation in interstate commerce of obscene material. It was favorably passed by the Senate and, during the course of these hearings, was favorably reported by the House Judiciary Committee and yesterday was passed by the House of Representatives.

Today we shall hear the attorney general of the State of North Dakota, Leslie Burgum, who will testify as to the recent legislation in the State of North Dakota which is effective in curtailing the manufacture and distribution of pornography.

Also, Mr. William C. O'Brien and Mr. Harry J. Simon of the United States Post Office Department will explain the procedures of the Post Office Department in curbing the distribution by mail of pornographic material and some of the problems that confront the Post Office Department.

A fourth witness will be Inspector Roy Blick, who testified in the New York hearings on the national picture but will present additional material that has occurred since the hearings in New York. He will also point out how effective law enforcement, through coordination of Federal and local officials, can bring results in apprehending producers, distributors, and sellers of pornography.

Since the hearings in New York, the subcommittee has been advised that two distributors of pornography have been apprehended through coordination of the subcommittee and the peace officers of the respective areas. Further details on these two matters will be brought out in future hearings.

It is gratifying to the subcommittee that the press, the radio, television, public officials, church leaders, civic leaders, and the very parents themselves all over the country have strongly backed the subcommittee's efforts on this drive against pornography and have urged the subcommittee to greater effort to clean up the traffic that has contaminated and will contaminate the minds of our youth and lead them into possible delinquencies. The subcommittee is dedicated to do everything in its power to protect the youth of the Nation from this insidious filth.

Senator LANGER. Call your first witness.

Mr. CHUMBRIS. The first witness will be Inspector Blick.

Senator LANGER. Do you solemnly swear that the evidence you are about to give in the pending matter shall be the truth, the whole truth, and nothing but the truth, so help you God?

Mr. BLICK. I do.

TESTIMONY OF ROY BLICK, INSPECTOR, METROPOLITAN POLICE DEPARTMENT, WASHINGTON, D. C.

Senator LANGER. You may proceed.

Mr. CHUMBRIS. Mr. Blick, would you please state your official title?

Mr. BLICK. Inspector, Metroploitan Police Department.

Mr. CHUMBRIS. And what division do you have?

Mr. BLICK. Sex and perversion.

Mr. CHUMBRIS. Mr. Blick, you testified in New York City last week; is that right?

Mr. BLICK. I did. Week before last, I believe.

Mr. CHUMBRIS. And since that time, Mr. Blick, have you had occasion to make an arrest of a distributor of pornography?

Mr. BLICK. I have.

Mr. CHUMBRIS. And would you please explain at this time the manner of the arrest, and the person involved, and the modus operandi?

Mr. BLICK. Back in November of 1954, I had received confidential information that a man by the name of Alfred Peter Selmer, from Nanticoke, Pa., was bringing pornographic material, films, into the District of Columbia, or carrying them through the District of Columbia.

On 2 or 3 occasions I had information that he was coming to the District of Columbia, but we did not locate the gentleman. Yesterday I received the same information, that he was entering the District of Columbia, and I sent a lookout over the radio for a green Packard bearing Pennsylvania tags, driven by Alfred Peter Selmer, white, 5 feet 9½ inches, 172 pounds, blond hair, husky build.

Mr. CHUMBRIS. For the record, would you spell his last name?

Mr. BLICK. S-e-l-m-e-r. In about 45 minutes scout 83, driven by Officer Campbell—and I forget the other officer's name—notified me by phone that they had apprehended the automobile, and it was in No. 8 precinct.

I went out there, and on the back seat of the automobile was 14 reels of film, 8 reels of positive, 6 reels of negative, about 10,000 feet of film altogether. Now, the positive films are to make duplications of films.

And he was on his way to some place—would not divulge where he was going—to have 80,000 feet of film made from the positive film.

He was photographed, fingerprinted, and taken over. Due to the way the law is written today, we had no proof that he had them in his possession to show or to exhibit.

Mr. CHUMBRIS. Mr. Blick, may I ask you a question at this point: Where was Selmer from?

Mr. BLICK. Nanticoke, Pa.

Mr. CHUMBRIS. Do you wish to proceed?

Mr. BLICK. He was brought back to my office, and I made him put up a $300 bond. This morning he didn't show up in court. A cash bond.

Mr. CHUMBRIS. Was it a forfeiture?

Mr. BLICK. It was forfeited by the presiding judge that was on the bench.

Mr. CHUMBRIS. And can you state what the official charge against him was?

Mr. BLICK. I charged him with possession of pornographic films.

Mr. CHUMBRIS. So there won't be any mistake of what pornographic films mean, would you please define what you consider pornographic films to be?

Mr. BLICK. Male and female sexual relations, abnormal or cohabiting, in the nude.

Mr. CHUMBRIS. And have you examined this particular film that was picked up?

Mr. BLICK. One reel in his presence, to make definitely sure that it was obscene and indecent.

Mr. CHUMBRIS. And did that film have any specific description or name?

Mr. BLICK. It was called The Kinsey Report.

Mr. CHUMBRIS. How long have you been with the vice squad?

Mr. BLICK. Twenty-four years.

Mr. CHUMBRIS. And you have had great experience in indecent and obscene films and pornographic material; is that correct?

Mr. BLICK. I have.

Mr. CHUMBRIS. And you would be in a position to testify as to whether this particular film you saw was pornographic or not?

Mr. BLICK. Yes, sir.

Mr. CHUMBRIS. In your opinion, was this film that you received definitely pornographic film?

Mr. BLICK. It was filth.

Mr. CHUMBRIS. Could you tell from the film whether it was of recent origin or an old film?

Mr. BLICK. It would have to be of recent origin, for one reason: The Kinsey report has only been out recently; and all of the films were new films, because I had to rewind them on reels.

Mr. CHUMBRIS. And this one particular film, what would the footage be on that film?

Mr. BLICK. 400.

Mr. CHUMBRIS. 400 feet. I understand that your entire seizure was how many feet?

Mr. BLICK. Close to 10,000.

Mr. CHUMBRIS. 10,000 feet. You mentioned the 80,000 feet of film made.

Could you explain that further?

Mr. BLICK. He was going to take the positive film to have duplications of what he had. The positive film makes negative film.

Mr. CHUMBRIS. All right, sir.

For the record, will you please explain the procedure usually followed by these persons in first making a negative, then a positive, and then another negative; will you please explain that procedure?

Mr. BLICK. There is only one positive that is made, unless someone is stealing the film themselves. Then from the positives you make all the negatives you wish.

Mr. CHUMBRIS. And that goes on so that the production is almost unlimited?

Mr. BLICK. You can make a billion feet of film all from one positive if you wish to do so.

Mr. CHUMBRIS. Now, this person Selmer; has he ever been prosecuted and convicted of any type of pornographic activity previous to this offense?

Mr. BLICK. Not to my knowledge. He stated that he was doing this for a friend of his up in Wilkes-Barre, Pa.

Mr. CHUMBRIS. And would you please give the name and the address of that person?

Mr. BLICK. Chester Wesensky.

Mr. CHUMBRIS. And the address.

Mr. BLICK. He runs the Big Chief Store in Wilkes-Barre, Pa.

He further stated—upon his person he had $1,485 on him, and he stated that was the money to have the films made from the positive prints.

Mr. CHUMBRIS. Did he have a little black book, or name and address book on him?

Mr. BLICK. He had two.

Mr. CHUMBRIS. And were you able to obtain some of the names and addresses from those two books?

Mr. BLICK. I glanced through the book, but I have been so busy I haven't had a chance to analyze the book like I would like to.

Mr. CHUMBRIS. Now, from your glancing through the book and from the known distributors and producers of pornography throughout the United States that you know of your own knowledge and that came out in our hearings in New York, did you recognize any of the names and addresses of those persons in those two books?

Mr. BLICK. Not connected with the factions up there; no, sir. This seems to be another outfit.

Mr. CHUMBRIS. Now, may I ask you this, that when you make a more detailed study of those two books, would you please submit to the subcommittee the names and addresses from those two books?

Mr. BLICK. I will be glad to.

Mr. CHUMBRIS. Did he say where he was going from Washington?

Mr. BLICK. He did not.

Mr. CHUMBRIS. Did he say where he had been, other than from his home town?

Mr. BLICK. He had left that morning on his way to wherever he was going.

Mr. CHUMBRIS. And he wouldn't tell you where he was going?

Mr. BLICK. No, sir.

Mr. CHUMBRIS. Now, as far as this man's particular case is concerned, he forfeited the bond; is that correct?

Mr. BLICK. Yes, sir.

Mr. CHUMBRIS. And do you consider any further action against this particular person at this time?

Mr. BLICK. Only a misdemeanor; that is all we can hope for.

Mr. CHUMBRIS. Now, this Chester Wesensky, of the Big Chief Store, in Wilkes-Barre, Pa., have you had any previous knowledge as to his operations?

Mr. BLICK. I had not. He has a brother, under another name of Stanley Wayne. Stanley Wayne is supposed to be the brother of Chester, and he also goes under the name of Stanley Wesensky.

Mr. CHUMBRIS. And you know of his operations?

Mr. BLICK. Yes; I understand he is a big operator.

Mr. CHUMBRIS. Now, do you have any approximation of the value of the merchandise that was taken from Selmer yesterday?

Mr. BLICK. It is according to who wants it. To me it would be worth 5 cents. To the ones that want it, to get the positive film, they would pay a large price for it. But the negative films sells for $25 on up, for 100 feet.

Mr. CHUMBRIS. $25 for 100 feet?

Mr. BLICK. On up.

Mr. CHUMBRIS. On up. Inspector, I would like to ask you a few other questions, supplementing the testimony that you gave in New York that there were 34 cases in the past 2 years involving pornographic activities that came to the attention of your office; is that right?

Mr. BLICK. That is correct.

Mr. CHUMBRIS. Now, I would like to ask you specifically of one case where a person was apprehended between Sixth and Seventh Streets, on Pennsylvania Avenue SE., in a second-story apartment. Do you recall that case?

Mr. BLICK. I do. I was on the raid.

Mr. CHUMBRIS. And would you please explain to us—first, isn't it a fact in that particular case and the one across the way in Alexandria, Va., involving the same person, that a juvenile was involved?

Mr. BLICK. Yes.

Mr. CHUMBRIS. And would you explain the nature of that man's activity and what he was caught doing?

Mr. BLICK. Him and his partner—and his partner was an innocent victim, he had no knowledge of what was going on, on the second floor——

Mr. CHUMBRIS. First, would you give his name, for the record?

Senator LANGER. Wait a minute. If that partner is innocent, we don't want to use him.

Mr. CHUMBRIS. Not the partner. The person we are talking about. Is it Borgard?

Mr. BLICK. That is right.

Mr. CHUMBRIS. Would you please explain, then, what this person was involved in doing, and the action you took?

Mr. BLICK. I think the best thing to do is to tell you how I came in touch with him.

Mr. CHUMBRIS. Yes.

Mr. BLICK. I had a young lady come to my office and she stated that she had been a fool, she had a couple of drinks too many, and she had had picture taken in the nude, over this radio shop. She asked for the pictures, and they stated that the pictures didn't turn out.

I talked to her for a long time, and she stated that is all it was.

Upon her statement, we got a search warrant for the premises and went up there and searched the place. We found the young lady's picture more than in the nude. I also found out that this man had a trailer over in Alexandria, and I got in touch with the Alexandria police immediately and told them the trailer number, and they went over, and I believe they got a suitcase full of pornography or pornographic material.

Mr. CHUMBRIS. Inspector, may I inject at this time that the person's name—I mentioned the name of Borgard, Marion Virgil Borgard. I show you his picture. Is that the person that you are discussing at this particular time?

Mr. BLICK. I think it is; yes.

Mr. CHUMBRIS. Would you read into the record the identifying features that are imprinted in the mug that you have there of him?

Mr. BLICK. P. D. No. 143191, taken August 10, 1954. Charged with possession, with intent to exhibit obscene pictures, Fochet, M. D., 35 years old, 5 feet 10, 162 pounds, medium build, blue eyes, medium complexion, brown hair, good teeth, small flesh-colored mole left temple. Born in Chuluota, Fla. Address 22719 Temple, Trailer Village.

Mr. CHUMBRIS. Before I injected the name, were you through giving your participation in the raid?

Mr. BLICK. Yes, sir.

Mr. CHUMBRIS. And there was also a raid in Alexandria; is that correct?

Mr. BLICK. Yes, sir.

Mr. CHUMBRIS. And the Alexandria Police Department not only obtained suitcases full of obscene material, but they impounded his trailer, as well as some of his equipment; is that correct?

Mr. BLICK. That I don't know.

Mr. CHUMBRIS. Do you know of your own knowledge whether after the matter was disposed of in court, they returned his equipment and the trailer?

Mr. BLICK. The equipment that we had was returned to him.

Mr. CHUMBRIS. Why was the equipment that you had returned to him?

Mr. BLICK. By order of the court. There is no law to hold the equipment or to confiscate the equipment.

Mr. CHUMBRIS. Now, Inspector Blick, I understand that you have been vitally interested in having such a law introduced in the Congress and passed by the Congress of the United States; is that correct?

Mr. BLICK. I have.

Mr. CHUMBRIS. And if such a law were passed, would that be an effective means in curtailing the production and manufacturing of this obscene material?

Mr. BLICK. Very much so.

Mr. CHUMBRIS. Would you please explain, in a few words, how it would curtail it?

Mr. BLICK. Well, when you seize a sound-projection machine—it sells for anywhere from $450 to $1,100. And the other equipment that goes with it for the projection, you might have $1,400 invested in the projection equipment alone. The film, you have 1,600 feet of film that would be shown; it would cost you, if you know how to get it, about $100 or $125. For a stag affair, you could get anywhere from $2.50 to $8 admission charge. $3.50, and 150 people there—100 people, I should say, to make it easy for me—that would be $350 that would be taken in, and the cost of the film would be $125. That would be $225 profit.

Now, if the police walked in, he could be fined anywhere from $50 to $500 on a misdemeanor charge. And what other material that we would seize, the projection machine, chairs, and whatnot, the owners could come and claim them, and we would have to return same to them. We would retain the film only.

Mr. CHUMBRIS. Now, when you were referring to a stag party— your testimony in New York referred to a particular stag party where there were boys from 11 to 17, 197 of them, to be exact; is that correct?

Mr. BLICK. I believe that was the figure; yes.

Mr. CHUMBRIS. And these stag parties are affecting juveniles as well as adults; isn't that correct?

Mr. BLICK. Yes, sir.

Mr. CHUMBRIS. Now, getting back to these girls who pose for people, like Borgard that you mentioned, would you explain within your own knowledge the method of operations of persons like Borgard who take these juvenile pictures, these indecent and lewd pictures, and nude pictures?

Mr. BLICK. Now, Mr. Chumbris, I will not explain Borgard, or take any particular one, because——

Mr. CHUMBRIS. Take any one. Their usual method of operation.

Mr. BLICK. But there are quite a few people that will go ahead and pose in the nude, or cohabit with the opposite sex, or put on an act of perversion, and when they get home they will think about it, and then they will go back and say to the photographer, "I made a fool of myself; I want my negative and the pictures."

And the photographer says, "Look, it didn't come out."

And, of course, that satisfies the mind of the individual.

And those pictures, the negatives, there can be thousands and thousands of pictures taken from the negatives and sold in other parts of the country unbeknown to that individual who had her picture or his picture taken.

Mr. CHUMBRIS. So there won't be any mistake in the record, when you say "it didn't come out," it means that the negative didn't take satisfactorily enough so that any pictures could be reproduced from it?

Mr. BLICK. That was his reason, but the negative was perfect.

Mr. CHUMBRIS. Always the negative was perfect, and the girl went away thinking that the picture was destroyed, but instead it was distributed throughout the country; is that correct?

Mr. BLICK. Yes, sir. I have around five or six hundred of those in my possession in the suitcase.

Mr. CHUMBRIS. Now, is that a common practice with these types of pictures?

Mr. BLICK. I would say "Yes."

Mr. CHUMBRIS. Now, directing your attention to nude pictures taken by photographers of young girls, wasn't there a recent case in the District of Columbia, last year, around July 9, 1954?

Mr. BLICK. Are you speaking about the Chucosky case?

Mr. CHUMBRIS. I am referring now particularly to the Murry Levy case at 2 Thomas Circle.

Mr. BLICK. Yes, that is the 17-year-old girl.

Mr. CHUMBRIS. Would you please explain that for the record, whatever facts you have at your command?

Mr. BLICK. The only facts that I have is that the picture was taken. By whom, I don't know.

Mr. CHUMBRIS. You don't know who took the picture?

Mr. BLICK. No, sir.

Mr. CHUMBRIS. Who was apprehended for that?

Mr. BLICK. I believe his name was Murry Levy.

Mr. CHUMBRIS. And was his address 2 Thomas Circle NW?

Mr. BLICK. Yes, sir.

Mr. CHUMBRIS. And about this other case you were just mentioning before I brought up the name of Murry Levy, the Chucosky case, would you please explain to us that case?

Mr. BLICK. That was where a man was taking pictures of his wife in the nude, and the children watching it, actual perversion that Mrs. Chucosky was performing on herself.

Mr. CHUMBRIS. Would you get the correct spelling of that name, if you have it with you?

Mr. BLICK. You have it on there.

Mr. CHUMBRIS. On this particular exhibit?

Mr. BLICK. I think so.

Mr. CHUMBRIS. Would you please look at it and see if you can pick it out of that group?

Is that also the same case where there was a card index of 600 negatives?

Mr. BLICK. Those were the negatives I was speaking to you about. It is C-h-u-c-o-s-k-y.

Mr. CHUMBRIS. The full name and the address.

Mr. BLICK. Vincent W. is the man's name. The address was 607 Fourth Street NW, apartment 1. He was charged with sale and possession of indecent and obscene pictures.

Along with him was a George Fodor, who was a wholesaler in the city.

Mr. CHUMBRIS. I think George Fodor was a witness in the hearings in New York City; is that correct?

Mr. BLICK. I saw him up there. I did not hear him testify.

Mr. CHUMBRIS. He was a wholesaler of pornography; is that correct?

Mr. BLICK. Yes, sir.

Mr. CHUMBRIS. And I believe Fodor testified that he is now living in Florida.

Mr. BLICK. Yes, sir.

Mr. CHUMBRIS. Now, the person that you just mentioned, do you know whether they still live at the same address that you just gave?

Mr. BLICK. They do not.

Mr. CHUMBRIS. They have moved; is that correct?

Mr. BLICK. Yes, sir.

Mr. CHUMBRIS. Do you know the present address?

Mr. BLICK. I have heard—I don't know whether this is authentic or not.

Senator LANGER. We do not want the address used. The people have left there and it might be embarrassing to the present occupants of that locality.

Mr. CHUMBRIS. Do you have anything further on this particular case, Inspector, that you would like to state to the subcommittee at this time?

Mr. BLICK. No.

Mr. CHUMBRIS. Do you have a card index with you?

Mr. BLICK. I do.

Mr. CHUMBRIS. And would you please present them to the chairman with the various categories that are listed?

Mr. BLICK. The first one are girls performing fellatio—but that is not the way it is written here.

The second one, men performing cunnilinguism—of course, that is not the way it is written here, either.

The fourth section, sexual relations.

Mr. CHUMBRIS. These are negatives in these various categories; is that right?

Mr. BLICK. Yes, you can make a hundred thousand prints off of one of them.

Mr. CHUMBRIS. In other words, a person could take that negative and make a hundred thousand prints; is that right?

Mr. BLICK. Yes, sir; and still make more.

Mr. CHUMBRIS. And you have 600 in there.

Mr. BLICK. Approximately. I have never sat down to count them.

Mr. CHUMBRIS. Do you have anything on bestiality?

Mr. BLICK. Sadistic bestiality, yes. I have any type of perversion that you wish.

Mr. CHUMBRIS. Now, Inspector, getting back to this confiscation of equipment, isn't it true that sometimes the police department loses money on the fact that the time and the preparation of confiscating this equipment, when you make raids such as this, is large in comparison to the penalty that is imposed on the offender?

Mr. BLICK. Many times, for this reason: Some of this equipment is not so easy to handle, and man can hurt himself taking this out and putting it in the wagon and then taking it out and marking it and taking care of it as he should to protect the property as long as it is in the custody of the police department, and then to have it turned back, and we keep nothing but the film that has to be destroyed by a bonfire.

Mr. CHUMBRIS. Then you, in your opinion, would definitely recommend that the law in the District of Columbia be amended so that the property can be impounded, confiscated, and not returned to the offender; is that correct?

Mr. BLICK. Absolutely.

Mr. CHUMBRIS. Now, what is your opinion as to the severity of the penalties for these various offenses in the District of Columbia as a deterrent to future criminal activity by these people? Do you think the penalties are severe enough?

Mr. BLICK. I do not.

Mr. CHUMBRIS. And would you comment on that, please?

Mr. BLICK. Well, when you can make such an amount of money as the average run of these people make on this material that they sell, and they work their own hours, and ride around in beautiful cars, and the penalty is anywhere from $100 to $500 fine, or a year in jail, they are willing to take chances on it.

Mr. CHUMBRIS. Now, I have noticed this exhibit that you have presented to us. You may refer to it, if you so please. You have one in front of you.

Just give us an idea of the nature of the disposition of some of those cases, the amount of the fine, or the jail sentence that is given.

Mr. BLICK. $250 or 90 days; $100 or 60 days; nol-prossed; nol-prossed; nol-prossed; $100 or 60 days; $100 or 60 days; not guilty; nol-prossed; $100 or 90 days; $100 or 90 days.

Mr. CHUMBRIS. Then, in both of those instances, the fines, in your estimation, are light in comparison to the nature of the offense; is that correct?

Mr. BLICK. To my belief it is. Very much so.

Mr. CHUMBRIS. I believe you testified in New York that you think a person who sells and distributes pornographic material to a juvenile is doing a more harmful act than if he were selling or distributing narcotics.

Would you like to comment on that?

Mr. BLICK. I stated in New York, if my memory serves me right, that pornography was worse than narcotics.

Mr. CHUMBRIS. And the reason?

Mr. BLICK. The reason why would be this: That if an individual had one capsule of narcotics, he would use it and no one could take it after him. With these pamphlets, these pictures, and whatnot, they can be passed around from one person to another and 500 or a thousand can see the same booklet over a period of time.

Mr. CHUMBRIS. Therefore, since pornography affects so many, that makes it much more effective?

Mr. BLICK. Yes, sir. They are getting so bold that, as long as we are talking about it, I would like to show 2 or 3 of the latest ones that are out.

Mr. CHUMBRIS. Yes, sir. Would you please exhibit them to the chairman?

Senator LANGER. These are the very latest ones, are they, Inspector?

Mr. BLICK. Yes, sir. These are the latest pictures that are being sold to the public today. You can see they have gone from black and white into color. You can see the idea. This young lady here— I don't believe she is over 18 or 19, is she?

Mr. CHUMBRIS. Inspector, I believe some of the witnesses in New York testified that the sentences and fines imposed are so light that they don't even amount to a license fee; is that correct?

Mr. BLICK. Yes, sir.

Mr. CHUMBRIS. In the raid that the 196 boys were involved in, how many men did you use on that raid?

Mr. BLICK. I could be mistaken, but I think it was close to around 30. I could be mistaken, because I used everybody that I could get my hands on.

Mr. CHUMBRIS. For that particular raid alone, what cost would you say it was to the city of Washington, D. C., to apprehend that one person, for those involved for the stag party?

Mr. BLICK. Of all the work and everything, including the time of building the job up, I would say close to $1,200 easily.

Mr. CHUMBRIS. And what was the fine the person who plead guilty received?

Mr. BLICK. I would have to refer to the records, because I think it was——

Mr. CHUMBRIS. Would $200 sound like the correct fine?

Mr. BLICK. No, sir. It was around $100 or 60 days.

Mr. CHUMBRIS. $100 or 60 days. And it cost you over $1,200.

Mr. BLICK. If you want to consider our time that was consumed.

Mr. CHUMBRIS. And that doesn't involve the judicial processes involved, also, the cost for judicial processes?

Mr. BLICK. I am just speaking about the police department.

Mr. CHUMBRIS. Now, in the taking of these nude pictures of some of these young girls, was a promise made to them that they would be used for calendars and post cards, and things like that, legitimate ones?

Mr. BLICK. That I cannot answer, Mr. Chumbris, because I don't know.

Mr. CHUMBRIS. Inspector, could you state how many of these 2-by-4 booklets get into the high schools and junior high schools here in Washington? Have you made any specific survey on that?

Mr. BLICK. The only way that we can go on that would be just the complaints. Now, we had a complaint this week that a 17-year-old boy had gotten hold of some of this obscene and indecent material, and we talked to the boy last night. The only way that we can get hold of that is what comes to us through the parents, or the wonderful cooperation that we are receiving from the schools here in Washington.

Mr. CHUMBRIS. Now, Inspector, were you in New York when we read the comments from the various chiefs of police throughout the Nation as to the amount of pornography that is being sold and the amount that is getting to the children? Were you there at that time?

Mr. BLICK. I don't believe I was in the room at that time.

Mr. CHUMBRIS. While we read into the record numerous replies from chiefs of police to indicate that pornography is getting to the children—as a matter of fact, in one instance, they were found on children in the elementary schools as well as junior high schools. And we received a letter this morning from the chief of police in one of our States in the country which pointed out that in about six schools they had a great amount of traffic in pornography, and they sent a picture to illustrate the type of material that is coming in, and that was some of the material that you are showing, and some of these.2-by-4's.

Would you please look at that picture and see if that is the type of pornographic material that gets around to the children in the schools?

Mr. BLICK. This, and worse.

Mr. CHUMBRIS. This, and worse?

Mr. BLICK. Yes, sir.

Mr. CHUMBRIS. I would like to have that marked as an exhibit.

Senator LANGER. It will be so marked.

Mr. CHUMBRIS. We will mark this exhibit 28.

Senator LANGER. It will be made a part of the record.

(The photograph was marked "Exhibit No. 28," and is on file with the subcommittee.)

Mr. CHUMBRIS. Is there anything further that you would like to comment on, Inspector Blick?

How about some of these titles? Do you have any titles of the films themselves?

Mr. BLICK. Do you want me to read them off?

Mr. CHUMBRIS. I would leave that with the chairman.

Senator LANGER. You don't have to read them. Just file them.

Mr. CHUMBRIS. Just file the list of titles.

Mr. BLICK. I can't, because that is my receipt that I sent to the——

Mr. CHUMBRIS. I show you a mimeographed list that was picked off of the Simon Simring case in Orangeburg, S. C., that was mentioned in the New York City hearings, and so if some of these titles are similar to those that you have in your possession, we will file that for the record.

Mr. BLICK. Yes, sir.

Mr. CHUMBRIS. They are similar?

Mr. BLICK. Yes, sir.

Chairman KEFAUVER. That will be filed as an exhibit.

(The list of film titles in the possession of Simon Simring were marked "Exhibit No. 29," and are on file with the subcommittee.)

Mr. CHUMBRIS. I would like to ask you one other question: What was the value of the material that you impounded from George Fodor's place when you arrested him, in the last year or so?

Mr. BLICK. I think the record will show—I forget what I said.

Mr. CHUMBRIS. I think you did mention it in the New York hearing.

Mr. BLICK. Yes.

Mr. CHUMBRIS. And, as a matter of fact, I think you mentioned the fact that he had a cellar full of that material at his home; is that correct?

Mr. BLICK. That is correct.

Mr. CHUMBRIS. He operated out of his home; is that correct?

Mr. BLICK. Yes, sir.

Mr. Chumbris. Now, as I understand your testimony—and I would like for you to repeat it—the law in the District of Columbia now as to the manufacture and distribution and sale of pornography is not as effective as it should be; is that correct?

Mr. Blick. That is the way I feel about it; yes, sir.

Mr. Chumbris. No further questions, Mr. Chairman?

Senator Langer. I want to thank you again very much for your kindness in helping us out, Inspector, your kindness in New York, and taking time this afternoon.

Mr. Blick. Yes, sir.

Senator Langer. Mark this "Exhibit 30." It shows children 4, 6, and 10 years old.

Mr. Chumbris. This will be exhibit No. 30.

(The photos of indecent acts by children were marked "Exhibit No. 30." and are on file with the subcommittee.)

Mr. Chumbris. And this is definitely an obscene and lewd and pornographic picture; is that correct?

Mr. Blick. I would say it is about the worst that a person could take.

Mr. Chumbris. Thank you very much, again, Mr. Blick.

Senator Langer. Inspector Blick, I appreciate very much your coming down.

Mr. Chumbris. Solicitor O'Brien and Inspector Simon.

Senator Langer. Do you solemnly swear that the evidence you are about to give in the pending matter shall be the truth, the whole truth, and nothing but the truth, so help you God?

Mr. O'Brien. I do.

Mr. Simon. I do.

TESTIMONY OF WILLIAM C. O'BRIEN, ASSISTANT SOLICITOR, POST OFFICE DEPARTMENT, ACCOMPANIED BY HARRY J. SIMON, INSPECTOR, POST OFFICE DEPARTMENT, WASHINGTON, D. C.

Senator Langer. You may proceed.

Mr. Chumbris. Mr. O'Brien, will you give us your full name and your address, and your official title, for the record?

Mr. O'Brien. My name is William C. O'Brien. I am Assistant Solicitor of the Post Office Department, in charge of Fraud and Mailability Division. Of course, my official address is Post Office Department, Washington, D. C. My home address is Chevy Chase, Md.

Mr. Chumbris. And Mr. Simon, will you give your full name, address, and official title?

Senator Langer. Just a moment.

You have had 43 years' experience in this, haven't you?

Mr. O'Brien. Just 41, sir.

Senator Langer. That is your background, 41 years?

Mr. O'Brien. That is right, sir.

Mr. Chumbris. Mr. Simon.

Mr. Simon. Harry J. Simon, post office inspector. I am domiciled in Washington, D. C., in the Post Office Department Building, and reside in Washington, D. C.

Mr. Chumbris. How long have you been in your present position?

Mr. Simon. I have been with the Post Office Inspection Service since 1925, approximately 15 years as a post office inspector.

Mr. Chumbris. And you are one of their experts, I understand, on testifying before congressional hearings; is that right?

Mr. Simon. Not an expert, but a post office inspector who has been investigating cases of dealers in obscene and indecent matter in connection with the mails for 7 or 8 years.

Mr. Chumbris. And you have testified previously before congressional committees?

Mr. Simon. I have.

Mr. Chumbris. I understand, Mr. O'Brien, that you have a statement that you would like to proceed with.

Mr. O'Brien. I have a general statement which I prepared, not knowing that you were going to examine witnesses by questions. But whichever way you wish to proceed, it will be all right with me.

Mr. Chumbris. Mr. O'Brien, we are particularly interested in the legal procedure under which the Post Office Department operates in detecting and curbing pornographic, obscene, and lewd material from going through the mails, and whatever else is under your jurisdiction.

Mr. O'Brien. I may say at the outset that the Post Office Department is receiving a great many complaints from parents whose children have been the recipients of obscene advertising of various kinds. On the cardboards which have been brought in to the committee room and which are now being opened up by one of your assistants, we have attached samples of advertising matter which has been sent through the mails and complained about, and some copies of the letters from parents complaining about the advertisements exemplified on those boards, which were received by those children, some sent to very young children, and some sent to teen-agers.

The mailing volume of these advertisements is steadily growing. The volume of complaints we are receiving is steadily growing, and in my long experience, it has never heretofore been equaled in volume or as to the character of advertising.

The advertising is becoming more daring. It is already a menace in itself to public morals, and especially to the morals of children.

I think, in my judgment, the increase of this traffic is due to several principal factors.

One, I believe, is the ready availability of pornography in wholesale lots, made by such persons, I think, as Inspector Blick has talked about previously this afternoon, and the fact that an obscene dealer can go into business on a comparatively small capital—he needs only to begin to circularize advertisements, sometimes they are periodical advertisements of small size, and sometimes they are circular advertisements more ambitiously prepared, as you see on the board over there. And that one in the left-hand corner at the top is an example of one used by the Male Merchandise Mart in Hollywood. The advertisements which the man is just now putting up are advertisements of Samuel Roth. I think he appeared before you in New York briefly. And of other purveyors——

Senator Langer. Both of them claimed the fifth amendment, didn't they, or did Roth testify?

Mr. O'Brien. Yes; he did.

Senator Langer. And Klaw did?

Mr. O'BRIEN. Yes.

We have examples of Klaw's advertisements and various others: the Stag Shop, the Tourlanes Publishing Co.——

Mr. CHUMBRIS. Mr. O'Brien, so that the record may be straight, the person you are referring to that sends out the material that is now on the board there is Samuel Roth, of New York; is that right? 110 Lafayette, New York; is that right, eighth floor?

Mr. O'BRIEN. That is correct, sir. We have issued numerous orders against various enterprises, but he is a very active man, and invents a new name for his business every time we issue an order against the one he is using.

Mr. CHUMBRIS. You are referring to Sam Roth?

Mr. O'BRIEN. Sam Roth.

Mr. CHUMBRIS. I would like to get that straight. You say he invents a new name every time you put a stop order against the old name?

Mr. O'BRIEN. That is right.

Mr. CHUMBRIS. Now, I believe he testified in New York that he had as many as 15 or 20 trade names registered with the county clerk in New York at one time.

Mr. O'BRIEN. I think that would be true.

Mr. CHUMBRIS. Do you know the size of Mr. Roth's mailing books and pamphlets, and also these circulars that go throughout the country to youngsters?

Mr. O'BRIEN. He came into my office first after he appeared before your committee in New York and told me he had a mailing list of 400,000 names.

Mr. CHUMBRIS. Did he tell you where he gets his mailing list from?

Mr. O'BRIEN. Well, he accumulates the mailing list by, I think, the random circularization of names he finds in various books, telephone directories, or what not.

Mr. CHUMBRIS. I think he did mention in his testimony that he bought over 100,000 name lists from one Mr. Vallon, in Brooklyn, N. Y.

Mr. O'BRIEN. They all buy these names.

Senator LANGER. 180,000?

Mr. CHUMBRIS. 180,000, to be exact.

Mr. O'BRIEN. As in the case of Samuel Roth, so in the case of other persons that we have had to deal with in the mail order business, the facility with which they can change names and also locations is quite a problem for our Department in dealing with these enterprises.

Mr. CHUMBRIS. That is one of your biggest headaches; isn't it, Mr. O'Brien?

Mr. O'BRIEN. One of our biggest headaches.

Mr. CHUMBRIS. What is the recommendation of the Department to correct that difficulty that you have?

Mr. O'BRIEN. The recommendation of the Department is incorporated, I think, in a bill which was introduced by Congressman Rees, of Kansas, H. R. 174. That bill would authorize the Post Office Department, the Postmaster General, to temporarily impound mail of companies whose sale of indecent literature through the mails is the subject of a proceeding.

Mr. Chumbris. Mr. O'Brien, I think I would like to point out at this time that the Senate Juvenile Delinquency Subcommittee has voted to support a similar measure in the Senate of the United States, which will be introduced on Monday by the chairman, Senator Kefauver.

Mr. O'Brien. I am very happy to hear that, sir, and I know the Postmaster General will be gratified.

Senator Langer. Now, in that measure, you remember in the New York hearings, we had a gentleman up there who had been convicted 6 or 7 times, and it seems that each time he got convicted, the fine he received was less. At that time we instructed the chief counsel to draw up a bill providing for a more severe penalty for the second offense and for the third offense.

Do you recall that?

Mr. Chumbris. Yes, sir.

Senator Langer. Has that bill been prepared for introduction?

Mr. Chumbris. That bill has been prepared for introduction, and it will be ready within a few days.

Senator Langer. We may adjourn by the 15th of July, you know.

Mr. Chumbris. We will have it in next week.

Senator Langer. Would you be in favor of that?

Mr. O'Brien. Yes, although the prosecution end of it is more Mr. Simon's field. Certainly anything that would tend to lessen this greatly growing and steadily worsening traffic in obscenity would be a great help to the Post Office Department.

Senator Langer. Well, in New York, for example, the fourth felony means life.

Mr. O'Brien. Yes.

Senator Langer. In other words, the penalty is progressively higher and more severe for each offense.

Mr. O'Brien. I think, of course, that is a very strong deterrent if you can put it into effect.

Mr. Chumbris. Isn't it true that the State of Minnesota has a statute along that particular line?

Mr. O'Brien. I am sorry, counsel, I don't know that.

Now, you asked me a few minutes ago if I would discuss the legal situation, the laws which we have to use and which we try to enforce in the Post Office Department to prevent the dissemination of obscene matter.

Of course, the principal and oldest law is the one now incorporated in title 18 of the United States Code, known as section 1461. It is a law which was passed in 1872, I believe, and amended several times since, and it has a twofold character. It provides that no obscene, lewd, indecent, or filthy matter shall be carried in the mails. It says that if they are carried in the mails, they shall not be delivered by any post office or letter carrier. And it also provides a penalty for whoever knowingly deposits such matter in the mails, or knowingly causes it to be taken from the mails. The penalty is $5,000 fine or 5 years' imprisonment, or both.

That, of course, is very strong law, both in the scope of the matter it embraces and also in the penalty it carries. The difficulties of enforcement, of course, are very numerous.

Now, as far as the criminal provisions are concerned, Mr. Simon can tell you more about it. We have had the experience of not being able to prosecute offenders where it would do the most good—in other words, where the obscene matter has been directed for delivery. That is because a fellow may live in a liberal or ultraliberal typical jurisdiction, either on the west coast or the east coast. We do not regard the mailing of some of the stuff we consider obscene as very serious, and as Inspector Blick has shown you, the fines or penalties imposed are not commensurate with the injury that such matter does to the public, and especially to the juveniles.

Therefore, the Post Office Department is advocating and presently trying to obtain approval for additional legislation which will authorize prosecution of offenders in the communities where the matter is delivered and where it actually inflicts injury upon the recipient. I think such legislation would be of great help in deterring some of this traffic.

Mr. CHUMBRIS. Is there such a bill pending before Congress?

Mr. O'BRIEN. The bill has not been introduced. It is presently being drawn and submitted to the Budget Bureau, and it hasn't come in yet, but I believe it will be offered.

Mr. CHUMBRIS. I say, No bill has been introduced in Congress at this time?

Mr. O'BRIEN. No.

Mr. CHUMBRIS. Could we get a copy of that proposed bill, Mr. O'Brien?

Mr. O'BRIEN. I think you will have to wait until the administration clears it through the Budget.

Senator LANGER. You see, Mr. O'Brien, we are doing this year what we have done during all the years that I have been in the Senate. We will go along, in January we will meet, nothing is done, February nothing is done, March nothing is done, April nothing is done, May nothing is done—you and I have had that matter up before, as you know, and I think you and I are in full agreement.

Now, we will introduce this bill, and we will get it in in the middle of June, and finally when the House will pass on it, it will never be considered by the other House, and therefore it will die, and next year we will come back with all this testimony over again.

You and I have had that up in connection with other postal matters, in connection with the small loans, insurance frauds, and so on.

Mr. O'BRIEN. That is true.

Senator LANGER. Is there any way we can get this bill in next week that you know?

Mr. O'BRIEN. I believe I would have to find out what progress has been made on it before I could answer that, Senator. My last information is that it is imminent, but not actually in the hopper yet.

Next week we are going to have an exodus of some kind.

Mr. CHUMBRIS. You may continue.

Senator LANGER. Before you continue, I am very much interested in this, because our New York testimony shows that some of these fellows make a million or a million and a half or $2 million a year.

Mr. O'BRIEN. That was Mr. Klaw.

Senator LANGER. It is to their interest to do all they can to keep these bills from being passed. Certainly this subcommittee ought to find some way to get these bills in so that they can be passed without being killed year after year.

Mr. O'BRIEN. I think you will find very strong support of that. Mr. Simon can speak for it.

Senator LANGER. We fool around and we don't get it in here until the 24th or 25th of June. It is in the Subcommittee of the Judiciary, and 2 weeks the full committee, the Senate Judiciary Committee, and it will lay around a week before anything is done, and all the time July 15 is approaching, and by the time we adjourn nothing is done, and the bill is dead.

Mr. CHUMBRIS. I might point out one gratifying thing. This bill that was reported out of our subcommittee, the one which prohibits interstate transportation by private car of pornographic material, it has also passed the House, so now that one bill that has been pending for 3 or 4 years has now finally passed.

Senator LANGER. That has been pending for 7 or 8 years, and I am glad to hear that.

How is the runaway-fathers bill?

Mr. CHUMBRIS. That bill is reported out of the Senate.

Senator LANGER. That will have to go to the full committee in the Senate.

Mr. CHUMBRIS. That is another bill that has been defeated each year since 1948 and 1949.

Senator LANGER. It was put in by Congressman Pope or Congressman Jacobs 15 years ago, and it still isn't passed. There certainly ought to be some provision made so that we can get action on these bills.

Mr. O'BRIEN. As to this man who is making the million or million and a half dollars from the sale of this pornography, at least one of these is Irving Klaw, who refused to testify. I have a copy of the charges we have pending against him, and if we supported the charges—I am the complainant—if we support these charges, an order can be issued that will stop all mail addressed to Irving Klaw. That means, of course, his mail-order business in this type of pornography, what I call pornography, in which he has been indulging, these pictures, photographs, slides, and so forth, will be in the past.

Senator LANGER. You have just told us that 1 fellow has got 20 different corporations. They will slip it over and put it in the name of somebody else.

Mr. O'BRIEN. We are not too slow about following it. It is something that we can handle effectively by impounding this mail.

Senator LANGER. If you impound the mail they will use an automobile or airplane.

Mr. O'BRIEN. We only have the mail to deal with.

Senator LANGER. I understand that.

Mr. CHUMBRIS. At this time you don't have the impounding statute to operate under. That is one of the bills you are trying to get through?

Mr. O'BRIEN. I have an opening and impounding authority as to a fictitious name, with which I have had some success and some failure.

Mr. CHUMBRIS. Is that what you term the unlawful order or the stop order?

Mr. O'BRIEN. The unlawful order is pursuant to 290 United States Code 55, by which the Postmaster General can stop the mail of persons obtaining obscenity through the mail.

Mr. CHUMBRIS. That hasn't proved 100 percent effective?

Mr. O'BRIEN. It is 100 percent effective where the courts would leave the order in effect.

Mr. CHUMBRIS. What is the difficulty there?

Mr. O'BRIÉN. I say, 100 percent effective as to each order. Now, in the case of the woman up in Connecticut and around there, Mrs. Tagger was her name. She ran a business which could operate in 1 place under 1 name for a few weeks or months, and then skip to another. She was constantly moving along. We finally did put an end to her use of the mail for obscenity; 100 percent effective, I think, is too strong.

Mr. CHUMBRIS. Let's strike the words "100 percent effective," and use the word "effective."

Mr. O'BRIEN. I can say that in most of these cases where we have complaints on a 259 (a) and obtain an order, I think in a very high percent of the cases there has ben no revival of that business. However, there is this: we have to deal with the intricacies of procedure as prescribed by the Administrative Procedure Act. A man can postpone and fool around with our procedures for many months. Mr. Roth here, in one case, has managed to do that for 12 months.

Mr. CHUMBRIS. In the meantime, he has already profited on that first advertisement he has sent out; is that correct?

Mr. O'BRIEN. Yes.

Mr. CHUMBRIS. And by the time this procedure was put into operation——

Mr. O'BRIEN. We did use the fictitious name procedure against some of Mr. Roth's enterprises, and the court refused to give any relief, and that was the place where impounding action was very useful, but nevertheless the delays which are incident to complying with all the prescriptions of the act can be very bad when you come to enforcing the law against fly-by-night operations, which, when they close up after they have taken all the money they can, are indifferent to the order.

Senator LANGER. Did you get that batch of literature I got from North Dakota last week?

Mr. O'BRIEN. Have I received it yet?

Senator LANGER. Yes.

Mr. O'BRIEN. I probably have. If I did, I replied to you, and sent it back, probably.

Senator LANGER. I sent it to Mr. Summerfield.

Mr. O'BRIEN. It comes over to me.

Senator LANGER. It came from Dickey County, N. Dak.

Mr. O'BRIEN. I bet it was Good Times advertisements, if I were betting on which case it was, because Good Times and similar publications are demanding circularization at the present time.

Mr. CHUMBRIS. Do you want to get back to your statement, Mr. O'Brien?

We have injected some questions into this that you probably covered later on.

While we are still on the question of recommendations, a question was raised in New York concerning the envelope not containing a sufficient identification of the person who puts this material into the mails.

Do you have any suggestions of a law that should be enacted to take care of that?

Mr. O'BRIEN. Requiring a person who mails indecent matter to disclose his identity on the envelope?

Mr. CHUMBRIS. That is right.

Mr. O'BRIEN. It never occurred to me that we could do that.

Mr. CHUMBRIS. Is it possible that it can be done? You notice we get a lot of these envelopes, and it just mentions some fictitious company, without any individual name attached to it, with some address; that is the only identifying feature on it.

Mr. O'BRIEN. I might say that it will probably be a statute which will be difficult to enforce as a mailability statute. It might be one, if constitutional, which would be enforceable as a criminal statute. The reason is, of course, that if a man mails first-class matter in a plain envelope and we have no way of going into that mail, it would go through without challenge. Another thing, if it were possible to issue an order by the Postmaster General in such a case, we have the problem of willfully mailing obscene matter without putting his address on the outside, I don't know whether it would mean anything beneficial. I haven't thought anything about it.

Mr. CHUMBRIS. Would you please give that thought, and give whatever recommendations that you may have to the subcommittee at a later time, because this matter was raised during the course of the New York hearings, and if there are suggestions that you can make on that particular point, I am sure the subcommittee would greatly appreciate it.

Senator LANGER. Can we set a day when we are going to get that? Can you get it in a week.

Mr. O'BRIEN. Next week is a bad week.

Senator LANGER. You have got a bunch of assistants. You have got millions and millions of dollars in the Post Office Department. I realize that you can't do all of that, but you must have some assistants that can prepare that and get it in here in the week or so; is that right?

Mr. O'BRIEN. I will try to comply with your request, Senator.

Getting back to this discussion of law, the nonmailability statute is one which is most often employed by the Post Office Department, because, of course, it is readily applicable to all matter which is not under seal. That would enclose all circular matter which is third class and all publications which are not mailed under seal. Therefore, most of our post cards, most of our work, comes under that statute. And we do exclude from the mails under that statute great quantities of nonmailable obscene matter, mainly in the form of periodicals, sometimes two or three hundred copies of a magazine may be declared unmailable, because it is obscene. The publishers are pretty well acquainted with that fact, and consequently we find not many of them willing to take a risk when they have a bad issue, they probably send it by some other means of conveyance. Sometimes you will find publications scattered around the country which have indicia on them indicating entry as second-class matter, but that doesn't mean that it was disseminated by the mail, it could have been delivered by private carrier, common carrier, or some other form of transportation.

And then, of course, we have a number of lawsuits arising from our efforts to exclude obscene matter from the mails. We have some very close questions on what obscenity constitutes. The battle is an unceasing one between those who want to make a living out of this pornographic matter, and law enforcement officers and the public, which objects to having the mail used for the distribution of such material.

Mr. CHUMBRIS. Mr. O'Brien, do you know, of your own knowledge, the method of operation of these people obtaining mailing lists and how they could screen these mailing lists for whether the person is an adult or a minor?

Mr. O'BRIEN. No, sir; I don't.

Mr. CHUMBRIS. Now, Mr. Samuel Roth admitted in his testimony in New York City that his office procedure could be improved to a great extent in determining whether the name lists that he buys or rents contain names and addressse of minors.

Mr. Chairman, in conjunction with the name lists, I have a letter here from Congressman Blatnik, of Minnesota, which was sent to us this morning, with some material, and some of this——

Mr. O'BRIEN. I might say we proceeded against Tourlanes.

Mr. CHUMBRIS. Tourlanes Publishing Co., 229 West 28th Street, New York City, N. Y.

Mr. O'BRIEN. I entered charges against them several months ago. The case has been tried and heard. The hearing examiner has recommended an order stopping their mail. And of course they have the right to appeal, under the Administrative Procedures Act, which they will no doubt pursue.

Mr. CHUMBRIS. Mr. Chairman, may I read into the record the Congressman's letter, because it is an interesting sidelight.

Senator LANGER. Yes.

Mr. CHUMBRIS. It says:

DEAR MR. CHUMBRIS: My assistant told me of his conversation with you yesterday and your desire to see the material which was sent to Mr. Peter McHardy of Hibbing, Minn. Peter is a young man now serving with the Armed Forces in Germany, and his father wonders whether or not his mailing address was obtained through his Army enlistment.

Any information you can give me on this matter will be greatly appreciated.

The reason why I say this is unusual is because this is the first time we have had any inkling that a mailing list can be made up of young men who enlist in the armed services.

Do you have any comment to make on that? Is there any such possibility, that you can think of?

Mr. O'BRIEN. We haven't heard of that before. As a matter of fact, I don't get information concerning mailing lists.

Mr. CHUMBRIS. I would like to have that introduced into the record and marked "Exhibit No. 31."

Senator LANGER. That may be done.

(The letter referred to was marked "Exhibit No. 31," and is as follows:)

CONGRESS OF THE UNITED STATES,
HOUSE OF REPRESENTATIVES,
Washington, D. C., June 8, 1955.

Mr. PETER CHUMBRIS,
   Room 900, HOLC Building,
      Washington 25, D. C.

DEAR MR. CHUMBRIS: My assistant told me of his conversation with you yesterday and your desire to see the material which was sent to Mr. Peter McHardy of Hibbing, Minn. Peter is a young man now serving with the Armed Forces in Germany, and his father wonders whether or not his mailing address was obtained through his Army enlistment.

Any information you can give me on this matter will be greatly appreciated.
Sincerely yours,

JOHN A. BLATNIK, *Member of Congress.*

Mr. O'BRIEN. Here is our complaint against the Tourlanes Co., which was filed on February 15, this year.

Senator LANGER. How many complaints have you filed, Mr. O'Brien, on subject matter of this kind, this year?

Mr. O'BRIEN. This is the sixth month. I would say perhaps 200. I can't tell you offhand. I am just estimating, as well as I can.

Senator LANGER. What is the disposition of them?

Mr. O'BRIEN. I would say most of them quit when they are confronted with charges.

In other words, they say, "We quit, we won't do it any more, we agree to go out of business." More than half of them.

Mr. CHUMBRIS. Would you say that your complaints filed have stepped up within the last year?

Mr. O'BRIEN. Yes, sir.

Mr. CHUMBRIS. To what extent? What is your average number of complaints per year that you filed, would you say?

Mr. O'BRIEN. Now, the average number of complaints over a period of years—remember, in the first place, the statute was passed in 1950, this 259 (a), and we started off pretty slowly on it, because we didn't get too many cases, of course. And there weren't so many concerns at first.

Mr. CHUMBRIS. In other words, there were many more concerns that have opened up business since 1950?

Mr. O'BRIEN. Yes, sir.

Mr. CHUMBRIS. How many more concerns, would you say, have opened up since 1950?

Mr. O'BRIEN. You mean in excess over the average number in existence?

Mr. CHUMBRIS. Yes.

Mr. O'BRIEN. I don't know.

Mr. CHUMBRIS. Percentagewise.

Mr. O'BRIEN. I don't really know that, sir. You see, you have the fellow coming and going and opening here and there, and one does, and another crops up.

Mr. CHUMBRIS. Can you explain the reason why so many are cropping up since 1950?

Mr. O'BRIEN. I tried to explain that before, that availability of this type of picture—you can buy it, go into these studios where they have a bin of it, just like a bin of junk, and you can go in and take a handful of these and buy them, and then you are in business.

Mr. CHUMBRIS. And, in your opinion, since 1950 this business of obscene literature and bondage pictures and fetish pictures and nude pictures, all those that have been determined as obscene, has jumped up tremendously in its manufacture, distribution, and sale throughout the United States; is that correct?

Mr. O'BRIEN. In my opinion?

Mr. CHUMBRIS. Yes.

Mr. O'BRIEN. I can't answer that question.

All I can say is that I see more of them. Perhaps we have been more effective in rooting it out.

Mr. CHUMBRIS. You see more of it, and there are more concerns that are cropping up every day to get into this particular type of business?

Mr. O'BRIEN. More concerns are cropping up every few days.

Mr. CHUMBRIS. And therefore that must be an indication that that business is increasing; is that correct?

Mr. O'BRIEN. I think it is generally increasing, yes.

Senator LANGER. The reason for that is that nobody is ever put in jail. When they get a prosecution, all they do is tell them to stop it, and the fellow says, "Yes, I will do it no more."

Mr. O'BRIEN. Senator, I can't put them in jail. I wish I could. All I can do is stop their mail. When I say stop it, that may mean the mails go back marked "Out of Business." And that is a measure I am willing to adopt, because it saves the Government trial time and money.

In other words, if a man agrees to go out of business now rather than prolong the hearings 6 months, the Government and the public gain by having the business stop quickly, and also less expensively.

Senator LANGER. Can't these people be prosecuted?

Mr. O'BRIEN. They can be prosecuted if the United States attorneys feel they have cases of sufficient strength, but very often we can stop them, Senator, in cases where the United States attorney would probably not undertake the prosecution.

Mr. CHUMBRIS. You have heard of the Solliday case in Baltimore, where the United States attorney obtained a conviction for the distribution of this type of pictures we are talking about—the fetish, the bondage, the strip-tease.

Mr. O'BRIEN. One of my men testified in that case.

Mr. CHUMBRIS. In that case, the common carrier was used, and still a conviction was obtained, under the common-carrier provision, which is 1462 of title 18.

Mr. O'BRIEN. Right.

Senator LANGER. How many fellows have gone to jail since 1950?

Mr. O'BRIEN. I don't know. Mr. Simon is the man who handles the prosecutions.

Senator LANGER. Can you tell us?

Mr. SIMON. I have some statistics on the number of arrests in comparison to the number of cases we have issued for investigation. That is based on the mailing of all types of nonmailable matter, including threatening letters and postal cards. During the fiscal year ending 1954, we had issued for investigation 5,233 cases, which is quite an increase, and the statistics in our possession at the present time indicate that there will be a tremendous increase during the current fiscal year.

Now, arrests for mailing obscene matter during the fiscal year ending June 30, 1954, there were 136 arrests and 112 convictions.

During the current fiscal year ending April 1955, there were 166 arrests and 137 convictions.

Senator LANGER. What is the average amount these gentlemen get?

Mr. SIMON. My experience has been that the penalty is very small in most obscenity cases; they get $50 or $100 fine. Most of them are probation and frequently there is not even a fine. The most excessive fine—I just experienced three cases that were tried in California, in San Francisco, the northern district of California, involving mail-fraud photographs. They were jury trials in each case. After previous prosecution the promoters had continued to operate. But a year ago I took the matter up with the present United States attorney.

We obtained indictments in each case and convictions in each instance. These defendants were given suspended jail sentences from 6 to 9 years and fines were $1,500—1 got a $3,000 fine, 1 a $4,000 fine, and 1 a $5,000 fine, which is quite excessive—and those are the only adequate sentences we have experienced in this particular type of case.

Senator LANGER. Don't you think the law should be changed to make it compulsory that the judge had to give them at least 90 days or a year in jail?

Mr. SIMON. The penalty is adequate if the judges would only——

Senator LANGER. The Congress has the power to say to the judge, "You have got to give him at least a year."

Mr. SIMON. I think there should be more adequate sentences to deter these people.

Senator LANGER. Would you draw up a law in this omnibus statute you are drawing up to say that the judge has no discretion; when he convicts, he has to give him at least a year? When you stop this stuff, you have got to have some kind of adequate penalty to stop it. When a man is making a million dollars a year and gets $100 or $50 fine, it makes the whole law ridiculous.

Mr. CHUMBRIS. Mr. Simon, are you familiar with the case in which a Federal judge in Newark, N. J., last summer issued a year-and-a-day penalty to this person for his first offense in sending an obscene picture through the mails?

Mr. SIMON. I don't recall that particular case; no, sir.

Mr. CHUMBRIS. Some of our material from the hearings in New York have not come to Washington and have been forwarded to another part of the country for the hearings. I don't have the exact name of the person involved, but the judge issued this statement, that from here on in any case that comes before his court of obscene literature, obscene pictures, lewd pictures, was going to get the full penalty of the law.

Mr. SIMON. That was in a Federal case.

Mr. CHUMBRIS. In a Federal court.

Are you in accord with that type of meting out punishment?

Mr. SIMON. No, sir; I hadn't heard about it.

Mr. CHUMBRIS. Are you in accord with it?

Mr. SIMON. I am; yes, sir.

Mr. CHUMBRIS. Could you believe that that would definitely act as a deterrent to future traffic in pornographic literature through the mails?

Mr. SIMON. I certainly do.

Mr. CHUMBRIS. As a matter of fact, it would be the same for any other provisions, such as 1462, through common carrier, and the other provisions of the law?

Mr. SIMON. Yes, sir.

Mr. CHUMBRIS. If the punishment were greater?

Mr. SIMON. I agree.

Mr. O'BRIEN. Of course, you could amend 1461 and say:

* * * shall be fined not less than $1,000 or less than one year in jail.

Senator LANGER. And providing further that the judge cannot suspend the sentence, and get away from all the suspending business.

We ran across that, as you will remember, during the war, where they had defective wiring in the airplanes, and a lot of our soldiers were killed. And we had a judge in Indiana that suspended the sentence, even though there had been several mechanics and soldiers killed. You remember that. The judge finally resigned when they started making an investigation.

Mr. SIMON. I might say that since I have been engaged in this type of work I only know of one instance where a man has received a maximum penalty of 5 years in prison for mailing obscene matter.

Mr. O'BRIEN. Of course, where we stop these people, or they quit, they did suffer financially; they probably have a lot of money invested in their advertisements.

Senator LANGER. If your theory is right, then if a man enforces a prohibition law, a fellow can sell liquor all year long, or 2 years or 3 years or 4 years, and when you finally convict him, if he says he won't sell any more liquor——

Mr. O'BRIEN. No; that is not my theory.

Senator LANGER. That is the way the things works.

Mr. O'BRIEN. No, sir.

Our function in the Post Office Department is not punitive. Our function is to stop the use of the mails for the distribution of obscenity. When it comes to the prosecution and penalty, that is up to the Department of Justice. But we try to stop the channel of the mails from being used in order to let this matter flow into the houses of the public and contaminate the minds of these children that you are here trying to protect.

If you can effect that, then after we have done that, the avenues are still open for prosecution of the offender.

Senator LANGER. As Mr. Simon says, they issued 5,280 arrests.

Mr. SIMON. Those are cases issued for investigation. And that is all types of nonmailable matter. We don't have any breakdown as to the dealers in obscene matter. It is all types of nonmailable matter.

Mr. CHUMBRIS. Mr. O'Brien or Mr. Simon, while we are on the question of the nature of the offense and the penalty involved, what is your opinion on a statute which provides that the equipment that the pornographer has would be confiscated and not returnable to the offender? Are you in favor of such legislation? That would definitely cut off the production end of the business, as well as some of the distributing end.

Would you be in favor of such legislation? In other words, if the photographic equipment were confiscated and if the projector, the movie projector and the processing of film, that equipment that he uses for that work confiscated, like it is under the narcotics law and under the old prohibition law, would you be in favor of such a provision in the law, whether it be Federal or State?

Mr. SIMON. I would, in connection with criminal cases, because I have experienced such situations where these offenders have been taken into custody, in using a search warrant and material is confiscated, and thereafter the court ordered the material returned, and they are back in business again.

Mr. CHUMBRIS. Then, if the equipment were taken away from them, they couldn't produce these pictures fast enough, and therefore they couldn't distribute them through the mails; is that right?

Mr. SIMON. It would at least put them to considerable expense in duplicating them.

Senator LANGER. I want to call your attention to the fact that a man brings in wool from Canada and doesn't pay this duty, or brings in some of the Selkirk wheat; if he does that, they don't arrest him and punish him, but they take his trucks, customs takes the trucks, the automobiles, everything involved in bringing that Selkirk wheat in, and they sell them. And there is nothing you can do to stop it. And so some of these men lose trucks costing six or seven thousand dollars.

We have 70,000 cases up in North Dakota, some are pending right now in the district court of North Dakota. That is the way to stop violations of the customs law. Why wouldn't it work here?

Mr. SIMON. I agree with you.

Senator LANGER. If an automobile carried some of this obscene literature, if that automobile could be confiscated, or an airplane carried it and an airplane could be confiscated, why wouldn't that be a good law to have?

Mr. CHUMBRIS. A similar law to that has been introduced, Senator.

Senator LANGER. But there hasn't been any action on it. You did a good job of introducing stuff, but nothing has been passed.

Mr. CHUMBRIS. Mr. Simon, on the same issue, we have with us the Honorable Leslie Burgum, the attorney general of the State of North Dakota, whose State legislature in 1955, this recent legislature, enacted such a provision in its law, which he will testify to in a short while.

Senator LANGER. Let's have him testify now.

Would you come up, Mr. Burgum. It is not necessary to swear you in this matter.

(The prepared statement, in full, submitted by Mr. O'Brien is as follows:)

STATEMENT BY WILLIAM C. O'BRIEN, ASSISTANT SOLICITOR, FRAUD AND MAIL-
ABILITY DIVISION, OFFICE OF THE SOLICITOR, POST OFFICE DEPARTMENT, WASH-
INGTON, D. C.

The Post Office Department receives numerous complaints made by parents whose children have received advertisements of pornographic books, pictures, movies, slides, photographs, and other items including trashy sex and crime stories, filthy novelties and other miscellaneous dirt.

The mailing volume of such advertisements is large and is steadily growing. The daring and indecency of the advertisements themselves, apart from the indecent nature of the items sold, is a menace to public morals both adult and juvenile.

The increase in this traffic is due to several principal factors. The ready availability of the pornography in wholesale lots, the ease and simplicity of setting up business with comparatively small capital investment and the reluctance of the courts to sustain administrative orders denying use of the mails to such enterprises.

Purveyors of pornography with little to lose by changing name and location can easily, and securely accumulate quick profits while the law takes its leisurely course.

At this point, the committee may wish some discussion of the laws available to the Post Office Department in dealing with the traffic in obscene matter through the mails. The laws usually invoked are section 1461 of title 18 United States Code and section 259a of title 39 United States Code.

Section 1461 declares nonmailable every obscene, lewd, lascivious or filthy book, pamphlet, letter, writing, print, or other publication of an indecent character. The statute provides that such matter "shall not be conveyed in the mails or delivered from any post office or by any letter carrier." This law also provides penalties of $5,000 fine or 5 years imprisonment or both, for knowingly depositing obscene matter for mailing or delivery, or for knowingly taking same from the mails for the purpose of circulating or disposing thereof.

There have been several convictions under the criminal provisions (as Post Office Inspector Simon will tell you) but compared with the vast volume of the trafflic in obscenity, such convictions have not proven to be significantly deterrent to the growing volume and worsening character of that traffic, nor have such convictions prevented purveyors of pornography from circularizing and selling to children.

Criminal law enforcement, however, is a limited deterrent where action can be taken but some of the worst offenders are domiciled in jurisdictions where indictments and convictions are difficult to obtain. Thus, secure in the well founded belief they are immune from criminal prosecution, or that jail sentences are less likely than fines in their home jurisdictions, dealers in pornography use the mails to advertise and sell their filthy merchandise to people in more conservative distant States.

The present law, title 18, United States Code, section 1461, allows prosecution of obscenity mailers only at the point of mailing but not at the points where delivery is made and where the real harm to the community is done.

The Post Office Department is studying legislation to correct this defect in the law. Such legislation, if passed will amend title 18, United States Code, section 1461, so as to permit prosecution of dealers in obscenity in the jurisdictions where obscene advertisements and other indecent matter are delivered, or at the place of mailing.

The passage of this legislation should greatly help to end the comparative security from prosecution which now encourages and to a degree protects the owners of many enterprises peddling obscenity to children as well as adults throughout the country.

The provisions of title 18, United States Code, section 1461, relating to the non-mailability of obscene matter are administered by the Solicitor's office, in cooperation with the postmasters throughout the country. It is the postmaster's duty to inspect matter offered for mailing and if he is in doubt as to whether it should be accepted for mailing, he is required to submit the question to the Solicitor for the Post Office Department for advice and ruling. Of course, postmasters cannot open or inspect sealed first-class matter. Consequently, a great deal of obscenity both in advertising and in the form of nude or otherwise indecent pictures can escape detection at the point of mailing if sent as first-class matter. Criminal prosecution is one remedy for such misuse of the mails. The post office inspectors investigate such mailers and are usually able to secure evidence for prosecution purposes. Mr. Simon, who handles most of this work is here and can explain his problems, including his experiences where juveniles are concerned.

Another remedy for the traffic in obscenity through the mails is provided by 39 United States Code 259a, which authorizes the Postmaster General to issue orders against parties who are obtaining or attempting to obtain money or property through the mails for obscene, lewd, lascivous, indecent, filthy, or vile matter or give information as to how, where or from whom such matter may be obtained. This law was passed by Congress in 1950. Its enforcement is subject to the provisions and requirements of the Administrative Procedures Act (5 U. S. C 1001 et seq.). Therefore, formal charges must be served upon the person or concern accused of violating the law, who is entitled to a formal hearing before a hearing examiner. Respondents may avail themselves of procedural measures which roughly parallel those of a civil court proceeding, including the right to appeal from the hearing examiner's initial decision and from the Department's final order.

Skillful maneuvering by a respondent in these cases can cause long delays of weeks or months before an order finally becomes effective. These protracted delays sometimes augmented and increased by court orders enable those engaged in selling pornography by mail to accumulate profits without hindrance and to such an extent that when the Department's order stops the use of the mails and cuts off their revenue, the exploiters are little concerned and can start another enterprise, providing a repetition of the same long drawn out proceeding.

Procedural red tape is a great obstacle to the enforcement of a law which could swiftly end much of the mail order traffic in obscenity.

All of these enterprises affect juveniles, some by direct appeals to their growing sexual curiosity and by sensationalism stimulating of abnormal and character-destroying sensuality. The advertising samples which have been brought here for the inspection of the committee typify the approach of some of these dealers about whose use of the mails to circularize children, we receive complaints.

Only a few of such complaints from parents have been presented. They represent, in my experience an insignificant fraction of those who have just cause for complaint. In my opinion, based upon several years association with this work, not more than one person in several thousand who could complain, will actually do so. Consequently, the frequency with which we are now receiving such complaints from parents indicates to me a tremendously wide distribution of obscene circulars and letters advertising dirty books, pictures, movies, slides, novelties, et cetera, to children as well as to adults.

Returning to the enforcement of 39 United States Code 259a, and the problem of procedural delay, I believe the Post Office Department has some hope of solving this problem if Congress enacts into law H. R. 174 introduced by Congressman Rees of Kansas. This bill would authorize the Postmaster General to impound the mail of dealers in obscenity pending decision of their cases before the Post Office Department, in circumstances where the protection of the public warrants such action. Last year we had cases against such a dealer, whom we called the alphabetical lady. She began her operations with a fictitious name, such as Afton Publishers. When this was challenged she moved and sent out circulars under a B name such as Buffton and down the alphabet she went from place to place, securing mail delivery service for a few weeks until that phase of her scheme was worked out. Of course, we followed right along but she was usually a jump ahead. Mail addressed to each new name was impounded temporarily on the ground that it was fictitious, as it was, and we finally ended that scheme. Had she used corporate or true personal names, we would have been practically impotent without express impounding authority such as provided by H. R. 174.

The committee may be interested to learn that we have issued a complaint charging Irving Klaw, New York, with violating the provisions of 39 U. S. Code 259a, copy of the complaint is here available to the committee, with some of his circulars. I am convinced that the charges are sound and sustainable and that the evidence will warrant and support the issuance of an order against Klaw's scheme. An increasing number of complaints against Klaw are being received by the Department.

I also have here complaints issued and pending against Male Merchandise Mart, Hollywood, Calif.; The Stag Shop, Los Angeles, Calif.; and Tourlanes Publishing Co., Great Neck, N. Y.

I also have here, as a sample of completed proceeding the case against Gargantuan Books, and Rise & Shine Books, New York, one of the many such enterprises conducted by Samuel Roth, whose circular advertisements have aroused parents to protest against his use of the mails.

Besides the direct order sales of indecent movies, photographs and slides, there is the big problem of the sex books which purport to be designed and intended for proper sex instruction but are really advertised and sold by means of advertising which is plainly designed to arouse the curiosity of the prurient. Court decisions have, I think, sufficiently excluded from application of the postal obscenity statutes, the legitimate texts for adults, which discuss sex and advise mature persons concerning their problems in married life. But the young and immature are frequently assailed by publicity sensationally dwelling on the purely carnal and lascivious aspects of sex and by means of advertisements in girly type magazines solicit the small sums for which such book—and pamphlets may be obtained through the mails. Of course, direct mail advertising is also used to sell not only tracts about normal sexual life but also concerning abnormalities and deviations therefrom which, I am informed by court officers, psychologists and others are extremely detrimental to the morals of juveniles as well as adults. This evil we deal with as well as we can with the authority now conferred on the Department by existing laws.

And last but not least we have the constant and rapidly growing problem of paper back novelties and cheap, trashy, sexy, periodical literature. I may say that the Post Office Department is gravely concerned about the use of the mails to distribute such indecent literature. We resist to the utmost the efforts of those who daily seek to send such matter by mail and great quantities are excluded by Solicitor's rulings that it may not be carried in the mails under the provisions of 18 U. S. Code 1461. Moreover, the Department has refused to grant second-class rates to such publications.

Numerous publications containing sexy illustrations and text dwelling lasciviously on sex episodes and sex crimes reach the public through newsstand sale. But most of them were distributed by some means of transportation outside of the mails, including of course, many entered as second-class matter.

In conclusion, I may say, that the Post Office Department, despite the handicaps, which I have mentioned, is fully employing its authority under the law to protect the public from obscenity of all kinds. And may I again commend to the favorable consideration of the committee such legislation as I have mentioned which will greatly assist the Postmaster General, the Solicitor and the Chief Post Office Inspector in dealing with this problem.

Would you state your full name and your address and your official title, for the record?

STATEMENT OF LESLIE R. BURGUM, ATTORNEY GENERAL OF THE STATE OF NORTH DAKOTA, BISMARCK, N. DAK.

Mr. BURGUM. Leslie R. Burgum, attorney general, Bismarck, N. Dak.

Mr. CHUMBRIS. And how long have you been the attorney general for the State of North Dakota?

Mr. BURGUM. Since January 3, 1955.

Mr. CHUMBRIS. And, Mr. Attorney General, you were the Attorney General at the time that House bill No. 825 was introduced and passed by the Legislature of the State of North Dakota and written into law?

Mr. BURGUM. Yes; I was, at the time of the passage of House bill No. 825.

Mr. CHUMBRIS. And the provisions of said law, does it deal with confiscation of the equipment of a person dealing in pornography?

Mr. BURGUM. Yes; it does; section 4:

Seizure and confiscation of equipment used in production or manufacture of indecent literature or articles and of vehicles used in distribution of indecent articles.

Senator LANGER. Mr. Attorney General, would you mind reading that whole section.

Mr. BURGUM (reading):

Any peace officer of this State may seize any equipment used in the printing, production, or manufacture of indecent and obscene literature, matter, or articles, of whatever nature, and may seize any vehicle or other means of transportation used in the distribution of such indecent and obscene literature, matter, or articles, and may arrest any person in charge thereof. The procedure prescribed in chapter 29–31 of the North Dakota Revised Code of 1943 relating to confiscation of equipment used in the commission of crimes shall apply and shall be followed in carrying out the provisions of this section.

Senator LANGER. That would mean, would it not, that if a truck or an automobile was used in hauling this literature, and he was arrested, convicted, you could confiscate the truck?

Mr. BURGUM. That would be my interpretation, Senator.

Senator LANGER. An airplane or anything else that is used?

Mr. BURGUM. That is correct.

Section 1 refers to films. And I assume—and the title here refers to pictures. This confiscation section doesn't mention films or pictures, but I assume that "articles of whatever nature" would mean that you could seize films and projectors, or anything else you could get ahold of. I certainly would try it.

Mr. CHUMBRIS. Do you believe that such a law would act as a deterrent to the manufacture, production, and distribution of obscene material?

Mr. BURGUM. Yes; I believe it would.

Mr. CHUMBRIS. It would certainly put a lot of people out of business, wouldn't it?

Mr. BURGUM. Yes; that confiscation section is rather deadly, because some of that stuff, the projectors, for instance, automobile, or whatever they were using, is expensive.

Mr. CHUMBRIS. And, Mr. Attorney General, I believe that your State is the first State in the United States that has placed the confiscation of pornographers' equipment into law.

Mr. BURGUM. That may be. I couldn't say as to that. I notice that this bill was introduced by seven members of the house of representatives, and one of them is Mr. Brooks, State's attorney of Cass County. That is the county in which the city of Fargo is situated.   He was State's attorney there for a number of years, with Senator Knowles.

Whether or not he had experience with this thing, I am not prepared to say.   But as State's attorney of Stutsman County—we use the term "attorney" there, in a good many States they use the designation "county attorney" or "prosecuting attorney"—but I had a little run-in with it.   It comes back to my mind after listening to this testimony here.

Two women were returning from church.   They were both mothers, and they found on the street a card addressed to any young girl who might be interested in posing in the nude for a calendar, and that this party could be reached in a certain way.   And they turned it over to the police.   They ran it down, and I think the party left town before they got anything done about it.

But it comes back to me after listening to this testimony here.   That, evidently, was an operation along this line.

Mr. CHUMBRIS. I might point out at this time, Mr. Burgum, that from the hearings that we held in New York, we found very little, if none at all, of actual distribution from the State of North Dakota to other parts of the country, and the stiffness of that particular law might be the deterrent that brought that result about.

Senator LANGER. All we did find was that some was being shipped into North Dakota.   We found a man that had an office in Fargo and another office in Minot and another in Grand Forks.

But if any evidence is presented to you, I am sure that you will make short shrift of the fellow that is doing it, knowing your reputation for law enforcement out there.

Mr. BURGUM. That is right.

These representatives definitely felt there was some danger, some possibility of this thing developing, because several of them introduced this bill.   And it was not introduced at my suggestion.   But it is on the statute books there now.

And the penalty, by the way, is $1,000 fine or a year imprisonment. And there is a saving clause, too, in the bill:

Any person who violates any of the provisions of this act shall be punishable by a fine not to exceed $1,000—

that is the maximum—

or by imprisonment not to exceed 1 year, or both such fine and imprisonment.

Mr. CHUMBRIS. And a survey of the State statutes would show that the penalty provisions under the new law of North Dakota are much more stringent than in most of the States?

Mr. Burgum. I would suspect that that is the case. I would not be prepared to say, though.

Mr. Chumbris. We have introduced this into our New York hearings, Mr. Attorney General, the brief of the laws dealing with pornography of the 48 States. And our survey indicates that North Dakota does have one of the most stringent laws, especially in view of the confiscation provision in its statute.

Mr. Burgum. Well, that is the measure that is on the books now.

Senator Langer. Any objection to making that law a part of the record, Mr. Burgum?

Mr. Burgum. No.

Senator Langer. Then it is ordered to be made a part of the record.

Mr. Chumbris. That will be marked "Exhibit No. 32."

(The bill of the North Dakota legislature was marked "Exhibit No. 32," and reads as follows:)

THIRTY-FOURTH LEGISLATIVE ASSEMBLY OF NORTH DAKOTA

HOUSE BILL NO. 825

(Introduced by Representatives Vinje, Roen, Gefreh, Schuler, Langseth, Brooks, and Haugland)

A BILL For an act relating to the prohibition of the buying, selling, distribution, designing, or disseminating in any way, of obscene writings and pictures and providing for the enforcement and administration of this act and penalties for its violation; and to repeal sections 12–2107, 12–2109, and 12–2111 of the North Dakota Revised Code of 1943

Be it enacted by the Legislative Assembly of the State of North Dakota:
SECTION 1. SALE, EXHIBITION AND DISTRIBUTION OF LEWD AND OBSCENE MATTER TO PERSONS UNDER TWENTY-ONE PROHIBITED.—No obscene, lewd, salacious or lascivious book, pamphlet, picture, paper, letter, magazine, newspaper, writing, print, printing, film, negative, transcription, wire or tape recording, or other matter of indecent character, shall be sold, loaned, given away, shown, exhibited, distributed, advertised or offered for sale, loan, gift or distribution, or be held in possession with intent to sell, loan, give away, show, exhibit, or distribute, to any one under the age of twenty-one. Any person, firm, copartnership, or corporation who hires, uses, or employs any one under the age of twenty-one to sell, give away, or in any manner distribute such matter, and any person who, having the care, custody, or control of a person under the age of twenty-one years, permits such person to sell, give away, or in any manner distribute such matter, shall also be guilty of a violation of this Act. The trial court shall take into consideration and give due weight to the approval by the national association known as the "Comics Code Authority," or such associations successors, of any comic books or publications in question under this Act.

SEC. 2. BUYING, SELLING, DISTRIBUTING, EXHIBITING, PREPARING, POSSESSION OF, OR BRINGING INTO STATE ANY EQUIPMENT FOR PREPARING, LEWD AND OBSCENE MATTER.—No person, firm, copartnership, or corporation shall buy, sell, cause to be sold, advertise, lend, give away, offer, show, exhibit, distribute, cause to be distributed, or design, copy, draw, photograph, print, etch, engrave, cut, carve, make, publish, prepare, assist in preparing, solicit or receive subscriptions for, or hold in possession with intent to sell, lend, give away, offer, show, exhibit, distribute, or cause to be distributed or bring or cause to be brought into the State any obscene, lewd, salacious, or lascivious book, pamphlet, picture, paper, letter, magazine, newspaper, writing, print, printing, film, negative, transcription, wire, or tape recording, cast, cut, carving, figure, image, or other matter, article, or instrument of indecent character or immoral use, or any equipment, machinery, or devices used or intended to be used in the preparation, manufacturing or producing of such obscene matter and material. The trial court shall take into consideration and give due weight to the approval by the national association known as the "Comics Code Authority," or such associations successors, of any comic books or publications in question under this Act.

SECTION 3. DISTRIBUTION OF INDECENT ARTICLES: TIE-IN SALES.—No person, firm, co-partnership or corporation shall as a condition to a sale or delivery for resale of any paper, magazine, book, periodical, or publication require that the purchaser or consignee receive for resale any other article, book, or other publication reasonably believed by the purchaser or consignee to be obscene, lewd, lascivious, filthy, indecent, or disgusting.

SECTION 4. SEIZURE AND CONFISCATION OF EQUIPMENT USED IN PRODUCTION OR MANUFACTURE OF INDECENT LITERATURE OR ARTICLES AND OF VEHICLES USED IN DISTRIBUTION OF INDECENT ARTICLES AUTHORIZED.—Any peace officer of this state may seize any equipment used in the printing, production, or manufacture of indecent and obscene literature, matter, or articles of whatever nature, and may seize any vehicle or other means of transportation used in the distribution of such indecent and obscene literature, matter, or articles, and may arrest any person in charge thereof. The procedure prescribed in Chapter 29–31 of the North Dakota Revised Code of 1943 relating to confiscation of equipment used in the commission of crimes shall apply and shall be followed in carrying out the provisions of this section.

SECTION 5. PENALTY.—Any person who violates any of the provisions of this Act shall be punishable by a fine of not to exceed one thousand dollars, or by imprisonment for not to exceed one year, or by both such fine and imprisonment. The term "person" herein shall include any firm, co-partnership, or corporation.

SECTION 6. SEVERABILITY.— Should any part of this Act be adjudged invalid or unconstitutional, such adjudication shall affect only the part of this Act specifically covered thereby and shall not affect any other provisions or parts of this Act.

SECTION 7. REPEAL.—Sections 12–2107, 12–2109, 12–2111 of the North Dakota Revised Code of 1943 are hereby repealed.

Senator LANGER. And I wish, Mr. Chumbris, that you would mail a copy of that law to every attorney general in the United States, so that they may have the benefit of the North Dakota legislation, and they may draw up statutes similar to or even more stringent, if they want to, so that they will have a guide to go by. Tell them we would like to have them acknowledge receipt of a copy of that law, if you would.

If the attorney general of North Dakota can't furnish such copies, we will have it duplicated and mailed out to them. Also send a copy to the Attorney General of the United States.

Mr. CHUMBRIS. I might point out, Mr. Chairman, that during the session that passed this legislation, 1955, our subcommittee was in North Dakota on official business and other matters. And the Judiciary Committee was very much interested in this problem, and asked our subcommittee staff members to coordinate the efforts.

That was one instance of excellent coordination between Federal and State committees, legislative committees, in working on a bill that would be a deterrent to this pornographic filth that gets to our children throughout the country.

Senator LANGER. Senator Kefauver took a great interest in that, and I remember that he asked the staff particularly to go up to the Judiciary Committee on North Dakota, they were in session at that time, and bring it to the attention specifically of the judiciary committee.

Senator Kefauver told me that there wasn't any objection—I believe you were out ther, Mr. Chumbris—on the part of a single legislator. The matter was presented to them out there at one of their meetings of the judiciary committee of the house—I believe it was the joint meeting of the house and senate out there. It passed without a single vote in opposition to it.

Senator Kefauver is very proud of the fact, and he has a right to be, that in that State we helped the legislature to set an example for other States to follow.

Mr. BURGUM. Of course, there is one thing out there, the distances are great, and the population is comparatively sparse. There are a lot of wide open spaces, and you probably don't have the available market, as readily as you would have it in some of the congested areas.

Mr. CHUMBRIS. Mr. Attorney General, you have heard the testimony of Inspector Blick here earlier this afternoon as to some of the problems that the police department has in dealing with this pornographic material, first, in apprehending the culprit, and then in seeing that he is prosecuted, and then after being prosecuted, if convicted, given sufficient penalty.

In view of the legislation that was introduced and passed by the State of North Dakota, would you like to comment further, so that whatever the experience of North Dakota has, it might be transmitted to the other 47 States in the United States.

Mr. BURGUM. Well, of course, we haven't had any experience under this new bill, but I think there is a general tendency to make penalties too light, to give suspended sentences, or to treat the whole matter so that it doesn't justify the evidence that is put into the prosecution.

As the inspector pointed out, you make a very sincere effort to run down a crime, and you spend the money of State, and then there is a suspended sentence given, or a very light penalty, and a promise gotten from the defendant that he will be good in the future.

Mr. CHUMBRIS. Would you state that much of the failure to give stiffer penalties for this offense can be attributed to the fact that the general public has not yet been apprised of the seriousness of this filth and the fact that it gets to so many children in our Nation?

Mr. BURGUM. I think so, very definitely.

To be perfectly frank about it, I didn't realize until I heard the inspector and the gentlemen here who have been testifying how widespread was the circulation and the money that is involved in this sort of thing.

Of course, I can remember when I was a boy—and that is a long time ago—seeing pictures, but it was unusual, it was a rare thing. Now apparently it is resorted to on a pretty well organized basis.

Mr. CHUMBRIS. And the magnitude of this particular production and distribution throughout the country has hit a proportion beyond the vision of even people who are actively engaged in tracking down this type of crime; is that correct?

Mr. BURGUM. I think so.

I think that most people, including law enforcement officers out in our State, have no idea as to the way this is being carried out in, for instance, some of the large metropolitan centers.

Mr. CHUMBRIS. There was an exhibit introduced here a moment ago that I would like for you to see. I would like for you to take a look at that, Mr. Burgum, and see how debased some people have gotten in this pornographic matter, and how it affects children.

That is a picture portraying a mother and her three children. And every one of those are under 10 years of age, or even less, as was testified to by Inspector Blick. I can understand the reason for the great care that this subcommittee has taken in going into this particular problem.

Now, nothing went on in our days as a child like that.

Mr. BURGUM. No; it is a new field to me, I am frank to say. I think that the Federal enactment certainly is justified in a situation of this kind.

Mr. CHUMBRIS. Now, as I was pointing out, the magnitude of this particular business, during the course of our investigation in New York, through the cooperation——

Senator LANGER. Mr. Chumbris, it isn't only in New York; we have had hearings in California, Palm Springs, showing the literature pouring in from Mexico. And San Diego has produced a lot of this. We have had hearings all over the United States, and the situation isn't any worse in New York than it is other places.

Mr. CHUMBRIS. That is correct.

I wanted to point out, for comment from the Attorney General, that while we were conducting hearings in New York that two large raids were made, one in the southeastern part of the United States, and one in the southwestern part of the United States, which indicated the tremendous amounts of money that is being made in the exportation of this pornographic material.

It goes to point out that the magnitude of this particular distribution and the manufacture of pornography is unlimited. And we are gaining more and more information day by day as we proceed with this particular investigation.

In our opinion, with legislation such as was introduced in North Dakota, and also discussed by Inspector Blick, which is being submitted by the subcommittee to the Senate on Monday, do you believe that legislation along that line will act as a deterrent?

Senator LANGER. Just one minute. Not introduced in North Dakota, but passed in North Dakota, signed by the Governor.

Mr. BURGUM. I believe so. I believe it would in our State, I am sure, if it were enforced.

Mr. CHUMBRIS. Are there any other comments that you would like to make at this time, sir?

Mr. BURGUM. I do not know of any, I don't believe.

Senator LANGER. Mr. Attorney General, you are familiar with the fact that in North Dakota during the last 3 years we haven't had a single murder; you are familiar with that fact, which was sent out by J. Edgar Hoover a while ago.

Would you say that perhaps one reason that we have had such a splendid record out there is due to the fact that we haven't had literatuer of that sort out there in large quantities? We have had very little of that sort of stuff there; isn't that true?

Mr. BURGUM. I think that is generally true. You have a pretty free and open country out there, you know. But I think there is a little difference—not that the people are any better, but they are nearer to the hills and to the rivers, and that sort of thing.

Mr. CHUMBRIS. Mr. Attorney General, I would like to point out that we have received replies from chiefs of police who state that the traffic in pornography and obscene literature is hitting the rural areas at a much greater percentage than it is hitting the local areas in the past few years.

And therefore, North Dakota, not being confronted with it at this time, it isn't necessarily true that it will not be confronted with it, since in other parts of the country in rural areas this has become a serious problem.

Mr. BURGUM. Of course, it may be more prevalent than I think. It may be that it just hasn't come to my attention. But I was assistant State's attorney for a couple of years, and then State's attorney, and I never had a prosecution for the thing. It may be that this just didn't head up the right way.

Mr. CHUMBRIS. Other than the incidents referred to by the chairman, we have had very little information of this particular pornographic material getting into or getting out of North Dakota, so our information is similar to the information that you are giving the committee.

But I did want to point out that the rural areas of the United States have been faced with an increase in this particular traffic.

Senator LANGER. Of course, North Dakota is a very religious State. Some time ago the Saturday Evening Post wrote up North Dakota from a religious angle, and it showed, for example, in Traill County, in 3 townships they have 12 churches. And they had photographs of some of those churches, and we are very proud of the religious atmosphere out there in that State.

These churches, as I remember it, are all Lutheran Churches. You are familiar with Traill County, you have been up there a great many times, and you know the very fine religious atmosphere that we have up there. I believe you yourself were at one time head of the Methodist Angle, isn't that true?

Mr. BURGUM. That is right; yes.

Senator LANGER. And I think you will agree with me that the people up there are perhaps more religious than they are in most States?

Mr. BURGUM. Well, the Lutheran Church, for instance, is very strong in that State, because it was settled by people from northern Europe, German, Scandinavian. The Catholic Church is also strong.

But, as I said about the passage of this bill, you know it was almost unanimous. Parents—most parents, certainly—are death against this sort of thing, the parents of children—it would be the last thing they would want the children to get hold of.

Mr. CHUMBRIS. I would like to make one further comment, Mr. Chairman, that the testimony in our hearings on pornography showed that one distributor had 171 distributing points in 14 States, most of which were in rural areas. So it indicates that there is an increased traffic in rural areas, as well as in the larger cities, throughout the United States.

Mr. Simon, hearing the testimony of the attorney general from the State of North Dakota, and also the testimony of Mr. Blick, would you like to comment on the advisability of stiffer penalties in the statutes, not only on the Federal level but also on the State level?

Mr. SIMON. As far as the Federal is concerned, I feel that there should be a minimum sentence imposed, although I don't know how that could be worked out.

There are a lot of factors that are taken into consideration before a man is sentenced, such as a presentence investigation, and extenuating circumstances involved in the individual case. But I do feel that this considerable traffic is probably responsible for the fact, of course, that there aren't stiffer penalties imposed.

TESTIMONY OF WILLIAM C. O'BRIEN AND HARRY J. SIMON—
Resumed

Mr. CHUMBRIS. Now, Mr. O'Brien, we asked several questions of Mr. Simon so that it would answer the particular questions that were coming in from this side of the table.

Would you like to add anything further? I know we distracted you from your prepared statement. Would you like to add anything further at this time before we move on to Mr. Simon for a complete statement from him as to the investigative procedures of the Post Office Department?

Mr. O'BRIEN. Well, I can say this: That our problem in dealing with these matters comes into a great variety of indecent matters. For instance, we not only have these obscene movies which you have heard a lot about today, these photographic records of indecent conduct, both between men and women, and sometimes between persons of the same sex, these deviate activities, but what you might call the very lowest and most heinous kind of indecency, but you have other categories of indecent matter which are a great problem, I think, and which predispose the mind to accept, and perhaps embrace, the more horrendous forms of obscenity.

You have the beginning of obscenity introduced to the young, and I presume to the susceptible adult in certain types of periodical literature, which deal in sex crimes and strip-tease picture, and also in the sale of slides and post cards, and all kinds of printed matter, drawings, and pamphlets and books about sex, which are often sold under the guise of education, which really are sold and advertised in such a manner as to lead the readers to buy them as pornography.

One of these on the border, Illustrated Sex Facts, we have a pending matter on that. We are proceeding in the Congress and all over the country.

As Mr. Simon brought out, there are a great quantity of complaints against that very company, which I won't name, but you can see it illustrated. That is part of a page.

The left-hand page is the advertisement of a sex book, and the right-hand page is part of the contents of the girlie striptease type of magazine in which these people love to advertise, which Irving Klow advertises in, and a great many people advertise who want to make money out of selling these types of so-called educational matter.

So you have what you might call a pseudo educational sex book, which is really something to describe sex, describe the intimacies of normal and abnormal intercourse.

And of course, I understand and appreciate, and I have recognized and so said, that sex educational texts have their place, but.not in the indecent. This is a different approach. This uses that which it is proper to know for improper purposes.

Then we have a sex crime magazine, a little pocket sized magazine which is sometimes borderline. We have a great deal of trashy, obscene literature which, little by little, breaks down the resistance of the decent minded, the very worst type of stuff we have to deal with here.

And we in the Post Office Department are trying effectively to enforce a law against the use of the mails for such matter, if we can hold it to be indecent and be supported by the courts.

That comprehends, in my view, as great and as pernicious a volume of obscenity, and as pernicious an attack upon the morals of the young as you will find in the more expensive—perhaps more than the various expensive filthy matter that you have to confront, because it breaks down the general moral fiber, as I say, and the resistancy which the normal mind has to indecency.

Mr. CHUMBRIS. Now, Mr. Sam Roth, who is the publisher of the matter which you explained in this particular chart, and who was explaining, for instance, this particular exhibit, which shows a drawing of a naked man and a naked woman in a very, very compromising embrace, and is this particular advertisement which did get into the hands of minor children, which was sent to our subcommittee by the irate parent; he pointed out that such a drawing, even though it got into the hands of a juvenile, would not have any effect on them, although it would have an effect on somebody over 25 years of age. Would you agree with his thinking on that particular point?

Mr. O'BRIEN. No; I do not agree with his thinking on that particular point, or any point, for Mr. Roth has been a constant source of trouble to the Post Office Department for a long period of years.

And while he tells me that he is in effect an apostle of propriety, I am unable to accept his statement, because every circular, pamphlet, book or picture which has emanated from his establishment has been of the nature which I have considered tending to degrade the morals of the public.

Mr. CHUMBRIS. Are there any other particular charts there, Mr. O'Brien, that you would like to explain to us at this time? I see that you have some very beautiful charts, and one that has taken quite a bit of effort on the part of the Post Office Department to put together.

Mr. O'BRIEN. Well, we tried to assemble—I am afraid rather hastily—some sample of the literature about which we have complaints from juveniles being the addressees.

This is the Tourlanes case.

I don't know any others that I can talk about, because some of them are still pending cases.

Mr. CHUMBRIS. Would you like to read a sample letter from an irate parent?

Mr. O'BRIEN. Well, there are a lot of them here.

Mr. CHUMBRIS. This is merely a cross-section of what the Post Office Department has received; is that correct?

Mr. O'BRIEN. Very small sample; yes, sir.

I have one here which was sent to a 12-year-old girl, and to a 15-year-old girl, a 13-year-old boy—I don't know whether these people are willing to have their complaints incorporated in the record, or their names.

Mr. CHUMBRIS. You can omit the names; just read the contents.

Most of these were mailed to teen-age boys, 17, 13, and 1 was mailed to a 12-year-old child. In fact, one child wrote in and said, "I am a 16-year-old girl, and I received the sex advertisement in the mail, and I want to know why it was sent to me." The children themselves resented this.

And, of course, another thing that I should mention is that apparently the mailing lists which are used by many of these people include the names of those that are registered at prep schools and academies, and such places. And they hope that some of the boys will buy sets of these dirty pictures and dirty pamphlets and circulate them among the student body, and thereby make a lot more sales.

Mr. CHUMBRIS. Mr. O'Brien, there was testimony adduced at our previous hearing which indicated that Mr. Irving Klaw, whom you mentioned earlier in your testimony, had at least, I think, 60 percent of his mailing list made up of young girls between the ages of 6 to 16 for the movie stills.

He is known as one of the kings of the pinup girls.

Now, that means that Mr. Klaw could use that mailing list also for the distribution of his circulars, such as the circulars you have on these various exhibits.

Mr. O'BRIEN. Yes, sir.

And I might say that Mr. Klaw is the most prolific producer and the most regular printer of illustrated circulars showing these torch pictures and so-called pinup—women wrestling; women, of course, in suggestive attitudes; women boxing; women strolling with each other; women tearing each other's clothes off—we have movies which we can show the committee.

Mr. CHUMBRIS. Mr. O'Brien, the technical name for some of those pictures is fetish, bondage pictures; is that correct?

Mr. O'BRIEN. They are bondage, or fetish pictures, where the girls are tied up or being spanked or beaten, or where they wear heavy leather boots, or other equipment which tends to exhibit the activity of their limbs.

That, of course, is his principal stock in trade.

Mr. CHUMBRIS. I show you here an exhibit which was introduced in the previous hearings, showing a catalog put out by Irving Klaw, the pinup king.

Are these examples of the type of advertisements that go throughout the country, and many of them reach minors?

Mr. O'BRIEN. Yes, sir. This is a very good sample of a large catalog.

He also sells a smaller catalog frequently.

Mr. CHUMBRIS. Would you please read into the record some of the types of pictures as he personally describes them in his own catalog?

Mr. O'BRIEN. Well, one caption here is entitled "New Cheesecake Photos," photos of models showing various poses. Movies No. 254, "Chris Strips for Bed;" "Our new high heel movie entitled 'Chris Strips for Bed," starring new model Frisk Penneas." And it is available in both 8-millimeter and 16-millimeter size.

Mr. CHUMBRIS. About some of the bondage pictures, does he have some of those portrayed in that catalog?

Mr. O'BRIEN. May I say, before I answer that, that I just had a day-long conference with a psychiatrist attached to one of the larger courts in this country, who discussed these pictures and pointed out the fetish aspects, the sexually stimulating fetish features like the high heels and the boots.

Mr. CHUMBRIS. Would you give that doctor's name, please.

Mr. O'BRIEN. I want to use him as a witness. Do you mind if I don't give it right now?

Mr. CHUMBRIS. Might I point out, in the testimony on these particular pictures Dr. George Henry of Cornell University testified to the fact that these particular pictures have a greater effect, an impact, on certain sudden persons than a nude picture or a picture with slight clothing.

Would you agree?

Mr. O'BRIEN. My information, from many cases involving conferences with psychiatrists and others, is that they incite people to crime.

Mr. CHUMBRIS. That is the bondage and fetish people you are referring to?

Mr. O'BRIEN. That is right.

As I said before, I have issued a complaint against Mr. Klaw, and I have a copy here.

Senator LANGER. I think you have read the testimony of J. Edgar Hoover on this matter, too.

Mr. CHUMBRIS. Mr. Simon, we didn't get to your particular statement but asked certain questions of you. We would like for you to make whatever comments you would like to make at this particular time on your activity on behalf of the Post Office Department to curtail pornographic matters from getting into the mails.

Mr. SIMON. We subscribe to a large number of magazines, and also purchase a number of magazines on the newsstands. These magazines are examined for ads of suspect dealers in obscene matter, and such advertisements are used as a basis for a large number of our investigations.

These investigations are conducted through the use of fictitious names and what is known as test correspondence. As a result of such correspondence, I have used, oh, possibly 200 names in connection with this work. As a result, these names have gotten on mailing lists of various dealers in obscene matters, and we have seen a large number of circulars from all parts of the country.

Such circular matter is also made the basis of investigation. In addition, we get thousands of complaints from the public during the course of the year, from persons who have received such literature, and including a large number from parents of juveniles.

We examine our files, and if there is no investigation under way, we do institute an investigation. So we do make an investigation of every case that is brought to our attention, either in the form of advertising or, either through periodical advertising or unsolicited circular matter, as well as complaints from the public.

We don't have any particular difficulty with the extremely pornographic matter, such as Inspector Blick described this morning. Most United States attorneys don't prosecute in that type of case. But we very rarely will get a United States attorney to authorize prosecution in connection with this type of matter, over which we have most of our difficulty.

Senator LANGER. The United States attorneys have got to obey the Attorney General. What is the attitude of the Attorney General on it; do you know?

Mr. SIMON. They are quite upset over a lot of complaints that have been received, and it is left up to the individual United States attorneys as to whether they desire prosecution. But most United States attorneys, with respect to this type of matter, feel that they will not be successful in prosecuting.

Most of our difficulty is in the larger cities, and we feel that if we could get legislation that would permit prosecution at the offices of address, we would be able to curb a number of these.

I have for the past 6 or 7 years been endeavoring to obtain a conviction at the office of address in connection with the mailing of obscene matter, that is, prosecute the mailer at the office of address under sections 1461 and 3237.

Section 3237 states that where the mails are used, it is a continuing offense, and prosecution can be instituted at the office of mailing address or any point through which it passes.

We have obtained a number of indictments in various jurisdictions, but almost invariably the defendants have entered a plea of guilty. And we have had very few contested cases. But in one case of the larger dealers in obscene matter, we had an 82-count indictment returned in the State of Kansas approximately 4 or 5 years ago, against one of the larger dealers in this type of material, stuff such as is displayed here. They were completely nude, but not the action type of photograph, or motion picture film.

The judge in the district court held that the offense was complete when the matter was deposited in the mails in California, and he dismissed the indictment. The case went up to the court of appeals at Denver, and the court of appeals sustained the lower courts.

Now, we have introduced legislation, as Mr. O'Brien mentioned, which is pending before the budget now, as I understand, to permit prosecution at the office of mailing address or any point through which it passes, that is, amended the basic law of 1461, which would overcome the objection raised by the court of appeals.

Senator LANGER. Would you write a letter to Budget Bureau—ask Senator Kefauver to send a letter to the Budget Bureau, enclosing some of these pictures? I think it would influence the Bureau to give its consent to favorable legislation on this.

Mr. SIMON. I think that legislation was introduced last session and never left the budget.

Mr. CHUMBRIS. Do you remember the number of the bill?

Mr. SIMON. No, unless Mr. O'Brien has that.

Mr. CHUMBRIS. What was the number of that bill during the last legislature?

Mr. O'BRIEN. Which bill?

Mr. CHUMBRIS. The one which makes it an offense on both ends.

Mr. O'BRIEN. I don't know.

Mr. SIMON. I might possibly have that confused with the impounding bill.

Mr. O'BRIEN. The impounding bill is 174 of this Congress.

Mr. SIMON. That is in this Congress, too?

Mr. CHUMBRIS. Mr. Simon, on this question of the United States attorneys being reluctant to prosecute on the Klaw type of a picture that is being sent through the mails, since the Soliday investigation and conviction in Baltimore in May of this year, don't you think that that would encourage their action also against pictures put out by Klaw that are sent through the mails?

Mr. SIMON. Since that hearing up in New York I am beginning to notice more sympathy from the United States attorneys.

Mr. CHUMBRIS. You will note that Mr. Klaw did not testify as to his activities, but took advantage of the immunity clause of the fifth amendment when he was called as a witness in the hearings in New York.

Mr. SIMON. I recall that.

Mr. CHUMBRIS. Have you anything further to add at this time, Mr. Simon?

Mr. SIMON. I might mention a case which just came to my attention about 6 weeks ago. It is the first time in my experience where I have found a minor involved in the sale and distribution through the mails of extremely pornographic matter.

In the middle of April I caused the arrest of a 16-year-old high-school boy, who had just turned 16 in April, for engaging in the sale of extremely pornographic matter. He mimeographed and sent through the mails a large number of lists of approximately 51 pornographic post picture films.

And that boy came from a very fine family, mother and father separated. The mother knew that the youngster was engaged in the mail-order business, but he developed this extremely pornographic business about last August, I think he said, the latter part of August, and since then up to the time of his arrest he sold over $3,000 worth of pornographic film.

We have ascertained from the boy his source of supply, and that matter is now before the United States attorney at Los Angeles, in which district the supplier was located.

Mr. CHUMBRIS. Mr. Simon, I would like to ask you, the testimony that you are receiving now, the psychiatric testimony, has it been to the effect that the fetish and the bondage type of a picture is one that is sufficient to come within the definition set forth by our courts as to what constitutes obscene and lewd?

Mr. SIMON. Well, there has been considerable difference of opinion on that particular score. I have spoken to several psychiatrists, and while they feel that it has a demoralizing effect on the persons whose minds are open to such type of material, they have been reluctant to testify.

Now, as Mr. O'Brien said, we discussed this matter with one of the leading psychiatrists in the country, who will testify for us in this Klaw case.

Mr. CHUMBRIS. May I point out that in the Soliday case in Baltimore, the psychiatrist definitely testified it was upon his testimony that the jury brought in a verdict of conviction; that bondage pictures and fetish pictures were sufficient to incite lust, and thereby came within the. definition of the court.

And also, the psychiatrist, Dr. George Henry, from Cornell University, testified to the same effect. And I believe, if you examine the testimony of Dr. Karpman, from St. Elizabeths Hospital, you will find that this testimony was supporting the position of the other two psychiatrists, which would indicate that the trend of psychiatric thinking would be sufficient to obtain convictions in the type of pictures that are being sent through the mail by Mr. Klaw.

Mr. SIMON. I have discussed the Klaw case with Dr. Karpman on several occasions. I had also interested the United States attorney over in Baltimore in the prosecution of Klaw in the district of Maryland.

But after the decision of the court of appeals in Denver, holding that you can't prosecute the mailer at the post office of address, we had to give up that particular phase.

The United States attorney at New York has declined to proceed.

Mr. CHUMBRIS. Could you give us the sort of material that this 16-year-old boy was distributing that you are referring to?

Mr. SIMON. It is a dealer in the vicinity of Los Angeles. The matter is now before the United States attorney at Los Angeles. The man has not been arrested, to my knowledge, and is awaiting action of the grand jury.

Under those circumstances, I don't think you want to make his name public.

Senator LANGER. We do not.

Mr. SIMON. I will be glad to tell you his name in private.

Mr. CHUMBRIS. I have no further questions.

Senator LANGER. I want to thank everybody that was here today. I want to thank especially the attorney general from North Dakota for coming down here. I want to thank him for giving us the benefit of his experience.

I want you to know, on behalf of Senator Kefauver, that we appreciate your cooperation.

I want to thank the post office authorities. We appreciate the kind of cooperation we have received from you everyplace, whether it has been Los Angeles, New York, or wherever it was, we found we could rely upon you to help us out.

Mr. SIMON. The chief inspector is anxious to cooperate with everybody.

Senator LANGER. This hearing is adjourned.

(Whereupon, at 4:10 p. m., the hearing was adjourned.)

JUVENILE DELINQUENCY

(Obscene and Pornographic Materials)

SATURDAY, JUNE 18, 1955

United States Senate,
Subcommittee To Investigate Juvenile
Delinquency, of the Committee on the Judiciary,
Los Angeles, Calif.

The subcommittee met, pursuant to recess, at 9:40 a. m., at room 518, United States Post Office and Court House Building, Los Angeles, Calif., Senator Estes Kefauver presiding.

Present: Senator Kefauver.

Also present: James H. Bobo, counsel; and William Haddad and Carl Perian, consultants.

Chairman Kefauver. This morning the subcommittee will study the relationship of pornographic materials to juvenile delinquency. Hearings on this subject have already been held in New York City and Washington.

Last year the subcommittee, during its community hearings, discovered that pornography was getting into the hands of children. When the work of this subcommittee was resumed this year, we decided that a further study of this situation was long overdue.

Our contention was fortified by letters from every section of this country, complaining about the pornographic materials reaching children.

Psychiatrists called before the subcommittee testified that a direct relationship between pornography and juvenile delinquency existed. A 110-percent increase in sex crimes may be attributed, in part, to these materials.

Undoubtedly, pornography is one of the contributing factors to the increase in juvenile delinquency and sex crimes in the United States.

This business thrives on the young inquisitive mind, and the pornographers slant much of their materials to children.

Society is often derelict in providing the proper sex education for our youngsters. When a child doesn't have this proper sex education, he is forced to search in the gutter for his information. In the gutter he finds this filth.

The abnormal is portrayed as the normal. Adults engage in illicit acts, lending prestige to the situation and creating the wrong impression in the child's mind.

One shocking fact uncovered by this subcommittee is that pornography is big business in the United States. Conservative estimates place the gross sale of these materials at three to four hundred million dollars a year. Much of this money comes from the lunch and allowance money of our children.

This traffic exists because of gaping loopholes in Federal legislation.

Under present laws, a pornographer cannot ship his materials through the mails. But he can load up a truck and move his filth across State lines with complete ease.

If the Congress acts on our recommendations, this situation will be cleared up.

Postal and custom laws must also be tightened. After these hearings, our recommendations will be presented to the Congress.

But not only has the Federal Government been derelict in its duties; local communities have failed to protect our children from these pornographic materials.

These big-business pornographers are often let off with slight fines and suspended jail sentences. One of the biggest operators in the country—a man our subcommittee investigators have tracked throughout the East—was recently released on a $50 bail which he forfeited. He will soon be arrested in another community, if the pattern of his past activities is any indication. And he will probably be let off with another slight fine. Most communities have no way of knowing about this man's vicious activities.

Every community in this country must look at its own laws and investigate its own situation. Only through an alert public opinion can these pornographers finally be stopped.

Here in California the subcommittee is exploring another phase of this vast business—that of the mass mailing of pornographic and semipornographic materials.

Our preliminary investigations indicate that much of these materials are mailed here in California.

Numerous reports have reached our office complaining that these materials were mailed to children as young as 10 years. The post office, too, has received similar reports.

Several witnesses appearing before us in New York City used the privilege of the fifth amendment in refusing to answer our questions. Members of the subcommittee felt that this privilege was improperly used and we have recommended that certain witnesses be cited for contempt of Congress. Certain other witnesses will be charged with perjury.

I hope that our witnesses today will consider very carefully their decision on whether or not to cooperate with the subcommittee's investigation.

Pornography is a difficult subject to talk about. Certain dangers arise from spotlighting this situation. But do we hide our heads in the sand like an ostrich? Or do we bring out the facts in the most candid manner, and have the warm sunlight of public opinion act to stop this menace? I think we must proceed forward with this study and rely upon the good judgment of our citizenry. It is far better to see and stop than to close our eyes and let this business grow and grow.

At this point I want to thank very much the Los Angeles Police Department and also the postal inspectors who have been of great help to us. They have cooperated wonderfully with our subcommittee, and they are very alert to the problem that is with us out here in southern California; have been taking active and affirmative measures to do something about it. They have been very thorough and painstakingly helpful to the staff of our subcommittee in working up the hearing today. Also the sheriff's office and several of his deputies have been very fine to us.

Mr. Bobo, who is our first witness this morning?

Mr. Bobo. Mrs. Mary Dorothy Tager.

Chairman Kefauver. Mrs. Tager, will you come around and will you hold up your hand.

(Mrs. Tager was sworn.)

Chairman Kefauver. All right, Mr. Bobo. We want to give everybody a chance to be heard and develop our case as fully as possible. This is Saturday and I know that everybody would like to get away as soon as we possibly can, so you interrogate Mrs. Tager.

TESTIMONY OF MARY DOROTHY TAGER, BALBOA, CALIF.

Mr. Bobo. Mrs. Tager, would you state your full name and your address and where you are presently living for the record?

Mrs. Tager. Mary Dorothy Tager, 2100 Ocean Boulevard, Balboa, Calif.

Mr. Bobo. Mrs. Tager, are you married? Do you have a family?

Mrs. Tager. I am not married; I am divorced. I have a family. I have a girl, Dorothy, 17. I have a boy, David, 15.

Mr. Bobo. Mrs. Tager, have you ever been engaged in a mail order business of sending photos and other things through the mail?

Mrs. Tager. Yes, sir; I have.

Mr. Bobo. At what time did you begin in this business?

Mrs. Tager. Well, I would say some time later in 1948, and I was active in the business up, oh, until some time in 1951.

Mr. Bobo. Were you in the business by yourself?

Mrs. Tager. No; I was in with my ex-husband and a partner.

Mr. Bobo. And under what trade name did you operate this business?

Mrs. Tager. Well, actually, under several. We operated under Stand-Out Products, Novel Arts, T and R Sales. They are the main names we operated under. We also operated under, oh, many hundreds, I guess, of fictitious names.

Mr. Bobo. In this business what was the merchandise which you sold, Mrs. Tager?

Mrs. Tager. I sold nudes, straight nudes, nothing pornographic, consisting of slides, black and white films, 8 and 16 millimeter, 50, 100, 400-foot reels.

Mr. Bobo. Would you put the microphone over closer to you?

Mrs. Tager. My nudes were nudes. I mean, as you would see on any calendar. It was not nothing——

Chairman Kefauver. Mrs. Tager, will you talk a little louder so we can all hear? Pull the microphone a little closer to you.

Mrs. Tager. As I say, my nudes were straight nudes. They weren't what you could classify as pornographic. They were no different than you would see on any calendar or any magazine you pick up on a newsstand.

Mr. Bobo. In these nudes which you sold, many of them were in various suggestive poses. Would you mean by the fact that they were not pornographic, was that they might not be considered under the present laws pornographic?

Mrs. Tager. Well, no. Personally I don't consider a picture of a nude woman as pornographic. I think it definitely depends on the way the woman is posed or—now, to me pornographic material would be more in a strip sequence that would be very suggestive, more so than a straight nude.

Mr. Bobo. Did you sell these particular nudes and novelty cards through the United States mail?

Mrs. Tager. Yes, sir.

Mr. Bobo. How would you secure the names of customers to whom you were sending this?

Mrs. Tager. Well, there are many sources. Of course, magazine advertising is one of the main sources of your names. There are many ads appearing even today in magazines or comic books, which is more or less a come-on actually for nude picture buyers. So over a period of time from the replies you get from these various magazines, you accumulate a very large mailing list.

Mr. Bobo. Do you buy these mailing lists from other persons, from the publishers of so-called legitimate magazines?

Mrs. Tager. Yes; that can be done. That can be done.

Mr. Bobo. Did you ever purchase any mailing addresses from any of the so-called legitimate magazines?

Mr. Tager. No. I purchased mailing names from Mosley, who was—well, that is a legitimate place of business where they——

Chairman Kefauver. I didn't understand that name. Mosley?

Mrs. Tager. Mosley.

Chairman Kefauver. How do you spell it?

Mrs. Tager. M-o-s-l-e-y, I believe.

Chairman Kefauver. And where is Mosley's establishment?

Mrs. Tager. Well now, he is through the Middle West somewhere. Offhand I couldn't tell you.

Chairman Kefauver. You mean——

Mrs. Tager. I have forgotten just where it is; it has been so long.

Chairman Kefauver. What is the official name of the company, Mosley?

Mrs. Tager. Mosley Mailing Lists, I imagine.

Chairman Kefauver. Mosley Mailing Lists?

Mrs. Tager. Yes. That is a legitimate house where they sell mailing lists to anyone that has anything to sell.

Mr. Bobo. You don't know what city in the Midwest he is located in?

Mrs. Tager. Offhand, I don't. I don't—it's been so long since I have contacted this concern.

Mr. Bobo. In buying mailing lists from Mosley or from others, was there any specification as to the names that would appear on these mailing lists, as to the type of people whom you wanted to mail to?

Mrs. Tager. Well, yes. If you were going to buy a mailing list, naturally you would buy a list of men buyers who were interested in similar merchandise.

Mr. Bobo. Did you make any effort to determine, when you received the mailing list, as to just who the people were; whether these were men buyers? Included on these mailing lists would be names of men and women both, wouldn't there?

Mrs. Tager. Yes; that is true.

Mr. Bobo. Most of these mailing lists were really just compilations of names and addresses without any specification that they be people who purchased nude photographs?

Mrs. Tager. Oh, that is true. That is true. I mean there would be no actual way of knowing. You would only have the person you bought the names from, you would only have their word that they were buyers of merchandise that would be similar to what you were selling.

Mr. Bobo. Mrs. Tager, I want to get back to the mailing lists in just a moment; but, first, in securing these nude photos which you sent out through the mail, also the other novelty items, where would you secure the models for these photos?

Mrs. Tager. Well, there are various places where models are gotten. I believe most of the models we used came from U. C. L. A., the college here.

Mr. Bobo. In using these girls, who did the photography work?

Mrs. Tager. Well, there were photographers working for us. In other words, we would buy the negatives from the various photographers.

Mr. Bobo. The age of these girls which you used to pose for the pictures, were there any specifications as to the age that the girl would be?

Mrs. Tager. Well, naturally, we weren't going out—I don't believe any photographer with any conscience is going to photograph a minor. I would say most of the girls run from 21 to maybe 25.

Mr. Bobo. Did you secure any of the models yourself at any time?

Mrs. Tager. No; I never did. Mr. Tager used to shoot when we first went into business—he used to do his own shooting of the models, but then as we grew it wasn't profitable to spend time shooting the models. It was much more profitable to just buy the negatives.

Mr. Bobo. Did you ever purchase any negatives of nude photos from Andy's Agency here in Los Angeles?

Mrs. Tager. No.

Mr. Bobo. Have you ever done any business whatsoever in purchasing photographs from an Andy Anderson?

Mrs. Tager. No; I have never purchased anything from Andy Anderson. In fact, I know the man by sight only. I know very little about him.

Mr. Bobo. Have you ever secured any models through Mr. Anderson, or do you know whether or not your husband ever secured any models through Mr. Anderson?

Mrs. Tager. I never did. Now, whether Mr. Tager did or not, that I could not say.

Mr. Bobo. On these negatives that you would buy from a photographer, who would do the printing of these materials for you?

Mrs. Tager. Well, most of our printing was done at Quantity Photos. That is at Sunset and Western.

Mr. Bobo. Here in Los Angeles, Calif.?

Mrs. Tager. Yes, sir; but most any—I found that most any photographic house that is set up to do work in quantity will do your work for you.

Mr. Bobo. Have you ever done business with any other photoshop?

Mrs. Tager. Well, yes. In fact, there has been actually, I guess over a period of time, there has been quite a few.

Mr. Bobo. Do you have the names of any others with whom you might have done business?

Mrs. Tager. Well, yes.   There is quite a few.   Frank Rode, he did some of our prints for us.

Mr. Bobo. Where is he located?

Mrs. Tager. Well, I believe he is still at Keystone Studios on Olive right now.

Mr. Bobo. Here in Los Angeles?

Mrs. Tager. Yes; and his place of business on East 12th Street.   I know there were several others, but offhand I can't truthfully think of their names.

Mr. Bobo. What was the cost to you of the photographs which you would send out in a mail package?

Mrs. Tager. Well, I am afraid I don't understand you on that. You would have to specify.

Mr. Bobo. You were selling a package.   You advertised that you would sell a package of 6 nude photographs, or in whatever quantity you sold them, 1 photograph.   What would be the cost to you of that photograph.

Mrs. Tager. Well, that would be kind of difficult to break down. It could be done, but there would be quite a time to break that down in this respect.   You would have to take your—after all, you have your employees, you have a terrific overhead.   You have your advertising costs and everything.   Of course, that is all——

Mr. Bobo. Well, Mrs. Tager, I was meaning from the producer of the photograph, the studio from which you bought it.

Mrs. Tager. Yes.

Mr. Bobo. What was the cost to you of that photograph?

Mrs. Tager. Well, I used to pay two-fifty a negative.

Mr. Bobo. Two-fifty a negative?

Mrs. Tager. For one negative.

Mr. Bobo. From the negative, what was the cost of the finished and developed picture?

Mrs. Tager. Well, various prices.   One time I was paying $11, and it was broken down as far as $7 for a hundred.

Mr. Bobo. $11 and $7 a hundred?

Mrs. Tager. Yes.   At various prices.

Mr. Bobo. You bought them in large quantities?

Mrs. Tager. Yes.   Depending on the quantity, there would be a terrific breakdown.

Mr. Bobo. What was the quantity you usually purchased from them?

Mrs. Tager. Oh, I might possibly go in with 25, 30, or 40 sets of 8, and have a thousand of each made up.

Mr. Bobo. You sold these——

Mrs. Tager. Sometimes more, sometimes less, depending upon how the stock was depleted.

Mr. Bobo. And from these sets of 8 which you sold, they cost you $7 a hundred?

Mrs. Tager. Yes.

Mr. Bobo. And you sold them for what, Mrs. Tager?

Mrs. Tager. $2 a set.

Mr. Bobo. $2 a set?

Mrs. Tager. Of eight, yes.

Mr. Bobo. Mrs. Tager, in mailing these photos through the mail, although you did not regard them as pornographic, you had a great deal of difficulty with the post-office authorities; is that right?

Mrs. Tager. That is right.

Mr. Bobo. You attempted in many ways to avoid the various postal regulations dealing with mailing this type of material out to the country?

Mrs. Tager. That is correct.

Mr. Bobo. When you would set up a business, such as I think at one time you operated the Paragon—was it Paragon Books?

Mrs. Tager. No.

Mr. Bobo. What was the name of one of your businesses?

Mrs. Tager. Stand-Out Products.

Mr. Bobo. The Stand-Out Products, would you rent office space?

Mrs. Tager. For them?

Mr. Bobo. Yes.

Mrs. Tager. Oh, yes; post office boxes, mailing addresses, post office space.

Mr. Bobo. Would you place advertisements in magazines or newspapers or any other media of advertising?

Mrs. Tager. Yes.

Mr. Bobo. With whom would you place this advertising, would you place it with an agency or directly with the magazine.

Mrs. Tager. No; through an agency, through an agency.

Mr. Bobo. What advertising agency did you use to place your advertising?

Mrs. Tager. Well, at the time—most of my business was given to McKee, Burns & McKee.

Chairman Kefauver. Have her spell these names.

Mrs. Tager. McKee, M-c-K-e-e, I believe.

Mr. Bobo. McKee——

Mrs. Tager. Burns & McKee.

Mr. Bobo. Let's get that name clear, Mrs. Tager. It is McKee, Burns & McKee?

Mrs. Tager. & McKee.

Mr. Bobo. Burns, B-u-r-n-s?

Mrs. Tager. Yes.

Mr. Bobo. McKee, Burns & McKee?

Mrs. Tager. That is correct.

Mr. Bobo. Where are they located?

Mrs. Tager. They were on Western Avenue when I did business with them. Where they are today I couldn't say.

Mr. Bobo. You don't know whether or not they are still in business?

Mrs. Tager. No; I don't know.

Mr. Bobo. At what date did you do business with them?

Mrs. Tager. Well, I would say through, oh, somewhere around the end of '49, '50, and possibly part of '51.

Mr. Bobo. Did you prepare the advertising copy that would be used in the various magazines?

Mrs. Tager. Both my husband and I.

Mr. Bobo. Was there ever any question asked you as to the type of merchandise which you were selling through this advertising?

Mrs. Tager. No; I can't say that truthfully we were questioned too much about what we were selling.

Mr. Bobo. In drawing these ads and preparing the advertising copy, it was your idea to make them as sexually suggestive and as sexually attractive as possible, would you say?

Mrs. Tager. Oh, yes. After all, we were advertising material that the buyer hadn't seen. Any ad has to be—well, an ad is a come-on to buy the materials, so naturally our ads, we would go as far as possible with them.

Mr. Bobo. In this ad there was a suggestion, generally, that it might be pornographic in nature or be more than just a plain strip photo?

Mrs. Tager. No. I more or less don't believe that. I do believe that when a person, an individual, answers an advertisement, a magazine, say, for a pinup, I believe he expects eventually to get nudes; but I don't believe that he completely expects to get pornographic pictures. I think a great majority are satisfied with just a nude.

Mr. Bobo. Do you know the names of any of the magazines in which your advertisements have appeared?

Mrs. Tager. Yes; there are many. I mean, all of the girlie magazines they have appeared in.

Mr. Bobo. You speak of girlie magazines. You are speaking of what type of magazine?

Mrs. Tager. Well, you have got Pic and See and Hit and Miss and Male and Man and all that.

Mr. Bobo. That type of publication?

Mrs. Tager. All that type of magazine.

Mr. Bobo. Did they play in any so-called romance magazines?

Mrs. Tager. We have had a few ads in those magazines, but they never proved profitable.

Mr. Bobo. Did they ever appear in any of the comic-book type of magazine?

Mrs. Tager. Not that I know of; no.

Mr. Bobo. Did you specify any particular type of magazine in which they would appear?

Mrs. Tager. Well, naturally a magazine that would be full of pinups is the best medium for you to get your customers from. Where they have magazines that are full of pinups, if they want more they would answer your ad and then you have a buyer for your nudes.

Mr. Bobo. You also advertised, in addition to the strip series of photos which you made, movies of nude girls?

Mrs. Tager. Yes, sir.

Mr. Bobo. Weren't some of these movies of nude girls in rather suggestive poses or rather suggestive or sexual or sensual actions?

Mrs. Tager. Well now, that would be debatable. To my way of thinking, no.

Mr. Bobo. Well, they don't just have the girl standing there with a movie camera.

Mrs. Tager. No, but actually there aren't too much on those movies.

Mr. Bobo. The girls go through some sort of contortions or dances or some type of action?

Mrs. Tager. Yes. I had one that did a swimming act in the water. That to my way of thinking was quite—it was very good. I mean, there was nothing that could be classed—I mean, you could go to a moving picture show and see practically the same thing today.

Mr. Bobo. Except for the fact that they would be dressed?

Mrs. Tager. Well, sometimes they are not always dressed completely.

Mr. Bobo. Would this particular ad be a representative ad of the type of ad which you used in your magazine?

Mrs. Tager. Yes.

Mr. Bobo. And that would be designed more or less to show various girls in various acts, dances, and so forth?

Mrs. Tager. Well, that could be, yes.

Mr. Bobo. And it was designed not to appeal particularly to the patrons of the arts, but more to those who prefer some emotional stimulation from these pictures?

Mrs. Tager. Well, that again is debatable, because my mailing list, over 60 percent of my customers were doctors.

Mr. Bobo. Do you know how many——

Mrs. Tager. They are professional men, so——

Mr. Bobo. Excuse me.

Mrs. Tager. So I kind of doubt—I mean, that—well, maybe a picture like that would tend to excite them. I really don't know.

Mr. Bobo. This particular type of picture appearing in a magazine, do you think that might attract a sexually inquisitive youngster to buy something to find out about sex?

Mrs. Tager. Well, it is possible. Of course, I have always been on the theory, when I was in business, that a child—if your prices were high enough, a child would not have the money to come ahead and send for your material. A quarter he would have, or 50 cents or a dollar; but if your material is high enough, I think that in itself more or less scares some of the children away from buying the material. Of course, most children today have quite a bit of money.

Mr. Bobo. Well, your strip series set, the photos sold from what, $2 a set?

Mrs. Tager. But they weren't strip. I didn't handle strip photos. Mine were strictly nudes.

Mr. Bobo. Well, a strip of nudes?

Mrs. Tager. Yes.

Mr. Bobo. And here you have a special, 48 different photos for $10.

Mrs. Tager. No.

Mr. Bobo. Which would not be out of reason of any of the children in this country today?

Mrs. Tager. Well, that is true.

Mr. Bobo. And on your order form which I have here there is no request that the person sending in for any of your photos list his name or, I mean, list his age?

Mrs. Tager. Well, even if he did, it wouldn't do much good; because you can take a boy 17 years old and it is pretty hard to tell if you get an order from him through the mail whether he is 17 or 70. He is not, naturally, going to put his age down as 17; so I never felt—well, for a while there, in fact, I sent out an inquiry slip before I ever sold any of my nudes. When I would get a reply from a magazine, I would send a pinup in reply to that ad, and before I would send a person a come-on letter like that for the nudes I would send a letter of inquiry with the age and everything on it, and I always asked if they were photographers or artists, sculptors; and it was amazing all the doctors were artists.

Mr. Bobo. Mrs. Tager, what you mean is that every one you received from an ad like this you would send out an inquiry to determine whether he was a doctor or a lawyer?

Mrs. Tager. No; to determine his age. To determine his age, what he was interested in, whether it was film, slides, or black and whites.

Mr. Bobo. For what reason would you like to determine the age of the customers?

Mrs. Tager. Well, I only had one purpose at that time. I felt that if I was ever in trouble and I was accused of selling to minors, these coupons that I kept with the ages of the different individuals, I always felt that they would be more or less in my favor. In other words, that I was trying to keep children out of my files.

Mr. Bobo. That was in the mailing lists in which you bought. Suppose a child had sent—this was a letter that you sent out; this wasn't a magazine ad; would that be correct?

Mrs. Tager. No; this is not one of mine, unless this was sent out after I retired from the business. That is quite possible.

Mr. Bobo. Did any of your ads ever suggest such as this: You must have Georgia in the nude. Georgia has been named the showgirl of the year because she has so much to show and she knows how to show it. You will sit and sigh over her beautiful figure and what she does with it. She is your open door to a girl's private life.

Mrs. Tager. No; I am afraid my advertising wasn't quite that strong.

Mr. Bobo. Well, most of the advertising that you see in this particular business, that would give the idea that these are just not straight nude scenes?

Mrs. Tager. That is true. That is very true.

Mr. Bobo. And for a sexually inquisitive youngster of 12 or 16——

Mrs. Tager. Well, he would really think he was getting something.

Mr. Bobo. Yes, ma'am. This is another copy of a letter. Is that one of the particular types of mailing advertising which you sent out?

Mrs. Tager. No. I am afraid this is another one that was sent out after I left the business.

Mr. Bobo. Are you acquainted——

Mrs. Tager. Although I have seen this before.

Mr. Bobo. Are you acquainted with the Mr. Ross to whom these orders are addressed to?

Mrs. Tager. Yes. He was associated with my husband and I.

Mr. Bobo. What is Mr. Ross' full name?

Mrs. Tager. I believe his true name is Rosenblatt, Rubin Rosenblatt. We know him under the name of Roy J. Ross.

Chairman Kefauver. Get that spelled.

Mr. Bobo. Rubin, R-u-b-i-n?

Mrs. Tager. I believe that is his name.

Mr. Bobo. How do you spell Rosenblatt?

Mrs. Tager. Well, I imagine R-o-s-e-n-b-l-a-t-t.

Mr. Bobo. And you knew him as what?

Mrs. Tager. Roy J. Ross.

Mr. Bobo. Where did Mr. Ross reside?

Mrs. Tager. Well, that I could not tell you right now. I don't— the last address I had was 4100 Goodland Avenue.

Mr. Bobo. What was that street again?

Mrs. Tager. 4100 Goodland, G–o–o–d–l–a–n–d, Avenue in North Hollywood; but whether he is still there or not I wouldn't know.

Mr. Bobo. The original mailings, in receiving the orders and so forth from the various magazines in which your ad appeared, there was no effort upon your part to determine the age or the type of person that was getting the material?

Mrs. Tager. Well, yes; there was.

Mr. Bobo. If I sent in an order to you from one of these magazines and enclosed my $10——

Mrs. Tager. Yes.

Mr. Bobo. Would I get a letter of inquiry back as to my age, or would I get the strip photos or whatever other merchandise you had to sell?

Mrs. Tager. Well, no. When you place an ad in a magazine—of course, I am going by my own experiences; what some of the others do might be entirely different. When an ad is placed in a magazine and you, perhaps, answer the ad, you send me a dollar. Well, naturally, for that dollar you are not going to get nudes. You get four pinup pictures. Your name is kept on file, and in order for me to keep or try to keep children out of my files, I would send them a letter of inquiry as to their age, and I would get that letter of inquiry back from them before I would attempt to send them any of these advertising pieces for nudes.

Mr. Bobo. The original was just a come-on?

Mrs. Tager. That is right.

Mr. Bobo. And actually it was more or less a fraudulent ad because the person got not what he thought he was asking for?

Mrs. Tager. Well, that is very true.

Mr. Bobo. Because the material which was sent to him did not meet the description——

Mrs. Tager. But if you had sent it through the mail with a description, you would have been closed by the Post Office Department, too; so you had it one way or the other.

Chairman Kefauver. Well, when you would finally send the real thing, the nudes, did you send those through the mail?

Mrs. Tager. Yes, sir.

Chairman Kefauver. You said that you tried to keep the age of children or secure it for a while. Did you give up that effort?

Mrs. Tager. I did because I found, oh, several would come back to me in a handwriting that you could more or less tell that it wasn't a grownup's handwriting, and on the coupon the age might be marked as 26 or 30; so I finally felt that—I mean, it was kind of a useless cause, so I dropped it.

Chairman Kefauver. From that time on you would mail back to anyone who wrote in without inquiring whether they were kids or adults?

Mrs. Tager. Well, of course, the girls that opened the mail were instructed to watch out for handwriting that did look juvenile; but, as I say, if they were 17 or 18 years old, he is still a juvenile, but yet you could not determine from his handwriting his age.

Chairman Kefauver. Well, if it looked like juvenile handwriting, would the dollar be sent back to him?

Mrs. Tager. It would be sent back to him.

Chairman Kefauver. What explanation would you make?

Mrs. TAGER. "Out of business."

Senator KEFAUVER. All right.   Go ahead, Mr. Bobo.

Mr. BOBO. You say you made a survey as to the number of juveniles that you would receive mail from.   Did you receive mail from quite a number of people of the young age?

Mrs. TAGER. Well, now, of course, as I say, I am judging by the handwriting.

Mr. BOBO. You actually——

Mrs. TAGER. That would accompany the orders.   There were quite a few.   There were quite a few.

Mr. BOBO. What would be the size of the mailing which you would send out?   What was the size of the business you did in the mail-order business?   If you were attempting to send out any mailing at one time, what would be the number of mailings that you would make?

Mrs. TAGER. Well, now, that could vary anywhere from 20,000 pieces up to a couple of hundred thousand; even more.

Chairman KEFAUVER. And what is the biggest one you ever sent out?

Mrs. TAGER. Well, you see, I believe the biggest mailings from the business I was associated with, oh, I believe they were sending maybe a quarter of a million pieces a month.

Chairman KEFAUVER. A quarter of a million a month.   Do you have a sample of the kind of things that were sent?

Mr. BOBO. Would this be a representative sample of the copy matter?

Mrs. TAGER. Yes.

Chairman KEFAUVER. Let those be made exhibits so we can have an idea what they were.

(The samples referred to were marked "Exhibit No. 33," and are on file with the subcommittee.)

Chairman KEFAUVER. How would they be sent, by postal permit or did you put stamps on each one?

Mrs. TAGER. Well, to begin with we were using the coil stamps, and then we went into the Pitney-Bowes machine with the permit.

Chairman KEFAUVER. First-class mail?

Mrs. TAGER. Yes, sir.

Chairman KEFAUVER. All first-class mail?

Mrs. TAGER. Yes, all first-class.

Chairman KEFAUVER. You had just one of these machines that printed the permit on it?

Mrs. TAGER. Yes.

Chairman KEFAUVER. Were they mailed here—of course, you did business in a lot of places.   Some were mailed here—you will go into that, Mr. Bobo?

Mr. BOBO. Yes, sir.

Chairman KEFAUVER. All right.   I see.

Mr. BOBO. What would be the average return from a mailing, percentage return on the mailing that you would make?

Mrs. TAGER. Well now, that, too, is a little difficult to answer in this respect: It would depend entirely on the mailing list that it was sent out on.   On one mailing list you might expect 10 or 12 percent returns.   Another mailing list you may get 4 or 5 percent returns.

Mr. Bobo. On the business which you did in sending out and the percentage of returns, what would be your figure as to the gross annual business which you did in a year's time for the year 1952 or the last year in which——

Chairman Kefauver. Say the peak year.

Mr. Bobo. The biggest year that you had, your peak year.

Mrs. Tager. Well, of course, the peak came actually—actually the peak to this business came right after I walked out on the business and my husband and Mr. Ross, through my instructions and through another party's instructions, went all out; and I believe it is on record in the bank, something like $750,000 in a period of a very few months.

Mr. Bobo. That is your husband and Mr. Ross?

Mrs. Tager. Yes.

Mr. Bobo. And the third party was whom?

Mrs. Tager. Well, I just say on the advice of a third party.

Mr. Bobo. Who was this third party? That was advice to you from a third party?

Mrs. Tager. Yes. Yes.

Mr. Bobo. Well then, the biggest peak year in which you were connected with the business, what was the largest amount of deposits which you made in that year; your gross business?

Mrs. Tager. Well, offhand that would be a little difficult to pin down right to a figure.

Chairman Kefauver. Well, just approximately; your best remembrance.

Mr. Bobo. Is it true that you did approximately $3,000-a-day business?

Mrs. Tager. During this peak, yes. As I say, we were taking in from three to four thousand dollars a day in the mails.

Mr. Bobo. That was on strip photos and movie films?

Mrs. Tager. That is right.

Chairman Kefauver. What was it, a million-dollar-a-year business, you did, approximately that?

Mrs. Tager. I would say so. Of course, as I say, the peak to this came after I was out of it due to illness.

Mr. Bobo. Mrs. Tager, in this particular business you organized a great number of companies under a great many different names, is that correct?

Mrs. Tager. That is correct.

Mr. Bobo. Would each one of these companies be set up and have an office and be licensed to do business?

Mrs. Tager. No, sir.

Mr. Bobo. Actually would it just be a name for the purpose of receiving mail?

Mrs. Tager. That is correct, for possibly one mailing.

Mr. Bobo. And the address to which this mail would be sent, how did you determine the spot to where the mail would be sent and addressed?

Mrs. Tager. Well, it would be—it is very easy to get a post office box. There are many legitimate telephone answering services or mail receiving services. There are many offices where you can rent desk space very cheaply. So we just went from one to the other until we finally ran out of them.

Chairman Kefauver. I don't understand. Until you ran out of what?

Mrs. Tager. Of addresses around here locally.

Chairman Kefauver. You mean you just used up all the addresses you could find.

Mrs. Tager. That is right.

Chairman Kefauver. How many did you use in the course of your business, do you know?

Mrs. Tager. Well, I imagine the figure would probably run possibly 200 in the course of a couple of years.

Chairman Kefauver. 200 different addresses. These companies that you formed, were they corporate companies, were they required to register under the California law?

Mrs. Tager. No.

Chairman Kefauver. In other words, you just pick up—you had a Stand-Out Co. Is that one of your companies?

Mrs. Tager. Yes. That was registered.

Chairman Kefauver. But most of them would just be names that you would pick up and get a post office box and some kind of office space and address?

Mrs. Tager. Yes, that is correct; but, you see, that address would only be used for one mailing.

Chairman Kefauver. Used for one mailing, and then you would get your mail there and move on somewhere else?

Mrs. Tager. That is correct.

Chairman Kefauver. How long would it take to handle one mailing when you did get one of these addresses?

Mrs. Tager. Well, by the 10th day you have most of your returns in from the day that your mail is mailed, so a mail address is good for approximately 2 weeks. Then you have no more use for it.

Chairman Kefauver. Then after you got your replies back, where would you respond from; the same address?

Mrs. Tager. Well, yes. On your orders going out to the individual you would use the same address.

Chairman Kefauver. I know, but actually the orders were filled from your central office somewhere, weren't they?

Mrs. Tager. Yes.

Chairman Kefauver. You only use the mail address to get the orders in and you took the orders to your central office for the fulfilling of them?

Mrs. Tager. That is right.

Chairman Kefauver. Where was your central office?

Mrs. Tager. We had several. We were at 141 North La Brea; we were at 14006 Ventura Boulevard; we were—let me see. We had another office on Ventura Boulevard, a large one. I can't think of the number right now.

Chairman Kefauver. And those offices would be where you had the supply of films and cards and all the mailing machinery?

Mrs. Tager. Yes, sir.

Chairman Kefauver. How many did you have working in those central offices?

Mrs. Tager. Well, of course, gradually as we grew we kept adding on help. I believe at the height of this operation there were close to 50, 51, 52; in that vicinity; of girls working for us outside, of outside typists.

Chairman KEFAUVER. You mean you had that many people in the office mailing out things and typing up, and then used a lot of outside typists, too?

Mrs. TAGER. Yes.

Chairman KEFAUVER. Where would you get the outside typists?

Mrs. TAGER. Well, through any agency. I mean, women that will type names in their homes, name lists, and things like that.

Chairman KEFAUVER. Excuse me, Mr. Bobo.

Mr. BOBO. So that we may clarify some of the profits that were made in this particular business, Mrs. Tager, would you say that these prices were the approximate prices paid and the approximate prices for which the material sold: That color slides cost you two and three-quarters cents each in 100 lots, and they were sold for $3 for 6 slides?

Mrs. TAGER. That is correct.

Mr. BOBO. And that 50 feet of black and white 8-millimeter film cost 65 cents, which you sold for $4?

Mrs. TAGER. That is correct.

Mr. BOBO. And 100 feet of 16-millimeter film cost you $1.65 and sold for $7?

Mrs. TAGER. That is right.

Mr. BOBO. And color film with sound sold for as much as $70?

Mrs. TAGER. That is right.

Chairman KEFAUVER. What would that sound be?

Mrs. TAGER. Music.

Chairman KEFAUVER. You mean music to accompany the dancing or whatever they were doing?

Mrs. TAGER. Yes.

Mr. BOBO. And the volume of your business reached such a great extent at its peak, that the post office in—what is that, in Encino, Calif.—was raised from a fourth-class post office to a second-class post office?

Mrs. TAGER. That is true.

Mr. BOBO. Do you have any idea as to the amount of money spent for stamps by you in your organization in a year's time in the peak year?

Mrs. TAGER. Well, of course, I don't have any records or anything with me. I mean——

Mr. BOBO. Just approximately.

Mrs. TAGER. Well, there were many thousands of dollars. I mean, I really and truly couldn't give you an approximation on that.

Mr. BOBO. And the reason, Mrs. Tager, for the forming of all these companies and changing your address was so that you might avoid the unlawful orders and stop orders that the Post Office Department put out against you; is that correct?

Mrs. TAGER. Yes and no. Using all the different addresses had a different purpose, too. Naturally, a customer, when he buys material from you if it is not quite as risque as what he expects, he is not going to be a repeat buyer. Our purpose in using many fictitious names was for the purpose, more or less, to keep that customer buying.

Mr. BOBO. But if the post office——

Chairman KEFAUVER. Well, let's pursue that a minute. In other words, under one name, under one mailing address you would get a lot of names, and then you would sell them their orders, and you would use those same addresses with another name, maybe with a little different approach, to secure orders from the same people; they thinking that it was another company?

Mrs. TAGER. It is another company, that is correct.

Chairman KEFAUVER. And you had a lot of repeat buyers, I suppose?

Mrs. TAGER. Oh, yes, many.

Chairman KEFAUVER. How large a territory did your mailing list cover?

Mrs. TAGER. It was nationwide. Worldwide, in fact.

Chairman KEFAUVER. You mean you got orders from all States in the Nation?

Mrs. TAGER. All over the world.

Chairman KEFAUVER. All over the world? You mean Canada, Mexico?

Mrs. TAGER. Even Ceylon.

Chairman KEFAUVER. Even Ceylon. Wherever the mazaine went, why, you would get orders back?

Mrs. TAGER. That is correct.

Chairman KEFAUVER. Could you give us any estimate, say, in a peak year, how many orders you had?

Mrs. TAGER. Well, that, too, would be very difficult. They ran way up into the ——

Chairman KEFAUVER. Hundreds of thousands?

Mrs. TAGER. Well, yes, I imagine they would, with all the increase from the different magazines; yes.

Chairman KEFAUVER. Hundreds of ,thousands of orders from the world over. Did you have special rates for orders from Ceylon and Canada?

Mrs. TAGER. Well, no. No. I received much, oh, an awful lot of foreign money; an awful lot of foreign money. Of course, much of it wasn't worth the paper it is written on. I mean, as far as the exchange, they would send the proper amount, but I would send the merchandise anyway.

Chaiman KEFAUVER. You received a lot of foreign money back and you would send the merchandise anyway and get what you could out of the foreign money?

Mrs. TAGER. Yes.

Chairman KEFAUVER. Where did you bank the foreign money?

Mrs. TAGER. I didn't. I kept it as souvenirs.

Chairman KEFAUVER. Do you still have a lot of it?

Mrs. TAGER. No. My son has a collection, and I have given it to several of this boy friends to start a collection with. It is pretty well scattered.

Chairman KEFAUVER. All right, Mr. Bobo.

Mr. BOBO. Then if the post office should happen to get out an unlawful order on one of the businesses which you had, it would in no way affect your main operation?

Mrs. TAGER. Well, I believe what you mean is not the unlawful, the fictitious, don't you? There is quite a difference there on that. The unlawful would pertain to a man in business using his correct name; but a fictitious order——

Mr. BOBO. A fictitious order, a stop order to keep you from using that mailing address?

Mrs. TABER. Yes. That was no trouble.

Mr. BOBO. That wouldn't interrupt your business at all?

Mrs. TAGER. No.

Mr. BOBO. And you would move on and change to another one and still continue doing business under all the other names?

Mrs. TAGER. That is correct.

Mr. BOBO. The Post Office Department made quite an effort to crack down on your business, as well as many of the other businesses of a similar nature?

Mrs. TAGER. That is true.

Mr. BOBO. You had a great deal of trouble receiving all the mail that you were getting to answer to your advertisements?

Mrs. TAGER. Yes, sir.

Mr. BOBO. Did you find it necessary or were you ever a part of any type of organization where people in this particular business organized to evade the Post Office Department officials?

Mrs. TAGER. Well, yes. I belonged to an organization that many of the operators in this business joined. We formed a group more or less to pool our notes and try to stay in business.

Mr. BOBO. Do you have the names of any of the persons who joined in this organization with you? Do you have the name of the organization, first? Did it go under a name?

Mrs. TAGER. Yes; it did. It was all initials. In fact, I couldn't even pronounce it.

Mr. BOBO. Do you know the address of that organization?

Mrs. TAGER. Well, we met at several places. There was no permanent address.

Chairman KEFAUVER. Well, give us the best—get the best name you can.

Mr. BOBO. All right.

Mrs. TAGER. We would have our meetings at different places.

Mr. BOBO. Well, the initials? If you can't pronounce it, could you give us a close description of what the name might be?

Mrs. TAGER. No; offhand I can't. I believe it was A. S. C. A. something .

Mr. BOBO. Was it the Associated Photographers of Strippers and Nudes?

Mrs. TAGER. Well, that sounds— that could be. That could be.

Chairman KEFAUVER. Say that again.

Mr. BOBO. The Associated Photographers of Strippers and Nudes.

Mrs. TAGER. That could be.

Mr. BOBO. It was not listed under a name, but under the letters of it.

Mrs. TAGER. Yes. Yes.

Mr. BOBO. Who were some of the members of this particular organization?

Mrs. TAGERS. Well, as I say, there were several. Myself, Mr. Tager, Mr. Ross, Ann Walker.

Mr. BOBO. Do you know where Mrs. Walker lives?

Mrs. TAGER. At present, no.

Mr. BOBO. Is she in Los Angeles?

Mrs. TAGER. That I couldn't tell you. I haven't been in contact— in contact with any of these people in approximately 2 years.

Mr. BOBO. Give us some of the other names.

Mrs. TAGER. Well, there was Roy Howard.

Mr. BOBO. Do you know where he was living at the time?

Chairman KEFAUVER. I didn't understand the name.

Mrs. TAGER. Roy Howard.

Chairman KEFAUVER. Where is he now?

Mrs. TAGER. That I couldn't tell you.

Chairman KEFAUVER. In Mexico?

Mrs. TAGER. No; I understand he is back in town here somewhere, but I have not seem him.

Clayton W. Kirby.

Mr. BOBO. Is that K-i-r-b-y?

Mrs. TAGERS. That is right.

Mr. BOBO. Where does he live?

Mrs. TAGER. I imagine he is still over at Cinema Enterprises. That is on Hyperion.

Bill Door.

Mr. BOBO. Do you know where Mr. Bill Door is at the present time?

Mrs. TAGER. I believe he is in the courtroom.

Mr. BOBO. He is here. He lives in Los Angeles?

Mrs. TAGER. I couldn't tell you just where he lives.

Mr. BOBO. Well, is Mr. Door here?

Mrs. TAGER. I believe he is in the courtroom. I saw him.

Chairman KEFAUVER. He is here under subpena, I believe.

Mrs. TAGER. Yes.

Well now, there was Evan and Virginia Wilson.

Mr. BOBO. What was that first name?

Mrs. TAGER. Evan, E-v-a-n.

Mr. BOBO. Do you know where they are?

Mrs. TAGER. I believe Virginia is still in the San Fernando Valley.

Mr. BOBO. Do you know Russ Racine?

Mrs. TAGER. Yes; Russ Racine.

Mr. BOBO. How do you spell his name?

Mrs. TAGER. R-a-c-i-n-e.

Mr. BOBO. Russ Racine?

Mrs. TAGER. Yes.

Mr. BOBO. Is he still in this area?

Mrs. TAGER. I don't believe so. I believe he is up around the San Francisco area.

Mr. BOBO. Do you know Tom Cooper?

Mrs. TAGER. Yes.

Mr. BOBO. Was he a member of this association?

Mrs. TAGER. I believe—I believe he went to meetings, but the one night that he was there I wasn't there.

Mr. BOBO. Do you know Mr. Glied that might have been connected with this business?

Mrs. TAGER. Felix Glied?

Mr. BOBO. Felix Glied.

Mrs. TAGER. Yes.

Mr. BOBO. How do you spell that name, please?

Mrs. TAGER. G-l-i-e-d, isn't it? i-e-d or e-a-d. I think it is i-e-d.

Mr. BOBO. G-l-i-e-d?

Mrs. TAGER. I think so.

Mr. BOBO. Is he still in this area?

Mrs. TAGER. I believe so.

Mr. BOBO. Approximately how many members altogether did this association have?

Mrs. TAGER. Oh, I would say roughly maybe 20, because there were many that would have liked to have gotten into it, but we didn't want them in the organization.

Mr. BOBO. Well, there were approximately 20 in this association. Do you know from your association with this business how many people there are in this particular business, or were at the time that you were in it in this particular area?

Mrs. TAGER. Well, the figure is high. I believe when I was operating there must have been well over 200, at least 250 operators.

Mr. BOBO. That is all that you had knowledge of. Is that over the country or in California?

Mrs. TAGER. No. In the Los Angeles area alone.

Mr. BOBO. Do you have any idea as to the estimate of the number of people who might have been engaged in this business over the country?

Mrs. TAGER. Well, I imagine the figure is quite high because Los Angeles, I believe, is the main port for all this material. I think New York runs a close second. You have got many operators scattered through the Midwest. I would imagine several hundred operators.

Mr. BOBO. Several hundred. You are speaking of in this business, the business not of strip photos, but nude photographs and nude motion-picture films?

Mrs. TAGER. Yes.

Mr. BOBO. The purpose of this organization which the members got together and formed was what, Mrs. Tager?

Mrs. TAGER. Well, to pool our notes and more or less try to keep each other in business in the respect that when one person would be closed with a particular order from the Post Office Department, we planned on putting our heads together to see if we could come up to a solution to stay in business.

Mr. BOBO. Did you come up with a solution to stay in business as a result of this organization?

Mrs. TAGER. Well, yes and no. There were several things we learned in order to keep in business.

Mr. BOBO. What were some of these things, Mrs. Tager?

Mrs. TAGER. Well, keeping the post-office inspectors out of your files was one of them.

Mr. BOBO. How did you manage that?

Mrs. TAGER. Well, I think I was the one that stumbled onto that. I received two orders one day from separate parts of the country, the same handwriting on the signature; that is, the letter was typewritten on a standard size typewriter sheet of paper, but it had been torn in two. When I put the two pieces together they fit perfectly. The typewriter made the same mistakes. So that is what put me onto the code of how they had gotten into my files.

Mr. BOBO. In other words, mail that came in to you, you examined it very carefully?

Mrs. TAGER. Yes, sir, until we grew to the extent that I couldn't do that; but this was in the beginning.

Mr. BOBO. Some of the other methods which you arrived at from this organization to avoid the post office inspectors and to avoid the type of prosecution were what, Mrs. Tager?

Mrs. TAGER. Well, there were many things we learned. Not to drop all the mail in one particular box or one particular post office station, feeling that when a lot of mail came in it caused suspicion. If the mail was scattered it wasn't so apt to cause suspicion. I mean, there are many little things like that that were important to us to stay in business.

Mr. Bobo. Well, supose one of the members of the organization got into difficulty with either the Post Office Department or other police officials. Was there any effort made for group participation in his defense?

Mrs. Tager. Well, originally when the organization was formed, we planned on hiring an attorney to represent us if any one of us needed help. We would just pay a certain amount of dues.

Mr. Bobo. What were the dues to the organization?

Mrs. Tager. I believe it was $25 entrance fee and then I think it was agreed on $10 a month; but that agreement was made before we had contacted an attorney; in other words, not knowing what the retainer was he would want. Now, in the organization there was one stipulation made, however, that if anyone in our group was picked up for pornographic pictures, they could expect no aid from the organization; because the group at this particular time in the organization were handling just straight nudes.

Mr. Bobo. The group that you were associated with was handling none of the lewd and lascivious, really obscene perverted type of material?

Mrs. Tager. No. We were handling all more or less the same thing. That is why, as I say, there were several that would have liked to have gotten into the organization and we just didn't want them in with us.

Chairman Kefauver. Mrs. Tager, you said at that time. Did the organization deteriorate as time went on?

Mrs. Tager. Yes; it was very short-lived; very short-lived.

Chairman Kefauver. Pornographers did get into the organization?

Mrs. Tager. Yes; I believe a couple did.

Mr. Bobo. Did your dues increase at a later time? You said originally it was $25 and $10 a month. What was the final arrangement?

Mrs. Tager. Well, we made no final arrangement. I mean, the organization, we did not make arrangements with an attorney that we expected to have represent us as a group, and the organization just died.

Mr. Bobo. Did you ever hire an attorney to represent the organization or to defend any of the members in any respect?

Mrs. Tager. We approached attorneys to represent us, but we did not have one attorney to represent the whole group.

Mr. Bobo. Did any attorneys ever set as a fee, for maybe the reason you did not hire them, a certain percentage of the gross business of the organization?

Mrs. Tager. Yes.

Mr. Bobo. They would represent you and for the organization for a certain percentage?

Mrs. Tager. No, not as a group. As an individual, yes, but not as a group.

Mr. Bobo. As an individual, that was you in busines, you and Mr. Tager and Mr. Ross in business, that you had difficulty with the Post Office Department? What was the reason, Mrs. Tager, for you leaving this particular business?

Mrs. TAGER. Well, I divorced Mr. Tager.

Mr. BOBO. Is he still in the business?

Mrs. TAGER. As far as I have been told, yes.

Mr. BOBO. Is he still in business with Mr. Ross?

Mrs. TAGER. Well now, that is a difficult question. I do not believe so. I do not believe so.

Mr. BOBO. When was the last time that you were connected with the business that you got into difficulty with the post office, Mrs. Tager.

Mrs. TAGER. Well, when I was connected with this business I believe it was back in 1951 when I had a tremendous mailing going out of Las Vegas, Tucson, and Phoenix.

Mr. BOBO. You went out on business to Las Vegas, Tucson, and Phoenix?

Mrs. TAGER. Yes. I had a mailing that went out with addresses bearing Las Vegas, Phoenix, and Tucson.

Mr. BOBO. Whom did you make this trip with?

Mrs. TAGER. Well, after I had difficulty with the Post Office Department, naturally, I tried to get the mail released. My mail was being—the replies were being held up in these various post offices, so I made this trip with my attorney.

Mr BOBO. What was the purpose of this, to make an all-out mailing to get the most out of the business that you could?

Mrs. TAGER. Well, no. No. No. The purpose was that I thought that there were too many people getting mail from operators in California at the time, and I thought maybe using another State for an address might revive some of the customers that I had lost.

Mrs. BOBO. Well, what happened when you went out to make your mailings in Las Vegas, Phoenix, and Tucson, did you get into further difficulty?

Mrs. TAGER. Well, yes. After the mail was out and the orders had come in, I received word from the Post Office Department that I was closed on a fictitious order. Well, at the time I had felt that there was approximately $40,000 tied up in those three mailings, so naturally I was going to fight for it. I was told to go to Las Vegas, Phoenix, and Tucson, identify myself and my mail would be released. Well, that is not the case.

Mr. BOBO. By whom were you told if you would go to Las Vegas, Phoenix, and Tucson, and identify yourself your mail would be released?

Mrs. TAGER. By the letter from the Post Office Department in Washington.

Mr. BOBO. Was it a signed letter?

Mrs. TAGER. A form letter that they sent out.

Mr. BOBO. Yes.

Mrs. TAGER. Well, naturally, I went to these post offices with my attorney, but then, after I identified myself, they said, "You still can't have the mail."

So we tried to fight further for it. In fact, I believe we made—well, it was another trip down there before they would release it to me, because, of course, that had to come out of Washington.

Mr. BOBO. What further fight did you make for this mail, Mrs. Tager, to have it released?

Mrs. TAGER. Well, I had identified myself. I mean, even though I was closed on a fictitious order, I was not fictitious, I was not using a fictitious name in order to hide my identity. I mean, that was not the intent.

Mr. BOBO. Did you ever in the entire matter receive any information or advice that you should get a cease and desist order so that you would have thereby a solution to your troubles?

Mrs. TAGER. Yes.

Mr. BOBO. By whom, from whom did this advice come?

Mrs. TAGER. Well, I believe that his citing the cease and desist did have quite a big bearing on this mail released.

Mr. BOBO. You believe what, Mrs. Tager?

Mrs. TAGER. I believe that by my signing this cease and desist order it had quite a great bearing on the Post Office Department releasing this mail that was tied up.

Mr. BOBO. Well, Mrs. Tager——

Mrs. TAGER. You see, at the time——

Mr. BOBO. Who was the attorney that represented you in receiving this cease and desist order?

Mrs. TAGER. Stanley Caidin.

Mr. BOBO. Is he here in Los Angeles?

Mrs. TAGER. Yes. I believe he is in the courtroom here.

Mr. BOBO. Did you have an agreement with him in representing you in this matter?

Mrs. TAGER. Yes.

Mr. BOBO. What was the agreement which you had with him?

Mrs. TAGER. Well, if he could get the mail released I was to pay him 25 percent of my gross take.

Mr. BOBO. Now, on the mail that you had tied up?

Mrs. TAGER. That is right.

Mr. BOBO. Was your mail released to you?

Mrs. TAGER. Yes, sir.

Mr. BOBO. Did the amount of the 25 percent of the mail that was released to you—was that in the sum of $1,329.95, represented by this check?

Mrs. TAGER. Yes, sir. Yes, sir; that is true.

Mr. BOBO. Is that the check with which you paid Mr. Caidin for his 25 percent?

Mrs. TAGER. Yes.

Mr. BOBO. It has also marked in the lower right corner "25%"?

Mrs. TAGER. That is right.

Mr. BOBO. And that is representative of that?

Mrs. TAGER. That is correct.

Chairman KEFAUVER. That will be marked as an exhibit; exhibit 34.

Mr. BOBO. Exhibit 34.

(The check was marked "Exhibit No. 34," and appears on p. 342.)

Chairman KEFAUVER. Is that the total payment, or is that on just one of the——

Mrs. TAGER. That was just on this mailing that was made in Las Vegas, Phoenix, and Tucson.

Chairman KEFAUVER. Were there others held up that he helped you get out?

Mrs. Tager. Well, not—no. Now, he naturally helped Mr. Tager and Mr. Ross after I was out of this, but that is the one he helped me on.

Chairman Kefauver. Did he go with you to Las Vegas?

Mrs. Tager. Yes.

Chairman Kefauver. Phoenix, and Tucson?

Mrs. Tager. Yes.

Chairman Kefauver. Did you get it released at all places?

Mrs. Tager. Yes.

Chairman Kefauver. How did you get the mail back here?

Mrs. Tager. In suitcases.

Chairman Kefauver. By plane?

Mrs. Tager. Yes.

Chairman Kefauver. You just picked up, you didn't examine it there, you brought it right back to California?

Mrs. Tager. Yes, sir.

Chairman Kefauver. Did you have some trouble with it in Las Vegas?

Mrs. Tager. Well, yes. Do you mean in the respect of who would have possession of it because of this 25 percent? Yes, Mr. Caidin didn't feel that he could trust me in a room overnight with this mail, even though the mail was mine; so we had quite a discussion over who would keep the key and who would keep the mail. In fact, he even went so far as to tie the suitcases up with rope with special knots, that if I had opened them, he would know about them. So the mail was being opened at my home. Out of pure meanness I cut all the ropes off of it to give him something to think about.

Chairman Kefauver. Did you get that difficulty resolved?

Mrs. Tager. Yes.

Chairman Kefauver. When you opened it at home—you opened it at your home, you say?

Mrs. Tager. Yes.

Chairman Kefauver. Who was there when you opened it?

Mrs. Tager. Well, there was Mr. Caidin, Mr. Cummins, Oscar Commins, Daniel Bloomgarden, Mr. Ross, Mr. Tager, and myself.

Chairman Kefauver. Who are these men that you have talked about?

Mrs. Tager. At that time they were connected with Mr. Caidin. The firm was Caidin, Cummins & Bloomgarden.

Chairman Kefauver. What happened when the mail was opened, did you divide up the mail?

Mrs. Tager. Well, that was quite a hectic day. Mr. Caidin naturally wanted his share right then and there. Of course, I had to explain that that mail had been held up for several months. Naturally, many of the checks that came in that mail—the payment had been stopped on them. Many of the money orders were outdated, they were old, so that I wouldn't know actually the total of that mailing for some time, until these checks and money orders had cleared.

Chairman Kefauver. What was the total amount as of that day in the checks and the money orders?

Mrs. Tager. Well, that is kind of hard. I wish I had brought some of these records with me.

Chairman Kefauver. Was it around——

Mrs. Tager. I know we took a terrible loss on it.

Chairman KEFAUVER. Was it around $26,000?

Mrs. TAGER. Somewhere in that vicinity, I would say.

Chairman KEFAUVER. Then you found that a lot of checks and mail orders had been stopped on you?

Mrs. TAGER. That is right.

Chairman KEFAUVER. So that after the amounts stopped and you got to the net, then this check represents 25 percent of the net?

Mrs. TAGER. Twenty-five percent of what we cleared.

Chairman KEFAUVER. All right. While we have a pause, you were talking about putting mail in different post offices. As a matter of fact, you would load up your car and just go from town to town up and down the coast here?

Mrs. TAGER. That is true.

Chairman KEFAUVER. And put mail in all the post offices?

Mrs. TAGER. That is true.

Chairman KEFAUVER. Spread it out. Did you go to Arizona, Nevada several times with mailings?

Mrs. TAGER. No. Just once that I went to Arizona. The first time to employ the services of these people running these mail addresses. Then I came back, prepared the mailing, and Mr. Tager and Mr. Ross took it to Arizona and Las Vegas and mailed it.

Chairman KEFAUVER. Did Mr. Caidin just represent the whole group, or did he have an independent arrangement with Mr. Ross and your husband aside from his arrangement with you?

Mrs. TAGER. Well, yes. The arrangement, as I say—now, this 25 percent to have this mail released for me, now, Mr. Caidin was to keep Mr. Ross and Mr. Tager in business for a percentage of their business.

Chairman KEFAUVER. Do you know what that arrangement was?

Mrs. TAGER. I believe 10 percent.

Chairman KEFAUVER. That was separate and apart from this check?

Mrs. TAGER. Well, yes. You see, after his episode took place it wasn't too long after that that I had many trips in and out of hospitals. Even though I knew what was going on in the business, I was not active in it.

Chairman KEFAUVER. Do you know how much this second arrangement paid Mr. Caidin about a month?

Mrs. TAGER. Well, you know, there are many things that a person knows, but you can't really prove.

Chairman KEFAUVER. Well, if you don't know——

Mrs. TAGER. This is one of these things.

Chairman KEFAUVER. If you don't know, don't say. If you don't know, why, then don't say.

Mrs. TAGER. I know there has been cash and checks. I would say Mr. Caidin was drawing $1,500 or better a month.

Chairman KEFAUVER. All right.

Mr. BOBO. Did you keep two sets of books in your operation, Mrs. Tager, when you were operating?

Mrs. TAGER. Yes, sir; I did.

Mr. BOBO. What was the purpose of keeping two sets of books?

Mrs. TAGER. Well, when this approach was made to keep us in business for a percentage, you know no one can stay in business and give someone 10 percent of their gross, especially where it is a partnership. When this percentage was arranged with Mr. Caidin, I spoke it over with Mr. Tager and I advised 2 sets of books, 1 for Mr. Caidin's benefit, because I felt if Mr. Caidin received $1,500 a month or better, he would be very satisfied, without receiving actually 10 percent of the gross.

Mr. Bobo. Did you show the same set of books to the Internal Revenue Bureau?

Mrs. Tager. No. The Internal Revenue Bureau had the proper books. This other set, as I say, was set up for Mr. Caidin's benefit only, and it was done at the proper time, because Mr. Caidin sent his auditors down to audit the books to make sure he was getting his 10 percent.

Chairman Kefauver. Which set of books did they audit?

Mrs. Tager. The ones put up for their benefit.

Chairman Kefauver. They didn't audit the other books?

Mrs. Tager. No.

Chairman Kefauver. What would be the difference in the income on the two sets of books, about? I mean, would one be twice as much income as the other one?

Mrs. Tager. Well, yes; possibly more. But, as I say, to give someone 10 percent of a gross business, that is quite a lot. It can't be done.

Chairman Kefauver. Go ahead, Mr. Bobo.

Who was president of this association you have been talking about?

Mrs. Tager. Of the organization?

Chairman Kefauver. Of the organization.

Mrs. Tager. Well, actually, I believe Merle Kennel was the president of it. Ann Walker was the treasurer-secretary.

Chairman Kefauver. Did you have an office in it?

Mrs. Tager. No; I did not.

Mr. Bobo. Did you ever receive any type of mailing lists from Mr. Caidin in his connection with the business? Did he ever present to you any mailing list of any sort?

Mr. Bobo. What type of mailing list did you receive from him?

Mrs. Tager. Well, it was supposedly a list that is kept by inspectors, of buyers of nude pictures, for their own benefit.

Mr. Bobo. Do you know what the origin of this particular list was?

Mrs. Tager. Well, as I say, it came out of Washington.

Mr. Bobo. Is just came—you don't know——

Mrs. Tager. No.

Mr. Bobo. Definitely the origin of this?

Mrs. Tager. That is what I was led to believe, anyway.

Mrs. Bobo. Mrs. Tager, how many times have you been in difficulty with the law?

Mrs. Tager. Once.

Mr. Bobo. Where was that?

Mrs. Tager. That was back in Rhode Island.

Mr. Bobo. Was it in connection with this business?

Mrs. Tager. Yes; it was.

Mr. Bobo. What were the circumstances surrounding that?

Mrs. Tager. Last September I was accused of mailing one obscene picture through the mails on or about the 18th of August. I was arrested. My bail was set at $2,000. Then four more counts were added to the original one, which that charge made up a count. In other words, the names of four people who I am supposed to have mailed pictures to were each considered a count. I did not do this thing, but, of course, that is not neither here nor there right now; but I know who did.   This particular person I sold some mailing lists to, because I needed the money at the time.   In fact, I did some typing for him in my home.

Mr. Bobo. Who is the person to whom you sold your mailing list?

Mrs. Tager. Calvin Sugarman.

Mr. Bobo. How do you spell it?

Mrs. Tager. S-u-g-a-r-m-a-n.

Mr. Bobo. Where does he reside?

Mrs. Tager. In Providence, R. I.

Mr. Bobo. Do you have his address there?

Mrs. Tager. On Hope Street.

Mr. Bobo. H-o-p-e.

Mrs. Tager. Hope.

Mr. Bobo. Did you ever engage in the business in Rhode Island?

Mrs. Tager. No, sir; I have not.

Mr. Bobo. Did you sell the mailing list which you had to any persons in any other part of the country?

Mrs. Tager. Not since I have been out of the business; no.

Mr. Bobo. Is that the only mailing list you sold within recent times?

Mrs. Tager. Oh, yes.   Yes.

Mr. Bobo. Did you ever, while you were in California connected with this business—you had numerous fictitious orders against you and your business?

Mrs. Tager. Yes, sir.

Mr. Bobo. That is the only difficulty you have had with any of the law-enforcement agencies or the courts on the coast?

Mrs. Tager. That is right.

Mr. Bobo. Are you on probation now?

Mrs. Tager. Yes, sir; I am.   I had to plead guilty to this charge, otherwise I would be in jail 5 months; and as it stands, circumstantial evidence plus the fact there is—well, Calvin Sugarman, his family is quite influential.   I was told before I went back to Rhode Island that I wouldn't stand a chance if I brought him in to it, because his family is not, if they can prevent it, going to have his name in the headlines.

Mr. Bobo. You are not engaged in this business in any way at the present time?

Mrs. Tager. No, sir.   I have not been since 1951.

Mr. Bobo. And Mr. Ross or Mr. Tager, your husband, and his partner, have they ever been in any difficulty with the authorities, even been charged with anything?

Mrs. Tager. Yes; they have had many charges, but I think—in fact, they have been arrested a few times, but as far as I know Mr. Tager has only paid a $600 fine.   Mr. Ross did serve a term, a short term for bribery.

Mr. Bobo. The $600 fine was involved in a case involving this type of material, or pornographic material?

Mrs. Tager. Yes, yes—no, this type of material.

Mr. Bobo. Has he ever served any time?   Mr. Tager has never served any time?

Mrs. Tager. Not that I know of.

Chairman Kefauver. Well, I believe that is all now, Mrs. Tager. Some matters that we might want to ask you about further might come up, so you stay around, will you?

Mrs. Tager. Yes.

Chairman Kefauver. We will have a 10-minute recess at this time. (Short recess taken.)

Chairman Kefauver. The subcommittee will come to order.

Expressing my thanks to some of you who have helped us so much this morning, I want to thank and express our appreciation for the help of the Los Angeles district attorney's office, Mr. Roll, and others of his staff. Also the United States attorney and his staff, Mr. Waters, and Mr. Billings, and many others. We are going to try to hear as many witnesses as possible today. Mrs. Tager and others possibly will mention other names. We don't want to do anyone an injustice. If anyone's name has been mentioned and they feel that they have not been correctly presented or if they have some statement they want to make, an explanation or a chance to be heard, if they will let the staff of the subcommittee know, we will see that they have a chance of being heard immediately, because we don't want any charges to go out without any explanation that anyone wants to make in connection with them.

Mr. Stanley Caidin's name has been mentioned. He is a member of the bar of Los Angeles and California. He is here and has asked to be heard next.

Mr. Caidin, would you come around, sir? Just come up here, Mr. Caidin, and have a seat.

Mr. Caidin. Well, in view——

Senator Kefauver. Well, if you——

Mr. Caidin. Can I request not to be photographed? I guess not. Do I have that right?

Chairman Kefauver. Well, I don't know, Mr. Caidin.

Mr. Caidin. Well, it doesn't matter. I am photographed.

Chairman Kefauver. Will you hold up your hand, sir, and be sworn. (Mr. Caidin was sworn.)

Chairman Kefauver. All right, Mr. Bobo, will you take over.

TESTIMONY OF STANLEY R. CAIDIN, ATTORNEY AT LAW, BEVERLY HILLS, CALIF.

Mr. Bobo. State your name and your address, and your occupation for the record.

Mr. Caidin. My name is Stanley R. Caidin. My business address is 9441 Wilshire Boulevard in Beverly Hills. My home address is 10383 Rochester Avenue in west Los Angeles.

Mr. Bobo. Mr. Caidin, you stated you wanted to reply to some of the things which Mrs. Tager has said.

Mr. Caidin. Well, of course——

Chairman Kefauver. Well, you just tell all about it, Mr. Caidin. Make any statements you want to make.

Mr. Caidin. I was, of course, quite shocked, sitting back there, to hear the nature and the type of accusations made by Mrs. Tager; and my primary purposes, actually, is not to answer point by point the testimony of Mrs. Tager, because to do that would be to dignify it with a certain amount of credibility. There is—there are some things I would like to say, since my name was mentioned in the manner it was.

Firstly, most of what Mrs. Tager said was false. There was a grain or a salt of truth in a portion of her testimony, and in a considerable portion of it from there on she went on a wild flight of imagination, and much of her testimony is false.

I regret that I have to be in a position where, frankly, the accusations of a woman who has been convicted of a crime and who was here for her own purposes, and having thrown about and made accusations against people which will undoubtedly receive publicity is very distressing. I don't think, very frankly, if I may criticize the committee, and do so respectfully, I would like to do so.

Chairman KEFAUVER. Well, you can criticize the subcommittee all you want to.

Mr. CAIDIN. And I do as I do respectfully, and I do it as follows: Of course, you are a Senator, Mr. Senator, and Mr. Bobo is a well-known attorney himself, and I think all people who are accused at this hearing—that an investigation should have been made as to the charges, so that this publicity could have been avoided. If there was any merit in the charges and the committee felt there was—but, the effects of wild accusations made by a woman of that type are in effect to intimidate attorneys and to prevent in large measure people of this—engaged in business from the right to counsel for this reason: Naturally, any attorney would not wish to be named as I have been named and dishonored publicly. My primary concern is this, that if this course of procedure is followed and other witnesses are permitted to make accusations of this type, knowing that publicity will follow, attorneys will be reluctant, and rightfully so, in going into court to defend the rights of these people.

Now, I would like one thing clear, and that is this: Although this has been designated as an investigation of pornographic material, there is no showing—there has been no introduction of any of the material to show it has been pornographic. Therefore, the public has been led to believe that this is an investigation of so-called pornographic material. Yet the facts are that this material has been passed upon by the courts, that these people have been engaged in business under an injunction granted by the courts and have been operating with the sanction of the courts and openly and publicly. This is not an underground operation. These people are operating a business. The courts have inspected and examined the merchandise.

Now, I am not saying that for all the people, but of the persons who are operating under court injunction.

Chairman KEFAUVER. Well, Mr. Caidin, what injunction are you speaking of, sir?

Mr. CAIDIN. Well, there are several injunctions that have been in effect. One was granted under which Mr. Tager was engaged in his business originally on the grounds—well, he was operating on a restraining order granted by the Federal court some years ago; and at the time that Mrs. Tager was testifying to, there was a restraining order in effect by which the business was permitted to continue without interference from the Post Office Department.

Chairman KEFAUVER. A restraining order against whom?

Mr. CAIDIN. Against Roy Ross—I am sorry. That is against the Post Office Department.

Chairman KEFAUVER. Who was this attorney in getting that restraining order?

Mr. CAIDIN. I was the attorney who got the restraining order.

Chairman KEFAUVER. Well, Mr. Caidin, we have had descriptions of the material which was involved. Do you disagree with the description of the pictures and the advertising and the method of operation described by Mrs. Tager?

Mr. CAIDIN. No. The materials sold were nude photographs of the Marilyn Monroe calendar type, that is correct, and the courts do not consider them obscene here in California, apparently.

Chairman KEFAUVER. Well, if it is all within the law, I don't see why you are excited about it.

Mr. CAIDIN. Well, I am excited because the testimony of Mrs. Tager taken by itself would lead people to believe that I was an ogre of some type, which I assure you I am not. I have tried to do——

Chairman KEFAUVER. Well, of course, lawyers very frequently represent the most heinous criminals—not saying Mrs. Tager is a criminal—but lawyers protect them in their rights. Courts always appoint lawyers to protect criminal defendants when they don't have lawyers of their own; so even if this has been a flagrant law violation and if you just acted as a lawyer in representing them, I don't see why you should be so excited about it, Mr. Caidin. I think Mrs. Tager's story, the testimony she has given, shows the flourishing of a very substantial business; and she has told about how you were connected with the business, what you did as her attorney.

What part of her story is not true, Mr. Caidin?

Mr. CAIDIN. Well, firstly, she stated that I was paid on a percentage basis and that I—that they kept two sets of books, one which was shown me and one which they showed for other purposes. That is absolutely false. Now, I will say this——

Chairman KEFAUVER. Well now, on the percentage basis, have you seen this check?

Mr. CAIDIN. I meant generally. Yes.

Let me go into that, if I may, although I don't think it is proper, again, for the reason that the arrangement between an attorney and his client is not the concern of this committee; but since it was mentioned as though it were an improper thing, I would like to explain these circumstances, then. Firstly, when the client first came to my office, I might point out that he was out of business. The Post Office Department had impounded all incoming mail.

Chairman KEFAUVER. Now, who is that, Mrs. Tager?

Mr. CAIDIN. No. This is Mr. Ross. Mr. Ross came to the office, advising me that he was out of business. He said the Post Office Department was impounding his mail. He had another attorney who had not had any success with the case.

Chairman KEFAUVER. About when was this, Mr. Caidin?

Mr. CAIDIN. It was maybe 4 years ago, I guess. I am not sure of the date. 1952, maybe.

Chairman KEFAUVER. About 4 years ago, then, all right.

Mr. CAIDIN. Approximately. Anyway, I was young and fresh out of law school at the time.

Chairman KEFAUVER. Well now, Mr. Caidin, was that the first connection you had with it, 4 years ago. This check seems to be dated June 13, 1950.

Mr. CAIDIN. Then that would be correct. It was before 1950, then. It was before that check.

May I see the check, please? It seemed like—4 years seems like a long time, but I guess it has been longer than that. May I see the check?

Chairman KEFAUVER. Let's see. It is dated June 13, 1950, apparently, but it seems to have been deposited on June 14, 1951.

Mr. CAIDIN. Well, that mistake is on the check, then. The bank mark would be correct, obviously.

Chairman KEFAUVER. Yes.

Mr. CAIDIN. The error was on the check, then.

Chairman KEFAUVER. That is unless it was held up in being deposited.

Mr. CAIDIN. Not for a year, no, no, I am certain it wasn't held up for a year, Senator. The 1951 date would be correct, and the date on the face of the check, then, would be incorrect; so my 4-year estimate would be very good. In fact, it is apparently exactly 4 years. The check was dated June 14, 1951. That is the bank stamp.

Chairman KEFAUVER. That is when it was deposited?

Let the check be an exhibit.

(The check was submitted earlier, marked "Exhibit No. 34," and is as follows:)

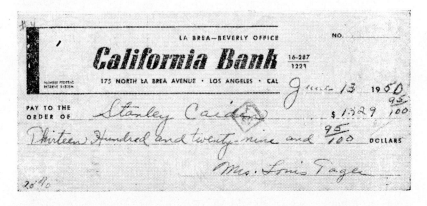

Mr. CAIDIN. Yes. At any rate, I was—this gentleman came to my office, told me briefly he had been in the mail-order business selling various types of merchandise, including lamps and novelties and pictures; that the post office had closed him off by cutting off all of his mail.

I said that seemed like a high-handed procedure, and I asked him what type of material he was selling, sending.

He showed me some photographs which were photographs of the Marilyn Monroe type picture which are seen frequently on calendars and are no more or less suggestive than the posters which the motion-picture companies, in my opinion, at least, were using for advertising their films. I told him I didn't think that material was obscene. In any event, it didn't seem to me that the Post Office Department in a unilateral action should determine it to be obscene; that if the Post Office Department had the right to impound mail on the belief of somebody that it might be obscene because someone in the post office didn't like it it didn't seem to me that that type of censorship was fair or proper. There had never been a hearing of any consequence and the mail had been seized.

Chairman KEFAUVER. Well now, Mr. Caidin, hadn't the Los Angeles Police Department secured convictions against people dealing in this type of material?

Mr. CAIDIN. Not to my knowledge, no, sir.

Chairman KEFAUVER. Against Mr. Ross? Wasn't Mr. Ross convicted here in Los Angeles?

Mr. CAIDIN. That was long, long after he came to my office, sir.

Chairman KEFAUVER. But it was over the same material, the same type of material you are talking about?

Mr. CAIDIN. I don't know whether he was convicted or whether he pleaded guilty, as a matter of fact.

Chairman KEFAUVER. Well, anyway, he was found to be guilty, either voluntarily or by conviction.

Mr. CAIDIN. That is correct.

Chairman KEFAUVER. All right, sir.

Mr. CAIDIN. But at the time he came to me he had no prior convictions of any kind, to my knowledge, certainly; and I told him that this was a matter which should be tested in the courts, as to whether the Post Office Department has the right to seize people's mail without a formal adjudication by any court that the material was unmailable; and I said it didn't appear to me that it was unmailable. So I filed a lawsuit and, incidentally, this was at the time the discussion of fees came into it. I hesitated to go into it because, as I say, I don't think the matter of an attorney's fees is relevant to a matter of juvenile delinquency. Mr. Ross told me he didn't have a dime, couldn't pay any money for attorney's fees, and couldn't pay attorney's fees. I told him if he couldn't pay attorney's fees, then I couldn't represent him.

He said, he just was broke, they just closed down his business. He didn't have 10 cents of money coming in, and he was completely destitute. In effect, that is what he told me.

I said, "Well, how do you expect me to take a case without any agreement for compensation?"

It was then that it was agreed upon that he would pay me a small retainer and 10 percent of the business if the case was successful; and that was agreeable to him, and, of course, in my mind if the courts held that the business was a proper one and that there was nothing wrong with it and that he would be operating under a court restraining order, I certainly saw and do not see any impropriety in any such arrangement. If there were, I never would have made it. I felt the pictures were not obscene, the court would not find them obscene; and since he couldn't pay attorney's fees and was entitled to representation, and this was a reasonable basis for proceeding, and we did proceed on this basis.

Chairman KEFAUVER. Let me see what your agreement was. Ten percent of the amount realized from gross sales?

Mr. CAIDIN. Yes. Of course, very frankly, I didn't know what the gross sales would be. I had no conception of what that fee would come to, whether it would be a high fee or a low fee. I didn't know whether we would be successful in the court action, although I believed we would because I thought the material was not obscene and I didn't believe the court would find it obscene.

Chairman KEFAUVER. Well, was it your understanding that if you won the case, it was going to be 10 percent from then on out as long as he was in business?

Mr. CAIDIN. I don't remember the exact terms of the retainer agreement. It has been 4 years. It either was for a period of time, so long as he shall continue in business, or for a specified period, whichever occurs first. I am not sure of the wording of the retainer agreement, but I don't have it with me; but it was for 10 percent for a period which hadn't expired, at any rate. I don't know what the exact term was; but, anyway, we were successful and obtained a restraining order in the court. As a matter of fact, it was a three-judge court hearing held here in the Federal Building, and the matter was taken under submission for some length of time.

The 10 percent agreement, incidentally, was never observed and I never saw any set of books, no set of books was ever submitted. It is true that some accountants did go into the business, but I never really did anything, I mean.

Chairman KEFAUVER. Well, Mrs. Tager said that you sent an auditor over to see the books and that she showed them the books with the lesser amount.

Mr. CAIDIN. Well, I have no knowledge of what books were shown the auditors.

Chairman KEFAUVER. Did you send auditors over to see the books?

Mr. CAIDIN. Yes, sir. According to the auditors I was being underpaid by either 25 or 35 thousand. By my own auditors, and, I don't know, it was agreed, at any rate, instead of a percentage, that a retainer agreement be made, which I think was $1,500 a month, and that was in substitution of any percentage agreement. I was satisfied because, very frankly, I didn't intend to—I didn't know what the percentage would be, and I felt that $1,500 a month was a fair fee, certainly, and I had no quarrel with it; and that was——

Chairman KEFAUVER. $1,500 a month?

Mr. CAIDIN. Yes.

Chairman KEFAUVER. Was that after the case had been settled?

Mr. CAIDIN. I beg your pardon?

Chairman KEFAUVER. Was that after the case had been decided and they were allowed to operate?

Mr. CAIDIN. Oh, yes.

Chairman KEFAUVER. How much did you get under this 10 percent arrangement?

Mr. CAIDIN. As far as I know, I got nothing under the 10 percent arrangement. I received a payment—this, of course, I am going way back now. I have to give estimates. I received a payment of, I think, $400 a month, $600, $800, and then $1,200; and then finally they settled on $1,500. They never—I was never submitted any accounting of the business. I would just get a check, and it would be for some amount like 6, 8, 700, I don't know what it was now; and finally at the end of the time we agreed on $1,500 as a retainer. I never enforced any 10 percent agreement and never tried to.

Chairman KEFAUVER. Well, did you get 10 percent as long as the business operated?

Mr. CAIDIN. I never got 10 percent, sir.

Chairman KEFAUVER. Well, I thought you said—well, you got $1,500 a month, then?

Mr. CAIDIN. Yes, sir.

Chairman KEFAUVER. As long as it operated, or do you still get it?

Mr. CAIDIN. No, no, sir. I haven't received it for years. I think I only received $1,500—I think for about 6 or 7 or 8 months, no more than that. Six or seven months, I think it was; and then the total I received was probably, from that phase of my representation, I think was about probably ten or twelve thousand dollars. I am not sure. It was in the neighborhood of $10,000.

But, as I say again, I hate to be here justifying what fee I charged. I don't think this has got anything to do with juvenile delinquency.

Chairman KEFAUVER. Well, I think the way this operation goes on is important from the viewpoint of our inquiry, Mr. Caidin.

Mr. CAIDIN. Well, I would be happy to cooperate and answer any questions.

Chairman KEFAUVER. Well, you go on and tell all about it. What was it you said about $35,000 that auditors found that you were being underpaid?

Mr. CAIDIN. I don't remember the figure. It was a substantial amount. I don't know whether it was 25,000, 35,000, or 20 or 40. I don't recall, frankly; but if the 10-percent agreement had been kept in effect, it would have been substantially more.

Chairman KEFAUVER. Yes.

Mr. CAIDIN. But, as I say, I never attempted to enforce that, and I think there was some testimony here that I turned over a list—was that the testimony of Mrs. Tager, sir? I missed it. Did you ask Mrs. Tager if I turned over some names to the business? Was that question asked?

Mr. BOBO. Yes, sir.

Mr. CAIDIN. That is absolutely false?

Chairman KEFAUVER. No. I think she said—I believe she said it came from Mr. Cummins.

Mr. BOBO. No. She said Mr. Caidin furnished a list of customers from Washington, D. C.

Mr. CAIDIN. If that is her testimony, that is absolutely false.

Chairman KEFAUVER. Let's get is straight, now. Where is Mrs. Tager. Just stand up.

Who was it you said in the law firm furnished you with a list of names?

Mrs. Tager. Mr. Caidin.

Chairman Kefauver. When was that?

Mrs. Tager. It was a list of 60,000 names. They supposedly came from Washington.

Chairman Kefauver. Did he bring them to you personally and give them to you?

Mrs. Tager. Yes. They were brought to the office, and I didn't want any part of them; but they supposedly came from the files in Washington.

Chairman Kefauver. From somebody in Washington?

Mrs. Tager. In other words, if I had sent out a mailing on these 60,000 names, they were supposedly people—repeat buyers that the Post Office Department had kept a file on. In other words, every one of those names would have ordered, they would have brought in money.

Chairman Kefauver. All right. Anyway, we are just interested in clarifying your testimony.

Mr. Caidin. That is absolutely false, 100—I never heard such false testimony in my life. It is completely and absolutely false. That is perjury, unquestioned perjury; and it is no more true than her fantastic statements about 60 percent of her customers being doctors.

This woman should not be permitted to make accusations like this. It is absolutely false. I have never heard—I am shocked even to think that that statement would be made, that I would submit a name. I not only have not submitted 60,000 names——

Chairman Kefauver. Well, Mr. Caidin, you have no objection to the business, so I don't see why submitting names should make any difference.

Mr. Caidin. Well, I have an objection to the business if the business were improper or judicially determined——

Chairman Kefauver. Well, you said it had not been judicially determined to be improper and you had no compunction about it, so I don't see why you are so excited about names. If a business is all right, why shouldn't you submit all the names you want to?

Mr. Caidin. Well, I certainly don't—I am not in business with any client. I don't submit names or I don't submit customers to any client, and the statement that I submitted names is just absolutely false.

Chairman Kefauver. Well, I mean, if you thought the business was all right, and you said you thought it was all right, I don't see why helping your client in the business wouldn't be—why you have any objection to that. After all, you were supposed to get 10 percent of the gross. It might enhance your business. It might enhance your fee.

Mr. Caidin. As I explained, Senator, I was not receiving 10 percent of the gross.

Chairman Kefauver. I know. You were supposed to.

Mr. Caidin. I never attempted to obtain 10 percent.

Chairman Kefauver. That was the agreement.

Mr. Caidin. Yes, sir, but I was not receiving 10 percent of the gross, and it was not to my benefit to increase business or help business or participate in business; and it just isn't so. That is all. If a person testifies——

Senator Kefauver. Well, if you didn't expect to receive 10 percent, what did you make an agreement to that effect for?

Mr. CAIDIN. Because that was the only basis upon which I could be compensated. I had no idea what 10 percent would be.

Frankly, I am not trying to apologize for 10 percent. If a client comes to me without any funds and I think he is entitled to representation, I will make a contingent representation with him.

Chairman KEFAUVER. All right, sir.

Mr. CAIDIN. Is there anything else?

Chairman KEFAUVER. No. You just tell anything you want to about it.

She particularly talked about the trip over to Las Vegas or somewhere.

Mr. CAIDIN. I think she testified that I went with her to Las Vegas when they made a mailing. That is false.

I did go to Las Vegas after the mail had been impounded, not for mailing.

Chairman KEFAUVER. No; she didn't say you went there to make the mailing, I don't believe. She said after the mailing was tied up, then you and she went to Las Vegas.

Mr. CAIDIN. That is true. I went with her to obtain the release of the mail.

Chairman KEFAUVER. And to Tucson and Phoenix.

Mr. CAIDIN. That is correct; and I appeared at the post office and presented legal affidavits. I appeared as her counsel before the inspectors in the Post Office Department to obtain release of the mail.

Chairman KEFAUVER. And you got some cease and desist order?

Mr. CAIDIN. That is correct.

Chairman KEFAUVER. In the courts, or where did you get it?

Mr. CAIDIN. From Washington. It was forwarded by the Post Office Department.

Chairman KEFAUVER. Then did you have some difficulty about tying up the bundles?

Mr. CAIDIN. I have no recollection of any difficulty in tying up bundles. I think there was a discussion——

Chairman KEFAUVER. That you ought to keep them, rather than she?

Mr. CAIDIN. Yes; there was such a discussion. I am just trying to recall exactly what happened.

Chairman KEFAUVER. Well, did you get a rope and tie the packages up?

Mr. CAIDIN. I have no recollection. It is possible. I don't deny that, though. I might have tied it. I don't remember getting a rope. I don't know where I could have gotten a rope.

Chairman KEFAUVER. Well, a big string?

Mr. CAIDIN. No. I don't recall tying up packages.

Chairman KEFAUVER. What was the discussion about who was going to keep the packages?

Mr. CAIDIN. Well, Mrs. Tager was so insistent that she keep the packages, that I told her I didn't see why she should be so insistent upon it; and she finally says that apparently she didn't trust me or I didn't—I don't know, or I didn't trust her. I don't know, but there was some discussion about where the suitcases would be.

Chairman KEFAUVER. Anyway, there was a lack of mutual trust in the matter somewhere.

Mr. CAIDIN. At that point, after my auditors' check, I think there was a certain amount of distrust crept into the matter. But, in any event, my statement has been lost here in the questioning; what I was trying to get at is this: I don't feel that as an attorney I have ever done anything except represent my clients properly and ethically, and at the hearing this morning, the way the charges and the nature of Mrs. Tager's testimony, contrary to her impressions, would be gleaned——

Chairman KEFAUVER. Well, Mr. Caidin, did you know they were operating under all these different names in getting mailings in different names?

Mr. CAIDIN. Yes; I knew that.

Chairman KEFAUVER. Do you think that was a little odd?

Mr. CAIDIN. No, sir; I knew why it was being done.

Chairman KEFAUVER. And why was it being done? You knew why——

Mr. CAIDIN. I am just trying to think. I am not so sure now. I am not so sure I knew why it was being done.

I will tell you, Senator, as I recall now, I didn't know that mailings were being made under these different names until after the mail had been impounded. In other words, they never consulted with me and said they were going to make a mailing under the name of Joe Smith in a certain territory. I did not know it prior to any mailings.

Now, what did happen was this: After a mail—after certain mail would be impounded, perhaps, then I would learn for the first time that a mailing had been made and had been impounded. Then I would learn that a mailing had been made under a different name. That would be the first time I would know about it.

Chairman KEFAUVER. That didn't make any difference to you?

Mr. CAIDIN. It was the same merchandise. If it was not obscene and it was proper merchandise under the law, no, I don't care what name they mailed it under.

Chairman KEFAUVER. You didn't stop representing them when you found that out?

Mr. CAIDIN. No, sir. I saw nothing wrong with it. As long as the merchandise was proper and could go through the mails properly, I saw no reason.

Chairman KEFAUVER. What was the reason they used so many different names? You said you knew. What was the reason?

Mr. CAIDIN. Well, Mrs. Tager—I am not so sure I knew, now. It might be—I don't know, to tell you the truth, except Mrs. Tager said it helps business. I really—I don't know. I do know, apparently, if Mrs. Tager's testimony is accurate.

Chairman KEFAUVER. You don't think it had anything to do with sort of avoiding postal inspectors?

Mr. CAIDIN. No, sir. I will tell you why. That is—I am not being facetious—I would say no, absolutely not, because they didn't have to use different names. They were operating under a court restraining order, and all the mail was being delivered to their home door, to the business there, and there was no use to use fictitious names to assure mail delivery, and all the mail was being received, so it is not true that they were doing this to avoid postal laws. There couldn't be a reason for it.

Chairman KEFAUVER. What name did you get the restraining order in?

Mr. CAIDIN. Roy J. Ross.

Chairman KEFAUVER. But there were a whole lot of other names where Mr. Ross' name didn't appear, weren't there; a lot of names and advertisements?

Mr. CAIDIN. I don't know.

Chairman KEFAUVER. When you got the restraining order, when did you get it, Mr. Caidin?

Mr. CAIDIN. I don't recall the date.

Chairman KEFAUVER. Then, what happened to Mr. Ross after this Nevada business? What happened to Mr. Ross?

Oh, yes. One other thing I think you ought to explain. Mrs. Tager said that you brought the mail back in suitcases and you came with her on the plane. That was true?

Mr. CAIDIN. That is true.

Chairman KEFAUVER. And then that you had a meeting, and I think you ought to explain this, at somebody's home; where she was there and you were there and others were there.

Mr. CAIDIN. That is correct.

Chairman KEFAUVER. Who all were there? Did she name the right people? What was the purpose of this meeting?

Mr. CAIDIN. To open the mail.

Chairman KEFAUVER. Were your partners there at the same time?

Mr. CAIDIN. I don't recall. No—I think she mentioned Mr. Bloomgarden's name. I don't know. He might have been there. If he was there, he didn't stay long. He might have dropped in. I don't think he was there during the meeting; no.

Chairman KEFAUVER. Then when you opened the mail, what did you do? I mean, who opened the mail?

Mr. CAIDIN. I don't recall. I was sitting there at a table when the mail was being opened.

Chairman KEFAUVER. Did all of you keep accounts as to how much the orders were?

Mr. CAIDIN. Probably. I didn't keep accounts. I mean I was there.

Chairman KEFAUVER. Well, who was keeping accounts for you.

Mr. CAIDIN. I don't recall. I might have. I might have made notes, too. I don't recall.

Chairman KEFAUVER. Was there some argument about the fact that since this mail was so old, that many checks might have had payment stopped on them?

Mr. CAIDIN. That was discussed, yes; because, as I said, the agreement was if I succeeded in releasing the mail, it was a percentage agreement on that; and they said that the checks might not be good. That is correct. There was such a discussion.

Chairman KEFAUVER. So it was finally agreed to wait until the checks cleared to see what it was?

Mr. CAIDIN. Yes, sir.

Chairman KEFAUVER. And that is when this check was made?

Mr. CAIDIN. Probably. Probably.

Chairman KEFAUVER. All right, sir. Then what happened to Mr. Ross? How long did you continue to represent him, Mr. Caidin?

Mr. CAIDIN. Oh, I don't know.

Chairman KEFAUVER. I mean, a year, 2 years?

Mr. CAIDIN. It might have been a year. I don't know. It might have been 6 months, a year. Actually, now, Senator——

Chairman KEFAUVER. Well, did he finally get indicted in Kansas?

Mr. CAIDIN. There was an action brought in Kansas which was dismissed.

Chairman KEFAUVER. Did you represent him there?

Mr. CAIDIN. No, sir; I did not. I counseled him.

Chairman KEFAUVER. We have here the indictment in Kansas, 89 counts. All the counts are sending material to children under 21 years of age; some of them 11, some 14. Did you know anything about that?

Mr. CAIDIN. I know there was an action filed in Kansas and Mr. Ross talked to me about it. The action was dismissed.

Chairman KEFAUVER. Why did it get dismissed?

Mr. CAIDIN. It was dismissed because the court in Kansas had no jurisdiction to try the case, and the case was later refiled here in the Los Angeles Federal court, and Mr. Ross went to trial and was acquitted. The merchandise was found by the court to be not obscene. It was heard right here, and the merchandise and the pictures and the films were seen by the Federal court judge here in Los Angeles, sir, and the court found that none of the material sent by Mr. Ross was obscene, and Mr. Ross was acquitted after a trial.

Chairman KEFAUVER. Did you represent him in that trial?

Mr. CAIDIN. No, sir; I did not.

Chairman KEFAUVER. Well, did Mr. Ross get convicted in the State courts here in Los Angeles, then?

Mr. CAIDIN. I have heard that to be the case.

Chairman KEFAUVER. But you didn't represent him?

Mr. CAIDIN. I did not represent him.

Chairman KEFAUVER. How did you happen to stop representing him?

Mr. CAIDIN. He stopped coming to see me. I don't recall. I never had a conversation in which he said, "You no longer represent me"; and I never told him, "I no longer represent you." It was just a parting of the ways, I guess.

Chairman KEFAUVER. He just got another lawyer?

Mr. CAIDIN. I presume. I mean——

Chairman KEFAUVER. Well, he had to have a lawyer to be in court, I guess.

Mr. CAIDIN. Yes. It was not an unfriendly termination. It was just a parting of the ways.

My judgment, apparently, has been completely vindicated insofar as the nature of the business. The court here having found that none of the merchandise was obscene, my judgment in the first instance appears to have been correct, when I said I didn't believe any of the merchandise was obscene. I don't want it to appear that I was handling—representing a client——

Chairman KEFAUVER. What do you personally think about that advertisement, Mr. Caidin? That was some of Mr. Ross', some advertisement of this group.

Mr. CAIDIN. I don't approve of the advertising.

Chairman KEFAUVER. Well, you knew they were sending out that kind of thing, didn't you?

Mr. CAIDIN. I didn't make it a point to inspect the advertising. I saw the merchandise that they were selling. I thought that under the statute, that the test of obscenity is what they were sending to the customers; whether the pictures they were sending were obscene.

Chairman KEFAUVER. Well, we are considering here our proposals to amend the postal laws on obscenity. Do you think they ought to be amended?

Mr. CAIDIN. That is a question I was hoping you would ask, Senator, and it is not one that I am going to be able to answer very well.

There are two public interests here to be served, and it is a very, very difficult question for this reason. Firstly, if the post office is given any broader powers than it has now, I think it would be extremely dangerous. The way the law is set up now, a hearing is held in Washington before the Post Office Department, by which merchandise is inspected by the Department, and if the Postmaster General in the exercise of his unlimited discretion should think the material is objectionable, he has the right to issue a stop order by which all incoming mail can be seized. Now, that is a power which is a dangerous power, because we are left to depend upon the Postmaster General's personal viewpoint as to what is objectionable and what is not objectionable; and we have much material that is along the line, or public morals or viewpoints might change, the sentiment of the country might be different at one time, or a particular man might think one set of photos is obscene and another man looking at the same set would think they are not obscene. Yet, if we give the Postmaster General the right in his own discretion to seize the mail, it could subject all the citizens of this country to a tyrannical power.

Chairman KEFAUVER. You mean, you think it might be a bad thing if the Postmaster General had the right to seize this stuff going through the mail?

Mr. CAIDIN. It depends on what the merchandise being sold is.

Chairman KEFAUVER. Well, do you think this ought to be declared obscene? That has been sent through the mail by your people, your clients.

Mr. CAIDIN. Well, it certainly is borderline. It is borderline.

Chairman KEFAUVER. Pretty close, you think?

Mr. CAIDIN. Yes. I would say that is borderline material; but I don't consider the merchandise sold in response to those ads as being obscene.

Chairman KEFAUVER. Well, the ads are just as important—more people see the ads than do the merchandise.

Mr. CAIDIN. Well, if you take those ads, I would say they were very poor taste. It is, as you say——

Chairman KEFAUVER. You wouldn't like your young children to be seeing too much of that.

Mr. CAIDIN. No. It is in poor taste. To say it is obscene, I don't know. I would have to look at the material with the ads, actually, to see if the material is obscene.

Chairman KEFAUVER. I know, but whether you get the material or not, here these are what they send out as a come-on for the others, and I expect more people see this than do the material.

Mr. CAIDIN. As I say, it is borderline. It is poor taste. I wouldn't say it is obscene. It is in poor taste.

Chairman KEFAUVER. Well, would you want your children to be reading this kind of stuff?

Mr. CAIDIN. No, sir; I wouldn't want my children to read anything in poor taste, including the comic books and much of our literature. I certainly wouldn't want that in my home; no.

Chairman KEFAUVER. Well, you wouldn't like your children to have these nude pictures around, would you, that they send out in response to this?

Mr. CAIDIN. I frankly—the nude pictures that I have seen——

Chairman KEFAUVER. Well, just answer the question. Do you want your children in possession of these nude pictures that your clients sent out?

Mr. CAIDIN. Well, I will have to make it a hypothetical answer, since my oldest child is 2½ years of age. I would answer the question "No"; I wouldn't want nude pictures personally around the house.

Chairman KEFAUVER. That is what we are getting at.

Mr. CAIDIN. Yes; but, as I say, it is a matter of taste; and if the pictures themselves are not obscene in the sense of being repugnant to a sense of morals or decency. I looked at the picture such as the Marilyn Monroe picture, and it doesn't seem obscene to me, sir. As I say, it is a question of morals and taste.

Getting back to the revision of the law——

Chairman KEFAUVER. Well, you appreciate the fact that young children are more impressionable than adults, aren't they?

Mr. CAIDIN. Yes, sir. I might say that I am sure we have all seen when we were youngsters pictures of—nude pictures and slides; and the point is——

Chairman KEFAUVER. But you don't advocate it, do you?

Mr. CAIDIN. I don't—I wouldn't want to make it a public platform that every child should receive nude films as part of his growing up; but they will get it, and I don't think it will do them any harm.

Chairman KEFAUVER. If they don't get too much of it?

Mr. CAIDIN. Well, as I say, the Marilyn Monroe picture in the hands of an adolescent isn't going to—I don't think it will have a bad effect on his future development or growth. I just don't see it.

But getting back, if I may, sir, to the question which you asked, which I suppose is the primary purpose of the committee——

Chairman KEFAUVER. Yes.

Mr. CAIDIN. As to recommendations in reference to legislation, I think that what we have are actually adequate laws, in this sense: I don't think the Post Office Department should be set up as a judge of the morals of the country, and if any broader powers would be given, that would be the case. I think the Postmaster General's powers are too broad now. I think we have criminal statutes that make it a criminal offense to send pornographic and lewd material through the mail. Penalty for violating that statute is a $5,000 fine and 5 or 10 years' imprisonment. Now, if that is not an adequate safeguard against pornography, I frankly don't know what would be. If a man violates the law, he will be given a substantial fine and a prison sentence and will be convicted of a felony under our present existing laws.

Now, if men are sending pornographic material through the mail, they should be brought to trial on such statutes; but I don't see that the expansion of the powers of the postmaster are any answer.

Chairman KEFAUVER. Well, I appreciate your views about it. Of course, one thing, there is a loophole in the law about carrying it in trucks and automobiles, which we hope to get tightened up.

Mr. Bobo, do you have any questions you want to ask?

Mr. BOBO. Mr. Caidin, I just wonder if this is the only arrangement you have had with people in this business, similar arrangement, with Ross and Tager? Have you had a similar arrangement with others in this same business, as to the matter of a fee for your representing them for a percentage of the business?

Mr. CAIDIN. It is possible. I may have.

Mr. BOBO. Do you know the names of who your clients might have been?

Mr. CAIDIN. Yes, sir. I think I had one other arrangement of that type.

Mr. BOBO. Who was that, Mr. Caidin?

Mr. CAIDIN. I refuse to answer the name of the party, except in closed doors, as a privilege between attorney and client. I am not privileged, as an attorney, to mention my client's name.

Mr. BOBO. Had you represented this person in a cease-and-desist order and received your contingency on the basis of that?

Mr. CAIDIN. Which person are you referring to now?

Mr. BOBO. This second person of whom you are speaking now.

Mr. CAIDIN. I don't believe so.

Mr. BOBO. Is the 10 percent fee—that attorney-client relationship that you are expressing there, is the 10 percent for services performed or is it a part of the business?

Mr. CAIDIN. No. No. I am not sure. Frankly, I am not sure that I had such an arrangement with another one. I might have had it with one other party, I am not sure. I would have to check my files. It might have been a straight retainer or straight percentage, but I think of another party that I might have had such an arrangement with. I am not sure.

Mr. BOBO. But it wasn't for past services performed?

Mr. CAIDIN. Yes. It was a combination of past services—it was for services being performed, if there was such an arrangement. I don't recall.

Mr. BOBO. Did you receive monthly payments on a gross part of the business that this other person did, gross monthly?

Mr. CAIDIN. I don't believe I had such an arrangement.

Mr. BOBO. Do you know what they amounted to, what the payments in this particular instance amounted to?

Mr. CAIDIN. Very small.

Mr. BOBO. You have no idea as to the approximate amount?

Mr. CAIDIN. Oh, it might have been a thousand five hundred—five hundred to two thousand dollars.

Mr. BOBO. That is per month?

Mr. CAIDIN. Oh, no. That is, I think, all I received.

Mr. BOBO. All you received at any time.

Chairman KEFAUVER. Did you have anything to do with this association?

Mr. CAIDIN. No, sir.

Chairman KEFAUVER. Do you know about it?

Mr. CAIDIN. This is the first I heard about it, was here.

Chairman KEFAUVER. Anything else, now, Mr. Caidin, you want to say?

Mr. CAIDIN. Well, no, except I don't think the committee should go into these problems between attorneys and clients and fees and all that business.

Chairman KEFAUVER. Well, Mr. Caidin, it appears to us that this was more than an attorney-client arrangement. You were actually— at least had a contract to get 10 percent of the business; 10 percent, as far as we know, just on and on. Well, maybe it didn't work out that way, but that looks more like a participation in the business rather than just a representation.

Mr. CAIDIN. As I say, sir, the agreement was not enforced. One, it was never observed. Second, as long as it is a proper business, like if it is no different than if it was Sears, Roebuck mail-order house, this is a mail-order business; and if there is any difference between a legitimate mail-order house and receiving a contingent fee from that and receiving a contingent fee in any other type of case, as long as the business is proper and approved by the courts, it is a proper business.

Chairman KEFAUVER. I don't hear many fees based—attorneys base fees upon the amount of recovery. If you have a negligence case, you get 25 percent or whatever the amount of recovery; but certainly it is uncommon to me that lawyers are paid by a corporation or business on the basis of a percentage of the gross sales of a business.

Mr. CAIDIN. I have handled many, many business deals, sir, outside of this field, in which I have a participating arrangement with the client for legal services; and I particularly refer, of course, to the motion-picture business. It is a frequent custom.

Chairman KEFAUVER. To get a percentage of the gross sales?

Mr. CAIDIN. Of the income from a motion picture; yes, sir. That is, producers—I have in the office now at least one motion picture, and I have had several television programs and other materials of that type in which our fee was a retainer plus a percentage of the income.

Chairman KEFAUVER. That would be for legal services on that one picture, wouldn't it?

Mr. CAIDIN. It would be for legal services on the picture; yes, sir.

Senator KEFAUVER. Here are these people operating under different names, over a long period of time, a general business. Do you know of any case like that?

Mr. CAIDIN. A television series would go——

Senator KEFAUVER. I am not talking about a series. A person has a X corporation, engaged in the hotel business, the theater business. Some lawyer gets a percentage of the gross sales, gross business. I have never heard of it.

Mr. CAIDIN. Well, sir, it is not an uncommon arrangement.

Chairman KEFAUVER. Well, have you had any arrangement like that?

Mr. CAIDIN. In the motion picture and television field I have.

Chairman KEFAUVER. I mean, of the gross sales of the whole company, a percentage of the gross sales of the whole company?

Mr. CAIDIN. Well, yes, sir. An independent production——

Chairman KEFAUVER. I am not talking about just some film, where it is just a 1 film or 1 production. I mean, XYZ motion picture company, you get 10 percent of the gross sales of the whole company?

Mr. CAIDIN. I personally haven't had it, but I am sure lawyers have had it.

For instance, to get back to motion pictures, if I may, where a company is formed, it might make 10 pictures and give a 10-percent running interest to the attorney for all the pictures they might take. That is not an uncommon arrangement.

Chairman KEFAUVER. All right, Mr. Caidin, Thank you, sir.

Mr. CAIDIN. Thank you.

Senator KEFAUVER. Now, who is our next witness?

Mr. BOBO. Mr. Stapenhorst.

Chairman KEFAUVER. Mr. Ralph E. Stapenhorst, please.

How are you, Mr. Stapenhorst?

All right, Mr. Bobo.

(Mr. Stapenhorst was sworn.)

TESTIMONY OF RALPH E. STAPENHORST, POSTAL INSPECTOR, GLENDALE, CALIF.

Mr. BOBO. Mr. Stapenhorst, would you state your full name and address and your position for the benefit of the record?

Mr. STAPENHORST. My name is Ralph E. Stapenhorst. I live at 409 West Lexington Drive, Glendale 3, Calif. I am employed as a post office inspector and domiciled at Los Angeles, Calif.

Mr. BOBO. As a post office inspector, what do your duties consist of?

Mr. STAPENHORST. Among other cases assigned to me for investigation at Los Angeles, are many involving possible dealers in obscene matter.

Mr. BOBO. In following through on these particular cases, have you ever dealt with any matters involved in sending nude photos through the mail, the type of material which we have been discussing here this morning?

Mr. STAPENHORST. Yes, I have; starting early in 1948.

Mr. BOBO. What is the position of the Post Office Department with regard to those engaged in the business of sending out advertising matter and in receiving orders back through the mail and mailing out these photo sequences?

Mr. STAPENHORST. The Postmaster General, postmasters, chief post office inspector and post office inspectors after a mailing has been made of the circular matter similar to that which has been shown to the committee, frequently receive complaints from both adults and the parents of juveniles who have received the advertising. Upon receiving such complaints, a case is issued for investigation by a post office inspector.

As is fairly well known, the post office inspector uses test names and addresses throughout the country to purchase this material. The evidence is then presented to the United States attorney for consideration of prosecution. We sometimes have cases involving what the dealers in this matter have called borderline material, in which a certain United States attorney does not wish to consider prosecution, but the inspector considers that it is sufficiently obscene and indecent to try to put the operator out of business. With material of this kind, the inspector submits a report to his inspector in charge, and it reaches the Department in Washington, and if the Solicitor, who is the legal authority for the Post Office Department, agrees, a hearing is held under the Administrative Procedures Act. If the evidence before the hearing examiner for the Department is considered such, the Post-master General issues an unlawful order.

Mr. BOBO. Mr. Stapenhorst, while you have been here in the Los Angeles office, have you become familiar with the Ross-Tager case which has been under discussion this morning?

Mr. STAPENHORST. I have considerable familiarity with parts of the Ross-Tager operation. I did leave Los Angeles for other assignments in February, 1950, and returned to Los Angeles in September 1953. So my knowledge of certain court actions and so forth with regard to Roy J. Ross and Louis Tager is partly from reading reports of other inspectors and partly from hearsay.

I did, however, cooperate with the United States attorney at Los Angeles in March, 1954, in the prosecution of Roy J. Ross and Louis Tager.

Mr. BOBO. From the file which you have and from your experience with that case, would you outline for us the operation of the Ross-Tager business that was revealed by your investigation and the Post Office Department investigation?

Mr. STAPENHORST. Another inspector determined the destination of numerous parcels mailed into the State of Kansas by Roy J. Ross and Louis Tager, and after interviewing many hundreds of addressees, we found that somewhere around 80 of them were juveniles, and those persons were willing to be witnesses in the prosecution of Ross and Tager in Kansas.

We have had testimony that that indictment was dismissed on the grounds that the court in Kansas did not have jurisdiction, as was a similar indictment in Detroit, Mich.

Chairman KEFAUVER. Against Ross and Tager there?

Mr. STAPENHORST. Against Ross and Tager in Detroit, Mich.

We had as witnesses in the Ross and Tager prosecution in Los Angeles five juveniles in the State of California who had purchased what we consider obscene material from Roy J. Ross and Louis Tager.

Mr. BOBO. What type of material is this, Mr. Stapenhorst?

Mr. STAPENHORST. Roy J. Ross and Louis Tager had an assortment of moving picture films that might have had 40 or 50 different titles. In the films were depicted—in one film, a female wearing an uplift brassiere and black panties, talking on the telephone and squirming around on a bed, in what some people would consider suggestive poses. In others females who have unusually large developed breasts take various provocative poses, and encircle the breasts with a rope, and otherwise call attention to their anatomy. In others 3 or 4 females in the nude might be playing baseball, and, of course, some people would get a lascivious reaction from such moving pictures.

Mr. BOBO. In addition to that were there still photos in color or slides?

Mr. STAPENHORST. Yes. Roy J. Ross and Louis Tager also sold through the mail in large quantities sets of photographs of females in the nude, and also color transparencies.

Mr. BOBO. You were telling us the outcome of the case here in Los Angeles before I stopped you, Mr. Stapenhorst.

Mr. STAPENHORST. Early in February, I believe it was, Louis Tager pleaded guilty to the first five counts in the indictment which charged mailing obscene matter, and to count No. 51, which charged con-spiracy to violate the law regarding obscene matter.

A trial was had before Federal Judge Peirson M. Hall on about March 29, 1954, and the judge, after viewing a number of the films and examining the slides and photographs, declared that the material he had viewed was not obscene; that Roy J. Ross was not guilty.

Mr. Tager then moved to have his plea of guilty set aside, which motion the judge accepted, and the United States attorney was ordered to proceed with the prosecution later that afternoon. When the United States attorney informed the court that he wished to have some of the juvenile witnesses here and needed time, the action against Louis Tager was dismissed for want of prosecution by the Government.

Mr. Bobo. In the operation——

Chairman KEFAUVER. I didn't understand. Did he first plead guilty?

Mr. STAPENHORST. Louis Tager first pleaded guilty to the first five counts in the indictment and to the 51st count charging conspiracy.

Chairman KEFAUVER. And then he decided to change his plea?

Mr. STAPENHORST. He decided to change his plea on the afternoon that he learned that his partner, Roy J. Ross, had been found to be not guilty in court.

Chairman KEFAUVER. And then the United States attorney asked time to get the juvenile witnesses, then?

Mr. STAPENHORST. That is correct.

Chairman KEFAUVER. And the case—they didn't come in?

Mr. STAPENHORST. The action against Ross concluded about 2 : 30, and the court recessed until 4 o'clock that afternoon when the trial of Louis Tager was to proceed. Naturally, since the juveniles lived anywhere from San Mateo to San Diego, Calif., a distance of 120 to 400 miles, we couldn't have them here in an hour and a half.

Chairman KEFAUVER. We have the transcript of the record in that case which will be made an exhibit to the hearings at this time.

(The transcript referred to was marked "Exhibit No. 35," and is as follows:)

IN THE UNITED STATES DISTRICT COURT

SOUTHERN DISTRICT OF CALIFORNIA, CENTRAL DIVISION

Hon. Peirson M. Hall, judge, presiding

No. 23340—Criminal

UNITED STATES OF AMERICA, PLAINTIFF V. ROY J. ROSS, DEFENDANT

REPORTER'S TRANSCRIPT OF PARTIAL PROCEEDINGS

Los Angeles, Calif., March 23, 1954

Appearances

For the plaintiff : Laughlin E. Waters, United States Attorney, Los Angeles 12, California : by Manuel Real, Assistant United States Attorney.

For the defendant : Burke Mathes, Esq., 453 South Spring Street, Los Angeles 13, California.

Los Angeles, Calif., March 23, 1954, 2 p. m.

*   *   *   *   *   *   *

The COURT. How long do you want to argue this case, Mr. Real?

Mr. REAL. Not too long, your Honor. I just want to point out a few things, and that is with relation to at least 4 of the movies which I thought, as I was watching, came within the purview of the statute. One was "Sheer Delight," and I think that goes beyond the art phase. In other words, we are going to have a basis of whether or not it is art or whether or not it is actually lewd, and then in between there will be the varying degrees.

The COURT. No; the statute does not say anything about art.

Mr. REAL. I know it doesn't.

The COURT. The prosecution did not say anything about art.

Mr. REAL. That is correct.

The COURT. The statute says that they are obscene, lewd, lascivious, and filthy.

Mr. REAL. As to the basis of obscene, I think most of the tests have been established on whether or not they are art or they are obscene, and in between there has been a number where nobody could decide whether it might have been art or might not have been, or might have been obscene or might not have been. I think Sheer Delight crosses that line with the carressing of the hands and breasts and private parts which I think goes beyond the line.

The COURT. There was no evidence of that.

Mr. REAL. I thought I saw that in Sheer Delight.

Then the picture Enough Rope, with the tying up of the breasts, and in Satan's Daughter, again the carressing of the breasts, and I think Busy Signal, I think, was the worst of the lot.

The COURT. Why?

Mr. REAL. That was the one with the suggestion of moving around.

The COURT. Maybe she had to.

Your argument reminds me of the Frenchman who came to New York and saw the Empire State Building, and someone wanted to know what he thought of it.

He said, "It reminds me of sex."

The other person asked him, "Why?"

"Well, everything reminds me of sex."

Mr. REAL. That is true. The human body reminds people of sex, but the thing is people don't normally sit and loll in a chair or on a bed, people don't normally do the things that were done in these particular films. It is not a normal reaction. It is not a normal result of any action of the human body; it is something that has been actually used to suggest the subject of sex to arouse people to sexual passions.

I think, Your Honor, in that respect there are two phases of this case. One phase is the phase about whether or not they are obscene; and even if Your Honor finds that they are not obscene, I might call Your Honor's attention to another one which is merely typical of the same one you saw, except it has more to it, and I am referring to Government's 49. I direct this particular part of the argument to the conspiracy count, which is count 51.

Of course, we can say this: That as far as intent goes there is no intent; that it is not necessary that they intend or that the person who is making the film intend that they be obscene; so whether or not they are obscene, whether he intended them to be obscene or not, is not a question so far as the substantive counts go.

I think we have here a little different question. Certainly the law has never punished intent alone. So even though they intend them to be obscene, if they are not in fact obscene, then you have gone beyond that, except in one situation, and I think the law provides this: that where somebody intends to violate a law of the United States under section 371, even though they don't accomplish their intent, if they make some act, whether it be an innocent act or a criminal act, toward that particular end, they are guilty of the conspiracy.

In that respect I might call Your Honor's attention to these exhibits—and there are many of them like this—in which it was an advertisement of the films themselves.

The COURT. That was the enclosure in those photographs?

Mr. REAL. No; this was another one. This was a circular that came out before.

The COURT. Was that the one that starts out with, "I have been a collector of nude pictures"?

Mr. REAL. No. This one starts with "Party films, private films, your films. These are my latest releases, made for you, just as you would have them for yourself, showing what you would have shown to be seen by yourself and your own personal friends," etc. And then they go on to describe the particular films that Your Honor saw.

I think from that you might conclude that even by their own admission in their own advertisements that these cannot be established as art films.

The COURT. What is obscene, lewd, lascivious and filthy about calling something a party film? That is a film for a party of people.

Mr. Real. I realize that, Your Honor, that it may not be, but after you see the films you begin to realize that they are not party films, and the distribution that was given to these particular advertisements is not one that would show that they were distributed for that particular purpose.

I might call your attention to the stipulation in which you might recognize the first 10 counts, these ads went unsolicited to minors and certainly unsolicited to many people who did not want them. I don't think that you can say that they are party films in the sense that people would show them at a birthday party for a 9-year-old child or a birthday party even for a 21-year-old child.

I think that that is on the basis of the conspiracy count and it shows at least the intent to violate the status, section 1461. These are not made for any other purpose except to arouse the passions of the person, that is, the sexual passion of the person.

The Court. And that makes it what?

Mr. Real. Obscene, Your Honor.

The Court. That makes it obscene?

Mr. Real. At least in my estimation what I have considered to be obscene from the tests that have been provided.

The Court. You mean sex is obscene?

Mr. Real. Not sex in itself, Your Honor.

The Court. What is it then?

Mr. Real. Under the proper circumstances sex of course is not obscene. It probably—well, it is the end result of our very existence really.

The Court. And the beginning too.

Mr. Real. And the beginning.

But I think there are ways and means that that is to be actually accomplished and those ways and means were not shown in these films.

The Court. No; I do not think it was shown in these films. I do not think anything was shown in these films.

Mr. Mathes. If the court please, if the arousing of sex was the intent I would be glad to submit it on that basis. But as they were being shown I watched the group here, and I think that was the last thing that anyone was thinking of. They aren't art, they aren't artistic in the least bit; I don't think the come within any of the tests laid down in the cases under the purview of the statute.

The Court. If the arousing of sex, sexual desires, is to be the test of whether or not it is obscene, lewd, lascivious and filthy, such pictures as these are incomparable compared to scenes in motion picture films——

Mr. Real. Yes, Your Honor.

The Court. Where, with a series of events and suggestions and conversation, and the triangle between a man and a woman, they finally wind up showing them going to the bedroom—they do not show anything more—but certainly if that is the test then I think that the Postmaster General ought to take on all of the motion picture companies, ought to pick on Life magazine, in which pictures appear that are absolutely no different from these except these are animated——

Mr. Real. And those are highly colored.

The Court. Highly colored, yes, and they are circulated not only by the millions of copies in magazines, Life and others, but there must be tens of millions of pictures that are distributed and find access to a 9-year-old child and a 21-year-old child so that people do not have to waste their money for these kind of pictures.

Mr. Real. Your Honor, I think the animation is what makes its obsence, not the mere showing of a picture.

The Court. It does not make it any more obscene than motion-picture films where they maybe have more clothes—not much—maybe have more clothing, but are certainly calculated to do nothing else but to arouse the sexual desires. If this defendant was up here on a charge of using the mails to defraud on the ground that he had represented to people that they were going to get some obscene and lewd pictures and sent them these, I think maybe you might have a case.

Mr. Mathes. Perhaps a much greater case than at present, Your Honor. But you don't have the presence of the mail fraud section at all which might contribute to coming within the purview of the statute. It is entirely a solo act and the best you can say of it is it might be a borderline case.

The Court. I do not think it is even a borderline case, counsel.

The whole case, in view of the stipulation of facts here, depends upon whether in the long run the pictures which I have seen, the motion pictures, the still films and the slides, are lewd, obscene, lascivious, and filthy, and by no means can I reach that conclusion.

The matter of what is obscene, lewd, lascivious, and filthy depends upon the mores of the times. No doubt there was a time when a picture of any woman of more than above her ankle, her knees and thigh, was considered indecent and was considered lascivious. It would not be, I do not think, considered obscene. But certainly in the past 50 years in the standards by which courts and everybody else has to do in the abdication of these words of the statute and the only standards you can go by is what is common and general.

In the oriental countries and in many European countries, but particularly in the oriental countries, people walk along the street and they think nothing at all of urinating on the sidewalk or off the sidewalk in the presence of everybody, or even performing the action of excreta. Here that would be obscence and it would be filthy. To them it is not.

Now our standards have not gone that far, but certainly the standards in the United States, which are the current standards, you cannot judge these by the standards of today when a woman could not show any more of her form than above her shoetop and could not even show her ankle, but certainly there is nothing in any of these pictures that I have seen that compares in suggestivity (if that is the word to be used) of pictures that have appeared in Life magazine, Look magazine, all kinds of art magazines that are for sale by the millions of copies, or calendars distributed free, post cards, photographs, found every place in every store, so that now it has become commonplace. The picture of a naked woman just does not arouse or attract attention anymore. In fact, they have to build it up with the kind of advertisements that you have here, so you think it is going to be something special, in order to get it.

Insofar as these pictures are concerned, I noticed there was not one single frame of the motion pictures where there was shown the sexual organs of a female. In fact, in every pose and posture they seemed to be careful to conceal it.

And insofar as showing the breasts of women, which these pictures mostly did—of course they have a freak of nature in there in one of them who probably should have been in a circus, or may be now for all I know—but as far as that is concerned, if there had been one one-hundredth of an inch more or less on women's dresses at parties that you and I and Mr. Real and post office inspectors—and no doubt the Postmaster General—see every day, why their breasts would be just as fully shown as they are here. I refer to one less wire, or stay, or whatever they call it.

There was nothing in the way of pornography here, which usually goes with these things that are regarded as obscene, lewd, and lascivious. There was no sodomy. There was no buggery, which has been shown in films of all kinds heretofore, and which have been condemned, and which I as a judge have condemned, and which everybody condemns because those are obscene, lewd, lascivious, filthy, and disgusting.

Then so far as these still photographs—well, if there were not more calendars given away with more of the human form shown and more lewd and suggestive than these are, and transmitted through the mails, I have not been living for a long time.

Now insofar as the other standards are concerned, I have no doubt but what there are people that would consider any picture of a naked women in any pose as obscene, lewd, lascivious, and filthy, but I do not think that that is the general standards and concepts of American life today. The concepts we had years ago have disappeared because things like that have become commonplace. And certainly here in this case I have not seen anything that would even justify in my judgment the expense to which the United States has been put up to this moment in the matter of the prosecution of this case.

I have no doubt but what, in view of the care and meticulous way with which the record has been taken in connection with the stipulation and in view of the fact that there has been no oral testimony but that it has resolved itself upon my judgment, that a record has been made here for the purpose of imposing upon my brethren in the circuit court of appeals an appeal in this case so that they must sit down and go through the experience which I have had today looking at these pictures.

But I cannot be deterred in that and I cannot give consideration to that. I am bound by my duty here and by every concept that I have. The pictures are not obscene, they are not lewd, they are not lascivious, and they are not filthy, and they are a waste of time to look at for anybody.

The judgment of the court is a judgment of not guilty for the defendant. His bond is exonerated and the defendant is discharged.

(Whereupon, at 3:55 p. m., court was adjourned.)

IN THE UNITED STATES DISTRICT COURT

SOUTHERN DISTRICT OF CALIFORNIA, CENTRAL DIVISION

UNITED STATES OF AMERICA, PLAINTIFF, *v.* LOUIS TAGER, DEFENDANT

No. 23340—Criminal

REPORTER'S TRANSCRIPT OF PROCEEDINGS

Los Angeles, Calif., March 29, 1954

Appearances

For the plaintiff: Laughlin E. Waters, United States attorney, Los Angeles 12, Calif.; by Manuel Real, assistant United States attorney.

For the defendant: Caidin, Bloomgarden & Kaiman, 9441 Wilshire Boulevard, Beverly Hills, Calif.; by Stanley R. Caidin, Esq.

Los Angeles, Calif., March 29, 1954, 10 a. m.

The COURT. Any ex parte matters?

Mr. CAIDIN. Your Honor, in the matter of *United States* v. *Ross and Tager,* I represent the defendant Louis Tager and at this time would like to ask leave of court to withdraw the plea of the defendant Louis Tager of guilty to counts 1 through 5 of the indictment and count 51, change the plea to not guilty, and ask that the court at this time dismiss the action as to this defendant.

The COURT. He pleaded to all counts, did he not?

Mr. REAL. No. Six counts, Your Honor.

The COURT. Your motion is to withdraw the plea of guilty heretofore made as to the six counts?

Mr. CAIDIN. Yes, Your Honor, counts 1 through 5 and count 51.

The COURT. Is the defendant here?

Mr. CAIDIN. No, Your Honor, he is not.

The COURT. I will not proceed unless he is here. I want to ask him about it.

Mr. CAIDIN. I will be back then with the defendant, Your Honor.

The COURT. Very well.

*   *   *   *   *   *   *

Los Angeles, Calif., March 29, 1954, 2 p. m.

*   *   *   *   *   *   *

Mr. CAIDIN. I have my client in court this afternoon, Your Honor, in the matter of *United States* v. *Ross and Tager.*

The CLERK. Case No. 23340, Your Honor.

Mr. CAIDIN. We should at this time like to ask leave of court to withdraw the plea of guilty of Louis Tager to counts 1 through 5 inclusive and count 51 of the indictment and substitute for that plea——

The COURT. Do you move to withdraw your plea heretofore entered for the purpose of entering another and different plea?

Mr. CAIDIN. Yes.

The COURT. Is the defendant here?

Mr. CAIDIN. Yes.

The COURT. Come forward.

You are the defendant Louis Tager?

The DEFENDANT. Yes, Your Honor.

The Court. You have heard the motion of your counsel to withdraw the plea of guilty and enter another and different plea. Is that your desire?

The Defendant. Yes, sir.

The Court. The motion is granted.

Mr. Real. Your Honor, may I be heard before Your Honor rules on the motion?

The Court. If he wants to withdraw his plea of guilty, a defendant may do that at any time and it is no business of the United States attorney.

Mr. Real. Well, Your Honor, I have a case that says otherwise.

The Court. He can withdraw his plea of guilty. He has not been tried. Now I will ascertain his plea and on the next move you can be heard on it. Ascertain the defendant's plea.

The Clerk. What is your plea to count 1 of the indictment?

The Defendant. Not guilty.

The Clerk. And as to all other counts up to and including count 51?

The Defendant. Not guilty.

The Clerk. A plea of not guilty as to all 51 counts, Your Honor.

The Court. Are you ready to set the matter for trial?

Mr. Real. Yes, we are, Your Honor.

The Court. I will try it this afternoon after I finish with the rest of my calendar. You may stand aside.

Mr. Caidin. Your Honor, I have a jury trial in Department 63 of the Superior Court.

The Court. When?

Mr. Caidin. Right now. They are holding it until 2 : 30.

The Court. I will set it for trial tomorrow morning.

Mr. Caidin. I will be in this jury trial for 2 or 3 days.

The Court. How long will it take to try? It is liable not to take very long, is it not?

Mr. Real. It depends on whether or not we are going to stipulate to this also, Your Honor, whether or not it is going to be tried by stipulation.

The Court. I will try it right now, if you are willing to stipulate that the stipulation filed in the case as to the defendant Ross may be stipulated to and that all of the evidence introduced in that case in behalf of the Government may be deemed to be introduced in this case. Is that your stipulation?

Mr. Real. That wasn't my stipulation. I thought we might go through the trial.

The Court. You mean listen to this all over again?

Mr. Real. At least the stipulation and possibly go through part of it again.

The Court. You mean show some of those same pictures over again?

Mr. Real. Very possible.

The Court. I understood the defendants were up for punishment, not the judges. What do you not want to stipulate to?

Mr. Real. We will stipulate to all the facts of the case, Your Honor, it is just that we want to go through the trial.

The Court. You mean you want to show those pictures over again?

Mr. Real. If Your Honor wants to see them.

The Court. I do not want to see them. Is there anything different about them than there was before last week?

Mr. Real. No; there isn't.

The Court. Are you willing to accept the stipulation?

Mr. Caidin. I would like to stipulate that the pictures heretofore introduced be deemed to be introduced at the trial of the defendant Louis Tager and that this case be disposed of on the same evidence.

The Court. That all of the evidence introduced on behalf of the Government be reintroduced?

Mr. Caidin. That is correct.

The Court. Will you stipulate to that?

Mr. Real. I can't do that, Your Honor.

The Court. Do you have additional evidence?

Mr. Real. No, but my instructions are not to do that.

The Court. Not to do that? Do you offer it all in evidence?

Mr. Real. We will offer it in evidence. I have it upstairs.

The Court. Will you stipulate that they may be deemed to be in evidence?

Mr. Real. As soon as I bring them down, Your Honor. I can't do that when they are up in my office.

The COURT. These are the same pictures that I saw last week?

Mr. REAL. They are, Your Honor.

The COURT. And you are under instructions not to stipulate that I have seen them once?

Mr. REAL. That this case may be tried on the evidence already introduced.

The COURT. Your instructions are not to do that?

Mr. REAL. That is correct, Your Honor.

The COURT. And what other evidence do you have?

Mr. REAL. We have none other than that, but we want to go through this evidence in this trial. We will make the stipulation and we will set up, you might say, the record.

The COURT. Set up the record?

Mr. REAL. Yes.

The COURT. That stipulation sets up the record for you now.

Mr. REAL. We have no objection to it being continued until Mr. Caidin can come over here again.

The COURT. If your only purpose in continuing it is to compel me to look at those horrible pictures again—or are you going to demand a jury trial?

Mr. REAL. No; we are not.

The COURT. Do you waive a jury trial?

Mr. CAIDIN. Yes; we waive a jury trial.

The COURT. You had better file a written waiver, then. You say you have to be in the superior court?

Mr. CAIDIN. Yes, Your Honor. I could be back here probably at 4:15.

The COURT. I will hold the matter on the calendar this afternoon.

Mr. CAIDIN. Thank you, Your Honor.

*　　　*　　　*　　　*　　　*　　　*　　　*

The COURT. Are you ready for trial?

Mr. REAL. We are not.

The COURT. Where are your motion picture operators?

Mr. REAL. They are upstairs.

The COURT. Get them down here. I am going to try this case if it take until midnight. I will set it for trial beginning at 9 o'clock tonight if you insist on trying it.

Mr. REAL. There are my instructions, Your Honor.

The COURT. Very well.

We will have a short recess.

(Short recess.)

The COURT. The motion was granted to vacate the plea of guilty and this matter was continued until this time for trial. Has the jury waiver been signed?

Mr. CAIDIN. No, Your Honor.

The COURT. It must be signed by Government counsel as well.

Mr. REAL. Your Honor, in that case the Government is not prepared to go to trial for the reason that we felt that the motion that was served on us on the 24th of March, 1954, should not have been granted because Mr. Tager entered his plea voluntarily and freely. There was no surprise or inadvertence or any mistake in the entry of the plea. He was represented by adequate counsel, and under the case of *Friedman* v. *United States* (200 F. (2d), p. 690), the motion should not have been granted.

We are not ready to go to trial. We do not have our witnesses here. They are witnesses that would have to come from all over the country and therefore we are not prepared to go to trial at this time, Your Honor.

The COURT. Is the jury waiver signed?

Mr. REAL. I have here a jury waiver signed by the defendant Tager and by his counsel Stanley Caidin and by myself on the part of the Government.

The COURT. It will be approved by the court.

Do you consent to a waiver of jury, Mr. Tager?

The DEFENDANT. Yes; I do, Your Honor.

The COURT. You have heard the statement of Government counsel, Mr. Caidin. Are you ready for trial?

Mr. CAIDIN. Yes, Your Honor. We will stipulate that all of the material heretofore introduced in this action on March 23, 1954, was sent through the mails by Mr. Tager.

The COURT. Will you accept the stipulation in writing which was filed on the trial of the defendant Ross?

Mr. CAIDIN. Yes, Your Honor. We accept that stipulation.

The COURT. Would you accept that stipulation, Mr. Real?

Mr. REAL. Your Honor, I cannot do that at this time.

The COURT. You mean the Government expects to bring all these witnesses here on all these accounts rather than to accept the admission by the defendant in this stipulation?

Mr. REAL. That is our position at the present time, Your Honor.

The COURT. Do you also offer to stipulate that all of the exhibits which were put in evidence—as I recall, there was no oral testimony——

Mr. REAL. That is correct.

The COURT. All the exhibits that were put in evidence in the case of *United States* v. *Ross* may be deemed to have been admitted in evidence against this defendant?

Mr. CAIDIN. Yes, sir.

The COURT. You offer to make that stipulation?

Mr. CAIDIN. Yes, Your Honor. And I hereby expressly agree to that stipulation.

The COURT. Well, counsel, there seems to me to be nothing else to prove. The stipulation in evidence here agrees to all of the allegations of the indictment concerning the mailing, the contents of mailing, and counsel here has agreed that all of the pictures and other material which were introduced in evidence may be introduced in evidence against his client in this case.

I have seen them once. I have seen them sufficiently recently that I am quite sure that I would see nothing different in them if I looked at them again, and for that reason I can see no reason why the Government should not proceed to trial forthwith because the trial could be over immediately.

Mr. REAL. Your Honor, it is the feeling of the Government that the Government has a right to have Your Honor hear the witnesses in the case and hear their testimony.

The COURT. Hear their testimony?

Mr. REAL. That is correct.

The COURT. Even though they stipulate that everything was done?

Mr. REAL. That is correct, Your Honor.

The COURT. Well, I think it is quite an unusual attitude on the part of the Government in view of the many trials that are set. The defendant admits that he did all of the things that he is charged with doing here, and under the previous trial the whole question of whether or not they are lewd, lascivious, obscene, and filthy, and I held that they were not.

If the Government is not ready for trial, the case will be dismissed for lack of prosecution. The defendant is discharged and his bond is exonerated.

Court is adjourned.

(Whereupon, at 4: 20 p. m., court was adjourned.)

CERTIFICATE

I hereby certify that I am a duly appointed, qualified, and acting official court reporter of the United States District Court for the Southern District of California.

I further certify that the foregoing is a true and correct transcript of the proceedings had in the above-entitled cause on the date or dates specified therein, and that said transcript is a true and correct transcription of my stenographic notes.

Dated at Los Angeles, Calif., this — day of April A. D. 1954.

———— ————, *Official Reporter.*

Mr. BOBO. In the operation of these businesses by Ross and Tager, on a post-office investigation of them where they are constantly changing names and addresses, what is the difficulty that the Post Office Department faces in that, Mr. Stapenhorst?

Mr. STAPENHORST. That many of the addresses used by these people we find that someone has come in and rented the privilege of receiving mail and paid a fee which ranges all the way from $2 or $3 a month to in some cases $25 a month. The operators of these secretarial services outside of Los Angeles are frequently not very careful in obtaining the true name, and a good address for the person who is using a fictitious name at the secretarial service. We frequently find that there is no such address, and if there is such an address, that it is a motel where the renter of the privilege may have stayed 1 night 3 months before, and similar circumstances.

Mr. Bobo. In other words, if you get a fictitious order out against the XYZ company, by the time you can move in and either stop the mail or return the mail to where it is coming from, their mail will be going over to another address?

Mr. Stapenhorst. That is correct. Mrs. Tager described rather clearly the plan of operation of some of these operators. It is to mail anywhere from 3,000 to 20,000 letters, perhaps; receive the orders at the mail receiving privilege or through the post office box for a period of 10 days or 2 weeks. At the end of that time, fill the orders, and possibly within a few days the person using that fictitious name is informed that his mail is being held from delivery and he should appear before some official in the post office to establish his identity. Now, one of the difficulties post office inspectors have had continuously with these operations is that we may receive a complaint 2 or 3 days after the mailing has been made. The inspector may promptly place an order for the merchandise, suspecting that it is obscene. He does not receive the merchandise until the operator takes it upon himself or herself to fil the orders received. After the inspector has received the merchandise, the operator has received the bulk of his orders and frequently has no interest in the 12 to 50 pieces of mail which arrive after the mail addressed to that fictitious name is held up.

Mr. Bobo. Mr. Stapenhorst, you stated that Mrs. Tager's testimony relative to that particular thing was rather clear and adequately described it. In your familiarity in reading the file of the Ross-Tager operation, would you say that basically the story which she told of this operation as revealed by your investigation was substantially correct?

Mr. Stapenhorst. My knowledge of the Roy J. Ross and Louis Tager and Dorothy Tager operations is rather sketchy. I was not in the area very much at the time, and my information about her operations is not very complete.

Mr. Bobo. Were you familiar with the cease and desist order that was gotten against the Post Office Department, or were you familiar with the details in the Las Vegas and the Phoenix and the Tucson cases, where Mrs. Tager had difficulty in having her mail released to her?

Mr. Stapenhorst. No, sir, I was not.

Mr. Bobo. Mr. Stapenhorst, do you have any suggestions as to how the fictitious order could be improved, where the post office inspectors could descend upon these people in a more rapid fashion?

Mr. Stapenhorst. I would strongly recommend that the Congress consider legislation authorizing the Postmaster General to order the impounding of mail addressed to a person, firm, corporation or partnership which is suspected of dealing in matter which may be in violation of law. The mail would be impounded, pending a proper hearing. If the hearing established that the business was legal and not in violation of any law, the operator could have his mail. If it was established that the business was in violation of law, the mail would then be returned to senders by the postmaster, suitably endorsed.

Mr. Bobo. In the Hollywood and the California area, the district covered by the Los Angeles office, is the volume or the number of people engaged in this business of selling nude photos and nude films—what would you say the extent of that operation is in this area?

Mr. Stapenhorst. Well, there may be deposited in the mails each day anywhere from a thousand to four or five thousand, perhaps more than that numbers of letters addressed to prospective customers.

As to the dollar volume, as to the total number of incoming orders every day, there are scores of operators, large and small, in these businesses, and I would have no way of knowing.

Mr. Bobo. Do you have any approximation? Have you ever worked on a case that would give you an idea as to the volume of business which an operator might do?

Mr. Stapenhorst. I am aware that at times, day after day or evening after evening, Roy J. Ross and Louis Tager would deposit for dispatch 30,000, 40,000, and 50,000 letters a day. There is a statement somewhere in the record that on one day 100,000 first-class letters were mailed to prospective clients.

I have also seen large quantities of the outgoing parcels mailed by Roy J. Ross and Louis Tager at the Van Nuys Post Office.

Mr. Bobo. From the complaints that the Post Office Department received in Los Angeles and of the complaints with which you have knowledge, what is the extent of the business?

Mr. Stapenhorst. You mean in——

Mr. Bobo. In relation to juveniles or in relation to any other person, people complaining that this material was sent to them from the Los Angeles area.

Mr. Stapenhorst. The business seems to maintain more or less of a level. I would doubt that at the present time all the dealers in obscene matter are mailing thirty to fifty thousand letters a day as Roy J. Ross was doing himself at one time. Other than that, I know there are scores of operators in this area, as revealed by the ads in the so-called girlie magazines.

Mr. Bobo. We have received a number of complaints in our office in Washington of the Male Merchandise Mart. Have you done any investigation on that particular case?

Mr. Stapenhorst. Yes, I have.

Oh, do you wish some details on the extent of the operation?

Mr. Bobo. Yes.

Mr. Stapenhorst. In February 1954, the Postmaster General received hundreds of complaints concerning the Male Merchandise Mart. On March 1, 1954, the Postmaster General——

Mr. Bobo. Where is this Male Merchandise Mart?

Mr. Stapenhorst. Male Merchandise Mart has an office and packing room at 8627 Melrose Avenue, Los Angeles 46, Calif.

The records of the county clerk of Los Angeles County reveal that the owner of the firm is V. E. Stanard. V. E. Stanard is known to me as Violet Evelyn Alberts, the wife of David Stephen Alberts, a man who has been convicted in both the State and Federal courts on charges of dealing in or mailing obscene matter.

Mr. Bobo. What type of obscene matter has that operation, the Alberts operation, been, Mr. Stapenhorst?

Mr. Stapenhorst. In March 1954 the mail was impounded upon order of the Federal judge. In August 1954 it was released to the plaintiff after a civil action had been filed and heard, because the evidence before the court consisted only of the advertising.

Before me I have a recently mailed circular of Male Merchandise Mart, and the circular starts out at the top:

BANNED BY BIGOTS WHO CAN'T STAND THE MEANING OF THE WORD "SEX," BUT AVAILABLE TO YOU IF YOU HURRY

The Male Merchandise Mart firmly believes that mature men of clean minds are entitled to choose their own literature. We have waged a relentless war against prudes and self-appointed censors who would keep these fascinating and enlightening books from you.

NOTE.—We make every possible effort to prevent these books from reaching young people or persons who would use them for the fulfillment of indecent desires.

At this point I would like to make an observation. Some years ago I made approximately 25 test purchases from David S. Alberts and from some of the firm names he was using at that time. I say under oath, and I could produce the records to prove it, that on every single one of the orders I sent to David S. Alberts I did not put anything in the space which called for the customer's age.

Inside the circular are described 26 books on every angle of sex. Some of the titles are:

Aphrodisiacs and Anti-Aphrodisiacs: Subtle, unusual methods of stimulating sex interest in yourself and your mate.

The History of Flagellation: Strange, lurid cases of men and women submitting to lash and fang for sex gratification. McCabe. $1.

Bestiality and the Law: The shocking prevalence of sexual relations between humans and animals. Niemoeller. 55 cents.

Bestiality in Ancient and Modern Times: Shameful revelation of why some women must have male animals under their roofs. Niemoeller. 55 cents.

What Is a Hermaphrodite?

Why Males Wear Female Attire.

Magical Secrets of Love: Sexual witchcraft.

William Heirens, Notorious Sex Maniac: Case histories of lust-crimes and their perpetrators. Cauldwell. 55 cents.

Petting as an Erotic Exercise: Precoital techniques among the unmarried and wedded discussed.

Revelations of a Sexologist.

Private Letters From Homosexuals to a Doctor.

The Intimate Embrace: Scientific discourse on the various positions of embrace. A recommended study for husband and wife. Cauldwell. 55 cents.

So much for the books on every angle of sex.

Are ordinary novels too tame for you? Here's exciting, intimate reading that gives you that thrill!

POCKET-SIZE EDITIONS, 15 CENTS EACH. MINIMUM ORDER, $1

Curious and Unusual Love Affairs.
Confessions of a Minister's Daughter.
Amorous Tales of the Monks.
The Love Affairs of a Priest and a Nun.
The Prostitute and Her Lover.
Art of Intimacy in Marriage.

All for 15 cents, mind you. Minimum order $1.

Then they have Sex in Prison, Wild French Cartoons, The Flimsey Report, and French Love Stories.

Rare Specials.—These are full-length unabridged hardcover books, that have been ordered out of print in this edition. Each one is a "must" for your very private collection. $2 each:
Naughty Bedtime Books.
Bedroom With a View.

There are 2 for $1, 5 for $2, or all 9 books for only $3:

Bed Time Girl.
Brutal Kisses.
Come Night, Come Desire.
Everybody Loves Irene.
Four Dames Named Sin.

Chairman KEFAUVER. We will make that an exhibit to your testimony, Mr. Stapenhorst.

(The circular referred to was marked "Exhibit No. 36," and is on file with the subcommittee.)

Chairman KEFAUVER. Go ahead, sir.

Mr. STAPENHORST. On the circular which accompanies the one printed in black on yellow paper is an announcement:

MEN . . . LET'S FACE IT!

There's a lot of "sock" that can be gotten from adult items dealing with our favorite subject . . . sex. But you've got to play by the rules, and that is restrict these items for adult use only. We can bring you these hard-to-get, genuine private stag items if you keep your pledge.

Among the items sold are:

Wow! Wolf Deck!! Sold to adults only!
$3.50 deck, 2 for $6.
A pack of beauty.
Art slides in natural color.
Body in art.
Peep show.
Real old-time cartoon booklets. A whole flock of 'em for $2—and a flock of "rare enjoyment" in every one!
Just the kind that dad used to carry around in his vest pocket and show the gang at the Saturday night poker session. They are rich!
All new and good—a big assortment, $2.
Beauty in Bondage: Whose heart would not thrill in pity at the poor, helpless, cruelly gagged and bound young creatures, completely at the mercy of their brutal captors.
Marilyn Monroe playing cards, $3 per deck. Special: Both decks, $5.50.
Banned before—now available for first time!
Banned from the mails as lewd . . . now, a special court ruling makes this great nude available to you for the first time. "Her nude, not lewd," says the judge!

Chairman KEFAUVER. We will make that an exhibit to your testimony, too.

(The announcement referred to was marked "Exhibit No. 37," and is on file with the subcommittee.)

Mr. BOBO. Along that same line, Mr. Stapenhorst, may I interject——

Chairman KEFAUVER. Well, Mr. Stapenhorst, I was interested in one picture here that we have had a lot of testimony about. That is this bondage testimony, Tina's Torture. We have had testimony of psychiatrists that these bondage pictures have a very deleterious effect upon young people. You didn't mention that one. That is one of the ones up here [indicating]. What does that say?

Mr. STAPENHORST. (Reading) :

Tina's Torture is advertised:
"Best bondage serial ever made."

Read what happens when a beautiful female spy captures Tina, innocent young daughter of a brilliant scientist, and attempts to force a secret formula from her sweet lips.

What terrors await Tina in the secret dungeons?

Tina couldn't understand why she was bound so strangely until her evil tormentor called in the assistant. How could Tina know why the French maid trembled eagerly as Tina's body heaved with pain?

Does Tina reveal her father's secret? We couldn't blame Tina if she did when one bondage and torture device after another subjected her to humiliation and pain.

You'll find all the answers graphically illustrated and fired with imagination in this amazing new series.

Episodes Nos. 1 and 2 are now ready. $3 per episode; $5 special.

Both episodes Nos. 1 and 2 (6 sensational scenes), each episode on 8 by 10 glossy photo.

Final 18 chapters of Tina's Torture are now ready. Special price for all 20 chapters is only $18 if bought at one time; 10 chapters for $12, 3 chapters for $5.

Mr. BOBO. I would like to interject just a moment, if I might, Mr. Stapenhorst, that the subcommittee answered a number of ads that appeared in magazines on stationery in a very scrawled hand; the stationery being headed "Eastern High School, Washington, D. C." We signed these with the names of "Claude Marvin" and "Peter Nicholas," represent the first names of two staff members of the subcommittee. We received an answer from the Male Merchandise Mart containing exactly the material which you have described there.

Chairman KEFAUVER. Let this be filed as an exhibit.

(The material referred to was marked "Exhibit No. 38," and is on file with the subcommittee.)

Chairman KEFAUVER. You mean that it was written on the letter-head of Eastern High School?

Mr. BOBO. Yes, sir; on student stationery with "Eastern High School" on the head of it.

Chairman KEFAUVER. And you got back the same material?

Mr. BOBO. Exactly the same.

Chairman KEFAUVER. The same material that Mr. Stapenhorst has been describing. All right.

Mr. BOBO. Mr. Stapenhorst, have you done any survey or received any data relative to the volume of business that was done by the Alberts operation?

Mr. STAPENHORST. In March and April of this year a count was kept of the number of pieces of mail which were delivered to Mrs. V. E. Standard and her husband, David S. Alberts, at the west branch of the Los Angeles post office. This count did not include in the totals the number of letters which were returned to the sender, which sometimes ranged up to two or three hundred pieces a day. The volume ran from 497 to 1,033 letters a day addressed to Male Merchandise Mart, Stag Shop; various other enterprises operated by David S. Alberts and his wife; for an average of 696 letters per day over a 7-day period.

I have no information concerning the volume at the present time, but I would assume that it is about the same, possibly a little greater, a little less.

Mr. Bobo. Do you have any information or have you received any information as to the amount of postage that might have been used by the companies which the Alberts operated?

Mr. Stapenhorst. In September 1954, Mrs. V. E. Standard had $4,000 worth of postage placed in the postage meter used by her. In October, $6,000; in November, $2,000; and in December, $7,000. All these settings are after the August 1954 court decision which released the mail to the Male Merchandise Mart.

In February, $4,000 was spent; in March, $3,500; in April, $2,000; and in May, $1,500.

Chairman Kefauver. Are they still operating?

Mr. Stapenhorst. They are still operating.

Chairman Kefauver. You described Tina's Torture. Here are some of the pictures from it. Is that what you were talking about, Mr. Stapenhorst?

Mr. Stapenhorst. Yes. Those are the serial described in the advertising of Male Merchandise Mart.

Chairman Kefauver. Whipping, torture, beatings, is that correct?

Mr. Stapenhorst. Stretching.

Chairman Kefauver. Now, you say Mr. Alberts has a criminal record?

Mr. Stapenhorst. Yes. David S. Alberts was arrested on November 14, 1949, by Los Angeles police officers, and in June 1950, he was found to be guilty as charged, violations of the State law. He was sentenced to 180 days in jail on condition that he serve 60 of them. He was placed on probation for 3 years and fined $500.

In February 1951, upon presenting proper evidence before a judge and with the support of his probation officer, that he was not in any improper business, the State of California probation was lifted.

Chairman Kefauver. Well, he was in business at that time, wasn't he?

Mr. Stapenhorst. It is my own observation and opinion that Alberts was at that time laying low. The only operation with which I am familiar was a business operated by himself and his wife which involved the sale of novelties, none of which an ordinary person would consider obscene.

Chairman Kefauver. How many other operators like that are there around here?

Mr. Stapenhorst. There may be 20, there may be 100. It would be hard to guess.

Chairman Kefauver. Somewhere between 20 and 100?

Mr. Stapenhorst. Somewhere between 20 and 100.

Chairman Kefauver. All about the same type of business?

Mr. Stapenhorst. All about the same type. I do believe that at the present time the business of V. E. Stanard and David S. Alberts may be the greatest in the southern California area.

Chairman Kefauver. Alberts has just been convicted again, hasn't he?

Mr. Stapenhorst. That is correct. He was arrested late in February or early in March 1955, at his place of business, as was his wife, Mrs. Violet Evelyn Alberts; and before a judge in the municipal court for the Beverly Hills judicial district he was found guilty of violating two counts of the State law regarding possessing and advertising obscene matter on June 10. He is to come up for sentence on the 24th of June, according to the information I have.

Chairman KEFAUVER. Mr. Stapenhorst, I am interested in this Ross case, where the man pled guilty and then changed his plea and the Government didn't have time to present its case. Is it not true that Mr. Morris Lavine was his attorney at the time he pled guilty?

Mr. STAPENHORST. I do not recall the name of Louis Tager's attorney.

Chairman KEFAUVER. I mean Mr. Tager's attorney.

Mr. STAPENHORST. At the time he pled guilty, Louis Tager's.

Chairman KEFAUVER. Well, anyway, his attorney saw the films and what not, and after seeing them advised his client to plead quilty, which he did.

Mr. STAPENHORST. I believe that is obvious.

Chairman KEFAUVER. And then when the other man was let off, when Ross was let off, he discharged his attorney and changed his mind and got another attorney and pled not guilty, and the judge threw the case out. Is that correct?

Mr. STAPENHORST. That is correct, I believe.

Chairman KEFAUVER. Do you know the names of either of the attorneys?

Mr. STAPENHORST. The attorney for Roy J. Ross was Mr. Burke Mathes.

Chairman KEFAUVER. And who was Mr. Tager's attorney?

Mr. STAPENHORST. I can't recall at the moment who was Mr. Tager's attorney on that March 29, 1954, date.

Chairman KEFAUVER. Your testimony has been very useful, sir, and we think from you we have gotten the fullest possible picture of what is going on in this section of the United States. Our staff has estimated that this general type of business has grossed from $300 million to $350 million a year in the country. When that figure was stated and released, there was a lot of discounting of it. It was hard for me to believe that a business of this kind could be so extensive, but what you have shown here indicates that that may have been a conservative estimate of the gross business in the Nation.

What would you think about it?

Mr. STAPENHORST. Well, I operate in one of the largest centers for the distribution of pornographic material, indecent, obscene moving pictures, films, cartoon books, and so forth. I do not have too much familiarity with the volume of business in and around New York City, Chicago, Detroit, St. Louis, San Francisco; other metropolitan centers; but I feel that the extent of the business is something which the people who are in it are anxious to hide because of the fact that knowing how lucrative the business is, others will be tempted to get into it, and the more competitors the less business there may be for all.

Chairman KEFAUVER. Well, we appreciate your cooperation very much with our committee, Mr. Stapenhorst.

Mr. STAPENHORST. If I may, Senator——

Chairman KEFAUVER. Do you have anything else you would like to tell us about?

Mr. STAPENHORST. Yes. I would like to read 2 of 3 typical complaints out of about 120 which were received by me in the 3-week period.

Chairman KEFAUVER. Yes; I wish you would read them.

Mr. Stapenhorst. May I retain these?

Chairman Kefauver. Yes.

Mr. Stapenhorst. Or may they become exhibits? I would rather retain them and not reveal the identity of the complainants and addressees.

Chairman Kefauver. Very well. You can retain them, but read the substance of them.

Mr. Stapenhorst. Attached for what action deemed advisable is a letter dated January 26, 1955, addressed to Mr. Jim Brennan, Columbus City, Ind., bearing the return address of Male Merchandise Mart. It was turned over to the inspector's office by local United States attorneys who stated that the addressee is a juvenile and the letter had been received from a juvenile's father.

May I have the name of the addressee stricken from the record?

Chairman Kefauver. Yes. The names of the people who sent in the complaints, do not read.

Mr. Stapenhorst. This is addressed to the Post Office Inspector in charge of Philadelphia, Pa., by the Postmaster at Flemington, N. J.

The enclosed literature considered obscene was turned over to this office by the county detective, Hunterdon County, Flemington, N. J. Addressee is a young boy, and his mother delivered the literature to the authorities for investigation.

This is also to the inspector in charge at Philadelphia from the Postmaster at Newfield. The mother of the addressee has asked the Post Office Department to check into the enclosed mail that was sent to her son, who was only 15 years of age. She contends that it is indecent and that it was not solicited by her son.

This is a letter from the postmaster in New Jersey. A doctor in Westfield, N. J., requested that I send the enclosed letter to you for investigation. The letter was addressed to and opened by his 12-year-old daughter, who claims she did not send for the information.

These are a few of the reasons post office inspectors are so zealous in attempting to keep this pornography from the hands of the juveniles.

Chairman Kefauver. Are those typical of letters about teenagers or from their parents that you have gotten all over the United States?

Mr. Stapenhorst. Those are typical of the scores and hundreds of complaints which inspectors all over the United States received. I might mention that——

Chairman Kefauver. And the police here in Los Angeles received the same complaints, too?

Mr. Stapenhorst. The police in Los Angeles and the sheriff and the Los Angeles County district attorney receive the same type of complaints. Sometimes in some numbers.

Chairman Kefauver. And there is really no effort in this industry, or whatever you call it, to—they want to get orders from anybody, whether they are kids or whether than are grownups?

Mr. Stapenhorst. That is my impression.

Chairman Kefauver. It seems to be well founded.

All right, sir. You go on, Mr. Stapenhorst.

Mr. Stapenhorst. I might mention that after quite an extensive investigation by other inspectors and myself, reports were submitted to the United States attorney in Los Angeles in February, May, July, and December 1949, with evidence concerning the use of the mails by

David S. Alberts, who is the husband of the woman who operates Male Merchandise Mart. After—the United States attorney frankly wished to wait until the conclusion of the State action against David S. Alberts, and that was concluded in June 1950.

So in October 1950, a Federal grand jury had no hesitation about indicting him for mailing obscene matter or information telling where, how, and from whom it might be obtained, seven counts.

In December 1950, David S. Alberts pleaded guilty to two counts and he was fined $100 on each count in the Los Angeles Federal court.

Chairman KEFAUVER. $100?

Mr. STAPENHORST. $100 on each count.

Chairman KEFAUVER. That is liable to put him out of business, isn't it?

So, so often they just pay their little fines as operating costs as a license to do business?

Mr. STAPENHORST. That is correct.

Chairman KEFAVUER. And go right on?

Mr. STAPENHORST. And in many instances a very inexpensive license.

I would like to introduce into the record as an exhibit a page from the Postal Bulletin of March 17, 1955, which contains in the right-hand column a three-paragraph notice to postmasters about Post-master General Arthur E. Summerfield's clean-up-the-mail campaign.

Chairman KEFAUVER. We are glad to receive that as an exhibit.

(The bulletin referred to was marked "Exhibit No. 39," and is as follows:)

EXHIBIT No. 39

[From the Postal Bulletin, March 17, 1955]

"CLEAN-UP-THE-MAILS" CAMPAIGN

On March 17, 1955, Postmaster General Arthur E. Summerfield stated in press release No. 63 that "A growing volume of unwanted lewd and obscene matter is being sent through the mails into American homes, and the Post Office Department is intensifying its 'Clean-Up-the-Mails' efforts to stop this offense against common decency."

Mr. Summerfield further announced "Citizens who wish to help the Post Office Department in its 'Clean-Up-the-Mails' campaign can do so by delivering, to their local postmaster, any material received through the mails which they consider obscene."

Postmasters are instructed to forward such material to the post office inspector in charge of the division in which the office of mailing is located.

Chairman KEFAUVER. Anything else, Mr. Stapenhorst?

Mr. STAPENHORST. That is all, I believe.

Chairman KEFAUVER. Thank you very much, sir.

Well, we have some other witnesses here we are not going to get to hear today, but we do want to hear some others. I think at this time, though, we will have to take a break for a short lunch. Suppose we recess now and try to get started again at 15 minutes after 2.

We will stand in recess until 15 minutes after 2.

(Whereupon, at 1:10 p. m., a recess was taken until 2:15 p. m. of the same day.)

AFTERNOON SESSION

(Whereupon the hearing was resumed at 2:15 p. m.)

Chairman KEFAUVER. The subcommittee will come to order.

Who will be our next witness, Mr. Bobo?

Mr. Bobo. Mr. David S. Alberts.

Mrs. V. E. Alberts. Mr. Alberts will be here in just one moment. He is on his way.

Chairman Kefauver. Who are you?

Mrs. Alberts. Mrs. Alberts.

Chairman Kefauver. You are Mrs. Alberts?

Mrs. Alberts. Yes.

Chairman Kefauver. All right. He will be here shortly?

Mrs. Alberts. Yes.

Chairman Kefauver. Mr. Barnes. Will Mr. Barnes come around? How are you, Mr. Barnes? We are glad to see you.

All right, Mr. Bobo.

TESTIMONY OF PHILLIP I. BARNES, POLICE OFFICER, CITY OF LOS ANGELES, ATTACHED TO THE ADMINISTRATIVE VICE DIVISON, PORNOGRAPHIC DETAIL

Mr. Bobo. Mr. Barnes, would you state your name, your address, and your position for the record, please?

Mr. Barnes. My name is Phillip I. Barnes. My business address is 1337 Georgia Street. I am a police officer for the city of Los Angeles, attached to the administrative vice division, the pornographic detail.

Mr. Bobo. How long have you been connected with the pornographic detail?

Mr. Barnes. For the past 18 months.

Mr. Bobo. Would you speak up just a little louder. Pull the microphone closer to you.

Mr. Barnes. For the past 18 months.

Mr. Bobo. Attached to the pornographic detail of the police department, it is your duty to investigate cases involving the sale of pornographic literature within the city of Los Angeles?

Mr. Barnes. That is true.

Mr. Bobo. Mr. Barnes, in your capacity as a policeman and in dealing with pornographic literature, have you ever discovered that pornographic literature gets into the hands of those of juvenile age?

Mr. Barnes. I have.

Mr. Bobo. What type of pornographic literature have you found prevalent?

Mr. Barnes. Pornographic literature of all forms; written, photographic, statues, and so forth.

Mr. Bobo. What are the ages of some of the children that you have found pornographic literature in the possession of?

Mr. Barnes. The youngest that I recall was 10 years old.

Mr. Bobo. Ten years old?

Mr. Barnes. Yes sir.

Mr. Bobo. In the investigation of cases involving pornographic literature, what is the type that is most prevalent in the hands of those of juvenile age?

Mr. Barnes. I would say the most prevalent would be the type known to us, or in the language of the people who deal in it, as the Tijuana Bible, which is a small booklet about 2 by 3 inches, of a cartoon type, that is very lewd and very obscene in its character.

Mr. Bobo. It shows all types of sexual perversions?

Mr. Barnes. Yes; it does.

Mr. Bobo. Have you ever developed any cases involving juveniles where lewd photographic film, movie film, was involved?

Mr. Barnes. Yes; I have.

Mr. Bobo. Would you tell us somewhat of the extent of the traffic in pornographic film, as well as stills and booklets?

Mr. Barnes. It would be better for me to describe first what I term as true pornography. There are basically two types of pornography we find here in Los Angeles. One, the true pornography which is of a very lewd and obscene type that it is easily discernible and without question lewd. The second is the gray matter that falls into the category of that which was just brought before the committee at the morning session.

In Los Angeles in the past 18 months, through the investigations that have been conducted by myself and the officers with my squad, the true pornography type has not been prevalent to the point where it is a problem. To that end, I mean that it is not readily sold on the streets or in bookstores and so on, as might be alleged.

However, the pornographic material such as was described earlier this morning is prevalent. That is a problem to us. It is a problem to us to this extent: Each and every case that is brought to our attention in the form of complaint is carefully analyzed and investigated. The results of this investigation are presented to the office of the city attorney or the office of the district attorney for the application of a complaint or for the application of obtaining a search warrant. If such complaint is forthcoming or if such warrant is forthcoming, then the actions that follow are quite clear. We make the arrest and present the same facts to the court. If the complaint is refused, we are stopped at its onset. Many times we have been refused complaints for this type of literature, particularly in obtaining search warrants, because it was felt by the courts and by the office of the city attorney that it is an interpretive fact; that if you believe what you are reading in the brochure, then you believe that there is pornographic literature awaiting you at the other end; that if you believe that the literature in the brochure is not true, then you will find that which would be construed legal at the other end. So therefore we have been very unsuccessful in prosecuting complaints of this nature.

The type of pornographic material of the true pornographic type, there has never been any problem whatsoever in prosecuting and getting convictions. The courts have been lenient in the type of sentences or fines that are dealt to the defendants in these cases.

Mr. Bobo. What is the usual fine in a case involving true pornographic literature?

Mr. Barnes. I would say that the average is a suspended jail sentence and a fine of roughly $150.

Mr. Bobo. Have you ever known of any pornographic film or pornographic pictures or pornographic books displaying pictures displaying those of juvenile ages in the poses for pornographic literature?

Mr. Barnes. Yes; I have, sir. We had one such case fairly recently involving a husband and wife, a man in Hollywood who was titled a producer of motion pictures and scripts for motion pictures. In this particular case there were two juveniles. One was a girl 16 and one a girl 17. All of the participants in this case were prosecuted, with the exception of the photographer, who was in residence in

Hawaii. We did obtain a warrant for her arrest, and that warrant was presented to the Honolulu Police Department in certified form, but extradition was not granted and the person is not prosecuted as of this date.

Mr. Bobo. Were these movie films you are talking about or still photos?

Mr. Barnes. These were 3-D still photos, color.

Mr. Bobo. They showed the persons in indecent acts?

Mr. Barnes. Acts of sexual perversion between men and women, women and women, and men and men.

Chairman Kefauver. Well, were some of them convicted?

Mr. Barnes. They were all convicted.

Chairman Kefauver. Since they have been convicted, give us their names and addresses.

Mr. Barnes. Mr. Paul George Horner, 5253 Fountain Avenue. I note that that address might be incorrect. It might be 6253 instead of 52.

Mr. Jack Richard Massey, 125 West Acacia Street, Glendale.

Mrs. Mildred Frances Massey, of the same address.

The warrant was obtained for a Mrs. Frederick Rackel, of Honolulu, T. H.

Each of the people mentioned was specifically charged with acts of sexual perversion, citing 3 counts in the case of Mr. Horner, 1 count in the case of Jack Massey, 3 counts in the case of Mildred Massey, and 5 counts in the case of Mrs. Frederick Rackel.

Chairman Kefauver. Is it true that these particular pictures have shown up all over the country and very widely?

Mr. Barnes. We have received reports that these same pictures or duplicates of these pictures have been received as far away as India, in Europe, in Cuba, and various parts of the United States.

Chairman Kefauver. So they get one picture; of course, they make millions of duplicates.

Mr. Barnes. Yes, sir; they can.

Chairman Kefauver. Go ahead.

Mr. Bobo. Did you discover anything among these people as to their distribution process for mailing out these slides?

Mr. Barnes. Mr. Horner explained to me that he was the president of an association whose interest, prime interest, was the furtherance of 3-D photography, and that he corresponded with these members who were located throughout the world; and that quite often they would exchange examples of their work. He did not and would not qualify the examples as being pornographic.

Mr. Bobo. Did he give you the name of the association?

Mr. Barnes. He might have, but I do not know; I do not have that with me.

Mr. Bobo. You do not have that?

Mr. Barnes. No, sir; I do not.

Mr. Bobo. Have you worked on any other case involving the taking of pornographic photos or pornographic film, its development and distribution in the Los Angeles area?

Mr. Barnes. Yes; I have.

A case of Mr. Richard Bush, of 422 Lincoln Boulevard, Santa Monica. Mr. Bush was arrested first for the sale of lewd film. We made the arrest after purchasing five reels of pornographic film, including one which is entitled "The Nun, or Something Old, Something New." The investigation continued in the way of searching the premises of Mr. Bush, which divulged numerous photographs of a very pornographic nature, including that of the man himself and a 16-year-old girl engaging in an act of sexual perversion.

Based upon this photograph we secured a complaint against Mr. Bush for violation of the State statute prohibiting sexual oral coitus, and prosecuted him for that charge. He was found guilty.

Mr. BOBO. Do you have another case that you can bring to our attention, Mr. Barnes?

Mr. BARNES. As to amounts of property confiscated in the way of pornographic material, probably the most outstanding one was made by myself and officers of the administrative vice division, along with the officers from Huntington Park Police Department. This involved the arrest of a man by the name of Joseph Winter, a woman by the name of Beatrice Burke. Their address at that time was 1301 Club View Drive, Los Angeles. At the time of their arrest we confiscated approximately $50,000 worth of lewd material, both photographic and written.

Mr. BOBO. From the people did you determine where they might have secured this material?

Mr. BARNES. Mr. Winter, following his conviction, was advised by his attorney to divulge to me the source of his material. Mr. Winter stated that he was making the delivery from the Star Book Shop in San Francisco and that he had been apprehended while in transit. He said that the material that he had received from Star Book Shop was only a very, very small portion of that which the operator of that shop had at his disposal.

Upon examining the contents of this material, we found that it originated from all over the country, with particular attention to New York, Philadelphia, and Los Angeles. From New York there was an exceedingly large amount of material supplied by Irving S. Klaw, whom I understand this committee has met.

Chairman KEFAUVER. Mr. Klaw calls himself the "Pinup King," and we are recommending that he be held in contempt of the Senate for not testifying in New York.

Mr. BARNES. Your action is commendable.

Mr. Klaw has been known to the members of this police department for a good number of years as a major distributor of the flagellation type of pornography.

Also in the same material that was confiscated was material that came from Mr. Edward Mishkin of New York City, whom I also understand you have talked to.

Chairman KEFAUVER. That is M-i-s-h-k-i-n?

Mr. BARNES. Yes. As this is the largest single confiscation that we have made, it was important to us to try to determine the origin of this production, rather than its distribution; and the areas that were found to be producing and distributing locally were taken into the investigation and appropriate action taken to the removal of that source. Part of that is still currently under investigation.

I would like to make a statement relative to the conditions of pornography in Los Angeles.

Chairman KEFAUVER. Before you do that, may I ask a question?

Mr. BARNES. Yes, sir.

Chairman KEFAUVER. You are a fine police officer, and I want to compliment you upon all you are doing under difficult laws and difficult situations; but in these cases of Mishkin and Klaw, for instance—this is a San Francisco case—Do you exchange memos about these people, that is, with the New York police force, with the San Francisco police force?

Mr. BARNES. Immediately after your departure from New York City I was given a letter of request from the New York City Police Department to investigate certain persons who were corresponding with Mr. Mishkin.

Chairman KEFAUVER. You mean that is after our hearing there about 3 weeks ago?

Mr. BARNES. Yes, sir. Prior to that date and since the time I have been assigned to this detail, I had not received communications from the New York City Police Department. I have received numerous communications from other law-enforcement agencies, and particularly in the Los Angeles County area; all of the agencies represented here who have requested information or requested that we conduct investigations, the office of the postal department, sheriff's office, district attorney's office. We constantly are getting together and comparing our notes and making mutual investigations in an attempt to stop the distribution of this material.

Chairman KEFAUVER. Mr. Barnes, this is aside from the subject slightly, but since our crime committee investigation of 4 or 5 years ago, I have been plugging very hard for some kind of a national agency, under at least the jurisdiction of the Federal Government, to act as an information exchange group and coordinating group and information group for police authorities, prosecuting attorneys, all around the country; so that when something shows up here in Los Angeles that affects New York or Chicago, they would have information about it. Doesn't this case rather prove that something like that is very badly needed?

Mr. BARNES. Before I answer you, Senator, I wonder if I might clarify my expressions. Any statement that I might give to you in the way of an opinion or observation is that of my own. I do not speak for the police department. I am not in a position to do that.

Chairman KEFAUVER. We understand that entirely. I was only asking your personal opinion.

Mr. BARNES. My personal opinion is that we need very much a central intelligence agency for the purpose of disseminating this information back and forth from one law-enforcement agency to another. I think there is a certain element of distrust that exists between law-enforcement agencies. Through this effort it might be a step in the right direction to abolish this distrust and create a better understanding, and results would therefore be better if such an agency was created.

Chairman KEFAUVER. I don't mean to underestimate the tremendous importance of the Federal Bureau of Investigation, but it has charge of enforcement of Federal laws and they do have the police records of people; but situations, conditions like you have found here, where in many cases there may not be any police records, the detailed information about this pornography operation here would not be available through the FBI or any other source of information that I know of.

Mr. BARNES. That is true. That is true.

Chairman KEFAUVER. Thank you, sir.

Mr. BARNES. I was requested to bring to the hearing a report relative to an arrest that we made in the city of Culver City. There has been no mention, as I understand, of recordings. This is the only arrest that I have made myself where I have personal knowledge of recordings being produced and distributed that were of a pornographic nature. This involved the arrest of one Erwin Beard. Mr. Beard was residing at 12230½ Washington Place, Culver City. We received information that Mr. Beard was engaged in the sale of pornographic recordings.

Upon learning of his address in Culver City, we contacted the Culver City Police Department and told them we had made contact with Mr. Beard under the guise that we were to purchase these records, and they recommended that we go ahead with our investigation and arrest, and then bring them before the Culver City Police Department for booking.

I purchased four records from Mr. Beard, all of which were of a very pornographic nature.

After the arrest had been effected, Mr. Beard surrendered the remaining part of his material, which was approximately 375 records and the two master disks from which they are made. In the interrogation of Mr. Beard following his arrest, he told me that he, in company with another gentleman, had created this business, had cut the original disks and were engaging in producing them until 3 years ago, when his partner was arrested and convicted; and that he immediately took his master disks and the remainder of his stock and put them in hiding until very recently. In fact, 2 weeks prior to the date of our arrest. He again attempted to make sales, and that the confiscation we made at this time completely obliterated his business.

Mr. BOBO. What was the value placed upon the records, Mr. Barnes?

Mr. BARNES. Mr. Beard was selling these for $20 for 2 disks and—$20 for 2 disks, and then he added 2 other disks as an incentive for further purchase.

Mr. BOBO. You speak of these as being pornographic records?

Mr. BARNES. Yes, sir.

Mr. BOBO. What kind of material is on the record?

Mr. BARNES. One was entitled "Mr. Big Dick." Without becoming embarrassing, I can say that it was completely pornographic in the way of its wording, the noise, sound effects that were used, the expressions that were used. It told of the sexual intercourse of a Mr. Big Dick and two daughters of a prostitute. It was of a type that we described as truly pornographic. There would be no question as to whether it was or it was not.

Mr. BOBO. There was no question as to the obscenity?

Mr. BARNES. No, sir; there was absolutely none.

About the largest global producer that we have taken in the way of still photographs was Mr. Kai Mortensen, Box 13, Newbury Park, Ventura County. Mr. Mortensen was engaged in producing 4 by 5 pornographic—of the true pornographic type photographs and distributing them throughout the United States, including Mr. Mishkin and Mr. Klaw, as I spoke of before. They were two of is clients. We confiscated about 5,000 photographs and negatives from Mr.

Mortensen at the time of his arrest. We prosecuted him here and convicted him of the sale and keeping for sale of this material. He was then prosecuted again in Ventura County for the same charge and convicted. His entire material was confiscated and ordered destroyed by the court.

At the time of his arrest we also took the list of names and addresses that he had of his clients.

Mr. Bobo. What was the sentence that Mr. Mortensen received?

Mr. Barnes. I cannot accurately say. It was not a jail sentence. It was a fine and a suspended sentence.

Mr. Bobo. Did you discover in your investigation how orders would be shipped to Mr. Mishkin or Mr. Klaw in New York City?

Mr. Barnes. Mr. Mortensen was associated with a man in Simi, Calif., and through this association he was able to distribute the mail from Simi, Calif., to the agents outside of the California area. As far as those in the Los Angeles area and immediate local area, he would deliver those in person. Those would include Mr. E. A. Smith, the operator of a book store on Main Street here in Los Angeles, who also has been arrested by us and convicted on two separate occasions, which included the photographs that were produced by Mr. Mortensen.

Mr. Bobo. Is it your understanding that they were sent by mail to Mr. Klaw and Mr. Mishkin in New York from the men in Simi, Calif.?

Mr. Barnes. That is the information given to us by Mr. Mortensen. As to the accuracy of it, I do not know.

That information was conveyed to both the office of the FBI and to the postal authorities locally.

Mr. Bobo. Did he——

Mr. Barnes. Pardon me.

Mr. Bobo. Did he give you the name of the man in Simi, Calif., which whom he was associated?

Mr. Barnes. Without referring to my notes, no, sir. At this time I don't think so. I think I would recognize the name if I heard it.

Mr. Bobo. Was the name——

Mr. Barnes. Yes, the name was Kish.

Mr. Bobo. K-i-s-h, Mr. Kish?

Mr. Barnes. Yes.

Mr. Bobo. In Simi, Calif. Do you know his first name?

Mr. Barnes. No, sir. Again, without referring to the notes that I made at the time of the arrest and investigation, I could not say his first name. I do recall going there to the location at Simi to ascertain whether or not this man was still residing there, with officers from the Ventura County sheriff's office, and we found that Mr. Kish was still residing there and we obtained the license numbers of the cars that were present at that time.

Mr. Bobo. Would the name of Ed Kish—would that refesh your recollection?

Mr. Barnes. That sounds correct, sir.

Mr. Bobo. Mr. Ed Kish?

Mr. Barnes. Yes.

Mr. Bobo. Of Simi, Calif.?

Mr. Barnes. Yes, sir.

Chairman Kefauver. Mr. Barnes, did this customer list indicate nationwide distribution?

Mr. BARNES. Yes, sir; it definitely did. It included most of the States.

Chairman KEFAUVER. Some foreign countries?

Mr. BARNES. As I recall, there were no foreign countries listed.

Locally we have another problem that is coming to our attention constantly. That is the so-called model studios and model agencies that we have, whereby an amateur photographer might rent the premises for the purpose of photographing nude females. Any person, regardless of their background photographically speaking, may do so.

Chairman KEFAUVER. You mean without a license?

Mr. BARNES. Yes, sir; they may. They pay a fee of anywhere from $2 to $10 an hour for the privilege of photographing such a person.

From these studios we have had numerous complaints and proof of illegal photographs or pornographic photographs being made and disseminated; but in each and every case where we can establish the time for the element of prosecution, we do prosecute. However, the control of the studio itself is still outside of the scope of the police department.

When I was given the assignment to make this investigation of these studios, I was told to submit recommendations as to municipal legislation for their control; and on the 26th of May, this year, I submitted to the police department a detailed recommendation as to the control of the legislation. This recommendation has not been approved as of this date. We believe that it will be approved; possibly not in its present form, but in a form like the one that we have recommended. That would be to place all of the model studios under license by the Police Commission and by the city of Los Angeles; that each and every model who poses in the nude for photographs will be registered with the police department; that each and every model agent and studio manager, owner, operator, will likewise be required to be registered with the police department; and that one of the prime requisites of this registration be that the man not be convicted or have any conviction of a felony or any crime against public morals.

Further, described in there are the types of photographs that will be permitted. Those are fairly interpretive as far as true type is concerned, to remove any element of possible interpretation of being anything other than pornographic.

It is also recommended in there that this does not infringe upon any legal and appropriate medical research or any other approach to the photographing of the nude form without due cause and due reason.

Mr. BOBO. May we have a copy of your recommendations for an exhibit to our record?

Mr. BARNES. You may have that, sir.

Chairman KEFAUVER. That will be made an exhibit.

(The document referred to was marked "Exhibit No. 40," and is as follows:)

LOS ANGELES POLICE DEPARTMENT

EMPLOYEE'S REPORT

Subject: Recommended municipal legislation.

Name and rank: Sgt. H. R. Keever, watch commander, administrative vice.

Date and time reported: May 26, 1955, 1:30 p.m.

In answer to your assignment, this squad has conducted an investigation and research into the field of nude model photography. This investigation indicated the following action is necessary and needed to properly supervise and maintain any degree of good moral standards for this activity.

1. Each studio that is rented, leased, or used for the purpose of photographing nude models should be required to be licensed by the city of Los Angeles as such. (This would not apply to private-owned studios that are used exclusively by the owner or his employee or to a studio rented or leased by an individual and his employees as a permanent photographic business location, and used exclusively by said individual or his employee.)

2. Each owner, manager, or operator of any studio; each agent or model representative of a model who is photographed in a state of nudity should be registered with the Los Angeles Police Department and obtain a police commission permit before engaging in the business of renting, leasing or loaning their studio for photographing nude models; or assigning, employing, hiring, or sending any model to any location for the purpose of being photographed in a state of nudity.

3. Every model that is to be photographed while in a state of nudity should be required to be registered with the Los Angeles Police Department and to have a police commission permit before engaging in such activity.

The foregoing recommended points are suggested due to the results of our investigations of nude model studios and are based on the conclusions drawn from this investigation and the interviews with those engaged in that business.

There are approximately eight studios in the city, as of this report, that are used exclusively for the purpose of allowing amateur photographers to photograph nude models. Some of these studios maintain inexpensive box-type cameras for the convenience of those amateurs who do not have cameras. The average charge for "group" photographers (three or more photographers, photographing the model simultaneously) is $4 for a 2-hour period. Private photography (one photographer) is at an average of $10 per hour. Model fees are basically $5 per hour, but sometimes obtain as much as $25 an hour if the photographing is done at a private location, i. e., the photographers' apartment, beach area, or mountain resort.

The reception room area of most studios is usually occupied by the owner, manager, or operator of the studio, thereby allowing the photographers to "shoot" without supervision. In most cases the owner, manager, or operator does not indicate a feeling of responsibility or concern as to what transpires in the studio proper. On occasion, we have found that the owner, manager, or operator is a sex deviate and arranges the studio sittings to accommodate his fellow deviates.

New model applicants generally fall into the category of 18- to 30-year-old females that are lacking in strong moral standards. Some are known prostitutes, some professional burlesque strippers, others are former juvenile-detention-home releasees, and some just indolent females seeking income without physical or mental effort.

Upon application for work, it becomes the owner's, manager's, or operator's responsibility to "inspect" the new applicant and determine if she "qualifies." Very few are refused employment. Age seems to determine the model's popularity. If she is in her upper teens, her physical attributes are usually still photographically attractive and by coincidence, usually her ability to cope with a promising line of conversation regarding future movie contracts, is not as sharp as it would be in later years.

Models we have interviewed have informed us that the studio operators have told them that big major studio producers, directors, and photographers are among the men who are "shooting" the models in his studio. Others relate that they were informed that unless they had intimate relations with the operator, they wouldn't get assigned to the high-paying private sittings.

Not always are the operators the corrupt participant. One operator related the story of a model who was charging $1 a picture for those who wished to make a closeup of her unclothed genital area. This practice is not uncommon, because the model feels she cannot be identified by such a photograph. Other models are conducting prostitution at their apartments with the photographers following the studio sittings. We have verified this fact.

Agents and model representatives usually operate at a $5 flat rate fee for all appointments they arrange for private sittings. We have made arrests for prostitution at such private "sittings" but were unable to prove the agent knew in advance that the sitting would result in an act of prostitution. One agent stated to our informant, "Be sure and carry a camera with you. That way you can prove you intended to take pictures and that the 'piece' you get will be the result, not the intent, then the police can't pinch you."

In the main, the photographers are not even semiprofessional. The photographs they take speak for themselves. One may show concentration on bust shots only, another will be of buttocks, and still another will concentrate on the groin area. "Sneak shots" (taken while the model is changing pose and is unaware) are very frequently taken. These photos are usually developed at home in an inexpensive developing tank and may not come to our attention for many months or until a print is circulated away from the photographer.

It is felt that it is next to impossible to control the photographer except by studio regulation and operator-model laws. If the regulation is strong enough, both the operator and the model will exercise voluntary control over the photographer.

Upon the completion of the investigation of the nude modeling business, we compiled three proposed statutes for consideration and a set of recommended rules to be followed for each police commission permit holder. We then interviewed all known studio operators and agents as well as numerous models regarding this proposition. It was the general opinion that such control is needed and the recommended rules were both reasonable and appropriate.

We, therefore, submit to you for consideration and approval the following recommended statutes and police commission rules for the operation of the nude photographic modeling business.

It is further suggested that the administrative vice division maintain the records and files of all applicants for police department permits and that the police commission endorse eligible applicants.

PROPOSED ORDINANCES
Nude modeling

1. Every studio, agency, or model representative that employs the services of any model to be photographed in a state of nudity by one or more photographers other than the licensed owner, manager, operator, or agent, shall be required to be licensed by the city of Los Angeles and to obtain a permit from the police commission. Any studio, agency, or model's representative that employs the services, or rents said services to any other person without being licensed and operating under a police commission permit, shall be guilty of a misdemeanor.

(a) "State of nudity" is that state that exposes the human form without covering to the genital area and/or the female breasts.

2. Any person who owns, operates, maintains, or controls any studio, agency or model's representative organization that employs the services of any model to be photographed in a state of nudity shall be required to be registered with the police commission before engaging in said business. Any person who owns, operates, maintains or controls any studio, agency, or model's representative organization that employs the services of any model to be photographed in a state of nudity without being first registered with the police commission is guilty of a misdemeanor.

3. Any person who engaged in the act of modeling or posing as a photographic subject while in a state of nudity shall be required to be registered with the police commission before engaging in said act. Any person who engages in such act of modeling or posing as a photographic subject while in a state of nudity and is not registered with the police commission is guilty of a misdemeanor. (This section does not apply to bona fide medical research.)

POLICE COMMISSION REGULATIONS
Nude modeling

1. Every studio, agency, or model's representative must operate under police department permit issued by the police commission, while engaging in the employment of services of any model who poses or models as a photographic subject while in a state of nudity.

(a) This permit will be displayed in a conspicuous manner so as to be visible from the reception room area of said business.

2. Every person who owns, operates, maintains, or controls any studio, agency, or model's representative organization that employs the services of any model to be photographed in a state of nudity shall be required to be registered with the police department and the registration card issued shall be displayed upon request by any police officer, by the person to whom it is issued.

(a) This registration card is not transferable and must be immediately accessible to the applicant, while engaged in the operation of his business.

3. Every person who engages in the act of modeling or posing as a photographic subject while in a state of nudity is required to be registered with the police

department and must display the registration card issued at the request of any police officer while said model is so employed.

(a) This registration card is not transferable and must be immediately accessible to the applicant while engaged in the act of modeling or posing in a state of nudity.

4. It shall be the responsibility of each owner, manager, or operator of a photographic studio as described in this section to maintain a photographer's registration book within the studio and that each photographer be compelled to sign his true name and correct address under the present date before engaging in photographing a model who is posing in a state of nudity. Model's name will also be placed by photographer's signature to denote model used.

5. It shall be the responsibility of each owner, manager, or operator of a photographic studio as described in this section to prohibit the consumption of any alcoholic beverages by models, photographers or other parties present during the course of business of photographing models in a state of nudity.

6. It shall be the responsibility of each owner, manager, or operator of a photographic studio as described in this section to maintain supervision over the conduct of models in their employ and to maintain professional standards in the issuance of directions to said models.

7. The following rules shall be followed in the photographing of any model in a state of nudity:

(a) No photographs shall be made which exposes the genitals or pubic hair of the model.

(b) No photographs shall be made which depicts any lewd or suggestive act or motion.

(c) No model shall be photographed while touching her breasts or genitals with her hand.

(d) No photographs shall be made which includes a man and a woman while either is in a state of nudity.

(e) Where two or more models of the same sex are used in the same photograph, there shall be no touching of the bodies between models.

(f) In any case where motion-picture photography is used, the model must wear a permanent nontransparent covering over the genitals and crease of the buttocks. The nipples of the breasts that have different pigmentation than the body of the breast must also be covered with like material.

(g) No photographer shall be allowed to make physical contact with the model while the model is engaged in posing or modeling.

(h) Upon completion of modeling and during recesses between modeling assignments, the model will retire to an enclosed dressing room or become clothed.

(i) Profanity and obscenity will not be permitted at any time during the conducting of photographic modeling.

(j) It shall be the responsibility of every owner, manager, operator, and model to report violations of this section to the police department immediately.

(k) There will be no photographs made in any order that may be assembled in sequence form depicting the dressing or undressing of a model.

(l) There will be no photographs made of a model in the process of removal of the undergarments such as brassiere or panties.

8. Each applicant for a police commission permit as owner, manager, operator, or model will be required to be photographed by the police department before engaging in business. Permits will not be issued to any person who has been found guilty of any felony or any crime involving public morals.

9. It is not legal for any person, below the age of 18 years, to be photographed in the state of nudity. Model applicants will be required to present positive proof of age before permit will be granted.

10. No person under the age of 18 years will be allowed to be present on the premises while models are posing in a state of nudity.

11. A complete copy of the foregoing rules and regulations shall be posted in a conspicuous location within the studio for the benefit of all concerned parties.

12. Each change of address by an owner, manager, agent, or operator, or model shall be reported by mail to the police department, within 5 days and suitable notations will be made on the applicant's registration card.

13. All outdoor photography of nude models within the city of Los Angeles will be conducted in such a way to eliminate all possibilities of observation by any party or parties to be offended. (See sec. 311.1 P. C.)

Respectfully submitted.

P. I. BARNES, No. 5454.
R. O. COLLINS, No. 6885.
R. E. ANDERSON, No. 5306.

Mr. BOBO. Mr. Barnes, have you had any occasion to investigate any pornographic cases wherein the use of male models might be used?

Mr. BARNES. Yes, sir; we have. We had such a case recently involving a Mr. Lyle Frisby, whose business address was 1438 Naud Street, Los Angeles. On the 16th of May 1954, by virtue of a warrant, we arrested Mr. Frisby and another gentleman, who is in the audience at the present time, a Mr. Robert Mizer. Mr. Mizer was distributing a magazine known as Physique Pictorial, which is a magazine containing photographs of male models of the muscle-men type. Included in this magazine were photographs under ads of male models. One of these ads was under the name Lyle of Hollywood. It showed a photograph of a man in a seated position, who appeared to be wearing a jock strap over the pubic area. We went to Mr. Frisby at the address he had advertised in this magazine and purchased the same photograph from Mr. Frisby, and the photograph was without any adornment in the area of the pubic region. It was a complete nude; the genitals were showing. Based on this purchase we made the arrest of Mr. Frisby and of Mr. Mizer. Both Mr. Frisby and Mr. Mizer were convicted in court. However, Mr. Mizer filed a notice of appeal through his attorney, and the case was reversed, following his sentence of 90 days in jail. The case was reversed and Mr. Mizer was released from that conviction under the appellate decision, that in the manner in which he sold the photograph he was not guilty.

Mr. Frisby was convicted and all his material confiscated and destroyed.

Mr. BOBO. What was the size of the amount of the material that you confiscated and destroyed, the quantity?

Mr. BARNES. There were many thousands of photographs, and basing it on the sale value as it was told to us, they were $2 a print, I would say close to $10,000 in that sense, in the sense that they sell it.

Mr. BOBO. Was his distribution entirely within this area, or did he have distribution in points outside of the California area?

Mr. BARNES. Mr. Frisby indicated that he sold throughout the United States and that he did have the sanction of the postal department for selling such material.

Chairman KEFAUVER. Now, that is just what he said about it?

Mr. BARNES. That is just what he said about it.

Chairman KEFAUVER. Well, I don't believe he had the sanction of the post office.

Mr. BARNES. I concur with your conclusions.

Mr. BOBO. Was there any evidence developed around Mr. Frisby that showed where he had sold these particular types of photographs, near schools and playground areas?

Mr. BARNES. Mr. Frisby's business location was backed up against a playground and within 300 yards was a school and school grounds. One of the charges in his complaint was keeping or, rather, possessing lewd photographs within 300 yards of a school, park, or playground.

During the investigation we found one man, who is now a marine, who had posed for such photographs when he was 17 years of age. He was not available at the time of the prosecution, so therefore his case was not brought up, other than through the investigation.

Mr. BOBO. Did you receive any evidence in your investigation whether these photographs may have been sold to any of the children on the playground or at the school?

Mr. BARNES. No, sir; I did not.

Chairman KEFAUVER. Well, Mr. Barnes, you and the other officers here are good men. I have been associated with many men in the Los Angeles police force, and you have good, conscientious men. You have been making a hard try at this thing. The laws and the decisions of the courts and other things have caused you a great many handicaps, haven't they?

Mr. BARNES. Yes; they have, sir.

Chairman KEFAUVER. I hope you don't become discouraged by virtue of the difficulty you have had.

Mr. BARNES. No, sir. We sit back and wait.

Chairman KEFAUVER. As I understand your testimony, your particular hardships and recommendations are, then, you have talked about the control of the studios; that is one thing.

Mr. BARNES. Yes, sir.

Chairman KEFAUVER. The wording of the statute, the State statute, is another difficulty you have had.

Mr. BARNES. Yes.

Chairman KEFAUVER. The light sentences are another difficulty.

Mr. BARNES. Yes, sir.

Chairman KEFAUVER. The absence of exchange of information between police departments is another national difficulty.

Mr. BARNES. Yes.

Chairman KEFAUVER. And then the strengthening that needs to be done of the postal regulation is still another difficulty.

Mr. BARNES. Yes, sir.

Chairman KEFAUVER. Do you have any other suggestions as to what might be done to help you clean out this filth, be able to enforce it better?

Mr. BARNES. The problem—pardon me.

Chairman KEAUVER. To be able to enforce the laws better.

Mr. BARNES. I think the problem that faces us now, that is probably the greatest problem, is the fact that each case must be tried on its own merits. That which we might bring in today and have a court adjudge guilty from the interpretation of the material, that same material can be sold by his next-door neighbor the following day and another arrest made, and a presentation to the second court or second jury would reverse the decision insofar as their interpretation might be; so that we are not—we do not have a standard to operate with. It becomes quite a problem to us when we make the same arrests at 10 or 12 different locations; 1 or 2 might be guilty and the balance would not, or vice versa.

Chairman KEFAUVER. And the final thing you need is better backing on the part of the people in your efforts.

Mr. BARNES. Yes, sir; definitely.

Chairman KEFAUVER. That is a big thing.

Mr. BARNES. Yes, sir.

Chairman KEFAUVER. Thank you very much, Mr. Barnes.

Mr. BARNES. Thank you.

Chairman KEFAUVER. We compliment you upon your work and we wish you continued success.

Mr. BARNES. Thank you very much, sir.

Chairman KEFAUVER. Mr. Alberts. Will Mr. Alberts come around now.

Get Mr. Fleishman a chair there.

Mr. FLEISHMAN. Thank you, sir. I have got one.

Chairman KEFAUVER. You are Mr. Alberts?

Mr. ALBERTS. I am Mr. Alberts.

Chairman KEFAUVER. Will you hold up your hand.

(Mr. Alberts was sworn.)

TESTIMONY OF DAVID S. ALBERTS, ACCOMPANIED BY COUNSEL, STANLEY FLEISHMAN, LOS ANGELES, CALIF.

Mr. FLEISHMAN. Mr. Senator, at the outset——

Chairman KEFAUVER. Let Mr. Alberts sit down.

Mr. FLEISHMAN. I have three short motions that won't take 3 minutes.

Chairman KEFAUVER. Just a minute, now, sir.

Mr. FLEISHMAN. Thank you.

Chairman KEFAUVER. Now, Mr. Alberts, what is your address?

Mr. ALBERTS. Sunset Palm Apartments, Los Angeles.

Chairman KEFAUVER. Sunset Palm Apartments?

Mr. ALBERTS. Yes, sir.

Chairman KEFAUVER. And your age, sir?

Mr. ALBERTS. Thirty-three.

Chairman KEFAUVER. And your wife is back there with you?

Mr. ALBERTS. Yes, sir.

Chairman KEFAUVER. Now, sir, tell us your full name.

Mr. FLEISHMAN. Stanley Fleishman.

Chairman KEFAUVER. Now, Mr. Fleishman, what is your address?

Mr. FLEISHMAN. 1741 North Ivar.

Chairman KEFAUVER. And you are an attorney at law of the city of Los Angeles, and you are the attorney for Mr. Alberts?

Mr. FLEISHMAN. I trust that won't be held against me, Mr. Senator.

Chairman KEFAUVER. No, sir. As a counsel you have a right to take any case that is within the canons of ethics.

Mr. FLEISHMAN. Thank you, sir. As I say, I have three short motions, if I may.

Chairman KEFAUVER. Pull that a little bit closer, sir.

Mr. FLEISHMAN. They won't take 3 minutes. The first is, we believe that Mr. Alberts ought not to be required to testify here now because, as you have been told, he is up for sentence a week from yesterday, and we can't help but feel that this must be an influencing factor upon the court, which it should not be on an open court. Moreover, there is a motion for a new trial set for the same time, and we feel that the motion may be seriously adversely affected; that he would not get the fair hearing that he would get otherwise. I am sure you are familiar with the Delaney case where this problem was faced very seriously by the court, so we feel that if the testimony is necessary, that it be put over to another time. That is our first motion.

Chairman KEFAUVER. Mr. Fleishman, let me see if I understand that sufficiently. Mr. Alberts has been convicted in the State court?

Mr. FLEISHMAN. That is true.

Chairman KEFAUVER. On a number of counts of possessing or selling——

Mr. FLEISHMAN. Well, there are two counts involved.

Chairman KEFAUVER. What are the counts?

Mr. FLEISHMAN. I was not the attorney there so that I am just familiar with it in a general sense and couldn't state it accurately. It does have to do generally with the subject that you are inquiring into today, though.

Chairman KEFAUVER. Who was the attorney in those cases?

Mr. FLEISHMAN. I believe it was Mr. Maddox of Beverly Hills—I know it was.

Chairman KEFAUVER. Anyway, those cases grow out of this matter we are discussing here; is that correct?

Mr. FLEISHMAN. It is certainly related sufficiently.

Chairman KEFAUVER. And when was Mr. Alberts convicted?

Mr. FLEISHMAN. I am not sure of the time. Within the last month, certainly.

Chairman KEFAUVER. Maybe Mr. Alberts would know.

Mr. FLEISHMAN. I wouldn't want him to answer that.

It was within the last month, sir.

Chairman KEFAUVER. Very well.

Mr. FLEISHMAN. I do believe——

Chairman KEFAUVER. I am just trying to get the date.

Mr. FLEISHMAN. Yes. The new trial is coming up on Friday, within a week, and we do feel that it has already been seriously adversely affected, and that to require him to proceed would make it even more serious. As a matter of fact, I spoke with Mr. Bobo briefly in the hope that so much wouldn't be said, because I am sure we all agree that a court case ought to be decided by the court uninfluenced by this type of proceeding, however necessary this type of proceeding may be.

Chairman KEFAUVER. Then, after the motion for a new trial is argued, if it is granted there will be a new trial; if it is not, there will either be a sentence or an appeal; is that correct?

Mr. FLEISHMAN. That is right.

Chairman KEFAUVER. What are your other motions, sir?

Mr. FLEISHMAN. The second one is on the subpena duces tecum. We feel that it is much too broad, amounting to a fishing expedition in a large part. It calls for all records of your interest and property, real, personal, or mixed. This is not a general investigating committee. Of course, it has a purpose, and it would seem that much of the material sought is outside of the purpose. I think this perhaps calls to mind what may have happened, and I think it is unfortunate. I have a feeling that these subpenas were signed in blank and handed over to investigators who came out here, and then completed it as they thought fit.

Chairman KEFAUVER. Mr. Fleishman, you are wrong about that. The subpenas were signed by me.

Mr. FLEISHMAN. With the material called for in the subpenas?

Chairman KEFAUVER. I am sure. I don't remember the particular subpena, but my ruling——

Mr. FLEISHMAN. Well, the newspaper accounts indicated that the investigators were coming out here to determine who to investigate and how to do it.

Chairman KEFAUVER. Well, of course, we have been here for some time and we are in pretty close communication with one another.

Mr. FLEISHMAN. Well, I may be in error.

Chairman KEFAUVER. Then, anyway, suppose we read the subpena into the record. Let it be printed in the record at this time. We have a copy of it.

(The subpena was marked "Exhibit No. 41," and reads as follows:)

UNITED STATES OF AMERICA

CONGRESS OF THE UNITED STATES

To DAVID S. ALBERTS, *Greeting:*

Pursuant to lawful authority, you are hereby commanded to appear before the Subcommittee To Investigate Juvenile Delinquency of the Senate of the United States, on June 17, 1955, at 9 a. m., at their committee room, 518 United States Post Office and Courthouse Building, 312 North Spring Street, Los Angeles, Calif., then and there to testify what you may know relative to the subject matters under consideration by said committee, and bring with you copies of your Federal and State income tax returns for the years 1950 to 1954, inclusive, bankbooks, canceled checks, check stubs, statements of accounts and liabilities, profit and loss statements, and other records pertaining to your business for the years of 1950 to 1954, inclusive, and all records of your interest in property, real, personal, or mixed.

Hereof fail not, as you will answer your default under the pains and penalties in such cases made and provided.

To _____ to serve and return.

Given under my hand, by order of the committee, this 10th day of June, in the year of our Lord one thousand nine hundred and fifty-five.

ESTES KEFAUVER,
Chairman, Subcommittee To Investigate Juvenile Delinquency,
Committee on the Judiciary.

[Endorsement]

JUNE 13, 1955.

I made service of the within subpena by serving in person the within-named David S. Alberts, at 8627 Melrose Avenue, Los Angeles, at 4:30 p. m., on the 13th day of June 1955.

P. I. BARNES.

Mr. FLEISHMAN. Yes, certainly.

Chairman KEFAUVER. Now, in response to the subpena are you bringing in any records and books?

Mr. FLEISHMAN. We have brought records, but we deem it to be an unreasonable search and seizure and also violative of the fifth amendment.

Chairman KEFAUVER. Either tell us whether you are complying with the subpena—

Mr. FLEISHMAN. Well, records have been brought, but we will not turn records over on the ground that we feel it is an unreasonable search and seizure and it is violative of the defendant's—you sound like a defendant when you come here a little bit—the witness' rights under the fifth amendment.

Chairman KEFAUVER. Then, what is your third motion, sir?

Mr. FLEISHMAN. The third motion is that we feel that this committee of one is improperly constituted. Much has been said, and correctly so, as to the impropriety of having committees of one; and I understand that there was a Senate rule pointing to the vice inherent in it and urging that there be no mores uch committees; so that we feel that this committee, being improperly constituted, has no power to compel any testimony.

Those are the three motions.

Chairman KEFAUVER. Well, dealing with your motions in the reverse order, I don't like committees of one, either. I have always advocated that there should be more than 1 Senator present at any meeting, but the rule of the Judiciary Committee is that if permission by the committee is given for a hearing to be held by 1 Senator, it is a legal hearing and is permitted. Such permission has previously been written into the record here.

As to the second part, your second motion, I would like to have permission for the staff to see just what records you might have brought in response to the subpena so that we can get a description if not the details of the records, but what they are, in the record; and then we will decide that question later on as to whether the subpena is too broad.

I think, frankly, that there is something to your suggestion or your objection that with the case pending that you are talking about, that we perhaps should not require Mr. Alberts to testify this afternoon. As much as I dislike the kind of business that has been described that he is in, I don't want to take an unfair advantage of him.

But, Mr. Fleishman, Mr. Alberts will remain under subpena. His case will be disposed of some time or another. This committee will be back in Los Angeles some time again, and eventually Mr. Alberts will be required to tell the committee such parts of the nature of his business as pertains to our investigation.

Mr. FLEISHMAN. That is understood, of course.

Chairman KEFAUVER. Can it be understood that he will remain under subpena, that he will appear upon notice either to you as his counsel or to him by telegram or by letter?

Mr. FLEISHMAN. Certainly. That would be agreeable.

Chairman KEFAUVER. Very well. We will excuse you at this time.

Mr. FLEISHMAN. Thank you.

May Mrs. Alberts be excused also? She was also involved in the same proceeding, and although she was——

Chairman KEFAUVER. Let's have Mrs. Alberts come around. We take people one by one as they appear.

TESTIMONY OF VIOLET EVELYN STANARD ALBERTS, LOS ANGELES, CALIF.

Chairman KEFAUVER. Now, you are Mrs. Alberts?

Mrs. ALBERTS. Yes; Violet.

Chairman KEFAUVER. What is your first name?

Mrs. ALBERTS. Violet.

Chairman KEFAUVER. What? I thought your name was Stanard.

Mrs. ALBERTS. You didn't ask me.

Chairman KEFAUVER. Ma'am?

Mrs. ALBERTS. You didn't ask me.

Chairman KEFAUVER. I thought I asked you what your name was.

Mrs. ALBERTS. You asked my first name. My whole name is Violet Evelyn Stanard Alberts.

Chairman KEFAUVER. I see. Now, you are the wife of the man who has just been here?

Mrs. ALBERTS. Yes.

Chairman KEFAUVER. Now, what is the situation relative to Mrs. Alberts. Mr. Fleishman?

Mr. FLEISHMAN. She was in the same trial and was acquitted, although we feel that the judge might just as well be influenced, perhaps, by this. The two of them were tried together in the court of the same trial.

Chairman KEFAUVER. You mean the transactions about which we would ask her you think have a direct relation to the business of her husband?

Mr. FLEISHMAN. The same thing, Your Honor. The same thing. They worked together.

Chairman KEFAUVER. They were tried on the same charges?

Mr. FLEISHMAN. Yes.

Chairman KEFAUVER. But the charges were dismissed as to Mrs. Alberts?

Mr. FLEISHMAN. That is true, after trial.

Chairman KEFAUVER. After trial?

Mr. FLEISHMAN. Yes.

Chairman KEFAUVER. You mean the jury dismissed her?

Mr. FLEISHMAN. The judge.

Chairman KEFAUVER. Well, is she under indictment?

Mr. FLEISHMAN. No.

Chairman KEFAUVER. Or a charge of anything at the present time?

Mr. FLEISHMAN. No, but I think it is the same business, and again the judge, I feel, would be as likely to be influenced as to Mrs. Alberts' testimony—almost, not quite as much—as he would with Mr. Alberts.

Chairman KEFAUVER. Well, frankly, Mr. Fleishman, legally I don't think you have much ground to stand on insofar as Mrs. Alberts is concerned. I am sure the judge will decide the case, the motion for a new trial and the sentence on the evidence and the facts before him without regard to what this lady might testify; but we don't want to —we would lean over the other way rather than take a chance on prejudicing his position.

Mr. FLEISHMAN. It would be agreeable——

Chairman KEFAUVER. But I think Mrs. Alberts might very well know, and I put you on notice, that you will be required to tell about this whole business.

Mrs. ALBERTS. I will be available, as my husband will be.

Chairman KEFAUVER. Then you will remain under subpena and we will notify you when we come here again.

Mr. FLEISHMAN. We will be agreeable to that. Thank you very much, sir.

Chairman KEFAUVER. Now, Mr. Fleishman, with Mr. George Martin here—we don't want to see the contents of what you produce, but we would like to at least have an inventory of what it is. Then you keep it in your possession, so that we can decide whether what you have brought in is responsive to the subpena which has been made in the record. If you will go over this with Mr. Martin?

Mr. FLEISHMAN. Yes.

Chairman KEFAUVER. Lieutenant Walter J. Sullivan.
Have a seat, sir.

STATEMENT OF LT. WALTER J. SULLIVAN, INVESTIGATOR FOR THE DISTRICT ATTORNEY, LOS ANGELES COUNTY, CALIF.

Chairman KEFAUVER. All right, Mr. Bobo.

Mr. BOBO. Lieutenant Sullivan, would you state to us your name, your address, and your present position?

Lieutenant SULLIVAN. Walter J. Sullivan; I reside at 4053 Farmdale Avenue, Studio City. I am an investigator working out of the office of District Attorney S. Ernest Roll.

Mr. BOBO. Mr. Sullivan, on or about March 1 of this year, 1955, did you participate in a police raid on the Alberts' establishment?

Lieutenant SULLIVAN. I think the date was, if I may refer to my notes—was on or about February 25. I am not quite sure, but I think that was the date, after——

Mr. BOBO. That was the establishment of David S. Alberts and Violet E. Stanard Alberts?

Lieutenant SULLIVAN. That is right, sir. Yes; it was on February 25, after obtaining a proper search warrant from Judge Charles Griffin of the municipal court of Beverly Hills, we proceeded to various addresses and took samples of some of the materials that the Alberts were mailing.

Mr. BOBO. Do you have a list of the addresses from which they were operating?

Lieutenant SULLIVAN. Yes. They have an office and some material at 8627 Melrose Avenue, Los Angeles; a warehouse at 8733 Santa Monica Boulevard; and officers also went to their home at that time located at 11064½ Strathmore Drive in West Los Angeles.

Mr. BOBO. Upon visiting these establishments, did you find any material of a pornographic nature, strip photos, or lewd films?

Lieutenant SULLIVAN. Yes. We found material that in our opinion was of that nature. We took samples of quite a number of the materials that they were mailing out, brought them back to the court. They were later reviewed by the district attorney's office, following which both Mr. and Mrs. Alberts were charged with four counts of violation of State law.

Mr. BOBO. Do you have with you any copies of pictures of the material which you actually seized in these raids?

Lieutenant SULLIVAN. With the consent of Judge Griffin, I have with me some of the material that we took at that time.

Mr. BOBO. In each establishment in which you visited, how many samples of the particular——

Chairman KEFAUVER. Well, let's see some of it up here.

Mr. BOBO. May we have copies of that?

Lieutenant SULLIVAN. Here is a box of stereotype pictures, consisting of pictures of nude women in color.

A bunch of pamphlets: Curious and Unusual Love Affairs, How To Be Happy Though Married, Prostitution in the United States, A Prostitute and Her Lover, Letters of the Courtesans, The Love Affairs of a Priest and a Nun, Amorous Tales of the Monks, Wild Women of Broadway, Confessions of a Minister's Daughter.

I think you gentlemen already have in your possession some of the—flagellation pictures of Tina and others of the same sort.

Mr. BOBO. These are pictures showing various types of torture between females, beatings?

Lieutenant SULLIVAN. Decks of playing cards, pictures of nude women on each and every playing card.

Mr. BOBO. These are large playing cards with lithograph full-color pictures of various women in nude poses.

Lieutenant Sullivan, on this one card here I notice an autograph on the bottom of the picture. Do you know the person, the photographer, who might have taken these pictures?

Lieutenant SULLIVAN. I do not, sir.

Mr. BOBO. A Mr. Felix Glied, Jr.

Lieutenant SULLIVAN. I know of him by name, but I am not personally acquainted with him. He is a local photographer.

I have quite a number of other things here. I don't know whether the committee would be interested in all of them or not, sir.

Mr. BOBO. In visiting these various establishments, you took just certain samples of the materials which were there?

Lieutenant SULLIVAN. That is correct, sir.

Here are a couple of bound books. One, Witch on Wheels; the other, Resort to Sin; which it is my understanding that the judge who tried them as the result of this raid thought that they were obscene.

Mr. BOBO. This Resort to Sin is a book by Mr. Clifford Forbes, published by the Arco Publishing Co., Inc., 420 Lexington Avenue, New York, N. Y.

The Witch on Wheels is a book by Bill Boltin, published by the same publishing company.

Both of those books, it is your understanding, were found to be obscene in the view of the judge in that case?

Lieutenant SULLIVAN. That is my understanding, sir.

However, I might say this, that the prosecuting attorney, Mr. James Nelson, is here present at the hearing and can better advise the committee as to the judge's findings.

That is two pictures of some of the evidence that was seized that is now under the court's jurisdiction, but in the hands of the district attorney.

Mr. BOBO. You have presented us two pictures of some of the evidence that was received. Am I to understand that in picking up this, did you pick up the entire contents of the buildings into which you raided?

Lieutenant SULLIVAN. No.

Mr. BOBO. How many samples of each particular type of literature would you confiscate?

Lieutenant SULLIVAN. I would estimate approximately six types of each piece of literature or book or picture that they had for sale out there, sir.

Mr. BOBO. In picking up six samples of each particular type of literature which they had, how was it transported back to the place of storage?

Lieutenant SULLIVAN. It was transported by truck. We reported to the judge what we had and it was then brought to the district attorney's office and placed in storage for use of the judge and the court.

Mr. Bobo. Approximately what quantity of material was seized, Mr. Sullivan?

Lieutenant Sullivan. I would say approximately—possibly a ton of it.

Mr. Bobo. A ton of it?

Lieutenant Sullivan. I would say approximately a ton.

Mr. Bobo. Did you place any approximate valuation upon the entire contents of the buildings which you visited? Was there a valuation placed upon them?

Lieutenant Sullivan. No; not to my knowledge, sir. We did see some records of the business which indicated to us that the business was grossing forty to fifty thousand dollars a month.

Mr. Bobo. Was there a method of operating according to the evidence which you picked up there? Was it by mail order business and solicitation?

Lieutenant Sullivan. Yes, sir; it was by mail order business. We found much of the advertising that was going out over the country in this particular warehouse which we raided.

Mr. Bobo. Were they operating under the name of the Male Merchandise Mart?

Lieutenant Sullivan. Yes, under that name, and one of their latest name was the Sailor Jock's.

Mr. Bobo. I believe you also have with you there a purchase order book which you confiscated in that raid. What does that purchase order book show as to the distribution of material? Does it show that purchases were made only in the Los Angeles area from the Male Merchandise Mart, or were there purchases made from points outside of California and other places in different parts of the United States?

Lieutenant Sullivan. They were made from outside of California. New York City and various other locations throughout the country. I have several purchase order books here if you want to look them over, sir.

Mr. Bobo. All right, sir.

Lieutenant Sullivan. We seized at the time some of their mailing lists, approximately 15 boxes of the mailing lists, which indicated that they were shipping at least advertising, possibly merchandise, to all sections of the country.

Mr. Bobo. Do you have any approximate count as to the number of names which might appear upon that mailing list?

Lieutenant Sullivan. I do not, sir.

Chairman Kefauver. Anything else you want to tell us about it, Mr. Sullivan?

Lieutenant Sullivan. Not at the moment, Mr. Senator. So far as the trial of the action is concerned——

Chairman Kefauver. We would like to have the opportunity of getting information from—you have been mighty cooperative with our people, but particularly the order books and the connections in other States showing interstate commerce and the type of interstate commerce. We would ask you to let us develop as much as we can. It would be helpful from this standpoint. That will be all right, won't it?

Lieutenant Sullivan. Yes, sir.

Chairman Kefauver. Thank you very much, sir.

Now, I said in the beginning that anyone's name who was here that had been brought out who wanted an opportunity to make any statement would have that opportunity. I don't believe anyone has spoken to our counsel or staff about it. Is there anyone whose name has been mentioned who would like to testify?

Mrs. Ray SUCHMAN. Mr. Chairman, you mentioned my name wrong. I wonder if I could just have a minute on this television issue.

Chairman KEFAUVER. Well, lady, we finished up our television hearing. What is it? You told me your right name this morning.

Mrs. SUCHMAN. Mrs. Ray Suchman.

Chairman KEFAUVER. What is the nature of your statement, Mrs. Suchman?

Mrs. SUCHMAN. I just wanted to say I am in 100 percent hearty agreement with all you are doing, but I don't think there has been enough stressed on television. If you go along all the streets, little houses that are ready to collapse have an antenna on them. That shows the power of television.

Chairman KEFAUVER. Yes.

Mrs. SUCHMAN. I just wanted you to take cognizance of that. It is a very important thing in our lives. I don't go to movies; I sit home. A lot of us old folks get all of our information and entertainment over the television. I just wanted that to go in the record.

Chairman KEFAUVER. Yes. Thank you very much.

Mrs. LETA MEYERS SMART. Mr. Chairman, I am hoping what I left with you will suffice.

Chairman KEFAUVER. Just a moment, now, good lady. Will you tell us your name?

Mrs. SMART. Leta Meyers Smart. I was interested because one of your reasons for this investigation was the juvenile delinquency among the Indian children.

Chairman KEFAUVER. Yes, ma'am.

Mrs. SMART. Since I have covered it in the material I left with you, and I think I have had your assurance that it is a subject that you are interested in, especially on account of the new drug that these children are taking and the letting loose of the liquor on the Indian reservations. That is all brought out, so I won't take up the time of the committee; but I have been asked to be sort of a spokeswoman for this lady here, whom I have just met this morning. She left a letter with you yesterday, and she will give you her own name. I haven't had time to go into it to see really what her suggestions would be to your committee; but the main difficulty here is now with this lady that she would like to know just what form her plan would have to be in so as to get the attention of your committee. I think you have her letter there.

What is your name? Give your name.

Mrs. NIVENANDA. I am Madam Nivenanda.

Chairman KEFAUVER. Well, Mrs. Nivenanda, if you have written us a letter, it will certainly get our attention; but what is it you have on your mind?

Mrs. NIVENANDA. I would like to know for what extent I could benefit for the juvenile delinquency? I have given consultations on many cases and have given a lot of time and prevented people from getting down on Skid Row, so to say, and I would like to know, since

I am of foreign descent, the sort of fear that I could have to un-American activity in my mind, and would not be beneficial for the children; and I would like to inquire as to what extent I could serve.

Chairman KEFAUVER. Well, we appreciate your willingness to serve. You write us fully just how you can serve and in what ways you think you will be helpful, and we will let you know.

Mrs. NIVENANDA. Thank you.

Chairman KEFAUVER. As to the Indian children, we have had some hearings in North Dakota. Senator Langer has been out to New Mexico and Palm Springs; Arizona, too; and we are aware of the sad plight of our Indian children, with bad housing, schooling sanitary conditions; the fact that they are being subjected to not very healthy influences. We hope we can do something about it. We appreciate your interest. I think we understand one another about the Indian children.

Mrs. LETA MEYERS SMART. One thing I want to bring especially to this—I am not trying to stir up a hornet's nest nor turn a Democrat against a Republican—but if you read my material, you will see that I referred to Public Law 277. Now, if it hadn't been for that law having come into effect August 15, 1953, which turned the liquor loose to the Indians, we wouldn't have as great a juvenile delinquency or adult delinquency problem among them; but that happened. Try as we could, when some of us were in Washington, to advise that special Congressman who drafted that H. R. 1055, that to do that would be absolutely unconstitutional, Harold Patton, of Arizona, his name was; and he didn't know about the situation that the Indians themselves would have to amend certain provisions in their treaties before the President or Congress could bring that about legally.

Now, I think an Indian should have the same right as everyone else, it is not that; but until the tribes themselves——

Chairman KEFAUVER. Well, now, lady——

Mrs. SMART. And I bring that out in my material.

Chairman KEFAUVER. We will study your material.

Mrs. SMART. Yes. It is very serious. It has to be undone some way or another.

Chairman KEFAUVER. All right. Thank you, ma'am.

Mrs. SMART. The repeal of Public Law 277.

Chairman KEFAUVER. We appreciate your interest and the interest of everyone else who has been here to our hearings.

I particularly wanted to see if there is anyone whose name has been mentioned in the hearings who wanted to make an explanation or present their side of any controversy that has come up here.

Now, Mr. Bobo, there are undoubtedly witnesses here who have been subpenaed, whom we are not going to be able to hear this afternoon. Do you want to read any of them out so we can see if they are here?

Mr. Bobo. Yes, sir.

Chairman Kefauver. Mr. Martin, you read out the names of any witnesses that we have not called.

Mr. Martin. William Door.

Mr. Door. Here.

Chairman Kefauver. Mr. Door, where are you, sir?

Mr. Door. Here.

Mr. Martin. William Miller.

Mr. Miller. Here.

Chairman Kefauver. Is Mr. Miller here?

Mr. Miller. Here.

Mr. Martin. Mr. and Mrs. Glied?

(No response.)

Mr. Martin. Andy Anderson?

Mr. Anderson. Here.

Mr. Martin. Mr. De Muth.

Mr. De Muth. Here.

Chairman Kefauver. Well, gentlemen, can we have your willingness that you will remain under subpena, and that by notice by letter or by telegram you will reappear at the time we notify you? Is that all right with you, sir, Mr. Door?

Mr. Door. Yes.

Chairman Kefauver. Mr. Anderson?

Mr. Anderson. Yes.

Mr. Miller. I would like to say a word.

Chairman Kefauver. All right, sir. Come up here. What is your name, sir?

Mr. Miller. William Miller.

Chairman Kefauver. All right, Mr. Miller. You hold up your hand and be sworn.

(Mr. Miller was sworn.)

TESTIMONY OF WILLIAM J. MILLER, HOLLYWOOD, CALIF.

Chairman Kefauver. I believe there is also Miss or Mrs. Helene Block. Is she here, too?

Mrs. Block. Yes.

Chairman Kefauver. Will you come back at the time we notify you?

Mrs. Block. Yes.

Chairman Kefauver. Mr. Miller, what is your full name?

Mr. Miller. William J. Miller.

Chairman Kefauver. Where do you live, sir?

Mr. Miller. 2829 Beachwood Drive.

Chairman Kefauver. All right, Mr. Miller, what is it you want to tell us now?

Mr. Miller. I was subpenaed to bring my records down here and to appear. For what reason, I would like to know. I have never been in this business at all in my life, and why should I be subpenaed?

Chairman Kefauver. Well, if we have done you an injustice, I certainly want to apologize. What is the situation about Mr. Miller?

Mr. Bobo. Mr. Miller, have you ever been involved with any photographic or model agencies or the securing of models for taking of photographic pictures?

Mr. Miller. I am very friendly with Mr. Anderson, but as far as having anything to do with his business or ever supplying models for anybody else, never.

Mr. Bobo. Have you ever—excuse me.

Mr. Miller. I have never been connected with his business financially or any other way.

Chairman Kefauver. Get up closer to the microphone.

Mr. Miller. I have never been financially or any other way connected with Mr. Anderson outside of being a friend. Why I was brought—I would like to know why, because I know many attorneys, I know fellows that are in the butcher business, automobile business, doctors; and I am not associated with being a doctor because I am around with them.

Mr. Bobo. Have you ever had any type of business arrangement, either financial or otherwise, with Mr. Anderson?

Mr. Miller. No.

Mr. Bobo. With Mr. Tom Cooper?

Mr. Miller. No.

Mr. Bobo. Do you know Mr. Tom Cooper?

Mr. Miller. Very well.

Mr. Bobo. Have you ever had any type of business arrangement or financial arrangement or otherwise with Mr. Gerald Duke?

Mr. Miller. I sold him some equipment and lent him $100 at one time to pay rent on a building that he opened, and gave him supplies at that particular time when I was running an auction business with photographic equipment. This was several years ago.

Mr. Bobo. Mr. Duke was engaged in a photographic studio?

Mr. Miller. He opened one on Sunset Boulevard.

Mr. Bobo. What type of equipment was it that you furnished?

Mr. Miller. I sold him a printer, a developing tank, some darkroom lights, and I think some paper, if I am not mistaken.

Mr. Bobo. Were you paid for that material at the time at which you sold it to him?

Mr. Miller. Not yet.

Mr. Bobo. You haven't been paid?

Mr. Miller. I was paid $40 on $180.

Mr. Bobo. When was it you gave him this material or sold him this material?

Mr. Miller. I think approximately 3½ or 4 years ago.

Mr. Bobo. You also lent him $100 with which to establish his business?

Mr. Miller. To pay the rent, which was paid back to me.

Mr. Bobo. Have you ever received from either Mr. Anderson or Mr. Tom Cooper or Mr. Gerald Duke any of the girl photographs from them?

Mr. Miller. Yes; plenty of them.

Mr. Bobo. You received these for your own personal use?

Mr. Miller. Absolutely.

Mr. Bobo. How many photographs would you say you had received from Mr. Anderson?

Mr. Miller. Well, I couldn't say that because I have got pictures of practically every model that was ever in the city.

Mr. Bobo. Are these pictures of the nude variety or strip variety of pictures?

Mr. Miller. Some are and some aren't. A lot of it is color and third dimensional.

Mr. Bobo. Approximately how many photographs of girls and models would you say that you had in your possession, Mr. Miller?

Mr. Miller. Probably 10,000.

Mr. Bobo. Have you also in your possession or have you received from Mr. Anderson, Mr. Cooper, or Mr. Duke any moving-picture films?

Mr. Miller. Never.

Mr. Bobo. Do you have in your possession any moving-picture films showing a nude woman?

Mr. Miller. No. Pinup models. I have maybe 5 or 6 hundred-foot reels.

Mr. Bobo. Five or six——

Mr. Miller. With a hundred feet on each one of them, because I haven't got a projector and I don't use them.

Mr. Bobo. May I ask you, Mr. Miller, what do you do with all these pictures?

Mr. Miller. I got them as a collection, because I shoot a lot of pictures myself.

Mr. Bobo. Do you also, yourself, shoot pictures of models and women?

Mr. Miller. Very seldom. I have, but I haven't—I wouldn't say over a dozen models in my life.

Mr. Bobo. Have you ever shot pictures of women in the nude?

Mr. Miller. Yes.

Mr. Bobo. What was the purpose of these pictures?

Mr. Miller. I took them as pinups and also as calendar color shots.

Mr. Bobo. Have you ever either given or sold any of these thousands of pictures that you have away?

Mr. Miller. I have given them to some friends of mine, but never sold one in my life.

Mr. Bobo. Mr. Miller, do you also go under the name of Mr. G. L. Seymour?

Mr. Miller. No.

Mr. Bobo. Have you ever gone under the name of G. L. Seymour?

Mr. Miller. That may have been on a check maybe years ago. I wouldn't say that. That has been many years ago, if it was.

Chairman Kefauver. Well, did you ever? That is the question. Was that ever an alias that you had?

Mr. Miller. I won't say "Yes" and I won't say "No," because I really don't remember.

Mr. Bobo. Have you ever gone under an alias?

Mr. Miller. That was—yes, years ago.

Mr. Bobo. Have you ever gone under the alias of Fred Williams?

Mr. MILLER. Well, I don't think I will answer any more questions like that without an attorney. That has got nothing to do with what this particular thing is about, and I know nothing about it, what you called me for.

Chairman KEFAUVER. Well, Mr. Miller, you came up here and wanted to testify.

Mr. MILLER. I wanted to know why I was called up here.

Chairman KEFAUVER. We wanted to give you a chance.

Mr. MILLER. I have a perfect right to ask that question, I think.

Chairman KEFAUVER. Well, Mr. Miller, I will tell you why you were called. We have information of your activities with these people, and you have a record back here beginning in Elizabeth, N. J., on November 14, 1918.

Mr. MILLER. That is correct.

Chairman KEFAUVER. And you are very closely associated with these people in this business. Mr. Bobo has some other questions to ask you.

Mr. MILLER. Well, I——

Chairman KEFAUVER. So we are not doing you any harm by just subpenaing you up here. You have been charged with everything in the books.

Mr. MILLER. That is why I want to make it clear that I have nothing to do with this particular business, and I would like you to know that. That is one reason——

Chairman KEFAUVER. What is your present business?

Mr. MILLER. Well, I deal in jewelry and appliances.

Chairman KEFAUVER. What is the name of your business?

Mr. MILLER. I am at Metropolitan Building, 315 West Fifth Street.

Chairman KEFAUVER. Have you got a big business?

Mr. MILLER. No. I work out of another office now. In my place the business was discontinued in 1950——

Chairman KEFAUVER. What is your annual income, Mr. Miller?

Mr. MILLER. Probably around six thousand, sixty-five hundred.

Chairman KEFAUVER. Would you be interested to know that you only reported $1,600?

Mr. MILLER. When was this?

Chairman KEFAUVER. 1954.

Mr. MILLER. That was after everything was deducted. I think you will find that.

Chairman KEFAUVER. That seems to be the gross amount you report.

Mr. MILLER. No. The auditors do it. Whatever it is, I wouldn't say.

Chairman KEFAUVER. $1,600, and you have got a 1954 Cadillac.

Mr. MILLER. I got what?

Chairman KEFAUVER. Don't you have a Cadillac?

Mr. MILLER. Yes.

Chairman KEFAUVER. A 1954 Cadillac?

Mr. MILLER. No.

Chairman KEFAUVER. 1953.

Mr. MILLER. But——

Chairman KEFAUVER. 1953?

Mr. MILLER. My particular things that was taken in the audit was over $6,000 last year. I brought my records. I wanted them looked over; but I don't know what it is all about, because I have nothing to do with this particular line of business at all. Never have had. I have never sold a picture in my life and don't have any financial dealings with them at all.

Mr. BOBO. But you have had an association with people who did deal with and sell this material?

Mr. MILLER. Well, I know them, but I have never—never was in the business myself.

Mr. BOBO. You did also furnish the photographic equipment——

Mr. MILLER. A sink——

Mr. BOBO. Some material to a man who 3 or 4 years ago—who hasn't paid you for it?

Mr. MILLER. Yes.

Mr. BOBO. What was the value of this material?

Mr. MILLER. It only came to $180—something, plus $100 that I lent him in cash, which was paid back to me.

Mr. BOBO. Were the pictures that you received in payment on the equipment which you had furnished to him?

Mr. MILLER. No. No. No. I was paid back $20 at a time.

Chairman KEFAUVER. Well, did you make plans to start a photography business with Ray Porter, Mr. Miller?

Mr. MILLER. Pardon?

Chairman KEFAUVER. Do you know Mr. Ray Porter?

Mr. MILLER. No.

Chairman KEFAUVER. You don't know him?

Mr. MILLER. Never heard of him.

Mr. BOBO. Mr. Miller, have you ever known or associated with a Mr. Jack Dragna?

Mr. MILLER. Yes, I know Mr. Dragna very well.

Mr. BOBO. What was the nature of your association with Mr. Dragna?

Mr. MILLER. I knew him many years ago in prohibition days.

Mr. BOBO. Have you ever done any business with Mr. Dragna?

Mr. MILLER. Never.

Mr. BOBO. Do you know a Mr. Momo Adamo?

Mr. MILLER. Yes, I do.

Mr. BOBO. What has been your association with Mr. Adamo?

Mr. MILLER. I haven't talked to the man 5 times in the last 10 years.

Mr. BOBO. Did you previously have an association or business arrangement with him?

Mr. MILLER. Never.

Mr. BOBO. Do you know Mr. Lou Cohen?

Mr. MILLER. Yes.

Mr. BOBO. Did you ever have any business association or connection with him?

Mr. MILLER. That was—he run the auction sales, if that is the Lou Cohen you mean.

Mr. BOBO. Which auction sales, auction sales for you and your company?

Mr. MILLER. Yes. That is when I went out of business.

Mr. BOBO. Do you know a Dr. William De Orgler?

Mr. MILLER. What is the name?

Mr. Bobo. Dr. William De Orgler, D-e O-r-g-l-e-r. He goes under the name of Captain Zita, Z-i-t-a.

Mr. Miller. I know who he is. He used to—he used to book acts at the old Florentine Gardens several years ago. I never——

Mr. Bobo. You never had any transactions with him at any time?

Mr. Miller. Just barely knew him to say hello to him.

Mr. Bobo. Mr. Miller, have you ever had any association with any of the girls who had posed for nude pictures or posed for nude moving pictures?

Mr. Miller. I have had lots of them to dinner; yes.

Mr. Bobo. Have you in any way ever offered any type of business arrangement with any of these girls?

Mr. Miller. No. What do you mean by "business arrangement?"

Mr. Bobo. Did you ever arrange with them to be photographed even by yourself or by others?

Mr. Miller. I have taken pictures of several of them; yes.

Mr. Bobo. How extensive has been your taking of pictures of nude models?

Mr. Miller. Only the ones that I still have in my own collection. That is all. The same as dozens of others that take them. I have never sold them, and of the ones that I got, I still have.

Mr. Bobo. Do you pay these girls for taking the pictures?

Mr. Miller. Naturally.

Mr. Bobo. What is the amount paid for the model?

Mr. Miller. $5 an hour. I haven't shot any for a couple of years.

Mr. Bobo. From whom do you receive the names of the girls who would pose for nude pictures?

Mr. Miller. Oh, there is the Andy Agency and several others.

Mr. Bobo. Who operates the Andy Agency?

Mr. Miller. Mr. Frank Anderson.

Mr. Bobo. Frank Anderson. Who else have you ever received or ordered a model from?

Mr. Miller. None in particular; only I have had them call me wanting to to know if I was going to shoot.

Mr. Bobo. You have never taken pictures of any girls other than from Frank Anderson, the Andy Agency?

Mr. Miller. I have taken pictures of other girls, but not from any other agency.

Mr. Bobo. How would you make your contact then?

Mr. Miller. They call you. The models call for work.

Mr. Bobo. What happens to the negatives of the pictures which you take, Mr. Miller?

Mr. Miller. Mine are all in color and there is no negative. It comes back from Eastman through the Eastman process laboratory; returns the film to you already done up.

Mr. Bobo. And you take pictures of nudes and forward them to the Eastman Kodak Agency and they return them to you in color, developed?

Mr. Miller. That is correct.

Mr. Bobo. Do you send these pictures through the United States mail?

Mr. Miller. It doesn't go through the mail at all. It is delivered down on Orange Drive and Santa Monica Boulevard.

Mr. Bobo. The Eastman Kodak Co. office?

Mr. Miller. The Eastman Kodak Co. office.

Mr. Bobo. On Orange Drive?

Mr. Miller. That is right. When you buy your film, it automatically goes back to them for development and is returned to you.

Mr. Bobo. Are they returned to you in slide form or in picture form?

Mr. Miller. In slide form.

Mr. Bobo. Have you ever done business with the Ansco Co. or any of the other film companies?

Mr. Miller. No; never.

Mr. Bobo. Have you ever had any difficulty in having any of the color shots which you might take—having them processed?

Mr. Miller. I haven't had any trouble with them. I get my slides back. I think once or twice they have punched holes in them; but outside of that, I have gotten all mine back. In fact, Eastman will not return it unless it is allowed to go through the mail if necessary.

Mr. Bobo. They are pictures of nude women?

Mr. Miller. Yes.

Mr. Bobo. Do you make any determined effort to see that certain parts of the anatomy are not shown?

Mr. Miller. If you didn't do that, you wouldn't have any pictures.

Mr. Bobo. Well, Mr. Miller, where did the girls who posed for these pictures for you receive your name, to know that you are photographing them?

Mr. Miller. Well, I think that gets around among the girls themselves. I know dozens of people, and if I want to get an attorney, I would know where to go and get him; or if I wanted to find any particular thing. Those girls, I imagine, would look up somebody that shoots pictures, the same as you would look up a certain grocer or someone else.

Mr. Bobo. Have you ever taken any pictures of any models that were under 21 years of age?

Mr. Miller. Not that I know of.

Mr. Bobo. Have you questioned them about their age?

Mr. Miller. Yes. They will all say that they are more than that or older and sign a slip to that effect.

Mr. Bobo. What is the nature of the slip which they sign?

Mr. Miller. They sign their model's release which says that they are 21 years of age.

Mr. Bobo. It also states on that that they have no objection to it being sold?

Mr. Miller. That is right; but I never sold a picture and wouldn't. I have them for my own collection the same as others.

Mr. Bobo. Did you draw up your own model's release?

Mr. Miller. No.

Mr. Bobo. From whom do you receive the model's releases?

Mr. Miller. You can get them most any place.

Mr. Bobo. How many girls did you say you thought you had photographed?

Mr. Miller. I will say all together, in a period of 5 years, I haven't photographed over 20.

Mr. Bobo. And you made extensive photographs of these 20, great numbers of photographs?

Mr. Miller. No; I wouldn't say that.

Mr. Bobo. And yet your name has gotten around among all the model agencies and among all the models in town that you pose people for pictures?

Mr. Miller. That is correct.

Mr. Bobo. How much of the total part of your total income in the past 5 years would you say you spent on model's fees?

Mr. Miller. In the last 5 years?

Mr. Bobo. Yes, sir.

Mr. Miller. Probably $250 or $300, possibly.

Mr. Bobo. And you pay them $3 an hour to $10 an hour?

Mr. Miller. No; never 10.

Mr. Bobo. What would be the value and what have you got invested in your collection of motion picture film and pictures that you have at your home in your collection?

Mr. Miller. Well, I have had a lot of pictures given to me. If you went into that, I wouldn't know. I couldn't say that exactly.

Mr. Bobo. You have also purchased great numbers of them, haven't you?

Mr. Miller. No. I have traded some of the ones that I have had for others.

Mr. Bobo. But you never——

Mr. Miller. In other words, if you would get several practically alike, you would trade them with someone else that shot a different model.

Mr. Bobo. Where would you get the ones that you would trade?

Mr. Miller. Ones that I had taken.

Mr. Bobo. Ones that you had taken, how would they be like some that other people had taken?

Mr. Miller. Well, it could be a different setting. It could be on the ocean beach or it could be up in Big Bear or somewhere else. It could be in dozens of different places.

Mr. Bobo. Approximately how many pictures do you have, Mr. Miller?

Mr. Miller. Probably 10,000.

Mr. Bobo. And you have taken all of those yourself except the few that have been given to you?

Mr. Miller. Oh, I wouldn't say—99 percent of the ones that I have, have been taken by someone else.

Mr. Bobo. And all of them given to you?

Mr. Miller. A lot of them have been given to me; yes.

Mr. Bobo. Have you ever purchased any of them?

Mr. Miller. No, I haven't.

Mr. Bobo. Where did the rest of them come from that you did not take yourself and were not given to you?

Mr. Miller. Say that over again?

Mr. Bobo. Well, you said that you had approximately 10,000; that 99 percent of them were taken by somebody else, that some of them had been given to you. The rest of them, where did they come from?

Mr. MILLER. The ones that I took myself.

Mr. BOBO. Which accounts for 1 percent?

Mr. MILLER. Well, I have taken more than 1 percent of them.

Mr. BOBO. All I am trying to arrive at, you have either had 9,000 given to you or 1,000 you have made yourself. Is that correct?

Mr. MILLER. That is about right.

Mr. BOBO. Who gives you all of these pictures?

Mr. MILLER. Well, Andy has given me some.

Mr. BOBO. How many has he given you?

Mr. MILLER. Copper has given me a lot.

Mr. BOBO. How many has Mr. Anderson given you?

Mr. MILLER. Several thousand.

Mr. BOBO. For what reason would Mr. Anderson give you several thousand pictures?

Mr. MILLER. Because I am around him all the time. I go out to his place quite often, practically every day.

Mr. BOBO. He is in the business of selling pictures, isn't he, sir?

Mr. MILLER. He doesn't sell pictures.

Mr. BOBO. There is a value placed on these pictures, cost to him?

Mr. MILLER. Well, I gave him a lot of paper at one time when I was in the auction business; but, of course, a 4 by 5 piece of paper costs approximately 1 penny.

Mr. BOBO. You gave Mr. Anderson quite a bit of photographic paper?

Mr. MILLER. When I run the auction places; yes, sir.

Mr. BOBO. Did he ever pay you for it?

Mr. MILLER. No.

Mr. BOBO. You had no arrangement with him, except to give him photographic paper?

Mr. MILLER. That is right; and I gave him what you would call paper that is outdated, which is still good. You can get it on the stands today, and buy a box of paper which is approximately worth $18 or $20 when it is in date. You can buy that same paper for $3.50 or $4.

Mr. BOBO. So for a small quantity of outdated paper he has given you three or four thousand photographs of nude women, for which he paid models to pose and which he developed himself?

Mr. MILLER. I don't think he has to pay the models to pose. He runs their agency and he has their agency and books the girls for photographers; and they carry their pictures in the place as more or less an exhibit.

Mr. BOBO. Well, from whom else have you received pictures?

Mr. MILLER. I have received pictures from dozens of different ones, the photographers that take them. Tom Cooper.

Mr. BOBO. Well, for what reason does Mr. Cooper give you pictures?

Mr. MILLER. Well, for the same reason that if I had anything that he wanted, he could have it, too.

Mr. BOBO. That is a rather loose arrangement. Do you think I could go down and he would give me some, too?

Mr. MILLER. Chances are he would; yes.

Mr. BOBO. What is the purpose of the taking of these pictures?

Chairman KEFAUVER. I didn't understand. You say you gave him pictures?

Mr. MILLER. I have given him pictures.

Chairman KEFAUVER. Did you give Andy pictures, too?

Mr. MILLER. Pardon?

Chairman KEFAUVER. Do you give the other people pictures, too?

Mr. MILLER. I have given pictures, too.

Chairman KEFAUVER. So your pictures are getting circulated around, too?

Mr. MILLER. They don't get circulated around like that. They are making a collection of them. They are not for sale.

Chairman KEFAUVER. Do you keep these for showing at parties that you have at your house? Is that the purpose of it?

Mr. MILLER. No. I don't know just exactly why I have ever kept them. I have got a hobby for saving pictures. I have taken pictures in Florida since 1912 up until now with an old three-eight Eastman years ago and still have them.

Chairman KEFAUVER. Do you have them in a file box, indexed so you know exactly who they are?

Mr. MILLER. Who they are?

Chairman KEFAUVER. Indexed by their names.

Mr. MILLER. Yes.

Chairman KEFAUVER. 10,000 in an index?

Mr. MILLER. I think so. Close to that. I have never counted them, so I don't really know.

Chairman KEFAUVER. Do you have a couple of big safes or file cabinets?

Mr. MILLER. I have a filing cabinet.

Chairman KEFAUVER. Do you keep it locked?

Mr. MILLER. Sure.

Chairman KEFAUVER. What do you keep in these safes, just pictures?

Mr. MILLER. They are not safes, they are filing cabinets.

Chairman KEFAUVER. Just full of pictures?

Mr. MILLER. Yes.

Chairman KEFAUVER. Don't you have a couple of safes, too?

Mr. MILLER. I have one safe in my store.

Chairman KEFAUVER. You don't have one at your home?

Mr. MILLER. I have one that is empty. You can go up and look at it. They searched the place the night that the subpena was issued. They came to my door and asked me if I had any pictures, with an excuse that they wanted to investigate a robbery that was in my home a year ago last October. When they came in I said, "What do you want?"

They said, "We really want to know about your pictures."

I said, "Go right through the house and look at anything you want"; which they did.

Chairman KEFAUVER. Are you acquainted with Mr. Door?

Mr. MILLER. I know who he is. I don't know the man well. I have seen him several times. Don't know him personally, no.

Chairman KEFAUVER. Do you know the Tagers?

Mr. MILLER. Never seen them until this morning.

Chairman KEFAUVER. Or the Alberts? Do you know them?

Mr. MILLER. Don't know them at all.

Chairman KEFAUVER. Do you want to look this over, sir, and see if you think it is substantially correct?

Well, let's see. We have one——

Mr. MILLER. This is something I know nothing about, what you have here [indicating]. What is this?

Chairman KEFAUVER. Well, that is just the stenographer's name that copied it down here. Maybe we had better hand you the original. Maybe you will recognize that better.

Mr. MILLER. This is all correct. What is the last? What is the last page?

Chairman KEFAUVER. Well, the last page, I will read it. Well, the last page on this one is the allegation that you have been——

Mr. MILLER. Subpenaed here.

Chairman KEFAUVER. No; that you have been engaged in this pornographic material, that you have been partners in this business with Andy Anderson, Tom Cooper, Gerald Duke; that you have two filing cabinets full of pictures, card indexes; that you exchange them with other people; that you have parties at your home, bringing them in to see the pictures; that——

Mr. MILLER. That is a lie.

Chairman KEFAUVER. That you take a lot of lewd pictures and nude pictures.

Mr. MILLER. I said that's a lie.

Chairman KEFAUVER. But outside of this part at the bottom, you think that this is fairly correct?

Mr. MILLER. This is absolutely correct.

Chairman KEFAUVER. Well, let's take this one that is correct. Then this one also says that among the films that you have stockpiled, including one, "Gentleman in Paradise," is that correct, do you think?

Mr. MILLER. It is not correct.

Chairman KEFAUVER. Well, this what you say here is correct——

Mr. MILLER. In that [indicating], yes.

Chairman KEFAUVER. Starts you back at Elizabeth, N. J., on November 14, 1918?

Mr. MILLER. I won't answer any more questions in regard to that. I think I can stand on my rights to that effect. That has nothing to do with this.

Chairman KEFAUVER. Well, anyway, in New Jersey and Massachusetts and Ohio and Illinois?

Mr. MILLER. I am aware of that, Senator. I told you that is correct.

Chairman KEFAUVER. Very well. This is correct. We will let it be filed as an exhibit to your testimony.

(The police record of William Miller was marked "Exhibit No. 42," and reads as follows:)

Miller, Bill, LA No. 138057.
True name: Miller, William J.
Alias: Seymour, G. L.
Alias: Williams, Fred.

Record

	Number	Date	Charge and disposition
Police Department, Elizabeth, N. J.	------------	Nov. 14, 1918	Charge of fugitive; turned over to police department, Boston, Mass.
		Nov. 22, 1918	Arrested Boston, Mass., on charge of larceny of auto.
State Reformatory, Concord Junction, Mass.	21659	Jan. 11, 1920	R. S. G., 5 years, indicted; paroled Jan. 9, 1920; TOT Columbus, Ohio, No. 4551; Mar. 31, 1920, committed to Ohio State Reformatory for larceny.
Police Department, Columbus, Ohio.	5258	Mar. 31, 1920	Grand larceny, WEGJ $1,000 and taken to Franklin County, Ohio, jail; on Jan. 12, 1920, sent to the State reformatory.
Police Department, Philadelphia, Pa.	53384	June 23, 1922	Attempted larceny—larceny of auto, for New York City Police Department. Escaped while being taken into custody; apprehended June 23, 1922.
Police Department, Aurora, Ill.	------------	Jan. 26, 1924	Confidence game (bogus checks). Sent to the State penitentiary.
State Penitentiary, Joliet, Ill.	9001	Mar. 5, 1924	Confidence game; 1-10 years; Mar. 8, 1929, discharged.
Police Department, Brazil, Ind.	16	Apr. 1, 1929	Forgery; broke jail Apr. 4, 1929.
Police Department, Fitchburg, Mass.	------------	Jan. 9, 1931	Uttering, 15 counts; 18 months House of Correction, Worcester, Mass.
Police Department, Tampa, Fla.	3092	Jan. 17, 1932	Inv. fugitive and jail break.
Police Department, Boston, Mass.	33490	Nov. 14, 1933	Larceny, worthless checks; released to Springfield, Mass.
Police Department, Springfield, Mass.	4740	----do-------	Forgery; 60 days House of Correction.
Jail and House of Correction, Springfield, Mass.	------------	Nov. 15, 1933	Forgery; Dec. 26, 1933—60 days and released.
Police Department, Holyoke, Mass.	------------	Feb. 8, 1934	Larceny by check; sent to House of Correction for 2 months.
Police Department, New Haven, Conn.	4349	Apr. 21, 1934	Fraud, checks, 3 counts; 1 month on each count.
Police Department, Cleveland, Ohio.	42678	May 5, 1934	Issued check to deft; June 16, 1934, Ohio State Penitentiary.
State Penitentiary, Columbus, Ohio.	68440	June 20, 1934	Check to defraud; 1-3 years.
Police Department, Dayton, Ohio.	13404	June 19, 1937	Fraudulent check; July 23, 1937, 1 year; paroled.
Police Department, Miami, Fla.	CR-248	Nov. 26, 1939	Crim. Reg. (Vol.); released.
Do	20214	Nov. 28, 1939	Vol. Crim. Reg.; released.
Sheriff's Office, Miami, Fla.	CR-331	----do-------	Crim. Reg.; released.
Police Department, San Diego, Calif.	17589	Jan. 10, 1943	Sec. 593B, Tariff Act; released to U. S. Customs.
Sheriff's Office, San Diego	84479	Jan. 11, 1943	Smuggling; released on bond posted with U. S. Commissioner.
Police Department, Los Angeles	2097-W-18	July 27, 1943	Sec. 242, Police Code, battery; dismissed.
Sheriff's office, Los Angeles	A-49435	Oct. 25, 1944	Burglary; relaesed on bail.
Do	B-39359	Oct. 22, 1947	Suspicion, Dangerous Weapons Act, sec. 2.
Do	B-40067	Oct. 28, 1947	Violating dangerous weapons control law of 1923, Dangerous Weapons Act 19.70; 2 counts.

In addition to the connections of Bill Miller shown in the rundowns of Andy Anderson and Bill Door, the following information is from observance of his activities over a period of approximately 6 years.

He first came to attention upon information received as to his being involved in receiving of stolen jewelry. In investigating this activity, it was discovered that subject was a constant associate of known prostitutes and persons involved in lewd and perverted activities. It is believed that he first made associates of photographers and model agencies, in order to obtain girls for the many parties and entertaining that took place at his house. Later, subject became more aware of the possibility of financial gains in this field; consequently, backing persons such as Andy Anderson, Tom Cooper, and Gerald Duke in model agencies and photo studios.

Subject has stockpiled in filing cabinets in his home and 2 safes what appear to be many thousands of photographs of girls listed alphabetically by name, which includes anywhere from 5 to 50 pictures of each pose, which would tend to show that this is more than a collection of a hobbyist; also many rolls of moving picture films, including one entitled "Gentlemen in Paradise."

At present it is known that subject owns most of the equipment used by Andy Anderson.

Mr. MILLER. But what about the other evidence that you have on the back page? I would like to know about that.

Chairman KEFAUVER. Well, if you want me——

Mr. MILLER. Who gives that information and says that I am connected with them? Because I am friendly with them, does that say that I am in business with them?

Chairman KEFAUVER. Well, this is information that has been gotten up.

Mr. MILLER. Well, by whom?

Chairman KEFAUVER. Well, anyway, it is in our files, Mr. Miller. If you want me to read it to you, I will read it to you.

Mr. MILLER. I would love you to read it.

Chairman KEFAUVER. This explains, I suppose, in addition to this general criminal record, in 8 or 9 states, everything from burglary to larceny——

Mr. MILLER. There is no burglary. I beg your pardon.

Chairman KEFAUVER. Forgery, worthless checks——

Mr. MILLER. I refuse to answer any more of your questions.

Chairman KEFAUVER. Smuggling. Is this true, that the 31 arrests or convictions in many, many States? Isn't that about right?

Mr. MILLER. I have told you that is correct, but why is that——

Chairman KEFAUVER. I will read this——

Mr. MILLER. You are trying to bring up things that I know nothing about.

Chairman KEFAUVER. This may give you some indication of why you were called, and I will read it, and then you can say whether it is true or not.

Mr. MILLER. That is right. That is all I want to find out.

Chairman KEFAUVER (reading):

In addition to the connections with Bill Miller shown in the rundowns of Andy Anderson and Bill Door, following information is from observances of his activities over a period of approximately 6 years:

First came to the attention upon information received as his being involved in receiving stolen jewelry.

I suppose that is not——

Mr. MILLER. Was I ever tried or brought up to arrest?

Chairman KEFAUVER. Well, is that correct?

Mr. MILLER. I asked you a question. You may answer me. Did I ever——

Chairman KEFAUVER. Well, you asked me to read this to you, and I am going to read it to you. Do you want me to read it to you?

Mr. MILLER. Yes.

Chairman KEFAUVER (reading):

Investigating this activity it was discovered that subject was a constant associate of known prostitutes and persons involved in lewd and perverted activities.

If you want to make any comments along as I read, you can do so.

Mr. MILLER. Well, I resent that.

Chairman KEFAUVER. Well, you asked me to read it, sir.

Mr. MILLER. No. I say I want you to read it, but you told me just now to answer you on it, and that is what I did.

Chairman KEFAUVER. All right. You say you resent that. [Reading:]

It is believed that he first made associates of photographers and model agencies in order to obtain girls for the many parties, entertainment that took place at his house.

Any comment?

Mr. MILLER. That isn't so. I know a lot of girls and go out with a lot of them. I don't see any harm in that; do you?

Chairman KEFAUVER. Well, you asked me to read it, and you answered.

Later he became more aware of the possibility of financial gains in this field, consequently backing persons such as Andy Anderson, Tom Cooper, and Gerald Duke——

Mr. MILLER. Wait. Where did they get the idea that I backed them, can you find that out? Bring them up here for that investigation.

Chairman KEFAUVER. Well, you rented them a place, you sold them film.

Mr. MILLER. I lent him a hundred dollars. If you lend a man $100, regardless of what he does with it is none of my business.

Chairman KEFAUVER. You gave him photographic equipment.

Mr. MILLER. I sold him equipment. Don't every store sell them?

Chairman KEFAUVER. They haven't paid you for it?

Mr. MILLER. I still have got it coming, I guess.

Chairman KEFAUVER. Gerald Duke——

Mr. MILLER. I have been paid part of it. That is the only man that never paid me.

Chairman KEFAUVER. Well, you just asked me to read this, and you make any explanation that you want. [Reading:]

And Gerald Duke and model agencies and photo studios. He has stockpiled in filing cabinets in his home and two safes what appear to be many thousands of photographs of girls listed alphabetically by name, which includes anywhere from 5 to 50 pictures of each pose, which would tend to show that this is more than a collection of a hobbyist.

Do you have different pictures of each pose?

Mr. MILLER. Mr. Senator, with due respect to you, I think one of our most prominent men in the country today has a much finer and a bigger collection than I will ever have.

Chairman KEFAUVER. We are just talking about you. I am just talking about what you have. [Reading:]

Also many reels of moving-picture film, including one entitled "Gentleman in Paradise." It is alleged that he owns most of the equipment used by Andy Anderson.

Now, most of this is not true?

Mr. MILLER. I didn't say that. I said that I gave Andy the equipment that is in there. The equipment that was taken from Duke's place was turned over to Mr. Anderson, because they were together at that particular time.

Chairman KEFAUVER. Do you own your own home?

Mr. MILLER. That is right.

Chairman KEFAUVER. You do have a large, elaborate home, don't you?

Mr. MILLER. I wouldn't say that it is elaborate.

Chairman KEFAUVER. How large is it?

Mr. MILLER. What you can get for eighty-five hundred. Eight thousand seven fifty is what it cost me when I bought it in 1942.

Chairman KEFAUVER. What do you think it is worth today?

Mr. MILLER. I don't know. I never wanted to sell it. It isn't paid for to begin with. I took a loan on it, though, of eleven thousand here 2½ years ago.

Chairman KEFAUVER. Anything else you——

Mr. MILLER. Which I was obliged to do.

All I want to do is find out why they bothered me about these things.

Chairman KEFAUVER. Well, Mr. Miller, it ought to be quite apparent to you why you have been called here. You have a criminal record going back to 1918.

Mr. MILLER. Everybody else that——

Chairman KEFAUVER. Consisting of thirty-odd arrests or convictions of all kinds of things.

Mr. MILLER. Was I ever arrested for anything like you are calling for?

Chairman KEFAUVER. I haven't gone over these closely. I really don't know. But I can go over them closely if you want me to.

Mr. MILLER. It isn't necessary; but all I say is that the thing that is here, that I don't think I should have been called up here. I don't see any reason for it.

Chairman KEFAUVER. What is this smuggling conviction here?

Mr. MILLER. For bringing perfume across the border from Mexico.

Chairman KEFAUVER. Well, you don't want me to read all these, do you?

Mr. MILLER. It isn't necessary.

Chairman KEFAUVER. Here is another one: San Diego, United States Customs, Tariff Act.

Mr. MILLER. That is the very same thing.

Chairman KEFAUVER. Here is another one, 1947. That was in 1943. Here is 1947. Was that the same thing?

Mr. MILLER. It couldn't be 1947.

Chairman KEFAUVER. I mean, the same kind of charge?

Mr. MILLER. It couldn't be in 1947; I beg your pardon.

Chairman KEFAUVER. Well, 10–22–47—no; that is DW. That is the Dangerous Weapons Act; isn't it?

Mr. MILLER. That is right.

Chairman KEFAUVER. What was this?

Mr. MILLER. There was a gun in my home because I had been robbed 3 different times and burglarized 4 times, and I got a rifle in my home and a pistol in case I was held up again or stuck up.

Chairman KEFAUVER. You came out here from Miami, Fla., in 1939; didn't you?

Mr. MILLER. That is right.

Chairman KEFAUVER. And you went from Ohio to Florida; is that right?

Mr. MILLER. That is right.

Chairman KEFAUVER. And you went from Connecticut to Ohio; is that right?

Mr. MILLER. That is right.

Chairman KEFAUVER. And you went from Massachusetts to Connecticut.

Mr. MILLER. That was all in one series, without being released.

Chairman KEFAUVER. And you went from Illinois to Massachusetts; is that correct?

Mr. MILLER. Well, has that any bearing on this case?

Chairman KEFAUVER. I am just asking you about it.

Well, of course, the reason you were called is that you were shown to have close associations with these people. You have a very large collection—10,000 pictures.

Mr. MILLER. I don't see any harm in having those.

Chairman KEFAUVER. That is unusual. Well, it is a little unusual.

Mr. MILLER. Other people make a collection of having stamps or coins.

Chairman KEFAUVER. And you take pictures, you give them out to other people. They might get them in circulation.

Mr. MILLER. I take pictures of the Rose Bowl and the bullfights.

Chairman KEFAUVER. So I think that we were quite justified in calling you, Mr. Miller. We are glad to have your explanation about them.

Mr. MILLER. About those things, I know nothing about them, only what I have told you now. I will make it clear that I do not have any affiliation with them so far as the business end is concerned.

Chairman KEFAUVER. You are just not in that sort of business?

Mr. MILLER. Pardon?

Chairman KEFAUVER. That is just not one of your businesses?

Mr. MILLER. That is correct.

Chairman KEFAUVER. All right, Mr. Miller. Thank you for saying you will testify.

Is there anybody else who wants to testify today?

Well, our final witness——

Mr. DE MUTH. Mr. Senator——

Chairman KEFAUVER. Yes, sir.

Mr. DE MUTH. Would it be possible to get this over with today? Is that what you are asking?

Chairman KEFAUVER. What is your name?

Mr. DE MUTH. De Muth.

Chairman KEFAUVER. Mr. De Muth, there hasn't been very much said about you here, has there?

Mr. DE MUTH. No, sir; but, see, I am gainfully employed as a carpenter to support my family. It does take time.

Chairman KEFAUVER. Well, Mr. De Muth, we would rather let you know when to come back again sometime.

Mr. DE MUTH. That is perfectly all right, sir. You asked the question.

Chairman KEFAUVER. You were subpenaed here. You will get, I guess, a per diem for the time you have been attending.

Our last witness will be Mr. James F. Nelson.

All right, Mr. Bobo. You ask Mr. Nelson.

TESTIMONY OF JAMES F. NELSON, DEPUTY DISTRICT ATTORNEY, COUNTY OF LOS ANGELES

Mr. Bobo. Mr. Nelson, would you give us your name, your address, and your present position for the record?

Mr. Nelson. James F. Nelson. I reside at 11732 Missouri Avenue in West Los Angeles.

I am now a deputy district attorney for the County of Los Angeles.

Mr. Bobo. Working in the district attorney's office of Los Angeles County, did you handle the case involving Mr. Alberts and his wife, Mrs. Alberts?

Mr. Nelson. I did, sir.

Chairman Kefauver. Suppose we don't repeat the testimony that has been given before, only new matters to be brought up. Mr. Bobo is trying to get a plane, I think, here at 5 o'clock.

Mr. Bobo. Thank you.

In investigating and determining this case, Mr. Nelson, did you receive complaints or letters of complaints from parents that their children had been receiving advertisements for this particular type of literature?

Mr. Nelson. Yes, sir; through the office of District Attorney S. Ernest Roll on the 18th day of February 1955, I was contacted by Mr. Roll, who brought to me at that time a packet of letters which he had through the latter months of 1954 received from various parts of the country, and many of which included reference to the receipt by juveniles of brochures of advertising from the Male Merchandise Mart, operated by Mr. Alberts. It was at that time that Mr. Roll instructed me to take action in connection with this matter.

Mr. Bobo. In the prosecution of this case, to what extent would you say the Alberts business was, financially?

Mr. Nelson. From the records that we had obtained as a result of the search warrants that were issued for the three premises which were searched, we have been able to estimate that approximately a gross of $40,000 to $50,000 a month business was done by Mr. Alberts and his wife under the name of APR Industries, Inc. He also operates——

Chairman Kefauver. You mean $600,000 a year, something like that?

Mr. Nelson. Approximately, sir, yes; and I think we can say from the records that we had that this could be a conservative estimate.

The business, as I have stated, was in the name of APR Industries. He also operated under various other names, to wit, Paragon Enterprises, Male Merchandise Mart, Sailer Jock's Stag Shop, and I think there are one or two others which I can't recall at this time.

Mr. Bobo. In the prosecution of this case Mr. Alberts was convicted and Mrs. Alberts was released?

Mr. Nelson. That is correct, sir.

Mr. Bobo. What is the reason on this particular case, was she involved in the business with him?

Mr. Nelson. She actually, according to the records of APR Industries, was the only member of the family connected with the corporation. I believe she was secretary-treasurer and was definitely involved in the business. However, there is a case in California dealing with the prosecution of misdemeanors, which the counts that we had alleged against Mr. and Mrs. Alberts were, that where the evidence shows that a wife is involved in a misdemeanor under the direction and control of the husband, it is presumed that she has been coerced by the husband; and for that reason the judge dismissed the counts as against Mrs. Alberts.

Mr. Bobo. Under this indictment which they were brought, it was a misdemeanor, would it be of help to people in a position such as yourself, if the penalties could be strengthened and the charge for this raised to a felony or a more serious crime?

Mr. Nelson. Speaking for myself and the information that was gained through this experience, I can say definitely that it would be of considerable benefit if the penalties were made more stringent. As has been brought here before in these hearings, the usual type of penalty is a fine less than a thousand dollars, perhaps some suspended jail sentence; and when there is a gross business of the amount that has been mentioned here, a small fine is not enough to stop the enterprise.

Mr. Bobo. In the handling of this case was there any question in your mind, your own mind, that the material which you were presenting to the court was of a pornographic or of a lewd nature?

Mr. Nelson. We had, in conjunction with the members of the Los Angeles Police Department and the sheriff's office, considered the volume of evidence that was picked up pursuant to the search warrants and considered them thoroughly in the office, and were definitely of the opinion that in the application to which these brochures and mailing pieces were being applied, that they were obscene; and especially as applied to juveniles that were more or less impressive or impressionable, of that age. There were items that are before this committee now which we had considered obscene in originally determining to file a complaint, and which the court has declared obscene as of this moment, "Tina's Torture," which is before the committee, having been one of them.

I have here also a book which was not mentioned, and was specifically mentioned by the court, entitled "Sword of Desire," by Robert W. Tracy, which was a part.

Mr. Bobo. Who is the publisher?

Mr. Nelson. I believe that is also published by Arco——

Mr. Bobo. Arco Publishing Co., New York 17, New York.

Mr. Nelson. The judge as well passed upon some of the stereo slides which I believe this committee has, which we had previously determined went beyond the mere artistic values, and he has pronounced a portion of the box of slides which you have there in his opinion as being obscene.

Chairman Kefauver. Mr. Nelson, anything else you want to add for our benefit?

Mr. Nelson. I think that we have covered pretty much through Mr. Sullivan's testimony and my own what we are able to submit about Mr. Alberts, and in deference to Mr. Bobo and his airplane, I think that would be all.

Mr. Bobo. Don't let that bother you, sir.

Mr. Nelson. I don't know of anything else that needs to be brought out at this time.

Chairman Kefauver. Well, we thank you very much for your cooperation for your effort as a good law enforcement officer.

Well, thise closes our hearing for the time being in California. It will be our intention to visit California again during the life of this committee, and hear the witnesses who were not heard today, who will remain under subpena, and to take up other aspects of problems of juvenile delinquency. We will, of course, watch with interest what happens out here between now and the time our committee has the opportunity of returning.

I think these hearings have been among the most valuable that our subcommittee has held in any part of the country. In these 4 days we have heard about 3 separate phases of the juvenile-delinquency problem.

On Wednesday distinguished Californians told us about the outstanding work done here with juvenile delinquency; about the programs for the welfare of young people, about the interests in the youth in the State of California. I think the enlightened program approach to rehabilitation of youngsters which we heard about deserves commendation, and we hope that it will be promulgated in other States and other sections of the Nation.

I have been particularly impressed with the youth-authority and the forestry and ranch type rehabilitation programs; with indications in all parts of California that people are gathering together themselves at the grass-roots level to consider and to deal with and do something about this problem.

We can say that the witnesses who have appeared here from Los Angeles have shown a keen awareness of what should be done. They are working at it hard and intelligently, making good headway.

In the city of Los Angeles I think we have a good police force of good, thoughtful people who are doing the best they can under the circumstances. They themselves admit many difficulties they have had. I think the suggestions made by Mr. Barnes should be given a great deal of consideration locally. Greater public backing is, of course, necessary and will be the greatest cure; and the same goes with the information we have had about the sheriff's office, about the prosecutors, the district attorney's office. I think I can say without hesitation if other States would emulate California, particularly in the rehabilitation, the youth authority and other constructive programs, that we would be farther along in clearing up crime among our young people.

While there has been a substantial increase in juvenile delinquency over the Nation, Governor Knight wired us that California was holding its own. There has been apparently some increase in Los Angeles, but Chief Parker has told us that the increase has not been as large as the percentage increase of population.

We find present here about the same general problems in connection with housing, schooling, recreation that we have found in other parts of the country. I have been impressed with the awareness that adolescents must have something more than slides and swings, and that these places for their cars, the fact that clubs have been formed, have been fine steps in the right direction.

Here in Los Angeles we have heard from people who understand the complicated problem, and they express a willingness to do something about it. They are working at it hard. They are to be commended, and we want to give all possible encouragement to the good city officials and county officials who appeared here before us.

On Thursday the movie industry explained to us the problems that they have had in making and selling a motion picture. We have had many criticisms from the public generally about crime and violence and overplaying sex in some movies. This is not to be taken as a condemnation of the movie industry generally. I recognize the fact that movies have been a great and good force in the education and entertainment of people. I was impressed by the statement about children's movies in the school, travel movies, made by Mr. Albright who came here from Washington. I am impressed generally by the sincerity and the willingness of the people in the movie industry to cooperate with the findings of this committee; that they themselves recognize that there has been too much crime, violence, brutality just for brutality's sake in some pictures; and that beginning some time back they have determined on their own to do something about it. I think that generally the association of which Mr. Eric Johnston is head and all parts of it is an outstanding organization. This, I believe, is the best example of self-regulation of an industry of its own accord that I know of, done because of public interest. I hope that it will receive the fullest cooperation of producers and the members of the industry all the way through.

The responsibility of the movie industry is a tremendous one. We all understand the tremendous impact movies have upon our people, upon our young people. It is not sufficient that they do a fairly good job or mediocre job or even a good job, they must do an outstanding one. Our study of the movie code was both penetrating and revealing. l think the industry is to be commended for applying a code of morals to themselves, and generally both of these codes are well considered, good codes. It is this type of regulation that prevents censorship, a word that is repugnant to most of us, and certainly to me, at all times. I want to make it clear that as far as the chairman is concerned, that I am not in favor of censorship of the movies. I don't like censorship. I think self-regulation, focusing public opinion so as to bring about improvement is, however, the surest guaranty that we have against the increasing demand for some kind of censorship. Unless the industry continues to improve the quality of its pictures and gives full awareness to what the public needs in the field of children's pictures particularly, there will be an increasing demand for censorship.

There was a large body of well thought out opinion that while the codes are in the main effective, there have been many instances of violations of both the advertising and the motion-picture codes. The fault does not lie entirely with the men who are called upon to administer the code. There is a difficult problem, one which is complicated by many factors. It is evident that there is a good deal of influence, and sometimes pressure, to make them see things a certain way in close cases; maybe to approve something that they have some question, some misgivings about. Some of the fault seems to be in a rather loose interpretation of responsibility by some of the movie producers. Judging by their testimony to us, I am aware that this is a situation which they are attempting to rectify, and I think they are making headway. I hope they make more headway as soon as possible. Mr. Shurlock impressed me as being a sincere man in his work with the code. Personally I am a little disturbed about the type of movie advertising is allowed to reach the public. I realize that the advertising administration has a difficult time reviewing all of the advertisements sent to it, and a difficult time proving to some people that a new approach to selling their products should be used. It is not easy to give a story of a picture in advertising. I think some of the advertising has gone definitely too far and is not excusable.

Mr. White, who is in charge of this part of the code, impresses me as a sincere, earnest, conscientious man who has been under pretty severe difficulties in carrying out the administration of the code just as he would like for it to be carried out. I hope now that our hearings are over, that both as to the production code, the picture code and the advertising code, that these gentlemen, with the support of the industry, will continue more vigorously their attempts to correct what I feel to be at least poor selling taste in some instances. We will continue our consideration of movie problems, and all of this testimony will be studied by the members of the committee and the staff in Washington. Later on we will issue a report.

I want it understood that our report is not for the purpose of condemning; we want to recognize the good with the bad. Our purpose is to work with the movie industry to try to see that it is better from the viewpoint of its influence upon the child, and we hope that the people in the industry will understand that and will give us their confidence.

Today we have heard about one of the filthiest rackets in the United States. Pornography is often directed at young people. It has been getting into the hands of kids in schools. All of the testimony that we have had in other places shows that it is a degrading influence that it has been striking at the moral foundation of youth, and undoubtedly has contributed to juvenile delinquency substantially. It is one of the principal causes for outrageous sex murders and sex crimes.

The mail order business in nude and obscene photographs and movies has been shown here to be substantial, and it covers what goes on here, the whole of the United States. I think that from today's hearings we will be able to frame Federal legislation that will help clamp down on some of these pornographers and purveyors of filth. One of our newspapers here carried on a commendable campaign of exposing what has been going on here. The police have worked on it hard, but I think it is quite evident that there needs to be larger fines, revision of State statutes, many other matters, including a more interested public, if it is really going to be cleaned up.

Now, I want to urge the people in every community, and certainly here in California, to take another look at their own laws and make sure they are adequate to cope with a business that runs into three or four hundred million dollars a year. Our staff made that estimate based upon preliminary hearings in New York and eastern cities. I think what we have heard here shows that this is a fair estimate of the size of the gross business of this obscene and questionable literature. A fine of $50 or a suspended sentence won't keep this filth out of your community.

We have been derelict in the Federal Government level in dealing with this. I think it is quite obvious that our postal laws must be strengthened, that laws relative to the transportation of pornography by private automobiles and what not must be looked into. There are other Federal approaches to the problem that should be considered.

We will between the time now and when we hear other witnesses, follow with much interest what is done here in Los Angeles. In spite of the fine efforts of police authorities and others here in Los Angeles, it is quite evident that Los Angeles is one of the substantial, one of the largest centers for the making, producing, and distribution of this kind of obscene literature, films, in the whole United States. What it would have been without the good efforts of our police authorities, it is, of course, quite evident.

There are other big cities in the United States that have just about the same general kind of problem. I am impressed also by the fact that this is a nationwide business, that customers here, people here do business with those in New York and other places.

In closing, let me commend all of those in this area who have taken the trouble to write this committee, presenting their views and their feelings about our investigation. We have had an interested audience, and I want to thank them for their suggestions, participation, and some of the observations that they have made.

We appreciate very much the fair treatment that the press has given us since we have been here, and radio and television. Let me assure all of you that we on the subcommittee are going to continue to search for methods for solving the problems of juvenile delinquency.

I want to thank again Mr. Stillwell, Mr. Campbell, Mr. Fee, our engineer, Mr. McKeeney, many others in the GSO, Attorney General's Office, and many friends who have been so helpful to us here.

I would like to say I think our staff has done an outstanding job. Few people have been here a very short time and have developed the testimony that has been brought out, and much of the testimony that could have been brought out. They have been very diligent and hardworking. I think they have done a very good—a mighty fine job in this hearing.

Is there anything else, Mr. Bobo, before you catch that 5 o'clock plane?

Mr. BOBO. No. That is it.

Chairman KEFAUVER. The meeting will not adjourn. We will stand in recess and the hearing will be continued. Let me make it clear to you again that all witnesses, those here and those not here who have been subpenaed, who have testified, will remain under subpena. We may want to call some of you back. Those who have not testified will be notified when to come back at a later time.

Thank you very much. We now stand adjourned.

(Whereupon, at 4:25 p. m., Saturday, June 18, 1955, the hearing was adjourned.)

JUVENILE DELINQUENCY
(PROVIDENCE COMMUNITY HEARINGS AND OBSCENE AND PORNOGRAPHIC MATERIALS)

HEARING

BEFORE THE

SUBCOMMITTEE TO INVESTIGATE JUVENILE DELINQUENCY

OF THE

COMMITTEE ON THE JUDICIARY UNITED STATES SENATE

EIGHTY-FOURTH CONGRESS

FIRST SESSION

PURSUANT TO

S. Res. 62

INVESTIGATION OF JUVENILE DELINQUENCY IN THE UNITED STATES

PART 2

NOVEMBER 8, 1955

Printed for the use of the Committee on the Judiciary

COMMITTEE ON THE JUDICIARY

HARLEY M. KILGORE, West Virginia, *Chairman*

JAMES O. EASTLAND, Mississippi
ESTES KEFAUVER, Tennessee
OLIN D. JOHNSTON, South Carolina
THOMAS C. HENNINGS, JR., Missouri
JOHN L. McCLELLAN, Arkansas
PRICE DANIEL, Texas
JOSEPH C. O'MAHONEY, Wyoming

ALEXANDER WILEY, Wisconsin
WILLIAM LANGER, North Dakota
WILLIAM E. JENNER, Indiana
ARTHUR V. WATKINS, Utah
EVERETT McKINLEY DIRKSEN, Illinois
HERMAN WELKER, Idaho
JOHN MARSHALL BUTLER, Maryland

SUBCOMMITTEE TO INVESTIGATE JUVENILE DELINQUENCY IN THE UNITED STATES

ESTES KEFAUVER, Tennessee, *Chairman*

THOMAS C. HENNINGS, JR., Missouri
PRICE DANIEL, Texas

WILLIAM LANGER, North Dakota
ALEXANDER WILEY, Wisconsin

JAMES H. BOBO, *General Counsel*

II

CONTENTS

Statement of—   Page
  Cronin, John P., director of recreation, city of Providence, R. I_____   435
  McCage, Judge Francis J., judge of the juvenile court, Providence,
    R. I_____   443
  Murphy, John A., chief of police, Providence, R. I., accompanied by
    Lt. William E. May, chief, juvenile bureau, Providence Police
    Department, Providence, R. I_____   437
  Reynolds, Mayor Walter H., mayor of Providence, R. I_____   431
  Roberts, Gov. Dennis J., State of Rhode Island_____   422
  Williamson, Arnold, assistant United States attorney, district of
    Rhode Island_____   505
Testimony of—
  Caporicci, Nicholas, Cranston, R. I_____   519
  Murphy, Detective James, Poughkeepsie Police Department,
    accompanied by Detective Francis Doerr, Poughkeepsie Police
    Department, Poughkeepsie, N. Y_____   511
  Simon, Harry J., postal inspector, United States Post Office Depart-
    ment, Washington, D. C_____   498
  Tacy, N. A., district manager, bureau of post-office operations,
    Providence, R. I., accompanied by E. A. Craugh, postal inspector,
    and Edgar La Vault, postal inspector_____   454
  Temkin, Jacob, former United States district attorney, district of
    Rhode Island_____   479

EXHIBITS

Number and summary of exhibit

1. Report of the Third Annual Governor's Conference of Children and
  Youth_____   [1] 424
2. Sound mental health—good moral standards_____   [1] 424
3. Copy of S. Res. 89, 83d Congress, 1st session, and copy of the resolution
  authorizing the subcommittee to hold hearings in Providence, R. I__   [2] 450
4. Copy of a check payable to Calvin Sugarman in the amount of $450
  and signed by Robert Adams_____   [2] 459
5. Affidavit made by Mary Dorothy Tager_____   [2] 471
6. Letter dated October 31, 1955, addressed to Hon. Herbert Brownell, Jr.,
  from Senator Estes Kefauver_____   [2] 477
7. Affidavit of Leo Vine, dated December 10, 1955_____   [2] 524
8. Statement of Jacob S. Temkin, made under oath on December 12,
  1955_____   [2] 525
9. Letter of H. J. Simon, postal inspector, dated December 20, 1955____   [2] 528
10. Letter of E. R. LaVault, postal inspector, dated December 27, 1955__   [2] 529
11. Letter of E. A. Craugh, postal inspector, dated December 27, 1955___   [2] 529
12. Letter of Nelson A. Tracy, district operations manager and for post
  office inspector_____   [2] 530

---

[1] On file with the subcommittee.
[2] Printed in the record.

JUVENILE DELINQUENCY

(Providence Community Hearings and Obscene and Pornographic Materials)

TUESDAY, NOVEMBER 8, 1955

UNITED STATES SENATE,
SUBCOMMITTEE OF THE COMMITTEE ON THE
JUDICIARY TO INVESTIGATE JUVENILE DELINQUENCY,
Providence, R. I.

The subcommittee met, pursuant to notice, at 9:50 a. m., in the courtroom, Federal Building, Providence, R. I., Senator Estes Kefauver (chairman) presiding.

Present: Senator Estes Kefauver.

Also present: Representative John E. Fogarty; Peter N. Chumbris, associate counsel; H. Patrick Kiley, investigator; George Martin, investigator; and William Haddad, consultant.

Chairman KEFAUVER. The meeting will come to order.

This is a subcommittee of the Senate Judiciary Committee, charged by the Senate of the United States with the purpose of investigating problems of juvenile delinquency and of reporting to the United States Senate on what conditions we find, what Federal legislation or what action by any of the executive departments might be helpful in giving our children a better opportunity and in curbing the juvenile delinquency about which all of us know so much.

This is about the 20th hearing that we have had over a period of 2 years and we are very glad to be in Providence with you at this time.

The subcommittee is composed of Senator Langer of North Dakota; Senator Wiley, of Wisconsin; Senator Hennings, of Missouri; and Senator Daniel, of Texas; and myself.

Unfortunately, because of illness or other subcommittee hearings, it has been impossible for any of the other members of the subcommittee to be here today. I do not like holding one-man committee hearings, but there was no alternative to doing so today.

We have had some members of our very competent staff here for a few days to arrange for the hearing. On my right is Mr. Chumbris, our associate counsel. Mr. Haddad is on his right. Mr. Kiley, who is with my personal staff, and Mr. George Martin, who is a member of the staff of the Senate subcommittee.

This morning our mission is a pleasant one—to find out the details of the many fine programs originating here to curb and control juvenile delinquency. I have taken occasion already to refer to some of the things that are being done in Rhode Island, and in Providence, in the field of citizen and government participation at the local level to curb and control juvenile delinquency.

On several occasions both of your respected Senators, Senator Green and Senator Pastore—and we are very glad to have had the help and cooperation of your Senators and their administrative assistants, Pat Maisono is here, who is Senator Pastore's administrative assistant—and your two forthright Representatives, Representative Fogarty and Representative Forand, have sent information to our subcommittee on Rhode Island's delinquency control projects and what is being done here. Hundreds of Rhode Island citizens have written to us and have received and commented upon our subcommittee's literature. Here we have an alert audience and a receptive audience. This is not always the case in some places we have been.

In our work to reduce juvenile delinquency we have all too often come against the stone wall of public apathy But that is not so here. Your forward-looking officials and your outstanding newspapers, your good churches and many school people and public officials have led the fight against this apathy.

Governor Roberts, when he was mayor of Providence, initiated programs which are bearing fruit today His belief in proper recreational facilities as a preventive for juvenile delinquency is largely responsible for the State's many active recreational programs.

If every city and State in the Union had the outstanding leadership in the fight against juvenile delinquency as you have here in Rhode Island, we would not be faced with a steadily growing delinquency rate.

The vast majority of our children are fun-loving, honest, and talented; 96 or 97 percent of our kids are the best that any ever had, God-fearing, anxious to get an education and to assume their responsibility as citizens.

Yet for all of this, last year almost half a million children came before our courts A million and a third youngsters got into trouble with the police The rate has been constantly increasing over the past 5 years Those under 18 years of age committed 58 percent of all the automobile thefts in the country; 49 percent of all of the burglaries. This was a 10 percent increase over 1953 and marked a 58 percent increase in juvenile delinquency since 1948.

It is distressing to find, as one study has found, that the largest number of delinquents come before the courts for the first time when they are merely 10, 11, 12, or 13 years old For them, this was their first step along the road to a warped life. This was the time society should have come forward to help them. Too often society missed this challenge.

I honestly believe most delinquents can be saved through understanding treatment. Certainly at the tender age of 11, there is still time to correct a child's antisocial conduct.

Much of this needed help must come from within the family circle. But help must also come from the community, and from the school, and from the church. That is why it is so important to operate programs on the neighborhood, the city, and the State level.

Many sections of this Nation are groping around, attempting to find the right answer to their juvenile-delinquency problems. This subcommittee feels that we have been of some help and that we can help them find the right answers by promulgating the details of projects which have successfully solved delinquency in other sections.

This afternoon our mission is a lot less pleasant. At that time we will continue our investigation of one of the worst rackets in the United States today, that of pornography—and in talking about pornography I am not talking about the borderline cases where freedom of the press might be involved; I am talking about plain dirt and filth which is degrading to our adults, let alone to our young people.

At our New York and Los Angeles hearings psychiatrists told us that certain forms of juvenile delinquency were definitely linked to pornography. We found that not only do children readily obtain this filth, many times it is peddled to them even at schools when they are taking their recreation, but they all too often actually are tempted into making pornographic films and pictures. Their youthful innocence is being exploited by unscrupulous adults who are willing to pervert the youth of this country in order to make a few fast dollars.

Our hearings have helped reveal the scope of this business, and it is an alarmingly big business. Early estimates place the yearly traffic in this insidious filth at from three to four hundred million dollars. When I first heard that figure I was astonished, I couldn't believe it; but, as we have found, businesses in several places where the business amounts to more than a million dollars, some places two or three million dollars, it is easy to understand. Our subcommittee staff now speculates that the yearly business may run as high as half a billion dollars.

Some pornographers enjoyed immunity from proper punishment because of gaping loopholes in the Federal law. Some of these loopholes have already been closed. For instance, we found that while there were Federal laws against using the mails to send certain types of literature from one State to the other, that there was no law against placing a bundle in an automobile or a truck and carrying it from one State to the other. Fortunately, as a result of the work of this subcommittee, that loophole has now been plugged.

Legislation that will close other loopholes has also been suggested to the Congress and several bills are now pending in the Senate.

Our investigations also revealed how this pornography reaches the hands of our children. It is this phase of the investigation that brings us particularly to Providence.

During our California hearings in June of this year, we found that mail-order pornography accounted for a sizable share of this pornography business. We found, also, in June of this year that an operation in Providence was closely tied in with a national operation, and at that time I stated we would have a hearing in Providence during this year.

Nine-year-old children have received these materials through the mails. The psychiatrists have said that the unsuspecting children all too often believe the abnormal acts they view in the literature; they believe that they are normal.

We have also found that in 10 years there has been something like a 90 percent increase in sex crimes, which psychiatrists lay to a considerable extent to this traffic in pornography. Of course, pornography is but one small part of our entire study. A committee like ours can only throw the spotlight of public opinion on some subjects. We have neither the money nor the time to devote to following through on all the revelations. Others, in and out of Government, must finish

the job. Those out of Government can plead "no action," and pay
only the penalty of their conscience; those in Government who have
responsibilities have other penalties to pay. There can be no excuse
for them not doing their duty.

I want to express my appreciation to Judge Edward W. Day,
and the clerk of the court, Mr. Murphy, for the use of the courtroom
and for other help that they have given us; and to Judge John P.
Hartigan for the use of his court chambers. Then to Mr. Proctor,
the United States marshal; Mr. Pyne, the deputy marshal; Edward
Curran and Edward Brennan, the deputy United States marshals,
and many others, whose names I will mention later, our thanks for
their help and their cooperation.

Mr. Chumbris, who is our first witness?

It is a great pleasure to have with us today as our first witness the
distinguished Governor of Rhode Island, whom I have had the honor
of knowing for many, many years, and whose work in this field and
in other fields I have kept in touch with. Governor Roberts, we are
certainly honored to have you and we appreciate your cooperation
with our committee.

You have a prepared statement and after that we might have some
discussion about particular subjects.

Governor ROBERTS. Fine, Senator.

Chairman KEFAUVER. Governor Roberts, do you have some copies
of your statement?

Governor ROBERTS. I think there are some copies. We will have
them in a few minutes; they are on their way down, Senator.

STATEMENT OF GOV. DENNIS J. ROBERTS, STATE OF RHODE ISLAND

Chairman KEFAUVER. All right, sir. If you will proceed.

First, Governor, tell us, before becoming Governor of Rhode
Island you were the mayor of Providence for a number of years;
were you not?

Governor ROBERTS. That is right. I was mayor of Providence
from 1941 to 1950. And then Governor of the State of Rhode Island
from 1951 until the present time, Senator.

I have a prepared statement to read to the subcommittee, but
before doing that, as Governor of the State of Rhode Island, I would
like to welcome you and the members of your staff to our State. The
work of this subcommittee for the past 2 years has been followed by
me and many people throughout the country, as there is no more
important concern of Government than the children of our country
and our State, their well-being, and their potential as mature, well
adjusted, God-loving citizens.

The children and youth of our communities today will be those
who will make our laws, operate our factories, run our businesses, and
populate our professions tomorrow. Our basic moral and family
concepts as formulated today will in large measure determine the
heritage they pass on to the next generation.

We in Rhode Island are proud of our children and youth. Less
than 1 percent of them become violators of our State's laws. The
positive, healthy attitudes and actions of our youth have clearly
demonstrated time and time again through the activities of boys'

clubs, Catholic Youth Organizations, YMCA, YWCA, summer camps, 4–H Clubs, little league baseball, junior police, and a multitude of other activities in which the children of our communities are participating.

The junior activities of the youth of our community clearly demonstrate that they have the imagination, the diligence, and the fortitude necessary to the development of mature and substantial adults.

I think it is unfortunate that there are so many critics who publicly vilify and indict the youth of this country as a collective unit. A more timely and hopeful viewpoint was recently enunciated by the Most Reverend Russell J. McVinney, bishop of Providence, when he said:

If some youths do not live up to the high ideals given them at home and in school, it does not mean that the entire generation is wrong.

In support of this view, we in Rhode Island were recently treated to a most remarkable observance of Halloween, in which evidence of destruction and vandalism was almost totally absent. This splendid achievement is due to positive programs for the entertainment of the youngsters by numerous public, private, and church groups, and an emphasis by parents on a positive approach to the celebration of this occasion.

Chief Judge Francis J. McCabe of our statewide Rhode Island juvenile court, defines juvenile delinquency in a most profound and substantial manner. Justice McCabe said, and I quote:

Juvenile delinquency in legal term denotes only that a young individual has committed a certain act in violation of the law. The label "juvenile delinquency" is no more enlightening about the basic difficulty handicapping the child than the term "insane" is for the mentally disordered * * *. Neither term is any indication of the dynamics of his behavior, it merely serves to describe his condition. With regard to delinquency, it ignores the cultural patterns and mores, all of which are relevant to the causation of the behavior so described. Child behavior is the product of many diverse forces which stem from within the child's own makeup as well as from the environment in which he lives. It is generally agreed that delinquent behavior is not the result of any single factor within the personality of the child or of any single influence of his environment. Juvenile delinquency constitutes an individual, complex, and many-sided phenomenon arising out of individual needs and desires. Its roots reach deep into the conditions that cause social and personal maladjustments.

I have taken time to read into the senatorial record these expressions of Judge McCabe, for therein he has succinctly stated the problem in accordance with our views in Rhode Island.

Three years ago, as Governor of the State of Rhode Island, I recognized the need within our State of bringing together all people concerned with the subject of children and youth. I did this, not because of my great alarm or apprehension over the incidents of delinquency among our children, but rather to do some stock taking and self-evaluation on a statewide basis. This was done through the medium of the annual Governor's conference on children and youth. The first such conference was entitled "Juvenile Delinquency."

The purpose of our annual Governor's conference on children and youth is to stimulate interest within our communities in the various problems of children and youth and to aid in interpreting and publicizing the problems relating to all Federal, State, local, and private agencies serving our young people. Experts from many sections of the country participate in these conferences.

Such was the spontaneity of the response to the committee responsible for collection of the material used that we followed with a second program last year centered about sound mental health—good moral standards. This year, only 2 weeks ago, our annual conference concerned itself with opportunities and responsibilities of children and youth in Rhode Island.

I have with me copies of the reports which contain the activities of the annual conferences for the first 2 years. I would appreciate their being introduced into the record. At this time I would like to offer them, if it is permissible.

Chairman KEFAUVER. We are glad to have them, Governor. They will be filed as exhibits to our record.

Governor ROBERTS. Thank you, Senator.

(Report of Third Annual Governor's Conference on Children and Youth, was marked "Exhibit 1.")

(Sound Mental Health—Good Moral Standards, report of the Fourth Annual Governor's Conference on Children and Youth, was marked "Exhibit 2.")

Governor ROBERTS. Your committee will note that these reports are designed to highlight the accomplishments and the services, both public and private, to children and youth throughout our State.

I believe that the problem of juvenile delinquency is the concern of all. It can and must be dealt with, in an intelligent, understanding, and constructive manner. The forces of education, psychiatry, social service, police, courts, recreation, housing—all have their impact on children, either positive or negative. We must make their impact positive. Many of these same forces when applied to the children in the setting of their homes, the church, and the school, form the culture and behavior patterns of their whole lives. To this end we need not only well-trained personnel but also dedicated people in all areas providing service to children.

It is my firm belief that every child has a need of, and a right to, a homelife embracing the positive qualities of love, security, and guidance. These qualities are strong and real. If they are provided in abundance, combined with spiritual direction, as obtained through religious activities and love for one's God, the children will possess the basic ability to withstand the pressures that make for delinquency.

Within the framework of the State government, substantial contributions can be made in the preventive field of juvenile delinquency. We had this in mind in Rhode Island when we established the division of mental hygiene services within the department of social welfare 5 years ago. Many of the activities of this division in developing a sound mental-health program are concerned with services to children. Let me review briefly some of these activities.

First, two psychiatric clinic teams are engaged in a broad education program throughout the State. They meet with civic groups, such as the Parent Teachers Association, and nursing groups and discuss with them how to recognize emotional problems of our children in the early stages and what to do about them. In this way professional people engaged in mental hygiene are actively creating an awareness among our general citizenry of behavior symptoms that frequently lead to delinquency.

Second, within the mental-hygiene services of our State government are provided consultative services to school departments throughout the State. Working with school personnel, such as teachers, attendance officers, principals, and superintendents, the need for early recognition of behavior disorders is brought out. After recognizing symptoms of such behavior problems in children, and discussing these matters with their parents, referrals are made to our mental-hygiene community clinic for prompt professional diagnosis and treatment.

Third, the mental-hygiene community clinics which are part of our mental-hygiene services provide psychiatric and psychological services to our children wherever the need is indicated. The sources of referral are varied. Children come to the clinic largely through school departments, social agencies, local physicians, the clergy and, in many instances, through parental referrals. Other children are referred to the clinic by the juvenile court, the departments of health and education, and the division of probation and parole. The community clinical team, including the clinical psychiatrist, psychiatric social worker, and other thoroughly trained personnel, participate in evaluation conferences on each case referred, in order to determine the kind of help that might be best for the child. Most cases are accepted for treatment or for psychological or psychiatric testing.

Fourth, Rhode Island also has a child-guidance clinic in operation at the Dr. Patrick I. O'Rourke Children's Center in Providence. The children's center is a State institution providing group living experience for dependent and neglected children, and also serves as an agency for diagnosis. The juvenile court utilizes the services of this agency for placement of many children prior to legal disposition of the child's immediate or future plans for living. The child-guidance clinic develops a social portrait of the child pointing up his needs, strengths, and weaknesses. This study is made available to the court and to the social worker working with the child.

By means of these services and in individual care and treatment many children, who otherwise might become delinquent, are placed in foster homes or in other suitable living arrangements and are able to develop in a normal and healthy manner. We consider this emphasis on mental-hygiene services as a positive, aggressive, and preventive program with respect to juvenile delinquency.

Other State agencies play an important role in this field. Our statewide probation and parole services of the department of social welfare also carries on a preventive program. We have hundreds of boys and girls referred each year to the probation and parole council located in this section of the State. Such referrals come from schools, clergy, parents, and the police department. These children have not been formally presented to the juvenile court as delinquents but are considered by the source of the referral as in need of some guidance and supervision over and above that which they are receiving in their homes. Probation and parole personnel utilize the services of the mental-hygiene clinic for diagnosis and guidance in developing a constructive program for each child.

We have found an excellent response to this program and we consider it to be of great value.

There are approximately 15 probation and parole counselors assigned to the juvenile court for both preventive and corrective services. They have developed close liaison with judges, local civic leaders, Parent-Teachers Associations, and other community groups interested in the problems of juvenile delinquency.

The juvenile court itself employs a coordinator for juvenile delinquency, who conducts an additional program throughout the community by means of radio, television, press, and meetings with interested groups.

In 1951, Rhode Island established an alcoholic-treatment clinic within the department of social welfare. It is utilized by the division of probation and parole for services to many of the older predelinquent youths of our State who are in danger of becoming involved in further delinquency because of their use of alcoholic beverages. Medical psychiatric and psychitherapeutic services of the alcoholic-treatment unit have been most helpful in this preventive field of public service.

I think you may be interested in several pieces of legislation recently enacted by the Rhode Island General Assembly which bear on this problem. Because I believe that the role played by trained personnel in law enforcement is vital, I recommended to the last session of our general assembly, and it was passed, creation of a municipal police-training school. This school is located at the University of Rhode Island, and is under the direction and supervision of the Rhode Island State police. Any city or town within the State of Rhode Island may, upon application, send candidates for police training to this school and, what is more important to this hearing is, a course in juvenile delinquency is provided.

Last year the general assembly also took steps to strengthen our State laws regulating the sale and distribution of barbituates and other hypnotic drugs. Legislation was enacted which makes the illegal sale to or possession by any person under 21 years of age of any such substance a very serious offense.

Two other pieces of legislation which were passed by the last general assembly should be mentioned in connection with protecting our children. The first is a revision of the Rhode Island adoption law, strengthening the role of the juvenile court and other child-welfare services in the adoption and home-placement procedures.

The other is an act creating a special commission to study the whole field, within the State, of the publication, sale, distribution, or possession of comic books, magazines, and publications, with particular reference to its effect upon minors. I appointed this commission in July and it is now studying a preliminary report and preparing recommendations to be presented to the general assembly not later than February 15, 1956.

Preventive programs, as we all agree, can be best initiated at the municipal level. Our cities and towns are engaged in a concentrated effort to meet the problem. Providence, for example, has an outstanding and comprehensive program of organized recreation which integrates the use of all appropriate municipal facilities. This programed activity includes the utilization of schools, playgrounds, swimming pools, parks, social agencies, and a police-sponsored summer camp.

Despite these efforts, there are still many unmet needs in providing organized recreation. Expansion of municipal facilities is vital. I believe that one method of meeting these needs would be to provide multiple-use recreational facilities in conjunction with our new schools. Provisions should be made for the acquisition of sufficient land and equipment for community recreation in conjunction with the building of the school proper.

To this end, I strongly urge that your committee seek legislation enlarging the proposed Federal aid-to-education program for school construction to include the acquisition of additional land and facilities for organized recreation. I recognize that this plan involves multi-million-dollar appropriations, but I submit that it is a positive approach to the basic problem. In this way, we will guarantee recreation, not only for the schoolchildren while in school, but a total community program for children after school hours.

I think this is extremely important, Senator, for this reason:

Many of our children become delinquent because of environment circumstances—they are living in substandard dwellings, crowded conditions; they have no opportunity for guidance or training within the home; they are put on the streets. An adequate recreational program in a community, with sufficient plant and trained personnel meeting the standards of the National Recreation Association, will give that child direction, guidance, and strength, and will eliminate the vulnerability that exists in the environmental circumstances that confront many children in the urban areas of the United States.

I see also in this proposal a recreational outlet not only for our youth, but also for the aged and handicapped, as well, who are equally in need of leisure time activity.

Senate bill 728, introduced by you and Senators Hennings and Langer, providing for raising the level and expanding the function of the United States Children's Bureau, the creation of a Federal Advisory Council on Juvenile Delinquency and the granting of Federal assistance in cooperation with the States, should be considered and enacted at an early date. I feel that this legislation would greatly assist in diminishing the incidence of juvenile delinquency.

I have not attempted to review all we in Rhode Island are doing in the field to help our young people live better lives. It has been my purpose to point out to you and your committee some of the programs in which we are engaged for the prevention of juvenile delinquency. The Federal Government can provide support, encouragement, and leadership in this field. Our children and youth possess great strength, ability, and the basic drive to move in a positive direction.

Government at best plays a secondary role to the home, the church, and the school in the development of the character of our youth. This role is, nevertheless, of vital importance in the prevention of juvenile delinquency. It is our duty to constantly review and improve governmental programs and activities in this field. In Rhode Island, this is our aim and our goal.

Rhode Island is grateful to you and your committee, and eagerly looks to your recommendations to the Congress to alleviate the problems and the conditions that induce delinquency in the youth of this community and this country.

Chairman KEFAUVER. Governor Roberts, you have made a good statement of a very excellent program. I want to thank you very much.

The program that you have here in Rhode Island, the accomplishments that you have made, will be contained in our hearings and in our report which will, of course, be disseminated and studied and read by public officials all over the United States. I think you are doing many things here from which others will secure an inspiration.

I think I should comment that your statement that only 1 percent of the youth of Rhode Island has come in contact with the courts or might be placed in what we would call a juvenile delinquency class is,

I believe, the best we have heard of any State in the Nation, and the people here are certainly to be congratulated upon it.

I should have said in the beginning that the committee, early in its work, secured on a loan basis from Governor Roberts and the State of Rhode Island, the services of Mr. Harold Langlois, of your department of social welfare. He has helped us a great deal in our early work.

Governor Roberts, I want to ask you 1 or 2 questions.

Governor ROBERTS. Yes, Senator.

Chairman KEFAUVER. I am glad of your interest in Senate bill 728 to which you referred on page 6 of your statement.

About the only thing the Federal Government can do outside of the field of interstate commerce and narcotics and things of that sort, is to try to furnish some guidance and some example; and this bill, I think, as you have set forth here, would be of some assistance.

Mrs. Elliott of the Children's Bureau is doing an excellent job, but the Children's Bureau is a branch of a branch of the Department of Education and Welfare. The welfare of our children, in our opinion, makes it necessary for us to first bring together all of the groups dealing with children and to give them status so that they can perform; and we appreciate your support of that.

We want you to know, also, that this committee has strongly recommended Federal aid program for school construction. We had a hearing devoted entirely to education down at Nashville, Tenn. There the consensus was that unless we spent money for schools we were going to spend money for penal institutions in the years to come.

I am very much interested in the State law that you have and the course that you have for municipal police training school, and the fact that you do have a juvenile delinquency division.

Woud you tell us, sir, some more details about how your law handles the barbiturate problem, which you referred to on page 5 of your statement?

Governor ROBERTS. The law that is referred to there, Senator, was passed in the last session of the general assembly, and it places greater responsibility upon those who legally dispense with the barbiturates and material of that type, and puts a very severe penalty upon it. The emphasis was on the penalty, in the theory that it would deter the indiscriminate sale and ability to get into the possession of people who should not have the barbiturates or other hypnotic drugs.

Chairman KEFAUVER. We have read with much interest the fact that you have strengthened your adoption laws in Rhode Island. We had a hearing about 7 or 8 months ago in Chicago, in which we found that in some States there was no regulation whatsoever of placement agencies, no requirement for an examination of the home or the character of the adoptive parents, the suitability of the parents for the child, and we found that many thousands of children were being placed in homes where they were simply not suited; on a black-market basis.

You have adopted what I believe is substantially the national uniform adoption law; is that correct?

Governor ROBERTS. That is correct, Senator.

Chairman KEFAUVER. Requiring, first, examinations of the homes and supervision, and then a checkup before and after adoption?

Governor ROBERTS. That is right, Senator.

Chairman KEFAUVER. That would certainly do a lot of good.

I notice, also, the commission that you have to study comic books. I don't know if the public here generally knows, but in our hearings on the comic book industry we found that every month 100 million comic books are passed around, being printed and distributed. Of those 100 million, about 80 million are all right; some of them are truly funny and some of them may be even helpful; but about 20 million of them are, up to some time back, depicting death or violence or brutality, disrespect for the police, for parents.

We had testimony in several places that juvenile crimes could be traced back exactly to reading some comic book. Of course, usually the law comes out successfully, but that is in the end and in very fine print.

The comic-book industry is apparently trying to clean its own house, but I hope that your commission here will come up with some worthwhile legislation which certainly is needed.

Governor ROBERTS. We have as chairman of the commission, Senator, Mr. Clarence Sherman, who is librarian of the central library in the city of Providence, and a group of men and women who have displayed a rather deep interest in the welfare of our youth in this area. They are about to publish a report there, going over the rough draft of the report. It should be available in another 2 weeks. I am certain that they will make available the report in sufficient copies for your committee.

Chairman KEFAUVER. We would like very much to have a copy.

Governor ROBERTS. I had experience with practically the same group when I was mayor of Providence some years ago, and they did a very thorough job. They had to recognize their limitations as a committee; they didn't get into censorship. They were cognizant of the freedom of the press and so forth, but they did by calling in the representatives of the industry that distributed their books here in the State of Rhode Island, they got pretty good cooperation in most instances. I think out of 7 or 8, only 1 was reluctant to give full cooperation. It was a great improvement.

That same group, not identical, but the majority of them are now working and will have that report.

Chairman KEFAUVER. We certainly would like to have a copy, because many States have tried laws on the subject of comic books; some of their laws have been good and some laws have been bad. So I think it is a pretty good idea to study the whole problem before trying to get into the field of legislation.

I am interested, also, in the governors' conference on children and youth. When was this established, Governor Roberts, and tell us something about the makeup of the membership of the conference, how it is selected?

Governor ROBERTS. The governors' conference, originally the concept comes out of the White House Conference on Children and Youth that was called by President Truman some 4 years ago. As a result of that conference each State was supposed to set up a governors' conference on children and youth.

Here in Rhode Island we did it under the leadership of Father Lamb, who was head of the Diocesan and Social Service. The composition of the commission is made up of people who deal with youth, school, parent-teachers, juvenile court, those in the mental health program, those in the service clubs. It is a representative group making up the governors' commission, and then down below that each community has a group made up of people who have an interest and an ability through their positions and their activity in the community to have an effect on the children and youth, whether it be in the psychiatric, the medical, social, recreational, school, home, church, or whatever the activity might be.

They coordinate and evaluate the services in a community, and they try to create a grassroots movement to improve these various services that will in time give opportunity to youth and prevent delinquency.

If I may, Senator——

Chairman KEFAUVER. How is it financed, Governor?

Governor ROBERTS. It is financed by the State. The cost is very nominal. The effort and the greatness of the committee is the dedication of its membership. They have a sincere interest, and they give their time and effort and their accomplishments have been good in my opinion.

If I may say, Senator, they point up, or this governors conference has pointed up, and I think all individuals that have a concern in this area in the State of Rhode Island have come to a realization that the child in a normal home, with the love and affection and the guidance and the direction of sound parents, the religious training, good school activity and so forth, does not become a delinquent; he has the basic strength that is given to him in the home and the church and the school.

Delinquency many times come about because of a physical vulnerability or a mental vulnerability, or because the child just does not have opportunity in his community by reason of his environment, because of low income, because of habits of the parents, and so forth, the child may have a very poor environment. There are many areas of the great cities of the United States where the child is living 7 and 8 in 2 rooms. He has no opportunity for homelife. He eats and sleeps at home and then he is sent to school; then he is put on the street.

Now, the cure for that is adequate recreational facilties and personnel that are trained, that are not merely going into the recreational field for a job, but that have an interest and a dedication, a little more than a recreational worker, who has the capacity, perhaps, of a social worker, if I amy use that term.

If you have that in a community, you make up for the loss, or you make up for the vulnerability that exists in the lack of proper environment for our children. If you meet that need, why then, I think you will cut doen the incidents of juvenile delinquency in the urban areas of the United States of America greatly.

That is why I have emphasized and why I perhaps presume upon your time to mention this again. I think if the Federal Government, with its school program, would consider in the construction of school plant sufficient gymnasium space, locker space, rooms where arts and crafts and other programs can be carried out after school hours by a personnel known as recreational workers and meeting the standards of the national associatiln, that then you will provide the child with the opportunity, with the incentives and with the outlets that he needs in his formative years, in his school years, here in this community and other communities.

I think it is one of the greatest contributions the Federal Government can make. The local communities cannot do it because they are having a difficult time to finance their general operations at present.

Chairman KEFAUVER. Governor, in my opinion, at least half of the bigtime racketeers and criminals would have been good citizens if they had had different environments, a little different chance early in their lives. They cost society a great deal now. A little money spent then might have saved society not only a lot of grief but even substantial amounts of money which now has to be spent for penal institutions.

We certainly are grateful to you, Governor Roberts.

Governor ROBERTS. Thank you very much, Senator.

Chairman KEFAUVER. This is an excellent statement, and I thank you for it.

Governor ROBERTS. I am grateful for the opportunity.

Chairman KEFAUVER. Won't you sit with us as long as you can here today. We would be glad to have you sit here and listen.

Governor ROBERTS. If I may, I will sit through Mayor Reynolds' statement.

Chairman KEFAUVER. Hon. Walter H. Reynolds, the distinguished mayor of Providence.

STATEMENT OF WALTER H. REYNOLDS, MAYOR OF PROVIDENCE, R. I.

Mayor Reynolds, we thank you very much for your cooperation with the staff of our subcommittee and with our subcommittee. They have told me of your helpfulness to them.

We know already of some of the things you are doing here, and I am certain your statement will be of much interest, not only to us but to mayors and people everywhere who read it.

Do you have a prepared statement?

Mayor REYNOLDS. Yes, Senator.

Chairman KEFAUVER. I don't seem to have any copies of it here. Can you pass them around?

Mayor, do you want anyone to sit with you while you testify?

Mayor REYNOLDS. No. I think they can appear later on and answer any specific questions you may have, Senator. They are more familiar with it than I am.

Chairman KEFAUVER. Mr. Mayor, how long have you been mayor of this good city?

Mayor REYNOLDS. This is my third 2-year term, Senator.

Chairman KEFAUVER. You mean you have 2-year terms here?

Mayor REYNOLDS. Two-year terms. You might be able to do something about that in your committee.

Senator KEFAUVER. I used to be familiar with that problem in the House of Representatives. It comes around awfully often.

Mayor REYNOLDS. I understand, Senator.

Chairman KEFAUVER. Before becoming mayor, Mr. Reynolds, what did you do?

Mayor REYNOLDS. I happened to be with the city about 20 years, Senator, in various capacities.

Chairman KEFAUVER. By the way, how large is Providence now, according to their chamber of commerce?

Mayor REYNOLDS. It has a quarter of a million people.

Chairman KEFAUVER. All right, Mayor Reynolds.

Mayor REYNOLDS. Thank you, Senator.

Governor Roberts, and ladies and gentlemen, I appreciate the opportunity to appear here this morning to testify before this committee on the matters of juvenile delinquency. No subject could be more serious; no subject could be more immediate for it affects directly our hearts and our homes.

I shall confine my testimony to the broad aspects of the delinquency picture as I see it here in Providence. I shall leave it to those who may follow me here to cite the majority of the statistics and to reply to questions of detail, as these persons are likely, from their professional and constant contact with their subject-matter, to have a more intimate and specific knowledge than that which I possess.

I am informed that there are approximately 40,000 persons within the city of Providence falling within the juvenile-age brackets. Approximately 1,500 arrests are made annually, and of these some 500 or slightly more are deemed sufficiently serious to be referred to our juvenile court. This means that gross delinquency rate is less than 4 percent and serious delinquency involves annually less than 1½ percent of our juvenile population. I believe that compared to national trends and to trends in delinquency in other cities, this reflects a fairly good situation in this city.

At this point I should like to make it clear that I think there is no such thing as a satisfactory rate of delinquency. So long as we have delinquency, whether in greater or lesser degree, we are still confronted with the delinquency problem. We feel, however, that this is a front upon which we have made some progress in Providence, and I would like to cite for this committee some of the positive measures which have been undertaken in the community in our efforts to decrease delinquency.

We have under the jurisdiction of the State of Rhode Island an excellent juvenile court to which I have referred previously. The personnel of this court are trained and experienced individuals who have dealt with the problems of youth over the years with firmness and understanding.

We have within the Providence Police Department a division of juveniles which is manned by specialists and which is assigned exclusively to work with juveniles. Comprising a strength of 22 men and 4 policewomen, this division is on duty 24 hours a day, and constitutes a powerful deterrent to prospective delinquents. The record of delinquencies and crimes cleared by arrests through the work of this division and through cases referred to this division appears to me to illustrate both its constant vigilance and its continued value.

We have had no experience and no problems with the drug traffic which in this city does not appear to involve juveniles. Sex crimes and crimes of violence are, on the whole, an extraordinary occurrence. Organized gangs and gang warfare of which we read in other cities are here practically unknown.

We have, as do all communities, continuing problems with motor-vehicle offenses, theft, breaking and entering, larceny of automobiles— most frequently where a careless driver leaves a key in the ignition—

and with vandalism. We seek earnestly to combat and reduce the commission of crimes in these categories.

Up to this point I have directed my remarks chiefly to the detection of delinquencies and crimes, to apprehension of the offenders and to the disposition of cases cleared by arrest. I would like to call your attention briefly to the prevention of delinquency and crime, which to us here in Providence is a matter of paramount interest.

The Providence Junior Police Camp, a resident summer camp maintained by our recreation department in cooperation with the police department, gives to nearly 400 boys in the underpriviledged group, many of whom might become problem cases, a healthful period of good food and good environment. The opportunity to work constructively with boys which is afforded by this venture has proved extremely worthwhile.

During the summer of the city of Providence operates some 42 neighborhood playground programs and throughout the year 5 indoor centers, and 6 school centers during fall, spring, and winter, all dedicated to keeping youth constructively employed. In connection with these centers our recreation department has developed a unique program through which the division of juveniles actively enlists many problem-area juveniles for specific sports and projects, thus channelling their interests and activities along healthful and socially oriented lines.

Over the past years of my own administration, and that of my predecessor, new playgrounds and playfields have been acquired, and the city's appropriation for recreational operations and programing has been sharply increased with the dual purpose in mind of providing both the usual and normal recreational activities and affording at the same time a particular and productive method of working with the problem youth.

While I am upon this subject of prevention of delinquency and crime, I should be remiss, indeed, if I did not admit the tremendous debt of gratitude to the many private, religious, and other nongovernmental agencies in this city, which, through cooperation with us, and in their own private and individual programs, have done an admirable amount of work in the prevention of delinquency and crime. I shall not take your time to enumerate each of these agencies. All have taken a vital interest in the problems of delinquency in this city and have worked tirelessly for the benefit and welfare of youth.

Approximately a year ago, a Providence committee composed of members of our city council and citizens of this city, including both clergy and laity, undertook a study of the delinquency problem in Providence. From the report of this committee which has now been submitted, I find very little pointing with alarm and a great deal of good common sense.

It may interest this committee to learn that perhaps the most damaging criticism included in this report was directed to the failure of the public-housing projects to provide recreational and community-center facilities in large housing developments. The report makes certain recommendations, such as a committee to screen literature and comic books which has since been appointed by the Governor of this State. Additional recommendations were made with respect to the place of the school in the delinquency problem and the role of the parent and the home. All of these are important matters and will receive continued attention.

In conclusion, permit me to say that while we are in no sense satisfied with the juvenile delinquency problem in Providence, we feel that we are approaching it in a positive and a constructive manner. It is my hope that this testimony and our results may be of interest to your committee and perhaps also to other cities which have been less fortunate than ourselves.

Chairman KEFAUVER. Mayor Reynolds, thank you very much for giving us a good review of what you are doing here in Providence, and of the enlightened programs, and also for admitting that you are not fully satisfied with everything and that there are more things to be done.

Mayor REYNOLDS. Right.

Chairman KEFAUVER. I am interested in your attitude toward public-housing projects not providing sufficient recreational and community-center facilities. We have had that same complaint in other places.

Whose responsibility, whose fault is that; what should be done about it?

Mayor REYNOLDS. A bigger appropriation by the public-housing officials, of course, could accommodate that. But maybe the city should pick up in those places where there are no adequate facilities for recreation.

Chairman KEFAUVER. There has been a tendency both in the administration in the Congress down in Washington to just think only or largely about room space in connection with public-housing projects and cut down on what I think is equally important, the recreational facilities, which I think is a very shortsighted viewpoint. Don't you think so?

Mayor REYNOLDS. Yes, Senator.

Chairman KEFAUVER. But then, of course, the city itself could do something about that if it would pick up the——

Mayor REYNOLDS. I believe if we had sufficient funds we probably should do that.

Chairman KEFAUVER. How do you get along in getting funds for your youth programs here? Do you find apathy of the citizens and the appropriating bodies, or do you get as much money as you want?

Mayor REYNOLDS. I think we get all the money that is available, Senator. We have a budget of about $30 million, and I think it is proportionately well financed for the recreation department.

I think about 8 or 10 years ago we spent $30,000 on recreation; and since Governor Roberts came into the picture, I think we are spending now over $300,000.

Chairman KEFAUVER. $300,000 in the city now?

Mayor REYNOLDS. Yes. And 10 years ago, it was about $30,000.

Chairman KEFAUVER. You said here you had 42——

Mayor REYNOLDS. 42 play areas.

Chairman KEFAUVER. Neighborhood playgrounds. What are those?

Mayor REYNOLDS. They are regular ball fields and recreational fields.

Chairman KEFAUVER. Slides?

Mayor REYNOLDS. I think Mr. Cronin, my recreational adviser, would be more familiar with the details of this, Senator, if you have any specific questions to ask.

Chairman KEFAUVER. Mr. Cronin, why don't you come around and tell us about it. We are glad to have you here. Tell us about your recreational program and what you would like to do.

STATEMENT OF JOHN P. CRONIN, DIRECTOR OF RECREATION, CITY OF PROVIDENCE, R. I.

Mr. CRONIN. Well, Senator, in our recreation program, as Mayor Reynolds has pointed out, we have advanced to a great extent over the past 8 years. That was due to our new development on a year-round basis, which was instituted during the regime of Mayor Roberts. At that time, there was developed a recreation advisory committee, which has advised Mayor Reynolds and myself in the development and help of our program.

We have 42 playgrounds, and some of them are large playfields with 2 major diamonds on them, and 2 little league or softball fields, and also tot park areas.

We have a master plan——

Chairman KEFAUVER. Who supervises these playgrounds and what is your arrangement about that?

Mr. CRONIN. In the supervision of the playgrounds, Senator, we have people whose standards are high. Every person that is a director of our playground must have a college degree. It is my intent and we hope to raise recreation to the dignity of education, and then we feel that our program will have the highest type leadership possible, which to my mind is more important than facilities.

I inherently believe that our leaders must not be worried by a situation that exists today through the media of television, the press, and the radio, which tend to compound the weaknesses of our youth instead of consolidating the strengths of our youth. It is our job and our leadership's job to consolidate the strength, and in that leadership we try to imbue in all our workers a desire to lead, not by force, but by the subtle force of attraction—their attractiveness. So that we can bring people into our program.

Chairman KEFAUVER. That is a very noble ambition.

You have five indoor centers. What kind of centers are those that the mayor spoke of?

Mr. CRONIN. Our indoor centers are akin to community centers in character. We carry out a highly diversified program in those centers. We operate them, some of them, on a year-round basis; others are school centers. We have a wonderful liaison with the school department. All the schools are available for our use.

I think one major factor is this, that in the last year of Governor Roberts' administration as mayor a school was planned in which the recreation department was called in so they could work, then, with the planning division in the technical development of the school; so that the school would be community in character, in its use; that during the schoolday its physical education facilities could be used, in the evening, or in the afternoon and evening, by our recreation department, and that project has worked out very well indeed.

We hope that all schools in the future can be developed that way, as has been recommended by Governor Roberts in his talk this morning, sir.

Chairman KEFAUVER. Is Chief Murphy going to tell us about the junior police camp; will that come under his discussion later on?

Mayor REYNOLDS. Mr. Cronin is in charge of that.

Chairman KEFAUVER. The chief is going to testify.

Are you going to tell us about the junior police camp or do you want Mr. Cronin to?

Mr. MURPHY. I think my assistant here, who is in charge of the juvenile bureau, will be capable of answering that question.

Chairman KEFAUVER. We will save that for him, then.

Mayor REYNOLDS. I think the camp will be more properly explained by Mr. Cronin; it is more under his jurisdiction.

Chairman KEFAUVER. You just explain it a little bit, and let's save some explanation for our friend over here.

Mr. CRONIN. In 1946, the junior police camp was developed, during the mayoralty of Governor Roberts. The purpose of the junior police camp was to give boys an opportunity for camping who did not have the economic means to do so.

The camp is divided into three categories as far as the youngsters are concerned. They are all selected by the police department, the division of women and juvenile. I operate the camp technically, sir.

Now, the purpose of the camp is to prevent delinquency. In these three categories I would like to state that we do not publish two of the categories of youngsters, but I will give it here.

First, one-third of the youngsters of the 400 boys are underprivileged; they are in lower income and economic circumstances.

Another third is in the so-called twilight zone of delinquency. And that probably needs a work of explanation. Boys who are, let us assume, 12 years of age, have the physical development of a 16-year-old boy. They are immediately sought by boys of that age level, although their emotional development is not commensurate with the development of a boy of 16 years of age.

There they learn expressions that they do not have adequate ability to comprehend, yet they go back into the classroom with boys and girls of their chronological age of 12. We do what we can to channelize those boys in the proper paths of citizenship through good leadership.

The final third of the boys have unfortunately been before the courts. I have worked closely with Judge McCabe who is the chairman of our recreation advisory committee, and who has worked with me a long while in this work. In so doing, we are able to live with those boys at camp, we get to know them, and therefore provide a program for them and then follow it up in our recreation department once they leave the camp.

The junior police department work very, very closely with me in this particular field. We coordinate, we integrate our work; and we integrate the junior police camp with our recreation department. I have been able to do this more successfully in the last 2 years, when we have developed a fieldworker system, outstanding men who go through the streets at night and bring youngsters into our program who are reluctant to come into our program because they do not want to enter the group or the society pattern.

Therefore, we have been able to use the junior police camp directly in preventing delinquency, and to follow up the work there on a year-round basis in our recreation department.

I believe that answers the question unless, Senator, there are some others.

Chairman KEFAUVER. Thank you, Mr. Cronin, very much. I like your enthusiasm for what you are doing.

Now, Mayor, do you have any others? Mr. Murphy and Judge McCabe are going to testify.

Mayor REYNOLDS. Mr. Murphy will testify, I believe.

Chairman KEFAUVER. Do you want to have any of your other people come around?

Mayor REYNOLDS. No; I think that is sufficient.

Chairman KEFAUVER. Mr. Mayor, we have heard something about a Lorenzo report in connection with housing here in Providence; what is that?

Mayor REYNOLDS. That is a committee just referred to.

Chairman KEFAUVER. We will be glad to have a copy of that report.

Mayor REYNOLDS. I will be very happy to send it to you.

Chairman KEFAUVER. Thank you very much, Mayor.

We will have about a 10-minute recess and resume at 20 minutes after 11.

(A recess was taken.)

Chairman KEFAUVER. It has been called to my attention that Mr. John Frabotta, the sociology instructor at the Uxbridge High School, is here with members of his sociology class. Where did you go to, Mr. Frabotta?

Mr. FRABOTTA. Here, Senator.

Chairman KEFAUVER. They are standing in the back. We certainly appreciate your interest and your presence here today.

I met the members of your class, about 18 or 20 boys, bright-looking high school boys, and I note that there weren't any girls in the class. I don't know why; but we certainly do appreciate your being here today, and your interest.

There are some chairs and seats around if some of you want to sit down.

Our next witness is the Honorable John A. Murphy, the chief of police of Providence, R. I.

Mr. Murphy, you come around, and if you have Lieutenant May with you, of whom we would like to ask some questions and who will join in the discussion, have him come around, too.

STATEMENT OF HON. JOHN A. MURPHY, CHIEF OF POLICE, PROVIDENCE, R. I., ACCOMPANIED BY LT. WILLIAM E. MAY, CHIEF, JUVENILE BUREAU, POLICE DEPARTMENT, PROVIDENCE, R. I.

Chairman KEFAUVER. Lieutenant May, what is your first name?

Mr. MAY. William E., Senator.

Chairman KEFAUVER. What are you with the department?

Mr. MAY. I am in charge at the present time of the juvenile bureau, under the direction of Comdr. Walter E. Stone.

Chairman KEFAUVER. Mr. Stone is here?

Mr. MURPHY. Not now; but he will be here later.

Chairman KEFAUVER. Chief Murphy, how long have you been chief of the police department of Providence?

Mr. MURPHY. A little over 2 years, Senator.

Chairman KEFAUVER. And have you been with the department for some time previous to that?

Mr. MURPHY. Since 1924, sir.

Chairman KEFAUVER. That is in the neighborhood of 31 years?

Mr. MURPHY. Thirty-one years, sir.

Chairman KEFAUVER. Chief Murphy, we are very glad to have you and Lieutenant May with us. Do you have a prepared statement, sir?

Mr. MURPHY. A very short one, sir.

Chairman KEFAUVER. Do you have some copies of it you can pass around?

Mr. MURPHY. No; I haven't sir; just one copy.

Chairman KEFAUVER. All right, sir. You tell us about the problems of juvenile delinquency here in Providence and what you as chief of police are doing about it.

Mr. MURPHY. The juvenile bureau of the Providence Police Department was organized in November 1945 by Gov. Dennis J. Roberts, who at that time was mayor of the city of Providence.

At the time of its inception, there were 3 sergeants and 7 patrolmen. The present strength of the juvenile bureau is 26 police personnel— 1 lieutenant, 2 sergeants, 4 policewomen and 19 patrolmen, 1 civilian clerk and 5 matrons.

It has proven to be a valuable bureau in the Providence Police Department. The bureau operates a 24-hour-day schedule. This bureau works very closely with the juvenile court, school department, and various social agencies of the city of Providence.

We are very happy to report that there are no juveniles involved in any form in the use of narcotics in the city of Providence. However, several complaints have been investigated which revealed no foundation for a complaint.

There is very little drinking of intoxicating liquors by juveniles here, and we feel that this is due to the continued patroling in the cafes, bars, and public amusement places where young people congregate, by the policewomen and plainclothesmen who check on all youthful looking patrons.

Another notable feature in this city in which there are approximately 40,000 boys and girls of juvenile age, is the absence of organized gangs, and we feel this is due in part to the juvenile officers who maintain a helpful and friendly attitude toward the youths in the schools, where they give safety talks, organized sport programs with the boys, and then arrange competitive games between the different sections of the city.

During the summer months the juvenile officers assist the recreation department in operating and maintaining the Providence Junior Police Camp where over 360 underprivileged and predelinquent boys are given a 2-week vacation at the seashore at no cost to their parents; the entire expense of this camp is paid by the city of Providence.

On Halloween the juvenile officers run parties for the boys and girls of the city. Since their inception, these parties have proven eminently successful, resulting in a drastic reduction in complaints relative to the willful destruction of property, so prevelant in other places.

Over 9,000 children were provided with refreshments, wholesome entertainment, and prizes were donated by the merchants of the city. These children might otherwise have been out in the street, causing damage to property and performing other mischievous pranks.

Chairman KEFAUVER. That is a great advancement, Chief Murphy. When was it you had 3 sergeants and 7 patrolmen?

Mr. MURPHY. 1945, sir.

Chairman KEFAUVER. And now you have 26 policemen——

Mr. MURPHY. Twenty-six personnel altogether, sir.

Chairman KEFAUVER. That is 4 women, 1 lieutenant——

Mr. MURPHY. Two sergeants, 19 patrolmen, 5 matrons, and 1 police clerk.

Chairman KEFAUVER. What is the difference in the budget that you had in 1945 and at the present time for this special juvenile work?

Mr. MURPHY. We operate directly on the police department budget. I cannot answer that question as far as the police department budget is concerned; I think that would have to come from the commissioner.

Chairman KEFAUVER. We found in some places that personnel assigned to the juvenile squad don't like it very much; they feel that that is a softie work, or is not a very good assignment.

Do your people have pride in the fact that they are on the juvenile squad?

Mr. MURPHY. They are very anxious to get into the juvenile squad. Right now I have applications for about 15 to get into the juvenile squad.

Chairman KEFAUVER. And so it is regarded as a special privilege if they have that opportunity?

Mr. MURPHY. That's right. And they don't like to get out of there.

Chairman KEFAUVER. That's fine.

Mr. MURPHY. If they seek promotion, they really don't want to get out, but they have to get back into the uniformed force, and give somebody else a chance to move into the juvenile bureau.

Chairman KEFAUVER. And you have a special period of training for those who go into the juvenile division?

Mr. MURPHY. Well, they are trained as they go along, from the sergeants and the lieutenants who head the division.

Chairman KEFAUVER. These 19 patrolmen, do they go largely on foot or are they motorized?

Mr. MURPHY. Mostly all on foot, sir.

Chairman KEFAUVER. We have had ever so many people tell us that as respects the juvenile, that officers on foot are much better influence than those who go by car; that an officer on foot who talks with the boys, the boys look up to him, and he has a chance to counsel them and become good friends; but if they go by in an automobile the boys are liable to say, "Well, that fellow has gotten to be a big shot, and you can't stop him and he can't stop and talk with us."

Mr. MURPHY. I think that Lieutenant May would be the one to answer that question. He is sitting right at my side here, and I would like to have him explain his department.

Chairman KEFAUVER. You tell us about it, Lieutenant May.

Mr. MAY. Senator, we have 14 of the 19 patrolmen who work days. They are in and out of the school all day long. They give 4 different safety talks to each school throughout the entire city, 4 times a year, 2 times for each term.

Chairman KEFAUVER. What are these safety talks, what does that consist of?

Mr. MAY. Crossing highways, obeying rules and regulations. They give them small courses in the laws, in the ordinances of the city. They are in and out of the schools.

As you mentioned about the boys being acquainted with the officers, they are very well acquainted with the juvenile men. In fact, on many occasions they come down asking for references when they get to be 16 and they are looking for employment. They come down looking for a reference from the men. They know them all by their first names.

Chairman KEFAUVER. Kids are going to look up to somebody, and if they look up to a good officer that is a fine thing, you think?

Mr. MAY. That is the way we have it operating now, Senator; yes, looking up to these juvenile officers.

Chairman KEFAUVER. How about these four policewomen, you have, what do they do?

Mr. MAY. They investigate all cases where a woman is involved, or a young girl. A woman or a girl is never questioned by a man unless that policewoman is present.

In addition to that, she covers all the cafes with the police officers in civilian clothes. They cover all the cafes, bus terminals, union station, any place where juveniles might congregate. It has quite an effect on this drinking problem, which we have very little of in the city of Providence.

Chairman KEFAUVER. What is your law about serving alcoholic beverages to juveniles?

Mr. MAY. The law is that no one is to be served any alcoholic beverage under the age of 21.

Chairman KEFAUVER. Is that pretty well enforced in Providence?

Mr. MAY. Yes, sir.

Chairman KEFAUVER. That sounds like you are doing pretty well. I was interested in what you said about there being no narcotic violations. Does that include marihuana?

Mr. MAY. I have been connected with the juvenile bureau, Senator, for the past 8 years, and up until the present time we have not had one case involving any form of narcotics or barbiturates of any form at all.

As the chief has mentioned, we have investigated several complaints which, after investigation, proved there was no foundation to them.

Chairman KEFAUVER. Lieutenant May and Chief Murphy, I am very much interested in your junior police camp. You say that is down at the seashore, and you send 360 children down for 2 weeks vacation every year?

Mr. MURPHY. That is the camp that Mr. Cronin explained to you previous to me.

Chairman KEFAUVER. Who pays for that camp?

Mr. MURPHY. The city of Providence pays for that.

Chairman KEFAUVER. Do all the kids who want to go have a chance to go?

Mr. MURPHY. Not all that want to go. Only those that are underprivileged and wouldn't have a chance to go otherwise.

Chairman KEFAUVER. Do you have more that should go than you are able to take care of?

Mr. MURPHY. Yes. I would say there are more that should go, but we cannot take care of the whole number.

Chairman KEFAUVER. How many do you think would like to go who should be entitled to go?

Mr. MURPHY. I think you could answer that question.

Mr. MAY. Probably another hundred or two hundred, probably.

We start off at the beginning of the camp season to send 360 boys there. But we usually end up by sending 400 to 420.

At the camp, you will always find one youngster who is down there and his friend is going, and he would like to be going, too. The way we have been operating, we send that boy.

The camp only has facilities for about 400 boys now.

Chairman KEFAUVER. That is certainly a wonderful thing for an underprivileged kid to have a chance to have a 2 weeks camping vacation.

Mr. MAY. The biggest percentage of the boys, sir, when they came back, they all gained from 4 to 9 pounds.

As the chief said, there is no cost to the boy at all.

Then during the camp, we have two police officers down there who are assistants to Mr. Cronin. And we keep changing that policeman every 2 weeks so all the boys will get acquainted with all the juvenile men.

Chairman KEFAUVER. Chief Murphy, you said something about your officers organizing games for the kids. Where is that done and how is it done?

Mr. MURPHY. That is done by the juvenile bureau, too, Senator.

Mr. MAY. We have all the seasonal sports. At the present time, we have a touch football game which is in operation. We compete with the different sections of the city. Members of the juvenile bureau operate those, conduct those games.

When the touch football season is closed, we go into the basketball season, which runs until the spring. Then when the basketball season is completed, we go into baseball. We run that until the junior police camp opens up in the latter part of June, and it keeps us busy with sports all the year round.

It has a tendency to keep the boys in with the police. We usually pick out a kid that possibly looks like he may be getting into trouble. We stick him on the team and keep him busy like that; and it has proved very successful.

Chairman KEFAUVER. Do you need more personnel to organize these recreational activities?

Mr. MAY. At the present time, we have a sufficient number of personnel to operate properly, Senator.

Chairman KEFAUVER. The mayor said that only about 1 percent of the youth or less than 1 percent—actually less than 1½ percent get into serious delinquency problems. What do you call a serious delinquency problem?

Mr. MAY. That is something, Senator, where we would send a boy to juvenile court.

As the mayor has mentioned, we apprehend about 1,500, that is both boys and girls, in the course of a year, and approximately 500 of those boys and girls are referred to juvenile court.

Chairman KEFAUVER. What is the breakdown, sexwise, what percentage of boys and what percentage of girls; or will Judge McCabe tell us about that?

Mr. MAY. I think he could, Senator, much better than I could on that.

Chairman KEFAUVER. What are usually the types of offenses which account for this 1½ percent?

Mr. MAY. We have breaking and entering, larceny, and after larceny would be assault, which mostly are simple assaults, no aggravated assaults; and in the fourth place comes the driving off without the consent, of which our mayor has already spoken and said that the driving off is done with a lot of help from the motorist who conveniently leaves his key in the switch.

Chairman KEFAUVER. The Chair is very happy to see an old friend with whom I served in the House of Representatives back in the dark, dark ages, here, Congressman Fogarty. Won't you come around and sit with us up here? We would be glad to have you, Mr. Maisono. Would you come up?

Speaking of recreation, Congressman Fogarty and I used to play paddle ball and handball down at the gymnasium.

Chief Murphy and Lieutenant May, what in your opinion are the reasons for these few number of offenses that you have? What do you think are the principal causes for this theft and what not?

Mr. MAY. For holding it down, Senator?

Chairman KEFAUVER. I.mean what causes the kids to commit the offenses that they do?

Mr. MAY. Broken homes, and boys that don't have enough recreational facilities, that get out. When they are not busy, an idle mind, chances are, will bring on some kind of offense. That is why we stress the programs to keep the boys busy.

Chairman KEFAUVER. Has there been a decline in the percentage of juvenile offenses in the last few years since you have had a larger police force?

Mr. MAY. Yes; there has, Senator.

Chairman KEFAUVER. What percentage decline; do you have that?

Mr. MAY. I haven't got the percentages here, Senator. But in the past year, we have probably stepped up a lot on the motor-vehicle violations, which have increased, but that is just due to the fact that we have stepped up on the program and sent more to court, as the juvenile court welcomes referrals on a boy or a girl, and we thought this might be a means of slowing it down.

Chairman KEFAUVER. Your policemen and women on the juvenile squad, do they work with the probation officers from the juvenile court?

Mr. MAY. At times, Senator, they do; yes, sir.

Chairman KEFAUVER. Mr. Chumbris, do you have any questions you want to ask?

Mr. CHUMBRIS. I just wanted to ask one question. We found throughout the country that any area near a large body of water, either the ocean or the bay, would have difficulty with the narcotics problem.

I would like to know what means you use to keep the narcotic problem to such a low level that you do here in Providence, R. I.?

Mr. MAY. We never had any of those yet.

Mr. CHUMBRIS. Do you have an adult problem of narcotics?

Mr. MAY. I wouldn't know too much about that. I doubt that there is much of that.

Mr. MURPHY. Not too much; no.

Mr. CHUMBRIS. It does not affect either the adult or the juvenile?

Mr. MAY. That's right. We have had none with juvenile.

Mr. CHUMBRIS. Do you have your statistics there before you, Lieutenant, your statistics dealing with the overall juvenile delinquency problem?

Mr. MAY. I have the first 9 months of this year. Is that what you mean?

Mr. CHUMBRIS. Yes. Well, we would like to have you submit it as an exhibit to your testimony this morning.

Mr. MAY. Yes.

Chairman KEFAUVER. Anything else, Chief Murphy, that you want to tell us about?

Mr. MURPHY. That is all I know of, Senator.

Chairman KEFAUVER. Lieutenant May, is there anything else you want to tell us about?

Mr. MAY. No, sir.

Chairman KEFAUVER. I certainly want to commend you on your work. I want to commend the people of Providence on having the foresight to appropriate enough money to enable you to build up your special juvenile squad as you have in these 10 years. It is certainly bringing good results.

I think it should be pointed out that the money spent for this squad is paid back many, many times over in law enforcement, less criminality, better citizenship. Don't you think so?

Mr. MURPHY. Very much so, Senator.

Chairman KEFAUVER. We are glad to have you with us.

Mr. MURPHY. Thank you very much.

Chairman KEFAUVER. Judge McCabe, we would like to have you come around.

STATEMENT OF HON. FRANCIS J. McCABE, JUDGE OF THE JUVENILE COURT, PROVIDENCE, R. I.

Judge Francis J. McCabe, the judge of the juvenile court.

Mr. McCABE. That is correct, sir.

Chairman KEFAUVER. You are the chief judge of the juvenile court?

Mr. McCABE. Yes, sir.

Chairman KEFAUVER. We have heard a great deal about your court, Judge McCabe, and we appreciate the information you have given our staff and our committee from time to time. We know of your work with the National Association of Juvenile Judges.

Mr. McCABE. Thank you, Senator.

Chairman KEFAUVER. Judge McCabe, will you tell us how long you have been the chief judge of the juvenile court; how it is composed, something about your work, any recommendations to this committee.

Do you have a prepared statement, Judge?

Mr. McCABE. In answer to your specific question, no; I haven't any prepared statement. I didn't know whether I was to have a prepared statement or whether I was to answer any specific questions that might be given to me.

I personally prefer the latter, and may be following my own preference. I came here without the prepared statement.

Chairman KEFAUVER. That is all right.

Mr. McCABE. In reference to your second question as to how long I have been chief judge, I have been chief judge of the juvenile court in Rhode Island here since July 1, 1944, about 11½ years.

Chairman KEFAUVER. You have jurisdiction over the entire State? Your court has?

Mr. McCABE. Territorially, we cover the whole State of Rhode Island.

The subject matter, we have jurisdiction over any boy or girl who might become delinquent, wayward, dependent, or neglected. That is as far as the juvenile jurisdiction of subject matter is concerned.

We in the juvenile court have further jurisdiction over adults, such as nonsupport, contributing to delinquency, adults who are charged with neglect, and fathers who are charged with nonsupport, either criminally or civilly under the reciprocal enforcement and support law.

We have jurisdiction, also, over all adoptions under 18 years of age, that is, where the children are under 18 years of age; all child-marriage cases; and also jurisdiction over all children that are committed to the extra school—that is the school for the feebleminded children.

In a broad way, that is the scope of our jurisdiction. In other words, our court, I believe, was primarily set up to take care not only of the problems that might immediately affect youth but all other branches and ramifications of the problem, where it originates and where it goes, namely within the family unit itself.

I think that our law is unique in its provisions insofar as we are one of the three States in the Nation that have a statewide juvenile court; so that in many ways our court has the aspect of a family court dealing with the child who might be delinquent, a child who might be dependent or neglected, a husband who doesn't support and, outside of the community, the person who might contribute to the delinquency of this child.

We have two judges in the court; my associate, Judge Booth. We have a clerk of the court. We have three intake supervisors, and we have a prevention coordinator whose duties were mentioned previously this morning, by the Governor.

We have assigned to us from the director of probation and parole, Mr. Hagan, about 23 or 24 probation councilors, who are assigned to the various areas throughout the State. The majority of these people handle juvenile cases exclusively.

We like to think of our court as a hub of a wheel, the court being the hub and the various spokes being the public and private agencies that go out to this great thing we call the community or the State, the rim of the wheel.

Our court operates as a two-way street. Cases into court come through these spokes, or agencies, and cases are redirected to various agencies, or spokes, those agencies being equipped more adeptly than some others, or than the court itself, to effect a curative, or treatment process, for the various subjects that come before it.

In other words, our court in this State is pretty much the clearance center for many of the problems affecting children. Sometimes some people feel in this State, and as in other States, that a juvenile court in and of itself is the answer to the juvenile-delinquency problem.

The court is not an answer; the court does not sit in any ivory tower. We are accessible, both to the clients that come before us and to the general public, trying to explain to them what we are trying to achieve. But we do sit high enough in this seat for a panoramic view of just what is happening all over this State, as far as the problem is concerned.

I, too, feel very fine about the situation as far as boys and girls, and the adults, are concerned in this State; but, on the other hand, I think in this State, as in any other State in the Nation, during this era, that either we have a delinquency problem or we deny it; either we admit that we have one and try to do something about it, or else we shut our eyes to the problem and it will come to visit us in more terror at some subsequent date.

It has been our aim and our philosophy that if we could get at the so-called vulnerables at as early a stage as possible, and if we could educate a public to the understanding of the problems that confront these children, and the circumstances under which they grow in the home and in the community, that we might go a long way to cut down this delinquency picture to a minimum.

To my way of thinking, it can be done; but it cannot be done by retaliation and calling names. We have got to face up to the proposition that there is this problem and that talking will not solve the problem, that we have to do something about it.

If typhoid strikes in the city of Providence today, that case is not only treated but every medical force within the immediate environments of this city is called into play. There is isolation processes that go in, and there is antitoxins that are given to others who might be near this thing. In other words, we try to eliminate causes. I think that we have developed far enough in this child-behaviour problem to do something about it. I think that there are many places that we have to start; but it would be a wonderful thing if we first started with the adult, on a thorough understanding of what the problem is.

Chairman KEFAUVER. Will you say that again, please? I don't think that many of the people here heard that. "It would be a wonderful thing if we first started with the adult."

Mr. McCABE. That is correct; and his point of view.

I feel that we could raise the moral tone of our community, and all communities, and I think that we as adults are exemplars either for good or for evil of the children who are imitative of what the adult has done.

I think if we sit down some afternoon and have an examination of our own consciences as to what we are doing in this cause, that maybe we would come up with some remedies.

To be specific, Lieutenant May has mentioned the fact that we have jurisdiction over automobile violations and thefts of automobiles. Now, to me a simple traffic offense is a very serious thing. Either we respect the law or we disobey it as adults; and many adults speed if they can get away with it. It isn't a question of whether it is right or wrong, but "If the policeman is not watching me, it is perfectly all right to get away with it." And some adults and some parents, in cases that we have found, have even had their children watching out the back window of the car to see whether the policeman was following them in a certain zone.

So now if this same child, when he gets a car at 16 or 18, decides to speed, he will feel it is all right because Dad taught him that.

And then it is too much bother for us adults to take a key out of a car. We ask each boy and girl, that steals an automobile, that comes before us, "Well, how did this thing happen?" We have very few experts that can do the job with tinfoil or a coin. The majority of cases are that they found the key in the ignition, over the visor, or in the pocket of the car. The press and radio have cooperated with us to the fullest extent on various announcements requesting people to take these keys from the car.

Now, if you are logical about this you may say that McCabe is arguing wrongly here. I may be. I am just saying this, that we can help the occasion of delinquency by not placing some of these temptations before these children by a little cooperation.

Then at home, Senator, I might be a little bit busy some afternoon when I come home, maybe I like to take a nap, from all these hearings and various things that we run into. The telephone rings, and I say to my youngster, "Well, shush, shush, don't tell them I am here." I am teaching my child to lie, whether I know it or not.

Well, maybe some of us bigger businessmen might brag about the fact that we are able to cut a little corner and, well, fool Uncle Sam on that one. And then we wonder why the children take on these things, and many of these things become a way of life.

These are just a few specific examples where we could start a little tuning up within our own lives.

Now, when you come to the question of the physical disabilities of a child, it is a dramatic thing——

Chairman KEFAUVER. Judge, before you get to another subject matter, I have heard that you and also Judge Booth do meet with parents in the schools and other places and talk with them in the same vein that you are talking with us here today.

Mr. McCABE. That is right.

Chairman KEFAUVER. Tell us about that program. How often do you do it and how are the meetings organized, and what response you have?

Mr. McCABE. Well, there is little or no organization to the programs that we have. We have no press agents, but we are booked up until about June.

Any number of civic groups, like parent-teachers groups, Kiwanis groups, civic clubs, church groups and so forth invite us to speak to them at night. We have representative groups. Over the course of a year, maybe, we would talk to 150 or 160 on different occasions.

We invite representative groups to come in and see us. We hold a question-and-answer period afterward and try to answer some of the difficulties of these people. We try to urge them to set up at the grassroots a civic center or a community center where many of these problems that they have can be screened, and we, through the prevention coordinator, try to give them advice on the setting up of certain organizations that might be conducive to the best interests of that community. We feel that if we can get our story home to enough people, and I think we have made tremendous progress as far as education is concerned, to a thorough understanding of what we are trying to achieve, that we can mold public opinion to the point where citizens will be willing to pay for services to the schools that meet this child early and where the child might be detected; that the citizens will be able to permit and give to the legislature funds that they might appropriate for mental hygiene, recreation, and all the things that might help to round out this child; but to say that recreation in and of itself, to say that any one of these things that I mentioned is an answer to juvenile delinquency, to me that is erroneous because it is such a complex proposition that we definitely have to hit at every segment of it; and it needs a combined and united attack.

What we have tried to do in this State here is to recognize that, to teach that and to have a full understanding on the part of the public and private agencies, that our one aim is this child, or this family, and that child or that family is not a dismembered part of our organization, but rather that this child is a unit and has to be treated as a unit, and that our services have to be integrated and coordinated; that I cannot work on the child's leg, somebody else on the head, somebody else on the finger; we have got to attack this problem on a community level, on an all-out level, everyone doing what they can, and the product is going to be the result of the weakest link if we do not work together.

Chairman KEFAUVER. Judge McCabe, in connection with your educational program, I have been advised that you had a very successful youth panel program here a number of years ago. Would you tell us about that?

Mr. McCABE. We have had that. When Governor Roberts was here this morning he did not go into too much detail. I think one of the grandest things I ever saw, and enjoyed thoroughly, was a panel of youngsters that we had in the court a few years back. We had had the representatives of the various schools pick out representative children, boys and girls, not only those particularly who were high scholastically, but a well-rounded child in school, and we met monthly and sometimes twice a month with these children to obtain their point of view on current problems and what we should do and how we might be able to make goodness and right living more attractive for this so-called 1 or 2 percent that we run into.

We also had a panel such as that at the commission meeting of children and youth, and I think it brings out very, very vividly that the boy and girl of today is a grand person; that the boy and girl of today is much brighter perhaps, if we wanted to admit it, than we were in our day; and that the boy and girl of today is the same human being that they were 50 years ago, or 100 years ago; but they are set in different settings, perhaps, and these settings are made by the adult world; and these children have ideas about these things.

Fortunately, predominantly the large percentage of our children are outstanding.

When we seem, to me, to place so much emphasis on this word called "delinquency," and many of these children, of the 99 percent, feel that they are condemned because they happen to be placed in this category called teen-agers at this particular time. It has always been my impression that we never can forget the tragedy that juvenile delinquency is in this age. But we also should never forget that we have millions of our children who are doing a sterling job today and who are going to do a very, very excellent job tomorrow, a much better job, if we provide the means for them to do it.

But never let the tail wag the dog. I should be tremendously proud of the boys and girls of this era, and I think that, as you say the age limit has dropped down, 21 to 17, it is all right for them to go into service. Many of them that we meet have wonderful records. Look at the last war, look at the Korean incident. These are all products of this age. And who are we to condemn the many for the faults of the few?

I still feel that the answer lies within ourselves, if we want to look at this problem correctly. If we want to look at the philosophy that is underlying this whole thing. We have had difficulty in explaining to people and trying to make them understand that these children, under our law, are not considered criminals. We try to show that our law is that retaliation is not the answer, nor is it the law, because punishment and retaliation up to this point in history has achieved nothing.

Nor, on the other hand, do I feel that we should be cream puffs and coddle these children. I think punishment is a salutary form of treatment, but I don't think that punishment, in and of itself, is an end or cures anything.

I think that we have to consider the philosophy that each child is a human being, should be treated as such, and we do everything within our power to bring out the potentialities that are in this child so that these potentialities, when they are developed, might be an asset and an attribute to the community. In that way I feel that we definitely can cut down to a minimum this question of juvenile delinquency if we as a unit, individuals, corporate entities, private agencies, municipal agencies, State agencies, and Federal agencies, want to work together at the task.

Chairman KEFAUVER. I think that is an excellent summation of the whole problem and what we should do about it.

Now, judge, in the last few years what has been your rate of increase or decrease of delinquency and of the number of children coming into your court?

Mr. McCABE. I have statistics here which I will be only too glad to give to you and which I will offer the committee.

Statistics can mean one of many things, or can mean nothing, as far as I am concerned—all these opinions of mine are personal, by the way.

I had a case that would come in this morning where 8 boys stole 1 automobile. Well, I would report that, you would agree, as eight boys involved. Now, tomorrow I have 1 boy that is involved in stealing 8 automobiles. Am I going to count that 1 boy or 8 cases? It is 1 boy I have to treat, not 8 automobiles.

Some recording would count that as 8 cases; 8 cases interpreted to the public would mean 8 children.

I feel that we are in business to treat children, not automobiles, or homes that are broken into, et cetera, et cetera. We count a boy, no matter how many things he is involved in, as one case, and it is on that basis that our statistics have been set up.

Now, we have shown general decreases since about 1952. These are small. There has been a little increase over the last year, that is, from last year's report, but one thing that pushes our statistics up is the fact that we do have speeding of juveniles, and traffic offenses, which sometimes, as the public says, "It's just a traffic offense."

They don't consider that as a delinquent act or as a wayward act; yet they are counted and asked for as delinquent or wayward, whatever the case might be; yet I think that there are very few courts around the country that have jurisdiction in juvenile courts of the traffic offender.

We had about 956 children who were adjudicated either wayward or delinquent last year. That is about 100 more than the year before.

We held about 3,500 hearings, court hearings, on all our cases last year. In answer to your question to Lieutenant May as to the ratio between boys and girls, we have about 7½ to 8 boys to the 1 girl; we would run about 7½ to 1, or 8 to 1, it would vary from year to year.

Again, to just state on this question of statistics, we have urged and we have gotten cooperation to this extent, that any child that has shown any maladjustment that comes within the purview of our law be referred to the court as quickly as possible so that we in turn could make a proper referral to an agency that might do some remedial work with the child.

Our experience has shown us, our knowledge, our reading and so forth, that the earlier that we can get a child, and the earlier we can put into cooperation an effective therapy, the sooner we are going to do something for the child, and perhaps save a more serious offense later on and make a much happier life for the child.

If you want specific figures, I could read them into the record, or I would be glad to leave them with you, Senator.

Chairman KEFAUVER. Suppose you just furnish us with the figures, Judge McCabe.

Mr. McCABE. All right.

Chairman KEFAUVER. Judge, do you have any recommendations as to what the Federal Government, Congress, or what this committee can do to be of assistance?

Mr. McCABE. Yes; I have. I do hope that that bill of yours passes, and I do hope that we are able to get money from the Federal Government here so that the school program, as mentioned by the Governor, might be helped.

More particularly, in my field we are able to have a better mental-hygiene program for the child. That is, as I read your bill some time back, there is one provision for mental hygiene clinics.

It might be well at this point for me to mention that many of our agencies have been hard hit because of the expense of personnel for this type of work, and whether or not in your bill there might be provision whereby these funds might be given to recognized private agencies in the community for the carrying on of this child-guidance work and a mental-hygiene program, in addition to what might have been given to the various State and local organizations, hoping that we would be able to again hit on a twofold basis, both the public and the private.

Chairman KEFAUVER. Judge, I interrupted you a few minutes ago. You started to say something about the physically handicapped child.

Mr. McCABE. The physically handicapped child is a dramatic incident. You see the polio child, or the child that is with broken limbs, and maimed, and you put this placard up here, it draws a person's attention, it is attractive. So, as a consequence, we take and give our money for these campaigns.

But it is a very, very difficult thing for the average person to see a child who is emotionally upset, to see whether there is anything the matter with this child. Many say, "He is just a hellion," or "He is just a brat," or "He hasn't had the proper bringing up," and "A good crack over the some place might help him out." But that's a little bit further north of where the treatment should be given to him. We have to recognize these facts.

But it is a pretty hard proposition to get the person who hasn't seen a child of this type to recognize it and do something about it. Whatever we see, whatever is dramatic, yes, we will pay for it; but what is hidden and what might be latent and yet be very, very open a few years hence, well, it's too late to meet it then, even with dollars.

I think we should recognize it now, not only with dollars, but with an understanding sympathy toward a rehabilitation of this child at this point where something can be done for the child.

Chairman KEFAUVER. Mr. Chumbris, do you have any questions you wish to ask Judge McCabe?

Mr. CHUMBRIS. No; I do not, Senator.

Chairman KEFAUVER. Judge, we thank you very much for a very enlightened statement. I want to say that I think you are one of the fine juvenile judges of our entire country. You and Judge Booth are not only doing your jobs as judges, but you are doing extrajudicial work of a very important nature. We want to keep in touch with you.

We appreciate your appearance here today.

Mr. McCABE. Thank you very much, Senator. It was a pleasure.

Chairman KEFAUVER. The subcommittee will stand in recess until 2 o'clock, and we will meet sharply at 2.

(Whereupon, at 12:25 p. m., a recess was taken until 2 p. m.)

AFTERNOON SESSION

Chairman KEFAUVER. The subcommittee will come to order.

At this point in the record we will have read into the record the Senate resolution establishing this subcommittee.

We will also have read into the record the authorization of the members of the committee for this hearing to be held by the chairman. They will be incorporated in the record.

(The documents referred to follow:)

EXHIBIT No. 3

[S. Res. 89, 83d Cong., 1st sess.]

RESOLUTION

Resolved, That the Committee on the Judiciary, or any duly authorized subcommittee thereof, is authorized and directed to conduct a full and complete study of juvenile delinquency in the United States. In the conduct of such investigation special attention shall be given to (1) determining the extent and character of juvenile delinquency in the United States and its causes and contributing factors, (2) the adequacy of existing provisions of law, including chapters 402 and 403 of title 18 of the United States Code, in dealing with youthful offenders of Federal laws, (3) sentences imposed on, or other correctional action taken with respect to, youthful offenders by Federal courts, and (4) the extent to which juveniles are violating Federal laws relating to the sale or use of narcotics.

SEC. 2. The committee, or any duly authorized subcommittee thereof, is authorized to sit and act at such places and times during the sessions, recesses, and adjourned periods of the Senate, to hold such hearings, to require by subpenas or otherwise the attendance of such witnesses and the production of such books, papers, and documents, to administer such oaths, to take such testimony, to procure such printing and binding, and, within the amount appropriated therefor, to make such expenditures as it deems advisable. The cost of stenographic services to report hearings of the committee or subcommittee shall not be in excess of 40 cents per hundred words. Subpenas shall be issued by the chairman of the committee or the subcommittee, and may be served by any person designated by such chairman.

A majority of the members of the committee, or duly authorized subcommittee thereof, shall constitute a quorum for the transaction of business, except that a lesser number to be fixed by the committee, or by such subcommittee, shall constitute a quorum for the purpose of administering oaths and taking sworn testimony.

SEC. 3. The committee shall report its findings, together with its recommendations for such legislation as it deems advisable, to the Senate at the earliest date practicable but not later than January 31, 1954.

SEC. 4. For the purposes of this resolution, the committee, or any duly authorized subcommittee thereof, is authorized to employ upon a temporary basis such technical, clerical, and other assistants as it deems advisable. The expenses of the Committee under this resolution, which shall not exceed $44,000, shall be paid from the contingent fund of the Senate upon vouchers approved by the chairman of the committee.

RESOLUTION

Resolved by the Subcommittee of the Committee on the Judiciary To Study Juvenile Delinquency in the United States, That pursuant to subsection (3) of rule XXV, as amended, of the Standing Rules of the Senate (S. Res. 180, 81st Cong., 2d sess., agreed to February 1, 1950) and committee resolutions of the Committee on the Judiciary, adopted January 20, 1955, Senator Estes Kefauver (Democrat, of Tennessee), and such other members as are present, are authorized to hold hearings of this subcommittee in Providence, R. I., on November 8, 1955, and such other days as may be required to complete these hearings, and to take sworn testimony from witnesses.

Agreed to this 7th day of November 1955.

THOMAS C. HENNINGS, Jr.,
PRICE DANIEL,
WILLIAM LANGER,
ALEXANDER WILEY,
Members of Subcommittee to Study Juvenile Delinquency.

Chairman KEFAUVER. Mr. Chumbris, who is our first witness?

Mr. CHUMBRIS. Mr. George Morrow.

Chairman KEFAUVER. Mr. Morrow, will you come around? Inasmuch as the testimony this afternoon may involve some conflicts and whatnot, I will have to ask all of the witnesses to be sworn.

You are not Mr. Morrow?

Mr. McGUIRE. No; I am not.

Chairman KEFAUVER. What is your full name, sir?

Mr. McGUIRE. My name is Joseph T. McGuire. I am an attorney from Worcester, Mass. I am here on behalf of a brother attorney, Allen McDonald, Esq., of 340 Main Street, Worcester, Mass., who requested of me yesterday afternoon, to appear for him on this matter, as he has a case in Boston today.

I wish to submit, Senator, a statement from a Dr. Wolfson with reference to the physical condition of Mr. Morrow and why he is not present at this time [handing].

Chairman KEFAUVER. Who does Mr. Morrow represent?

Mr. McGUIRE. Mr. Morrow is under a summons from the United States of America, Congress of the United States [handing].

Chairman KEFAUVER. Mr. Morrow is not an attorney?

Mr. McGuire. He is not. Mr. McDonald is Mr. Morrow's attorney, and Mr. McDonald was unable to be here today; so I have the office right next to his and he requested that I come down in his place.

Chairman Kefauver. We will let the statement be read or copied into the record.

(The letter referred to above is as follows:)

WORCESTER, MASS., *November 7, 1955.*

To Whom It May Concern:

I, Irving N. Wolfson, M. D., on oath depose and state that I am a practicing physician residing in the city of Worcester, Mass., with an office at 37 Fruit Street, and that on November 5, 1955, I examined Mr. George Morrow. I found he had (1) congestive heart failure, (2) coronary artery disease with angina.

These diagnoses were supported by physical examination which revealed pulmonary basal rales and ankle edema. Fluoroscopy revealed generalized cardiac enlargement, and electrocardiograph revealed the following:

(1) Coronary artery disease with (?) old anterior infarction;
(2) Incomplete left bundle branch block;
(3) (?) Cor pulmonale.

The patient was treated by digitalization, mercuhydrin, and advised to restrict his physical activities in the future. I believe that he is too ill to travel or testify at this time.

Signed and sealed this 7th day of November 1955

(Signed)   IRVING N. WOLFSON.

STATE OF MASSACHUSETTS,   NOVEMBER 7, 1955.
        Worcester, ss:

Personally appeared before me, Irving Norman Wolfson, M. D., on oath stated that the above is a true statement of the condition of George Morrow to his best knowledge and belief.

(Signed)   JOSEPH E. McGUIRE,
                                                        Notary Public.

My commission expires September 26, 1958.

Chairman KEFAUVER. Do you know Mr. Morrow?

Mr. McGuire. I have met him on one occasion. I met him yesterday afternoon.

Chairman KEFAUVER. Is Mr. Morrow in the hospital, or is he——

Mr. McGuire. He is not in the hospital. I met him in his home.

Chairman KEFAUVER. Is he going around?

Mr. McGuire. The only time that I observed him, he was in his home, and he had an oxygen tank next to him. I was with him for approximately 15 to 20 minutes.

The reason that I went to his house was to pick up a retainer for coming down here.

Chairman KEFAUVER. That is a very pertinent reason.

The next question is, did you pick it up?

Mr. McGuire, is it a physical disability or fear of retaliation that Mr. Morrow is worrying about?

Mr. McGuire. I believe there are two reasons for Mr. Morrow not being present here. I think primarily, from my conversation with Mr. McDonald, it is an apprehension of his physical condition and the effect that it would have upon him to be present.

I think, secondarily, from my conversation with Mr. McDonald, he fears retaliation.

Chairman KEFAUVER. What kind of retaliation? Not naming names, but by what group of people?

Mr. McGuire. I have no knowledge of that, sir.

Senator KEFAUVER. Did he tell you that?

Mr. McGuire. No; he has not told me that.

Chairman Kefauver. Did he tell you he was afraid of retaliation?

Mr. McGuire. He did not tell me himself; I was told that by Mr. McDonald.

Chairman Kefauver. Mr. McDonald is the other counsel?

Mr. McGuire. Yes; he is.

Chairman Kefauver. From this physical report, there seems to be a number of things which apparently Mr. Morrow has had for a long time; there doesn't seem to be any immediate acute physical defect. He seems to have been able to do business with what latent physical defects he has.

I will have to ask you to tell Mr. Morrow that apparently he is not confined, and——

Mr. McGuire. I believe that Captain Henry of the Worcester police force could probably testify as to his physical condition from his knowledge and observation of Mr. Morrow. I believe that from Mr. McDonald's conversation with me, that Mr. Morrow in the past has been able to travel, but that the physical pressure upon him in answering questions here would certainly be detrimental to his heart condition.

Chairman Kefauver. Mr. McGuire, Mr. Morrow will have to testify sometime; if not today, he will have to testify sometime before this subcommittee.

Mr. McGuire. Yes, sir.

Chairman Kefauver. You might advise him of that situation.

Mr. McGuire. Yes, sir.

Chairman Kefauver. And see if he wants to come on down.

In the meantime, I will have the staff of the committee select a competent physician and make an examination of him up there this afternoon.

Mr. McGuire. Certainly.

Chairman Kefauver. And report back to us.

Mr. McGuire. I believe you will find him at his home.

Chairman Kefauver. But he is an important witness in this inquiry, one of the key ones. So you consult with him and see if he does not want to come on down and testify. In the meantime we will be in contact with some physician and have him examined, and we will appreciate your cooperation.

Mr. McGuire. Thank you, Senator.

Any further questions, Senator?

Chairman Kefauver, That is all.

Let this statement be put in the record.

Who is our next witness?

Mr. Chumbris. Mr. N. A. Tacy and Mr. E. A. Craugh.

Chairman Kefauver. Are you Mr. Tacy?

Mr. Tacy. Yes.

Chairman Kefauver. And you are Mr. LaVault?

Mr. LaVault. Yes.

Chairman Kefauver. And you are Mr. Craugh?

Mr. Craugh. Yes, sir.

Chairman Kefauver. You do solemnly swear the testimony you will give will be the whole truth, so help you God?

[In unison, "I do."]

TESTIMONY OF N. A. TACY, E. A. CRAUGH, AND EDGAR LaVAULT

Chairman KEFAUVER. Sit down, gentlemen.

Mr. Chumbris, will you ask any questions of these gentlemen; and will you speak loudly, please.

Mr. CHRUMBRIS. Mr. Tacy, I understand you are going to be the spokesman?

Mr. TACY. I think Mr. Craugh probably will be the spokesman.

Mr. CHUMBRIS. Now, Mr. Craugh——

Chairman KEFAUVER. First identify each one of them who they are and what they do.

Mr. CHUMBRIS. First give your full name, your address, and your official capacity.

Mr. CRAUGH. Edward A. Craugh, Worcester, Mass.; postal inspector.

Chairman KEFAUVER. How long have you been a postal inspector?

Mr. CRAUGH. Over 13 years.

Chairman KEFAUVER. And how long have you had something to do with this jurisdiction?

Mr. CRAUGH. In Rhode Island, you mean?

Chairman KEFAUVER. Yes.

Mr. CRAUGH. I came down on this case in July 1954.

Chairman KEFAUVER. You have been here on this case since July 1954?

Mr. CRAUGH. At various times.

Chairman KEFAUVER. All right.

Mr. Tacy, what is your full name and you home address?

Mr. TACY. Nelson A. Tacy, Middletown, R. I. My office is in Providence, R. I. I am district manager, Bureau of Post Office Operation.

Chairman KEFAUVER. What is your district, Mr. Tacy?

Mr. TACY. The State of Rhode Island, southeastern Massachusetts.

Chairman KEFAUVER. And you were formerly a post office inspector?

Mr. TACY. Prior to January 16 of this year; yes, sir.

Chairman KEFAUVER. As in charge of this district and as a postal inspector, you are here to testify about a matter that has come under your official jurisdiction?

Mr. TACY. As a post office inspector.

Chairman KEFAUVER. Yes, sir.

Mr. TACY. Prior to January 16 I was a post office inspector.

Chairman KEFAUVER. Mr. LaVault, what is your name?

Mr. LAVAULT. Edgar R. LaVault. 39 Mountain Avenue, Riverside. I am a postal inspector.

Chairman KEFAUVER. How long have you been a postal inspector?

Mr. LAVAULT. Over 13 years.

Chairman KEFAUVER. Very well. Proceed, Mr. Chumbris.

Mr. CHUMBRIS. Mr. Craugh, will you please explain to the subcommittee the matter which you have under investigation and give us the preliminaries to that investigation.

Mr. CRAUGH. This investigation related to the mailing of circulars advertising pictures which were probably obscene. In one step of the operation, a sample obscene picture was actually sent.

Mr. CHUMBRIS. Will you give the approximate date when this investigation started?

Mr. CRAUGH. I started in it about July 20. Prior to that——

Mr. CHUMBRIS. Of what year?

Mr. CRAUGH. Of 1954. Prior to that, Inspector Tacy and Inspector Egan had made some investigation at Providence and Pawtucket. My investigation started at Worcester, was found to be related to their investigation; so we got together and correlated our efforts.

Mr. CHUMBRIS. When was it that you first dealt together on this investigation?

Mr. CRAUGH. I would say J talked to Mr. Tacy on the telephone about the 23d or 24th of July. That is approximate. And I came down here, I believe it was July 27.

Mr. CHUMBRIS. How did you first come into this investigation, what was the first lead?

Mr. CRAUGH. I happened to stop at the detective bureau of the Worcester Police Department, and the deputy chief had a letter postmarked Washington, D. C., that contained a circular describing these pictures, the envelope on which an order could be placed, and a portion of the original circular envelope with the address removed.

He showed it to me, and since it was mail matter, I agreed to see what I could find out about it.

Mr. CHUMBRIS. Do you have any exhibits with you that you would like to introduce into evidence which would indicate the first lead to this investigation?

Mr. CRAUGH. I have here—there is a photostat of the circular and a photostat of the envelope in which this original complaint was received at Worcester, and a photostat of the order envelope by which an order could be returned [exhibiting], addressed to this name in Worcester.

Mr. CHUMBRIS. We would like to have that introduced as exhibit No. 4.

Chairman KEFAUVER. It will be introduced, but it is probably a file that you have to keep in your records?

Mr. CRAUGH. I have to keep those papers.

Chairman KEFAUVER. So I think it is probably better, Mr. Chumbris, if you can summarize it some way, and if we need it as an exhibit we can get it back from you.

Mr. CHUMBRIS. Is that the photostat that you need for your records or could you leave a copy of it with us?

Mr. CRAUGH. These papers are papers of the Inspection Service, and we are required to keep them in our custody.

Chairman KEFAUVER. We will work that out with you later. If you have additional photostats, that may be helpful; but you may ask any questions you wish.

Mr. CHUMBRIS. Will you summarize this particular exhibit and explain it to the subcommittee?

Chairman KEFAUVER. Mr. Brennan, we appreciate your handing these exhibits. Tell us briefly what it is about, sir.

Mr. CRAUGH. This is addressed "Dear Friend." [Reading:]

Your name has been given me by a personal friend that you bought nudes from in the past. He is not able to give you the type of photos you were wanting. Knowing that I have the stuff you are looking for, he feels we can do business.

The pictures I have are not the ordinary run of the mill. Art photos. To say these are risque is to put it mildly. The models are good but secondary to the poses.

A little more along the same line. Then—

I have an assortment of 48 pictures now. You can have all 48 for $15. Eight photos for $3, or 32 for $10. Place you order as soon as possible so I can prove to you my photos are all I claim they are.

And then the order blank for any interested person to fill out and submit.

Mr. CHUMBRIS. Do you have any letters of complaint from minors concerning advertisements of that type?

Mr. CRAUGH. I have one letter of complaint, and I have the details on another complaint that wasn't received by letter.

Chairman KEFAUVER. Mr. Craugh, you did not say who that was mailed to or what happened to the exhibit. That was mailed out to where, and what happened?

Mr. CRAUGH. This particular one was mailed to the chief of police at Worcester by some person who received one of these circulars and was evidently offended by its receipt; so he mailed it to the chief of police at Worcester, and the deputy chief brought it to my attention when I stopped in there.

Chairman KEFAUVER. In other words, it is a general mailing that was sent out by somebody?

Mr. CRAUGH. That's right.

Chairman KEFAUVER. Who was it sent out by, and from where?

Mr. CRAUGH. I investigated that and found out that it was mailed principally in the Providence area, the original mailing containing this circular. I found that out from return cards, or from the post mark on undeliverable circulars that were returned to the Worcester address by the letter carrier.

Chairman KEFAUVER. To whom is it supposed to be sent back, the $15 or what-not?

Mr. CRAUGH. The name was John E. Carter.

Chairman KEFAUVER. Mr. Chumbris says that will come in later, so you develop the matter in your own way.

Mr. CHUMBRIS. Now will you please explain the letter of complaint from the minor?

Mr. CRAUGH. This letter was received through a postmaster in California. It was referred to the postmaster by the parents, by the mother of a 16-year-old boy who received one of the later mailings, the one that contained a sample picture which is obscene. That was referred to our Service.

Mr. CHUMBRIS. Was that complaint in connection with the exhibit you have just been discussing?

Mr. CRAUGH. No; that's under a different name. The actual mailing was made under a different name.

Mr. CHUMBRIS. Under a different name?

Mr. CRAUGH. Yes.

Mr. CHUMBRIS. Do you have a copy of that letter of complaint from the parent of the 16-year-old boy?

Mr. CRAUGH. No; there was no letter submitted. There was a letter from the postmaster referring the matter to our Service.

Mr. CHUMBRIS. How did you know, relate how you knew it was a 16-year-old boy that made the complaint, or the parent of a 16-year-old boy?

Mr. CRAUGH. Here is the letter from the postmaster. [Reading:]

This was submitted to me by the mother of the addressee who is 16 years of age. Both the boy and his mother reside at a certain address in California.

Mr. CHUMBRIS. All right. Do you have any other exhibits relating to the preliminary of your investigation into this matter?

Mr. CRAUGH. Yes. I have one other complaint relative to mailing of this matter to a boy of 15 in a suburb of Boston. This was brought to my attention first by the Worcester police, who received a call from the Massachusetts attorney general's office that he had received some of these circulars, received one of these same circulars advertising these pictures.

I interviewed the boy's father later and found out that he had received one more of this series; but he did not receive one of the obscene pictures.

Mr. CHUMBRIS. Who are the people that you were investigating in this investigation?

Mr. CRAUGH. I was trying to determine the identity of the person who set up the mail drop at Worcester, Mass.

Mr. CHUMBRIS. Fine. Now will you please explain that?

Mr. CRAUGH. I went up, after I had investigated and found out that the person who had the service where this mail was being delivered was reputable, I first discussed it with the Worcester police at the time. The person who operated the secretarial service believed that this man, of whom she gave a general description, would call. We waited there, the lieutenant of the Worcester police and myself waited there all that day but he never showed. Eventually the owner of the secretarial service received a letter asking that the mail be forwarded to Narragansett, R. I., 11 Rose Court.

We then determined that 11 Rose Court was the residence of Dorothy M. Tager.

Mr. CHUMBRIS. Continue, please.

Mr. CRAUGH. I got in touch with Mr. Tacy as soon as I realized that the mailing for this particular drop had been made in Providence, Pawtucket, North Attleboro, Mass., and learned that a similar case, similar cases bearing on Pawtucket and Providence, whereby fictitious names were used to get remittances for selling pictures, advertising pictures of the same general type.

Mr. CHUMBRIS. Will you please continue.

Mr. CRAUGH. We eventually learned, Mr. Tacy, I believe, learned that on the first two operations in Providence and Pawtucket, that bank accounts had been opened under the fictitious names that were used at the mail drops, and through the efforts, cooperation of bank employees we were able to get an idea who the person was that had arranged, the man who had arranged these mail drops. And it developed that it was Calvin Sugarman, of Providence.

Mr. CHUMBRIS. What was that name again?

Mr. CRAUGH. Calvin Sugarman.

Mr. CHUMBRIS. And you say he lives in Providence?

Mr. CRAUGH. He lives in Providence.

Mr. CHUMBRIS. Do you have his address?

Mr. CRAUGH. 108 Woodbine Street.

Mr. CHUMBRIS. All right. Continue.

Mr. CRAUGH. We later learned that another mail drop had been set up at Hartford, Conn., and a subsequent one at New Britain, Conn., under different names.

Chairman KEFAUVER. Tell, sir, what you mean by a mail drop. I understand, but what is a mail drop?

Mr. CRAUGH. A person wishing to receive mail at an address other than his own residence can obtain the services of a public secretary, and in some cases private detective agencies do have that service whereby, by payment of the fee, the mail will come to that place and can be picked up by them at any time later.

Chairman KEFAUVER. In other words, the envelope and the address on the advertisement is given the same as that mail drop?

Mr. CRAUGH. That's right.

Chairman KEFAUVER. And then some of the mail, the letters may be mailed there or anywhere else?

Mr. CRAUGH. They are addressed to the place where the service is hired.

Chairman KEFAUVER. All right. Go ahead.

Mr. CHUMBRIS. Let's get this first mail drop. Give the name in which the mail drop was registered.

Mr. CRAUGH. That was rented in the name of Robert Adams Co.

Mr. CHUMBRIS. And where was that mail drop?

Mr. CRAUGH. That was at the Busy Bee, 86 Weybosset Street, in Providence. The Abbey Telephone Service was the name of the concern to which this service was obtained.

Mr. CHUMBRIS. Do you have any further details on that mail drop, to whom you traced it?

Mr. CRAUGH. On June 1 the man who arranged for these mail drops called and requested service under the name of Robert Adams. He paid a fee, and mail came in large quantities for several days. He called for it for a few days.

Chairman KEFAUVER. What do you mean by "large quantities"?

Mr. CRAUGH. I don't have the figures here, but I would say at least 100 letters, I would estimate at least 100 letters a day, including returned circulars that were undeliverable because of poor addresses.

Mr. CHUMBRIS. Have you been able to determine who the person was under the Adams mail drop at 86 Weybosset Street, Providence?

Mr. CRAUGH. He was identified as Calvin Sugarman.

Mr. CHUMBRIS. And how did you identify him as Calvin Sugarman?

Mr. CRAUGH. One of the ladies who operated the service at that address recognized, thought she recognized Calvin Sugarman, and called his home and told him there was some Adams mail there. He came down later that day and picked some up.

Mr. CHUMBRIS. Do you have any exhibits which would make the connection between the Adams mail drop and Sugarman?

Mr. CRAUGH. Well, I have affidavits that I took from these people.

Mr. CHUMBRIS. Will you summarize the affidavit that you have before you?

Chairman KEFAUVER. Don't read it; just tell us what is on it.

Mr. CRAUGH. All right. This one is, I believe, a principal owner, where she states about the opening of the business, the engaging of the service, and then her sister thought she recognized this Mr. Adams and called his home. She kept no record of the number of pieces received, and she picked out a photo, a picture of Calvin Sugarman from six others that were shown to her. The fact that he engaged the service and called for mail there was also corroborated by another person who engaged office space in there, they are in the insurance business, and she recognized the photo, reeognized him from the photo, too. And also one from the sister wherein she details recognizing him and calling up his home, Sugarman's home, and telling him there is Adams mail there. But then later that day he called for some of the mail.

Mr. CHUMBRIS. Now, was there an Adams bank account that you investigated?

Mr. CRAUGH. I am aware that there was an Adams bank account.

Mr. CHUMBRIS. Can you give us any more information on that?

Mr. CRAUGH. Here are photostats of the Adams bank account that was opened on June 15 with a deposit of $100. Subsequent deposits between June 18 and June 29 total $742, of which $123 was cash and the rest checks and money orders. $450 was withdrawn on June 25, $247 on June 29, and its was practically closed out on July 7, there was only $1.40 left.

Mr. CHUMBRIS. Do you have a check drawn by Robert Adams— before I get to that, do you have a withdrawal exhibit there that you would like to submit to the subcommittee?

Mr. CRAUGH. There is the amount of $450 shown as a check against the account on June 25, 1954.

Mr. CHUMBRIS. Do you have an exhibit in the form of a check?

Mr. CRAUGH. Yes. Here is a photostat of a check drawn June 24, 1954, in the amount of $450.

Mr. CHUMBRIS. And who is the maker of the check?

Mr. CRAUGH. Robert Adams.

Mr. CHUMBRIS. And who was the payee?

Mr. CRAUGH. Calvin Sugarman.

Mr. CHUMBRIS. And was that check endorsed by Calvin Sugarman?

Mr. CRAUGH. His name appears on the reverse.

Chairman KEFAUVER. You have a copy of it, Mr. Chumbris. Let's make it an exhibit, exhibit 4.

(The check above referred to was marked "Exhibit No. 4," and is as follows:)

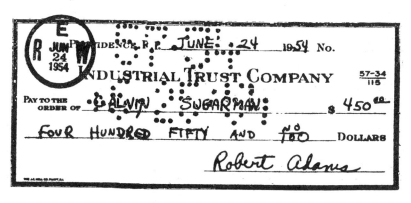

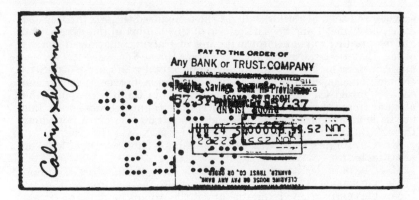

Mr. CHUMBRIS. Aside from the Adams mail drop, are there any other mail drops?

Mr. CRAUGH. The next one was Joseph V. Bush, or J. V. Bush.

Mr. CHUMBRIS. Would you relate as concisely as possible the background for this Bush mail drop?

Mr. CRAUGH. Mr. LaVault will tell that.

Mr. LAVAULT. I called on Miss Mary A. Hanna, who operates the Busy Bee Secretarial Service at 547 Broadway in Pawtucket. She told me that on or about June 30 an individual stated he was J. V. Bush called on her, saying he represented the J. V. Bush Co., and that he wished to use that address as a mail drop. He paid Miss Hanna a fee of $2 for that month. He called approximately every other day for the first 30 days to pick up the returns as well as the mail received.

I had with me that day seven photos, one of whom was the photo of Mr. Calvin Sugarman. Miss Hanna identified Mr. Sugarman's photo as the person who represented himself as J. V. Bush.

Mr. CHUMBRIS. Was there any other identifying feature, such as a bank account?

Mr. LAVAULT. I didn't go into that particular feature myself, but there was another identifying feature.

Sometime around August 1 the Pawtucket Police Department had made an inquiry of Miss Hanna regarding a complaint they had received on the circular mailings, and at their request she took the auto registration of J. V. Bush and she turned it over to the police. Later, out of curiosity, she also called the registry of motor vehicles herself and learned that the auto was registered in the name of Sugarman.

Mr. CHUMBRIS. Was that Calvin Sugarman?

Mr. LAVAULT. She didn't recall that at the time I discussed it with her; but we later identified it as the auto of Calvin Sugarman.

Mr. CHUMBRIS. Who will relate the bank account of Bush?

Mr. CRAUGH. I have the details on that. This account was opened July 2, 1954, with a $5 cash deposit. The deposit slip is marked "Watch this account closely, allow no overdrafts."

Between July 6 and August 5 a total of $1,069 was deposited, $600 in cash and the remainder in money orders.

There were two withdrawals of $200 on the 8th and the 12th of July and $132.60 on the 12th of July, which apparently relates to a bill for printing in connection with this operation.

Mr. CHUMBRIS. Do you have anything further?

Mr. CRAUGH. The check, the account, between August 1954—September 22, 1954, had $59.41 as a balance. There is no further activity until July 11, 1955, when a $55 check was drawn against the account, leaving a balance of $3.98. Here is a photostat of this check [exhibiting], that $55 check, signed "Joseph V. Bush," payable to cash.

Mr. CHUMBRIS. Who endorsed that check?

Mr. CRAUGH. Calvin Sugarman.

Mr. CHUMBRIS. That date to which you were referring, July 11, 1955, can that be identified with any other happening just before that time as a part of this investigation?

Mr. CRAUGH. July 11——

Mr. CHUMBRIS. Referring to Mrs. Tager, specifically.

Mr. CRAUGH. July 11, 1955, bears no relation.

Mr. CHUMBRIS. What I was referring to is this: Was it in June of 1955, wasn't there something referring to Mrs. Tager?

Mr. CRAUGH. Oh, that's right. I believe her case was finally disposed of.

Mr. CHUMBRIS. Her case was disposed of in June of 1955 and this account was closed in July of 1955; is that correct?

Mr. CRAUGH. In July of 1955; correct.

Mr. CHUMBRIS. Do you know whether that $55 check that you are referring to went into Calvin Sugarman's private account?

Mr. CRAUGH. I haven't been able to; I don't think we could determine that.

Mr. CHUMBRIS. Do you have a deposit there of approximately $55 to Calvin Sugarman's account?

Mr. CRAUGH. I believe this is it, on July 8. The bank number corresponds with the bank number on the check that was drawn against the account.

Mr. CHUMBRIS. Take a look at the face of that check of July 11, I believe, and see if there isn't a notation in the left-hand corner of the savings account of Calvin Sugarman.

Mr. CRAUGH. They are the same number.

Mr. CHUMBRIS. Would you read that number?

Mr. CRAUGH. 155886.

Mr. CHUMBRIS. And that notation is on that last check; is that correct?

Mr. CRAUGH. That is on this last check, and it is also on the deposit slips in the savings account.

Mr. CHUMBRIS. Was there another mail drop in this investigation?

Mr. CRAUGH. The third mail drop was the one established at Worcester.

Mr. CHUMBRIS. All right, sir.

Mr. CRAUGH. Under the name of John E. Carter.

In that case the person who established the account called on July 2 and engaged the services, paying $15 in cash for mailing service for 1 month. He told the person operating this secretarial service that he would return, but he never did.

Subsequently, the secretary received a large envelope from John E. Carter, with a letter instructing the mail to be forwarded to John E. Carter, care of 11 Rose Court, Narrangansett, R. I.

Subsequently, the secretary received $20 more in cash and throughout a period when that was in operation there were 641 pieces of mail received, 201 of which were apparently orders for the pictures advertised under the name of John E. Carter.

Mr. CHUMBRIS. Let's get the identifying features so that you connect the Carter mail drop with Calvin Sugarman.

Mr. CRAUGH. I followed the same practice there. I showed several photographs to the secretary in Worcester, and she picked out the one which was Calvin Sugarman's.

Mr. CHUMBRIS. Then as far as you were able to determine, Carter and Calvin Sugarman were one and the same person?

Mr. CRAUGH. Yes.

Chairman KEFAUVER. Wasn't that the one where Mrs. Tager came into the picture?

Mr. CRAUGH. She made a phone call, I believe, he apparently wrote the letter of instructions asking that the mail be forwarded, although it is signed John E. Carter.

Chairman KEFAUVER. For the record at this point, do you want to tell who Mrs. Tager is, or, Mr. Chumbris, you tell who Mrs. Tager is?

Mr. CRAUGH. Near the beginning of my investigation, when I found out that this mail from these various sources was going to 11 Rose Court, and that the resident there was Mary D. Tager, or D. Mary Tager, I recall that we had received some information from 2 or 3 years prior to that relative to the operations known as Tager and Ross on the West Coast. The name came to mind. I looked up the information we had and found out that it was a large-scale operation on the west coast.

We made inquiries then and discovered that it was apparently the same Mrs. Tager who had operated in the nude-picture business in the Los Angeles area on the west coast.

Chairman KEFAUVER. I think by way of summary it might be stated that in the early part of this year the staff of this committee made an investigation preparatory for a hearing. At our hearing in early June of this year Mrs. Tager and others testified at Los Angeles that she had a large business in excess of $1 million a year, she and her husband—at that time they were divorced—had a business in excess of $1 million a year, operating on the west coast in various and sundry assumed names, with drops at Los Angeles, Las Vegas, Nev., Phoenix, Ariz., Tucson, and many, many other places. The only time she had ever been in any difficulty was the operation here in Providence, R. I., or in Rhode Island.

We also got some information from her about her operations here. At that time, as chairman of this committee, I stated that we would investigate and find out what we could about the operation in this part of the country and have a hearing here at Providence.

She sent her literature to every State in the Union, to many foreign countries. It was a very vast operation that she had on the west coast, one of the biggest. Is that your information about it?

Mr. CRAUGH. That's how I connected her with the operation.

Chairman KEFAUVER. Go ahead, Mr. Chumbris.

Mr. CHUMBRIS. Then there was no question in your mind about the Carter and Calvin Sugarman being one and the same person; is that correct?

Mr. CRAUGH. That is right.

Mr. CHUMBRIS. Now, is there another mail drop that you wish to describe?

Mr. CRAUGH. The next mail drop was operated under the name of Earl Drake, 647 Main Street, Hartford, Conn.   The operator at that place was primarily, her business was primarily dispatching, handling the dispatching of trucks, but she did a little mail-drop work on the side.

He paid a fee of $10, and he called again, he called first on July 16, 1954.   He called again on August 9, 1954, after making a call on the telephone, and he picked up what mail there was, which I understand was very small at that time.

He called again one other day briefly, but didn't stay long; she couldn't remember the date.

She also picked out a photo of Calvin Sugarman as the person who represented himself to be Earl Drake.

Mr. CHUMBRIS. Now will you please explain hcw you connected Calvin Sugarman to the Drake mail drop?

Mr. CRAUGH. The description that we had at first tallied with that of the others.   Then I took the photo with several other photos we might have——

Mr. CHUMBRIS. Were any bank accounts or checks——

Mr. CRAUGH. There were no bank accounts on Carter or Drake, as far as we could ascertain.

Mr. CHUMBRIS. Was there another mail drop?

Mr. CRAUGH. The next one was set up in New Britain, Conn. Arrangements were made on July 15 under the name of Jeff Ellis. He stated that at that time he would call and pick up the mail, but about the end of July the operator, the secretary, received a letter asking that all mail be forwarded to 11 Rose Court, Narragansett, R. I.   Not too much mail was received there at that time.   About 2 or 3 pieces of mail a day.

Before July 30 there were 2 or 3 pieces.   Subsequent to that it averaged about six pieces a day.

On or about August 9 the man representing himself to be Jeff Ellis called at the office asking about the amount of mail, and later that day detectives from the New Britain Police Department called, because they had received a complaint through the mail of one of his circulars, I believe.

Mr. CHUMBRIS. You said the mail was transferred to 11 Rose Court, Narragansett?

Mr. CRAUGH. That is right.

Mr. CHUMBRIS. Who was at that address?

Mr. CRAUGH. That is the address, that was the residence of Mary D. Tager.

Mr. CHUMBRIS. Is that the same person as Mary Dorothy Tager?

Mr. CRAUGH. Mary Dorothy Tager; yes.

Mr. CHUMBRIS. Will you make the connection between Sugarman and the Ellis mail drop?

Mr. CRAUGH. The operator of the service in New Britain also identified a photo of Calvin Sugarman as the person who represented himself to be Jeff Ellis.

Mr. CHUMBRIS. And you were satisfied that that was one and the same person?

Mr. CRAUGH. I was.

Mr. CHUMBRIS. Now, are there any other mail drops?

Mr. CRAUGH. The next mail drop was under the name of M. Miller. That was set up at 11 Rose Court, Narragansett. The mail addressed to M. Miller came to 11 Rose Court.

We questioned delivery employees at the Narragansett branch of the Wakefield, R. I., post office, and one recalled having some mail addressed to M. Miller, and he stopped at the house, rang the bell, and a boy answered, Mrs. Tager's son. When the carrier asked about M. Miller, the boy asked his mother, "Who is this M. Miller?" and Mrs. Tager answered, "It's all right. I will answer it. It goes here."

Other employees have made statements relative to the delivery of mail under the various names at 11 Rose Court, forwarded from John E. Carter, Jeff Ellis, and Earl Drake.

Mr. CHUMBRIS. Were there any other identifying features in this instance other than you have just explained?

Mr. CRAUGH. In this particular case this was apparently arranged solely by Mrs. Tager, we had no connection with Calvin Sugarman in this particular fictitious name, M. Miller.

Mr. CHUMBRIS. Do you have any other mail drops that you wish to describe?

Mr. CRAUGH. The next one was set up at 18 Tremont Street, Boston, Mass., under the name of G. Wallis. This was arranged for by telephone. The proprietor of the secretarial service at that point received a telephone call on August 17, 1954, and the nature of the call, which was from a woman, was that she was establishing a cosmetic business in Boston and wished to receive mail at this secretarial service.

Subsequently a money order for $12.45 issued at Narragansett branch of the Wakefield post office was received by the proprietor of the secretarial service in payment for the mail drop.

Shortly after that we received from various sources specimens of this G. Wallis mailing, which contained a short circular and the sample obscene picture that I referred to before.

Mr. CHUMBRIS. Do you have any of those exhibits?

Mr. CRAUGH. We do have one here [handing].

Chairman KEFAUVER. All these are just plain lewd and obscene, and in clear violation of the postal laws?

Mr. CRAUGH. That's the only picture. I consider it a very filthy one.

Chairman KEFAUVER. There is no question but what this is in violation of the law.

Mr. CRAUGH. That's right.

Chairman KEFAUVER. Is that your private file?

Mr. CRAUGH. That is my private file.

Mr. CHUMBRIS. Now, Mr. Craugh, do you have any exhibits of the circulars that you wish to introduce at this time?

Mr. CRAUGH. Yes.

Mr. Chumbris. Or that you want to read into the record?

Mr. Craugh. I have a specimen, I believe, of all these circulars that were mailed or used under the different names.

Chairman Kefauver. So they will be privileged to the press, if they want to reproduce any part of them in writing their story, let them all be made a part of this record.

Mr. Craugh. Do you want me to read them?

Chairman Kefauver. Just describe them; but they will all be made a part of this record. If you want to read part of them, that is all right.

Mr. Craugh. The first one was the Adams circular, headed "All Nude Photo Collectors." [Reading:]

I have just completed shooting the finest nude model photos in my entire career, and I am offering them to you for the first time. These are 4 by 5 glossy prints, made expressly for the collector who is satisfied with only the unusual. I have shot these models in the poses that a true collector would appreciate. There are no drapes or shadows hiding the charms of these lovely creatures. They are completely nude. I, too, was a collector before I started shooting my own models, as I never got what I wanted.

Then there is a description of nine of these sets, entitled "Miss Unbelievable." [Reading:]

Make your friends gaze with envy at this sexsational female. With a 38-inch bust, 34-inch waist, and hips of 36. For you who like the busty gal, she is unbelievable.

The other descriptions on the other eight sets are along the same line.

This is a limited offer, and these sets are only available while they last. They will never be offered again. These sets are available for $2 per set, $10 for 6 sets, $15 all 9 sets, plus a special set not mentioned. All the orders for $6 or more sent airmail immediately.

And the bottom is an order blank.

The next one, the Bush circular, is printed in red. That starts out:

NUDE FOR THE CHOOSEY COLLECTOR

After seeing the type of picture sent out by the operators all over the country, I believe my collection of nude women is the best yet.

A similar description of the 4 by 5 glossy prints:

Not a flat-chested gal in the lot. Someone once claimed that the beautiful women in the country were all in Hollywood. I disagree. These are east coast models, and terrific. Complete assortment of blondes, red heads, and brunettes. Tall and short. I have a hundred different pics which can be yours for $20. I have 48 different pics for $10; also 20 pics for $5. If you want the whole collection of 168 pics, they are yours for $30. First come, first serve. These will be sent express.

The next one is the John Carter circular, which I read part of previously. Do you wish it repeated?

Chairman Kefauver. Are they all about the same?

Mr. Craugh. They are all about the same. The first four, up to Drake, they are all printed. The Ellis one is typewritten, and in the form of a' letter.

I received your name from a west-coast firm. I can supply you with the spicy pics you need for your own use. I have had the negatives sent to me from Germany, Sweden, and Mexico, where everything goes. First-class action shots. These are sold 10 pics for $5, 30 for $10. No samples given. All orders filled within 10 days.

The M. Miller one, most of them were on a half sheet of plain stationery, were handwritten.

I have the kind of pictures you are looking for, the hard-to-get kind.   6 for $3, 25 for $10; one 8-millimeter movie $7.   Offer is limited.

Chairman KEFAUVER. What is that 8-millimeter movie?

Mr. CRAUGH. We never saw it. That's the only description. It doesn't give any description of what might be on it.

The next one is the G. Wallis mailing. This was typewritten in green ink.

Men, the enclosed sample is proof I have what you are looking for.   Assortment of 35 for $10, or a larger assortment of the best for $15.   These will never again be offered.   Offer good only 2 weeks.   Also I have shorts, action shots of Tom Neal and Barbara Payton, shots Franchot Tone divorced her for.   These are a special gift with all $15 orders.

Mr. CHUMBRIS. Mr. Craugh, identify the basic information received from Technoprint which covers the orders of printing of the envelopes and circulars.

Mr. CRAUGH. Mr. LaVault will do that.

Mr. LAVAULT. I spoke to the operator of Technoprint Co. in Providence here. He informed me that on or about June 4 a woman who identified herself as Dorothy Tager, 11 Rose Court, Narragansett, called at his place of business and placed an order for printed matter. She had with her a typewritten sample of the circular she desired printed. They printed 5,000 of that particular circular, including the 2 envelopes, the 1 for mailing and the 1 for the return.

Subsequent to June 4 two other orders were received from Mrs. Tager. The three were in the name of Robert Adams, John E. Carter, and J. V. Bush.

Mr. CHUMBRIS. Do you have any information as to where the Drake circulars were printed?

Mr. LAVAULT. They were obtained from the same place, also.

Chairman KEFAUVER. I didn't understand from where they were obtained.

Mr. LAVAULT. Technoprint, sir.

Chairman KEFAUVER. Is that here in Providence?

Mr. LAVAULT. Yes, sir. On Empire Street, in Providence.

Mr. CHUMBRIS. Do you know what the cost was for the circulars?

Mr. LAVAULT. Yes; I have a record of that there, I believe. The first order for Robert Adams was $132.60.

Mr. CHUMBRIS. Do you have any exhibit there that identifies that with the Calvin Sugarman operation?

Mr. LAVAULT. Not in this particular record. But it was——

Mr. CHUMBRIS. I think Mr. Craugh has something on that.

Mr. CRAUGH. Yes; I have something on that [looking through records].

Chairman KEFAUVER. You have a check there for payment of it, I take it, have you?

Mr. CRAUGH. There is a check issued against the Bush account on July 12 for $132.60.

Mr. CHUMBRIS. Which is the exact amount that you referred to?

Mr. LAVAULT. That's right, sir.

Mr. CHUMBRIS. All right, sir. Now, do you have any other identifying features as to—I think you mentioned that some of these circulars were printed, others were typewritten, and others were handwritten; is that correct?

Mr. CRAUGH. That's correct.

Mr. CHUMBRIS. Some had green ink, and some had black ink?

Mr. CRAUGH. The first were printed. The Ellis one had black ink. The Miller one was handwritten on a half sheet of paper, and the Wallis one was typed in green ink.

Mr. CHUMBRIS. Do you wish to make any significance of that particular point as to the different type of circular sent out?

Mr. CRAUGH. Well, apparently to have the person receiving them, if they received more than one, think they were doing business, or receiving them from a different concern, different operator.

Mr. CHUMBRIS. Seven different operations; is that correct?

Mr. CRAUGH. Yes.

Mr. CHUMBRIS. Now, did any you three gentlemen talk to Calvin Sugarman personally?

Mr. CRAUGH. Mr. Tacy and I did.

Mr. CHUMBRIS. Do you have any affidavits from Mr. Sugarman pertaining to this operation?

Mr. CRAUGH. Yes.

Mr. CHUMBRIS. Would you summarize the contents of the affidavit?

Mr. CRAUGH. We first went to Mr. Sugarman's home on August 24, 1954, and asked him if he would come down to our office, we wanted to talk to him. He demurred at the time; but he did—at first, but he did come down that afternoon.

We told him what we were investigating, and that he appeared to be involved. This was not an affidavit; we just asked him questions, but we didn't administer the oath.

He told us, briefly, that he had begun, he admitted that he was involved to this extent, but he was doing it for an unidentified man from New York City as a favor. He said the man's name was Adams, that he had met him at the Biltmore Hotel in Providence, but would give him no further information. He denied that he knew Mary Tager, Mrs. Tager.

Subsequent to that date he did appear at the office with his attorney, Mr. Adelson, on September 3, and related that he had become acquainted with Mrs. Tager at Kingston Inn; that she wished to publish a book but needed some money. The amount of $4,000 was the amount she stated would be necessary.

Later she gave him details about this nude picture business, and he went around to set up the drops at the various places, the first five. He disclaimed any knowledge of the Miller or Wallis operation.

Mr. CHUMBRIS. Did you talk to Mrs. Tager?

Mr. CRAUGH. I did.

Mr. CHUMBRIS. And what was the substance of your conference with Mrs. Taber, relating to this operation?

Mr. CRAUGH. On August 25, 1954, Mr. Tacy and I called at her home at 11 Rose Court, Narragansett, and after identifying ourselves, told her we wanted to, we asked her if she would tell us about the mail coming to her address under the various names.

She said she was doing work for a Myron Miller, an M. Miller who was not around and was traveling in the South. She would not otherwise identify the person she was doing business with. She claimed that she was not responsible for mailing, preparing or mailing any of the circulars, and was hired by Miller solely for the purpose of addressing envelopes for the mailings.

We asked her about the various names. At first she indicated she wasn't familiar. For instance, she claimed not to recognize the name Robert Adams. She claimed she forwarded all the mail she received for Miller to West Virginia. We checked that out and there was no Miller at the place in West Virginia that she gave us.

Mr. CHUMBRIS. Did Mrs. Tager become suspicious of Sugarman's operations?

Mr. CRAUGH. According to Mr. Sugarman's statement, apparently she did, because she sent letters to at least two of the drops whereby she gave them instructions to forward the mail rather than to let him pick it up when he would call at a later date.

Mr. CHUMBRIS. Do you have any information as to Mary Dorothy Tager's bank account?

Mr. CRAUGH. This account was opened at a branch of the Providence Union National Bank in Narragansett, on July 7, 1954. A cash deposit of $150. From July 12 to July 21, cash of $244 and checks of $269 were deposited. To August 9, cash of $45 and checks and money orders of $823. From August 16 to September 28, cash of $155 and checks of $143. Total cash, $594; checks totaling $1,085; or a grand total of $1,679 deposited.

Mr. CHUMBRIS. Do you have anything further on that point?

Mr. CRAUGH. On June 28 a check was drawn to the order of Dorothy Tager by Robert Adams. I believe that is shown on a deposit slip. That was signed on the back, on the reverse, Dorothy Tager.

Chairman KEFAUVER. Is that the same signature on the Robert Adams check that is endorsed by Mr. Sugarman?

Mr. CRAUGH. Where the name Adams appears to be the same.

Chairman KEFAUVER. The same bank account?

Mr. CRAUGH. It is the same bank account.

Mr. CHUMBRIS. Now we have a reference to an Old Division letter. Would you please comment on that point?

Mr. CRAUGH. In an effort to obtain more evidence on the extent of the operations, we did request assistance from inspectors throughout the country and asked them to interview people who might have been engaged, or who might have received orders from these various names.

Mr. CHUMBRIS. In your investigation of the matter had you become convinced that fraud had been committed?

Mr. CRAUGH. We could find no evidence that anybody had received any pictures for the money they had remitted, money or other values they had remitted.

Mr. CHUMBRIS. Would you explain that a little bit more? People sent in money with the orders; is that correct?

Mr. CRAUGH. That is right.

Mr. CHUMBRIS. And from your investigation no one had received any material for that money sent?

Mr. CRAUGH. That is right

Mr. CHUMBRIS. Is that what your investigation showed?

Mr. CRAUGH. That is what was indicated at that time.

Chairman KEFAUVER. Was this literature sent all over the United States, various and sundry States?

Mr. CRAUGH. Yes; it was including Alaska, I believe.

Chairman KEFAUVER. All over the United States and Alaska?

Mr. CRAUGH. Yes.

Chairman KEFAUVER. Something over 30,000?

Mr. CRAUGH. I beg your pardon?

Chairman KEFAUVER. Did you find where 30,000 had been sent, or something of that sort?

Mr. CRAUGH. No; not in this particular exhibit. It was indicated that, well, at least 30,000 letters, approximately 30,000 letters of all types had probably been sent, soliciting orders for merchandise, for the pictures.

Chairman KEFAUVER. How many remittances did you get evidence had been sent back or can you estimate it?

Mr. CRAUGH. The closest one I had was on the Worcester operation, where there were apparently 241 orders there. Some of the others were difficult to tell because they had no—they kept no records of how many pieces of mail, either.

Chairman KEFAUVER. They sent their money and did not get anything back?

Mr. CRAUGH. That's right.

Mr. CHUMBRIS. You developed the fraud angle of this investigation; did you?

Mr. CRAUGH. Well, briefly, I can give you a few examples of what people sent in, how much they sent in, and didn't receive anything in return.

Pennsylvania: a $10 money order to the name of Drake and a $10 check to Adams. The check in that case bore, in addition to the Adams endorsement, also a J. V. Bush endorsement.

Three checks in the amounts of $3, $3, and $5 to Carter, Miller, and Ellis. That was from the same person.

Mr. CHUMBRIS. From the same person?

Mr. CRAUGH. Yes, sir; a total of $11.

This is from Georgia. Earl Drake, $10 money order; Wallis, a $15 money order. No pictures.

Pennsylvania. Carter, $10; Wallis, $15. Both cash in that instance.

Mr. CHUMBRIS. Did you have any instances where 1 person was defrauded more than 1 time?

Mr. CRAUGH. That one I just mentioned, there is 1 there with 3.

Mr. CHUMBRIS. How many instances of that do you have?

Mr. CRAUGH. There must be, well, 40 or 50 at least that we have evidence of.

Mr. CHUMBRIS. Are you going to submit any of those as exhibits for the record, or is this part of your file?

Mr. CRAUGH. This is all part of our files.

Mr. CHUMBRIS. Let's see, how many do you have in your hand there?

Mr. CRAUGH. I must have approximately 25 or 30 here.

Mr. CHUMBRIS. And how many did you receive altogether?

Mr. CRAUGH. It was well over 100, I would say, approximately 150 at least.

Mr. CHUMBRIS. 150?

Mr. CRAUGH. I think that was about the amount.

Mr. CHUMBRIS. That is of those people who have complained; is that correct?

Mr. CRAUGH. No; not necessarily. Some complained but most of these did not complain.

Mr. CHUMBRIS. I mean, through your investigation.

Mr. CRAUGH. We took action to see if they had received anything from return addresses we noted on the mail, going to the various drops.

Mr. CHUMBRIS. On this all-division letter, was that subsequently countermanded?

Mr. CRAUGH. We did receive instructions that a further study would be made of the matter and that we wouldn't send out any more for the time being, making more requests for the time being.

Mr. CHUMBRIS. I understand there was a reference to paragraph 5 of the all-division letter. Will you please explain that?

Mr. CRAUGH. We stated, "The investigation strongly indicates violation of the mail fraud statutes in addition to the obscene statute."

Chairman KEFAUVER. You felt two statutes had been violated, the obscene statute and the mail fraud statute?

Mr. CRAUGH. Yes.

Mr. CHUMBRIS. Then after you came to that decision, what was your next step?

Mr. CRAUGH. I think we discussed the matter with—we had discussed the matter prior to this with the United States attorney, and I kept him informed of——

Mr. CHUMBRIS. When was that?

Mr. CRAUGH. I think right from the, almost from the beginning of the investigation.

Mr. CHUMBRIS. And continuing on until what period?

Mr. CRAUGH. Until the arrest of Mrs. Tager.

Mr. CHUMBRIS. What was Mrs. Tager arrested for?

Mr. CRAUGH. Mailing obscene pictures, using the mails to send an obscene picture.

Mr. CHUMBRIS. Was any charge lodged against her for fraud?

Mr. CRAUGH. No.

Mr. CHUMBRIS. Was there any charge lodged against Calvin Sugarman at that time for either fraud or for mailing obscene literature?

Mr. CRAUGH. No.

Mr. CHUMBRIS. That takes it up to what date?

Mr. CRAUGH. She was arrested on September 10, 1954—no; she was arrested on the 13th, September 13. A warrant was issued on September 10, 1954.

Mr. CHUMBRIS. And her case was disposed of in June 1955?

Mr. CRAUGH. That's right.

Mr. CHUMBRIS. Up to June 1955 had any complaint been lodged against Calvin Sugarman?

Mr. CRAUGH. No; not to my knowledge.

Mr. CHUMBRIS. When I refer to "complaint," I am referring to an official complaint through the United States attorney's office. I believe you said you took it up with the United States attorney's office?

Mr. CRAUGH. We had apprised him of the facts.

Mr. CHUMBRIS. Do you know whether that matter had ever been presented to a grand jury up to June 1955?

Mr. CRAUGH. You mean the case of——

Mr. CHUMBRIS. Either the question of fraud or the question of mailing obscene literature, against Calvin Sugarman?

Mr. CRAUGH. There was a grand jury session on December 27.

Mr. CHUMBRIS. Of what year?

Mr. CRAUGH. 1954.

Mr. CHUMBRIS. Was that the Sugarman case, Calvin Sugarman?

Mr. CRAUGH. That was the Tager case.

Mr. CHUMBRIS. I am referring to Calvin Sugarman.

Mr. CRAUGH. There is no case against Calvin Sugarman.

Mr. CHUMBRIS. There was no case against Calvin Sugarman through June 1955; is that correct?

Mr. CRAUGH. That's correct.

Mr. CHUMBRIS. You said the case against Mrs. Tager wsa disposed of in June 1955. How was it disposed and on what charge?

Mr. CRAUGH. I believe she pleaded guilty to several counts of mailing obscene literature, or mailing obscene pictures, and she received 2 years' probation.

Mr. CHUMBRIS. Was there any fine attached to that?

Mr. CRAUGH. No fine that I know of.

Mr. CHUMBRIS. Getting back to Mrs. Tager, you say, what was the date of her arrest on the west coast?

Mr. CRAUGH. I think it was September 13, 1954. That was the date she was picked up by the marshals.

Mr. CHUMBRIS. I am referring to in April of 1955 on the west coast.

Mr. CRAUGH. She didn't appear for trial called here at Providence on April 20, and Inspector Egan and I had a lead and sent word to the west coast to see if she could be located there. Inspector Stapenhorst and Inspector Schneringer located her the night of April 30, and she was eventually brought back here by the marshals.

Mr. CHUMBRIS. Did she submit an affidavit around that time?

Mr. CRAUGH. Inspector Schneringer and Inspector Stapenhorst did obtain an affidavit from her.

Mr. CHUMBRIS. Do you have a copy of that affidavit in your file?

Mr. CRAUGH. I do.

Mr. CHUMBRIS. Do you have a copy that you could submit for the record?

Mr. CRAUGH. I just have this copy here.

Mr. CHUMBRIS. You have submitted a copy to the staff. I wish to introduce a copy of that affidavit.

Chairman KEFAUVER. Let it be admitted.

(The affidavit referred to above is as follows:)

Following is a sworn statement given by Mrs. Tager at the time of her arrest on April 30, 1955:

"I, Mrs. Mary Dorothy Tager, having been duly sworn depose and say:

"The following statements are made freely and voluntarily, without any promises or threats, and with the knowledge they may be used for or against me. It is my desire that all the facts relating to my activities during my residence in Rhode Island the last 2 years be brought to light, and these following statements are a true and accurate account of them, including the circumstances leading up to my arrest at Narragansett, R. I., last September.

"I can say at the beginning that it has been fairly well known I sold through the mails in California pictures of the so-called art variety. Some were alleged to have been in the category of obscene pictures, but I know I never handled or sold squeamish pictures, or any which in my opinion could be (called) considered obscene. I was never arrested prior to September 1954. These activities of which I speak were during 1949 and 1950.

"I separated from my husband, Louis Tager, and then divorced him in 1951. I was quite broken up, and my health was poor. I therefore returned to my mother's home at Narragansett, R. I., in December 1952. I was very ill, and remained confined in the house until some time in March 1953. I then secured employment at the Coast Guard House, Narragansett, R. I., as a waitress, and worked there until September 1953. I then worked for the same employer, William Bolster, at another of his restaurants in West Greenwich, R. I., from September to November 1953. I collapsed at work and spent the next 6 weeks in the South County Hospital, Wakefield, R. I. I was operated on in November for an intestinal ailment (malignant growths) and got out of the hospital about Christmas 1953. I was unable to work or do anything until about April 1954. I applied for employment at the Kingston Inn, and there I met a Mr. Carl Sherman whose correct name I was later to learn is Calvin Sugarman. We dated a few times. I had been writing a book about the nude picture business. Carl (Calvin) read part of my completed manuscript, and became interested in selling pictures. He had been in some sort of mail order business (merchandise) but lost a lot of money. He wanted and needed negatives and mailing lists. I needed money. I sold him a total of $1,800 for a number of negatives and about 50,000 to 60,000 names. I sold the negatives, as I recall, for $2.50 each set of eight. The mailing list names were $15 per thousand. These negatives and mailing lists were part of the old Ross-Louis Tager operation material.

"My health was still not good, and I had lost any desire to actively engage in the old picture business. Therefore I was content to advise and help Calvin Sugarman to some extent in his operating the picture business through the mails. I did some of the stuffing and sealing of the envelopes containing the advertising literature. I did this at my home and was paid $6.50 per thousand by Sugarman. Miss Shirley Barber (age about 20) of Wakefield, R. I., also did some of the typing, stuffing, and sealing. Some of this work she did at my home; some at her home. I did not receive any compensation from Sugarman. I did not receive any profits or percentage from the operation which was actually his. The first money I received from Sugarman was three or four hundred dollars, in the form of his own personal check drawn against his account at the Industrial Trust Co., Hope Street branch bank, which was in his neighborhood. After the elapse of a few weeks he began paying off the balance of the $1,800 by giving me $50 or $100 every night or so, although there were days when I received nothing from him. Sugarman still owes me a couple hundred dollars. Now when he paid me these additional amounts, the payment was in the form of currency and checks which he had received in orders for pictures. I can positively state that the negatives I sold Sugarman were the strictly art photo type. I did not sell him any that are of the pornographic type. I have never handled any of the pornographic or real obscene kind.

"Sugarman arranged for his own mail drops and selected the various fictitious names which were used in the operation. In stuffing the envelopes I of course had occasion to see the names and addresses he used for his return orders. I don't remember them except that he used the name Busch; also Adams and possibly Drake. As a matter of fact, I had reason to believe that Sugarman opened a bank account in the name of Busch. I am of the recollection this account was at the main office of the Industrial Trust. He issued a check payable to me in a substantial sum of, I believe, $200, and I deposited it in my bank account at the Wakefield-Narragansett branch of the Industrial Trust. Sugarman had secretarial addresses in Connecticut, Massachusetts, and Rhode Island. I did not, as mentioned above, arrange for any of those mail drops. However, without my knowledge and consent Sugarman must have arranged for some of these drops to forward bundles of returns from the mailings to my home, and he picked them up there. My residence at that time was 11 Rose Court, Narragansett. One time he asked me to pay the next month's bill for a mail drop at Boston, which was in the name of Wallis. I asked the boy friend of my daughter if he would buy and mail the money order for me. His name is Joe Problod, and he usually resides at Providence, but spends the summer in Narragansett.

"I do not know where Sugarman had the picture positives made, but I rather believe it was through some commercial place in Providence which does not ordinarily do that sort of work. I should mention that I never filled any orders and did not know what type of photos Carl was mailing. In all truth I must say he showed me a pornographic picture (Barbara Peyton-Tom Neal) which appeared to me to be a copy print about 14 by 20 inches in size. I must also say I saw some other pornographic type photos in his possession, but I never considered for a moment he should be so stupid as to sell and send them through the mails.

I should have suspected something when I became aware he was mailing out a short 'pitch' to the effect that if the addressee bought a certain amount of the regular photos a photo of Barbara Peyton-Tom Neal would be sent free. I did some of the addressing of envelopes for the mailing of that 'pitch.' I believe 3,500 to 4,000 of these were mailed. Carl (Sugarman) had us (Shirley and me) leave the envelopes unsealed, and he handled them thereafter, presumably stuffing and later filling and mailing the orders.

"I believe Sugarman was obtaining his pornographic pictures from an Italian fellow who had a small pickup truck and had some regular business with the commissary at the Quonset Point Naval Air Base which enabled him entrance to that base. This fellow, whose name I have heard but do not recall now, sells large quantities of those photos.

"I understand one of the indictments relates to a Wallis transaction, and that I deposited the check for the order in my own bank account. The one Wallis check I received was received by me from Sugarman. During the period alleged in my indictment I was very ill and required shots of Demerol every 4 hours. Some of these shots were administered by my doctor, Dr. Thomas Nester, Narragansett. Another person who may be able to corroborate my statements that the enterprise was really operated by Sugarman is Dot Bolster, a neighbor on Rose Court, Narragansett. She has seen Carl engaged in the activity and she has helped, for free, stuff some of the envelopes.

"I returned to California and resided around Orange County since the first part of this year. My case was to come to trial in Federal District Court, Providence, R. I., April 20. The reason I did not return was principally because I was of the opinion this whole deal was a coverup for Sugarman and I was to be left holding the bag for everything and much of which I was not responsible. I might say I was advised by an attorney to 'take off.'

"These statements are made in good faith and are true. Under the circumstances in which I am now placed there would be no particular reason to lie or misrepresent what actually happened."

Mr. CHUMBRIS. Would you summarize the contents of that affidavit?

Mr. CRAUGH. Yes. She summarizes her activity in the nude picture business in California back in 1949 and 1950, separated from Louis Tager, her husband, and divorced in 1951. She was ill for some time, and later came back to Rhode Island in March 1953.

She worked at various restaurants around there, and about April 1954, she met Calvin Sugarman, with whom she went out a few times.

She details her writing a book about the nude picture business, which she intended to publish, and got him interested in. She claims he had been in a sort of mail-order business, but lost a lot of money, and that she sold him a total of negatives and a large mailing list, 50,000 names, for mailing advertisements, apparently, to those who wanted nude pictures.

She said the mailing lists and the negatives were part of the old Ross-Tager operations. She claims she had lost any desire to engage in the old picture business, therefore, she just advised and helped Calvin Sugarman. She did some of the stuffing and sealing, and was paid $6.50 per thousand for the circulars.

"I did not receive any profits or percentage," but she says she got three or four hundred dollars from Sugarman in the form of his own personal check.

Chairman KEFAUVER. What is the date of that affidavit, sir?

Mr. CRAUGH. April 30, 1955.

Chairman KEFAUVER. Now, sir, from the information you got, letters and investigation, how many people sent money in, or what is your best estimate, where they received nothing back?

Mr. CRAUGH. I would say, this is just an outright estimate, I would say at least 2,000 people. I would estimate close to 2,000 people.

Chairman KEFAUVER. And that is in all parts of the country?

Mr. CRAUGH. That is in all parts of the country.

Chairman KEFAUVER. How many States are involved, do you know?

Mr. CRAUGH. Well, pretty nearly every one of the 48 States.

Chairman KEFAUVER. And the Post Office Department officials. felt that there were two laws violated, the law against obscenity and the mail-fraud statute?

Mr. CRAUGH. Yes.

Chairman KEFAUVER. Was Mrs. Tager indicted in connection with this matter or with some other matter? She mailed out some- thing obscene, apparently, and she was indicted for that?

Mr. CRAUGH. For that.

Chairman KEFAUVER. Was that in connection with one of these operations? That was the Boston operation, was it not?

Mr. CRAUGH. That was the Boston operation; yes. Wallis, G. Wallis.

Chairman KEFAUVER. That is the G. Wallis, 18 Tremont Street,. in Boston. She pled guilty and got a suspended sentence.

What happened to Mr. Sugarman?

Mr. CRAUGH. Nothing happened to him.

Chairman KEFAUVER. Didn't something happen the other day?

Mr. CRAUGH. I read in the papers that he had been indicted.

Chairman KEFAUVER. All right. Go ahead, Mr. Chumbris.

Mr. CHUMBRIS. Then as far as your investigation is concerned,. that brings the Tager-Sugarman matter up to date; is that correct?

Mr. CRAUGH. That's right.

Mr. CHUMBRIS. Do any of you three gentlemen have anything additional to add to what you have already told us?

Mr. LAVAULT. Nothing.

Mr. TACY. I have nothing.

Mr. CHUMBRIS. When you discussed the matter with the United States attorney, you presented to them the entire picture as you have presented it here, both as to Sugarman and as to Tager?

Mr. CRAUGH. That's correct.

Mr. CHUMBRIS. And only Mrs. Tager was the one who was charged,. and she was charged with mailing obscene matter?

Mr. CRAUGH. Yes.

Mr. CHUMBRIS. And no charge was lodged against either Sugarman or Tager for the fraud charges; is that correct?

Mr. CRAUGH. That's correct.

Chairman KEFAUVER. Did you ask for action on the matter?

Mr. CRAUGH. We discussed the matter with them.

Chairman KEFAUVER. That was the purpose of presenting it, I take it, to the United States attorney, to get some action on it; is that it?

Mr. CRAUGH. We presented the facts.

Mr. CHUMBRIS. Did you determine during your investigation whether there was a violation, also, of the State of Rhode Island fictitious address statute?

Mr. CRAUGH. Yes. We had, in our investigation, checked to see whether any of these names, the two names used in Rhode Island, were registered according to State law. We found no record.

Here is the letter from the deputy secretary of state [exhibiting], addressed to Mr. Tacy:

After searching our corporate files we do not find record of Robert Adams Co., nor Joseph V. Bush, either as domestic or foreign corporations. We enclose copy of chapter 386 which you requested—

the law that applies.

Mr. CHUMBRIS. What is the citation of that statute?

Mr. CRAUGH. Chapter 386, General Laws, 1923, chapter 214. I believe that is the full citation.

Mr. CHUMBRIS. And what is the penalty for that, do you have it there?

Mr. CRAUGH (reading):

Any person violating this shall be imprisoned not exceeding 1 year or be fined not exceeding $500.

Mr. CHUMBRIS. When you presented this matter to the United States attorney's office, did you make any recommendation with submitting the facts and the testimony and the exhibits?

Mr. CRAUGH. We don't dictate to the United States attorney; we present all the facts at our disposal. We don't make recommendations.

Mr. CHUMBRIS. You say you don't make any recommendations. You just submit the facts and you——

Mr. CRAUGH. We submit the facts.

Mr. CHUMBRIS. And I think you stated a moment ago that what you have submitted to the subcommittee now is the same type of material you submitted to the United States attorney; is that correct?

Mr. CRAUGH. That's right; yes, sir.

Chairman KEFAUVER. Anything else, gentlemen?

Mr. CRAUGH. No, sir.

Mr. TACY. No, sir.

Mr. LAVAULT. I have nothing.

Chairman KEFAUVER. Stay around a while; something might come up.

The committee will stand in recess for 5 minutes.

(A recess was taken.)

Chairman KEFAUVER. The committee will come to order.

Mr. CHUMBRIS. Mr. Craugh, just one question. A little earlier you stated there was a violation of the Rhode Island statute and you turned the matter over to the United States attorney. Now, did you turn that same material over to the attorney general of the State of Rhode Island, or to any of the——

Mr. CRAUGH. No. We made inquiry to see if those names had been registered in Rhode Island.

Mr. CHUMBRIS. But you did not turn whatever material you had over to the State for the State to prosecute; is that correct?

Mr. CRAUGH. That's right.

Mr. CHUMBRIS. You only turned material over to the United States attorney's office?

Mr. CRAUGH. That's correct.

Chairman KEFAUVER. Who is our next witness?

Mr. CHUMBRIS. Arnold Williamson.

Mr. MAINELLI. Senator, my name is Joseph Mainelli. I am the United States attorney for the district of Rhode Island.

In view of the fact that Mr. Sugarman now stands indicted in an indictment that was returned in the Federal district court, and having in mind the case of *Delaney* v. *The United States*, reported in 199 Federal Reporter, second series, I believe it is at page 507—I am not quite sure of the page number—and anticipating that some of the charges made in the Delaney case might be made in the case of Calvin Sugarman, and some court might have to pass upon whether or not some of the testimony given before this committee will be prejudicial to the defendant, and I feel that Mr. Williamson, as one of my assistants, might be assigned to the trial of this case, and certainly would not like the charge to be placed against him as the prosecutor of having delivered any inflammatory material here, especially in view of the fact that the case is pending, it is my considered judgment that in order to further the ends of justice that it would be better for him not to appear to testify.

I have so instructed him, and I am willing to assume the responsibility in the matter.

Chairman KEFAUVER. Mr. Mainelli, when did you become a United States attorney here?

Mr. MAINELLI. I was nominated by President Eisenhower on July 3, I believe it was, and I was appointed by the court on July 5 of this year as an interim appointment until confirmation by the Senate.

Chairman KEFAUVER. July 5, 1955?

Mr. MAINELLI. That's right, Senator.

Chairman KEFAUVER. When was Mr. Sugarman indicted?

Mr. MAINELLI. Mr. Sugarman was indicted last Friday afternoon.

Chairman KEFAUVER. What date was last Friday?

Mr. MAINELLI. Today is the 8th. I would say it was November 5.

Chairman KEFAUVER. This committee wrote the Attorney General of the United States some days previous to that, asking permission for Mr. Williamson and Mr. Temkin to testify. You are aware of that?

Mr. MAINELLI. I am not, Mr. Senator.

Chairman KEFAUVER. On October 31 I wrote Mr. Brownell a letter setting forth the facts of the case that had been developed here, as secured by our staff, asking permission for these gentlemen to testify, Mr. Temkin and Mr. Williamson.

Five days later an indictment was returned. Why was not something done about this case before this time? You have been here since July 5.

Mr. MAINELLI. Yes; I have. I had contemplated action in this case much before the time that action did take place, but because of other matters I had to defer it; but because of the fact, and having in mind that the ruling in the case of *Delaney* v. *The United States*, wherein the charge was made that the matters presented at a congressional hearing were inflammatory, and an objection was made to the court in its refusal to dismiss the indictment in that case, the court held that that was not a valid objection because the hearing was held after the grand jury had met to consider the case, and therefore it could not be stated that the matter was inflammatory insofar as procuring the indictment is concerned.

Chairman KEFAUVER. The indictment has been secured here already.

Mr. MAINELLI. That is correct.

Chairman KEFAUVER. You did not act until you were ordered to act after the Attorney General received this letter, did you?

Mr. MAINELLI. Well now, I don't know anything about the Attorney General receiving that letter.

Chairman KEFAUVER. Were you ordered by Washington to proceed against Sugarman?

Mr. MAINELLI. I will not answer that question because any conversation I had with Washington was confidential, as far as I am concerned.

Chairman KEFAUVER. I don't want to have any trouble with you, Mr. Mainelli. Did you act on your own volition or did you receive instructions?

Mr. MAINELLI. Let me say that the ultimate result was of my own volition, because I had called in the postal inspector in this case 2 weeks after I assumed office, and I gave them my view of the matter and told them how I felt about it.

If you will question those gentlemen, I think that they will express to you just what my views were.

I found myself in a position where this subcommittee had scheduled a certain hearing.

Chairman KEFAUVER. Yes; and I have an idea that nothing would have happened if we had not scheduled hearings, too.

Mr. MAINELLI. That is your opinion, Senator. Of course you are entitled to it.

Chairman KEFAUVER. The letter to the Attorney General will be marked "Exhibit 6."

(The letter above referred to is as follows:)

OCTOBER 31, 1955.

Hon. HERBERT BROWNELL, Jr.,
    Attorney General of the United States,
        Department of Justice, Washington, D. C.

DEAR MR. BROWNELL: The United States Senate Subcommittee To Investigate Juvenile Delinquency is contemplating a hearing on November 8, 1955, in Providence, R. I. Aside from various community aspects of the juvenile delinquency problem, the subcommittee is desirous of inquiring into the manufacture, distribution, sale, and possession of pornographic, indecent, and lewd material.

One of the serious situations in pornography revolves around the partnership of Mary Dorothy Tager and Calvin Sugarman. The use of the United States mails to transmit pornographic and obscene materials in three States in New England was investigated by our staff several weeks ago. In addition, the subcommittee conducted an investigation concerning some 30,000 pieces of advertising that was transmitted through the mails for pornographic material by said Tager and Sugarman, which resulted in their receiving numerous payments for this obscene material, none of which was delivered to the potential purchasers. There appear to be a least 200 counts on a mail fraud charge which were never prosecuted.

In connection with the above, the subcommittee, at its hearings in Providence, desires to hear the persons concerned in this matter, particularly former United States Attorney Jacob Temkin and present Assistant United States Attorney Arnold Williamson who prosecuted this case. The post office witnesses have signified their intention to testify, but both Messrs. Temkin and Williamson stated that they would not testify without prior approval and permission from your office.

The subcommittee intends to subpena both Messrs. Temkin and Williamson, as it feels that their testimony is vital to the investigation and hearings contemplated in Providence, R. I., as previously mentioned.

We would appreciate an early reply from your office as to whether Messrs. Temkin and Williamson will be given permission from your office to testify.

With kindest regards, I am
    Sincerely,

ESTES KEFAUVER, Chairman.

Chairman KEFAUVER. Mr. Mainelli, if you will come and sit down, please.

How many assistant district attorneys do you have here?

Mr. MAINELLI. Two.   That is 1 less than the office had 2 years ago.

Chairman KEFAUVER. Mr. Williamson, and who is your other?

Mr. MAINELLI. Samuel Tanzi.

Chairman KEFAUVER. Do both of them try criminal cases?

Mr. MAINELLI. Mr. Tanzi has only been in the office since last ecember, I believe.   I don't know how extensive his trial practice as been in criminal cases in the office.

Chairman KEFAUVER. How long has Mr. Williamson been in the office?

Mr. MAINELLI. I am just guessing at this.   About a year and a half.

Chairman KEFAUVER. He is a young lawyer; is he not?

Mr. MAINELLI. They are both young men, Senator.

Chairman KEFAUVER. Both are experienced, are they not?

Your objection is on the basis that you might assign Mr. Williamson to try this case, and in that event, why, he might be prejudiced in connection with it; is that your objection?

Mr. MAINELLI. Well, no, Mr. Senator.   My objection is to the subject matter of this hearing.   I feel that so long as there is an indictment pending, the charge might be made in open court that inflammatory matter of such a nature as to prejudice the defendant's right may be adduced as a result of this hearing.

I will, of course, be in a position where I will have to contest any such allegation.   I certainly——

Chairman KEFAUVER. That is for the court to pass on, whether a change of venue should be granted; is it not?

Mr. MAINELLI. That is correct, Mr. Senator.

Chairman KEFAUVER. This case is not on all fours with the Delaney case, is it, Mr. Mainelli?   I have forgotten that case, but it seems to me that in that case the Attorney General of the United States in Washington asked that the witnesses not testify.

Mr. MAINELLI. As far as the facts in that case are concerned, I am not concerned with what transpired at the hearing, because I know nothing about that.   But as far as the facts in the case are concerned, as reported in the opinion, in my opinion they are analogous.

Chairman KEFAUVER. They held that it could not be prejudicial in connection with the securing of the indictment because the hearing was held afterward?

Mr. MAINELLI. That's correct.

Chairman KEFAUVER. Isn't that the same thing here?

Mr. MAINELLI. No; I beg to differ with you, Senator, because the conviction was reversed on the ground that matters prejudicial to the defendant were adduced at a hearing before the Senate subcommittee after the indictment had been returned.

Now we find ourselves in the same situation here, identically.

Chairman KEFAUVER. What the court held was that under the particular situation in that case there should have been a change of venue; isn't that correct?

Mr. MAINELLI. I don't say that the court held there should have been a change of venue.   I know that the conviction——

Chairman KEFAUVER. That is a case that arose in Boston?

Mr. MAINELLI. That's correct. The conviction was reversed on the ground that——

Chairman KEFAUVER. On the refusal of the judge to grant a change of venue under the particular facts of that case. Isn't that correct?

Mr. MAINELLI. No; I don't think so, Senator. If my recollection serves me, there was a motion, or rather the case had been assigned for trial and a motion was made to defer the trial to some later time so as to permit enough time to elapse to sort of wear out whatever prejudicial matter had been presented at that subcommittee hearing.

The court of appeals held that that motion should have been sustained and that the trial should have been deferred until such time as whatever prejudicial matter had been adduced at the hearing might have worn off so that the defendant there might have received a fair trial.

Chairman KEFAUVER. I think it was on a matter of change of venue under the particular facts of that case.

In any event, we have heard your statement about it, and thank you very much, Mr. Mainelli.

Mr. Williamson, will you come around, sir.

Mr. MAINELLI. I will have to send for him, sir. He is downstairs.

Chairman KEFAUVER. Well, send for him.

Mr. MAINELLI. All right.

Chairman KEFAUVER. Mr. Craugh, when did you turn substantial information over to the United States attorney and to whom did you turn it over here?

Mr. CRAUGH. It was about September 17.

Chairman KEFAUVER. 1954?

Mr. CRAUGH. 16th; 1954. And that was mailed to the office of Mr. Jacob Temkin, who was then United States attorney.

Chairman KEFAUVER. Your investigation then was substantially completed and the information turned over at that time?

Mrs. CRAUGH. Yes, sir.

Chairman KEFAUVER. September 16, 1954?

Mr. CRAUGH. Yes. I think that was the date, sir.

Chairman KEFAUVER. Who is the next witness?

Mr. CHUMBRIS. Mr. Jacob Temkin.

Chairman KEFAUVER. Mr. Temkin, do you solemnly swear the testimony you will give at this hearing will be the whole truth, so help you God?

Mr. TEMKIN. I do.

TESTIMONY OF JACOB TEMKIN

Chairman KEFAUVER. Mr. Temkin, do you want to tell us about this matter, or, what is your position?

Mr. TEMKIN. I think perhaps, Senator, you put me on the defensive by posing it that way.

I think you will be interested, nevertheless, in my position.

Chairman KEFAUVER. I don't mean to put it in the way that causes you any effrontery, Mr. Temkin. I just wanted to know if you wanted to tell us about the matter.

Mr. TEMKIN. It seems to me the other witnesses in this particular case, Senator, were called, they were asked to give their names, their background, and then submit themselves to questioning.

Chairman KEFAUVER. All right, sir. We will do with you that way.

Mr. TEMKIN. I think you ought to proceed in an orderly manner. I don't want to be critical, but it seems to me if you are going to follow an orderly procedure, I would like to proceed in that manner.

Chairman KEFAUVER. Very well, Mr. Temkin.

Mr. TEMKIN. I will give my name and my address.

Chairman KEFAUVER. If you will give your name and address, sir.

Mr. TEMKIN. And background.

Chairman KEFAUVER. ·Yes, sir.

Mr. TEMKIN. My name is Jacob S. Temkin. I am an attorney. My office is at 540 Hospital Trust Building, Providence, R. I. I reside at 15 Harwich Road, Providence, R. I.

My background is as follows. I was born in Providence——

Chairman KEFAUVER. Do you want to sit down?

Mr. TEMKIN. I think I am a little more comfortable standing up, if it doesn't make any difference to you, sir.

Chairman KEFAUVER. All right, sir.

Mr. TEMKIN. My background is as follows. I was born in Providence, attended the public schools here. I am a graduate of Brown University, the class of 1926, with the degrees of bachelor of arts and master of arts in that year. I am a graduate of Harvard Law School with the degree of bachelor of laws in the year 1929.

I was admitted to the bar of the State of Rhode Island in 1929, and I have continuously practiced in this jurisdiction since that time. I am a member of other bars, including Federal bar, circuit court of appeals bar and the Supreme Court of the United States bar.

In 1939 and 1940 I was an assistant attorney general for the State of Rhode Island. In 1942 through a portion of 1944 I was the chief legal officer of the Rhode Island office of OPA. A portion of that time I was acting regional enforcement attorney of IPA in New England, and I was a special assistant to the United States attorney for the district of Rhode Island, handling OPA matters.

From June 30, 1953, through July 2, 1955, I was the United States attorney for the district of Rhode Island.

Chairman KEFAUVER. I did not understand those dates, Mr. Temkin.

Mr. TEMKIN. Am I talking loud enough for you, sir?

Chairman KEFAUVER. Yes; but this June 1953, you said?

Mr. TEMKIN. June 30, 1953, through July 2, 1955, I was United States attorney for the district of Rhode Island.

My interests have not been strictly legal, and I would like to mention them because they have a direct bearing on the content of the case under discussion and because of their relevancy to the subject matter of this particular subcommittee, of which you are the chairman.

For many years I have been interested in social welfare activities of various kinds. For 25 years I have been in an executive position with the Jewish Family and Children's Service, 10 years of which I was president of that organization.

For more than 15 years I have been a trustee of the Jewish Children's Home of Rhode Island, which operated the Jewish Orphanage, and later when that was closed, operated a camp for underprivileged children.

For more than 10 years I have been a director of the Narragansett Council Boy Scouts of America, which has jurisdiction in the State of Rhode Island, parts of Massachusetts.

For several years I was associated with the Council of Social Agencies of the city of Providence, and I have been chairman of that organization.

I have been on various committees of one kind or another having to do with civic functions and public welfare.

For more than 10 years I have been actively associated with the Miriam Hospital during that time, and now I am on its executive committee.

Mr. Chairman, you will be interested to know—I don't have to call it to your attention—prior to saying that let me say this, that for 2 years I was on the executive committee of the bar association. For 2 subsequent years I was chairman of the executive committee of the Rhode Island Bar Association. Now I will come back to what I was referring a moment ago.

Mr. Chairman, in 1951, you headed a committee known as the Kefauver committee, which was interested in investigating organized crime in interstate commerce. In August of 1951, you submitted your report as chairman of that committee. That report in due course was submitted to the Governor of the State of Rhode Island, Dennis J. Roberts, who testified here this morning. Governor Roberts, through the Attorney General, asked the bar association, the Rhode Island Bar Association, to appoint a committee to consider the recommendations of the Kefauver committee, so-called, as they applied to conditions in the State of Rhode Island. I was privileged to be the chairman of that committee, which held hearings and submitted a report to the Governor of the State of Rhode Island in connection with organized crime in this State. As the same, they had been at that time taking into account the recommendations which your committee, of which you were chairman, had submitted recommendations to the Senate of the United States; and on that committee, sir, were the present president of the Rhode Island Bar Association, the president-elect of the Rhode Island Bar Association, and former president of the bar association, two other highly respected members of the bar who had practiced at least 25 years in this State, a young lawyer as secretary, and myself as chairman.

Now, I mentioned to you, sir, a short time ago that my background would have relevancy to the subject matter with which you are concerned, and I as a private citizen am concerned. You will recall this morning, Judge McCabe spoke of a wheel, of a hub, and spokes. Sir, I call to your attention that the organizations with which I have been affiliated are the spokes in the wheel to which Judge McCabe referred this morning.

If you care to hear further about my background, I will be glad to elaborate further. I have given it to you in summary fashion, but I think it is important for you, sir, to know, and the record should contain these facts, because my background, both as a lawyer and as a citizen of this community, would not stand some of the inferences that have been implied in newspaper accounts and in the testimony presented here this afternoon.

I am prepared now, sir, and I give you this statement. You asked me what my position is, I will read this statement.

The reason that I am here is in connection with this Sugarman case. I want to make my position clear. I would like to advise this subcommittee that in my opinion there is serious doubt as to the propriety and legality of questions directed to one who has knowledge of a criminal case which arose during his tenure as United States attorney. I believe this to be true whether an indictment has been returned or not.

I also want to make it clear, however, that I have no hesitancy in answering such questions if this subcommittee holds that it has a right to ask them and is willing to assume the responsibility for the same.

Chairman KEFAUVER. Very well. This subcommittee assumes responsibility for any questions it asks.

I appreciate your statement about your background, a statement of lots of good public service. The only question I wanted to ask is, what was your position about doing something in connection with the Sugarman case?

Mr. TEMKIN. Do you want it in narrative form, sir, or do you want to ask me questions?

Chairman KEFAUVER. I just asked you a question. The matter was presented to you, and what did you do about it?

Mr. TEMKIN. I heard the statements that were given a short time ago——

Chairman KEFAUVER. September 16, 1954.

Mr. TEMKIN. That is not the first date, sir, that the matter was presented to me. I will tell you when the matter was presented to me, and I have to make a preliminary statement in connection with it.

I have not sought the file in this case because I felt it was improper for me to ask for the file in the office of the United States attorney in connection with any matter. I am testifying to the best of my recollection.

Sometime during the summer of 1954, it may have been in July or it may have been in August, Mr. Nelson Tacy, a postal inspector, came to my office. He told me, sir, that he had a matter with reference to using the mails for, or mailing obscene literature through the mails. Naturally I was concerned about such a matter.

He said that Mr. Craugh in Worcester also had some evidence in connection with that case, and the two of them were working together; that Mr. Craugh had consulted the office of the United States attorney in Massachusetts in connection with it. I told him that the jurisdictional matter ought to be straightened out, either Massachusetts would handle it or I would handle it, depending upon the postal inspectors and the evidence that they had.

He also asked me if I knew one Calvin Sugarman. I said I did not. He said, "Do you know Calvin Sugarman of Hope Street?" I said, "I do not." I said, "The only Sugarman that I associate with Hope Street is the Max Sugarman Funeral Home on Hope Street in Providence." He said, "Well, that's the one. Calvin is Max Sugarman's son."

I said, "I do not know Calvin, I know Max Sugarman. He is the only Jewish funeral director in the State of Rhode Island." Such members of my family and relatives who have passed away have been buried by Mr. Max Sugarman. As I understand his father before him was a funeral director, and he succeeded his father in that line of endeavor.

He told me that he was having trouble with Calvin Sugarman; that he went over to see him, couldn't get him to come down to the office; called up several times, and Calvin Sugarman just did not come down to the office. I told him that in my opinion what he ought to do is to continue his efforts to see if he could not get Calvin Sugarman down to the office.

Calvin Sugarman finally came down to his office, and as I understand the situation——

Chairman KEFAUVER. Is that the father of Calvin Sugarman you are talking about?

Mr. TEMKIN. I am talking about Calvin Sugarman, sir.

Chairman KEFAUVER. I say, this is the father, Max Sugarman, that you are talking about?

Mr. TEMKIN. No; I am not, sir. I am talking about Calvin Sugarman.

Chairman KEFAUVER. But you were talking with Max, the father?

Mr. TEMKIN. I have not mentioned talking with Max Sugarman. And that's one of the things, sir, that I resent. Not your bringing it up now, but the fact that there has been too hasty a decision by certain individuals in connection with this case. I would like to ring it along in sequence, sir, if I may.

Chairman KEFAUVER. I am just trying to get the facts, sir. You went down to the funeral home and talked to somebody; who was it?

Mr. TEMKIN. What is that, sir? I told Nelson Tacy.

Chairman KEFAUVER. All right, sir.

Mr. TEMKIN. He is the man who came in to see me and asked me about Calvin Sugarman. I told him I didn't know Calvin Sugarman, but I knew his father, the funeral director, the only Jewish one in this State. And I told Tacy to continue his efforts to try to get him down to Tacy's office. And he did continue his efforts to bring him down there.

When he got down there, as I understand it from Mr. Tacy later, the interview was not productive; it was a denial, and my recollection is that there was no signed statement in connection with it.

Mr. Tacy then came to me and said, "We are getting nowheres. We are getting a runaround."

I said, "Well, I told you"—I am talking to Tacy now in my office—"I told you, Mr. Tacy, that I know Max Sugarman. If you feel that I can be of assistance to you I will be glad to do it. I will be glad to talk to Max Sugarman to see if I can prevail upon him to have his son come down to your office"—Tacy's office—"to be interviewed, and to cooperate with the postal authorities."

Mr. Tacy said, "I would be very happy if you did that."

Now, Mr. Max Sugarman had a reputation in this community of deep religious convictions, and I felt that if I spoke to someone with that kind of background he might be persuaded to prevail upon his son to cooperate with the postal authorities.

I wrestled with the problem for a few days, for these reasons. I was asking a man—and, sir, may I mention that I know of no other instance where a United States attorney went out of his way in this manner to assist a Federal agency in the prosecution of a case, and that's why I resent the inferences that have been brought before you with relation to my conduct in this case.

As I say, I wrestled with the problem for a few days because I was going to ask a man to expose his son to what I thought was clear criminal prosecution, or what I was told. Everything that I knew about the case up until that time was the information that Mr. Tacy had given me, and secondly, I had heard that Max Sugarman's days were numbered, that he was suffering from a fatal illness.

I wrestled with that problem, and it is a serious problem. Finally, one Saturday afternoon I reached the conclusion as to how I was going to act and handle this matter. I called up the Max Sugarman Funeral Home and I asked for Mr. Max Sugarman, and he wasn't there. I left my name, I left my telephone number. He called me back later that afternoon at my home, it was a very hot summer's day, and he said, "Mr. Temkin?" I said, "Yes, Mr. Sugarman." He said, "Did you call me?" I said, "Yes. I have a very important matter that I would like to speak to you about."

That's as far as I got. And he said, "Where are you?" And I said, "I am at my home." And he said, "Where do you live?" I said, "387 Coe Avenue, Providence, R. I.," and that is where I was residing at that time.

He said, "I will be right over."

He came to my home in response to my telephone call, and he sat down at one of my chairs—he was an elderly man, I knew he was sick. I had trouble breaking the story to him, as you would or anybody else in my position; but I did break it to him. And I asked him if he knew what his son was doing and whether he understood the involvements that his son was in. And he said, "No," he had no knowledge of it at all. The poor old man broke down in my home. Then I had a job on my hands.

Well, a short time later he left. He came back to my home with another son of his, saying—the son spoke and said he was all upset, he wanted to get more information, he couldn't get it from his father, the father was so upset.

I gave him the information. I wanted him to have his brother Calvin Sugarman go down to the inspector's office and cooperate with him. I made no promises; I know better than that. I was merely trying to be of assistance.

As a result of that situation Calvin Sugarman was down at the cape that weekend. He didn't come home until the following day. And when he came home, his father, as any father would have done, brought him over to my house and he said, "Now you tell Mr. Temkin the whole story." And I refused to listen to it. I said, "You go down to the postal inspectors and tell your story to the postal inspectors."

The next thing that I know, sir, an appointment was made by Mr. Adelson, who represented the Sugarman family, in behalf of Calvin Sugarman, with the postal inspectors, and they went down there, gave their statement. I understand that that statement—and I don't know the contents of the statement, because I have never seen the statement—I understand that statement was dictated for a day and a half, or something like that, was typed off and Calvin Sugarman came in and then signed it.

Then Mr. Tacy came to my office and said, "We got what we wanted, we were stymied up until this point. We couldn't make any progress, we knew certain things but we didn't know everything about this thing, and we didn't have enough on anybody." And he said that in his opinion Mr. Sugarman was telling the whole truth to him.

Now, sir, following that, this is what happened: I had some men in the office, and at that time—although you asked, sir, as to how many assistants there were—I will tell you, sir, that when I came into office there were three assistants. Before long there were only two assistants. The Department of Justice saw fit to eliminate one position in my office.

During the summer of 1954 one of my assistants submitted his resignation, to be effective in the early part of September. Accordingly, from that time on there were just two of us in the office, Mr. Williamson, to whom Mr. Mainelli just referred, and myself.

I had a search of the law made to determine under what sections of the code we could proceed against anybody involved in this case. They were some law clerks whom I had brought into the office that summer.

As I recall the situation, and as I say I am testifying from the best of my recollection, because I have never looked at the file, and that is going to be important to you, sir, in a minute—I had an examination of the law made because I wanted to determine how we could proceed against those who were involved in this particular scheme, which was as repulsive to me then as it is now, and as it has always been to me. We determined other than conspiracy there were 3 sections, then we boiled it down to 2 sections, 1, using the mails to defraud, and the other, mailing obscene literature.

On that particular day Mr. Tacy called me and he said he wanted to come over and see me; and he did. And I thought it was one of the periodic visits he was going to make.

May I interrupt for just one moment. In the course of this investigation there was an account in the Industrial Bank under the name of Dorothy M. Tager. There were checks in that account which at the end of the month, which had gone through clearance, sir, and which at the end of the month would have been returned to Mrs. Tager, the depositor of the account, the drawer of the checks. Mr. Tacy was concerned as to how we could grab those checks, lay our hands on them.

I asked him if he had any experience along those lines, and he said no. Finally, I conceived the idea that we serve a subpena on the bank, returnable before the grand jury, and that's what I did, and that's why those checks are here, I mean in the office of the United States attorney, subject to scrutiny by the grand jury, and that's the only reason we were able to grab them.

Now coming back to the story, where on a particular day Mr. Tacy called me. Mr. Tacy used to come in to my office frequently. When I say frequently, I mean that there was a slight interruption because, as you will recall, sir, on August 31 of 1954 Hurricane Carol paid this section a visit, and this building was closed down for a week.

It was shortly after that Mr. Tacy called me—it may have been the 10th of September or the 13th, something like that—before I say that may I also interject this: Mr. Tacy told me that he had endeavored to interview Mrs. Tager down at Narragansett pier; that he was unable to get any information from her; that he had no confidence in what she had to say; that he didn't believe anything she had to say; that the evidence was against anything that she had said.

In any event, on this particular day Mr. Tacy called me and said he would like to come in and see me, and, sir, at no time, as long as I was United States attorney, did I postpone an appointment with any Federal agent of any bureau which he had with me; my office was always open to any one of them at any time to come in and see me.

Chairman KEFAUVER. Mr. Temkin, nobody has accused you of postponing any engagements.

Mr. TEMKIN. No; but I want to come to the important point.

I told him to come right over. The inference in this particular case at this point, I mean prior to the time of my testimony, was that a case was not brought against a particular individual. I want to explain that, and I am coming to it now.

Mr. Tacy did not come over alone; he came over with Mr. Craugh, the man who testified here at length a short time ago, and one Mr. Simon of the Postal Inspector's Office at Washington. I never met Mr. Simon before.

Mr. Tacy brought in the file, put it down on the side of my desk. He said, "We want you to prepare a complaint against Mrs. Tager. We think she is going to leave the jurisdiction. We want to arrest her."

Up until that point, sir, I had an examination of the law made with a view of bringing prosecution not only against her, but anybody in connection with that case.

I said, "What about Mr. Sugarman?"

And Mr. Simon, who seemed to be the spokesman at that point— I never met Mr. Simon, and I said, "What about Mr. Sugarman?"

And he said, "We have no case against him."

Chairman KEFAUVER. Who was that said that?

Mr. TEMKIN. Mr. Simon, Mr. Tacy, and Mr. Craugh. I make that categorical statement, recognizing that I am under oath when I am making it.

And I said, "Are you sure?"

And they said, "Yes."

I said, "Are you sure that you only want to arrest Mrs. Tager?"

And they said, "Yes."

And I said, "Mr. Simon, what is your experience in this field?"— because at that I had read the circuit court opinions, I think one out in the west coast and one out in the Midwest, in which Mrs. Tager's former husband had been involved, and upon which the circuit courts had turned down prosecution.

He said that this was his speciality, that he traveled all over the country, that he did nothing but this. I think he may have said— I asked him whether he was a lawyer, he may have said he was; I am not sure of that.

But he said, after my questioning, "We have gone over this case thoroughly. There is no need to bring any action against Sugarman because we don't have a case against him. We can't tie him up with the obscene matter, and we don't have a case against him on the other matter."

Whereupon, I prepared the form of complaint for Mr. Tacy to sign. I called the girl in to dictate it, and also the form of warrant which was to be signed by the United States commissioner.

I never saw the file, I never looked at the file, to that point or since that point, and that's also important so far as I am concerned in this case.

Chairman KEFAUVER. Well, sir, why didn't you look at the file?

Mr. TEMKIN. I will come to that. Because I was relying upon these men, and I had every reason to rely on statements of qualified men, or people that I thought was qualified and what is more, sir, it isn't necessary that a Federal agent come to United States attorney to have a form of complaint filled out; it can be filled out by himself before a commissioner and then it can be brought before the court of the United States commissioner, and the United States Attorney's office would represent the Government.

I relied on the statements of those men up until that point. While we were there, until the complaint and warrant were prepared, I said to Mr. Simon, because he appeared to be the spokesman, the man who knew all about this particular type of offense, and he convinced me that he was speaking with authority. I asked him if he had any forms in other jurisdictions, and he said, "Yes," he would send me one; and he did send one later.

I said, "Now, gentlemen, this is the practice of my office. I recognize that an indictment can be brought with any number of counts. With my training as an assistant attorney general in Rhode Island, and my experience in the office of the United States attorney, led me to believe that it was best to follow this policy, that it wasn't necessary to bring every single type of count available; you brought the most important, a reasonable number of the most important counts, and you proceeded on that basis."

And I said, "Gentlemen, while this is fresh in your minds, let me have, and I will jot them down, the most important cases that you feel are the most important and the ones upon which we can establish the guilt of the defendant." And they enumerated some and I jotted them down.

Mrs. Tager in due course was arrested. I appeared in this very room, the United States commissioner, sir, was sitting just where you are. I appeared here in behalf of the Government and asked for bail, proceeded upon a one-count, which was the practice in the office on complaints and warrants, and that was enough for the rest. Bail was set, and I understood that she subsequently furnished the bail.

In my office, as soon as these three gentlemen left, I turned the file over to Mr. Williamson and told him to handle it from there on; I told him what the situation was, what the recommendations of the inspectors were; I told him everything I knew about the case, every fact as I knew it in complete detail; and I turned it over to him to handle.

Now you may ask, sir, at this point if I recognized that this was a serious matter, and I did, why did I assign the case to Mr. Williamson? I think, sir, there is sufficient answer to that. There were two of us in the office at the time, and I am not relying on numbers or lack of assistance as any excuse in this case. I was concerned at that time with matters affecting organized crime in this community, the very thing, sir, that I referred to when I said I was chairman of a committee considering the recommendations of the Kefauver committee, so-called, and not for 1 month or 1 week or 1 day, but for months on end I was concerned with such a matter, and there was publication of that matter in the Evening Bulletin of August 18, 1954, and it concerned what the newspaper described as a one-time public enemy, and that was a racket, and it involved organized crime, and that was one of the matters that I was concerned with. I brought before the grand jury more than 40 witnesses, notwithstanding that there were only 2 of us in the office.

I tried to break them down, and I worked hard on them. There were two sets of transcripts prepared of the evidence produced at that time. One set I sent to the Department of Justice in Washington. I corralled all the agencies around here, the Internal Revenue, the police departments, local and State, the FBI, anybody that had any kind of relationship to a matter of this kind, I called them in my office, I spoke to them, I got information from them.

I brought those people, the witnesses, 40 or more of them, and I didn't take any vacation that summer, I brought them before the grand jury, and I worked hard, and I sent one of those sets of transcripts down to Washington, because they had set up a special unit in the Department of Justice called Organized Crime, and I felt this thing, felt right within the purview of that particular unit.

Unfortunately, we couldn't produce the evidence, and the grand jury returned no indictment.

I will point out, sir, that in my opinion that was the first time that a grand jury in this jurisdiction had remained beyond its ordinary 6-month term. I recognize that under the Federal Rules of Criminal Procedure that a grand jury is in existence for 18 months, but the practice in this jurisdiction is to clean up everything in 6 months for a grand jury and dismiss it. I kept that grand jury in existence for much more than that because I wasn't satisfied to leave that particular case involving organized crime until I was satisfied I couldn't proceed further with it.

Another matter I handled at that time was one—and I had to investigate it, it involved tax evasion by a very notorious bookie in this community. I spent half of the summer trying to get the evidence in that case. Finally, I did get some evidence. I proceeded against him and I convicted him.

I was also concerned with a very serious tax evasion case sent down by New York jurisdiction where they had already received, where an indictment had already been returned in a case involving some $3 million in civil liability, and I took that case and I proceeded to work on it, and I tried that case—there were only 2 of us in the office at the time—I tried that case for 3 weeks, and I was successful in getting a conviction, and there were 40 different types of appeals and other kinds of documents that were filed after that in connection with that case, and I handled them all successfully.

That was why, sir, if I have spoken loudly up to this moment, I have spoken loudly because I resent, and I resent it deeply, any implication arising out of irresponsible statements from anybody.

Now let me proceed further. I think you have a picture of my office at the moment, and what we were doing there. We were handling not only criminal cases but civil cases as well. Two of us, and I am not making an issue of that, because I say we did our work and we did it well; and the results prove it.

Arnold Williamson was in charge of that case. I had nothing to do with it after that unless he wanted to ask me a question. He sat down with the investigators, the inspectors; he prepared with them the list of witnesses, and the witnesses—I am making this statement, sir, so you will know to the best of my recollection every detail where I had any connection with this case.

Chairman KEFAUVER. Are you talking about the Tager case now?

Mr. TEMKIN. I am, sir. That's what I am coming to right now.

Chairman KEFAUVER. All right.

Mr. TEMKIN. I had to tell you, sir, what the situation was in the office. Now I am coming back to the Tager case.

The witness subpenaes, subpenaes duces tecum, for many years in this office were issued over the name of the United States attorney. As it applies to the Tager case, the witness subpenaes were issued over my name. There was somebody out in Michigan who claimed he had a heart condition and couldn't come here. He wrote a letter in to that effect, it was addressed to me, but I didn't know who he was. I asked one of the girls to find out who he was. It was somebody in connection with the Tager case, and I wrote him a firm letter that he had to be here, and he was here.

There was somebody in Philadelphia who wrote in to say that there was a case of mistaken identity. I didn't know the name, because no name meant anything to me in connection with that case. I wasn't handling the details of it. I responded to that letter, after getting the information, I said "There is no case of mistaken identity; that the person to whom the subpena was directed is the person to whom it should have been directed." I said, "You appear here. Otherwise, you will be in contempt of the grand jury"; and he did appear.

I think there was somebody else along the same line.

In due course, the case was presented before the grand jury. Mr. Williamson took up with me the matter of the indictment. I did not recall whether I prepared the indictment or reviewed his draft of the indictment. I will say that during the period of time that I was United States attorney I prepared or reviewed every indictment, every criminal information that was presented in court. This was just for technical accuracy, to see that the indictment, or the information, conformed with the requirements of the statute with relation to charging the offense properly.

The grand jury returned the indictment, and I will tell you, sir, what my policy and practice was. Always present the best and primary evidence to the grand jury; leave it up to them as to whether they feel that an indictment should be returned or not. There were strict instructions to me on that account. There were strict instructions they were to bring in anybody that they thought could contribute to the case, or that the grand jury thought could contribute to the case. Those were my strict instructions. It was the policy that I pursued throughout.

The grand jury returned the indictment. In due course, Mrs. Tager was arraigned.

Before, however, the grand jury met in connection with this case, there was another incident with which I ought to familiarize you, sir. A man by the name of Mr. Brady, who had gone bail on the bond, the commissioner's bond of Mrs. Tager, said that he feared she was going to leave the jurisdiction, and he wanted to be relieved. I gave instructions to Mr. Williamson that we had nothing to do with a commissioner's bail bond, that it was a matter that would have to be taken up with the United States commissioner. That may be a technical point, sir, but I merely point it out to you because it is something I am coming to in a moment.

In due course, she was surrendered, and provisional bail was procured.

I think that the grand jury returned its indictment sometime the latter part of December 1954. I think the first Friday of January 1955 was arraignment day, and this was an open indictment, sir. I think that whatever that date was, she came in along with others to be arraigned. Her counsel was one Norman LaSalle, a lawyer of high repute in this community, who had come into the case on a referral basis from some other attorney, he told me.

In any event, the matter took its natural course. I instructed Mr. Williamson to arrange to send out notices to the defendant, to her counsel, and to the surety on the bond that that case would be tried first on the April calendar, I think it was April 20, the third Wednesday, if I recall it, in the month of April. My reason for setting it down so quickly was because of the nature of the offense and because witnesses would have to be coming from various parts of the country.

A few weeks before that time Mr. LaSalle came to me and said he wouldn't be ready to go on with the case because he couldn't prepare it. Mrs. Tager had left town without any forwarding address, but she had left a note, and that note said, "I am not guilty. A lawyer advised me to leave town," and something to the effect that Sugarman had influence.

When Mr. LaSalle brought that to my attention, Mr. Williamson was with me, and the three of us were in the library of the United States attorney's office, I said, "Now, Norman, did you tell her not to leave?"

He said to me, "Do you think I am crazy?"

I said, "I know you to be a reputable lawyer and I know you wouldn't do it." And I said, "Do you think that the lawyer that referred the case made any such statement?"

He said "No."

And I said, "Mr. Williamson, you inquire about that and get the facts on that from this other attorney"; and Mr. Williamson did. He reported that there wasn't any basis for that at all.

I was troubled by the matter of that accusation of influence, and I sat down and I thought about it, and I took that problem home with me——

Chairman KEFAUVER. Just what was the accusation of influence, Mr. Temkin?

Mr. TEMKIN. I don't recall specifically. The file will indicate precisely what she said. Because later on I gave instructions to go out and get that letter, or that note. Something about the influence of Mr. Sugarman.

I had complete confidence in the postal inspectors, and I knew that they weren't involved in influence, or at least I felt that way. I knew I wasn't involved in influence; I am the one that broke the case against Sugarman. And I had complete confidence in Arnold Williamson, and everybody in my office, and I know that there wasn't any influence.

In any event, when she failed to appear, when she was supposed to appear, I insisted, notwithstanding a long plea by her counsel for a postponement, that we wanted a default in a case like that. And Mr. Williamson, acting upon my instructions, presented that view to Judge Day; default was granted; a bench warrant was issued.

Thereafter, I was concerned about her bail jumping. As you will recall, sir, in August of 1954, as a result of the Communist jumping——

Chairman KEFAUVER. Mr. Temkin, I don't want to cut you short. We have a lot of witnesses to be heard. I want you to take all the time you want, but we are not particularly interested in the details of Mrs. Tager's case. What we want to know is about what happened to Mr. Sugarman. But if you are getting to that, why, all right.

Mr. TEMKIN. That is the case, sir, from then on.

Chairman KEFAUVER. You are talking in some detail about Mrs. Tager.

Mr. TEMKIN. Because there is another reference, and there was introduced as an exhibit just before I testified, a certain document. I think I would like to work up to that point.

Chairman KEFAUVER. All right, sir. What happened to Mrs. Tager? Let's get that out of the way.

Mr. TEMKIN. That's right. I want to state what the situation was at that moment, because of the Communists jumping bail, the Congress of the United States saw fit to make it an offense to jump bail. There was some problem of jurisdiction between the postal inspectors and the FBI on that matter. I called them both in, and I told them I wanted Mrs. Tager, and I didn't care who got her.

I gave immediate instructions to get that note to which I just referred. That note was procured, and I believe by a postal inspector.

On April 30, Mrs. Tager was apprehended out in the west coast.

Now, I recognize that the worst criminal can be truthful at times, and I don't want to discount it. As a prosecutor, I recognize that you have got to rely upon the testimony, sometimes, of people that you wouldn't associate with but who, nevertheless, will bring forth certain points necessary for the success of a trial.

Mrs. Tager made some statements in that statement, made some remarks in that statement, and I have only a vague recollection of them——

Chairman KEFAUVER. That is the affidavit of Mrs. Tager dated April 30, 1955, to which you refer. You saw that affidavit, I take it?

Mr. TEMKIN. Yes; I saw it.

Mr. Egan brought it over to my office, and I told him either to make a copy of it or leave that one with me and I would make a copy, or he would make a copy, one of the two; I wanted a copy, because at that time the case against Mrs Tager had not been concluded.

Chairman KEFAUVER. Did you have a copy of it made? What did you do with the affidavit, Mr. Temkin?

Mr. TEMKIN. What is that, sir?

Chairman KEFAUVER. What action——

Mr. TEMKIN. It was turned over to Mr. Williamson who was handling the case.

Chairman KEFAUVER. You read the affidavit, I take it?

Mr. TEMKIN. Oh, yes.

Chairman KEFAUVER. And that was shortly after it was taken, before she was sentenced; is that correct?

Mr. TEMKIN. That affidavit came in, I don't know, a few weeks after April 30. I couldn't say when. I turned it over to Mr. Williamson. We couldn't proceed under the bail jumping statute because 30 days had not elapsed, which was a requirement under the statute.

Chairman KEFAUVER. Mr. Temkin, the thing that I wanted to ask about in connection with the affidavit, I have it here——

Mr. TEMKIN. I haven t seen it since then.

Chairman KEFAUVER. You saw it then. She recites in a great deal of detail how in all of these matters she was just working for Mr. Sugarman.

Mr. TEMKIN. That's right. And I am going to——

Chairman KEFAUVER. And Mr. Sugarman had the accounts, that he had the drops, and he was the one who had the pictures, and that he was a——

Mr. TEMKIN. That statement doesn't say, however, who the attorney was, or name the attorney who told her to beat it away from Rhode Island. That statement doesn't specify who was subjected to influence, and you read it, sir. This is my recollection.

Chairman KEFAUVER. No. I am just saying that——

Mr. TEMKIN. That's right. Why didn't the statement say that? I would like to know.

Chairman KEFAUVER. Just a minute, Mr. Temkin. The point I am making is that she recites in a great deal of detail how each one of these operations with which she was connected were Mr. Sugarman's operations, that he got the money, that she was just working for him, that he had the printing done, and that he saw about the drops. Sugarman arranged for his own mail drops and selected the various fictitious names that were used in the operation. You had this shortly after April 30.

Mr. TEMKIN. That's right. You want to know what I did with that?

Chairman KEFAUVER. Yes.

Mr. TEMKIN. I saw to it that Mr. Williamson got it. Because at that time when she was returned here, the case against her was not concluded, and it was necessary——

Chairman KEFAUVER. Mr. Temkin, it is your responsibility. You were the District Attorney, were you not?

Mr. TEMKIN. Yes, sir.

Chairman KEFAUVER. And——

Mr. TEMKIN. My responsibility to do what?

Chairman KEFAUVER. Your responsibility to enforce the law.

Mr. TEMKIN. Exactly. And this is the way I did it. I turned it over to Mr. Williamson, who was handling the case. My recollection is that he called in Mr. Sugarman and went over every bit of detail in connection with the case. His conclusion was, and I didn't even see Sugarman in the office, I don't know whether he came there, Mr. Williamson told me that he was there, he had gone over the matter with him, that he still believed Mr. Sugarman was telling the truth.

In due course, Mrs. Tager was sentenced. That is as much as I know about the case, sir.

Chairman KEFAUVER. Did he go over the matter with Mrs. Tager to see whether she had sworn to the truth or not?

Mr. TEMKIN. Who had gone over it with Mrs. Tager?

Chairman KEFAUVER. Mr. Williamson.

Mr. TEMKIN. She was a defendant in the case. How would he go over the case, discuss the case with a defendant, sir? A defendant who was incarcerated at the time.

Chairman KEFAUVER. He went over it with the man for whom she was working, and I just thought——

Mr. TEMKIN. That would be highly improper, sir, for him to do that.

Chairman KEFAUVER. Did he question the affidavit of Mrs. Tager?

Mr. TEMKIN. Did he question it?

Chairman KEFAUVER. Yes; the truthfulness of this affidavit? Did you question the truthfulness of this affidavit?

Mr. TEMKIN. Certainly I questioned it. I questioned it at all times, and for these reasons——

Chairman KEFAUVER. Mr. Temkin——

Mr. TEMKIN. I think you ought to permit me to continue.

Chairman KEFAUVER. I just wanted to make this observation, that her affidavit in fact is almost identical to what these gentlemen have testified on the record; that is, the dates, the names, the amounts of money, the checks.

Did you compare this affidavit with the record that these people had?

Mr. TEMKIN. No, sir; I did not know what the case said. I turned the matter over to Mr. Williamson.

Chairman KEFAUVER. You took the record home 1 night with you?

Mr. TEMKIN. I did?

Chairman KEFAUVER. Yes.

Mr. TEMKIN. Never did, sir.

Chairman KEFAUVER. Let's see. I had a letter here I was just reading.

Mr. TEMKIN. What does it say?

Chairman KEFAUVER. That Mr. Tacy was writing Mr. Simon, I don't know, Mr. Tacy; is this correct?

The United States attorney took all the papers home with him last night, and I have not heard from him since.

September 17, 1954; is that correct?

Mr. TACY. That's correct, if I wrote it, sir. Yes, sir. I wrote the letter to Mr. Simon. That's the way I understood it.

Chairman KEFAUVER. Is that this gentleman here?

Mr. TACY. That's this gentleman right here, sir [indicating Mr. Temkin].

Mr. TEMKIN. I never took that folder home. I never read it. That isn't my letter, sir, and you as an attorney should recognize that there is no value to that statement.

Chairman KEFAUVER. That is what this gentleman said.

Mr. TEMKIN. Well——

Chairman KEFAUVER. In any event, Mr. Temkin——

Mr. TEMKIN. I think that you have to consider the probabilities, sir.

Chairman KEFAUVER. In any event, you were the attorney, you were the district attorney. The file was in your possession, it was in your custody, whether you assigned it out to Mr. Williamson, or whoever you assigned it to, it was your responsibility to do what that file indicated you should do; was it not?

Mr. TEMKIN. Personally, sir?

Chairman KEFAUVER. Well, as district attorney.

Mr. TEMKIN. Certainly. I did what any district attorney would do. I was handling matters, and I assigned the case to him, and he handled the case.

Chairman KEFAUVER. I just want to get this straight. Is it your statement here that nothing was done because Mr. Williamson didn't act?

Mr. TEMKIN. What do you mean, sir?

Chairman KEFAUVER. I mean, are you passing the buck to Mr. Williamson? That's what I want to know.

Mr. TEMKIN. No; I am not passing the buck. But I don't like the inference.

I told you categorically, sir, that when the three inspectors came in to my office, they said they had no case against Sugarman. And I turned the matter over to Mr. Williamson to handle it as a routine matter.

Chairman KEFAUVER. Mr. Temkin——

Mr. TEMKIN. Yes, sir.

Chairman KEFAUVER. Even if they had said that, and we will ask them about that in a minute, you apparently thought you had a case against Mrs. Tager, and you have her affidavit which is at least evidence of what she would testify, of amounts, places, and in which she says Mr. Sugarman was the principal, and she was only working for him.

Mr. TEMKIN. Well, Mr. Williamson was handling the matter. That is April 30. When those gentlemen came into my office, it was the beginning of September 1954. This is April 30, 1955, that the statement was given to which you refer, sir, and which has been introduced as an exhibit in this case.

Chairman KEFAUVER. You were still the district attorney, and you were for 3 months afterward.

Mr. TEMKIN. I certainly was. And the fact that I was in office only 3 months after that didn't mean to say that I didn't continue to work with the same degree of vigor and zeal in behalf of the Government.

Chairman KEFAUVER. All right, sir.

Mrs. Tager got a suspended sentence; is that correct?

Mr. TEMKIN. No. She was put on probation for 2 years.

Chairman KEFAUVER. How did that happen; did she come out here?

Mr. TEMKIN. Yes. She was returned here.

Chairman KEFAUVER. Did you recommend the 2 years, or agree to it?

Mr. TEMKIN. I did not recommend it and I did not agree to it. What happened was that Mr. Williamson, who had been handling the case, spoke with Mr. Normal LaSalle. As a result of that conversation, Mr. Williamson came to me and said, "The facts are these. A first offender. A woman in poor physical condition. I think because she has been in jail for some 2 months that a probation would be a proper disposition."

I said, "That is your recommendation?" And he said, "I want to recommend it."

I said, "You are close to the case. While I personally wouldn't do it, you are close to the case, it is your considered judgment. If you feel that that's what it should be, then I will stand back of you."

Chairman KEFAUVER. Anything else, Mr. Temkin?

Mr. TEMKIN. Not unless you decide to ask me further questions, sir.

Chairman KEFAUVER. Mr. Temkin.

Mr. TEMKIN. Yes, sir.

Chairman KEFAUVER. Mr. Tacy, I believe, had testified that the investigative trial and whatnot was turned over to you on September 16, 1954. Is that about the time?

Mr. TEMKIN. No, sir. That investigative file was put on my desk the day that the three gentlemen came in and the date that the complaint was sworn to. Whatever that date was, that is the date.

He didn't bring in a file subsequent to that time. It was right in the corner of my desk, because—and this, sir, is the verification of it. While the complaint was being typed and the form of warrant, and I asked the gentlemen while the matter was fresh in their minds what were the best cases upon which they could proceed, and I recognize the proceeding under obscene literature is a more serious offense than proceeding under the charge of using the mails to defraud, when it is $5,000 and 5 years in jail, my recollection is that on the other it is 5 years in jail and $1,000 fine——

Chairman KEFAUVER. Mr. Temkin——

Mr. TEMKIN. I want to answer that particular thing.

I told them to let me see the names of the parties upon whom they had the best cases, and they went to the file and they picked out the names, Mr. Morofsky out in Michigan, somebody out in—two people out in New York. One was a drop of the postal department itself out in the Midwest somewhere. I think one was up in the northern part of New England.

I think that when it came down ultimately to Mr. Williamson to dispose of the case, Mr. Williamson moved to dismiss that particular count in which the postal authorities themselves had used a fictitious name.

Now, there is one thing, sir, before I finish, and I would like to comment on it if you will permit me.

Chairman KEFAUVER. All right. You go ahead. I have been trying to be patient.

Mr. TEMKIN. Well, I recognize your patience, sir, but if you were in the same position that I am at the moment, with my background and my record, being called upon to account for this thing here, you would understand the feelings, I am sure you would. You would recognize, sir, that anybody in your position would have to be patient. If I overstepped the bounds, I apologize to you, sir. I don't feel I have.

Chairman KEFAUVER. You talk and take all the time you want.

Mr. TEMKIN. I want to tell you that another matter has come up that I would like to discuss.

The inferences in view of the evidence that has gone in by the three inspectors, there was a violation of the Rhode Island law with the use of trade names, and I will explain that, and I will tell you, sir, as a lawyer, and you will recognize that the letter that was introduced in evidence was a letter addressed to the secretary of state with reference to corporate names, and if you will look at the letter you will see it.

Chairman KEFAUVER. Mr. Temkin, I don't want to interrupt you, but the purpose of this discussion right here and now, I don't think that is part of this particular hearing.

Mr. TEMKIN. But it was brought out, sir, by you and by counsel for the committee.

Chairman KEFAUVER. All right. Go ahead, then.

Mr. TEMKIN. I didn't bring it out.

Chairman KEFAUVER. Say anything about it you want to, sir. You mean you don't think the Rhode Island law applies to this situation?

Mr. TEMKIN. I didn't say that, sir.   I said that the letter that went in was a letter from the secretary of state with reference to a corporate name as distinguished from a fictitious trade name.   And fictitious trade names are not recorded in the office of the secretary of state in this State, but in each town clerk's office or in the recorder of deeds of each city and town.

I told Mr. Tacy when he came to me with that proposition that the only way that you could proceed—and I am talking now as an experienced prosecutor, having been an assistant attorney general of the State of Rhode Island—the only way that you could proceed in that manner is to go to each city and town to see whether any of these names were recorded as names under which Calvin Sugarman, or Dorothy M. Tager, or anybody else operated.

Do I make myself clear, sir?

Chairman KEFAUVER. Yes, sir.

Mr. Temkin, do you or do you not assume responsibility for what Mr. Williamson did with the case?

Mr. TEMKIN. I am the head of the office, sir.   Whatever is done in connection with the matter I recognize is my responsibility as head of that office.   I can't tell it to you any differently. sir.

I am sure that you, as chairman of this subcommittee, also feel the responsibility for what your staff does or does not do in this particular case.

Chairman KEFAUVER. That's right.

Mr. TEMKIN. And as the head of any body or agency, the head must assume the responsibility, and I have got to assume it.

Chairman KEFAUVER. We have that clear.   Now the second question is, when you were securing an indictment against Mrs. Tager, why did you not also secure an indictment against Mr. Sugarman?

Mr. TEMKIN. Mr. Williamson had the file.   If the evidence as he went over it—he was assigned to the case—if the evidence as he went over it warranted the procuring of an indictmnet, I feel confident, and I have confidence in him—and he is sitting right here—that he would have brought it.

Chairman KEFAUVER. All right.   The third question, assuming that the evidence against Mr. Sugarman may have been weak in the beginning, before Mrs. Tager came up for sentence she made an affidavit that she was only working for Mr. Sugarman and that he was the principal. Why were not steps taken then to secure an indictment against him?

Mr. TEMKIN. The grand jury, sir, had met on April 20. The grand jury was in recess. If there was any evidence to proceed against Mr. Sugarman, Mr. Williamson was still in charge of the case, I am sure if he felt that way about it, he would have proceeded against Sugarman.

Chairman KEFAUVER. But, sir, you read the affidavit yourself, and——

Mr. TEMKIN. Well now, just one second.

Chairman KEFAUVER. All right.

Mr. TEMKIN. I want you to understand that I had no knowledge of the details of this case. I admit I read an affidavit, and I don't know what the relevancy is of one statement that she may make or the relevancy of another statement, and I think you, sir, in my position would realize that.

Naturally, you don't know the significance of it, the importance of it, and the relevancy of it. Naturally, you turn it over to the man who is handling the matter. He is familiar with the details, with the facts, and he is the one that would reach a conclusion in connection with it.

Chairman KEFAUVER. I must say, Mr. Temkin, that it would bother me slightly, I think, if I had a woman up for sentence and before she was sentenced, filed an affidavit, if I had that affidavit from her that she was only working for a person who did all these operations and I was recommending that she be sentenced without doing anything about the principal, I must confess that would bother me a good deal.

Mr. TEMKIN. Does there say anything in that statement, sir, that she is not guilty?

Chairman KEFAUVER. Well, she is——

Mr. TEMKIN. Does there? I don't have it.

Chairman KEFAUVER. She admits her guilt. But she gives the details of how he got the money, the bank account was opened in his name, that he arranged his own mail drops, selected the various fictitious names which were used in the operations.

Mr. TEMKIN. Did she say that she is guilty or not guilty?

Chairman KEFAUVER. The main thing she did was stuff envelopes for him.

Mr. TEMKIN. Did she say, sir, that she was guilty or not guilty?

Chairman KEFAUVER. She states the facts.

Mr. TEMKIN. Is there any conclusion about the guilt?

Chairman KEFAUVER. She doesn't say "I am guilty" or "I am not guilty." She just told how it started.

Mr. TEMKIN. May I, sir, just glance at it for a moment?

Chairman KEFAUVER. Yes; read it over [handing].

It is not for people to come in and say "I am guilty" or "I am not guilty." When facts are presented to the district attorney——

Mr. TEMKIN. Yes; but when she appeared before you, sir, out in Los Angeles, she said she was not guilty. Nonetheless, she pleaded guilty in this court, in this very building. If she was not guilty, why did she plead guilty?

Chairman KEFAUVER. Anyway, she states certain facts there.

Mr. TEMKIN. You are assuming, sir, that what she says here, sir, are necessarily facts. I wouldn't reach that conclusion.

Chairman KEFAUVER. I don't know whether they are facts or not. But she made an affidavit and she apparently testified.

Mr. TEMKIN. Yes; but you have to understand the person with whom you are dealing, And that's why I am bringing out——

Chairman KEFAUVER. I don't want to argue with you. These gentlemen have bank accounts, bank checks, deposits, which coincide exactly with what she said. They are in their possession right here now. They were in your possession then.

Mr. TEMKIN. Yes. But what of it, if these men came in and said they had no case, I had every reason to rely on their recommendation.

Chairman KEFAUVER. Then at that point let's hear from these gentlemen for a while.

Mr. Simon, you come around here a minute, please, sir; and come around, Mr. Tacy.

TESTIMONY OF HARRY J. SIMON, N. A. TACY, AND E. A. CRAUGH

Chairman KEFAUVER. Mr. Simon, tell how long you have been in the Post Office Department, something about your background.

Mr. SIMON. I have been connected with the Post Office Department in the Inspection Service since November 1925, and since January 16, 1941, as a postal inspector.

Chairman KEFAUVER. 1941 as a postal inspector?

Mr. SIMON. Yes, sir.

Chairman KEFAUVER. And you gentlemen have given your backgrounds, I believe.

Now, Mr. Simon, was this case brought to your attention that we are involved in here? Just tell what you know about this case and what recommendations, if any, did you make, what did you do about it.

Mr. SIMON. My first information about this investigation came from Inspector Craugh, who was investigating one of these, I think it was the Adams or Carter operation in Worcester, Mass.

I also learned then that Mr. Tacy and Mr. La Vault were handling cases involving similar operations, and they had reason to think that they were being handled by the same individual.

I came up to Providence in September 1954 at the request of the Chief Inspector to act in an advisory capacity with these inspectors who were investigating the Dorothy Tager operation in this area.

The main reason for coming up here——

Chairman KEFAUVER. In September at that time did they have their investigation completed and the file was finished up?

Mr. SIMON. Yes. When I came up here, their investigations were complete, I believe, except for the report to the United States attorney.

Meanwhile, I had also had some correspondence, I think, from Mr. Tacy with respect to proceeding against some of these names under an unlawful order through the Solicitor's Office. I assisted them in every way possible because of my experience in handling this type of case.

Chairman KEFAUVER. You did what?

Mr. SIMON. I assisted them in preparing their case for the Solicitor for the Post Office Department from an unlawful order standpoint, that is, with respect to denying them the use of the mails.

Chairman KEFAUVER. Did you go to see Mr. Temkin about it?

Mr. SIMON. Yes. On September 10, I believe it was, I accompanied Mr. Tacy and Mr. Craugh to Mr. Temkin's office, and we discussed the facts in the case. It is my recollection that Mr. Temkin asked my advice in the matter.

I told him that it wasn't our function to make any recommendations to the United States attorney, but on the basis of the information that I gathered from these inspectors I felt that we had a very strong case on the obscene standpoint, because you didn't have to prove intent.

Chairman KEFAUVER. Are you talking about a strong case against Mr. Sugarman?

Mr. SIMON. I mentioned that we had a case against Mr. Sugarman on the basis of fraud, unless they could show that they had made some effort to furnish the pictures.

On the basis of my past experience with Dorothy Tager, she had always furnished pictures, and I was familiar with her operations running back to about 1949, I believe it was, and we had any number of proceedings in Washington, to deny them the use of the mails.

I was also instrumental in getting indictments returned against Louis Tager, the former husband of Dorothy Tager, and Roy J. Ross, in three different jurisdictions. And we had no complaints at that time of failure to furnish merchandise.

I felt that Sugarman was strongly involved in this case on the basis of the evidence, in the possession of the inspectors but I made no recommendation to Mr. Temkin as to whether or not he should proceed on fraud or obscenity; I merely express that point, I thought he should be aware or familiar with the possibility, point of intent in a fraud case, with which I was thoroughly familiar.

Chairman KEFAUVER. So I understand it, you said you presented the matter, that you thought this was a strong case, but it was not your province to try to make a recommendation as to what he would do about it, how he would proceed?

Mr. SIMON. I felt that Sugarman was involved in this very deeply on the basis of what evidence these inspectors had gathered, and I further suggested to Mr. Temkin that we also include the entire chain of letters in the indictment so as to bring in Sugarman.

Chairman KEFAUVER. Was that done?

Mr. SIMON. No, sir. I understand—well, I came up, there were two visits I made up here to Providence. The first time was this discussion with Mr. Temkin. The second time he asked me to come up to assist in preparing the indictment, and Mr. Temkin at that time, it was about the middle of December, as I recall, Mr. Temkin in my presence dictated the indictment to a stenographer in the presence of two other assistant attorneys in his office, I don't recall who they were at this time.

Chairman KEFAUVER. When you had your conference in the beginning about it, did you recommend that Mr. Sugarman be brought into the case?

Mr. SIMON. I made no recommendation one way or the other. Mr. Temkin——

Chairman KEFAUVER. But you asked that all the letters be included so as to include his being in the case?

Mr. SIMON. Yes. That would necessarily have included Mr. Sugarman as a defendant had those entire chain of letters been included in the indictment.

Chairman KEFAUVER. Have you at all times felt and so stated that you had a strong case against Mr. Sugarman?

Mr. SIMON. I mentioned it to the inspectors. I had correspondence with Mr. Craugh I think back in August. And I think back at that time I told him that if we could get a United States attorney to prosecute a failure to furnish merchandise in this type of case, the thing to do would be to get a warrant in he will go along with it.

Chairman KEFAUVER. You heard Mr. Temkin say that he didn't proceed because you said just as positively you didn't have any case; is that correct?

Mr. SIMON. I have no recollection of ever having made any such statement to Mr. Temkin. I merely advised him about this point of intent and related——

Chairman KEFAUVER. Mr. Simon, with your feeling about it, would you have suggested or indicated that you did not have any case against Mr. Sugarman?

Mr. SIMON. No, sir.

Chairman KEFAUVER. Was it ever so indicated by any of you?

Mr. SIMON. No, sir. I have no recollection of any of these inspectors ever indicating they had no case against Sugarman.

Chairman KEFAUVER. Mr. Tacy, is that correct?

Mr. TACY. That is substantially as Mr. Simon stated.

Chairman KEFAUVER. Were you there?

Mr. TACY. I was there.

Chairman KEFAUVER. Did you ever recommend that you did not have a case against Sugarman?

Mr. TACY. No; I did not, sir.

Chairman KEFAUVER. Is your feeling, too, that he was deeply involved in the matter?

Mr. TACY. I wrote the United States attorney a résumé of the case under date of September 16, and submitted the exhibits with that report, and stated in it, or stressed in it the continuity of the scheme from the first mail drop, the Adams drop—they run in alphabetical order, you will note—down to the Wallis drop. And that's all we could do under our instructions, to present the evidence to him for his decision.

Chairman KEFAUVER. You have here a copy of the letter you wrote. This is the Post Office Department. Then you wrote the other division. You sent a letter up here outlining the whole thing?

Mr. TACY. I sent a letter to my inspector in charge—no; I sent a letter to the United States attorney; I am sorry.

Chairman KEFAUVER. Yes, sir; and you said in pretty plain words that you thought you had a strong fraud case?

Mr. TACY. I expressed the continuity of the schemes; yes, sir.

Chairman KEFAUVER. Mr. Craugh, is that your feeling?

Mr. CRAUGH. That's right. In that letter we include some names of people who had not received the Wallis circular containing the obscene picture, in other words, to show the continuity up to that point.

Chairman KEFAUVER. So none of you gentlemen said anything or gave any indication that you did not have any case against Mr. Sugarman; is that correct?

Mr. TACY. That is correct, Senator.

Mr. CRAUGH. Yes, sir.

Mr. SIMON. Yes, Senator.

Chairman KEFAUVER. Is that your opinion, Mr. Simon?

Mr. SIMON. That is correct.

Chairman KEFAUVER. And you have heard Mr. Temkin testify here that he did not proceed, among other things, because you told him you did not have a case; is that correct?

Mr. TACY. No, sir.

Chairman KEFAUVER. That is not the case; is that the case, Mr. Simon, or not?

Mr. SIMON. That is not the case, as Mr. Temkin testified.

Chairman KEFAUVER. And you, Mr. Tacy?

Mr. TACY. That is not the case as I understand it, sir.

Chairman KEFAUVER. Mr. Craugh?

Mr. CRAUGH. That is not the case.

Chairman KEFAUVER. Thank you very much, gentlemen.

Let me ask this further question. Did anything change the case you had back in September 1954, when the whole file was turned over and the case that was presented to the grand jury the other day, or November 5, on which an indictment of 21 or 22 counts was secured? Is it the same case now as it was then?

Mr. SIMON. I might say it is much stronger, then, because up to this time there has been no merchandise furnished.

Chairman KEFAUVER. There wasn't then, either?

Mr. SIMON. No, sir.

Chairman KEFAUVER. So it is the same case?

Mr. SIMON. Yes, sir; to that extent.

Chairman KEFAUVER. Thank you, gentlemen.

Mr. Temkin, I would like to ask you, what has changed the case between September and November of this year?

Mr. TEMKIN. September of 1954, sir, and this year?

Chairman KEFAUVER. Yes.

Mr. TEMKIN. The statement of Mr. Simon, just now, and you as an attorney, sir, would recognize two things——

Chairman KEFAUVER. Mr. Temkin, just 1 minute, now.

Mr. Simon is a career man, and I don't think he would have any particular motive in saying anything evil about you.

Mr. TEMKIN. I am not talking about motive, because I told you, sir, that I had confidence in the postal inspectors, and I relied on their recommendation.

But Mr. Simon just now said that they could not establish that no merchandise was not sent to these various people that ordered it, and therefore, if you couldn't establish that, you couldn't establish one of the elements, which was obtaining money under false pretenses, and if merchandise was sent, then there was no case. And he made that statement just now.

Chairman KEFAUVER. Mr. Temkin, you laid great stress that they recommended that they didn't have a case.

Mr. TEMKIN. Precisely. And he said it just now, when he said he didn't know whether merchandise had been sent.

Chairman KEFAUVER. Mr. Temkin, they said just the opposite.

Mr. TEMKIN. Well, sir, I respectfully disagree, and I dispute that conclusion. I would like to have the record read on that.

Chairman KEFAUVER. We will ask him to come back again. Come back, Mr. Simon.

Mr. TEMKIN. I think, sir, that the record ought to be read, never mind Mr. Simon.

Chairman KEFAUVER. Mr. Temkin, I am running this hearing.

Mr. TEMKIN. I understand, sir, and I don't want to be disrespectful; and I apologize if I appear to be that way.

Chairman KEFAUVER. Mr. Temkin has disputed your word as to what you said, whether you stated you did not have a case back in September 1954 against Mr. Sugarman. Did you tell him that you did not have a case against him?

Mr. SIMON. I positively did not.

Chairman KEFAUVER. Your recommendation and your feelings were exactly the other way?

Mr. SIMON. Yes, sir. I made no recommendations as to what should or should not be done.

Chairman KEFAUVER. Did you feel you had a strong case against Mr. Sugarman?

Mr. SIMON. What is that?

Chairman KEFAUVER. Did you feel you had a strong situation against Sugarman at that time?

Mr. SIMON. Yes; on the basis of what evidence we had. But I was talking to Mr. Temkin about Dorothy Tager's background and her past experience with her, and mentioned the point of intent. I did not express myself, and we did not, that we did not have a case against Sugarman, because I felt he should be involved.

Chairman KEFAUVER. But on this intent matter you were talking about Dorothy Tager?

Mr. SIMON. Yes. I was referring back to the experience with Dorothy Tager in the past.

Chairman KEFAUVER. She had usually sent the pictures?

Mr. SIMON. Yes. We had no complaints with the thousands of circulars she had mailed out——

Chairman KEFAUVER. You were talking about her past, you were not talking about Sugarman's past?

Mr. SIMON. I knew nothing about Sugarman until this case.

Chairman KEFAUVER. Thank you again, Mr. Simon.

Mr. TEMKIN. Sir, may I point out, I don't want to cross-examine Mr. Simon, because that is your prerogative, and this is not that kind of a hearing. I would like to have produced by the postal inspectors any document where they called, asked me why I didn't proceed against Sugarman.

The reason I say that, sir, is, I want to point out something in connection with the practice in the United States attorney's office. At any time a matter is presented to the United States attorney where a party is involved, the postal inspectors want a letter from the United States attorney for their records that prosecution was declined, and I defy them to produce such a letter, if that was the case in connection with Mr. Sugarman.

And now, sir, this statement here, and I am referring to the statement of April 30:

I can positively state—

and this is the statement of Mrs. Tager—

I can positively state that the negatives I sold Sugarman were the strictly art photo type. I did not sell him any that are of the pornographic type. I never handle any of the pornographic or real obscene kind.

Well, why did she plead guilty? That's what I am arguing with you about, sir, and I want to press my point on that. If she was not guilty she said she had nothing to do with obscene literature, why did she plead guilty then?

Chairman KEFAUVER. If you had this, why didn't you hear the evidence and prosecute her for perjury?

Mr. TEMKIN. Pardon, sir?

Chairman KEFAUVER. I say, if you thought that he or she was making a false affidavit, why didn't you prosecute her for perjury?

Mr. TEMKIN. Senator, she was a troubled woman, and I say that, if you will bear with me for a few minutes, sir, the inspectors told me they could not rely on her information. She was a sick woman. She had her own children—this is from the inspectors—mailing this sort of stuff out. She had her own children's friends mailing this sort of stuff out. Before the case came on for trial a Mrs. Mostin came into the office. She and her attorney came into the office complaining that Mrs. Mostin's children were taken by Mrs. Tager somewhere, and she didn't know where they were, and Mrs. Tager wasn't a fit person.

Chairman KEFAUVER. It is a heinous situation to get someone to mail out this sort of literature.

Mr. TEMKIN. Absolutely. And to have your own children do it.

Chairman KEFAUVER. Isn't that what she said that Mr. Sugarman was doing to her?

Mr. TEMKIN. Mr. Sugarman was what?

Chairman KEFAUVER. Getting her to mail out this literature. That is what she says in her affidavit.

Mr. TEMKIN. She is not a person to be believed. I am giving you the background of this woman.

Chairman KEFAUVER. No; but the proof that she has, the documentary proof. Here is a check, Mr. Temkin. What more proof do you ever want to the operation of this Adams thing? Here is the check [exhibiting]. Signed by Adams and endorsed by Sugarman.

Mr. TEMKIN. May I explain it, sir?

Chairman KEFAUVER. Yes.

Mr. TEMKIN. When the inspectors came to me they told me the only drop upon which there was any obscene literature was G. Wallis. All this other stuff apparently, all these other drops referred to mailable material.

Now, as I understand it from the inspectors, what happened was this: Sugarman opened up certain drops, as testified to by these gentlemen. Others received orders. G. Wallis, using the Mrs. Tager alias G. Wallis, as we had the information from the inspectors, used the names that came in for this mailable material, apparently, and sent out this filth, and the only drop, according to my recollection of the testimony, the evidence that the inspectors gave me, was the G. Wallis drop, that she was the only one connected with it.

Chairman KEFAUVER. All right. Is there anything else you have, Mr. TEMKIN?

Mr. TEMKIN. No, sir. I want to say, finally, that I stand ready at any time, here or in Washington, or elsewhere, if you feel you want additional evidence in connection with this matter, to submit it to you, because I feel so strongly about it.

On my record, on my background, to be called here, I deeply resent it, and I defy the postal inspectors to produce a letter from me, or anybody in my office, declining prosecution so far as Sugarman is concerned. I defy them to do that. And that's practice.

Chairman KEFAUVER. All right, Mr. Temkin. These gentlemen of the Post Office Department are doing their duty.

Mr. TEMKIN. I know it, and so was I. I want you to recognize it.

Chairman KEFAUVER. I still don't understand the testimony.

Mr. TEMKIN. I think, sir, that you ought to consider this.

Chairman KEFAUVER. Just a minute. I just want to ask you, are there any other reasons why you did not bring, present to the grand jury the facts on Mr. Sugarman?

Mr. TEMKIN. Mr. Williamson had this case. If he felt——

Chairman KEFAUVER. I am not talking about him, I am talking about you, sir. Are there any other reasons why you didn't?

Mr. TEMKIN. Well, yes.

Chairman KEFAUVER. What are they?

Mr. TEMKIN. I have already explained them. I told you what I was doing at the time.

Chairman KEFAUVER. Besides what you have explained?

Mr. TEMKIN. I am only one person, sir.

Chairman KEFAUVER. I must say, Mr. Temkin, your explanation is highly unsatisfactory to me.

Mr. TEMKIN. It may be unsatisfactory to you, sir, but I will tell you, and I will publicly state that when I was in the office of the United States attorney not less than 14 hours a day was spent by me in that office in connection with that work. Saturdays and Sundays included. And you have no right, sir, to say to me that you dispute it.

Cnairman KEFAUVER. I don't dispute it——

Mr. TEMKIN. Because I think you ought to examine the facts and look at the record. When you do you will be satisfied. You say now, sir, you are not satisfied.

I want to say, sir, I recognize this hearing. I recognize I am appearing before a Senate committee. And if I may go on to a tangent, sir, you may be the President of the United States. You are going to be looked up to as a fair individual. And if you are President, I hope that that fairness will carry through. And if you have the reputation for being fair——

Chairman KEFAUVER. Mr. Temkin, just a minute. You have gone mighty far afield. I am not a candidate for any office, and I am not here as such. We have been running this investigation for about 2 years now, and this is a matter that came up in California. I am here as a result of the revelations in California.

Mr. TEMKIN. Precisely. And I ask you, sir, to get all the facts in the case, and that's why I appeared before you, sir. I could have stood behind a cloak and refused to testify; I didn't do it.

Chairman KEFAUVER. All right, Mr. Temkin. That is all for now. Mr. Williamson, do you want to have something to say?

STATEMENT OF ARNOLD WILLIAMSON, ASSISTANT UNITED STATES ATTORNEY

Mr. WILLIAMSON. The hour is getting late, Senator. I don't know how long you intend to sit here this evening.

Chairman KEFAUVER. We had intended to go home tonight.

Mr. WILLIAMSON. My statement will be very brief and to the point.

Of course you can appreciate, as a United States Senator, that every criminal or every defendant is innocent when he appears before the court, and——

Chairman KEFAUVER. Mr. Williamson, the present district attorney made a point that you might be called on to testify to handle this case. I don't want to embarrass you.

The main thing I want to know is, was Mr. Temkin responsible for this case and what did you do with his consent, and were you acting for him in what you did in connection with this case?

Mr. WILLIAMSON. Sir, I will have to answer you in this manner: As I started to say, every defendant who appears before a court in this country is presumed to be innocent until proven guilty. There is a present indictment against the gentleman who is sitting in this courtroom today, presently pending before the United States district court for this district.

You may be acquainted, Senator, with the case of Dennis W. Delaney——

Chairman KEFAUVER. Yes; I am acquainted with it.

Mr. WILLIAMSON. The former internal revenue district collector for the district of Massachusetts, who was discharged by President Truman in 1951 because of certain failures of his in office, and that case was recently reviewed, or I should say in 1952 it was reviewed by the First Circuit Court in this district, and Judge Frank Magruder, who is an outstanding jurist, commented there upon certain of the dangers that occurred during the course of the investigative committee's hearing immediately subsequent to the indictment of Mr. Delaney. And you will recall, Senator, that the district court——

Chairman KEFAUVER. I have the case here, Mr. Williamson. Go ahead, though.

Mr. WILLIAMSON. Thank you, Senator.

You will recall, Senator, that defense counsel in that case presented several motions to the district court, presided over by Judge Wyzansky, and that the court denied those motions, and the defendant went to trial, and the defendant was found guilty by the district court.

An appeal was taken to the First Circuit Court of Appeals in this district, and the circuit court, in a brilliant decision by Judge Magruder some time in 1952, overturned the district court's finding and remanded the case to the district court.

Here again, Senator, we have the groundwork laid where we have almost an identical situation. The Government——

Chairman KEFAUVER. Mr. Williamson, let me ask you right at that point. Our investigators have been up here working on this matter for several weeks. After the hearing had been set, why, then, last week an indictment was brought about. Of course on that basis I suppose any hearing like this, you would just call it off, whether there had been a dereliction of duty or not, by the final bringing of an indictment.

Mr. WILLIAMSON. I think Judge Magruder in his decision handled that situation very well, Mr. Senator, by indicating that those hearings before the Senate subcommittee could have been held in closed session; but that is not my point, Senator.

I wish to comment and continue my statement for the purposes of clarifying the record, and merely state this, that it is not only the duty of the Justice Department to prosecute the criminals, not only in this district, but throughout the United States, but it is also the duty of each and every United States attorney, and his assistants, and it is spelled out in the United States Attorney's Manual, that they must see that fair play and justice is done to not only the defendant but everyone.

Until this man who is seated in the courtroom with his two counsel appear before Judge Day for trial, we cannot presume as to whether or not he is guilty or innocent. Our Constitution and our American heritage sets out clearly what his rights are. And we presume he is an innocent man.

Chairman KEFAUVER. Just a minute——

Mr. WILLIAMSON. Please, Senator.

Chairman KEFAUVER. No one doubts that. The only question is, presenting a matter to a grand jury, for a grand jury to say whether there is a probable cause or not, that is not trying to adjudge the man. I don't want to get into any details with you, Mr. Williamson, other than what you want to get into, but simply to ask you whether what you did was with Mr. Temkin's counsel or direction, whether you were following his advice, whether you were acting for him or not?

Mr. WILLIAMSON. Senator, prefaced by the statements—I am saying this very respectfully to you, sir, and very humbly—prefaced by the statements that I have made, and in view of the findings and the publicity that may be given this hearing, this man's rights in our Federal court may be seriously in jeopardy. He may have been seriously prejudiced here in this hearing today. Many of the key witnesses who would necessarily have to appear in trial have testified before you today, and have laid bare the Government's case before these two gentlemen here [indicating], who are counsel for the defendant.

Chairman KEFAUVER. That might help them. They know what the Government's case is.

Mr. WILLIAMSON. It may help the defendant, Senator, but I respectfully submit that it may defeat the very purpose that your committee is attempting to do, and that is to prosecute successfully, I presume, a crime of this type. And in view——

Chairman KEFAUVER. Just a minute. You misunderstand our purpose here, sir.

Mr. WILLIAMSON. Well, I may misunderstand——

Chairman KEFAUVER. Our purpose here is we want to put a stop to this passing around of pornographic literature in the United States.

Mr. WILLIAMSON. Senator, I——

Chairman KEFAUVER. This business of sending out this sort of stuff and hiring many names and drops, and trying to get around the mail statute, has had a very deleterious effect upon the youth of our Nation. It is a nationwide operation; we have seen it in this very case, the relationship between this man and Mrs. Tager. And when district attorneys are not doing their duty in at least presenting to a grand jury the kind of thing we have had described here today, we want to find out why. That is why we are here.

Mr. WILLIAMSON. Senator, I can only add this to my comments that I have already stated. I am under instructions from the United States attorney for this district not to testify before this committee relative to the present indictment, and that is a secret indictment that is pending in the United States district court for this district.

For the record, as to your inquiry, I can merely add that I found Mr. Temkin to be a very vigorous prosecutor. I deemed it an honor to work under him. I know that he went to great lengths and worked all hours of the night and day and Saturdays and Sundays, if necessary, to stamp out all possible crime in this area.

He had a tremendous backlog of cases, both criminal and civil, when he came into office. He removed that backlog, and our calendar is current.

I also, Senator, have a congratulatory letter from you with reference to matters pertaining to the use of narcotics, and I only can add, Senator——

Chairman KEFAUVER. That's right. I remember it very well.

Mr. WILLIAMSON. Thank you, sir.

Chairman KEFAUVER. Let me ask you, Mr. Williamson——

Mr. WILLIAMSON. I would like to just point the situation, Senator.

Chairman KEFAUVER. Go ahead.

Mr. WILLIAMSON. That that matter of narcotics, not merely 1 case, but 2 cases, 1 case involved 5 defendants and the other case a single defendant, came into our office in November of 1954. The grand jury sat, an indictment was returned, the requests of the defendants who were languishing in jail without bail, a trial was held, and the three defendants in that case were found guilty after trial which I handled myself. One of the defendants who went to trial received a maximum sentence of 5 years under the act, and the other 2 defendants received the minimum sentence under the act of 2 years.

The other case, the defendant desired to plead subsequent to the trial of other narcotics cases. He entered a plea, and he received the 2-year minimum sentence.

I can only press upon you once again, Senator, the fact that Mr. Temkin and I, during a good part of the year 1954, were alone in that office. We had a tremendous amount of work. We worked to the highest degree of our capacity. It was always my attitude and his that we should present every case to a grand jury fairly, and let the grand jury determine what the facts were.

The witnesses who have testified here today testified before the grand jury. Other than that, Senator, I cannot add any further statements because, as I say, I am under instructions from the United States attorney for this district, and if you wish to ask any questions pertaining to the file, or any other questions pertaining to my position here, I humbly suggest that you address them to the United States attorney, Mr. Joseph Mainelli.

Chairman KEFAUVER. Just this question: Mr. Temkin was a man responsible for the running of the office of the district attorney, is that correct, at the time this matter happened?

Mr. WILLIAMSON. Well, Mr. Temkin was the United States attorney, as he stated; yes, sir.

Chairman KEFAUVER. He was the responsible official in charge of the office; is that correct?

Mr. WILLIAMSON. He was in charge of the office; yes, sir.

Chairman KEFAUVER. Did you get the indictment here the other day, Mr. Williamson?

Mr. WILLIAMSON. I beg your pardon, Senator?

Chairman KEFAUVER. Did you present the matter to the grand jury the other day; was it you that did it?

Mr. WILLIAMSON. I don't think that that is a proper question, Senator. I think that is a question that Mr. Mainelli can answer. I think the press reported his name as being the party who presented it, and I don't think it is proper proceeding now to inquire as to what went on before that grand jury matter.

Chairman KEFAUVER. I am not asking you what went on. I just wondered if you had a case to present to the grand jury last week, what was the difference between them and last June?

Mr. WILLIAMSON. I don't know as there was any difference, Senator. I think that clearly Mr. Simon indicated here that, if anything, the case would be stronger now as to fraud. Now, I can't add any more to that, Senator.

Chairman KEFAUVER. All right. That is all right, Mr. Williamson.

Mr. WILLIAMSON. Thank you, very much.

Chairman KEFAUVER. May I ask the court officials, the bailiff and the marshal, and also you gentlemen and ladies of the press; we are going to have to go on about 2 hours more. Would you prefer, say, to come back at 7:30 and carry on then, or carry on now?

Mr. TEMKIN. May I ask a question, sir?

Chairman KEFAUVER. Very well, sir.

Mr. TEMKIN. I would like to know whether I am dismissed and the matters that you are going to consider later are matters in connection with this case or other matters?

Chairman KEFAUVER. I will tell you what. Counsel advises me that he does not think that the other witnesses bear on the matter we have been discussing. If that does happen and anyone starts to have anything to say about it, we will defer the matter until you can be here to be present.

Mr. TEMKIN. I didn't get the last part, sir.

Chairman KEFAUVER. I say, if any witnesses do start to discuss the matter about which you have been talking, we will ask them to defer it until we can notify you so you can be present.

Mr. TEMKIN. I will leave word with counsel where I am.

Chairman KEFAUVER. Very well. Suppose we stand in recess until——

Mr. CHESTER. May I, Senator. I represent a man who is under summons. I have been sitting here all day hoping he would be called. I am here to report that he can't be here because he is in the hospital. He was operated on yesterday, he is in the Miriam Hospital. I refer to Chester Szlashta.

Chairman KEFAUVER. What was he operated on for?

Mr. CHESTER. He was operated on for a hernia, I understand. His doctor is Dr. Migliaccio, of 196 Broadway, in Providence. He was admitted to the hospital Sunday and operated on yesterday.

Chairman KEFAUVER. Do you have the doctor's certificate?

Mr. CHESTER. No. I have been waiting for that. I called last night and talked with the nurse, and she said it would be in the mail. It hasn't been in the mail. But I can't——

Chairman KEFAUVER. You were served last week. It would seem that if you had some matter like this, he might have put it off until after the hearing.

Mr. CHESTER. I can't explain that, Senator. I am here only to report what I have been asked to report by this man.

Chairman KEFAUVER. What hospital do you say he is in?

Mr. CHESTER. Miriam Hospital.

Chairman KEFAUVER. When did he go to the hospital?

Mr. CHESTER. I understand he went to the hospital Sunday.

Mr. CHUMBRIS. What is your name, sir?

Mr. CHESTER. My name is Benjamin C. Chester. I am a partner of Crowe & Heatherington, 255 Main Street, Pawtucket.

Mr. CHUMBRIS. Do you know of your own knowledge that he received a subpena on the 2d day of November?

Mr. CHESTER. I have the subpena here with a return of the deputy marshal. It doesn't say what day he received it.

Of my own knowledge, no, I don't know.

Mr. CHUMBRIS. When were you retained by Mr. Szlashta?

Mr. CHESTER. I personally was not retained. He is an employee of a company in Pawtucket that is represented by Mr. Crowe, and the employer of the man called Mr. Crowe, I would say Sunday or Monday.

Chairman KEFAUVER. It looks like, sir, he just went to the hospital to get out of coming down here.

Mr. CHESTER. That, sir——

Chairman KEFAUVER. If he thinks he is going to get by with that, you tell him he is badly mistaken. He will remain under subpena and he will be heard.

Mr. CHESTER. All right. I will report that, Senator. But I didn't want to have to come back after the recess.

Chairman KEFAUVER. All right.

We will stand in recess until 7:30, and we will try to finish in about an hour and a half.

(Whereupon, at 6:10 p. m., a recess was taken until 7:30 p. m.)

EVENING SESSION

Chairman KEFAUVER. The subcommittee will come to order.

I want to apologize for inconveniencing so many people here by having a night session, but I have a hearing in the morning with Senator O'Mahoney on the monopoly problem affecting General Motors which I promised to be back for in the morning; so we have no alternative.

It is our policy to give anyone whose name has been mentioned an opportunity to be heard if they want to. I know that Mr. Sugarman is here. I am not going to require him to testify in view of the situation, but I did want him to know that if he had anything to say and he wanted to say it, that he had an opportunity to do so.

Mr. SUGARMAN. I decline under the fifth amendment, sir.

Chairman KEFAUVER. What is that? Mr. Sugarman, come around
Let's identify you. You have been subpenaed. For future reference,
you have been subpenaed and you will continue under subpena.

You are going to make some statements, so I guess you might as
well be sworn. Will you hold up your right hand.

Do you swear the testimony you give will be the whole truth, so
help you God?

Mr. SUGARMAN. I do.

Mr. ADELSON. Mr. Senator, may I make a statement? I am the
attorney for Mr. Sugarman.

Chairman KEFAUVER. Yes, indeed, sir.

Mr. CHUMBRIS. Will you please give your name and your address
for the record?

Mr. ADELSON. My name is Joseph E. Adelson.

Chairman KEFAUVER. Let the record show that Mr. Adelson is a
practicing attorney for the past 28 years.

Mr. ADELSON. Correct, Senator.

Chairman KEFAUVER. And that Mr. Adelson and I went to law
school together at Yale Law School a long, long time ago. I don't
think I have seen you until today.

Mr. ADELSON. That is correct, sir.

Chairman KEFAUVER. We were in the same class.

Mr. ADELSON. Our paths haven't crossed until today.

Chairman KEFAUVER. That was a fine class we had. Former
Senator Brien McMahon from Connecticut; Judge Joe J. Smith,
who is a United States judge in Connecticut; Herbert Brownell, who
is our Attorney General; and many, many others. So it is good to
see you again, Joe.

Mr. ADELSON. Thank you very much. It is good to see you.

Chairman KEFAUVER. We will go from the friendly side to the
legal side.

Mr. ADELSON. As I said, I am the counsel for Mr. Sugarman.
I just want to make a short statement to explain his position in today's
hearing.

In the fall of 1954 I was retained to represent him; and after listening
to his story, cross-examining him myself for several days, I took the
responsibility to communicate with the postal inspectors and told
them that we wished to have a conference with them, at which time
I was prepared to have Mr. Sugarman disclose all the facts in his
possession in reference to the so-called Tager case.

We did have such a conference. It lasted almost 2 days. At that
time, although we were not required to, I had my client make a statement under oath, and he, in my opinion, made a full disclosure of
everything that he knew in reference to the case. He answered all
questions that were put to him, both by myself and by the postal
inspectors.

When he was subpenaed to appear before this committee it was
my intention to have my client follow the same procedure; but as
you know, Mr. Senator, there is an indictment that was returned last
Friday, quite unexpectedly, and because of that I have now advised
my client to refuse to answer any questions that may be put to him
that may incriminate him, and have advised him to claim his constitutional rights under the fifth amendment.

I want to make this statement because it is inconsistent with the former position we took before the postal inspectors.

Chairman KEFAUVER. Thank you, Mr. Adelson.

Mr. ADELSON. Thank you, sir.

Chairman KEFAUVER. I shall not ask Mr. Sugarman about any of the details of the case. I do want to identify him for the record and ask that he be—as I understand it, he will plead the privilege of the fifth amendment?

Mr. ADELSON. That is correct, Mr. Senator.

Chairman KEFAUVER. What is your first name, Mr. Sugarman?

Mr. SUGARMAN. Calvin Sugarman.

Chairman KEFAUVER. And what is your address?

Mr. SUGARMAN. 108 Woodbine Street.

Chairman KEFAUVER. How old are you, sir?

Mr. SUGARMAN. Thirty.

Chairman KEFAUVER. What is your business? I mean, in what business are you now?

Mr. SUGARMAN. I am employed in the funeral home.

Chairman KEFAUVER. Funeral home with your father?

Mr. SUGARMAN. Yes.

Chairman KEFAUVER. Is that the Sugarman Funeral Home?

Mr. SUGARMAN. Yes.

Chairman KEFAUVER. Mr. Adelson, I think there is merit in your position. Unless Mr. Sugarman wants to make any statement, unless he wants to testify, at the present time we are not going to require him to do so.

Mr. ADELSON. We respectfully decline to testify, Mr. Senator.

Chairman KEFAUVER. You don't have to decline anything unless you are required to.

Mr. ADELSON. We will take the opportunity not to testify, Mr. Senator.

Chairman KEFAUVER. Very well.

Mr. Detective James Murphy and Detective Francis Doerr, will you please come around.

Do you solemnly swear the testimony you give will be the whole truth, so help you God?

Mr. MURPHY. I do.

Mr. DOERR. I do.

TESTIMONY OF DETECTIVE JAMES MURPHY; ACCOMPANIED BY DETECTIVE FRANCIS DOERR, POUGHKEEPSIE POLICE DEPARTMENT, POUGHKEEPSIE, N. Y.

Chairman KEFAUVER. You are Detective James Murphy?

Mr. MURPHY. Yes, sir.

Chairman KEFAUVER. And you are Detective Francis Doerr?

Mr. DOERR. Yes, sir.

Chairman KEFAUVER. Your chief is John L. Martin, Jr.?

Mr. DOERR. That is correct, sir.

Chairman KEFAUVER. I want you to convey a message to him that he has been very cooperative with our staff in the matter of this inquiry, and we are very grateful.

Mr. DOERR. Thank you, Senator.

Chairman KEFAUVER. You are detectives with the Poughkeepsie, N. Y., police force?

Mr. DOERR. Yes, sir.

Mr. MURPHY. Yes, sir.

Chairman KEFAUVER. How large a city is Poughkeepsie?

Mr. DOERR. About 50,000, sir.

Chairman KEFAUVER. Mr. Chumbris, will you carry on.

Mr. CHUMBRIS. Which of you two gentlemen is going to be the spokesman?

Mr. MURPHY. Detective Doerr.

Mr. CHUMBRIS. Detective Doerr, have you discussed the matter under investigation with members of our staff?

Mr. DOERR. We have not, sir. Our chief has contacted your staff and discussed this situation.

Mr. CHUMBRIS. Will you please state——

Chairman KEFAUVER. When you talk about your chief, say Chief Martin.

Mr. DOERR. Chief John Martin; yes, sir.

Mr. CHUMBRIS. Did this matter deal with pornographic material?

Mr. DOERR. Yes, sir.

Mr. CHUMBRIS. Will you please relate in your own words the name of the party involved, or parties involved, the approximate date, the area covered.

Mr. DOERR. Yes, sir. This investigation is the *People* v. *William John O'Connell*.

Chairman KEFAUVER. State that again so we can all hear.

Mr. DOERR. *People* v. *William John O'Connell*.

Chairman KEFAUVER. How do you spell O'Connell?

Mr. DOERR. O'-C-o-n-n-e-l-l.

Chairman KEFAUVER. This is a matter in Poughkeepsie, N. Y.?

Mr. DOERR. Yes, sir.

Chairman KEFAUVER. All right, sir.

Mr. DOERR. And William O'Connell resides at 497 Main Street, the Clinton Hotel, Poughkeepsie, N. Y. He is 29 years of age, and he is an electrician by trade.

Our investigation started on July 12, 1955, when we received information that William O'Connell had in his room at the hotel pornographic pictures, lewd literature, and obscene pictures.

On the 12th day of July we attempted to question William O'Connell, but he was out of town, and we could not question him until July 14, which was a Wednesday.

We went to the place where he was employed, a construction job at the Hudson River State Hospital, and we requested of him that he come to our police station to give us information about his having possession of these pornographic pictures, which he readily did.

We took him to the police station and received from him a statement of admission that he had many pornographic pictures, lewd literature, and obscene prints in his room at the Clinton Hotel.

Chairman KEFAUVER. Mr. Doerr, everything you testify to is admitted by Mr. O'Connell; is that correct?

Mr. DOERR. That is correct, Senator.

Chairman KEFAUVER. All right, sir.

Mr. DOERR. After we received this statement of admission from him we asked permission if we could go to his room and confiscate all obscene materials that he had in his possession.

Receiving his permission, we went to his room at 487 Main Street, and we collected in large quantities many obscene prints and materials.

Mr. CHUMBRIS. When you say "large quantities," just how many?

Mr. DOERR. We confiscated several rolls of pornographic film, thousands of pictures of nude posed women, many obscene prints, many cartoons, 2 by 4 comic cartoons.

Chairman KEFAUVER. Did you say "many cartons of them?"

Mr. DOERR. Cartoons, 2 by 4 picture books.

Chairman KEFAUVER. You mean boxes?

Mr. DOERR. No; individual books, Senator.

Mr. CHUMBRIS. How many would you say you had in that group, 1,000; 2,000?

Mr. DOERR. No; I don't think that many, not of the comic books, pornographic books.

Mr. CHUMBRIS. When you referred to 2 by 4's, for the record please explain what a 2 by 4 is?

Mr. DOERR. It is a small comic book illustrated with pornographic pictures.

Mr. CHUMBRIS. Very indecent type; is that correct?

Mr. DOERR. Indecent acts; that is correct.

Mr. CHUMBRIS. They usually have about eight pages?

Mr. DOERR. That is correct.

Mr. CHUMBRIS. And they are caricatures rather than actual pictures?

Mr. DOERR. That is correct. We also confiscated pamphlets of lewd literature and manuscripts of lewd literature from his room. All this was taken to the police department, identified by O'Connell, and identified for later identification.

Mr. CHUMBRIS. When you refer to manuscripts, are you referring to that item that is later produced into printed books; is that correct?

Mr. DOERR. This size [exhibiting].

Chairman KEFAUVER. What you show here, can you leave that as an exhibit? It is about 4 inches by 6 inches.

Mr. DOERR. This is the other side, sir, to that.

Chairman KEFAUVER. This is interesting. You say you had the manuscript of these things that later got into books?

Mr. DOERR. They were a larger volume than that, Senator, along the same lines, lewd literature. Some of them were illustrated, some were not.

Chairman KEFAUVER. This says on the front here, "500 francs." It is printed in English, and we found a lot of these people have put on here that they are printed in France, although they are printed in the United States, on the theory that they think that will be more interesting.

Mr. DOERR. Most of the books that we confiscated were printed just like that, sir.

You may also have this, sir, in evidence, if you wish [handing].

Mr. CHUMBRIS. Can you leave these various exhibits with us?

Mr. DOERR. Yes, sir. And here also is obscene prints which you may have [handing].

Mr. CHUMBRIS. Did you determine from him where he sold these pornographic articles?

Mr. DOERR. Yes; we did. He had been employed before he became an electrician as a cabdriver in the city. Among his various cabdrivers and other acquaintances of his he sold some of these obscene prints, lewd pictures, pornographic pictures.

Also, on his job as an electrician, there was an electrician where he worked, he also distributed and sold amongst his fellow employees these same obscene materials.

Mr. CHUMBRIS. Did you proceed with that investigation any further to determine if he had people working with him or working the same type of operation?

Mr. DOERR. Yes, sir; we did.

Mr. CHUMBRIS. And did you learn of any other names that he would like to reveal to the subcommittee at this time?

Mr. DOERR. Yes, sir. During the course of our——

Chairman KEFAUVER. Let's don't reveal the names unless you have proof. Do you have documentary proof of what they had been doing?

Mr. DOERR. We have statements of admission, sir. They have all been arrested and convicted of this crime.

Chairman KEFAUVER. Arrested and convicted?

Mr. DOERR. Yes, sir.

Chairman KEFAUVER. All right. You tell us about it, then.

Mr. DOERR. We have another man involved in this case, Nathan Van Wagenen. Age 70 years, residing at 11 South Hamilton Street, in the city of Poughkeepsie, employed as a taxi driver with the Veteran Cab Co., Poughkeepsie, N. Y.

In the course of our investigation we learned through O'Connell that Mr. Van Wagenen also was involved in this case. We went to the cab office where he worked, requested of him to come to the police station to question him further on this. After he came to the station with us we got an admission from him that he was involved, and he had made a partial living by showing these pornographic films to different organizations.

We requested of Mr. Van Wagenen that we go to his house and confiscate any pornographic literature, or obscene prints, lewd literature, which he gave us permission to do.

We went to his home, 11 South Hamilton Street, and confiscated several rolls of pornographic films; also 2 or 3 suitcases which were filled with lewd literature, small comic books, as you have there, along the same lines.

Mr. CHUMBRIS. Did you determine from whom Van Wagenen purchased this material?

Mr. DOERR. Yes, sir; we did. Talking with Mr. Van Wagenen, and where he came into possession of these obscene materials, he stated to us that a year prior he became acquainted with an ex-con from Sing Sing by the name of Philip D'Amelio. He is an ex-con from Sing Sing. He made his home in Poughkeepsie at the time, 14 Talmadge Street, Poughkeepsie.

Mr. CHUMBRIS. Do you know if he uses an alias?

Mr. DOERR. He had an alias. "Philly New Yorker." He was widely known throughout the State.

New Yorker at the time was a fugitive from justice at Poughkeepsie, wanted for grand larceny.

Detective Murphy and I apprehended D'Amelio in Oswego County, State of New York, and brought him to Poughkeepsie. We questioned him thoroughly on the matter of obscene materials, offensive materials. We have a statement of denial from Philly New Yorker ever operating with obscene materials.

Mr. CHUMBRIS. You say you do have a statement?

Mr. DOERR. Of denial; yes, sir.

Mr. CHUMBRIS. From whom did you receive that statement?

Mr. DOERR. D'Amelio, alias Philly New Yorker.

Mr. CHUMBRIS. When was that?

Mr. DOERR. Friday, August 12, 1955.

Mr. CHUMBRIS. That was previous to his being a fugitive from justice; is that correct?

Mr. DOERR. Yes, sir; that's correct.

Mr. CHUMBRIS. At this time he is a fugitive from justice?

Mr. DOERR. He was until that day, Friday, August 12, when he was apprehended.

Mr. CHUMBRIS. But now he has been in custody——

Mr. DOERR. He is free as of now. His trial has come up. It was reduced to petit larceny. He was fined, restitution was made, and he is now free.

Mr. CHUMBRIS. Are there any other persons whom you have investigated and found that have sold pornographic materials to Van Wagenen?

Mr. DOERR. Yes, sir; another person, Richard Wallace Booth, 26 years of age, living at 18 Fox Terrace, Poughkeepsie. He also is an electrician by trade. At the present time he is employed at the Hudson River State Hospital, Poughkeepsie, N. Y.

He became involved in this investigation with O'Connell. He was introduced to O'Connell a few months prior, and through his association with O'Connell he learned that O'Connell had access to pornographic film. He also learned that O'Connell had a projector set, and from being acquainted with him he borrowed films, and a projector set, from O'Connell, took it to his home at 18 Fox Terrace, and showed it to numerous people.

In this investigation Booth was also arrested under 1140 of the penal law. He pleaded guilty. It was reduced to 722, and he was fined $25 in the city court, Poughkeepsie, N. Y.

Mr. CHUMBRIS. Are you through with the Booth matter at this time?

Mr. DOERR. Unless you have more questions to ask me; yes, sir.

Mr. CHUMBRIS. You say he received a $25 penalty; is that correct?

Mr. DOERR. That is correct?

Mr. CHUMBRIS. Do you know the circumstances under which the charge was reduced, and the reason for it, if you can relate that?

Mr. DOERR. Through the assistant district attorney.

Mr. CHUMBRIS. We have received testimony in our New York hearings, particularly, from police chiefs and other police officials that they went to a lot of trouble to break a pornographic case involving hundreds and sometimes thousands of pornographic articles, maybe take 6 months to do so, and costing the State or the city thousands of dollars, and then have the matter presented to court where only a reduced charge was made and a small fine was given.

Is that the situation that you found in this case?

Mr. Doerr. Sir, I think the district attorney, the assistant district attorney felt that Booth was involved in this not trying to sell or peddle any of these obscene materials, just the fact that he had a few friends that he wanted to show in his private home.

Mr. Chumbris. And he wouldn't be an operator in the same category as O'Connell; is that correct?

Mr. Doerr. No, sir; that is correct.

Mr. Chumbris. All right, sir. Are there any other persons who deal in pornography, either through O'Connell or through Van Wagenen?

Mr. Doerr. Yes, sir; we have another subject involved in this investigation, Robert C. Fuller, 33 years of age, residing at 104 Mansion Street, Poughkeepsie, N. Y. A machine operator employed at the Fargo Manufacturing Co., Poughkeepsie, N. Y.

We have a signed statement before a notary public, admission from Fuller that he became acquainted with O'Connell through other friends, and through his acquaintance he learned that O'Connell had pornographic film, and he borrowed a few of these pornographic films to show at his home to friends of his.

We feel as though he is not an operator as O'Connell is; that he just got this for his own private affairs.

Mr. Chumbris. Now, from O'Connell did you obtain a little black book or a name list?

Mr. Doerr. Yes, sir; we did.

Mr. Chumbris. Did that name list indicate connections with people in the pornographic racket, as we may call it?

Mr. Doerr. Yes, sir; it did.

Mr. Chumbris. Would you relate just what you found from that name list?

Mr. Doerr. When we confiscated this little black book that O'Connell had in his possession, we found many names, addresses and telephone numbers of girls in New York City. We questioned him as to the identity of these girls, his contacts with these girls and how he came to have all these names, addresses, in his possession.

O'Connell stated that in New York he made the acquaintance of Doris Garcia, 270 West 77th Street, apartment 2, New York, N. Y., telephone SU-7-1705.

He also stated that this girl was a call girl; that he met her at the Hotel Peerless—that address I have here also, 45th Street and Broadway, New York City.

Mr. Chumbris. Without going into each individual name, were any of the girls who are listed in that list in any way connected with morals cases or pornographic racket?

Mr. Doerr. He had telephone numbers of many girls that were connected with the Jelke case.

Mr. Chumbris. That is the famous Jelke case in New York City?

Mr. Doerr. Yes. Names like Pat Ward, Pat Thompson, Barbara Harmon, Erica Steel, Sylvia Kiig. He stated to us that through Doris Garcia, a call girl, he gained these other addresses and telephone numbers.

Mr. CHUMBRIS. Were you able to determine whether O'Connell was a producer of pornographic material, or merely a distributor and seller of pornographic material?

Mr. DOERR. We feel that he was not a producer of pornographic material.

Mr. CHUMBRIS. Could you tell where he was receiving this material?

Mr. DOERR. Yes, sir; he admitted to us that he had contacts in New York City; that he was receiving a good deal of pornographic material.

Mr. CHUMBRIS. And did he relate how he received it, what method he used in getting it back to Poughkeepsie?

Mr. DOERR. He made personal contacts, he made personal visits to New York City to gain this material.

Mr. CHUMBRIS. Did you obtain the names and addresses from him or from any other substantial means in determining who these people might be?

Mr. DOERR. We endeavored to, sir, and he could not remember the places that he obtained this material from, only the fact that it was in the vicinity of Times Square, New York City. He did state—pardon me, sir.

Mr. CHUMBRIS. Go ahead.

Mr. DOERR. He did state that he carried on a good deal of correspondence with Irving Klaus in New York City.

Chairman KEFAUVER. Claw, you mean.

Mr. DOERR. Claw, pardon me.

Mr. CHUMBRIS. Were there any other references from where he may have received this material?

Mr. DOERR. Not O'Connell, sir. O'Connell also stated that he received some of this obscene material from Nathan Van Wagenen at different times also.

Mr. CHUMBRIS. Did he mention the name of Al Stone as a source of material in New York City?

Mr. DOERR. Sir, he did not admit that to us.

Mr. CHUMBRIS. When you asked him, did you have any key people in New York who are known throughout the country as distributors of pornographic material, and ask him if he did or did not receive any of this pornographic material from them?

Mr. DOERR. He mentioned the name of Stone, and he did not say that he had any contacts with him.

Mr. CHUMBRIS. But he knew Al Stone; is that correct?

Mr. DOERR. Yes, sir; that is correct.

Mr. CHUMBRIS. Did you know that Al Stone was mentioned in the course of our New York hearings on pornography in May of this year?

Mr. DOERR. I believe I read about it, sir; yes, sir.

Mr. CHUMBRIS. In which he pled the fifth amendment?

Mr. DOERR. Yes, sir.

Mr. CHUMBRIS. Now, did you get from the subcommittee the list of seizures from Al Stone, where his name was mentioned on various name lists?

Mr. DOERR. No, sir.

Mr. CHUMBRIS. You have not received that from our subcommittee?

Mr. DOERR. No, sir.

Mr. CHUMBRIS. Are there any other known persons in New York City in the distribution of pornographic material that O'Connell might have mentioned?

Mr. DOERR. We have the names of many publishing houses in New York and different parts of the country that O'Connell was corresponding with. He did not admit that he was getting obscene material from them. We have——

Chairman KEFAUVER. Let's don't mention them unless you can tie them up.

Mr. DOERR. They were in his possession, and that's all we know about it.

Mr. CHUMBRIS. Are there any other cases dealing with pornography that you have investigated?

Mr. DOERR. During the course of the investigation we also apprehended one subject, Edward D. Manning, 46 years of age, residing at 51 Smith Street, in the city of Poughkeepsie.

Manning, in a statement of admission to us, said that about 3 years ago be worked for an electrical company in the city of Poughkeepsie, and he received, through a man by the name of Al, 3 or 4 films, pornographic films, for which he paid a total of $50 from this unidentified person.

Subsequently Mr. Manning sold these films to Nathan Van Wagenen.

Mr. CHUMBRIS. Now, I believe you investigated a case regarding a 19-year old boy. Could you relate that, please?

Mr. DOERR. Sir, Detective Murphy will tell about that.

Chairman KEFAUVER. You tell us about it, Mr. Murphy, and speak up, will you, please.

Mr. MURPHY. I think you are referring to the Mrs. Cifarelli case. That happened in August 1951. Mrs. Cifarelli——

Mr. CHUMBRIS. 1951?

Mr. MURPHY. Yes, sir. I believe that is the one you mean.

Mr. CHUMBRIS. Well, state it briefly. That goes a little far back, 1951.

Mr. MURPHY. Well, she complained that her son was present at a showing of a movie in the cellar of her home. We found out that her son, Frank, age 16, along with 3 or 4 other young boys about the same age, obtained a film from a certain veteran, a man by the name of Fred Vetter, of Poughkeepsie, N. Y.

We took statements from all the boys involved in the case, and from those statements we took them to the district attorney, and a warrant was issued for the arrest of Vetter.

At that time he refused to give a statement. Since that time we have had him under pretty strict surveillance, and we know he is not in the business any more.

Mr. CHUMBRIS. Did you have a 1953 case involving minors also, in which a $250 fine was levied? A person showing obscene prints to minor children?

Mr. MURPHY. Yes. We have a park in Poughkeepsie called Pulaski Park. At that time we had 2 or 3 complaints that a man was hanging around the park and showing pictures of nude persons right on the back of playing cards.

Subsequently, officers picked this particular man up, and at first he denied it, but they found this deck of cards under the front seat of his car. At that time this man was fined $250. His name was Chester Allard.

Mr. CHUMBRIS. I understand within the last 24 hours there was a case that you investigated?

Mr. MURPHY. Right now, just outside of Poughkeepsie, it is in the town of Poughkeepsie, our detectives, also the town police, are investigating a case involving a man committing certain immoral acts with 5 high school girls, at least 5 high school girls, and at the same time he has in his possession certain pornographic film that he is showing to these young ladies. He has been arrested at the present time.

Mr. CHUMBRIS. You say he has been arrested?

Mr. MURPHY. He has been arrested. At the moment he is out on bail, but the case is still under investigation.

Mr. CHUMBRIS. Was this a large quantity seizure?

Mr. MURPHY. No. They found two rolls of pornographic film in his house. They found a projector; and they found other articles that are definitely for sex means and measures.

Mr. CHUMBRIS. Of course you have not completed your investigation on that particular case?

Mr. MURPHY. That's right. It is still under investigation right now.

Chairman KEFAUVER. Mr. Murphy and Mr. Doerr, we thank you very much for coming and telling us about this. It is quite apparent you are staying on the job up there. You seem to have a lot of violations, however.

Mr. DOERR. Senator, we have a picture of the subject, O'Connell, and if it will mean anything to you, you may have it.

Chairman KEFAUVER. I wish you would leave it with us, if you will.

Mr. DOERR. Yes, sir [handing].

Chairman KEFAUVER. What do you gentlemen recommend in connection with this whole problem; do you have any recommendations?

Mr. MURPHY. We think that you are making a move in the right direction and that something should be done to curb this influx of this kind of material. You seem to be doing a very nice job on it.

Chairman KEFAUVER. All right, sir. Thank you, Mr. Murphy and Mr. Doerr.

Who is our next witness, Mr. Chumbris?

Mr. CHUMBRIS. Nicholas Caporicci.

Chairman KEFAUVER. Mr. Caporicci, do you solemnly swear the testimony you give will be the whole truth, so help you God?

Mr. CAPORICCI. Yes, sir.

TESTIMONY OF NICHOLAS CAPORICCI, CRANSTON, R. I.

Chairman KEFAUVER. We will get down to the point in question. Tell us your name, sir.

Mr. CAPORICCI. Nicholas Caporicci, 15 Connecticut Street, Cranston.

Chairman KEFAUVER. Cranston, R. I.?

Mr. CAPORICCI. Yes, sir.

Chairman KEFAUVER. All right, Mr. Chumbris. Do you want to ask the gentleman some questions?

Mr. CHUMBRIS. Yes, sir.

Mr. Caporicci, do you want advice of counsel?

Mr. CAPORICCI. Advice of a counsel?

Mr. CHUMBRIS. Yes. Do you want to have a lawyer to be with you when you appear here now?

Mr. CAPORICCI. Well, if I need one; yes.

Mr. CHUMBRIS. What is that?

Mr. CAPORICCI. If I need a lawyer.

Chairman KEFAUVER. Do you want to just tell us about the matter that you are here about?

Mr. CAPORICCI. Yes.

Chairman KEFAUVER. We want to know who it is you have been dealing with in New York in this film business.

Mr. CAPORICCI. Well, like I said before, I wouldn't know him if I see him again.

Mr. CHUMBRIS. Will you relate, just where did you meet this person?

Mr. CAPORICCI. It was in a restaurant, sir.

Mr. CHUMBRIS. Where?

Mr. CAPORICCI. In a restaurant on the corner of 48th or 49th Street.

Chairman KEFAUVER. In Providence?

Mr. CAPORICCI. New York.

Chairman KEFAUVER. You went down to New York? How do you happen to go to New York?

Mr. CAPORICCI. I had a few days off, and I took a couple of days off.

Chairman KEFAUVER. You went down there on something else, or did you go down there to meet him?

Mr. CAPORICCI. No; just for pleasure.

Chairman KEFAUVER. And you got a 1,600-foot film; is that right?

Mr. CAPORICCI. Yes.

Chairman KEFAUVER. You spliced them together, several films together?

Mr. CAPORICCI. Yes.

Chairman KEFAUVER. Where did you meet this man; who was he?

Mr. CAPORICCI. I met him in a restaurant at the corner of 48th or 49th Street.

Chairman KEFAUVER. Did he just walk up to you or did you walk up to him?

Mr. CAPORICCI. No. He was selling booklets.

Chairman KEFAUVER. He was what?

Mr. CAPORICCI. Selling the small books.

Chairman KEFAUVER. Selling books?

Mr. CAPORICCI. Yes.

Chairman KEFAUVER. You mean on the horse races?

Mr. CAPORICCI. No.

Chairman KEFAUVER. Books on what?

Mr. CAPORICCI. Well, pictures.

Mr. CHUMBRIS. How was it that you were arrested for this offense?

Mr. CAPORICCI. I bought a small radio, a stolen radio from a boy.

Mr. CHUMBRIS. How old was the boy?

Mr. CAPORICCI. About 13, I guess.

Mr. CHUMBRIS. And then after you purchased this, did you know that it was a stolen radio?

Mr. CAPORICCI. Well, I presume it was stolen, but I never asked him whether it was stolen or not.

Mr. CHUMBRIS. You presumed it was stolen?

Mr. CAPORICCI. Yes.

Mr. CHUMBRIS. How did they find the pornographic material on you?

Mr. CAPORICCI. I had it locked in a compartment of a car.

Mr. CHUMBRIS. In your car?

Mr. CAPORICCI. Yes.

Mr. CHUMBRIS. When you spliced together this 1,600 feet of film, how did you make use of that film? Did you rent it out?

Mr. CAPORICCI. No.

Mr. CHUMBRIS. What did you use it for, then?

Mr. CAPORICCI. I didn't use it. I showed it once, and that was all I did, show it.

Mr. CHUMBRIS. Where did you show it?

Mr. CAPORICCI. What?

Mr. CHUMBRIS. Where was it that you showed the film?

Mr. CAPORICCI. In a friend of mine's house.

Mr. CHUMBRIS. Just you and he together?

Mr. CAPORICCI. Yes.

Mr. CHUMBRIS. And you didn't have stag parties and show the film at these stag parties?

Mr. CAPORICCI. No.

Mr. CHUMBRIS. Are you sure about that?

Mr. CAPORICCI. I am positive.

Mr. CHUMBRIS. And you say you wouldn't know who this person in New York was if you saw him again?

Mr. CAPORICCI. No.

Chairman KEFAUVER. Did he just come up to you and say he had something to sell?

Mr. CAPORICCI. No. Like I said, he was selling books.

Chairman KEFAUVER. Did you buy some books?

Mr. CAPORICCI. He asked me if I wanted to buy books. I says, "No." Then we started talking and he said he had some films. So that's when I bought films.

Chairman KEFAUVER. All right. Thank you very much.

Mr. CHUMBRIS. Mr. McGuire.

Mr. McGUIRE. Yes, sir?

Mr. CHUMBRIS. Mr. McGuire, are there any later developments in Mr. Morrow's matter?

Mr. McGUIRE. No. As a matter of fact, I haven't communicated with the office at all. I just stayed on to hear the rest of the testimony.

I understand that you were having a doctor examine him.

Chairman KEFAUVER. We have been trying to make arrangements. I don't know what the situation is.

Mr. McGUIRE. All I can do is reiterate the position that I took before, that I came down for counsel; that the basic reasons that he is not here is, one, in apprehension of his physical condition, based upon the medical testimony that was submitted in affidavit form, together with the fear of retaliation which he expressed to Mr. McDonald.

Chairman KEFAUVER. We will have Mr. Morrow and he will have to be heard, either in Washington or up at Worcester.

Who is our other witness who is not here?

Mr. CHUMBRIS. Mr. Schlessler.

Chairman KEFAUVER. All right. Thank you very much, Mr. McGuire.

Mr. McGUIRE. Thank you, sir.

Chairman KEFAUVER. We had certain police officers here who would testify in connection with certain matters relating to Mr. Morrow and Mr. Schlessler, but since they could not be here we have sent the officers home also.

We will have to continue this hearing until a later date to come back and hear these witnesses, and such others as we may have.

We will conclude our hearing of witnesses this evening.

I think I should say by way of summing up, I felt that our hearing this morning was quite productive in the description by the Governor and the mayor, the chief of police and Judge McCabe of the juvenile court, of the awareness of the problem of dealing with young people and with juvenile delinquency in the State of Rhode Island and in the city. Affirmative steps have certainly been taken in the matter of recreation, education. I think the juvenile judge and his assistant, Judge Booth, not only handle their juvenile court intelligently, but they have gone out to secure the cooperation in a larger program of the people.

I have been impressed with the increase in the division of police dealing with juveniles here in the city, with the low rate of juvenile delinquency, less than 1½ percent, I believe, is the lowest of any State that we have come across in the country.

The Commission to deal with comic books should come up with some worthwhile legislation.

I was delighted to find that there has been a uniform adoption law passed by the Legisture of Rhode Island.

The boys camp, the recreational facilities, seem to be forward-looking.

So I think some of the programs here will certainly be useful to people in other parts of the country studying what they can do in various cities to help with youth and youth opportunity and in curbing juvenile delinquency.

Our hearing this afternoon in connection with the Sugarman case and the Tager case, as I said, we determined to come here last June when we had testimony about it out in California.

I think some people may not realize the deleterious effect that the circulation of this lewd, lascivious, indecent literature has upon the youth of our country.

I am glad to say that some of the traffic has been broken up. We found when we started our investigation that over the Nation the fellows who would be on probation one place, and maybe would be convicted 2 or 3 times somewhere else other than the place where they were on probation, and they would never find out about it.

We find also that while there are a lot of little people in the business, there are some big ones, and they all seem to be tied together. It is hard to understand how anyone can get into this sort of business. We do have laws to prevent it from being sent through the mail.

I hope that there can be an increased interest on the part of the public and our law-enforcement officers in stamping out and stopping the interstate shipment, printing, sale to minors of the kind of junk we have been talking about here this afternoon.

I don't want to appear to be unkind, but it is very difficult for me to see how, with these postal inspectors who spent months and months and months putting all the men in their division, building up a case, getting the facts, feeling that they have a strong case against a person or against people who have not only been in the business in one place, but get over in 3 States with different drops, or 4 States, with all that information in the hands of the district attorney over a period of 9 or 10 months, I think that there is a substantial dereliction of duty in not at least presenting the evidence to a grand jury.

I think that is particularly true when the evidence concerning the agent was presented, but not the principal.

It is furthermore particularly true when the case was made airtight by a signed affidavit on the part of the agent. I am entirely unsatisfied with the explanation Mr. Temkin has given. Be he ever so good a man, I am afraid he did not discharge his duty in this matter. The matter has at long last been presented. I feel it is within the jurisdiction of this committee to expose the distribution of this kind of filth. Where we find that anyone connected with the Government of the United States is not doing his duty, we expect to let the public know about it.

We do expect to be back in this section some time later, and have a further hearing of these witnesses. I want to again thank the judges who have been so good to us here, and Mr. Proctor, the marshal, Mr. Brennan, who has been very fine in helping us out, and many, many others who have cooperated with the staff of our committee.

For the record I would like to put their names in the hearing of the record. I won't take up the time in reading all of them.

Judge Edward W. Day, and clerk of court Neale D. Murphy, for the use of the courtroom, and other favors.

Judge John P. Hartigan, for use of his chambers; and the following for their excellent cooperation in serving subpenas, finding office space, supplies, help and assistance.

Howard S. Proctor, United States marshal; Patrick Pyne, chief deputy United States marshal; Edward Curran and Edward Brennan, United States marshals.

Raymond A. Creegan, postmaster, and his staff.

Special mention: Comdr. Walter Stone, Lt. Thomas Healey, Sgt. William Cummings, and Sgt. William Cahill, of the Providence Detective Bureau.

Chief of Police John L. Martin Jr., Poughkeepsie, for making available to the committee Detectives James Murphy and Francis Doerr.

Deputy Chief of Police P. Frank Carroll, Worcester, Capt. Lawrence W. Henry, and Lt. James F. Daly, of the Worcester Detective Bureau.

Lt. Anthony Lecaire, Massachusetts State Police.

Lt. James Waters and staff. North Attleboro Police.

Deputy Chief of Police Vincent Hourigan, Pawtucket, and Lieutenant Henchen.

Chief of Police Louis B. Fonchecourt, Cranston; and Lieutenant Morretti.

Harold V. Langlois, division of correctional services, State of Rhode Island.

William W. Dickenson, superintendent of post office buildings.

Margaret Butler, secretary.

Edward Bell, custodial foreman; and Edward Doyle, custodial force.

Chairman KEFAUVER. With that, the subcommittee will stand in recess until further call.

(Whereupon, at 8:30 p. m., the subcommittee was adjourned until further call.)

(Subsequent to the hearing, Chairman Kefauver ordered that the following exhibits, Nos. 7 through 12, be made a part of this printed record:)

EXHIBIT No. 7

AFFIDAVIT OF LEO VINE

STATE OF CONNECTICUT,
    County of Fairfield:

In Shelton, Conn., on the 10th day of December 1955, before me personally appeared Leo Vine who, having been sworn, deposed as follows:

1. I am a private in Support Company, 506th Regiment, 101st Airborne Infantry Division at Fort Jackson, S. C.

2. During the spring of 1954 I was a second-year student at the Harvard Law School, Cambridge, Mass. Like many of my classmates I was seeking summer employment. At this time I saw a notice posted on the law school bulletin board stating that the United States attorney in Rhode Island would be interested in interviewing second-year law students for summer work in his office in Providence, R. I. The notice was signed by the student employment office of the law school.

3. I completed an application for this position and subsequently was interviewed by Mr. Jacob S. Temkin, the United States attorney in Rhode Island at that time. I knew Mr. Temkin at that time by reputation. I did not know him personally. Mr. Temkin informed me at a later interview in June 1954 that the position of student legal assistant in his office would be without compensation. He approved my application and I accepted the position.

4. I occupied an office adjoining that of Mr. Temkin. The intervening door was generally open and I was invited to attend conferences concerning cases arising that summer. I was made to feel part and parcel of the office that summer. I was usually informed as to each stage of development of any particular case. The fact situations of each case were presented to me and I did legal research necessary to prepare memorandums of the law relevant to these cases.

5. The Tager case, involving the use of the mails for the sale of obscene literature, was one of those which came up during the course of that summer. I remember seeing the photographs which were used as bait for the prospective purchaser. Also, there was literature which, as I recall, promised to show why Franchot Tone and Tom Neal were fighting over Barbara Payton. The snapshots I saw seemed definitely to fit the "obscene" category. I recall the indignation of the postal inspectors and Mr. Temkin at this use of the mail service. I further recall Mr. Temkin's express statements to the effect that whoever had mailed the pictures and literature would pay the legal penalty. At no time did I ever hear or see anything which would suggest that Mr. Temkin had deviated from his intention to bring the offender or offenders into court for punishment.

6. I did research on this case. I do not recall the exact references of the applicable law, but I believe that there were at least 2 and possibly 3 different sections of the United States Code which were relevant, dealing with the use of the mails to transmit obscene materials and to defraud. I was present during various conferences dealing with this case. The principals were Mr. Temkin and the postal inspectors. I never met either Mrs. Tager or young Sugarman.

7. During these conferences I recall the anxiety of the postal inspectors stemming from the fact that Mr. Tager had been implicated in similar offenses in the Western States and had escaped conviction because of some legal technicality. They did not want the same thing to happen with Mrs. Tager. Those are the general outlines of the case as I now recall them.

8. In the early part of September 1954, just before I returned to law school, I recall a conference which took place in Mr. Tempkin's office. He and the postal inspectors who had been working on the case were present. The conversation focused on the difficulty of tying Sugarman in with the available evidence; that is, the evidence was such that the inspectors seemed to feel that they could not bring Sugarman within the relevant sections of the United States Code. They were

apparently ready to proceed against Mrs. Tager—or have Mr. Temkin proceed against her with the evidence which they had obtained—but the case against Sugarman had loopholes. They agreed that the case against Sugarman was not strong enough to bring into court. These are the general impressions which I have retained of that particular conference. It is my recollection now that Mr. Temkin was at all times ready and willing to proceed against young Sugarman and any other person connected with this crime.

9. This is a true statement of what I recall about this case.

LEO VINE.

Subscribed and sworn to before me the day and year first above written by Leo Vine.

LOUIS KREIGER, *Notary Public.*

EXHIBIT No. 8

STATEMENT OF JACOB S. TEMKIN

STATE OF RHODE ISLAND,
    County of Providence:

In Providence on the 12th day of December 1955, before me personally appeared Jacob S. Temkin, who having been sworn, deposed as follows:

1. The conference with the three postal inspectors took place in the office of the United States attorney for the district of Rhode Island on September 10, 1954, the day on which the complaint was filed with the United States commissioner against Dorothy Tager.

The letter of transmittal, from the testimony, was dated September 16, 1954, and apparently was forwarded on that day.

It is not unusual to have reports and letters of transmittal follow actual arrests by a matter of days or weeks.

The session of September 10, 1954, was without benefit of the letter of transmittal; and all exposition, explanation, and recommendations except as the postal inspectors consulted the file, were oral. All decisions of the actions to be taken were based upon the oral presentation.

The majority of prosecutions begun through the office of the United States attorney are commenced upon oral presentation by investigators of a Government agency, of what they purport the facts to be and the violations they have uncovered, together with their recommendations as to the issuance of complaints. The investigators themselves sign these complaints under oath before the United States commissioner.

2. The file was delivered to my office on September 10, 1954, and may have been removed by the postal inspector after the conference in order to prepare the report and transmittal letter.

Before the receipt by my office of the transmittal letter, I had assigned the case to Mr. Arnold Williamson, Jr., an assistant United States attorney in my office.

I never read the transmittal letter; and to my knowledge no one has said that I read it or that I examined the case file. I have done neither to this day.

3. Reference was made to the file by the inspectors on September 10, 1954, in my office in order to obtain the name of the party in Michigan to whom the obscene material was sent. This information was necessary because it had to be incorporated in the complaint which was lodged with the United States commissioner. It was not possible for me to prepare the complaint without obtaining from the postal inspectors the small amount of factual matter necessary for this purpose.

4. Mr. Craugh, as spokesman for Mr. Tacy and himself, during part of the hearing (p. 133 et seq. of the transcript) testified the inspectors merely submitted the facts and made no recommendations.

I affirm that the postal inspectors asked for a complaint to be issued against Mrs. Tager. I affirm that they did not ask for a complaint to be issued against Mr. Sugarman. The postal inspectors, to my knowledge, have never denied either of these points.

I affirm that the reason a complaint was issued against Mrs. Tager on September 10, 1954, is that the postal inspectors asked for it and they stated they had the evidence to support it. I know of no stronger recommendation they could make.

I affirm that I prepared a complaint against Mrs. Tager on the recommendation of the postal inspectors.

I affirm that a complaint would have been prepared against Mr. Sugarman if the postal inspectors has asked for it. However, in addition to not asking for a complaint against Mr. Sugarman, they informed me they had no case against him and maintained this position at the conclusion of a series of searching questions on my part concerning the role of Mr. Sugarman in this case.

All of these actions took place on September 10, 1954, when I had only the word of the postal inspectors upon which to proceed. The transmittal letter was not yet written. I could not secure an iota of information concerning this case from any other individual than the postal inspectors then sitting in my office.

Mr. Simon testified (p. 193 et seq. of the transcript) that he made no recommendations and presented only the facts contained in the file to me. Yet, he also testified that I sought and he gave his advice as an expert concerning the necessity to prove specific intent in the crime of using the mails to defraud and the absence of this requirement in the crime of mailing obscene material. Mr. Simon gave his expert advice on this aspect of the case for only one reason: to explain why the postal inspectors were unable to establish a case of using the mails to defraud against Mr. Sugarman.

5. Mr. Simon (p. 194 of the transcript) testified there was a case against Mr. Sugarman on the basis of fraud unless "they could show that they had made some effort to furnish the pictures".

I affirm that on the contrary, the burden is on the Government to prove that no effort was made to furnish pictures and that, if shown, this alone does not prove the requisite criminal intent. The intent required to be proved in the crime of using the mails to defraud is that the scheme to defraud or the intention to devise such a scheme existed at the time of mailing and that the mailing was in furtherance of the scheme. Unless this intent can be shown, not as of September 10, 1954, but as of the date of the mailing, criminal intent as to Mr. Sugarman cannot be proved (title 18, U. S. C. A. 1341).

6. Independently, the affidavit of Mr. Leo Vine substantiates my position.

7. It is not necessary for a Federal agent to consult with the United States attorney on the issuance of process. He himself may swear out a complaint before a United States commissioner, without initial reference to a United States attorney.

In many districts it is the approved procedure for the Government investigators to go directly to a United States commissioner and swear out complaints without any knowledge of the complaints or of the case or cases to which they apply on the part of the United States attorney. The postal inspectors never asked me and, so far as I am aware, never asked an assistant of mine to issue a complaint against Mr. Sugarman. To my knowledge the postal inspectors have never sworn out a complaint against Mr. Sugarman before a United States commissioner.

8. So far as I am aware to this day, the only drop with which obscene material is connected and through which obscene material was sent was the so-called G. Wallis drop at 18 Tremont Street, Boston, Mass.

The postal inspectors informed me of exactly the same thing on September 10, 1954—that the G. Wallis drop was the only one that they could tie in with obscene material and Mrs. Tager was the only person they could link with that drop. The postal inspectors gave this identical testimony at the hearing (p. 112 et seq. of the transcript). They informed me that they could not connect Mr. Sugarman with this drop or with obscene material in any way. I am informed and believe that the transmittal letter confirms this statement.

9. Mr. Simon (p. 195 of the transcript) said he came to Providence and spoke with me in December of 1954. He did not make any inquiry about a case against Mr. Sugarman at that time for the reason he himself told me in September of 1954 that there was no case against Mr. Sugarman and he knew the inspection service had presented nothing more in the way of evidence against Mr. Sugarman to December 1954.

10. It is practice that when the Postal Inspection Service submits a case and there is refusal by the United States attorney to prosecute, the Postal Inspection Service demands a written declination of prosecution. As to Mr. Sugarman, no such letter was requested and none was given.

11. It is practice that when the Postal Inspection Service submits a case, it periodically corresponds with the office of the United States attorney and requests status reports. As to Mr. Sugarman, no such correspondence took place and no reports were requested and none was given.

12. There was no denial by the inspectors of the assistance I gave the postal inspectors in speaking with Mr. Max Sugarman, father of Calvin Sugarman, and despite a delicate situation, prevailing on him to have his son, Calvin Sugarman, cooperate with the postal inspectors, after he initially rebuffed them. Without this assistance the Postal Inspection Service would have had no case against Mrs. Tager.

13. There was no denial by the inspectors of the other assistance I gave the inspectors in connection with this case.

14. There was no denial by the inspectors of my testimony as to Mr. Tacy advising me Mr. Sugarman was telling the whole truth to him in the Sugarman statement (p. 160 of the transcript).

15. There was no denial of my testimony that Mr. Tacy told me he was unable to get any information from Mrs. Tager; that he had no confidence in what she had to say; and that the evidence was against anything she had said. (p. 161 of the transcript).

There was no denial of my testimony that Mrs. Tager was a bail jumper.

There was no denial of my testimony that the inspectors told me Mrs. Tager was a troubled woman, a sick woman who had her own children and the friends of her children mailing out filth (p. 203 of the transcript).

16. Upon information and belief, I state the postal inspectors submitted a written document in which are listed names of persons as witnesses to testify against Mrs. Tager and that this document includes the name of Calvin Sugarman as a witness. Even the postal inspectors are astute enough to know that Mr. Sugarman would not be recommended as a witness for the Government against Mrs. Tager, if they considered him to be a possible defendant.

17. There is no refutation of the statement as to my policy to present the facts to the grand jury, to bring before the grand jury the best and primary evidence, and any other evidence which the grand jury desires and which is obtainable.

18. Mr. Arnold Williamson, Jr., assistant United States attorney, testified the policy of the office was to present every case to a grand jury fairly and to let the grand jury determine whether to return an indictment.

19. The opening statement of Senator Kefauver (p. 108 of the transcript) mentioned that the only time Mrs. Tager, despite her previous brushes with the law, was in difficulty was in Rhode Island.

Mrs. Tager admitted, in a widely circulated magazine article about the dirty pictures racket, that she headed a million dollar mail order business on the west coast, that she had several brushes with the Postal Inspection Service, and that this operation extended throughout the United States and abroad. Yet she was never convicted until she began her operations in Rhode Island. The conviction took place during my tenure as United States attorney.

20. The affidavit of Mrs. Tager of April 30, 1955, states, among other things, that she had nothing whatsoever to do with obscene material. On June 3, 1955, approximately 45 days later, Mrs. Tager pleaded guilty to the charge of causing obscene material to be mailed.

I affirm that on September 10, 1954, and in prior conferences, the postal inspectors told me Mrs. Tager was not worthy of belief concerning anything she said. All that I know of the actions and statements of Mrs. Tager since that date convinced me that no reasonable man could place any faith in or credence upon the statements of Mrs. Tager, unless they were corroborated.

21. This case was assigned in the ordinary manner to Mr. Arnold Williamson, Jr., an assistant in my office; he reviewed it with the inspectors; and he prepared it for the grand jury. I was not in the grand jury room at any time during his presentation of the case.

22. Mr. Williamson testified that some of the witnesses who testified at the hearing also testified before the grand jury in December 1954.

23. Mrs. Tager's affidavit of April 30, 1955, was turned over to Mr. Williamson as a matter of course, since he was still handling the case. I have no doubt that if there was credible evidence against Mr. Sugarman at that or any other time while he was in charge of the case, Mr. Williamson would have proceeded against him. I have no knowledge of facts which would make me critical of the methods of Mr. Williamson in handling this case.

24. I recognize my responsibility as head of the office of the United States attorney for the district of Rhode Island during my tenure. I also recognize my duty in regard to the official position which I occupied. I discharged that duty fully and properly with all the vigor that I command. There is no basis whatsoever for any findings which reflect upon or even hint of a question concerning my conduct in office.

JACOB S. TEMKIN.

Subscribed and sworn to before me by Jacob S. Temkin the day and year first above written.

WILLIAM J. SHEEHAN,
Notary Public.

EXHIBIT NO. 9

POST OFFICE DEPARTMENT,
INSPECTION SERVICE,
OFFICE OF INSPECTOR,
Washington 25, D. C., December 20, 1955.

Mr. JAMES H. BOBO,
   General Counsel, Subcommittee to Investigate Juvenile Delinquency,
      Washington 25, D. C.

DEAR MR. BOBO: Reference is made to your letter of December 1, 1955, with which you transmitted a copy of a letter dated November 28, 1955, from Mr. Jacob S. Temkin, former United States attorney, Providence, R. I., together with a copy of your reply of November 30. This correspondence has reference to hearings held by your subcommittee at Providence on November 8, 1955.

It is felt that the testimony which I gave under oath before the subcommittee on November 8 clearly showed what transpired during the conference with Mr. Temkin on September 10, 1954, in which I participated, and there is nothing which I could add by affidavit.

Several statements are made in Mr. Temkin's letter to which some comment appears essential. It is alleged by Mr. Temkin that the "postal inspectors had been stymied in their investigation" prior to the time Sugarman submitted a sworn statement; that as a consequence of his contacting the father of Calvin Sugarman, the latter called at the office of the inspectors and gave them a complete statement; and that it was his (Temkin's) "assistance which resulted in the break of this case." I regret to tell you that such statement is not in agreement with the facts. Prior to the time the inspectors secured a sworn statement from Calvin Sugarman, they had developed evidence from various other sources to positively link Dorothy Tager to the mailing of the obscene pictures under the name of G. Wallis. Disregarding Sugarman's affidavit, the inspectors were in possession of evidence obtained without any assistance from Sugarman to implicate both him and Dorothy Tager in the use of the mails in a scheme to defraud; in fact, such involvement was indicated in the inspectors' report to the United States attorney pertaining to Mrs. Tager.

In referring to the conference with the three inspectors in his office on September 10, 1954, Mr. Temkin stated in part: "I questioned the postal inspectors closely on charges which might be placed against Calvin Sugarman and was advised that, in their opinion, he was not involved in mailing obscene material and that they could establish no case against him on a charge of using the mails to defraud." No such opinion was expressed by me or the other inspectors who participated in the conference. It is not our function to decide prosecutive features, but rather to present to United States attorneys facts and evidence resulting from our investigations.

The "transmittal letter" of the postal inspector mentioned by Mr. Temkin has reference to the inspectors' formal report to the United States attorney, setting forth the facts and outlining the evidence. Such a report dated September 16, 1954, names Dorothy Tager as the offender and Sugarman as a prospective witness; however, this report was prepared after Mr. Temkin indicated that he would proceed only against Dorothy Tager on the charge of mailing obscene matter and that no action would be taken against Sugarman.

The letter from Mr. Temkin also contains the following statement:

"The committee should know that it is the practice of the Postal Inspection Service to require a letter from the United States attorney if he declines to prosecute matters turned over to him for action. No such letter was requested by the potal inspectors in this case and none was sent."

Frequently inspectors present informally to United States attorneys violations of the postal laws, and such officials advise verbally that prosecution will be declined. There are no mandatory instructions to inspectors to require a letter from the United States attorney if he declines prosecution.

In connection with your request for a copy of the transmittal letter referred to in Mr. Temkin's communication, it is respectfully felt that request therefor should be made upon the United States attorney or the Department of Justice.

Sincerely yours,

H. J. SIMON,
Postal Inspector.

EXHIBIT No. 10

POST OFFICE DEPARTMENT,
INSPECTION SERVICE,
OFFICE OF INSPECTOR,
Providence, R. I., December 27, 1955.

Mr. JAMES H. BOBO,
General Counsel, Subcommittee to Investigate Juvenile Delinquency,
United States Senate, Washington 25, D. C.

DEAR MR. BOBO: Your letter of December 1, 1955, transmitting copy of a communication dated November 28, 1955, from Mr. Jacob S. Temkin, former United States attorney, Providence, R. I., and a copy of your reply of November 30, 1955, which relate to hearings held by your subcommittee at Providence, R. I., on November 8, 1955, has been received.

In his letter Mr. Temkin dwells principally on conversations which took place during the course of the investigation between him and certain postal inspectors. I was not present at those conferences; therefore, I am unable to testify as to what was said by the parties involved.

Mr. Temkin also stated in his letters, "The postal inspectors had been stymied in their investigation. It was my assistance which resulted in the break of this case." I am aware of the reply submitted to you by Inspector H. J. Simon, in which he answers Mr. Temkin's allegation by stating "such statement is not in agreement with the facts." I concur in Mr. Simon's reply. Mr. Temkin was furnished several affidavits dated prior to the Sugarman affidavit which indicate Mr. Sugarman was implicated in the postal violations disclosed in our investigation. These affidavits are mentioned in the transmittal letter to the United States attorney.

There are no other additional comments which I wish to make regarding Mr. Temkin's letter and there appears to be no necessity for furnishing an affidavit for the record.

Sincerely yours,

E. R. LAVAULT,
Postal Inspector.

EXHIBIT No. 11

POST OFFICE DEPARTMENT,
INSPECTION SERVICE,
OFFICE OF INSPECTOR,
Worcester, Mass., December 27, 1955.

Mr. JAMES H. BOBO,
General Counsel, Subcommittee to Investigate Juvenile Delinquency,
First Street and Indiana Avenue, NW., Washington, D. C.

DEAR MR. BOBO: Receipt is acknowledged of your letter of December 1, 1955, to which was attached a copy of a letter from Mr. Jacob S. Temkin referring to a hearing before the subcommittee on November 8, 1955, at Providence, R. I., and a copy of Senator Kefauver's reply to Mr. Temkin.

Concerning the letter submitted by Mr. Temkin, I can say that the United States attorney is the postal inspector's counselor and determines all preliminary questions of law and procedure, including appearances before the grand jury. The United States attorney also determines the competency and sufficiency of the evidence presented.

When an investigation by a postal inspector discloses evidence of a violation of a Federal law, he presents the facts to the United States attorney, and that official then makes decision as to prosecution. In this case, Mr. Tacy and I kept Mr. Temkin verbally informed of the results of our investigation on several dates. At the conference of September 10, 1954, it was Mr. Temkin's decision to proceed against Dorothy Tager alone. Under date of September 16, 1954, Mr. Tacy and I submitted a letter to Mr. Temkin containing a complete recital of the facts relating to the activities of Dorothy Tager and Calvin Sugarman.

I am aware of the substance of the letter submitted to you by Inspector H. J. Simon in answer to your letter of December 1, 1955, and I agree with his statements. In view of the above, there does not appear to be any necessity for furnishing an affidavit for the record.

Sincerely yours,

E. A. CRAUGH,
Postal Inspector.

EXHIBIT No. 12

POST OFFICE DEPARTMENT,
DISTRICT MANAGER,
Providence, R. I., December 27, 1955.

Mr. JAMES H. BOBO,
General Counsel, Subcommittee to Investigate Juvenile Delinquency,
United States Senate, Washington, D. C.

DEAR MR. BOBO: I wish to acknowledge the receipt of your letter of December 1, 1955, enclosing copies of one from Mr. Jacob S. Temkin, former United States attorney at Providence, R. I., and of your reply in reference to the hearings in Providence held by your subcommittee on November 8, 1955.

There is little further that I can add of value than has already been submitted in a letter of presentation of facts to the former United States attorney, Mr. Jacob S. Temkin, under date of September 16, 1954, signed by Post Office Inspector E. A. Craugh and myself and testified to in your subcommittee hearing at Providence, R. I., on November 8, 1955. I have been made aware of the report of Inspector Harry J. Simon to your subcommittee in this matter and fully concur therein.

Mr. Temkin discussed with me and on occasion with Inspector Craugh present practically every angle of the case. There is no question in my mind but that Mr. Temkin was thoroughly familiar with every step taken by all of the investigators in the entire investigation, and it was not until very shortly before the Federal grand jury proceedings began on December 27, 1954, that discussions of the case were had with the assistant United States attorney, Mr. Arnold Williamson. My best recollection is that Mr. Williamson telephoned me at the Postal Inspection Office at Providence suggesting that I call at his office to review this case with him in preparation for the grand jury. Mr. Williamson appeared not to be as familar with the case at that time as Mr. Temkin.

Because of the background if Mrs. Mary D. Tager in similar questionable enterprises in several States in the West several years previous, Mr. Temkin's advice was sought early in our investigation. Postal inspectors have always considered the United States attorney advisor in legal procedure and we did not wish to waste time on unessential angles. The former United States attorney followed the investigation of this case very closely from the beginning and requested me on numerous occasions to come to his office in the Federal building for a discussion of the current aspects. On occasion, he telephoned me at my home late in the evening for information as to progress and to suggest further procedure. When the facts had been gathered and the case was ready for prosecutive action in this instance, it appears to have been turned over to the assistant United States attorney for handling in the grand jury

We did not, to my knowledge, advise the United States attorney, as alleged by him, that we could establish no case against Mr. Calvin Sugarman on a charge of using the mails to defraud; that had to be the decision of the United States attorney.

The presentation letter of September 16, 1954, referred to by the former United States attorney, plainly sets forth the continuity of the operations of Mrs. Mary D. Tager and Mr. Calvin Sugarman under the various fictitious names preceding that of G. Wallis, which it was presumed might have been considered as a basis for prosecution of use of the mails to defraud and possibly conspiracy. This phase of the investigation (the continuity of the operations involving Mrs. Mary D. Tager and Mr. Calvin Sugarman) was discussed with the former United States attorney in a conference in his office on September 10, 1954, at which Inspectors Craugh and Simon, as well as myself, were present. With a knowledge of all the evidence pointing to the use of the mails to defraud in these operations of both Mrs. Tager and Mr. Sugarman, the United States attorney decided to prosecute only the case of G. Wallis involving the operations of Mrs. Mary D. Tager under that fictitious name. Notwithstanding this verbal decision of the former United States attorney at said conference it was deemed advisable because of the character of the evidence to set forth the facts pointing to the use of the mails to defraud in the letter of presentation under date of September 16, 1954, as I felt that the letter of presentation should embody the full facts as developed in our investigation.

As to the statement of Mr. Temkin in his letter of November 28, 1955, to your subcommittee that at my request he undertook to speak to the father of Mr. Calvin Sugarman in an effort to have the father prevail upon his son to cooperate with the postal inspectors, the fact is that Mr. Temkin requested me by telephone to come to his office on August 27, 1954. I did so and made a note of what was said. He stated: "I have a clue for you—the best clue yet—Sugarman's father." I told the former United States attorney that we, the inspectors, had already discussed that angle. He then asked me whether he should talk to the father. I told him that as he had a legal mind I would have to depend on his judgment in such a matter. He, Mr. Temkin, then stated that he would like to have my opinion and I agreed that it might be a very good idea—that it might cause Mr. Calvin Sugarman to come in and tell us the true story, which we believe he later did. The evidence will show that up to this point the inspectors were not in any sense "stymied in their investigation" as alleged by Mr. Temkin.

As to the statement of the former United States attorney that "I also testified that I had, as a routine procedure, assigned the case to an assistant who thereafter handled it, including the presentation to the grand jury and that I at no time had read the postal inspectors' report in the case," the fact is that on December 3, 1954, I addressed a letter to Mr. Temkin as United States attorney, referring with particular emphasis to pages 8 and 9 of our letter of presentation of September 16, 1954, and listing witnesses and their testimony, and also to my interview with him, Mr. Temkin, in his office on December 2, 1954, in this connection. The witnesses mentioned in that letter of December 3, 1954, were the selection of the former United States attorney, Mr. Temkin, made during the visit to his office on December 2, 1954, after thorough discussion of the evidence each witness would be expected to testify to. I recall making shorthand notes of the witnesses he decided to be important. The information set forth in the letter of December 3, 1954, was set forth in the manner Mr. Temkin had indicated to me he wished it.

Very sincerely,

NELSON A. TACY,
District Operations Manager and former Post Office Inspector.

JUVENILE DELINQUENCY

(TELEVISION PROGRAMS)

HEARINGS

BEFORE THE

SUBCOMMITTEE TO INVESTIGATE
JUVENILE DELINQUENCY

OF THE

COMMITTEE ON THE JUDICIARY
UNITED STATES SENATE

EIGHTY-FOURTH CONGRESS

FIRST SESSION

PURSUANT TO

S. Res. 62

INVESTIGATION OF JUVENILE DELINQUENCY IN THE
UNITED STATES

APRIL 6 AND 7, 1955

Printed for the use of the Committee on the Judiciary

COMMITTEE ON THE JUDICIARY

HARLEY M. KILGORE, West Virginia, *Chairman*

JAMES O. EASTLAND, Mississippi
ESTES KEFAUVER, Tennessee
OLIN D. JOHNSTON, South Carolina
THOMAS C. HENNINGS, JR., Missouri
JOHN L. McCLELLAN, Arkansas
PRICE DANIEL, Texas
JOSEPH C. O'MAHONEY, Wyoming

ALEXANDER WILEY, Wisconsin
WILLIAM LANGER, North Dakota
WILLIAM E. JENNER, Indiana
ARTHUR V. WATKINS, Utah
EVERETT McKINLEY DIRKSEN, Illinois
HERMAN WELKER, Idaho
JOHN MARSHALL BUTLER, Maryland

SUBCOMMITTEE TO INVESTIGATE JUVENILE DELINQUENCY IN THE UNITED STATES

ESTES KEFAUVER, Tennessee, *Chairman*

THOMAS C. HENNINGS, JR., Missouri
PRICE DANIEL, Texas

WILLIAM LANGER, North Dakota
ALEXANDER WILEY, Wisconsin

JAMES H. BOBO, *General Counsel*

CONTENTS

Statement of—   **Page**
  Banay, Dr. Ralph S., research psychiatrist, Columbia University,
    New York, N. Y_____   79
  Fellows, Harold E., president and chairman of the board, National
    Association of Radio and Television Broadcasters; accompanied by
    Edward H. Bronson, director of Television Code affairs, NARTB,
    and Thad H. Brown, vice president for television, NARTB,
    Washington, D. C_____   44
  Heffernan, Joseph V., vice president, National Broadcasting Co., Inc.,
    RCA Building, Radio City, New York 20, N. Y_____   121
  Hennock, Frieda B., member of the Federal Communications Com-
    mission, Washington, D. C_____   24
  Lazarsfeld, Dr. Paul F., professor of sociology, Columbia University,
    New York, N. Y_____   87
  Maccoby, Dr. Eleanor E., lecturer, department of social relations,
    Harvard University, Cambridge, Mass_____   4
  Walker, Mrs. Louise S., supervisor of audio-visual education, Mont-
    gomery County, Md., schools_____   117
  Wood, William A., general manager, metropolitan Pittsburgh educa-
    tional television station WQED, Pittsburgh, Pa_____   104

EXHIBITS

(Number and summary of exhibit)

1. Television and Our Children; the Experts Speak Up, article by Robert
   M. Goldenson, appearing in the December 1954 issue of Parents
   magazine_____   [2] 49
2. Copies of Facts About TV, published by the television information
   committee of the National Association of Radio and Television
   Broadcasters during October, November, and December 1954_____   [2] 55
3. Information relative to juvenile delinquency published by the National
   Association of Radio and Television Broadcasters_____   [1] 67
4. Excerpts from mail received by Children's Corner from viewers who
   watch WQED TV at Pittsburgh, Pa_____   [2] 114

[1] On file with the subcommittee.
[2] Printed in the record.

JUVENILE DELINQUENCY
(Television Programs)

(This is a continuance of hearings held June 5 and
October 19 and 20, 1954)

WEDNESDAY, APRIL 6, 1955

United States Senate,
Subcommittee of the Committee on the Judiciary,
to Investigate Juvenile Delinquency,
Washington, D. C.

The subcommittee met, pursuant to call, at 10:10 a. m., in the Old
Supreme Court Chamber, United States Capitol Building, Senator
Estes Kefauver presiding.

Present: Senators Kefauver and Wiley.

Also present: James H. Bobo, general counsel; Carl L. Perian, and
William Haddad of the subcommittee staff.

Chairman Kefauver. The subcommittee will come to order.

This is a continuation of the television hearing held in April and
October of last year, at which time Senator Hendrickson presided.

Due to the time limitation of witnesses and also the illness of one
witness, we were not able to hear from the type of witnesses that are
important in an investigation of this kind. That is, the social scientists who have done much work in the field of television upon the
effects of its audiences.

In these hearings we hope to fulfill this void and thereby enable us
to complete our report on—the subcommittee's special report on—
television. We have established in previous hearings there has been
an increase in television programs that have as their theme crime and
violence.

We now hope to hear from witnesses who are concerned with television research and what the long-range effects of television may be on
the Nation's youth.

Our investigation has resulted in an ever-increasing amount of correspondence from parents and organizations over the possible detrimental effects of some of these programs.

(Excerpts from a few of the many letters concerned with TV programs read as follows:)

The New Jersey Congress of Parents and Teachers, in convention assembled, do
hereby request * * * that the Congress of the United States be requested to
take action against the showing of television programs on crime, sex, and horror
stories detrimental to health, moral character, and spiritual development of our
youth.—New Jersey Congress of Parents and Teachers.

While I am writing may I also suggest that in the work of your subcommittee
to study the influence of comic books and television crime programs on juvenile

1

delinquency, you might find a good opportunity to analyze the effect of beer and wine commercials on young TV viewers. Certainly if crime programs have an effect on young people the constant repetition of entertaining and appealing advertisements for alcoholic beverages could create appetites which it would be illegal to satisfy.—Mr. Roger Burgess, Washington, D. C.

As a mother of 2 boys, ages 7½ and 9 years, I do not favor these films with scenes of violent actions * * * I do feel frustrated when I have to deprive the children from observing the TV shows that they enjoy. If these films were not shown and other educational as well as entertaining films were substituted, all parents would be pleased.
Thank you again for your committee's good work.—Mrs. Harold Monchick, West Palm Beach, Fla.

I, for one, will appreciate anything you can do to improve the programs and if possible improve the whole phase of TV operation. It's pretty low, in my opinion.—Mr. B. C. Delahoussaye, Crowley, La.

We learned that efforts are being made nationally to curb the sale of comic books, and to censor radio and television programs as one means to stop the publicity of horror stories.
The women at the meeting signed a roundrobin to assure you of our deep and abiding interest in your work * * *.—Greater St. Louis Regional Women's Guild, St. Louis, Mo.

TV and radio crime programs are directly responsible for most of the appalling increase in juvenile crime in our Nation.
The great American public is applauding you.—Mr. Bennett L. Williams, Los Angeles, Calif.

It has been our observation in talking with many boys who are now coming before the board of the California Youth Authority that the modus operandi used in crimes of violence and aggressive crimes against persons has frequently been taken directly from a crime television program. * * *
It is the studied opinion of some of us working in this field that programs that fail to promote respect for law and order are often injurious to young persons; likewise, programs showing someone being knocked out in every episode tend to make that type of behavior acceptable on impressionable young minds.—Heman G. Stark, California Youth Authority.

May I comment that many children's programs on television also show excessive violence, terror, and brutality.
I would greatly appreciate * * * an inquiry into the possible harmful effects of television violence on our young people. * * *—Mrs. Fay Grad, Bronx, N. Y.

We wish to commend you and your committee for the many things that you have done in improving television and radio programs for our children.—Kiwanis Club of Hammond, Ind.

This organization, which is interdenominational and represents thousands of sincere and intelligent people, greatly appreciates your stand against the present demoralizing influences of television. We thank you and may God bless you and strengthen you.—Christian Guidance Bureau, Grand Rapids, Mich.

Something should be done to do away with radio, TV, and movies that teach childhood delinquency, and crime.—Mr. J. Richard Feeley, Amesbury, Mass.

I do not have a television in my home because it grieves me so to see what the children are being fed.
May God bless you and your committee and guide you a solution to such an important consideration.—Mrs. Edna Street Barnes, Savannah, Ga.

We strongly urge that unfavorable effects of television viewing be remedied.—Arden, Del., Parent Teachers Association, Wilmington, Del.

We are pleased that you hold public hearings on television "crime and violence" programs. It has a great share in juvenile delinquency.—Mrs. E. Sala, Detroit, Mich.

I really believe that a lot could be and should be done for the bettering of radio and TV.—A. Robinson, Quincy, Ill.

I would greatly appreciate your consideration of these television programs.—Myrna Fuller, Quincy, Ill.

We, as mothers and as members of a church organization strongly interested in the welfare and mental health of our children, hereby go on record as approving the work of your committee, investigating the sale of comic books, and the fare offered on television for our children to view.—The Evening Circle, St. John Evangelical and Reformed Church, Caseyville, Ill.

Please continue to do all you can to give us more wholesome TV programs for our children.—Mrs. George Holl, Germantown, Wis.

I write to express our interest in the work of the committee that is investigating TV programs, comic books, and lascivious literature as they affect children. We are hopeful that the investigation will bring action.—Mrs. Hugo Schuessler, Bethel Women's Guild, Evansville, Ind.

I happen to believe that everyone connected in any way with the media reaching youth (and education [teaching] is not confined within the four walls of a classroom) must have ideals, morals, and values beyond reproach. However, I am not idealistic enough to believe this to be true. * * *

The TV industry is not interested in honesty or it would have produced more programs of quality rather than 75 percent or more, by actual count, of sheer tripe by objective standards of criticism. * * *

The views expressed by members of the TV industry represent in essence all that America has never been, or must not become. Communication at the lowest level is the antithesis of all that is beautiful, moral, valuable in life, and significant in the esthetic sense. * * *

I urge that the FCC get tough with the television companies and take any steps which seem necessary * * *.—Julius J. Hubler, professor of art education, State University of New York, Buffalo, N. Y.

Chairman KEFAUVER. However, if we should find that too many other factors go into the making up a delinquent to make television viewing of any consequence, then we can assure the parents of its harmlessness.

On the other hand, if the opposite is indicated, we will try to find a way toward a solution of the problem here in the next 2 days.

In other words, we are objectively going into these hearings to look into the research projects that have been done to determine how much we can generalize from them, determine why there has been very little done in this area, and also to find out how we on the subcommittee can aid in bringing about planning for research and possibly lay out the framework of necessary funds and personnel.

We will also hear from people who have concerned themselves with educational television, and the development of children's programs.

We feel that this very new and important media of information that has done a whole lot to bring many families together, to furnish home information; and we hope that the people of the country, the viewers of television, can have the fullest cooperation of the television and broadcasting industries in trying to see that this important medium of information is used for the best possible purpose, for not only the entertainment but for the education of our young people.

I think public discussion by people who have made a study of this matter will be of importance to the television industry as well as to the general public.

Senator Wiley, do you wish to make any statement or observations before we call our first witness?

Senator WILEY. Mr. Chairman, I am happy to be seated at this table with you again. I remember what valiant services you performed in the Crime Committee.

My own idea is that out of these hearings there should come light and information for all of us in the field of what might be called intercommunication.

After all, the human mind is the receiving set, and it gets the ideas that are impacted upon it. Youth itself is traveling from the cradle to maturity, and during that course it is being impacted by millions of ideas, and some great leader has said the idea is the thing.

Long before that, a Great Teacher said that as a man thinketh in his heart, so is he.

Now, these youngsters of ours are receiving these ideas. How can we best, in this age of propaganda as we call it, help shape the human mind into constructive thinking so that the youngsters of today can be the real guiding force of tomorrow in this period when our own country has been called to leadership?

To me, I think everyone should join in pursuing that particular thing we have in mind, and that is, to find the way to aid this television business and other communication means to the human mind.

Chairman KEFAUVER. Thank you, Senator Wiley.

Mr. Bobo, our counsel, and Karl Perian, who is with our staff, have secured and suggested the witnesses for this hearing.

At the end of the hearing tomorrow, or, if that is not possible, then at some other time, we will give anyone who has any contribution to make, any public witness, an opportunity of being heard.

We have extended invitations to all of the broadcasting companies and the television industry, and of course we want to present all points of view.

Mr. Bobo, who is our first witness?

Mr. BOBO. Dr. Eleanor Maccoby.

Chairman KEFAUVER. Dr. Maccoby, will you come around?

Glad to have you with us, Dr. Maccoby. Mr. Bobo, do you wish——

Mr. BOBO. Dr. Maccoby, would you state your name and your affiliation and your address for the benefit of the record?

STATEMENT OF DR. ELEANOR E. MACCOBY, LECTURER, DEPARTMENT OF SOCIAL RELATIONS, HARVARD UNIVERSITY

Dr. MACCOBY. Yes. I am Eleanor Maccoby, Harvard University, a lecturer there, and my field is child psychology.

Mr. BOBO. Dr. Maccoby, I think you have a statement which you would like to present to the subcommittee?

Dr. MACCOBY. Yes; that is right.

Chairman KEFAUVER. Dr. Maccoby, how long have you been with Harvard University?

Dr. MACCOBY. Five years.

Chairman KEFAUVER. And you are a specialist and you teach child psychology?

Dr. MACCOBY. I teach child psychology and public opinion. I have done some work in the mass media.

Chairman KEFAUVER. And have you made a special study on the impact of various television programs upon youthful viewers and listeners?

Dr. MACCOBY. Some study, Senator; not as much as I wished.

Chairman KEFAUVER. Are you familiar with—have you studied a great deal of the writing and research on this subject?

Dr. MACCOBY. A good deal of it, Senator. I will try to speak up, then.

Chairman KEFAUVER. Dr. Maccoby, you will have to speak as loud as you can. Do you wish to read your statement, or do you want to speak orally?

Dr. MACCOBY. I will do some of both. I will ad lib as I go along, if I may.

Chairman KEFAUVER. Very well, you go in your own way.

Dr. MACCOBY. Well, I have been asked to testify to you gentlemen on a study on television children which we did in Cambridge, Mass., about 4 years ago.

Now, you will recognize, of course, that television has changed a great deal since that time.

There was a virtue of doing it in the winter of 1950–51, however, because at that time there were many families which did not have television, and it was possible for us to compare the activities of children in families which did have television with families which did not have it.

Now, at that time, about two-thirds of the families of the area which we were studying had no television. We worked with families who had children between the ages of 4 and 17, and we drew a sample of families at random from the city of Cambridge.

We talked to about 332 mothers, and these mothers had 622 children. So we asked the mothers to describe to us exactly what each one of their children had been doing on the schoolday immediately preceding the interview, that is, through the afternoon and into the evening, and also during each hour of the day on the last Sunday before the interview took place.

Now, in the families which did have television we found the children were spending 2½ hours per weekday and 3½ per Sunday watching television.

One thing that interested us was the fact that children watched as much as this, regardless of how long they had their sets. Many people had told us that television was sort of a new toy and that the interest in it would wear off after the child had had a chance to see all the kind of things there were and had sort of settled down.

We did not find that to be the case. Even the children who had had their television sets as long as 2 years were still watching the viewing as much as those who had just gotten their sets. We have had results in just this last week which are not fully tabulated yet, but it looks as though the 3-hour average per day still stands up pretty well as the amount of time that the average child does spend watching TV.

Now, we also found that children of ages 4 and 5 spend as much time watching television as children who are 9, 10, and teen-aged, and we did not investigate how early it starts. We do know that by the age of 4 the TV habit is pretty well established.

I remember interviewing 1 mother whose child of 16 months was in a playpen in the living room at the time I was interviewing, and the child kept saying "Kate, Kate," and pointing to the television set, and the mother said she kept the playpen in front of the TV set because the child enjoyed the television set so much and had learned her first word, "Kate," to stand for a TV star, so I am convinced that it begins very early.

We were interested to note, too, that the majority of children of all ages watch programs which are not primarily intended for children. I think you can see that must be the case, since the major television viewing hours, especially for children, are between 5 and 6, and children are watching programs well after dinner, well up to bedtime, watching much fare that is not specifically children's programs.

Now, this means that almost any program on television is seen by some children, and that includes programs as late as the night-owl theaters.

I know of one case of a child of four whose mother is living alone with the child, and keeps the child up with her for company until 11:30 or 12, and they watch television together most of that time.

Now, we did find that children in homes which have television go to bed later than the nontelevision homes.

The difference there is about a little less than a half hour difference in bedtime, the TV children going to bed on the average a half hour later.

Now, that half hour is kind of a deceptive figure, because some parents guard the bedtime of their children very closely whether they have television or not, so their children go to bed anyway, but other parents allow themselves to be wheedled. What happens is, a child wants to stay up just this once to see a special program, and then it happens again and again and finally gets to be the pattern in the family.

Now, it has been assumed in some quarters that it is safe enough to show programs that might be unsuitable for children so long as they are put on the air after 9 or 10 o'clock.

Now, it is true, of course, that a large proportion of children are in bed by these hours, but many are not, and no matter when a program is on, some children will see it.

This might be important if we remember that TV children who see late programs tend to be the ones for whom home controls are somewhat weak. The parents are not getting them in bed, you see, and therefore they are the ones who would, in any case, be most apt to pick up whatever undesirable material there was on these late programs.

Well, one question that we felt to be important was, What is television taking the place of?

If children are spending 3 hours a day watching television, they must be doing it instead of what they would have been doing in those 3 hours if they didn't have television, and we are interested in this question of substitution of activities. So we compared the children who did have television and were spending their 3 hours a day watching it with the children who didn't yet have it to see just exactly what they might have been doing if they were not watching television.

We found some television time is a direct transfer from radio listening, movie going, comic book reading, and regular book reading. We found, however, that television watching is so much greater in time than the time that used to be spent on those other media that the child's total exposure to mass media is just about doubled when the family gets television. That is, the television takes away a good deal of time from other mass media, but it also takes time from hobbies, from playing outdoors, from helping mother around the house, and all the other kinds of children's activities that would go on. As I say, the total exposure to mass media is just about doubled with the advent of television in the home.

It is interesting, too, to note that TV children who watch television a great deal are the ones who read comic books a great deal. They are not the ones who read books. There is a negative relationship there, and the more a child watches television, the less he is likely to read books.

Some of the television time, incidentally, is taken from sleep time, as I have said, because the bedtimes are later.

All right; now what about the impact of having a television set upon family life?

You are all familiar with the statement that Henry Ford took the American family out of the home and scattered them and that television has brought them back together again. That is true, in a certain sense. We found in our study that the amount of time children spend actually in the physical presence of their parents and their other family members goes up when they get television because the family spends a good deal of time sitting together and watching television.

However, the amount of time a child spends with his family, not counting television time is very drastically reduced. It is about half as great, and what happens then is that the parents and children are sitting together watching something jointly, but they are not talking together nor playing together nor working together. They are only doing that half as much time as they used to before they got television.

Now, the meaning of this was brought home to me in a particular interview that I remember. I was talking to the mother in the dining room of a little apartment because her husband was sitting in the living room watching television, and we did not want to disturb him. So we were sitting there and I was interviewing her about her children's activities and while we were there the little boy came home from school and he went up to the living room and went up to his father and he had brought home a drawing he had made at school. He said, "Look, Daddy; see this drawing?" that he had. His father said, "Sssh." He pushed him away because the father was in a particularly crucial part of the story, so the child sat down and watched the program.

But here was an opportunity for the parent and child to interact, and for the father to say something to his boy about the accomplishment; but here was an opportunity that was missed because of the father's absorption in TV. I assume tihs is happening at a lot of times.

Particularly interesting, was, of course, the family dinner hour, which has always been a time of the family life when they discussed the doings of the day and the parents have a chance to discuss with children about telling them what was right or wrong about what happened. In the families we studied, one-sixth of the children had their supper in front of the television set every night, and almost half had their supper in front of television 2 or 3 times a week; so that the family dinner hour, in some families at least, has sort of evaporated because of the advent of television.

Please don't misunderstand me. I know there are some families where the family dinner hour is not all sweetness and light and instruction to children, and I imagine that television is better than what one finds in the situation at the dinner table; but there is no doubt that television is cutting into that time of interaction.

Now, one final point about the matter of family influence. When children are watching television with their parents the parents may not be exercising much active influence in the sense of guiding and instructing the children, but at least they know where the children are. The children are not out on the streets unsupervised.

We find that many parents are quite at a loss to know how to control teen-age youngsters and they are thankful when there is something as interesting as television to keep them at home without an argument.

I have a quotation here from one mother who said in an interview:

> I think television tends to hold a family together. There are a lot of things to say for TV in that way. I find I don't have to go looking for my daughter at dinnertime and she stays home in the evening. She never goes out evenings now, and TV has safeguarded my daughter.

Now, another mother of a younger child, this boy was about 8 years old and very active and mischievous boy, was very pleased with television because it kept her son out of mischief and she said it is just like putting him to sleep. She can sit him down in front of the television set and he will be absorbed and happy, and will not be in the way. As a matter of fact, that is what we found mother thought best about television; it is a wonderful babysitter before the dinner hour when the children are tired and cranky and it is a great relief for her to send the children up before the television set and let them be quiet. This means she will let them watch anything on television at that hour. She is not there to monitor them because she is elsewhere, and she is simply using television as a sitter.

Now, I would like to turn to a question which is in some ways more interesting and more important than the question of how much time children spend watching TV or under what circumstances they watch.

I would like to discuss the question of the effects on children of the kind of thing that they see on television programs.

Now, I would like to say at the outset that this is a question about which we have very few solid facts. I know this committee has received contradictory evidence from different sources. Some witnesses have felt that the acts of violence that children see on TV and in comic strips simply provide a harmless outlet for the aggressive impulses that all children have anyway.

Others have felt that constantly viewing violent episodes must leave a lasting mark on the child, sometimes even providing the stimulus for outright acts of delinquency.

Now, I am sorry to have to hedge on this point, but I believe there is some truth in both points of view because some kinds of TV content does have lasting effect on some children, under some conditions, but we are just now beginning to find out what some of the conditions are that are important.

Incidentally, I would like—the American Medical Association has given to a small group of us at Boston University and Harvard a small amount of money for research in this area. The American Bar Association has talked to us and is interested in it, and one of the studies I will refer to was supported by the United States Public Health Services.

Now, the first question we must ask ourselves about television is why children are interested in it in the first place. That may seem a strange question to ask because, of course, it seems as though the programs are intrinsically interesting. But when one says a program is interesting, he is saying something about the viewers as well as about the program, because the program is not interesting unless it strikes a responsive chord in a person.

Now, the child sometimes views television just because he has got curiosity about the world around him, a natural, understandable thing.

There is another motive, though, and that is a desire for escape from whatever unpleasant situations there are in real life around him.

Now, most of us are familiar with the impulse to pick up a mystery story to take our mind off our worries, and this impulse holds for children, too.

We did a study in 2 parts of the Boston metropolitan area in which we interviewed about 400 mothers to find out a lot of details about the way they trained their children, how much they punished them, what kind of punishment they used, whether they would let them make noise in the house, whether they would allow them to go out unsupervised, whether they required them to be very neat and careful, and so on.

(The study appears at the end of Dr. Maccoby's statement on p. 20.)

Dr. MACCOBY. We found the children who were most punished and most restricted were the ones who spent their time, more time, watching television, from which we concluded that there is an element of escape in the motivation for the child to watch television. He goes to it because other things are unpleasant, and that makes television more pleasant. I am not saying this detracts at all from the value of television to the child, but it is one of the reasons that he does look.

Now, sometimes the child is escaping from frustration, in other words, when he watches TV, and sometimes he is just simply bored. But when he sits down to watch a program, he puts himself in imagination in the hero's place.

He feels a pride when the hero is threatened, and he has a sense of power when the hero does something to defeat an enemy.

We come to this very important question of TV programs as being simply a harmless outlet for aggression. Basically, as I understand it, the idea is this: If a person is thirsty and takes a long drink of water, there is a period of several hours when he won't want a drink of water again. His need has been satisfied.

Now, the theory goes that when a person is frustrated or angry, if he does something aggressive, this will discharge his anger and he will be more quiet and peaceful afterward. The next step in the theory is that it is possible to discharge one's anger indirectly or vicariously through the activity of somebody else by watching a prize fight, for example, or watching a gun battle on television.

Now, a number of questions come to mind about this point of view: First of all, if it is true that a child can get some discharge of his aggressive feelings by viewing violent activity on television, how long does the relief last?

Presumably, if he reenters a frustrating situation when the TV situation is over, he can be made angry again and will be just as ready for relief aggression as he ever was before.

Another question is this: If a child sits down to watch a television show when he is not angry, but merely sits down out of habit or because he is bored, is there any danger that aggressive feelings will be aroused rather than quieted?

Now, the research on this question has yet to be done, so I am only guessing here. I expect when we do the research that we will find that aggressive feelings are sometimes increased rather than reduced by aggressive scenes on television or in the movies.

Mothers have reported to me a number of instances where, after a violent television show, there has been a flurry of quarreling among the children in the home. Some of my students have told me about watching a wresting show on television and then getting down on the living room rug and wrestling. I don't mean to say this a harmful activity. This is just sort of a spillover into relief from some of the impulses that are aroused by the material that they see on television. Sometimes the activity that spills over can be perfectly harmless and sometimes it may not be.

Now, here is a final question: Let's assume it is true that some children do experience a certain relief for their aggressive feelings when they see fighting and murder on television. Is it not true that while they are having this experience, they are practicing what the hero does, and adding his acts to their own repertoire of possible future behavior?

There is not any doubt that children pick up all sorts of content from the programs they watch. Teen-age girls watch the movie stars and the TV stars to see very carefully what is the proper thing to wear to the theater or nightclub or how to act at a wedding or what you are supposed to do when you ride on an airplane, whether you are supposed to tip the stewardess or not, these things these girls have never had in a situation of having to experience, and some time they may, so they want to be ready so they wouldn't be unsophisticated, so they watch closely and store up these little items of information which the television offers them for future reference if the situation ever comes up when they need it.

Now, just at the present time, we are doing a little experiment at Harvard where we are testing children for what they remember out of a movie. What we have done is to compare children who were angry and upset at the time they saw the movie with children who were not, and we have found that when a child sees a movie, this was a Dead End Kids movie, by the way, one with lots of action and violence, when a child sees a movie of that sort while he is upset and angry, he remembers the aggressive content better than if he were not angry when he saw the program. He remembers the quiet, mild material much less well, if he saw the movie while he was angry, which means, then, that what a person sees and remembers out of a television show depends upon the mood he was in at the time that he saw it.

There is a kind of selection here, and the very children who are going to be most in danger, perhaps, of using aggressive activity, are the ones who focus right on that kind of activity when they see it in a show, whereas other children might see the same material and not notice that at all.

Now, please understand that I am not claiming that every child who sees a murder on a television show is going to rush right out and make use of the information he has gained by committing a relief murder. For most children, the situation will never arise in which the knowledge could be put to use, because the relief restraints on the expression of aggression are very great indeed.

But for some children it can be incorporated into action. I know of an instance in which two boys saw a movie in which a character hung up an enemy by his hands in order to make him confess some misdeed. Now, these two boys had been suspecting their little brother of stealing from their piggy bank, so when they got home from the movie they took their little brother down into the basement and hung him up from a pipe in the basement by his hands in order to get him to confess. He didn't confess. His mother found him there about a half hour later and he was scared but not much hurt. He had been stealing from their piggy bank to this day, and he is proud to this day that he did not confess it.

But here you have an instance where these boys had a motivation to deal harshly with their little brother. They simply picked up from a movie they had seen. They probably would have picked it up from something else if not by the movie. The movie added to their repertoire of possible things one can do to their little brother and it triggered off activity which already had a strong potential behind it.

Now, all this means is that a TV program or a movie can have one function for one child and an entirely different function for another child, depending upon what particular elements in the program fit in with the child-relief situation.

I have been talking about how children can have aggressive feelings aroused or quieted by TV programs and have also indicated that under some circumstances certain aggressive actions can be learned from television.

We must not overlook the fact that a child can also learn from television that wrongdoing will be punished.

Some of the things he learns from programs, in other words, may operate to inhibit aggression by providing the child with warnings about the possible consequences of his actions.

The child may learn that aggressive action is permissible in some conditions, for instance, in a battle where the action is directed against an enemy, but he can also learn that unprovoked aggression against members of one's own society or family will bring retribution. It becomes important, then, to know about television; not only how many killings there are in the programs the child sees but who does the killing, why he does it, and what the consequences are for the person who does it. The television industry, of course, has recognized the importance of the outcomes of stories for the moral training of children and it has adopted a code which requires that criminals shall always be punished in television.

This is a standard which should certainly help to prevent some of the possible undesirable effects of violent programs. But beyond this, it appears to me as important whether the criminal is punished by an agent of the law or by a private citizen who adopts the role of Robin Hood and takes the law into his own hands.

We are all familiar with the fact that some of the most popular characters on television for children's programs are the private citizen who has more power than the agents of the law and goes out and brings the criminal in when the law could not do it unaided.

Now, in some stories, too, the punishment for the criminal comes as a kind of an afterthought with little emphasis, while in others the moral consequences are woven into the very heart of the story in such a way as to make a more lasting impression on the child.

Now, we do not know, actually, how much attention children pay to the consequences of evil deeds on television programs. The industry has made a strong effort to see to it that evildoing is punished.

We know, however, that children remember some things and not others out of programs, and we do not know exactly how much they remember the consequences. There is a group at Boston University now who have been doing a study in which they cut up films, Hopalong Cassidy films, and rearranged them so that the film can have a different ending. Sometimes the hero wins and sometimes he loses, and although their research is not completed yet, it looks quite clear that the effect upon the child and what he remembers is influenced by who wins in the movie, and the person the child admires most is influenced by who wins. So all we can say at this point is outcomes make a great deal of difference. We do not want to take the position that all aggression in movies is bad and something that should be filtered out, but rather it makes a great deal of difference how it is woven into the story.

Now, as a final point, I would like to say that it has been a sobering experience for me to be asked to give so-called expert testimony to the members of this committee about the kind and amount of influence television has on children.

I have been forced to take stock of what we know and the amount is not very impressive. Perhaps it is not surprising that we know relatively little about television. Scientific knowledge accumulates very slowly, and television is very new.

We do know a great deal about some of the psychological processes that are involved in the way children learn new material in general, and we know something about the functions of phantasy life for children's personalities.

But the specific applications of this knowledge to the problems of television and its effect have not yet been made. They should be made for the problem is an extremely important one, and it is my hope that one result of this committee's work will be to focus attention upon the need for more research in the area.

Chairman KEFAUVER. Thank you very much, Dr. Maccoby. I think your statement has been very fair, objective, and helpful. I think it establishes a good base for other testimony we will hear. Senator Wiley, do you have any questions?

Senator WILEY. I have been very much interested in the dissertation here. Being a father and a grandfather and seeing these grandchildren of mine before television, I am particularly interested, because, of course, I have good grandchildren, in what I would say would be the instructive value of television. I can remember as a boy looking at colored pictures, books, and so forth, pictures out of the Old Testament, and historical illustrations.

Now I see these youngsters learning history, learning morals, if you please, the utilization of the moral code, really, through some of these pictures.

I see them being instructed in Government out of some of these pictures, and what I call it, it is a package system of impacting the young mind so that it feels an impact such as we never felt when we were youngsters. We never heard a sermon, never heard any kind of a preachment that would compare with what some of these pictures will do.

At the same time, I feel that there are certain improvements, particularly relating to the youngsters. Of course, we are all youngsters, some of us are not grown up yet. We take Hopalong Cassidy and some of those things and we enjoy them yet at times. But what we are really interested in here, as I understand it, is to find if there is to be any improvement, an improvement of a way of impacting the youth, the mind of the youngster.

When he gets above a certain age, he has got to use his discretion about what he wants to see. Until he arrives at that age, the parent has got the responsibility, together with the moving-picture industry.

But I want to thank you, also, for a very interesting, challenging dissertation.

Dr. MACCOBY. Thank you.

Chairman KEFAUVER. Mr. Bobo, do you have any questions?

Mr. BOBO. Yes; Dr. Maccoby I was interested in the last point which you gave there. Isn't it true that some children, viewing television, or is it true, would remember a scene where there was crime and violence or sensationalism more than they would remember who it was that finally brought the criminal to justice?

Dr. MACCOBY. Yes, I think that would be true.

Mr. BOBO. That, regardless of the end result of the program, that the thing which would ring true in his mind would be the sensational part of the picture?

Dr. MACCOBY. For some children, yes.

Mr. BOBO. Do you find that there is an individuality of television viewing that one child is affected one way and one child is affected another way?

Dr. MACCOBY. We suspect so because of things they remember, depending upon the mood they were in when they saw the material. Some children are generally more upset and frustrated than the others and they will be the ones who will select the information from the media that fits their mood.

Mr. BOBO. Now to the vicarious results of television. A constant exposure to scenes of aggression or scenes of violence, would that continue to build up in that child, he being satisfied with the television program, not having another outlet for his aggression, and eventually, even though he might have started as a normal child, as a constant buildup of watching the aggressive scenes; might it result in a more serious aggression when the outlet does come on a personal basis?

Dr. MACCOBY. I think we should remember what Senator Wiley has just said. We don't want to give the impression all the things that children see are crime and violence. They get constant exposure to television but a lot of it is not of that sort.

Now, a child who is upset and takes television as a way out when he has no relief outlets, I think such a child might simply develop the habit of getting all his satisfactions through phantasy. That is not a very happy thing psychologically, but it does not mean he is going to rush out and commit murder in relief. The problem of transfer of the things you learn in television to relief activity is the big question and we cannot be sure exactly when this is going to happen. It does happen, sometimes, but by no means always.

Mr. BOBO. There was another question that Senator Wiley's statement brought up in my mind; about the marvelous effects of these pictures on teaching children certain things. How would that affect your schoolteacher in the educational system in providing a program interesting enough for children after they have been home 3 hours a day watching television?

Dr. Maccoby. Well, it means she has a lot of competition. She has to do a better job, I think.

Mr. Bobo. I have heard of numerous instances—I would not say numerous, but I have heard of a few instances, where schoolteachers threw up their hands and left because they could not compete with television visual effect.

Dr. Maccoby. I know that has happened, and I know some teachers are grateful for the fact that children become interested in school-work. Our own 13-year-old ward saw Romeo and Juliet in the movies and has been memorizing the balcony scene the last 2 weeks. She never would read Shakespeare before, so I think teachers are going to find that is a kind of help.

Mr. Bobo. Now, as to crime and violence, which I think during the last hearings it was stated by some witness that 25 to 15 percent of the programs viewed during the normal children's hours were crime and violence programs. Suppose that only this was reduced to 2 percent, but the child had a deep interest in crime and violence programs. Would he seek out that 2 percent of the programs and still get about the same percent of crime and violence?

Dr. Maccoby. He would seek them out. He might get a slightly reduced fare because of the fact he could not be in front of the television set all those moments, but, yes, he would certainly seek out the things that interested him because of his own problems.

Senator Wiley. May I interrupt there?

Chairman Kefauver. Yes, Senator Wiley.

Senator Wiley. I just want to take that idea you brought up because it is very challenging. It is like food. You get—you reduce 15 percent to 2 percent. Then you have 13 percent for something else. If you have something else in there, the question is, Will it neutralize, will it—what effect will it have upon the standards, the morals, the mental standards of the child? It seems to me that the child has to learn to be discriminating. That is part of life's education. And, on the other hand, the way the shrub is bent, the tree will grow.

Dr. Maccoby. Yes.

Senator Wiley. You have to bear that in mind with these youngsters.

Dr. Maccoby. Yes, this question of the children learning to be discriminating is, I think, an important one, and what I personally wish is that parents would spend more time watching with their children and reacting to the programs. The children have not any way of telling whether the things they see are good, bad, or proper morally, and the place they have to get that training from, essentially, is their parents, after all. Most parents, as far as I can tell, sit side by side with their children and nobody talks and I think the parents should comment about the outcomes of situations, and say, "Now, that is not the way it really would be," or "I would hate to see a child of mine do that," or something of that sort to try to keep the reality element alive for the child and use this as a way of moral training.

Chairman KEFAUVER. Anything else, Mr. Bobo?

Mr. BOBO. I just wanted to build this one point, Senator, and it will just take a moment.

This survey was conducted with 662 families; is that correct?

Dr. MACCOBY. No, 662 children, but only three-hundred-and-thirty-some families. They had more than one child.

Mr. BOBO. An area-type survey, where you spot check one person per block?

Dr. MACCOBY. That is right.

Mr. BOBO. To get the overall viewpoint of the whole city?

Dr. MACCOBY. That is right.

Senator WILEY. Were they American children, or were they foreign born?

Dr. MACCOBY. Almost entirely American children. There were a few foreign-born families, whatever proportion there is living in the town of Cambridge. But almost all the children themselves were American born.

Mr. BOBO. Did you have a chance to find out any way their so-called I. Q., or what grades they were in in school?

Dr. MACCOBY. No; we did not go into that.

Chairman KEFAUVER. It is often said a parent does not want a child to see a television program; they just turn it off.

Dr. MACCOBY. That does not happen very much.

Chairman KEFAUVER. To what extent did you find parents did use some selectivity as to programs that their children would see?

Dr. MACCOBY. We found that most of the parents took a very strong position that the children should finish their schoolwork before they looked at programs. And they wouldn't allow them to study in the same room as the television set, which we thought was a good thing. Most of the parents thought most of the fare on television was perfectly all right for the children to see, and they made little effort to censor the kind of things the children could see so long as they had finished their homework.

Chairman KEFAUVER. So when television time came, that is, after the homework was finished, there was not any substantial selectivity?

Dr. MACCOBY. Very little.

Chairman KEFAUVER. Don't you think that parents, if they did use some judgment about programs, that it would be wholesome in considering the psychological makeup of their own children and that might be of some help in this matter?

Dr. MACCOBY. I think it would. I think it is a difficult task for parents, because children can wheedle very effectively, but I think they should do it, all the same.

Chairman KEFAUVER. When will the research by the American Medical Association and the American Bar Association and the Children's Bureau that you have been engaged to do, when will that be completed?

Dr. MACCOBY. Well, we are just actually beginning. By the end of the summer, there will be the pilot studies ready and then it is a question of whether we apply for financing to support a larger program on the basis of what has been finished.

Chairman KEFAUVER. Did you do any research as to whether the children who were television watchers made higher or lower grades in the school?

Dr. MACCOBY. I have not investigated that.

Chairman KEFAUVER. Or whether it improved their school standing or not?

Dr. MACCOBY. I don't know that, Senator.

Chairman KEFAUVER. I suppose the same principles that you talked about as to television would also apply to movies; would it?

Dr. MACCOBY. Movies and comic books; yes.

Chairman KEFAUVER. And comic books.

Dr. MACCOBY. But not book reading, which is quite a different phenomenon as far as we can tell.

Chairman KEFAUVER. I was interested in your statement that most of the children who were avid television watchers were also readers of comic books. Is that true?

Dr. MACCOBY. Yes.

Chairman KEFAUVER. By comic books are you talking about the better comic books or the worse ones?

Dr. MACCOBY. Some of both, depending on the child.

Chairman KEFAUVER. Dr. Maccoby, from the viewpoint of creating a wholesome influence for the children who watch television, and if there is a television in the home they are going to watch it, are they not?

Dr. MACCOBY. Yes.

Chairman KEFAUVER. From the viewpoint of being helpful or more helpful to children, what suggestions would you give the producers of television shows and the television industry? I suppose more educational pictures, more travel pictures, or ·what would be your suggestion?

Dr. MACCOBY. That would help. I would not want to suggest that all aggressive material should be filtered out of programs. I think aggression is the very heart of some of the best art, the best literature that we have ever had. If any of you saw the Iliad on Omnibus last Sunday, you will recognize that.

I think that, therefore, we will want to be very careful about trying to censor out such material, but that it does make a great deal of difference, the kind of theme that the material is imbedded in, and that this is a matter that we could give a great deal of attention to.

Chairman KEFAUVER. Then you have already indicated that if the hero is going to win, and if the villain is going to be punished, that it is important that the person who wins and the person who punishes the villain is not just a private citizen who has taken the law into his own hands, but it is better if he is an officer of the law; is that correct?

Dr. MACCOBY. Yes.

Chairman KEFAUVER. Of course, it is often said the reason there are not more educational television shows or historical or travel shows is that the TV industry puts on what the people want. Do you think that is true?

Dr. MACCOBY. I think it is true, but I am not a believer in the notion that every program we have on television should be one that has a very high Hooper rating. I believe in diversity of fare on television, and I think one of the sad things about the industry's own efforts at self-censorship, why, there have been some good ones, too, but what has happened is that the material has been sort of homogenized. It is too much alike. There is not variety. There is not material for the small groups of people who are interested in the special kind of things. I would like to see more variety made available and I think once new things are tried interest in them will develop, but it could not be expected to exist in the form of a large audience until people have had a longtime chance to see it.

Chairman KEFAUVER. Then you feel as I do, that the television industry has a right, by virtue of the channel having been given to them by the Federal Government, that it is their obligation in return for that to see that programs that will be helpful are shown and not just those that have the highest Hooper rating?

Dr. MACCOBY. I certainly do.

Chairman KEFAUVER. You must take into consideration that the shows are going to have an impact upon our children, their morals, either for good or bad, and that they are not justified in just showing those shows that have the largest watching audience.

Dr. MACCOBY. It may be asking a lot of them, considering that they are, after all, people who are there to make money.

Chairman KEFAUVER. Well, that is the purpose of the Federal Communications Commission, to see that the morals of our people are not adversely affected by the grant of this franchise; is it not?

Dr. MACCOBY. Right.

Chairman KEFAUVER. So I do not think it is asking too much of them. If they don't want to take their channel on that basis, they do not have to, and they know in advance the obligation that goes with it. Is that not correct?

Dr. MACCOBY. Yes.

Chairman KEFAUVER. Do you feel the shorter sleep that children get as a result of those who watch television is an adverse element?

Dr. MACCOBY. I suspect it is for some children. Perhaps the half hour delay does not make much difference, but, as I say, that is an average of some children going to bed later, 3 hours later, than they would otherwise, and for children who lose 3 hours of sleep I think that is quite serious.

Chairman KEFAUVER. You say there was less reading. What would these children be reading if they were not watching television?

Dr. MACCOBY. When I said reading, I meant to, incidentally, exclude comic books from that. They do less reading of books when they watch television. Some of the books that they might read are probably not much better than what they see on television. Some would be, and they would certainly have more variety, so that we would not have this homogeneity that I worry about.

Chairman KEFAUVER. Do you find that watching television, or children watching television, increases their desire to read comics?

Dr. MACCOBY. I don't know that. All I know is, children who watch television a lot read comics a lot.

Chairman KEFAUVER. Mr. Bobo, Senator Wiley—do you have any other questions?

Senator WILEY. Do you want to be specific on those comics? Are they good comics, bad comics, or in between comics?

Dr. MACCOBY. It depends on the child. Some children read only animal comics and Little Lulu, and others are interested in only the horror and crime ones.

Chairman KEFAUVER. It is interesting to note that in Cambridge, in Boston, there is a society that has done a great deal in getting the news stands to leave out the horror and crime comics and also the filthy literature, and they have been very successful, I would say.

Dr. MACCOBY. I wanted to say, two summers ago a colleague of mine wanted to do research and he was looking for comic books and he had to look far and wide in the Boston area to find them, so we felt encouraged.

Chairman KEFAUVER. I was talking with Father McNeill—what is the name of the organization that has done such a good job in Boston in cleaning up the comics?

Dr. MACCOBY. I don't remember the name.

Chairman KEFAUVER. Anyway, it is very impressive.

Dr. MACCOBY. Yes.

Chairman KEFAUVER. Mr. Bobo, do you wish to carry on; do you have any more questions?

Mr. BOBO. I have just 2 or 3 more. Do you believe, Dr. Maccoby, that the needs of some children, it may be the vicarious reduction of aggressive impulses by watching or identifying them with the so-called TV hero as Hopalong Cassidy or Roy Rogers?

Dr. MACCOBY. Do I believe what of them?

Mr. BOBO. Do you believe some of the needs of some of these children for acting out of their aggression are met by identifying them by these television heroes?

Dr. MACCOBY. Yes, momentarily, but perhaps not in a lasting fashion.

Mr. BOBO. When the show is over, he is still in the same position he might have been so far as his aggressive tendencies are concerned?

Dr. MACCOBY. If he goes back to that same position, his aggressive tendencies will be rearoused.

Mr. BOBO. Therefore, none of his causes of frustration would be removed by what he sees on television?

Dr. MACCOBY. Probably not until he gets the habit of rushing to the television and going outside instead of having a fight.

Mr. BOBO. Do you think there is a probability that after identifying himself with these TV heroes, that he might have a tendency to act out his relief aggression as the television hero acted out his?

Dr. MACCOBY. For some children, as the case of these two boys who took their little brother in the basement, I think this has happened, but it is built upon a relief desire to do this thing anyway, so I don't think these children were made into naughty children by what they saw in the movie.

Mr. BOBO. So we come back to the premise that television might affect one child one way and another, another way.

Dr. MACCOBY. Yes.

Mr. BOBO. So we could not say that crime involvements on television necessarily was a cause for delinquent action?

Dr. MACCOBY. That is right.

Senator WILEY. That brings up this thought in my mind. I was in an airplane the other day and I noticed that a clergyman was reading a very exciting detective story. I am wondering if there is any comparison between a boy who might be studying Latin or American history or reading grammar in school and coming home and seeing

Roy Rogers and that clergyman who has just preached a sermon and gets on a plane and reads this detective story.

Dr. MACCOBY. Very much the same thing.

Senator WILEY. The same thing?

Dr. MACCOBY. I think so.

Senator WILEY. In other words, someone has said, the breakfast that you ate this morning, if you fed it to an Eskimo, he would be dead before he got up from the table. And we human beings have different food physically and we also have different food mentally. But I am really interested in that reaction because the child wants a little excitement, if it is good and he gets it that way. In fact, I know some adult children that get excited looking at Roy Rogers, too.

Well, you think there is just a difference of years, that is all, between the clergyman and the boy of 10?

Dr. MACCOBY. Yes; I think it serves the same function.

Senator WILEY. Thank you.

Chairman KEFAUVER. Dr. Maccoby, I suppose you would not want to, on the information you have, say whether you think on the whole that television, putting the plus against the other, is a contributing factor to juvenile delinquency or emotional instability among our young people?

Dr. MACCOBY. This would be going a good deal beyond my information. To guess about it, I would say that television probably is not a basic cause, that it sometimes provides ammunition for the children who are looking for ammunition for bad deeds. It also provides it for good deeds.

Chairman KEFAUVER. But it would be definitely put on the plus side, on the good side, if there was more consideration of the programs that were shown; is that correct?

Dr. MACCOBY. Yes.

Chairman KEFAUVER. I have always been interested in knowing, after seeing a show where there is a lot of shooting and I see a lot of them, of course, because I have four children that watch television a great deal——

Senator WILEY. You used to have it down in Tennessee.

Chairman KEFAUVER. Children?

Senator WILEY. No, shooting.

Chairman KEFAUVER. Of course, Davy Crockett. [Laughter.] But some of the shooting, really, I must confess, gets a little rough even for a hardened person like myself. I wonder whether it does keep children from sleeping or whether they are emotionally upset so that they do not relax as well when they go to bed.

Dr. MACCOBY. I will tell you one interesting thing that was told to me by a child psychiatrist who deals with very aggressive, delinquent, disturbed boys. He says when he takes these boys to see a western, they are better and more relaxed afterward than they are at practically any other time. When he takes them to see Snow White, it disturbs them terribly, and if they see a television show in which a nice little boy goes outdoors and falls down and bumps his knee and his other bandages his knee, these boys give in to a terrific flurry of breaking furniture and what not because the thing that is wrong with those boys is that they have never been able to establish the proper kind of love relationship with the mother figure. And here they see that thing on television and it worries them to death, makes them nervous. This is the thing they could not sleep over.

Whereas just seeing somebody shoot, if he is on the right side and has a good excuse for it, it does not disturb the child.

Chairman KEFAUVER. Those were delinquent children, but, I suppose, the opposite would tend to be true if they were normal?

Dr. MACCOBY. I think it would depend on the outcome.

It seems to me the villain in one of these westerns is a wonderful character because he provides an excuse for being aggressive and for the aggression to be all right. The child is not frightened by aggression, and does not fear punishment if he can feel that he is shooting in the interest of law and order and morality, which is what all the westerns are about. The things which keep the children from sleeping, I think, are the horror programs or the programs that come out in such a way that he fears punishment because he has done an aggressive act that was not justified.

Chairman KEFAUVER. We certainly are grateful to you for coming down and giving us the benefit of your study and your great knowledge on this subject.

Dr. MACCOBY. Thank you, Senator.

Chairman KEFAUVER. We would like to have, as time goes on, further reports from you.

Dr. MACCOBY. Thank you.

(The study referred to on p. 9 reads as follows:)

WHY DO CHILDREN WATCH TELEVISION?[1]

(By Eleanor E. Maccoby, Harvard University)

Television, as we know, can be deeply absorbing to children of all ages, but we know little about the reasons why this is the case. A related problem is the question of why some children become enthusiastic television fans while others are uninterested or even bored. It is evident that if educators and parents should wish to guide the quantity and quality of TV viewing in young children, they must know something about the motives which lie behind the childrens' interest in this medium.

To some, the answer may appear obvious: Children like TV because the material presented on the TV screen is intrinsically interesting or exacting. But to say that a television program is "interesting" is to make a statement not only about the program but about the viewer. If it is interesting, it strikes a responsive chord in him—satisfies a particular need, provides wanted information, or perhaps offers release from general tension. When we attempt to understand the relationship of the child to his favorite TV programs, we are face to face with a larger question which is of great importance to present-day psychology: Namely, what are the functions of fantasy for the individual? The child spends much of his waking life in daydreaming, imaginative play, and exposure to mass media (fairy stories, comic books, radio, and TV). There have been several suggestions concerning the child's motives for this active fantasy life. The first is that fantasy provides a child with experience which is free from real-life controls so that, in attempting to find solutions to a problem, he can try out various modes of action without risking the injury or punishment which might ensue if he experimented overtly. Another function of fantasy is as a distractor. Readers are doubtless all familiar with the impulse to pick up a detective story to escape temporarily from the pressures of real life; similarly

[1] The material presented in this report is drawn from a larger study of identification in young children, conducted by the Laboratory of Human Development at Harvard University. The group primarily responsible for planning the study, gathering data, and analyzing results are Prof. Robert R. Sears, former director of the laboratory; Prof. John W. M. Whiting, present director; and Drs. Harry Levin, Edgar L. Lowell, Eleanor E. Maccoby, and Pauline S. Sears. This investigation was supported by a research grant (M–461) from the National Institute of Mental Health of the National Institutes of Health, Public Health Service.

for children, if the environment imposes strain, we may assume the child will be motivated to "get away from it all" by immersing himself in fantasy. A third function of fantasy, which was emphasized by Freud in connection with his analysis of dreams, is the wish-fulfillment function. According to this point of view, fantasy provides an outlet for impulses which are not allowed free expression in real life. Supporting this view is the fact that young children take an especially great interest in stories depicting violence and sudden death (reflecting perhaps the inhibition of aggressive impulses in their daily life) while adolescents are more interested in themes of romantic love.

In connection with the last type of explanation, it should be noted that the vicarious satisfactions provided by fantasy are presumably of a lower order than real-life satisfactions, so that fantasy outlets are chosen only as second-best solutions when real-life satisfactions are lacking.

The present study represents an effort to provide data bearing upon some of the above-presumed functions of fantasy. Specifically, the following hypothesis is tested: Children will spend more time watching television if they are highly frustrated in real life than if they are not. It will be recognized that this prediction would be made on the basis of either the distraction explanation of fantasy or the wish-fulfillment explanation. Of course, no implication is intended here that the desire to escape from an unpleasant real-life environment or obtain satisfactions vicariously which are denied in real life are the only reasons for children's interest in television. The present study is focused upon only one of many possible explanations of interest in television.

During the winter of 1951-52, 2-hour interviews were conducted with 379 mothers residing in the Greater Boston metropolitan area. Each of these mothers had a child in kindergarten (aged about 5½ years old), and was asked to describe in detail her methods of training the child. Among other things, she was asked about methods and severity of punishment, permissiveness in the areas of sex, dependency, and aggression, and the nature and degree of restrictions imposed upon the child in connection with noise, neatness, going away from the house alone, etc. On the basis of the entire interview, the mother was rated on the degree of emotional warmth which characterized her relationship with the child. Each mother was also asked how much time each day the child watched television, on the average, and whether she attempted to impose any restrictions on the total amount of TV he could see or upon any particular programs.

The median length of time which the children spend watching TV daily, according to the mothers' report, was 1½ hours. There is reason to believe, from previous studies, that this may be an underestimate of the time the children actually spent watching television. For the following analysis, we must assume that even though most mothers probably underestimated their children's TV time somewhat, the rank order has some validity, so that differences in amount of TV watching among children from different kinds of home environments may be relied upon even if the absolute figures on hours of viewing may not.

A first approach to analyzing the study's hypothesis would be to correlate measures of frustration the child undergoes at home with his hours of television viewing. But both the number of hours of TV watching and the frustrations experienced by the child are functions of social class, as are the attitudes of mothers toward television itself. Mothers in the upper brackets of the socioeconomic scale more often impose restrictions on the number of hours their children may watch television, and the particular programs they may see, than do the mothers in the lower groups, and (perhaps in consequence) the children in the families from the lower socioeconomic levels spend more time on the average watching television. At the same time, the lower-SES mothers are less permissive and more restrictive in general in their child-training practices than the mothers in the upper middle class group. Because of these relationships, the analysis has been carried out separately for the two main social-class groups included in the study.[2]

Nine characteristics of the parents' treatment of the child were selected, each of these nine characteristics being presumably related to the amount of frustration the child experiences in his home environment. Each of the characteristics

---

[2] Social class was measured in this study by giving a weight of 2 to a score on Warner's index of occupational status, and a weight of 1 to the family's annual income. Our "upper-middle" group are mainly business and professional families, who would be classed 1-3 on Warner's 7-point scale. Our "upper-lower" group are primarily skilled and semiskilled workers' families, with some service and clerical occupations represented, and would fall in categories 4-7 on Warner's scale.

was then related to the amount of the child's daily television viewing, within the two social-class groups. The results are shown in table 1.

TABLE 1.—*Mean number of hours per day of television viewing for children subject to varying degrees of frustration in the home*

Characteristics of home training of child	Upper-middle class			Upper-lower class		
	Hours TV	Number of cases	Significance level [1]	Hours TV	Number of cases	Significance level [1]
Punishment for aggression toward parents:						
1. Mild	1.4	25	$t_{12:3}=2.00$	1.6		
2. Moderate	1.3	93	$p=<.03$	1.6		
3. Severe	1.6	42		1.7		
Permissiveness of sex behavior in child:						
1. Highly permissive	1.0	24				
2. Moderately permissive	1.4	59	$t_{1:34}=2.23$	1.5	34	$23:4=2.34$
3. Slightly permissive	1.5	52	$p=<.02$	1.5	46	$p=<.01$
4. Not at all permissive	1.4	33		1.8	79	
Mother's response to dependent behavior in child:						
1. Positive, rewarding	1.3	74	$t_{1:3}=1.88$	1.7		
2. Neutral	1.4	37	$p=<.05$	1.7		
3. Negative, punishing	1.5	57		1.6		
How far away from home is child allowed to go along?:						
1. Fairly far (across streets)	1.3	19		1.6	32	
2. Own block only	1.4	71		1.6	72	
3. Restricted to own yard	1.4	75		1.7	53	
How frequently mother checks on child's whereabouts:						
1. Seldom or never checks	1.4	24		1.3	11	
2. Occasionally checks	1.4	67		1.7	65	
3. Fairly often checks	1.4	35		1.5	40	
4. Constantly checks	1.3	39		1.8	43	
Level of obedience demands:						
1. Child not expected to obey promptly	1.2	43	$t_{1:3}=1.77$	1.6	52	
2. Moderate obedience demands	1.4	98	$p=<.05$	1.7	76	
3. Child expected to obey instantly	1.6	26		1.6	30	
Level of demands for quiet, neatness, good table manners, and going to bed on time:						
1. Few demands	1.1	44	$1:3=2.27$	1.9	37	
2. Moderate demands	1.4	72	$p=<.02$	1.6	56	
3. Severe demands	1.5	52		1.6	67	
Extent of use of physical punishment:						
1. Child seldom or never spanked	1.2	35	$t_{1:4}=1.58$	1.5	16	$t_{12:4}=1.88$
2. Spanked occasionally	1.4	71	$p=<.06$	1.5	50	$p=<.04$
3. Spanked fairly often	1.4	40		1.7	53	
4. Spanked often	1.5	21		1.8	42	
Affectional relationship, mother to child:						
1. Extremely warm	1.1	22	$t_{1:4}=2.88$	2.1	9	
2. Quite warm	1.4	63	$p=<.01$	1.7	50	
3. Matter of fact	1.4	54		1.5	57	
4. Cold	1.6	29		1.7	45	

[1] For these p values, a 1-tailed test has been used, since the test is for a difference in a predicted direction. It should be noted that a t test is not in ideal measure of the significance of differences here, since it was designed to test differences between 2 groups (usually an experimental and control group) and it is difficult to know what combinations of groups may be legitimately made for t tests when there are more than 2 groups. Therefore, the individual p values in the above table should be interpreted with caution, and the meaning of the table should rest more upon the series of tests considered jointly.

Among the upper middle-class group, it appears that the more frustrating a child's home experiences, the more he watches television, a finding consistent with the prediction. Seven out of the nine measures of frustration employed show a relationship with TV viewing in the expected direction (six of the differences being significant at less than the 0.05 level), and there is no instance in which frustration is associated with low TV watching.[3] As for the magnitude of the relationships: the children who are coldly treated by their mothers watch television a half hour more per day than the children who are warmly treated— an increase of nearly 50 percent in the amount of TV watching from one group to the other. Other measures show an increase of from 15 to 40 percent in the amount of television watching with increases in frustration.

[3] It is not permissible to combine these probabilities statistically since the nine measures employed are not fully independent of one another.

In the lower-class group, however, the situation is different. It is true that severe physical punishment and lack of permissiveness in the sex sphere appear to be associated with high interest in television. However, the children who are frustrated in the sense of being required to be neat, quiet, and mannerly and go to bed at a rigidly enforced bedtime spend less time watching television than the chilren who are given more freedom in these matters. And six of the frustration measures show no relationship with TV viewing.

How can one explain the fact that frustration is associated with extensive television viewing in upper middle-class children but not among the upper lower-class children? A possible explanation lies in the differential patterns of TV viewing among the parents in the two class groups. Previous research has shown that the adults in upper-middle homes spend considerably less time watching TV than do the adults in the lower socioeconomic brackets. Possibly, the children in the lower-SES families, when they are frustrated, tend to escape to television. But when they are not frustrated, they do what their parents do, namely, watch television. To put it another way: if the parents of a lower-class child are permissive, warm, and nonpunitive with him, he tends to imitate them and want to be with them, which makes him a TV fan, since that is what his parents are. If he does not have a warm relationship with his parents, he may seek television as an escape and a source of vicarious satisfaction. Thus the amount of frustration does not differentiate the children who are greatly interested in television from those who are not in the lower-class groups. In the upper-middle groups, however, the parents are busy doing other things. If the child is motivated to be like them and be near them, he will not spend as much time at television, while coldness on the part of the parents (along with other frustrations) will increase the attractiveness of television as an escape and a source of vicarious satisfaction.

It might be pointed out here that the relationship between the upper-middle-class child's interest in television and his home frustrations is perhaps even stronger than it appears in table 1. For the mothers who are strict and nonpermissive with their children tend to disapprove of television and place restrictions upon the amount of time their children may watch in a given day. This means that in the upper-middle class the frustrated children spend time watching television despite the fact that their mothers make efforts to limit their exposure to television. As a matter of fact, an effort was made to analyze the relationship between television watching and the mothers' demands for quiet, orderliness, etc., holding constant both social cla s and the mother's restrictions of TV itself. While the number of cases for this analysis is small, it appears that among the upper-middle families, the children who are highly restricted at home spend the most time watching television, except when the mother places great and rigidly enforced restrictions upon television itself, in which case, presumably the child seeks other forms of vicarious satisfaction which are not directly restricted.

SUMMARY AND CONCLUSIONS

The extent of a child's interest in television has been studied as a symptom of a need for vicarious satisfaction through fantasy, when the child is frustrated in his efforts to obtain satisfaction in real life. The findings are:

1. In the upper-middle class, the children who are highly frustrated in their current home life (subject to many restrictions and not treated permissively or warmly) spend the most time viewing television programs.

2. In the upper-lower class, there is little or no relationship between frustration and TV viewing in children.

The differences between the classes has been interpreted as meaning that in the upper-lower class, where the parents themselves spend a good deal of time watching TV, there is more positive motivation for a child to watch television, so that a child will be drawn to it even in the absence of frustration because it is a dominant activity of the family circle. In the upper-middle class, the effects of frustration may be seen more clearly, because in the absence of frustration, the child is drawn away from television.

Chairman KEFAUVER. We will divert the program some, because Commissioner Hennock has a meeting of her Commission, and will have to attend it, so we will call Commissioner Frieda Hennock as our next witness.

Miss Hennock, we are happy to have you with us this morning.

STATEMENT OF HON. FRIEDA B. HENNOCK, MEMBER OF THE FEDERAL COMMUNICATIONS COMMISSION

Commissioner HENNOCK. I am very happy to be here.

I want to say that your public-address system is very bad. I cannot hear you. I heard you ask some questions about the Commission, but I did not hear what they were.

Chairman KEFAUVER. This is not a public-address system, and I am sorry you did not hear us; I am sorry I did not speak louder.

Since this is a television hearing, the television boys would like to take some pictures of you while you are testifying. Do you object?

Commissioner HENNOCK. Not at all. I have objection to televising other types of hearings, not these.

Chairman KEFAUVER. Well, if they annoy you, you say so.

Commissioner HENNOCK. No, I think the public should get in on the act here, Senator; that is one of the missing links, the most important missing link.

I have a statement that I prepared yesterday, and I have one that I prepared some time ago. I have two statements here.

Since I am not very good at reading statements, Senator, and since you have so many statements read before you and put in the record, perhaps I will just skip through the two statements quickly, and then subject myself to questioning by you, as chairman, and your fellow Senators.

Chairman KEFAUVER. That will be all right.

We will have both of your statements printed in full in the record, but you go through them as you wish, and then we will have some questions to ask you.

Commissioner HENNOCK. Thank you very much.

I found it necessary to write this 2-page summary last night because I felt it better pointed up the relationship of the FCC to the broadcasting industry, and also to your committee and the work they are doing here, and so I will go on quickly.

Chairman KEFAUVER. First, for the record, Miss Hennock, when did you come to the Federal Communications Commission?

Commissioner HENNOCK. I have been a Commissioner since July 1948.

Chairman KEFAUVER. Prior to that time you were——

Commissioner HENNOCK. I was a practicing lawyer up in New York.

Chairman KEFAUVER. I know that you have always taken a great deal of interest, however, in social work, and problems of children.

Commissioner HENNOCK. Yes, sir; I have.

I am no expert in this field, however, and I am glad—I notice that you are calling experts, but I do want to testify here as a member of the Commission.

Our function, under the Communications Act and what the Supreme Court has construed as our function in the field of programing, so that my position is very clearly defined, is—I will quickly refer to a few sentences in the several pages, and then subject myself to questioning.

As I state on the first page, I know of no field where there is more important work to be done by the Senate than in juvenile delinquency, and the attention this committee is giving to this critical problem is most timely. Nowhere can this committee be fore effective in stemming the excessive, concentrated and exaggerated portrayal of crime and violence than in radio and television. For the air waves over which broadcasters send their signals are in the public domain. The broadcasters acquire no vested interest in the air waves, and are issued licenses of no more than 3 years' duration.

The FCC requires broadcasters to operate in the public interest, and it must take programing into full account in issuing and renewing their licenses.

Here I want to say, Mr. Chairman, that in 1938 the Senate Interstate Commerce Committee was opposed to superpower, large AM broadcasting stations.

Senator Wheeler was then the chairman. By the mere passage of the resolution of that committee, which the FCC has ever since honored, the FCC never has gone in for superpower AM stations—just the mere passage of a resolution of that committee.

Now, this is the public domain, and I am going on from here as to what your committee can do as far as we are concerned, the FCC and the broadcasters and the public.

Broadcasters who apply for station licenses and for license renewals are required to report in detail the percentage of time devoted to different types of programs such as entertainment, religion, news, education, discussion—I did not list them all—and those that are sustaining and commercial, and so forth; that is when they apply for a license.

Now, the objective is to insure balanced programing responsive to the needs, interests, and tastes of the communities served by the licensees.

In addition to the foregoing, the FCC should have a brand-new requirement which we do not now have, but which is clearly indicated as a result of the hearings you have had here, and that is, I think, we should require the broadcasters to tell the number of acts and threats of crime and violence on all their programs throughout the broadcast day.

Moreover, the FCC should pursue a rigorous policy of refusing renewal of the licenses of offending stations which disregard their public-service responsibilities by continuing to victimize immature audiences with a concentrated and profuse deluge of crime, brutality, sadism, and outright murder.

The programing standard set out in the code of the National Association of Radio and Television Broadcasters are excellent, but they have little effect on programing as the code is voluntary and the NARTB is not in a position to enforce it effectively.

I see my good friend, Mr. Fellows, back there, who is the president of that association, and I know how keenly he personally feels about cleaning up the programing with all the crime on it.

But I know he cannot do the job effectively, as sincere as he is, and as competent, and I know how hard he works.

Now, the networks supply a large amount of TV programing and should be held responsible for its quality. The profusion of crime and violence in TV films mounts continuously.

The responsibility of the licensees is clear. With 35 million television sets and 120 million radio sets pouring out an unending stream of crime and violence, it is important for the FCC to take positive corrective steps.

The broadcasting licensees are most sensitive to the policies of the FCC. With an alerted public and an active Senate committee, the FCC, if it takes the appropriate steps, cannot fail to obtain almost immediate results; and that is why I urge your committee to study the possible resolution that I have in mind. I do not have it here to submit it, but I have it drafted, if you would like to have it.

In addition, I urge the following steps:

1. Women's organizations and all other civic, educational, welfare, and religious groups should supplement the activities of established monitoring organizations in viewing and listening to TV and radio programs. All such groups should press the stations, the networks, the program sponsors and the FCC itself to bring to a halt the broadcast of pernicious programs which are making a significant contribution to the rise of juvenile delinquency.

2. These public-service groups should study the reports of the FCC licensees.

After we get this new provision in, so they have to tell us how many acts of violence and crimes they have daily, I want these public study groups to study their reports to us, and file complaints against these licensees.

That just takes a short time, and I will help them.

3. A National Radio and TV Children's Week should be proclaimed during which there should be an evaluation of all radio and television programs in terms of their suitability for children.

4. An alert and articulate public should, as of right, present positive and constructive suggestions to licensees and sponsors as to its radio and TV program preferences for adults and children alike.

I think Dr. Mccoby's testimony was excellent, and I wish women in her category would come and give us a positive program, and say, This is the kind of program to have beteen 3 and 5 in the afternoon for children, and this is the kind to have between 7 and 8."

I feel the licensees have been neglected. It is not altogether their fault. I think there has been a very deaf public and a very blind public here, and I am very glad to see women of that training in here to testify.

The public should no longer take its radio and TV programing for granted, or continue to accept passively anything the networks and broadcasters choose to offer.

5. Since radio and TV operate in the public domain, the FCC should set up proper programing standards for both as soon as possible, and insure their implementation by rigorous enforcement.

I am sure the industry knows what I mean when I say that. We just have never set up standards for television.

We have never said there should be so much commercialism and so much sustaining programing which will be in the public interest in television.

We did that in radio. We have been so busy getting television off the ground, and since the lifting of the freeze in 1952, when we only had 108 stations, to get these 420-some-odd television stations on the air, we have never really gotten into the programing as a Commission, and we should do that, set up standards, so the licensees themselves know what to do.

I cannot blame them altogether because when I go out to talk to them they say, "What do you want us to do? What percentage of time shoud be religion, what percentage public service, what percentage discussion, what percentage good story telling, and what time for children?" I could not give them the answers because we have not done it.

I might say—I am just saying this not to criticize the Commission, but we just have not gotten around to it; we have been so busy getting these stations on the air.

And, last, of course, you expected me say something about educational television, I am sure.

We have 252 channels, television channels, reserved for educational television affording an unprecedented opportunity for guiding the young and enriching the lives of all. Such noncommercial stations should be built immediately. They could arouse and stimulate interest in the arts, music, history, literature and science, to an extent heretofore unknown. Moreover, these stations can be built at a most reasonable cost and operated very economically.

The enemies of educational television really do not present the right figures. You can build a station for as little as $50,000 to $100,000 to cover this entire area, and you can operate it very economically, and that could be a schoolhouse of the air, day and night, with no commercialism, and operated by the finest educators in this vicinity.

Imagine what that would mean if you could turn the dial and tune in to a completely noncommercial educational station in 250 cities?

Let me go on to the rest of my statement and just read one paragraph that I have which shows our authority as a Commission which has been sustained by the Supreme Court to look at programing.

In Justice Frankfurter's own inimitable way, he stated it in a very important case—on page 4 of my succeeding statement—in *National Broadcasting Company* v. *U. S.* (319 U. S. 190):

But the act does not restrict the Commission merely to supervision of the traffic. It puts upon the Commission the burden of determining the composition of that traffic.

The Commission's licensing function cannot be discharged, therefore, merely by finding that there are no technological objections to the granting of a license. If the criterion of public interest were limited to such matters, how could the Commission choose between two applicants for the same facilities, each of whom is financially and technically qualified to operate a station? Since the very inception of Federal regulation by radio, comparative considerations as to the services to be rendered have governed the application of the standard of public interest. convenience, or necessity.

In other words, we have to look at the traffic. We are not just traffic cops; we have to look at what it consists of.

Then, at the bottom of the page I say while self-regulation by the industry is desirable, to the extent that it falls down, the regulatory body responsible under the law to insure that broadcasters operate in the public interest, must act.

Then I wind up and ask for a set of hearings by the FCC to determine what goes on in these children's programs.

That can be done in short order by a rule-making proceeding, Mr. Chairman, which we do every week, and a short notice; and we can get exactly how much goes on by way of threats and violence and in every station of the country.

We can just send a questionnaire in, and they can answer us and have some witnesses in to collate the facts and then, of course, we should announce an immediate policy as to what we think is good and what is bad in television programing.

Thank you very much.

Chairman KEFAUVER. Well, your statement is direct and to the point.

It is good to have a public servant who has a definite position and an idea about what should be done to improve the operation of the programs of the Commission, of which you are a member.

Senator Wiley, do you have some questions to ask Commissioner Hennock?

Senator WILEY. I do feel that the Commissioner has not only issued a challenge to the Commission itself but to the public and to this committee.

You are talking about setting up some standards that would be the result of consultation with your group and the public-spirited citizens and with the industry; is that the idea?

Commissioner HENNOCK. Yes, sir.

I have always wanted the industry in on this, Senator Wiley, because I do not feel they have had the guidance that they need.

I feel the public has been very deaf and blind. They just refuse to look at the airwaves, and what goes on them.

The airwaves belong to them. They just turn the dial, and they let it go on. They never let the sponsors hear from them.

Just imagine what a sponsor would do if he were to hear from others as to the revolting nature of these programs when he is trying to build up good will with the public. Immediately he would change, would he not?

He does not want that kind of public reaction. And yet the public is not in here doing a job, and that is why I think your hearings are so beneficial.

Senator WILEY. Well, you think the same course would apply to some of the newspapers in reporting crime also?

Commissioner HENNOCK. I think so. But, of course, you see, the newspapers are not in the public domain; that is why I think you could do such fine work in radio and television, because there you have created us—the Senate, the Legislature, has created us—an administrative body to regulate in the public domain radio and television.

Newspapers are not in our domain.

Senator WILEY. Oh, no; I was thinking about responsibility; that was all I was thinking about.

Whether you felt while you are within the public domain, you claim there is the responsibility, but I was just trying to get your answer. I am not giving the answers as to whether there is any responsibility on the press also in relation to you, in reporting crime.

Commissioner HENNOCK. Well, I think there is, but according to Dr. Maccoby they do so little reading that I do not even think they read the papers. I think they only read comic books, unfortunately.

Senator WILEY. I was interested in your comment on educational television.

Did I understand that you wanted public stations by the States? Is that what you are getting at?

Commissioner HENNOCK. Well, I believe, because we are an administrative body and you are the Senate and we are very sensitive to what you want, you are really our bosses in a way because you have created us, and if you passed a resolution in the public interest and asked us to look into this and do something about it as the licensing agency—they only get a 3-year license, and they have to show they are operating in the public interest at the end of 3 years—I think you could accomplish a great deal, Senator, and very effectively right through us.

Senator WILEY. In some States they do have State-operated stations, do they not, radio and television?

Commissioner HENNOCK. No, sir; not by the State. I know of none—well, outside of the city of New York, which was Fiorello LaGuardia's——

Senator WILEY. What about the University of Wisconsin?

Commissioner HENNOCK. Well, that is a university in your own State that has done a wonderful job in radio for many years. But while they use State funds to run a 7-station network in FM and radio, and they have 1 television station, they are licensed as an educational institution, not as a State; and under our provisions, only an educational institution or a group of them can come in to use our educational channels, and so they come in as educators in your State, and that was a very good question because there is a very fine distinction there because they do use State funds.

Senator WILEY. Sure.

Commissioner HENNOCK. Yes, sir; and they do an excellent job.

Senator WILEY. What I was really driving at—I did not quite get your testimony in that connection—did you mean that in your opinion, it was your opinion, that in order to probably even arrange competition between the industry and a State-operated station or whether you want to call it educational operated or paid for, that it would be well to get more of these public stations?

Commissioner HENNOCK. I mean by noncommercial educational television stations, stations that are operated by educators like the University of Wisconsin, like the station in Houston, the University of Houston, which it operates, like the stations at Harvard and MIT, that whole area of educators in the Boston area, who are coming in.

We have a State movement on in Alabama, and the movement is going on every day, and I am hoping to hear soon of a new station in Tennessee, but there is a question of the educators doing it with either private or public funds operating on a cooperative basis among all segments of education; that is what they usually do, make it available to all educators.

Now, the advantage of that, Senator, is twofold: First, you get the educators interested in the programing and in the use of the people's airwaves.

The impact of television is so tremendous that they ought to be in here trying to use it and finding out how to use it, and spreading culture and education, both in class and at home.

Secondly, I think it will be very helpful to the commercial broadcasters—I do—and I think also it will give the public a program choice.

I do not think they are going to be competitive, because those who want to listen, to tune in and watch Milton Berle or I Love Lucy are going to watch those programs.

But if you can still get a small percentage of, let us say, of 100,000 people watching a great Shakespearean program or watching Dr. Baxter teach college Shakespeare—I was out in Los Angeles when, I understood, he had the second highest rating on a Saturday morning on a Columbia Broadcasting station.

If we can expose that many people to Shakespeare, and the more of those programs we have, the better off we are.

We may not always get the largest audience; even the smallest audiences are worth while. We do not want to compete with them; we just want to get on the air and spread culture and education free of charge to as many people as possible.

Senator WILEY. It is your idea that you could, by setting up a code or some standards, to bring about quite a beneficial result as far as programs, particularly for the youth, are concerned?

Commissioner HENNOCK. Yes, sir; we already have a code.

The industry has an excellent code, and the National Association of Broadcasters is doing what they can, but I tried to say that they are very limited.

It is a voluntary code, and you and I know how very difficult it is to enforce these things among the members; and there is an agency that can do the enforcement here—if they fall down, and I think they have fallen down miserably among themselves—I am not saying the NARTB has fallen down, but I am talking about the broadcasters.

I think the public has fallen down, and I think the FCC should do more; and I think if these hearings do nothing more than to get a concerted effort by the FCC and the public, to get after the licensees and the sponsors, I think you have accomplished a great deal.

Senator WILEY. I think the other point, Mr. Chairman, that the witness expressed, particularly just now, is the responsibility of the average citizen or, you could say, the public, in calling attention to any delinquencies in the matter.

I think the public opinion is a big factor, and we do not utilize it enough at times.

Commissioner HENNOCK. Very true.

Senator WILEY. All right.

Chairman KEFAUVER. Commissioner Hennock, I wish you would read, in order to put your evidence in proper perspective, the last paragraph on page 2, ending on page 3 of your statement.

Commissioner HENNOCK. Yes, sir. Did you say the last paragraph?

The six suggestions I have——

Chairman KEFAUVER. No; on page 2 of the second statement.

Commissioner HENNOCK. I see.

Chairman KEFAUVER. Beginning with "Some mention has been made."

Commissioner HENNOCK. Yes, sir. As for the extent to which——

Chairman KEFAUVER. No. "Some mention has been made of the need for more study"——

Commissioner HENNOCK. Yes, sir.

Chairman KEFAUVER. You read it.

Commissioner HENNOCK. As for the extent to which children are exposed to television——

Chairman KEFAUVER. No; the next paragraph.

Commissioner HENNOCK. Some mention has been made of the need for more study and research. While I think all those concerned with the problem will welcome further research, there would seem to be little doubt in the minds of parents all over the country as to the effect of TV programs on children. In a recent coast-to-coast survey conducted by the American Institute of Public Opinion—more popularly known as the Gallup poll—7 out of 10 of the men and women who were asked whether they thought any of the blame for teen-age crime could be placed on the mystery and crime programs on television and radio, answered "Yes." Fewer than 1 out of every 4 persons queried felt that no blame was attached to TV and radio. These views are amply supported by 37 comments from leading psychiatrists, psychologists, public officials, child specialists and others which were submitted for your record by Mrs. Logan.

Mrs. Logan is head of the Los Angeles NAFTRB, I think the initials are.

Chairman KEFAUVER. Yes, we had her testimony, I think, on the 20th of October last year.

Commissioner HENNOCK. Did you want me to read the next one?

Chairman KEFAUVER. Yes, read the next one.

Commissioner HENNOCK. Yes, sir.

As I stated before, the solution to this problem rests with the broadcasters, the public and the Federal Communications Commission. All three, in my opinion, have the duty to come to grips with an intolerable situation and take the necessary steps to improve the programing to which the children of this country are being subjected.

Chairman KEFAUVER. I think that statement is very pertinent and challenging and, as Senator Wiley said, it places a challenge on our people, parent-teachers associations, groups everywhere, but it immediately places a very definite one on the Federal Communications Commission, does it not?

Commissioner HENNOCK. Yes, sir; in my opinion, it does. I only have one vote, Senator.

Chairman KEFAUVER. Yes, I appreciate that.

Senator WILEY. But what a vote.

(Laughter.)

Commissioner HENNOCK. I might say this, Mr. Chairman.

Chairman KEFAUVER. I am sure you are not only influential as a formulator of public opinion, but your views in the FCC.

Commissioner HENNOCK. I do not know, Mr. Chairman, my term expires June 30; I may not be there after then. I am only a Democrat, you know.

Chairman KEFAUVER. As just another Democrat, I hope you are there.

Senator WILEY. There are quite a few of them around yet.

(Laughter.)

Commissioner HENNOCK. They are right down at the bottom.

Chairman KEFAUVER. Before we get off on a political discussion, what I want to know, Miss Hennock, is when the Commission is going to initiate investigatory proceedings for the purpose of assembling all the facts as to what kind of programs the TV broadcasters are giving to our people.

Commissioner HENNOCK. Well, I have been hoping for one ever since 1952 and; as a matter of fact, 1950.

We were going to have a conference with the broadcasters then, because we realized from some of the applications for renewal, how highly commercial television was getting, and the back-to-back commercials that they were putting on, the amount of commercialism, which was mounting daily, and I voted for an immediate—as a matter of fact, there was a time there when we did not know whether we would renew their licenses.

We thought we would keep them on temporary licenses until we looked into the programing. That was in 1950; and this is 1955, and I do not know when we are ever going to call that conference.

We decided to call a conference, and never did. I just have one vote.

Chairman KEFAUVER. You mean, Commissioner Hennock, that the FCC does not have submitted to it the programs and at least some synopsis of what the contents of these various programs is?

Commissioner HENNOCK. We have submitted to us a classification, a broadcast classification, showing how much of the programing is, as I said, religious or entertainment or news, education, discussion, and so forth, in those categories. We have figures showing how much of it is sustaining and how much of it is not, how much is commercial.

We have all kinds of data submitted to us, and the amount of commercialism would surprise you, as it did me; but that is all. Nothing has been done about it.

Chairman KEFAUVER. You mean as to how many of these programs have violent acts and shooting and crime?

Commissioner HENNOCK. We have none of that now. We have no such classification, and that is what I seek in this third paragraph.

In the third paragraph of my summary on the first page, you will see that is what I seek. I want this new classification showing how many acts and threats of crime and violence there are on these programs.

We could get that very readily if we just put it in these application forms, which is very simple.

Chairman KEFAUVER. I certainly hope that your position about that prevails, because I think that is information that should not only be given to the FCC, but I think the public should know about it; do you not think so?

Commissioner HENNOCK. Yes, sir; I think it would be very helpful, Senator, and that is why I was very glad to come here and testify.

Those 2 or 3 little things that could be done quickly without national legislation—they are just cooperation between your committee and our Commission, that could be very effective.

Chairman KEFAUVER. Then, as to the NARTB, that is the voluntary code, and as is the case with many voluntary codes, you have difficulty with some members, getting them to comply.

Commissioner HENNOCK. That is right.

Chairman KEFAUVER. Does the association report to the FCC on noncomplying members or members who give difficulty in carrying out the code?

Commissioner HENNOCK. I never have heard from them, no. But I know that the association itself is very much concerned with the problem, and I know that Mr. Fellows, in working on the code with a staff and the entire association, they try to do it on a voluntary basis; and you know what that means.

Chairman KEFAUVER. Does it not seem that a report should be made as to the extent of compliance with the code by this voluntary association to the FCC, which would be part of the evidence presented to the FCC when a renewal application comes up?

Commissioner HENNOCK. I do not think so, because I think that would not be good, Mr. Chairman, and for one reason; perhaps you might agree with me, I do not know.

I feel that one of the best provisions of the act is that we keep a licensee directly responsible to the FCC. Each licensee is individually responsible to us.

Now, the association is not one of our licensees. I would rather have jurisdiction over our own licensees, whom we give licenses to, and whom we renew licenses for every 3 years. These are very valuable franchises, as you know. They carry a great amount of value and power with them.

I would not want to see an industry association step in here between us and our own licensees. I think it would be bad for the licensees and for the Commission.

Chairman KEFAUVER. I agree with you; you have direct responsibility and direct control.

Commissioner HENNOCK. That is right; I think your idea is a good one, though.

Chairman KEFAUVER. But as matters stand now, you really do not know what kind of programs they are putting on?

Commissioner HENNOCK. No, sir.

Chairman KEFAUVER. You do not know whether they are wholesome programs or in the public interest or not.

It seems to me, not by way of control or direction of the industry, but as a matter of information to the FCC, that the record of compliance, as gotten up by the code association, would be of some benefit.

Commissioner HENNOCK. I agree with you, Senator, it would be. But I have never seen such submission of evidence, and if that is your recommendation for the NARTB, I think that is a very good one.

Chairman KEFAUVER. I only meant to you as evidence as to whether the stations were complying with the code or not.

Commissioner HENNOCK. Yes, sir. I think that would be very helpful.

Chairman KEFAUVER. I am interested in the National Children's Radio and TV Week. It seems to me that has a great deal of merit, by pointing up to people what they themselves could do about this problem.

How do you think we could get that started?

Commissioner HENNOCK. Well, if you just got on television, Senator—I saw you, you are very good [laughter]—and you demand time across the board on all four networks, and you declared next week or the week after as National Children's Week for Radio and Television, to wipe out all viewing of crime and acts of violence, and so forth, and ask all the parents and public service groups to cooperate—I do not know of a better way that it could be done.

I think it would be very effective, and I think you would get the time if you asked for it; you would certainly be entitled to it.

Chairman KEFAUVER. I did not know that my request was coming back as a suggestion for me, Miss Hennock, but if I could get you to come on with me——

Commissioner HENNOCK. I will certainly do that, but I think you would be much better alone.

What about Senator Wiley? Did I leave you out, Senator? I am sorry.

Chairman KEFAUVER. Now, why can't substantially the same standards that you have in radio be applied to television?

Commissioner HENNOCK. Well, I would be delighted with that in a way; but, of course, it is another medium.

It lacks the—the addition of sight to sound makes television the most important medium of mass communications. It is a synthesis of the news and the movies, and its public acceptance is almost unbelievable.

I remember during the freeze when we had 108 stations, when we first started the freeze, there were not even three-quarters of a million sets in the hands of the public.

We were talking about changing our basic standards; we were talking about going to color; we were talking about moving all television to ultra high so that your present sets might have been affected very substantially.

Nevertheless, the public continued to buy these sets at an almost unprecedented rate. They never went for radio as they did for television.

It has a public acceptability that is unbelievable. They bought 17 million sets by April 1952, with just 108 stations on the air.

Now we are up to 35 million sets. This is a different medium. I think that the impact is greater on children and adults of these crime programs, and I think that something should be done that is very basic here, and really on a national basis.

It is beyond us, really almost as a Commission, except where our own licensees are concerned. Unless you get on here as a national hookup— I am not kidding, I am very serious—and get on all the stations and just tell them that these homes can either be beer halls or barrooms or they can be places of culture, these 35 million sets or 35 million beer halls and places of crime and violence too often every day— and it is just heartbreaking to see this happening, particularly when you realize the immediacy of the art and the importance of it.

Chairman KEFAUVER. But your radio code or standards have to do with generally the kind of program that eliminates disrespect for law. Not to have it so that it is emotionally upsetting to children.

Commissioner HENNOCK. We do not get into that, Senator. Under section 326—I think I ought to make my position clear—we are prohibited from censoring under that section. We do not tell a licensee, "Put on Jack Benny and not Milton Berle."

Chairman KEFAUVER. I did not mean that. But you did have those general standards set up.

Commissioner HENNOCK. Yes, general standards as to commercialism.

I think it was 80 percent commercial and 20 percent had to be sustaining under our radio requirements. That was the famous Blue

Book that was issued in 1945. We have not issued any standards since then.

Chairman KEFAUVER. Why don't we have standards for television?

Commissioner HENNOCK. That is exactly what I am advocating, Senator, having a set of standards. You are absolutely correct.

Chairman KEFAUVER. Is the Commission doing anything about it?

Commissioner HENNOCK. No, sir.

I think they hope that the—I want to state the mitigating circumstances here, Senator. I do not want to be in the position of making it all black where the Commission is concerned.

As I said, we have been all tied up in processing and in licensing these new television stations since the freeze. We have been busy doing that.

We have not looked at the programing, as such, and we have not set up new standards.

But I do feel that the Commission should do it now and, of course, also the Commission has been hoping that the industry would do something about it themselves, and that they would attend to it themselves. But that has not been taking place, I am sorry to say.

Chairman KEFAUVER. Well, it would certainly seem long past the time when standards should have been set up, and I think they would help the control of the Federal Communications Commission over the industry for good.

Commissioner Hennock, I have always been interested in the educational programs and, of course, they would do a tremendous amount of good, the information, to be informative and be educational for our children; and it has been disappointing to me that more headway has not been made for educational stations and channels.

What is the hold-back?

Commissioner HENNOCK. Well, Senator, the first year we had 47 applications for these 250 channels by institutions throughout the country.

We reserved these channels because educators need more time to go to their legislatures and their fiscal bodies to get their funds. You know how public funds are, how difficult it is to obtain them.

Unfortunately, the various legislatures, the educators went to, turned a deaf ear in various communities, but I think we have made great progress.

It is not true that we have not made progress. More and more stations are going on the air, and those that are going on are having great success with the programs that they are putting on.

I wish I could devote much more time to helping these licensees. It is a very long process.

You take the city of Washington: there they have to go to Congress for the public school funds. They went. The District school system here applied, filed an application, and they were turned down, although the President did include the funds in his own budget; I think President Eisenhower included them 2 years ago.

Now they have to go back and get private funds.

Now, getting all the educators in any community together in a cooperative venture on one station means that you have the private schools, public schools, higher and lower education, and your public service groups, all cooperating in one organization or corporation, which is usually the applicant—that is a very complicated structure, and takes a very long time to get going.

I mean, it is not like a private licensee calling a lawyer and saying, "File an application for me tomorrow. Here is $100,000 in the bank, and show them my credit."

You know, it just is not done that easily, but I think we have made great progress, and I think the press have not given us due credit for it here and there.

By and large, the press throughout the country have been very nice about educational television, but in some areas they just seem to neglect the tremendous efforts.

These educators—I went out to Denver, for instance, they have an application on file, and they had, I think, funds in the budget, and then they had a taxpayer's suit to deter the educators from going ahead with the application, and they had to take that suit up to the higher courts. I mean, you have all these things to contend with, but we will straighten this out.

The public-school system of this country was not built overnight, and we will build these stations, Senator, as long as these channels are kept intact.

Chairman KEFAUVER. One trouble is, you mentioned the enemies of educational TV. They are trying to take the channels away, are they not?

Commissioner HENNOCK. Yes; they have been, Senator; but, very fortunately——

Chairman KEFAUVER. Who are these enemies of educational TV?

Commissioner HENNOCK. Well, there are just a few selfish interests, Senator. I cannot name them, Senator. I would not attempt to do that. They are just some selfish interests who covet these channels. Some of them are very, very valuable, and they are very scarce, and you know, and very desirable, and in various communities there are different interests who would like to take them away and come in with these applications to take that channel away.

But they do not get anywhere with the Commission. They have not gotten anywhere so far. We have not taken a single channel away, and the late Senator Tobey said that there should be an 11th commandment, "Do not covet thy neighbor's educational TV channel," and when he was chairman of that Interstate and Foreign Commerce Committee——

Chairman KEFAUVER. Senator Tobey spoke with great wisdom.

Commissioner HENNOCK. He was a great admirer of your efforts in this field and other fields.

Chairman KEFAUVER. He was a great friend in this and other things.

About how many applications have been filed to try to take away an educational channel?

Commissioner HENNOCK. Well, quite a few, Senator.

They are filed here and there, and I do not have an account of them. They come in all sorts of forms.

They want to use the channel part-time, and they come in all kinds of ideas for solving everything in the community if they give them one of these channels. I do not have the figures, but I would look them up for you.

Chairman KEFAUVER. Has the Commission been unanimous in turning them down, in disrupting educational channels?

Commissioner HENNOCK. Yes; they have.

Chairman KEFAUVER. Mr. Bobo, do you wish to ask Commissioner Hennock any questions?

Mr. BOBO. I would like to ask one question.

Do you think the public is aware of the role of the FCC in granting licenses to television broadcasters?

Commissioner HENNOCK. Well, from the number of applications we have for television stations and radio stations, I sometimes think they are only too much aware of it. But as regards public surveillance of the field of programing, there are very, very few complaints, and they are not in touch with the FCC, to speak of.

Mr. BOBO. That is what I was getting at for my next question.

Do you receive complaints?

Commissioner HENNOCK. When they want a station they are in here, believe me, they know we are here. But somehow they are not performing their share when it comes to programing.

Mr. BOBO. The reason I asked the question is I wondered about the statement that was made on the first page as to television causing a tremendous increase in juvenile delinquency because of the viewing of crime and violence in television.

Commissioner HENNOCK. Well, I just base that on the record or such portions of it that were here.

I have some of that material with them, and I am prepared to state the basis of my opinion. I am not an expert in this field. I can only take the opinions of experts.

As I state, I am just a lawyer, but I do know that just my own commonsense—if I am supposed to have any as a bureaucrat—tells me that the looking at crime day and night is not good for children.

Chairman KEFAUVER. I think it would be well for Mr. Bobo to go over the material that you have.

Do you have any which is not in our present or past hearings, and which will not be produced in these hearings? If you do, I think it should be included in the record.

Commissioner HENNOCK. Thank you, Senator; I would be glad to produce it.

Mr. BOBO. Do you think it would materially aid the Commission in setting up standards if the public—we have received hundreds and thousands of letters from parents—if the public generally wrote to the FCC asking——

Commissioner HENNOCK. I think the Chairman's suggestion and your question is a good one.

I think if you took your own material and your own letters from the public and used them by submitting them to us and showed us your ideas, I mean the ideas of the public as expressed to you, I think they would have a great effect on my fellow commissioners.

I am sure they would read them with great interest, and I know we could take it up in commission session to see what we could do about using them.

Senator WILEY. Mr. Chairman, I would like to get the witness' reaction to one very serious situation.

Chairman KEFAUVER. Senator Wiley.

Senator WILEY. As you well know, this matter of television is playing and will continue to play more and more an important part, a larger and more important part, in elections.

The costs on the utilization of television stations is something prohibitive from the standpoint of any poor man.

If some group could get hold of stations in a State they could dominate for the time being virtually every impact of that kind upon the minds of the electorate.

Has any consideration been given to something that would be in the nature of providing, well, let us say, a barrier against such a situation?

In a number of States—take my State: In a primary a man running for Senator is limited to an expenditure personally of $5,000. That would not buy over the stations of the State 15 minutes.

Now, to get around that at times, organizations organize separate groups; candidates are not supposed to know anything about it.

What I am getting at is that certain groups could simply put one candidate out of business, and another candidate could have plenty of funds to buy up all the television stations and their time.

I am thinking now in terms of the public interest, the rights that we have always found were American rights for individuals to get a fair play before the electorate. This system makes it so he cannot get a fair play before the electorate.

Has there been any thought given to that in relation to, say, Federal officers running for office?

Commisisoner HENNOCK. Senator, I have given it a great deal of thought and, of course, I realize you are a Republican, and you talk about a poor man not being able to run for the Senate; and I keep wondering about why so many people in the administration do not do something about it.

I do feel that these airwaves belong to the people, and I may be a Democrat, but I fight for your right to appear on television, believe me, especially during campaign time, free of charge on the people's airwaves.

There are 35 million sets, there are 35 million political meeting halls, too, you know, potential political meeting halls, and 2 years from now there will be 50 million potential meeting halls.

I know of nothing more important than to assure your appearance on the television screen as a candidate, regardless of party, and using the people's airwaves free of charge, not having you beholden to any large or small interests in your State.

I think that if you, in the Senate, the most important legislative body in the world, got together and called on this industry, and the Commission, to see to it that this time was released to the people, to bring them their candidates—there are new habits in this country. People do not go to political halls as they used to. They want their candidates at home after a hard day's work on their television screens.

What you raise is probably one of the most basic problems in America today, to give you, to give all candidates, the freedom of the use of these airwaves.

I know of no more important use in the public interest than to bring the people their candidates.

If you gentlemen of the Senate, just a handful of you, would do something about it, you would get a very quick answer and a very responsive one.

Senator WILEY. Will you be a little more definitive in that last statement of yours.

Commissioner HENNOCK. Yes. I think a gentleman with your fine debating powers could get on the floor of the Senate and make a speech, when it convenes next week, to this effect, and alert your brother Senators to this problem, and I think, perhaps, a resolution to the FCC and a call on the industry to see how much time is available across the board to all parties for use in political campaigns and all during the year, to keep an informed electorate, would bring very good results.

Senator WILEY. You apparently have very definite ideas on the subject, and if you want to put them in more concrete form any time, I would suggest to the chairman that you be privileged to communicate them to us.

Speaking about Republicans and Democrats, generally for many years when we got to the water's edge, we were neither; we were Americans first.

Commissioner HENNOCK. That is right.

Senator WILEY. And on the large plain of fair play and the right of the public, and the right of the candidate, we should be Americans first always; and to me it presents a situation in many places that is very dangerous.

It means that not only power but a few with tremendous money assets can do what we used to say the bosses did, and then we got the primary and the people had a right to speak, but now you have got this great instrument that we never thought of as probably being the overwhelming dominating influence in an election, which can be placed in the hands of those who have the money.

Commissioner HENNOCK. That is right, Senator.

Senator WILEY. And it is a very serious situation, it seems to me, that calls for serious thought and serious remedy.

Thank you for your contribution.

Commissioner HENNOCK. I might suggest one other thing, to be specific: If you would wire every station in your State for immediate time to discuss any of the issues that you think are important in your State on television, of course, you would have to give equal time to the opposing views or they would have to give it; they would be subject to that, and that is right, as they should be under the law, under our editorialization policy.

But if you find if you do not get any response, if you will communicate with me, I will take it up with the Commission, and we will be in touch with your licensees or—I am speaking now for myself, not the entire Commission; but I should certainly move the entire Commission to be in touch with them to get an answer.

Senator WILEY. Well, I am not talking simply about myself or any particular individual.

Commissioner HENNOCK. You are talking about the whole problem.

Senator WILEY. I am talking about a situation that is only too apparent because I have seen when I was not a candidate in recent years, where I have seen all radio time is bought, and it took money to buy that; in other words, the fellow that is preferred by the group that has the money or the power gets the time: so the station is closed against one who, perhaps, the people would like to hear.

Again I say I am making these remarks in the public interest because, to me, the public are the ones who are being deprived of the right, not simply the candidate. The public is being deprived of that right.

Commissioner HENNOCK. Yes, sir.

Senator WILEY. That is why I am very happy to get your reaction and your fine sense of cooperation in the matter.

But it has got to take more than that, because once these stations have this license, they control it also with power. They say the time is sold, so there you have got it.

Commissioner HENNOCK. Well, Senator, that is why I suggested your making the approach on a nationwide basis on the floor of your own forum.

I think every Senator has a feeling about this that I have talked about, rich or poor.

I think most Senators resent the fact that they have to worry about such huge expenditures of campaign funds as are required for television; and I think Senators should be given free time to bring their issues and themselves as candidates to the people, regardless of party or importance of State or anything else.

I think that right on the Senate floor, if you gentlemen—I hope I am not being too forward, but I think that is where your best sounding board is, and I think you will get a great deal of support there, and it will have a great effect on us and the industry.

Senator WILEY. Thank you very much.

Chairman KEFAUVER. Commissioner Hennock, we do appreciate your appearance.

I want to say to you that personally I think you have made an excellent effort for the welfare of our people since you have been a member of the FCC.

Commissioner HENNOCK. Thank you very much, Mr. Chairman; and please know that I am there to serve all of you.

Chairman KEFAUVER. We will insert your entire statement in the record at this point.

(The prepared statement of Commissioner Hennock follows:)

STATEMENT OF COMMISSIONER FRIEDA B. HENNOCK OF THE FEDERAL
COMMUNICATIONS COMMISSION

Thirty-one million television receivers are pouring an unending stream of crime, violence, outright murder, brutality, unnatural suspense, and horror into the living rooms of America where, in constantly increasing numbers, the children and youth of the country are found before the screen. The suggestions which have been made before this subcommittee that there is no discernible relationship between these programs and the recent appalling increase in juvenile delinquency, in my opinion, flout commonsense and rudimentary sound judgment. The crime and brutality saturating TV programs day and night present a critical problem to the broadcasters, the FCC and the public alike.

It is no answer to point to some of the genuinely edifying and wholesome programs which are available for children. They are too few and far between, although they serve to illustrate the splendid opportunity afforded by the great new medium of television, to give a vivid portrayal of the great principles on which our society is founded, to awaken interest in the rich cultural heritage of our civilization, to develop understanding of the problems of the world in which we live, and on the lighter side, to entertain wholesomely.

There is wide concern in many responsible quarters over the saturation of children's programs with assorted blood and thunder. The outraged objections of parents over the whole country are joined by expressions of concern on the part of parent-teacher associations, editors, child specialists, sociologists, and psychiatrists, as well as by public officials.

A study by the Purdue Opinion Panel of programs carried over the seven New York City television stations in a sample week (January 25-31, 1954) disclosed 7,065 acts and threats of violence—more than twice the number monitored during the test week in 1953, and 2½ times as many as noted in 1952. This means an average of 10.7 acts and threats of violence per hour of programing in 1954, as compared with 6.2 in 1953. Stated differently, the incidence of acts or threats of violence was every 6 minutes in 1954. This was the general count. But what of the children's programs? There the figure was over 6 times as high—38.2 per hour to be exact, in children's dramas.

While corresponding figures are not available for the country as a whole, it may be assumed that they are not far different, since most of the programs were carried over the networks.

Your record contains the reports of other studies disclosing the incredibly mounting incidence of crime and violence as the staple diet of television audiences. Mrs. Clara Logan of the National Association for Better Radio and Television has cited a typical case. In Los Angeles, in 1951, there were five TV crime serials on the air. In 1952 this had increased to 9, and in 1953 to 15. Now there are 20.

As for the extent to which children are exposed to television, the figures which have been assembled will come as a surprise to no parent. The New York Parents Association discovered in their recent survey that children in the elementary grades average from 22 to 27 hours a week before the television screen— a time equivalent to what they spend in school. The heaviest viewers were aged 5 to 6. High-school students, it was found, averaged 15 to 20 hours of viewing per week. There is little room left for doubt that television is already one of the major influences molding the oncoming generation, which has been aptly described as the first TV generation.

Some mention has been made of the need for more study and research. While I think all those concerned with the problem will welcome further research, there would seem to be little doubt in the minds of parents all over the country as to the effect of TV programs on children. In a recent coast-to-coast survey conducted by the American Institute of Public Opinion—more popularly known as the Gallup poll—7 out of 10 of the men and women who were asked whether they thought any of the blame for teen-age crime could be placed on the mystery and crime programs on television and radio, answered "Yes." Fewer than 1 out of every 4 persons queried felt that no blame was attached to TV and radio. These views are amply supported by 37 comments from leading psychiatrists, psychologists, public officials, child specialists, and others which were submitted for your record by Mrs. Logan.

As I stated before, the solution to this problem rests with the broadcasters, the public and the Federal Communications Commission. All three, in my opinion, have the duty to come to grips with an intolerable situation and take the necessary steps to improve the programing to which the children of this country are being subjected.

The public must make its objections and its desires known. The parents, the parent-teacher associations and all interested civic, welfare, and religious groups should register their views with the broadcasters, the sponsors and the Commission.

The broadcasters who have the primary responsibility should act at once to rectify the serious imbalance in their programing, which cannot help but convey to the minds of the immature viewers and listeners the impression that crime, violence, brutality, and horror are the most conspicuous features of life. There is no other impression which can be gained by children who are subjected to a relentless and increasing barrage of crime and violence on the television screens in their homes. The lofty expressions and exemplary standards formulated in the industry codes have little actual relationship to the programing offered on television. The codes recognize the public-service responsibility of the broadcasters. That responsibility is not being met.

This brings me to the question of the role of the FCC in relation to programing. As Commissioner Hyde has stated to the subcommittee, the Communications Act expressly prohibits the Commission from exercising any censorship over broadcast programs. And, apart from its illegality, I fully agree with those who feel that it would be undesirable and repugnant to our American system for the Government to prescribe specifically what programs broadcasters shall or shall not put on the air.

This is not to say, however, that the FCC is devoid of any function or responsibilities relating to programs. The airwaves over which broadcasters send their signals are in the public domain. The use of these valuable public resources is permitted, under the Communications Act, only by broadcasters licensed by the Commission, on a finding that they will serve the public interest, convenience, or necessity. These licenses can be of no more than 3 years' duration. The broadcasters acquire no vested interest in the airwaves and the Commission must make a finding each time a license is renewed that the public interest will be served thereby.

The courts have affirmed the Commission's responsibility as regards programing. In *National Broadcasting Company* v. *U. S.* (319 U. S. 190, 215 et seq.) the United States Supreme Court:

"But the act does not restrict the Commission merely to supervision of the traffic. It puts upon the Commission the burden of determining the composition of that traffic.

"The Commission's licensing function cannot be discharged, therefore, merely by finding that there are no technological objections to the granting of a license. If the criterion of public interest were limited to such matters, how could the Commission choose between two applicants for the same facilities, each of whom is financially and technically qualified to operate a station? Since the very inception of Federal regulation by radio, comparative considerations as to the services to be rendered have governed the application of the standard of public interest, convenience, or necessity."

The final and ultimate test of whether the broadcaster is discharging the public trust he assumes as a licensee is his programing. It is what reaches the ears and eyes of the listening and viewing public which determines whether the interests of the public are served or not.

The Commission cannot, of course, direct its licensees not to broadcast particular programs, except in regard to such matters as obscenity, indecency, profanity, lotteries, or fraudulent advertising which the law specifically prohibits. Programing must be viewed as a whole, to ascertain whether the licensee has discharged his obligations to the public. But that is precisely what is involved in the questions which have been raised over the country about programs for children. Each outraged complaint about individual scenes of brutality, murder, crime, or horror acquires added significance for the FCC in the light of the broad picture of concentrated, unrelenting, and constantly increasing saturation of the programs with offensive content.

While self-regulation by the industry is desirable, to the extent that it falls down, the regulatory body responsible under the law to insure that broadcasters operate in the public interest, must act. Allowing for all the gaps in our information on this subject at this state, in my opinion there has been a convincing demonstration that the broadcasters have generally fallen far short of the minimum standard which the public and the FCC have the right and the duty to require of them in the matter of programing for children. In these circumstances I feel it is incumbent on the Commission to take positive remedial steps.

First, the Commission should initiate immediately an investigatory proceeding for the purpose of assembling all the facts. It should conduct hearings to afford the public, the broadcasters, and all other interested parties an opportunity to submit their comments. The Commission should then announce to the broadcasters the adoption of a firm policy against the future renewal of the licenses of any broadcasters who persist in failure to meet their responsibilities to the public by continuing to subject the children and the youth of this country to the concentrated and unbalanced fare of violence, brutality, crime, and horror from which there is little escape under present programing.

SUMMARY OF THE STATEMENT OF FRIEDA B. HENNOCK OF THE FEDERAL COMMUNICATIONS COMMISSION

I know of no field where there is more important work to be done by the Senate than in juvenile delinquency, and the attention this committee is giving to this crucial problem is most timely. Nowhere can this committee be more effective in stemming the excessive, concentrated, and exaggerated portrayal of crime and violence than in radio and television. For the airwaves over which broadcasters send their signals are in the public domain. The broadcasters acquire no vested interest in the air waves, and are issued licenses of no more than 3 years' duration. The FCC requires broadcasters to operate in the public interest, and it must take programing into full account in issuing and renewing their licenses.

Broadcasters who apply for station licenses and for license renewals are required to report in detail the percentage of time devoted to different types of programs such as entertainment, religion, news, education, discussion, etc. The objective is to insure balanced programing responsive to the needs, interests, and tastes of the communities served by the licensees.

In addition to the foregoing, the FCC should impose a new requirement for reports by broadcasters of the incidence of acts and threats of crime and violence on all programs throughout the broadcast day. Moreover, the FCC should pursue a rigorous policy of refusing renewal of the licenses of offending stations which disregard their public service responsibilities by continuing to victimize immature audiences with a concentrated and profuse deluge of crime, brutality, sadism, and outright murder.

The programing standards set out in the code of the National Association of Radio and Television Broadcasters are excellent, but they have little effect on programing as the code is voluntary and the NARTB is not in a position to enforce it effectively. The networks supply a large amount of TV programing and should be held responsible for its quality. The profusion of crime and violence in TV films mounts continuously.

The responsibility of the licensees is clear. With 35 million TV sets and 120 million radio sets pouring out an unending stream of crime and violence, it is important for the FCC to take positive corrective steps.

The broadcasting licensees are most sensitive to the policies of the FCC. With an alerted public and an active Senate committee, the FCC, if it takes the appropriate steps, cannot fail to obtain almost immediate results.

In addition, I urge the following steps:

1. Women's organizations and all other civic, educational, welfare, and religious groups should supplement theactivities of established monitoring organizations in viewing and listening to TV and radio programs. All such groups should press the stations, the networks, the program sponsors, and the FCC itself to bring to a halt the broadcast of pernicious programs which are making a significant contribution to the rise of juvenile delinquency.

2. These public service groups should study the reports of the FCC licensees, note the incidence of acts and threats of crime and violence and file complaints against offending licensees.

3. A National Radio and TV Children's Week should be proclaimed, during which there should be an evaluation of all radio and television programs in terms of their suitability for children.

4. An alert and articulate public should, as of right, present positive and constructive suggestions to licensees and sponsors as to its radio and TV program preferences for adults and children alike. The public should no longer take its radio and TV programing for granted, or continue to accept passively anything the networks and broadcasters choose to offer.

5. Since radio and TV operate in the public domain, the FCC should set up proper programing standards for both as soon as possible, and insure their implementation by rigorous enforcement.

6. And finally, the 252 channels reserved for educational television afford an unprecedented opportunity for guiding the young and enriching the lives of all. Such noncommercial stations should be built immediately. They could arouse and stimulate interest in the arts, music, history, literature, and science, to an extent heretofore unknown. Moreover, these stations can be built at a most reasonable cost and operated very economically.

Chairman KEFAUVER. We have Mr. Harold Everett Fellows, president, National Association of Radio and Television Broadcasters, and we have Dr. Ralph Banay of Columbia University.

Gentlemen, it is 12 o'clock, and I apologize for scheduling you this morning and not getting to hear you.

I wonder if it would be convenient if we would recess until 1 o'clock, and then come back at that time?

(Discussion off the record.)

Chairman KEFAUVER. We will stand in recess until 1 o'clock.

(Whereupon, at 12:05 p. m., the subcommittee recessed, to reconvene at 1 o'clock p. m. of the same day.)

Chairman KEFAUVER. The subcommittee will come to order.

Our next witness is Mr. Harold Everett Fellows.

Mr. Fellows is president of the National Association of Radio and Television Broadcasters, 1771 N Street NW., Washington, D. C.

The subcommittee is glad to have you here, Mr. Fellows.

In our hearings on this subject, we want to get all angles and all sides of the problem, and we appreciate your cooperation in coming to testify.

STATEMENT OF HAROLD E. FELLOWS, PRESIDENT AND CHAIRMAN OF THE BOARD, NATIONAL ASSOCIATION OF RADIO AND TELE-VISION BROADCASTERS, ACCOMPANIED BY EDWARD H. BRONSON, DIRECTOR OF TELEVISION CODE AFFAIRS, NARTB; AND THAD H. BROWN, VICE PRESIDENT FOR TELEVISION, NARTB

Mr. FELLOWS. Thank you, Mr. Chairman.

Chairman KEFAUVER. Will you identify the gentlemen with you?

Mr. FELLOWS. This is Mr. Thad Brown, vice president of the association, in charge of television.

Chairman KEFAUVER. I do not think we understood you, sir.

Mr. FELLOWS. Mr. Thad Brown on my right is vice president of the association, in charge of television; and on my left is Mr. Edward Bronson, who is the director of all our television code affairs.

Chairman KEFAUVER. Mr. Brown is vice president of the association in charge of television?

Mr. FELLOWS. Television; that is right.

Chairman KEFAUVER. And Mr. Bronson?

Mr. FELLOWS. He is director of television code affairs.

Chairman KEFAUVER. Director of television?

Mr. FELLOWS. Of code affairs; in other words, the operation of the NARTB Code.

Mr. Bronson will give testimony very shortly, and then Mr. Bronson and Mr. Brown will assist me in helping to answer any questions you may have.

Senator WILEY. I suggest that you lift up your voice; I have difficulty hearing you.

Mr. FELLOWS. I find the accoustics are difficult here. There is difficulty in hearing anywhere in the room.

Senator WILEY. Throw your voice out.

Mr. FELLOWS. Right.

Chairman KEFAUVER. This is an old historical room.

Senator WILEY. Webster had no trouble here.

Chairman KEFAUVER. This room has had some historical debates.

Mr. FELLOWS. Well, you certainly give us something to shoot at.

Senator WILEY. Shoot at us; that is what we want.

Chairman KEFAUVER. Mr. Fellows, do you wish to further identify yourself before proceeding with your evidence and testimony, or do you——

Mr. FELLOWS. No, I think you have identified me properly for the purpose.

Chairman KEFAUVER. How long have you been president of this association?

Mr. Fellows. I have been president of the association for the past 4 years.

I have been a broadcaster for better than a quarter of a century, about 27 years.

Chairman Kefauver. Did you succeed Justin Miller as president?

Mr. Fellows. I did, Mr. Chairman.

Chairman Kefauver. And you were a broadcaster before that time?

Mr. Fellows. That is right.

Chairman Kefauver. Where?

Mr. Fellows. In Boston.

Chairman Kefauver. At what station?

Mr. Fellows. WEER.

Chairman Kefauver. Do you devote all of your time to the affairs of the NARTB?

Mr. Fellows. I do, sir.

Chairman Kefauver. How large an office and staff do you have here?

Mr. Fellows. We have here—our headquarters are here in Washington, and we have personnel or a staff of 70.

Chairman Kefauver. How is the association supported?

Mr. Fellows. Supported by dues from the members of various radio and television stations and associated members, various members who sell equipment and supplies.

Chairman Kefauver. Are all of the television stations members?

Mr. Fellows. Not all of them.

Chairman Kefauver. How many of them are not?

Mr. Fellows. There are about 60 percent of the television stations which are members of the association; all of the networks are members of the association.

Chairman Kefauver. There are just three networks?

Mr. Fellows. That is right—four, I am sorry, sir.

Chairman Kefauver. Why don't this other 40 percent belong? What is the problem?

Mr. Fellows. Some of them are not very old on the air. A lot of them we have not been able to properly solicit.

Some of them do not feel that it is necessary, do not feel that there is, perhaps, enough to be gained. They do not all see eye to eye on that. We are constantly increasing.

Chairman Kefauver. Do the dues depend upon the size of the station?

Mr. Fellows. They do indeed; yes, sir.

The dues are proportioned in accordance with the size of the station. The small stations pay the smaller amount.

Chairman Kefauver. In your statement, do you go into how the association was formed, and its purposes?

Mr. Fellows. The association is just over 30 years old; but I do not go into it in this testimony, Senator.

Chairman Kefauver. What is the general purpose of the association?

Mr. Fellows. The general purpose of the association we have declared in policies which I can submit to you in great detail; but the general purpose of the association is to effect a unity for better broadcasting throughout the country, and it has been so since it started.

It is an attempt together to find the way to make better broadcasting and a better business under the free-enterprise system for broadcasting as we know it in America, which is quite unusual, which is to exchange ideas and information.

It is to keep the members completely informed of the developments here and elsewhere, their obligations, their responsibilities.

We meet throughout the country from time to time. We reduce ourselves to districts and regions where several of us go out into the field and have common meetings.

Senator WILEY. Is it a union of the stations or the corporations or of those who broadcast?

Mr. FELLOWS. The stations entirely. This is on the business and management side, Senator.

Senator WILEY. It is a union of those who have the license to broadcast?

Mr. FELLOWS. That is correct, sir.

Senator WILEY. Not the broadcasting chaps or women?

Mr. FELLOWS. No.

Senator WILEY. O. K.

Mr. FELLOWS. Not the talent; it is on the business and management, ownership side.

Chairman KEFAUVER. Do you get out a weekly or monthly publication?

Mr. FELLOWS. We get out several, Mr. Chairman.

Chairman KEFAUVER. What is the nature of these?

Mr. FELLOWS. Informative, what is going on, what developments there are.

Chairman KEFAUVER. Just for the information of the committee, not to be printed in the record, but as an exhibit, will you file samples of the different kinds of publications you put out?

Mr. FELLOWS. We will indeed, sir.

Would you like for us to cover, for instance, a period of time, say, a month, so you would get an idea of what is contained and for how long a period of time?

Chairman KEFAUVER. Yes; file those you put out last month, during the month of March.

Mr. FELLOWS. Fine; during the month of March.

Chairman KEFAUVER. All right.

Mr. Fellows, you may proceed in your own way.

Mr. FELLOWS. The National Association of Radio——

Chairman KEFAUVER. Do you have copies of your statement?

Mr. FELLOWS. I do indeed, sir, and I thought they had been given to you.

Chairman KEFAUVER. Yes; here they are. All right.

Mr. FELLOWS. The National Association of Radio and Television Broadcasters is a business association of the radio and television industry representing the majority of radio and television stations and all television networks, providing industry services of a wide variety, but not supplying program material either to stations or networks.

In the interests of expedition and ready reference, I will cite the previous testimony on behalf of the NARTB upon this subject and before this continuing subcommittee.

Mr. Ralph Hardy, vice president for Government relations of the association, presented testimony and was subject to examination before this subcommittee on Saturday, June 5, 1954.

At that time there was introduced into the record a copy of the television code and copies of other material relating to the industry's effort to affirmatively combat juvenile delinquency.

On October 20, 1954, I presented testimony and was subject to examination, along with Mr. Edward H. Bronson here, director of television code affairs, and Mr. Thad H. Brown, vice president for television of the association. My direct testimony related specifically to three matters:

(1) The television code.

(2) The positive effort of the association to develop television programing that can assist various school and civic organizations in their attempts to reduce the incidence of juvenile delinquency.

(3) A summary of plans for the future.

To complete the historical record, representatives of the NARTB appeared in full and exhaustive hearings before a subcommittee of the Committee on Interstate and Foreign Commerce, House of Representatives, in its investigation of radio and television programs, the principal subject of which related to programing and the child audience.

In these proceedings, held on Monday, September 15, and Tuesday, September 16, 1952, the testimony was presented by Mr. John Fetzer, chairman of the television code review board. Mr. Ralph W. Hardy; and Mr. Thad H. Brown, previously referenced; and myself.

Commercial television broadcasting was initiated only 10 years ago, but I believe it safe to say that no other industry has so quickly and completely captured the attention, imagination, and interest of the American people.

The television industry, charged with the tremendous responsibility for this medium in an attempt to guarantee that its forward path be the good path, adopted the television code March 1, 1952.

In the previous testimony last year before this subcommittee we went into an exhaustive explanation of the code. Prior to that hearing we had also presented (in 1952) lengthy testimony, particularly in connection with the television code and the programing of radio and television stations, before a House subcommittee of the Committee on Interstate and Foreign Commerce.

This subcommittee, pursuant to House Resolution 178, was authorized to conduct a—

full and complete investigation and study to determine the extent to which radio and television programs * * * contain immoral and otherwise offensive matter, or place improper emphasis on crime, violence, and corruption.

Therefore, as I am sure you realize, we are distinctly aware of past and present congressional interest in the programing of radio and television stations. We are also aware of the overwhelming acceptance of television by the American people, as evidenced by their purchase and use of approximately 35 million receiving sets.

This fact emphasizes to us the weighty responsibilities that are ours—responsibilities that are assumed with what we trust is a full realization of the impact of our actions. Television broadcasting stations are fully cognizant of the fact that good programs attract large audiences. They also know that bad programing in this free market place of ideas will rapidly toll the demise of any television station. Therefore, it is incumbent upon a station to learn the desires of its listeners, both present and potential, because it is the public preference which, in the final analysis, controls this industry, rather than any network, station, agency, or advertiser.

In view of this fact, the industry, obviously, is as concerned about its acceptance in the home as any group possibly could be. We are gratified that its acceptance has been so widespread and enthusiastic.

As we have indicated in our previous testimony, however, we are aware of the allegations that have been made against certain mystery and adventure programing. Only a few of these allegations have been to the effect that television is a major cause of juvenile delinquency, but there have been numerous comments to the effect that television may be a contributing factor.

The NARTB has attempted to inform itself regarding opinions of the experts on this matter and has passed along its findings to the broadcasters to guide them in their programing and to suggest ways in which they can combat juvenile delinquency in their own communities.

For example, we learned several months ago that the youth bureau of the Detroit Police Department was probing deeply into the possible causes of juvenile delinquency. We sent a member of our staff there to interview the officials and to write a report which was sent to all broadcasters and to many public opinion leaders around the country.

In Detroit, television was found not to be a cause or stimulus of juvenile delinquency, but was found instead to be a useful measure in controlling it. Inspector Ralph Baker, chief of the youth bureau, said—

the local television stations in Detroit have been exceedingly helpful in carrying programs which will tend to educate parents and children alike in social behavior that will minimize our task.

Last October, Television magazine decided to check with some of the most respected psychiatrists of the American Phychiatric Association to see if they felt that television was actually warping young minds. They found complete agreement that—

there is no scientific body of facts in existence that could in any way prove that television is one of the causes of juvenile delinquency.

Dr. Nathan Ackerman, psychiatrist specializing in children's problems, said that he does not believe that television is responsible for the increase in juvenile delinquency. "Television," Dr. Ackerman stated, "merely reflects the values of our current social life."

Dr. Abraham Bernstein, Columbia University psychologist, said:

I don't see how television can be singled out as the factor causing the increase of juvenile delinquency. Maybe it was caused by the sensation of the war. There's been an increase in automobiles too, but no one is blaming that on television * * *

Parents magazine, a highly respected publicaation, recently carried an article entitled "Television and Our Children—The Experts Speak Up." The article summarizes the replies to a questionnaire sent out by Dr. Robert M. Goldenson, assistant professor of psychology at

Hunter College, to child-behavior specialists in various parts of the country.

In response to the question of whether television programs are responsible for juvenile delinquency, the great majority gave a flat "no." The few who answered more or less affirmatively qualified their replies as "mere suspicions," with "no definite proof."

The authorities whose answers comprise the Parents' article are: Lauretta Bender, chief, children's division, Bellevue Hospital, New York City; Clark W. Blackburn, general director, Family Service Association of America, New York City; Gunnar Dybwad, director, Child Study Association of America, New York City; George Edwards, judge of probate, juvenile division, Detroit, Mich.; Nelson Foote, professor of sociology, University of Chicago; Lawrence K. and Mary Frank, authors of How To Help Your Child at School; Sheldon and Eleanor Glueck, Harvard Law School, Cambridge, Mass.; Frances L. Ilg, Gessell Institute, New Haven, Conn.; J. Edgar Hoover, Director, Federal Bureau of Investigation; Alice V. Keliher, professor of education, New York University; Paul Popenoe, director, American Institute of Family Relations, Los Angeles; William C. Menninger, the Menninger Foundation, Topeka, Kans.; Herman Scheibler, superintendent of schools, Indianapolis, Ind.; Benjamin Spock, Western Psychiatric Institute and Clinics, Pittsburgh, Pa.; George Stevenson, medical director, National Association for Mental Health; and Luther Woodward, New York State Department of Mental Hygiene.

At this point, Mr. Chairman, with the approval of the committee, I would like to submit this article for inclusion in the record.

Chairman KEFAUVER. How long is the article?

Mr. FELLOWS. It is not too long, sir.

Chairman KEFAUVER. Let it be marked "Exhibit No. 1" and printed in the record.

Mr. FELLOWS. Printed in the record?

Chairman KEFAUVER. Yes, sir.

Mr. FELLOWS. Thank you.

(The document referred to was marked "Exhibit No. 1," and reads as follows:)

EXHIBIT No. 1

TELEVISION AND OUR CHILDREN—THE EXPERTS SPEAK UP

Here is one of the most important articles we have ever published on TV and children. Eighteen prominent authorities from the fields of health, education, welfare answer the TV questions which are on every parent's mind. Their statements add up to a concrete though flexible guide to help regulate your child's TV viewing.

(By Robert M. Goldenson, Ph. D., assistant professor of psychology, Hunter College)

(The author bases this article on replies received from the questionnaire he sent to the following authorities: Lauretta Bender, chief, children's division, Bellevue Hospital, New York City; Clark W. Blackburn, general director, Family Service Association of America, New York City; Gunnar Dybwad, director, Child Study Association of America, New York City; George Edwards, judge of probate, juvenile division, Detroit, Mich.; Nelson Foote, professor of sociology, University of Chicago; Lawrene K. and Mary Frank, authors of How To Help Your Child At School; Sheldon and Eleanor Glueck, Harvard Law School, Cambridge Mass.; Frances L. Ilg, Gesell Institute, New Haven, Conn.; J. Edgar

Hoover, director, Federal Bureau of Investigation; Alice V. Keliher, professor of education, New York University; Paul Popenoe, director, American Institute of Family Relations, Los Angeles; William C. Menninger, The Menninger Foundation, Topeka, Kans.; Herman Scheibler, superintendent of schools, Indianapolis, Ind.; Benjamin Spock, Western Psychiatric Institute and Clinics, Pittsburgh, Pa.; George Stevenson, medical director, National Association for Mental Health; Luther Woodward, New York State Department of Mental Hygiene.)

Not long ago I opened the door of my living room and almost stumbed over the shadowy figures of four youngsters grouped, wide-eyed and silent, around the television set. Suddenly one of them shouted, "It's time for the fight! Here they go! Yippee!" The other three screamed and clapped in delight as the villain and the marshal began to slug it out with murderous intent. The two powerful men rolled over and over, threw chairs at each other, landed resounding blows, and by the time the fight was over, the four youngsters were literally jumping up and down with excitement.

Were these children—and thousands like them—little demons, taking delight in homicidal assault? Or was television debasing the taste and arousing—or instilling—violent impulses in decent American children?

In an effort to round up some definite opinions on these questions and several others that occurred to me, I drew up a brief questionnaire and sent it around to colleagues in various parts of the country. On my mailing list were a child psychiatrist at a leading hospital, the director of an important research project on juvenile delinquency, an executive of the Child Study Association of America, a pediatrician and author of a best seller on child care, the medical director of a national mental health organization, superintendent of schools, sociologists, psychologists, family life experts.

The answers I received turned out to be so comprehensive and yet so concrete that they will, I believe, clear the television air and help all of us achieve a more level-headed and constructive approach to the medium. The following is a faithful presentation of these answers, made up almost entirely of quotations from the authorities.

IN YOUR JUDGMENT, ARE TELEVISION PROGRAMS RESPONSIBLE FOR JUVENILE DELINQUENCY?

The great majority answered "No." Most typical were the following replies: No, the argument is the same as for comics, movies, radio—no evidence that delinquent acts have been due to any of these alone. Delinquency is due to deep-seated conflicts, discrepancies, and deficiencies in the personality. Children are too complex to react directly and only to some one immediate stimulus such as a TV program" * * *. "Because of the complex interplay of numerous forces—largely those of parent-child emotional interrelations—I cannot say that television programs are responsible for juvenile delinquency" * * *. "No, although an occasional program may be provocative to an already disturbed, antisocially motivated youngster."

The few who answered more or less affirmatively qualified their replies as mere suspicions or impressions, with no definite proof. Says one, "I have no firsthand information, but I cannot see how continual presentation of patterns of crime and violence to impressionable younsters can fail to have a harmful influence."

ARE TELEVISION PROGRAMS RESPONSIBLE FOR EMOTIONAL UPSETS OR DISTURBANCES IN CHILDREN? IF SO, WHAT TYPES OR EXAMPLES?

In general the respondents felt that some programs do provoke mild upsets; occasionally, too, deeper disturbances are brought to the surface in sensitive children, but their basic causes lie elsewhere. A psychiatrist for children writes: "In general, no. If a child has good and sufficient reasons for being emotionally upset, TV programs may precipitate an immediate reaction—increase anxiety, or lead to some open expression (not necessarily bad)," and a mental hygiene expert says, in similar vein, "not primarily responsible. An already anxious or fearful child may not be able to take some TV portrayals and exposure may heighten his anxiety."

An educator separates older from younger children, writing, "for the very young, yes, I feel they do create emotional upsets. Loud noises, gun battles, strange photography all create an emotional disturbance," while another expert reminds us that "other children, however, have seen the same programs without apparent disturbance," and adds this suggestion: "Perhaps the positive approach would be better—do programs of these types build emotional stability and social adjustment?"

WHAT IS YOUR IDEA OF A GOOD PROGRAM FOR CHILDREN?

A typical recommendation was the following: "Programs designed for children with understanding of their growth and development, and which give, if possible, some opportunity to the child for participation—current affairs programs for various age levels, adapted dramatic presentations, science, geography," Other examples were programs of an educational nature, a circus variety, adventure stories with a good plot, and one for all ages. In one answer the point was made that children should watch any lively presentation of human problems within their range of experience or understanding, or programs dealing with facts of the physical world, or life in any form, facts or fantasy, that deal openly with the situation. In other words, they need not be limited to programs that are created specifically for child audiences. Children profit from any programs that widen their horizon in a desirable way.

TO WHAT KIND OF TV PROGRAMS SHOULD CHILDREN NOT BE EXPOSED?

All authorities felt that though no one program is disturbing to all children, nevertheless it is best to steer them away from murder, horror, terror, from anything that appears to be unduly anxiety-producing, depressing, or deliberate propaganda of any sort," from "destruction, torture, cataclysm, especially that involves children, with whom they readily identify themselves. A child specialist remarks: "Apart from crime and violence, there is a large proportion of mere triviality and trash. A little of this goes a long way, I feel." Another adds, "neither should children be exposed to situations from which false sets of standards may be derived."

HOW DO YOU FEEL ABOUT WESTERN FILMS FOR CHILDREN'S TELEVISION FARE?

Opinions here were also uniform. Although not always enthusiastic about westerns, the authorities generally found them acceptable. One correspondent writes: "See no harm in reasonable amount. Suspect the release value (release of hostility) exceeds their stimulation effect." In other words, the four youngsters mentioned at the beginning of this article were probably getting quite normal feelings of belligerence out of their systems in a healthy way. Another rates them as fairly innocuous for stable children. One answer puts the pro's and con's in this way, "some parents to whom I have talked feel there is too much gunplay and ruffian conduct; others point out that they are stereotyped to the point where the good always comes out ahead, that sex is played down and that the children do not get too excited about them because they know the hero will win."

HOW DO YOU FEEL ABOUT CRIME AND DETECTIVE PROGRAMS AS CHILDREN'S TELEVISION FARE?

On this question opinions were fairly scattered. Only one authority, a superintendent of schools, said flatly, "I am definitely against these." A psychiatrist and a mental hygienist grouped them with westerns as "fairly innocuous for stable children" and "see no harm in reasonable amount," while a specialist on juvenile delinquency cautiously remarks, "depends on the nature of the materials and on the age and type of children." A family relations expert warns that it is very difficult not to make the criminal into the real hero of the piece—as John Milton did with Satan in Paradise Lost. Another psychiatrist discounts this point by remarking, "I marvel at how many of these programs children can view and digest without the anxiety which I may feel. They say to me, 'don't you know it's just TV?'"

Nevertheless, judging by the general tenor of their responses, the great majority of these questioned would probably agree with this more extended statement: "From the reports of surveys which I have seen, I would say that too many children are seeing too many of them. Parents and teachers to whom I have talked would like to see them at least relegated to the later hours of the day, although it is not certain that even this would deter some children's seeing them. Not too much progress is being made in getting hours changed, or in getting these programs off the air, either in television or in radio. Perhaps we need to get parents to give more supervision to the programs their children see."

The head of the FBI puts it this way: "It is of course recognized that improperly and unintelligently prepared presentations on the radio and television which recognize no restraint in producing in young minds pictures of torture, fantastic acts of violence, and brutality may have a harmful effect on receptive young minds. However, we feel that programs that portray crime in its proper light and which, through educational means, awaken Americans to action have a proper place on the radio and television."

HOW CAN WE HELP CHILDREN DEVELOP GOOD VIEWING TASTE?

Practically all put the responsibility on the shoulders of the parents. Says one, "so often parents blame the child for poor viewing taste, but actually most parents look to the TV set as an excellent babysitter. If they would watch the children's programs and discuss the points with their children they would soon become more viewing conscious." In the same general vein others write, "try to select programs carefully and discuss freely in the family circle all the programs seen, pointing out why some are good, others not," and "we can only hope to cultivate good taste in our children by developing good taste ourselves and helping our children to be sure to see the programs that are good programs. It's a teaching process, as anything about rearing children is. Parents can accomplish a lot by pointing out sequences of bad taste, by reacting themselves to elements of bad taste, by appreciating aloud or indirectly programs which are in good taste. We do this with clothing, manners and in other connections all the time. Why not in connection with television programs?" Note that' this does not imply a close censorship that prevents the child from sampling many types of programs; for, as one expert put it, "children cannot be protected, in life, from exposure to unwholesome influences, but they can be taught how to recognize and deal with them when they are exposed."

WOULD YOU ADVOCATE LABELING OR PUBLICIZING CERTAIN PROGRAMS "FOR ADULTS ONLY"?

"No," said all but one. "This would only add to their lure for children; they have a great need to be adult" * * *; "children would watch them anyway or even more and those parents alert enough to forbid would forbid them anyway." * * * It would only lead to secret evasion on the part of the children." One respondent makes the further point that it would license in those programs labeled "adult" the elements of questionable merit which we do not want our children to see.

WHAT EFFECT DO YOU BELIEVE TELEVISION IS HAVING ON CHILDREN'S SCHOOLWORK?

As a whole, the authorities did not view with alarm the effect of television on schoolwork, but recognized good as well as bad effects. Even the head of a school system recognizes that television can be a great aid or a great hindrance. If the programs and time are supervised well, then I think TV can help the child's outlook and work in and out of school. But if he is left to watch all programs then it can be a definite hindrance. A psychologist and father of three finds that TV adds considerable information on certain aspects of modern life. As to reading, there seem to be two views, both expressed by the same individual, "I assume that the predigestion of literary classics in the movies and TV programs may lead to superficiality in reading such classics. On the other hand, first-rate presentations of Shakespearean films might well stimulate greater interest and motivation to read the classics. Only carefully designed research can supply the answers."

But perhaps the fullest and most representative answer is the following: "I think it is difficult to generalize. Homework is suffering among some children who are watching television too many hours a day. On the other hand, some teachers report many pupils are doing better work in the classroom as a result of television which stimulates the children's interest. Many thoughtful parents are saying their children are watching programs which give them a better general background for social adjustment and cultural development. * * * There seems to be some indication that children of higher ability are profiting from television, while those of lower intelligence are not. There seems to be some correlation, too, between parental supervision and greater benefits from televiewing."

SHOULD PARENTS CONTROL THE AMOUNT OF TIME THE CHILD SPENDS ON TELEVISION?

A unanimous "Yes" to this question. Here are some typical comments: "Same rationale as limiting number of desserts and requiring reasonable number of hours of sleep." "For same reasons the parents are accustomed to use in every other area of their children's lives." "In my opinion a certain amount of well-planned and constant discipline of children is highly desirable; and if parents properly explain the need of this to children it will do more good than harm."

The answer from the Child Study Association makes some particularly helpful points: "In those homes where the children seem to profit most from television, the family has worked out both the amount of time which the children normally watch television, the types of programs—in some instances, the specific programs * * *. It would seem that a balanced life—school, active participation in recreative sports and activities, work in the home and homework—is desirable, and that parents should try to help their children achieve that balance."

HOW MUCH FREEDOM SHOULD CHILDREN BE ALLOWED IN CHOOSING THEIR OWN TELEVISION PROGRAMS?

Though advocating parental control over the time spent on television, most of the experts would give the children a good deal of leeway in the choice of programs. This answer is fairly representative: "Compromise is necessary, with guidance from parents and exposure of children to a large amount of suitable adult material, which they are quite able to appreciate—just as the children of a century ago could enjoy Dickens as much as they now enjoy comic books." Another put it this way: "As much freedom as possible, restricted only if there is evidence that the child is upset by some programs." Note that these answers do not give the child complete license, excluding the parent from the picture: "Obviously parental control is necessary just as it is necessary for parents to teach children not to eat harmful foods," says one; and "Parents should supervise, especially for young (under 7) and for sensitive children," says another.

One answer, however, seems to present all aspects of the question of freedom: "In general, quite a lot of freedom should be given, in my opinion. This does not mean that I think children should be turned loose to a steady diet of crime programs, for example. But I think they should be permitted to sample a wide variety of programs and should be helped to choose discriminatingly. If there is a limitation on the amount of time children may watch television, then they can be helped to choose wisely the programs to fit that time limit."

So there you have them: the thoughtful opinions of a varied group of professional people, all of whom are making the study of children a lifelong concern. They are provocative, too, for what they do not say. Not one of them took the occasion to berate televisin, blaming it for many of the ills of society. Not one brushes it aside as unimportant or advocates keeping it out of the home. They realize that it is here to stay and recognize the rich resources and even richer potentialities of the medium.

In pondering over these questions it occurred to me to reconstruct the programs which my 11-year-old boy had seen during a single week—and I was amazed at the result. They included a film on the production of aluminum in Canada and another on lion hunting; a family comedy whose plot centered around the complicated preparations of a husband for a fishing trip—further complicated by his wife's calculated interference; a daily "space" serial in which the operation of a rocket ship was accurately explained; 3 westerns, 1 of which dealt with rights of oil land, a second with a heartless confidence man who mulcts old people and a third (which I looked in on for a moment) contained some of the most beautiful scenery imaginable; a 1-hour variety show that included an excellent scene from an opera; a science program on the use of the sun's energy as a source of power; several news programs, combining on-the-spot film with commentary; and a comedian who acted out that hilarious old slapstick scene of the awkward painter who interrupts a lavish party to carry out his job. All in all, my boy had a week of good entertainment, exciting though vicarious adventure, information, artistic inspiration (I hope)—and got the subject matter for a school essay from the program on the sun's energy. A medium that can provide all this, and more, is not to be lightly dismissed.

The replies to the questionnaire are more than scattered opinion. They add up to a concrete, though flexible, guide for the 20 million families who live with television. Put in very few words here is the advice these authorities offer parents:

1. Encourage your child to explore many types of programs—but keep an eye on what he sees and what is available. Discuss this in the family.

2. If a child becomes overwrought by some programs, eliminate them for the time being at least—but don't fail to see whether or not there might be a deeper cause for his reaction.

3. Don't merely limit the time spent on television—help the child plan his entire week so that he will have time for all kinds of activities.

4. Discourage regular viewing of programs that might set false standards— but explain why they are undesirable.

5. Realize that children need children's fare: thrills, action, sheer nonsense— but that they also have an urge to grow and be like adults, and will appreciate many adult programs.

6. Individually and through organizations, offer constructive suggestions to broadcasting stations and producers for better television programs.

7. In general, use the same kind and amount of intelligent guidance with regard to television that you use in other spheres of your child's life—and have faith in his ability to manage himself well.

Mr. FELLOWS. You may recall that two of these authorities, Dr. and Mrs. Sheldon Glueck, testified before your committee on November 20, 1953; and in response to a question by Senator Hennings, Professor Glueck stated that television, movies, radio, and comic books are all social influences important to our entire culture, but that no one has, as yet, done any sound research as to their impact. He further stated that certainly television is a social influence—but one which is neither all good nor all bad. He said it was matter of how you use it and how you digest it.

Another witness before your committee at that time was Dr. Edward W. Greenwood, child psychiatrist at the Menninger Clinic in Topeka. He pointed out that no one can authoritatively say that radio, television, or comic books create harmful effects upon children. He said he sometimes wished it were possible to blame juvenile delinquency on these media, since it would make the problem of correction so much simpler.

I would also like to submit for the record several pertinent fact sheets which we have issued to broadcasters and public opinion leaders since the last time we appeared before this committee.

I have one here dated March 1955, and it deals with children's programing. There is one dated December 1954, which deals with juvenile responsibility; one dated November 1954, which deals with education; and one for October 1954, dealing with commercial television as an instructor.

I would like to submit those.

Chairman KEFAUVER. At this point—are the same ones we have?

Mr. FELLOWS. These are the same ones, Mr. Chairman. They give you an indication of some of the information in which you are interested. You said you would like to see what we gave out during the last month.

It would be much more comprehensive than this, but this is in the nature of some of the things we distributed.

Chairman KEFAUVER. I think we might have these printed in the record, also. They are not very long. Let that be exhibit No. 2.

Mr. FELLOWS. Fine.

(The documents referred to were marked "Exhibit No. 2," and read as follows:)

EXHIBIT No. 2

[Facts About TV, October 1954—The Television Information Committee of the National Association of Radio and Television Broadcasters, Washington, D. C.]

EDUCATION : COMMERCIAL TELEVISION AS AN INSTRUCTOR

For fund solicitors : In the Nation's Capital, the Community Chest is employing television to train its door-to-door volunteer fund solicitors. Before distributing campaign supplies, more than 400 team captains invited workers to their homes to witness a television playlet in which the volunteer worker met and handled three types of Community Chest presentations. The programs were broadcast simultaneously over WTOP-TV and WMAL-TV, Washington. In a half-hour, television exposed thousands of workers to a training course which might well have consumed months in any other fashion.

For history teachers : October's issue of the Civic Leader (teacher's edition of the American Observer) contains a listing of nationally televised programs which can be employed as "homework assignments" and teaching aids by instructors in current history. Listed are NBC's American Forum, American Inventory, Camel News Caravan, Hall of Fame, Meet the Press, Youth Wants To Know ; CBS's Television News, Chronoscope, See It Now, You Are There, Youth Takes A Stand ; Dumont's Author Meets the Critics, Meet Your Congress, Youth Forum ; ABC's Answer for Americans, At Issue, Cavalcade of America, Junior Press Conference, Open Hearing.

Says the article : "Television can be a powerful motivating instrument in the current history program. With the help of a few pointed questions (pupils) can be taught to look at a given telecast with critical eyes. And, thus motivated, they should be interested in analyzing and interpreting what they saw and heard on the TV screen. The analysis and interpreation must be done in the classroom. There, in free discussion based on factual information, we learn why certain events are taking place, what alternative courses of action are open to us, and what, if anything, we can do to solve our problems."

For mail users : It isn't only philatelists who can learn more about the stamp world from the ABC network's new series of half-hour dramatizations from the Post Office Department files (Thursday, 8 p. m., e. s. t.). Postmaster General Arthur Summerfield, who introduced the series on the air, sees the entertaining instruction as valuable to all users of the mails—both in protecting against losses of money and materials and in finding new and economical ways in which the postal service can be employed.

———

[Facts About TV, November 1954]

A SEARCHING LOOK PAYS EDUCATIONAL DIVIDENDS

An examination of the log listings of a local television station—no matter how exhaustive—does not often give a true reflection of the location station's—educational contributions to the community.

A Milwaukee, Wis., viewer—for example—might have set out 6 months ago to make a study of the educational features offered on Station WTMJ ; and, he might well have pursued a method of noting, in newspaper listings, those programs which "seemed to be" educational in character and then watching them as a check.

But, had this been the "way of doing it," chances are that the researcher would have completely overlooked—"Man Next Door : Bob Heiss," "Ask Esther Hotton," "Woman's World"—all of which are daytime "master of ceremony" shows, varied in their nature.

Yet, in those same 6 months, here is a partial list of the educational fare worked into these three shows :

Historical : Feature of Lincoln-Douglas debates ; review of book on Civil War ; dramatization of origin of Labor Day ; life story of Will Rogers ; feature on development of American prairies ; Wisconsin historical review.

Gardening : Film tour of flower show ; how to grow geraniums, philodendron ; park commission demonstration on bulb planting ; how to protect roses ; advice on fall work in yard and garden ; demonstration of various arrangements of cut flowers ; how to raise house plants.

Dramatics : Playlets by amateur groups ; description of little theater movement in America.

Arts and crafts: Ideas for making Christmas gifts; demonstration of pottery making; telecast of sidewalk arts and crafts show; exhibits from amateur art show; State fair crafts demonstration; demonstration by sculptor.

Hobbies: Feature on sports cars and how to use them; interview on model aviation; talk on hiking and exploring by YMCA official; interview with collector of diamonds; hobby show and demonstration.

Geography: Demonstration of Hawaiian culture by local Hawaiian-American club; illustrated travel talks on Europe, Haiti, India, British Honduras, Scotland, Japan, Nigeria, Thailand, Switzerland, Canada, Alaska, Iraq; interview with young American tourists just back from Sweden; interview with United States counsel general in Western Germany; feature on youth of various nations.

Homemaking: Hints on interior decoration; interview with soap company official on handling of laundry; demonstrations of new methods in needlework; showing of new appliances for the home; demonstration on proper use of washing machines; talk on household budgeting; discussion of functional and esthetic aspects of exterior house planning; colorcast on use of color in the home.

Health: Series of public health hints; interview with pediatrician; film on health clinics; talk and demonstration on nutrition; film on care and treatment of infantile paralysis.

Industry: Film on American transportation; look inside business management of a State fair; talk on the paper business; interview with a nylon industry official; how a research institute operates; camera tour of apothecary shop; demonstration of ice cream manufacturing; feature on electroplating.

Professions: Interview with members of American Institute of Architects; panel of lawyers from local bar association answering questions of viewers; interview with Texas jurist; feature on nurses.

Religion: Book review of God's Wonderful World for children; interview with retired Lutheran minister and philosopher; feature on the Anglican church; camera report on National Liturgical Conference.

Agriculture: Interview with county home agent; feature on making of cheese; interview with livestock farmer; feature on uses of dry milk; feature on rabbit farming; demonstration on growing of Indian wild rice; feature on mushroom raising; horticulture show.

Behavior: Instructions in the art of human relations; recreation ideas for Halloween; interview on social etiquette and manners; demonstration of courteous telephone techniques by a consultant to the phone company.

Government: Clubwomen's panel on International Children's Emergency Fund; analysis of recent changes in the Social Security Act; demonstrations and instructions on registration and voting; feature on youth aid bureau of police department; interview with city alderman; interview of maintenance of roads with State highway official; interview with State Department official.

Music: Instruction in music appreciation; selections by local choral group.

Literature: Book review on biography; demonstration of effective letter writing by library staff members; stories for children; talk on writing of poetry; introduction to great classics.

Science: Interview with University of Wisconsin instructor in anthropology; talk on insects by museum biologist; interview with geologist; interview with physicist; program honoring jubilee of light by State utilities association; feature on distillation.

Schooling: Feature on how to get children ready for school; demonstration of how to improve speed of reading; panel discussion on problems of the local schools; introduction to adult education classes in the vicinity; telecast of activities at a private school.

Charity: Interview with Volunteers of America official; demonstration of need for and handling of overseas CARE packages.

Pets: Interview on birds with president of local Audubon Society; ideas on locating lost dogs; instruction in building and maintaining a home aquarium; demonstration on care and training of dogs by Humane Society.

National Defense: Demonstration of home methods of civil defense; films on activities of Armed Forces stationed in area; demonstration by members of Army Signal Corps; interview with senior United States Marine officer in Wisconsin; feature on Air Force Reserve; award of Bronze Star to Milwaukee veteran who resisted Communist indoctrination; film on the Marines; interview with commandant of Wisconsin Military District.

Miscellaneous: Demonstration of Travelers' Aid Society services and how to employ them; introduction to new electrical fixtures and hardware for home use; showing of sketches of upcoming Paris fashions; demonstrations of various types of hair styling; interview with Grand Knight of Knights of Columbus.

In other words—at least 131 separate educational features worked into 3 entertainment programs over the 6-month period.

This case example suggests the desirability of the television station issuing to thought leaders in the community—as WTMJ–TV does—a weekly direct mail listing of educational inserts in local programs.

It also suggests the wisdom of educators and parents checking with the station—and through on the air observance—to gain awareness of inserts which can be employed for classroom and fireside training and discussion. And, possibly, for certain homework assignments.

[Facts About TV, December 1954]

JUVENILE RESPONSIBILITY AND BROADCASTING: DETROIT

The Youth Bureau of the Detroit Police Department approaches juvenile delinquency with an understanding attitude. It is even more interested in the correction required by full appreciation of the problem than it is in the punishment required by law.

Because of this attitude, the youth bureau probes deeply into the possible causes of juvenile delinquency, and possible measures that will tend to curb it.

Television has not been found to be a cause or stimulus. Television has been found to be a useful measure in control.

According to Inspector Ralph Baker, chief of the youth bureau: "In all the juvenile offenders whom we have talked to as they are brought into the detention home, there has only been an occasional mention of TV. On the other hand, the local television stations in Detroit have been exceedingly helpful in carrying programs which will tend to educate parents and children alike in social behavior that will minimize our task. The less arrests we have to make, the better we like it."

WHAT POLICE EXPERIENCE SHOWS

A 16-year-old holdup man—who robbed a doctor in his car—is one of the few who said he got the idea from a detective show on television. On further questioning, however, the boy admitted that he "probably would have committed some sort of crime anyway."

He thought that "the television program made the crime look easy, even though the villains were caught."

Two other boys were questioned. One had stolen a watch from a home; another had committed a sexual offense. They both had television receivers in their homes. Neither felt that television had anything to do with the situation.

"This 1-in-3 ratio over a half-day period is not typical," according to Inspector Baker. The holdup boy was brought to the inspector's office because he was the first juvenile offender in a long time to have mentioned television at all.

Lt. Francis Davey of the youth bureau believes that television has decreased juvenile delinquency by "keeping kids closer to home and off the streets at night." This is in spite of the fact that the frequency of juvenile offenses has been climbing in Detroit for several years.

The lieutenant's reasoning is as follows: "There has been a tremendous increase in juvenile population which has not been matched by a corresponding increase in social and corrective facilities for them. Naturally, there has been an increase in juvenile delinquency, but it has not been as large an increase as would have been experienced had not television provided a new reason for children sticking close to home and sharing experiences with their parents."

The chief factors causing juvenile delinquency in Lieutenant Davey's opinion are: too many working mothers, broken homes, and adult circumvention of certain laws by organizing into pressure groups which leads children to discover that they may be successful in circumventing laws by organizing into gangs.

Patrolman Allen Hartz of the 15th precinct seconds this opinion. He finds only a rare mention of TV in all the arrests he makes.

"Television is a very minor factor in juvenile delinquency—if a factor at all," according to Harlan Ringelberg, assistant chief probation officer of the Wayne County Juvenile Court. "As a matter of fact, parents of children on probation are encouraged to devote attention to certain TV programs. The difficulty comes in getting them to watch enough of the TV fare which educates, informs, and inspires."

"Television needs a drama that will train parents in their responsibilities and still be as compelling as the ordinary family comedy or detective script," says Eugene Moran, Negro probation officer who handles an area where the incidence of juvenile delinquency is prevalent. "Television stations and networks put on good instruction," he says, "but the audience is largely composed of those adults who do not need the training."

RECOMMENDATIONS FOR PARENTS AND BROADCASTERS

Carelessness of parents in knowing whom their children are associating with, in knowing where they are at night, in inspecting the places which they frequent, in enforcing a curfew when they must be home—these are the factors which worry Mr. Moran the most. He also finds that too many churches in his area do not provide any sort of community and recreational activities for children in the congregation, and that too many ministers are not in a position to counsel their people because they are engaged in a commercial job during the week between Sabbaths.

"If television has any effect on juvenile dissatisfaction," Mr. Moran says, "it is only in presenting so many admirable and personable characters with which the child does not feel that his own parents measure up."

The Detroit Youth Bureau is scientific in its approach—so much so that the Columbia Broadcasting System has selected it for a sequence on its cultural television series entitled "The Search." Dr. William Wattenberg, professor of educational psychology at Wayne University, consults with the officials of the youth bureau regularly and examines many of the offenders brought into the detention home.

Some months ago, Dr. Wattenberg suspected that there might be some link between the television programs juveniles watched and their tendency to be delinquent. He conducted a study. The results showed that the favorite program of delinquents and nondelinquents was the same one—I Love Lucy.

Although none of Dr. Wattenberg's findings have disclosed any link between television and delinquency, it is his opinion that producers of television detective, mystery, and western shows are best advised to be extremely cautious about showing any reenactments of crimes in detail.

YOUTH PROGRAMING BY DETROIT TV STATIONS

The positive contribution of Detroit broadcasting stations to the problem with which the youth bureau deals is cited as follows:

WWJ–TV has recently launched a 15-week series from the University of Michigan entitled "The Teenager"—a study of adolescent behavior. This is a course in which the instructor is Dr. William C. Morse, associate professor of educational psychology and director of the university's gresh air camp. It involves discussion of questions of special interest in the area of adolescence and dramatizes situations which teach through example.

For instance, in one of the sequences, a sympathetic mother tries to help her teen-age daughter, who finds it difficult to talk to boys on the telephone. Topics covered by the series are as follows:

1. What Is A Teen-ager?
2. Manners and Mores
3. Psychological Implications of Physical Changes
4. Adjustment to Personal and Social Problems
5. The Adolescent in the Family
6. The Adolescent in School
7. The Adolescent in Group Activity
8. Sex and Adolescence
9. Dating Habits
10. Delinquency and What To Do About It
11. Normal and Abnormal Behavior
12. Getting Ready for Adulthood.

WWJ–TV's Traffic Court frequently devotes some of its cases to the youth driving problem. The program provides actual reenactments of cases appearing before the court. The telecast is presided over by Detroit Traffic Judge John B. Watts, and has been officially endorsed by the Traffic Safety Association and the Michigan Bar Association.

To orient viewers with recreational facilities available in the city, WWJ-TV inserts material on parks and playgrounds in its weekly series of films entitled "City Affairs."

At WXYZ-TV, half of a 2-hour Saturday program (known as Ed McKenzie's Saturday Party) is devoted to teen-age talent contests cosponsored by the Detroit Parks and Recreation Commission and the Detroit Public Schools. Master of Ceremonies McKenzie has been awarded a plaque in recognition for his work in combating juvenile delinquency and effecting racial understanding.

A weekly quiz show known as Headline Hunters is telecast on WXYZ-TV in cooperation with public and parochial schools. The purpose of this program is to stimulate interest of youth in world, national, and local affairs.

Guests from the Detroit Police Department appear weekly on WXYZ's Heart of Detroit telecast to demonstrate police equipment, show the work of the patrolmen, and deliver advice on law observance and safety.

Children from the United Foundation sponsored agencies appear on Dinner Theater, a daily TV show. They eat a meal on camera and demonstrate the activities and services of their agency. During Girl Scout Week, a baking contest for girls is conducted on camera by the station.

Off-camera activities of WXYZ are numerous. Talent is made available for teen-age functions, PTA meetings, and school assemblies. Executive directors of the station teach television classes at Wayne and Detroit Universities and appear as guest speakers at high-school meetings. Each year, the station serves as the publicity unit for the city's Junior Achievement program. WXYZ's public-service director represents the station at all meetings of Detroit youth and social agencies.

RADIO'S INFLUENCE ALSO EMPLOYED

Both of the above stations also tie their radio facilities into the program.

WWJ radio has long cooperated with the public schools in presenting 2 weekly programs written, directed, and produced by students. Frequently these programs inspire good conduct and general behavior.

Weekly radio time is devoted to a Boy Scouts' report. Youth concerts by the Detroit Symphony Orchestra are broadcast. In association with Junior Achievement, the radio station has carried a series of 13 programs entitled "Careers Unlimited," with the general theme: "Busy hands do not get into trouble."

In cooperation with the National Broadcasting Co., WWJ radio is making a number of tape recordings by inmates at Jackson Prison on the general theme— "Crime doesn't pay"—which are being used by NBC as spot announcements and inserts in documentaries on the entire network.

On a year-round basis, WXYZ radio produces a weekly show entitled "Sandlotters," in cooperation with the Detroit Traffic Safety Department. The show includes sports stories, sports news, and traffic safety messages from Judge Watts of traffic court.

The School Music Hour, radioed by WXYZ, combines entertainment value with information designed to interest more teen-agers in activities sponsored by schools. Local high schools are featured on a rotating basis.

MORE CONTRIBUTIONS BY CAMERA

Station WJBK-TV has assigned Production Manager Glenn Boundy, Jr., to be a member of the Detroit Mayor's Youth Committee; and its Public Service Director Kenneth Boehmer as an officer in the Businessmen's Youth Club. Other members of the staff are active in instructing evening classes at local universities.

On Sundays, WJBK-TV carries a number of programs helpful to teen-agers and their parents. Appointment With Age, which is devoted to problems of retired life, places particular emphasis on youthful respect toward older folks. Each Sunday noon, the University of Detroit telecasts a half-hour feature in which problems of the youngsters are discussed by leading educators and students. Two additions of The Christophers film series are shown; and This Is the Life, another religious family feature, is televised.

Michigan State College presents a program for teen-agers and parents over WJBK-TV each Saturday at 9:45 a. m. Wayne University has a similar program—also on Saturday morning.

[Facts About TV, March 1955]

CHILDREN'S PROGRAMING

A recent study reveals that parents and children watch and enjoy many of the same programs and that we make a mistake when we think of television's influence on children only in terms of so-called children's programs. The results of this study are quite significant for they show that (1) the family is drawn together by this common ground, watching and discussing programs as a group; (2) the tastes of children may be somewhat higher than hitherto believed; and (3) the vocabulary and intellectual curiosity of children develop faster and they turn to books, music, etc. to satisfy this interest that is piqued by TV.

It may be well to remind ourselves of something we've always suspected; namely, that children are part of the family and that TV shows labeled "family" are for them too. Our occasional forgetfulness may be forgiven on the grounds that many programs are called "children's programs," perhaps justly so because they have few if any adult viewers. This tends to mislead many critics of "children's programs," whose comment often lead us to conclude that they themselves may not be getting the full picture even if the children are.

The New York Herald Tribune education department recently completed a survey of television tastes of 1,200 school children. In an article, "Kids Aren't Kids When it Comes to TV," Nancy Moltke-Hansen finds that "The kids don't like programs designed for them as much as programs designed for their parents. Their favorite show is I Love Lucy. Next on the list comes Topper, then Disneyland and Superman. No more than 40 percent of the children's favorites are actual children's programs. For the rest their votes cover the range of adult shows—from You Are There and Hall of Fame, through Dragnet, The Big Show, and Medic, to Jackie Gleason, Life With Riley, and Beat the Clock."

Miss Moltke-Hansen finds the term "children" ambiguous in classifying programs, because many "children's shows" are slanted toward kids from 3 to 7 years old while their older brothers and sisters of 8 and 9 go for Roy Rogers and Disneyland. At 13, however, they want Dragnet and the above-mentioned popular comedies.

In quizzing several TV network executives on their opinions as to who was viewing what, it was found that they were generally unaware of the extent to which children watched the situation comedies and other shows designed for older people.

The adult mind, properly typified by network executives, community leaders, and parents themselves, is not to be blamed for its incomplete understanding of children's pleasures and motivations. It is hard to recall one's own specific reaction to children situations; nevertheless, children have their own valid reasons for their likes and dislikes.

For example, one little girl in the grade said she liked Mr. Peepers because "my mother and father like it too and so do our next door neighbors," demonstrating a need to feel at one with the other members of her social group. Children feel cozy and grown up when they share laughter with their parents and their parents' friends, the study found.

Topper offers the fascination of ghosts that you can't see, My Little Margie presents the appealing spectacle of someone else getting into trouble in a comical way, Mama is "such a sweet program—when you watch it you can laugh at some things and feel sad at others." These are the reactions of children in the third, fourth, and fifth grades.

Children apparently like to feel they are learning while being amused and they don't insist on happy endings. Medic's attraction is that it tells about hospitals; it's a true story and the person doesn't always live. On the Carousel tells very interesting things like how they make shoes. You Are There is a favorite because it gives historic facts and legends from many countries and shows the details of famous historical events.

What do these findings mean? For one thing, they show that the tastes and preferences of children may be somewhat higher than hitherto believed. It tells sponsors that much of their audience consists of youngsters, toward whom a programmatic as well as an advertising eye must be at least partially cocked.

But much more than this is suggested.

Children enjoy, through television, the same entertainment as their parents, thus creating a common ground for the whole family that is the very basis of a healthy society. Family life becomes more than a mere peaceful coexistence.

There are things to talk about, to compare with one another, to explain and to have explained. Stimulus and ferment, cultural curiosity, a parent-child interchange of feelings and ideas are created during the common leisure of both parents and their children—something of as much cultural validity as the father's playing baseball with his son or the mother's teaching her daughter how to cook and keep house. For TV creates ideas—the "how to do it" of the mind—as much as techniques—how to bake a cake, improve your golf, etc.

A case in point is the opportunity for children to ask "why?" when presented with a TV situation. Here the parent performs his role as teacher and guide. In company with a 5-year-old, a 7-year-old, and a 10-year-old, Dr. Willard Abraham, professor of education at Arizona State College, watched a television program, taking note of some of the words used in the script. They were: "Chapter, laboratory, surrounded, extinguished, devise, venture, instrument, audience, ceremony, domain, universe, influence, circuit, disappear, destination, expedition, desolate, inspection, squadron, adventure, crater, short wave."

After the program was over, Dr. Abraham talked it over with his young friends and was surprised to discoved that they had understood it. He concluded that "their vocabulary had grown through hearing the words used often in correct ways." So he writes in the March issue of Family Circle magazine.

In considering the relationship between TV-watching and book-reading Dr. Abraham asserts that television is more an aid to reading than a hinderer of it, because it builds young vocabularies and stimulates curiosity on matters of detail that are suggested on TV but which cannot be presented as fully as in a book.

This thinking is strongly seconded by Commissioner John C. Doerfer of the Federal Communications Commission, the Government body whose responsibility it is to license radio and television and observe how well the public interest is served.

Speaking in San Francisco recently, Mr. Doerfer declared, "The head librarian of a large metropolitan city recently was quoted as saying that 'TV is tending to become more of an ally than a competitor.' When the people closely associated with these manifestations of the cultural growth of the American people publicly testify that broadcasting is no longer considered a competitor but an ally, it bears an imprint of more reliability than the subjective appraisals of broadcast programs by casual observers."

Furthermore, Mr. Doerfer pointed out, the audience for concert music rose from 3,680,000 to 4,203,000 last year, the sale of musical instruments shows a big rise, and the number of children studying music has greatly increased. He quoted the dean of a conservatory of music and a director of choral music to the effect that a child seeing one of his own contemporaries give an outstanding recital on TV makes the youngster want to learn music himself.

Where but on television, he asked, could so many young people watch Yehudi Menuhin play the violin and take time to discuss what he was doing and why he enjoyed it so much. This he did on a recent Omnibus program one Sunday afternoon recently when millions of children and their parents were watching TV.

Mr. FELLOWS. In addition to these positive comments, the NARTB also attempts to keep the industry fully informed of criticism through the issuance of regular reports.

The members of the television industry recognize that they, as do all of us, have an affirmative obligation to contribute to the public welfare of this country and its citizens. At our previous appearance before the subcommittee we outlined various steps which the National Association of Radio and Television Broadcasters contemplated taking in order to help serve the public interest in television programing.

Among these were a broadening of the monitoring of television stations by the television code affairs staff. The subcommittee was informed of our plans to employ a professional research organization to expand the amount of actual monitoring of television programing in various areas.

We also indicated plans for a pilot study to determine public attitudes toward television programing. We informed the subcommittee of our plans to enlarge the staff of the television code affairs department.

All of these plans have been activated and, at the same time, we have continued our activity in providing stations with all information coming to our attention in regard to suggestions for advancing the fight against juvenile delinquency in their respective communities. We have found the television broadcasters anxious to do their part in cooperating with any soundly organized campaign to reduce delinquency.

As I said before, I have accompanying me today Mr. Bronson and Mr. Brown, whom I introduced earlier.

Mr. Brown and Mr. Bronson will be here with me if you want to ask various questions, after Mr. Bronson has given his side of the picture here, directly reporting on the code operation.

Thank you, Mr. Chairman.

Chairman KEFAUVER. I think the best way to proceed is to allow Mr. Bronson to make a statement now.

Mr. BRONSON. May I proceed, Mr. Chairman?

Chairman KEFAUVER. Yes, you may proceed.

Mr. BRONSON. I have already been identified, so I will not repeat the opening paragraph.

I am deeply appreciative of the opportunity to appear before this committee and present to you the activities and progress of the television code since we reported to this committee on October 20 of last year. Already Mr. Fellows has reviewed much of the code board's administration to that date, so I shall confine this report to activities expanded and instituted since that time.

A most important part of this activity is that of monitoring television programing and advertising. This activity conducted by the code board staff of NARTB falls into two categories. First, is the review of television network organizations and the second is that of the schedules offered by local stations in individual cities across the country.

It should be noted at the outset, by way of review, that this monitoring project is conducted among code subscribing stations and networks only and is purely for the information and guidance of the code review board and the individual station or network to which such monitoring may relate.

Network monitoring, for the most part, is conducted by three of the four code board staff members working at NARTB headquarters here in Washington and by four auxiliary monitors operating under the direct supervision of the director of television code affairs and his assistant, Mr. Charles S. Cady.

Our current schedule of network monitoring provides reports on approximately 260 hours of programing each month. This is an increase of 300 percent over the figure reported to this committee last October.

The second category, that of local station review, provides monthly reports on approximately 280 hours of programing and covers an average of 24 stations a month. It might be interesting to note here that in our last report we recorded 231 stations as subscribers to the television code. There are now 245 as well as all four of the national television networks.

For this second category of monitoring, the code review board, through NARTB, retains a nationally known and recognized research firm with monitoring facilities in over 200 cities to do the actual monitoring. This, incidentally, is an increase of more than 500 percent over the same activity 5 months ago.

Mr. Fellows testified last October that our monitoring activity had been largely exploratory to that time. While we now have in operation a full scale monitoring service, the results of which are retained in confidence by the code review board and reported only to the individual code subscriber concerned, we are continuing to explore new methods and techniques and to widen the scope of reported coverage.

A special monitoring program is now being conducted relating to children's programing and covering 22 stations in 9 cities. Because much of the information to be reported in this survey is of a subjective nature, particular care was taken in the preparation of the survey forms and the accompanying instruction and, in some instances, duplicate monitors were assigned to each time period to be covered.

I have reported the foregoing in some detail to demonstrate that our monitoring is expanding in 2 areas, both quantity and quality.

Coincident with this I should like to point out that the code board staff at NARTB has been enlarged to 4 full-time persons working on the affairs of the code board and their administration.

Also, plans are provided for additional staff personnel when, and, as they are needed to provide for the code board's expanding activity. With regard to monitoring, however, the most significant growth is not in the number of full time staff personnel, but is a result of retaining a national research firm to assist in this work and thus adding the services of more than 600 trained monitors in over 200 cities throughout the United States.

One phase of television programing that seems to have caused some interest in the past, was that of film product available to television and its relationship to the code. I am sure the committee will be interested in knowing that the code board staff has contacted nearly 140 producers and distributors of film for use on television. This is but a part of a continuing and widening educational program to acquaint producers and distributors with the code, the activity of the code review board and the need for care in development of the product they offer to code subscribers.

Personal visits by the director of television code affairs and his assistant, have been instituted and will be continued. Through these activities, we feel the producers and distributors of film are more conscious of the need for code conformance in the preparation and presentation of their product.

A corollary activity in the film picture is stepped up assistance to the individual code subscriber upon the part of the code board and the code board staff. After careful study, a recommended clause for use in film contracts by code subscribers was sent out to all subscribers from the code review board. This clause reads:

Station ——— is a subscriber to the NARTB television code, and reserves the right to alter or to reject a film, in accordance with the appropriate provisions of this contract, if, in the opinion of the station, said film is contrary to the code.

Not only was this language furnished to the code subscribers, but an imprinted hand stamp containing this language was sent to each subscriber. Each subscriber may use this at his own option in the course of contracting for film to be presented over his television facilities.

A concluding note should cover the pilot study of viewer attitudes the television code review board had in the field at the time we appeared before the Senate subcommittee investigating juvenile delinquency last October.

I wish to point out that this survey was just what its name implies—a pilot study. It was conducted by a nationally known and accepted survey firm long active in broadcast survey work for the guidance and information of the code review board and staff to determine what might be done along similar lines and in greater detail in the future. This pilot study now is being reviewed by a subcommittee of the code review board for this purpose.

The foregoing statement has been an effort to detail for you some of the expanding activity of the television code review board and the NARTB staff assigned to carry out the policies of that board. As you know, this is a program of industry voluntary self-regulation. It improves and widens in an evolutionary manner and seldom is dramatic. The suggestions and criticisms of this committee, as well as those of responsible organizations and of the general viewing public always are welcome and have proved to be most helpful.

Thank you very much for the opportunity to make this report and for your courteous attention.

Chairman KEFAUVER. Thank you very much, Mr. Fellows and Mr. Bronson.

As I understand it, Mr. Bronson, you are the chairman of the code board?

Mr. BRONSON. No, sir. I am a member of the NARTB staff. The chairman of the code review board is Mr. John A. Fetzer, a station owner and operator.

Chairman KEFAUVER. Mr. Fetzer?

Mr. FELLOWS. F-e-t-z-e-r.

Chairman KEFAUVER. Where is Mr. Fetzer; where does he live?

Mr. BRONSON. He is located in western Michigan, Kalamazoo, Mich., and he has radio and broadcasting properties in western Michigan, and also Nebraska. His headquarters are, sir, in Kalamazoo, Mich.

Chairman KEFAUVER. How much time does Mr. Fetzer give to the code board, code review board?

Mr. BRONSON. Well, he gives considerable time comparatively from his personal business, sir. He is not a member of our staff, naturally.

The code review board itself, if I may explain, is composed of five persons from the broadcasting industry who are owners or management operators of broadcasting properties, that is, television properties.

This code board meets on a minimum of four times a year, and its record has been much more than that in the past.

I might say beyond that we are in contact with Mr. Fetzer from time to time regarding affairs of the code, even though he may not be with us in Washington.

The code board staff, which I head, is located at the NARTB headquarters, reporting to Mr. Fellows as president, and carrying out the policies of the code board.

Chairman KEFAUVER. Senator Wiley, do you have any questions you wish to ask these gentlemen?

Senator WILEY. The statements that these gentlemen have made seem to point up the fact that they are giving earnest study to the problem before us.

When you got the reaction from these numerous people to the effect that their judgment, in substance, was that television, I think the language was, in response to the question of whether television programs were responsible for juvenile delinquency, the majority gave a flat "no," and a few who answered affirmatively qualified their answers by a reply that it was mere suspicion, but no definite proof.

I do not think, of course, it requires any specialist to know that the mental food some of these children get, outlined to a large extent their course, whether it is in the television or the church or the schools or in their contacts. I presume you all realize that?

Mr. FELLOWS. We do, indeed, Senator.

Senator WILEY. Realizing that, then, operating under your code, the idea is that you feel it your obligation to screen those things that might have a negative effect upon the young minds?

Mr. FELLOWS. That is right.

Chairman KEFAUVER. Mr. Fellows, you gentlemen speak out louder, because we have some newspaper people here and reporters, and an audience who cannot hear you unless you speak up.

Senator WILEY. Now this code that you speak of, have you got a copy of that code?

Mr. FELLOWS. We have, indeed, Senator.

Senator WILEY. It is in the record; all right.

Mr. BRONSON. It is already in the record.

Would you like copies, Senator, for the moment?

Senator WILEY. I would like to see it, of course.

Chairman KEFAUVER. Here is one for Senator Wiley.

Senator WILEY. I notice, among other things, that you say the presentation of the technique of crime in such detail as to invite imitation should be avoided; the use of horror for its own sake will be eliminated. Law enforcement shall be upheld, and other provisions that seem very educational and worthwhile.

Well, now we come to this:

Responsibility toward the children: The education of children involves giving them a sense of the world at large. Crime, violence, and sex are a part of the world they will be called upon to meet, and a certain amount of proper presentation of such is helpful in orienting the child to his social surroundings. However, violence and illicit sex shall not be presented in an attractive manner nor to an extent such as will lead a child to believe that they play a greater part in life than they do. They should not be presented without indications of the resultant retribution and punishment.

Well, that is a large order. How often do you take a television subject, or whatever you want to call it, and apply this particular section to it? How often is this considered?

Mr. FELLOWS. It is considered in connection—that or whatever particular phrases apply, are considered in connection with every single criticism that comes before the television code review board.

Those are the ideals, the principles upon which we intend and, we hope, and we continue to build, so far as the television industry is concerned, and those of the television industry who subscribe to and participate in the operation of the code.

The document was prepared, Senator, by about 20 leading broadcasters working as a committee, and in subcommittees, over a period of, Thad, it was something in excess of a year, was it not?

Mr. BROWN. That is right.

Mr. FELLOWS. And is in some degree the result of some 20 years of experience in the radio field.

I can remember years ago when I myself was a member of the committee working on radio standards of practice, and we learned a great deal about reactions and preventive measures that we should set up or philosophy which we should incorporate into such a going code.

Then we had, of course, the impact of television, and it was pointed out this morning it adds another dimension, which is sight, and that is really—I do not think it is unbecoming for me to say—a tremendously well thought out document directed toward what we think is realism and practicality, and what we think should be done by the television industry in protecting the public interest, and we are particularly aware of the problems with regard to children's audiences.

It is for home consumption, this business of television, and it is a problem all apart and by itself, and we recognize that.

Senator WILEY. What I was getting at was, after reading that provision, that apparently those who wrote this code thought that part of their business consisted of educating children as to these subjects.

Mr. FELLOWS. I think that is an interpretation, Senator, if you do not mind my saying so.

I also think I should add that that code is activated daily by each broadcaster.

The networks that we mentioned have great amounts of people, sometimes 20 and 30 in the large networks, who devote themselves to this business of program screening and program preparation in accordance with that code.

Many people are involved and activated daily throughout this country.

Senator WILEY. Is there an extra copy of this?

Mr. FELLOWS. There is indeed.

Senator WILEY. I would like to have one for my own use. I would be very happy to—this is yours? Thank you. I would have liked to have seen it before.

I think that is all at this time, Mr. Chairman.

Chairman KEFAUVER. Mr. Fellows, have you reached a conclusion— you stated in your testimony that you do not think that these programs of violence and shooting and what-not, some of them, have any substantial effect upon juvenile delinquency. And how do you account for the surveys of parents in which they express the belief that it does?

Mr. FELLOWS. Mr. Chairman, if you will permit me, I did not attempt to reach a personal conclusion. I was attempting to quote confusion or conflict that there is in a great many people in this field of endeavor, such as psychology and child study, who have determined in their own right, to their own satisfaction that there is no great contribution on the part of television to juvenile delinquency.

I know that others have——

Chairman KEFAUVER. Why don't you put the others in your statement, too?

Mr. FELLOWS. I think they have been included in various testimony which your committee has had.

Chairman KEFAUVER. Well, in looking over your releases to the television industry, you only present the side apparently——

Mr. FELLOWS. In those releases which we have given you, sir.

We will give you other material where we attempt to keep the broadcasting industry completely informed, and tell them of the criticism, as well.

Chairman KEFAUVER. Look these over and see if you find where you have given the other side of the picture.

Mr. FELLOWS. In these we may not have. I was supporting my testimony with these. We have others which will be in the documents which you asked us to send along, indicating the extent to which we have informed our own people.

Chairman KEFAUVER. Do you have them with you?

Mr. FELLOWS. I do not think we do. They are as far away as the office. We will get them to you shortly.

Chairman KEFAUVER. Will you have them in the morning?

Mr. FELLOWS. We will have them for you in the morning.

Chairman KEFAUVER. Those will be marked "Exhibit No. 3," and placed on file with the subcommittee.

(The information was submitted the following day, April 7; was marked "Exhibit No. 3," and is on file with the subcommittee.)

Chairman KEFAUVER. The Gallup poll is that 7 out of 10 of the men and women who were asked whether they thought any of the blame for teen-age crime could be placed on television programs answered, "Yes."

Are you aware of that?

Mr. FELLOWS. I heard the quotation this morning; I had not heard it before, sir.

Chairman KEFAUVER. Did you send that around to your broadcasters?

Mr. FELLOWS. I do not think we have it yet.

Chairman KEFAUVER. This was a long time ago.

Mr. FELLOWS. Yes, but I mean the details, we put it in a code— I think in our last code—bulletin.

Mr. Bronson tells me it was included in the last code bulletin.

Chairman KEFAUVER. I cannot hear you, sir.

Mr. FELLOWS. Mr. Bronson thinks it was in our last code bulletin.

Chairman KEFAUVER. Will you bring that, Mr. Bronson?

Mr. BRONSON. I will look it up; I am not certain it was included. As I recall, the Gallup survey to which you refer appeared last fall; I do not think it was within the last few months, although my memory may be incorrect, if it is the same one to which you are alluding there.

Chairman KEFAUVER. I wonder why in your statement or in your information you do not set forth these experts who have concluded that while there are beneficial effects of television, such as keeping more children at home and some of the educational programs, all of which we appreciate, why don't you include some of the authorities who take a different point of view?

Mr. FELLOWS. May I speak to that, Mr. Chairman?

Chairman KEFAUVER. Yes; that is what I am asking for.

Mr. FELLOWS. We were told, at least we understood we were being told, that you would like up to report on what we had done since the hearing last October, about the various progress that we were in, right in the middle of making, and that is what I understood that you and the committee wanted at this point.

You wanted us to come back and tell you what we had done about increasing monitoring, what we had done about stepping up various procedures, and what had happened betimes on the thing, and I think we devoted ourselves almost entirely to that.

Chairman KEFAUVER. Well, we did want the progress you had made, and I congratulate you upon the greatly increased activity since you were here last fall.

But in your statement, sir, you went beyond that, and in order to try to prove the conclusion that you have reached that television programs, certain of them, do not have an adverse effect upon juvenile delinquency; that is in your statement on page 5.

I think, in order to give a rounded-out picture, and not to mislead the public or your television people, that after listing these 35 or 40 people who reach one conclusion, you might well have set forth the other side as shown by what the parents themselves thought, and also many experts who have opinions other than this.

In other words, what we want are the facts, and I am sure that is what you want or should want your broadcasters to get.

Mr. FELLOWS. Indeed; that is why I regret in any way if we have given any impression that what we do not want are facts. If I gave that impression I am entirely wrong. We seek them at all times.

We have said in the testimony before that the broadcasters of this country, if they could really feel they were contributing to juvenile delinquency, I am sure, as good citizens, they would be, as anyone else, interested and concerned with the problem.

I think I did add, Mr. Chairman, on page 6—Mr. Bronson has called my attention to it—in addition to positive comment, the NARTB attempts to keep the industry fully informed of criticism through the issuance of various reports, and we do have a record of these various reports and polls.

I have not given you a direct answer as to the Gallup report.

There are a great many reports which have come to bear on the problem of juvenile delinquency; there are 1 or 2, and I can name them if you want me to, but they have been refuted, they have been fundamentally amateur reports in too many cases, which have not been substantiated, which have been used to some degree in open testimony, and such a situation existed in Chicago along about a year or two ago.

We do not want to officially or authoritatively use or quote any of these things unless we feel that they are substantially correct.

I have no doubt but what of a group of people interviewed, possibly 75 would immediately say that they felt that television had some influence in the field of juvenile delinquency.

We do not say, Mr. Chairman, that it does not. We hope to find out. along with you, whether it does.

We have not been convinced; it has not been proved to us, that generally speaking it is a major factor. To what extent it is a factor we certainly want to eliminate it; I can assure you of that.

Chairman KEFAUVER. Well, parents would be the best people to judge, would they not?

Mr. FELLOWS. We use the Parents magazine article because we thought it would quite nearly reflect a parental opinion.

The publication is devoted and directed to that, and we felt that we are somewhat better off——

Chairman KEFAUVER. I am not talking about the Parents article, which is written by so-called experts, 2 or 3 of whom I do not have any confidence in. I am talking about the actual parents of young people; I mean, they are the ones who live with the young people and who know.

Mr. FELLOWS. We listen to them, sir, and we work with them. We work with minority groups and we work with organized groups. We are concerned about it.

But we have not been able to find, beyond what we are doing in our code—our code expresses what we try to do, and we think so far that we are making a definite contribution, and that if there is an area of juvenile delinquency involved in most television programing to which you would refer as possibly being involved in the thing, we think that we are making an awful lot of progress, and that the industry itself has been growing up tremendously.

As I said, we are just 10 years old.

Chairman KEFAUVER. You are, of course, familiar with the fact that psychiatrists, such as Dr. Frederick Wertham, in actual child study cases, both in the case of comics and TV shows, has found where crimes or misdeeds have in actual cases been laid directly to what they saw on television or what they read?

Mr. FELLOWS. We find, as you are pointing out, great disagreement among the psychiatrists and among the various authorities in the field.

Chairman KEFAUVER. I do not see that you set out the disagreement. You set out——

Mr. FELLOWS. I have not set it out in this testimony, sir, but I assure you we have.

Chairman KEFAUVER. You have not set it out in this testimony you are giving us, and I think you would be rendering a better public service if you would not let your television stations and industry feel that this is just nothing to this. But if you would set forth the fact that 7 out of 10 parents, many great psychiatrists and child students, I mean students of children's affairs, feel that as to some children there is a connection and an adverse effect.

Mr. FELLOWS. I really think, Mr. Chairman, that when you get the material you are going to get that you have asked for, and get it tomorrow, you will see that we continually attempt to give whatever is developed on both sides to the industry, to our members.

Chairman KEFAUVER. What control do you try to exercise or any influence over those who prepare the scripts and the taking of the pictures that go over television?

Mr. FELLOWS. Well, I will let Mr. Bronson tell you something of his day-to-day efforts, in his day-to-day operations in that field.

Mr. Bronson. Mr. Chairman, I think the simplest answer to your question regarding individual stations as to scripts is that the individual station management appoints or designates persons responsible within their organization at the local level, I am speaking now, for the preparation of the program material or scripts, as you have stated.

It is that assignment, in conformance with the television code, if that station subscribes to the code.

At the network level I think I can speak of some great assurance of a tremendous activity in the area of review or, if you prefer, preview of material, upon the part of the originating point of the network service in television.

There are specific department heads or executives assigned to that project.

They have competent and adequate staffs.

I might say from my own experience and, as an observation in talking with these people, that a great deal of the material from time to time has been eliminated and is regularly eliminated or changed at those points.

The preparation of television film itself, Mr. Chairman, I believe you are aware, for the greater part is produced outside of our own industry—that is the reason I made a reference to our effort in my statement, sir——

Chairman Kefauver. That is produced by the movie industry?

Mr. Bronson. By independent producers, I believe; not necessarily the movie industry, as you might——

Chairman Kefauver. I know, but by movie studios.

Mr. Bronson. Yes; and there are many studios now, Mr. Chairman, that are producing specifically for television programing.

(Discussion off the record.)

Chairman Kefauver. Will you proceed?

Mr. Bronson. Yes, sir.

As I was mentioning the studios to which you refer, Hollywood studios, normally, I think, you consider as film product for theater consumption.

I think I should state at this point that with the advent of television there are many producing agencies now producing film only for television use, and not necessarily for theater use.

Chairman Kefauver. Do you try to get them to comply with the code?

Mr. Bronson. Yes, sir; we do.

Chairman Kefauver. What do you do about fellows who do not comply with the code?

Mr. Bronson. Are you referring to film producers, or to stations, sir?

Chairman Kefauver. Well, of course, you only have direct association with the stations.

Mr. Bronson. Stations and the networks; that is correct.

Chairman Kefauver. And the networks.

Do all of the shows we see on television meet your code?

Mr. Bronson. Do all the programs that you see, sir, or that the public sees?

Chairman Kefauver. I mean that anyone sees.

Mr. BRONSON. I think there are exceptions to the code, being very honest about it, and I think we are endeavoring to correct those exceptions, sir.

Chairman KEFAUVER. What do you say about it when you see exceptions?

Mr. BRONSON. We bring it immediately to the attention of the individual station or the network and the properly designated executive, discuss it with him.

In some instances, I might even point out that code review board, sitting as a reviewing board, looks over program material and has called in executives concerned with it.

Chairman KEFAUVER. Then what if, after bringing it to their attention, it is not corrected; what do you do then?

Mr. BRONSON. We have a very good record, sir, I believe. We have yet to find any serious violations that have continued and have not been corrected.

Chairman KEFAUVER. But what recourse do you have if they do not correct them?

Mr. BRONSON. May I ask Mr. Brown to speak to that?

Mr. BROWN. Mr. Chairman, we have regulations and procedures which were drafted to perform a step-by-step function with regard to either complaints or with regard to a monitoring result which appeared to be in violation of a particular code.

Mr. Bronson has already told you of the first several steps.

In the event that corrective measures are not taken, and in the event that the staff feels that the matter is of serious enough consideration, it is taken to the television code review board, which has already been specified, with a membership of five.

Should that board find that, in its opinion, as a type of grand jury, that there has been a continual and willful violation, it certifies a complaint to the television board of directors of the NARTB which, in effect, sits in judgment upon it.

The television code review board takes it before the television board of directors, and should the television board of directors find that there has been a violation of the code, there are a number of things that it can do.

First of all, it is able to suspend its right to exhibit the seal—I do not know whether the seal has been referred to before or not—but if you subscribe to the code, and if you are a subscriber in good standing, you have the right to use a seal on your screen, or in any other appropriate way on your correspondence, and so forth, which specifies to the public that you are a member in good standing of the television code.

Should the board find that you are in violation, it can either suspend your right for 30 days, or 6 months, or forever, to exhibit that seal, which evidences that you are a member in good standing of the Television Code.

Chairman KEFAUVER. Do you make any finding or give any evidence or any report to the Federal Communications Commission in connection with persistent violators?

Mr. BROWN. No, sir; this is completely industry self-regulation. There is no relationship at all with the Federal Communications Commission.

Chairman KEFAUVER. If you had a persistent violator, would you feel that it would be in the public interest to call that matter to the attention of the FCC in connection with a renewal of a license?

Mr. BROWN. Well, I will just answer insofar as the intent of the draft of the code is concerned, which I happen to have handy, as draftsman, and the intent was definitely, no. Perhaps Mr. Fellows would like to say something more about that.

Mr. FELLOWS. If I may be permitted to do so, Mr. Chairman, there are one or two things in the testimony today that I would like to point out.

First of all, I think it would be becoming to give back to Commissioner Hennock her remarks about her sincerity, and to say that she was equally sincere. But she was appearing in her own behalf, and I simply want to get into the record that Commissioner Hennock's opinions with regard to many of the things in connection with the operation of the FCC and the success of this code, her opinions are not shared by most of the other members of the Commission.

Chairman KEFAUVER. She said she thought it was a good code.

Mr. FELLOWS. She spoke particulary—she felt, I am quite sure she indicated, that it had not been successful in its operation.

I think she was a little stronger about that. We have been publicly commended by past Commissioners and present Commissioners, whom we can name, by the Chairman of the Commission, for the excellent work and the progress that has been made under the code, and doing the very things that we propose to do.

Commissioner Hennock also spoke—and this is directly to the question that you asked Mr. Brown—also spoke of the matter of the Commission's being interested in our findings.·

The majority of the opinion of the Commission is that they are not engaged in censorship in any way; they make that proclamation very clear.

Chairman KEFAUVER. Mr. Fellows, I was not bringing that out for the purpose of engaging the Commission in censorship. But when an application comes up for renewal, the Commission has the responsibility of determining whether the public interest is going to be served——

Mr. FELLOWS. They do indeed.

Chairman KEFAUVER. By the renewal of this application.

Mr. FELLOWS. That is right.

Chairman KEFAUVER. And if a station has been consistently violating the code, if they have been encouraging—if they have been, rather, discouraging law-enforcement officers, as I know one station did, then those are matters that the Commission ought to know about, it seems to me. That is no matter of censorship.

It is just a question of whether they are carrying on their station in the public interest.

Mr. FELLOWS. Well, do you feel, Mr. Chairman, that we should of our own will and volition voluntarily send to the Commission whatever we are attempting to do with the particular station?

Chairman KEFAUVER. I do not know. I am just here to try to find out, but it would seem to me——

Mr. FELLOWS. We have not felt——

Chairman KEFAUVER. If I were a member of the FCC which, of course, I am not, and I am sure I never will be, but if the question came before me, if I had to decide a question, as to whether to renew station XYZ, renew its franchise, and a fight was being made on the station as to whether it had been a good station, operating in the public interest, just as an evidentiary matter, I would be very much interested in knowing whether they had lived up to the code, whether they had violated it.

Mr. Fellows. If I got your question to Mr. Brown correctly, in the first place, I want to echo what Mr. Bronson said a few moments ago.

Fortunately, you were speaking, I think, of the misdemeanor which continued, and which came to this part of the process that Mr. Brown was reading about.

We have not had one of those yet. We have been successful enough so that we have had the proper response from the various criticisms and the things that were going on, so we have not faced this issue yet at all, sir.

I might add that I think the Commission would know well enough about it by the time that it arrived——

Chairman Kefauver. Speaking of you have not had a misdemeanor that had not continued, are you talking about radio as well as television?

Mr. Fellows. Yes, sir; we have a radio standards of practice, too, sir, which operates on a different basis.

Chairman Kefauver. You do not think the Mickey McBride station in Miami was a continuing misdemeanor?

Mr. Fellows. I do not remember the Mickey McBride, Mr. Chairman. We do not have the same policing power, if it may be called that, incorporated in the radio standards of practice that are incorporated in the Television Code.

Chairman Kefauver. Do you remember, Mr. Bronson?

Mr. Bronson. I do not think I do, Mr. Chairman.

My work, may I say, sir, is devoted entirely to the Television Code, on that side, on that particular side, of the industry.

Chairman Kefauver. Well, it would seem if you are keeping up with radio stations, you would have remembered that instance down there, where for over a long period of time, the Miami Crime Commission was criticized, and the matter was taken before the Federal Communications Commission as to whether or not they had given some encouragement to having a wide open town. You do not recall that?

Mr. Fellows. How long ago was this, Mr. Chairman?

Chairman Kefauver. It has not been so long ago.

Mr. Fellows. I do not recall it, sir.

Chairman Kefauver. Four or five years ago.

Mr. Fellows. That is what I was wondering, because I came here 4 years ago, and I was wondering—I think it would have come to my attention, and I would be able to respond.

Chairman Kefauver. How long have you been with this organization, Mr. Brown?

Mr. Brown. I have been with this organization 4 years, too, Mr. Chairman.

I have heard of the situation, I have heard something about it, but I know very little about it, being on the television side.

Chairman KEFAUVER. I want to make myself clear. I think I have been familiar with what you have done, particularly during the time Justin Miller was president. I think you have a good association.

But I think you have a tremendous responsibility, and I think you are going to have to stay right on top of it; and it seems to me that you are going to have to take the gloves off, and not just present the positive side to your stations and networks, but you are going to have to be critical when it is necessary to be critical, and firm; otherwise the public will not give you the backing that you have to have.

I think your code reads like a good one; I have not gone over it closely.

I have 1 or 2 more questions.

You say you have had no violations that you were not able to correct?

Mr. FELLOWS. That is correct.

Chairman KEFAUVER. Is that correct?

Mr. FELLOWS. That is right.

Chairman KEFAUVER. Are you entirely pleased with all of these TV shows for children?

Mr. FELLOWS. No, sir.

Chairman KEFAUVER. You are not pleased?

Mr. FELLOWS. Not with all of them, you said.

Chairman KEFAUVER. Yes. What is it that does not please you?

Mr. FELLOWS. Why, there are some specific shows we reviewed for your committee, our Television Code Review Board reviewed some 3 or 4, segments of programs that they had monitored, and we found in 2 instances what we considered violence in excess, beyond the provisions of the code.

We think it is all moving in the right direction, but we do not, by any means, think we have eliminated all the possibilities yet.

We think we are getting stronger and stronger all the time, but if you ask us if we are entirely pleased, the answer is, "No, we are not."

Chairman KEFAUVER. What did you do about those two instances?

Mr. FELLOWS. What did we do about them?

Chairman KEFAUVER. Yes, sir.

Mr. FELLOWS. We reported back immediately to the committee, and the stations on which these programs occurred.

Chairman KEFAUVER. Are they discontinued?

Mr. FELLOWS. They have been, sir, or improved. Mr. Bronson properly adds "or improved."

Dr. Maccoby, I think, if I may be permitted this observation, she, too, hit this morning very effectively upon the business of attempting to see, if there were aggression of any sort, that it was approached in the proper manner; that the reason why it was there and how it occurred is what is important, not the elimination of aggression entirely; but a control of how it comes about, how it is handled, and that, we think, is terribly important; and we do not think we have arrived at anywhere near a hundred percent educational or developing recognition of that necessity at all sources.

Chairman KEFAUVER. Do you invite viewers, parents, the public generally, to write you?

Mr. FELLOWS. Yes, sir; we do all the time, sir.

Chairman KEFAUVER. So you know what they think about your programs?

Mr. FELLOWS. We go into the field and work with them, Mr. Chairman.

Mr. Bronson, in an aside here is reminding me that you might be interested in knowing the extent to which we work with educational and religious groups. We call on them and share the problems with them.

Chairman KEFAUVER. When will this special work, this monitoring of programs on 22 stations, relating to children's programing, when will that be completed?

Mr. BRONSON. I would hope, Mr. Chairman, that that could be reviewed and in our hands, may I say firmed up, within a month—I mean 30 days from today, may I say.

Chairman KEFAUVER. We would like to get the report of that study as soon as possible to be included in the record.

Mr. BRONSON. I am sure we would be very happy to furnish it for you, sir.

Chairman KEFAUVER. Is there any objection to giving the name of the nationally known and recognized research firm——

Mr. BRONSON. No, sir.

Chairman KEFAUVER. That is doing this monitoring?

Mr. BRONSON. No, sir. It is the American Research Bureau. It has been active in the field of survey work in television programing since 1949, which is considerably back in television age, as I think you will agree, sir.

I might add to that that this particular research firm has instituted a special staff within its organization for our purposes, which has not been in any way in conflict or activity with the regular research projects which it undertakes for other enterprises.

Chairman KEFAUVER. On page 3——

Mr. FELLOWS. Is that of the code, Mr. Chairman?

Chairman KEFAUVER. No, on page 3 of Mr. Bronson's statement——

Mr. BRONSON. Yes, sir.

Chairman KEFAUVER. In the middle of the page you say:

I am sure the committee will be interested in knowing that the code staff has contacted nearly 140 producers and distributors of film for use on television.

Does that mean that this is since last October that you have contacted that many?

Mr. BRONSON. That is correct, Mr. Chairman; yes.

Chairman KEFAUVER. How many producers and distributors are there?

Mr. BRONSON. Well, there are several hundred, if you count isolated producers of individual products, sir.

We are attempting, first, to contact those particular producers or distributors who are primarily serving the large majority of the product to the industry. The exact number at this point I cannot quote.

Chairman KEFAUVER. What are you doing when you are contacting them, encouraging them to have more educational programs or higher type programs?

Mr. BRONSON. In my own particular contact, Mr. Chairman, it is primarily relative to the code, and urging their recognition of the code and conformance to it in the production of their material.

We have endeavored to do that.

Chairman KEFAUVER. Did you contact them because they were violators, or is this just a routine contact?

Mr. BRONSON. I think that in my statement, I believe, Mr. Chairman, I indicated that this was part of our educational program among those groups, or that particular group, sir.

Chairman KEFAUVER. Yes.

Mr. BRONSON. And it is with that particular intent in mind that we call upon them.

Chairman KEFAUVER. Tell me again what is this pilot study that you speak about on page 4 of your statement?

Mr. BRONSON. Well, that primarily, Mr. Chairman, was a pilot study of viewer attitudes, it is just that, a pilot study.

Its primary purpose was to indicate what type of survey might be undertaken in a larger vein.

This was a very small sample, but it was set up first to sound out which, as I understand, is an accepted research method, what type of thing might be involved in a greater scale, sir, and to a wider area.

This includes only one area; and, as I say, it is not a very large sample, but its purpose was purely that of a pilot analysis or study of viewer attitudes to TV programing and advertising as offered in that area.

Chairman KEFAUVER. Now, this 40 percent, Mr. Fellows, who are not members of the association, and I think it is unfortunate that all of the industry is not in the association——

Mr. FELLOWS. We are trying to come closer and closer to that, Mr. Chairman.

Chairman KEFAUVER. What can be done about them?

Mr. FELLOWS. We are constantly soliciting them and educating them.

There are many among them who, as I remarked before, are comparatively new, and we are getting at them as soon as we can.

There are many who do very little local originating, and consider that the source of their programing, such as the networks and the film producers, a large part of their program content, comes to them from outside.

They do very little local originating, and they believe they are reasonably protected in program structure by the fact that those who serve them, some of them are directly committed to the code, and some of the others in philosophy, at least, assure them as they purchase or negotiate for films, and they reason they do not need to belong.

There are many stations in the country who consider that to their own locally adopted philosophies and code of ethics are sufficient; that they are equal to the television code as we publish it.

Those are the three major difficulties that we have. But Mr. Bronson has indicated to you that we had gone in these 5 months from 231, I think it was, up to 245; that is about the extent of the progress that we are making.

Some 3 years ago our initial subscription to the code was only 58 stations, and it has been brought up to 245 by now.

We are hopeful that it will be over 300 in the course of the next 3 or 4 months. We cannot guarantee that, obviously.

Chairman KEFAUVER. Mr. Fellows, I heard many people say that they think an individual show might be all right and meet the provisions of your code, and the children could take 1 show or maybe 2 of a type.

But, on some stations anyway, given a certain time in the afternoon and on through bedtime, just one shooting play after another, and they claim it is given to them in too big a dose, although any one of the performances might be according to the provisions of your code, and it is the amount and extent that has the bad effect.

Is that a question that you go into?

Mr. FELLOWS. It is a question that we go into and, fortunately, we do not encounter it very much. But if I am saying this properly, we do not condone it.

That partly arises from some development in the industry quite a while ago, Mr. Chairman, called block programing, and we certainly feel that in this area a continued source of programing which follows the same pattern hour after hour, with exposure such as you indicate, is not healthy, not right. That is the position we take in the individual instances that we face.

Chairman KEFAUVER. You are trying to do something about it?

Mr. FELLOWS. We are indeed, sir; the code board is itself doing something about it.

Chairman KEFAUVER. Is the block programing still in existence?

Mr. FELLOWS. In a great many cases it is still in existence, particularly so in radio; it has not developed in television to the degree it has in radio.

Chairman KEFAUVER. Mr. Bobo, do you have some questions?

Mr. BOBO. Yes, sir.

Mr. Bronson, this pilot study, is that study devoted to determining the type of programs that the person wants? Is that the idea behind that study?

Mr. BRONSON. I think it might be better stated, Mr. Bobo, that it is the reaction of the persons participating to what they had seen in all categories as we have broken it down or as the research company conducted the study.

It was not an indication, although I think the question may be in there, as to the type of thing they might wish to see more of, if I might put it that way.

Mr. BOBO. I was wondering about that because Mr. Fellows pointed out that a number of psychiatrists, as you pointed out, who appeared before our committee, Dr. Greenwood, for instance, said that no one can authoritatively say that radio or television has any effect either way.

As you pointed out, the Gluecks pointed out, in answer to Senator Hennings' question, that they had not done the kind of detail they would have liked to do, and they say that a consistent hammering away influence of an exciting or salacious kind of story day in and day out must have a corrosive effect on the minds of youth.

Dr. Banay stated this morning that she had only been able to accomplish a very small survey.

Mr. FELLOWS. You mean Dr. Maccoby.

Mr. BOBO. I am sorry, Dr. Maccoby; and I was just wondering if the television board would be interested in conducting a survey by psychiatrists to determine what the actual effect of television would be on youngsters.

Mr. Fellows. We are definitely interested in that, and if I may just go a little further than Mr. Bronson has gone, that is the purpose of the pilot study, to attempt to determine just what procedure you will follow.

This was fundamentally what the researchers call a methodological study, to attempt to find out what the real impact was, what the reactions to the various types of programing were, so that you might be guided by such information.

It was a pilot study because I do not think we are wrong in assuming that there has not yet been a broad overall study which will authoritatively, just as the gentleman there said, establish this.

We looked to it, almost all branches of our industry look to it, ultimately from all sources.

We were very grateful to the doctor this morning—we are grateful because of the fact that Dr. Maccoby referred to it this morning—the American Medical Association study, the one they are connected with, we look forward to the ultimate research in this field that will truthfully bespeak what is happening, what is television doing. We do want to know it very, very much.

I think, Mr. Chairman, I could have added and, perhaps, it would have seemed much more fair to you if I added, that it has not been authoritatively proved that television is a major factor in delinquency problems.

It equally has not been authoritatively proved, sir, that it is not. We do not go at all on the assumption that there can be no harm in what is going on; that is not our approach.

Chairman Kefauver. Well, it is apparently your approach from your statement, because you reiterate several times that it is not a factor.

Mr. Fellows. I think I am quoting most of the time other people, sir.

Chairman Kefauver. Well, you could have quoted some the other way if you wished to.

Mr. Fellows. Yes, I understand; I accept your correction.

Chairman Kefauver. Dr. Maccoby this morning made two suggestions that I wish to cite. One is the one we were just talking about, the recurring one program after the other; and the other was that it would seem to me that this is by way of suggestion, at least it would be worth mentioning in your code, that while any one program might comply with the code, that several of them running together might have an adverse effect.

The other suggestion she made was that it is important who captures the villain.

Mr. Fellows. I noticed the observation.

Chairman Kefauver. That impresses children better in the field of law enforcement if it is an officer of the law who finally captures the villain rather than someone taking the law into his own hands.

Is that a matter to which you have given consideration?

Mr. Fellows. Yes.

Chairman Kefauver. Is that in the code?

Mr. Fellows. By still giving consideration to—Mr. Bronson might quote, if you do not mind, sir——

Mr. Bronson. Mr. Chairman, if I may, some relevance of the statement you just made on page 3 of the code under the topic acceptability of program material, section (t):

"Law enforcement should be upheld and officers of the law are to be portrayed with respect and dignity," has, at least, I think, an indirect reference to what you have in mind.

Chairman KEFAUVER. Yes, it does.

Mr. BRONSON. It is not quite as far as you go, sir.

Chairman KEFAUVER. Except I hardly think this would apply to the idea of law-enforcement officer is not to be made fun of or treated lightly.

Mr. BRONSON. That is correct.

Chairman KEFAUVER. It does not infer that they should be the heroes in a contest with the villain .

Anything else, Mr. Bobo?

Mr. BOBO. There was just one question that I had, Senator, if I could ask it.

Do you know whether or not in your facts about TV that you send out—have you ever brought to the attention of the industry and the stations Dr. Maccoby's report on her study?

Mr. FELLOWS. We have not, have we?

Mr. BRONSON. You mean the 1951 report?

Mr. FELLOWS. You mean the 1951 report to which he referred this morning? I do not believe we have reported it in detail.

Mr. BOBO. There have been two reports.

Mr. FELLOWS. I think it was printed in the Educational Quarterly; I think you are right.

Chairman KEFAUVER. Thank you very much, gentlemen.

You will bring these other records up in the morning?

Mr. FELLOWS. We will.

Mr. BRONSON. Yes, we will.

Chairman KEFAUVER. As we go along with your study of this matter, we would like to keep in contact with you and work with you, and I do not want anything I have said to suggest that I do not think your association is not a good one.

You certainly have the right idea, and you have done effective work. Of course, always when we are aiming at perfection there is much more to be done, as you very well realize.

Dr. Banay, Ralph Steven Banay, research psychiatrist, Columbia University, New York.

We are glad to have you with us, Dr. Banay.

Dr. BANAY. Thank you.

Chairman KEFAUVER. Do you want to further identify yourself by telling about your work and your qualifications to testify on this subject?

STATEMENT OF DR. RALPH S. BANAY, RESEARCH PSYCHIATRIST. COLUMBIA UNIVERSITY, NEW YORK

Dr. BANAY. Yes. I am a qualified psychiatrist by the American Board of Psychiatry and Neurology.

Chairman KEFAUVER. You will have to speak louder. We do not have a loud-speaker system here.

Dr. BANAY. I am a qualified psychiatrist by the American Board of Psychiatry and Neurology.

I am a director of the clinic which is affiliated with the district attorney's office in Kings County, N. Y., and I am a consulting psychiatrist to the United States Bureau of Prisons in Washington.

Chairman KEFAUVER. You are a consulting psychiatrist for the United States Bureau of Prisons, and you are associated with the attorney general's office, the district attorney's office in Kings County?

Dr. BANAY. Yes.

Chairman KEFAUVER. Is that the office in which Mr. Miles McDonald used to be——

Dr. BANAY. Yes; Mr. Silver is the head.

Chairman KEFAUVER. Mr. Silver is now the district attorney, Mr. Edward Silver?

Dr. BANAY. Yes.

Chairman KEFAUVER. How long have you been a psychiatrist?

Dr. BANAY. Over 25 years.

Chairman KEFAUVER. And of what schools are you a graduate of?

Dr. BANAY. The University of Budapest, Hungary.

Chairman KEFAUVER. How long have you been practicing in the United States?

Dr. BANAY. From 1927.

Chairman KEFAUVER. All right, sir. We would appreciate hearing from you.

Dr. BANAY. Yes.

The visual images which are impinged on the mind of young spectators through the medium of television have two significances. One, the content of the images and, two, the length and frequency of exposure to them. Most children nowadays spend several hours watching their set, sometimes indiscriminately without supervision of parents or their selection of the program to be viewed.

Frequent knob turning by children usually leads to a presentation which is saturated with action, fights, gunplay, murder, or other manifestations of violence.

A subconscious identification with the personalities and events of the show make the children more susceptible to permanent impression, suggestion, and conditioning effect of these presentations.

Children might even see the images out of sequence as isolated events paying no heed to the conception of the good being rewarded and the evil punished. They might be under the spell of the drama and absorbed so completely that their own aggressive tendencies become activated not just in fantasy life, but in reality.

A 13-year-old girl in the heat of the excitement and resentment toward her mother, who turned off the television and her favorite murder story, grabbed a kitchen knife and attempted to stab her mother as an aftereffect of the violence she had witnessed. The bipolarity of human emotions, the love and hate of aggressivity and passivity, good and evil can be enhanced or impeded by constant conditioning with images of violence.

The child whose overall knowledge of life and experiences is restricted and is exposed by the control of parents builds up subterranean hate and fantasy of retribution. When he or she views images of retribution, a gratification unknown heretofore occurs, and he feels encouraged to act out his hostilities. Thus the belief forms that aggression is a way of life and demonstration of power.

Murder is the very stock in trade of TV and radio drama and to a lesser extent of film and stage thrillers. The gun is perhaps the commonest toy. A travesty of killing is the most popular form of play.

"This will kill you," is a popular conversational cliche. "Drop dead," is a devout injunction heard constantly. A psychologist studying our culture might fairly deduce that we were obsessed with the idea of sudden violence and retributive death.

Murder, of course, is the very essence of drama; book and play have always found dalliance with death a sure formula for profitable popularity. But no generation prior to ours has taken so intimate or universal a role in foreshortening doom, in fact or by fantasy. It would seem that the decreasing percentage of the population that is not actively engaged in killing is occupied a good part of the time in musing upon the murder theme. The adolescent mind being the delicately suggestible mechanism it is, can we wonder that young people so often carry into effect the violent action pattern that is so persistently entertained in thought and in play.

We adults can better understand youth and its problems, needs and anxieties if we take the trouble to recall the circumstances of our own adolescence. A healthy boy or girl is a torrent of often chaotic energy. Without purpose or direction that plethora of priceless vigor can go astray in any number of chance channels, and many of these can be deleterious, destructive and even vicious. Exposing them to persistent viewing of violence and creating false images and conceptions of life and its mores and customs we allow an unfavorable subconscious conditioning of children in our homes by an instrument which could be under different circumstances the most progressive and unlimited disseminator of culture, education and moral conditioning.

I have been analyzing——

Chairman KEFAUVER. You have some more statements?

Dr. BANAY. Yes. I would just like to refer to the fact that I have been analyzing a 1-week program schedule on the radio at the time when the children have the availability of the program.

Chairman KEFAUVER. Is this radio or television?

Dr. BANAY. Television, excuse me.

Chairman KEFAUVER. Yes.

Dr. BANAY. And then find that on the hour, by the hour, there are crime stories.

In one Saturday program, there was Hopalong Cassidy, when he wipes out a gang.

Chairman KEFAUVER. So far as the committee is concerned, tell us what station it is.

Dr. BANAY. These are the local stations; these programs when analyzed by the program, are receivable by Washington, D. C., stations.

Chairman KEFAUVER. That is all the television stations?

Dr. BANAY. All the television stations available here in Washington, D. C.

Chairman KEFAUVER. Very well; I would be very interested to see just how you analyzed them.

Dr. BANAY. Well, Hopalong Cassidy at 9 o'clock wipes out a gang.

The next program, Buffalo Bill, Jr., there is a false accusation of murder; at 11 there is a crooked insurance deal.

At 1 o'clock there is a story of kidnaping; at 1:30 there is a western story with cattle rustling; the sheriff is either shot in the back or is in cahoots with the gang.

At 2:15, 3 pirates, revenge; at 3 o'clock, a western story again with violence; at 5 o'clock, Roy Rogers; 2 desperadoes blow up the train; at 5:30, an orphan boy eludes the authorities.

Chairman KEFAUVER. Orphan boy does what?

Dr. BANAY. Eludes the authorities.

Chairman KEFAUVER. Yes.

Dr. BANAY. At 6 o'clock, a cowboy G–men story; at 6:30, the Black Phantom; at 7 o'clock, a vicious sabotage ring by Gene Autry.

At 8 p. m., a western, young man ruthlessly runs the cow country; then there is The Lineup, a crime story, safe robbery, and mugging.

At 10 o'clock there is International Police. I do not want to read it any further, because probably by that time most of the children are in bed.

Chairman KEFAUVER. Read a little further.

Dr. BANAY. All right; I will.

At 11:30, Man Behind the Badge, Mr. District Attorney; at 11, The Crooked Way; at 11:15, a western, with a lot of action and shooting; at 12 o'clock, Hit and Run, a man convicted and framed on a hit and run accident; Danger, several murder investigations. That was 1 day's programs.

The next day is Sunday, which is relatively free of crime stories.

At 10 o'clock western movies; at 11 o'clock a reluctant burglar, jilted rich girl plots revenge; at 1:30, Roy Rogers—a double-feature movie, western plus an ex-convict attempt to expose loan sharks.

Five-thirty, Captain Gallant, gang attacks a caravan; at 6 o'clock, Sky King, saboteur blows up a secret desert project; 7 o'clock, Big Town, crime drama; 7:30, steamship captain robs and deserts passengers; 9 o'clock, Watch Me Die, a man seeks a perfect method of murdering his wife, divorce won't do; he wants her money.

Nine-fifteen, Public Prosecutor, seeks out murderers and other criminals.

Nine-thirty, Front Page Detective; 10 o'clock, Ellery Queen, mystery; 10:30, Ellery Queen, mystery.

Do you wish to have a further recital?

Chairman KEFAUVER. Well, suppose we put it in the record.

Dr. BANAY. Should I read it?

Chairman KEFAUVER. No; do not read them now.

Dr. BANAY. I will turn it over to the reporter.

Chairman KEFAUVER. Let them be continued at this place in the record.

Dr. BANAY. Yes.

Monday: 4 p. m., Gene Autry, Law of the West, film; 4:30 p. m., Black Phantom, serial; 5:30 p. m., western film; 6 p. m., 5 westerns and Superman; 7 p. m., movie, chorus girl murdered. Ramar of the Jungle; 11 p. m., movie, murder; 11:15 p. m., drama, gangsters shoot cops; 11:25 p. m., mystery, a young woman is charged with poisoning her husband.

Tuesday: 4 p. m., Gene Autry, Lone Shark; 4:30, Black Phantom, serial; 5:30, western; 6 p. m., 4 westerns and prison drama; 7 p. m., Superman, the Cisco Kid, western; 9:30 p. m., The Circle Theater, western, Mack Saber, and the Crime Man, and the Elgin Theater, a western with bigamy; 10 p. m., Danger, dueling; 10:30 p. m., Badge 714, beating and robbing; 11:15 p. m., Danger, escape murder, et cetera, the Signet Theater, a woman leaves her crooked husband.

Wednesday: 4 p. m., Gene Autry and western film; 4:30 p. m., Black Phantom, serial; 5 p. m., Studio 7, drama, guide accuses boss of murder, and western; 5:30 p. m., western; 6 p. m., four westerns, movie, avenging a father's death; 7 p. m., Ramar of the Jungle, Superman; 10 p. m., Follow That Man, mystery; 10:30 p. m., Big Town; 11:15 p. m. Signet Theater, suspense thriller about a murder epidemic; 11:25 p. m., western prison film.

Thursday: 4 p. m., Gene Autry, western movie; 4:30 p. m., the Black Phantom, serial; 5 p. m., western; 5:30 p. m., western; 6 p. m., three westerns; 7 p. m., Wild Bill Hickok; 7:45 p. m., movie, the Creeper, "serum turns people into cloying murderers"; 8:30 p. m., Justice, "wiretapping" and T-Men in Action; 9 p. m., Dragnet, Counterpoint, drama, "foolproof way to steal"; 10 p. m., the Public Defender; 10:30 p. m., Public Prosecutor, the Falcon, mystery, Paris Precinct, "a French dragnet"; 11 p. m., western.

Friday: 4 p. m., Gene Autry, and western; 4:30 p. m., the Black Phantom, serial; 5 p. m., Studio 7, drama, "doctor kills a patient," western; 5:30 p. m., western; 6 p. m., four westerns; 7 p. m., Badge 714, and two westerns; 9 p. m., the Big Story, "stealing and terrorizing"; 9:30 p. m., Paris Precinct, the Vise, drama; 10 p. m., the Line-Up, Mr. District Attorney; 10:30 p. m., mystery movie; 11:15 p. m., Signet Theater drama, "man discovers crime of his future father-in-law," crime movie.

Saturday: 95 TV hours; 23 hours of programs obviously having crimes, 24 percent.

Sunday: 110½ TV hours; 15¼ programs containing crime, violence, et cetera, 14 percent.

Monday, 4 p. m. to 10 p. m.: 48 TV hours; 8½ TV hours containing crime, et cetera, 18 percent.

Tuesday, 4 p. m. to 10 p m: 48 TV hours; 11½ TV hours with crime, violence, et cetera, 24 percent.

Wednesday, 4 p. m., to 10 p. m.: 48 TV hours; 8½ hours with crime or violence, 18 percent.

Thursday, 4 p. m. to 10 p. m.: 48 TV hours; 11¾ hours with crime or violence, 24 percent.

Friday, 4 p. m. to 10 p. m.: 48 TV hours; 12 hours with crime or violence, 25 percent.

Inasmuch as juvenile delinquency is primarily a problem of emotional health or emotional disturbance, I feel very much inclined to put on the record that the effect of this violence on emotionally disturbed children is much greater, and they are the ones who are candidates for delinquency.

If the proverb is true that prison is college for crime, I believe for young disturbed adolescents, TV is a preparatory school for delinquency.

Chairman KEFAUVER. I did not quite understand it.

Dr. BANAY. If a prison is a college for crime, I believe that for young emotionally disturbed children, viewing violent television pictures is preparation for delinquency and crime.

Chairman KEFAUVER. Then your testimony is that overall you think the violent TV programs or some of our TV programs, do increase juvenile delinquency?

Dr. BANAY. Yes. I believe so.

Chairman KEFAUVER. And you think that is especially so in the case of emotionally disturbed children, to begin with?

Dr. BANAY. Yes, because they are the ones who more likely commit delinquent acts in the future.

Chairman KEFAUVER. That is a normally stable child might take it in stride, but one that is already upset or not stable, it would be easier— he would be easier prey or it would be a greater influence?

Dr. BANAY. Yes. The emotionally secure and stable child, able to absorb the shock of violence and either repress it successfully, either act it out harmlessly or either sublimate it—but the emotionally impaired child, unable to do any of this, unable to repress it success- fully, unable to act it out harmlessly, and unable to sublimate it.

Chairman KEFAUVER. Dr. Banay, you are associated with a great many psychiatrists, you know them?

Dr. BANAY. Yes, I do.

Chairman KEFAUVER. And you talk with them about this problem, do you?

Dr. BANAY. Yes, I do.

Chairman KEFAUVER. What is the attitude of most of the profes- sional psychiatrists and psychologists on this subject?

Dr. BANAY. It is very difficult to say because relatively a small number of psychiatrists are specializing in preventing, treating and analyzing delinquent children. But those who have profound experi- ence in this field, they feel that prevention or causation of delinquency is associated with images which are created either with pictures or television presentations.

Chairman KEFAUVER. In other words, it is your testimony that those who have had great experience in the matter agree with your con- clusion about it?

Dr. BANAY. Yes, I do.

Chairman KEFAUVER. As for yourself, sir, I take it that as consultant to the Bureau of Prisons, Federal Bureau of Prisons, of which Mr. James Bennett is the director——

Dr. BANAY. Yes, sir.

Chairman KEFAUVER (continuing). And in your work with the district attorney's office of Kings County, of which Mr. Edward Silver is the district attorney, you have talked with and examined and treated and reported upon the experience of many, many young people?

Dr. BANAY. Yes; I did. Besides, for 3 years I was in charge of the psychiatric clinic of Sing Sing Prison.

Chairman KEFAUVER. I did not understand that now.

Dr. BANAY. For 3 years, from 1940 to 1943, I was director of the psychiatric clinic of Sing Sing Prison, which gave me thorough opportunity to examine, analyze, and investigate the emotional back- ground of a great many delinquents and criminals.

Chairman KEFAUVER. And so your testimony is based upon your actual contact and study and reaction of juveniles who have been accused of crime?

Dr. BANAY. Yes. My testimony is based on clinical experience of a great number of individuals who got into delinquency or crime.

Chairman KEFAUVER. Could you give us any estimate of the number of delinquents or young people that you have come in contact with over a period of, say, a year?

Dr. Banay. Over a year, I would say about four or five hundred.

Chairman Kefauver. And you have been in this business for many, many years?

Dr. Banay. Over 15 years, in very close contact with this problem.

Chairman Kefauver. Mr. Bobo, do you have any questions?

Mr. Bobo. No, sir; I have not.

Chairman Kefauver. Have you written extensively on this subject, Dr. Banay?

Dr. Banay. Yes. I published a book on Youth in Despair, which was prominently concerned with juvenile delinquency and crime, and I wrote about 50 articles in different magazines on delinquency and crime.

Chairman Kefauver. Have you talked about this impact of television?

Dr. Banay. Yes; I was on the program with Mr. Bennett in Philadelphia just about a month ago, I believe.

Chairman Kefauver. I mean, have you written about it in your articles and in your books?

Dr. Banay. Yes; I did.

Chairman Kefauver. These books are well known, are they not?

Dr. Banay. Yes.

Chairman Kefauver. And these articles?

Dr. Banay. Yes.

Chairman Kefauver. Have you talked with the National Association of Broadcasters or these people who were here about them?

Dr. Banay. I received some correspondence recently as a reaction to a quote which appeared somewhere.

Chairman Kefauver. You say you saw a quote from them?

Dr. Banay. No. they wrote me of a quote of mine which appeared in the Annals of the American Academy of Social Sciences, and they were inquiring of the origin of this quotation which I wrote in an article.

Chairman Kefauver. Which you denied?

Dr. Banay. No, I did not deny it. They were asking me where did the article appear.

Chairman Kefauver. I see. You gave them that information, did you?

Dr. Banay. Yes.

Chairman Kefauver. Well, then, in the statement here of Mr. Fellows—I do not know if you have a copy of his statement. Do you have one?

Dr. Banay. Yes, I have a copy of the statement.

Chairman Kefauver. Do you have it there?

Dr. Banay. I have it in the back.

Chairman Kefauver. On page 5 and going over to page 6, I see a lot of people who are listed as authorities for the subject, and for the conclusion that television programs are not responsible, have no connection with an increase in juvenile delinquency. I do not see any statements made by you on either one of those pages.

Dr. Banay. I was not asked; at the time my opinion was adverse; maybe that was the cause.

Chairman Kefauver. Will you name for us some of the best known child psychologists who have made clinical studies of this particular problem?

Dr. BANAY. I cannot name—my acquaintance is among the criminal psychiatrists, psychiatrists who practice in the field of delinquency or crime, and not child psychiatrists.

Chairman KEFAUVER. I mean that is what I am talking about, psychiatrists who deal with crime and criminals, and that includes juvenile criminals, does it not?

Dr. BANAY. Yes. I will be able to send a long list of men because I am the chairman of the psychiatric section of the Academy of Forensic Sciences, and secretary of the Medical Correction Association. That has about two or three hundred members, mostly psychiatrists who work in this field.

Chairman KEFAUVER. And you are the chairman of that section?

Dr. BANAY. I am chairman of the psychiatric section of the American Academy of Forensic Sciences.

Chairman KEFAUVER. Has the American Academy, the group of which you are a chairman, made any conclusion about this problem that we are discussing here, I mean any formal conclusion?

Dr. BANAY. I do not remember having made any formal conclusion.

Chairman KEFAUVER. Very well. Do you have anything else, Mr. Bobo?

Mr. BOBO. No.

Chairman KEFAUVER. We thank you very much for your testimony, Dr. Banay.

The subcommittee will stand in recess until 10 o'clock in the morning, at which time Senator Hennings will preside.

(Whereupon, at 2:50 p. m., the subcommittee adjourned, to reconvene at 10 a. m., Thursday, April 7, 1955.)

JUVENILE DELINQUENCY
(Television Programs)

THURSDAY, APRIL 7, 1955

United States Senate,
Subcommittee of the Committee on the Judiciary,
to Investigate Juvenile Delinquency,
Washington, D. C.

The subcommittee met, pursuant to call, at 10:20 a. m., in the Old Supreme Court Chamber, United States Capitol Building, Senator Thomas C. Hennings, Jr., presiding.

Present: Senators Hennings, Langer, and Wiley.

Also present: James H. Bobo, general counsel; Peter Chumbris, associate counsel; William Haddad and Carl L. Perian of the subcommittee staff.

Senator HENNINGS. The subcommittee will please come to order.

Dr. Paul Lazarsfeld is to be our first witness according to the schedule handed me by counsel. Is Dr. Lazarsfeld here?

Good morning, Doctor.

I believe it has been the practice not to swear in the witness on testimony of this character.

So you may proceed, if you will, Mr. Bobo.

Mr. BOBO. Dr. Lazarsfeld, would you state your name and address for the record, please, sir?

STATEMENT OF DR. PAUL F. LAZARSFELD, PROFESSOR OF SOCIOLOGY, COLUMBIA UNIVERSITY, NEW YORK

Dr. LAZARSFELD. My name is Paul F. Lazarsfeld, and at this moment I live in Los Altos, Calif., for a year of leave of absence, but usually I live at 52 West 85th Street, at Manhattan.

Mr. BOBO. And, Dr. Lazarsfeld, would you give us your professional background?

Dr. LAZARSFELD. Well, at this moment I am professor of sociology at Columbia University, and a great part of my teaching has to do with studies of mass media. I was born and raised in Vienna, Austria; got my Ph. D. there; and did early studies on radio in Austria. That brought me forth nationally to the attention of the Rockefeller Foundation.

In 1932 I got a fellowship to come here to do some comparative work, and I found the situation here much more attractive. I have stayed here ever since and have been in charge of a variety of research projects in the mass media field; have done certain work for foundations and for industry.

Mr. Bobo. What schools did you receive degrees from, Doctor?

Dr. Lazarsfeld. I have my Ph. D. from Vienna, and now I am professor at Columbia.

Mr. Bobo. Have you written any books on the subject of mass media, any articles?

Dr. Lazarsfeld. I probably wrote half a dozen books, and I wrote two scores of articles on this.

Mr. Bobo. Dr. Lazarsfeld, we are interested in determining the impact of television upon juvenile delinquency. I wonder, do you have a statement that you would like to make to the committee about what is known about the impact or what knowledge we have of the impact of television?

Dr. Lazarsfeld. Yes; I would like to do that very much. I was only told a few days ago that I would have the privilege to be a witness here, and so I will have to put my written statement in later.

But the reason I was so pleased that you would listen here is that in all the 30 years of work in this field, I have always been very startled by a paradox from what came clearly out of what I read of your old hearings, that in view of this question of the effect of the mass media on young people, everyone says how terribly necessary it would be to have a great deal of knowledge and, at the same time, only very little knowledge is available; and why it is that when everyone comes for data, then no one has any, has worried me a great deal; and I thought I would point out why I think this situation exists and what could be done about it. If you will permit me, I would like to make five points.

I would tell you a little bit about what I know about the history of research in this field, and then give you whatever opinion I have that it would make a difference if you knew something.

But what is it really we should look for and should know, and then I would warn you a little bit that one should not be too optimistic.

Finally, if I am permitted, to express an opinion of what this hearing could help.

Now, as to the history of the situation, why, there is such general demand for knowledge and so little available, I think you have to look at three different factors here: First, we students in the field; you had yesterday a distinguished scholar, Dr. Maccoby from Harvard. There is more very good work done at Rutgers by the Reillys, at Yale by Hofland. But, it is traditional in academic work, a professor picks up a topic; he drops it when he gets bored with it; or he drops it if he is not a good student and as far as the academic goes, that is all right, because a hundred years more or less does not make much difference for us.

Slowly it will accumulate. But if you do not look at it only from the point of view of progress of academic work but as a burning social issue, then I think it is not possible to leave it just to the accidental initiative of scholars. I do not want to make an invidious comparison, but we certainly would not have an atomic bomb today if the development had been merely left to Ph. D. dissertations.

I don't think that we exactly need a Los Alamos Laboratory to study the effects of television, but we need, if it is an urgent social problem, then some central planning and central organization, and some pressure; some priority has to be put on it.

At what point you leave a problem to academic free enterprise and at what point you try to organize it is, of course, a very serious question. But it might very well be that the topic you are discussing here needs at this moment somewhat more planning and organization.

Now, planning and organization obviously requires funds, and the question is, where should they come, and they have mostly come from foundations.

There is now the second point; I think that a few words should be said about it.

At several points, foundations have played——

Senator WILEY. I was asking whether or not we had your written statement, because it is very difficult up here to hear everything.

Dr. LAZARSFELD. No; I am sorry; it will come, but I had no time to prepare it.

The foundations have played several times a crucial role in this field. When in the—soon after the war, you had the biggest commotion about the movies, and the fact which the movies would have out of which, then, the movie code developed, as you know—there were smaller foundations, the Payne fund, which did very intensive work on the effect of movies.

Then, when radio came up and everyone was curious as to what it should do, the Rockefeller Foundation created two major projects: One at Ohio, to study how radio should be used in schools; and one in Princeton, to study what effect radio would have on the political and social life of the country.

Now, the question is, why has the foundation work not taken on this continuity and planning which might be necessary in this field? And that has to do with a definite policy foundations have in this matter, and which might be of interest for you to discuss.

The foundations feel two things: One, that they should never give permanent directions to academic work. They spend funds for a few years to stimulate a new field, but they then throw it back to the universities and professors to go on with it or not.

There is definite and probably very reasonable discontinuity in foundation work which makes it difficult to accumulate knowledge.

Unfortunately, the foundation field, as you probably know—there has been considerable discussion whether foundations should do work in controversial fields and the foundation has become more cautious recently, which I, as a professor, consider a very regrettable development. While, when radio came up, the Rockefeller Foundation was still quite willing to finance large-scale study of what radio does to this country, now that television is here, no foundation has dared to do—to invest considerable funds in necessary investigation.

I was, for about a year and a half, the chairman of a committee to advise one of the large foundations whether they should do considerable research in television, and, to my regret, while our committee advised them strongly to do it, they have decided not to do this kind of work because it might be misunderstood as meddling, while actually exactly this kind of support would be necessary.

Finally, a third factor in this research picture is the industry itself.

As you probably know, and you know it from your hearings on comics, that television, the television industry, like most communications industry, do spend research money and work with academic groups. I can testify that there is certainly never any influencing of the scholar by the industry, but, again, the industry has to do the

kind of research which is close to their immediate operational problems.   They can never lay out large-scale plans.   The people go from
one little study to the next, and while industry has contributed great
knowledge to this field, it could not contribute to any continuity and
to any systematic work.

So, reviewing the situation over the last 30 years, and I have for a
great part of it lived through it, everything has militated against
the kind of systematic building and relatively quick building of
knowledge which would be necessary in a field of social concern like,
let us say, cancer, or, in this case, criminalogy.

Now, if I now turn briefly to what kind of knowledge do I refer to,
then it is quite clear that what is missing from what I just mentioned
is not individual fine studies, which we have in large number, and
you have heard a good example of it yesterday, but this kind of
knowledge, where there is large fund, or continuing work is necessary.
Let me give you a few examples.

For instance, we are all concerned with, do the programs we have
now have bad effects, and there is great controversy whether the
programs are bad or not.

Now, undoubtedly, the much more provocative problem would be
to experiment with good programs.

Now, a network, the way the American broadcasting television
system is built, cannot experiment very much.   I think there is great
need for experimentation on a small scale with completely different
kind of programs for young people, and you ought to be aware that
this is a difficult matter.

We do not know whether there is any talent; we do not know
whether anyone has any ideas what good programs are.   I know very
little about it.   We do not know whether children would listen to what
I call good programs and we should study, if they listen, whether it
would have good effect.

But the strange thing is that all the discussion is the programs are
bad, and do they have bad effects?   Instead of experimenting, what do
we really mean by a good program?   I don't think anyone really
knows.   Who is there, anyone around who can write it, and then what
would the poor children do if they had to listen to good programs?
I think it is not as bad from my experience with my children; they
don't resent good stuff as it is said, but experiments have to be made,
and that is obviously something which is very important.

Let me give you a second example.

All the studies which we can do on small funds in universities are
short term.   We put kids into a laboratory and do it this way, and
do it that way, and then look for the effect.

But probably the real problems are the long-term effects.   There
have been some ideas on cumulative effect.   What do those things do
6 years later, not 6 minutes later?

The opposite idea is, as you probably have heard, too, that it might
very well be that the children are infatuated at 13 with comics, and
read them in terrible amount, and at 15 they find it completely silly.
Just as they do not like to eat children's food when they are 14, they
might not like to read children's stuff, like comics.   I don't know.
Don't quote me as having said the one or the other, but the whole
question of what those media play in the development of children
over a period of 6, 8 years, and not in a short experimental situation,

is very important, and again obviously you need funds and central planning for that.

One third example of needed research which, again, due to the situation described, has been omitted, is very often overlooked. How do those controversial programs get on the air? No one seriously thinks that a president of a network is a malefactor who sits here and thinks how he can corrupt little children.

It comes about, supposing that those programs are bad, by a variety of circumstances. For instance, there is a legend that children like bad programs, so here is one good reason to put them on. But maybe it is not true. We do not know.

Then it is easier to write stupid programs than good programs, and everyone overlooks the tremendous amount of stuff which has to go on television. I mean scores of hours every day. Now, there just are not enough good people in the world to write so many good programs. So you have mediocre people who use stereotypes, and very often they do not know it.

So the question of how do programs get on the air, at what point would it be possible to influence, do you have to influence advertisers, do you have to get a better writer, should you have some special educator who worries at every network? No one really quite knows how programs get on the air, because there are scores of people involved in those decisions, and, again, if that were studied, one can very easily capitalize on the good will which the industry undoubtedly has, to be cooperative.

And it is at this point that I would like to say a word on something which is quite important, I am sure, for all of you: Suppose we had all this knowledge and we spent a lot of money and planning; would it make any difference? Would the industry really act on it?

I think there is good reasons to suppose that that will actually be the case. We have a variety of examples that a great deal of industry practices have been changed when actual data were available.

We know that it is not really anywhere a bad will, but kind of the mechanics and the lack of clarity in the situation which leads to all this debate, and I can only express my conviction on the basis of much experience that if more knowledge were forthcoming more quickly, then I do not think there are any real evil forces in the picture, and the situation would be a much less controversial one.

Now let me, however, before closing, make one fourth point: I do want to warn you that, while it is my duty here to say how little we know, and how urgent it would be to know more about it, and to know what should be done about it, one should not look to research as a kind of a panacea which now will solve all your problems. You should not do it on two points:

First, in this whole matter of the mass media, there are questions of convictions and taste which can never be settled by research.

You canot settle by research whether people should read good books rather then bad books, or whether they should listen to good music. You have to have certain convictions on the dignity of men, on the importance of the matters of the mind, and you have to stick to them irrespective of research.

If I see a cruel picture in a comic, or if I hear a stupid television program, and they exist, undoubtedly, then I do not want them and I get away from them irrespective of whether I have research data or not.

Secondly, there is a great danger that research is being used as an alibi. Let us just wait until we have enough research and then we will do something.

Now, that is not what the real role of research is. People have to make decisions; they act. We do some studies; we improve their action; their actions improve our studies because they raise new questions. There is an interaction between the responsible decisions of the policymaker and the research man. While we do not want to be drowned by your decisions, we also do not want to be used as an alibi.

Now, that brings me to the final question: Do I have any reason to think that appearing before this committee will change the situation?

I am very sorry that Senator Kefauver is not here today, because one of the interesting studies we have done was on the effect of the Kefauver hearings on crime several years ago, and one of my colleagues made a study of what effect did the television crime hearings have on the audience. Did they really become aware of the problem of crime? The finding was that it had a very great effect in making them worried, but then there was not anything they could do about it, and therefore their worry was either dissipated or even converted into intention and a desire to get away from the situation. So one of the great dangers is to say something is bad and not to say what concretely can be done about it.

Let me end by saying if I do not misunderstand a committee like yours, there are three things which can come out in direct or indirect way from your work here. First, and I have purposely not mentioned it so far, your legislative committee might have influence on the National Science Foundation which is, after all, a Federal agency. The National Science Foundation restricts itself so far almost exclusively to matters of the physical sciences, and it has only one officer who is supposed to worry whether nonphysical sciences should be included.

I have regretted that all the time. I feel you have here a very interesting example, that you have a powerful Federal agency that could help clarify this matter. You could call it measurement of the facts and then it is near enough to mathematics so that you do not need to call it social sciences. But I think if this committee were to approach the National Science Foundation to see whether they could not extend their work into research in a crucial area like yours, you would do a good turn to yourselves, to the problem, and also the interest—academic interest I refer to, here.

The second thing is, and which I have already mentioned, that planning is obviously necessary, and it is in the academic tradition that planning is frowned upon, and correctly so. And only if a public body states. So radio is a signal danger, like, well, look, now cancer is so important. Let us ask the medical school to concentrate on cancer. In that situation, then, the academic community does not mind to take policy directions, and if you consider that importantant enough, you have a great number of devices. There always have been White House conferences; there can be many such ways by which the coordination of work, the speeding up of work, the stressing of emphasis on one specific research problem could be done.

Finally, there is, of course, the matter of funds, and there I have mentioned before that just as there are no evil doers in the industry, I am quite sure there are no evil doers in the foundations. But everyone is a little bit scared of everyone else, and the foundations, by unfortunate legislative incidents last year, are especially scared because one committee has told them they should stay with themselves and not study controversial matters, and if another committee came around and say maybe there are 1 or 2 they should be investigating and spend their fund, it would redress, a little bit, the balance, and would again help the problem you are concerned here with.

Senator HENNINGS. Dr. Lazarsfeld, on behalf of the subcommittee, I want to thank you for a very excellent and thoughtful and profound statement. I think some of us may have some questions to have by way of further expansion on your thesis, if you will indulge us. Counsel, Mr. Bobo, do you have any questions?

Mr. BOBO. No questions.

Senator HENNINGS. Senator Langer, do you have any questions to ask?

Senator LANGER. In your opinion, what is the effect of these western movies on children?

Dr. LAZARSFELD. You know, having focused my whole testimony on that we know so little and what can we do to know more, I would have to preface an answer to any such question that quite honestly no one knows anything about that, and I can give you the pattern of the discussion and it will apply to everything.

Some people say it is a transitory experience, and they had Indian novels 40 years ago and then had western movies, and some people say it all goes by. Some people have pointed out, we have evidence on that, it makes kids quite excited at the time when they listen, and there is good reason to assume that if you work them up emotionally, it might, for some children, have a bad effect later.

Permit me to put it this way: It rained yesterday. If you were to ask me what is the effect of rain, I could not tell you because if I was playing tennis, the effect was very bad. If I was just raising a crop, the effect might have been very good. It might be good for fishing and bad for camping, and in this general question of the effect, really cannot be answered here just like the effect of rain. They are different on different people, under different conditions.

Senator LANGER. Well, of course, you know that little children, 6, 7, 8 years old, the boys especially, now have belts with guns. Do you think that is due to the fact that they are seeing these western movies and seeing all this shooting?

Dr. LAZARSFELD. Oh, undoubtedly; it is part of it. And part of it is that, I meant to mention that, if there were more attention to that, the toy industry might have different kinds of ideas. And it does not just have to be guns.

Senator LANGER. What is your opinion on this beer advertising? There will be a big football game and in the intermission a lot of beer advertising; what is your idea about that?

Dr. LAZARSFELD. In what respect?

Senator LANGER. Well one beer company will get up and say what beautiful, fine beer they are manufacturing, and they say, "Oh, boy, what a beer."

Dr. LAZARSFELD. Well, look; I have definite opinions on it: If someone is a tetotaler, then the answer is very simple. If you are engaged in beer drinking, then the effect of that beer drinking is very bad.

If you are an artist, then some of those advertising effects are very good because they are very amusing and others are very bad because they are very stupid.

If you are a psychologist or a market research man, then you say by and large the effect is good, because it sells a lot of beer, you see, and it undoubtedly does. So really, there is no way to answer that.

Senator LANGER. How old were you when you left Vienna?

Dr. LAZARSFELD. I was 30.

Senator LANGER. Thirty?

Dr. LAZARSFELD. Thirty.

Senator LANGER. Well, now, what is your opinion in comparing the children in Vienna with the children in the United States? What is the difference in thinking?

Dr. LAZARSFELD. Oh, tremendous. Well, again, I am comparing, now, middle-class children.

Senator LANGER. Yes?

Dr. LAZARSFELD. With each other.

I think that the American children are socially much more developed. They know better how to get along with each other. They know better how to handle themselves in public life. They have a better civic education. And, if you don't mind my saying so, the Austrian children know more; they have learned more. It is really two completely different educational systems. We become socially adjusted and educated as European children and the American child becomes a citizen, but does not know so much homework as we do.

Senator LANGER. In what way do the Austrian children know more, the children in Vienna, than the children in New York City, for example?

Dr. LAZARSFELD. In straight matters of—my children were raised here, and I cannot talk with them about Homer, and I can't talk with them about the medieval times—but why should I, come to think of it? I mean, it is a whole world of traditional knowledge, which you don't have any use for. But you gain—you know, when I was a child, you could not edit a newspaper. You were forbidden to have a newspaper. Debates, campus life, nothing of that sort exists.

Senator LANGER. I am interested in getting your answer. Why do the children in Austria know more than the children in the United States?

Dr. LAZARSFELD. Because the whole tradition of the educational system is different. When I was young, we had drill schools. We were drilled 6 hours a day to know those things, and had no campus life, no fraternities, no debates, no self-government at schools, nothing.

Senator LANGER. That is all, Mr. Chairman.

Senator HENNINGS. Thank you, Senator Langer. Senator Wiley?

Senator WILEY. Do you think it is possible, by any group of men, to arrive at definite recommendations as to the impact of certain pictures upon all the minds of children, or are the children's minds different, depending upon human heredity and background, economic conditions, and maybe some political conditions having something to do with it? What is food for one is poison for the other. Is that true?

Dr. LAZARSFELD. Absolutely, Senator.

Senator WILEY. If that is true, is it possible that we are talking about creating an index in relation to pictures affecting the morals of children? Is anyone smart enough to say all these pictures or this category, or that category, should be put on the index?

Dr. LAZARSFELD. No, but that is not the problem. No one, no reasonable person looks at it this way. First, just because children are so different, by all those factors you mentioned, one of the problems would be the balance of the schedule. You see——

Senator WILEY. The what?

Dr. LAZARSFELD. What is called a balanced program. You see, you do not want to have everything of one kind, but you can acquire a great deal of knowledge how you get the right combinations, as stations do in many respects. They have light comedy, they have serious drama. You can have the same kind of balance that you develop in children's programs.

Senator WILEY. Well, could you lay down a definite rule and say that any picture that is lewd, any picture that puts a premium on dishonesty, any picture that puts a premium on immorality, that those pictures might have the same effect upon all young minds?

Dr. LAZARSFELD. Senator, this is what I meant by my point 4: I think you should put down the rule that there should never be a premium on dishonesty, but you should say that out of your conviction and not claiming that it has this or that effect because we do not even know that, you see.

I will come out straight, here, that on children's programs dishonesty should not be rewarded, but I say it as a citizen, if you please, but not because I claim that it makes children dishonest. One has to have the courage of his convictions, even as a research man.

Senator WILEY. But, of course, you know that in New York, for instance, they have agreed or disagreed on what pictures should or should not be?

Dr. LAZARSFELD. Yes.

Senator WILEY. However, I think that you can get into the problem of where you got, say, a very sensitive, nervous child, if you were to show him a lot of shooting pictures before he went to bed, he would not get any sleep, possibly.

Dr. LAZARSFELD. Yes.

Senator WILEY. What are you going to do about it? Are you going to say if a picture itself points a good moral, that that is the duty of the parent, to see that the child does not get that dose any more than he should get a big hunk of meat before he goes to bed?

Dr. LAZARSFELD. Well, correct, Senator. But isn't that a problem we have, generally? Take automobiles. If you put a car into the hand of a crazy boy, he does harm.

Senator WILEY. You are stealing my figure of speech. I have used that politically many times.

Dr. LAZARSFELD. I take it as a compliment.

Senator WILEY. I am complimented.

Dr. LAZARSFELD. And you coordinate safety devices, safety councils, school influence, parent influence, but you also make sure that the car does not contain dangerous parts. I mean, it is a coordination, and where research can play a very great role, a progressively great role.

Senator WILEY. Well, Mr. Chairman, I remember making a note here, after listening to the distinguished witness, as to if he could answer the question, What is knowledge?

Dr. LAZARSFELD. Well, if I try to answer that in the specific context, I would say it consists of a number of steps: The first is to ask good questions. If you do not raise good problems, you will never have knowledge.

Secondly, you have to be always aware that you know only a very small part of whatever you want to know.

Senator WILEY. You know, the Scripture says that man's knowledge is foolishness with God. Do you agre with that? We are getting a little far afield, but I am just wondering.

Dr. LAZARSFELD. No, Scripture is always a matter of interpretation. I would interpret it as saying it is a little step away from foolishness, rather than——

Senator WILEY. I think that is all, Mr. Chairman. Thank you.

Senator HENNINGS. Thank you, Senator Wiley.

Senator LANGER. Just one question. What do you teach in Columbia?

Dr. LAZARSFELD. What is called social research.

Senator LANGER. You are a professor of social research there?

Dr. LAZARSFELD. Well, I am a professor of sociology, it is called, but it is a department. But my work is what is the effect of radio, why people elect presidents, I have made large studies, and always, why people buy certain products. I am—my main, exclusive field is what is called study of mass behavior, voting, listening, buying, and such things.

Senator LANGER. You are a full professor there?

Dr. LAZARSFELD. Yes. I am chairman of the department.

Senator LANGER. How long were you in California?

Dr. LAZARSFELD. I am in California now. I am now on a year's leave of absence. I just happened to be down here.

Senator HENNINGS. Dr. Lazarsfeld, I suppose you know that Senator Langer is a distinguished alumnus of Columbia University?

Dr. LAZARSFELD. I did not.

Senator WILEY. I thought there was something common between you.

Senator HENNINGS. And that is why he has the interest in your activities there.

I found your statement exceedingly interesting because, with my very sparse knowledge of this subject, what you have said is about coincidental with the views I thought I held, although my own mind is not closed on the subject, either. I feel we know so very little about the impact of not only television and radio but of books, even the classics, throughout the ages, that it is very difficult to suggest that we may appoint a grand censor to determine what shall be seen or shall not be seen.

There are questions of taste involved. There are questions of choice involved, are there not, Dr. Lazarsfeld? That is to say that we know that we all, children and adults alike, and adults are not far removed from children, really, in many respects, may profit more by things that have intrinsic worth and merit, whether it be from the literary or the stage production point of view, good plays, good books, good movies, good programs. They seem to bring something perhaps the meretricious, the less worthy only in terms of taste, may bring.

Of course, we get into the question of taste, which is not like Senator Wiley's question of what is knowledge.

I was very much interested in your suggestion about the difficulty of this, too, because we know that boys in the United States, for example, have been exposed to all sorts of literature long before television and radio, and the mass media came into being: The Nick Carter series, the dime novels of our fathers' days, back in a period following the Civil War. Those were the old-fashioned desperado stories, lots of gunplay, lots of shooting, virtue always triumphed and the hero married the girl, and so it was with the Oliver Optic books, which were written shortly after the Civil War. They related to stories about drummer boys and the Union Army. There was a lot of blood and work with the bayonets and on a gunboat down in the Mississippi, and all manner of things dealing with war and bloodshed and violence.

We will never know what result those have had on perhaps our acceptance of war as the last step of diplomacy, so to speak, containing the ends of a given power or combination of powers.

Senator WILEY. If the chairman will pardon me, they said it made possible the recruiting of the Rough Riders.

Senator HENNINGS. Well, some of us used to read Horatio Alger behind our geographies because it was said he was said to be trash. There was nothing in Alger that was obscene.

Dr. LAZARSFELD. May I make a comment on that?

Senator HENNINGS. I would be delighted to have you do that, sir.

Dr. LAZARSFELD. I think you bring up a very important point, but it has another side.

While there might be no difference between these earlier products and the modern media, they certainly deserve more attention and more study for several reasons.

First, you see, there is so much more of it.

Senator HENNINGS. That is right.

Dr. LAZARSFELD. This is one thing which might make a difference.

Senator HENNINGS. Enormous volume.

Dr. LAZARSFELD. Secondly, you do not need to know how to read, you see. It is just you hear it, while you——

Senator HENNINGS. You have read John Steinbeck's piece in the Reporter magazine 2 or 3 weeks ago about television and its effect upon his family?

Dr. LAZARSFELD. I think I heard about it.

Senator HENNINGS. He says as his children watched television their jaws dropped and their eyes became glazed and they acquired what he called the television face. They were enraptured by these wonderful things that were going on before their eyes, and in which they could change and choose among by the flick of a dial.

Your observation about long-term effects is interesting. I was in Scotland Yard last summer, and spent a good part of an afternoon with the commander in charge of the criminal bureau there, and he called a number of his assistants in and among other questions I asked him about the juvenile delinquency rate insofar as figures can reflect such things, and we looked askance at all figures, all statistics and such.

Senator LANGER. Mr. Chairman, may I ask another question? Before you came over in this country——

Senator HENNINGS. I want to complete my question, but it is all right.

Senator LANGER. What countries in Europe did you travel in?

Dr. LAZARSFELD. Well, I studied in France for a year, and I know a little bit of the Continent, but I have spent, except for my year in France, most of my life in Vienna, Austria. But I have to say that several years ago I was invited by the Norwegian Government; I spent a term teaching at the University of Oslo; so I know Norway.

Senator LANGER. Senator Wiley will be interested in that. How long were you in Norway?

Dr. LAZARSFELD. One term; about 6 months.

Senator WILEY. What?

Senator LANGER. He said he was in Norway for about 6 months, which would interest you very much.

Senator WILEY. I am interested in that, because what he got there would counteract what he didn't get in Columbia. Excuse me.

Dr. LAZARSFELD. I was visiting professor at Oslo.

Senator HENNINGS. May I continue with my question? The director of the bureau at Scotland Yard said their juvenile rate was dropping, and had over the past few years, and I asked him what had attributed to that. And he said television. I said, Why? Indeed, many people in our country believed if we just got rid of the television sets, and just got rid of them, they would not have any juvenile delinquency. Many people oversimplify it at that point.

Well, he said, of course you know the BBC does screen the programs, and perhaps is a little more careful about crime and violence than yours, but, he said, it keeps them off the streets. He said they stay at home at night and watch television, and they are not on the streets of London getting into trouble, so there is another side of the coin.

Well, we could, with profit, certainly, discuss this matter with you the rest of the day and perhaps the rest of the week, Dr. Lazarsfeld. I wonder if counsel has any questions, if no other members of the subcommittee have?

Mr. BOBO. I just have one that arose, Senator. I notice you have avoided expressing an opinion one way or another, Dr. Lazarsfeld. This is not to put on the spot in any way, because of lack of knowledge, but you spoke of your own children. I wonder how you feel about your own children watching TV.

Dr. LAZARSFELD. Yes; I can certainly say by what policy I am guided. Most of all, I was concerned with competition. I kept on and still do play chamber music at my house, for instance, so that I have a supply of good music for the children by demonstration and not by preaching.

We try, Mr. Chairman, to have whatever books we can think of in the rooms of the children so they read.

So that one idea is that you provide them with alternative possibilities so they have more choice.

The second is you try to talk with them, whenever possible. For instance, my daughter was afraid of crime films, and it was very important to talk it out when she happened to see something. So talking about it is not so dangerous, that is not so real, and so on, is very important; and every psychologist knows that children do not talk very easily with parents, but you do your best.

Senator HENNINGS. Are there any further questions?

(No response.)

Senator HENNINGS. If not, thank you very much, Dr. Lazarsfeld, for giving us the opportunity of hearing you today, and for your contribution to this work that we are undertaking.

(Subsequent to the hearing the following statment was submitted by Dr. Lazarsfeld and ordered made a part of the record:)

WHY IS SO LITTLE KNOWN ABOUT THE EFFECTS OF TELEVISION ON CHILDREN AND WHAT COULD BE DONE ABOUT THE MATTER?

(By Paul F. Lazarsfeld, Columbia University and Center for Advanced Study in the Behavioral Sciences)

I am glad that I can testify before this committee because this permits me to discuss a paradoxical and bothersome situation. In the course of your hearings, and wherever else television is discussed, one always hears the complaint that so little is known about the effects of this new medium on children. Even people who express strong opinions must concede that their feelings are derived from more or less casual observations. At the same time, the topic is obviously of considerable importance; this can best be seen from the fact that a whole congressional investigation is devoted to it. Usually when something becomes a matter of national concern there is a concentrated effort to acquire relevant knowledge. Why isn't that the case in regard to the effects of television in general, and its effect upon children in particular?

With your permission I should like to discuss this paradoxical situation from five points of view.

1. What are the factors which retard the accumulation of useful knowledge in this field?
2. What kind of research is most needed?
3. What difference would it make if such research were carried out?
4. What would be the inevitable limitations of this research?
5. What could this Senate committee do to improve the situation?

THREE REASONS FOR THE LACK OF KNOWLEDGE

Yesterday you heard a distinguished witness, Dr. Maccoby, from Harvard, who told you about some interesting studies which she has done. A few other persons, like the Rileys at Rutgers, Hovland at Yale, Brodbeck at Boston University, have also carried out investigations in this same general area. But it all adds up to very little, and the work of the various scholars is not coordinated. This is good academic tradition. A professor picks up a topic and sticks with it for a while; but he drops it when something else interests him more or when he can't find a good student to carry out further experiments. From a professional point of view this is all right, because there are many things which deserve to be studied. We are used to the idea that knowledge on any specific topic accumulates slowly. From the point of view of scientific progress a few decades more or less do not make too much difference.

But if some problems become a burning social issue then it might be a mistake to leave research progress to the accidental initiative of individual scholars. I don't want to overdo this comparison, but we certainly would not have a polio vaccine or an atomic bomb today if most of the research departments had been left to doctor-of-philosophy dissertations.

We obviously do not need anything of the magnitude of a Los Alamos Laboratory to study the effects of television. But if it is an urgent social problem then we need some central social planning; priorities have to be set up, and some central organization is needed to coordinate research work and to press it forward. At what point a problem is best advanced by academic free enterprise and at what point more definite organization becomes desirable is a difficult question to decide; but it might very well be that the topic your committee is discussing needs at this moment more systematic and overall planning than it would get in the normal course of academic affairs.

Now, planning and organization obviously require funds. The question is where they should come from. Up until now, the little research which has been done in the field of television has generally been supported by foundations. Several times, in the history of mass media research, foundations have played a crucial role. Soon after the First World War, as you know, there was great public excitement about motion pictures—the self-imposed code which still controls most of the studios was one of the resulting developments. At that time a small foundation, the Payne Fund, sponsored a number of experiments to study the effects of movies on children. Dozens of studies, coordinated by the late W. W. Charters, helped to give the whole discussion an element of rationality, even though some of the research was controversial. Then in the late thirties, when radio had come on the scene, the Rockefeller Foundation, through John Marshall, organized a number of interlocking studies. One major project, located at Ohio State University, has permanently affected educational broadcasting, especially its use in schools. Another, located at Princeton, set the style for much of the mass media research which is going on today.

Why has no foundation stepped in and helped to clarify the new role which television is likely to play? There are two reasons for this, one intrinsic to foundation policy, and the other the unfortunate result of an external situation. Foundations have always felt that they should not give prolonged support to any one field. They provide funds for a few years to stimulate a new type of activity; but then they leave it to the universities and professions to go on from there. In general, this policy of discontinuity, so characteristic of foundation grants, makes good sense. But just as in the case of the private scholar, when a topic develops into a social concern a more sustained financing policy might become necessary.

Unfortunately, the chances for such a turn of affairs are small at this moment, because of the kind of criticism which has been leveled against foundations in recent years. Another congressional committee has scared the foundation boards, which are regrettably cautious to begin with, and none of them now wants to provide funds for a controversial field. When radio appeared on the scene the Rockefeller Foundation was still quite willing to finance large-scale studies as to what effects the new medium might have on American life. Now that television is here, with presumably even more intense effects, no foundation has dared to sponsor the necessary research. For about a year and a half I was chairman of a committee of prominent citizens who had been asked by a large foundation to advise what that foundation could contribute to desirable developments in television programing and research. Just as our committee submitted a detailed plan, endorsed by the industry as well as by critical reform groups, the attacks on foundations began, and the sponsoring organization decided to drop the whole matter.

One word might be added regarding the role of the industry itself in the research picture. The television industry does spend some money on research and there is some constructive collaboration with academic groups. I can testify that I have never heard of any undue influence of the industry upon the scholars. But the broadcasters usually do research which is close to their immediate operational problems. They cannot lay out large-scale plans. As a result, while industry research has contributed considerable knowledge on a few specific points, it cannot contribute to it systematically.

Reviewing the situation over the last 30 years—and I have lived with it closely for most of that time—it seems apparent that everything has militated against a coordinated and relatively quick buildup of knowledge of the sort which is necessary to deal with topics of social concern.

SOME EXAMPLES OF DESIRABLE AND MISSING RESEARCH

I am sure that by now you are impatient to hear some examples of the kind of research I feel is getting squeezed out as a result of the situation I have described to you. The answer is very simple: any research which needs the collaboration of groups which are usually not in contact with each other, or which takes a considerable amount of time, or which is unusually expensive, or any combination of the three.

As an instance of the first, let me draw your attention to the fact that everyone talks about bad television programs and the effects which they have; but actually it would be much more constructive and enlightening to experiment with good programs. Why shouldn't it be possible to get reformers and writers together and have them devise programs which everyone thinks would be desirable and beneficial? Would children listen to them? Would they have good effects? And even prior to that, do we really know what we mean by a good program? Are there people around who could write them? It is such a simple idea, but consider what has to be done to carry it out. You have to get psychologists and writers to meet and work together. You have to have funds to produce programs for experimental purposes, regardless of whether a television station or network is willing to put them on the air. But the aridity and the negativism of much of the discussion which takes place today can be overcome only if it is shown that there is something like a good program, that there are people who can be trained to write and produce them, and that children are willing to listen to them.

Let me give you a second example. We in the universities, with our limited funds, can only do short-term studies. We put kids into laboratories, have them listen to programs, and then find out what they think or feel a few minutes later. But the real problem is the cumulative effect of television, what it does to children 6 years, not 6 minutes, later.

There are all sorts of speculations on this point. Some feel that while children are infatuated with overly dramatic stories at 13, they find them silly at 16; another argument is that children who have had a chance to release their aggressions and fears in a make-believe way will grow up to be more creative and balanced adolescents 5 years later. Don't quote me as having stated that as a fact. What I am trying to argue is that we probably have to follow up all sorts of children for a period of 4 to 8 years to get a real picture of what role television plays in the development of personality. This has been recognized in other fields. For example, at the time when progressive education was a matter of great concern, an 8-year study was organized to investigate what kind of elementary-school education makes for greater success in college and on the first job. I submit that only such long-term studies would give us a realistic picture of the role of television in a child's personality development.

Nor is the role of parents as clear cut as it may look. A growing child needs to have material around from which he can build up his developing world. Do the parents know how to provide it? Can they invent enough stories to satisfy the children's curiosity? Do they provide toys or books which are as satisfying as a bad television program? We need to study the extent to which parents understand the emotional needs of their children. We need studies which would result in ideas as to how the average family can create an atmosphere which will compete with television. The difficulty of these problems should not be underrated. It is hard enough for a mother of several children just to keep the household going. We cannot expect her to be a creative psychologist all day long in addition. And just exhortation to be a good mother won't help. Only detailed and large-scale studies of what actually goes on in the home will lead to advice which is concrete enough so that the average mother can utilize it.

A fourth example of needed research leads us to the other side of the fence. People who dislike today's television fare never raise the question: How do these controversial programs get on the air? No one seriously thinks that the president of a network is a malefactor who wants to corrupt little children. Obviously these programs appear because of a variety of circumstances. We know that certain legends as to what children like develop in the industry. We also know that it is easier to write a stupid and stereotyped program than to make a creative contribution. We often overlook what a tremendous amount of script has to be written to fill scores of hours on hundreds of television stations. If we want to have better programs we should know at what point the decisions are made to put on the programs we don't like. Where could influence be exerted? With the advertiser? With the writer? Would it help if every network had an educator who advised on children's programs? We definitely need studies on the life history of programs; how they are commissioned, how they are written, why they are finally put on the air. Only very skilled people, who would have to be paid well, could provide this picture, which, incidentally, I don't think even the telecasters themselves have.

I have given four examples of unorthodox kinds of studies which would add to our understanding of the effects of television. At the same time, I want to stress that even the research which is going on now on a small scale could be greatly helped by better coordination and better financing. We have some indication from existing studies as to how children influence each other in their listening habits. We have some inkling as to why television has such a hold on children. But what might be called a psychological theory of television is still missing, and will continue to be so unless we make collective efforts to help it along.

WHAT WOULD BE THE VALUE OF MORE KNOWLEDGE

I have already mentioned that I don't think that broadcasters are men of bad will. They just follow the line of least resistance. But that still leaves the question as to whether they could make use of knowledge which a more extensive and systematic research effort could provide. I happen to be fairly optimistic on this point. During the last war some of my associates at Columbia University were asked by the War Writers Board to do a study of magazine stories. A committee of writers had become worried about the stereotypes which many of these stories contained: gangsters always had Italian names; the money sharks were all Jewish ; and the Negroes were always cast in the role of submissive servants. For a man who has to condense a story into a few pages these stereotypes are of great help ; but their effect on the audience might be bad. The committee who wanted us to analyze the stories felt that if these practices were brought to the attention of writers in a dramatic fashion they would stop making use of stereotypes. When our content analysis was finished it turned out that one of the men on the executive committee of the War Writers Board was one of the main offenders ; he just hadn't known that he himself made use of the practice which he was anxious to stop in others. I am confident that the kind of research we all have in mind would greatly influence writers if they were provided with concrete suggestions. The executive officers of the broadcasting industry are also likely to be influenced. After all they are in business to get large audiences. They have never been shown that they can get large audiences with different kinds of programs. If research can do that then one of the main pressures toward the present policy would be relieved.

Take as another avenue of change the toy industry. The present type of television program may very easily parallel the traditional production of toy guns and cowboy suits. Is it possible to think of different tie-ups between television programs and toys? Would children be interested in building toy cities if programs were to dramatize the problems of modern industrial living? Would it be possible to construct simple scientific toys which might be asked for if there were interesting science programs for children, and which in turn would reinforce the interest in such programs? I do not know whether all this is possible ; but I am pretty sure that no one can tell until appropriate experiments have been carried out with programs as well as with new types of toys. The very fact that we can only speculate on such matters shows how primitive our thinking in this field still is.

Finally, I think that more knowledge would affect the behavior of parents. As I have mentioned before, children do not listen to television programs in a social vacuum. They tie the programs in with the games they play with each other. They use programs as substitutes for what their parents cannot give them for lack of time, energy, and insight. It might be possible to develop programs which dramatize family situations ; these could give parents more ideas as to what to do with their children, and, at the same time, provide the children with chances to find their own daily lives more interesting and satisfying.

I am aware that when I am optimistic about what differences more knowledge would make I can give you little evidence that I am right. But it seems to me a fairly obvious maxim that it isn't enough just to prohibit programs which children seem to like and parents disapprove of. Only if constructive substitutes are found for the present situation can we really count on a change.

THE LIMITATIONS OF RESEARCH

So far I have stressed how little we know and how urgent it would be to know more about the effects of television on children. It is now my duty to warn you that one shouldn't view research as a kind of panacea which will solve all your problems. You should not do so on two grounds. First, in the whole matter of the mass media there are questions of convictions and taste which can hardly be settled by research. At least for the time being research cannot decide whether people should read good books rather than bad books, or whether they should listen to good music. One has to have convictions on the dignity of man, on the importance of matters of the mind, and one has to stand up and be counted on these convictions. If I see a cruel picture in a comic, or if I hear a stupid television program, I react negatively, even though I may not be able to back up my conviction with research findings.

Secondly, there is a great danger that research will be used as an alibi. Some people say we should do nothing until we have enough research. But this is not the way research should be called upon. We must make decisions all the time, regardless of how much detailed evidence we have. As a matter of fact, there is a very productive interrelation between action and research. We do some studies; they improve the soundness of our decisions; conversely, actions raise new questions which lead to better research. The responsible policymaker uses whatever research findings are available, and when he has no data he makes the best decision he can. The responsible research man is guided in his work by his own intellectual appraisal of the whole problem; but wherever possible he gives priority in his work to those issues which are in the foreground of social concern.

This brings me to my final question: Do I have any reason to think that appearing before this committee will do any good? Here again I am inclined to be optimistic.

WHAT THIS COMMITTEE CAN DO

I am afraid that witnesses before such committees usually expect the Senators to act like benevolent gods, and to perform the miracles which the witness would like to see come about. I hope I don't share this illusion. I think, however, that there are at least three developments which could evolve from the present investigation.

First, and I have purposely not mentioned it so far, your committee might have influence on the National Science Foundation which is, after all, a Federal agency. It is true that, so far, the National Science Foundation has restricted itself almost exclusively to matters in the physical sciences; it has only one officer concerned with the question as to whether nonphysical sciences should be included.

I think the topic with which you are dealing represents a good example of why the Foundation, at least at certain critical points, should extend its activities into what is justifiably called the social sciences. This committee could approach the National Science Foundation and ask them to extend their work, and to support research on the crucial area of the effect of mass media on young people. By such a directive you could get great help on the problem you are concerned with, and, at the same time, you would make an important contribution to the interests I am informally representing here—the social scientist who would like to make a contribution to the welfare of his country. If a problem of jurisdiction arises, you could call it the measurement of the effects of the mass media; this is near enough to mathematics so that the National Science Foundation would be the proper agency for action.

Secondly, your committee could raise an emergency flag. In general, as I have mentioned before, the academic community doesn't like to take directives as to what they should be concerned with. But if a public policy body decides that a problem has high priority then we do not mind such directives. There are many ways in which you could coordinate the work of scholars. The White House conferences, which I think were started by President Hoover, represent one way in which the coordination and collaboration of scientists around a specific problem can be obtained. Your committee should be able to do something of this kind to concentrate interest and to speed up research on the effects of television on young people.

Finally, your committee could try to undo some of the harm which resulted from another investigation last year. This, again, is a point I have made before but it deserves reiteration. Big foundations of the kind we have in this country are virtually unknown in other parts of the world, and they are most characteristic of the American way of life. Through them great wealth can join with academic skill to solve important problems. If the foundations are scared into innocuous sidelines, then the efforts of the donors, as well as of the scholars, are wasted. I hope that your report will tell the foundations that they should spend part of their funds are matters which are controversial. The effect of television on children is controversial not because some people are against crime and others for it; it is controversial because so little is known that anyone can inject his prejudices or his views into the debate without being proven wrong. If the foundations were encouraged to sponsor research on this kind of controversy then the result might very well be a shift from empty debate to well-directed action.

Senator HENNINGS. Now, Mr. William A. Wood is the next witness, according to our list, Mr. Counsel.

Mr. Wood, have you a prepared statement?

Mr. Wood. Yes, Mr. Chairman, I have.

Senator Hennings. You may proceed in your own way, sir, either reading from your statement or speaking extemparaneously or interspersing your statements with such observations as you like.

Mr. Wood. Thank you.

Senator Hennings. Proceed, Mr. Wood.

STATEMENT OF WILLIAM A. WOOD, GENERAL MANAGER, METROPOLITAN PITTSBURGH EDUCATIONAL TELEVISION STATION WQED

Mr. Wood. My name is William A. Wood. I live at 4216 Centre Avenue, Pittsburgh, Pa. I am the general manager, of Metropolitan Pittsburgh Educational Television Station, WQED. I am here today to speak for WQED. I am not authorized to speak for other educational television stations although some of the points covered may apply to them.

Mr. Bobo. Excuse me, Mr. Wood, do you have copies of your statement?

Mr. Wood. They will be available shortly. They are being mimeographed now, and there will be a number of copies reaching the committee room in a few minutes.

I might insert here, so far as educational television is concerned, by May there will be 12 stations on the air, with a potential audience of 25 million viewers; 12 more are building, and 100 more than that are in the planning stage.

Let me begin by saying that at WQED we are telecasters with problems as various and persistent as those of other television broadcasters who have appeared before this committee, although they are not in all cases the same problems.

There are two fundamental differences between commercial and educational TV stations: (1) We are not supported by the sale of air time for advertising purposes, and (2) attracting the largest audience is not an overriding objective with us.

Television as a business—as an instrument of advertising has taken the pattern it has for sound economic reasons. At the present time at least, more people will look at the entertainment programs offered by commercial television than any other kinds of programs. And quantity of audience is a basic essential in advertising.

The basic theory which is behind this movement for ETV stations goes like this: So far television is primarily a recreation medium—a spectator medium. Sports, drama, variety, popular music, quiz games. Television can be used a lot more than it has been to date. It is as though since the invention of printing, printing was confined to the light and recreational and seldom used to record serious material, the Bible, the classics. Man's knowledge in a thousand fields of learning.

Television does not have to stop where it is now any more than printing need be confined to only the subject matter which will draw maximum readership. Television can go into any field—the only limitations are the technical limitations of the medium itself.

So the educational TV movement approaches television with a different motivation than commercial TV. Ours is a specific attempt to use television for purposes other than entertaining maximum audiences. What stations like WQED are doing on their air is not in competition with nor incompatible with what commercial stations are doing any more than Homer's Odessy is with the story of Lassie. Both can well have a place in your library and both kinds of TV programs may well be available on your viewing receiver.

As with its sister educational stations, WQED is nonprofit, noncommercial, and dedicated to the use of television for educational purposes. WQED is supported financially by foundation grants, funds from the public schools, and contributions from the general public in the southwestern Pennsylvania community.

WQED seeks to serve its community in somewhat the same way the community is served by its schools, its universities, its art galleries, its libraries, its symphony orchestra, its legitimate theater. We attempt to offer some of the same opportunities such institutions offer but by the use of electronics to bring these things right to the family fireside. We are not a substitute for these other institutions but we serve sometimes where they are inaccessible and also we provide stimuli designed to further the community's use of these other institutions. In this way I suppose educational television is selling something, as commercial television does. It is selling educational and cultural resources instead of commercial products.

WQED does not claim any exclusivity in what it is doing. Some of the finest educational TV programs are on commercial air. But whereas such programs must occupy a small part of the total program schedule on a commercial station, such programs are the totality of our schedule. It then follows, I think, that in concentrating our whole attention on educational programing, we can give exposure to a greater proportion of untried and promising uses of TV because we need not stick to the proven audience getters.

How does what WQED does relate to the question of juvenile delinquency today?

A recent poll taken by the University of Pittsburgh indicates that the juvenile delinquency problem is considered to be of primary importance by the people of our community. That is all we need to know. Then it automatically takes a priority as we plan our whole program schedule. Instead of conflicting with the economic necessities of the station's operation, it complements them in our case because we operate on contributions from our community. If we provide the community with programing relating to a field of their expressed interest, juvenile delinquency, we stand to continue to receive the contributions we need to keep going.

At present, WQED has no program on the air dealing exclusively with juvenile delinquency as a problem, although we will by fall, but it is probably that everything on our air could have a bearing on the problem in that the content of the programs, and even the way they are presented, is calculated to motivate the viewer in a constructive direction. We try to give a positive motivation to all our programs. I do not believe that merits any especial commendation. Since we are not under the compulsions of a business with time for sale, we have no reason for existing unless we offer such motivations.

On WQED school programs make the educational experience richer and more stimulating to youngsters. Appreciation shows such as good music, ballet, and art motivate worthwhile interests and pastimes, courses in history, English, science enable people of various ages to improve their minds and better their positions in life. And programs in family relations, scout training, presenting teen-age views and activities and homecrafts and hobbies are all designed as direct deterrents of delinquency.

Some programs of these types are available in Pittsburgh on other stations, of course. But to the television intermittently available in such serious categories in our area we are able to add the entire output of a station—of our station. They are available, and our community has them to draw upon to whatever extent it cares to—8 hours a day for a total of 40 hours a week.

Here is 1 day's output at WQED—as an example. This is the program scheduled for yesterday, April 6. Two inschool shows—one to stimulate interest in the wonders of nature (4th grade), a second documenting the story of workers in industry (7th grade and 8th grade), dressmaking for homemakers, the saga of America's westward expansion, how America's military sea transport works, a visit—on film—to the old churches of Virginia. The Children's Corner, featuring a children's Easter story and instruction in dancing. How glass bottles are made—a program in the basic fundamentals of music appreciation, the mechanics involved in the rebuilding of a DC–6 airplane. High school for adults, "heat" as a section in basic physics. How newspaper comic strips are created, for a teen-age audience. Flower arranging, the Paris ballet performance of the Swan Song, a film of Charles Laughton reading from Dickens, and a panel show on current issues featuring undergraduates from the University of Pittsburgh. That is 1 day's program.

Senator HENNINGS. Mr. Wood, that not only has variety and substance, but it sounds intensely interesting.

Mr. WOOD. Well, Mr. Chairman, I think I can speak to that right at this point.

Senator WILEY. How many hours?

Mr. WOOD. Sir?

Senator WILEY. How many hours?

Mr. WOOD. That is 8 hours.

Senator HENNINGS. Forty hours a week, did you say, Mr. Wood?

Mr. WOOD. Forty hours a week.

Senator HENNINGS. This schedule sounds good.

Senator LANGER. Is part of that in the evening?

Mr. WOOD. Yes, sir; it starts at 1 : 30 p. m. until 9 : 30 p. m.

Senator WILEY. What do you do with the rest of your time?

Mr. WOOD. I wish we could be on the air longer, Senator.

Senator HENNINGS. What do you do with the rest of your time, Senator Wiley?

Senator WILEY. Committee work. [Laughter.]

Mr. WOOD. This schedule sounds good, but not if we are just talking to ourselves. Does anybody look? Viewing to stations like ours is selective. Not as many people look nor do they look as many hours as they do to other stations. I think you cannot expect anyone, no matter how serious minded, to set himself to learn during every leisure hour he has. But they do look. And those who look encompass all walks of life in the Pittsburgh area.

The University of Pittsburgh survey says nearly 50 percent of the set owners turn some time to WQED. The bulk of these look at us an hour or so per day. Our high-school programs, English, history, physics, get 8 percent of the audience. Our serious music programs, 6 percent. Our home do-it-yourself program received over 1,000 fan letters last week and claims 10 percent of the viewers.

Let me dwell for a moment on WQED's High School of the Air. The High School of the Air is designed to allow adults who didn't graduate from high school to acquire the credits they lack and earn a diploma. The State department of education accepts these credits if our students can pass the State examinations. The air programs are presented in collaboration with the Pittsburgh public schools.

Four hundred and ninety-nine students enrolled for credit last fall; 71 percent of the examinations taken at the close of the semester were passed. But of especial interest to this committee might be the fact that correctional institutions in western Pennsylvania are using the High School of the Air. The Allegheny County Workhouse had some of its inmates in the class and they passed 95 percent of their examinations, a considerably higher percentage than the general public.

This semester we also have enrollments at the Western Penitentiary, a State prison. Prison authorities are interested in the response shown by some of their charges and there would seem to be some encouraging signs about the rehabilitation possibilities of a delinquent who is interested enough in schooling to take a course and study hard enough to get passing grades. At least 2 of the workhouse class will, if they pass their next examinations, be ready for high-school graduation this June. There is some question as to where they will go to receive their diplomas.

These high school courses on the air are accelerated courses. As we go ahead with them, it will become possible for an adult who applies himself to complete high school in 1½ years.

By next year we hope to provide summer makeup courses for regular high-school students who have failed to subject during the school year. This too, we think, has its place in helping to curb delinquency.

The WQED program which should be of great interest to this committee, if I have correctly judged your interests by previous testimony, is a daily hour-long offering at 4:30 every afternoon on channel 13 known as the Children's Corner.

This program has not missed a day since WQED began broadcasting 1 year ago this last Tuesday. It is a continuing experience for children featuring a spritely young lady named Josie Carey in the center of a highly varied land of fantasy and fact—adroitly presented instruction and fun; song and story. Its audience ranges in age from 2 to 12 years. It counts an extraordinary number of adult viewers and its rating in the Pittsburgh area is 30 percent of the available television audience.

On the Children's Corner there has never been an act of violence of any kind. There are no cowboys, Indians, or space men. Adult conflict has no place there. The audience is there, though. The show receives 4,000 letters a week.

Learning is dispensed throughout this hour of programing, even though it is not for learning that the kids tune it in. They learn numbers, how to tell time, some words and phrases in French, simple nursery songs, creativeness through art contests, poetry, zoology with live creatures, home hobbies and crafts, children's stories, instruments of the orchestra and even a little juggling and prestidigitation. I have with me excerpts from Children's Corner fan mail which testifies to its power as a teaching program.

Senator HENNINGS. Mr. Wood, at that point, may I ask you, sir, do you pitch the program on a median or an average age?

Mr. WOOD. Mr. Chairman, I think——

Senator HENNINGS. How do you meet that problem?

Mr. WOOD. I think the program, frankly——

Senator HENNINGS. You mentioned telling time, for example. That would not be of any particular interest to a youngster who can tell time.

Mr. WOOD. The teaching on the program, some of it, is useful for preschool age, some for older children.

The show, frankly, just grew, and items were added to it; that where interest was indicated, and it seems from what our audience says, that though there are different ages involved in different segments of the program, that all of the age groups look through the whole hour.

Those who are looking for something for 10-year-olds will sit through the telling time, which is for the 4-year-olds, in order to get to their part of the program.

It was not set up for any particular age. In fact, we have some reason to think that you cannot be certain when you start what age will be attracted by a prtculr childreni's program.

We have some fan mail such as something like this:

"I am 39; have 5 children. I enjoy the program as much as they do."

And there is a child aged 47 here who asks if it is all right for him to look. So it has run quite a gamut, and I think, perhaps, the charm of the program is more important to the viewer than whether it hits his particular age.

There seems to be growing evidence in our town that Children's Corner is becoming a means of putting worthwhile things into the minds and behavior patterns of young viewers.

Not all the programs which educational stations can create and air can have the magic that this one seems to have. But here is a successful example which shows that with enough ingenuity and imagination and with creative people, programs which have high value as to content can get audiences.

An audience on shows like this is steadily exposed to actions and ideas and truths which would be patently incapable of having any detrimental effect on it, and there is some indication they have a salutary effect on the youngsters at the other end. I do not by saying this mean to take any position against other TV programs for youngsters at all, but we are finding that it is good to offer this kind—to have it there if the kids want it, and in Pittsburgh they want it.

I have a half-hour film of this program if the committee at this or any other time would care to look at it.

WQED is just 1 year old as a television broadcaster. We are poverty stricken, but our year has convinced us that there is a place for community educational TV. This movement is going to succeed because it fills a need and the community recognizes that it fills a need. ETV is a very definite step toward the realization of television's broad potential which includes entertainment but which includes a great deal more, too.

Thank you, Mr. Chairman.

Senator HENNINGS. We thank you very much for your very fine statement; and, if I may, as one member of the subcommittee, make the observation, that you are doing an admirable job.

Mr. WOOD. Thank you.

Senator HENNINGS. I am sure that Pittsburgh is very proud of this station, and they cannot have anything but good from it. That is the sort of thing we know cannot have a very bad effect if, I say, we know as much as we know.

Senator Langer?

Senator LANGER. What does it cost you to put on this program during the last year?

Mr. WOOD. You mean, Senator, the Children's Corner program?

Senator LANGER. Yes; these 8 hours a day for 1 year; what did it cost?

Mr. WOOD. The 8 hours a day for the first year came to a total of operating costs close to $280,000.

Senator LANGER. I think you are doing a mighty fine job there.

Senator WILEY. How much did the station cost?

Mr. WOOD. Senator, the station, that is, getting started and having the physical equipment, came to in the neighborhood of $225,000.

Senator WILEY. What territory do you cover?

Mr. WOOD. We cover a part of the 10 counties surrounding Pittsburgh, although with our present power we do not completely cover all of the 10 counties. We have a potential viewing audience of well over a million.

Senator WILEY. Is it operated by the university?

Mr. WOOD. No, sir; this is a nonprofit corporation which was organized—it was first brought to the attention of Pittsburgh leadership by Mayor David Lawrence, of Pittsburgh, who gathered some representative citizens together, and this group eventually formed a nonprofit corporation of citizens representing only the community rather than their own particular companies or educational institutions.

The board of directors, which is the ultimate authority for our station, includes in its ranks the presidents of the local universities, the superintendents of schools, certain leading attorneys and businessmen, and industrialists of the Pittsburgh area.

Senator WILEY. How do you get your operational costs?

Mr. WOOD. There are three sources: One through foundations which have helped us and continue to help us; one through schools which vote funds to the station for the school programs; and one through the community at large, where we actually ask our families in the community to contribute $2 or more per year toward our operating costs. At present there are 63,000 families who have contributed to us.

Senator WILEY. Are you meeting your overhead?

Mr. WOOD. Just barely, sir.

It means, if we are to be able to continue at a rate of, say, a quarter of a million dollars a year operating costs, we have to be able to get the kind of money we have received so far on a regular and continuing basis.

At the present time, we do not have very much ahead, and it all depends on whether our sources, the foundations, the schools and

61227—55——8

the public, will continue to contribute at least to the extent they have up to now.

Senator WILEY. Is there any opposition by the regular licensed stations?

Mr. WOOD. No, sir; we have the finest of support from all of the commercial broadcasters in our area; it has been an extraordinary thing.

Senator WILEY. Were you previously in the business?

Mr. WOOD. Yes, sir; I was with CBS television here in Washington before I went to Pittsburgh, and I began broadcasting a good many years ago with NBC, so I have been with both of the top networks.

Senator WILEY. You have been here all morning, have you?

Mr. WOOD. No, sir; I did not arrive until nearly the end of Mr. Lazarsfeld's testimony.

Senator WILEY. You did not hear the previous testimony, then?

Mr. WOOD. Not entirely.

Senator WILEY. Well, out of your experience, because we are talking about the impact of ideas and visual education on the young mind, out of your experience, what could you tell us is the course that should be pursued, not only by institutions like your own, but others, recognizing that you are all simply licensees of a public right in the public domain? You recognize that?

Mr. WOOD. Yes, Senator.

Senator WILEY. So what direction or directive or suggestion would you give out of your experience that might be of benefit, say, toward—well, we do not want to say siphoning, but giving right direction to the young mind because, after all, delinquency is wrong thinking and is the result of wrong ideas, and sometimes the result of maybe physical conditions.

My real question is, what light can you give us that might be profitable for all others engaged in the business of televising?

Mr. WOOD. Senator, I think this: I think that we are finding in our field of television—but this is not a new discovery, it is also being discovered by the men in commercial broadcasting—that it is possible to get positive motivations into broadcast programs which will keep an audience and do for that audience, perhaps, a little more than just to entertain it.

I think that all serious-minded men in the field of broadcasting would like to do that, and I think that most of them are doing it.

It is a slow proposition, perhaps, and there are very sound economic reasons why it must be slow.

But I believe that in some ways educational television can help to explore more thoroughly than the commercial broadcaster has time to explore, just how you can combine positive motivations in programing with programs that are good audience getters, too, and that the more the way to do that can be discovered, the more such programs will find their way into program schedules.

They are there already. They will, perhaps, increase in quantity and in proportion to the total program schedule, as it can be shown how to do them.

It is our basic problem and, I suppose, it is one of the basic problems of anyone in broadcasting—it is not the easiest thing in the world to take a program that has the greatest of objectives and be sure that it is going to get an audience, and if you have a great program so far as its objectives go, and nobody looks at it, you are nowhere.

So you have to find a way to put those two things together, the ability to draw and hold an audience, and something worthwhile in the way of a message when you get it.

I think that the whole industry is moving in that direction, and it is possible that the pace of moving in that direction may accelerate. If in any way stations like ours can help in that acceleration, we feel that it is part of our job to do that.

Senator WILEY. I like that phrase, "positive motivation."

During the 8 hours that you broadcast, do you figure out that there are certain hours where you can best impact the young mind, for instance, after school or whatever it is? I am just trying to figure out whether now that we are talking about children, whether we are now giving thought to the time when they are most easily impacted.

Then, do you give thought to the kind of a program that would do the job that you are talking about, positive motivation?

Mr. WOOD. The time we pick for the Children's Corner was determined a good deal on the basis of the pattern of family schedule in the Pittsburgh area.

It is an early-at-night dinner town. People eat their dinners at 5:30, 6 o'clock at the latest. The mothers like their kids to be occupied just before dinner.

It is a good time for the kids, too, and I think it is as good a time as any to have the children in a receptive mood for this kind of a program; that is why we are on the air from 4:30 to 5:30 with this program.

Senator WILEY. Will you pardon me—were you finished?

Mr. WOOD. I was just going to add, as to the motivations in the program, in the preparation of it at all times that is one of the things we try to keep in mind, how we can introduce in any element of the program something that will be a stimulus in a positive direction as a result of looking at the program.

Senator WILEY. You apply the rule that so many of these commercial advertisers do, of just suggestion, suggestion, suggestion?

Mr. WOOD. Senator, it is hard to explain that. It would be a lot easier if, at some time in your busy schedule, you had a minute to look at that film, how the kids on that program—they are only youngsters themselves—get across what they get across; that is hard to put into words. It just happens, and in a good many cases there is no sign put up which says, "Now we are teaching you something."

Very much to the contrary. There is a puppet, a tiger, who came from France, and who speaks only French, and when he comes on the program, because he has no other language he must needs speak in French, and we find out the youngsters at the other end are learning a good many French words and phrases not because we are teaching them, but because the poor little puppet can speak no other language, so it behooves the audience if they are polite to learn his tongue.

Senator WILEY. Again I return to the original question: Out of your vast experience, just what suggestions, concrete suggestions, have you got now, or what lessons have you learned, outside of what you have testified to, that would be of benefit for others if they were to get on the bandwagon 100 percent seeking to answer the question of juvenile delinquency?

Mr. Wood. Well, Senator, this is purely my own opinion, and I do not speak here for WQED, but I think if there is indignation in the community about the effects or possible effects of broadcasting on children, that this might well be turned into positive channels.

For instance, where there is an educational station or, even lacking that, where there is any station, responsive to a constructive approach, it seems to me that the community itself can do something, not about tearing down what is on the air, but about seeing if it can bring something imaginative and good and attractive, that is so good and attractive that, perhaps, it eventually will replace some of the things that are on the air now.

There is much indication in our area that the Children's Corner program will be sought after as a national program instead of being seen just in our area. This is a good thing.

It means that a program with good motivations is good enough so that there is demand for it, perhaps across the whole country.

If we have any faith in good programs on television, they should be able to stand up in competition, and if they do then, perhaps, the community, by making available or helping to give access for programs of this kind, can eventually see them reach their full use by having them available in all the cities of the United States instead of just one.

Senator Wiley. Well, I think that, of course, from my own personal observation—I must say that when there is a good program I am a television fan, at night—that is, at 10 o'clock at night—and the rest of the day is filled with the worries of the day.

I think some of the funny things are worthwhile. A man does not live just by food alone, and you can say a man does not live alone by being inculcated with positive motivation alone. He has got to have a little variety and good humor, something that suggests, perhaps, that life is really worthwhile.

I feel that out of many of these programs these youngsters, if they are really what they should be—and many of them are—really are exalted and trying to do something.

The chairman spoke of the Henty books and other books. I remember that the theme of those books was to love our country, and which were so selflessly devoted to the preservation of our country.

Well, these youngsters—and I have 10 grandchildren—and when I can I watch them to see how they react, and I see the youngsters out with a gun shooting "bing, bing, bing," they have had that influence, and trying to tell them that that is something they have got to be careful with.

I have also seen them as they have stood before programs and cried, there were tears, with respect to some fine picture, some situation where they were taught to be gentlemen and to exemplify the characteristics of gentlemen, and so forth.

Of course, to me it is the greatest result in the world, particularly for youngsters, and I suggest, as the chairman says, that most of us are youngsters and not yet grown up at this time.

So we are looking for a way to protect the youngsters who will be the men of tomorrow.

I want to thank you personally for a very fine presentation, sir.

Mr. Wood. Thank you, sir.

Senator HENNINGS. Senator Wiley, I take it you believe that real life is earnest but the grave is not its goal.

Senator WILEY. That is right.

Senator HENNINGS. There is time for a little lightness.

You said, Mr. Wood, that you did not countenance any violence on these programs. Did I so understand you?

Mr. WOOD. Mr. Chairman, I was referring to the children's program.

Senator HENNINGS. Yes, to the children's program.

A good many of us were raised on such things as Hans Christian Andersen, Grimm's Fairy Tales, Jack and the Beanstalk, Snow White, and Rose Red, all of those things which were——

Senator WILEY. And a little Wisconsin cheese, too; do not forget that. [Laughter.]

Senator HENNINGS. You have a good deal of overtone, overlay of violence, do you not, in those books?

Mr. WOOD. It appears on channel 13, too, not in this particular program, but in some others.

Senator HENNINGS. I was not undertaking to cross-examine you on that point, except to ask you whether you think such violence as may necessarily be a part of some of the classics, fairy tales and the more advanced stories, as you go up along through the early teen years—do you think violence is in and of itself to be avoided on programs of this kind?

Mr. WOOD. No, Mr. Chairman.

I feel that it is a question of how it is handled, whether it is handled tastefully and wisely.

Certainly, it would be a very bland and innocuous presentation that would eliminate violence where violence was a part of what you were presenting.

Senator HENNINGS. It is not your view that the children should be entirely divorced from reality and some of the less happy and more unfortunate phases of life?

Mr. WOOD. No, sir.

Senator HENNINGS. You do not try to shield them from all suggestion that there is evil in the world, and evildoers?

Mr. WOOD. No, sir.

Senator HENNINGS. Your suggestion that the program has to have interest, and sustained interest to be successful in the marketplace, entertainment, whether it be education under the guise of entertainment, where you infiltrate, so to speak, to teach them something in spite of themselves—is it not quite true that a child does tend to shy away from anything that says, "Now, this is education; you are going to be educated?"

Mr. WOOD. I cannot testify thoroughly as to that, but we assume that.

We feel that if we can make it attractive for itself, that we are likely to get a better audience and hold their attention better.

I might say, though, Mr. Chairman, that the programs we do for the schools, which are looked at in the classroom on television receivers, the teachers tell us hold the class interest even though they are very frankly and straightforwardly a teaching medium.

They do, the teachers in the studio do, their very best to make the presentation attractive, but it is teaching and it is known to the child to be teaching because it is coming to him in his classroom. But there is no slackening of his interest in watching the television screen during these periods.

Mr. Bobo. Do you have any evidence or has your station done any research, speaking about the children's program, that these positive motivations about which you spoke, transfer themselves to the children, that they actually put into effect the positive motivations that you show on the program?

Mr. Wood. Nothing conclusively, sir.

We have, as I pointed out earlier there is a 3-typewritten-page presentation here of excerpts from fan letters from the children, and in many cases from their parents, writing for them, which are some evidence that the kids learn, and take stimulation from what they see. But we have no research, no survey that follows this up. We have been too poor and too busy to do it, although I wish we could do it.

Mr. Bobo. But your letters do show from parents and from the children that they have in some instances, at least—I wonder, could we have those letters just inserted in the record, if you have a copy there, and we will insert the extracts of letters from the parents and children in the appendix of the record?

Mr. Wood. Yes, sir.

I will not bother the committee with reading any of them now, but, in general, they all speak to the point of what happens positively to the viewer having looked at this program.

Senator Hennings. That may be entered into the record at this point. Let it be exhibit No. 4.

(The material was marked "Exhibit No. 4," and reads as follows:)

Exhibit No. 4

Excerpts From Mail Received by Children's Corner From Viewers

Prince Charming's dance lessons do so much to overcome youngsters shyness and self consciousness. Dancing becomes a pleasure all of a sudden. Imagination you use is actually contagious for me too.

Would like a copy of your list of French words and translations. There is another little girl in our neighborhood who came from France and we have fun talking in French.

Folks on your program are now a part of our family life. My 4½-year-old daughter has become very interested in learning how to tell time. Along with your help this project is very successful. Also, it would do your heart good to tiptoe into her room when she is singing one of the songs you teach the children.

If more children's programs were like yours we would have less juvenile delinquency today.

Most grateful for your good program. Son's interest in counting and telling time has been stimulating to all of us.

I am in my second year of Latin in high school and I thoroughly enjoy your program when I am able to watch it. One of the nicest children's programs on TV. Would like a list of your French words so as to compare the languages of French and Latin.

My little daughter 3, is learning to draw pictures thanks to your efforts. Also learning all your little songs.

Daughter 4 loves the show. I do too.

I am one of those grownups who certainly would never miss the Children's Corner. It's a must every day.

I like the way your program brings in a few spiritual elements at times. I personally feel that the spiritual side of a child's life is very important.

I think your program is just wonderful. I suppose you allow kids 47 years old to watch, for I enjoy it as much as I would as if I was 7.

I am 39 and have 5 children—oldest 17, youngest 7—and I enjoy your program immensely.

I teach third-grade pupils and look forward to reading your book Small World to the children on Friday afternoons. I thoroughly enjoy your program.

Your program is entertaining and educational and also extremely relaxing to my youngsters nerves in comparison to other children's programs. Believe it or not, I relax too. Wish you were on longer.

When an adult feels the charm you radiate to children, you really have something.

As new owners of a TV set, we have enjoyed your particular contribution to better programs for the younger folk and the young at heart.

My children have learned many things from your program and they get a lot of fun out of it too. I also join in their praises.

Features on your show are outstanding. Both my son Robby, 3½, and I have become real fans. It is certainly network caliber. We, of course, are very Pittsburgh-minded and feel it to be very exciting having such a fine show on our excellent educational channel.

I think your program proves that TV for children can be interestingly handled without talking down to the children.

Mother has to write for me because I am too young but I am old enough to know that your show is very good for children.

Appeals to children of all ages as well as their parents.

My children simply sit spellbound during your program. I must admit that I also enjoy your imaginative little characters. Keep up the good work.

My sister and I watch your program. Mummy and daddy do too. Daddy especially likes grandpere (probably because he used to teach French) and always asks me what new words I've learned.

I am a parent, sincerely grateful you produce the type of program you do. I am sure my son gains something every day from your show.

The Children's Corner is No. 1 on our list for TV education.

My husband and I think it is the best children's program on TV.

Not only is the program well organized and performed, it is also original and of intense interest to all—not only children.

Even though my son is only in kindergarten he is fascinated by grandpere and enjoys the French lessons.

When my young daughter started to speak the French phrases as they sounded to her, I suddenly realized just how very much a child learns from what he or she sees or hears on TV. It is nice to know that there is one program that teaches along the right lines and does it in such a nice manner.

Your program is just delightful. I wouldn't have believed it was possible to present so many educational facts and fancies with such warmth and appeal for the children, and wonder of wonders in this day and age—mother does too.

The mother and father of the tame tigers mentioned appreciate very much the entertainment and education you folks at WQED are giving our children in just the proper dosage to make them eager for more. Tame tiger father manages to infiltrate the tame tiger ranks in front of the TV set when the Animal Alphabet and King Friday holds sway and Tame Tiger Cathy is in charge of summoning mother when Pat Hamilton is on.

I feel that the level of your program is higher than most TV entertainment designed for children and yet holds the attention of boys and girls. I am not alone in this conviction, as it is shared by my wife and four neighborhood families, all of whom are college grads or college level and parents of sub-school-age children. This letter is written by one who is not easily prompted to such dissertations.

So varied that the children don't want to miss a minute of it. Your contests are very stimulating and encourage children to draw and originate.

Having moved here from the District of Columbia I have seen many and varied children's programs and having four tame tigers of our own I think I know what appeals to them. The Children's Corner ranks at the top. It is a wonderful program, original and clever.

My thanks to you and all who work with you for the bewitching fantasy and educational instruction presented on the Children's Corner. It is a delight to have the world of fun and make-believe so expertly portrayed to our children. It is sorely needed in this workaday factual life.

I taught kindergarten and the primary grades and I think your program is tops. Thank you for bringing such a variety of ideas to the children in this area.

You are teaching languages as if they were games and I hope to have the children writing them too. Thank you, too, for the disguised lessons in manners and morals which are truly absorbing.

My youngster astounds his relatives by speaking French as it is quite an accomplishment for a 7-year-old to greet you in French.

My son, 2, watches with his young sister. What a liberal education he is receiving for his tender years, besides counting to 12 via X's number song, he is able to count to 10 in French and sings the Tame Tiger song.

Thank Daniel for us, before she became interested in the Tame Tiger Torganization my little girl wouldn't even look at hamburgers.

At our home we have three grandsons. Each evening your program is a must. The pleasure we get out of watching their reaction to your program does us a lot of good.

I have watched your program many times with my children and I have recommended it to everyone I know and shall continue to do so. You seem to understand children perfectly in every phase of the planning of the program.

My husband and I are very enthusiastic about the Children's Corner and think the introduction of foreign languages is a first rate idea. Even little Alice, 3½ years old, is becoming bilingual.

You have a very clever way of bringing lessons of courtesy, introductions, making appointments, etc., into your program. I know my three children can learn much that is valuable for their character training and be entertained at the same time.

As a mother of three children I would like to say how much we all enjoy your program. We only wish there were more of the better programs such as yours on the air for the children. We get quite a bit of amusement out of some of the older children who call the Children's Corner kid stuff because they are usually in the front row on the floor at 4:30. This includes even high school friends of my son.

Mr. Bobo. I was interested in some testimony we had yesterday about the enemies of educational television. No one was specified as being an enemy of educational television.

You, being in educational television, do you have any knowledge of any known enemies to WQED in Pittsburgh?

Mr. Wood. No, sir.

Mr. Bobo. Did you have any known enemies as the station was building, and did you have a concerted drive to keep you from building your station?

Mr. Wood. I know of none.

I think this, and it is very natural, there have been skeptics, and there still are, and we probably have to be around a lot longer before we can completely eliminate that skepticism, but that is all right with us.

Mr. Bobo. But there is no one trying to take your channel away from you?

Mr. Wood. No, sir.

Mr. Bobo. Or in some way blocking your activities?

Mr. Wood. No, sir.

Mr. Bobo. Thank you very much.

Senator Hennings. Mr. Wood, thank you very much for coming here and giving us this splendid testimony, and to point out to us some of the problems and, as well, some of the constructive steps being taken by you and your station.

You mentioned a film which you were good enough to suggest we might have the benefit of.

I wonder if counsel would arrange sometime at the convenience of the subcommittee to get the film. It would not require Mr. Wood to come here again, but, of course, we would always be glad to have him.

Mr. WOOD. I would appreciate it, Mr. Chairman, if you would look at it and, perhaps, it might answer a question or an allusion of Senator Wiley's as to whether there is any fun and laughter in this kind of television. I believe if you look at the film, you will laugh a little.

Senator HENNINGS. Thank you very much.

Mr. WOOD. Thank you, Mr. Chairman.

Senator HENNINGS. Mr. Heffernan was the next witness on our list. However, he has very graciously yielded, I understand, to Mrs. Walker.

Mr. Heffernan, I will ask you to bear with us. Counsel has informed me that he told Mrs. Walker that she would be the next witness, so if we may ask your indulgence.

We would like to hear from you, Mrs. Walker.

We are very glad to have you here this morning.

On behalf of the subcommittee, I want to express our appreciation for your having come to be of assistance to us.

Will you proceed, please, in any way that you would like to. You may read your statement or you may make a statement.

STATEMENT OF LOUISE S. WALKER, SUPERVISOR OF AUDIOVISUAL EDUCATION, MONTGOMERY COUNTY, MD., SCHOOLS

Mrs. WALKER. Well, I have no statement to read, so I will have to make it.

Mr. BOBO. You are connected with the audiovisual education of——

Mrs. WALKER. Supervisor of audiovisual education for the Montgomery County, Md., schools.

Mr. BOBO. I believe you have some opinion, Mrs. Walker, on the effect of audiovisual education on children as you have determined it in the Montgomery County schools?

Mrs. WALKER. Yes; I do. I have some very definite opinions.

Senator HENNINGS. Perhaps, before you proceed, Mrs. Walker, it might be helpful if you would give us something of your background and previous experience in this or related fields.

Mrs. WALKER. Yes. I am a graduate of Teachers College in Texas.

Senator WILEY. Will you speak a little louder, please.

Mrs. WALKER. I am a graduate of Teachers College in Texas, with a B. A. degree; a master's degree in education at the University of Texas; I have done graduate work in several universities, the University of California, Columbia, Harvard, Maryland, American University, George Washington, and so on.

Senator HENNINGS. Graduate work in what field?

Mrs. WALKER. Largely in the field of education, but more recently in the field of audiovisual education.

I have had experience in the studio, working in studios, and have produced educational shows, produced educational programs.

Senator HENNINGS. Thank you.

Mrs. WALKER. I am affiliated with a number of educational organizations all related to audiovisual education. There are a number of those.

Mr. BOBO. Have you done any work in the field of educational television?

Mrs. WALKER. Yes. I am one of the incorporators of the Greater Washington Educational Television Association, Inc., channel 26, which has been allotted to this area, and we have done some experimental programs in this area.

We did a series of 13, and then a series of 6; the last 1 ended a week ago last Sunday.

We do not have immediate plans for another series.

Mr. BOBO. I believe you also have had some experience in producing programs for educational purposes over the regular TV channels.

Mrs. WALKER. Yes; over a commercial station. I had three seasons of in-school programs. Those were programs that came in the evening.

They were for community information to enlighten our own parents on what modern education is, and to take them right into the classroom, unrehearsed. They were classroom productions, not remote although they were done in the studio.

Mr. BOBO. Do you think that on the regular television channels that there is a need for audiovisual education as you have seen it in Montgomery County schools, of that type of program?

Mrs. WALKER. Well, definitely there is need. Now, we would much prefer having our own station, such as the one you just heard described, because—well, for a great many reasons.

We can control the programing; we can beam the programs at the time we want them; we can eliminate commercials, and we can do a great deal, we think, in relation to in-service training of teachers.

Mr. BOBO. What are the difficulties that you have faced here in Washington in putting on an educational television station?

Mrs. WALKER. Well, I think we are very grateful for what we have had; but the time that has been given to us, community-service time, that time we were never sure of, that is one thing. It is changed frequently, and that is the reason we are not on at this time, because we were given a very undesirable time on Saturday, one that we did not feel we could use with the type programs we were producing.

There are a number of other difficulties. There is very little, if any, time allotted for rehearsal. The direction of a program is very important, that is the program, and sometimes the directors are not very conversant with educational methods.

Mr. BOBO. I notice yours is audiovisual education in the Montgomery County schools. Do you think that educational programs such as you are mentioning here are an important adjunct to the school program of the schools with which you are connected?

Mrs. WALKER. Yes; I certainly do. I think we are very proud of our audiovisual program in our schools, and when I say "audiovisual," I am not just speaking of television; certainly I am speaking of the motion picture, the use of the educational motion picture, slides, both the standard and the two-by-two's, use of opaque projectors; use of recordings, of various types of recordings, and so forth; the total program is what I am referring to. Definitely, I think, it enriches and certainly does a great deal toward making all of our learning and all of our teaching more effective in the classroom.

Mr. Bobo. Do you have any research or any evidence or any opinion on the fact that the positive motivations behind the type of program with which you are connected, do transfer themselves over to the children?

Mrs. Walker. Definitely and, of course, I am very much interested in children participating in programs, not just the viewing of programs. That is an important thing, giving them experience. In preparing programs, there is a great motivation in an English class to write a script for television or radio, that is going to be used—in other words, try to give them realness in their learning.

Mr. Bobo. You say it definitely did transfer itself. I wondered in what respect that has been shown.

Mrs. Walker. Would you explain what you mean by saying "transfer itself"?

Mr. Bobo. If you put on a program that has a positive motivation for honesty, does it transfer itself over to the child, so that the child becomes more honest because of having seen that program?

Mrs. Walker. Well, I certainly would not be one to answer that "Yes" or "No." I certainly believe that all good influences are all to the good, and I believe that, as one of the Senators pointed out, we do live in a very real world, and that it is important that children see not only the good but that when they see the bad they know it is bad.

It is a question of interpretation, and there, I think, we have a three-way responsibility. I think the network has a responsibility to the public, I think certainly the parent has a responsibility, and I think the school has a tremendous responsibility; and I do not believe that the school is being provided the materials and the equipment to handle that or take on that responsibility that it should have.

Mr. Bobo. When I spoke a moment ago about the difficulties of educational television, I was not referring to the normal channels.

You said you were one of the incorporators of the educational television station for Washington and the Washington area?

Mrs. Walker. Yes.

Mr. Bobo. What difficulties has that faced?

Mrs. Walker. Well, of course, we are not on the air; we have not picked up the station. That is a UHF station, and our committee, our group, our organization, right now we have no money, and we are not even producing experimental programs at this point.

Mr. Bobo. There is no concerted drive to keep this station from getting its channel?

Mrs. Walker. Do I know of any drive?

Mr. Bobo. There is no drive by anyone to prevent it from getting its channel, the only difficulty is getting funds?

Mrs. Walker. Right; and I have never heard criticism of educational programs. That is one thing we feel safe, if we can draw any conclusion at all, and I can say they are on the positive side, and my experience was always that we did get very glowing commendation from the public on educational programs, and saying, "We hope you stay on," but that, of course, does not pay for the program.

Senator Hennings. Senator Wiley?

Senator Wiley. No questions.

Senator HENNINGS. Mrs. Walker, I want to thank you very much for coming here to present your excellent statement and to aid us in the work of our subcommittee.

Do you have any further questions, Mr. Bobo?

Mr. BOBO. I have no further questions. Thank you very much.

Senator HENNINGS. Thank you, Mrs. Walker.

(Subsequent to the hearing the following statement was submitted by Mrs. Walker and ordered made a part of the record:)

STATEMENT OF LOUISE S. WALKER, SUPERVISOR OF AUDIO-VISUAL EDUCATION, MONTGOMERY COUNTY, MARYLAND, CHAIRMAN, VISUAL EDUCATION AND MOTION PICTURES FOR THE NATIONAL CONGRESS OF PARENTS AND TEACHERS

To the Committee on Juvenile Delinquency:

In the years in which I have produced educational television programs as a part of a total audiovisual program for my schools, I have been constantly impressed by the great interest children have manifested in this medium. I have been made aware, through their discussions with me and among themselves, of the impact the various programs make upon them. I have, all too often, been made aware of the little control and supervision which parents have exerted in relation to the types of programs their children are viewing. Many children are seeing programs day after day the contents of which, to say the least, are either too advanced or depict episodes which need interpretation by aduts. A program may or may not be harmful in itself but in the interpretation ascribed it. As an example, a program dealing with wrongdoing must be accepted on the part of the viewer as evil. It is here that the adult is given a wonderful opportunity to point out or teach the child to discriminate between what is acceptable and what is not acceptable in his society since he must live with both factors. It is consequently unfortunate when these opportunities are overlooked or ignored. Closing one's eyes to reality does not insure protection from what one does not wish to experience. Both good and evil exist and it is only through the realization of their existence that one can learn to safeguard himself from the harmful effects. What may be termed a bad program could well be termed a good program when seen and interpreted in the spirit in which it was written and produced. All experiences are educational, either for good or for evil, and certainly television is one means of communication which provides audio and visual experiences which should have controls to minimize the harmful effects on young people.

I am not among the believers that television is a major cause for juvenile delinquency. To recognize the potential effects which programs have on the young child one has only to understand something of how children learn, the means by which they learn and, add to this the areas or content fields which attract them. Certainly the fact that environment does affect behavior is accepted by most people. To live too much in a world of gangsters, murderers, and evildoers will no doubt make its impact on many children. How great this impact may be will be determined through time, but the question remains, "Do we want to take the risk?" Since the causes of behavior are multiple, one must deduct that undesirable television programs will leave their imprint.

My personal concern is not so much to get rid of the bad of the present-day programs as it is to find a way to stimulate children, parents, and teachers to demand a higher standard of programing. Of course, this would of itself, squeeze out the undesirable. Good taste in viewing can be developed just as we know good taste in all the arts can be developed—through education. Children tend to enjoy what they are taught to enjoy. As habits and discrimination are developed in relation to food (sense of taste being involved here) so can they be developed in relation to all the senses. Any music teacher, recreation teacher, librarian, or dietitian can vouch for the veracity of this statement. Therefore, I feel that the home, the school, the church, and all agencies responsible for the education and general welfare of children have a tremendous responsibility in providing experiences (including television programs) for children which will enable them to develop into the most successful citizens.

Senator HENNINGS. Now, Mr. Heffernan, please. Mr. Heffernan, I want to thank you very much for coming here this morning. Have you a statement?

Mr. HEFFERNAN. I have, Mr. Chairman.

Senator HENNINGS. Do you have a statement that you would like to read and, perhaps, later we will ask some questions, both the subcommittee and the counsel? If you have a statement, we will be very glad to hear it.

STATEMENT OF JOSEPH V. HEFFERNAN, VICE PRESIDENT, NATIONAL BROADCASTING CO., INC.

Mr. HEFFERNAN. My name is Joseph V. Heffernan. I am a vice president of the National Broadcasting Co. I appear here at the invitation of the subcommittee to furnish information with respect to television services provided by NBC. Many of the points in my statement were presented last October. They are given again now since none of the members of the subcommittee was in a position to attend the hearing in October.

Juvenile delinquency: The problem of juvenile delinquency is properly a matter of concern to all Americans. The citizens of our country should feel grateful to this subcommittee for having undertaken the laborious task of exploring this difficult and at times tragic subject.

The problem is difficult because the causes of juvenile delinquency appear to be complex and deep rooted. Most experts in the field agree that juvenile delinquency does not result from a single cause.

The pursuit of simple solutions has nevertheless continued on some fronts. These can delay rather than advance the resolution of a problem so complex. We feel that the report of this subcommittee will recognize these points, and that, on the positive side, the work of the subcommittee can contribute importantly to a deeper understanding of this subject.

The creation of NBC: I would like, first of all, to tell you about NBC and some of its activities.

NBC is in the business of broadcasting and of supplying programs for broadcast. NBC is the first network broadcaster. It was founded 29 years ago under the leadership of David Sarnoff, now chairman of the board of NBC and of RCA, to bring to the public—

* * * the best programs available for broadcasting in the United States. * * *

And, Mr. Chairman, I should like to say here that we, having been organized for the very purpose of raising the standards of broadcasting, greatly appreciate the activity of any group such as your subcommittee, which interests itself in the general problem of raising program standards.

I want you to know that we are happy to appear here and to cooperate with any group and, particularly, a group of distinguished Sentors, such as this subcommittee, who undertake work in the field, the general field, of raising the standards of programing.

Senator HENNINGS. Thank you, Mr. Heffernan.

Mr. HEFFERNAN. We are an organization of human beings. We make no claim to perfection in every program we broadcast. But we take real pride in the purpose of our organization— to bring the best to the public—and feel that our record justifies the conclusion that our programs as a whole have been and are superior.

NBC's operations: The television operations of NBC are conducted in three major divisions: The television network, the television stations owned by NBC itself, and the NBC film division.

In the operation of its television network NBC provides a program service to more than 180 stations throughout the country, all but 5 of these are independently owned and receive the NBC programs under affiliation contracts between them and NBC.

These network programs are provided during part of the broadcast day and the stations present their own programs during the remainder of the day. To a large extent the sponsors of network commercial programs select the programs they want and the stations in turn may accept or reject the network programs in accordance with the terms of their affiliation contract with NBC.

Senator WILEY. What does that last statement mean, "in accordance with the terms of their affiliation contract with NBC"?

Mr. HEFFERNAN. Well, Senator, taking your own State as an example, station WTMJ–TV, which is one of the finest stations in the United States——

Senator WILEY. So is the State, of course.

Mr. HEFFERNAN. That is correct, sir. (Continuing.) Has under its affiliation contract with NBC the complete right on its own to determine whether it regards any particular program offered by NBC as being in the public interest.

The station itself makes that decision, and if, in its own judgment, it regards any program as not in the public interest, the station has a right to reject that program, and that is not a violation of its affiliation contract, to accept programs from us.

In other words, it can accept programs from us, but is not obligated to take any program which itself feels is not in the public interest.

Senator WILEY. How does it apply to competitive stations?

Mr. HEFFERNAN. You mean do other networks operate on the same basis?

Senator WILEY. Yes, within the same cities.

Supposing you have two stations there; can they get the same program from you?

Mr. HEFFERNAN. Well, in general, the networks operate on the basis that while we do not have an exclusive affiliation in general, WTMJ–TV in Milwaukee takes NBC programs, and it happens that CBS owns its own station in Milwaukee and puts CBS programs on its own station there.

The ABC Network is affiliated with another station in Milwaukee so that, in general, in the larger cities the programs of each separate network go on separate stations. That is not invariably true, but, in general, that is the way it works.

Senator WILEY. Well, if NBC has program X and it relates, say, to a commercial product, it is a good program, WTMJ gets it.

Can any other station make application for it to get it?

Mr. HEFFERNAN. It cannot, Senator, in that our contract with our affiliates gives the station the first right of refusal for that program in the area which it serves.

Taking, for example, the Peter Pan program, which is one of the great programs of recent times, perhaps of all times, the Peter Pan program was offered out in Milwaukee to WTMJ in Milwaukee.

They took it and, having accepted it, under our contract no other station in Milwaukee was entitled to it.

Senator WILEY. Well, you are a licensee of the Government. I was just wondering now, as a one-time lawyer of many, many years ago—I used to practice law—I am just wondering on what authority you have to say that you will only sell your goods to one station.

Mr. HEFFERNAN. Well, in general, Senator, I think that is the way most businesses operate; that is the way the automobile business operates. General Motors——

Senator WILEY. Wait a minute; do not say the automobile business is consistent with Government licensee business.

I wonder if you have the answer? It just came to me because I have seen some litigation at times over these things, apparently, and I was just wondering when you used the phrase "according to the terms of the affiliation contract," it just came out of a clear sky to me.

I know how you operate now, and I am just wondering on what authority you can say if another station, if two stations also have licenses from the Government, just how you can simply say that you are just going to sell to one station rather than the other.

Mr. HEFFERNAN. This takes us into a rather fundamental part of the Communications Act of 1934, which provides that the broadcasting business is not a common-carrier business; it is a competitive-enterprise business, a competitive-enterprise business, under which one station competes with another station.

We offer our product, as a competitive enterprise, to a distributor in Milwaukee just, as for example, as there are several automobile companies, each of which has his own outlet in Milwaukee, and there are several competing networks, each of which has his outlet.

Being a competitive enterprise, and so defined by statute, it is true that the Government licenses us, but the function and the purpose of the Government coming in to license this business was to avoid electrical interference as between one station and another; that was the need and purpose and reason for the Government's coming in to license the stations.

In doing that, however, they recognized the value of competitive enterprise as such, and expressly provided by statute that the business of broadcasting should continue to be a free-enterprise competitive business, and would not be a common-carrier business, and it is expressly so stated in the act.

Senator WILEY. WTMJ, let us take that; let us take that station, and let us take any particular picture, and let us assume that it is a picture that is of vital interest to combating moral delinquency of minors, acting as an antidote.

Now, WTMJ gets that over what station, how does that come? Does it come in the shape of a film or is it——

Mr. HEFFERNAN. No. Most of our programs, Senator, particularly—most of our programs are carried via the lines of the American Telephone & Telegraph Co., the radio relay lines, and the coaxial cable lines.

Senator WILEY. From where?

Mr. HEFFERNAN. From the point of origination, which may be New York or Chicago or Los Angeles, for the most part, or Washington.

Our news programs originate in large part, as you gentlemen know because you gentlemen make the news, in Washington.

So, the point of origination, let us say, is Washington. It is picked up on the lines; it is picked up by NBC, created into a program, and fed out on the lines which we lease from the telephone company across the United States to our affiliates throughout the United States, more than 180 of them.

Senator WILEY. It is not sent, say, from the general station like WTMJ, transmitted from WTMJ?

Mr. HEFFERNAN. I am sorry, Senator, I did not understand that.

Senator WILEY. My ignorance is so immense on how these things are operated——

Mr. HEFFERNAN. I did not hear your question, sir.

Senator WILEY. Is the particular television program sent from a station, another station, to WTMJ?

Mr. HEFFERNAN. It is not sent from a station, as such. It is picked up by a camera in a studio and transmitted simultaneously to all stations throughout the United States affiliated with NBC.

It is a simultaneous broadcast in our principal programing. Let us take Peter Pan as the great example: that originated in our studio in Brooklyn, and was transmitted simultaneously to the stations throughout the United States affiliated with NBC, and which had agreed to accept that particular program.

Senator WILEY. I think you have made it clear to me.

Senator HENNINGS. Did you see the program, Senator Wiley, the Peter Pan program?

Senator WILEY. I do not think I did.

Senator HENNINGS. With Miss Mary Martin?

Senator WILEY. I cannot remember all these women like you do. [Laughter.]

Senator HENNINGS. They may get to Wisconsin one of these days. [Laughter.]

At any rate, it was one of the most, I thought, one of the trancendentally fine things I have ever seen over television during the entire course of the medium's existence.

Mr. HEFFERNAN. Thank you very much, Mr. Chairman.

NBC programs which are not sponsored are available to all stations on the network at their election.

NBC itself owns and operates five television stations. These carry the network programs during certain hours of the broadcast day and present their own local programs during the remainder. The stations owned by NBC are in New York, Chicago, Los Angeles, Cleveland, and Washington.

The NBC film division provides film programs to television stations and to advertisers who use the programs in purchasing time on stations of their own selection.

NBC television programs come from various sources. Some are produced by NBC itself, at the network or local level, or are provided by producers under contract to NBC. Some are purchased by NBC from outside producers or talent agencies. Others are provided by advertisers themselves who have purchased time on our facilities. Some of the programs on the stations owned by NBC consist of film produced specifically for television. Others are films produced originally for motion-picture release.

Economics of Broadcasting: The broadcasting industry is based on the American system of competitive enterprise. It is free to the public and seeks its support in advertising revenue.

As a network we compete with other advertising media such as newspapers, magazines, and national spot for the dollars spent by national advertisers. In this competition we offer advertising for sale in programs broadcast on our own and on independently owned stations affiliated with us and located throughout the country.

In supplying these programs on a national basis we offer the advertiser national distribution of his advertising message. If the advertiser feels that one of our programs best meets his requirements he may buy it. But if he feels that newspapers or magazines or national spot or direct mail or billboards or another network will serve his particular needs better, he can and does buy them.

I wish we could claim that network broadcasting outsells other media in this competitive race. But the fact is that, on the basis of figures for 1954, newspapers still get the biggest slice of the advertisers' dollar and magazines, national spot and direct mail campaigns take a big slice, too. This is the kind of competition we have to meet.

The effectiveness of television as an advertising medium, and its ability to provide high-quality programs at substantial cost, depends on its success in reaching and holding a mass audience. The maintenance of this audience depends in turn upon offering a service which meets public need and interests. Thus the public-service objectives and the commercial objectives of television as a medium are interlocking.

The degree to which the television industry has met these twin objectives is indicated by its amazing growth. Public enthusiasm for television has brought it to the point where it now serves 34 million American families, or nearly three-fourths of all those in the Nation.

Television and the presentation of ideas: In providing a television service NBC is one of the media engaged in the presentation of ideas. These media include newspapers, magazines, books, radio, and motion pictures. But in dramatic ways television differs from the others. It is the only one which brings into the homes of the Nation the magic combination of sight plus sound plus motion plus color.

The first problem of the broadcaster is to reach the public. No one is obligated to turn on his set or, if on, to tune our stations or, if tuned, to stay with us.

People will tune our stations and stay tuned only if they like what we offer. One of the ways we reach them is through their common interests in being entertained.

But this does not mean we seek the lowest common denominator of taste. We expressly reject that approach. This was never more dramatically demonstrated than by our televison presentation of Peter Pan. This program, which was seen over NBC on March 7, was viewed by more than 67 million people—the largest audience ever to witness any single television program. As most of you know, the star of the show was Mary Martin; the story is based on that of Sir James M. Barrie; and the program was presented in compatible color and black-and-white.

'Peter Pan received an ecstatic reception from the program critics. The Chicago Tribune said:

Sheer magic * * *. This was surely the most rewarding telecast of the season and one of the finest of any year * * *. Through this children's classic, TV came of age.

The New York Herald Tribune commented:

* * * as close to perfection as we've got yet, conceivably the most polished, finished, and delightful show that has ever been on television.

Once we have established the audience habit to tune to NBC in order to get the hit shows, it is more likely the audience will stay tuned to see our programs of information, enlightenment, and culture. It is in this way that we have gotten large audience for such great cultural and informational programs as the NBC Opera Theater, Victory at Sea, Meet the Press, Youth Wants To Know, Mr. Wizard, and special documentaries like our recent Three-Two-One-Zero, which related the story of the development of nuclear energy.

We presented on the NBC television network the Maurice Evans production of Hamlet, Richard II, and Macbeth. Each of these masterpieces played to an audience of nearly 20 million viewers.

Through this approach, the whole audience, over the course of time, is exposed to the best in literature and music and the fine arts. It becomes acquainted with the sciences, both the physical and social sciences. Religious services are brought into the home. The audience sees the news as it is happening all over the country and all over the world. It knows the issues and events and leaders of our times, because it has seen them on television.

The test of program policies is of course how they reflect themselves in concrete examples. NBC's record of great programing in the past is well known. It includes the Dr. Walter Damrosch broadcasts to schoolchildren, the University of the Air, the many years during which the Metropolitan Opera was broadcast by NBC, and the NBC Symphony Orchestra under Maestro Arturo Toscanini.

Here is a partial list of our current television network programs:

Regular programs: A cornerstone of our Sunday schedule is Frontiers of Faith, the NBC religious program, produced in cooperation with the National Council of the Churches of Christ in the United States of America, the National Council of Catholic Men, and the Jewish Theological Seminary.

Also on Sunday are: American Forum of the Air, one of the oldest and best known forum programs on television.

Youth Wants To Know, in which juveniles actually participate in asking questions of outstanding personalities of our time.

Zoo Parade, one of the finest instructional programs on the air.

The Hallmark Hall of Fame program, one of the finest dramatic shows we have and the program on which such magnificent successes as Amahl and the Night Visitors, Hamlet, and Macbeth were originally seen.

At 6 is one of the great programs of the week—Meet the Press.

From 7 to 9 a. m. each weekday, Monday to Friday, we open our network programing with Today. This program features news and special events, including interviews on issues of public interest and book reviews.

At 10 a. m. each weekday, Monday to Friday, we have the children's educational program Ding Dong School. In all the discussions of television this is one show which has almost universally been acclaimed as one of the finest children's programs on the air.

At 11 a. m. each weekday, Monday to Friday, we have Home. This is a service-type program built especially for the woman in the home. While it deals principally with points relating to homemaking, it includes discussions of juvenile delinquency and a regular series on civic problems entitled "What We Are Doing About It."

At 7:45 p. m. each weekday, Monday to Friday, we have the News Caravan, produced by NBC and narrated by John Cameron Swayze. It includes integrated film and live pickups from various cities whenever and wherever occasion warrants it. It is, we believe, the outstanding news program on the air and the public response supports this view.

On Saturday we have Mr. Wizard, a children's educational program based on a study of the sciences, chemistry, and physics, described in language that junior high-school children can understand. It is presented in cooperation with the Cereal Institute.

Integration in regular programs: In addition to these regular daily or weekly programs, we have presented from time to time a number of classics, documentaries, and other educational elements which were integrated into the schedule of regular programs. In this way the large audience which these programs regularly attract is available to view these features. This is an illustration of how we have brought the best to all the people and not just the minority groups to whom programs of a classical nature might otherwise be limited.

Senator Wiley, this is an illustration of the point you made that people do like to be entertained, and we feel that we should take advantage of that point and, at the same time, bring in light doses of educational matter within the entertainment program, and in that way reach a much broader audience than we would otherwise reach.

Examples of these programs are:

Rip Van Winkle, by Washington Irving; the Scarlet Letter, by Nathaniel Hawthorne; Romeo and Juliet, by William Shakespeare; and Kidnaped, by Robert Louis Stevenson, presented on the Kraft Television Theater.

Othello, by William Shakespeare, and Holiday Song, by Paddy Chayefsky, presented on the Philco Television Playhouse.

Cakes and Ale, by W. Somerset Maugham; Appointment in Samarra, by John O'Hara; Great Expectations and David Copperfield, by Charles Dickens; and the Hunchback of Notre Dame, by Victor Hugo, presented on the Johnson's Wax and American Tobacco programs.

I have already referred to the Maurice Evans' production of Amahl and the Night Visitors, Hamlet, and Macbeth, which appear on the Hallmark Hall of Fame program.

Eome examples of the NBC policy of enlightenment through exposure in children's programs are:

The Howdy Doody program has begun a series designed to interest youngsters in good music. It first explains musical instruments and musical forms, then gradually raises its sights.

Pinky Lee has begun a Prodigy Series to stimulate an interest in studying music. Young musicians of unusual talent are invited to perform on the program and are rewarded with an opportunity to appear with the California Junior Symphony Orchestra.

The Paul Winchell and Jerry Mahoney show introduced educational elements when it first went on the air last fall. One device it uses is a song describing some natural phenomenon or scientific principle. The lyrics, illustrated by a series of pictures, are sung by one of the dummy characters to answer such questions as: "What makes the stars shine?" "What makes a snowflake?" "Where does electricity come from?"

That program, by the way, of enlightenment through exposure, was commented upon, with respect to these children's programs, commented favorably, just last night by the Scripps-Howard paper in New York, the New York World-Telegram.

PROGRAMS IN THE PUBLIC INTEREST

Of the many programs in the public interest which NBC has produced, we take special pride in three series. It happens that in presenting these on the network we have found no sponsor for them. This has not diminished but in a sense increased our feeling of pride in having gone forward with them.

NBC Opera Theater: The first of these series is the NBC Opera Theater, which presents operas in English, under Samuel Chotzinoff as producer and Peter Herman Adler as musical director.

The operas which have been presented are—and the list is here which the reporter can copy into the record.

Opera	Composer
Amahl and the Night Visitors	Menotti
The Marriage	Martinu
Sister Angelica	Puccini
Der Rosenkavalier	Richard Strauss
Carmen [1]	Bizet
Macbeth	Verdi
The Marriage of Figaro	Mozart
The Taming of the Shrew [1]	Giannini
Pelleas and Melisande	Debussy
Salome	Richard Strauss
Abduction from the Seraglio [1]	Mozart
La Tosca	Puccini

[1] In color.

Schedules for the near future are:

The Would-be Gentleman, and Ariadne Auf Naxos	Richard Strauss
Grifflekin	Lucas Foss
The Saint of Bleecker Street	Menotti
La Grande Breteche	Holingsworth

You will note, Mr. Chairman and Senator Wiley, that a number of these operas are of special appeal to children: Amahl and the Night Visitors, for example; the Story of the Three Wings, and Carmen is always of great appeal to children; Macbeth, Verdi's opera, based, of course, on Shakespeare's play; The Taming of the Shrew, La Tosca, The Saint of Bleecker Street, which is coming to be presented, and one not mentioned here is Hansel and Gretel, which was also presented.

All of these operas were presented in the afternoon or early evening. The New York Times, in commenting on the NBC Opera Theater, said this:

The most vivid laboratory example of a program that meets the ultimate qualitative test for TV is probably the NBC Opera Theater. This company's aim has not been merely to do "opera on television." Instead, with excitement, imagination, and a magnificent refusal to compromise its artistic integrity, it has widened the horizons for all of opera and made a cultural contribution that transcends mere media.

Is it too rash to hint that the NBC opera, in terms of its national influence, now is the equal and conceivably even the peer of the Metropolitan? * * *

We feel very proud of those words, Mr. Chairman, and we feel very proud that NBC in this way can bring opera to people who otherwise would have no opportunity whatsoever to get to New York and attend the Metropolitan and hear and see the fine opera which we have brought to them.

Senator HENNINGS. Mr. Heffernan, I happen to have seen a great many of these things that you were talking about and I am surprised to hear that you cannot find a sponsor for some of these excellent programs. What is the problem?

Mr. HEFFERNAN. Well, Mr. Chairman, I am glad you raised that point because it is one of the suggestions I have here in connection with the great many activities of women's organizations which we are happy to see and to cooperate with.

The basic problem of getting a sponsor is that advertising, and the spending of advertising budgets, is a cold-blooded, business proposition. The advertisers, such as the large companies, who spend their money, do so on the advice of advertising agencies.

They get out their slide rules, they look to the number of people the program reaches, and they divide the cost of the program into the number of the people to get the cost per thousand people reached. Let's go back to Peter Pan; 67 million people, with as large a cost as that was, the actual unit cost per thousand persons reached is low, so that there is no problem.

The cost is not an absolute cost. It is a unit cost. There is no problem to sell a Peter Pan that reaches 67 million people, but unfortunately, in raising the sights of the public, here to view opera, we do not yet get an audience large enough that advertisers have been willing to pay the cost per thousand involved.

Now, we think that happens to be one of the areas where the networks themselves make a great contribution in that they undertake the cost of putting on the program nevertheless, to bring and lead the tastes and standards of the people up to the point where this audience, as it has, gradually increases and builds.

As the audience builds, the cost per thousand of such a program goes down, and the advertiser may get interested. We are still hopeful that this program will get a sponsor, because actually let us take the example of Toscanini and the NBC Symphony Orchestra. We produced that for 17 years; in 2 years out of the 17 we had a sponsor, but Toscanini and the NBC Symphony Orchestra was as magnificent a program whether it did have a sponsor or did not have a sponsor, so the quality is not affected basically.

Senator HENNINGS. As a corollary to that, Mr. Heffernan, would it not be true, that if you choose to do so you could have a cheaper program and very likely get a sponsor for it?

Mr. HEFFERNAN. That is undoubtedly so, sir. I appreciate that observation.

61227—55——10

Senator HENNINGS. Are your rates and is your method of entering into these contracts so rigid that you could not, that is get a sponsor even though you lost some money in the production of such things as the NBC Symphony Orchestra?

Mr. HEFFERNAN. Rigidity may well express it, sir, in that the network consists, for the most part, of independently owned stations and our contract with them is that we will sell. whenever we sell a program, it will be sold at a rate applicable to the station itself.

Taking again Senator Wiley's example or taking your own example in St. Louis, KSD–TV, there is a particular rate applicable to KSD–TV so that there is an element of rigidity in it with respect to the sale.

When we make a sale, it must meet a certain price applicable to St. Louis, Milwaukee, and each of the cities composing the network so that there is a substantial, it is a relatively high hurdle, whereas if you do not sell it, then the problem of cost does not come in.

Now if your question is: Could we cut that price in half and thereby move it, to do so would mean a delicate renegotiation with each of the independently owned stations who adjust at the rate applicable.

Senator HENNINGS. That is what I was getting at, whether you could minimize or rather ameliorate, let us say, the burden upon the stations for a worthwhile program presently not sponsored.

Mr. HEFFERNAN. Well, I will say this: That we do attempt to do so, and I am sure that if a fellow came along and made an offer for the NBC Opera Theater that did not fully meet our cost, that it would find sympathetic interest in NBC because wherein we did sell Toscanini and the NBC Symphony Orchestra, we did not in any instance fully recover our cost by any means.

Senator HENNINGS. I suppose taxwise, it could be charged off to advertising or good will?

Mr. HEFFERNAN. It is an expense of doing business and to the extent we do not recover those costs, they are applicable against other areas where you hope to make a profit.

Senator HENNINGS. Yes.

Senator WILEY. Now if you have got—you mentioned several fine pictures, whatever you want to call them, supposing you have not got a sponsor for X, but it is a wonderful thing that should go out. Does WTMJ pay you anything for it?

Mr. HEFFERNAN. If it is a nonsponsored show, they do not, sir. We provide the programs such as, take the NBC Opera Theater. NBC itself pays the cost of that program, and lays it down at WTMJ in Milwaukee, and they put the program on the air over their facilities, and so do our affiliates.

Senator WILEY. That is true in all cases where you haven't any sponsor.

Mr. HEFFERNAN. That is correct, sir. They do not pay us for the program. We provide the program to them, these unsponsored programs, without charge although that fact is taken into account in determining the general economic arrangements as between the independently owned stations and NBC.

Senator WILEY. Mr. Chairman, I have got to leave. I am going to take this gentleman's statement. I have listened to him with profit, and I am now late for another meeting. I know you will understand, sir.

Senator HENNINGS. I am sure Mr. Heffernan understands that most of us are late to other meetings at other times. We are sorry you have to leave, Senator Wiley.

You may proceed, Mr. Heffernan.

Mr. HEFFERNAN. Victory at Sea: This series is a film documentary presented in cooperation with the United States Navy. It was produced by Henry Salomon and coordinated by Robert W. Sarnoff. Victory at Sea dramatically depicts the wartime naval operations of the United States and other navies, based on film obtained from the files of 10 different governments, including films captured from wartime enemies. The symphonic score for the production—the longest symphonic score ever written—was composed by the distinguished contemporary musical composer, Richard Rodgers—under commission from NBC.

Wisdom Series: This consists of conversations with distinguished persons. Those who have appeared on the program so far are Carl Sandburg, Frank Lloyd Wright, Bertrand Russell, Robert Frost, Wanda Landowska, Rabbi Louis Finkelstein, Alfred P. Sloan, Jr., Sir Osbert Sitwell, and Eamon de Valera.

Among those who are scheduled for future broadcasts are Arnold Toynbee and Pablo Casals.

Procedures for program development: In seeking new ways to serve the public, we constantly and critically measure our performance against our objectives. An internal procedure we started sometime ago will illustrate this.

Under this procedure we examine every program to determine whether it can contribute to our objective of providing programs of culture as well as entertainment, and ask each producer to file a "responsibility report" on what he has done with the shows under his charge to contribute to this objective.

Although there are some programs which do not lend themselves to this, there is a number of entertainment shows which can incorporate significant material of culture and enlightenment, and thus contribute to broadening public taste and understanding. An outstanding example was the presentation by NBC of ballet in our recent color production Sunday in Town.

Local community service: I have mentioned many examples of programs in the public interest taken from our network schedule. In addition, the five television stations we own have developed individual projects of special interest to the local communities they serve. There are many examples of these. I shall mention just a few.

Our television station in New York has a special program each Saturday aimed at combating juvenile delinquency. This is Junior Champions. And for an hour each Saturday it also presents Children's Theater—a program of education and entertainment which features the natural sciences, geography, and history. It has also a daily service program for children, which gives instruction on safety, hobbies, and weather and school information. Each Sunday it has a program of musical instruction for children.

Our television station in Washington is conducting a series of special educational programs in cooperation with the Board of Education. One day each week science is taught, another day is devoted to civics and current events, another to the background of the news, another to Spanish lessons, another to French.

Standards of taste in broadcasting: I have tried to give you a broad background picture of how we are using television affirmatively as a constructive social influence. In a moment, I will turn to the other aspect of our responsibility—the procedures we follow to keep our programs free of offensive material. Before doing so, I would like to state our position on one matter that has been raised in these hearings.

We want to make it clear that in our opinion programs which include crime and mystery are a proper and legitimate part of the broadcast schedule. The subjects of crime and violence have been part of our literature in the Old Testament, in the Greek classics, in Shakespeare, in the opera, in the modern novel.

Of course we recognize that special care must be taken in presenting crime and mystery on the air. The NBC code of standards outlines policies we follow in connection with programs which include crime and mystery.

When properly presented, programs of this type educate against crime and delinquency. They can be used to impress upon millions of Americans that lawbreaking is a sordid business in which the criminal cannot win. This is the lesson which is driven home in programs like Dragnet, based on the files of the Los Angeles Police Department, and Big Story, which exposes rackets.

Programs which include crime and mystery are in fact only a small part of our diversified program structure. On the basis of our current schedules such programs account for 2.5 percent of the programing on our television network. This figure does not include Westerns, which do not belong in the category of such programs. If Westerns were included the figure would be increased by 0.6 percent.

The NBC code: I would like to turn to specific procedures we follow for establishing proper standards of taste in broadcasting, and for insuring compliance with these standards.

First, we have formulated our own program code to serve as a guide for ourselves and our advertisers. The original NBC Code was the first in the industry, and was adopted 21 years ago—in 1934. It has been strengthened and revised from time to time to meet new developments.

Copies of the NBC program code have been furnished to the members of the subcommittee. You will see that it is comprehensive and far reaching. A recent report published by UNESCO characterizes the NBC Code as "very strict."

In addition to our own code, we adhere to the program code of the National Association of Radio and Television Broadcasters.

A code of standards is an important first step, but it must be carried through with sincerity if it is to be effective. One of the means of carrying out our code is through our continuity acceptance department. This consists of an experienced staff of 32 people and is responsible to the company's top management. It reviews all radio and television scripts, all television film, and all advertising copy in advance of broadcast. The television director on all live broadcasts has the responsibility for calling continuity acceptance to attend television rehearsals wherever there are questions about the presentation of visual elements.

The cost to NBC of its continuity acceptance function is approximately a quarter of a million dollars a year.

Children's program review committee: As a separate means of maintaining high standards in NBC programs, we have established the NBC Children's Program Review Committee. This consists of three persons of outstanding reputation who have agreed to review our programs from the standpoint of suitability as children's fare. It is I believe the first such committee ever formed within our industry. We hope and expect that this committee will make a significant contribution toward the maintenance of high program standards for the millions of American youngsters who watch television.

The chairman of the committee is Mrs. Mildred McAffee Horton, (Mrs. Douglas Horton), a vice president of the National Council of Churches of Christ in the United States of America, a director of NBC, and formerly president of Wellesley College and head of the WAVES during World War II.

Another member of the committee is Dr. Frances Horwich, the distinguished educator who is so well known for her incomparable program, Ding Dong School. Dr. Horwich's teaching experience began with an assignment in the first grade of an Evanston, Ill., school. Her experience ranges from director of kindergartens in the Winnetka, Ill., schools to Croton-on-Hudson, where she was director of the Hessian Hills school; from counsellor of student teachers in Chicago's City Teachers' College to visiting professor of education at the University of North Carolina. As an author of articles and texts in her field, Dr. Horwich is known to educators everywhere for her human approach to the problems of children and to young teachers preparing to work with small children.

The third member of the committee is Dr. Robert Goldenson, a graduate of Princeton, Pittsburgh and Harvard, who is an assistant professor of psychology at Hunter College and a specialist in family relations. He served as president of the Tri-State Conference on Family Relations in 1953 and was a member of the International Congress for Mental Health. Dr. Goldenson is the author of many articles and books in the field of child study.

Supervisor of children's programs: In addition to the review by this committee, Dr. Horwich has been appointed by NBC as supervisor of children's programs. In this capacity, Dr. Horwich is giving the benefit of her firsthand knowledge of child psychology to each producer, director and others engaged in the day-to-day preparation and presentation of programs which reach the child and the adolescent.

Other concepts of responsibility: Still another method of maintaining high standards of taste in NBC programs is in effect in our company. Four years ago Mr. Weaver, who was then head of the NBC television network, and is now the president of NBC; issued a directive to all producers of shows which states in part:

* * * we must watch all dramatic shows for violent portrayals which might offend or overfrighten any part of our audience. In comedy shows we must avoid humor that is offensive or embarrassing to any groups.

While our continuity acceptance department is supposed to eliminate offensive material, I shall personally hold the individuals running the shows responsible for the content of those shows. You are all adult, know the power of this medium, and must develop a sense of responsibility for what you do in it.

These policies are applicable to the programs we ourselves produce and as well to programs produced by others which are to be shown on NBC facilities.

In addition we pay careful attention to the public's reaction to our programs, as expressed in the audience mail we receive. The commendations and criticisms which our listeners and viewers send in are valuable guides to us, and we use them constructively in determining our policies.

Television and juvenile delinquency: As a responsible medium for the presentation of ideas, NBC is deeply conscious of its position in relation to social problems of the day. It does not turn its back on them. It welcomes an opportunity to help in their solution.

We have reflected this in the treatment of juvenile delinquency on our television network. We have dealt there on many occasions with this difficult subject. Our speakers have included distinguished public officials, judges, psychiatrists and criminologists. They have discussed juvenile delinquency or ways of combating that problem in 151 programs or segments since the beginning of 1954.

One of these programs was the play Diary, written by the distinguished American author Robert E. Sherwood. John Crosby, the television critic of the New York Herald Tribune, wrote that Mr. Sherwood's play:

* * * tackled one of the largest social problems of our times, juvenile delinquency, with sympathy, intelligence and stunning dramatic effectiveness.

We are aware of no responsible scientific data or opinion which fixes television as the cause of juvenile delinquency.

Dr. Goldenson recently consulted 18 distinguished authorities in this field. They are listed in the footnote.

To his question, "In your judgment are television programs responsible for juvenile delinquency?", the great majority answered "No." His full report of the views of these experts appears in the December issue of Parents Magazine.

Senator HENNINGS. Mr. Heffernan, of course the question put that way would not, to anyone who has any smattering in his field, the answer would have to be "No," would it not? I think what disturbs some people, some members of this committee, is not, are television programs responsible for juvenile delinquency, but do they through their impact have any effect upon young people, and if so, how and to what extent.

Mr. HEFFERNAN. I think your observation, Mr. Chairman, is a fair one.

Senator HENNINGS. I don't think anybody, except a street corner, curbstone expert on these very complicated subjects, would undertake to say that juvenile delinquency is caused by television or by comic books or broken homes or by slums or by lack of playgrounds or by any one of a variety of factors which some of us feel do have a bearing upon it.

I am one member of the subcommittee. I do not know about the feeling of the others, but I believe that this medium is one that perhaps has little effect upon the misfortunes of young people and the growing tide of young people in trouble, getting in trouble with the law and other kinds of trouble.

So if I may make that one comment by way of criticism, I believe the question is leading and suggestive and does not permit of an explanation of the thing that we are really trying to get at.

Mr. Heffernan. I think your comment is a very fair and sound one, Mr. Chairman. I only would say that: That in the context of some discussion in the press, and others in which there had been, I think, some irresponsible references to television as the cause of juvenile delinquency, it was rather to meet that context that Dr. Goldenson asked the question in this way.

It is true the article proceeds to discuss the subject in what I believe is a scientific and a sound basis and the views of these experts, and I am referring to the full text of the article.

Senator Hennings. Yes.

Mr. Heffernan. Dr. George D. Stoddard, former president of the University of Illinois, has this to say in respect of films and juvenile delinquency:

> There is little evidence that the motion picture has much effect upon the behavior of children and youth. When a healthy high-school boy chooses to spend 3 hours on a sunny Saturday in a world of make believe, the trouble is not in the motion picture, but in the quality of home and neighborhood life.
> Anyone who is anxious about the contents of motion pictures should analyze Homer, The Old Testament, Shakespeare, Mother Goose, or the modern novel. Terrible things happen to men. It is inevitable that they find a place in dramatic art.

Another authority in this field is the distinguished head of the Federal Bureau of Investigation, Mr. J. Edgar Hoover. He has said this:

> A youngster old enough to commit a crime is old enough to listen to an anti-crime program which plainly and convincingly teaches him that the criminal, an enemy of society, is playing a losing game.

Senator Hennings. You see Dragnet now and then, do you not, Mr. Heffernan?

Mr. Heffernan. Yes, I do.

Senator Hennings. I see it and enjoy it very much. I am a great television fan when I have an opportunity to see it. I was once a district attorney, as you may know.

Mr. Heffernan. I know you were.

Senator Hennings. I spent a good many years in criminal courts, but one thing that I might observe about some of these programs, and I quite agree with what others have said, in the general suggestion that we cannot insulate children from the troubles in the world, nor can we attempt by any medium or any variety of media, to convince them that there are not evildoers and that there are not immoral people, that there are not those who are at war with society, to put it one way, but I do believe that in Dragnet they use the name "Mo," which means modus operandi, I do believe that children may be given ideas about that, as to how to break into a house, how to—I recall one show particularly where a boy was taught to push a key in a door, put a thin strip of paper under the door, push the key that was on the inside of the door out of the lock, pull the key out from the inside. Now that would be helpful to a young burglar, if he had not been taught that elsewhere.

There are a good many—there is a professional criminal class in this country and they have a good many techniques that are mighty well developed, and some of them are experts and very proficient.

Now I am not saying at all that we should not know about these particular things. There is the other side of the coin; it may enable people to guard against such encroachments upon their property or upon their person or their safety, but I do think sometimes you can give youngsters ideas by books, comic books and magazines, and moving pictures and television. I am not saying it is a necessarily bad thing. But I do wonder about just that one phase of it at times.

Mr. HEFFERMAN. What you say, Mr. Chairman, undoubtedly is correct.

Senator HENNINGS. But you cannot cut everything out just because it might teach somebody something he should not know about. I fully appreciate that. I do not mean to interrupt you, except this is one of the things that is giving me a little pause on some of the crime and mystery programs that have been presented. But for the most part, they do show that crime is sordid, and if you sat, as I have, for a good many years across the table from young robbers and stickup men and murderers, and thieves of all varieties, and seen them as they confront the court, the district attorney, you then have an opportunity to see what happens and how they feel about things, it would be the greatest object lesson that I can think of.

Or go to the penitentiaries—I am a member of that committee that inspects the penitentiaries and reformatories—and see what happens afterward, and I think that television as well as the moving-picture industry, as well as radio, have all done a pretty good job on that. They have shown this business of crime for profit is not a very durable, or in the long run, a very profitable nor happy pursuit. Those are just some of the things we think about.

Mr. HEFFERMAN. There is no doubt, Mr. Chairman, that knowledge can be used against man as well as for man. The airplane is perhaps the prime example, the invention of the airplane, a great boon to man. but is used as an instrument for warfare.

Senator HENNINGS. Yes.

Mr. HEFFERNAN. We try to be mindful of the point you make to this extent: That in general, we program, and beginning with the network at 7:30, light music and news. We try as a general matter not to schedule a matter of crime or anything involving mystery before 9 o'clock so that there is a substantial part of the children that will be in bed by that hour. Now there are exceptions.

Senator HENNINGS. Most of us learn plenty about the modus operandi from our reading of Conan Doyle and Sherlock Holmes and the forerunners for many of these present things long before radio and television were thought of.

Some of the most ingenious schemes were perpetrated by the criminals that were ultimately run down by the eminent Sherlock Holmes.

Mr. HEFFERNAN. I come now, Mr. Chairman, to a point referred to by Dr. Lazarsfeld, and I believe yesterday by Dr. Maccoby. Some experts on juvenile delinquency have suggested that a definitive answer to the causes of juvenile crime can come only from a research project carried out on a very large scale and over a number of years by psychologists and sociologists attached to a university or foundation. They have said that such a project should deal broadly with the behavior patterns of children, and that it cannot confine itself to media influences, since other factors such as the influence of parents, economic conditions, and worldwide tensions are clearly relevant.

If a university or foundation should undertake such a project we should be glad to supply information and cooperate with them. That is the point Dr. Lazarsfeld was making this morning and I thought very wisely and soundly.

I should like to start here, Mr. Chairman, with one suggestion that is not in my text, and that is this: As I indicated, there are a number of producers of programs for television other than networks and stations themselves, independent packagers, they are called in the trade, many of them on film and some live.

My first suggestion is that those independent producers of television programs should themselves be subject to the television code, which will give one additional source of check on the standards of programs available to children.

Senator HENNINGS. Do you buy any of the independent products?

Mr. HEFFERNAN. We do. We do not ourselves produce anything like all the programs that go on NBC. But when we buy them, we send them to our continuity acceptance department to process them and check them. But there are more than 400 stations throughout the country——

Senator HENNINGS. Generally, they are not live television, are they?

Mr. HEFFERNAN. For the most part, they are on film.

Senator HENNINGS. Yes.

Mr. HEFFERNAN. For the most part they are film, and many stations are not equipped with a separate department as we have, to check the content of the programs. I do not say they do not check, but they do not have a staff of 32 people. They are obviously not that— I have dealt at some length with some positive aspects of NBC programs. I have done this because I believe that in this difficult area many broadcasters have done a better job than they are given credit for.

The broadcasting industry has in a span of 30 years gone through the dual revolution of the coming of radio and now television. It has established itself as one of the major industries, and is providing a service unequaled throughout the world.

It is only human that it should have made some mistakes. But it has shown an awareness of its responsibility to serve the public as an influence for good and to avoid material in bad taste which goes beyond other media for the presentation of ideas. NBC is proud of the fact that the adoption by it 21 years ago of its code of broadcast standards provided the leadership in this area.

The significance of this leadership by NBC is indicated in a recent report of a New York State joint legislative committee. This committee had studied a number of subjects, including the effect of television on minors. Its report referred to the adoption of the NBC code, quoted the NBC code at length, and concluded in part:

That the radio and television industry is making a sincere, honest, and effective effort to assure the presentation of wholesome entertainment and that legislation in this field is not necessary at this time.

We agree with this. But fundamentally we believe that, apart from the constitutional problem, it is better for Government to stay out of the business of regulating program content.

Senator HENNINGS. By constitutional problem, you mean the first amendment?

Mr. HEFFERNAN. That is right. We are opposed to Government censorship and to any device by which Government is empowered to check the expression of opinion. We believe that in the long run any attempt to regulate program content by Government decree will prove both unwise and unworkable.

In taking this position we feel it puts more, and not less, responsibility on the broadcaster himself. It puts the control over program content squarely up to him.

I would like to add, Mr. Chairman, that in making these observations about the constitutional problem, I do not mean to imply that we feel this committee does not properly concern itself in holding these hearings with programs and with their possible effect upon children, because we feel that any responsible body which will lend its weight to the raising of program standards is operating in the area that we like to see it operate in, and we welcome help from any area in the raising of program standards.

Senator HENNINGS. Perhaps even beyond that, too, Mr. Heffernan, you might feel that as a result of these hearings some of the public may be disabused of the view that these programs are solely responsible for some of the difficulties in which our young people find themselves in terms of society in general.

Mr. HEFFERNAN. That is a very wise observation.

Senator HENNINGS. Thank you.

Mr. HEFFERNAN. The adoption by NBC of its code of broadcast standards was a recognition of the responsibility we bear as a broadcaster. This system of self regulation, which the industry as a whole has followed in the industry code, is one alternative to Government regulation of program content.

Another is the basic process of education itself. Our schools and colleges give substantial time to the encouragement of higher standards for books and literature generally, as they should. We have schools of journalism in many of our great universities. But television has already surpassed the printed word in its hold on the public mind. Should not our schools and colleges keep pace by striving in that field also to encourage higher standards of listener demand for television programs?

There is also the public itself. This country has now had compulsory education for more than a hundred years. Are not the literate people we have developed capable of a large measure of direct program control by the simple device of tuning some stations in and tuning others out? Our Government does not tell them what to read. I don't believe it need tell them what to see or what to hear.

The direct-program control exercised by the public itself will be as effective as it is informed and discriminating. The newspapers have been helpful in this respect. Most of the metropolitan papers carry the daily logs of all television stations in their area. Parents are afforded an opportunity in this way to guide the viewing habits of their children.

If parents will respond to this opportunity and if they exercise discrimination in the selection of the superior programs over others, those broadcasters who offer superior programs will get the kind of listener support they need in order to continue to offer better programs.

The obligation to be discriminating attaches as well to the findings of those who make industry surveys. Broad, shotgun condemnations of an industry as a whole, without recognition of the superior programs produced by many in that industry, serve only to discourage those who have struggled to do something better.

May I say, Mr. Chairman, that I compliment this committee for the scientific approach of the witnesses who have appeared here. I have in mind particularly Dr. Lazarsfeld and Dr. Maccoby, who came yesterday, and I could not have been more gratified in the scientific, painstaking, fact-seeking, openminded attitude that they brought to this committee on this subject.

Our country was founded on the faith that the people themselves are capable of making the decisions which will determine their future. To make this faith effective, Americans have placed special values on education, on the broadest access to information, on the wide dissemination of the arts.

In securing these values our media of communication play a major role. And among these media television has a foremost part. Its influence for good is beyond calculation, and its freedom to serve the public must be preserved.

Senator HENNINGS. Mr. Heffernan, I want to thank you very much on behalf of this subcommittee for having come here, this is your second appearance before this subcommittee and I believe you were good enough to come before the Elections Committee on another occasion.

Mr. HEFFERNAN. That is right, sir; that was 4 years ago.

Senator HENNINGS. So you have made many journeys here, and you and your organization have devoted considerable time to the preparation of material for the benefit of the committees of the United States Senate in their effort to arrive at some solution to these various problems.

It has been an excellent presentation. I would like to ask Mr. Bobo if he has any questions.

Mr. BOBO. I just have one, Senator, and Mr. Heffernan. I have read the testimony from the previous hearings, and listened to the testimony of the psychiatrists and sociologists that we have had during this series of hearings, and the general opinion seems to be, of those that have appeared, that the individual crime and violence program, if we should take Dragnet as an example, has no effect or probably has no effect upon a child, on juvenile delinquency, but where you have four stations in a city, each one of those stations carrying at a time crime and violence, then they say that the constant hammering away of crime and violence without any selection or choice might have a detrimental effect.

Now my question is aimed at this: Is there any cooperation, or could there be any cooperation between the stations in a city or between the networks so that crime and violence programs might be staggered, because I realize that you in NBC might schedule your programs in such a way to avoid putting on too much crime and violence, but CBS's schedule might fill in the void during the hour when you are having entertainment, with a crime program, and ABC and Dumont the other way.

I wonder is there a possibility within the industry of an interstation or internetwork cooperation to stay away from all four channels carrying the same type of program where there is no choice.

Mr. HEFFERNAN. May I see if I understand your question, Mr. Bobo. Would it be your thought, for example, that at 9 o'clock at night, all stations, if they are to carry a program that involves scenes of crime and violence, it would all be at the same time?

Mr. BOBO. No, I was getting at just the reverse of that, Mr. Heffernan, rather than all four stations having crime and violence at the same time.

Mr. HEFFERNAN. I would think that would be the way to avoid it because the child could not possibly watch all 4, whereas if you put the 4 on at different half-hour intervals, he could watch them all going from one to the other as they came on.

Mr. BOBO. The point that I was attempting to make—I guess I didn't make myself clear. If he is attempting to look at NBC and there is a crime and violence program on and he is told to turn it off that station, but if he goes to another station he still finds the same kind of program, a program of crime and violence, then there is no choice or selectivity.

Mr. HEFFERNAN. Your suggestion, sir, has merit. Unfortunately, the business is so extremely competitive that we hardly talk to our competitors at all about anything, and when we do, it is not always in a cooperative spirit, and the antitrust laws don't permit too much cooperation. I am not saying that they would forbid this. But scheduling is a very difficult and complicated thing.

Senator HENNINGS. There we get down to a definition of terms again. What is crime and violence. Man's inhumanity to man, for example, may be even more distressing than a predatory individual going out and enriching himself at the expense of the social organization. There are all sorts of things other than the crime and violence itself that might have an impact, it would seem to me.

Mr. HEFFERNAN. I should think, Mr. Bobo, that one possible answer to your approach—I sympathize with the objective you are seeking, that is, I have suggested in my statement there that parents exercise discrimination, ask the child perhaps to turn it off. Now taking our network schedule as such, on Monday night we have no program at all involving crime or mystery; Tuesday night, none; Wednesday night, none until 10:30; Thursday night, we start at 8:30—we do have Justice, and at 9 o'clock Dragnet. Justice is a program produced in cooperation with the Legal Aid Association, at their request. It is a special program designed to make a point that many people do not appreciate, that they should, the individual citizen should, cooperate with the administration of justice, and that is the specific purpose of this program. We regard it, while it does include references to crime, it is inherent in it, in the program——

Senator HENNINGS. It is a very good program, I might say.

Mr. HEFFERNAN. It is inherent in the program that it should.

On Friday night at 10 o'clock, we have a half hour, and on Saturday night, none, and on Sunday night, none.

Now in view of that, 4 nights of the week, none at all, and on a fifth night none until 10:30 and on the other nights, at 9, I should think that if the parents were trying to exercise discrimination in guiding their child even if he were concerned about those programs, which are basically aimed for adults in any event, it would be possible to select— in fact, I personally have the feeling that if a parent will exercise discrimination in the selection of programing, there is much more fine quality programing on in NBC alone than any one child could possibly find, or should find time to look at. There is so much good being offered, that if the parent will just take the trouble to look up the newspapers and see when these good programs are offered, expose the child to those, the child will get as much as any normal child should look at in the way of television fare.

Now coming back to your specific suggestions——

Mr. BOBO. I think you have answered that, Mr. Heffernan. I did not ask that as a suggestion of my own.

Mr. HEFFERNAN. I think we have had that suggestion in the record previously and I wanted to clear the record as far as you were concerned.

In other cases we put on a fine dramatic program Monday night and one of the competing networks has a program that overlaps. One of the critics will say, "Why don't they get together and not compete?" But you cannot get together and not compete because the Sherman Antitrust Act forbids it.

Senator HENNINGS. Is that all, counsel?

Mr. BOBO. Yes, sir.

Senator HENNINGS. Thank you, Mr. Heffernan. The subcommittee now stands adjourned subject to the call of the Chair.

(Whereupon, at 1:15 p. m. the subcommittee adjourned, subject to the call of the Chair.)

X